February 23–27, 2013
Shenzhen, China

**Association for
Computing Machinery**

Advancing Computing as a Science & Profession

I0027571

PPoPP'13

Proceedings of the 2013 ACM SIGPLAN Symposium on
Principles and Practice of Parallel Programming

Sponsored by:
ACM SIGPLAN

Supported by:
***National Science Foundation, IBM Research, Huawei, Intel,
Loongson Technology, Elsevier, Institute of Computing Technology,
and State Key Laboratory of Computer Architecture***

Association for Computing Machinery

Advancing Computing as a Science & Profession

The Association for Computing Machinery
2 Penn Plaza, Suite 701
New York, New York 10121-0701

Notice to Past Authors of ACM-Published Articles
ACM intends to create a complete electronic archive of all articles and/or other material previously published by ACM. If you have written a work that has been previously published by ACM in any journal or conference proceedings prior to 1978, or any SIG Newsletter at any time, and you do NOT want this work to appear in the ACM Digital Library, please inform permissions@acm.org, stating the title of the work, the author(s), and where and when published.

ISBN: 978-1-4503-1922-5 (Digital)

ISBN: 978-1-4503-2091-7 (Print)

Additional copies may be ordered prepaid from:

ACM Order Department
PO Box 30777
New York, NY 10087-0777, USA

Phone: 1-800-342-6626 (USA and Canada)
+1-212-626-0500 (Global)
Fax: +1-212-944-1318
E-mail: acmhelp@acm.org
Hours of Operation: 8:30 am – 4:30 pm ET

Printed in the USA

Chairs' Welcome

It is our great pleasure to welcome you to the 18th ACM SIGPLAN Symposium on Principles and Practice of Parallel Programming (PPoPP'13). PPoPP continues its tradition of serving as a leading forum for research in all aspects of parallel software, including theoretical foundations, programming models, programming languages, compilers, algorithms, applications, and systems software.

PPoPP'13 received 146 complete paper submissions. In addition to the 29 program committee members, 85 members of the external review committee plus an additional 33 individuals reviewed these papers. We carried out two rounds of reviewing, with at least three reviews being obtained in the first round and additional reviews being obtained in the second round for papers where needed. After extensive discussions at an in-person program committee meeting in Atlanta, Georgia, USA, 26 full papers were selected for presentation at the conference. The program committee also invited 47 high quality submissions that could not be accepted as full papers as poster presentations and 19 accepted this invitation.

PPoPP'13 is excited to take place in the dynamic city of Shenzhen, China, our second visit to Asia in recent times. The conference will be co-located with the International Symposium on High-Performance Computer Architecture (HPCA) and International Symposium on Code Generation and Optimization (CGO), allowing attendees of one conference the option of attending talks at the other.

PPoPP'13 is a result of the efforts of a large number of people. We thank the authors of all the submissions, and workshop and tutorial presenters, for providing an intellectually stimulating and cutting-edge program. We are grateful for the tireless efforts of the program committee and external review committee, Arun Kejarwal, web and publicity; Harry Xu, workshops and tutorials; Rui Hou, local arrangements; Kun Wang, finance. We are grateful to Lisa Tolles and the team at Sheridan Communications for an efficient and streamlined publication process, as well as to Adrienne Griscti and the team at ACM. Finally, we offer our thanks to ACM SIGPLAN for its ongoing sponsorship; to the steering committee (Keshav Pingali, Calin Cascaval, Mary Hall, David Padua, J. Ramanujam, P. Sadayappan, Pen-Chung Yew) for their guidance; and to our partners for their financial support.

Alex Nicolau   **Saman Amarasinghe**
Xiaowei Shen   **Richard Vuduc**
General Chairs   *Program Chairs*

Table of Contents

Session 1: Papers

PPoPP 2013 Symposium Organization

General Chairs: Alex Nicolau *(University of California, Irvine, USA)*
Xiaowei Shen *(IBM Research, China)*

Program Chairs: Saman Amarasinghe *(Massachusetts Institute of Technology, USA)*
Richard Vuduc *(Georgia Institute of Technology, USA)*

Web and Publicity Chair: Arun Kejariwal *(Netflix, Inc., USA)*

Workshops and Tutorials Chair: Harry Xu *(University of California, Irvine, USA)*

Local Arrangements Committee: Rui Hou *(Chinese Academy of Sciences, China)*

Finance Chair: Kun Wang *(IBM Research, China)*

Steering Committee Chair: Keshav Pingali *(University of Texas at Austin, USA)*

Steering Committee: Calin Cascaval *(Qualcomm, USA)*
Mary Hall *(University of Utah, USA)*
David Padua *(University of Illinois at Urbana-Champaign, USA)*
J. (Ram) Ramanujam *(Louisiana State University, Baton Rouge, USA)*
P. (Saday) Sadayappan *(The Ohio State University, USA)*
Pen-Chung Yew *(Academia Sinica, Taiwan)*

Program Committee: Kunal Agrawal *(Washington University in St. Louis, USA)*
Rajeev Barua *(University of Maryland, USA)*
Chris Batten *(Cornell University, USA)*
Martin Burtscher *(Texas State University, USA)*
Calin Cascaval *(Qualcomm, USA)*
Wenguang Chen *(Tsinghua University, China)*
Yifeng Chen *(Peking University, China)*
Brian Demsky *(University of California, Irvine, USA)*
Dave Dice *(Oracle Labs, USA)*
Isaac Gelado *(Barcelona Supercomputing Center, Spain)*
Phillip B. Gibbons *(Intel Labs Pittsburgh, USA)*
Ganesh Gopalakrishnan *(University of Utah, USA)*
Naga Govindaraju *(Microsoft Corporation, USA)*
R. Govindarajan *(Indian Institute of Science, India)*
Ziang Hu *(Huawei, USA)*
Laxmikant Kale *(University of Illinois at Urbana-Champaign, USA)*
Paul H. J. Kelly *(Imperial College London, UK)*
Duane Merrill *(NVIDIA Research, USA)*
Mayur Naik *(Georgia Institute of Technology, USA)*
Ryan Newton *(Indiana University, USA)*
Dimitrios S. Nikolopolous *(Queen's University of Belfast, UK)*
Jens Palsberg *(University of California, Los Angeles, USA)*
Yoonho Park *(IBM Research, USA)*
Vijay Reddi *(University of Texas at Austin, USA)*

Program Committee (continued):   Michael L. Scott *(University of Rochester, USA)*
Nathan Tallent *(Pacific Northwest National Laboratory, USA)*
Philippas Tsigas *(Chalmers University, Sweden)*
Peng Wu *(IBM Research, USA)*
Binyu Zang *(Fudan University, China)*

External review committee:

Virat Agarwal	Allen Malony
Gagan Agrawal	Naoya Maruyama
George Almasi	Maged Michael
Nancy Amato	Sam Midkiff
Scott Baden	Eliot Moss
Guy Blelloch	Trevor Mudge
Ras Bodik	Frank Mueller
Greg Bronevetsky	Madan Musuvathi
Dhruva Chakrabarti	Satish Narayanasamy
Barbara Chapman	Vijay Pai
Arun Chauhan	Scott Pakin
Albert Cohen	Santosh Pande Pande
Guojing Cong	Victor Pankratius
Timothy Davis	Srini Parthasarathy
Bronis de Supinski	Louis-Noel Pouchet
Jim Dinan	Rodric Rabbah
Mattan Erez	Sanjay Rajopadhye
Thomas Fahringer	J. (Ram) Ramanujam
Sasha Fedorova	Lawrence Rauchwerger
Wilfried Gansterer	E. Jason Riedy
Guang Gao	P. (Saday) Sadayappan
Alex Garthwaite	Daniel Sanchez
Maria Garzaran	Peter Sanders
Mahantesh Halappanavar	Rob Schreiber
Tim Harris	Martin Schulz
Yuxiong He	Arrvindh Shriraman
Stephan Herhut	Stelios Sidiroglou-Douskos
Torsten Hoefler	Marc Snir
Mark Hoemmen	Ravi Soundararajan
Wei Hsu	Mike Spear
Costin Iancu	Michelle Strout
Sanath Jayasena	Kenjiro Taura
Mahmut Kandemir	Martin Vechev
Sam King	Uzi Vishkin
Jens Knoop	Jeremiah Willcock
Milind Kulkarni	Eran Yahav
Patrick Lam	Sudha Yalamanchili
Jaejin Lee	Rio Yokota
Zhiyuan Li	Antonia Zhai
Ben Liblit	Xiaodong Zhang
Kamesh Madduri	Qin Zhao
	Huiyang Zhou

Additional reviewers:

Sriram Aananthakrishnan
Daniel Cederman
Sunita Chandrasekaran
Bapi Chatterjee
Haibo Chen
Wei-Fan Chiang
Nhan Nguyen Dang
Xiaoning Ding
Yin Huai
Herbert Jordan
Changhee Jung
Hongjune Kim
Jungwon Kim
Klaus Kofler
Da Kuang
Rubao Lee
Jun Lee
Sangho Lee

Guodong Li
Ran Liu
Abid Malik
Mario Mendez-Lojo
Leo Meyerovich
Rupesh Nasre
Ioannis Nikolakopoulos
Molly O'Neil
Vitaly Osipov
Jungho Park
Simone Pellegrini
Kaushik Ravichandran
Sangmin Seo
Peter Thoman
Kaibo Wang
Hongtao Yu
Liang Yuan

PPoPP 2013 Sponsor & Supporters

Sponsor:

Supporters:

A Peta-scalable CPU-GPU Algorithm for Global Atmospheric Simulations

Chao Yang[1,5], Wei Xue[2,3], Haohuan Fu[3], Lin Gan[2,3], Linfeng Li[2], Yangtong Xu[2,3],
Yutong Lu[4], Jiachang Sun[1], Guangwen Yang[2,3] and Weimin Zheng[2,3]

1. Institute of Software, Chinese Academy of Sciences, Beijing, China
2. Department of Computer Science & Technology, Tsinghua University, Beijing, China
3. Ministry of Education Key Laboratory for Earth System Modeling, and Center for Earth System Science, Tsinghua University, Beijing, China
4. Department of Computer Science & Technology, National University of Defense Technology, Changsha, Hunan, China
5. State Key Laboratory of Space Weather, Chinese Academy of Sciences, Beijing, China
yangchao@iscas.ac.cn, {xuewei,haohuan}@tsinghua.edu.cn, {lin.gan27,linfeng.li1986,xuyangtong}@gmail.com,
luyut@sina.com, sun@mail.rdcps.ac.cn, {ygw,zwm-dcs}@tsinghua.edu.cn

Abstract

Developing highly scalable algorithms for global atmospheric modeling is becoming increasingly important as scientists inquire to understand behaviors of the global atmosphere at extreme scales. Nowadays, heterogeneous architecture based on both processors and accelerators is becoming an important solution for large-scale computing. However, large-scale simulation of the global atmosphere brings a severe challenge to the development of highly scalable algorithms that fit well into state-of-the-art heterogeneous systems. Although successes have been made on GPU-accelerated computing in some top-level applications, studies on fully exploiting heterogeneous architectures in global atmospheric modeling are still very less to be seen, due in large part to both the computational difficulties of the mathematical models and the requirement of high accuracy for long term simulations.

In this paper, we propose a peta-scalable hybrid algorithm that is successfully applied in a cubed-sphere shallow-water model for global atmospheric simulations. We employ an adjustable partition between CPUs and GPUs to achieve a balanced utilization of the entire hybrid system, and present a pipe-flow scheme to conduct conflict-free inter-node communication on the cubed-sphere geometry and to maximize communication-computation overlap. Systematic optimizations for multithreading on both GPU and CPU sides are performed to enhance computing throughput and improve memory efficiency. Our experiments demonstrate nearly ideal strong and weak scalabilities on up to 3,750 nodes of the Tianhe-1A. The largest run sustains a performance of 0.8 Pflops in double precision (32% of the peak performance), using 45,000 CPU cores and 3,750 GPUs.

Categories and Subject Descriptors D.1.3 [*Programing Techniques*]: Concurrent programming; J.2 [*Physical Sciences and Engineering*]: Earth and atmospheric sciences; F.2.1 [*Analysis of Algorithms and Problem Complexity*]: Numerical Algorithms and Problems

Keywords parallel algorithm; atmospheric modeling; GPU; heterogeneous system; communication-computation overlap; scalability

1. Introduction

Numerical simulation of the global atmosphere, as a key component in climate modeling, is one of the most computationally challenging problems in scientific computing. As scientists inquire to understand dynamic behaviors of the global atmosphere at increasingly fine resolutions [9, 16, 19, 27], the development of highly scalable algorithms for global atmospheric modeling is becoming an urgent demand. Scalable atmospheric solvers not only enable high-fidelity simulation of realistic problems but also lead to dramatic reduction in time-to-solution and substantial increase in accuracy.

Nowadays, heterogeneous architecture based on both CPUs and GPUs is becoming an important solution for large-scale computing. Successes have been made in applying efficient hybrid algorithms to some top-level applications, such as N-body simulations [7, 8, 11], biofluidics simulations [3] and phase-field simulations [26]. Although some promising approaches have been proposed to take advantage of GPU accelerations in regional weather predictions (e.g., [10, 14, 24, 25]), studies on fully exploiting heterogeneous architectures in global atmospheric modeling are still undergoing.

There are several difficulties in efficiently running a global atmospheric model on a petascale heterogeneous supercomputer. One comes from the reality that the global atmosphere is defined on a large computational area (i.e., the Earth) and exhibits a broad range of different spatial and temporal scales. These characteristics of the atmosphere require a global or stencil-based method instead of a particle-based method which is favorable on reducing the coupling of the system (e.g., [8]).

As a success in GPU-accelerated stencil computing, a petaflop performance in single precision has been achieved by Shimokawabe et al. [26] for phase-field simulations on the TSUBAME 2.0 supercomputer (2011 Gordon Bell Prize); but the double-precision performance (260 Tflops) in the same work, which is essential for atmospheric modeling, is relatively low. In order to conduct large-scale global atmospheric modeling on modern heterogeneous systems, we propose a scalable algorithm that works well for a global shallow-water model and sustains promising petascale performance in double precision. In the new algorithm, we apply an adjustable partition between CPUs and GPUs to achieve a balanced utilization of the entire system. And based on that, systematic optimizations for multithreading on both GPU and CPU sides are performed to enhance double-precision computing throughput as well as to improve memory efficiency.

Another difficulty in petascale simulation of the global atmosphere is the selection of the computational mesh for the Earth. The traditional latitude-longitude (Lat-Lon) mesh has been serving the atmospheric community for several decades. However, as the resolution becomes finer, the Lat-Lon mesh becomes unable to maintain satisfying load-balance due to the non-uniformity. For example, it has been claimed by Putman [18] that the Lat-Lon mesh may only scales to a few thousand processors at $0.1°$ horizontal resolution. In this study we use the cubed-sphere mesh among several choices [13, 22, 23, 28] primarily because: (1) it provides a good load-balance even when the number of processors is substantially large; and (2) each patch of the partition helps improve the overall performance in aligned memory access.

Due to the intrinsic curvilinear nature of the sphere, message passing pattern on the cubed-sphere is complicated compared to structured stencil computations such as the work of Shimokawabe et al. [26] in which the computational domain is a three-dimensional cube. To that end, we propose a "pipe-flow" communication scheme for the rearrangement of send/receive pairs across sub-block boundaries in order to maximize communication-computation overlap for the cubed-sphere geometry and to dramatically reduce communication overhead.

The rest of this paper is organized as follows. In Section 2, we introduce the mathematical model and numerical methods used in our global atmospheric simulation. Major algorithms proposed in this paper are presented in Section 3 in detail, after which some key implementation and optimization strategies on the Tianhe-1A are given in Section 4. We then show by several large-scale numerical tests in Section 5 that the proposed hybrid algorithm is petascalable on the Tianhe-1A. The paper is concluded in Section 6.

2. Equations and Discretizations

Among several equation sets that can be used to model the global atmosphere, shallow-water equations (SWEs) exhibit most of the essential characteristics of the atmosphere, thus can be used as a test bed for the development of new algorithms. The SWEs on a rotating sphere can be written as a system of conservation laws:

$$\begin{cases} \dfrac{\partial h}{\partial t} + \nabla \cdot (h\mathbf{v}) = 0, \\ \dfrac{\partial (h\mathbf{v})}{\partial t} + \nabla \cdot (h\mathbf{v} \otimes \mathbf{v}) = \Psi_C + \Psi_G, \end{cases} \quad (1)$$

where h is the thickness of the atmosphere, $\mathbf{v}$ is the velocity vector defined on the surface of the sphere. The two source terms $\Psi_C = -fh(\hat{\mathbf{k}} \times \mathbf{v})$ and $\Psi_G = -gh\nabla(h + b)$ are due to the Coriolis force and the gravity force, respectively. Here $\hat{\mathbf{k}}$ is the unit outward normal on the sphere, f is a Coriolis parameter, g is the gravitational constant and b is the height of the spherical surface describing a variable bottom topography (e.g., mountains).

In this study, we employ a cubed-sphere mesh that is defined by mapping an inscribed cube of the sphere to the surface, as shown in Fig. 1. The computational domain is the six faces of the cube, corresponding to the six patches on the sphere. An advantage of the cubed-sphere geometry is that the SWEs, when written in local coordinates, have an identical expression on the six patches; that is

$$\frac{\partial Q}{\partial t} + \frac{1}{\Lambda}\frac{\partial(\Lambda F^1)}{\partial x^1} + \frac{1}{\Lambda}\frac{\partial(\Lambda F^1)}{\partial x^2} + S = 0, \quad (2)$$

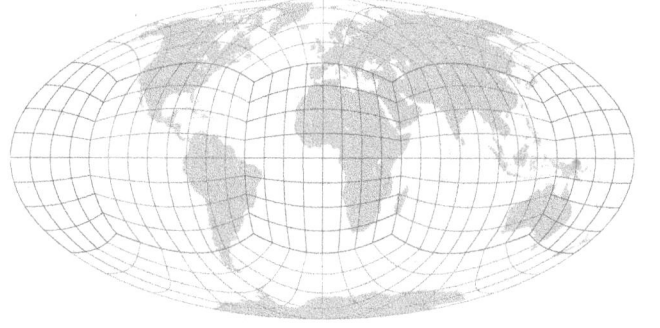

Figure 1. A cubed-sphere mesh on the sphere. The cubed-sphere is obtained by mapping an inscribed cube of the sphere to the surface. Mesh lines on the cubed-sphere coincide with great circles.

where $(x^1, x^2) \in [-\pi/4, \pi/4]$ are the local coordinates of a patch, $Q = (h, hu^1, hu^2)^T$ is the prognostic variable, $F^i = u^iQ$ ($i = 1, 2$) are the convective fluxes and $S = (0, S_1, S_2)^T$ is the source term. Note that the two contravariant components of the velocity, u^1 and u^2, are non-orthogonal. The source term becomes more complicated due to the non-orthogonality of the cubed-sphere, e.g.,

$$S_1 = -\frac{f}{\Lambda}\sum_{i=1}^{2}\left(g_{2i}hu^i\right) + gh\sum_{i=1}^{2}\left(g^{1i}\frac{\partial Z}{\partial x^i}\right) + \sum_{i,j=1}^{2}\Gamma_{ij}^1(hu^iu^j),$$

where $Z = h + b$ is the surface level of the atmosphere. Variable coefficients found therein such as Λ, Γ_{ij}^k, g_{ij} and g^{ij} all have fixed expressions that only depend on their geometric positions; details can be found in, e.g., [20, 21].

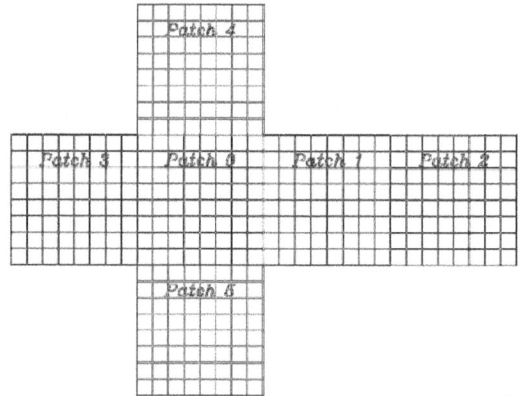

Figure 2. The computational domain of a cubed-sphere consists of six patches that are mapped from the six faces of a cube. Each patch is covered by a uniform rectangular mesh.

Suppose the cubed-sphere is equal-distantly meshed in the computational domain, with $N \times N$ mesh cells in each patch, as seen in Fig. 2. Then we may spatially discretize the SWEs (2) by using, for instance, a cell-centered finite volume method. All prognostic variables h, hu^1 and hu^2 are simultaneously approximated within each mesh cell as a single vector variable

$$Q_{ij}^k(t) = \frac{1}{\Lambda_{i,j}^k}\int_{C(i,j,k)}Q(t)d\sigma, \quad \Lambda_{i,j}^k = \int_{C(i,j,k)}d\sigma,$$

where $C(i, j, k)$ is a mesh cell with index (i, j) in patch k and $d\sigma = \Lambda dx^1 dx^2$. Then a solution vector is composed as $X(t) = [Q_{ij}^k(t)]$ at time frame t. Integrating (2) over each mesh cell leads to a semi-discrete system:

$$\frac{\partial X(t)}{\partial t} + \mathcal{L}(X(t)) = 0, \qquad (3)$$

where $\mathcal{L}(X(t)) = [L_{ij}^k(t)]$ and

$$L_{ij}^k(t) = \frac{4N}{\Lambda_{ij}^k \pi} \int_{\partial C_{i,j,k}} (F^1(t), F^2(t)) \cdot \mathbf{n} ds + S_{ij}^k(t), \qquad (4)$$

with $\mathbf{n}$ being the outward unit normal.

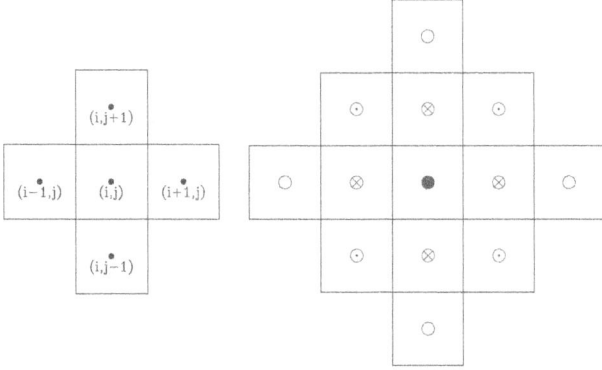

Figure 3. Left: State reconstruction in cell (i, j), values in the adjacent four cells are needed. Right: The 13-point stencil exhibits a diamond shape. Each dot represents a mesh cell on which the three prognostic variables are evaluated.

Cell edge integrations of F^i in (4) are done in a two-step manner. The first step is to reconstruct Q on each cell edge from both limit sides using the value of Q_{ij}^k on several adjacent neighbors. For example, as shown in the left panel of Fig. 3, two reconstructed states of q in the x^1 direction are obtained via

$$q_{i-1/2,j}^+ = \frac{16}{24}q_{i,j} + \frac{1}{24}(q_{i,j-1} + q_{i,j+1} + 3q_{i-1,j} - q_{i+1,j}),$$

$$q_{i+1/2,j}^- = \frac{16}{24}q_{i,j} + \frac{1}{24}(q_{i,j-1} + q_{i,j+1} + 3q_{i+1,j} - q_{i-1,j}).$$

The second step is to calculate F^i on any cell edge using a modified Osher's Riemann solver ([17]) as

$$\int_{\partial C_{i,j,k}} (F^1, F^2) \cdot \mathbf{n} ds \approx \left(\int_{\partial C_{i,j,k}} ds \right) (F^1, F^2) \big|_{Q^*} \cdot \mathbf{n}, \qquad (5)$$

where Q^* is calculated from a nonlinear combination [31] of Q^- and Q^+ on the same edge. Putting the two steps together, the stencil used in the calculation of (4) exhibits a diamond shape, with 13 points in total, as shown in the right panel in Fig. 3. Due to the hyperbolic nature of the SWEs, the computation of Q^* could not be done without a proper upwinding mechanism; that is, "if-else" statements are used in the code to calculate stencils. This type of dependency complicates the problem studied here from those in other applications (e.g., [26]).

To properly pass information between neighboring patches, a two-point linear interpolation is used to calculate corrected values on halos (i.e., ghost cells) across patch interfaces. Velocity components are transformed into a same coordinates system on each patch interface in the calculation of the numerical fluxes to maintain mass conservation, which is important for long-term integrations in climate modeling.

We integrate the SWEs using a second-order accurate total variation-diminishing Runge-Kutta method [6] that reads

$$\overline{X}(t^{(m)}) = X(t^{(m-1)}) - \Delta t \mathcal{L}(X(t^{(m-1)})),$$

$$X(t^{(m)}) = \frac{1}{2}\left\{ X(t^{(m-1)}) + \overline{X}(t^{(m)}) \right\} - \frac{1}{2}\Delta t \mathcal{L}(\overline{X}(t^{(m)})), \qquad (6)$$

in which there are two stencil evaluations at each time step.

3. Algorithms

Before describing the algorithms, we first decompose each patch of the cubed-sphere into small sub-blocks along both dimensions in a same way. Each sub-block is managed by an MPI process that corresponds to a computing node in a CPU-GPU cluster. Halo information from neighboring sub-blocks is updated before computing the stencils in each sub-block, as shown in Fig. 4.

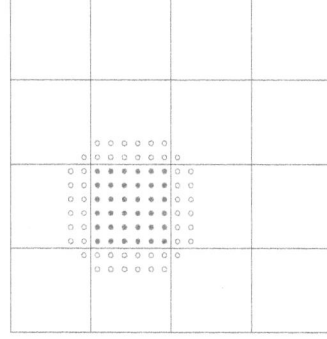

Figure 4. The halo updating pattern for a sub-block that is obtained by decomposing a patch of the cubed-sphere. Mesh cells in a sub-block are shown as solid dots and halo cells required by the sub-block are shown as empty dots.

3.1 CPU-only algorithm

In the CPU-only algorithm, the two stencil operations in (6) are carried out in a same procedure, which is described in Algorithm 1. MPI processes are utilized to manage all sub-blocks in the algorithm. In addition to that, by employing multi-threading techniques such as OpenMP, another level of parallelism can be added within each sub-block in order to further exploit the multi-core CPUs in each computing node.

Algorithm 1 CPU-only algorithm for each stencil cycle.

1: **for** all six patches **do**
2:     **for** all sub-blocks in each patch **do**
3:         Update halo information
4:         Interpolation on halos when necessary
5:         **for** all mesh cells in each sub-block **do**
6:             Compute stencil for the h component
7:             Compute stencil for the hu^1 component
8:             Compute stencil for the hu^2 component
9:         **end for**
10:     **end for**
11: **end for**

The workflow of Algorithm 1 for each stencil cycle is shown in Fig. 5, which consists of four stages: ① halo updating, ② data copying, ③ halo interpolating, and ④ stencil computing. Based on the framework of PETSc (Portable Extensible Toolkit for Scientific computation [2]), we make use of a pair of neighboring communication functions (VecScatterBegin/End) to update halo information. Right after that, an extra data copy is required to fill the buffer for later use. Then a linear interpolation is carried out on the halos across patch interfaces to prepare proper ghost-cell information for stencil computations. Since halo updating needs to be done before the stencil computation part, the communication can not be hidden and will eventually degrade the scalability when the number of MPI

3

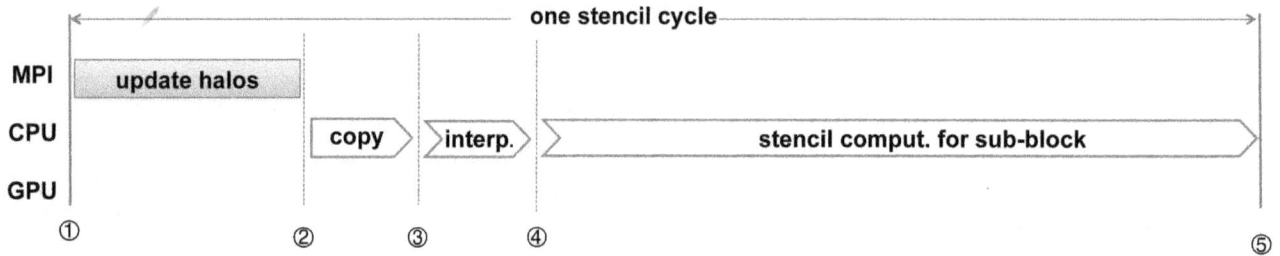

Figure 5. A CPU-only algorithm for the stencil computations. Halo updates are performed with MPI. An extra data copy is needed to prepare data for this stencil cycle before the stencil computations.

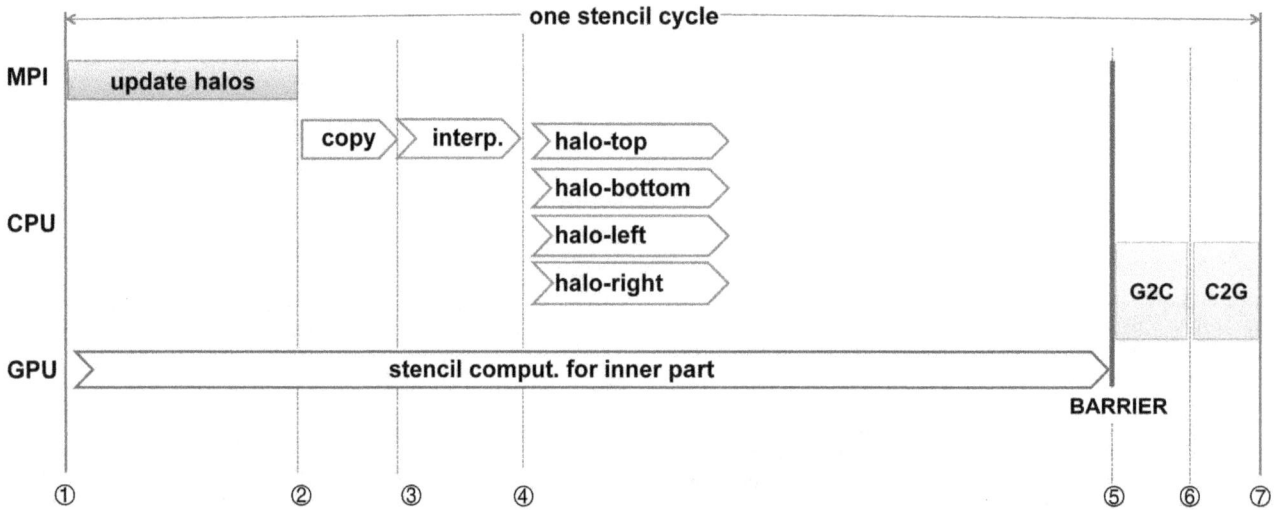

Figure 6. A hybrid CPU-GPU algorithm for the stencil computations. In the figure, "interp." refers to the interpolation on halos; "halo-top/bottom/left/right" refer to the stencil computations for the four halo areas in the outer part of the sub-block; "G2C" refers to the data movement from GPU to CPU and "C2G" refers to the data movement from CPU to GPU.

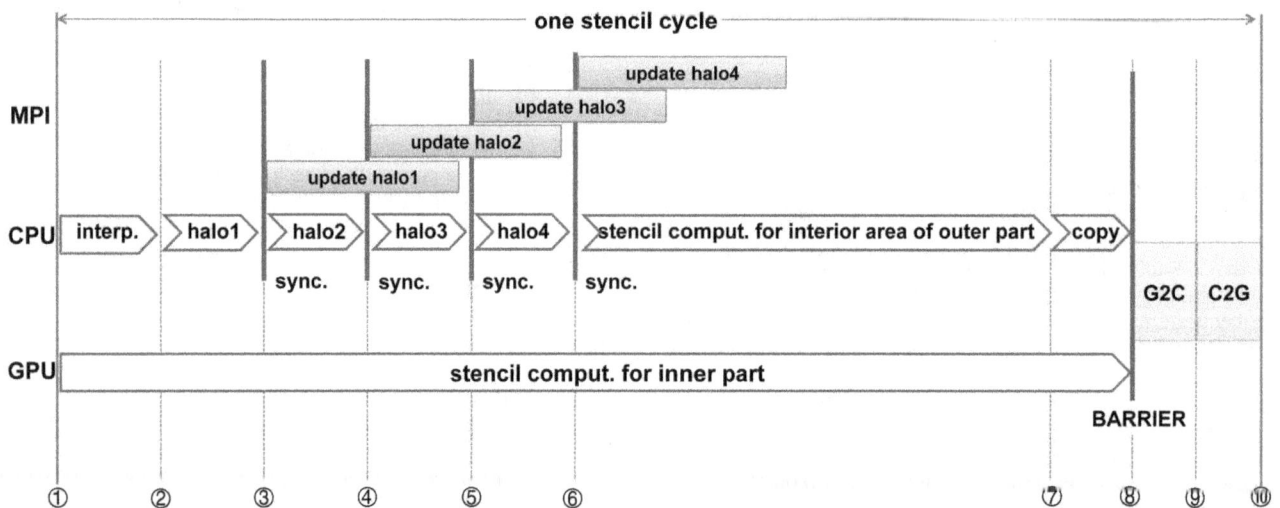

Figure 7. An optimized hybrid CPU-GPU algorithm for the stencil computations. The partition between CPUs and GPUs is adjusted to balance different computing resources and communication-computation overlap is applied in the optimized algorithm. In the figure, "halo-1/2/3/4" refer to stencil computations inside the four halo areas of the outer part.

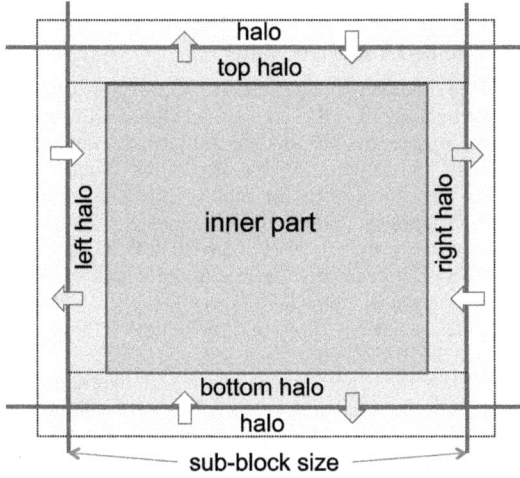

Figure 8. Each sub-block can be decomposed into an inner part that does not need halo information and a 2-layer outer part that is close to the four boundaries of the sub-block.

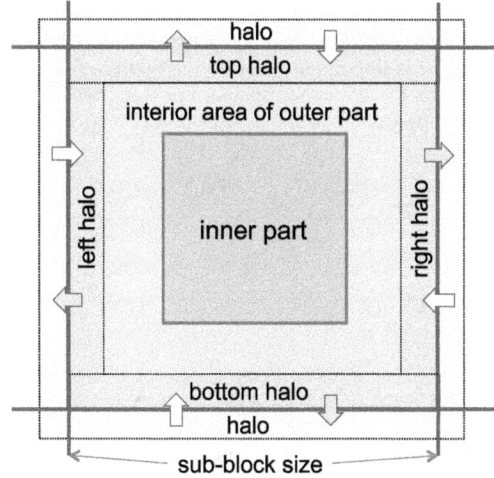

Figure 9. An adjustable partitioning of a sub-block between the CPUs and the GPUs. Compared to the original two-layer outer part, an interior area is introduced in the extended outer part. Accordingly, the size of the inner part assigned to the GPU becomes smaller.

processes becomes large. Besides, the CPU-only approach does not benefit from the GPU resources in a hybrid CPU-GPU system.

3.2 Hybrid CPU-GPU algorithm

In this subsection, we present a hybrid algorithm that is similar to the one employed by Shimokawabe et al. [26] in phase-field simulations. After decomposing the whole domain into sub-blocks, we separate each sub-block into an inner part that does not require halo information and an outer part that contains two layers of halos needed by neighboring sub-blocks, as seen in Fig. 8. Then for each computing node, we assign the GPUs to process the inner part and the CPUs to the outer part. To efficiently process the outer part with multi-threading, we divide it into four areas spanned along the four boundaries of the sub-block, as shown in the same figure. The values computed in the four areas of the outer part are halos needed by neighboring sub-blocks.

A workflow of the hybrid CPU-GPU algorithm for each stencil cycle is given in Fig 6. In the hybrid approach, the CPU code and the GPU code are executed concurrently in two OpenMP sections. While the inner part is processed by the GPUs, the CPUs perform: ① halo updating, ② data copying, ③ halo interpolating, and ④ stencil computing in the outer part. At ⑤, when the calculations on both sides are finished, data exchanging across the interior boundaries between CPUs and GPUs are carried out. The stencil computations for the outer part can be parallelized by utilizing OpenMP threads according to the four divided areas along the boundaries.

3.3 Adjustable partition between CPUs and GPUs

As shown in Fig. 8, when the GPUs are handling the inner part, which is a very large portion of the sub-block, the CPUs process a 2-layer outer part that only contains a very small portion of the sub-block (less than 1% for a $1,024 \times 1,024$ mesh). To make better use of the CPU resources and to improve the overall computing efficiency, we further propose an adjustable partition between CPUs and GPUs.

In the new algorithm, we increase the number of mesh layers in the outer part assigned to the CPUs, and decrease the size of the inner part correspondingly. In addition to the four areas that the original outer part owns, there is an extra interior area in the extended outer part, as shown in Fig. 9. This area is now processed by the CPUs instead of the GPUs to better balance the

computational loads on the two sides. There are several advantages to divide the outer part into an interior area and four two-layer halo areas. Firstly, after stencil computations inside a halo area are finished, the newly calculated values in this halo area can be sent to the neighboring sub-block, which can be done in parallel with stencil computations inside the next halo area. Secondly, stencil computations in the interior area can be performed in parallel with any unfinished halo updating, right after stencil computations in the four halo areas are done. Thirdly, the code to compute stencils for the interior area is more efficient since no judgments are needed to deal with the sub-block boundaries.

Fig. 7 illustrates the workflow of the optimized hybrid algorithm for each stencil cycle. In the new algorithm, because communications and computations are overlapped, proper halo information is already available at the beginning of the stencil cycle. So while the GPUs are processing the inner part, the CPUs: ① do halo interpolation (if necessary); ② conduct stencil computations for halo area-1; ③ conduct stencil computations for halo area-2 and send the computed results to the neighbor sub-block at the same time (similar for ④ and ⑤); ⑥ perform stencil computations in the interior of the outer part after finishing computing halo area-4; ⑦ copy necessary data to the buffer. At ⑧, when the calculations on both sides are finished, data are exchanged between GPUs and CPUs by the end of the stencil cycle.

In the new algorithm, all communications for updating halos are overlapped by the computations on CPU side, which leads to good scalability as well as efficient use of the CPU computing capacity. In addition to that, we can dynamically adjust the partition of a sub-block to achieve a balanced utilization of both CPUs and GPUs. The optimal ratio to partition the sub-blocks is searched automatically by analyzing the critical path in order to minimize the elapsed time.

3.4 "Pipe-flow" scheme for the cubed-sphere

The six patches of the cubed-sphere have different communication patterns that require a carefully designed communication strategy to conduct a conflict-free message passing. For example, as seen in Fig. 2, we should avoid concurrent sending of data from patches 0-3 to patch 4; otherwise both the number of message and the volume of data received by patch 4 are much larger other patches, which results in an imbalanced usage of the network.

Therefore, it is important to specify an optimized sequence of communications for the cubed-sphere. For that purpose, we propose a new "pipe-flow" scheme as shown in Fig. 10. In the "pipe-

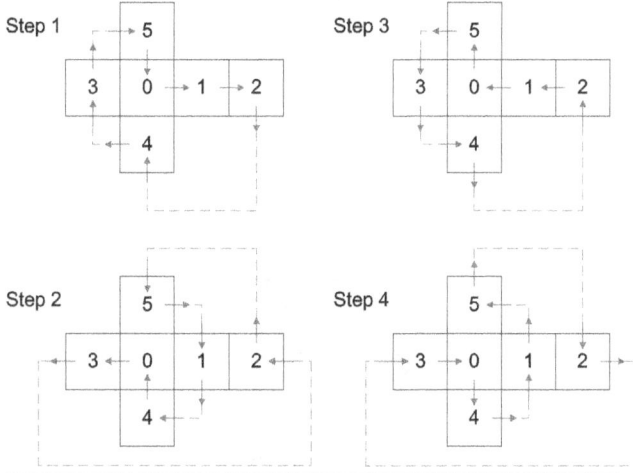

Figure 10. A "pipe-flow scheme to handle the complicated communication pattern of the cubed-sphere. There are four different steps in the arrangement of communications, shown as four panels in the figure. The arrows indicate the directions that data enter and exit the six patches like a flow.

flow" scheme, there are four different steps in the arrangement of communications. Communications are done like a flow going along a closed loop covering the six patches of the cubed-sphere, with inlet/outlet directions of the flow on each patch showing in the figure.

The direction of the "pipe-flow" inside each patch is decided by the inlet and outlet directions. The flow goes straight if the inlet and outlet of the flow are on opposite sides of the patch. Otherwise, directions of the flow are more complicated, as shown in Fig. 11.

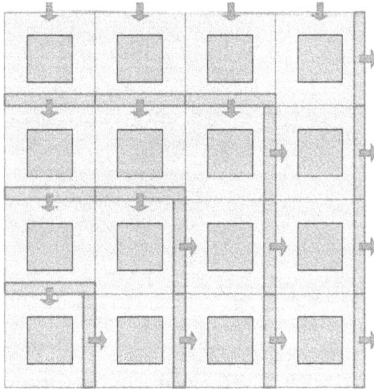

Figure 11. Directions of the "pipe-flow" inside a specific patch of the cubed-sphere. The square shaded regions represent the inner parts of sub-blocks, and the narrow shade regions represent the halos to be sent.

At any step of the "pipe-flow" scheme, each process only has one "send" and one "receive" to communicate with other processes. In this way, balanced and efficient message exchange steps are achieved for inter-process communication, leading to substantial improvement of the parallel performance when the number of processes is large.

4. Implementation & Optimization on Tianhe-1A

4.1 The Tianhe-1A supercomputer

As a petascale supercomputer, Tianhe-1A [32] features an MPP architecture of hybrid CPU-GPU computing. Unlike GPU-rich petascale systems such as the TSUBAME 2.0 [26], the deployment of CPUs and GPUs is different in the design of the Tianhe-1A supercomputer. In the system, there are totally 7,168 computing nodes, each of which consists of two six-core Intel X5670 CPUs with 32GB local memory and one NVIDIA M2050 GPU with 3GB onboard memory. The peak performance of the whole system is 4.7 Pflops in which the 100,352 GPU cores (i.e., 3,211,264 CUDA cores) provide around 3.7 Pflops and the other 1.0 Pflops are provided by the 86,016 CPU cores.

A proprietary high-speed interconnection network, the TH-net [30], is designed and implemented to enhance the communication capabilities of the system. The topology of the TH-net is an optoelectronic hybrid, hierarchical fat tree. The MPI implementation on the Tianhe-1A is customized to achieve high-bandwidth and low-latency data transfers, and the inter-node bandwidth of point-to-point unidirectional MPI operations is as high as 6,340 MB/s.

4.2 Optimization of the GPU stencil code

In the Tianhe-1A, each node is equipped with an NVIDIA Fermi M2050 GPU consisting of 14 streaming multiprocessors (SM) and 3 GB onboard memory. Each SM contains 32 streaming processors that can compute concurrently in a similar flavor to vector processors. Meanwhile, each SM also provides 64 KB local storage that can be configured as either 48-KB shared memory plus 16-KB L1 cache (the default mode) or 16-KB shared memory plus 48-KB L1 cache. To exploit the computing capacity of the GPUs in the Tianhe-1A, we employ CUDA version 4.0 for GPU programming.

According to (6), for each time step, there are two stages of stencil calculations that can be performed in a similar way. The only differences are the input/output vectors and their coefficients. The output vector of the first stencil calculation is used as the input vector of the second stencil calculation. Therefore, instead of copying the result back to the host (CPU) memory after the first stage is done, the data can remain in the GPU memory for the later use in the second stage. Only the information across interior boundaries needs to be exchanged with the host in between of the two stages. For that purpose, we map the two stages of stencil calculations in (6) into two CUDA kernel functions on the GPU in order to reduce the cost of data transfer. In addition to that, we implement another two kernels to reorder and transpose the interior boundary data that are needed by the CPUs.

On the GPU side, the two stencil kernels are clearly the most time-consuming part. A systematic optimization is performed on both the computation and memory operations to maximize the throughput for the stencil kernels. To provide a detailed description about different optimization techniques that we have considered, we go through a number of different versions of the CUDA codes in what follows.

4.2.1 Baseline

As a starting point, a baseline GPU code can be directly implemented by parallelizing the stencil computations inside the inner part of the sub-block. As shown in Fig. 12, for a NX by NY sub-block, we employ a thread grid that contains BX by BY thread blocks. Each thread block consists of TX by TY different threads. The configuration of the grid and block should satisfy that TX·BX=NX and TY·BY=NY. In this way, each point in the mesh is processed with a GPU thread. Note that for the GPU side, we do not need to compute the stencils for the mesh cells that are in the halo (shown as empty dots in Fig. 12). Therefore we can store all mesh

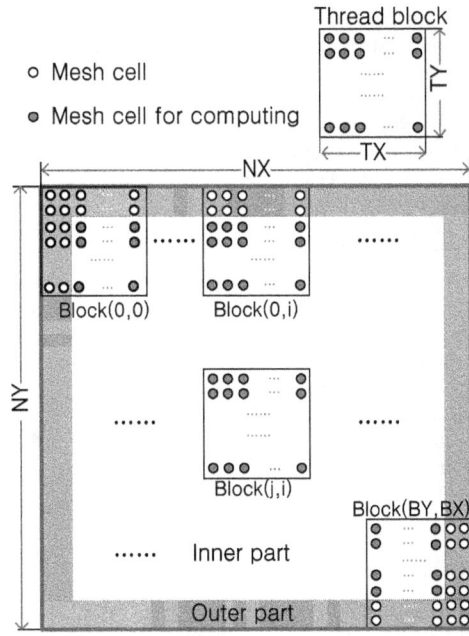

Figure 12. Strategy to compute stencils for the inner part of a sub-block using concurrent GPU threads. Mesh cells in the inner part are drawn as solid dots. And mesh cells in the halo which are needed by the inner part are drawn as empty dots.

cells of a sub-block in the GPU memory but only perform stencil calculations for the mesh cells owned by the inner part (shown as solid dots in Fig. 12).

Choosing the right size for the thread block is important for achieving a high parallel performance on the GPU platform. A general rule is to keep both TX and TY as multiples of 16. This is mainly because, on the NVIDIA M2050 GPU, threads are scheduled and executed in the unit of half-warp (16 threads). Therefore, by grouping and aligning both the arithmetic operations and memory accesses in the multiples of 16, we can generally achieve a more efficient utilization of both the 32 cores in each SM and the 16 memory banks of the shared memory.

For our specific kernels of computing nonlinear stencil terms, our experiments show that 16 by 16 is a proper thread block configuration (one thread per each point) that provides a good balance among different resources. As shown in the first point of Fig. 13, our baseline code processes a 1,024×1,024 sub-block in 117 ms.

4.2.2 Computing auxiliary vectors in run time

Several variable coefficients such as the tensor terms, the Coriolis source term and the topographic term, are needed in the evaluation of the nonlinear stencils. Note that those coefficients are only dependent of their geometry positions and remain unchanged during the whole calculation. Therefore it is a standard practice to compute and store them as auxiliary vectors for reuse. However, on the GPU side, the kernel functions need to read in up to 20 different auxiliary vectors, which is a large bandwidth requirement to the system. As a result, in the baseline implementation, only around 11% of the GPU computing capacity is utilized.

Therefore, in the new implementation, we adopt the strategy of computing 18 out of the 20 auxiliary vectors in run time rather than accessing them in global memory. Only the Coriolis force and the topographic data are stored as auxiliary vectors. Although the total computing amount is increased significantly, the actual processing time for a 1,024×1,024 sub-block is reduced from 117 ms to 48 ms,

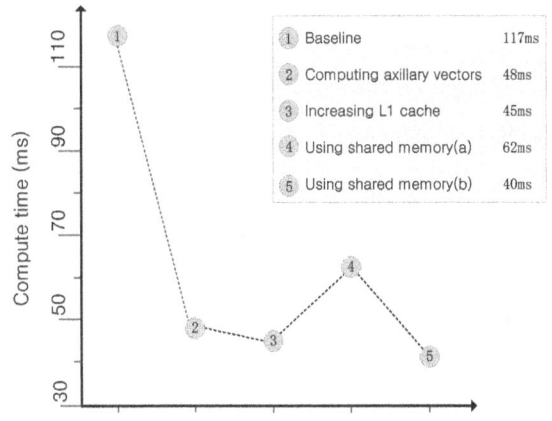

Figure 13. Comparison among different optimization techniques applied in the GPU stencil kernels.

shown as the second point in Fig. 13. Computing most auxiliary vectors in run time leads to great improvement of performance due to the substantial reduction of memory bandwidth requirements on the GPU side.

4.2.3 Increasing L1 cache

To further reduce the cost of the memory access, we can choose either to increase the size of the L1 cache or to use the shared memory. By increasing the size of the L1 cache from the default 16 KB to 48 KB, we further reduce the computation time from 48 ms to 45 ms, shown as the third point in Fig. 13.

4.2.4 Using shared memory

We can also move some of the frequently-used (especially the ones used by different threads in the same block) data into the shared memory to further improve data reuse. Due to the memory hierarchy of CUDA, shared memory can be accessible to all threads in the same block and temporarily store data during the lifetime of corresponding thread block. Compared with the global memory, the shared memory provides a much higher memory bandwidth and enables data reuse among all the threads in the same block. Applying a similar idea to the 3D stencil work by P. Micikevicius [15], we can load all the points in a thread block and the corresponding halos into the shared memory at the beginning of the computation, so that all the threads can reuse the neighboring points in the computation afterwards. For computing the 13-point stencil as shown in Fig. 3, each point in the middle of the block can be reused by 8 threads on average.

However, by adding the technique for using shared memory into our previous version, instead of achieving a better performance, the computation time for a 1,024×1,024 sub-block increases to 62 ms, shown as the forth point in Fig. 13. This is later found out to be a result of a low occupancy of the SM. In a 16 by 16 thread block, we need 12 KB shared memory to store all the points of the thread block and the halos. As the SM is under the configuration of 48-KB L1 cache and 16-KB shared memory, we can only support one thread block in one SM. By switching to the configuration of 16-KB L1 cache and 48-KB shared memory, we lose some cache hits but can then support more thread blocks in one SM. After switching the configuration, the shared memory version provides a computation time of 40 ms, shown as the fifth point in Fig. 13.

4.3 Optimization of the CPU stencil code

As shown in Fig. 7, a number of operations including halo updating, data copying, halo interpolating, stencil computing and data trans-

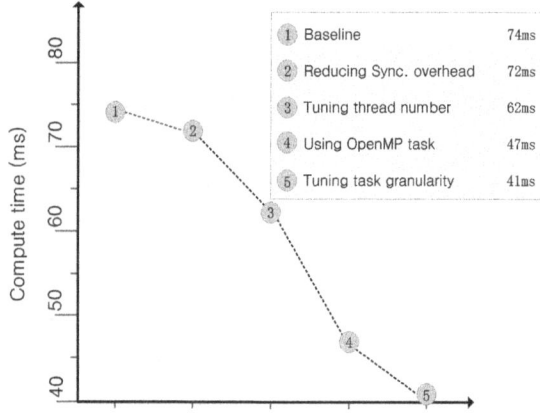

Figure 14. Comparison among different threading optimization techniques applied in the CPU stencil kernels.

ferring between CPUs and GPUs need to be performed on the CPU side. Among them, the most time-consuming part is to compute the stencils for the outer part within each sub-block. To improve the performance of stencil computation on the CPU side, we follow the idea from Datta et al. [5] by using array padding and in-loop vectorization techniques that help increase the in-core computing efficiency. In addition to that, we investigate several threading optimization techniques to maximize the computing throughput of the multi-core CPUs in each computing node.

As a starting point, we divide the interior area of the outer parts into four chunks along the four boundaries of the sub-block and parallelize them with separate parallel regions. To avoid false sharing and to reduce scheduling overhead, the OpenMP *for* worksharing construct is invoked at the outer loop of the stencil computation with static scheduling strategy over 12 threads. In addition to that, thread affinity is introduced to minimize the overhead of context switching. As mentioned in 4.2.2, instead of accessing the 20 auxiliary vectors, we compute 18 of them in run time so that the memory bandwidth requirement is substantially reduced. For our baseline CPU code, 74ms are needed to process the steps from ① to ⑧ in Fig. 7 for each stencil cycle, shown as the first point in Fig. 14. In the test, the sub-block size is $1,156 \times 1,156$ and the width of the outer part is adjusted to 66.

In the baseline implementation of the optimized hybrid algorithm, there are four barriers after processing each of the four interior chunks of the outer part, as seen in Fig. 7. The first three barriers are responsible for unexpected synchronization overhead, and can be eliminated by using the OpenMP *nowait* clause. Shown in Fig. 14 as the second point, by eliminating the three implicit synchronizations, the time cost is reduced from 74ms to 72ms.

Although most auxiliary vectors are calculated in run time in stead of being accessed from memory, there are still thirteen 3-component variables and two auxiliary coefficients needed during each 13-point stencil calculation, which may lower the computing throughput. To effectively hide the memory access latency, we increase the number of threads to twice as the number of CPU cores and the time cost is further reduced to 62ms, shown in Fig. 14 as the third point.

Since the four interior chunks of the outer part exhibit different data layouts (i.e., vertical v.s. horizontal) which might lead to load imbalance between threads, we try to schedule the threads dynamically and to reduce task granularity for each thread in order to maintain good load balance. However, no improvement has been observed. We then employ the OpenMP *task* construct [1] to achieve better scheduling efficiency. As a result, the time cost is

reduced to 47ms, shown as the fourth point in Fig. 14. To further balance the trade-off between scheduling overhead and load imbalance, we search for the best task granularity for different chunks of the outer part and the time cost is eventually reduced to 41ms, shown as the fifth point in Fig. 14. Here we find the optimal number of threads is 12, which is equal to the number of CPU cores in each computing node of the Tianhe-1A.

5. Parallel Performance and Analysis

In this section, we first present numerical results on a model problem to validate the code and then conduct a more realistic simulation using real topographic data. Both strong and weak scaling results on the Tianhe-1A are presented and comparisons among the CPU-only and the hybrid approaches are provided.

To conduct an accurate performance measurement of our hybrid application that uses both CPUs and GPUs, we count the number of double-precision arithmetic operations in the code using three different methods:

- A manual count of the double-precision arithmetic operations in the code. We count "$+, -, \times, \div$" as one flop, while counting trigonometric computations as five.

- A direct measurement by running the CPU version of the code (the GPU version uses identical code for computing) with Performance API (PAPI) [4].

- An estimate of the double-precision arithmetic operations based on analysis of the GPU assembly code generated from the CUDA tool "cuobjdump".

The second and the third methods provide almost identical flop count of the application, while the result of the first method (manually counting) is around 10% higher. This is possibly due to compiler optimizations. In our study, we employ the second method (measurement by PAPI) to analyze the performance of our code.

5.1 Model validation and simulation results

We start the numerical tests from a model problem, zonal flow over an isolated mountain, which is taken from the benchmark test set of Williamson et al. [29]. In this test, a geostrophically steady-state flow impinges from west to east over a compactly supported mountain of conical shape. Fig. 15 shows the surface level distribution of

Figure 15. Surface level distribution of the atmosphere at day 15 in the isolated mountain test. Results are obtained on a $10,240 \times 10,240 \times 6$ cubed-sphere mesh using 1,536 nodes of the Tianhe-1A. The conical mountain is outlined by the dotted circle in the figure.

the atmosphere at day 15 using a $10,240 \times 10,240 \times 6$ cubed-sphere mesh (around 1-km resolution) on 1,536 nodes of the Tianhe-1A. In the figure, a Rossby-type gravity wave propagates all around the

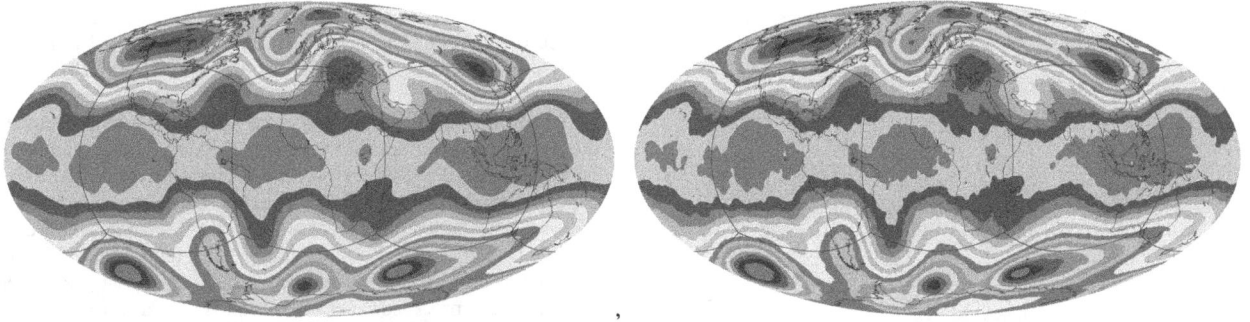

Figure 16. Surface level distribution of the atmosphere at day 15 in the real-topography test. We compare results at a 40-km resolution (left panel) and a 1-km resolution (right panel).

globe due to the presence of the mountain, which is in good agreement to published results (e.g., [12]).

We then conduct a more realistic simulation of the global atmosphere by inputing real topographic data of the Earth. The initial condition in this test is similar to that of the isolated mountain except that the surface level of the atmosphere is raised to avoid negative flow thickness due to the high elevations of some mountain ranges such as the Himalayas. Comparisons between results at a low-resolution of 40 km and a high-resolution of 1 km are given in Fig. 16, which clearly shows that as the resolution becomes finer, more details at small scales are discovered in the simulation.

5.2 Weak scaling results

In the weak scaling tests, we fix the mesh size on each sub-block to be $1,024 \times 1,024$ and then run the tests with different numbers of computing nodes (MPI processes). Configurations of the mesh size and the peak performance of available CPUs and GPUs in the Tianhe-1A are listed in Table 1. As the number of computing nodes increases from 6 to 3,750, the total number of unknowns is raised from 18.8 millions to nearly 12 billions.

Table 1. Configurations for the weak scaling tests.

Number of nodes	Mesh size	Peak of (CPU, GPU)
$6 = 6 \times 1 \times 1$	$6 \times 1024 \times 1024$	$(0.8, 3.1)$ Tflops
$24 = 6 \times 2 \times 2$	$6 \times 2048 \times 2048$	$(3.3, 12)$ Tflops
$96 = 6 \times 4 \times 4$	$6 \times 4096 \times 4096$	$(14, 49)$ Tflops
$384 = 6 \times 8 \times 8$	$6 \times 8192 \times 8192$	$(54, 198)$ Tflops
$864 = 6 \times 12 \times 12$	$6 \times 12288 \times 12288$	$(121, 445)$ Tflops
$1536 = 6 \times 16 \times 16$	$6 \times 16384 \times 16384$	$(216, 791)$ Tflops
$2400 = 6 \times 20 \times 20$	$6 \times 20480 \times 20480$	$(337, 1236)$ Tflops
$2904 = 6 \times 22 \times 22$	$6 \times 22528 \times 22528$	$(408, 1496)$ Tflops
$3750 = 6 \times 25 \times 25$	$6 \times 25600 \times 25600$	$(527, 1931)$ Tflops

In Fig. 17, we show the weak scaling performance of the proposed algorithms tested on the Tianhe-1A. In the tests, we compare four different algorithms, namely: the single-core CPU-only approach, the CPU-only approach with multi-threading, the hybrid CPU-GPU approach, and the optimized hybrid CPU-GPU approach with the adjustable partition between CPUs/GPUs and the "pipe-flow" scheme for communication-computation overlap. Except for the first approach in which there is no multi-threading, all the 12 CPU cores in each computing nodes are utilized in the tests.

As shown in the figure, not surprisingly, without using multi-threading, the CPU-only approach provides the lowest aggregate performance, which is improved by about 9.95 times when multi-threading is turned on. The hybrid CPU-GPU approach sustains an

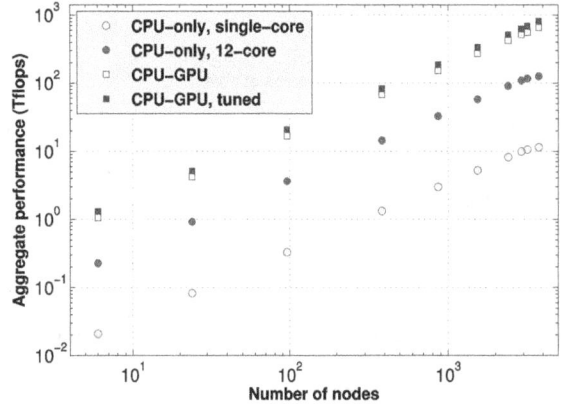

Figure 17. Weak scaling results on the Tianhe-1A. Shown in the figure are aggregate performances obtained by using: (○) the single-core CPU-only approach, (●) the multi-threaded CPU-only approach, (□) the hybrid CPU-GPU approach, and (■) the optimized hybrid CPU-GPU approach.

aggregate performance of about 658 Tflops, which is around 56 times better than that of the single-core CPU-only approach. When the optimized hybrid CPU-GPU approach is employed, thanks to the adjustable partition between CPUs and GPUs and the "pipe-flow" scheme for communication-computation overlap, the aggregate performance is further improved to 809.7 Tflops, which is around 32.8% of the peak performance.

The weak scalability of the CPU-only approach, no matter whether multi-threading is turned on or off, slightly suffers from higher communication overhead when larger number of nodes are utilized. On the other hand, the hybrid CPU-GPU approaches are able to achieve nearly ideal parallel efficiency even when the number of nodes is exceedingly large. This is because communications are totally hidden behind computations on the GPU side in the two hybrid approaches.

5.3 Strong scaling results

In the strong scaling tests, we fix the total problem size and increase the number of computing nodes. The total compute time should decrease as more computing nodes are utilized. However, because the computation-communication ratio becomes smaller at a higher node count, which will eventually affect the scalability, ideal strong scaling results are hard to obtain. Even a small fluctuation in the MPI communication will degrade the performance in the strong scaling tests. Therefore, successful communication-computation overlap is a key to achieve expected scaling results.

Number of nodes	384	1536	2400	3750
Time (s)	56.9	14.4	9.4	5.9
Efficiency	1.00	0.99	0.97	0.98
Agg. Tflops	84.5	335.1	513.4	809.6

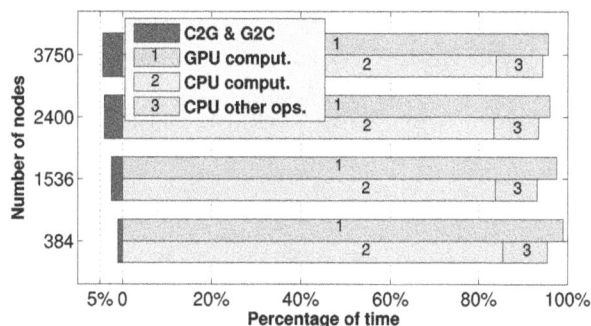

Figure 18. Strong scaling performance of the optimized hybrid CPU-GPU approach. The test results are obtained by running the code for 100 time steps using a $25{,}200 \times 25{,}200 \times 6$ mesh on the Tianhe-1A. The upper table shows the parallel efficiency and the aggregate performance in the strong scaling tests. The lower figure provides a breakdown of elapsed time.

We run the strong scaling tests using a $25{,}200 \times 25{,}200 \times 6$ mesh on the Tianhe-1A. Fig. 18 shows the strong scaling performance of the optimized hybrid CPU-GPU approach. For each node count, we calculate the averaged mesh size on each computing node and assign a proper portion of the outer layers to CPUs so that optimal performance can be achieved. As indicated in the top table of Fig. 18, nearly ideal strong scaling efficiency is sustained and an aggregate performance of 809.6 Tflops is delivered when 3,750 nodes are utilized.

There is only a very slight loss of scalability in the strong scaling tests, for which the reason is analyzed in the bottom figure of Fig. 18. In the figure, we can see that the computations as well as other operations (including interpolations and buffer preparations) on the CPU side (marked as "2" and "3" respectively) are totally hidden behind the computations on the GPU side (marked as "1"). The only part in the algorithm that could not be overlapped is the data transfer between CPUs and GPUs. Although this part only takes a small portion (less than 5%) of the total computing time, it still affects the parallel efficiency at larger node counts. We would like to point out here that both the parallel efficiency and the aggregate performance in the strong scaling results are superior to those in [26], in which communications were not totally overlapped with computations and the computing capacities from the CPUs were not fully exploited.

6. Concluding remarks

In this paper, we present a peta-scalable CPU-GPU algorithm for global atmospheric simulations. The major contributions of our work include: (1) an adjustable partitioning method that makes an equally-efficient utilization of both CPUs and GPUs in a heterogeneous system; (2) a "pipe-flow" communication scheme that conducts balanced and conflict-free message passing on the cubed-sphere geometry; and (3) systematic optimizations of the GPU and CPU codes that provide excellent performance for double-precision atmospheric simulation. With the above techniques combined, we manage to achieve nearly-ideal strong and weak scalabilities (both

over 98%) on the Tianhe-1A. Our largest run sustains a performance of 0.8 Pflops in double precision to solve 12-billion unknowns using 3,750 nodes (45,000 cores and 3,750 GPUs) of the petascale system.

According to the strong and weak scaling results presented in the paper, the communication is totally hidden by the computation on CPUs and GPUs. Therefore, the proposed hybrid algorithm is expected to maintain a similar level of scalability when running with an even larger number of nodes on the Tianhe-1A. We also remark here that: (1) the basic idea of the adjustable CPU-GPU partition is not only applicable to other heterogeneous systems with different processor/accelerator ratios, but also extendable to a homogenous many-core system by redefining the partition; (2) although the new "pipe-flow" communication scheme is specifically designed for the cubed-sphere for conflict-free communication, similar ideas can be applied to other semi-structured geodesic meshes (e.g., [23, 28]) that are also becoming increasingly popular in global atmospheric modeling.

Acknowledgments

This work was partially supported by NSF China under grants 91130023 & 61170075, by 973 and 863 Programs of China under grants 2010CB951903, 2011CB309701 & 2010AA012301, and by Specialized Research Fund for State Key Laboratories in China. We would like to thank Xiao-Chuan Cai for insightful discussion on scalable algorithms in climate modeling, thank Paulius Micikevicius for giving suggestions on optimizing the CUDA kernel, and thank NSCC-TJ for providing access to the Tianhe-1A. This research received loads of supports from Guoxing Yuan, Canquan Yang, Guang Suo, Min Xie, Juan Chen, Xiangfei Meng, Jinghua Feng and Bin Xu. The authors are also grateful to the anonymous reviewers for valuable comments that have greatly improved the paper.

References

[1] E. Ayguade, N. Copty, A. Duran, J. Hoeflinger, Y. Lin, F. Massaioli, X. Teruel, P. Unnikrishnan, and G. Zhang. The design of OpenMP tasks. *IEEE Transactions on Parallel and Distributed Systems*, 20(3): 404–418, march 2009.

[2] S. Balay, K. Buschelman, W. D. Gropp, D. Kaushik, M. Knepley, L. C. McInnes, B. F. Smith, and H. Zhang. *PETSc Users Manual*. Argonne National Laboratory, 2010.

[3] M. Bernaschi, M. Bisson, T. Endo, S. Matsuoka, M. Fatica, and S. Melchionna. Petaflop biofluidics simulations on a two million-core system. In *Proceedings of 2011 International Conference for High Performance Computing, Networking, Storage and Analysis (SC '11)*, pages 4:1–4:12, New York, NY, USA, 2011. ACM.

[4] S. Browne, J. Dongarra, N. Garner, G. Ho, and P. Mucci. A portable programming interface for performance evaluation on modern processors. *Int. J. High Perform. Comput. Appl.*, 14(3):189–204, Aug. 2000.

[5] K. Datta, M. Murphy, V. Volkov, S. Williams, J. Carter, L. Oliker, D. Patterson, J. Shalf, and K. Yelick. Stencil computation optimization and auto-tuning on state-of-the-art multicore architectures. In *Proceedings of the 2008 ACM/IEEE conference on Supercomputing (SC '08)*, pages 4:1–4:12, Piscataway, NJ, USA, 2008. IEEE Press.

[6] S. Gottlieb, C.-W. Shu, and E. Tadmore. Strong stability preserving high-order time integration methods. *SIAM Review*, 43:89–112, 2001.

[7] T. Hamada and K. Nitadori. 190 TFlops astrophysical N-body simulation on a cluster of GPUs. In *Proceedings of the 2010 ACM/IEEE International Conference for High Performance Computing, Networking, Storage and Analysis (SC '10)*, pages 1–9, Washington, DC, USA, 2010. IEEE Computer Society.

[8] T. Hamada, T. Narumi, R. Yokota, K. Yasuoka, K. Nitadori, and M. Taiji. 42 TFlops hierarchical N-body simulations on GPUs with

applications in both astrophysics and turbulence. In *Proceedings of the Conference on High Performance Computing Networking, Storage and Analysis (SC '09)*, pages 62:1–62:12, New York, NY, USA, 2009. ACM.

[9] K. Hamilton and W. Ohfuchi, editors. *High Resolution Numerical Modelling of the Atmosphere and Ocean*. Springer, 2008.

[10] T. Henderson, J. Middlecoff, J. Rosinski, M. Govett, and P. Madden. Experience applying Fortran GPU compilers to numerical weather prediction. In *Proceedings of 2011 Symposium on Application Accelerators in High Performance Computing (SAAHPC 2011)*, pages 34–41, 2011.

[11] Q. Hu, N. A. Gumerov, and R. Duraiswami. Scalable fast multipole methods on distributed heterogeneous architectures. In *Proceedings of 2011 International Conference for High Performance Computing, Networking, Storage and Analysis (SC '11)*, pages 36:1–36:12, New York, NY, USA, 2011. ACM.

[12] R. Jakob-Chien, J. J. Hack, and D. L. Williamson. Spectral transform solutions to the shallow water test set. *J. Comput. Phys.*, 119:164–187, 1995.

[13] A. Kageyama and T. Sato. Yin-Yang grid: An overset grid in spherical geometry. *Geochem. Geophys. Geosyst.*, 5, 2004.

[14] J. Michalakes and M. Vachharajani. GPU acceleration of numerical weather prediction. In *Proceedings of IEEE International Symposium on Parallel and Distributed Processing (IPDPS 2008)*, pages 1–7, 2008.

[15] P. Micikevicius. 3D Finite Difference Computation on GPUs using CUDA. In *Proc. 2nd Workshop on General Purpose Processing on Graphic Processing Units*, pages 79–84, 2009.

[16] H. Miura, M. Satoh, T. Nasuno, A. T. Noda, and K. Oouchi. A Madden-Julian Oscillation event realistically simulated by a global cloud-resolving model. *Science*, 318:1763–1765, 2007.

[17] S. Osher and S. Chakravarthy. Upwind schemes and boundary conditions with applications to Euler equations in general geometries. *J. Comput. Phys.*, 50:447–481, 1983.

[18] W. M. Putman. *Development of the finite-volume dynamical core on the cubed-sphere*. PhD thesis, The Florida State University, 2007.

[19] W. M. Putman and M. Suarez. Cloud-system resolving simulations with the NASA Goddard Earth Observing System global atmospheric model (GEOS-5). *Geophys. Res. Lett.*, 38, 2011.

[20] C. Ronchi, R. Iacono, and P. Paolucci. The cubed sphere: A new method for the solution of partial differential equations in spherical geometry. *J. Comput. Phys.*, 124:93–114, 1996.

[21] J. A. Rossmanith. A wave propagation method for hyperbolic systems on the sphere. *J. Comput. Phys.*, 213:629–658, 2006.

[22] R. Sadourny. Conservative finite-difference approximations of the primitive equations on quasi-uniform spherical grids. *Mon. Wea. Rev.*, 100:211–224, 1972.

[23] R. Sadourny, A. Arakawa, and Y. Mintz. Integration of the nondivergent barotropic vorticity equation with an icosahedral-hexagonal grid for the sphere. *Mon. Wea. Rev.*, 96:351–356, 1968.

[24] T. Shimokawabe, T. Aoki, C. Muroi, J. Ishida, K. Kawano, T. Endo, A. Nukada, N. Maruyama, and S. Matsuoka. An 80-fold speedup, 15.0 TFlops full GPU acceleration of non-hydrostatic weather model ASUCA production code. In *Proceedings of the 2010 ACM/IEEE International Conference for High Performance Computing, Networking, Storage and Analysis (SC '10)*, pages 1–11, Washington, DC, USA, 2010. IEEE Computer Society.

[25] T. Shimokawabe, T. Aoki, J. Ishida, K. Kawano, and C. Muroi. 145 TFlops performance on 3990 GPUs of TSUBAME 2.0 supercomputer for an operational weather prediction. *Procedia Computer Science*, 4: 1535 – 1544, 2011. Proceedings of the International Conference on Computational Science (ICCS 2011).

[26] T. Shimokawabe, T. Aoki, T. Takaki, T. Endo, A. Yamanaka, N. Maruyama, A. Nukada, and S. Matsuoka. Peta-scale phase-field simulation for dendritic solidification on the TSUBAME 2.0 supercomputer. In *Proceedings of 2011 International Conference for High Performance Computing, Networking, Storage and Analysis (SC '11)*, pages 3:1–3:11, New York, NY, USA, 2011. ACM.

[27] S. Shingu, H. Takahara, H. Fuchigami, M. Yamada, Y. Tsuda, W. Ohfuchi, Y. Sasaki, K. Kobayashi, T. Hagiwara, S.-i. Habata, M. Yokokawa, H. Itoh, and K. Otsuka. A 26.58 Tflops global atmospheric simulation with the spectral transform method on the Earth Simulator. In *Proceedings of the 2002 ACM/IEEE conference on Supercomputing (SC '02)*, pages 1–19, Los Alamitos, CA, USA, 2002. IEEE Computer Society Press.

[28] D. L. Williamson. Integration of the barotropic vorticity equation on a spherical geodesic grid. *Tellus*, 20:642–653, 1968.

[29] D. L. Williamson, J. B. Drake, J. J. Hack, R. Jakob, and P. N. Swarztrauber. A standard test set for numerical approximations to the shallow water equations in spherical geometry. *J. Comput. Phys.*, 102:211–224, 1992.

[30] M. Xie, Y. Lu, K. Wang, L. Liu, H. Cao, and X. Yang. The Tianhe-1A interconnect and message passing services. *IEEE Micro*, 1, 2012.

[31] C. Yang and X.-C. Cai. Parallel multilevel methods for implicit solution of shallow water equations with nonsmooth topography on the cubed-sphere. *J. Comput. Phys.*, 230:2523–2539, 2011.

[32] X.-J. Yang, X.-K. Liao, K. Lu, Q.-F. Hu, J.-Q. Song, and J.-S. Su. The Tianhe-1A supercomputer: Its hardware and software. *J. Comput. Sci. Tech.*, 26, 2011.

Adoption Protocols for Fanout-Optimal Fault-Tolerant Termination Detection

Jonathan Lifflander, Phil Miller, Laxmikant V. Kale

University of Illinois Urbana-Champaign
{jliffl2,mille121,kale}@illinois.edu

Abstract

Termination detection is relevant for signaling completion (all processors are idle and no messages are in flight) of many operations in distributed systems, including work stealing algorithms, dynamic data exchange, and dynamically structured computations. In the face of growing supercomputers with increasing likelihood that each job may encounter faults, it is important for high-performance computing applications that rely on termination detection that such an algorithm be able to tolerate the inevitable faults. We provide a trio of new practical fault tolerance schemes for a standard approach to termination detection that are easy to implement, present low overhead in both theory and practice, and have scalable costs when recovering from faults. These schemes tolerate all single-process faults, and are probabilistically tolerant of faults affecting multiple processes. We combine the theoretical failure probabilities we can calculate for each algorithm with historical fault records from real machines to show that these algorithms have excellent overall survivability.

Categories and Subject Descriptors D.1.3 [*Concurrent Programming*]: Parallel & distributed programming; D.4.5 [*Reliability*]: Fault-tolerance

Keywords Termination Detection, Fault Tolerance

1. Introduction

As parallel programs scale to larger systems, the occurrence of faults becomes increasingly likely to impact their execution [9]. At the same time, the popularity of distributed parallel programming systems that implement high degrees of dynamic behavior, such as asynchronous tasks [1], work stealing [4, 11, 12], and message-driven execution [8, 18, 19], are increasing. Unlike in bulk synchronous parallel programs, and even in dynamic data exchanges within BSP programs [7], there is often no clear global indication of when some particular distributed computation is complete. Thus, they instead rely on *termination detection* algorithms to provide that indication.

Termination in a distributed system is the state in which all processes are idle, and no message is in flight that may cause a process to become active [3]. There are many different approaches to termination detection (TD), which have been surveyed by Mattern [13].

Several researchers have constructed fault-tolerant algorithms for TD [10, 15, 16]. The past work in the area of fault-tolerant TD has focused on the problems of arbitrary failures in general distributed systems. These previous approaches handle failures of nearly the entire system, but at the cost of substantial complexity and non-scalable operations when faults occur. For instance, one algorithm routes and replicates all information used in termination detection through a constant number of processes, creating a sequential bottleneck that will grow with the system and problem sizes [16].

We approach the problem of fault tolerance (FT) from a different perspective: we should expect to experience faults, and pay only scalable and local costs to recover from faults that are likely to occur and unlikely to necessitate job termination. Specifically, in HPC systems, a large fraction of faults affect only a single node, and the likelihood of a fault decreases with the number of nodes it affects [14]. Thus, we explore several schemes to make TD tolerant of all single-process failures, and probabilistically tolerant of larger failures. The cost of recovery in our algorithm is very low, scalable relative to application behavior, and local to the communication neighborhood of the failed process. For applications whose behavior is scale-invariant [6], our algorithm is scale-invariant as well. We also show through experiments that our overhead on fault-free execution is minimal.

The primary contributions of this paper are as follows:

- We describe a new theoretical metric for TD, *process fanout*, that is used in analyzing our algorithms (§ 5.2).

- We characterize the (in)applicability of various fault-tolerant TD mechanisms to HPC applications (§ 3).

- We describe a series of three FT termination detection mechanisms (INDEP, RELLAZY, & RELEAGER) that present low theoretical overhead (both process-optimal and equal to or better than the cost of the message-optimal termination detector itself) on fault-free execution and do not impose non-scalable costs when recovering from faults (§ 5, § 6).

- We relate our algorithms' failure probabilities to fault data from real systems, to demonstrate their high practical survivability (§ 5.4, § 6.4, Table 1).

- We provide empirical measurements showing that the overhead costs of these schemes in a highly-scalable parallel runtime are low in practice (§ 7).

2. Background: Parental Responsibility Termination Detection

In constructing our fault tolerant termination detection algorithms, we build on the seminal work of Dijkstra and Scholten in defining the *parental responsibility* approach to termination detection [3, 13]. Our algorithms are constructed in terms of extensions to their original scheme. In this section, we introduce a concrete implementation of their algorithm, the invariants that they proved it obeys, and how those invariants provide for its correctness. We omit proofs of these invariants, since they can be found in their paper.

The computation is distributed among *processes* in a system. It is assumed to start at a particular *root process* which will eventually signal termination. All other processes are initially idle, or passive, and cannot be activated except by receiving a message from an already active process. This structure is generally known as a diffusing computation [3].

The general intuition of parental responsibility termination detection is that every message the application sends (also referred to as basic or primary messages) will eventually be *acknowledged*, and when all messages have been acknowledged, then termination is detected. The key to detecting termination using message acknowledgment is that some acknowledgments cannot be sent immediately, but must be delayed until the recipient can be sure that all work its messages have initiated in the system is complete.

To accomplish this, some processes are characterized as *engaged*, which means it or some process that was transitively activated by it is actively working, and all other processes are unengaged. The root is initially engaged, and all others are initially unengaged. An unengaged process becomes engaged upon receiving a message. An engaged process becomes unengaged when it has processed and acknowledged all messages sent to it and all messages it has sent have been acknowledged.

Every message carries an indication of its origin, denoting for the recipient who it must acknowledge, and when an unengaged process receives a message, that sender process becomes its *parent*:

```
def gotMsg(Endpoint predecessor):
  if (cornet.size() == 0):
    parent = predecessor;
    cornet.insertParent(parent, 1);
  else:
    cornet[predecessor].acksOwed++;
```

Dijkstra and Scholten describe storing the acknowledgments a process must send in a structure called a *cornet*, which distinguishes the first element placed in it to be removed last, and all other entries can be accessed or removed arbitrarily. In other words, it is 'very first in, very last out' and otherwise unordered. The subset of processes that are engaged form a directed tree determined by their parents, which is called the *engagement tree*. We describe an engaged process with parent p as *engaged to p*.

As processes consume messages that they receive, they may send messages to other process. That creates a debt of acknowledgments that must be repaid before the process can disengage, stored in D, which is initially zero:

```
def willSendTo(Endpoint successor):
  D++;
```

When these messages are acknowledged, the debt is reduced:

```
def gotAck(Endpoint successor, unsigned int count):
  D -= count;
  tryDisengage();
```

Once a process consumes a message, the process gains credit which can be used to acknowledge a message, stored in C, which is initially zero:

```
def processedMsg():
  C++;
  tryAck();
  tryDisengage();
```

With credit in hand, it is possible that the process may safely acknowledge some messages. The process checks whether it has consumed enough messages to acknowledge some source other than

its parent (chosen arbitrarily), and if so, transmits that acknowledgment and reduces its available credit:

```
def tryAck():
  if (cornet.size() <= 1): return;
  Endpoint predecessor = cornet.chooseNonParent();
  int a = cornet[predecessor].acksOwed;
  if (C >= a):
    C -= a;
    @predecessor { gotAck(self, a) };
    cornet.remove(predecessor);
```

We use the notation @proc { foo(); } to indicate sending a message to process proc asking it to execute the enclosed code. These messages are assumed to be processed between basic messages, and not in a preemptive manner, such as in an interrupt.

When a process has no one left to acknowledge but its parent, it may try to disengage:

```
def tryDisengage():
  if (cornet.hasNonParent()) return;
  if (D == 0 && C == 1):
    if (isRoot()) rootTerminated();
    else:
      @parent { gotAck(self, 1); }
      cornet.clearParent();
    C = 0;
```

In order to do so, all messages it sent must have been acknowledged ($D = 0$), and the only acknowledgment debt it still owes must be to its parent ($C = 1$).

INVARIANT 1. $C_p \geq 0 \wedge D_p \geq 0$

Both accounting variables are non-negative on all processes.

INVARIANT 2. *Process p being engaged is equivalent to* $\sum_{pred \in cornet_p}$ cornet[pred].acksOwed > 0

INVARIANT 3. $D_p > 0 \rightarrow$ *process p is engaged.*

A process must be engaged in order to send messages, and thus increase D above zero.

During execution, we denote the number of messages the application sends by M. The Dijkstra-Scholten algorithm sends an additional $\mathcal{O}(M)$ messages to accomplish its purpose.

The correctness of this TD algorithm is defined by two properties: it does not detect termination while any process is still engaged, and it detects termination when all processes have disengaged. For purposes of fault tolerance, we generalize this correctness to mean that the algorithm does not detect termination while any process is still engaged, and it either detects termination when all surviving processes have disengaged or reports a fatal error when it can no longer determine when that has occurred. When faults occur, it is still the application's responsibility to determine what work was lost in the fault and how to address that loss.

3. Related Work

The goal of the present effort is to describe an algorithm that is scalable – no single process or narrow subset of processes should be burdened with work that grows disproportionately from the effort it expends in executing the client application. Existing algorithms do not satisfy these desires, either during fault-free execution or during fault recovery.

Venkatesan's algorithm designates a number of 'leader' processes that are responsible for declaring termination [16]. To tolerate k-process faults, it must have at least $k+1$ leaders. Each of those leaders receives termination detection signals from all of the processes in the system, and must store and simulate the state of all of those processes to track when they have terminated. This presents a clear sequential bottleneck, and a potential memory overload, that is impractical in a high performance computing environment.

The protocol described by Lai and Wu [10] avoids all overhead during fault-free execution. However, in the event of a fault, every surviving process communicates directly with a designated root process. While the total number of messages necessary does not scale beyond the system's scale, the root process becomes a sequential bottleneck that will take $\mathcal{O}(N)$ time to receive these messages, process them, and respond. As systems scale up, this will lead to recovery taking longer than the time between failures, and thus ultimately does not achieve its goal.

Much recent research in fault-tolerant parallel computing has focused on *algorithmic fault tolerance* [6]. This approach does not generically try to make entire parallel applications fault-tolerant, but instead addresses itself to single component algorithms and libraries, with the expectation that these can later be composed to construct applications that derive their fault tolerance from that of the underlying pieces. Algorithmic fault tolerance has gained particular traction in numerical linear algebra [2], where the problems have structural characteristics that provide low-cost recovery mechanisms. Our work can be viewed as providing a fault-tolerant version of a scalable termination detection component, which can be readily integrated with other resilient components.

One particular environment where the need for fault-tolerant termination detection appears is work stealing with idempotent updates to global data [12]. That paper describes a mechanism to write distributed work stealing code that reads and writes global array structures, which are commonly used in computational chemistry applications. The work stealing mechanism provides load balance across the system, and relies on a termination detector to determine when there is no work left in the system. The tasks are arranged and programmed such that their execution is idempotent with respect to the global data. Thus, when a process fails, any potentially affected tasks are simply re-executed. The work stealing machinery maintains sufficient records to identify the subtrees that were stolen by a failed process, and can restart them. The system described in that paper is implemented in terms of a termination detector that is not itself fault tolerant. Thus, while it can be shown to survive simulated faults, it was not suitable for production use. We provide the necessary implementation of a fault-tolerant termination detector, and measure its overhead using a similar set of benchmarks.

4. System Model

In describing a fault-tolerant termination detection scheme, we make a number of assumptions about the parallel computer and interconnection network that it will run on. We do not rely on synchronized delivery of messages between sender and receiver, but instead let processes transmit message asynchronously and obliviously. The network may then deliver these messages in any order. We assume the network itself does not fail, or that such failures are accepted as leading to complete job failure.

We require a sort of 'network send fence' that permits us to conclude that a particular message has been successfully transmitted (but not necessarily received or processed) before sending another. This is a weaker assumption than some other schemes that depend on transmitting pairs of messages simultaneously [16]. However, a network satisfying such an assumption meets our own as well.

We assume that failures are *fail-stop* - i.e. failed processes do not recover [5], and do not behave maliciously (no byzantine failures). We make no assumption regarding process replacement after failure, since a fresh process is free to engage just like the initial set of processes do, by receiving a message.

In the event of a failure, we require two things of the underlying system. The first is that communication partners of failed processes

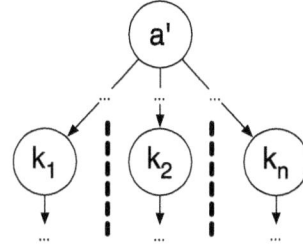

Figure 1: The INDEP protocol (§ 5) handles independent failures: k_1, $k_2 \ldots k_n$ can all fail simultaneously as long as they do not communicate.

receive notifications of the failure, so that they can react accordingly. In a closely-coupled HPC environment, it is reasonable to assume that an out-of-band mechanism such as the system's resource manager can provide this facility. The second requirement is a primitive to ensure that all messages sent by a failed process to a particular recipient have been received. Venkatasan refers to this facility as *fail-flush* [16].

To avoid undue complication of the descriptions, we do not explicitly address the failure of the root process. This could be mitigated in the protocol by electing or designating a backup process to take its place, which can be done with low execution-time cost but substantial implementation complexity. It would also be possible for the (assumed reliable) environment to take on the root's responsibilities, either initially, or in the event of its failure. As a single process in a prospectively large system, randomly distributed faults are unlikely to include the root process. For it to be worthwhile for our protocols to handle root failure, any parallel application or programming environment using our scheme must also be tolerant of the root failing, which imposes a similar complexity burden on them as well. Given our starting assumption that some unrecoverable faults are acceptable, as long as they are rapidly and reliably reported, we thus do not consider this vulnerability to be of fundamental importance.

5. INDEP: Tolerating Independent Failures

Our general approach to making these termination detection algorithms fault tolerant is to make potential parents of a failed process responsible for retaining and exploiting the information necessary for recovery. Who these children are and how they relate to a failed process is communicated through additional control signals. When processes fail, their parents delay termination until recovery has progressed far enough to take stock of their children and reattach them to the engagement tree as appropriate. If that is found to be impossible, our protocols reliably and rapidly report overall failure.

We begin by describing INDEP, a protocol for recovery from the failure of any single process or sets of independent processes that are not related by direct communication, as shown in Figure 1. These cases are always recoverable, and the completion of the recovery process is clearly delineated by the receipt of particular control signals between surviving processes.

The intuition behind INDEP is that any time a process p is about to send a message to a new recipient p_c, p ensures that its grandparent p_p will receive a message informing it of the possibility that p_c was a child of p should p fail. When a failure of p occurs, p_p will exchange messages leading it to adopt the children p_c as its own.

5.1 Modifications to Fault-Free Execution

When sending a message, each process records how many unacknowledged messages it has sent to each destination. For messages

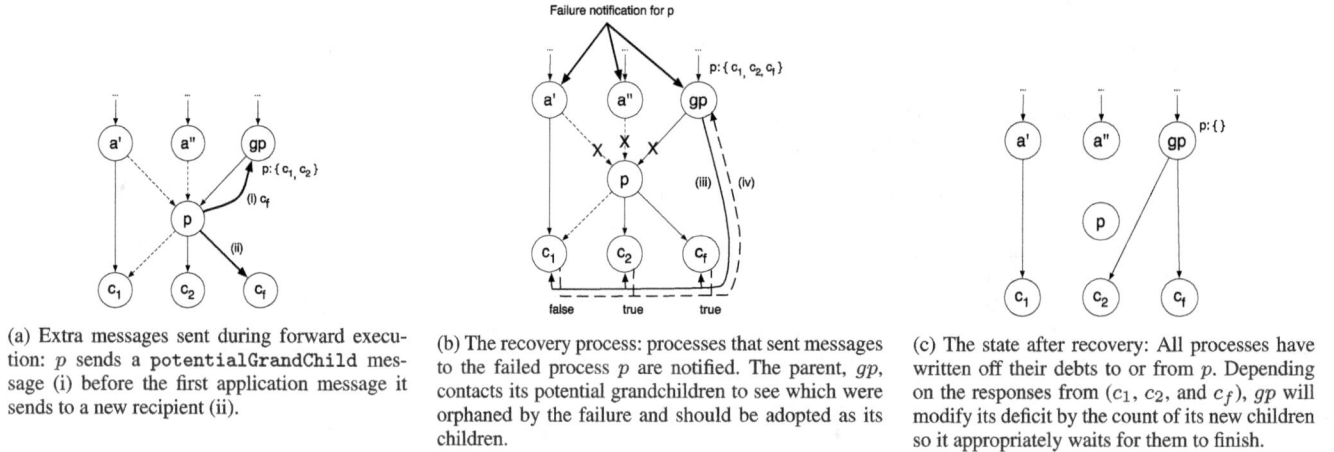

(a) Extra messages sent during forward execution: p sends a `potentialGrandChild` message (i) before the first application message it sends to a new recipient (ii).

(b) The recovery process: processes that sent messages to the failed process p are notified. The parent, gp, contacts its potential grandchildren to see which were orphaned by the failure and should be adopted as its children.

(c) The state after recovery: All processes have written off their debts to or from p. Depending on the responses from (c_1, c_2, and c_f), gp will modify its deficit by the count of its new children so it appropriately waits for them to finish.

Figure 2: The INDEP fault tolerance protocol.

that might engage a child, it also notifies its parent of the new prospective child (Figure 2a). This is where we depend on a network fence – if the child process receives the application message, that child's potential grandparent process must have been sent a notice regarding its presence.

```
def willSendTo(Endpoint successor):
  D++;
  successors[successor].acksOwed++;
  if (successors[successor].acksOwed == 1):
    @parent { potentialGrandchild(self, successor) };
    requestFailureNotice(successor);
    sendFence();
```

Because of the potential fault recovery responsibility that comes with sending a message to a process, the termination detector must request failure notifications regarding that process as well.

During forward execution, the grandparent processes record these notifications on a per-child basis:

```
def potentialGrandchild(Endpoint child, Endpoint gc):
  successors[child].potentialChildren.insert(gc);
```

During fault-free operation, the grandparents' records are never consulted. When process p receives an acknowledgment from process q, p's corresponding debt counter for messages to q is decremented. When q's debt goes to 0, indicating disengagement, its failures are no longer of interest, and any potential grandchildren it might have introduced are forgotten, since they are guaranteed to have previously disengaged from the child process:

```
def gotAck(Endpoint successor, unsigned int count):
  D -= count;
  successors[successor].acksOwed -= count;
  if (successors[successor].acksOwed == 0):
    dropFailureNotice(successor);
    successors.erase(successor);
  tryDisengage();
```

We also introduce a counter of pending recovery events named `pendingRecoveryEvents`, which is initialized to zero. The condition guarding disengagement must additionally check that this is zero. Its use is described below.

LEMMA 5.1. *In the absence of faults, termination is detected correctly.*

Proof. The additional messages and data structures are irrelevant, with the exception of the pending recovery event counter. This is initialized to zero and is never changed during fault-free execution. Thus, when termination would otherwise occur, the added condition that this counter is zero is satisfied. Therefore, we conclude that there is no change in the fault-free operation of the fault-tolerant variant of our termination detector, and the original algorithm's proof of correctness continues to hold. □

5.2 Fanout Bound

For every process, there is some number of other processes that it will send messages to over the course the computation. In scalable applications, this number is typically limited, and should not grow with the size of the computer system or the problem being solved. In particular, within a given phase or step of a computation that is run with termination detection, each process is only likely to communicate with a reasonably small subset of the system, and we refer to the size of the largest such subset as the application's *fanout* during that phase or step. For example, in preparing the data exchange necessary to obtain column data in sparse matrix-vector multiplication, this would be the number of processors having entries on that column [7].

We use the fanout, denoted f, to describe the bounds on our algorithms' costs. Note that $f \in \mathcal{O}(M)$ – it can never exceed the number of messages the application itself sends. In practice, it may be much lower. Where that is the case, we will see that our FT overheads scale more slowly than the cost of TD itself. The fanout is also bounded by the number of processes – it is impossible for any one process to send to more destinations than exist in the system.

Fault-free execution of INDEP sends additional control messages corresponding to the cumulative fanout of the system, distributed according to the engagement structure that the application's messages create. Each process stores its potential grandchildren in a structure with entries corresponding to its own fanout, and each entry lists grandchildren according to that child's fanout. Thus, it will occupy space that is $\mathcal{O}(f^2)$ in the worst case. These structures can be implemented as hash tables, allowing constant-time lookup.

5.3 Fault Recovery

When a fault occurs that kills process p_f, the processes that have interacted with it cooperate to use the extra information they have

16

stored to effectively 'contract' around its vertex in the engagement tree (Figure 2b). All of the processes that sent primary messages to p_f will receive notifications from the environment, indicating the failure and complete flushing of messages. These processes can all write off any debt p_f owed them, and ignore further acknowledgments from p_f:

```
def failureHappened(Endpoint failedProcess):
  if (successors.contains(failedProcess)):
    D −= successors[failedProcess].acksOwed;
    foreach (Endpoint grandchild
              : successors[failedProcess].potentialChildren):
      pendingRecoveryEvents++;
      willSendTo(grandchild);
      @grandchild { tryEngageGrandchild(self, failedProcess) };
    successors.erase(failedProcess);
```

One of the processes that sent p_f messages will discover that it was the failed process's parent, and is thus responsible for waiting on the termination of its children. The recovery counter is increased by the number of potential grandchildren that must be dealt with (zero for non-parent processes). The parent p_g informs each of them that p_f has died and tries to engage them.

Each of p_f's potential child processes will receive a message from the failed process's parent p_g notifying it of the failure. All of these processes write off any acknowledgment debt they owed p_f. If p_f was their parent, they then adopt p_g as their parent, and replace their debt to p_f with a parental debt of 1 to p_g. They then each send a message to p_g indicating what new debt, if any, they owe it, and any new potential grandchildren that p_g must be aware of as a result of having adopted an additional child.

```
def tryEngageGrandchild(Endpoint gp, Endpoint failedParent):
  if (cornet.contains(failedParent)):
    C −= cornet[failedParent].acksOwed;
    cornet.erase(failedParent);

  if (failedParent == parent):
    parent = gp;
    C++;
    cornet.insertParent(parent, 1);

    @gp { replyToGrandparent(self, 1, keys(successors)) };
    tryDisengage();
  else:
    // Potential grandparent expects a response, even if we don't
    //     engage it
    @gp { replyToGrandparent(self, 0, {}) };
```

When p_g receives these responses, it decrements the recovery counter, notes any additional debt new children owe it, and records their associated potential grandchildren:

```
def replyToGrandparent(Endpoint child, unsigned int debt,
                        set<Endpoint> children):
  if (debt != 0):
    D += debt;
    successors[child].acksOwed += debt;
    successors[child].potentialChildren.insert(children);
  pendingRecoveryEvents−−;
  gotAck(child, 1);
```

As each potential child's response is received, there is the possibility that termination has been reached, and so we test for it.

Note that there is a potential race between an affirmative response from a former child of p_f to p_g and a subsequent disengagement acknowledgment message from that child to p_g. Without treating each outstanding potential child as a message send, this race may cause the value of D on p_g to reach zero unexpectedly, or even become negative. By incrementing and decrementing D

along with the recovery counter, we ensure that Dijkstra's $D > 0$ invariant is maintained.

LEMMA 5.2. *In the presence of faults, this system does not report termination when it has not occurred.*

Proof. Consider a process p_f that fails while it is engaged to parent p_p. After the failure, p_f is effectively passive, but any processes that received messages from it may still be active. When the failure notification reaches p_p, it is aware of all such potential recipients, because of the send fence before the first message to each new recipient and the fail-flush before the failure notification. If p_f had no potential children, then its subtree of the engagement tree is complete at its failure, and p_p can disengage when its other debts are repaid. If p_f had children, p_p is prevented from disengaging until each of those children responds by the non-zero recovery counter. There are four possibilities for each child's state when the message from p_p arrives:

1. It is passive and not engaged: it responds indicating that it presents no cause for p_p to wait before disengaging.

2. Engaged to some other process: it responds indicating that another process is already prevented from disengaging until it does. Thus, p_p does not have to wait on it before disengaging.

3. Engaged to p_f: it responds that p_p is its new parent, which causes p_p to increase its outstanding debt by 1. This prevents p_p from disengaging until the newly acquired child disengages.

4. Failed: p_p is notified of the failure after requesting failure notices regarding it, and aborts the job.

Thus, any process that would have had to disengage before p_f could disengage must disengage or indicate its independence from p_p before p_p can disengage. We therefore conclude that termination cannot be reported prematurely. □

LEMMA 5.3. *In the absence of related-process faults, every surviving process will eventually disengage, and termination will be detected.*

Proof. A failure of a process that is not engaged will not prevent disengagement of any surviving process.

Every engaged failed process p_f has a parent p_p, some (possibly empty) set of other processes that sent it messages, and some (possibly empty) set of other processes to which it sent messages. The parent p_p and all of the other senders will receive failure notifications regarding p_f, allowing them to disregard its debt. All of the non-parents are then free to disengage despite p_f's failure.

The parent p_p must not disengage until all potential children of p_f are definitively engaged to another parent or have themselves disengaged. By the hypothesis, all of these processes are alive to receive and respond to the parent's query.

Their responses are as follows:

1. Not engaged: they do not engage as a result of the query, and their reply releases the obligation p_p had to them.

2. Engaged to some process besides p_f: they dispose of their debt to p_f and ignore further messages that may arrive from it, allowing them to eventually disengage from their own parent when appropriate, and their reply releases the obligation of p_p.

3. Engaged to p_f: As above, their past interaction with p_f is written off and will not impede their eventual disengagement. Their reply to p_p indicates that when they disengage, their acknowledgment to p_p will satisfy its obligation to wait for them.

17

Thus, all recipients of messages from p_f will be able to disengage when appropriate. When those that were engaged to p_f disengage, they will free p_p to disengage as well. □

LEMMA 5.4. *In the presence of a fault involving a process p_{send} and a process p_{recv} to which p_{send} has sent a message, the system will report failure.*

Proof. If p_{send} has sent messages, then it is engaged to some parent p_p, and has sent notifications about all potential p_{recv} to p_p. Thus, after flushing from p_{send}, p_p will have knowledge of the complete set of potential p_{recv}, and will attempt to contact each of them. These contact attempts will either garner an eventual response, indicating that child is not involved in a related-process fault, or an eventual failure notice will reach p_p, at which point it will abort. □

THEOREM 5.5. INDEP *is a correct fault-tolerant termination detection protocol.*

Proof. By lemmas 5.1, 5.2, 5.3 and 5.4, INDEP is correct. □

5.4 Survival Probability

An application using INDEP can survive the concurrent failure of any processes that do not share any communication edges between them. The probability that the protocol can survive the failure of a uniformly random selected set of processes is given by

$$\left[\frac{\binom{n-k}{f}}{\binom{n-1}{f}} \right]^k$$

where n is the number of processes in the job, k is the number of failed processes, and f is the application's fanout [14]. We can combine this formula with failure records from real systems to predict the practical survivability of our protocol. Table 1 shows data from the Cray XT5 system Jaguar at Oak Ridge National Laboratory[1] in combination with the failure probabilities for the protocols presented in this paper with an assumed job size of $n = 1024$. For each algorithm/fanout-parameter combination, we multiply the fraction of faults of a given size by the probability that the termination detector fails to recover from a fault of that size to compute a failure probability from faults of that size, and subtract the sum of those probabilities from 100% to calculate the survivability shown. Other systems for which we have less data available show single-node faults representing 70%–98%, and conservative survivability estimates (taking failures of more than 4 nodes as fatal) ranging from 85% (15% large failures) to 99.98% [14].

The assumption of uniformly distributed faults is an uncertain one. In applications with communication patterns optimized for network locality, this may be problematic. In others settings, such as work stealing, the randomness of the stealing process itself decorrelates the communication graph from system structure.

5.5 Recovery Costs

When an engaged process p_f fails, its parent will (after flushing) have a complete set of the processes to which p_f potentially sent messages prior to its failure. The parent will send a number of recovery messages equal to the size of the set of its potential adoptees, and each of them will send a response message back to the parent. The size of the potential orphan set is bounded by the fanout. Thus, INDEP will send $\mathcal{O}(f)$ control signals in order to recover from each failure.

[1] Personal communication with Terry Jones, ORNL

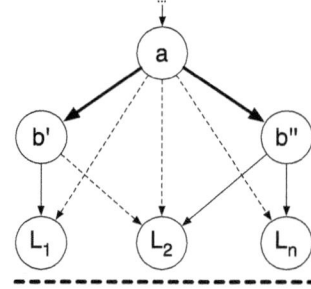

Figure 3: The RELLAZY and RELEAGER protocols handle related process failures providing parent-child interior pairs do not fail simultaneously. In the case depicted, any subset of these processes can fail as long as the failure set does not contain $\{a, b'\}$ or $\{a, b''\}$. $L_1 \ldots L_n$ are exterior processes in the communication graph.

6. Handling Related-Process Failures

We now turn to the problem of faults affecting processes that communicated directly before failing. Given some additional information conveyed in both basic messages and control signals sent during forward execution, the majority of these cases are recoverable (see Figure 3). The non-recoverable case, in which our algorithm reliably reports failure, is one in which it appears to a recovering grandparent that a failed process had a child that was *interior* to the communication graph that also failed.

We define an interior process to mean one that has sent messages to any recipients that have not fully acknowledged them. An exterior process is any process that is not interior. Interior processes must be engaged, by dint of invariant 3, and thus must have a well-defined parent and grandparent. Exterior processes may be engaged or unengaged; if they are engaged, they are leaves of the engagement tree, since they cannot have sent any message that would cause a child to engage to them.

The length of the interval in which the failure of a process and an interior child of that process would be fatal (the vulnerability window) depends on a tradeoff against additional control signals during recovery. In the RELLAZY protocol (§ 6.2), recovery uses the same control signals as in INDEP, but with fewer multi-process fault cases ending in failure, and full recovery is achieved when adopted processes disengage. The RELEAGER protocol (§ 6.3) sends more control signals than INDEP or RELLAZY, but it achieves full recovery once those control signals are processed.

During forward execution, each process process p sends messages to its grandparent p_p indicating its transitions from exterior to interior or vice versa. If p and its parent fail concurrently, p_p flushes those messages from p and checks whether it received an equal number of the two types of messages, or one more interior than exterior, to determine the condition of p when it failed. As we will describe, failed exterior processes can be safely written off, but failed interior processes can not, and are thus fatal.

6.1 Modifications to Fault-Free Execution

In these variants of the protocol, every message carries a note not just of the sender, but also of the sender's parent, so that the recipient knows what process is its grandparent if the sender becomes its parent. This is necessary because each process now transmits additional control signals to its grandparent during forward execution. Those signals convey sufficient information for the grandparent p_p to reconstruct whether the potential grandchild p_c was engaged to a failed child process, and if so, whether p_c was also potentially an interior process.

Nodes Failed	1	2	3	4	5	6	7	8	9	10	11	15	18	26, 86, 126, 338	Survival
Fault %	92.3	3.672	0.942	0.753	0.565	0.094	0.094	0.377	0.094	0.188	0.188	0.282	0.094	$4 \times 0.094 = 0.377$	%
INDEP $f = 2$	0	1.4e-4	1.1e-4	1.8e-4	2.2e-4	5.4e-5	7.4e-5	3.9e-4	1.2e-4	3.1e-4	3.7e-4	9.6e-4	4.3e-4	3.5e-3	99.315
$f = 8$	0	5.7e-4	4.3e-4	6.8e-4	8.2e-4	2.0e-4	2.7e-4	1.3e-3	4.1e-4	9.6e-4	1.1e-3	2.3e-3	8.6e-4	3.8e-3	98.633
$f = 32$	0	2.3e-3	1.6e-3	2.4e-3	2.7e-3	5.8e-4	6.9e-4	3.1e-3	8.5e-4	1.8e-3	1.8e-3	2.8e-3	9.4e-4	3.8e-3	97.466
$f = 512$	0	2.8e-3	9.3e-3	7.5e-3	5.6e-3	9.4e-4	9.4e-4	3.8e-3	9.4e-4	1.9e-3	1.9e-3	2.8e-3	9.4e-4	3.8e-3	93.210
REL*	0	7.2e-5	5.5e-5	8.8e-5	1.1e-4	2.7e-5	3.8e-5	2.0e-4	6.4e-5	1.6e-4	1.9e-4	5.3e-4	2.5e-4	3.3e-3	99.495

Table 1: Distribution of the node counts of concurrent failures on Jaguar, the probability the protocol sees a fault of the given size and fails to recover, and the probability a 1024-process job survives the distribution of concurrent failures using the various algorithms presented.

When a process sends its first message after engaging or after all of its recipients have fully acknowledged it, the process informs its grandparent:

```
def willSendTo(Endpoint successor):
  D++;
  if (D == 1):
    @grandparent { informGrandparentInterior(self, parent) };
    sendFence();
  successors[successor].acksOwed++;
  if (successors[successor].acksOwed == 1):
    @parent { potentialGrandchild(self, successor) };
    requestFailureNotice(successor);
    sendFence();
```

There are two places a process might send `informGrandparentExterior`. The most aggressive is when it receives an acknowledgment that brings its outstanding message count to zero:

```
def gotAck(Endpoint successor, unsigned int count):
  D -= count;
  successors[successor].acksOwed -= count;
  if (successors[successor].acksOwed == 0):
    dropFailureNotice(successor);
    successors.erase(successor);
  if (D == 0):
    @grandparent { informGrandparentExterior(self, parent) };
    sendFence();
  tryDisengage();
```

This creates the shortest intervals in which the failure of both an apparently interior process and its parent would be reported as fatal by the recovering grandparent process. However, it also creates a potentially large number of additional control signals (up to $\mathcal{O}(M)$), depending on how aggressively acknowledgments are transmitted. The other possibility is when it sends an acknowledgment to disengage from its parent, which is also $\mathcal{O}(M)$ in theory, but likely to be lower in practice.

Note that in either case, an exterior signal from process p_c to its grandparent p_g labeled with its parent p_p is always preceded by a similarly labeled and directed interior message, and two interior messages with the same label and destination cannot be sent without a single corresponding exterior signal intervening between them.

At the point of failure of a process p_f, its parent p_p must be able to distinguish whether each of p_f's message recipients p_c was an interior process engaged to p_f, even if p_c fails as well. Using the pairing property between the interior and exterior messages from p_c to p_p, p_p can compute whether p_c was engaged to p_f and interior at the time of its failure by flushing from p_c and then examining the parity between interior and exterior messages. Even parity indicates that every interior message p_c sent was followed by a exterior message, while odd parity indicates that p_c sent one last interior message that was never balanced by a exterior message.

LEMMA 6.1. *In the absence of faults, the related process protocol detects termination correctly.*

Proof. As before, the additional messages and recorded data do not affect detection of termination when no fault occurs. Thus, the correctness of the basic algorithm is maintained. □

6.2 RELLAZY: Lazy Multiprocess Recovery Protocol

The recovery process proceeds as before, but with an increase in the range of failures that a recovering parent p_p can accept from the children of its failed child p_f. In addition to processes that reply to p_p telling of their own non-engagement to p_f, p_p can now write off any process p_c that fails with even parity of interior and exterior messages to p_p after flushing but hasn't responded to the engagement query from p_p. This is safe because it guarantees that p_c was either not engaged to p_f (it sent no interior/exterior messages to p_p) or it was engaged to p_f but had no children of its own (interior and exterior messages from p_c to p_p balanced out). If any p_c fails and flushes out odd parity to p_p, then p_p must report failure because it cannot contract around a failed process for which it was newly responsible.

In this setting, each child p_d of p_c has no knowledge that p_p is its new grandparent, even though p_p successfully adopted p_c as its child and learned about all of p_c's children. Thus, if p_c were to fail in concert with one of its children p_d, p_p would not be able to safely determine whether p_d was an interior process or not, and thus must conservatively report failure. In order to do this, p_p must keep a record that p_c was adopted until p_c disengages. The subsequent failure of such a marked child will be reported as an error. The window of vulnerability in which the system cannot uniformly recover therefore extends from the failure of p_f through the disengagement of all its children p_c from p_p.

LEMMA 6.2. *In the presence of faults, RELLAZY does not report termination when it has not occurred.*

Proof. We follow the reasoning of the proof of lemma 5.2, with a change in the handling of failed children of p_f by p_p. When such a child has failed, it is effectively passive for purposes of termination detection. However, its transmissions prior to failure determine whether recovering parents will be allowed to terminate, or report failure. If the interior and exterior messages create odd parity at p_p, then p_p reports failure, and so does not allow early termination. If those message create even parity at p_p we are left with two possible cases:

1. p_c was not engaged to p_f at the time of its failure: if p_c was still engaged at all, it was to some other process that is responsible for its recovery. That process will not disengage and allow termination until its recovery around p_c is complete. This corresponds to case 2 of lemma 5.2.

2. p_c was engaged to p_f at the time of its failure: the even parity indicates that it was not an interior process. Thus, it was not responsible for waiting on any descendants to disengage before it disengaged. The recovering parent p_p has fulfilled its responsibility to delay termination until after p_c disengaged, and can safely disengage without leading to premature termination. □

LEMMA 6.3. *In the absence of apparent parent/interior-child faults, every surviving process will eventually disengage, and termination will be detected.*

Proof. Consider each process p that receives failure notifications regarding a set of processes. For each of those processes, p has some set of potential grandchildren p_c that it must address. The p_c come in the following varieties:

1. Still alive: they respond to the query from p, and the eventual disengagement of p and these grandchildren is as described by lemma 5.3.

2. Dead, with the resulting flush of messages providing

   (a) Even parity: p_c was not engaged to p's child at the time of failure, or was so engaged but had no potential children and so could not be interior. p can safely write them off, as it has no obligation to await disengagement of any children they may have had.

   (b) Odd parity: the hypothesis that the fault did not involve an apparent parent/interior-child pair was violated, and p will report an error.

In all cases satisfying the condition, p and all recipients of messages from failed processes are therefore allowed to disengage when their other obligations are satisfied, and termination will be reported. □

LEMMA 6.4. *In the presence of a fault involving a process p_{send} and an interior process p_{recv} which was engaged to p_{send}, the system will report failure.*

Proof. The parent p_p of p_{send} will receive a notification that p_{send} failed with a flush of messages. In the recovery process, p_p will request failure notification from all processes to which p_{send} sent messages, including p_{recv}. By the construction of the message sending code and the pairing property of the interior and exterior messages, p_{recv} must have transmitted odd parity of these messages to p_p. Upon flushing, p_p will observe this odd parity, conclude that the fault included a parent/interior-child pair, and report failure. □

THEOREM 6.5. RELLAZY *is a correct fault-tolerant termination detection protocol.*

Proof. By lemmas 6.1, 6.2, 6.3 and 6.4, RELLAZY is correct. □

6.2.1 Recovery Costs

The recovery communication resulting from a failure in RELLAZY is the same as in INDEP. Thus, RELLAZY sends at most $\mathcal{O}(f)$ control signals in order to recover from each failure.

6.3 RELEAGER: **Eager Multiprocess Recovery Protocol**

We now address recovery from failures of the following form:

- a process p_f fails, causing its parent p_p to initiate recovery,

- a process p_c was a child of p_f, and is adopted by p_p,

- p_c sent one or more messages to an exterior process p_d before the failure of p_f and subsequent recovery steps, where

- p_c and p_d subsequently fail concurrently.

As noted earlier, the challenge in this situation is that p_p will never have been sent the information necessary to determine whether its adopted potential grandchild p_d is an interior child of p_c or not. To correct that deficiency, the recovery protocol can exchange additional signals that convey the necessary information.

This eager recovery protocol variant still begins the same way, with processes that sent messages to a failed process p_f being informed of the failure and flushing from it, and its parent p_p querying each of its potential grandchildren p_c. We depart from the lazy recovery protocol in that the responses from p_c will no longer be returned immediately. Instead, they send a message to each of their own potential children p_d indicating their new potential grandparent p_p.

Each of those p_d respond to p_c indicating whether they are engaged to p_c, and if so, whether they are interior. The p_d that are engaged to p_c update their grandparent record to point to p_p instead of the now-dead p_f. When p_c receives all of those responses, it sends an aggregated response to p_p with the list of actually engaged children and an indicator of which of those children are interior.

When p_p receives the response message from p_c, the list of grandchildren is recorded as before, but with the interior bits used to initialize its view of each grandchild's interior/exterior parity. Essentially, this reconstructs the unpaired interior messages that those p_d would have sent to p_f before its failure. When p_p receives responses from all of its adopted children p_c, the system is no more susceptible to failure than it was prior to the failure of p_f— the window of vulnerability is closed.

Note that this recovery protocol races with potential disengagement of the affected processes. This race is not only tolerated, but actually aids resilience. Any process that disengages before the protocol finishes recovery is one fewer process whose failure will bring down the entire job.

THEOREM 6.6. RELEAGER *is a correct fault-tolerant termination detection protocol.*

Proof. The reasoning of lemmas 6.1, 6.2, 6.3 and 6.4 applies to RELEAGER as well, and thus RELEAGER is correct. □

6.3.1 Recovery Costs

Each failed engaged process will cause its parent to send a message to each of the failed processes' potential children. Failures among those children do not increase the message count. Each of the actual grandchildren sends a message to their own potential children (i.e. the potential great-grandchildren), and gets a response from each. The grandchildren then each send a response to the grandparent. Each of the grandparent and grandchildren may have $\mathcal{O}(f)$ messages to send, and there may be up to f grandchildren, giving a total message count bound of $\mathcal{O}(f^2)$. These messages are distributed such that each process handles at most $\mathcal{O}(f)$ of them.

6.4 Survival Probability

Out of an N-process job, consider a failure of k processes. By lemma 6.3, the algorithm can survive the failure of any one process, as long as its parent does not also fail with it. Out of the failed subset, consider the probability that a single process v has failed along with its parent. The number of k-process failure sets containing v is

$$\binom{N-1}{k-1}.$$

The number of these that also contain v's parent is

$$\binom{N-2}{k-2}.$$

Thus, the probability that the failure set will contain v's parent, given that it contains v, is given by their ratio

$$\frac{k-1}{N-1}.$$

20

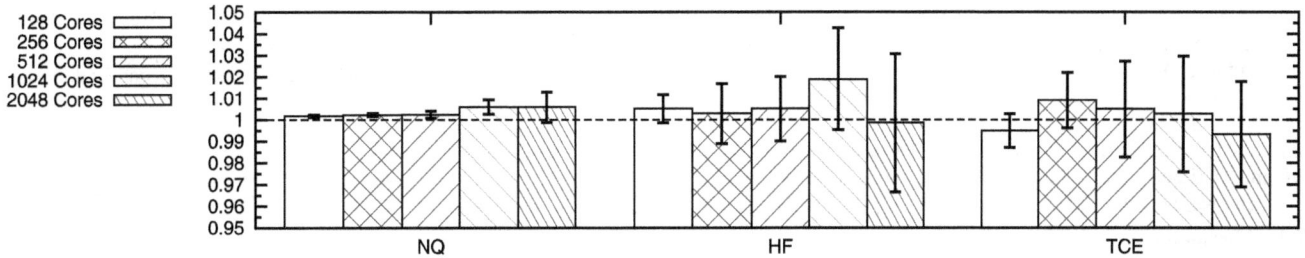

Figure 4: The overhead of our related-process fault tolerance protocols (RELLAZY or RELEAGER). Each bar shows the ratio of the average execution time using the protocol vs. average execution time without. Sample size is 24 runs of each application, at each scale, both with and without our protocol enabled. The whiskers represent the error in the difference of means at 99% confidence, using a Student's t-test.

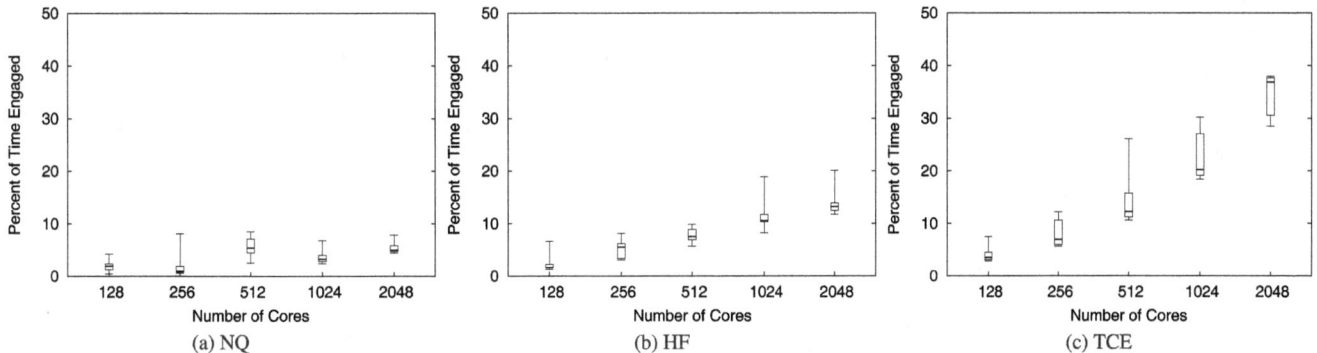

| (a) NQ | (b) HF | (c) TCE |

Figure 5: For three benchmarks, the percent of total execution time (in terms of processor-seconds) spent engaged: the time when a process is interior in the communication graph. For the RELLAZY and RELEAGER schemes, a process and its parent cannot fail simultaneously during this time or the protocol will not survive the fault. The vertical lines stretch between the minimum and maximum values; the box spans between the 25th and 75th percentile; the horizontal line spanning the box indicates the median.

The probability that the system survives this process's failure is then $1 - (k-1)/(N-1)$. Note that this directly reproduces the qualitative result that the algorithm always survives single-process failures (i.e. $k = 1$ fails with probability 0).

Given that k processes failed, and pessimistically assuming that none of them shares a parent (i.e. maximizing the cases that would lead to failure), the probability that the entire system survives is

$$\left(1 - \frac{k-1}{N-1}\right)^k$$

As with INDEP, we can combine these probability estimates with real failure data to determine how resilient the algorithms will be in practice. The results are shown in Table 1. Unlike INDEP, RELLAZY and RELEAGER do not become more vulnerable as fanout increases, because each process may have many communication partners, but has at most one parent. As the table shows, the two related-process protocols are more resilient than INDEP even in the most lenient fanout-2 case.

7. Experimental Results

7.1 Experimental Setup

We performed our experiments on Intrepid, a 40960-node IBM Blue Gene/P. Each node consists of a four-core 850MHz PowerPC 450 processor and 2 GB of DDR2 memory. We compiled our code with the IBM XL C/C++ Advanced Edition for Blue Gene/P, V9.0.

Our codes use an active-message-based runtime [17] implemented using MPI primitives with distributed-memory work stealing to balance work between cores during an iteration. We run one process per SMP node in a multi-threaded configuration, with one thread per core. One core is used as a server that polls the network and executes active messages. The other three cores maintain

a local deque of tasks that is optimized for efficient remote steal attempts and local task execution [4, 11].

7.2 Benchmarks

We evaluate our fault tolerance scheme with three benchmarks that involve parallel task collections. For the N-Queens benchmark (NQ), each task at depth d recursively tries to place the next queen at depth $d + 1$ creating up to N new tasks. At a certain depth s, a task stops producing more tasks and executes sequentially. The Hartree-Fock (HF) method is an algorithm from computational chemistry that forms the basis for several higher-level theories such as Coupled Cluster theory and Møller-Plesset perturbation theory. Our benchmark is comprised of the two-electron contribution component of Hartree-Fock. The matrices used for the computation (schwarz, fock, and dens) are distributed using a global address space and each task reads/writes the necessary portions. Tensor Contraction Expressions (TCE) constitute the entirety of Coupled Cluster methods, used in accurate descriptions of many-body systems in diverse domains. We benchmark a tensor contraction where the matrices are also distributed in a global address space.

7.3 Fault-free Execution Overhead

Our fault-tolerance protocols incur extra message sends during fault-free execution. All three protocols (INDEP, RELLAZY, RELEAGER) require a given process to send a message to its parent informing it of a potential grandchild before it actually sends a message to a new child. The related-process failure protocols RELLAZY and RELEAGER require a process to send a message to its grandparent before it possibly engages a child by sending it a message. We measure and plot the overhead of the related-failure case in Figure 4. The slightly less overhead induced in the INDEP protocol is statistically indistinguishable from the related-process case so we omit it. Figure 4 displays the ratio of execution time using the fault tolerance protocol versus normal execution without any fault tolerance.

For the NQ benchmark, the overhead is under 0.5% and is mostly within the error. The NQ benchmark is very well-behaved since the tasks are fairly uniform and do not access global data. The HF and TCE benchmarks have higher run-to-run variation, and the overhead we induce with our protocol is clearly within the error.

7.4 Measuring Exterior Processes

The RELLAZY and RELEAGER protocols can recover from a fault when the processes that fail do not include a parent/interior-child pair. Whether a process is an interior child is transient over time: processes may switch between exterior and interior over the course of a run depending on the communication patterns of the application. For the three benchmarks that are presented, we measure the amount of time that processes are in the exterior state compared to the total execution time of the application. The communication of these applications is primarily driven by the random work stealing employed, but varies depending on the duration of tasks and parallel slack available in different regions of the computation.

Figure 5 displays the percent of total execution time spent engaged after sending a message, which is an upper-bound on time spent as an interior process. Recall that a failed process can only be part of an unhandled related-process fault while it is interior. We show for all three benchmarks that this percentage of time is under 40 percent, but it is application dependent in terms of scaling behavior.

8. Conclusion

We have described a new approach to producing a fault-tolerant termination detection algorithm based on the original parental-responsibility algorithm described by Dijkstra and Scholten [3]. The three algorithms we describe have worst-case overhead and recovery costs measured in terms of the application's *process fanout*, which is upper-bounded by the DS algorithm's provably-optimal $\mathcal{O}(M)$ bound and by the number of processes in the system. In practice, especially in scalable HPC applications, it is often much smaller. Thus, the overhead for making termination detection fault tolerant is lower than the overhead of termination detection itself. Additionally, all overhead costs are distributed in a localized, scalable manner, avoiding the centralization that makes other fault-tolerant termination detectors unsuitable for HPC.

Through benchmark results, we have shown that the practical overhead costs are minimal. We use real system fault data to show that our algorithms are highly survivable in the face of the faults they are likely to encounter. Therefore, we conclude that our algorithms are well-suited to large-scale parallel applications.

Acknowledgements

The authors were supported by DOE grant DE-SC0006706 and NSF grants ITR-HECURA-0833188 and OCI-0725070. This research used resources of the Argonne Leadership Computing Facility at Argonne National Laboratory, which is supported by the Office of Science of the U.S. Department of Energy under contract DE-AC02-06CH11357.

References

[1] G. Bikshandi, J. G. Castanos, S. B. Kodali, V. K. Nandivada, I. Peshansky, V. A. Saraswat, S. Sur, P. Varma, and T. Wen. Efficient, portable implementation of asynchronous multi-place programs. In *PPoPP '09: Proceedings of the 14th ACM SIGPLAN symposium on Principles and practice of parallel programming.* ACM, 2009. ISBN 978-1-60558-397-6. doi: 10.1145/1504176.1504215.

[2] G. Bosilca, R. Delmas, J. Dongarra, and J. Langou. Algorithm-based fault tolerance applied to high performance computing. *Journal of Parallel and Distributed Computing*, 69(4):410 – 416, 2009. ISSN 0743-7315. doi: 10.1016/j.jpdc.2008.12.002.

[3] E. W. Dijkstra and C. S. Scholten. Termination detection for diffusing computations. *Inf. Proc. Letters*, 11(1):1–4, 1980.

[4] J. Dinan, D. B. Larkins, P. Sadayappan, S. Krishnamoorthy, and J. Nieplocha. Scalable work stealing. In *Proceedings of the Conference on High Performance Computing Networking, Storage and Analysis*, SC '09, pages 53:1–53:11. ACM, 2009. doi: 10.1145/1654059.1654113.

[5] F. Freiling, M. Majuntke, and N. Mittal. On detecting termination in the crash-recovery model. In A.-M. Kermarrec, L. Boug, and T. Priol, editors, *Euro-Par 2007 Parallel Processing*, volume 4641 of *Lecture Notes in Computer Science*, pages 629–638. Springer Berlin / Heidelberg, 2007. ISBN 978-3-540-74465-8.

[6] A. Geist and C. Engelmann. Development of naturally fault tolerant algorithms for computing on 100,000 processors, 2002.

[7] T. Hoefler, C. Siebert, and A. Lumsdaine. Scalable communication protocols for dynamic sparse data exchange. In *Proceedings of the 15th ACM SIGPLAN Symposium on Principles and Practice of Parallel Programming*, PPoPP '10, pages 159–168. ACM, 2010. doi: 10.1145/1693453.1693476.

[8] L. Kalé and S. Krishnan. Charm++ : A portable concurrent object oriented system based on C++. In *Proceedings of the Conference on Object Oriented Programmi ng Systems, Languages and Applications*, September 1993.

[9] P. Kogge, K. Bergman, S. Borkar, D. Campbell, W. Carlson, W. Dally, M. Denneau, P. Franzon, W. Harrod, J. Hiller, S. Karp, S. Keckler, D. Klein, R. Lucas, M. Richards, A. Scarpelli, S. Scott, A. Snavely, T. Sterling, R. S. Williams, and K. Yelick. Exascale computing study: Technology challenges in achieving exascale systems, 2008.

[10] T.-H. Lai and L.-F. Wu. An $(N-1)$-resilient algorithm for distributed termination detection. *Parallel and Distributed Systems, IEEE Transactions on*, 6(1):63–78, Jan 1995. doi: 10.1109/71.363410.

[11] J. Lifflander, S. Krishnamoorthy, and L. V. Kale. Work stealing and persistence-based load balancers for iterative overdecomposed applications. In *Proceedings of the 21st international symposium on High-Performance Parallel and Distributed Computing*, HPDC '12, pages 137–148. ACM, 2012. doi: 10.1145/2287076.2287103.

[12] W. Ma and S. Krishnamoorthy. Data-driven fault tolerance for work stealing computations. In *Proceedings of the 26th ACM international conference on Supercomputing*, ICS '12, pages 79–90. ACM, 2012. doi: 10.1145/2304576.2304589.

[13] F. Mattern. Algorithms for distributed termination detection. *Distributed Computing*, 2:161–175, 1987. doi: 10.1007/BF01782776.

[14] E. Meneses, X. Ni, and L. V. Kale. A Message-Logging Protocol for Multicore Systems. In *Proceedings of the 2nd Workshop on Fault-Tolerance for HPC at Extreme Scale (FTXS)*, Boston, USA, June 2012.

[15] N. Mittal, F. C. Freiling, S. Venkatesan, and L. D. Penso. Efficient reduction for wait-free termination detection in a crash-prone distributed system. In *Proceedings of the 19th international conference on Distributed Computing*, DISC'05, pages 93–107, 2005.

[16] S. Venkatesan. Reliable protocols for distributed termination detection. *Reliability, IEEE Transactions on*, 38(1):103–110, Apr 1989. ISSN 0018-9529. doi: 10.1109/24.24583.

[17] T. von Eicken, D. Culler, S. Goldstein, and K. Schauser. Active Messages: a Mechanism for Integrated Communication and Computation. In *Proceedings of the 19th International Symposium on Computer Architecture*, Gold Coast, Australia, May 1992.

[18] J. J. Willcock, T. Hoefler, N. G. Edmonds, and A. Lumsdaine. AM++: a generalized active message framework. In *Proceedings of the 19th international conference on Parallel architectures and compilation techniques*, PACT '10, 2010. doi: 10.1145/1854273.1854323.

[19] J. J. Willcock, T. Hoefler, N. G. Edmonds, and A. Lumsdaine. Active pebbles: parallel programming for data-driven applications. In *Proceedings of the international conference on Supercomputing*, ICS '11, pages 235–244. ACM, 2011. ISBN 978-1-4503-0102-2. doi: 10.1145/1995896.1995934.

Array Dataflow Analysis for Polyhedral X10 Programs *

Tomofumi Yuki

Colorado State University

yuki@cs.colostate.edu

Paul Feautrier

LIP (ENS Lyon, INRIA, CNRS, UCBL)

paul.feautrier@ens-lyon.fr

Sanjay Rajopadhye

Colorado State University

Sanjay.Rajopadhye@colostate.edu

Vijay Saraswat

IBM Research

vijay@saraswat.org

Abstract

This paper addresses the static analysis of an important class of X10 programs, namely those with finish/async parallelism, and affine loops and array reference structure as in the polyhedral model. For such programs our analysis can certify whenever a program is deterministic or flags races.

Our key contributions are (i) adaptation of array dataflow analysis from the polyhedral model to programs with finish/async parallelism, and (ii) use of the array dataflow analysis result to certify determinacy. We distinguish our work from previous approaches by combining the precise statement instance-wise and array element-wise analysis capability of the polyhedral model with finish/async programs that are more expressive than doall parallelism commonly considered in the polyhedral literature. We show that our approach is exact (no false negative/positives) and more precise than previous approaches, but is limited to programs that fit the polyhedral model.

Categories and Subject Descriptors D.3.4 [*Programming Languages*]: Processors — Compilers, Debuggers; D.3.3 [*Programming Languages*]: Language Constructs and Features — Concurrent programming structures; D.2.4 [*Software Engineering*]: Software/Program Verification — Validation

Keywords X10; Parallelism; Non-determinism; Array Data-flow Analysis; Polyhedral Model; Happens-Before; Race Detection; Execution Partial Order

1. Introduction

Because parallelism has gone mainstream, the problem of improving parallel programmer productivity is now increasingly important. It was the goal of the DARPA HPCS program, initially for the supercomputing niche, but is no longer a niche problem. A number of new parallel programming languages are being actively developed and explored [2, 6, 8, 18, 22, 30]. These languages all employ new programming models to ease the parallel programming effort.

* This work was funded in part by the National Science Foundation, Award Numbers: 1240991 and 0917319

While designing and writing parallel programs is significantly harder than its sequential counterpart, debugging is even harder. This is due to the non-deterministic nature of parallel execution, and the accompanying difficulty of reproducing errors. Therefore the problem of static analysis of parallel programs is becoming critical. Some recent parallel languages also attempt to ease the debugging effort. For example, Titanium [30] can check for possible deadlocks at compile time. Most parallel constructs in X10 [22] are designed such that no (logical) deadlocks occur.

In this paper, we present static race detection for a subset of X10 programs. By providing race-free guarantee, we can prove determinacy of a program. The ability to detect races statically will allow programmers to correct them as they write the program, greatly improving their productivity. The subset of X10 we consider includes its core parallel constructs, `async` and `finish`. We also require that the loop bounds and array accesses to be affine to fit the *polyhedral model*, a mathematical framework for reasoning about program transformations [13]. Although it considers a restricted class of programs, this model has proven very effective and has found widespread use in automatic parallelization in high performance computing.

We improve upon previous techniques for static data race detection in two key directions:

- Our analysis is statement *instance-wise* and array *element-wise*. Most existing approaches (e.g., [9, 15]) analyze race of static statements and conservatively flags as race if two statements that may happen in parallel access the same variable. Our analysis will find sets of statement *instances* (i.e., statement executed when loop counters take specific values) that may happen in parallel, and only flags as race if they access the same *element* of an array.

- In comparison with other methods that support both instance-wise and element-wise analysis [5, 7], our work supports parallelism based on finish/async constructs, which are more expressive than *doall* type parallelism considered in prior work.

Consider the following code fragment that uses the `async` construct of X10. An async spawns a new activity to execute the enclosed statement. The spawning activity cannot proceed beyond the end of an enclosing `finish` block—another of X10's constructs—until all activities that it has spawned have terminated.

```
for (i in 0..N) {
    S0
    async S1
}
```

The above code sequentially executes S0 at each iteration of the loop, and after executing S0, spawns a new activity to execute an instance of S1. Such parallelism cannot be expressed as *doall* type parallelism, and no clean way to express it as a *schedule* in the polyhedral model is currently available.

Our race detection is based on an adaptation of array dataflow analysis [11] from the polyhedral model. This allows us to have the same level of precisions as other work based on the polyhedral model, but is applicable to finish/async based parallelism. Specifically, the key contributions of this paper are:

- A very simple formulation of the operational semantics for this fragment of X10, significantly simplifying [16, 23]. This directly leads to a simple definition of the "happens-before" (HB) and "may-happen-in-parallel" (MHP) relation on statements.

- Characterization of the HB relation as an *incomplete lexicographical order*. This is the key to reuse techniques from the polyhedral model for X10 programs.

- Adaptation of Array Dataflow Analysis [11] for X10 programs. Array dataflow analysis answers the question, which instance of which statement produced the value being used for each statement instance. We have extended this analysis to handle X10 programs.

- Race Detection using array dataflow results. The key idea is that once we have solved the dataflow problem, we can identify the set of instances that cause a race by pinpointing the set of array cells which have multiple producers.

- Prototype implementation of a verifier for our subset of X10. If a program has races, our tool can tell precisely which statement instances are involved.

2. A Subset of X10

Our main interest is in intra-procedural analysis, and we wish to address the integration of finish/async concurrency with loops over array based data-structures in a pure form. Hence we will only consider assignment statements, sequencing, finish, async and for loops, and variables that range over integers and arrays of integers. This allows us to state certain properties of the key relations— Happens Before and its closely related May Happens in Parallel— in a pure form. Our formal treatment of the semantics can be extended *mutatis mutandis* with conditionals, local variables, potentially infinite loops, method calls, objects and functions etc., but we restrain ourselves to the subset we can analyze with polyhedral machinery.

The subset of X10 [22] we consider consists of the following control constructs:

- Sequence ($\{S\,T\}$): Composes two statements in sequence.

- Sequential for loop: We assume all loops have an associated loop iterator. X10 loops may scan a multidimensional iteration space. However, we assume that such loops have been expanded into a nest of unidimensional loops.

- Parallel activation, async: The body of the async is executed by an independent lightweight thread, called activity in X10.

- Termination detection, finish: An activity waits for all activities spawned within the body of finish to terminate before proceeding further. In addition, each program has an implicit finish as its top level construct.

We also require the program to fit the polyhedral model. The polyhedral model requires loop bounds, and array access to be affine expressions of the surrounding loop indices. Multidimensional arrays in X10 and Java are in fact trees of one-dimensional

arrays. As such, they support many operations beyond simple subscripting. An example is row interchange in constant time. Detection of such uses is beyond the scope of this paper; see for instance [29] for an abstract interpretation approach.

Note that the full language permits some additional constructs: for instance the (conditional) atomic block (when(c) S) . This construct permits data-dependent synchronization in general and barrier-style *clocks* [23] in particular. The at construct permits computation across multiple places. We leave the integration of these statements into the analysis of this paper for future work.

2.1 Operational Semantics

We provide a simple, concise structural operational semantics (SOS) for the fragment of X10 considered in this paper. This semantics is considerably simpler than [23] because it eschews the "Middleweight Java" approach in favor of directly specifying semantics on statements. Unlike [16] there is no need to translate the statement to be executed into different kinds of tree-like structure; the information is already contained in the lexical structure of the statement and can be elegantly exploited using SOS based structural rules.

In this section, we present the semantics, characterize certain syntactic properties of statements (the happens-before and the may-happen-in-parallel relation), and relate them to behavioral properties. For simplicity of exposition, we chose to use a sequentially consistent memory model. In future work we expect to apply the methods of [24] to adapt the analysis techniques developed in this paper to relaxed memory models.

We assume that a set of (typed) locations Loc, and a set of values, Val, is given. Loc typically includes the set of variables in the program under consideration. With every d-dimensional $N_1 \times \ldots \times N_d$ array-valued variable a of type array are associated a set of distinct locations, designated a(0,...,0), ..., a(N_1-1, ..., N_d-1). The set of values includes integers and arrays.

A *heap* is a partial (finite) mapping from Loc to Val. For h a heap, l a location and v a value by $h[l = v]$ we shall mean the heap that is the same as h except that it takes on the value v at l. By $h(l)$ we mean the value e to which h maps l.

DEFINITION 2.1 (Expressions). *We assume that a set of* RHS *expressions (ranged over by $e, e', e_0, e_1, \ldots$) that denote values is defined.* RHS *expression include variables (e.g., x), literals (e.g., 0), array accesses (e.g., a(p)), and appropriate operations over integers (e.g., addition). We also assume that a set of* LHS *expressions (ranged over by $a, a', a_0, a_1, \ldots$) that denote locations is defined. These include variables and array accesses.*[1] *We extend h to a map from* RHS *expressions to values and from* LHS *expressions to locations in the obvious way.*

DEFINITION 2.2 (Statements). *The statements are defined by the productions:*

(Statements)	S	::=
T		Execute T.
$\{T\,S\}$		Execute T then S.

	T	::=
$a = e;$		Assignment.
for(x in $e1$ $e2$) S		Execute S for x in $e1 \ldots e2$.
async S		Spawn S.
finish S		Execute S and wait for termination.

---

[1] Thus, as is conventional in modern imperative languages, the notation a(i) is ambiguous. When used on the LHS it represents a location and when used on the RHS it represents the contents of that location.

DEFINITION 2.3 (Paths). *The set of paths $\mathcal{P}[\![S]\!]$ corresponding to a statement S is given as follows. For a set of paths U, we let xU stand for the set of paths xs, for $s \in U$.*

$$
\begin{aligned}
\mathcal{P}[\![a = e]\!] &= \{\varepsilon\} \\
\mathcal{P}[\![\{S\,T\}]\!] &= \{\varepsilon\} \cup 0\,\mathcal{P}[\![S]\!] \cup 1\,\mathcal{P}[\![T]\!] \\
\mathcal{P}[\![\texttt{for}(x\ \texttt{in}\ e1..e2)\ S]\!] &= \{\varepsilon\} \cup x\,\mathcal{P}[\![S]\!] \\
\mathcal{P}[\![\texttt{async}\ S]\!] &= \{\varepsilon\} \cup a\,\mathcal{P}[\![S]\!] \\
\mathcal{P}[\![\texttt{finish}\ S]\!] &= \{\varepsilon\} \cup f\,\mathcal{P}[\![S]\!]
\end{aligned}
$$

The statements for which the operational semantics is defined are assumed to satisfy some static semantic conditions (e.g., well-typedness). We omit the details. Note that in a `for` loop the index variable is considered bound. To avoid dealing with alpha renaming, we assume that in the statement under consideration no two loop index variables are the same.

Note that the set of paths for a statement is non-empty and prefix-closed, hence defines a tree. A path $p \in \mathcal{P}[\![S]\!]$ is *terminal* if it is not a proper prefix of any other in $\mathcal{P}[\![S]\!]$. For example, in Fig. 1 $[0, f, 0, i, a]$ is the (terminal) path for statement $S0$, and $[0, f, 1]$ is a (non-terminal) path.

From the definition of statements and paths, the only place that two paths may diverge is at a sequential composition. For a statement S, let sx and sy be two distinct paths in $\mathcal{P}[\![S]\!]$. Note that paths in $\mathcal{P}[\![S]\!]$ are *symbolic*, since loop iterators are variables. We define an *instance* of a path as $t = s\theta$, where θ is a substitution applied to $s \in \mathcal{P}[\![S]\!]$ mapping index variables to integers.[2] Now, two *path instances* sx and sy can diverge either when they follow different branches via sequential composition, or when they have different values of loop iterators.

PROPOSITION 2.1. *For a statement S, let sx and sy be two distinct instances of paths in $\mathcal{P}[\![S]\!]$. Then either $x < y$ or $y < x$.*

We also introduce a notation to denote sub-statements. Let S be a statement and $s \in \mathcal{P}[\![S]\!]$. We use the notation $S\hat{\ }s$ to refer to the sub-statement of S obtained by traversing the path s from the root. Given a path instance $t = s\theta$, we define $S\hat{\ }t$ to be $(S\hat{\ }s)\theta$, that is, θ applied to the statement obtained by traversing the path s from the root of S. This definition is justified by the fact that θ is unique for each path instance.

DEFINITION 2.4 (Read and write set). *Let S be a statement, and $s \in \mathcal{P}[\![S]\!]$ a terminal path (or path instance). We let $rd(S, s)$ denote the set of locations read by $S\hat{\ }s$ and $wr(S, s)$ the set of locations written in $S\hat{\ }s$.*

Let s, t be two paths or path instances for S. We say s write-affects t if $wr(S, s) \cap (rd(S, t) \cup wr(S, t))$ is non-empty. We say that s and t conflict if s write-affects t or vice versa. We say that t self-conflicts if $rd(S, t) \cup wr(S, t)$ is non-empty.

For instance, let S be the statement $\texttt{for}(i\ \texttt{in}\ 0..10)\ a(i) = a(i) + 1$. Then the path $[\varepsilon]$ self-conflicts, as does $[i]$. But the path (instance) $[0]$ does not. In fact the paths $[i], [j]$ do not conflict if i, j are distinct integers (in the given range.)

Note that $S\hat{\ }s$ may be a statement with free variables (e.g., parameters), hence the set of locations read/written may be symbolic (i.e., heap-dependent at run-time.)

Execution relation. As is conventional in SOS, we shall take a *configuration* to be a pair $\langle S, h \rangle$ (representing a state in which S has to be executed in the heap h) or h (representing a terminated computation.)

---

[2] Usually, we will be concerned only with path instances that satisfy the bounds conditions for the index variable. Note that given S, $s \in \mathcal{P}[\![S]\!]$, and an instance $t = s\theta$ note that θ can be recovered uniquely.

The operational execution relation $\longrightarrow$ is defined as a binary relation on configurations. We use the "matrix" convention for presenting rules compactly. A rule such as:

$$
\frac{\begin{array}{c} c_0, \ldots, c_{p-1} \\ \gamma \longrightarrow \gamma_0 \mid \ldots \mid \gamma_{n-1} \end{array}}{\begin{array}{c} \gamma^0 \longrightarrow \delta_0^0 \mid \ldots \mid \delta_{n-1}^0 \\ \ldots \\ \gamma^{m-1} \longrightarrow \delta_0^{m-1} \mid \ldots \mid \delta_{n-1}^{m-1} \end{array}}
$$

(with $p \geq 0, m > 0, n > 0$) is taken as shorthand for $m \times n$ rules: infer $\gamma^i \longrightarrow \delta_j^i$ from $c_0, \ldots, c_{p-1}, \gamma \longrightarrow \gamma_j$, for $i < m, j < n$.

The axioms and rules of inference are:

$$
\frac{l = h(a), v = h(e)}{\langle a = e, h \rangle \longrightarrow h[l = v]} \tag{1}
$$

$$
\frac{\langle S, h \rangle \longrightarrow \langle S', h' \rangle \mid h'}{\begin{array}{rcl} \langle \{S\,T\}, h \rangle & \longrightarrow & \langle \{S'\,T\}, h' \rangle \mid \langle T, h' \rangle \\ \langle \texttt{async}\ S, h \rangle & \longrightarrow & \langle \texttt{async}\ S', h' \rangle \mid h' \\ \langle \texttt{finish}\ S, h \rangle & \longrightarrow & \langle \texttt{finish}\ S', h' \rangle \mid h' \\ \langle \{\texttt{async}\ T\,S\}, h \rangle & \longrightarrow & \langle \{\texttt{async}\ T\,S'\}, h' \rangle \mid \langle \texttt{async}\ T, h' \rangle \end{array}} \tag{2}
$$

One can think of these rules as propagating an "active" tag from a statement to its constituent statements. The first rule says that if $\{S\,T\}$ is active then so is S (that is, any transition taken by S can be transformed into a transition of $\{S\,T\}$). The second rule says that if $\texttt{async}\ S$ is active, then so is S. The third rule says the same thing for $\texttt{finish}\ S$. The fourth rule captures the essence of $\texttt{async}$ (we call it the *"out of order"* rule). It says that in a sequential composition $\{\texttt{async}\ T\,S\}$, the second component S is also active. Thus one can think of $\texttt{async}\ S$ as licensing the activation of the following statement (in addition to activating S).

The first `for` rule terminates execution of the `for` statement if its lower bound is greater than its upper bound.

$$
\frac{l = h(e_0), u = h(e_1), l > u}{\langle \texttt{for}(x\ \texttt{in}\ e_0..e_1)\ S, h \rangle \longrightarrow h} \tag{3}
$$

The recursive rule performs a "one step" unfolding of the `for` loop. Note that the binding of x to a value l is represented by applying the substitution $\theta = x \mapsto l$ to S, rather than by adding the binding to the heap. This is permissible because x does not represent a mutable location in S.

$$
\frac{\begin{array}{c} l = h(e_0), u = h(e_1), l \leq u, m = l + 1, T = S[l/x] \\ \langle T, h \rangle \longrightarrow \langle T', h' \rangle \mid h' \end{array}}{\begin{array}{l} \langle \texttt{for}(x\ \texttt{in}\ e_0..e_1)\ S, h \rangle \longrightarrow \\ \quad \langle \{T'\ \texttt{for}(x\ \texttt{in}\ m..u)\ S\}, h' \rangle \mid \langle \texttt{for}(x\ \texttt{in}\ m..u)\ S, h' \rangle \end{array}} \tag{4}
$$

We now define appropriate semantical notions.

DEFINITION 2.5 (Semantics). *Let $\xrightarrow{\ *\ }$ represent the reflexive, transitive closure of $\longrightarrow$. The operational semantics, $O[\![S]\!]$ of a statement S is the relation*

$$
O[\![S]\!] \stackrel{def}{=} \{(h, h') \mid \langle S, h \rangle \xrightarrow{\ *\ } h'\}
$$

Sometimes a set of observable variables is defined by the programmer, and the notion of semantics appropriately refined:

$$
O[\![S, V]\!] \stackrel{def}{=} \{(h, h'\big|_V) \mid \langle S, h \rangle \xrightarrow{\ *\ } h'\}
$$

where for a function $f : D \to R$ and $V \subseteq D$ by $f\big|_V$ we mean the function f restricted to the domain V.

Note in the above definition we have chosen not to restrict the set of variables over which the input heap is defined. In a more complete treatment of the semantics, we would introduce the new operation which permits dynamic allocation of memory, and define the program as being executed in a heap that is initially defined over only the input array of strings containing the command line arguments.

DEFINITION 2.6 (Determinacy). *A statement S with set of observables V is said to be* scheduler determinate over V *(or just* determinate *for short) if* $O[\![S,V]\!]$ *represents the graph of a function, rather than a relation.*

S is said to be scheduler determinate *if it is scheduler determinate over the set of its free variables.*

2.2 Happens Before and May Happen in Parallel relations

We now establish two structural relations on statements, and connect them to the dynamic behavior of the statements.

DEFINITION 2.7 (Happens Before). *Given a statement S, two terminal path instances i,j in $\mathcal{P}[\![S]\!]$, we say that i* happens before j, *and write $i \prec j$, if for some arbitrary label sequences s,t,u, some sequence c over integers, and integers m_0, m_1 with $m_0 < m_1$:*

$$i = sm_0c \wedge j = sm_1u$$
$$or, \quad i = sm_0c\,ft \wedge j = sm_1u$$

The definition does not explicitly mention async nodes. The label a may occur in i, but only in s or in t. In the first case the occurrence can be ignored because we are considering two paths that lie within the same async. In the latter case the occurrence may be ignored because it is covered by a finish. The intuition is that the "asyncness" of a node can never cause it to happen before some other node. But the "finishness" of a node can—it suppresses all downstream asyncs. This intuition is formalized in the next section.

The following proposition is easy to establish by reasoning about sequences.

PROPOSITION 2.2. *(Transitivity) If $i \prec j$ and $j \prec k$ then $i \prec k$. (Asymmetry) If $i \prec j$ then it is not the case that $j \prec i$. (Irreflexivity) For no i is it the case that $i \prec i$.*

Thus $\prec$ is a strict order. But it is not total. Consider $i = 0a$ and $j = 1$. It is not the case that $i \prec j$ or $j \prec i$.

DEFINITION 2.8 (May Happen In Parallel). *Given a statement S, two terminal path instances i,j in $\mathcal{P}[\![S]\!]$, we say that i* can start with j running, *if for some arbitrary label sequences s,t,u, some sequence c over integers, and integers m_0, m_1 with $m_0 < m_1$:*

$$i = sm_0c \text{ at, and,}$$
$$j = sm_1u$$

We say that i may happen in parallel *with j, and write $i\#j$, if i starts with i running, or i starts with j running.*

PROPOSITION 2.3. *Let S be a statement with two paths q,r. Then $q\#r$ iff $\neg(q \prec r) \wedge \neg(r \prec q) \wedge q \neq r$.*

The proof of the forward direction is easy. In the backward direction we need Proposition 2.1.

DEFINITION 2.9 (Race). *Given a statement S and two sub-statements T and U, we say that there is a* race *involving T and U, if for some legal instances $t = T\theta_t$ and $u = U\theta_u$, $t\#u$ and memory accesses by t and u conflict.*

2.3 Correspondence

We now establish the relationship between the HB and MHP relations and the transition relation. The formal language we are working with does not have conditionals, or local variables, or infinite loops. This means that every sub-statement will execute in every

initial heap. Hence it is possible to characterize the MHP and HB relations in very simple terms.

The key idea in establishing the correspondence is to surface the path/time stamp of a statement in the transition relation. We label each step by the "reason" for the step—the path (from the root) to the substatement that triggers (is the base case for) the transition.

We proceed as follows. First we define *labeled statements*—each substatement is labeled with the path from the root. Next we label transitions. The rules are a straightforward adaptation of Rules 1—4. The only point worth noting is that in the recursive rule for for, the substitution $S[l/x]$ replaces x by l in the labels of all substatements of S as well.[3]

$$\frac{l = h(a), v = h(e)}{\langle a = e^s, h \rangle \longrightarrow^s h[l = v]} \quad (5)$$

$$\frac{\langle S,h \rangle \longrightarrow^s \langle S',h' \rangle \mid h'}{\begin{array}{rcl} \langle\{ST\},h\rangle & \longrightarrow^s & \langle\{S'T\},h'\rangle \mid \langle T,h'\rangle \\ \langle\{\text{async } TS\},h\rangle & \longrightarrow^s & \langle\{\text{async } TS'\},h'\rangle \mid \langle\text{async } T,h'\rangle \\ \langle\text{async } S,h\rangle & \longrightarrow^s & \langle\text{async } S',h'\rangle \mid h' \\ \langle\text{finish } S,h\rangle & \longrightarrow^s & \langle\text{finish } S',h'\rangle \mid h' \end{array}}$$
$$(6)$$

$$\frac{l = h(e_0), u = h(e_1), u > l}{\langle \text{for}(x \text{ in } e_0..e_1) \ S^s, h\rangle \longrightarrow^s h} \quad (7)$$

$$\frac{\begin{array}{c} l = h(e_0), u = h(e_1), l \leq u, m = l+1, T = S[l/x] \\ \langle T,h \rangle \longrightarrow^s \langle T',h' \rangle \mid h' \end{array}}{\begin{array}{c} \langle \text{for}(x \text{ in } e_0..e_1) \ S,h\rangle \longrightarrow^s \\ \langle\{T' \text{ for}(x \text{ in } m..u) \ S\},h'\rangle \mid \langle \text{for}(x \text{ in } m..u) \ S,h'\rangle \end{array}}$$
$$(8)$$

Clearly this transition system is conservative over the previous one—it merely decorates each step with extra information.

THEOREM 1 (Characterization of HB). *Let S be a statement and q,r terminal paths in $\mathcal{P}[\![S]\!]$.*

If $q \prec r$ then for any heap h, in any labeled transition sequence starting from $\langle S,h \rangle$ containing q and r, (the transition labeled with) q occurs before (the transition labeled with) r.

(Converse) If for all heaps h and all transition sequences started from $\langle S,h \rangle$ containing q and r it is the case that q occurs before r then $q \prec r$.

The forward direction is proved by structural induction on S. The key case is sequential composition $U \equiv \{ST\}$ in which q is a path leading into S and r into T. Here, the only "out of order" transition possible is because of the "out of order" rule, which requires S be an async. But since $q \prec r$ we know that $q \equiv s0c$ or $q \equiv s0cft$ and $r \equiv s1u$ (with s being the label for U). Hence S cannot be an async since its type is specified by the first label of cft. In the converse direction, without loss of generality, let $q \equiv s0t$ and $r \equiv s1u$. If the first symbol in t that is not an integer is an a, then we show in the proof that the "out of order" rule can be used to construct an execution sequence in which r precedes q, contradicting our assumption. Hence $q \prec r$.

The proof of the following theorem is similar.

THEOREM 2 (Characterization of MHP). *Let S be a statement and q,r terminal paths in $\mathcal{P}[\![S]\!]$.*

If $q\#r$ then for any heap h there is a transition sequence starting from $\langle S,h \rangle$ containing q and r s.t. q occurs before r and another such that r occurs before q.

(Converse) If for all heaps h there is a transition sequence starting from $\langle S,h \rangle$ containing q and r s.t. q occurs before r and another such that r occurs before q, then $q\#r$ or $r\#q$.

---

[3] In Rule 7, s is the label for the whole for statement.

PROPOSITION 2.4. *Let S be a statement. If no two sub-statements are in a race, then S is determinate.*

The converse is not true. There may be a race but it may be *benign*, i.e., it does not affect the outcome of the program. Consider:

```
finish {
  async x=1; // S0=[f0a]
  x=1;       // S1=[f1]
}
```

Statements S0 and S1 are in a race (they may happen in parallel and their write sets overlap), however, the statement is determinate, it will always yield a heap which is the same as the initial except that maps x to 1.

3. The "Happens-Before" Relation as an Incomplete Lexicographic Order

In this section, we formulate the "happens-before" relation, in a manner familiar from polyhedral analysis. In the polyhedral analysis of sequential languages, statement instances in a program are given unique time stamps represented as *integer vectors*. These vectors are ordered lexicographically—this order is sufficient to capture the idea of "happens-before" for a sequential language.

The strict lexicographic order is defined for two distinct such integer vectors u and v as follows:

$$u \ll v \quad \equiv \quad \bigvee_{p \geq 0} u \ll_p v, \tag{9}$$

$$u \ll_p v \quad \equiv \quad \left(\bigwedge_{k=1}^{p} u_k = v_k \right) \wedge (u_{p+1} < v_{p+1}) \tag{10}$$

As we saw in Section 2.1, the happens-before order in X10 must be sensitive to the presence of finish and async nodes. To take these constructions into account, we will use the paths of Section 2.1—vectors of integers, loop counters and the letters a and f—as time stamps. Polyhedral analyses can take loop counters symbolically, but reason about path instances, where loop counters take some integer value.

We will consider only terminal paths. The lexicographic order may be extended to paths simply by specifying how to order the additional symbols a and f, for instance by assuming that $a < f$ and that they occur later than integers and loop counters. This convention is irrelevant, since, by Proposition 2.1, we will never have to compare a or f to any other item in a path provided, we only compare *distinct* vectors.

Given a time stamp q, $|q|$ is its dimension, $q_i, 1 \leq i \leq |q|$ (sometimes written $q[i]$) is its i-th component, and $q[i..j], i \leq j$ is the vector whose components are $q_i, q_{i+1}, \ldots q_j$. A common shorthand for $q[i..|q|]$ is $q[i..]$.

A time stamp in which the loop counters have been replaced by integers denotes at most one instance of an elementary statement or *operation*. The admissible values are constrained to be within the enclosing loop bounds, which are assumed to be affine. The set of admissible values for the time stamps of statement S, the *iteration domain* of S, is written $\mathcal{D}_S$. Under the above hypothesis, $\mathcal{D}_S$ is a polyhedron.

We now reconstruct the "happens-before" relation as a "relaxed" lexicographic order. We start from the observation that:

$$\mathbf{true} \equiv (q \ll r) \vee (q = r) \vee (r \ll q).$$

This suggests that $q \prec r$ be constructed as a case distinction:

- $q \ll r \rightarrow ?$
- $q = r \rightarrow \mathbf{false}$
- $r \ll q \rightarrow ?$

The case $q = r$ is obvious, since an operation cannot execute before itself. Let us now show that if $r \ll q$, then $q \prec r$ is impossible. In the notations of Definition 2.7, let s be the common prefix of q and r: $q = s.x.u$ and $r = s.y.v$. By Proposition 2.1, either $x < y$ or $y < x$ is true, and $r \ll q$ implies that $x > y$. Then, Definition 2.7 implies that $q \prec r$ cannot be true.

The conclusion is that in the above disjunction, only the first case has to be considered. This in turn can be expanded according to the definition (9) of $\ll$:

- $q \ll_0 r \rightarrow ?$
- $q \ll_1 r \rightarrow ?$
- $\ldots$
- $q \ll_n r \rightarrow ?$

The case distinction extends until $q \ll_k r$ is obviously false, i.e., when q_k and r_k are different integers, since all predicates $q \ll_{k'} r, k' \geq k$ contains the constraint $q_k = r_k$.

Let us now consider one of the cases $q \ll_p r$. The two time stamps have a common prefix $q[1..k] = r[1..k]$, and by the same reasoning as above, $q_{k+1} = 0$ and $r_{k+1} = 1$. We are then in a position to apply Definition 2.7. If the first letter in the vector $q[k+1..]$ is an f or if there is no letter, then $q \prec r$ is true, and otherwise is false.

The discussion above can be summarized by the following algorithm:

Algorithm H

- **Input**: Two paths q, r.
- **Output**: The constraint h in the loop counters of q, r (if any) which captures the precise conditions under which $q \prec r$.
- $h := \mathbf{false}$
- $b := \mathbf{true}$
- for $k = |q|$ downto 1:
  1. if $q_k = a$ then $b := \mathbf{false}$
  2. if $q_k = f$ then $b := \mathbf{true}$
  3. if $b \wedge k \leq |r|$ then $h := h \vee (q \ll_{k-1} r)$

Here, h denotes a disjunction of affine constraints, which is initialized to **false**, is augmented each time line (3) is executed, and is the "happens-before" predicate when the algorithm terminates.

In what follows, in the interest of compactness, we will allow sequences with more that two items, and timestamps containing integers larger than 1.

Example

Let us apply algorithm H to the example shown in Figure 1. The time stamps associated with each statement are as follows: S0: $[0, f, 0, i, a]$, S1: $[0, f, 1, j]$, and S2: $[1]$.

We first ask if $S0 \prec S1$. Then $q = [0, f, 0, i, a]$ and $r = [0, f, 1, j]$.

- We start from $k = |q| = 5$, $b = $ true, and $h = $ false.
- At $k = 5$, b becomes false, since $q_5 = a$.
- Since q_k does not point to an f until $p = 1$, no changes occur. At $k = 1$, $q \ll_0 r \equiv q_1 < r_1$ is false, and hence $S0$ does not happen before $S1$.

Let us now ask the question if $S0 \prec S2$. Then $q = [0, f, 0, i, a]$ and $r = [1]$. Since $|r| = 1$, line (3) is never executed until $k = 1$. We reach $k = 1$ in the same state as in the previous example, but in this case $q \ll_0 r \equiv q_1 < r_1$ is true, and hence $S0 \prec S2$.

Although we have illustrated the algorithm with an example, the algorithm is not used in this fashion in the following sections.

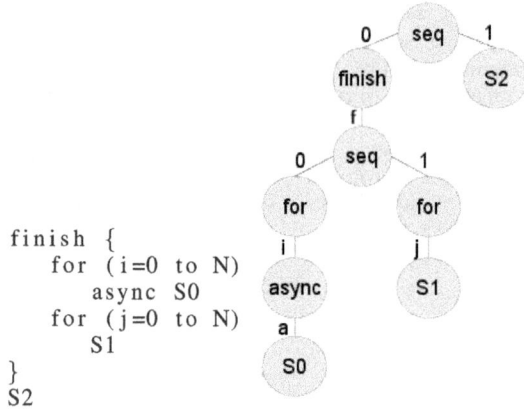

```
finish {
    for (i=0 to N)
        async S0
    for (j=0 to N)
        S1
}
S2
```

Figure 1: Example X10 code and its corresponding AST.

The important observation is that the algorithm only executes line (3) at a subset of the dimensions. Moreover, the subset is determined purely structurally, i.e., given the AST and two statements, one can find a subset I where lexicographic comparison should be performed. This leads to the following re-formulation of the algorithm as an *incomplete* lexicographic order:

$$q \prec r \equiv \bigcup_{k \in I} q \ll_k r, \qquad (11)$$

It is well known that the $\ll_p$ are disjoint. A pair q, r being given, there is at most one k such that $q \ll_k r$. k is the rightmost index such that $q[1 \dots k] = r[1 \dots k]$. From this follows that $\prec$ is transitive.

The observation that the "happens-before" relation is an incomplete lexicographic order becomes important in the next section. Because of this property, we can formulate the dataflow analysis questions for X10 programs in a way that can be efficiently solved.

Lastly, the way we have constructed algorithm H clearly implies that:

PROPOSITION 3.1. *Algorithm H exactly implements the "happens-before" relation of Definition 2.7*

4. Dataflow Analysis

In this section, we present an adaptation of array dataflow analysis [11] for X10 programs, based on the "happens-before" relation as defined in the preceding section. The analysis is outlined in Figure 2.

Dataflow analysis aims at identifying, for each read access to a memory cell x, the *source* of the value found in x, i.e., the operation which wrote last into x. If the program is sequential, and fits into the polyhedral model [13] each read has a unique source which can be identified exactly [11].

However, the situation is different for parallel programs, since the actual execution order of operations may differ from run to run, due to scheduler decisions or hardware clock drifts. As a consequence, the content of some memory cell at a given step in the execution of a program may differ across runs. In other words, the answer to the dataflow question, which operation wrote last into x may be different.

This is called a race in software, or a hazard in hardware. The presence of a race condition in a program is usually a bug [4], which may be very difficult to diagnose and to correct, as it may manifest itself with very low probability.

---

[4] It ultimately depends on the intension of the programmer.

Input:
R, A, f_R: A read in a statement R. R reads from a shared array (or scalar) A with access function f_R.
$\mathcal{W}$: Set of statements W that write to A with access function f_W.
Output:
Q: Quast (Quasi-Affine Solution Tree [10]) that gives the producer of read by instances of R.
Algorithm:

1. **foreach** $W \in \mathcal{W}$

   (a) Compute Potential Sources $\Sigma_W(v)$ of W; the set of statement instances that (i) write to the same memory location, and (ii) the read do not happen before the write, parameterized by instances of R, v.

   (b) Compute Self Overwrites $\Sigma_W^-(v)$ of W; the set of writes overwritten by another instance of the same statement, parameterized by instances of R, v.

2. **foreach** $W \in \mathcal{W}$

   (a) Compute Validity Domain $Valid_W$ of $v \in R$; the set where v is valid for $\Sigma_W(v)$. An instance v becomes invalid if its write is overwritten by other statements.

3. Compute Q:
   $Q := \emptyset$
   foreach $W \in \mathcal{W}$

   (a) $Q := Q \cup \big((\Sigma_W(v) / \Sigma_W^-(v)) \wedge v \in Valid_W \big)$
   A write W is a producer of v if (i) it is a potential source, (ii) not overwritten by other instances of W, and (iii) not overwritten by writes of other statements.

Figure 2: Overview of array dataflow analysis for our X10 subset.

4.1 Potential Sources

Let us focus on an instance of statement R at time stamp v, which has a read of array A at subscript(s) $f_R(v)$. The potential sources are instances of a statements W at time stamp w, which write into A at subscript(s) $f_W(w)$. f_R and f_W are vector functions of the same dimension as A. The set of potential sources is defined by:

$$v \in D_R, \qquad (12)$$
$$w \in D_W, \qquad (13)$$
$$f_W(w) = f_R(v), \qquad (14)$$
$$\neg(v \prec w) \wedge v \neq w \qquad (15)$$

Constraint (12) and (13) respectively constraints v and w to set of legal time stamps (iteration domain) of R and W. Constraint (14) restricts to those with conflicting memory accesses; those access the same *element* of the array A. Lastly, constraint (15) removes writes that happen after reads ($v \prec w$), and write by the same statement instance ($v = w$). In a sequential program, $\prec$ is total, hence $\neg(v \prec w) \wedge v \neq w \equiv w \prec v$, which is the usual formulation [11].

Let $\Sigma_W(v)$ be the set of potential sources as defined by (12-14) and (15). If the source program fits in the polyhedral model, all constraints are affine with the exception of (15), which can be expanded in Disjunctive Normal Form (DNF). Hence, $\Sigma_W(v)$ is a union of polyhedra.

4.2 Overwriting

Let x be a write to the same memory cell as w. x overwrite w if in all executions, x happens between w and v, or $w \prec x \prec v$. It is clear that if an overwrite exists, v will never see the value written by w. Both conditions are necessary: if one of them were not true, there would exists executions in which x happens before w, or v happens before x, and the value written at w would still be visible at v. This step is analogous to restricting the set of candidate sources to the most recent write in the original array dataflow analysis [11]. However, since the order is not total, the most recent write is not unique.

4.2.1 Self Overwrites

Write by a statement may be overwritten by other instances of the same statement. An instance w in $\Sigma_W(v)$ is a real source only if no other instance of W, x, overwrite w, i.e.,

$$w \in \Sigma_W(v) \land \neg \exists x \in \Sigma_W(v) : w \prec x. \qquad (16)$$

This is exactly the definition of the set of upper bounds of Σ_W according to $\prec$. When $\prec$ is total, in the sequential case, (16) defines the unique maximum of P_W. In extreme cases, $\prec$ may be empty, and all tentative sources must be kept.

One possibility is to eliminate the existential quantifier in formula (16) using any projection algorithm, compute the negation and simplify the resulting formula. The drawback of this approach is its complexity: quantifier elimination in integers may generate expressions of exponential size, and so does negation.

Another possibility is to exploit the special form (11) of $\prec$. Since existential quantification distributes over disjunction, one has to compute $\exists x : w \ll_p x$ for each term which is present in $\prec$. Due to the very simple form of $\ll_p$, this set can be computed very efficiently using Parametric Integer Programming [10]. Simply solve the problem $\min\{x \in \Sigma_W(v) | w \ll_p x\}$ parametrically with respect to v and w. The result is a conditional expression (a *quast*) whose nodes bear affine constraints in the parameters, and whose leaves are either affine forms or the special term $\perp$, indicating that for some values of the parameters, the set above is empty. The disjunction of the paths leading to leaves not bearing a $\perp$ is the required projection. Then take the union of all such sets, denoted Σ_W^- in Figure 2, and subtract it from Σ_W.

4.2.2 Group Overwrites

Another case of overwrite happens when, for a given read, there are two possible writing statements, W_1 and W_2. A candidate source $w_1 \in \Sigma_{W_1}(v)$ is not visible to v if there exists $w_2 \in \Sigma_{W_2}(v)$ where $w_1 \prec w_2$.

This condition can be checked by inspecting the AST and Σ_W. In the AST, the paths from the root to W_1 and W_2 diverge at some seq or async or finish node. Assume that W_1 is to the left of W_2, then for each $w_1 \in \Sigma_{W_1}(v)$, one may associate w_2 such that $w_1 \prec w_2$. Let p be the common prefix of time stamps labeled to W_1 and W_2. Then $\forall k, 1 \leq k \leq p, w_1[k] = w_2[k]$ and $w_1[p+1] < w_2[p+1]$. Regardless of the remaining values beyond $p+1$, $w_1 \ll_p w_2$ holds. According to algorithm H, $w_1 \prec w_2$ if the uppermost parallel construct in W_1 below the common node is not an async, and hence w_1 is overwritten by w_2. Otherwise, w_1 and w_2 can happen in any order and w_1 is not overwritten. Similarly, there is no w_2 where $w_1 \prec w_2$ if W_2 is to the left of W_1, since we obtain $w_2 \ll_p w_1$.

However, this construction fails if for the considered value of v, $\Sigma_{W_2}(v)$ is empty. As a set, $\Sigma_W(v)$ is a function of v, and it may be empty for some values of v, i.e., for some values of v, R may have no sources from W. Let us define the *range* of W as:

$$\Omega_W = \{v | \Sigma_W(v) \neq \emptyset\}.$$

The source is in $\Sigma_2(v)$ if $v \in \Omega_2$, and in $\Sigma_1(v)$ if $v \in \Omega_1 \backslash \Omega_2$.

In the general case we must consider more than two writing statements. Let us define an order on the writing statements by the definition: $W < W'$ if W is to the left of W' in the AST, and if the uppermost parallel construct in the path to W from the common node is not an async. It is easy to prove transitivity of $<$. For each

W, one may define a validity by the rule:

$$Valid_W = \Omega_W \backslash \bigcup_{w < W'} \Omega_{W'}.$$

The source is in Σ_W only if $v \in Valid_W$. Maximal elements in the $<$ order have no successors, hence for them $Valid_W = \Omega_W$, while some other statements may have empty validity sets, indicating complete overwriting.

5. Race Detection

Once we have Σ_W, Σ_W^-, and $Valid_W$ for all writers W, the output quast of the dataflow analysis may be computed. However, the resulting quast may not be well-defined: a read may have multiple sources when the program contains races. The detection of races using the array dataflow analysis result is discussed in this section.

5.1 Race between Read and Write

The set of potential sources $\Sigma_W(v)$ can be split in two sets according to whether $w \prec v$ is true or not. If $\neg(w \prec v)$, $\neg(v \prec w)$ and $v \neq w$ (recall constraint (15)), then the read and the write may happen in parallel. In other words, v and w are not ordered, and thus v may execute before w in some execution but w may precede v in the other. Hence there is clearly a race in this case.

Let $\Sigma_W'(v)$ be like $\Sigma_W(v)$ with (15) replaced by $\neg(w \prec v) \land \neg(v \prec w) \land v \neq w$. A non empty $\Sigma_W'(v)$ indicates a race. The emptiness of Σ_W' may be tested in many way, for instance by expanding its constraints to DNF and applying linear programming, or by submitting its definition to an SMT solver, like Yices, Z3, or CVC among others. If Σ_W' is found to be non empty, the compiler may issue a warning about statement R, and no further analyses are needed.

5.2 Race between Writes

Let $\Sigma_W^*(v)$ the set of sources after self overwrites have been removed. Then the source of a read at v is $\Sigma_W^*(v)$ if $v \in Valid_W$. However, the source may not be unique if the program has races. There are two types of races:

- Race between multiple writes by the same statement. If there exists a solution to the problem $v \in Valid_W, x, y \in \Sigma_W^*(v), x \neq y$, then x and y are involved in a race.

- Race between multiple writes by two statements. Two statements W_1 and W_2 have a race if: $Valid_{W_1} \land Valid_{W_2} \neq \emptyset$.

Both conditions can be checked by any SMT solver.

It is also important to note that it is not necessary to do all the above checks. For instance, if $W_1 < W_2$, their validity sets are disjoint by construction. Race detection of the first kind may be performed as we construct the sets, and the analysis may stop as soon as a race found. This approach may greatly reduce the complexity of the method.

5.3 Detection of Benign Races

The above approach is already sufficient to certify determinism of a program. However, additional analysis may be performed to flag questionable behavior of the program as warnings. For instance, our analysis detect array elements which are read but never written.

Another questionable behavior is *benign races*—races that do not influence the program determinacy. If two potential writes x and y may happen in parallel, x and y are in a race. However, if these writes are overwritten later or are not seen by any read, they are harmless. It might nevertheless be useful to warn the programmer of such behavior: a benign race can be taken as the indication of dead code. A way to handle them is therefore to do a backward recursive analysis starting from the output of the program.

5.4 Kernel Analysis

It is often the case that the full program is not polyhedral, while the core kernels are. In addition, due to the high cost of polyhedral analysis, it may not be practical to analyze the entire program.

The usual approach is to find "polyhedral parts"—subtrees in the AST that fit in the polyhedral model, and analyze them independently. Polyhedral methods are obvious candidates for such code fragments. For a finish/async language like X10, one must be more careful, since a subtree or a method may terminate but leave un-finished activities behind. Hence, to be handled with our methods, the sub-tree must satisfy the following properties in addition to the constraints of the polyhedral model:

- The uppermost parallel construct (in the path from the root of the sub-tree to each statement must be a finish if there is one.

- Similarly, let S be a statement that dominates statements in the sub-tree. Then the uppermost parallel construct in the path from the common prefix of S and the sub-tree to S must be a finish if there is one.

The above follows from algorithm H, and ensures that all statements before and after the sub-tree are ordered by the happens-before relation, with respect to the statements in the sub-tree.

6. Examples

In this section, we illustrate by examples the importance of two key strength of our approach; statement instance-wise, and array element-wise analysis. We specifically compare with the work by Vechev et al. [27] and with other polyhedral approaches [5, 7]. We are not aware of any other state-of-the-art static analysis techniques for race detection that perform instance-wise or element-wise analysis.

6.1 Importance of Element-wise

Let us first use an example similar to the one used by Vechev et al. [27]. The following code is a simplified example of a common case in parallel programming, where a shared array is accesses by multiple threads.

```
finish {
  async for (i in 1..N)
      B[i] = C[i];          // S0
  async for (j in N..2*N)
      B[j] = C[2*i];        // S1
}
for (k=1:2N)
     ... = foo(B[k], ...); // S2
```

The time stamps and iteration domains are:

- $S0$: $[0, \mathtt{f}, 0, \mathtt{a}, i]$, $\mathcal{D}_{S0} = \{i | 1 \leq i \leq N\}$
- $S1$: $[0, \mathtt{f}, 1, \mathtt{a}, j]$, $\mathcal{D}_{S1} = \{j | N \leq j \leq 2N\}$
- $S2$: $[1, k]$, $\mathcal{D}_{S2} = \{k | 1 \leq k \leq 2N\}$

The only read in the program is the read of B by $S2$. Our analysis returns the following answer to the question: which statement produced the value of B[k] at $S2$:

- If $1 \leq k \leq N \wedge k \leq 2N$ then $S0[k]$ is a producer.
- If $1 \leq k \leq 2N \wedge N \leq k$ then $S1[k]$ is a producer.

where $Sn[v]$ denote the instance of Sn when its loop counters take the value v. It concludes that there is a race by two writers since the two sources overlap at $k = N$.

For this example, both of the other approaches will find the race with similar precision. However, if an analysis is not element-wise, then the analysis only finds that there is a race with the entire array B. Assuming that the programmer is warned of this race and change

the lower bound of the j loop to $N+1$, making the program race free, statement based approaches will still conservatively flag the array B to be in conflict.

6.2 Element-wise with Polyhedral

However, element-wise analysis in the work by Vechev et al. [27] is limited compared to polyhedral approaches, since they use an over-approximation. They require that any multi-dimensional arrays is reshaped into a 1D array, and the range of the 1D array to be represented with affine constraints. Furthermore, the renaming must be relative to what is called the taskID that identify an iteration of the loop ran by a thread.

For example, write to array A in the following code is expressed as writes to $\mathtt{A_i[j]}$, where i is the taskID.

```
for (i in 0..(N-1))
  async
      for (j in 0..(N-1))
          A[i][j] = ... // S0
```

Approaches based on the polyhedral model, including ours, represents the write to A as an affine function $(i, j \rightarrow i, j)$ from the iteration domain $\mathcal{D}_{S0} = \{i, j | 0 \leq i, j < N\}$.

Let us illustrate the difference with a slight modification to the first example.

```
{ finish {
  async for (i in 0..(N-1))
      B[2*i] = C[i];        // S0
  async for (j in 0..(N-1))
      B[2*j+1] = C[2*i];    // S1
  }
  ... = foo(B[N]); // S2
}
```

The difference is in the writes to B, which now do not conflict. Our analysis returns the following answer to the question, which statement produced the value read by read B[N] at $S2$:

- If $\exists e : 2e = N \wedge N \geq 2$ then $S0[N/2]$ is a producer.
- If $\exists e : 2e = N - 1 \wedge N \geq 1$ then $S1[(N-1)/2]$ is a producer.

Note that the parametric integer linear programming [10] step (Section 4.2.1) introduces a "new parameter" (existentially quantified variable). The intersection of the two validity sets is empty, and we conclude that the program is race free.

However, the over-approximation by Vechev et al. [27] will approximate the write by $S0$ to be $0 \leq i \leq 2N - 2$, and the write by $S1$ to be $1 \leq i \leq 2N - 1$. Clearly, the two approximations overlap, and hence their approach would conservatively flag the program to have race.

6.3 Importance of Instance-wise

The examples above can also be implemented using *doall* loops. When implemented as parallel loops, previous approaches [5, 7] based on the polyhedral model can verify its determinacy, and does not require extensions proposed in this paper.

Our work can also detect races in finish/async programs that cannot be expressed with *doall* parallelism. The following is a simplified example of a case when such parallelism may be used. The example is based on Gauss-Seidel stencil computation that performs updates in-place, and uses some of the values (A[i-1][j] and A[i][j-1]) computed at the current time step and others from the previous time step.

The following code fragment illustrates a possible use of async in a way that cannot be expressed as loop parallelism. Detail of the statement S1 is not given to simplify the presentation, but some code corresponding to an asynchronous send is the motivation behind this example.

```
for (t in 1..T)
   finish for (i in 1..N-2) {
      //boundary conditions omitted
      for (j in start..end)
         A[i][j] =
            update(A[i-1][j], A[i][j-1],
            A[i][j], A[i+1][j], A[i][j+1]); // S0
      async S1(A[i][end]);                  // S1
      //boundary conditions omitted
   }
```

The point we illustrate with this example is the importance of statement instance-wise analysis. At the granularity of (static) statements, the pair of statements $S0, S1$ may happen in parallel. This is a conservative approximation because $S0[t, i]$ may happen in parallel with $S1[t', i']$ when $t \geq t'$ and $i > i'$. With this precision, our approach find that the read of A[i][end] by $S1$ is always the value written by $S0$.

6.4 Benefits of Array Dataflow Analysis

Array dataflow analysis is, strictly speaking, an overkill for detecting races. The formulation used by Vechev et al. [27] focuses on finding conflicting memory accesses. Dataflow analysis goes one step further by eliminating some of the accesses that are guaranteed to be overwritten from the consumer's perspective. Consider the following example:

```
finish{
   async{
      x = f(); //S1
      x = g(); //S2
   }
   async{
      x = h(); //S3
      x = k(); //S4
   }
}
t = x;       //S5
```

The approach by Vechev et al. [27] will find that statements $S1$, $S2$, $S3$, and $S4$ are all in race since they all may happen in parallel and writes to x. In contrast, array dataflow analysis will show that the read of x at $S5$ has two potential sources, $S2$ and $S4$.

The output by Vechev et al. [27] grows in size as the number of statements in async increases, while the output of dataflow analysis does not. When our analysis is integrated to a programming environment, we believe that the preciseness and compactness of our analysis result will help the programmer more than simply detecting races.

Moreover, once the statement $S5$ is removed from the above example, the approach by Vechev et al. [27] would still detect a race, while our analysis would detect that the race is benign, and hence the full finish block is dead code.

7. Implementation and Evaluation

We have implemented[5] our analysis for the subset of X10 described in Section 2. We take a representation of the AST, where statements only specify arrays (or scalars) being read or written, disregarding the what the operation is. Once we detect polyhedral regions in X10 programs, equivalent information can easily be extracted from the internal representation of the compiler.

Analysis of loop programs to detect regions amenable for polyhedral analysis, frequently referred to as Static Control Parts (SCoPs), or Affine Control Loops (ACLs) is well established through efforts to integrate polyhedral parallelizers into full compilers [14, 19]. In addition, we require that array accesses a[i] and

---

[5] Our implementation is available at www.cs.colostate.edu/PolyhedralX10/

a[j] point to the same memory location iff $i = j$. In general, such guarantee require pointer analysis, which is outside the scope of this paper.

We use the Integer Set Library [28] in our implementation to perform polyhedral operations and to solve parametric integer linear programming problems. The analysis itself is written in Java, and Java Native Interface is used to call ISL.

Java Grande Forum Benchmark Suite

Although our key contribution is verification of finish/async programs, we are not aware of any set of parallel benchmarks that use the extra expressive power of finish/async in their polyhedral parts. We have demonstrated how our technique can handle such programs earlier with examples. In this section, we use Java Grande Forum benchmark suite [26] also used by Vechev et al. [27] to compare performance and applicability of our proposed analysis to their approach. The results are summarized in Table 1.

Out of the 8 benchmarks, 3 that were not handled by Vechev et al. [27] cannot be handled by ours either. SPARSE includes indirect array accesses, which falls out of the polyhedral model. Similarly, MONTECARLO and RAYTRACER cannot be handle by polyhedral analysis. All of the remaining 5 fit the polyhedral model, at least partially, and we were able to verify the determinacy of all parallel blocks. In fact, MolDyn has data dependent conditionals, which we approximate by assuming that both branches are always taken. Clearly, this gives a superset of the set of races, which the analyzer proved to be empty.

Although we present execution times of our method, and that of Vechev et al., we do not claim that our approach is more efficient. Their implementation is not directly comparable to ours, due to many reasons. For instance, they work on a lower level representation of the program (Jimple,) which create a large number of scalar variables, and necessitates loop and array re-construction. In Section 6, we have demonstrated that our method can detect races in more program instances.

8. Related Work

Our work may be placed in two different contexts, (i) as an extension to the polyhedral model for analyzing finish/async programs, and (ii) as an approach for statically verifying determinism of finish/async programs.

Array dataflow analysis was introduced by Feautrier [11] and further expanded by Pugh and Wonnacott [20]. Extensions beyond the polyhedral model were proposed by Pugh and Wonnacott [21] and by Barthou et al. [3]. As far as we know, time stamps were first introduced by Feautrier [12] as a trick for proving the existence of schedules for well-structured sequential programs. They were further exploited for specifying complex program transformations by Bastoul [4]. They are similar to the *pedigrees* proposed by Leiserson et al. [17], with the difference that pedigrees are computed at run time, while time stamps exist only at compile time.

Since the emphasis in the polyhedral literature is placed on automatic parallelization, there has been very little work on verifying already parallel programs. The work by Collard and Griebl [7] that presents array dataflow analysis for programs with *doall* parallelism is most closely related to our work. The key distinction is that we handle finish/async programs that can express parallelism not expressible by doall loops.

In the other context, one key question in reasoning about determinism is the question which statements (or statement instances) have a clearly defined order of execution. Analyses to answer this question for finish/async programs, closely related to our "happens-before" relation, have been presented by Agarwal et al. [1] and by Lee and Palsberg [16].

Benchmark	while loop[1]	data-dep. if[2]	Time (s)[4]	Reference[5] Time (s) [27]
CRYPT	Y		7.6	54.8
CRYPT1	Y		0.24	-
CRYPT2	Y		0.24	-
SOR			1.85	-
SOR1			0.29	0.41
LUFACT1			0.35	1.94
SERIES	Y		1.25	-
SERIES1	Y		0.06	55.8
MOLDYN1[3]			0.35	24.6
MOLDYN2		Y	0.92	2.5
MOLDYN3			0.14	0.32
MOLDYN4			0.08	1.01
MOLDYN5		Y	0.08	0.34

Table 1: Performance of our implementation on JGF benchmarks [26]. Entries with the name followed by a number are verification of a parallel block that each contain a parallel loop surrounded by finish. All programs/blocks were verified to be determinate.

[1] Indicates that while loops were converted to for loops. These while loops are of the form:
```
n=100; do { ... n--;} while (n>=0);
```

[2] Indicates that data-dependent if statements were over-approximated by assuming both branches were always taken.

[3] MOLDYN require a final variable *pad* to be constant propagated due to expressions like: $i2 * pad$.

[4] Our experiments were conducted with 4-core Intel Core2Quad (2.83GHz) and 8GB of memory. We used Java 1.6, and ISL 0.10.

[5] These timing results are taken from their article [27] and were conducted with 4-core Xeon (3.8GHz) and 5GB of memory.

While Lee and Palsberg work at the level of a statement, Agarwal et. al. try to increase precision by exhibiting conditions on loop counters that guarantee (or forbid) parallel execution. However, these conditions use only equality and inequality, instead of the full power of affine constraints. The algorithms in these two papers are surprisingly complex when compared to algorithm H.

There is a separate body of work that address race detection with multi-threaded programs with locks (e.g., [9, 15]). These methods are not directly applicable to modern parallel languages where locks are rarely used.

The work by Vechev et al. [27] goes beyond the evaluation of the "may happens in parallel" relation and attempt to verify determinism of finish/async programs. Their analysis is also instance-wise and element-wise. The main difference is that their work use over-approximations of memory accesses, where our analysis is exact. In addition, we use array dataflow analysis to find races, but the information given by the analysis, which is more than enough to find races, can be used for other purposes.

Dynamic race detection (e.g., [25]) is a complementary technique to static analyses, and is more broadly applicable. However, dynamic analysis requires significant run-time overhead, and is subject to the well-known Dijkstra saying, that they can be used to prove the existence of races, not their absence.

The main drawback of our methods, compared to other approaches, is their restricted applicability; we require loops to be affine. Affine loop programs can be frequently found in scientific applications, which is an important target for emerging parallel programming languages. We believe that the increased precision more than compensates this restriction.

9. Conclusion and Future Work

This paper is a first step towards applying polyhedral analysis to finish/async programs. It has been written in the context of the X10 language. However, we expect our approach to be applicable to other languages with similar parallel constructs. For programs that fit in the polyhedral model, the analysis is exact, and as precise as can be. There are neither false positives nor false negatives. As a side effect, one can exploit the results of dataflow analysis for many other tasks, like scheduling and locality improvement, undefined variables detection, constant propagation and semantic program verification.

The approach in this paper can be extended in two directions:

- The X10 language has several control constructs which may create (or remove) races. Among them are clocks, a generalization of the classical barriers, the atomic modifier, and the at statement, which delegates a calculation to a remote place of the target system. Basically, all these constructs necessitate a new definition of the "happens-before" relation. The question is whether algorithm H can be extended to take care of them.

  Handling atomic and at constructs is a minor extension to the results presented here, but space constraints preclude an elaborate explanation. We are currently working on extending our analysis to handle clocks.

- Like all polyhedral analyses, our method applies only to a limited class of programs. Is there a possibility to remove some of these restrictions? A classical approach is to deal only with polyhedral subtrees of the AST, provided they don't interfere with the remnants of the program.

  One may also resort to approximations. The difficulty here is that since the source computation uses set *differences* (see for instance Section 4.2.2) over- and under-approximations are both needed. Depending on the quality of the approximations, the resulting analysis may have both false negatives and false positives. The problem will be to minimize their number.

References

[1] Shivali Agarwal, Rajkishore Barik, Vivek Sarkar, and Rudrapatna K. Shyamasundar. May-happen-in-parallel analysis of X10 programs. In *Proceedings of the 12th ACM SIGPLAN symposium on Principles and practice of parallel programming*, PPoPP '07, pages 183–193, New York, NY, USA, 2007. ACM.

[2] E. Allen, D. Chase, J. Hallett, V. Luchangco, J.W. Maessen, S. Ryu, G.L. Steele Jr, S. Tobin-Hochstadt, J. Dias, C. Eastlund, et al. The Fortress Language Specification. *Sun Microsystems*, 139:140, 2005.

[3] Denis Barthou, Jean-François Collard, and Paul Feautrier. Fuzzy array dataflow analysis. *Journal of Parallel and Distributed Computing*, 40:210–226, 1997.

[4] C. Bastoul. Code generation in the polyhedral model is easier than you think. In *PACT'13 IEEE International Conference on Parallel Architecture and Compilation Techniques*, pages 7–16, Juan-les-Pins, september 2004.

[5] V. Basupalli, T. Yuki, S. Rajopadhye, A. Morvan, S. Derrien, P. Quinton, and D. Wonnacott. ompverify: polyhedral analysis for the OpenMP programmer. *OpenMP in the Petascale Era*, pages 37–53, 2011.

[6] B.L. Chamberlain, D. Callahan, and H.P. Zima. Parallel programmability and the Chapel language. *International Journal of High Performance Computing Applications*, 21(3):291–312, 2007.

[7] Jean-François Collard and Martin Griebl. Array dataflow analysis for explicitly parallel programs. In Luc Bougé, Pierre Fraigniaud, Anne Mignotte, and Yves Robert, editors, *Euro-Par'96 Parallel Processing*, volume 1123 of *Lecture Notes in Computer Science*, pages 406–413. Springer Berlin / Heidelberg, 1996.

[8] UPC Consortium et al. UPC language specifications. *Lawrence Berkeley National Lab Tech Report LBNL–59208*, 2005.

[9] D. Engler and K. Ashcraft. Racerx: effective, static detection of race conditions and deadlocks. *ACM SIGOPS Operating Systems Review*, 37(5):237–252, 2003.

[10] Paul Feautrier. Parametric integer programming. *RAIRO Recherche Opérationnelle*, 22:243–268, September 1988.

[11] Paul Feautrier. Dataflow analysis of scalar and array references. *Int. J. of Parallel Programming*, 20(1):23–53, February 1991.

[12] Paul Feautrier. Some efficient solutions to the affine scheduling problem, II, multidimensional time. *Int. J. of Parallel Programming*, 21(6):389–420, December 1992.

[13] Paul Feautrier and Christian Lengauer. The polyhedral model. In David Padua, editor, *Encyclopedia of Parallel Programming*. Springer, 2011.

[14] T. Grosser, H. Zheng, R. Aloor, A. Simbürger, A. Größlinger, and L.N. Pouchet. Polly–Polyhedral optimization in LLVM. In *IMPACT 2011 First International Workshop on Polyhedral Compilation Techniques*, 2011.

[15] V. Kahlon, N. Sinha, E. Kruus, and Y. Zhang. Static data race detection for concurrent programs with asynchronous calls. In *Proceedings of the the 7th joint meeting of the European software engineering conference and the ACM SIGSOFT symposium on The foundations of software engineering*, pages 13–22. ACM, 2009.

[16] Jonathan K. Lee and Jens Palsberg. Featherweight X10: a core calculus for async-finish parallelism. In *Proceedings of the 15th ACM SIGPLAN Symposium on Principles and Practice of Parallel Programming*, PPoPP '10, pages 25–36, New York, NY, USA, 2010. ACM.

[17] Charles E. Leiserson, Tao B. Schardl, and Jim Sukha. Deterministic parallel random-number generation for dynamic-multithreading platforms. In *PPOPP'12*, pages 193–204, 2012.

[18] Robert W. Numrich and John Reid. Co-array fortran for parallel programming. *SIGPLAN Fortran Forum*, 17(2):1–31, August 1998.

[19] S. Pop, A. Cohen, C. Bastoul, S. Girbal, G.A. Silber, and N. Vasilache. GRAPHITE: Polyhedral analyses and optimizations for GCC. In *Proceedings of the 2006 GCC Developers Summit*, page 2006, 2006.

[20] W. Pugh and D. Wonnacott. Eliminating false data dependences using the Omega test. In *ACM SIGPLAN PLDI*, pages 140–151, 1992.

[21] W. Pugh and D. Wonnacott. Going beyond Integer Programming with the Omega Test to Eliminate False Data Dependencies. Technical Report CS-TR-3191, U. of Maryland, December 1992.

[22] Vijay Saraswat, Bard Bloom, Igor Peshansky, Olivier Tardieu, and David Grove. X10 language specification version 2.2, March 2012. x10.sourceforge.net/documentation/languagespec/x10-latest.pdf.

[23] Vijay Saraswat and Radha Jagadeesan. Concurrent clustered programming. In *CONCUR 2005 - Concurrency Theory*, pages 353–367, London, UK, 2005. Springer-Verlag.

[24] Vijay A. Saraswat, Radha Jagadeesan, Maged Michael, and Christoph von Praun. A theory of memory models. In *Proceedings of the 12th ACM SIGPLAN symposium on Principles and practice of parallel programming*, PPoPP '07, pages 161–172, New York, NY, USA, 2007. ACM.

[25] S. Savage, M. Burrows, G. Nelson, P. Sobalvarro, and T. Anderson. Eraser: A dynamic data race detector for multithreaded programs. *ACM Transactions on Computer Systems (TOCS)*, 15(4):391–411, 1997.

[26] L.A. Smith, J.M. Bull, and J. Obdrizalek. A parallel Java Grande benchmark suite. In *Supercomputing, ACM/IEEE 2001 Conference*, pages 6–6. IEEE, 2001.

[27] Martin Vechev, Eran Yahav, Raghavan Raman, and Vivek Sarkar. Automatic verification of determinism for structured parallel programs. In *Proceedings of the 17th international conference on Static analysis*, SAS'10, pages 455–471, Berlin, Heidelberg, 2010. Springer-Verlag.

[28] S. Verdoolaege. isl: An integer set library for the polyhedral model. *Mathematical Software–ICMS 2010*, pages 299–302, 2010.

[29] Peng Wu, Paul Feautrier, David Padua, and Zehra Sura. Instance-wise points-to analysis for loop-based dependence testing. In *International Conference on Supercomputing (ICS 2002)*, pages 262 – 273, June 2002.

[30] K. Yelick, L. Semenzato, G. Pike, C. Miyamoto, B. Liblit, A. Krishnamurthy, P. Hilfinger, S. Graham, D. Gay, P. Colella, et al. Titanium: A high-performance Java dialect. *Concurrency Practice and Experience*, 10(11-13):825–836, 1998.

Betweenness Centrality: Algorithms and Implementations *

Dimitrios Prountzos   Keshav Pingali

The University of Texas at Austin, Texas, USA
dprountz@cs.utexas.edu, pingali@cs.utexas.edu

Abstract

Betweenness centrality is an important metric in the study of social networks, and several algorithms for computing this metric exist in the literature. This paper makes three contributions. First, we show that the problem of computing betweenness centrality can be formulated abstractly in terms of a small set of *operators* that update the graph. Second, we show that existing parallel algorithms for computing betweenness centrality can be viewed as implementations of different schedules for these operators, permitting all these algorithms to be formulated in a single framework. Third, we derive a new asynchronous parallel algorithm for betweenness centrality that (i) works seamlessly for both weighted and unweighted graphs, (ii) can be applied to large graphs, and (iii) is able to extract large amounts of parallelism. We implemented this algorithm and compared it against a number of publicly available implementations of previous algorithms on two different multicore architectures. Our results show that the new algorithm is the best performing one in most cases, particularly for large graphs and large thread counts, and is always competitive against other algorithms.

Categories and Subject Descriptors   D.1.3 [*Programming Techniques*]: Concurrent Programming—Parallel Programming; G.2.2 [*Discrete Mathematics*]: Graph Theory—Graph algorithms

General Terms   Algorithms, Performance

Keywords   Concurrency, Parallelism, Amorphous Data-parallelism, Irregular Programs, Optimistic Parallelization, Betweenness Centrality.

1. Betweenness Centrality

Centrality metrics are essential in understanding network structure, since they capture the relative importance of individual nodes in the overall network. In this paper, we examine Betweenness Centrality (BC) [20], a commonly used metric that is based on shortest path computation. If $G = (V, E)$ is a graph and s, t are a fixed pair of graph nodes, the betweenness score of a node v for this node pair is the fraction of shortest paths between s and t that include v. The betweenness centrality of v is the sum of its betweenness scores for all possible pairs of s and t in the graph. More formally,

* This work was supported by NSF grants 0833162, 1062335, 1111766, 1218568, and 1216701 as well as grants and equipment donations from NVIDIA, IBM, Intel and Qualcomm Corporations.

let σ_{st} be the number of shortest paths between s and t, and let $\sigma_{st}(v)$ be the number of those shortest paths that pass through v. The betweenness centrality of node v is defined as: $BC(v) = \sum_{s \neq v \neq t \in V} \frac{\sigma_{st}(v)}{\sigma_{st}}$.

Applications of BC include study of sexual networks and AIDS [28], lethality in biological networks [17, 25], identifying key actors in terrorist networks [15, 27], organizational behavior [11], contingency analysis for power grid component failures [26], and analysis of transportational networks [23]. BC is also used as a heuristic in other algorithms; for example [22] proposes an algorithm for community detection and clustering in large networks, based on the BC of the network edges.

1.1 Brandes' Algorithm: a Basis for Parallel BC Algorithms

An efficient sequential algorithm for computing BC was proposed by Brandes [9], and it has been the basis for many parallelization approaches [5, 16, 19, 29, 36]. Below, we outline the main ideas behind Brandes' algorithm. We define the *dependency* of a source vertex s on a vertex v as: $\delta_s(v) = \sum_{t \in V} \frac{\sigma_{st}(v)}{\sigma_{st}}$. The betweenness centrality of a vertex v is then expressed using Eq. (1). The key insight is that $\delta_s(v)$ satisfies the recurrence (2), where $pred(s, w)$ is a list of immediate predecessors of w in the shortest paths from s to w.

$$BC(v) = \sum_{s \neq v \in V} \delta_s(v) \tag{1}$$

$$\delta_s(v) = \sum_{w \,:\, v \in pred(s,w)} \frac{\sigma_{sv}}{\sigma_{sw}}(1 + \delta_s(w)) \tag{2}$$

Brandes' algorithm uses this insight and it works as follows. Each $s \in V$ is considered as a source of shortest-paths and the contribution of s to $BC(v)$, for all $v \neq s$ is computed in two phases. In the first phase, a shortest-path computation is performed from s, that computes $pred(s, v)$ and σ_{sv} for all nodes. The predecessor lists induce a DAG D over the graph G. In a second phase, D is traversed backward (in non-increasing distance order) and for each $v \in V$, $\delta_s(v)$ is computed based on (2), and the contribution to $BC(v)$ is computed based on (1). The process is described in Fig. 1. Between processing successive sources, node and edge attributes are reset.

1.2 Understanding Parallelism in BC

This algorithm has parallelism at multiple levels. First, we can process multiple source nodes in parallel (loop in line 3 in Fig. 1). In this coarse-grained parallelization strategy, each thread picks an arbitrary graph node s and computes its contribution to the betweenness values of other nodes. Each of these computations is independent, and the updates on each $BC(v)$ form a simple reduction. This parallelization strategy is simple and effective, but each outer loop iteration that is performed in parallel requires its own storage, so the space overhead of this scheme can be substantial. Therefore, it is used only for relatively small graphs. We will refer to approaches

```
 1  Graph G = /* read input graph */
 2  Worklist wl = {v : v ∈ G.nodes}
 3  foreach s : Node ∈ wl {
 4      forall  v : Node ∈ G : // Compute shortest−path DAG D
 5          compute σ_sv
 6          compute pred(s, v)
 7      forall  v : Node ∈ D : // Traverse DAG D backward
 8          compute δ_s(v)
 9          BC(v) += δ_s(v)
10      forall  (u, v) : Edge ∈ G : // Reset graph attributes
11          reset (u,v)
12  }
```

Figure 1. Pseudocode for Brandes' algorithm.

using this strategy as *outer-level* schemes. Alternatively, we can expose parallelism by focusing on processing a single source node and performing each of the computation steps in parallel (loops in lines 4, 7, 10 in Fig. 1). This fine-grained, *inner level* approach is more space-efficient since we only need to maintain a single graph instance, but poses a more challenging goal for parallelization due to non-trivial data dependencies. Finally one can combine the two techniques by processing several source nodes in parallel and performing the per-node computations in parallel.

1.3 Previous Work

Examples of the outer-level approach are [12, 26, 41]. Parallel performance is excellent, as expected, but the size of the input graph is very small or a big distributed cluster is used [12]. Bader et al. in [5] were the first to present an approach that targets both outer-level and inner-level parallelism. This work focuses on unweighted graphs, where the shortest path exploration can be performed by a breadth-first-search (BFS) exploration. Both of the main phases of the algorithm are performed in a level-parallel manner. Within level i all nodes are processed in parallel but only edges between nodes in levels i and $i + 1$ are allowed to be processed. Similarly, in the backward DAG traversal, only nodes between levels i and $i - 1$ are processed in parallel. The strong ordering between levels is achieved by using barriers. Subsequent work by Madduri et al. [29], improves the algorithm to use successors instead of predecessors in the computation of the DAG D, which produces a more efficient, locality-friendly algorithm. [16] targets outer-level parallelism and also performs prefetching and appropriate re-layout of the graph nodes to improve locality. [39] presents a variation of [5] where the graph is logically partitioned among processors, locking is coarsened to a lock per partition, and the predecessor lists are distributed across partitions; [38] extends this work with architecture specific optimizations for the IBM Cyclops64 processor. Similarly, in [36] a GPU level-synchronous parallelization is presented, where graph edges are partitioned among the threads.

Edmonds et al. [19] present an approach that targets fine-grained parallelism and focuses on a distributed memory environment. This work deals with both weighted and unweighted graphs. In the case of weighted graphs, the level-parallel BFS approach is not applicable. Their solution breaks up the DAG construction phase into a number of sub-phases, separated again by barriers. Initially a label-correcting single-source shortest-path (SSSP) algorithm is employed [30, 33] to compute the shortest path distances and predecessor lists. Then, using the predecessor lists the node successors are computed. Finally, a third sub-phase computes $σ_{sv}$ in a level-parallel BFS style, using the node successors. The backward traversal of the DAG is performed without using barriers by using the predecessor lists. [40] presents a serial adaption of Brandes that deals with weighted graphs by adding virtual nodes to turn

them into unweighted graphs, where a BFS exploration can be performed. These algorithms compute the exact value of BC. To reduce the computational cost, a number of approximation algorithms have been proposed [4, 10, 21]. For example, instead of computing the contribution of all source nodes $s \neq v$ to $BC(v)$ in Eq. (1), we can compute the contributions of a subset of source nodes.

1.4 Goals and Contributions

This paper makes three contributions.

- We show that the problem of computing BC can be formulated abstractly in terms of the *operator formulation* of algorithms [34].
- We show that existing parallel BC algorithms can be viewed as implementations of different schedules for applying the operators to the graph, permitting all these algorithms to be formulated in a single framework.
- The full set of our operators can correctly compute BC *under any arbitrary schedule* and can therefore be the basis for a new class of algorithms that can potentially mine more parallelism. This is especially true for the case of weighted graphs, where a purely level-synchronous approach cannot be used. Using these operators, we derive a new parallel algorithm by carefully controlling and optimizing the scheduling of operators. It is space-efficient because it targets fine-grained parallelism. It is able to expose a lot of parallelism because it breaks away from the level parallel mode of execution. It deals with both weighted and unweighted graphs, and, as we show experimentally, has good scalability. Our current implementation targets multicore systems; it is straightforward to adopt it to a distributed setting.

The rest of the paper is organized as follows. § 2 presents the operator formulation of BC and describes how existing algorithms for BC can be viewed as implementations of different schedules for applying the operators to the graph. § 3 describes how to derive and optimize a new asynchronous algorithm for BC by appropriately controlling operator scheduling. § 4 presents our experimental evaluation on two multicore architectures using inputs from multiple graph classes. § 5 concludes the paper.

2. A Framework for Expressing BC Algorithms

In this section, we formulate the computation of betweenness centrality in terms of the *operator formulation* of algorithms [34]. Operators act on graph nodes and edges and update their attributes. We describe a generic algorithm that computes BC by repeatedly applying operators in an unspecified order to the graph until a fixpoint is reached (that is, when no new operator applications can happen). We also show that existing algorithms for BC can be viewed as particular schedules for applying these operators.

To introduce the notion of operators, we consider the simpler problem of computing the breadth-first-search level of nodes in a directed graph. Each node u has a field $l(u)$ (for level), initialized to 0 for *Root*, and to ∞ for all other nodes. When the algorithm terminates, the level of a node will be equal to the length of the shortest path from *Root* to that node. The algorithm discovers paths from *Root* incrementally, so during the execution of the algorithm, the level of a node v is equal to the length of the shortest path to v that has been discovered so far.

Fig. 2 shows the operator formulation for BFS. Like all the operators we introduce in this paper, this operator is applied to a single edge of the graph and to the two nodes that are its end-points. An operator has a left hand side that specifies the precondition (predicate) under which it can be applied; an edge that satisfies this precondition is called an *active edge*. An active edge can be updated as shown in the right-hand side of the operator.

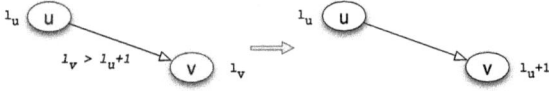

Figure 2. BFS expressed using a single operator for computing shortest paths.

The operator of Figure 2 can be described in words as follows: an edge (u, v) is active if $l(v) > l(u) + 1$; such an edge can be updated by setting $l(v)$ to $l(u) + 1$. If there are several active edges in a graph, an implementation is allowed to update them concurrently, provided that active edge attributes are updated atomically. It can be shown that as long as the scheduling of active edges is fair (that is, the selection of an active edge is not postponed indefinitely), (i) the computation will terminate within some finite number of steps, and (ii) upon termination, for each node u, $l(u)$ will be its BFS level.

2.1 Operators for BC

We now show how to express BC using a small set of operators. To keep the presentation simple, we focus first on unweighted graphs, and then extend our approach to the case of weighted graphs. Our solution operates in two phases. In the first phase, it builds the BFS DAG. As in the BFS computation described above, the first phase discovers and records paths from *Root* to other nodes incrementally. The second phase performs a bottom-up walk of the DAG to compute betweenness centrality.

For each node u we maintain a number of attributes:

- the shortest path distance ($l(u)$) of u,
- the number of shortest paths ($\sigma(u)$) of length $l(u)$ from *Root* to u,
- a list of nodes ($preds(u)$), each of which is the predecessor of u on a shortest path from *Root* to u, and
- a list of nodes ($succs(u)$), each of which is a successor of u on a shortest path from *Root*. Our implementation actually maintains only the number of the successors of a node and not the full list; for expository purposes we describe the operators using the successor list attribute.

Additionally, we associate with each edge (u, v) a level ($l(uv)$) and a path-count ($\sigma(uv)$) attribute; these are used for book-keeping during the algorithm execution, as explained below.

2.1.1 Operators for the DAG Construction Phase

The goal of the first phase is to construct the shortest-path DAG D and also compute the path-count $\sigma(u)$ for each node u. There are four operators, shown in Figure 3. Below, we discuss each in detail.

Shortest Path (SP): This is the same as the BFS operator except that it also resets $\sigma(v)$, $preds(v)$ and $succs(v)$ to their default values. This is the only operator that modifies levels of nodes. It is enabled when the following *guard* predicate $g_{SP}(uv)$ is true:

$$g_{SP}(uv) := l(v) > l(u) + 1$$

First Update (FU): This operator is applied to an edge connecting nodes at successive levels. It updates $\sigma(v)$ with the current value of $\sigma(u)$ and it also updates the predecessor and successor lists of v and u. The operator is enabled when g_{FU} holds:

$$g_{FU}(uv) := l(v) = l(u) + 1 \wedge l(uv) \neq l(u)$$

The second constraint ensures that the operator is applied only once, since after the operator application, $l(uv) = l(u)$ as long as $l(u)$ is stable. There may be several incoming edges to node

v at level $l + 1$ from nodes at level l, and this operator will be applied once for each such edge. These applications will be preceded by an application of the SP operator that brings node v to level $l + 1$.

Update Sigma (US): This operator is applied on an edge connecting nodes at successive levels, and it propagates changes to the path-count ($\sigma(u)$) of u to v. The previous update of $\sigma(v)$ from $\sigma(u)$ is stored in $\sigma(uv)$, which is used to compute the correct incremental update. The operator is enabled when g_{US} holds:

$$g_{US}(uv) := l(u) = l(uv) \wedge l(v) = l(u) + 1 \wedge \sigma(uv) \neq \sigma(u)$$

Correct Node (CN): This operator corrects the successor list of u in case its neighbor v moves to a lower level after having received some updates from u. Note that it is unnecessary to remove u from $preds(v)$ since $preds(v)$ would have been set to $\emptyset$ when v moved to a lower level as a result of applying *SP*. The operator is enabled when g_{CN} holds:

$$g_{CN}(uv) := l(u) \geq l(v) \wedge l(uv) = l(u) \wedge l(u) \neq \infty$$

Example 1 (Sample execution of the first phase). *In Fig. 4 we show a sample execution of the operators for the DAG construction phase of the algorithm. The Root node is s. Then, nodes a, b, c are at distance 1 and node d is at distance 2. Initially, all nodes other than s have distance ∞. First, we explore all nodes across the path (s, a, c, d). This results in a sequence of SP and FU applications that set $l(a) = 1, l(c) = 2, l(d) = 3$, update all path-counts to 1, and set successors and predecessors accordingly. Subsequently, we explore the path (s, b, c, d) and perform a similar sequence of operator applications. Note that, when we process (c, d), we apply US(cd) to correct c's contribution to d's path-count. When we explore path (s, c, d), the levels of c and d are lowered. Finally, we must also update the information of a and b to correctly reflect that c is no longer their successor. This is done by applying CN(ac), CN(bc). At this point, no more operators can be applied and thus we have reached the fixpoint.*

2.1.2 Operators for Backward DAG Traversal

The goal of the second phase is to update the dependency $\delta(u)$ and the contribution to the centrality $BC(u)$ for each node u, based on equations (2) and (1), respectively. This is achieved by applying the single operator in Fig. 5(a) until we reach a fixpoint. The operator is applied on a single edge (u, v) of the graph, such that $u \in preds(v)$. Hence, (u, v) is also an edge of the shortest-path DAG D. The operator guard is:

$$g := succs(v) = \emptyset \wedge u \in preds(v)$$

When the operator is applied, the value of $\delta(u)$ is updated based on the value of $\delta(v)$ as specified by Eq.(2), that is:

$$\delta(u) \stackrel{\pm}{=} \frac{\sigma_{su}}{\sigma_{sv}} (1 + \delta(v))$$

Additionally, v is removed from the successors of u, and u from the predecessors of v. Finally, $BC(v)$ is updated conditionally, based on $\delta(v)$. This happens during the update of the last predecessor u of v. The operator applies when $succs(v) = \emptyset$, that is, when v has no successors, or has received updates from all its successors. This way, the backward traversal of the DAG D is performed in a data driven manner, breaking away from a level-parallel implementation. In Fig. 5(b) we present a composite operator that is produced by merging together a number instances of the above backward traversal operator. This is an instance of an optimization we call *operator merging*, discussed in detail in § 3.3.

2.2 Operators for Weighted Graphs

In Fig. 6 we show the operators for the weighted case. We assume that each edge (u, v) has a strictly positive weight $w(uv)$. *SP*

Initial state: $\forall u \in V \setminus Root\colon [\sigma, l, preds, succs](u) = (0, \infty, \emptyset, 0)$, $[\sigma, l, preds, succs](Root) = (1, 0, \emptyset, 0)$
$\forall (u, v) \in E\colon [l, \sigma](u, v) = (\infty, 0)$

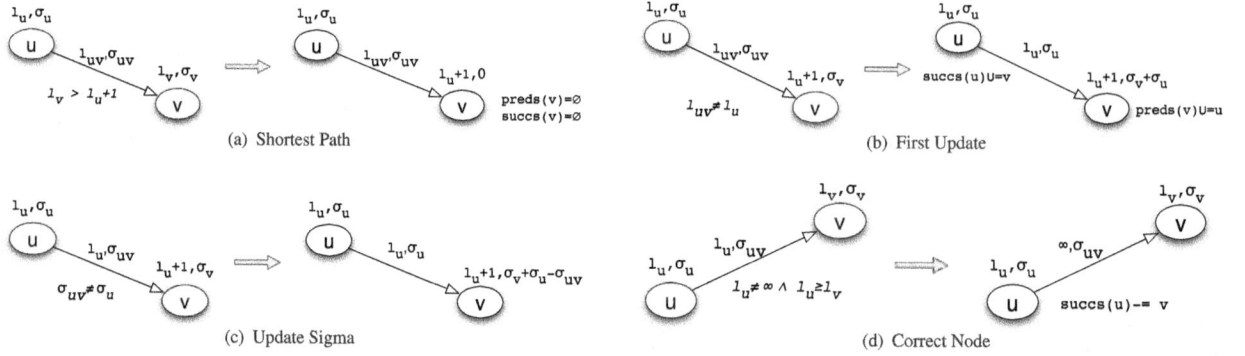

Figure 3. Operators for shortest-path DAG construction phase for unweighted graphs.

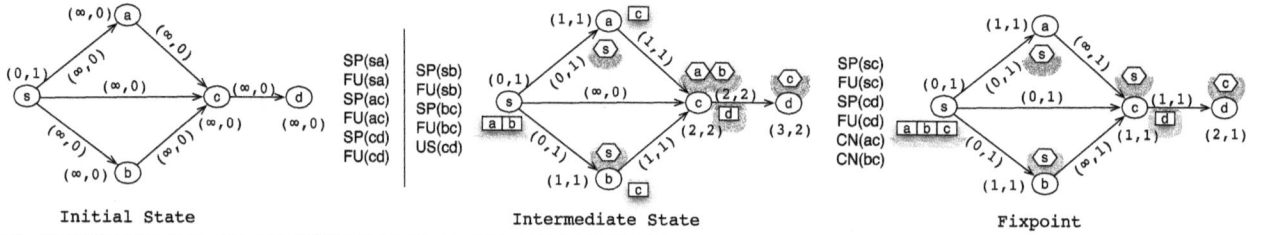

Initial State   Intermediate State   Fixpoint

Figure 4. Sample sequential execution of the algorithm. The graph state is shown before, during and after the algorithm execution. Each node u is decorated with $(l(u), \sigma(u))$. Square boxes represent $succs(u)$ and hexagon boxes represent $preds(u)$. In the first fragment, operators in the left column execute before the ones in the right column.

Initial state: $\forall u \in V\colon \delta_s(u) = 0$ **Initial state:** $\forall u \in V\colon \delta_s(u) = 0$

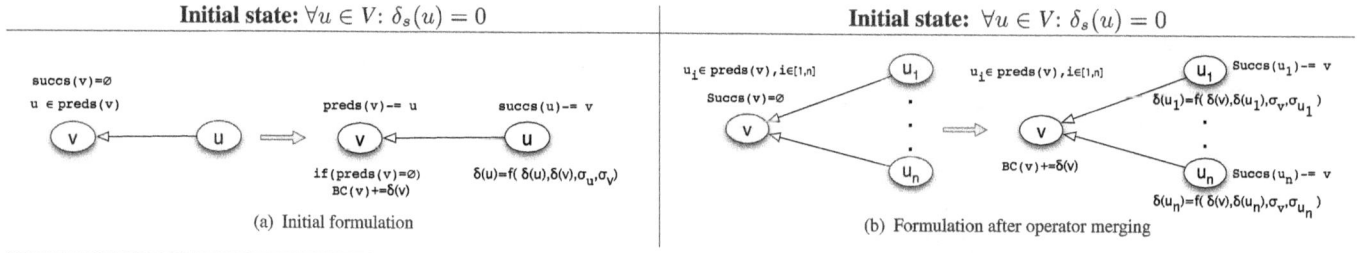

Figure 5. Operator for backward DAG traversal phase

discovers a new shortest path from $Root$ to v through u when $l(u) + w(uv) < l(v)$ and sets $l(v) = l(u) + w(uv)$. Similarly, g_{FU}, g_{US} are changed to properly identify successive nodes on shortest paths from $Root$. Finally, g_{CN} is modified to check for $l(u) + w(uv) > l(v)$ in order to capture the case when a shorter path v has been discovered after v has received an update from u. It is easy to see that the operators in Fig. 3 are derived from the ones in Fig. 6 by setting $w_e = 1$ for each edge e in the graph. The second phase is the same as in the unweighted case.

2.3 Characterizing BC Algorithms

Algorithms for BC in the literature can be viewed as implementations of particular schedules for the operators of Figures 3, 5 and 6. Some of the operators are not required for certain schedules.

Unweighted graphs: We first describe algorithms for unweighted graphs. The algorithms by Bader [5] and Madduri [29] build the BFS DAG level by level; each level is built in parallel, with barrier synchronization between levels. The construction of each level es-

sentially involves executions of the SP and FU operators of Fig. 3; US and CN are unnecessary in such level-by-level algorithms since nodes reach their final levels in a single step rather than being lowered to that level by relaxation, and the path-counts of nodes at the current level are finalized before moving to the next level. The second phase of [5], which traverses the DAG backward to compute betweenness centrality, can be described by applications of the operator in Fig. 5(b); once again, these applications are not performed in a data-driven manner but in a level parallel manner using an auxiliary stack data structure populated in the first phase. The second phase of [29] operates in a similar manner except that each node "pulls" information from all its successors instead of "pushing" information to its predecessors, and can be described by a similar operator. Approaches that exploit just coarse grained [16, 26] or both coarse and fine-grained parallelism [5] are also straightforward to describe with the same operators. An open question is what is the best policy for mapping operators from multiple iterations to the available computational resources. Approaches such as [36, 39] perform the level synchornous approach using the op-

38

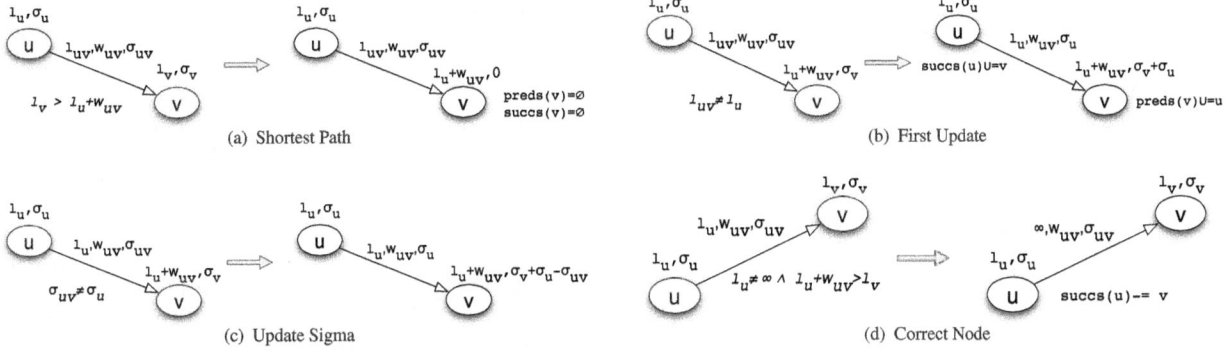

Figure 6. Operators for shortest-path DAG construction phase for weighted graphs. Initialization same as in Fig. 3

erators of Fig. 3. Logically partitioning the graph among threads and having each thread be responsible for its partition, is a different way of scheduling the operators and of achieving their atomic execution. Similarly, [12] can be seen as a SIMDization of the operators of Fig. 3. Data structure optimizations in the implementation of the graph abstract data type, such as the re-layout of graph nodes [16] or the distributed storage of the predecessor list [39], are orthogonal to our description of the algorithm and their effect on improving performance is complementary.

Weighted graphs: The algorithm for weighted graphs by Edmonds et al. [19] breaks down the forward pass in a number of sub-phases. It performs a first phase where applications of *SP* and *FU* are applied asynchronously in order to update the distance of nodes and the predecessor lists. Then in a subsequent phase, the path-counts are updated by using applications of the *US* operator in a level-synchronous manner. The *US* operator in that phase is simplified in that no corrections in the estimation of σ are necessary, due to the constraint on the schedule. Essentially, [19] acts as a label-correcting algorithm for only a subset of the node attributes $(l(u), preds(u))$ and as a label-setting algorithm for the rest $(\sigma(u), succs(u))$. Therefore, it is restricted to level-synchronous schedules for the computation of the latter. Our operators, on the other hand, provide a label-correcting capability for all node attributes and are able to merge the above two phases in a single, fully asynchronous phase, potentially exposing more parallelism. Finally, the backward DAG traversal is performed asynchronously using the operator in Fig. 5(b).

2.4 Correctness of BC Operators

In this section, we state the main correctness results of our operator formulation of BC.

Forward Pass We start with the operators for the forward pass, presented in Fig. 3. We prove that the first phase terminates, and that upon termination all node attributes have correct values. We consider the most general setting where operators are allowed to execute in any order. The computation is modeled by a *history*, which is a sequence of operator applications, each of which is considered to be an instantaneous event that changes the state of the graph. We denote an operator application on an edge (u, v) by $op(uv)$, $op \in \{SP, FU, US, CN\}$. To capture meaningful computations, we restrict attention to *well-formed histories*, which are histories where each time an operator is enabled on an edge, its execution cannot be postponed indefinitely. Correctness follows from the following two theorems.

Theorem 1. *(Termination) Any well-formed history H of events $op(uv), op \in \{SP, FU, US, CN\}$ of the operators in Fig. 3 to a graph $G = (V, E)$ has finite length.*

Theorem 2. *At the fixpoint, the following facts hold for an arbitrary node v:*
(a) $l(v)$ is equal to the length of the shortest path to v from Root. (b) u is the predecessor of v in a shortest path to v from Root $\iff u \in preds(v)$ and $v \in succs(u)$. (c) $\sigma(v)$ is the number of shortest paths from Root to v.

Due to lack of space, the proofs are presented in [35]. Here we briefly state the main ideas. Theorem 1 is proven by showing that each operator can appear only a finite number of times in an arbitrary history H. We prove that the *SP* operator appears only a finite number of times, and that successive *SP* applications partition H into "windows", within which we can only have a finite number of FU, US, CN applications. Theorem 2(a): We consider the partitioning of nodes $P = \{P_0 \ldots P_n\}$, where P_0 contains the *Root* and P_i contains nodes at shortest path distance i, that is, nodes directly connected to nodes in P_{i-1} but not to nodes in $P_0, \ldots, P_{i-2}$. We show that at the fixpoint the partitioning induced by our algorithm is equivalent to P. Theorem 2(b): ($\Rightarrow$) We examine an arbitrary history, and show that for an arbitrary edge (u, v) there always exists an *FU* application that updates appropriately $succs(v), preds(v)$ after u, v finally settle as successive nodes on a shortest path from Root. ($\Leftarrow$) Considering $u \in preds(v)$ and $v \in succs(u)$ at the fixpoint we show by induction on $l(u)$ that there exists a shortest path to v through u. Theorem 2(c): By induction on the shortest path length, using the fact that at the fixpoint $\sigma(v) = \sum_{u \in preds(v)} \sigma(u)$.

Backward Pass We now discuss the correctness of the operator in Fig. 5(a) for the backward pass. Proving termination is straightforward. Initially there is a fixed number of predecessor edges between the nodes comprising the shortest-path DAG. Each operator application depends on finding one such predecessor edge (u, v) and removes it from the graph. Therefore, the number of predecessor edges decreases monotonically and eventually becomes zero. At that point no more applications are enabled and the algorithm terminates. Correctness at the fixpoint follows from the theorem below (the proof is available in [35]):

Theorem 3. *Let $preds_{init}(v), BC_{init}(v)$ denote the values of the respective node attributes at the beginning of the backward pass. At the fixpoint, the following facts hold for an arbitrary node v: (a) $\delta(v) = \sum_{w \,:\, v \in preds_{init}(w)} \frac{\sigma_{sv}}{\sigma_{sw}} (1 + \delta_s(w))$ (b) if $v \neq Root$ then $BC(v) = BC_{init}(v) + \delta(v)$, else $BC(v) = BC_{init}(v)$.*

39

3. Derivation of New Asynchronous Algorithms

The operators in Figures 3, 6, 5(a) can be applied in any order, and as long as no enabled operator application is postponed indefinitely, the implementation will terminate and produce the right BC values. However, the number of operator applications, which is one measure of work-efficiency, may be very different for different orders. In addition, some orders may exploit locality better than others. Getting a scalable solution greatly depends on performing the right operator scheduling. Exploiting scheduling to improve parallelism is a well-studied area [6–8, 14]. Here, we derive asynchronous algorithms by choosing particular scheduling policies for operator execution.

A simple approach is to repeatedly scan all the edges of the graph in some order, applying all applicable operators to an edge when it is visited. This is inefficient since most edges will not have any operators that can be applied to them. Instead, we use a worklist-based approach. The unit of work in our setting is processing a single edge, which may trigger applications at neighboring edges. Therefore, we maintain a multiset of edges, implemented as a dynamic worklist Wl. At each step, we pick an edge e from Wl, apply an operator to it, and add to Wl new edges that may need processing. In a concurrent setting, Wl must support concurrent `add` and `poll` operations. Atomic operator execution is achieved by acquiring locks on the edge end-points during the operator execution.

In § 3.1 we discuss the most performance-critical aspect of our design: the policy for processing Wl elements. In § 3.2 we discuss how to incrementally update the Wl. In § 3.3, § 3.4 we describe key scheduling optimizations for improving the basic algorithm. Finally, in § 3.5 we present two algorithm variants that we can derive by exploiting all the scheduling insights.

3.1 Choosing a Worklist Processing Policy

During the algorithm execution, Wl will usually contain many edges where operators may be applied. An important design decision is picking a work-efficient order to process edges, since this will affect the convergence rate of the algorithm [24, 30, 31].

During the DAG construction phase, the shortest-path exploration (*SP* operator) is the backbone of our algorithm. The number of all other operator applications is ultimately a function of the times we mispredict the length of the shortest path to a node. Hence, a good ordering policy in our case is one that efficiently identifies shortest-paths, but which is also flexible enough to allow threads to optimistically try to expose parallelism. In the unweighted case, for example, a level-parallel approach allows only nodes within successive levels to be processed concurrently and can stifle parallelism if there are not enough nodes in a level. However, an approach that allows exploration of arbitrary paths on the graph may end up performing too much wasted work since it may mispredict the distance of nodes multiple times.

Our approach is loosely based on the Δ-stepping approach of Meyer *et al.* [30] and effectively tackles such problems. We partition the edges (u, v) in Wl into equivalence classes based on an approximation $l^*(v)$ of $l(v)$ defined as $l^*(v) := \frac{l(u)+w(uv)}{\Delta}$. The term $l(u) + w(uv)$ is the length of the path from the *Root* to v through u. Δ is a user specified parameter that defines a range of distance values that fall in the same equivalence class. Each equivalence class is associated with a bucket B_i. Each time an edge (u, v) is inserted in Wl, we compute $l^*(v)$ and place it in the appropriate B_i. Intuitively, we want to explore shorter paths before longer ones in order to minimize the number of mispredictions on the level of a node. Hence, our policy places these edges in lower-numbered buckets. Threads query the buckets for work in increasing order. The deviation from the classic Δ-stepping is that *there is no barrier between the processing of successive buckets*. Each thread queries

buckets in increasing order repeatedly until no more work is left, but different threads can be simultaneously operating on different buckets and, consequently, can extract more parallelism in case there is limited amount of work in a particular bucket. The role of Δ is to control the interplay between exposing parallelism, decreasing the probability of mispredicting levels, and controlling the overhead of iterating over and querying buckets in a concurrent setting. This strategy is enabled only because our operators are general enough to restore the correct values of attributes, in case of mispeculation. Note that the equivalence class of an edge can change after the point it is inserted in B_i. This however can only affect the performance and not the correctness of our algorithm. To mitigate the overhead even further, each thread gets a chunk of edges out of B_i each time it queries Wl.

The backward DAG traversal phase operates in a data-flow driven manner. When the δ value of a node is fully updated, we propagate changes backward by scheduling updates to its DAG predecessors. This scheme avoids a level-parallel traversal of the shortest-path DAG and can expose more concurrency in the case where the DAG contains independent components. Edges to be processed are inserted into a worklist. A FIFO or LIFO based worklist policy gave us the best performance.

The best value of Δ and of the other scheduling parameters varies across inputs. § 4 provides details about the chosen values.

3.2 Incrementally Maintaining the Worklist

We first discuss the policy for the DAG construction phase. Finding the minimal set of edges that need to be processed, and therefore need to be added to Wl, due to an operator application on edge (u, v) is challenging in a concurrent setting. This is because the immediate neighborhoods of u and v are, in general, unbounded. Therefore, we over-approximate the minimal set of edges by using the following policy: Whenever an operator changes the attributes of a node v, we add to Wl all edges adjacent to v that *may* need to be updated due to the change to v. We determine these edges for each operator as follows.

SP: An $SP(uv)$ moves v to a new level and identifies a new shortest path P to v. All outgoing edges of v are inserted to Wl so that the exploration along P continues. Additionally, incoming edges of v must be examined to correctly update neighboring nodes $w \neq u$ that lie on paths P' (longer than P). Such nodes may have recorded v as their successor. Hence, we add all adjacent edges to v to Wl.

FU, US: Both operators update $\sigma(v)$, so all outgoing edges of v are added to Wl to further propagate this update.

CN: This operator simply corrects the successor list of the source node u of the edge it is applied on and does not enable any other operators. Hence no updates to Wl are required.

To initialize Wl, we insert all outgoing edges of the *Root* to initiate the shortest-path explorations.

For the backward DAG traversal we use a data-flow driven policy that considers the minimal set of edges. Whenever $succs(v) = \emptyset$ an operator is enabled on each edge (u, v) between v and $u \in preds(v)$. In the baseline scheme, we add each such (u, v) to Wl. When operator merging is applied (see § 3.3), Wl can simply contain nodes; in this case we insert v to Wl. We initialize Wl with all (u, v) (or v), such that v is at the fringe of the DAG generated in the first phase. Such nodes are easy to identify after the first phase, since they have no successors. We perform a scan over all nodes and populate Wl appropriately, when this property is satisfied.

3.3 Optimization I: Operator Merging

In certain cases it is beneficial for performance reasons to merge multiple operators together and create a new composite operator. Operator merging is essentially a transformation that binds scheduling decisions at compile-time and provides benefits similar to classical loop optimizations. Co-scheduling the application of multiple operators can improve locality. Also, in a similar spirit to loop fusion, combining multiple operators together improves locality and reduces loop overheads. We identify two cases where merging is applicable and describe additional performance benefits it provides.

In the first phase, every $SP(uv)$ will lead to a subsequent $FU(uv)$. Merging the two firstly improves locality, since the data of v is already local to the thread due to $SP(uv)$. Second, it reduces the locking overhead, by eliminating locking for $FU(uv)$. Finally, it reduces the pressure on Wl, since we need insert the outgoing edges of v to Wl only once in the combined operator.

In the second phase, we can merge all applications of the operator between v and its predecessors u_i. The composite operator is shown in Fig. 5(b). Merging firstly permits all updates starting from v to be performed in a single operator application. Thus, we can avoid the removal of u from $preds(v)$, because now we do not need to keep track of whether processing v is over. In order to update $BC(v)$ correctly the composite operator needs to be applied once per node v and its predecessors. This can be achieved by simply inserting a single instance of v into Wl, upon receiving an update from the last successor. A special check to avoid updating $Root$ is also necessary. Note that we can perform fine-grained locking on each u_i and do not need to access atomically an unbounded number of nodes.

3.4 Optimization II: Improving the Worklist Update Policy

In § 3.2 we discussed a policy that over-approximates the set of edges that need to be processed after an operator application, and therefore need to be added to Wl. We identify various ways of improving that policy. Our optimizations reduce the number of redundant checks on parts of the graph for enabled operators and the number of add calls to Wl, thus leading to fewer accesses to shared resources. In practice they are important in speeding up the first phase of the algorithm.

First, when an $SP(uv)$ is executed, if $preds(v) = \emptyset$, then no incoming neighbor u of v needs to be processed, since $v \in succs(u)$ iff $u \in preds(v)$. Hence, we can avoid inserting incoming edges of v to Wl.

Second, when a $US(uv)$ is executed, if $succs(v) = \emptyset$, then we can avoid adding outgoing edges (v, w) of v to Wl. The reason is that in order for $US(vw)$ to be executed, w must already be a successor of v (an $FU(uv)$ must have been executed). Since v has no recorded successors, all (v, w) are already in Wl waiting to be processed, and we can avoid re-inserting them. This way, we expose opportunities to batch up all path-count updates and avoid redundant Wl population.

Third, when using the combined $SP(uv), FU(uv)$ operator, we can avoid adding outgoing edges (v, w) after an $FU(uv)$ if $succs(v) = \emptyset$, since they are already there due to the application of the combined operator. Note that all these optimizations are inexpensive since they require simple checks on operator-local state, and do not require acquiring extra locks.

3.5 Putting it All Together: Derivation of Two Asynchronous Variants

We now describe how to combine all the ideas presented in the previous sections in order to produce two asynchronous algorithms.

In the first algorithm, *async1*, during the forward phase (line 4 in Fig. 1), each thread extracts an edge out of the worklist and tries to find an operator to apply to it by checking the operator guards in some arbitrary order, while also merging applications of SP with FU. The order we chose is $[CN, SP \circ FU, FU, US]$. Note that the guards are mutually exclusive, therefore any order of checking the guards is guaranteed not to postpone an operator application in-

definitely. For the backward phase (line 7 in Fig. 1), each thread extracts a node out of the worklist and tries to perform the composite operator in Fig. 5(b) to all predecessor nodes. In Fig. 7 we show in pseudocode for the forward pass of *async1*.

```
1  Worklist Wl = {(srcNode, w) : (srcNode, w) ∈ G.edges}
2
3  foreach (u, v) ∈ Wl {
4      lock(u,v)
5      if (g_CN(u, v)) {
6          apply CN ; unlock(u,v)
7      } else if (g_SP∘FU(u, v)) {
8          apply SP ∘ FU; unlock(u,v)
9          Wl = Wl ∪ {(v, w) : w ∈ outNbrs(v)}
10         if (uHasPreds)
11             Wl = Wl ∪ {(w, u) : w ∈ inNbrs(u)}
12     } else if (g_FU(u, v)) {
13         apply FU; unlock(u,v)
14         if (vHasSuccs)
15             Wl = Wl ∪ {(v, w) : w ∈ outNbrs(v)}
16     } else if (g_US(u, v)) {
17         apply US; unlock(u,v)
18         if (vHasSuccs)
19             Wl = Wl ∪ {(v, w) : w ∈ outNbrs(v)}
20     } else { unlock(u,v) }
21 }
```

Figure 7. Pseudocode for forward pass of *async1*.

In the second algorithm, *async2*, we consider a node and all its immediate neighbors, and statically co-schedule operator applications on the edges connecting them. Additionally, we perform potential CN applications in place whenever we discover a new shorter path to a node. The motivation behind these design choices is to exploit spatial and temporal locality by having a a single thread work on an entire neighborhood. A potential issue with this design though is that it may be harder to load balance work, in case the node degrees are not evenly distributed. This can be more problematic in an environment with high degree of parallelism. The pseudocode for *async2* is presented in Fig. 8. Note that in this algorithm we insert nodes instead of edges into the worklist. The second phase is the same as in *async1*.

To guarantee atomic execution of operators we acquire fine-grained spinlocks on the end-points of each edge that an operator works on. The graph nodes are totally ordered based on their runtime (allocation) addresses. We acquire locks respecting this order to avoid deadlock between threads working on the same edge. To amortize locking overhead we acquire the locks in the beginning of the loop iteration and release them after the first successful operator application, or at the end if no operator is applicable. In case of a successful operator application we release a lock on a node immediately after the last access to a node attribute. Inserting edges/nodes in Wl after an operator application is done without holding any locks. This is because this action does not access any data attributes, and also because the graph structure is not mutated. This way we significantly reduce the length of atomic sections and allow more fine-grained thread interleavings.

4. Experimental Evaluation

We implemented two versions of the algorithm, based on the operators in Fig. 3 and Fig. 6 and compared their performance against a number of publicly available versions of BC algorithms for weighted and unweighted graphs. We ran our experiments on two architectures. First, an Intel Xeon machine (**Nehalem**) running Scientific Linux 6.3 with four 6-core 2.00 GHz Intel Xeon E7540

```
1   Worklist Wl = {srcNode}
2
3   foreach u ∈ Wl {
4     forall v ∈ outNbrs(u) {
5       lock(u,v)
6       if (g_{SP∘FU}(u,v)) {
7         apply SP ∘ FU; unlock(u,v)
8         Wl = Wl ∪ {v}
9         if (vHasPreds) {
10          // Inline CN applications
11          forall w ∈ inNbrs(v) {
12            lock(v,w)
13            if (g_{CN}(w,v)) { apply CN }
14            unlock(v,w)
15          }
16        }
17      } else if (g_{FU}(u,v)) {
18        apply FU; unlock(u,v)
19        if (vHasSuccs) Wl = Wl ∪ {v}
20      } else if (g_{US}(u,v)) {
21        apply US; unlock(u,v)
22        if (vHasSuccs) Wl = Wl ∪ {v}
23      } else { unlock(u,v) }
24    }
25  }
```

Figure 8. Pseudocode for forward pass of *async2*.

---

processors that share 128 GB of memory. Second, a Sun T5440 machine (**Niagara**) running SunOS 5.10. It contains two 8-core 1.4 GHz Sun UltraSPARC T2 Plus (Niagara 2) processors, and provides 128 concurrent hardware threads, sharing 32 GB of memory. On the Nehalem, the compiler used was GCC 4.7.1. On the Niagara, the compiler used was GCC 4.5.1. We report the average time (t) of 5 runs and the standard deviation (sd). We consider the following classes of input graphs:

- Real-world road network graphs of the USA from the DIMACS shortest paths challenge [2]. We use the full USA network (*USA-net*) with 24M nodes and 58M edges and the central USA network (*USA-ctr*) with 14M nodes and 34M edges.
- A network of scientific co-authorships [32] (*coauth*) with 391K nodes and 873K edges, where edge weights are converted to integers (by multiplying all weights by 1000).
- Scale-free graphs generated using the Recursive MATrix (R-MAT) scale-free graph generation algorithm [13]. The size of the graphs is controlled by a *SCALE* parameter; a graph contains $N = 2^{SCALE}$ nodes, $M = 8 \times N$ edges, with each edge having strictly positive integer weight with maximum value $C = 2^{SCALE}$. The RMAT graphs we used were generated using the tools provided by the SSCA v2.2 benchmark [3]. The parameters used for the graph construction were the default ones, as specified by the generator ($a = 0.55, b = 0.1, c = 0.1, d = 0.25$). For our experiments we removed multi-edges from the graphs. We denote a graph of $SCALE = X$ as *rmatX*.
- Random graphs containing $N = 2^k$ nodes and $M = 4 \times N$ edges. There are $N - 1$ edges connecting nodes in a circle to guarantee the existence of a connected component and all the other edges are created randomly, following a uniform distribution. A graph with $k = X$ is denoted as *randX*.

For large-scale graphs, it is computationally infeasible to compute BC by doing shortest path computations from every node of the graph. Therefore, like previous studies [4, 16, 19, 29], we perform shortest path computations for only a subset of nodes.

Nehalem	Forward		Backward
coauth	$\Delta = 512$	$CF128$	$CL256$
USA-net	$\Delta = 32768$	$CF64$	$CL256$
rmat25	$\Delta = 32768$	$CF256$	$CL256$
Niagara	Forward		Backward
coauth	$\Delta = 2048$	$CF128$	$CL256$
USA-net	$\Delta = 32768$	$CF128$	$CL256$
USA-ctr	$\Delta = 32768$	$CF128$	$CL256$

Table 1. Scheduling parameters for weighted graph experiments. CFx (CLx): Chunked FIFO (LIFO) with chunk size x.

4.1 Experiments on Weighted Graphs

We consider two algorithms for weighted graphs: (i) our algorithm *async1*, which is based on the operators of Fig. 6, with all scheduling optimizations enabled, and (ii) a serial reference implementation of Brandes' algorithm (**boost-s**) for weighted graphs, available in the Boost Graph Library [37] V. 1.47.0. The only parallel algorithm for weighted graphs with a publicly available implementation that we are aware of is [19]. However, that solution targets a distributed-memory environment while our implementation targets shared-memory multicores, so a direct comparison of performance is not meaningful.

4.1.1 Implementation Details

We parallelized *async1* in C++ using the Galois system [1]. Each of the two major phases of the algorithm in Fig. 1 is implemented as a parallel `foreach` loop over a worklist of edges and nodes, respectively. Below we discuss in more detail several aspects of our implementation.

Graph data-structure Our graph implementation is based on the compressed sparse row (CSR) format, with node and edge data stored in two different arrays. Our graphs were not initialized in a NUMA aware manner. In our experience this does not have an observable impact on our experimental machines, since they do not have deep NUMA hierarchies.

Worklist policies We use worklist implementations provided by the Galois system [1, 31]. In Tab. 1, we present the scheduling parameters that gave us the best performance. These values were obtained by performing a small manual search on the parameter space. A more exhaustive search can potentially lead to improved performance; we plan to examine this in future work. Recall that in the forward pass, we use a delta-stepping-like policy that prioritizes the work-items into buckets using the parameter Δ. Within each bucket, our scheme follows a `FIFO` or `LIFO` policy with additional chunking of work. For the backward pass, we use either a chunked `FIFO` or a chunked `LIFO` policy. For example, for the *coauth* graph forward pass on the Nehalem we use $\Delta = 512$ and each bucket is implemented using a `FIFO` policy with chunk size of 128 edges. For the backward pass we use a `LIFO` with chunk size 256.

4.1.2 Analysis of Results

Tab. 2 presents results for various real-world and one synthetic graph. Our algorithm scales very well on all graphs across both architectures. On Nehalem, *async1* achieves scalability of $9.5\times$ on both the USA road-network, and the *rmat25*. The high thread count on the Niagara, allows *async1* to mine the available parallelism through the fine-grained operator execution. For the two road-networks it achieves its best scalability, $32\times$ and $37\times$, at 64 threads. By exploiting cross-level parallelism *async1* is able to achieve scalability even on the really small co-author network ($4\times$ on Nehalem, $18\times$ on Niagara). We report the *boost-s* runtime to provide a reference against a publicly available serial implementation.

Nehalem	coauth (500 steps)		USA-net (10 steps)		rmat25 (10 steps)	
Threads	*t*	*sd*	*t*	*sd*	*t*	*sd*
boost-serial	68	0	510	4	3020	53
1	32	3	285	1	1493	102
4	12	0	78	0	383	27
8	10	0	43	1	223	6
12	10	0	34	0	170	8
16	8	0	31	0	163	6
20	8	0	30	0	159	10
24	8	0	30	0	157	15

Niagara	coauth (100 steps)		USA-net (10 steps)		USA-ctr (10 steps)	
Threads	*t*	*sd*	*t*	*sd*	*t*	*sd*
boost-serial	83	0	1872	107	1086	1
1	110	0	1583	6	981	5
16	9	0	115	0	69	0
32	6	0	65	0	37	0
48	6	0	53	0	29	0
64	7	0	49	0	26	0
96	10	0	53	1	26	0
128	15	0	61	2	31	2

Table 2. Average execution time (sec.) and stdv. of *async1* for weighted graphs

4.2 Experiments on Unweighted Graphs

We evaluated a number of BC algorithms for unweighted graphs. Below, we describe each of them and give details about the parallelization strategy and scheduling policy. We note that the graph format for all unweighted algorithms is based on the CSR format.

outer This is a parallelization only of the outer loop. The graph state is replicated P times, where P is the number of threads. Each thread performs an iteration of the outer loop which is mostly independent from other iterations. The updates on the betweenness value of each node form a reduction which is straightforward to handle. The serial algorithm executed in the inner loop by each thread uses the successor lists to represent the DAG, as discussed in [29]. The algorithm was implemented in the Galois system.

async1, async2 These are our algorithms based on the operators of Fig. 3 with all scheduling optimizations enabled. *async1* was used on the Niagara experiments, while *async2* was used on the Nehalem experiments. The algorithms were implemented in the Galois system following the same design choices as the weighted version in § 4.1.1. We now discuss the scheduling parameters that we used. On both architectures we select $\Delta = 1$. The intuition behind this is that in the case of unweighted graphs the diameter is low, which potentially increases the amount of work per level. Setting $\Delta = 1$ focuses the search for work in individual levels, while still allowing for cross-level speculation. We note that setting $\Delta = 1$ *does not make them level-synchronous algorithms*. As discussed in § 3.1 these algorithms allow threads to simultaneously work on an arbitrary number of buckets. Setting $\Delta = 1$ simply reduces the speculation window for the threads but does not restrict them to a single bucket. If bucket B_i becomes temporarily empty, threads move to buckets $T_j, j > i$, and can return later to T_i if new work exists there. This strategy is applicable only because our operators are general enough to restore the correct values of attributes in case of mispeculation. On the Nehalem, where *async2* is used, each bucket is processed using a LIFO policy. For rmat25 we use a chunk size of 8 nodes and for rand26 we use chunks of 32 nodes. On the Niagara, where *async1* is used, each bucket is processed using a FIFO policy with chunks of edges of size 512. The second phase uses a LIFO policy with chunk sizes of 16 (Nehalem) and 2048 (Niagara).

preds This algorithm is an inner-level, level-synchronous parallelization presented in [5]. The implementation is part of the SSCA v2.2 benchmark [3]. The implementation uses OpenMP directives to parallelize the loops and define their schedules, and OpenMP barriers for the synchronization of levels. The OpenMP scheduling policy for the forward phase is dynamic and for the backward phase is static.

succs/succs-serial This algorithm is an inner-level, level synchronous parallelization presented in [29]. The implementation is our adaption of the implementation provided in GraphCT v.0.5 [18]. GraphCT is a parallel toolkit for analyzing massive graphs on the massively multithreaded Cray XMT; the implementation is optimized for the Cray and uses compiler directives specific to that system. The algorithm, as presented in [29] admits a lock-free implementation. Our adaption is a parallelization using OpenMP. We replace the original atomic intrinsics with the equivalent ones provided by GCC to implement it. We experimented with various scheduling policies and present results for the guided policy, which performed the best. This algorithm also serves as the serial baseline that we compare all algorithms against.

4.2.1 Analysis of Results

In Tab. 3 we present the running time of all four algorithms for 100 iterations of the outer loop. Due to large running times, we present results only for high thread counts on the rmat25 graph, on the Nehalem. In Tab. 4, Tab. 5 we focus on the inner-loop parallelization strategies and present results for 10 iterations of the outer loop.

First, we discuss performance on the Nehalem (Tab. 3, Tab. 4). We can make a number of interesting observations. We note that for rmat25 *outer* is the best performing. We expect this to be the case when the graph fits in the available memory. However, this comes at the cost of high memory usage; for 24 threads *outer* requires about 63% of the 128 GB of main memory and it will exceed the machine's memory capacity for larger graphs. For this reason, we do not present results for *outer* on rand26 or on the Niagara, which has less memory and a larger number of threads. Second, *preds* starts by being more than 2× slower than *succs* (due to the locality benefits of *succs*), something that is in accordance with previous studies [29]. At higher thread counts, though, the performance gap between the two is reduced. Interestingly, on our system *preds* is sensitive to thread pinning. Avoiding pinning makes *preds* more than 2× slower than *succs* even on high thread counts (e.g. on 24 threads *preds* takes 174 sec. for 10 steps on rmat25 on Nehalem). Focusing on *async2*, on the Nehalem, we observe that it is slower than the other algorithms on the rmat25 graph, while it is the fastest on the rand26. We believe this is due to the structure of the input graphs. The average longest BFS level for the outer loop iterations we performed provides an approximation of the graph diameter. It is 15.9 (stdv. 0.7) on rmat25 and 20.1 (stdv. 0.57) on rand26. By increasing the "diameter" of the explored graph, hence decreasing the amount of work per level, an algorithm that tries to mine work from multiple levels becomes comparatively better.

On the Niagara, we experiment with a different variant of our algorithm, *async1*. In *async1* the unit of work is the processing of a single edge instead of a node and its immediate neighbors. Intuitively, this can lead to more fine-grained distribution of work, which can be more suitable for an environment with a high degree of parallelism. *async1* is able to scale to high thread counts on both inputs, as we see in Tab. 5. We do not report performance numbers on *preds*, due to execution problems on this platform. Regarding *succs*, its best running time is 325 seconds (stdv. 35) for rmat25 and 1044 seconds (stdv. 138) for rand26, both on 16 threads. *succs* did not scale beyond 16 threads. We believe this behavior is partly due to the poor exploitation of parallel resources by the level-parallel approach (more threads means less work per thread on each level) and partly to scaling issues in the OpenMP runtime on the Niagara.

4.3 Assessing the Effectiveness of Scheduling

To illustrate the effect of scheduling on the performance we consider one more experiment using *async2* on the *rmat25* unweighted graph on the Nehalem architecture. We execute two outer loop iterations and record the number of executed operators. We consider the following variants of *async2*: The first, Ord, is the version we already presented with all scheduling optimizations enabled. The second variant, Ord-d, is a de-optimized version of Ord where, the optimizations presented in § 3.4 are disabled. Both Ord variants use the same worklist policy. Finally, CF is a variant of *async2* with a FIFO worklist policy (with chunk size of 16 nodes) and all other scheduling optimizations enabled. Using a FIFO schedule for the unweighted operators gives us the optimal order of processing the edges in the sequential setting. The CF worklist policy maintains this FIFO order for each thread in the parallel setting, while relaxing the constraint of maintaining a total FIFO ordering among threads, to achieve better scalability. In Tab. 6, we report the average number of operator applications and runtime of the forward pass per outer loop iteration.

Firstly, note that for Ord and CF the operator counts for one thread are identical. This is natural since, with $\Delta = 1$, on one thread Ord emulates the best schedule (FIFO). Additionally, we see that the number of *US* applications and *CN* evaluations is zero. This is normal, since in the best schedule no corrections should be done to the path-count and we should never mispredict the level of a node. This is not the case for Ord-d, though, which disables some of the optimizations and performs unnecessary work. Also, we note that not all nodes and edges will be reachable from all possible roots, in a directed graph, therefore the number of operator applications will not, in general, match the node and edge count of the graph.

Focusing on runtime performance, we observe a correlation between the number of operator applications and the running time. CF deviates quickly from the optimal schedule in terms of operator applications. For 4 threads and above we observe an increase on the number of *SP* operators, which translates to increases in the number of other operators. Although we increase the number of threads, the extra work eliminates the gain from the increased degree of parallelism, something that hinders both scalability and absolute performance. Ord-d does not deviate from the best schedule in terms of *SP* applications, due to the use of the right scheduling policy, but lacking the worklist maintenance optimizations ends up performing much more work (observe the increased values of *e(CN)*, *None*). Ord, on the other hand, combines both a good policy for processing the worklist elements along with a careful policy for populating the worklist with new work, and manages to outperform both other variants. As the thread count increases it experiences a much smaller increase in the number processed elements (mainly manifesting as increased *e(CN)* and *None* values), but scalability is mainly hindered by a slower per-operator processing time.

Nehalem	async2		succs		preds		outer	
Threads	t	sd	t	sd	t	sd	t	sd
16	985	8	785	33	1051	4	275	2
20	1010	6	771	6	997	36	242	1
24	1063	6	802	73	960	8	209	4

Table 3. Execution time (sec) and stdv. for executing 100 outer-loop iterations on rmat25.

Nehalem	rmat25 (10 steps)						rand26 (10 steps)					
	preds		succs		async2		preds		succs		async2	
Threads	t	sd	t	sd	t	sd	t	sd	t	sd	t	sd
serial			261	16					601	44		
1	1014	7	385	1	806	11	1636	4	850	4	1449	24
4	309	2	155	1	205	1	515	4	308	7	364	0
8	161	1	92	1	115	1	266	1	199	8	191	1
12	120	1	80	3	101	1	206	4	202	27	144	0
16	101	0	78	4	99	2	195	5	191	19	128	0
20	91	0	76	2	101	1	187	1	191	18	125	0
24	86	1	74	1	106	1	183	0	190	9	126	0

Table 4. Average execution time (sec) and stdv on Nehalem.

Niagara	rmat25 (10 steps)		rand26 (10 steps)	
	async1		async1	
Threads	t	sd	t	sd
succs-serial	1794	39	3265	89
1	5019	81	6444	99
16	350	13	409	6
32	209	12	210	6
48	148	5	151	6
64	123	8	123	10
96	121	14	106	14
128	127	24	98	15

Table 5. Average execution time (sec) and stdv on Niagara.

5. Conclusion and Future Work

This paper presents a new formulation of BC in terms of the operator formulation of algorithms. This formulation captures the essence of the problem and allows us to not only express existing solutions as schedules of these operators, but also to derive new asynchronous algorithms that are able to extract large amounts of parallelism, are work-efficient, and work for both weighted and unweighted graphs. Our experiments show that our algorithms benefit from a high-degree of parallelism, achieve good scalability on real world inputs, and perform competitively against other solutions. As future work, we want to target a distributed memory environment. More importantly, our high-level operator formulation of BC opens up an avenue for automatically synthesizing different solutions. This will allow to perform a systematic design-space exploration in order to to find the solution that performs the best under the constraints of a particular input and architecture.

Acknowledgments

We would like to thank Professor Vijaya Ramachandran, the members of the ISS Group and the anonymous referees for their helpful comments. We are grateful to Andrew Lenharth and Xin Sui for many useful discussions.

References

[1] Galois system. http://iss.ices.utexas.edu/?p=projects/galois.

[2] 9th DIMACS Implementation Challenge. http://www.dis.uniroma1.it/~challenge9/download.shtml, 2009.

[3] D. Bader., J. Gilbert, J. Kepner, and K. Madduri. Hpcs scalable synthetic compact applications graph analysis (SSCA2) benchmark v2.2, 2007. http://www.graphanalysis.org/benchmark/.

[4] D. A. Bader, S. Kintali, K. Madduri, and M. Mihail. Approximating betweenness centrality. In *WAW*, Berlin, Heidelberg, 2007.

[5] D. A. Bader and K. Madduri. Parallel algorithms for evaluating centrality indices in real-world networks. In *ICPP*, 2006.

[6] G. Blelloch, J. Fineman, P. Gibbons, and H. Simhadri. Scheduling irregular parallel computations on hierarchical caches. In *SPAA*, 2011.

P	SP	FU	US	e(CN)	CN	None	Time/Iter.(sec)
				Ord			
1	25.3	43.5	0*	0*	0*	190.9	56.5
4	25.3	43.5	0.0	0.0	0.0	190.9	14.13
8	25.4	44.1	4.1	5.6	0.6	198.8	8.1
12	25.4	44.0	3.3	6.4	0.5	198.9	6.6
16	25.5	44.0	3.2	9.3	0.6	202.0	6.3
20	25.5	43.7	0.8	16.7	0.3	209.2	6.6
24	25.7	43.8	1.2	27.2	0.6	222.3	7.2
				Ord-d			
1	25.3	43.5	0*	265.2	0*	1934.0	332.2
4	25.3	43.5	0.0	265.5	0.0	1934.8	83.6
8	25.3	43.5	0.0	265.5	0.0	1934.9	50.5
12	25.4	43.5	0.0	265.7	0.0	1935.1	44.2
16	25.4	43.5	0.0	265.7	0.0	1935.2	42.5
20	25.4	43.5	0.0	265.9	0.0	1936.0	42.9
24	25.4	43.5	0.0	266.0	0.0	1935.8	44.5
				CF			
1	25.3	43.5	0*	0*	0*	190.9	55.2
4	26.4	44.2	9.8	23.1	1.8	497.6	24.6
8	28.3	47.1	18.6	68.9	6.1	979.5	25.6
12	28.6	47.0	17.9	77.2	6.3	995.6	23.2
16	29.4	47.6	19.4	104.3	7.2	1036.7	24.5
20	27.6	45.8	18.5	55.7	4.4	841.8	21.1
24	30.1	48.7	21.3	125.1	8.5	1188.7	29.7

Table 6. Average number of operator applications (millions) and runtime of the forward pass per outer-loop iteration, in an execution of 2 iterations on unweighted *rmat25*(Nehalem). *P*: thread count, *e(CN)*: is the number of *CN* evaluations, *CN*: is the number of actual *CN* applications. 0* denotes an absolute zero value. *None* denotes the number of checked edges for which no operator is enabled.

[7] R. D. Blumofe, C. F. Joerg, B. C. Kuszmaul, C. E. Leiserson, K. H. Randall, and Y. Zhou. Cilk: An efficient multithreaded runtime system. In *PPOPP*, 1995.

[8] R. D. Blumofe and C. E. Leiserson. Scheduling multithreaded computations by work stealing. *Journal of the ACM*, 46(5), 1999.

[9] U. Brandes. A faster algorithm for betweenness centrality. *Journal of Mathematical Sociology*, 25, 2001.

[10] U. Brandes and C. Pich. Centrality Estimation in Large Networks. *International Journal of Birfucation and Chaos*, 17(7), 2007.

[11] N. Bulkley and M. V. Alstyne. Does e-mail make white collar workers more productive? Technical report, University of Michigan, 2004.

[12] A. Buluc and J. Gilbert. The combinatorial BLAS: design, implementation, and applications. *Int. Journal of High Perf. Computing Applications*, 2011.

[13] D. Chakrabarti, Y. Zhan, and C. Faloutsos. R-MAT: A recursive model for graph mining. In *In SIAM Data Mining*, 2004.

[14] R. Chowdhury, F. Silvestri, B. Blakeley, and V. Ramachandran. Oblivious algorithms for multicores and network of processors. In *IPDPS*, 2010.

[15] T. Coffman, S. Greenblatt, and S. Marcus. Graph-based technologies for intelligence analysis. *Commun. ACM*, 47, 2004.

[16] G. Cong and K. Makarychev. Optimizing large-scale graph analysis on a multi-threaded, multi-core platform. In *IPDPS*, 2011.

[17] A. Del Sol, H. Fujihashi, and P. O'Meara. Topology of small-world networks of protein–protein complex structures. *Bioinformatics*, 2005.

[18] D. Ediger, K. Jiang, J. Riedy, D. A. Bader, and C. Corley. Massive social network analysis: Mining twitter for social good. In *ICPP*, 2010.

[19] N. Edmonds, T. Hoefler, and A. Lumsdaine. A space-efficient parallel algorithm for computing betweenness centrality in distributed memory. In *HiPC*, 2010.

[20] L. C. Freeman. A set of measures of centrality based on betweenness. 1977.

[21] R. Geisberger, P. Sanders, and D. Schultes. Better approximation of betweenness centrality. In *ALENEX*, 2008.

[22] M. Girvan and M. E. J. Newman. Community structure in social and biological networks. *Proceedings of the National Academy of Sciences*, 99(12), 2002.

[23] R. Guimerà, S. Mossa, A. Turtschi, and L. A. N. Amaral. The world-wide air transportation network: Anomalous centrality, community structure, and cities' global roles. *NAS*, 102(22), 2005.

[24] M. Hassaan, M. Burtscher, and K. Pingali. Ordered vs unordered: a comparison of parallelism and work-efficiency in irregular algorithms. In *PPOPP*, 2011.

[25] H. Jeong, S. P. Mason, A. L. Barabási, and Z. N. Oltvai. Lethality and centrality in protein networks. *Nature*, 411, May 2001.

[26] S. Jin, Z. Huang, Y. Chen, D. G. Chavarría-Miranda, J. Feo, and P. C. Wong. A novel application of parallel betweenness centrality to power grid contingency analysis. In *IPDPS*, 2010.

[27] V. Krebs. Mapping networks of terrorist cells. *Connections*, 2002.

[28] F. Liljeros, C. Edling, L. Amaral, H. Stanley, and Y. Åberg. The web of human sexual contacts. *Nature*, 411, 2001.

[29] K. Madduri, D. Ediger, K. Jiang, D. A. Bader, and D. G. Chavarra-miranda. A faster parallel algorithm and efficient multithreaded implementations for evaluating betweenness centrality on massive datasets. In *IPDS*, 2009.

[30] U. Meyer and P. Sanders. Delta-stepping: A parallel single source shortest path algorithm. In *ESA*, 1998.

[31] D. Nguyen and K. Pingali. Synthesizing concurrent schedulers for irregular algorithms. In *ASPLOS*, 2011.

[32] G. Palla, I. J. Farkas, P. Pollner, I. Derenyi, and T. Vicsek. Fundamental statistical features and self-similar properties of tagged networks. *New Journal of Physics*, 10, 2008. http://cfinder.org/wiki/?n=Main.Data#toc2.

[33] R. Pearce, M. Gokhale, and N. Amato. Multithreaded asynchronous graph traversal for in-memory and semi-external memory. In *SC*, 2010.

[34] K. Pingali, D. Nguyen, M. Kulkarni, M. Burtscher, M. A. Hassaan, R. Kaleem, T. Lee, A. Lenharth, R. Manevich, M. Méndez-Lojo, D. Prountzos, and X. Sui. The TAO of parallelism in algorithms. In *PLDI*, 2011.

[35] D. Prountzos and K. Pingali. Betweenness centrality: Algorithms and implementations. Technical Report TR-13-31, UT Austin, Jan 2013.

[36] Z. Shi and B. Zhang. Fast network centrality analysis using gpus. *BMC Bioinformatics*, 2011.

[37] J. G. Siek. and a. A. L. L.Q. Lee. *The Boost Graph Library: User Guide and Reference Manual (C++ In-Depth Series)*. Addison-Wesley Professional, 2001.

[38] G. Tan, V. C. Sreedhar, and G. R. Gao. Analysis and performance results of computing betweenness centrality on ibm cyclops64. *J. Supercomput.*, 56, 2011.

[39] G. Tan, D. Tu, and N. Sun. A parallel algorithm for computing betweenness centrality. In *ICPP*, 2009.

[40] J. Yang and Y. Chen. Fast computing betweenness centrality with virtual nodes on large sparse networks. *PLoS ONE*, 6(7), 2011.

[41] Q. Yang and S. Lonardi. A parallel algorithm for clustering protein-protein interaction networks. *Comp. Systems Bioinformatics*, 2005.

Compiler Aided Manual Speculation for
High Performance Concurrent Data Structures *

Lingxiang Xiang   Michael L. Scott

Computer Science Department, University of Rochester

{lxiang, scott}@cs.rochester.edu

Abstract

Speculation is a well-known means of increasing parallelism among concurrent methods that are usually but not always independent. Traditional nonblocking data structures employ a particularly restrictive form of speculation. Software transactional memory (STM) systems employ a much more general—though typically blocking—form, and there is a wealth of options in between.

Using several different concurrent data structures as examples, we show that manual addition of speculation to traditional lock-based code can lead to significant performance improvements. Successful speculation requires careful consideration of profitability, and of how and when to validate consistency. Unfortunately, it also requires substantial modifications to code structure and a deep understanding of the memory model. These latter requirements make it difficult to use in its purely manual form, even for expert programmers. To simplify the process, we present a compiler tool, CSpec, that automatically generates speculative code from baseline lock-based code with user annotations. Compiler-aided manual speculation keeps the original code structure for better readability and maintenance, while providing the flexibility to chose speculation and validation strategies. Experiments on UltraSPARC and x86 platforms demonstrate that with a small number annotations added to lock-based code, CSpec can generate speculative code that matches the performance of best-effort hand-written versions.

Categories and Subject Descriptors D.1.3 [*Programming Techniques*]: Concurrent Programming—Parallel Programming; D.3.4 [*Programming Languages*]: Processors—Code generation

Keywords Manual Speculation, Design Pattern, Concurrent Data Structure, Compiler Assistance

1. Introduction

Concurrent data structures play a key role in multithreaded programming. Typical implementations use locks to ensure the atomicity of method invocations. Locks are often overly pessimistic: they prevent threads from executing at the same time even if their operations don't actually conflict. Finer grain locking can reduce unnecessary serialization at the expense of additional acquire and release operations. For data that are often read but not written, reader-writer locks allow non-mutating methods to run in parallel. In im-

---

* This work was supported in part by National Science Foundation grants CCR-0963759, CCF-1116055, and CNS-1116109, and by an IBM Canada CAS Fellowship. Our Niagara 2 machine was provided by Oracle Corp.

portant cases, RCU [17] may additionally eliminate all or most of the overhead of reader synchronization. Even so, the typical concurrent data structure embodies an explicit compromise between, on the one hand, the overhead of acquiring and releasing extra locks and, on the other hand, the loss of potential concurrency when logically nonconflicting method calls acquire the same lock.

In a different vein, *nonblocking* concurrent data structures are inherently optimistic. Their dynamic method invocations always include an instruction that constitutes their *linearization point*. Everything prior to the linearization point is (speculative) preparation, and can be repeated without compromising the correctness of other invocations. Everything subsequent to the linearization point is "cleanup," and can typically be performed by any thread.

The usual motivation for nonblocking data structures is to avoid performance anomalies when a lock-holding thread is preempted or stalled. For certain important (typically simple) data structures, average-case performance may also improve: in the absence of conflicts (and consequent misspeculation), the reduction in serial work may outweigh the increase in (non-serial) preparation and cleanup work. Unfortunately, for more complex data structures the tradeoff tends to go the other way and, in any event, the creation of efficient nonblocking algorithms is notoriously difficult.

Transactional memory, by contrast, places the emphasis on ease of programming. Few implementations are nonblocking, but most are optimistic. With hardware support, TM may provide performance as good as—or better than—that of the best-tuned fine-grain locking. For application code, written by non-experts, even software TM (STM) may outperform coarse-grain locking. For concurrent data structures in libraries, however, STM seems unlikely ever to be fast enough to supplant lock-based code written by experts.

But what about speculation? Work by Bronson et al. [3] demonstrates that hand-written, data structure-specific speculation can provide a significant performance advantage over traditional pessimistic alternatives. Specifically, the authors describe a relaxed-balance speculative AVL tree that outperforms the java.util.concurrent.ConcurrentSkipListMap by 32–39%. Their code employs a variety of highly clever optimizations. While fast, it is very complex, and provides little guidance for the construction of other hand-written speculative data structures.

Our work attempts to regularize the notion of manual speculation (MSpec). Specifically, we characterize MSpec as a *design pattern* that transforms traditional, pessimistic code into optimistic, speculative code by addressing three key questions: (1) Which work should be moved out of a critical section and executed speculatively? (2) How does the remaining critical section validate that the speculative work was correct? (3) How do we avoid erroneous behavior when speculative code sees inconsistent data?

Using MSpec, we have constructed speculative versions of four example data structures: *equivalence sets, cuckoo hash tables, B^{link}-trees,* and a *linear bitmap allocator.* Our implementations outperform not only STM, but also pessimistic code with similar or finer granularity locking. The advantage typically comes both from reducing the overall number of atomic (read-modify-write) instructions and from moving instructions and cache misses out of critical sections (i.e., off the critical path) and into speculative computation. We note that unlike STM, MSpec does not require locking and validation to be performed at identical granularities.

In developing MSpec, our intent was to provide a useful tool for the construction (by experts) of concurrent data structures. We never expected it to be *easy* to use, but we expected the principal challenges to revolve around understanding the (data structure-specific) performance bottlenecks and speculation opportunities. As it turned out, some of the more tedious, mechanical aspects of MSpec were equally or more problematic. First, the partitioning of code into speculative and nonspeculative parts, and the mix of validation code and normal code in the speculative part, breaks natural control flows, making the source code difficult to read, understand, and debug. Second, since the original locking code must generally be preserved as a fallback when speculation fails, the programmer must maintain two versions, applying updates and bug fixes to both. Third, because naive speculation introduces data races, the programmer must deeply understand the memory model, and pepper the code with `atomic` annotations and/or memory fences.

To address these "mechanical" challenges, we have developed a set of program annotations and a source-to-source translator, CSpec, that generates speculative code automatically from annotated source. CSpec allows the programmer to continue to work on the (lightly annotated) original code. It eliminates the possibility of version drift between speculative and nonspeculative versions, and automates the insertion of fences to eliminate data races.

As a motivating example, we present our hand-constructed (MSpec) version of equivalence sets in Section 2, with performance results and implementation experience. We then turn to the CSpec language extensions and source-to-source translator in Section 3, and to guidelines for using these in Section 4. Additional case studies appear in Section 5, with performance results for both MSpec and CSpec versions. Our principal conclusion, discussed in Section 6, is that compiler-assisted manual speculation can be highly attractive option. While more difficult to use than STM or coarse-grain locking, it is substantially easier than either fully manual speculation or the creation of ad-hoc, data structure-specific nonblocking or fine-grain locking alternatives.

2. Motivating Example: Equivalence Sets

An instance of the data structure for equivalence sets partitions some universe of elements into a collection of disjoint sets, where the elements of a given set have some property in common. For illustrative purposes, the code of Figure 1 envisions sets of integers, each represented by a sorted doubly-linked list. Two methods are shown. The Sum method iterates over a specified set and returns some aggregate result. The Move method moves an integer from one set to another. We have included a set field in each element to support a constant-time MemberOf method (not shown).

2.1 Implementation Possibilities

A conventional lock-based implementation of equivalence sets is intuitive and straightforward: each method comprises a single critical section. Code with a single lock per set (lines 1–43 in Figure 1) provides a good balance between coding efficiency and performance. It is only slightly more complicated than a scheme in which all sets share a single global lock—the critical section in Move must acquire two locks (in canonical order, to avoid deadlock at line 25)—but scalability and throughput are significantly better. Given the use of doubly-linked lists, we do not see any hope for an efficient nonblocking implementation on machines with only single-word (CAS or LL/SC) atomic primitives.

STM can of course be used to create an optimistic version of the code, simply by replacing critical sections with transactions.

The resulting performance (with the GCC default STM system—see Figures 2 and 3) is sometimes better than with a global lock, but not dramatically or uniformly so. Even a specialized STM with "elastic transactions" [7], which provide optimization for the search phase in Move, still lags behind per-set locking. STM incurs non-trivial overhead to initialize a transaction and to inspect and modify metadata on each shared memory access. Additional overheads stem from two major lost opportunities to exploit application semantics. First, to avoid proceeding on the basis on an inconsistent view of memory, STM systems typically *validate* that view on every shared memory read, even when the programmer may know that inconsistency is harmless. And while heuristics may reduce the cost of validation in many cases, the fallback typically takes time proportional to the number of locations read. Second, STM systems for unmanaged languages typically perform locking based on hash-based "slices" of memory [6], which almost never coincide with program-level objects. In our equivalence set example, the commit code for GCC STM must validate all `head` and `next` pointers read in the loop in Sum, and acquires 6 locks (one per pointer) for write back in Move. Hand-written code can do much better.

2.2 A Manual Speculative Implementation

Our MSpec version of Sum exploits the fact that the method is read only, that it traverses only one set, and that nodes encountered in that traversal will never have garbage `next` pointers, even if moved to another set. These observations allow us to write an obstruction-free [10] MSpecSum that validates using a single version number in each set. Because locking and validation are performed at the same granularity, we combine the lock and version number into a single *sequence lock* field (`lck.v`) [14]. If we iterate over the entire set without observing a change in this field, we know that we have seen a consistent snapshot. As in most STM systems, failed *validation* aborts the loop and starts over (line 67).

The baseline critical section in Move begins by finding an appropriate (sorted) position in the target list s (lines 27–32). The element e is then removed from its original list (lines 34–35) and inserted into s at the chosen position (lines 37–41). The position-finding part of Move is read only, so it can be performed speculatively in MSpecMove—that is, before entering the critical section. The validation at line 83 ensures that the `pnext` element remains in the same set and no new element has been inserted between `pprev` and `pnext` since line 81, so that it is correct to insert e before `pnext`. The other validation, at line 79, ensures that the while loop continues to traverse the same set, and will therefore terminate. A set's version number is increased both before and after a modification. The low bit functions as a lock: an odd version number indicates that an update is in process, preventing other threads from starting new speculations. Version number increments occur implicitly in lock acquisition and release.

Under the C++11 memory model, any class field that is read during speculation and written in a critical section (in our case, three fields of `Element`) must be declared as an `atomic` variable to avoid data races. For reads and writes to atomics inside the critical section, since locks already guarantee exclusive modification, we can specify relaxed memory order for best performance. For sequence-lock based speculative reads, depending on the hardware, different methods for tagging memory orders add different overhead [2]. Since our experiments employ total store order (TSO) machines like the x86 and SPARC, in which loads are not reordered by the processor, atomic loads incur no extra costs under the sequential consistency memory order. So we simply skip tagging speculative reads and let them use `memory_order_seq_cst` by default.

```
1   struct Element {                      33   // remove e from its original set        66   }
2     int key;                            34   e→prev→next = e→next;                    67   if (v != s→lck.v) goto again;
3     Element *next, *prev;               35   e→next→prev = e→prev;                    68   return sum;
4     Set *set;                           36   // insert e before pnext                 69 }
5   };                                    37   e→next = pnext;
6   struct Set {                          38   e→prev = pprev;                          71 void ESets::MSpecMove(Element *e, Set *s) {
7     Element head;                       39   e→set = s;                               72   Set *oset = e→set;
8     Lock lck;                           40   pprev→next = e;                          73 again:
9   };                                    41   pnext→prev = e;                          74   Element *pprev = s→head;
                                          42   release_locks(oset→lck, s→lck);          75   Element *pnext = pprev→next;
11  int ESets::Sum(Set *s) {              43 }                                          76   while (pnext→value < e→value) {
12    int sum = 0;                                                                      77     pprev = next;
13    s→lck.lock();                       45   // manual speculative implementation     78     pnext = pprev→next;
14    Element *pnext = s→head→next;        46   // for TSO machines                      79     if (pnext→set != s)
15    while (pnext != s→head) {            47   struct Element {                         80       goto again;
16      sum += pnext→key;                 48     int key;                               81   }
17      pnext = pnext→next;               49     atomic<Element*> next, prev;           82   grab_unordered_locks(oset→lck, s→lck);
18    }                                   50     atomic<Set*> set;                      83   if (AL(pnext→set, MO_relaxed) != s || AL(
19    s→lck.unlock();                     51   };                                                pnext→prev, MO_relaxed) != pprev) {
20    return sum;                         52   struct Set {                             84     release_locks(oset→lck, s→lck);
21  }                                     53     Element head;                          85     goto again;
                                          54     SeqLock lck;                           86   }
23  void ESets::Move(Element *e, Set *s) {  55 };                                       87   AS(AL(e→prev, MO_relaxed)→next, AL(e→
24    Set *oset = e→set;                                                                          next, MO_relaxed), MO_relaxed);
25    grab_unordered_locks(oset→lck, s→lck);  57 int ESets::MSpecSum(Set *s) {          88   AS(AL(e→next, MO_relaxed)→prev, AL(e→
26    // find e's next element in s       58   again:                                            prev, MO_relaxed), MO_relaxed);
27    Element *pprev = s→head;            59     int sum = 0;                           89   AS(e→next, pnext, MO_relaxed);
28    Element *pnext = pprev→next;        60     int v = s→lck.v;                       90   AS(e→prev, pprev, MO_relaxed);
29    while (pnext→key < e→key) {         61     if (v & 1) goto again;                 91   AS(e→set, s, MO_relaxed);
30      pprev = next;                     62     Element *pnext = s→head→next;          92   AS(pprev→next, e, MO_relaxed);
31      pnext = pprev→next;               63     while (pnext!=s→head && v == s→lck.v) {  93   AS(pnext→prev, e, MO_relaxed);
32    }                                   64       sum += pnext→value;                  94   release_locks(oset→lck, s→lck);
                                          65       pnext = pnext→next;                  95 }
```

Figure 1. Per-set lock implementation of concurrent equivalence sets. The `key` field of each set's head is initialized to $+\infty$ to avoid loop bound checks in lines 16. For code simplicity, it's assumed that for any element, there is at most one thread calling `Move` on it at any time. `AL=atomic_load`, `AS=atomic_store`, `MO_*=memory_order_*`.

2.3 Performance Results

We tested our code on an Oracle (Sun) Niagara 2 and an Intel Xeon E5649. The Niagara machine has two UltraSPARC T2+ chips, each with 8 in-order, 1.2 GHz, dual-issue cores, and 8 hardware threads per core (4 threads per pipeline). The Xeon machine also has two chips, each with 6 out-of-order, 2.53 GHz, hyper-threaded cores, for a total of 24 hardware thread contexts. Code was compiled with gcc 4.7.1 (-O3).

To measure throughput, we arrange for worker threads to repeatedly call randomly chosen methods for a fixed period of time. We bind each thread to a logical core to eliminate thread migration, and fill all thread contexts on a given chip before employing multiple chips. Our mutex locks, where not otherwise specified, use test-and-test_and_set with exponential back-off, tuned individually for the two machines.

2.3.1 Test Configurations

We compare six different implementations of equivalence sets. **FGL** and **SpecFGL** are the versions of Figure 1, with set-granularity locking. (Code for the `Move` operation includes an extra check to make sure that `e` is still in the same set after line 25.) **CGL** and **SpecCGL** are analogous versions that use a single global lock. **Gnu-STM** uses the default STM system that ships with GCC 4.7.1; ε-**STM** employs elastic transactions [7], which are optimized for search structures. Loads and stores of shared locations were hand-annotated in ε-STM.

2.3.2 Performance and Scalability

Performance results appear in Figures 2 and 3. We use 50 equivalence sets in all cases, with either 500 or 5000 elements in the universe (10 or 100 per set, on average). We use 100% `Move` operations to simulate a write-dominant workload, and a 50/50 mix of

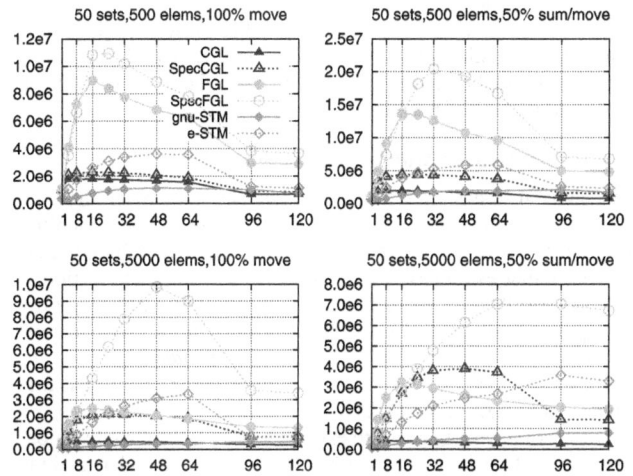

Figure 2. Throughput of concurrent equivalence sets on Niagara 2. The X axis is the number of concurrent threads; the Y axis is method invocations per second.

`Move` and `Sum` operations to simulate a mixed but higher-contention workload. The number of elements per set determines the amount of work that can be moved out of the critical section in `SpecMove`.

Figure 2 illustrates scalability on Niagara 2. As expected, FGL outperforms CGL in all tests, and SpecFGL outperforms SpecCGL. Since an invocation of the `Move` method holds 2 locks simultaneously, FGL reaches its peak throughput when the thread count is around 32. The sharper performance drop after 64 threads is due to cross-chip communication costs.

50 sets,500 elems,100% move

1.8e7	
1.6e7	CGL
1.4e7	SpecCGL
1.2e7	FGL
1.0e7	SpecFGL
8.0e6	gnu-STM
6.0e6	e-STM
4.0e6	
2.0e6	
0.0e0	

1 2 4   8   12   16   20   24

50 sets,500 elems, 50% sum/move

1.8e7
1.6e7
1.4e7
1.2e7
1.0e7
8.0e6
6.0e6
4.0e6
2.0e6
0.0e0

1 2 4   8   12   16   20   24

50 sets,5000 elems,100% move

1.4e7
1.2e7
1.0e7
8.0e6
6.0e6
4.0e6
2.0e6
0.0e0

1 2 4   8   12   16   20   24

50 sets,5000 elems,50% sum/move

1.2e7
1.0e7
8.0e6
6.0e6
4.0e6
2.0e6
0.0e0

1 2 4   8   12   16   20   24

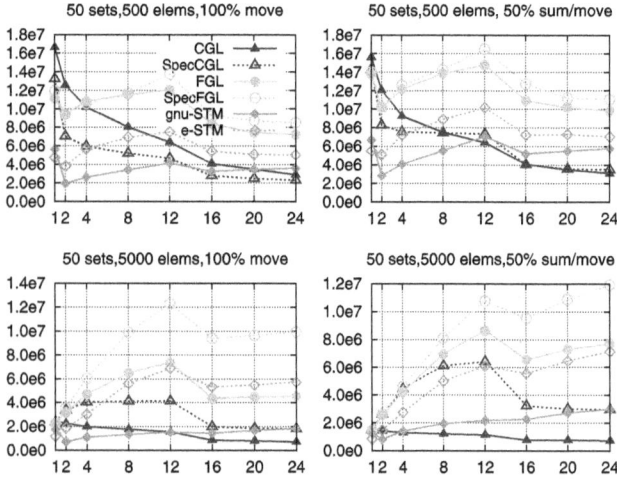

Figure 3. Throughput (invocations/s) of concurrent equivalence sets on Intel Xeon E5649.

Manual speculation improves scalability and throughput for both CGL and FGL. In the 5000-element, 50/50 sum/move case, SpecCGL even outperforms FGL, out to 80 threads. This suggests that simple coarse-grained locking with speculation could be an attractive alternative to fine-grained locking for workloads with significant work amenable to speculation. The baseline overhead of SpecFGL, measured by comparing to FGL on a single thread, is less than 10%. Therefore, even without contention, SpecFGL can deliver competitive performance. By contrast, both gnu-STM and ε-STM have significant baseline overhead (2–4× slower than CGL on a single thread), and can outperform only CGL.

Results on the Xeon machine resemble those on Niagara 2, with the interesting exception that single-thread performance is significantly higher in the 500-element case, where the data set can almost fit in the 32KB L1 data cache.

2.4 Limitations of Manual Speculation

The above results show that hand-written speculation can limit the cost of validation and yield significant performance and scalability improvements not only over STM, but also over lock-based alternatives. Other examples, summaries of which appear in Section 5, confirm that these results are not limited to a single data structure. The presence of general principles suggests, in fact, that manual speculation be thought of as a first-class *design pattern* for concurrent data structures. At the same time, our experience suggests that this pattern is not very easy to use.

Some of the challenges are expected, and are discussed in more detail in Section 4. To extract concurrency, one must understand the workload characteristics and concurrency bottlenecks that suggest an opportunity for speculation. To control the cost of validation, one must identify any data-structure-specific indications of consistency. To maintain correctness, one must insert validation before any operation that might produce anomalous results in the wake of mutually inconsistent reads.

Several challenges, however, are more "mechanical," and suggest the need for automation. First, the changed code layout and the mix of validation code and normal code break natural control flows, making the source code difficult to read, understand and debug. Second, if the original locking code co-exists with its speculative version (either as a backup when speculation fails or as an alternative when speculation is unprofitable), the programmer will have to maintain two separate versions of the code, and make sure that they track each other in the face of updates and bug fixes. Third,

manual speculation requires a deep understanding of the underlying memory model. Speculative loads, almost by definition, constitute data races with stores in the critical sections of other threads. In C++11, where data races are illegal, the programmer must identify and annotate all places where naive speculation would otherwise introduce a race. As discussed by Boehm [2], even the choice of annotation is nontrivial, and potentially architecture-dependent. In the equivalence sets example, the default sequentially consistent ordering is zero-cost for TSO machines, but has unacceptable overhead on PowerPC machines.

3. Compiler Aided Manual Speculation

We propose to overcome the difficulties in applying manual speculation with the aid of compiler. The key idea is to automatically generate speculative code from an annotated version of the lock-based code, allowing the programmer to focus on higher-level issues of what to do speculatively, and how and when to validate. This semi-automatic approach to speculation, which we call CSpec (*compiler aided manual speculation*), consists of (1) a simple but flexible set of annotations to specify the speculation method, and (2) a source-to-source compiler that transforms the annotated source into an explicitly speculative version.

3.1 Interface

The language interface is designed to be as simple as possible. It comprises the following directives:

- **#pragma spec**: tells the compiler to generate a speculative version for the following critical section. This directive should appear immediately before a lock acquisition statement, which must be the single entry point of its critical section.

- **#pragma spec consume_lock(lock0, lock1, ...)**: instructs the compiler to "consume" one or more locks (these should be a subset of the critical section's lock set) at a particular place in the code. Here, "consume" means that the lock is truly needed (to protect writes or to achieve a linearization point), and that speculation on data protected by the lock must end. Statements that cannot be reached from any consume_lock form the *speculative part* of a critical section. Multiple consume_lock directives are allowed in a critical section. It is also legal to consume a same lock more than once on a given code path: the compiler is responsible for acquiring each lock at the first consume_lock that names it.

- **#pragma spec set_checkpoint(id)**: marks a checkpoint with a specific integer id (id> 0). A checkpoint is a place to which execution can roll back after a failed validation. During rollback, all local variables modified beyond the checkpoint will be reset to their snapshots at the checkpoint. The default checkpoint (id=0) is located at the critical section's entry point.

- **#pragma spec validate_ver(ver0, ver1, ...[, cp_id])**: does a version number-based validation. If any version number has changed since checkpoint cp_id, roll back to that checkpoint.

- **#pragma spec validate_val(val0, val1, ...[, cp_id])**: is similar to validate_ver, but does value-based validation.

- **#pragma spec validate_cond(cond_expr[, cp_id])**: evaluates the expression cond_expr and rolls back to checkpoint cp_id if it is false.

- **#pragma spec waive_rollback(cp_id, var0, var1, ...)**: waives value rollback for specified variables at checkpoint cp_id.

Figure 4 presents a re-implementation of the equivalence set data structure using CSpec annotations. This new version is almost identical to the original lock-based code, except for seven embed-

```
1   int ESets::Sum(Set *s) {
2       int sum = 0;
3       #pragma spec
4       s→lck.lock();
5       Element *pnext = s→head→next;
6       while (pnext != s→head) {
7           sum += pnext→key;
8           pnext = pnext→next;
9           #pragma spec validate_ver(s→lck.v)
10      }
11      #pragma spec validate_ver(s→lck.v)
12      s→lck.unlock();
13      return sum;
14  }

16  void ESets::Move(Element *e, Set *s) {
17      Set *oset = e→set;
18      #pragma spec
19      grab_unordered_locks(oset→lck, s→lck);
20      Element *pprev = s→head;
21      Element *pnext = pprev→next;
22      while (pnext→key < e→key) {
23          pprev = pnext;
24          pnext = pprev→next;
25          #pragma spec validate_cond(pnext→set==s)
26      }
27      #pragma spec consume_lock(oset→lck, s→lck)
28      #pragma spec validate_cond(pnext→set==s && pnext→prev==pprev)
29      e→prev→next = e→next;
30      ...... // same as L35−41 of Figure 1
31      release_locks(oset→lck, s→lck);
32  }
```

Figure 4. Concurrent equivalence sets using CSpec.

```
1   int ESets::Sum(Set *s) {
2       ...... // same as L12−20 of Figure 1
3   }

5   int ESets::SpecSum(Set *s) {
6       int sum = 0;
7       int SPEC_tmp_var_0 = sum;
8   SPEC_label_1:
9       sum = SPEC_tmp_var_0;
10      int SPEC_ver_0 = spec::wait_ver(s→lck.v);
11      Element *pnext = AL(s→head→next, MO_seq_cst);
12      while (pnext != s→head) {
13          sum += pnext→key;
14          pnext = AL(pnext→next, MO_seq_cst);
15          if (AL(s→lck.v, MO_seq_cst) != SPEC_ver_0)
16              goto SPEC_label_1;
17      }
18      if (AL(s→lck.v, MO_seq_cst) != SPEC_ver_0)
19          goto SPEC_label_1;
20      return sum;
21  }
```

Figure 5. Automatically generated code for the Sum method. Memory ordering is optimized for TSO machines.

ded directives. Compiler output for the Sum operation appears in Figure 5. It includes both the original locking version and a speculative version. The speculative version includes appropriate tags on all atomic accesses, optimized for the target machine.

Compared with the pure manual speculation code in Figure 1, the CSpec implementation has the following advantages: (1) The language interface is concise. Usually, only a small number of directives is needed to describe the speculation mechanism; often, the original control flow can be retained, with no code motion required. The resulting code remains clear and readable. (2) Code maintenance is straightforward: there is no need to manage separate speculative and nonspeculative versions of the source. Any updates will propagate to both versions in the compiler's output. (3) The programmer is no longer exposed to low-level details of the memory model, as the compiler will handle them properly.

3.2 Implementation

Our compiler support is implemented as a clang [1] front-end plugin. The plugin takes user-annotated source code as input and does source-to-source transformation to create a speculative version. A nonspeculative version is also generated, simply by discarding all embedded directives. Alternative implementations, such as IR-based transformation or static and run-time hybrid support would also be possible; we leave these for future exploration.

We define a lock's *live range* as the set of all statements that are reachable from its acquisition statement but not reachable from its release statement. A *speculative code region* is defined as the union of all live ranges of the locks that appear in a critical section's *entry point*—the lock acquisition call immediately following **#pragma spec**.

Lockset Inference. A key part of the CSpec transformation algorithm is to identify the lock set that each consume_lock should actually acquire. The intuition behind the analysis is straightforward: we want every critical section, at run time, to acquire locks exactly once (this marks the end of speculation), and to acquire all locks named in any consume_lock directive that may subsequently be encountered on any path to the end of the critical section. Conservatively, we could always acquire the entire lockset at the first dynamically encountered consume_lock directive. To the extent possible with static analysis, we wish to reduce this set when possible, so that locks that are never consumed are also never acquired. Pseudocode of the algorithm we use to accomplish this goal appears in Algorithm 1.

Algorithm 1: Translating consume_lock directives

Input: a speculative code region R

1 // GetLiveRange(L, S): get L's live range assuming S is the acquisition statement;
2 $C \leftarrow$ all consume_lock directives in R;
3 **foreach** consume_lock cl in C **do**
4   **foreach** Lock l in cl.LockArgList **do**
5   cl.LiveRange $\leftarrow$ cl.LiveRange $\cup$ GetLiveRange(l, cl);
6   **foreach** Statement s in GetLiveRange(l, cl) **do**
7   s.LockSet $\leftarrow$ s.LockSet $\cup$ cl.LockArgList;
8 **foreach** consume_lock cl in C **do**
9   **foreach** Statement s in cl.LiveRange **do**
10   cl.LockSet $\leftarrow$ cl.LockSet $\cup$ s.LockSet;
11   **if** cl is unreachable from any other consume_lock in C **then**
12   replace cl with LockStmt(R, cl.LockSet);
13   **else if** cl is not dominated by another consume_lock in C **then**
14   remove cl;
15   **foreach** BasicBlock b in GetBasicBlock(cl).Parents **do**
16   **if** a path from R.entry to cl goes through b and the path does not contain any other consume_lock **then**
17   emit LockStmt(R, cl.LockSet) at the end of b;
18   **else** //cl is dominated by other consume_lock
19   remove cl;

The algorithm works in two phases. The first phase (lines 3–7) calculates the LockSet of each statement in code region R. These are the locks that must be acquired before the statement executes at run time. The second phase first infers the lock set for each consume_lock (lines 9–10) so that the set will contain all locks required by the consume_lock's live range. Then for each consume_lock, the algorithm decides how to handle it according to its reachability (lines 11–19). The generated lock acquisition calls use the same function name as the original call (the entry point of R) and the lock parameters appear in the same order as in the original call's parameter list. Thus, the output code is deadlock free if the original code was.

As an alternative to static lockset inference, we could allow locks to be acquired more than once at run time, and release each the appropriate number of times at the end of the critical section. This strategy, however, would be incompatible with source code using non-reentrant locks.

Checkpoint. A checkpoint serves as a possible rollback position. There are three kinds of variables a checkpoint may snapshot: (1) Live-in local variables. For a local variable that is declared before a checkpoint and may be modified after the point, our source transformation tool creates a local mirror for that variable and copies its value back when speculation fails (see sum in Figure 5). Nonlocal variables are assumed to be shared; if they need to be restored, the programmer will have to do it manually. (2) Version numbers. The tool finds validate_vers that may roll back to this checkpoint and, for each, inserts a wait_ver call to wait until the number is unblocked (line 10 in Figure 5). The values read (e.g., SPEC_ver_0) are kept for validation. (3) Validation values. Validate_vals are handled in the same way as validate_vers, except that no wait_ver is inserted.

Tagging Atomic Variables. After code transformation, our tool detects the class fields that are both written in write-back mode (after consuming a lock) and accessed in speculative mode, and re-declares them as atomic variables. Accesses to these variables are grouped into three categories: (1) accesses in write-back mode; (2) reads in validation; (3) other reads in a speculative phase. The tool selects an appropriate (target machine-specific) memory ordering scheme (including a fence if necessary) for each access category.

Switching Between Locking and Speculative Versions. The generation of two versions of a data structure opens the possibility of dynamically switching between them for the best performance. Since speculation doesn't win in all cases, it might sometimes be better to revert to the original locking code. The switch could be driven by user-specified conditions such as workload size or current number of threads. Switch conditions might also be automatically produced by the compiler based on profiling results, or on run-time information like the abort rate of speculation. These possibilities are all subjects for future work. In the experiments reported here, we use only the speculative version of the code.

3.3 Limitations

Our source-to-source tool currently faces three limitations, all of which suggest additional subjects for future work. First, the critical section must have a single entry point. In source programs with multiple entry points, it may be possible to merge these entry points by manually rearranging code structure. Second, we do not support nested speculation due to the complexity of nested rollbacks; inner directives will simply be discarded. Third, the analysis of locksets is static, and can be defeated by complicated data flow and re-assignment of lock variables. We argue that these are uncommon in concurrent data structures, and could be addressed through manual source code changes.

4. Principles of Coding with CSpec

Sections 2 and 3 presented an example of manual speculation and a compiler-based tool to assist in the process. In the current section we generalize on the example, focusing on three key questions that the user of CSpec must consider.

4.1 Where do we place consume_lock directives?

This question amounts to "what should be done in speculation?" because consume_locks mark the division between the speculative and nonspeculative parts of the original critical section. Generally, consume_lock(L) is placed right before the first statement that modifies the shared data protected by L on a given code path. Sometimes a modification to shared data A can only be performed under the guarantee that shared data B won't be changed; in this case B's lock should also be consumed. Since the speculative parts come from the original critical section, it may be profitable to rearrange the code to delay the occurrence of consume_locks. The principal caveat is that too large an increase in total work—e.g., due to misspeculation or extra validation—may change the critical path, so that the remaining critical section is no longer the application bottleneck.

In general, a to-be-atomic method may consist of several logical steps. These steps may have different probabilities of conflicting with the critical sections of other method invocations. The overall conflict rate (and hence abort rate) for the speculative phase of a method is bounded below by the abort rate of the most conflict-prone step. Steps with a high conflict rate may therefore best be left after consume_lock.

There are several common code patterns in concurrent data structures. Collection classes, for example, typically provide *lookup*, *insert*, and *remove* methods. *Lookup* is typically read-only, so there's no need to place any consume_lock in it. *Insert* and *remove* typically start with a search to see whether the desired key is present; we can make this speculative as well, by inserting consume_locks before the actual insertion/deletion. In resource managers, an *allocate* method typically searches for free resources in a shared pool before actually performing allocation. In other data structures, time-consuming logical or mathematical computations, such as compression and encryption, are also good candidates for speculation.

At least three factors at the hardware level can account for a reduction in execution time when speculation is successful. First, speculation may lead to a smaller number of instructions on the program's critical path, assuming this consisted largely of critical sections. Second, since the speculative phase and the following critical section usually work on similar data sets, speculation can serve as a data prefetcher, effectively moving cache misses off the critical path. This can improve performance even when the total number of cache misses per method invocation stays the same (or even goes up). Within the limits of cache capacity, the prefetching effect increases with larger working sets. Third, in algorithms with fine-grain locks, speculation may reduce the number of locks that must be acquired, and locks are quite expensive on many machines. We will return to these issues in more detail in Section 5.

4.2 How do we validate?

Validation is the most challenging and flexible part of CSpec programming. Most STM systems validate after every shared-memory load, to guarantee *opacity* (mutual consistency of everything read so far) [8]. Heuristics such as a global commit counter [23] or per-location timestamps [6, 21] may allow many validation operations to complete in constant time, but the worst-case cost is typically linear in the number of shared locations read so far. (Also: per-location timestamps aren't *privatization safe* [16].) As an alternative to opacity, an STM system may *sandbox* inconsistent transactions by performing validation immediately before any "dangerous" instruction, rather than after every load [5], but for safety in the general case, a very large number of validations may still be required.

Using the three validate_* directives provided by compiler-aided manual speculation, we can exploit data-structure-specific programmer knowledge to minimize both the number of validations and their cost. Determining when a validation is necessary is a tricky affair; we consider it further in the following subsection. To minimize the cost of individual validations, we can identify at least two broadly useful idioms.

Version Numbers (Timestamps): While STM systems typically associate version numbers with individual objects or ownership records, designers of concurrent data structures know that they can be used at various granularities [3, 12]. Regardless of granularity, the idea is the same: if an update to location l is always preceded by an update to the associated version number, then a reader who verifies that a version number has not changed can be sure that all reads in between were consistent. The `validation_ver` directive serves this purpose in CSpec.

It is worth emphasizing that while STM systems often conflate version numbers and locks (to minimize the number of metadata updates a writer must perform), versioning and locking serve different purposes and may fruitfully be performed at different granularities. In particular, we have found that the number of locks required to avoid over-serialization of critical sections is sometimes smaller than the number of version numbers required to avoid unnecessary aborts. The SpecCGL code of Section 2, for example, uses a single global lock, but puts a version number on every set. With a significant number of long-running readers (the lower-right graphs in Figures 2 and 3), fine-grain locking provides little additional throughput at modest thread counts, but a single global version number would be disastrous. For read-mostly workloads (not shown), the effect is even more pronounced: fine-grain locking can actually hurt performance, but fine-grain validation is essential.

In-place Validation: In methods with a search component, the "right" spot to look up, insert, or remove an element is self-evident once discovered: *how* it was discovered is then immaterial—even if it involved an inconsistent view of memory. Mechanisms like "early release" in STM systems exploit this observation [11]. In manual speculation, we can choose to validate simply by checking the local context. An example appears at line 28 of Figure 4, where `pnext→set` and `pnext→prev` are checked to ensure that the two key nodes are still in the same set, and adjacent to one another. When it can be used, in-place validation has low overhead, a low chance of aborts, and zero additional space overhead. In CSpec, it is realized as value-based validation (`validate_val`) or condition-based validation (`validate_cond`).

4.3 What can go wrong and how do we handle it?

In general, our approach to safety is based on sandboxing rather than opacity. It requires that we identify "dangerous" operations and prevent them from doing any harm. Potentially dangerous operations include the use of incorrect data values, incorrect or stale data pointers, and incorrect indirect branches. Incorrect data can lead to faults (e.g., divide-by-zero) or to control-flow decisions that head into an infinite loop or down the wrong code path. Incorrect data pointers can lead to additional faults or, in the case of stores, to the accidental update of nonspeculative data. Incorrect indirect branches (e.g., through a function pointer or the vtable of a dynamically chosen object) may lead to arbitrary (incorrect) code.

An STM compiler, lacking programmer knowledge, must be prepared to validate before every dangerous instruction—or at least before those that operate on values "tainted" by speculative access to shared data [4]. In a few cases (e.g., prior to a division instruction or an array access) the compiler may be able to perform a value-based sanity check that delays the need for validation. In CSpec, by contrast, we can be much more aggressive about reasoning that the "bad cases" can never arise (e.g., based on understanding of the possible range of values stored to shared locations by other threads). We can also employ sanity checks more often, if these are cheaper than validation. Both optimizations may be facilitated by using a *type-preserving allocator*, which ensures that deallocated memory is never reused for something of a different type [19].

5. Additional Case Studies

This section outlines the use of CSpec in three additional concurrent data structures, and summarizes performance results.

5.1 Cuckoo Hash Table

Cuckoo hashing [20] is an open-addressed hashing scheme that uses multiple hash functions to reduce the frequency of collisions. With two functions, each key has two hash values and thus two possible bucket locations. To insert a new element, we examine both possible slots. If both are already occupied, one of the prior elements is displaced and then relocated into its alternative slot. This process repeats until a free slot is found.

Concurrent cuckoo hashing was proposed by Herlihy and Shavit [9]. It splits the single table in two, with each having its own hash function. In addition, each table becomes an array of *probe sets* instead of elements. A probe set is used to store elements with the same hash value. To guarantee constant time operation, the number of elements in a probe set is limited to a small constant `CAPACITY`. One variant of the data structure (a *striped cuckoo hash table*) uses a constant number of locks, and the number of buckets covered by a lock increases if the table is resized. In an alternative variant, (a *refinable cuckoo hash table*) the number of locks increases with resizing, so that each probe set retains an exclusive lock. The refinable variant avoids unnecessary serialization, but its lock protocol is much more complex.

Since an element E may appear in either of two probe sets—call them A and B—an atomic operation in the concurrent cuckoo hash table has to hold two locks simultaneously. Specifically, when performing a *lookup* or *remove*, the locks for both A and B are acquired before entering the critical section. In the critical section of the *insert* method, if both A and B have already reached `CAPACITY`, then a resize operation must be done. Otherwise, E is inserted into one probe set. If that set contains more than `THRESHOLD` < `CAPACITY` elements, then after the critical section, elements will be relocated to their alternative probe sets to keep the set's size below `THRESHOLD`.

Speculation: Speculation makes *lookup* obstruction-free. We place `consume_locks` only before a modification to a probe set. This moves the presence/absence check in *insert*/*remove* out of the critical section. We illustrate the CSpec implementation of *remove* in Figure 6. If the element to remove is speculatively found in probe set A, *remove* needs to consume only A's lock instead of both A's and B's (case ①).

Validation: A version number is added to each probe set to enable `validate_ver`. In *remove* (and similarly in *lookup* and *insert*), to validate the presence of an element in a set (cases ①, ②), we only need to validate that set's version (lines 11, 16) after its lock is consumed. We don't do any validation in the `search` method, because linear search in a limited-sized (< `CAPACITY`) probe set will terminate in `CAPACITY` steps regardless of any change in set elements. To validate the absence of an element (case ③), both probe sets' versions should be checked (line 20). Though the two sets may be checked at different times, their version numbers ensure that the two histories (in each of which the element is not in the corresponding set) overlap, so there exists a linearization point [13] in the overlapped region when the element was in neither set. To support concurrent *resize*, a resize version number is associated with the whole data structure. At the checkpoint, that number is validated (line 7) to detect a *resize* which breaks the mapping between key and probe sets (line 5).

Performance: Our experiments (Figures 7 and 8) employ a direct (by-hand) C++ translation of the Java code given by Herlihy and Shavit[9]. We use a `CAPACITY` of 8 and a `THRESHOLD` of 4; this

```
1   bool CuckooHashMap::Remove(const KeyT& key) {
2       std::pair<Lock*, Lock*> lcks = map_locks(key)
3       #pragma spec
4       lock(lcks.first, lcks.second);
5       Bucket &setA = bucket0(key), &setB = bucket1(key)
6       #pragma spec set_check_point(1)
7       #pragma spec validate_ver(this→ver)
8       int idx = search(setA, key);
9       if (idx>=0) { // ① key is in setA
10          #pragma spec consume_lock(lcks.first)
11          #pragma spec validate_ver(setA.ver, 1)
12          setA.remove(idx);
13          unlock(lcks.first, lcks.second);
14      } else if ((idx = search(setB, key)) >=0) { // ② key is in setB
15          #pragma spec consume_lock(lcks.first, lcks.second)
16          #pragma spec validate_ver(setB.ver, 1)
17          setB.remove(idx);
18          unlock(lcks.first, lcks.second);
19      } else { // ③ key is not found
20          #pragma spec validate_ver(setA.ver, setB.ver, 1)
21          #pragma spec validate_ver(this→ver)
22          unlock(lcks.first, lcks.second);
23      }
24      return idx>=0;
25  }
```

Figure 6. CSpec tagged `Remove` method of cuckoo hash table.

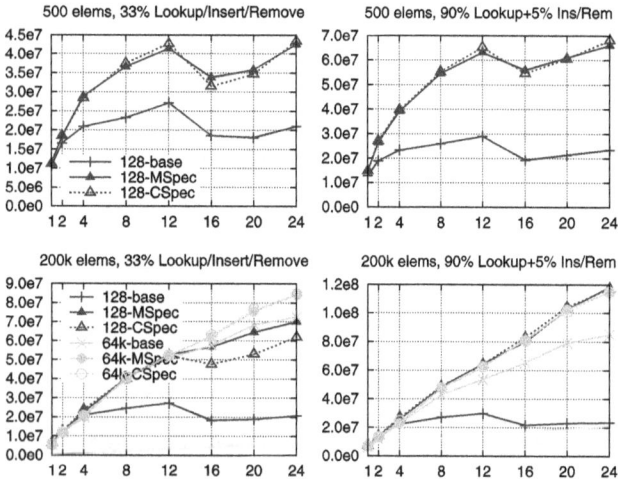

Figure 7. Throughput of cuckoo hash table on Intel Xeon E5649, for different data-set sizes and method ratios. The 128-* curves use striped locking; the 26k-* curves are refinable. *-MSpec are pure manual speculation implementations.

means a probe set usually holds no more than 4 elements. We ran our tests with two different data set sizes: the smaller (∼500 elements) can fit completely in the shared on-chip cache of either machine; the larger (∼200K elements) is cache averse. For the striped version of the table, we use 128 locks. For the refinable version, the number of locks grows to 64K. Before each throughput test, a warm-up phase inserts an appropriate number of elements into the table, randomly selected from a double-sized range (e.g., [0, 1000) for small tables). Keys used in the timing test are randomly selected from the same range.

For striped tables with 128 locks, CSpec code is 10%–20% faster than the baseline with 64 threads on the Niagara 2, and even better with 120 threads. The gap is significantly larger on the Xeon. Scalability in the baseline suffers from lock conflicts with increasing numbers of threads. CSpec overcomes this problem with fine-grain speculation, a shorter critical path, and fewer lock operations. For the same reason, CSpec is also useful for refinable tables in all configurations ("*-CSpec" vs "*-base"). For small data

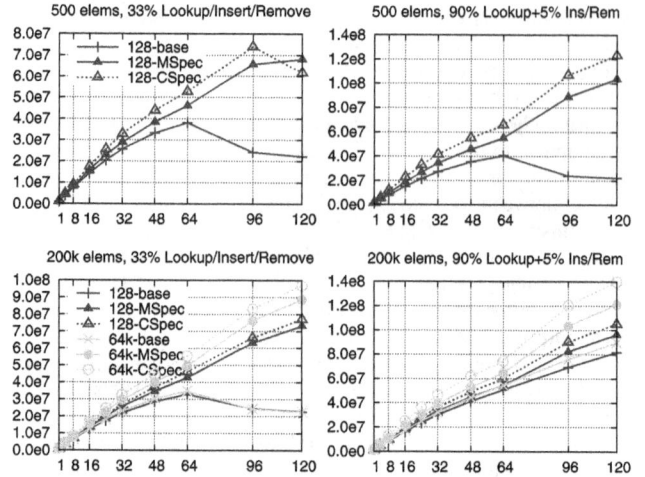

Figure 8. Throughput of cuckoo hash table on Niagara 2.

sets (upper graphs in Figures 7 and 8), refinable locking offers no advantage: there are only 128 buckets. For large data sets (lower graphs), baseline refinable tables ("64k-base") outperform baseline striped tables ("128-base") as expected. Surprisingly, CSpec striped tables ("128-CSpec") outperform baseline refinable tables and are comparable to CSpec refinable tables ("64k-CSpec"), because the larger lock tables induce additional cache misses.

This example clearly shows that fine-grained locking is not necessarily best. The extra time spent to design, implement and debug a fine-grained locking algorithm does not always yield superior performance. Sometimes, a simpler coarse-grained algorithm with CSpec can be a better choice.

A best-effort manual speculation version (MSpec) is also included in our experiments. For easy rollback, a critical section in MSpec is divided as a monotonic speculative phase and a non-speculative phase by reorganizing the code. Also, when a speculation fails, only one probe set has been changed in most cases, and we can skip the unchanged set in the next try. MSpec code, which adds 15% more lines to the baseline code, is considerably more complex than CSpec code. However, CSpec's performance matches MSpec's on Xeon ("*-CSpec" vs "*-MSpec"), and is even faster than the latter on Niagara 2, due to its simpler control flow and fewer instructions.

5.2 B^{link}-tree

B^{link}-trees [15, 22] are a concurrent enhancement of B^+-trees, an ordered data structure widely used in database and file systems. The main difference between a B^+-tree and a B^{link}-tree is the addition of two fields in each node: a *high key* representing the largest key among this node and its descendants, and a *right pointer* linking the node to its immediate right sibling. A node's high key is always smaller than any key of the right sibling or its descendants, allowing fast determination of a node's key range. The right pointer facilitates concurrent operations.

The original disk-based implementation of a B^{link}-tree uses the atomicity of file operations to avoid the need for locking. Srinivasan and Carey describe an in-memory version with a reader-writer lock in every node [24]. To perform a lookup, a reader descends from the root to a leaf node, then checks the node's high key to see if the desired key is in that node's key range. If not (in the case that the node has been split by another writer), the reader follows right pointers until an appropriate leaf is found. During this process, the reader holds only one reader lock at a time. When moving to the next node, it releases the previous node's lock *be-*

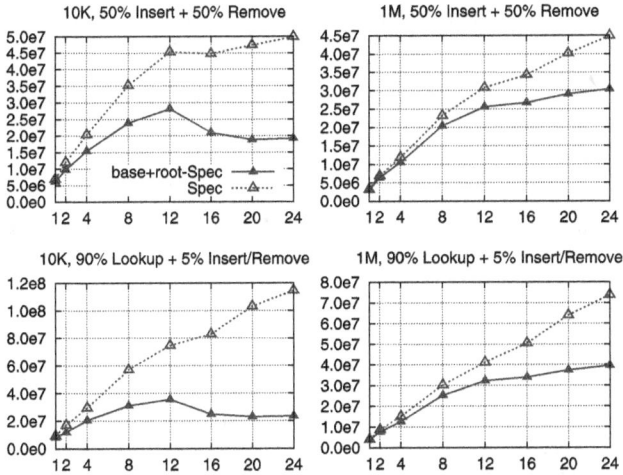

Figure 9. Throughput of B^{link}-tree methods on Intel Xeon E5649, for different tree sizes and method ratios.

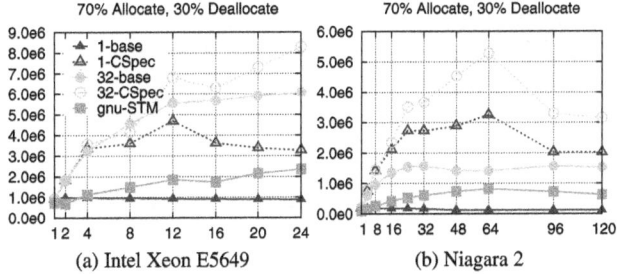

Figure 10. Throughput of linear bitmap allocator. The lock array uses a single lock in 1-* curves, 32 locks in 32-* curves.

fore acquiring the new one. In an insert/remove operation, a writer acts like a reader to locate a correct leaf node, then releases that leaf's reader lock and acquires the same leaf's writer lock. Because a node split may occur during the lock switch, the writer starts another round of search for the proper leaf using writer locks.

A full node A is split in three steps. First, a new node B is allocated with its right pointer linking to A's right sibling, and half the elements from A are moved to B. Second, A's right pointer is redirected to B, and A's writer lock is released. Third, A's new high key is inserted into its parent node. For simplicity, we employ the remove algorithm of Lehman and Yao [15], which does not merge underflowed leaf nodes; this means there is no node deallocation in our code.

Speculation: The B^{link}-tree algorithm already uses fine-grained locking. Its *lookup, insert* and *remove* operations contain two kinds of critical sections: (1) Critical sections protected by reader locks check a node's key range for a potential right move, or search for a key within a node. Not all of them can be transformed using CSpec, because the movement from one node to its right sibling or its child needs to hold two reader locks. CSpec cannot translate the overlapped critical section formed by the two locks. So, we manually convert the move step to speculation. (2) Critical sections protected by writer locks perform actual insertion and removal. If a node is full, a split occurs in the critical section. CSpec is able to handle these critical sections. The result of the transformation is that *lookup* becomes entirely speculative, and *insert* and *remove* start with a speculative search to check the presence/absence of the key to be inserted/removed. By performing searches in speculative mode, speculation eliminates the need for reader-writer locks. Simpler and cheaper mutex locks suffice for updates, and *lookup* operations become nonblocking.

Validation: Validation in a B^{link}-tree is relatively easy. Every speculation works on a single node, to which we add a version number. If (type-preserving) node deallocation were added to *remove*, we would use one bit of the version number to indicate whether the corresponding node is in use. By setting the bit, deallocation would force any in-progress speculation to fail its validation and go back to the saved parent (*not* the beginning of the method) to retry.

Performance: Figure 9 compares the original and CSpec versions of B^{link}-tree on the Xeon machine. Results on the Niagara 2 are qualitatively similar. The locking code uses a simple, fair reader-writer lock [18]. To avoid experimental bias, the CSpec code uses

the same lock's writer side. Each node contains a maximum of 32 keys in both algorithms, and occupies about 4 cache lines. To avoid a performance bottleneck at the top of the tree, the original algorithm uses speculation at the root node (only).

We ran the code with two different sizes of trees and two different mixes of methods. Small trees (10K elements) are more cache friendly than larger trees (1M elements), but suffer higher contention. The 90% *lookup*, 5% *insert* and 5% *remove* method mix simulates read-dominant workloads, and 0%:50%:50% simulates write-dominant workloads. As in the cuckoo hash experiments, we warm up all trees before beginning timing.

CSpec provides both greater throughput and greater scalability in all experiments, even with speculation at the root node in baseline locking code. CSpec scales very well even when running across chips (>12 threads). Comparing the left-hand and right-hand graphs in Figure 9, we can see that the advantage of speculation increases with higher contention (smaller trees). In separate experiments (not shown) we began with originally-empty trees, and ran until they reached a given size. This, too, increased the advantage of CSpec, as the larger number of node splits led to disproportionately longer critical sections in the baseline runs.

5.3 Bitmap Allocator

Bitmaps are widely used in memory management [25] and file systems. They are very space efficient: only one bit is required to indicate the use of a resource. A bitmap allocator may use a single flat bitmap or a hierarchical collection of bitmaps of different sizes. We consider the simplest case, where a next-fit algorithm is used to search for available slots. In the baseline algorithm, an array of locks protects the entire structure (one lock protects one segment of the bitmap). The data structure supports concurrent *allocate* and *deallocate* operations. To find the desired number of adjacent bits, *allocate* performs a linear search in its critical section, then sets all the bits to indicate they are used. *Deallocate* takes a starting position and size as parameters, and resets the corresponding bits in its critical section.

Speculation: Most of execution time is spent searching the bitmap for free bits. Since only one lock in the lock array is held at a time, we simply place a `consume_lock` directive before flipping the free bits.

Validation: After the lock is consumed, a `validate_cond` checks that the bits found during speculation are still available. No safety issues arise, as the bitmap always exists.

Performance: Our experiments (Figure 10) employ an array of 256K bits with a time-limited scenario in which a 70% *allocate*/30% *deallocate* mix consumes the bitmap gradually so it gets harder and harder to find a free slot. Allocation requests have the distribution 20% 1 bit, 30% 2 bits, 30% 4 bits, 15% 8 bits, and 5% 16 bits. Two lock array sizes, 1 (global lock) and 32, are used.

Data Structure	Locks	CSpec	Directives	Other changes
equivalence sets	CG, FG	2	5	No
cuckoo hash	CG, FG	3	23	No
B^{link}-tree	FG	3	17	hand-written speculative functions for moving between two nodes
bitmap allocator	CG	1	3	No

Table 1. A summary of the application of CSpec. CG/FG = coarse-/fine-grained.

On Niagara 2, CSpec-generated code ("*-CSpec") is significantly faster than the baseline as a result of a much shorter critical section in `Allocate`. Again, we see that coarse-grained locking with speculation ("1-CSpec") beats nonspeculative finer-grained locking ("32-base"). However, the benefit of CSpec is more modest on the Xeon machine. This is because the Xeon CPU can execute bit operations much faster than the simpler cores of the Niagara 2, leaving less work available to be moved to speculation. We also test a manual speculative version (not shown). Surprisingly, it is slightly slower than the CSpec version because its reorganized code contains more branch instructions. On both machines, the STM implementation is only faster than the single-lock baseline.

6. Conclusions

While fully automatic speculation, as provided by transactional memory, has the advantage of simplicity, we believe that manual speculation has a valuable role to play, particularly in the construction of concurrent data structure libraries. In support of this contention, we have presented four different structures—equivalence sets, a B^{link}-tree, a cuckoo hash table, and a bitmap allocator—in which speculation yields significant performance improvements. The principal challenges in their construction, as suggested in Section 4, were to identify the work that could profitably be moved to speculation, and to determine how and when to validate. To eliminate other, more mechanical challenges, we developed a set of compiler directives and a translation algorithm that partitions critical sections; identifies covering lock sets; and automates checkpointing, rollback, and the access tagging required to avoid data races and preserve sequential consistency.

Table 1 summarizes our four example data structures, comparing the baseline locking policies, the number of CSpec regions, the total number of added directives (excluding **#pragma spec**), and other changes to the source code. It clearly supports the claim that speculation can easily be added to existing lock-based code, with a small number of CSpec directives and few or no additional adjustments.

Our work suggests several avenues for future research, including a richer set of annotations, more sophisticated translation mechanisms, nested speculation, and dynamic selection among implementations with differing amounts of speculation.

References

[1] Clang: A C language family frontend for LLVM. http://clang.llvm.org.

[2] H.-J. Boehm. Can seqlocks get along with programming language memory models? *2012 ACM SIGPLAN Workshop on Memory Systems Performance and Correctness*, 2012.

[3] N. G. Bronson, J. Casper, H. Chafi, and K. Olukotun. A practical concurrent binary search tree. *15th ACM SIGPLAN Symp. on Principles and Practice of Parallel Programming*, Jan. 2010.

[4] L. Dalessandro and M. L. Scott. Sandboxing transactional memory. *21st Intl. Conf. on Parallel Architectures and Compilation Techniques*, Sep. 2012.

[5] L. Dalessandro, M. L. Scott, and M. F. Spear. Transactions as the foundation of a memory consistency model. *24th Intl. Symp. on Distributed Computing*, Sep. 2010.

[6] D. Dice, O. Shalev, and N. Shavit. Transactional locking II. *20th Intl. Symp. on Distributed Computing*, Sep. 2006.

[7] P. Felber, V. Gramoli, and R. Guerraoui. Elastic transactions. *23rd Intl. Conf. on Distributed Computing*, Sep. 2009.

[8] R. Guerraoui and M. Kapałka. On the correctness of transactional memory. *13th ACM SIGPLAN Symp. on Principles and Practice of Parallel Programming*, Feb. 2008.

[9] M. Herlihy and N. Shavit. *The Art of Multiprocessor Programming*. Morgan Kaufmann Publishers Inc., 2008.

[10] M. Herlihy, V. Luchangco, and M. Moir. Obstruction-free synchronization: Double-ended queues as an example. *23rd Intl. Conf. on Distributed Computing Systems*, May 2003.

[11] M. Herlihy, V. Luchangco, M. Moir, and W. N. Scherer III. Software transactional memory for dynamic-sized data structures. *22nd ACM Symp. on Principles of Distributed Computing*, July 2003.

[12] M. Herlihy, N. Shavit, and M. Tzafrir. Hopscotch hashing. *22nd Intl. Symp. on Distributed Computing*, Sep. 2008.

[13] M. P. Herlihy and J. M. Wing. Linearizability: A correctness condition for concurrent objects. *ACM Trans. Program. Lang. Syst.*, 12:463–492, July 1990.

[14] C. Lameter. Effective synchronization on Linux/NUMA systems. *Gelato Federation Meeting*, San Jose, CA, May 2005.

[15] P. L. Lehman and S. B. Yao. Efficient locking for concurrent operations on B-trees. *ACM Trans. Database Syst.*, 6:650–670, Dec. 1981.

[16] V. J. Marathe, M. F. Spear, and M. L. Scott. Scalable techniques for transparent privatization in software transactional memory. *Intl. Conf. on Parallel Processing*, Sep. 2008.

[17] P. E. McKenney, J. Appavoo, A. Kleen, O. Krieger, R. Russel, D. Sarma, and M. Soni. Read-copy update. *Ottawa Linux Symp.*, July 2001.

[18] J. M. Mellor-Crummey and M. L. Scott. Scalable reader-writer synchronization for shared-memory multiprocessors. *3rd ACM SIGPLAN Symp. on Principles and Practice of Parallel Programming*, Apr. 1991.

[19] M. M. Michael and M. L. Scott. Simple, fast, and practical non-blocking and blocking concurrent queue algorithms. *15th ACM Symp. on Principles of Distributed Computing*, May 1996.

[20] R. Pagh and F. F. Rodler. Cuckoo hashing. *J. Algorithms*, 51:122–144, May 2004.

[21] T. Riegel, C. Fetzer, and P. Felber. Time-based transactional memory with scalable time bases. *19th ACM Symp. on Parallel Algorithms and Architectures*, June 2007.

[22] Y. Sagiv. Concurrent operations on B-trees with overtaking. *4th ACM SIGACT-SIGMOD Symp. on Principles of Database Systems*, Mar. 1985.

[23] M. F. Spear, V. J. Marathe, W. N. Scherer III, and M. L. Scott. Conflict detection and validation strategies for software transactional memory. *20th Intl. Symp. on Distributed Computing*, Sep. 2006.

[24] V. Srinivasan and M. J. Carey. Performance of B+ tree concurrency control algorithms. *The VLDB Journal*, 2:361–406, Oct. 1993.

[25] P. R. Wilson, M. S. Johnstone, M. Neely, and D. Boles. Dynamic storage allocation: A survey and critical review. *Intl. Workshop on Memory Management*, Sep. 1995.

Complexity Analysis and Algorithm Design for Reorganizing Data to Minimize Non-Coalesced Memory Accesses on GPU *

Bo Wu*, Zhijia Zhao*, Eddy Z. Zhang†, Yunlian Jiang‡, Xipeng Shen*

*The College of William and Mary, Williamsburg, VA, USA
†Rutgers University, NJ, USA
‡Google, USA

{bwu,zzhao}@cs.wm.edu, eddy.zhengzhang@cs.rutgers.edu, yunlian@google.com, xshen@cs.wm.edu

Abstract

The performance of Graphic Processing Units (GPU) is sensitive to irregular memory references. Some recent work shows the promise of data reorganization for eliminating non-coalesced memory accesses that are caused by irregular references. However, all previous studies have employed simple, heuristic methods to determine the new data layouts to create. As a result, they either do not provide any performance guarantee or are effective to only some limited scenarios. This paper contributes a fundamental study to the problem. It systematically analyzes the inherent complexity of the problem in various settings, and for the first time, proves that the problem is NP-complete. It then points out the limitations of existing techniques and reveals that in practice, the essence for designing an appropriate data reorganization algorithm can be reduced to a tradeoff among space, time, and complexity. Based on that insight, it develops two new data reorganization algorithms to overcome the limitations of previous methods. Experiments show that an assembly composed of the new algorithms and a previous algorithm can circumvent the inherent complexity in finding optimal data layouts, making it feasible to minimize non-coalesced memory accesses for a variety of irregular applications and settings that are beyond the reach of existing techniques.

Categories and Subject Descriptors D.3.4 [*Programming Languages*]: Processors—optimization, compilers

General Terms Performance, Experimentation

Keywords GPGPU, Memory coalescing, Computational complexity, Thread-data remapping, Runtime optimizations, Data transformation

1. Introduction

Recent years have seen a rapid adoption of Graphic Processing Units (GPU) for high performance computing. As a massively

---

* Zhang and Jiang worked on this project before their graduations from The College of William and Mary.

```
(a) codelet
    // tid: the global ID of a thread
    // M: num. of neighbors per molecule
    ipos = pos [tid];
    for (j=0; j< m; j++){
        jpos = pos [ neighbors [ j*M + tid]];
        computeForce (f, ipos, jpos);
    }
    force [tid] = f;

(b) case 1: neighbors [0...3] = {4, 5, 6, 7}

(c) case 2: neighbors [0...3] = {9, 103, 23, 67}
```

Figure 1. (a) A simplified codelet of the force computation in a molecular dynamics simulation. The values in *neighbors* decides the access pattern of *pos*. (b) and (c) show a regular and irregular pattern respectively.

parallel architecture, GPU significantly accelerates many regular, data-parallel applications. But its benefits for irregular applications are far less substantial, especially when the application contains dynamic, irregular memory references.

The reason comes from the hardware properties of GPU. GPU organizes its threads in groups and memory in segments. Every W threads with consecutive ID numbers form a *warp*; every S consecutive bytes in the global memory form a *segment*. At a memory reference, the number of memory transactions needed to load the data accessed by a warp equals the number of segments the data fall onto. When that number is larger than the possible minimum, the accesses are called *non-coalesced memory accesses*.

Non-coalesced memory accesses are common in irregular applications. Figure 1 (a) shows a simplified codelet in the core computation in a molecular dynamics simulation. The underlined statement "pos [neighbors [j*M + tid]]" gets the coordinates of a neighbor of the current molecule. As a typical dynamic irregular reference, it may manifest various access patterns, determined by the values contained in *neighbors*. In the case of Figure 1 (b), all accesses by the warp are to a single memory segment; only one memory transaction is necessary, assuming a segment can contain four molecules' positions. But in the case of Figure 1 (c), because of irregular values in *neighbors*, the accesses are non-coalesced and require four memory transactions. This kind of irregularity is common in a molecular dynamics simulation, thanks to molecules' movements and their dynamic neighborhood. It is a key feature of many scientific simulations.

Non-coalesced accesses may result in memory transactions as many as W times of the minimum, leading to a throughput a number of factors lower than the peak of GPU [2, 5, 26]. They have been the focused target of some recent studies. However, most prior explorations [2, 12, 18, 20, 25] concentrate on static irregularities, where the memory access patterns are known at compilation time. The type of irregularity in our focus is dynamic: For instance, the content of the indexing array *neighbors* in Figure 1 depends on the input to the program and is updated throughout the simulation of the molecules movement.

Dynamic irregular accesses have to be treated during runtime. Some earlier studies [22] have relied on special hardware extensions that modern GPUs do not have. A recent study [26] shows the promise of pure software solutions. It develops a pipeline scheme that makes it possible for CPU to reorganize data and threads for a near-future GPU kernel invocation while GPU is working on the current kernel. A related study [5] demonstrates the feasibility of moving the reorganization to GPU so that CPU can also involve in workload processing.

Despite that these studies have shown promising speedups, the understanding to data reorganization for minimizing non-coalesced GPU memory accesses remains preliminary. The focus of the previous studies has been on coordinating CPU and GPU to allow runtime data reorganization. They have not explored fundamental issues on data reorganization and its relation with GPU memory performance. As a result, the reorganization algorithms they have adopted either lack performance guarantees or are effective to only some limited scenarios, as Section 3 reveals.

This current work provides the first principled understanding of GPU data reorganization for minimizing non-coalesced accesses. It makes four-fold contributions.

- **Complexity Analysis:** It systematically analyzes the relations between data reorganization and GPU memory accesses, and proves it infeasible to minimize memory transactions in polynomial time through just data repositioning, unless P equals NP. Furthermore, it proves that even if threads are allowed to be regrouped into warps, the complexity remains unchanged. The results indicate that it is virtually in vain to keep searching for a general, practical algorithm that can minimize GPU memory accesses, either with or without hardware extensions, through data repositioning, thread regrouping, or their combination— the three methods that have been pursued by most previous GPU memory optimizations. The strong theoretical results are essential for guiding the directions of the current research efforts. (Section 2)

- **Limitations and Essence:** This work points out the limitations of existing algorithms for optimizing GPU dynamic irregular references, and unveils that in practice, the essence for designing an appropriate data reorganization algorithm can be reduced to a classical tradeoff among space, time, and complexity. (Section 3.1 and 3.2)

- **Algorithms:** Based on the insights, this work develops two new data reorganization algorithms that complement prior algorithms with respective strengths. It shows that the new algorithms reduce space cost significantly with non-coalesced memory accesses kept minimized. (Section 3.3 and 3.4)

- **Comparison and Selection:** This work compares the various algorithms, unifies them into an assembly, and develops some selection guidelines and an automatic algorithm selector to address GPU dynamic irregular accesses in various scenarios. (Section 4)

- **Evaluation:** Experiments on a set of dynamic irregular applications show that the developed assembly, along with the al-

gorithm selector, circumvents the inherent complexity in finding optimal data layouts, making it feasible to minimize non-coalesced memory accesses for a variety of irregular applications and settings that are beyond the reach of existing techniques. Compared to existing techniques, the assembly produces up to 2X speedup (10-50% on average), demonstrating its promise as a comprehensive solution to dynamic irregular memory accesses in GPU. (Section 5)

2. Problem Setting and Complexity Analysis

In this section, we first provide some background on GPU that closely relates with the following discussions. We then describe the main approaches researchers have been pursuing to tackle non-coalesced GPU accesses. We finally reveal the fundamental challenges for such approaches by proving that using those approaches to minimize non-coalesced accesses for general irregular references is computational infeasible unless NP equals P.

2.1 Background on GPU

As a massively parallel device, GPU contains hundreds of cores residing on a number of streaming multiprocessors (SM). When a GPU kernel is launched, the runtime usually creates thousands of GPU threads running on these cores in parallel. These threads are organized hierarchically. A number of threads (32 in NVIDIA GPU) with consecutive IDs compose *a warp*, a number of warps compose *a thread block*, and all thread blocks compose *a grid*. (This paper uses CUDA terminology.) A warp is the unit in GPU scheduling; all threads in a warp proceed in lockstep.

GPU is equipped with several types of memory. The largest is off-chip main memory called *global memory*. It consists of a large number of segments (of 32, 64, or 128 bytes depending on the access mode.) For the large size and long access latency of global memory, its access efficiency is critical. GPU hence offers *memory coalescing*, a hardware-enabled feature that uses one memory transaction to load/store all the data in a memory segment that are requested by a warp at a load/store instruction. As a result, the execution of a load/store instruction by a warp incurs K memory transactions, where K equals the number of memory segments the requested data fall onto. Suppose the data to load/store by a warp at a reference contain D bytes and a memory segment is S-byte long. The reference is a *non-coalesced reference* when $K > \lceil D/S \rceil$. The corresponding memory accesses are *non-coalesced accesses*. Another type of memory on GPU worth mentioning is *shared memory*, which is on-chip with access latency comparable to that of register files. A thread can access an element that is loaded or stored into shared memory by another thread if and only if the two threads belong to the same thread block. In the following discussion, memory refers to global memory by default.

2.2 Objective and Complexity

The objective of non-coalesced access minimization is to minimize the number of non-coalesced accesses of a GPU kernel. The minimization, for its importance for GPU performance, has drawn lots of attentions. However, satisfying solutions are still limited to some special scenarios. In this section, we examine the inherent complexity of the previous approach and prove that in general cases, using the approach is infeasible to reach the objective unless NP equals P. The results may guide the direction of future research, and also lays the theoretical foundation for the rest of this work.

A GPU kernel may contain multiple references. We focus on one reference first and discuss other scenarios later.

2.2.1 Data Repositioning and NP-Completeness

Data repositioning has been the main direction pursued by previous work for minimizing non-coalesced accesses [2, 18, 22]. The essential idea is to reorder data elements on memory so that the data to be accessed by a warp can reside consecutively, covering the minimum number of memory segments. For the example in Figure 1 (c), the transformation would create a new array *Pos'* with the same elements as *Pos* has but in a different order, such that the four elements *Pos[9]*, *Pos[103]*, *Pos[23]*, *Pos[67]* fall into a single memory segment. Matrix transposing [22] is another example: By repositioning elements on memory to create a column-major data layout, it can minimize non-coalesced accesses for a column-wise reference to the matrix.

Although it seems simple, using data repositioning can be complicated when the data accessed by multiple warps overlap. Consider a reference $A[P[tid]]$, with P as follows
$P[]=\{$**8**, 23, 46, 93, **8**, **9**, 10, **67**, 5, 11, **41**, **67**, **9**, **41**, 55, 59$\}$.
Assume memory segment length $S = 4$ and warp size $W = 4$. The repetitive values in P (highlighted in bold font) dictate that some elements in A are accessed by multiple warps. Which segment to put those values is tricky. For instance, putting $A[8]$ into a segment with $A[23]$, $A[46]$, $A[93]$ would coalesce the first warp's accesses but leave the second warp's accesses non-coalesced.

The issue has been largely limiting the applicability of data repositioning. Despite many recent efforts, this approach has been effective for only the cases where each target data element is accessed by only one warp in a kernel. In an application with dynamic irregular references, that condition rarely holds: In a molecular dynamics, a molecule is often the neighbor of more than one molecule; in a sparse matrix multiplication, an element in the vector is often used to multiply multiple elements in the matrix; in a mesh simulation, a vertex is often shared by several triangles.

Complexity Theorem Prompted by the various difficulties people have so far encountered in finding a general data repositioning algorithm to guarantee minimum non-coalesced accesses, we conduct a systematic analysis on the inherent complexity of the problem. An important finding we obtain is that such an algorithm does not exist unless NP=P. Formally, we develop the following theorem:

Theorem 1. *Creating a new data layout through only data repositioning (which implies that each item in the original data structure has only one copy in the new structure) to minimize the non-coalesced accesses for an arbitrary data reference on GPU is an NP-complete problem.*

As this is the first strong claim on the complexity of non-coalesced access minimization, it is worth providing a formal proof, for verifying its correctness as well as offering insights that may be useful for analyzing the complexity of other GPU optimization problems.

Proof Assume that the irregular reference, when executed by all the GPU threads, accesses n unique data items. Let z be the length of a memory segment (in the unit of data items.) The goal of the repositioning is essentially to partition the n data items evenly into n/z clusters such that when each cluster is put onto a single memory segment, the total number of memory transactions at that data reference is minimized. To prove the NP-completeness, we use the following notations.

Δ : the set of all data items to be partitioned; $n = |\Delta|$; Ψ : the set of all warps; $m = |\Psi|$; $\Psi_{<x>} = \{w|w \in \Psi$ & w references $x\}$ ($x \in \Delta$); Ω : a complete partition of Δ with z data items per cluster; $r_C = |\bigcup_{x \in C} \Psi_{<x>}|$ ($C \subseteq \Delta, |C| = z$).

We can see that $\bigcup_{x \in C} \Psi_{<x>}$ essentially contains all and only the warps that each accesses at least one element in C. So, essentially, r_C is the number of memory transactions incurred by all data items in C when they are put into a single memory segment. Hence, totally there are $\sum_{C \in \Omega} r_C$ memory transactions for partition Ω if each cluster of data is put into one memory segment. The tar-

get problem is to find an Ω such that $\sum_{C \in \Omega} r_C$ is minimized. Its corresponding decision problem is: Given an arbitrary number u, whether an Ω exists such that $\sum_{C \in \Omega} r_C \leq u$. We call this decision problem **DLDP** (Data Layout Decision Problem).

Reduction from 3DM (three-dimensional matching), a known NP-complete problem [11], to DLDP is enough to prove that our target problem is NP-hard. **3DM** is defined as follows.

- Input: 3 disjoint sets $R, G, B, |R| = |G| = |B| = l$, and a set of 3-D vectors $T, T \subseteq \{< r, g, b > |r \in R, g \in G, b \in B\}$.
- Problem: Is there a set S meeting all these conditions (3DM conditions): (1) $S \subseteq T$; (2) $|S| = l$; (3) $\forall \langle r,g,b\rangle \in$ S, $\forall \langle r',g',b'\rangle \in$ (S - $\langle r,g,b\rangle$), $r \neq r'$, $g \neq g'$, $b \neq b'$.

From an instance of 3DM problem, we construct an instance of DLDP as follows: $\Delta = |B \cup G \cup P|$, $n = 3l$; $m = |T|$; $z = 3$; $u = l(m-1)$; Ψ : a set of m warps, with each warp having a unique ID equaling one element in T, and a warp with ID $\langle$r,g,b$\rangle$ accesses x if and only if $x \in \Delta$, $x \neq r$, $x \neq g$, and $x \neq b$.

We prove that a solution, represented as $\hat{\Omega}$, to the constructed DLDP solves the 3DM problem. Because $\hat{\Omega}$ is a partition of Δ, $|\hat{\Omega}| = l$; because $\hat{\Omega}$ solves the 3DM problem, $\sum_{C \in \hat{\Omega}} r_C \leq u$. From $\hat{\Omega}$ we derive a set of 3-D vectors $\hat{S}$ ($|\hat{S}| = |\hat{\Omega}|$). Each element in $\hat{S}$, $< y_1, y_2, y_3 >$, comes from one element in $\hat{\Omega}$, $\{x_1, x_2, x_3\}$, with "y_1, y_2, y_3" as an ascending sequence of "x_1, x_2, x_3" in R,G,B order (i.e., $\forall r \in R, g \in G, b \in B, r < g < b$).

We prove that $\hat{S}$ is a solution to the 3DM problem—that is, it meets all the 3DM conditions. It is obvious that $\hat{S}$ meets condition two and three given its derivation from $\hat{\Omega}$. To prove the first condition, we need to show $\forall \vec{v} \in \hat{S} \Rightarrow \vec{v} \in T$. This step uses the following lemma: $\vec{v} \in T \Rightarrow r_{\vec{v}} = m - 1$; $\vec{v} \notin T \Rightarrow r_{\vec{v}} = m$.

The correctness of the lemma is easy to see if one notices that $\vec{v} \notin T$ means all warps in Ψ must access at least one element in $\vec{v}$ (hence $\bigcup_{x \in \vec{v}} \Psi_{<x>} = \Psi$, $r_{\vec{v}} = m$), while $\vec{v} \in T$ means all but one warp whose ID equals $\vec{v}$ access at least one element in $\vec{v}$.

From the lemma, we see that if $\exists \vec{v}$ $\vec{v} \in \hat{S}$ and $\vec{v} \notin T$, then $\sum_{C \in \hat{\Omega}} r_C$ must be greater than u, $u = l(m-1)$, contradicting the initial condition that Ω is a solution to the DLDP. Thus, DLDP is NP-hard. Apparently, DLDP belongs to NP; the optimal data layout problem is hence NP-complete. Theorem 1 hence follows.

2.2.2 When Warp Reorganization is Allowed

The above proof assumes that only data repositioning is applied for reducing non-coalesced memory accesses. Some recent study [26] has shown that warp reorganization can help remove non-coalesced accesses as well, and can be used together with data repositioning for the optimization. In this subsection, we complement Theorem 1 by proving that using warp reorganization does not change the NP-completeness of the problem. That is, we prove the following strengthened complexity theorem:

Theorem 2. *It is an NP-complete problem to minimize the non-coalesced accesses for an arbitrary data reference on GPU through data repositioning, warp reorganization, or both.*

Warp reorganization is to swap threads across warps. It is also called *job swapping* because it exchanges the jobs of swapped threads and hence the data elements a warp accesses. The swapping may remove non-coalesced accesses. For instance, suppose that thread t_3 accesses $A[7]$ and thread t_7 accesses $A[3]$, while the other threads in the first two warps access $A[tid]$. After swapping t_3 and t_7, the new t_3 will do the work originally done by t_7 and access $A[3]$, while the new t_7 will take over the work of t_3 and access $A[7]$. Both warps' accesses become coalesced. Runtime warp reorganization has been shown to be feasible through either hardware extensions [9] or program transformations [26]. It may be used together with data repositioning in minimizing non-coalesced accesses [26].

We now prove that allowing warp reorganization does not change the computational complexity of the data repositioning problem. To prove it, it is enough to prove a special case of the problem to be NP-complete. The special case we use is when each data element is of the same size as the memory segment. In that case, data repositioning has no effect on the number of memory accesses as it does not change the clustering of data elements into memory segments. So if we can prove that using only warp reorganization to minimize non-coalesced memory accesses is NP-complete, Theorem 2 is proved.

Warp reorganization is equivalent to grouping the jobs of the threads into clusters with each cluster containing W jobs (W is the number of threads per warp). Without loss of generality, consider that a job contains just one irregular reference to an array. Let N stand for the number of threads, M represents the total number of memory segments that contain at least one data item requested at the reference. We claim that it is NP-complete (in regard to M) to partition N jobs evenly into N/W clusters such that when each warp takes one cluster of jobs, the total number of memory transactions at that data reference is minimized.

The proof is via a reduction from a known NP-complete problem, the **partition problem** [11] (represented as **PAR** to avoid confusion). All jobs can be classified into M categories based on which memory segment contains the data item requested in a job; we say two jobs are of the same type if they are in the same category. Let n_i ($i = 1, \cdots, M$) represent the number of jobs in the ith category. Apparently the total number of jobs N equals $\sum_{i=1}^{M} n_i$. In the PAR problem, the goal is to decide whether a given set S of integers can be partitioned into two subsets S_1 and S_2 such that the sum of the numbers in S_1 equals the sum of the numbers in S_2. The reduction to our problem is as follows. A special case of our problem is that the size of each warp (W) is $N/2$. Our remapping hence needs to assign the N jobs to two clusters. Apparently, the number of memory transactions for a job cluster is the number of types of jobs in the warp. It can be seen that the achievable lower bound of the number of memory transactions in our special-case problem is M. It is obtainable only when $M/2$ types of jobs fit exactly into one cluster; note that in this case, the integer set $S = \{n_1, n_2, \cdots, n_M\}$ is evenly partitioned. So, if we can find the best partition of threads into warps in polynomial time (in regard to M), we would be able to tell whether S can be evenly partitioned by checking whether the number of memory transactions resulting from our mapping is M. Hence, the PAR problem would be solvable in polynomial time, contradicting the well-established NP-completeness of the problem. Theorem 2 follows.

2.3 Discussion

This section has analyzed the computational complexity of using data repositioning for minimizing non-coalesced accesses. The proved NP-completeness should not rule out the possibility that through some heuristic algorithms, the approach may still yield good speedup on some special types of kernels. However, it does indicate the extreme challenge to use it for achieving the optimal for general cases. We next show that the challenge can be circumvented if a constraint assumed by the approach is relaxed.

3. Algorithms that Circumvent the Complexity

We design two new algorithms to circumvent the complexity facing data repositioning. The key observation is that the essential difficulty in data repositioning comes from an implicit constraint that the produced new data layout uses no more space than the original.

If we allow more space to be used, the complexity of the problem may reduce significantly.

Previous studies have not exploited this insight, except for the one by Zhang and others [26], which takes advantage of extra space but in an ad-hoc manner. In this section, we first review that previous method, reveal its limitation, and crystallize the analysis into an insight in the key tradeoff in designing a practical solution. We then describe the two new algorithms we design.

The following discussion is based on reference $A[P[tid]]$, a conceptual form of dynamic irregular references. It assumes the memory segment size (S) is a multiple of the working set size of a warp. This condition often holds given that the warp size and S are typically powers of 2. But even when it does not hold, the following discussions are still valid except that some preprocessing needs to be done to align data with memory segments.

3.1 Review of the *Duplication* Algorithm

The *duplication algorithm* is used by Zhang and others to optimize irregular memory accesses [26]. For an irregular reference, such as $A[P[tid]]$, the algorithm creates a new array A' such that $A'[tid] = A[P[tid]]$; the reference to $A[P[tid]]$ in the kernel is then replaced with $A'[tid]$. The algorithm naturally ensures that all accesses of a warp are to a consecutive memory region and there are no non-coalesced memory accesses, as illustrated by Figure 4 (b).

The algorithm is called "duplication" as it creates duplicated copies of a data element when the indexing array P contains repetitive values. Apparently, the new array A' is as large as the number of GPU threads (T), no matter how small the original array A is. Even worse is when there are multiple references to the same array (e.g., $A[P[tid]] + A[P[tid] + v]$), the algorithm creates a new T-long array for each of the references.

3.2 Limitations and Tradeoff

The duplication algorithm converts irregular accesses to regular ones. However, it may dramatically inflate space usage. For a K-element array referenced n times by T GPU threads, the space overhead is as much as a factor of $n * T/K$. In a modern GPU, T can be comparable with the number of bytes in the entire memory.

The large space overhead has two consequences. First, the basic duplication algorithm fails to apply when the space inflation exceeds the capacity of the memory. Second, the creation and transfer of the large volume of data may introduce substantial time overhead, throttling the optimization benefits. The previous work has used partial duplication to alleviate the issues [26]. The idea is to apply the transformation to only a fraction of the GPU threads. Although it can reduce the space overhead, it compromises the quality of the optimization proportionally. As Section 5 will show, it may result in substantially lower speedup than what is possible.

Figure 2 shows the conceptual positions of the previous approaches in a space of optimization quality, complexity, and space cost. Data repositioning and the duplication algorithm are at two extreme ends of the spectrum of space cost. The partial duplication lowers the space cost but also proportionally degrades the transformation quality and lengthens the kernel execution time. Data repositioning has the lowest space cost but the highest complexity. So the key for having a practical algorithm is to find a sweet design point that reduces the space cost without compromising the transformation quality and meanwhile possesses manageable complexity. We next describe two new algorithms towards that goal.

3.3 *Padding* Algorithm

The padding algorithm tries to avoid some unnecessary data copies made in the duplication algorithm without compromising the optimization quality. Its basic observation is that if two threads (t_1 and t_2) from the same warp access the same data element (a), there is

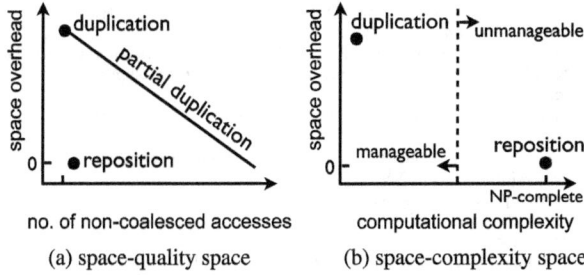

Figure 2. Positions of various algorithms in the space-quality-complexity coordinates. Graph (b) omits partial duplication for legibility.

```
// inputIndArray, outputIndArray: the original and produced indexing arrays
// inputArray, outputArray: the original data array and its new copy after padding
function Padding(inputIndArray, outputIndArray, inputArray, outputArray)
  inputIndArray = SortByFrequency(inputIndArray);
  for each warp w,
    uniqueRefSet = FindUniqueRefs(w, inputIndArray, inputArray);
    nRemainingSlots = FindRemainingSlots(currentMemSegment);
    if uniqueRefSet.size <= nRemainingSlots,
      for each e in uniqueRefSet,
        add element e to outputArray;
        update outputIndArray;
      end
    else
      pad dummy values to outputArray for memory segment alignment;
      for each e in uniqueRefSet,
        add element e to outputArray;
        update outputIndArray;
      end
    end
  end
end
```

Figure 3. The pseudo-code of the padding algorithm.

no need to create two copies of that data element. We can simply let them access the same copy of the data element. It will change the one to one regular mapping between data and threads created by the duplication algorithm, however, it will not create non-coalesced accesses since the two threads still access the same memory segment.

3.3.1 A Simple Design

A simple design is to just make the following modification to the duplication algorithm. When the algorithm is about to create a copy of an element in the new array A', it checks whether the current thread is the first of the current warp that accesses that element and avoids the creation if it is not. (An entailed change is that the original reference, say $A[P[tid]]$, needs to be replaced with $A'[Q[tid]]$ rather than $A'[tid]$, where Q contains the new mapping between a thread and the data it accesses in A'.)

Unfortunately, this simple modification is insufficient for two reasons. First, the avoided duplications cover only a small portion of all the duplications because the chance for two threads accessing the same data element to come from the same warp is often small. Second, the avoidance of some duplications often causes a misalignment between the working set of a warp and memory segments. As a consequence, the working set of a warp may span over the boundary of a segment, causing new non-coalesced accesses.

3.3.2 An Enhanced Design

Our enhanced design addresses the two problems of the simple design through sorting and padding. Figure 3 shows the pseudo code of the algorithm. It includes three steps.

Figure 4. An example that illustrates the algorithms of duplication, padding, and sharing. Assume 4 objects per memory segment, 4 threads per warp, and 4 warps per block.

The first step reorders data elements based on their access frequencies. At a data reference, the *access frequency* of a data element is the number of threads that access it. The second step reorganizes threads into warps. It reorders threads according to the order of data elements—that is, all threads accessing data X must precede all threads accessing Y if X precedes Y in the new data sequence. Starting from the first thread, every W adjacent threads form a warp in the resulting thread organization. These two steps address the first problem of the simple design: By making threads accessing the same data element locate closely and form warps, they reveal more opportunities for saving duplications.

The third step puts data elements into memory segments. Starting from the first data element in the new order, the data are greedily packed into a memory segment one after one. But when it finds that the current segment cannot hold all the data the current thread warp accesses (e.g., the first segment in Figure 4 (c)), it moves all the data accessed by that warp into the next memory segment, leaving some empty slots at the end of the previous memory segment. Data is duplicated only when necessary—that is, when one data element is accessed by multiple thread warps whose working data sets do not fall into the same memory segment. Examples are the two "c"s in the layout in Figure 4 (c). This step addresses the second problem of the simple design. By padding a memory segment with some empty slots when necessary, it aligns the working set of a warp with memory segments.

Analysis This padding algorithm guarantees zero non-coalesced access since it puts the working set of every warp into a single memory segment. Its space overhead comes from the padded empty slots and some duplicated data elements. If k threads in a warp access one single data element, the empty slot in a memory segment is at most as long as $mod(S, \lceil W/k \rceil)$, where $\lceil W/k \rceil$ computes the number of unique elements accessed by a warp and S is the number of data elements a segment can contain. Both S and W are usually power of two. So the worst case happens when k is small (hence the remainder is large) but is not a power of two. Specifically, when $k = 3$, the empty slot is the longest, up to $W/3 - 1$. But even in that case, the space cost is much lower than that of the duplication algorithm. The number of threads a memory segment serves in that

61

case must be no fewer than $t = (S - W/3 + 1)/(W/3)$. Following the assumption that S is the multiple of W, let $S = r * W$ with r being a positive integer. The number of threads served, t, must be no smaller than $3r - 1$, which is at least 2. In the duplication algorithm, these threads would use at least $2S$ memory (given that $r = 1$ means $S = W$), double what they use in the padding algorithm.

When analyzing the number of duplications in the padding algorithm, it is important to notice that among all the warps accessing the current memory segment, only the first of them may have some data elements duplicated. It is because only when the working set of a warp overlaps with the data elements in the previous memory segment, those overlapped elements may have a duplicate in the current memory segment (e.g., the second "c" in Figure 4 (c).) That overlap must be partial since at a complete overlap, the previous memory segment can already hold the working set of that first warp, and hence that warp would have corresponded to the previous rather than current memory segment. Due to the way threads are ordered, that partial overlap entails that the working sets of the other warps cannot overlap with the data in the previous segment, and hence have no duplicated data. Following the observation, we can see that in the case mentioned in the previous paragraph, the duplicated part of a segment is at most $W/3 - 1$, smaller than $1/3r$ of S. In comparison, the duplication algorithm creates at least 3 copies per data element in that case. The data element contained in one memory segment in the padding result would become $3 * (S - W/3 + 1)/S$ (which is greater than $3 - 1/3r$ and 2.67) segments in the result from the duplication algorithm.

Limitation Despite its appealing properties, the padding algorithm has one major limitation. Because it reorganizes not only data but also threads, it may cause side effects to other references in the kernel. For example, if a kernel contains "B[tid]+A[P[tid]]", after the third and ninth threads switch positions, they swap their jobs, and the accesses to B must also be swapped. In another word, $B[tid]$ must be replaced with $B[R[tid]]$ where, $R[3] = 9$, and $R[9] = 3$. Otherwise, the new thread 3 would add $A[P[9]]$ with $B[3]$ rather than $B[9]$, causing wrong computation results. As a result, the optimization of $A[P[tid]]$ makes accesses to B non-coalesced. So the padding algorithm is most beneficial when all references in a kernel follow the same access pattern (e.g., $B[P[tid]] + A[P[tid]]$.)

3.4 *Sharing* **Algorithm**

This algorithm overcomes the limitation of the padding algorithm by increasing duplication avoidance from a different angle. It uses the shared memory in GPU to enlarge the scope of duplication avoidance. Shared memory is a type of on-chip memory in GPU. Data written to shared memory by a thread is visible only to threads in the same thread block. Shared memory has an access latency a hundred times smaller than that of the global memory, and more importantly, its performance is largely insensitive to irregularities in accesses.

Insight The key insight of this algorithm is to shift irregular accesses from global memory to shared memory. As shared memory is visible within a whole thread block, the sharing algorithm enlarges the scope of duplication avoidance from a warp to a thread block. Its basic idea is to create a copy of all the data accessed by a thread block (a single copy per data element) and put them into a consecutive chunk of memory. Then, it loads these data in a consecutive (hence coalesced) manner into shared memory. It redirects memory accesses by the thread block to the corresponding copies in the shared memory. By keeping only one copy for all data elements accessed by a whole thread block, it avoids many duplications. By shifting irregular accesses to shared memory, it eliminates

```
// inputIndArray, outputIndArray: the original and produced indexing arrays;
// inputArray, outputArray: the original and produced data arrays;
// blockPos, blockSizes: the starting position and size of the working set of a thread block
function Sharing(inputIndArray, outputIndArray, inputArray, outputArray,
blockPos, blockSizes)
  [inputIndArray, inputArray] = DataClustering(inputIndArray, inputArray);
  for each thread block b,
    uniqueRefSet = findUniqueReferences(b, inputIndArray, inputArray);
    blockSizes[b] = uniqueRefSet.size;
    blockPos[b] = outputArray.size;
    for each e in uniqueRefSet,
      Add element e to outputArray;
      outputIndArray[e] = position(outputArray, e) - blockPos[b];
    end
    pad dummy values to outputArray for memory segment alignment;
  end
end
```

Figure 5. The pseudo-code of the sharing algorithm.

non-coalesced accesses to global memory. It uses clustering to further increase the opportunity for duplication saving. The detailed algorithm is as follows.

Algorithm Figure 5 outlines the pseudo-code of the sharing algorithm. It includes two steps. In the first step, it conducts clustering to swap threads among thread blocks so that the threads in a block have as many accesses to the same data elements as possible, while different blocks have as few as possible.

Many clustering algorithms can serve for the purpose. In our implementation, we use two. The first is a graph partition-based clustering [23], which is especially suitable for applications with a graph topology, such as the distribution of molecules in a molecular dynamics simulation, the structure of a mesh in a mesh simulation. In these applications, typically each thread is in charge of one node in the graph. The algorithm randomly selects some nodes as seeds and assign each of them a distinct cluster number. The nodes then iteratively propagate the cluster memberships to their neighbors. The threads are clustered by inheriting the cluster ID of their corresponding nodes. The second clustering algorithm is suitable for other cases. It uses the working set of a thread as its feature and applies the standard hierarchical clustering to build up the clusters.

After clustering, the second step prepares data to be loaded into shared memory and creates a new indexing array to reference them. Specifically, it places the data elements accessed by each thread block continuously into a global array. It is possible that even after the clustering, the working sets of two thread blocks may still overlap. In that case, some data will have to be duplicated across thread blocks. Some trivial padding fills up the final memory segment a thread block uses. Figure 4 (d) shows an example. The clustering switches threads 9 and 10 with threads 21 and 22. After that, each thread block accesses four unique data elements and there is no overlaps between the working sets of the two blocks and hence no duplications. Two meta-arrays, *blockPos* and *blockSizes*, record the starting offset and the number of accessed data elements in the new data array for each thread block. They add minor space cost. When the GPU kernel executes, each thread block loads the corresponding block of data to shared memory according to the meta-arrays.

Notes We make several notes. First, the clustering step is optional. It increases the chance for saving data duplications, but even if it is not used, the algorithm can still remove all non-coalesced accesses and avoid duplications inside a thread block.

Second, when clustering is used, threads in different blocks may get swapped. However, unlike the padding algorithm case, even with the swapping, the sharing algorithm can still apply to a kernel containing multiple references with different access patterns. It is because the sharing algorithm does not require data references to remain or become regular. Consider the example mentioned earlier, $B[tid] + A[P[tid]]$. After clustering-incurred thread swapping, the references may become $B'[Q[tid]] + A'[P'[tid]]$ and both references become irregular. However, the second step of the sharing algorithm ensures that both arrays will be loaded into the shared memory in a coalesced manner. Accesses to the copies in the shared memory may be irregular, but recall that the performance of shared memory is resilient to access irregularity. It is worth noting that for this algorithm to work properly, the clustering and data reorganization need to put all the references ($B[tid]$ and $A[P[tid]]$ in our example) into consideration.

Third, the usage of shared memory may have two side effects on the performance of the kernel. The first is the time overhead of the introduced accesses to shared memory, which is often negligible compared to the time incurred by global memory accesses, especially for the irregular applications that are often memory latency bound. The second effect is that because shared memory is partitioned to all active thread blocks on a streaming multiprocessor, a large usage of shared memory by a thread block may reduce the number of thread blocks that can be active at the same time (called GPU *occupancy*.) Our experimental results in Section 5 show that the effect is not obvious on irregular applications.

Finally, when a problem size is large, the working set of a thread block could be larger than the shared memory. Fortunately, we observe that for most kernels, when the problem size increases, the problem size per thread block often remains unchanged but more thread blocks are created. In exceptional cases, to apply the sharing algorithm, the kernel can be modified to break the task of one block into smaller tasks and assign them to more thread blocks.

Analysis Quality-wise, as described in the algorithm, after the sharing algorithm applies, the accesses to the global memory become consecutive and coalesced. It maintains the zero non-coalesced accesses guaranteed by the duplication algorithm.

Space-wise, the algorithm saves space cost by avoiding data duplications for threads inside a block. The maximum number of copies of a data element is the number of thread blocks, rather than the number of threads in the duplication algorithm. If on average k ($k < B$, B for the number of threads per block) threads access one data element, with a perfect clustering that puts threads accessing the same data element into a single block, the algorithm can virtually avoid all data duplications. In practice, the amount of savings depends on the clustering quality (or how frequently multiple thread blocks access the same data elements if clustering is not used.) Section 5 provides the empirical results.

3.5 Discussion

The two new algorithms introduced in this section guarantee zero non-coalesced access as the duplication algorithm does. Although they reduce the space overhead of the duplication method substantially, it should be noted that they do not guarantee minimum space cost. Designing an algorithm with that guarantee and zero non-coalesced accesses is not the goal of this work. In fact, that task is no easier than the data positioning problem (they form dual problems with each other.) Section 5 will show that the two algorithms do provide practical solutions to a variety of programs.

4. Algorithm Selection and Integration

The three algorithms described in the previous section have different strengths and weaknesses. In this section, we provide a qualitative comparison, and describe an automatic selector and its integration in a runtime library.

Qualitative Comparison We summarize the qualitative differences among the three algorithms as follows.

```
// T: # of threads;   D: the set of memory references;
// Dₗ: working set of a thread block;
// Z: the size of the irregularly accessed data;
if T is less or comparable with Z:
    use duplication;
else if D has a single access pattern:
    use padding;
else if Dₗ is smaller than shared memory:
    use sharing;
else:
    use duplication or change kernel to use sharing.
```

Figure 6. Guidelines for algorithm selection.

- **Applicability:** The padding algorithm is applicable to kernels that have a single reference pattern. While the other two algorithms do not have such a constraint, the sharing algorithm may need kernel modification when the working set of a thread block is too large to fit into shared memory, and the duplication algorithm may be applicable to only part of the data when the space limit is reached.

- **Space cost:** By avoiding unnecessary duplications, the padding and sharing algorithms use much less space than the duplication algorithm does.

- **Optimization capability:** All three algorithms have the capability to eliminate all non-coalesced memory accesses (in their applicable scenarios.) However, when being applied at runtime, the realizable benefits also depend on their runtime overhead.

- **Transformation overhead:** The time overhead of the duplication algorithm is in the creation and transfer of the new data copies, which can be substantial when the number of threads is very large or there are multiple references of different patterns to the same array. For the padding algorithm, the overhead includes the data and threads sorting time in addition to the creation and transfer of the new arrays. The overhead of the sharing algorithm consists of data creation and transfer time, the clustering time, the accesses to shared memory and the side effect on occupancy. Due to the large space reduction, the data creation and transfer in the two new algorithms usually take much less time than in the duplication algorithm. Data creation and transfer usually reside on the critical path of dynamic simulation applications, but the sorting and clustering in those two algorithms do not and hence can be largely hidden (e.g., through the CPU-GPU pipeline in G-Streamline [26].) We will come back to this point later in this section.

Algorithm Selection Based on the differences, we develop some simple guidelines, as Figure 6 shows, to help programmers select the suitable algorithm when writing a new program.

Meanwhile, we provide an automatic selector based on the online profiling and adaptive control offered by G-Streamline, a runtime library we previously developed [26]. The runtime library works when the GPU kernel is invoked in a loop. By profiling the initial several iterations during runtime along with some performance models of the system (e.g., the time to transfer a data from CPU to GPU, the time to create a data copy) built ahead of time through offline profiling, it estimates the kernel running time and optimization overhead to determine the suitable optimization algorithm to apply and the appropriate optimization parameters to use (e.g., the fraction of data to optimize in partial duplication.) Many irregular applications, including dynamic simulations and numerical calculations, are of that iterative pattern and are amenable for the runtime library to work. Our automatic selector employs the online profiling to estimate the amount of overhead of the algorithms and the kernel running time to pick the algorithm with the largest performance potential.

Integration with G-Streamline We integrate the selector and the reorganization algorithms into G-Streamline. G-Streamline uses a CPU-GPU pipelining scheme to allow runtime optimization of a future kernel invocation to happen on CPU when GPU is running the current invocation. However, if the future kernel's optimization depends on its previous invocation result, the optimization has to happen on the critical path. In that case, to make the optimization still happen asynchronously, kernel splitting is used so that the computations of a kernel are split and put into two parallel sub-kernels. The optimization of the second sub-kernel can run with the invocation of the first sub-kernel. The ratio between the amount of task between the second and first sub-kernel is called *transformation ratio*. The more costly the optimization is, the lower the ratio has to be so that the invocation of the first sub-kernel can hide the optimization overhead.

For all irregular applications we find, among the major operations in the three algorithms, sorting and clustering can happen across kernel invocations, but data creation and transfer are on the critical path due to dependences across kernel calls. They have to rely on kernel splitting to hide their overhead. In Section 5, we will see that the padding and sharing algorithms have much higher transformation ratio than duplication for their much smaller overhead in data creation and transfer. It is worth noting that G-Streamline uses its online profiling scheme to determine the suitable transformation ratio to ensure all overhead is hidden. If an optimization is infeasible to give benefits, G-Streamline shuts it down automatically to prevent any slowdown to the kernel.

Integrating the data reorganization algorithms into G-Streamline does not change the library's interface. It only adds a handful of functions as alternatives to the duplication algorithm already presenting in G-Streamline. The usage of the modified G-Streamline is the same as before [26]: Users insert several function calls into the GPU application to invoke the runtime asynchronous optimizations and online profiling; some minor changes to the kernel may be needed, including replacing old indexing arrays with new ones.

5. Evaluation

In this section, we evaluate the proposed algorithm assembly on eight benchmarks in Table 1, which all have dynamic irregular memory accesses. For comparing with the state of the art [26], they include all memory benchmarks used in the previous work: CFD is an unstructured grid finite volume solver; CG is a conjugate gradient method with sparse matrix-vector multiplication as its kernel; NN is for nearest-neighbor clustering; UNWRAP is for 3-D reconstruction. MD is a molecular dynamics simulation from the Shoc benchmark suite [7]; NBF and IRREG are derived from two irregular CPU applications heavily used by previous research [10]. The former is part of GROMOS, a force field simulation; the latter is the core of an iterative partial differential equation solver. The benchmark MERGE is a database update program. All code has gone through performance tuning to fit the execution models of GPU. The inputs to MD, IRREG, NBF and CFD consist of some nodes and neighbor lists generated randomly. The input to MERGE includes some indexing arrays of a set of data generated randomly. The inputs to CG contain a sparse matrix and vector. The locations of the non-zero elements in the matrix exhibit some patterns such that multiple rows of the matrix happen to multiple with a similar set of elements in the vector. The inputs to NN and UNWRAP come with the benchmarks.

We experiment on two types of GPU devices. One is NVIDIA Tesla C1060 hosted in a quad-core Intel Xeon E5640 machine, and the other is NVIDIA GTX480 hosted in a quad-core Intel

Table 1. Benchmarks and selected optimization algorithms (M1:Tesla C1060; M2: GTX480)

benchmark	description	alg. on M1	alg. on M2
MD	molecular dynamics	Sharing	Sharing
IRREG	partial diff. solver	Sharing	Sharing
NBF	force field	Sharing	Sharing
CFD	finite volume solver	Sharing	Sharing
CG	conjugate gradient	Sharing	Sharing
UNWRAP	3-D reconstruction	Dup.	(not runnable)
NN	nearest neighbor	Dup.	Dup.
MERGE	database update	Padding	Padding

unwrap cannot run on GTX480 for unknown reasons.

Table 2. Transformation ratios

benchmark	Dup.		Sharing	
	C1060	GTX480	C1060	GTX480
MD	0.25	0.1	0.85	0.65
IRREG	0.4	0.1	0.9	0.7
NBF	0.4	0.15	0.95	0.8
CFD	0.35	*	0.6	*
CG	0.45	0.15	0.5	0.2
UNWRAP	1	-	1	-
NN	0.7	0.4	0.7	0.4
MERGE	0.3	0.3	0.6	0.6

*: optimization is shut down; "-": not runnable.

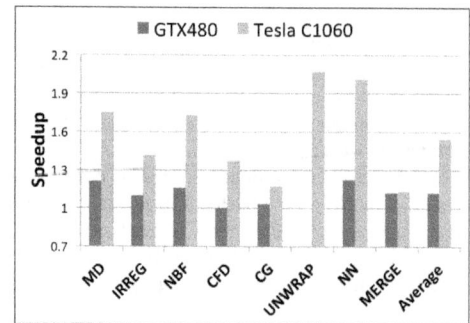

Figure 7. Speedup of selected algorithms

Xeon E5520 machine. Both machines have CUDA4.2 installed. We obtain hardware performance through the NVIDIA's CUDA profiler.

Results Overview Figure 7 reports the kernel speedups on both machines with the baseline as the execution time of the original GPU version. All overhead, including transformation and extra data transfer, is included. The selector-based algorithm assembly produces up to 21% speedup on GTX480. It gives even larger speedup (up to 109%) on C1060 because that device is more sensitive to irregular accesses for its lack of on-chip cache. (It is worth noting that having cache or not on massively parallel processors is still a debatable topic; some recent chips, such as Intel SCC, do not have cache for power efficiency.)

For further confirmation, we use the NVIDIA hardware performance profiler to measure the memory load efficiency. Load efficiency is defined as the ratio of requested global memory load throughput to actual global memory load throughput. As Figure 9

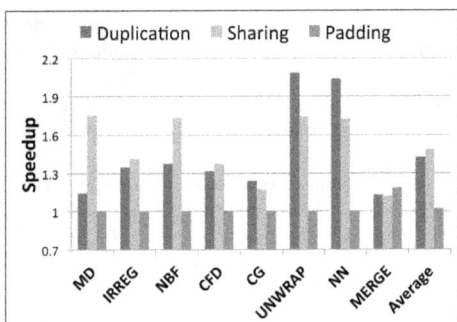

Figure 8. Speedup of all algorithms (Tesla C1060)

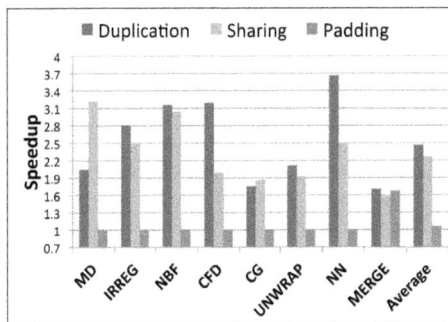

Figure 10. Potential speedups of all algorithms (Tesla C1060)

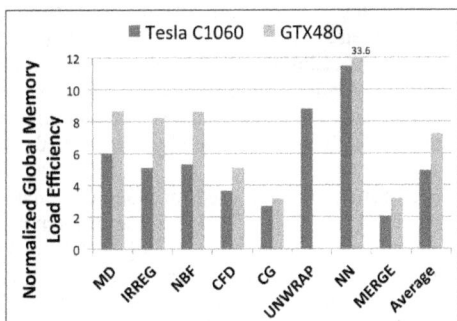

Figure 9. Memory load efficiency of selected algorithms.

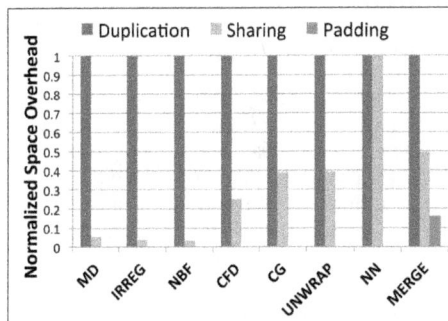

Figure 11. Normalized space overhead (*padding* is only applicable to MERGE.)

shows, the algorithm assembly improves the average efficiency by 4.9X on C1060 and 7.2X on GTX480 over the original version.

The two rightmost columns of Table 1 report the selected algorithms on the two machines. Figure 8 shows the speedups brought by each algorithm on Telsa C1060, confirming that all selections except for the one for CG on Telsa C1060 are correct. (We explain the selection error later in the detailed analysis on CG.)

Six of the eight benchmarks benefit the most from the newly designed algorithms on at least one machine. As Figure 8 shows, the new algorithms produce extra speedup as much as 8-60% over the duplication algorithm. It is mainly due to the larger transformation ratios (shown in Table 2) enabled by their large reduction of the overhead in data copy and transfer. The padding algorithm, due to its constraint on access patterns, is applicable to only the MERGE benchmark in the suite.

Overall, the results show that the two new algorithms significantly enhance the power of data reorganization for irregular memory optimizations. The algorithm assembly and online selector produce some promising speedups for most of the benchmarks. We next discuss each benchmark in further details.

MD, IRREG and NBF MD simulates the interactions of a number of molecules in a 3-D space. Two molecule nodes are neighbors if their distance is smaller than some predefined threshold. One thread is in charge of each node. In a simulation iteration, that thread traverses all its neighbors to calculate the force between each neighbor and that node. The inefficient memory references come from reading neighbors' positions.

The duplication algorithm improves the performance by duplicating position values to make sure adjacent threads load adjacent memory locations. Figure 10 shows that the full duplication can give 2X speedup on C1060 when overhead is not counted. But the overhead of data creation and transfer throttles the speedup to only 15%. The sharing algorithm has a higher performance potential than the duplication algorithm for the smaller working sets. Fig-

ure 11 reports that the sharing algorithm cuts the space overhead by 96%, which explains the seven times more speedup it creates than the duplication algorithm does when overhead is counted as Figure 7 shows.

The tremendous space reduction comes from two reasons. First, the irregular reference to data array is surrounded by a loop to traverse all neighbors, and in each iteration the memory access pattern of all threads is different depending on the topology of the interaction graph. The duplication algorithm, therefore, duplicates the same array the same number of times as the iteration number. Second, Sharing benefits greatly from clustering, which places adjacent nodes in topology closely in memory accessed by threads in the same block.

IRREG and NBF, like MD, have a graph topology. Figure 10 shows different potentials, because their kernels have different ratios of computation to memory accesses. Nonetheless, the sharing algorithm is also shown to be the best choice for them due to the reasons similar to MD. It is worth mentioning that the benefits of the optimizations also depend on the frequency of the neighbor list update in these simulation programs. When the update is frequent, the data transformations need to be applied often and hence lead to higher transformation overhead. When the overhead cannot be hidden completely, the runtime control of G-Streamline can adaptively adjust the fraction of data to transform to trade data layout quality for transformation efficiency [26]. A detailed study on various tradeoffs of the different algorithms in these frequent update scenarios are our future work.

CFD The program, CFD, computes force field of many particles. Each particle has substantially more features than the molecules in MD, and so each thread block processes more data. Figure 10 shows a potential of more than 3 times speedup from the duplication algorithm. But the data transfer overhead throttles the potential. The algorithm eventually produces 31% benefit with a 0.35

65

optimization ratio on C1060. The smaller space overhead of the sharing algorithm leads to a larger optimization ratio (0.6) and a higher speedup (37%.)

CG The kernel in CG does sparse matrix multiplication. The matrix is stored in the Compresses Sparse Rows (CSR) format. In the irregular kernel, one thread is in charge of one non-zero element in the sparse matrix. The accesses to the vector may not be coalesced depending on the sparsity in each row. The duplication and sharing perform similarly well in the potential graph. The best speedup on C1060 is 1.85 times, while the performance gain is around 20% on GTX480 due to the cache effects on the reuses of the elements in the vector. Figure 10 reports that the sharing algorithm has slightly larger potential than the duplication on C1060. The better algorithm, however, is duplication, because of the overhead caused by shared memory accesses. The subtle difference is not captured by the online algorithm selector, causing the sharing algorithm being selected. But the speedup lost is only less than 5%.

UNWRAP The kernel of this program is in a central loop, which transforms an image from the Cartesian coordinate system to the Polar coordinate system. Unlike the other programs, this program do not have data dependences carried by the different invocations of the kernel. The first tens of iterations of the program successfully overlap the overhead of both the duplication and sharing algorithms. The duplication was shown to be the better algorithm for its lack of the side effects in shared memory usage. (For unknown reasons, the benchmark cannot run on GTX480.)

NN The nearest neighbor identification program, NN, has a central loop to process an unstructured input file chunk by chunk. The kernel is launched once for each chunk, and calculates the Euclidean distances from the target location to each record in that chunk. At the end of the program, the main thread processes all distance results and obtains the K nearest neighbors. Figure 10 shows the large speedup potential on both C1060 and GTX480. The sharing algorithm does not reduce any space overhead as reported in Figure 11. The reason is that one record is only processed once, and the duplication algorithm essentially just transposes the data, creating no extra data copies. Like UNWRAP, there is no loop-carried dependence for NN, but the transformation and transfer overhead can not be fully overlapped, and we obtained 0.7 and 0.4 optimization ratios on C1060 and GTX480 respectively. On this special benchmark, the duplication algorithm is a better algorithm in both machines, producing higher speedup than sharing.

MERGE MERGE has the same access pattern for both loads and stores. Padding algorithm is applicable. As Figure 10 shows, Duplication and Padding have quite similar potential. Padding has a larger potential than Sharing because it needs no shared memory accesses. Padding reduces the size of transformed data significantly. Duplication, due to the memory size limit, only manages to transform 30% of data. Padding is the best choice on both GPUs for this program. The speedups on the two machines are quite similar on this program. The reason is that the program has few short reuse distances and hence does not benefit from cache much.

6. Related Work

Sections 1 and 5 have compared this work with previous studies [5, 22, 26] on optimizing dynamic irregular memory accesses on GPU. This section reviews some other related studies.

A number of studies have proposed compiler techniques to optimize GPU memory references. Examples include GPU optimizing compilers [12, 25], OpenMP-to-CUDA compilers [18], polyhedral models [2], performance tuning [20], and many others that cannot be listed for lack of space. All these techniques have focused on

static irregularities that are amenable for compiler analysis. The usage of shared memory in the design of our sharing algorithm is inspired by some of those previous work [2]. But to our best knowledge, the sharing algorithm is the first algorithm that uses clustering and shared memory to avoid data duplications for runtime data reorganizations.

There are some recent studies exploring the synergistic usage of CPU and GPU, including the execution strategies proposed by Huo and others [13], the exploitation of OpenCL [16], and so on. In this work, we use the CPU-GPU pipeline created in G-Streamline [26] as it meets the needs for hiding transformation overhead.

Thread divergence is another type of dynamic irregularity in GPU, defined as the threads in a warp follow different paths of a kernel. Some hardware extensions have been proposed to remove thread divergences from a kernel execution [9, 19]. Carrillo and others [3] have proposed loop splitting and branch splitting to alleviate register pressure caused by diverging branches. As pointed out by an earlier work [26], thread divergence and non-coalesced memory accesses essentially stem from the similar source, a mismatch between threads and data. It suggests that the findings from this study are potentially usable for helping eliminate thread divergences as well.

Data reorganization has been used for many CPU data locality enhancements (e.g. [1, 4, 6, 8, 15, 24].) Some of them have especially concentrated on irregular applications [10, 21]. Kulkarni and others have studied locality issues of irregular data structures in the contexts of optimistic parallelism [17] and scheduling [14]. As a massively parallel architecture, GPU displays different memory access properties from CPU, exemplified by the hierarchical thread organizations, hardware enabled memory coalescing, and the SIMT execution model. All these features create differences in the challenges and opportunities in applying data reorganization, triggering the new set of innovations in this paper on both complexity analysis and transformation techniques.

7. Conclusion

This paper presents some fundamental understanding in exploiting data reorganization for minimizing non-coalesced memory accesses on GPU. It reveals the complexity of the problem by proving that it is NP-complete to create a data layout through data repositioning to minimize non-coalesced memory accesses on GPU, no matter whether thread reorganization is allowed. It points out that it is possible to circumvent the complexity by relaxing the space constraint in data repositioning. It introduces two new algorithms for minimizing non-coalesced memory accesses while avoiding the space inflation problem of a previous algorithm. It compares the various algorithms, presents some selection guidelines, and develops an automatic selector in a runtime library. Experiments show that the new algorithms excel previous techniques especially under space pressure. The algorithm assembly, assisted by the algorithm selector, enhances the performance of a set of dynamic irregular applications significantly, providing promising solutions to a large class of dynamic irregular references.

Acknowledgment

We thank Weizhen Mao for her suggestions to one of the NP-completeness proofs. We owe the anonymous reviewers our gratitude for their helpful comments to the paper. Some of the devices used in this study were donated by NVIDIA. This material is based upon work supported by the National Science Foundation under Grant No. 0811791 and CAREER Award, DOE Early Career Award, and IBM CAS Fellowship. Any opinions, findings, and conclusions or recommendations expressed in this material are those of the authors and do not necessarily reflect the views of the National Science Foundation, DOE, or IBM.

References

[1] A. V. Aho, M. S. Lam, R. Sethi, and J. D. Ullman. *Compilers: Principles, Techniques, and Tools.* Addison Wesley, 2nd edition, August 2006.

[2] M. M. Baskaran, U. Bondhugula, S. Krishnamoorthy, J. Ramanujam, A. Rountev, and P. Sadayappan. A compiler framework for optimization of affine loop nests for GPGPUs. In *ICS'08*, pages 225–234, 2008.

[3] S. Carrillo, J. Siegel, and X. Li. A control-structure splitting optimization for gpgpu. In *Proceedings of ACM Computing Frontiers*, 2009.

[4] G. C. Cascaval. *Compile-time Performance Prediction of Scientific Programs.* PhD thesis, University of Illinois at Urbana-Champaign, 2000.

[5] S. Che, J. W. Sheaffer, and K. Skadron. Dymaxion: Optimizing memory access patterns for heterogeneous systems. In *SC*, 2011.

[6] T. M. Chilimbi and R. Shaham. Cache-conscious coallocation of hot data streams. In *PLDI*, 2006.

[7] A. Danalis, G. Marin, C. McCurdy, J. Meredith, P. Roth, K. Spafford, V. Tipparaju, and J. Vetter. The scalable heterogeneous computing (shoc) benchmark suite. 2010.

[8] C. Ding and K. Kennedy. Improving effective bandwidth through compiler enhancement of global cache reuse. *Journal of Parallel and Distributed Computing*, 64(1):108–134, 2004.

[9] W. Fung, I. Sham, G. Yuan, and T. Aamodt. Dynamic warp formation and scheduling for efficient gpu control flow. In *MICRO'07*, pages 407–420, Washington, DC, USA, 2007. IEEE Computer Society.

[10] H. Han and C.-W. Tseng. Exploiting locality for irregular scientific codes. *IEEE Transactions on Parallel Distributed Systems*, 17(7):606–618, 2006.

[11] D. S. Hochbaum. *Approximation Algorithms for NP-Hard Problems.* PWS Publishing Company, 1995.

[12] A. Hormati, M. Samadi, M. Woh, T. Mudge, and S. Mahlke. Sponge: portable stream programming on graphics engines. In *ASPLOS*, 2011.

[13] X. Huo, V. Ravi, W. Ma, and G. Agrawal. An execution strategy and optimized runtime support for parallelizing irregular reductions on modern gpus. In *ICS*, 2011.

[14] Y. Jo and M. KulKarni. Enhancing locality for recursive traversals of recursive structures. In *OOPSLA*, 2011.

[15] M. Kandemir. A compiler technique for improving whole-program locality. In *POPL*, 2001.

[16] J. Kim, S. Seo, J. Lee, J. Nah, G. Jo, and J. Lee. Opencl as a unified programming model for heterogeneous cpu/gpu clusters. In *PPoPP*, 2012.

[17] M. Kulkarni, K. Pingali, G. Ramanarayanan, B. Walter, K. Bala, and L. P. Chew. Optimistic parallelism benefits from data partitioning. In *ASPLOS*, pages 233–243, 2008.

[18] S. Lee, S. Min, and R. Eigenmann. Openmp to gpgpu: A compiler framework for automatic translation and optimization. In *PPoPP*, 2009.

[19] J. Meng, D. Tarjan, and K. Skadron. Dynamic warp subdivision for integrated branch and memory divergence tolerance. In *ISCA*, 2010.

[20] S. Ryoo, C. I. Rodrigues, S. S. Baghsorkhi, S. S. Stone, D. B. Kirk, and W. W. Hwu. Optimization principles and application performance evaluation of a multithreaded GPU using CUDA. In *PPoPP*, pages 73–82, 2008.

[21] M. M. Strout, L. Carter, and J. Ferrante. Compile-time composition of run-time data and iteration reorderings. In *PLDI*, San Diego, CA, June 2003.

[22] D. Tarjan, J. Meng, and K. Skadron. Increasing memory miss tolerance for simd cores. In *SC*, 2009.

[23] B. Wu, E. Zhang, and X. Shen. Enhancing data locality for dynamic simulations through asynchronous data transformations and adaptive control. In *PACT*, 2011.

[24] Y. Yan, X. Zhang, and Z. Zhang. Cacheminer: A runtime approach to exploit cache locality on *smp*. *IEEE Transactions on Parallel Distributed Systems*, 11(4):357–374, 2000.

[25] Y. Yang, P. Xiang, J. Kong, and H. Zhou. A gpgpu compiler for memory optimization and parallelism management. In *PLDI*, 2010.

[26] E. Zhang, Y. Jiang, Z. Guo, K. Tian, and X. Shen. On-the-fly elimination of dynamic irregularities for gpu computing. In *ASPLOS*, 2011.

Correct and Efficient Work-Stealing for Weak Memory Models

Nhat Minh Lê   Antoniu Pop   Albert Cohen   Francesco Zappa Nardelli

INRIA and ENS Paris

Abstract

Chase and Lev's concurrent deque is a key data structure in shared-memory parallel programming and plays an essential role in work-stealing schedulers. We provide the first correctness proof of an optimized implementation of Chase and Lev's deque on top of the POWER and ARM architectures: these provide very relaxed memory models, which we exploit to improve performance but considerably complicate the reasoning. We also study an optimized x86 and a portable C11 implementation, conducting systematic experiments to evaluate the impact of memory barrier optimizations. Our results demonstrate the benefits of hand tuning the deque code when running on top of relaxed memory models.

Categories and Subject Descriptors   D.1.3 [*Programming Techniques*]: Concurrent Programming;   E.1 [*Data Structures*]: Lists, stacks, and queues

Keywords   lock-free algorithm, work-stealing, relaxed memory model, proof

1. Introduction

Multicore POWER and ARM architectures are standard targets for server, consumer electronics, and embedded control applications. The difficulties of parallel programming are exacerbated by the relaxed memory model implemented by these architectures, which allow the processors to perform a wide range of optimizations, including thread-local reordering and non-atomic store propagation.

The safety-critical nature of many embedded applications call for solid foundations for parallel programming. This paper shows that a high degree of confidence can be achieved for highly optimized, real-world, concurrent algorithms, running on top of weak memory models. A good test-case is provided by the runtime scheduler of a task library. We thus focus on the Chase and Lev's concurrent doubly-ended queue (*deque*) [3], the cornerstone of most work-stealing schedulers. Until now, no rigorous correctness proof has been been provided for implementations of this algorithm running on top of a relaxed memory model. Furthermore, while work-stealing is widely used on the x86 architecture (an evaluation under a restrictive hypothesis of idempotence of the workload can be found in [10]), few experiments target weaker memory models.

Our first contribution is a correctness proof of this fundamental concurrent data structure running on top of a relaxed memory model. We provide a hand-tuned implementation of the Chase and

Lev's deque for the ARM architectures, and prove its correctness against the memory semantics defined in [12] and [7]. Our second contribution is a systematic study of the performance of several implementations of Chase–Lev on relaxed hardware. In detail, we compare our optimized ARM implementation against a standard implementation for the x86 architecture and two portable variants expressed in C11: a reference sequentially consistent translation of the algorithm, and an aggressively optimized version making full use of the release–acquire and relaxed semantics offered by C11 low-level atomics. These implementations of the Chase–Lev deque are evaluated in the context of a work-stealing scheduler. We consider diverse worker/thief configurations, including a synthetic benchmark with two different workloads and standard task-parallel kernels. Our experiments demonstrate the impact of the memory barrier optimization on the throughput of our work-stealing runtime. We also comment on how the ARM correctness proof can be tailored to these alternative implementations. As a side effect, we highlight that our optimized ARM implementation cannot be expressed using C11 low-level atomics, which invariably end up inserting one redundant synchronization instruction.

2. Chase–Lev deque

User-space runtime schedulers offer an excellent playground for studying low-level high-performance code. We focus on *randomized work-stealing*: it was originally designed as the scheduler of the Cilk language for shared-memory multiprocessors [4], but thanks to its merits [2] it has been adopted in a number of parallel libraries and parallel programming environments, including the Intel TBB and compiler suite. Work-stealing variants have also been proposed for distributed clusters [5] and heterogeneous platforms [1]. The scheduling strategy is intuitive:

- Each processor uses a dynamic array as a deque holding tasks ready to be scheduled.
- Each processor manages its own deque as a *stack*. It may only push and pop tasks from the `bottom` of its own deque.
- Other processors may not push or pop from that deque; instead, they steal tasks from the `top` when their own deque is empty. In most implementations, the stolen deque is selected at random.
- Initially, one processor starts with the "root" task of the parallel program in its deque, and all other deques are empty.

The state-of-the-art algorithm for the work-stealing deque is Chase and Lev's lock-free deque [3]. It uses an array with automatic, asynchronous growth. Assuming sequentially consistent memory, it involves only one atomic compare-and-swap (CAS) per *steal*, no CAS on *push*, and no CAS on *take* except when the deque has exactly only one element left.

We implemented and tested four versions of the concurrent deque algorithm, with different barrier configurations: (1) a sequentially consistent version, written with C11 seq_cst atomics, following the original description in [3]; (2) an optimized version, which takes full advantage of the C11 relaxed memory model, reported in Figure 1; (3) a native version for ARMv7, reported in Figure 2, and (4) a native version for x86. These native versions rely on compiler intrinsics and inline assembly to leverage architecture-specific assumptions and thus reduce the number of barriers required.

In our implementations of Figure 1 and Figure 2, we assume that the Deque type is declared as:

```
typedef struct {              typedef struct {
    atomic_size_t size;           atomic_size_t top, bottom;
    atomic_int buffer[];          Atomic(Array *) array;
} Array;                      } Deque;
```

In the code of Figure 1 the *atomic_* and *memory_order_* prefixes have been elided for clarity. The ARMv7 pseudo-code of Figure 2 uses the keywords R and W to denote reads and writes to shared variables, and **atomic** indicates a block that will be executed atomically, implemented via LL/SC instructions. The x86 version is based on prior work [10] and only requires a single **mfence** memory barrier in *take*, in place of the call to *thread_fence* in the C11 code.

2.1 Notions of correctness

The expected behavior of the work-stealing deque is intuitive: tasks pushed into the deque are then either taken in reverse order by the same thread, or stolen by another thread. We say that an implementation is correct if it satisfies four criteria, formalized and proven correct for our ARMv7 optimized code in Section 4:

1. tasks are taken in reverse order;
2. only tasks pushed are taken or stolen (*well-defined reads*);
3. a task pushed into a deque cannot be taken or stolen more than once (*uniqueness*);
4. given a finite number of push operations, all pushed values will eventually be either taken or stolen exactly once, if enough take and steal operations are attempted (*existence*).

These criteria hold because of the following assumptions and properties of the Chase–Lev algorithm:

- For any given deque, *push* and *pop* operations execute on a single thread. Concurrency can only occur between one execution of *push* or *take* in the owner thread, and one or more executions of *steal* in different threads.
- Newly pushed tasks are made visible to *take* and *steal* by the increment to bottom in *push*. As we shall see in Section 4, our ARMv7 implementation enforces this by placing a sync barrier before the update of bottom, guaranteeing that that the pushed element can not be stolen before bottom is updated.
- Taken tasks are reserved first by updating bottom; again, in our ARMv7 code, the sync barrier placed after the update to bottom will ensure that it will not be concurrently stolen.
- Stolen tasks are reserved by updating top. The only situation where *steal* and *take* contend for the same task is when the deque has a single element left; this particular conflict is resolved through the CAS instructions in both *take* and *steal*. This scenario was further optimized by Chase and Lev, making the CAS in *take* conditional upon the size of the deque being 1. The correctness of this optimization on a relaxed memory model depends on the presence of the two full barriers in *take* and *steal*, to ensure that at least one of the participants will have a consistent view of the size of the deque. Having just one *take* or *steal* seeing a consistent view of the size of the deque is enough: if it is *take*, that will force a CAS to be performed; if it is *steal*, the index reservation will ensure an empty return value.
- Finally, stolen tasks are protected from being concurrently stolen multiple times by the monotonic CAS update to top in *steal*. This CAS orders *steal* operations and makes them mutually exclusive. At the same time, *steal* operations that abort due to a failed CAS do not change the state of the deque.

2.2 Comparison of the C11 and ARM implementations

Our C11 implementation in Figure 1 is optimal in the sense that no C11 synchronization can be removed without breaking the algo-

rithm. However, if low-level atomics are compiled using the mapping of McKenney and Silvera [9] on ARMv7/POWER or the mapping of Tehrekov [14] on x86, the generated code contains more barriers than the hand-optimized native versions on both x86 and ARMv7. We show in Section 5 that this happens because of the need for *seq_cst* atomics to simulate ARMv7/POWER cumulative semantics. Concretely, on ARMv7, an extra **dmb** instruction is inserted before each CAS operation [11], compared to the native version where a relaxed CAS—coherent and atomic only—is sufficient. On x86, an **mfence** instruction is added between the two reads in *steal*. The fully sequentially consistent C11 implementation inserts many more redundant barriers [11].

3. The memory model of ARMv7

The memory model of the ARMv7 architecture follows closely that of the POWER architecture, allowing a wide range of relaxed behaviors to be observable to the programmer:

1. The hardware threads can each perform reads and writes out-of-order, or even speculatively. Basically any local reordering is allowed unless there is a data/control dependence or synchronization instruction preventing it.
2. The memory system does not guarantee that a write becomes visible to all other hardware threads at the same time point. Writes performed by one thread are propagated to (and become visible from) any other thread in an arbitrary order, unless synchronization instructions are used.
3. A dmb barrier instruction guarantees that all the writes which have been observed by the thread issuing the barrier instruction are propagated to all the other threads before the thread can continue. Observed writes include all writes previously issued by the thread itself, as well as any write propagated to it from another thread prior to the barrier. This semantics of barrier instructions is referred to as *cumulative*.

We build on the axiomatic formalization of POWER and ARMv7 memory model by Mador-Haim et al. [7], which has been proved equivalent to the operational semantics of Sarkar et al. [12]. A gentle introduction can be found in [8].

Axiomatic *execution witnesses* capture abstract memory *events* associated with memory-related instructions and internal transitions of the model. Unlike in stronger models such as x86, each memory access is represented at run-time by two distinct events: an issuing event—called sat for reads and ini for writes—eventually followed by a commit event when the speculative state of the instruction is resolved. Once a write instruction is committed, events that propagate it to other threads can be observed—propagation to thread A is denoted pp_A. All the relations part of an execution witness are listed in Table 1.

The core of the axiomatic model builds on the *evord* relation, modeling the *happens-before* order between events. This satisfies the fundamental property:

$$\xrightarrow{\text{evord}} \supset \xrightarrow{\text{after}} \cup \xrightarrow{\text{before}} \cup \xrightarrow{\text{comm}} \cup \xrightarrow{\text{insn}} \cup \xrightarrow{\text{local}}$$

and must be acyclic for an execution to be *consistent*.

We assume that the atomic sections, used to represent CAS-like behaviors, are executed atomically and obey a total order. We model them either as a single instance of a read instruction (failed CAS) or an atomic read–write pair of instruction instances (successful CAS). The atomicity of these accesses is captured by the $\xrightarrow{\text{po-atom}}$ relation. We do not assume any other property on these atomic sections (e.g., cumulativity). In practice, atomic sections can be implemented with LL/SC instructions.

We use several notation shortcuts. We refer to the deque global variables top, bottom, and array as t, b, and a. Elements of the buffer are written x_i, where i is the virtual index in natural numbers

```
int take(Deque *q) {
  size_t b = load_explicit(&q->bottom, relaxed) - 1;
  Array *a = load_explicit(&q->array, relaxed);
  store_explicit(&q->bottom, b, relaxed);
  thread_fence(seq_cst);
  size_t t = load_explicit(&q->top, relaxed);
  int x;
  if (t <= b) {
    /* Non-empty queue. */
    x = load_explicit(&a->buffer[b % a->size], relaxed);
    if (t == b) {
      /* Single last element in queue. */
      if (!compare_exchange_strong_explicit(&q->top, &t, t + 1, seq_cst, relaxed))
        /* Failed race. */
        x = EMPTY;
      store_explicit(&q->bottom, b + 1, relaxed);
    }
  } else { /* Empty queue. */
    x = EMPTY;
    store_explicit(&q->bottom, b + 1, relaxed);
  }
  return x;
}

void push(Deque *q, int x) {
  size_t b = load_explicit(&q->bottom, relaxed);
  size_t t = load_explicit(&q->top, acquire);
  Array *a = load_explicit(&q->array, relaxed);
  if (b - t > a->size - 1) /* Full queue. */
    resize(q);
  store_explicit(&a->buffer[b % a->size], x, relaxed);
  thread_fence(release);
  store_explicit(&q->bottom, b + 1, relaxed);
}

int steal(Deque *q) {
  size_t t = load_explicit(&q->top, acquire);
  thread_fence(seq_cst);
  size_t b = load_explicit(&q->bottom, acquire);
  int x = EMPTY;
  if (t < b) {
    /* Non-empty queue. */
    Array *a = load_explicit(&q->array, relaxed);
    x = load_explicit(&a->buffer[t % a->size], relaxed);
    if (!compare_exchange_strong_explicit(&q->top, &t, t + 1, seq_cst, relaxed))
      /* Failed race. */
      return ABORT;
  }
  return x;
}
```

Figure 1. C11 code of Chase–Lev deque, with low-level atomics

```
int take(Deque *q) {
  size_t b = R(q->bottom) - 1;            (a)
  Array *a = R(q->array);                 (b)
  W(q->bottom, b);                        (c)
  sync;
  size_t t = R(q->top);                   (d)
  int x;
  if (t <= b) {
    x = R(a->buffer[b % a->size]);        (e)
    if (t == b) {
      bool success = false;
      atomic /* Implemented with LL/SC. */
        if (success = (R(q->top) == t))   (f)
          W(q->top, t + 1);               (g)
      if (!success) x = EMPTY;
      W(q->bottom, b + 1);                (h)
    }
  } else {
    x = EMPTY;
    W(q->bottom, b + 1);                  (i)
  }
  return x;
}

void push(Deque *q, int x) {
  size_t b = R(q->bottom);                (a)
  size_t t = R(q->top);                   (b)
  Array *a = R(q->array);                 (c)
  if (b - t > a->size - 1) /* Full queue. */
    resize(q);
  W(a->buffer[b % a->size], x);           (d)
  sync;
  W(q->bottom, b + 1);                    (e)
}

int steal(Deque *q) {
  size_t t = R(q->top);                   (a)
  sync;
  size_t b = R(q->bottom);                (b)
  ctrl_isync;
  int x = EMPTY;
  if (t < b) {
    Array *a = R(q->array);               (c)
    x = R(a->buffer[t % a->size]);        (d)
    ctrl_isync;
    bool success = false;
    atomic /* Implemented with LL/SC. */
      if (success = (R(q->top) == t))     (e)
        W(q->top, t + 1);                 (f)
    if (!success) return ABORT;
  }
  return x;
}
```

Figure 2. ARMv7 pseudo-code of Chase–Lev deque

before any wrap-around is applied. Barrier instructions are omitted for brevity when implied by the presence of a $\xrightarrow{\text{sync}}$ or $\xrightarrow{\text{ctrl-isync}}$ relation. Irrelevant values in reads and writes are replaced with the placeholder "_" (e.g., $Rx,\_$). We do not label instruction instances individually, but decorate them with a disambiguating execution prefix, identified by a dot. These prefixes do not only distinguish between instruction instances, but also group related instruction instances within a same execution unit (usually an invocation of one of *push*, *take* or *steal*). For this, when no prefix is specified, the last prefix in left-to-right order is assumed.

4. Proof of correctness of the ARMv7 code

The proof is divided into five parts; it validates the criteria 2 to 4 enumerated in Section 2.1. Since *push* and *take* never execute concurrently and b is only ever modified in one of these functions, the proof of Criterion 1 does not involve reasoning about concurrency and we omit it here.

The proof builds on a precise analysis of all the possible execution witnesses of arbitrary invocations of the algorithm. We recall that an execution witness, as defined by the ARMv7 axiomatic model, is a graph capturing all memory events occuring during an execution (vertices), as well as the relations that link them (edges). Individual lemmas strive to narrow down the set of possible execution witnesses, based on properties of the algorithm and the architecture. To that end, we pinpoint specific subgraphs of an execution

witness (hereafter, *execution graphs*) that cannot occur together in the same consistent execution witness. We then show that all incorrect executions, such as those containing two instances of *steal* reading the same value added by a single instance of *push*, cannot have consistent execution witnesses and, as such, cannot happen.

The proof is structured as follows. In 4.1 we provide basic technical definitions and properties of the memory model, which are used throughout the proof. In 4.2 we describe all the possible execution graphs for each of the three operations (*push*, *take* and *steal*), following the control flow of the ARMv7 code in Figure 2. In 4.3 we show how the succession of dynamic arrays built by resizing can be abstracted as a single sequence of unique abstract values independent of resize operations, with strong coherence and consistency properties. Corollary 2 establishes Criterion 2 (well-defined reads). In 4.4 we build on the previous abstraction to prove Theorem 1, pertaining to the uniqueness of elements taken and stolen, which corresponds to Criterion 3 (uniqueness). Finally, in 4.5, we rely on all previous results to prove Theorem 2 establishing Criterion 4 (existence): the existence of matching *take* or *steal* operations for every pushed element, under the appropriate hypotheses.

4.1 Preliminary properties

Before delving into the details of the proof itself, we introduce some support definitions and related properties.

For convenience, we define the $\xrightarrow{\text{po-loc}}$ relation, which relates local (same-thread) accesses to the same memory location; $\xrightarrow{\text{po-loc}}$

Rl, α	read of value α from location l (_ stands for *any* value)
Wl, α	write of value α to location l (_ stands for *any* value)
sync	memory barrier (usually implied by $\xrightarrow{\text{sync}}$)
isync	instruction barrier (usually implied by $\xrightarrow{\text{ctrl-isync}}$)
$\text{sat}(X)$	*satisfy* (a.k.a. complete) event of a read instruction
$\text{ini}(X)$	*initialize* event of a write instruction
$\text{com}(X)$	*commit* event of an in-flight or speculative instruction
$\text{pp}_A(X)$	*propagate to thread of A* event
$\xrightarrow{\text{po}}$	*program order*
$\xrightarrow{\text{po-atom}}$	*atomic operation in program order* (for CAS; see below)
$\xrightarrow{\text{po-loc}}$	*same-location access in program order* (defined in 4.1)
$\xrightarrow{\text{co}}$	*write coherence*
$\xrightarrow{\text{rf}}$	*read from*
$\xrightarrow{\text{rff}}$	*read from far* (defined in 4.3)
$\xrightarrow{\text{fr}}$	*from read*
$\xrightarrow{\text{addr}}$	*address dependence* (usually implicit)
$\xrightarrow{\text{ctrl}}$	*control dependence* (usually implicit)
$\xrightarrow{\text{data}}$	*data dependence* (usually implicit)
$\xrightarrow{\text{dp}}$	*observable dependence* (defined in 4.1)
$\xrightarrow{\text{ctrl-isync}}$	*non-cumulative local ordering barrier* (see below)
$\xrightarrow{\text{sync}}$	*cumulative full barrier* (see below)
$\xrightarrow{\text{pp-sat}}$	*write-to-read propagation* (defined in 4.1)
$\xrightarrow{\text{after}}$	*after barrier edge*
$\xrightarrow{\text{before}}$	*before barrier edge*
$\xrightarrow{\text{comm}}$	*communication edge*
$\xrightarrow{\text{insn}}$	*intra-instruction order edge*
$\xrightarrow{\text{local}}$	*local order edge*
$\xrightarrow{\text{evord}}$	*event happens-before order* (usually typeset as $\rightarrow$)

On ARMv7, $\xrightarrow{\text{sync}}$ corresponds to a **dmb** instruction while $\xrightarrow{\text{ctrl-isync}}$ corresponds to a dependent conditional branch followed by an **isb** instruction.

Table 1. Summary of relations used in the ARMv7 axiomatic model

implies an instruction-level communication edge $\xrightarrow{\text{co}}$, $\xrightarrow{\text{rf}}$ or $\xrightarrow{\text{fr}}$. In particular, $\xrightarrow{\text{po-loc}}$ implies $\xrightarrow{\text{co}}$ between two writes.

We define the *dependence* relation $\xrightarrow{\text{dp}}$ as follows:

$$Rx,_{-} \xrightarrow{\text{dp}} Ry,_{-} \overset{\text{def}}{\Longleftrightarrow} Rx,_{-}(\xrightarrow{\text{addr}} \cup \xrightarrow{\text{ctrl-isync}})Ry,_{-}$$
$$Rx,_{-} \xrightarrow{\text{dp}} Wy,_{-} \overset{\text{def}}{\Longleftrightarrow} Rx,_{-}(\xrightarrow{\text{addr}} \cup \xrightarrow{\text{ctrl}} \cup \xrightarrow{\text{data}})Wy,_{-}$$

Lemma 1. *The following properties involving* $\xrightarrow{\text{dp}}$ *apply:*
$$Rx,_{-} \xrightarrow{\text{dp}} Ry,_{-} \implies \text{sat}(Rx,_{-}) \to \text{sat}(Ry,_{-})$$
$$Rx,_{-} \xrightarrow{\text{dp}} Wy,_{-} \implies \text{sat}(Rx,_{-}) \to \text{com}(Wy,_{-})$$

Proof. In the case the of an address or control dependence, the result is an immediate consequence of the definition of *intra-instruction* and *local orders*. It remains to be shown that the result holds for $\xrightarrow{\text{ctrl-isync}}$: a dependent conditional branch instruction, ctrl, followed by an isync barrier. Suppose $Rx,_{-} \xrightarrow{\text{ctrl-isync}} Ry,_{-}$. Then we have: $\text{sat}(Rx,_{-}) \xrightarrow{\text{insn}} \text{com}(Rx,_{-}) \xrightarrow{\text{local}} \text{com}(\text{ctrl}) \xrightarrow{\text{local}} \text{com}(\text{isync}) \xrightarrow{\text{local}} \text{sat}(Ry,_{-})$. $\square$

We define the relation $\xrightarrow{\text{pp-sat}}$ between instruction instances, $A.Wx,_{-} \xrightarrow{\text{pp-sat}} B.Ry,_{-}$, as follows:[1]

$$\begin{cases} Wx,_{-} \xrightarrow{\text{po}} Ry,_{-} & \text{if } A \sim B \\ \text{pp}_B(Wx,_{-}) \to \text{sat}(Ry,_{-}) & \text{if } A \not\sim B \end{cases}$$

where $A \sim B$ means that instruction instances grouped under prefixes A and B belong to the same thread.

Intuitively, $\xrightarrow{\text{pp-sat}}$ represents a "known-to" relation in the following sense: $A.Wx,_{-} \xrightarrow{\text{pp-sat}} B.Ry,_{-}$ means that, at the time of reading y, that specific write to x (as well as any write that is coherence-before it) is known to the thread executing B. It is clear that $\xrightarrow{\text{rf}}$ implies $\xrightarrow{\text{pp-sat}}$, by definition of communication edges (if threads are different) or uniprocessor constraints (if same thread).

---

[1] Note that $\xrightarrow{\text{pp-sat}}$ does not imply an *event happens-before order* on the events making up the related instruction instances.

Lemma 2. *The following properties involve* $\xrightarrow{\text{pp-sat}}$ *and* $\xrightarrow{\text{po-loc}}$:

(i) $A.Wx,_{-} \xrightarrow{\text{rf}} B.Rx,_{-} \xrightarrow{\text{po-loc}} B'.Rx,_{-} \implies A.Wx,_{-} \xrightarrow{\text{pp-sat}} B'.Rx,_{-}$

(ii) $A.Wx,_{-} \xrightarrow{\text{co}} B.Wx,_{-} \xrightarrow{\text{pp-sat}} C.Rx,_{-} \implies A.Wx,_{-} \xrightarrow{\text{rf}} C.Rx,_{-}$

(iii) $Wx,_{-} \xrightarrow{\text{pp-sat}} Ry,_{-} \xrightarrow{\text{dp}} Rz,_{-} \implies Wx,_{-} \xrightarrow{\text{pp-sat}} Rz,_{-}$

(iv) $\neg(A.Wx,_{-} \xrightarrow{\text{pp-sat}} B.Ry',_{-} \xrightarrow{\text{dp}} B.Wx',_{-} \xrightarrow{\text{pp-sat}} A.Ry,_{-} \xrightarrow{\text{dp}} A.Wx,_{-})$

Proof. We prove each point separately:

(i) If the write and the reads happen in the same thread, then all instruction instances belong to that thread, and *program order* prevails. Otherwise, either $A.Wx,_{-} \xrightarrow{\text{rf}} B'.Rx,_{-}$ and the result is immediate, or $A.Wx,_{-} \xrightarrow{\text{rf}} B'.Rx,_{-}$ and $B.Rx,_{-} \xrightarrow{\text{po-loc}} B'.Rx,_{-}$ implies the following: $\text{com}(B.Ry,_{-}) \xrightarrow{\text{local}} \text{sat}(B'.Ry,_{-})$, by definition of $\xrightarrow{\text{local}}$. Hence:
$$\text{pp}_B(A.Wx,_{-}) \to \text{sat}(B.Ry,_{-}) \xrightarrow{\text{insn}} \text{com}(Ry,_{-}) \xrightarrow{\text{local}} \text{sat}(B'.Ry,_{-})$$

(ii) Suppose $A.Wx,_{-} \xrightarrow{\text{rf}} C.Rx,_{-}$. Then $C.Rx,_{-} \xrightarrow{\text{fr}} B.Wx,_{-}$, and we have the following cycle in the *event happens-before order*:
$$\text{sat}(C.Rx,_{-}) \xrightarrow{\text{comm}} \text{pp}_Z(B.Wx,_{-}) \to \text{sat}(C.Rx,_{-})$$

(iii) Follows from Lemma 1.

(iv) Assume that:
$$A.Wx,_{-} \xrightarrow{\text{pp-sat}} B.Ry',_{-} \xrightarrow{\text{dp}} B.Wx',_{-} \xrightarrow{\text{pp-sat}} A.Ry,_{-} \xrightarrow{\text{dp}} A.Wx,_{-}$$
If $A \sim B$ then there is a cycle in $\xrightarrow{\text{po}}$. Otherwise, by Lemma 1, we have a cycle in the *event happens-before order*:
$$\text{pp}_B(Wx,_{-}) \to \text{sat}(Ry',_{-}) \to \text{com}(Wx',_{-}) \xrightarrow{\text{insn}} \text{pp}_A(Wx',_{-})$$
$$\to \text{sat}(Ry,_{-}) \to \text{com}(Wx,_{-}) \xrightarrow{\text{insn}} \text{pp}_B(Wx,_{-}) \qquad \square$$

Lemma 3. *The following properties involving barriers apply:*

(i) $(Wx,_{-} \xrightarrow{\text{sync}} Wy,_{-} \xrightarrow{\text{pp-sat}} Rz,_{-} \vee Wx,_{-} \xrightarrow{\text{pp-sat}} Ry,_{-} \xrightarrow{\text{sync}} Rz,_{-}) \implies Wx,_{-} \xrightarrow{\text{pp-sat}} Rz,_{-}$

(ii) $A.Wx,_{-} \xrightarrow{\text{rf}} B.Rx,_{-} \xrightarrow{\text{sync}} B.Wy,_{-} \xrightarrow{\text{pp-sat}} C.Rx,_{-} \implies A.Wx,_{-} \xrightarrow{\text{pp-sat}} C.Rx,_{-}$

(iii) *Let X stand for $A.Wx,_{-} \xrightarrow{\text{rf}} B.Rx,_{-}$ or $(A \sim B).Wx,_{-}$ and Y stand for $C.Wy,_{-} \xrightarrow{\text{rf}} D.Ry,_{-}$ or $(C \sim D).Wy,_{-}$ then the following holds:*
$$\neg(X \xrightarrow{\text{sync}} B.Ry,_{-} \xrightarrow{\text{fr}} C.Wy,_{-} \wedge Y \xrightarrow{\text{sync}} D.Rx,_{-} \xrightarrow{\text{fr}} A.Wx,_{-})$$

Proof. We prove each point separately:

(i) If $Wz,_{-}$ and $Rz,_{-}$ occur in the same thread, then all instruction instances belong to that thread and *program order* prevails. Otherwise, suppose $Rz,_{-}$ executes in A; we have two cases:
$$\text{pp}_A(Wx,_{-}) \xrightarrow{\text{before}} \text{pp}_A(\text{sync}) \xrightarrow{\text{before}} \text{pp}_A(Wy,_{-}) \to \text{sat}(Rz,_{-})$$
Or the other way around:
$$\text{pp}_A(Wx,_{-}) \to \text{sat}(Ry,_{-}) \xrightarrow{\text{insn}} \text{com}(Ry,_{-}) \xrightarrow{\text{local}} \text{com}(\text{sync}) \xrightarrow{\text{local}} \text{sat}(Rz,_{-})$$
In both cases, $\text{pp}_A(Wx,_{-}) \to \text{sat}(Rz,_{-})$.

(ii) Suppose $A \sim C$. If $A \sim B$, then *program order* prevails: all the instruction instances belong to the same thread. If not, suppose $C.Rx,_{-} \xrightarrow{\text{po}} A.Wx,_{-}$; then the *event happens-before order* contains the following cycle:
$$\text{pp}_B(A.Wx,_{-}) \xrightarrow{\text{comm}} \text{sat}(B.Rx,_{-}) \xrightarrow{\text{insn}} \text{com}(Rx,_{-}) \xrightarrow{\text{local}} \text{com}(\text{sync})$$
$$\xrightarrow{\text{local}} \text{com}(B.Wy,_{-}) \xrightarrow{\text{insn}} \text{pp}_C(Wy,_{-}) \to \text{sat}(C.Rx,_{-}) \xrightarrow{\text{insn}} \text{com}(Rx,_{-})$$
$$\xrightarrow{\text{local}} \text{com}(A.Wx,_{-}) \xrightarrow{\text{insn}} \text{pp}_B(Wx,_{-})$$
Otherwise, suppose $A \not\sim C$. If $A \sim B$, then $A.Wx,_{-} \xrightarrow{\text{sync}} B.Wy,_{-}$ and we have the result from (i). If not, we have:
$$\text{pp}_B(A.Wx,_{-}) \xrightarrow{\text{comm}} \text{sat}(B.Rx,_{-}) \xrightarrow{\text{insn}} \text{com}(Rx,_{-}) \xrightarrow{\text{local}} \text{com}(\text{sync})$$
Thus, we have $\text{pp}_C(A.Wx,_{-}) \xrightarrow{\text{before}} \text{pp}_C(\text{sync}) \xrightarrow{\text{before}} \text{pp}_C(B.Wy,_{-}) \to \text{sat}(C.Rx,_{-})$.

(iii) Suppose the contrary. If $B \sim D$, then $\xrightarrow{\text{rf}}$ and $\xrightarrow{\text{fr}}$ form a path that goes against $\xrightarrow{\text{po}}$: the graph is invalid according to uniprocessor constraints.
Otherwise, $B \not\sim D$ and the following holds (omitting intermediate steps in elaborating $\xrightarrow{\text{before}}$ for conciseness):
- $\text{com}(B.\text{sync}) \xrightarrow{\text{local}} \text{com}(C.Wy,_{-}) \xrightarrow{\text{local}} \text{com}(D.\text{sync}) \xrightarrow{\text{insn}} \text{pp}_B(\text{sync})$ if $B \sim C$.
- $\text{com}(B.\text{sync}) \xrightarrow{\text{local}} \text{sat}(Ry,_{-}) \xrightarrow{\text{comm}} \text{pp}_B(C.Wy,_{-}) \xrightarrow{\text{before}} \text{pp}_B(D.\text{sync})$ otherwise.

Either way, $\text{com}(B.\text{sync}) \to \text{pp}_B(D.\text{sync})$. By definition, we have an *after edge* between the two barriers: $\text{pp}_D(B.\text{sync}) \xrightarrow{\text{after}} \text{com}(D.\text{sync})$. Moreover, either $A \sim D$ or $A \not\sim D$:

- $\mathrm{pp}_D(B.\mathrm{sync}) \xrightarrow{\text{after}} \mathrm{com}(D.\mathrm{sync}) \xrightarrow{\text{local}} \mathrm{com}(A.\mathrm{W}x_{,-}) \xrightarrow{\text{insn}} \mathrm{pp}_B(\mathrm{W}x_{,-})$ if $A \sim D$.
- $\mathrm{pp}_D(B.\mathrm{sync}) \xrightarrow{\text{after}} \mathrm{com}(D.\mathrm{sync}) \xrightarrow{\text{local}} \mathrm{sat}(\mathrm{R}x_{,-}) \xrightarrow{\text{comm}} \mathrm{pp}_D(A.\mathrm{W}x_{,-})$ otherwise.

Thus, in all cases, we have a cycle:

$$\mathrm{com}(B.\mathrm{sync}) \xrightarrow{\text{before}} \mathrm{pp}_B(A.\mathrm{W}x_{,-})$$
$$\xrightarrow{\text{comm}} \mathrm{sat}(B.\mathrm{R}x_{,-}) \xrightarrow{\text{insn}} \mathrm{com}(\mathrm{R}x_{,-}) \xrightarrow{\text{local}} \mathrm{com}(B.\mathrm{sync}) \qquad \square$$

4.2 Execution paths

We consider the three operations of the work-stealing algorithm: *take*, *push* and *steal*. Each of them exhibits different execution paths depending on control flow. Data and address dependences are implicit in the notations and are omitted for brevity. Control dependences are implied by the guard conditions in each case and are also omitted, but we explicit the constraints on the b and t variables carrying the control dependence. Greek letters β, τ, ξ denote the memory values of b, t, and some x_i, respectively. Reads and writes are annotated with the corresponding line from Figure 2.

For *take* and *steal*, we say that an instance of the operation is successful if it returns one element; otherwise (including if it returns empty) it is considered failed.

4.2.1 Take

Two failure cases return no element (empty), and two success cases return one element from the deque. All four paths start with:

$$(a)\mathrm{R}b, \beta \xrightarrow{\text{po}} (b)\mathrm{R}a, \&x \xrightarrow{\text{po}} (c)\mathrm{W}b, \beta - 1 \xrightarrow{\text{sync}} (d)\mathrm{R}t, \tau$$

Specific continuations for each path are listed below.

Return empty without CAS, $\beta - \tau \le 0$: $\quad \cdots \xrightarrow{\text{po}} (i)\mathrm{W}b, \beta$
Return empty with (failed) CAS, $\beta - \tau = 1, \tau \ne \tau'$:
$\quad \cdots \xrightarrow{\text{po}} (e)\mathrm{R}x_{\beta-1}, \xi \xrightarrow{\text{po}} (f)\mathrm{R}t, \tau' \xrightarrow{\text{po}} (h)\mathrm{W}b, \tau + 1$
Return one without CAS, $\beta - \tau > 1$: $\quad \cdots \xrightarrow{\text{po}} (e)\mathrm{R}x_{\beta-1}, \xi$
Return one with (successful) CAS, $\beta - \tau = 1$:
$\quad \cdots \xrightarrow{\text{po}} (e)\mathrm{R}x_{\beta-1}, \xi \xrightarrow{\text{po}} (f)\mathrm{R}t, \tau \xrightarrow{\text{po-atom}} (g)\mathrm{W}t, \tau+1 \xrightarrow{\text{po}} (h)\mathrm{W}b, \beta$

4.2.2 Push

There are two paths: a straight case, and a resizing case which grows the underlying circular buffer.

Straight, $\beta - \tau < \mathrm{size}(x) - 1$:
$(a)\mathrm{R}b, \beta \xrightarrow{\text{po}} (b)\mathrm{R}t, \tau \xrightarrow{\text{po}} (c)\mathrm{R}a, \&x \xrightarrow{\text{po}} (d)\mathrm{W}x_\beta, \xi \xrightarrow{\text{sync}} (e)\mathrm{W}b, \beta + 1$
Resizing, $\beta - \tau \ge \mathrm{size}(x) - 1$: where x' refers to the new array
$(a)\mathrm{R}b, \beta \xrightarrow{\text{po}} (b)\mathrm{R}t, \tau \xrightarrow{\text{po}} (c)\mathrm{R}a, \&x \xrightarrow{\text{po}} \mathit{resize}$
$\xrightarrow{\text{sync}} (d)\mathrm{W}x'_\beta, \xi \xrightarrow{\text{sync}} (e)\mathrm{W}b, \beta + 1$
where $\mathit{resize} = \mathrm{R}x_\tau, \xi_\tau \xrightarrow{\text{po}} \mathrm{W}x'_\tau, \xi_\tau \xrightarrow{\text{po}} \cdots$
$\xrightarrow{\text{po}} \mathrm{R}x_{\beta-1}, \xi_{\beta-1} \xrightarrow{\text{po}} \mathrm{W}x'_{\beta-1}, \xi_{\beta-1} \xrightarrow{\text{sync}} \mathrm{W}a, \&x'$

4.2.3 Steal

There are three paths: two failure cases and one success case. Failure returns no element and success returns a stolen element.

Return empty without CAS, $\beta - \tau \le 0$: $\quad (a)\mathrm{R}t, \tau \xrightarrow{\text{sync}} (b)\mathrm{R}b, \beta$
Return empty with (failed) CAS, $\beta - \tau > 0 \wedge \tau \ne \tau'$:
$(a)\mathrm{R}t, \tau \xrightarrow{\text{sync}} (b)\mathrm{R}b, \beta \xrightarrow{\text{ctrl-isync}} (c)\mathrm{R}a, \&x \xrightarrow{\text{po}} (d)\mathrm{R}x_\tau, \xi \xrightarrow{\text{ctrl-isync}} (e)\mathrm{R}t, \tau'$
Return one with (successful) CAS, $\beta - \tau > 0$:
$(a)\mathrm{R}t, \tau \xrightarrow{\text{sync}} (b)\mathrm{R}b, \beta \xrightarrow{\text{ctrl-isync}} (c)\mathrm{R}a, \&x \xrightarrow{\text{po}} (d)\mathrm{R}x_\tau, \xi$
$\xrightarrow{\text{ctrl-isync}} (e)\mathrm{R}t, \tau \xrightarrow{\text{po-atom}} (f)\mathrm{W}t, \tau + 1$

4.3 Significant reads and writes

We define the sequence (β_n) of values taken by the variable b over the course of the program, according to the *write coherence* relation. Initially $\beta_0 = 0$. Since all *push* and *take* operations occur in a single thread, and *steal* operations never alter the value of b, the elements of (β_n) correspond to writes to b in program

order within the *push* and *take* operations. Similarly, we define the sequence (τ_m) of values taken by the variable t. We assume $\tau_0 = 0$. Furthermore, since all writes to t are from CAS instructions, which are sequentially ordered, and all such CAS instructions increment t by one, (τ_m) is monotonically increasing, and s.t. $\tau_m = m$.

For each index i, we define the sequence $(\xi_i^v)_{v \in \mathbb{N}}$ of successive values given to the element at index i in the deque by the last write $\mathrm{W}x_{i,-}$ of a *push* operation, regardless of the address $\&x$ of the underlying array. Only the last such write is called *significant* as it induces a new value in an (ξ_i^v) sequence, while writes due to resizing do not. For all i, ξ_i^0, the value before the first significant write to x_i location, is undefined: $\xi_i^0 = \bot$. Similarly, a read is *significant* if it occurs in a successful instance of *take* or *steal*.

Lemma 4. *For all i, (ξ_i^v) is globally coherent.*

Proof. Given two significant writes $\mathrm{W}x_{i,-}$ and $\mathrm{W}x'_{i,-}$ at index i (regardless of the address of the underlying array). If $\mathrm{W}x_{i,-}$ and $\mathrm{W}x'_{i,-}$ both write to the same memory location, then they are ordered by write coherence. If they do not, then there must be a resize operation after the first write and before the second (all writes happen in the same thread). Because of the cumulative barrier after a resize operation, threads that see the second value must have seen the first beforehand. Hence, there is a global coherence order on the writes, which corresponds to the order of *push* operations. $\square$

We define the relation *read from far* as follows: for some memory locations $m_0, \ldots, m_n$ and some value v, $\mathrm{W}m_0, v \xrightarrow{\text{rff}} \mathrm{R}m_n, v$ if $\mathrm{W}m_0, v \xrightarrow{\text{rf}} \mathrm{R}m_n, v$ or there exists a sequence of copies carrying the value of the write to the read:
$\mathrm{W}m_0, v \xrightarrow{\text{rf}} \mathrm{R}m_0, v \xrightarrow{\text{data}} \mathrm{W}m_1, v \xrightarrow{\text{rf}} \cdots \xrightarrow{\text{data}} \mathrm{W}m_n, v \xrightarrow{\text{rf}} \mathrm{R}m_n, v$.

For conciseness, we hereafter omit the variable name from reads and writes whenever the variable can be inferred from the value: e.g., $\mathrm{W}\beta_n$ stands for $\mathrm{W}b, \beta_n$. Let $\mathrm{W}\xi_i^v$ denote the vth significant write at index i, and $\mathrm{R}\xi_i^v$ a significant read s.t. $\mathrm{W}\xi_i^v \xrightarrow{\text{rff}} \mathrm{R}\xi_i^v$.

Lemma 5. *Given a write $\mathrm{W}x_{i,-}$ and a read $\mathrm{R}x'_{j,-}$,*

$$i \ne j \implies \mathrm{W}x_{i,-} \xrightarrow{\text{rf}}\!\!\!\!/\; \mathrm{R}x'_{j,-}$$

Proof. If the addresses of the underlying arrays differ, then the memory locations read and written are distinct and there can be no *read from* relation.

Otherwise, since old arrays are never reused, the addresses are the same and $i \equiv j \mod \mathrm{size}(x)$ $\mathrm{R}x'_{j,-}$ belongs to a successful instance of *take*, *push* (with resizing), or *steal*. Let X be that instance.

Let P be the instance of *push* to which $\mathrm{W}x_{i,-}$ belongs. In P, we have the following execution graph:

$$P.\mathrm{R}t, \tau_P \xrightarrow{\text{ctrl}} \mathrm{W}x_{i,-} \xrightarrow{\text{sync}} \mathrm{W}b, \beta_P + 1$$

where $\quad \tau_P \le i \le \beta_P \quad$ and $\quad \beta_P - \tau_P < \mathrm{size}(x) - 1$

Let us assume $i \ne j \wedge \mathrm{W}x_{i,-} \xrightarrow{\text{rf}} \mathrm{R}x'_{j,-}$ and show it is indeed impossible.

Assume X is a successful instance of *take* or *push*. Since X and P belong to the same thread, P must occur before X in program order (the order of loads and stores to the same location is preserved: $P.\mathrm{W}x_{i,-} \xrightarrow{\text{po-loc}} X.\mathrm{R}x'_{j,-}$).

If $j < i$, then $j \le i - \mathrm{size}(x)$. However, the following must hold in P:

$$\tau_P \le i \le \beta_P \wedge \beta_P - \tau_P < \mathrm{size}(x) - 1$$

hence $\quad j < i - \mathrm{size}(x) + 1 \le \beta_P - \mathrm{size}(x) + 1 < \tau_P$

Furthermore, if X is a *take* operation, $\mathrm{R}x'_{j,-}$ reads the last element of the deque, and $j = \beta_X - 1 \ge \tau_X$; if X is a *push* operation, $\mathrm{R}x'_{j,-}$ results from a copy operation of the resizing code, hence $j \ge \tau_X$. Since X occurs after P in program order and t is monotonically increasing, $P.\mathrm{R}t, \tau_P \xrightarrow{\text{po-loc}} X.\mathrm{R}t, \tau_X$ and $j < \tau_P \le \tau_X \le j$. Impossible.

If $i < j$, then, since $j \ge \beta_X$, b must increase from $\beta_P + 1$ to $j + 1$ between the write in P and the read in X. Hence, there must be an instance P' of *push* between P and X (in program order) that increments b to $j + 1$. Indeed, the only writes that increase the value of b occur in *push* and *take*; and the effect of *take* as a whole never increases the value of b since it first decrements the variable. We have:

$$P.\mathrm{W}x_{i,-} \xrightarrow{\text{po-loc}} P'.\mathrm{W}x_{j,-} \xrightarrow{\text{po-loc}} X.\mathrm{R}x'_{j,-}$$

hence $\quad P.\mathrm{W}x_{i,-} \xrightarrow{\text{co}} P'.\mathrm{W}x_{j,-} \xrightarrow{\text{pp-sat}} X.\mathrm{R}x'_{j,-}$

Thus, from Lemma 2 (ii), $P.\mathsf{W}x_i,_ \overset{\text{rf}}{\not\to} X.\mathsf{R}x'_j,_$.

Now, assume X is a successful instance of *steal*. We have the following execution graph for X:

$$X.\mathsf{R}t,\tau_X = j \xrightarrow{\text{sync}} \mathsf{R}b,\beta_X \xrightarrow{\text{ctrl-isync}} \mathsf{R}a,\&x' \xrightarrow{\text{po}} \mathsf{R}x'_j,_ \xrightarrow{\text{ctrl-isync}} \mathsf{R}t,\tau_X \xrightarrow{\text{po-atom}} \mathsf{W}t,\tau_X+1$$

If $j < i$, then $j \le i - \text{size}(x)$. However, the following must hold in P:

$$j < i - \text{size}(x) + 1 \le \beta_P - \text{size}(x) + 1 < \tau_P$$

Hence $\tau_X = j < \tau_P$. Since t increases monotonically, it must be that:

$$X.\mathsf{R}x'_j,_ \xrightarrow{\text{ctrl-isync}} \mathsf{R}t,\tau_X \xrightarrow{\text{po-atom}} \mathsf{W}t,\tau_X+1 \xrightarrow{\text{rf}} \mathsf{R}t,_ \xrightarrow{\text{sync}} \mathsf{W}t,_ \xrightarrow{\text{rf}} \cdots \xrightarrow{\text{sync}} \mathsf{W}t,\tau_P \xrightarrow{\text{rf}} P.\mathsf{R}t,\tau_P \xrightarrow{\text{ctrl}} \mathsf{W}x_i,_$$

Hence $X.\mathsf{R}x'_j,_$ must be committed before $\mathsf{W}t,\tau_X+1$. Since $\mathsf{W}t,\tau_X+1$ is (cumulatively) propagated to $\mathsf{W}x_i,_$, $X.\mathsf{R}x'_j,_$ must be committed before $\mathsf{W}x_i,_$. Formally: it follows from Lemma 3 (ii) that $\mathsf{W}t,\tau_X+1 \xrightarrow{\text{pp-sat}} P.\mathsf{R}t,\tau_P$. If $\mathsf{W}x_i,_ \xrightarrow{\text{rf}} \mathsf{R}x'_j,_$ then $\mathsf{W}x_i,_ \xrightarrow{\text{pp-sat}} \mathsf{R}x'_j,_$. We get:

$$X.\mathsf{W}t,\tau_X+1 \xrightarrow{\text{pp-sat}} P.\mathsf{R}t,\tau_P \xrightarrow{\text{ctrl}} \mathsf{W}x_i,_$$
$$\wedge\ P.\mathsf{W}x_i,_ \xrightarrow{\text{pp-sat}} X.\mathsf{R}x'_j,_ \xrightarrow{\text{ctrl-isync}} \mathsf{W}t,\tau_X+1$$

Lemma 2 (iv) tells that it is impossible. Thus $P.\mathsf{W}x_i,_ \overset{\text{rf}}{\not\to} X.\mathsf{R}x'_j,_$.

If $i < j$, then $i \le j - \text{size}(x)$, and there must be an instance P' of *push* s.t. $P'.\mathsf{W}b,j+1 \xrightarrow{\text{po-loc}} \mathsf{W}b,\beta_X \xrightarrow{\text{rf}} X.\mathsf{R}b,\beta_X$ (so that index j be accessible in X). P' cannot occur before P in program order because, as above, we would have $\tau_{P'} \le \tau_P \le i$ on the one hand, and $i \le j - \text{size}(x) < \tau_{P'}$ on the other hand. The underlying array also monotonically increases in size, so the inequality still holds if the sizes of P and P' differ. Hence P' occurs after P. Furthermore $\mathsf{W}x''_j,_ \in P'$. If x in P and x'' in P' refer to different arrays, then a resize operation R must precede P', s.t.

$$\mathsf{W}a,\&x \xrightarrow{\text{po-loc}} P.\mathsf{R}a,\&x \xrightarrow{\text{po-loc}} R.\mathsf{W}a,\&x'' \xrightarrow{\text{sync}} P'.\mathsf{W}x''_j,_ \xrightarrow{\text{sync}} \mathsf{W}b,j+1$$
$$\xrightarrow{\text{po-loc}} \mathsf{W}b,\beta_X \xrightarrow{\text{rf}} X.\mathsf{R}b,\beta_X \xrightarrow{\text{ctrl-isync}} \mathsf{R}a,\&x' \xrightarrow{\text{addr}} \mathsf{R}x'_j,_$$
$$\text{hence}\quad \mathsf{W}a,\&x \xrightarrow{\text{co}} R.\mathsf{W}a,\&x'' \xrightarrow{\text{sync}} \mathsf{W}b,\beta_X \xrightarrow{\text{pp-sat}} X.\mathsf{R}b,\beta_X$$

From Lemma 2 (iii), $\mathsf{W}b,\beta_X \xrightarrow{\text{pp-sat}} X.\mathsf{R}a,\&x'$; Lemma 2 (ii) concludes that $\mathsf{W}a,\&x \overset{\text{rf}}{\not\to} X.\mathsf{R}a,\&x'$. Since all resize operations allocate new arrays, $\&x' \ne \&x$, which contradicts our premises. Otherwise, x and x'' refer to the same array, hence $\mathsf{W}x_i,_ \xrightarrow{\text{po-loc}} \mathsf{W}x''_j,_$, and we get:

$$P.\mathsf{W}x_i,_ \xrightarrow{\text{po-loc}} P'.\mathsf{W}x''_j,_ \xrightarrow{\text{sync}} \mathsf{W}b,j+1 \xrightarrow{\text{po-loc}} \mathsf{W}b,\beta_X \xrightarrow{\text{rf}} X.\mathsf{R}b,\beta_X \xrightarrow{\text{ctrl-isync}} \mathsf{R}x'_j,_$$

It follows from Lemmas 3 (i) and 2 (iii) that:

$$P.\mathsf{W}x_i,_ \xrightarrow{\text{co}} \mathsf{W}x''_j,_ \xrightarrow{\text{pp-sat}} \mathsf{R}x'_j,_$$

Hence, from Lemma 2 (ii), $\mathsf{W}x_i,_ \overset{\text{rf}}{\not\to} \mathsf{R}x'_j,_$. □

Corollary 1. *Given a significant write* $\mathsf{W}\xi_i^v$ *and a significant read* $\mathsf{R}x'_j,_$*:* $\ i \ne j \implies \mathsf{W}\xi_i^v \overset{\text{rff}}{\not\to} \mathsf{R}x'_j,_$

Proof. If $i \ne j$, we know that $\mathsf{W}\xi_i^v \overset{\text{rf}}{\not\to} \mathsf{R}x'_j,_$. Furthermore, all copies, which happen during a resize operation, copy from and to the same index. Since there are less copies than the size of the expanded array, there can be no two copies writing to the same memory location in the new array. Hence, there can be no sequence of copies from $\mathsf{W}\xi_i^v$ to $\mathsf{R}x'_j,_$. □

Lemma 6. *Given a significant write* $\mathsf{W}\xi_i^u$ *and a significant read* $\mathsf{R}\xi_i^v$*:*

(i) $\mathsf{W}\xi_i^u \xrightarrow{\text{pp-sat}} \mathsf{R}a,\&x \xrightarrow{\text{addr}} \mathsf{R}x_i,\xi_i^v \implies u \le v$
(ii) $0 < u \le v \implies \mathsf{W}\xi_i^u \xrightarrow{\text{pp-sat}} \mathsf{R}x_i,\xi_i^v$

Proof. We prove each point separately:

(i) Suppose $v < u$. We define $W'.\mathsf{W}x_i,\xi_i^v$ as follows.

If $v = 0$, ξ_i^v is an undefined value; let $W'.\mathsf{W}x_i,\xi_i^0 \xrightarrow{\text{rf}} \mathsf{R}x_i,\xi_i^v$ be the initialization of x_i. $W'.\mathsf{W}x_i,\xi_i^0$ comes before $\mathsf{W}\xi_i^u$ in program order.

Otherwise, $0 < v < u$. Let $W.\mathsf{W}\xi_i^v$ be the significant write s.t. $W.\mathsf{W}\xi_i^v \xrightarrow{\text{rff}} \mathsf{R}x_i,\xi_i^v$. In other words, there exists a sequence of copies carrying the value of ξ_i^v to $\mathsf{R}x_i,\xi_i^v$. That sequence ends with a write $W'.\mathsf{W}x_i,\xi_i^v \xrightarrow{\text{rf}} \mathsf{R}x_i,\xi_i^v$. Moreover, according to the definition of (ξ_i^v) and the semantics of resizing, $W.\mathsf{W}\xi_i^v$ and $W'.\mathsf{W}x_i,\xi_i^v$ must come before $\mathsf{W}\xi_i^u$ in program order.

We have two cases: either $\mathsf{W}\xi_i^u$ and $\mathsf{R}x_i,\xi_i^v$ refer to the same memory location or they do not.

Assume that they refer to the same memory location x_i. Then it must be that $W'.\mathsf{W}x_i,\xi_i^v \xrightarrow{\text{po-loc}} \mathsf{W}x_i,\xi_i^u$, and we have:

$$W'.\mathsf{W}x_i,\xi_i^v \xrightarrow{\text{co}} \mathsf{W}\xi_i^u \xrightarrow{\text{pp-sat}} \mathsf{R}a,\&x \xrightarrow{\text{addr}} \mathsf{R}x_i,\xi_i^v$$

Hence, from Lemma 2 (ii), $W'.\mathsf{W}x_i,\xi_i^v \overset{\text{rf}}{\not\to} \mathsf{R}x_i,\xi_i^v$. Impossible.

Conversely, assume that they do not refer to the same memory location. Then there must be a resize operation between $W'.\mathsf{W}x_i,\xi_i^v$ and $\mathsf{W}\xi_i^u$:

$$\mathsf{W}a,\&x \xrightarrow{\text{sync}} W'.\mathsf{W}x_i,\xi_i^v \xrightarrow{\text{sync}} \mathsf{W}a,\&x' \xrightarrow{\text{sync}} \mathsf{W}x'_i,\xi_i^u \xrightarrow{\text{pp-sat}} \mathsf{R}a,\&x \xrightarrow{\text{addr}} \mathsf{R}x_i,\xi_i^v$$

Hence, from Lemma 3 (i), $\mathsf{W}a,\&x \xrightarrow{\text{co}} \mathsf{W}a,\&x' \xrightarrow{\text{pp-sat}} \mathsf{R}a,\&x$. And from Lemma 2 (ii), $\mathsf{W}a,\&x \overset{\text{rf}}{\not\to} \mathsf{R}a,\&x$. Since there is only one write $\mathsf{W}a,\&x$ that gives the value $\&x$ to a, we have a contradiction.

(ii) There exists a write $W.\mathsf{W}\xi_i^v$ s.t. $W.\mathsf{W}\xi_i^v \xrightarrow{\text{rff}} \mathsf{R}\xi_i^v$, and a sequence of copies carrying the value of ξ_i^v to $\mathsf{R}\xi_i^v$. That sequence ends with a write $W'.\mathsf{W}\xi_i^v \xrightarrow{\text{rf}} \mathsf{R}\xi_i^v$. Since $u \le v$, $\mathsf{W}\xi_i^u \xrightarrow{\text{po}} W.\mathsf{W}\xi_i^v$ by definition of (ξ_i^v). Thanks to the barrier after $\mathsf{W}\xi_i^u$ in *push*, $\mathsf{W}\xi_i^u \xrightarrow{\text{sync}} W'.\mathsf{W}\xi_i^v \xrightarrow{\text{rf}} \mathsf{R}\xi_i^v$. From Lemma 3 (i), we get $\mathsf{W}\xi_i^u \xrightarrow{\text{pp-sat}} \mathsf{R}\xi_i^v$. □

Corollary 2 (Well-defined significant reads)**.** *Given a significant read* $\mathsf{R}x_i,\xi$, $\xi = \xi_i^v$ *for some* $v > 0$.

Proof. Let X be the successful instance of *take* or *steal* s.t. $\mathsf{R}x_i,\xi \in X$.

Suppose $\xi \ne \xi_i^v$, then $\xi = \bot$ can only be an undefined value from the uninitialized array, prior to copying. Indeed, if x_i is not affected by copying, then it must be one of the new slots allocated by the resizing, hence its initial value is ξ_i^0. Let R be the *push* operation that allocates the array x. There exists a ξ_i^u such that:

$$\mathsf{W}x_i,\bot \xrightarrow{\text{co}} R.\mathsf{W}x_i,\xi_i^u \xrightarrow{\text{sync}} \mathsf{W}a,\&x \xrightarrow{\text{rf}} X.\mathsf{R}a,\&x \xrightarrow{\text{addr}} \mathsf{R}x_i,\xi$$

It follows from Lemmas 2 (iii), 3 (i) and 2 (ii) that $\mathsf{W}x_i,\bot \overset{\text{rf}}{\not\to} \mathsf{R}x_i,\xi$. Impossible.

Hence, $\xi = \xi_i^v$. We have $\mathsf{R}b,\beta \in X$ and $\beta \ge i+1 > 0$, for X is successful. Hence, there is an instance of *push* P s.t. $P.\mathsf{W}b,\beta \xrightarrow{\text{rf}} X.\mathsf{R}b,\beta$. Since $\beta \ge i+1$, either $\beta = i+1$ and $\mathsf{W}\xi_i^u \in P$, or there must be an instance of *push* that contains a significant write $\mathsf{W}\xi_i^u$ and comes before P in program order. In both cases, $\mathsf{W}\xi_i^u$ belongs to a *push* operation, hence $u > 0$. Moreover, thanks to the barrier after a significant write in *push*, $\mathsf{W}\xi_i^u \xrightarrow{\text{sync}} P.\mathsf{W}b,\beta$. If X is an instance of *take*, $P.\mathsf{W}b,\beta \xrightarrow{\text{po}} X.\mathsf{R}\xi_i^v$; otherwise, $P.\mathsf{W}b,\beta \xrightarrow{\text{rf}} X.\mathsf{R}b,\beta \xrightarrow{\text{ctrl-isync}} \mathsf{R}\xi_i^v$ and Lemma 3 (ii) gives $P.\mathsf{W}b,\beta \xrightarrow{\text{pp-sat}} X.\mathsf{R}\xi_i^v$. In both cases, $\mathsf{W}\xi_i^u \xrightarrow{\text{sync}} P.\mathsf{W}b,\beta \xrightarrow{\text{pp-sat}} X.\mathsf{R}\xi_i^v$, hence, by Lemmas 3 (i) and 6, $0 < u \le v$. □

4.4 Uniqueness of significant reads

The results from the previous section establish that two significant reads at different indexes cannot retrieve the same element ξ_i^v. The only possible cause of duplicate significant reads is thus reduced to the case where the reads access the same index i.

Theorem 1 (Work-stealing: uniqueness of significant reads)**.** *Given a worker thread executing a sequence of* push *and* take *operations, and finite number number of thief threads each executing* steal *operations, all against a same deque. If* X *and* Y *are two distinct successful instances of* steal *or* take*,*

$$\forall \mathsf{R}\xi_i^v \in X, \forall \mathsf{R}\xi_{i'}^{v'} \in Y, i \ne i' \vee v \ne v'$$

Lemma 7. *Given* S_1 *and* S_2 *distinct successful instances of* steal*,*

$$\forall \mathsf{R}\xi_i^v \in S_1, \forall \mathsf{R}\xi_{i'}^{v'} \in S_2, i \ne i'$$

Proof. All writes to t atomically increment it (by atomicity of CAS). Hence two successful *steal* operations cannot write (thus read) the same value of t. Reads from x in a *steal* operation access the index given by the value of the t variable. Hence $\mathsf{R}t,i \in S_1$ and $\mathsf{R}t,i' \in S_2$ imply $i \ne i'$. □

Lemma 8. *Given* T *a successful instance of* take *and* P *an instance of* push*. If* P *comes after* T *in program order, then:*

$$\forall \mathsf{R}\xi_i^v \in T, \forall \mathsf{W}\xi_j^u \in P, i \ne j \vee v \ne u$$

Proof. Assume $i = j \wedge v = u$. We have $\mathsf{R}\xi_i^v \xrightarrow{\mathsf{po}} \mathsf{W}\xi_j^u$; therefore $\mathsf{W}\xi_j^u \xrightarrow{\mathsf{pp\text{-}sat}} \mathsf{R}\xi_i^v$. From Lemma 6 (ii), it follows that $u > v$. We have a contradiction. $\square$

Lemma 9. *Given T_1 and T_2 distinct successful instances of* take,

$$\forall \mathsf{R}\xi_i^v \in T_1, \forall \mathsf{R}\xi_{i'}^{v'} \in T_2, i \neq i' \vee v \neq v'$$

Proof. We have the following execution graphs:

$$T_1.\mathsf{R}\beta_n \xrightarrow{\mathsf{po}} \mathsf{R}a_{,-} \xrightarrow{\mathsf{po}} \mathsf{W}b, \beta_n - 1 \xrightarrow{\mathsf{sync}} \mathsf{R}t, \tau \xrightarrow{\mathsf{po}} \mathsf{R}\xi_{\beta_n-1}^v \xrightarrow{\mathsf{po}} \cdots$$

$$T_2.\mathsf{R}\beta_{n'} \xrightarrow{\mathsf{po}} \mathsf{R}a_{,-} \xrightarrow{\mathsf{po}} \mathsf{W}b, \beta_{n'} - 1 \xrightarrow{\mathsf{sync}} \mathsf{R}t, \tau' \xrightarrow{\mathsf{po}} \mathsf{R}\xi_{\beta_{n'}-1}^{v'} \xrightarrow{\mathsf{po}} \cdots$$

And $\beta_n - 1 = i$ and $\beta_{n'} - 1 = i'$.

Since all instances of *take* occur in the worker thread, we have either:

$$T_1.\mathsf{W}b, \beta_n - 1 \xrightarrow{\mathsf{po\text{-}loc}} T_2.\mathsf{R}\beta_{n'} \quad \text{or} \quad T_2.\mathsf{W}b, \beta_{n'} - 1 \xrightarrow{\mathsf{po\text{-}loc}} T_1.\mathsf{R}\beta_n$$

Let us assume the first case as well as $i = i' \wedge v = v'$ and show it is impossible, the other case being symmetrical. We have $\beta_n - 1 = i = i' = \beta_{n'} - 1$, and $T_1.\mathsf{W}b, i \xrightarrow{\mathsf{po\text{-}loc}} T_2.\mathsf{R}b, i+1$.

Hence (β_n) must increase from i to $i+1$ between n and n'; there exists an instance P of *push* that writes $\mathsf{W}\beta_k \xrightarrow{\mathsf{po\text{-}loc}} T_2.\mathsf{R}b, i+1$, s.t. $n < k \leq n'$ and $\beta_{k-1} = i$ and $\beta_k = i + 1$ (as noted above, *take* as a whole does not increase the value of b). We get the following graph:

$$\mathsf{R}b, i \xrightarrow{\mathsf{po}} P.\mathsf{W}\xi_i^u \xrightarrow{\mathsf{sync}} \mathsf{W}b, \beta_k = i + 1 \xrightarrow{\mathsf{po\text{-}loc}} T_2.\mathsf{R}\beta_{n'} \xrightarrow{\mathsf{po}} \mathsf{R}a_{,-} \xrightarrow{\mathsf{addr}} \mathsf{R}\xi_i^{v'}$$

Lemma 3 (i) yields $P.\mathsf{W}\xi_i^u \xrightarrow{\mathsf{pp\text{-}sat}} \mathsf{R}a_{,-} \xrightarrow{\mathsf{addr}} \mathsf{R}\xi_i^{v'}$. It then follows from Lemma 6 (i) that $u \leq v'$ and from Lemma 8 that $v < u$. Impossible. $\square$

Lemma 10. *Given T a successful instance of* take *and S a successful instance of* steal,

$$\forall \mathsf{R}\xi_i^v \in T, \forall \mathsf{R}\xi_{i'}^{v'} \in S, i \neq i' \vee v \neq v'$$

Proof. We have the following execution graphs:

$$T.\mathsf{R}\beta_n \xrightarrow{\mathsf{po}} \mathsf{R}a_{,-} \xrightarrow{\mathsf{po}} \mathsf{W}b, \beta_n - 1 \xrightarrow{\mathsf{sync}} \mathsf{R}\tau_m \xrightarrow{\mathsf{po}} \mathsf{R}\xi_{\beta_n-1}^v \xrightarrow{\mathsf{po}} \cdots \xrightarrow{\mathsf{po}} S.\mathsf{R}\tau_{m'}$$

$$\xrightarrow{\mathsf{sync}} \mathsf{R}\beta_{n'} \xrightarrow{\mathsf{ctrl\text{-}isync}} \mathsf{R}a_{,-} \xrightarrow{\mathsf{po}} \mathsf{R}\xi_{\tau_{m'}}^{v'} \xrightarrow{\mathsf{ctrl\text{-}isync}} \mathsf{R}\tau_{m'} \xrightarrow{\mathsf{po\text{-}atom}} \mathsf{W}t, \tau_{m'} + 1$$

with $\beta_n - 1 = i$ and $\tau_{m'} = i'$.

Let us assume $i = i' \wedge v = v'$. Then $\tau_{m'} = i' = i = \beta_n - 1$. For S to succeed, we must have $\tau_{m'} < \beta_{n'}$. Hence, $\beta_n \leq \beta_{n'}$.

Also, for T to succeed, we must have $\tau_m < \beta_n$. Two cases:
- If $\beta_n = \tau_m + 1$, then a successful CAS occurs in T. Moreover, $\beta_n = \tau_m + 1$ implies $\tau_{m'} + 1 = \beta_n = \tau_m + 1$, hence $\tau_{m'} = \tau_m$. Impossible, since t is monotonically increasing and S must also contain a successful CAS with the same value of t.
- If $\beta_n > \tau_m + 1$, then no CAS occurs in T and $m' > m$. Since t monotonically increases, there must be two writes $A.\mathsf{W}\tau_m \xrightarrow{\mathsf{co}} B.\mathsf{W}\tau_{m'}$ s.t.

$$A.\mathsf{W}\tau_m \xrightarrow{\mathsf{rf}} T.\mathsf{R}\tau_m \xrightarrow{\mathsf{fr}} B.\mathsf{W}\tau_{m'} \xrightarrow{\mathsf{rf}} S.\mathsf{R}\tau_{m'} \xrightarrow{\mathsf{sync}} \mathsf{R}\beta_{n'}$$

If $S.\mathsf{R}\beta_{n'} \xrightarrow{\mathsf{fr}} T.\mathsf{W}b, \beta_n - 1$, then we have:

$$B.\mathsf{W}\tau_{m'} \xrightarrow{\mathsf{rf}} S.\mathsf{R}\tau_{m'} \xrightarrow{\mathsf{sync}} \mathsf{R}\beta_{n'} \xrightarrow{\mathsf{fr}} T.\mathsf{W}b, \beta_n - 1$$
$$\wedge \; T.\mathsf{W}b, \beta_n - 1 \xrightarrow{\mathsf{sync}} \mathsf{R}\tau_m \xrightarrow{\mathsf{fr}} B.\mathsf{W}\tau_{m'}$$

Impossible according to Lemma 3 (iii). Therefore $\mathsf{W}\beta_{n'}$, the source of $S.\mathsf{R}\beta_{n'}$ must come before $\mathsf{W}\beta_{n+1}$ (in *coherence order*, hence in *program order* as both occur in the same thread). Consequently, (β_n) must increase from $\beta_n - 1 = i$ to $\beta_{n'}$ between $n + 1$ and n'. Since T does not increment the value of b (execution without CAS), there must be an instance P of *push* that writes $P.\mathsf{W}\beta_k \xrightarrow{\mathsf{po}} \mathsf{W}\beta_{n'} \xrightarrow{\mathsf{rf}} S.\mathsf{R}\beta_{n'}$, s.t. $n < k \leq n'$ and $\beta_{k-1} = i$ and $\beta_k = i + 1$.

We get the following execution graph:

$$P.\mathsf{W}\xi_i^u \xrightarrow{\mathsf{sync}} \mathsf{W}b, i + 1 \xrightarrow{\mathsf{po}} \mathsf{W}\beta_{n'} \xrightarrow{\mathsf{rf}} S.\mathsf{R}\beta_{n'} \xrightarrow{\mathsf{ctrl\text{-}isync}} \mathsf{R}\xi_i^{v'}$$

Hence we have $\mathsf{W}\xi_i^u \xrightarrow{\mathsf{pp\text{-}sat}} \mathsf{R}\xi_i^{v'}$ from Lemma 3 (i) and Lemma 2 (iii). Finally, it follows from Lemma 6 that $u \leq v'$, and from Lemma 8 that $v < u \leq v'$. We have a contradiction. $\square$

Theorem 1 follows directly from Lemmas 9, 10 and 7.

4.5 Existence of significant reads

Theorem 2 (Work-stealing: existence of significant reads). *Consider a worker thread executing a sequence of* push *and* take *operations, and a finite number of thief threads each executing* steal

operations, all against a same deque. If the number of* push *is finite, then all threads reach a stationary state where $b = t$ in a finite number of transitions, and the following holds globally:*

$$\forall \xi_i^v, v > 0 \implies \exists! \mathsf{R}\xi_i^v \text{ in some thread before the stationary point}$$

Let P_F be the last instance of *push* in the worker thread, in program order. Let $\mathsf{W}\beta_{n_F} \in P_F$ and $\mathsf{R}\tau_{m_F} \in P_F$. We say that an instance X of *take* or *steal* is *trailing* if $\mathsf{R}\beta_{n \geq n_F} \in X$.

Lemma 11. *Given X a successful trailing instance of* take *or* steal: $\mathsf{R}\tau_m \in X \implies m \geq m_F$.

Proof. We have two cases:
- Assume X is an instance of *take*. X follows P_F in program order: $P_F.\mathsf{R}\tau_{m_F} \xrightarrow{\mathsf{po\text{-}loc}} X.\mathsf{R}\tau_m$, and $m \geq m_F$ by uniprocessor constraints.
- Assume X is an instance of *steal*. Since X is successful, X contains a successful instance of a CAS instruction, hence the two reads from t must yield the same value. Due to the barrier between $X.\mathsf{R}b_{,-}$ and the following read $X.\mathsf{R}t_{,-}$, and the barrier before $P_F.\mathsf{W}\beta_{n_F}$, we have:

$$\mathsf{W}\tau_{m_F} \xrightarrow{\mathsf{rf}} P_F.\mathsf{R}\tau_{m_F} \xrightarrow{\mathsf{sync}} \mathsf{W}\beta_{n_F} \xrightarrow{\mathsf{po\text{-}loc}} \mathsf{W}\beta_n \xrightarrow{\mathsf{rf}} X.\mathsf{R}\beta_n \xrightarrow{\mathsf{sync}} \mathsf{R}\tau_m$$

From Lemma 3 (ii), we have $\mathsf{W}\tau_{m_F} \xrightarrow{\mathsf{pp\text{-}sat}} X.\mathsf{R}\beta_n \xrightarrow{\mathsf{sync}} \mathsf{R}\tau_m$. It then follows from Lemma 3 (i) that $\mathsf{W}\tau_{m_F} \xrightarrow{\mathsf{pp\text{-}sat}} \mathsf{R}\tau_m$. Total order on CAS instructions and Lemma 2 (ii) guarantee that $\forall k < m_F, \mathsf{W}\tau_k \xrightarrow{\mathsf{co}} \mathsf{W}\tau_{m_F} \wedge \mathsf{W}\tau_k \xrightarrow{\mathsf{fr}} \mathsf{R}\tau_m$. Therefore, $m \geq m_F$. $\square$

Lemma 12. *Given X and Y distinct successful trailing instances of* take *or* steal, *then:* $\forall \mathsf{R}\xi_i^v \in X, \forall \mathsf{R}\xi_{i'}^{v'} \in Y, i \neq i'$.

Proof. Assume $i = i'$. According to Theorem 1, $v \neq v'$, hence there exist two distinct significant writes $\mathsf{W}\xi_i^v$ and $\mathsf{W}\xi_{i'}^{v'}$. Without loss of generality, let us assume $v < v'$; $P_F.\mathsf{W}\beta_{n_F}$ occurs after both writes, in program order. Furthermore, there is a cumulative barrier in *push* after each significant write, and before $P_F.\mathsf{W}\beta_{n_F}$. Since X reads from $P_F.\mathsf{W}\beta_{n_F}$, we have:

$$\mathsf{W}\xi_{i'}^{v'} \xrightarrow{\mathsf{sync}} P_F.\mathsf{W}\beta_{n_F} \xrightarrow{\mathsf{po\text{-}loc}} \mathsf{W}b_{,-} \xrightarrow{\mathsf{rf}} Y.\mathsf{R}b_{,-} \xrightarrow{\mathsf{dp}} \mathsf{R}\xi_i^v$$

Hence we have $\mathsf{W}\xi_{i'}^{v'} \xrightarrow{\mathsf{pp\text{-}sat}} Y.\mathsf{R}\xi_i^v$ from Lemma 3 (i) and Lemma 2 (iii). It then follows from Lemma 6 that $v' \leq v$; thus, $v < v' \leq v$. Impossible. $\square$

Corollary 3. *The combined number of successful trailing instances of* take *and* steal *is less than or equal to $\beta_{n_F} - \tau_{m_F}$.*

Proof. Let X be a successful trailing instance of *take* or *steal*, and $\mathsf{R}\beta_n \in X$ and $\mathsf{R}\tau_m \in X$. We know that $n \geq n_F$ (by definition) and $m \geq m_F$ (from Lemma 11). Hence $\tau_m \geq \tau_{m_F}$.

Furthermore, a *take* operation always contains one decrementing write to b (by one), which may be followed by one incrementing write to b (by one). Hence $n \geq n_F$ implies $\beta_n \leq \beta_{n_F}$.

Therefore, X can only read at an index i, s.t. $\tau_{m_F} \leq i < \beta_{n_F}$. Lemma 12 tells there can be no more than $\beta_{n_F} - \tau_{m_F}$ such X. $\square$

Lemma 13. *There is a finite number of successful (trailing or non-trailing) instances of* take *or* steal.

Proof. It follows from Corollary 3 that there is a finite number of successful trailing instances of *take* or *steal*.

Furthermore, there must be a finite number of non-trailing *take* operations, which come before P_F in program order.

Lastly, there is a finite number of *push* operations, thus (β_n) has a maximum, $\beta_{\max}$. Since two successful *steal* operations must read different values of t less than some value of b, there can be no more than $\beta_{\max}$ successful instances of *steal*.

Hence the finite number of successful instances of *take* or *steal*. $\square$

Lemma 14. *In each thread, there exists X a failed instance of* take *or* steal *s.t. $\forall \mathsf{R}\beta_n \in X, \forall \mathsf{R}\tau_m \in X, \beta_n \leq \tau_m$. Furthermore, each thread makes no more than $1 + m_F + \beta_{n_F} - \tau_{m_F}$ attempts at* take *or* steal *that result in a failed CAS instruction.[2]*

---

[2] Hence a thread eventually reaches a stationary state where $b = t$; it should be noted that the model does not guarantee progress; it is legal for a thread to end up looping on a non-final state where $b = t$ but $b \neq \beta_{n_F}$.

Proof. It follows from Lemma 13 that there is a finite number of successful instances, hence a finite number per thread. Thus, there must exist a failed instance of *take* or *steal*.

A failure can occur either because the deque is empty ($\beta_n \leq \tau_m$) or because of a failed CAS instruction. Suppose there is no X where $\beta_n \leq \tau_m$; then all failures must be due to a failed CAS instruction. A failed CAS occurs if the two values of t read during the instance X differ. Let Y_1 and Y_2 be two such failed instances executing in a same thread; let us assume that Y_2 follows Y_1 in program order, $n_1 \neq n_1'$ and $n_2 \neq n_2'$:

$$Y_1.R\tau_{n_1} \xrightarrow{\text{po-loc}} R\tau_{n_1'} \xrightarrow{\text{po-loc}} Y_2.R\tau_{n_2} \xrightarrow{\text{po-loc}} R\tau_{n_2'}$$

There exists a write $W\tau_{n_1'} \xrightarrow{\text{rf}} R\tau_{n_1'} \xrightarrow{\text{po-loc}} Y_2.R\tau_{n_2}$. Due to Lemma 2 (i), we have $W\tau_{n_1'} \xrightarrow{\text{pp-sat}} Y_2.R\tau_{n_2}$, and, as in the proof of Lemma 11, we deduce that $n_1' \leq n_2$.

Since $n_1 \neq n_1' \wedge n_2 \neq n_2'$, and t is monotonically increasing, it must be that $n_1 < n_1' \leq n_2 < n_2'$. Hence successive CAS-failing instances in a same thread read increasing values of t. It follows from Corollary 3 that t takes no more than $1 + m_F + \beta_{n_F} - \tau_{m_F}$ different values.

Therefore, there can be no more than $1 + m_F + \beta_{n_F} - \tau_{m_F}$ CAS-failing instances of *take* or *steal* per thread. Since there is also a finite number of successful such instances, any further *take* or *steal* operations must return empty, and the thread reaches its stationary point. □

Corollary 4. *The combined number of successful (trailing or not) instances of* take *and* steal *is equal to the number of* push.

Proof. A successful instance of *take* either decreases the value of b by one or increases the value of t by one; a successful instance of *steal* increases the value of t by one. An instance of *push* increases the value of b by one.

It follows from the previous lemma that the worker thread reaches a stationary point where $b = t$. Clearly, this cannot occur before all *push* operations and all successful instances of *take* have occurred.

Since $b = t$ at the stationary point and all increases to b precede, the sum of increases to t and decreases to b (the combined number of successful instances of *take* and *steal*) must be at least equal to the number of increases to b (the number of *push* operations). It is exactly equal, as otherwise there would be more significant reads than significant writes, which is impossible according to Theorem 1. □

One may finally prove Theorem 2. On the one hand, Corollary 4 tells that the number of significant reads (from a successful instance of *take* or *steal*) is equal to the number of significant writes (from an instance of *push*). On the other hand, Theorem 1 states that significant reads uniquely map to significant writes. By injectivity, there exists a unique significant read for each significant write.

5. On the C11 implementation

The sequentially consistent implementation is a direct translation of the original algorithm using C11 *seq_cst* atomic variables for all shared accesses. It is obtained from the code in Figure 1 by replacing all memory order constants with *seq_cst*; doing so makes fences unnecessary, hence they should be removed.

The optimized C11 implementation improves upon the previous version by replacing sequential consistency with release–acquire pairs where appropriate. It establishes happens-before relations between reads and writes, as required by the proof. Unfortunately, without relying on *seq_cst*, using only *release*, *acquire* and *consume* operations, we were unable to reproduce the required memory ordering constraints needed on the POWER and ARMv7 architectures while adhering to C11 semantics.

Although designed for ARMv7/POWER, most of the arguments developed in the proof informally translate to the rules of C11 in a straightforward fashion. In all cases that do not involve cumulativity, the $\xrightarrow{\text{pp-sat}}$ relation (defined in 4.1) combined with dependences, which form the core of the ARMv7/POWER proof, may be replaced with analogous properties pertaining to the C11 happens-before relation combined with release–acquire semantics. The one notable difference between the two models lies in the absence of cumulativity in the design of the C11 abstract machine: neither C11

fences nor C11 atomic accesses guarantee cumulativity. A similar effect can be achieved by chaining alternating release–acquire writes and reads, which form a happens-before path. But this device does not work in situations where propagation needs to be asserted between two reads, rather than a read followed by a write.[3] This situation occurs in the *steal* operation. Informally (see Lemma 10 for the formal description), it must be that two concurrent *steal* and *take* do not read "old" values of both bottom and top, where "old" could be defined as "older than the value known to the other party in coherence order". The presence of the two cumulative barriers in *steal* and *take* on ARMv7 guarantee such a condition:

- if the *take* barrier is ordered before the barrier in *steal*, then the program-order-previous write to *bottom* will be propagated to the instance of *steal*;
- conversely, if the *steal* barrier is ordered before the barrier in *take*, then value read by the program-order-previous read from top will be propagated to the instance of *take*.

In the second case, it is important to remark that the write that produced the value read in *steal* might belong to another thread, and thus not be sequenced before the barrier. In the absence of cumulativity, it need not be propagated to the instance of *take*.

To enforce this particular case of cumulativity in C11, we rely on the properties of sequential consistency. By making all writes (actually, CAS operations) to top sequentially consistent, we ensure that there is a total ordering between the two fences (in *take* and *steal*) and the write that produced the value of top read in the instance of *steal*. Furthermore, if that read uses *acquire* semantics, then there is a happens-before relation between it and the *steal* barrier. Hence, the write must come before said barrier in *sequential consistency total order*. Then, either the barrier in *steal* is ordered before the barrier in *take*, or the other way around:

- if the *steal* barrier is ordered before the barrier in *take*, then it follows from *seq_cst* barrier semantics that the value of top read by *take* cannot be older than the one read in *steal*;[4]
- conversely, if the *take* barrier is ordered before the one in *steal*, then the value of bottom read by *steal* cannot be older than the one written in *take*.[5]

6. Experimental results

We present experimental results on three current and widely used architectures: (1) a Tegra 3 ARMv7 processor rev 9 (v7l) with 4 cores at 1.3GHz and 1GB of RAM; (2) an Intel Core i7-2720QM machine with 4 cores (hyper-threading disabled) at 2.2GHz and 4GB of RAM; and (3) a dual-socket AMD Opteron Magny-Cours 6164HE machine with 2×12 cores at 1.7GHz and 16GB of RAM.

All tests were compiled with GCC 4.7.0, the first release of GCC to introduce built-in support for C11 atomics.

6.1 Synthetic benchmarks

We designed a synthetic benchmark to simulate the depth-first traversal of a balanced tree—with breadth b and depth d—of empty tasks by a main worker thread, reproducing the prototypical execution of a Cilk program. One or more thieves attempt to steal these tasks. For robustness and predictability, the worker always creates

---

[3] C11 defines a happens-before relation, which does not fully encapsulate the notion of cumulativity. The only inter-thread edges in happens-before come from write–read pairs with release–acquire semantics (see [6] 5.1.2.4p11 and p16). In the absence of a write instruction, no fence or other operation can propagate accumulated information to another thread—in other words, it is not possible to establish a happens-before path between two reads in different threads without an intervening write. Hence the reliance on *seq_cst* primitives, enforcing a *sequentially consistent total order*.

[4] See [6] 7.17.3p9.

[5] See [6] 7.17.3p11.

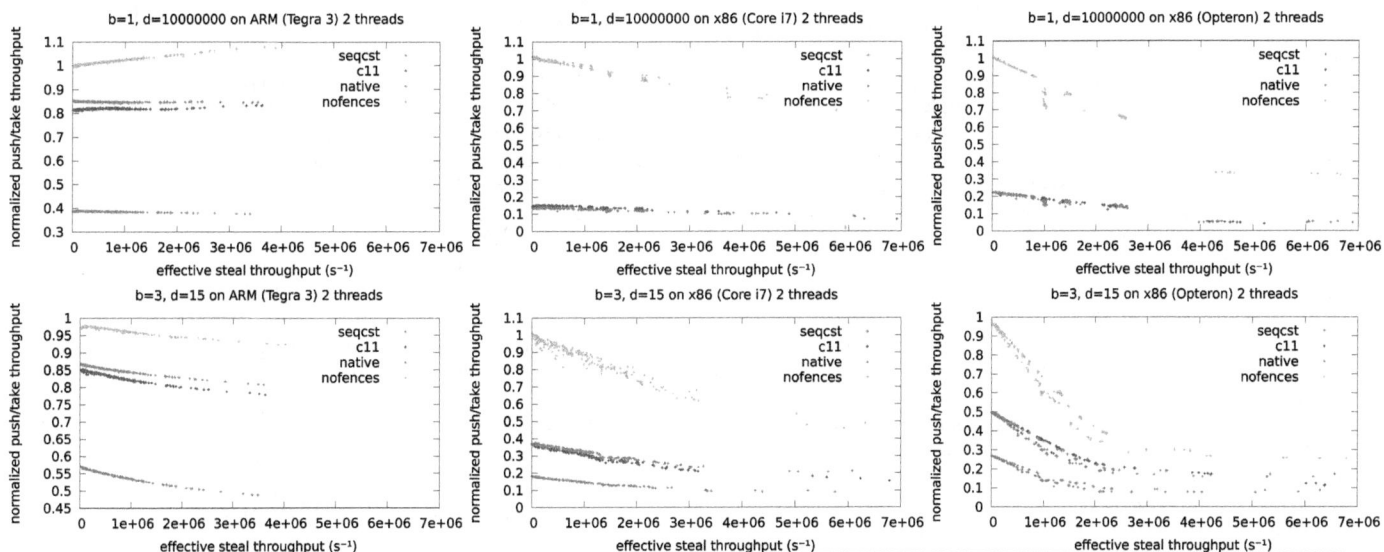

Figure 3. Synthetic single-thief benchmarks

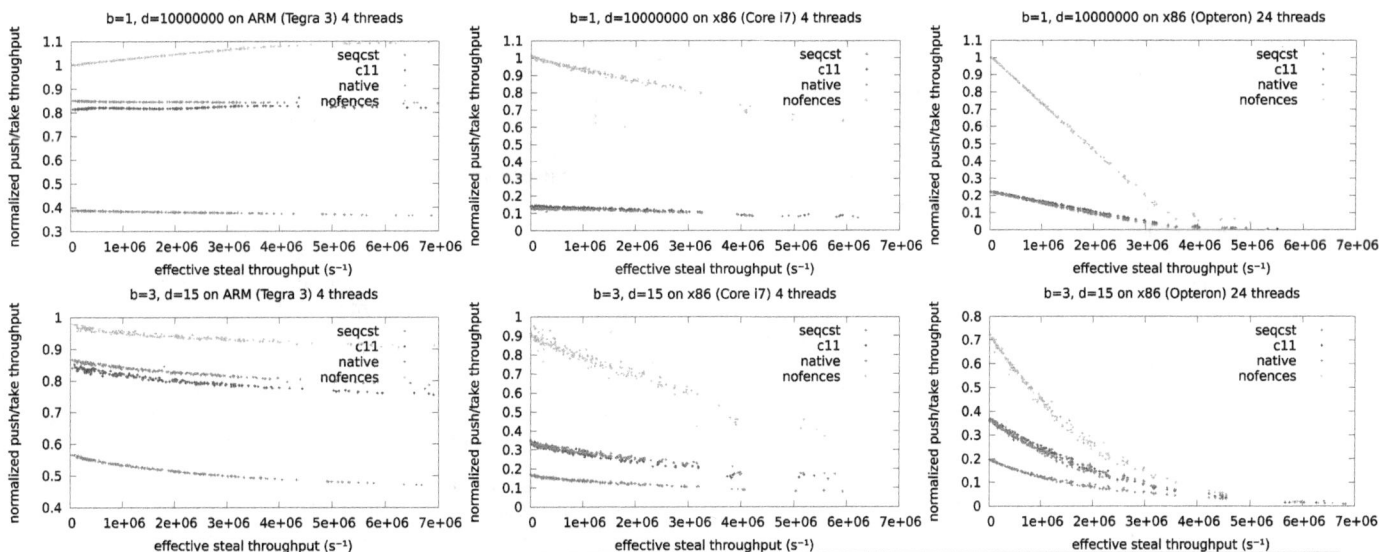

Figure 4. Synthetic multi-thief benchmarks

and pushes the same number of tasks in the deque, following the depth-first pattern, regardless of whether a specific continuation has been stolen by another thread (it is simply recorded as stolen, but subsequent tasks spawn normally and locally). The thieves perform *steal* actions at a configurable rate, and discard stolen tasks.

We have experimented with two different methods of *steal* distribution, the goal being to uniformly spread the contention over the entire life of the worker thread. The first method is based on the CPU clock of the core dedicated to each thief; with this technique, the clock is regularly sampled and the appropriate number of *steal* operations is performed accordingly. The second method relies on a random number generator, called in a busy loop, which allows *steal* operations with a set probability. While the clock-based approach produces more reliable results, it can only be used if a low-overhead CPU clock is available from user space, which is unfortunately not

the case on our ARM-based system.[6] Conversely, the second technique suffers from imprecision when targeting smaller ranges of frequencies, which is necessary on faster processors or when the number of cores increases.[7] Hence, the former is used on x86 and the latter on ARMv7, with appropriate empirical tuning to gather results over a common representative range of steal throughput.

We selected two workloads: a reasonably broad tree ($b = 3$; $d = 15$) and, as a special case, a degenerate comb-shaped tree ($b = 1$; $d = 10^7$). The former is meant to reproduce normal contention with *steal* operations alongside both *push* and *take*, while the latter illustrates a case of contention between *take* and *steal* only.

------

[6] The ARMv7 C15 cycle counter register can only be queried if first enabled from kernel mode, and is delegated to a monitoring co-processor, with unclear consequences for the bus, caches, and memory model as a whole.

[7] On higher end processors with multiple cores acting as thieves, higher steal probabilities can yield many times more steal attempts than there are tasks created over a set period.

We measure the time taken by the worker thread to complete the specified number of task creations and consumptions. This in turn serves to compute the *push/take* throughput—the combined number of of *push* and *take* operations completed per unit of time, as well as the *effective steal* throughput, defined as follows: the test protocol strives to perform a number of steals over time, at a fixed, nominal steal throughput; the *effective* throughput is the real throughput as could be observed after the experiment, i.e., how many steals were actually performed during the lifetime of the worker thread. These metrics provide a measure of the efficiency of the algorithm on its critical path at various levels of contention.

In order to assess the impact of the added barriers on the different architectures, raw throughput values have been normalized by the near-ideal throughput on the same workload (see Table 2), obtained on a single thread with no contention and no synchronization: memory barriers are replaced with simple compiler fences, and CAS operations with a simple branch and conditional assignment. These numbers provide a good approximation of the upper bound on the achievable throughput on each machine, though other minor factors can contribute to higher observable values. In particular, it should be noted that counting the throughput in number of operations per second is, by design, a generalization: the execution time of each operation depends on its nature and the exact control path taken; for example, an invocation of *take* returning empty will be faster than one returning a task.

In all diagrams, we have included a set of points labeled *nofences*, for comparison purposes. These correspond to the least common denominator among all the tested barrier placement strategies: only relaxed CAS operations are included, with otherwise no memory barriers. The *nofences* version violates the semantics of the work-stealing deque. Each of our proposed implementations of the algorithm can be seen as adding a different set of barriers to *nofences*, making it correct. Hence, results obtained with *nofences* should be taken as no more than a general baseline, as the complete lack of fences can lead to unexpected behavior. For instance, Figures 3 and 4 show greater throughput values at high contention for the comb-shaped workload on ARM. Those are the results of a long tail of fast empty *take* operations, an artifact due to the nature of the comb-shaped test and the absence of synchronization between empty *take* and *steal* (enabled by the lack of barriers in *take*).[8]

	$b=1; d=10^7$	$b=3; d=15$
Core i7 (2 threads)	4.87862×10^8	3.60838×10^8
Opteron (2 threads)	2.55142×10^8	2.04978×10^8
Tegra 3 (2 threads)	5.47223×10^7	4.12112×10^7
Core i7 (4 threads)	4.88018×10^8	3.66404×10^8
Opteron (24 threads)	2.56214×10^8	2.03235×10^8
Tegra 3 (4 threads)	5.48473×10^7	4.11242×10^7

Table 2. Near-ideal throughput (s^{-1})

All the results based on the mixed *push* and *take* "tree" workload show a marked improvement of the hand-written *native* and *c11* versions over the naive sequentially consistent translation of the original Chase–Lev algorithm, *seqcst*. While the relative gain remains stable at all levels of contention on the Core i7 and Tegra 3, it drops sharply on the Opteron, presumably because of the higher number of cores. Nevertheless, for low values, which more closely model realistic scenarios, the optimized implementations perform at least 1.5 times better than *seqcst* on both x86 and ARM.

Comparing x86 and ARM, we note that a higher relative throughput is achieved on ARM (peak at above 85%) than on x86

(peak at above 50%), indicating that the first serializing instruction introduced in the code is very costly on x86, especially if it is added to the critical path (as is the case in *native*, *c11* and *seqcst*, but not in *nofences*). This could suggest either the stronger guarantees of the x86 memory model—a full memory fence is required to linearize history in order to maintain *total store order* [13]—or aggressive local optimizations for single-thread execution without communication.

From these observations, we can postulate that advanced ARM architectures such as the Tegra 3 benefit the most from a well-written concurrent program that takes full advantage of the flexibility allowed by their memory model, and conversely struggle relatively more with literal interpretations of algorithms designed with stricter, simpler hypotheses in mind.

6.2 Task-parallel benchmarks

We further experiment on common task-parallel benchmarks, mostly extracted from the Cilk benchmark suite,[9] to evaluate the impact of the memory barrier optimization on realistic workloads and load-balancing scenarios.

Fibonacci is the tree-recursive computation of the 35th Fibonacci number; it illustrates the raw cost of the scheduling algorithm as each task only performs a single addition.

FFT-1D computes the Cooley-Tukey fast Fourier transform over a vector of 2^{20} elements.

Matmul is the blocked matrix multiplication, of size 256×256 on the Tegra 3 and Core i7 platforms, and of size 384×384 on Opteron to ensure a sufficient computation time.

Strassen is an optimized matrix multiplication algorithm, running on matrices of size 512×512 on the Tegra 3 and Core i7 platforms, and of size 2048×2048 on Opteron.

Knapsack is the usual resource allocation problem. A set of objects, each with a given weight and value, must be picked from a pool to fit a total weight constraint while maximizing value. We use 33 objects.

Seidel simulates heat transfer using the Gauss-Seidel method which iterates a 5-point stencil over an two-dimensional array. We used a resolution of 1024×1024 points with 20 iterations.

We compare the four implementations of the Chase–Lev deque presented in Section 2. The sequentially consistent, direct translation to C11 serves as a baseline to measure the speedups obtained with the three other implementations. We observe that the *nofences* version is inherently incorrect and generally results in erroneous executions. This version is only presented as a rough upper-bound on the performance gains of memory barrier optimization.

Figure 5 shows similar trends to the balanced tree synthetic kernel, with a clear advantage to the two optimized implementations (*native* and *c11*) over the *seqcst* baseline. *Fibonacci*, *FFT-1D*, *Matmul* and *Strassen* use a recursive divide-and-conquer pattern, leading to balanced binary trees. They appear in increasing order of granularity, ranging from a single addition to the multiplication of matrix blocks of size 16×16. On *Fibonacci*, the lowest granularity kernel, the results are very similar to the throughput achieved by the synthetic benchmark: the optimized versions show up to $1.19\times$ speedup on the Tegra 3 platform against the *seqcst* version, $1.3\times$ on Core i7 and up to $1.13\times$ on Opteron. These speedups gradually decrease as granularity increases, hiding the cost of the scheduling deque. Yet we still observe significant speedups on the *Matmul* kernel, with a granularity of 64 (vector) multiply-add operations per task: we obtain up to $1.03\times$ speedup on Tegra 3,[10] $1.1\times$ on Core

---

[8] In the case where the deque is empty, neither *take* nor *steal* needs to execute a CAS instruction; furthermore, in the absence of barriers, the ARMv7 memory model does not require successive decrements and increments of *bottom* in *take* to propagate to the thieves.

[9] http://supertech.csail.mit.edu/cilk

[10] The $0.95\times$ slowdown for the *native* version is a compiler artifact related with the usage of inline assembly.

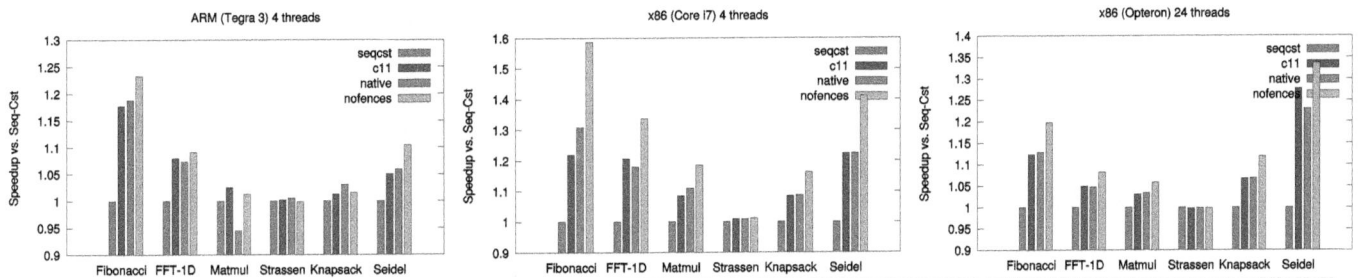

Figure 5. Task-parallel benchmark speedups against the C11 sequentially consistent baseline

i7 and 1.04× on Opteron. On *Strassen*, the largest granularity kernel, we no longer observe any significant improvement: the deque operations are entirely hidden by the work performed in each task.

The *Knapsack* kernel is also based on a divide-and-conquer pattern, yet it does not result in a balanced tree because of the non-deterministic, dynamic pruning of sub-optimal branches. Unsynchronized communications are used to share the best total value reached on any branch; this value is used to stop exploring branches known to represent sub-optimal prefixes. The *nofences* version shows lower performance, on Tegra 3, than our optimized *c11* and *native* versions because of longer delays until the best value is propagated to all cores, resulting in less pruning and more work. The performance improvement is reduced on this benchmark because additional barriers improve the accuracy on the current best value.

Finally, the *Seidel* kernel iterates on skewed wave-fronts of data-parallel tasks. A single main thread is responsible for spawning every task in a wave-front. It en-queues all tasks on its own work-stealing deque until it reaches a synchronization barrier. This scheme relies on stealing exclusively for the distribution of work among cores. This behavior puts a lot of strain on a particular deque, and induces a high level of contention. This explains the high performance gains of our optimized implementations on the 24-core Opteron platform: up to 1.3× speedup against the *seqcst* baseline, even higher than the speedups observed at a lower granularity on *Fibonacci*. However, despite its somewhat low granularity, corresponding to 16 additions and 4 multiplications of double precision floating point values per task, this benchmark only shows up to 1.05× improvement from our optimized versions on the Tegra 3 platform and up to 1.2× speedup on the Core i7. This is in line with the equivalent speedups observed for the similar granularity on *FFT-1D*, as the low number of cores on these platforms induce much less contention compared to the Opteron configuration.

Interestingly, our experiments show that the performance of our optimized versions is very close to the *nofences* version on the Tegra 3 platform. This validates our hypothesis about the benefits of an implementation that takes full advantage of the ARM relaxed memory model, rather than translating the classical sequentially consistent algorithm. Furthermore, the large performance gains on the two x86 platforms show that even in the case of stricter memory models such as *total store order* [13], relying on sequentially consistent algorithms represents a significant source of overhead.

7. Conclusion

We provided optimized implementations of Chase and Lev's concurrent deque, targeting the weak memory models of the POWER and ARM processors, as well as the C11 standard. Based on recent progress in the formalization of memory consistency, we established the first proof of the Chase–Lev deque for the weak memory model of a real-world processor. This paves the way for robust parallel library and programming language implementations based on a work-stealing scheduler.

Comparing our optimized implementation with portable C11 versions, we observed unrecoverable overheads in the interaction between atomic operations and the non-cumulativity of memory barriers in C11, a slight mismatch with the POWER and ARM memory models. We obtained strong performance gains on ARM and x86, and performance levels comparable to an (incorrect) fence-free version. This indicates that a high-throughput scheduler can be implemented efficiently on a weak memory model such as a multicore ARM, benefiting from its scalability and energy savings.

Acknowledgments This work was partly supported by the European FP7 projects PHARAON id. 288307 and TERAFLUX id. 249013, and by ANR grant ANR-11-JS02-011.

References

[1] C. Augonnet, S. Thibault, R. Namyst, and P.-A. Wacrenier. StarPU: A Unified Platform for Task Scheduling on Heterogeneous Multicore Architectures. In *Euro-Par*, 2009.

[2] R. D. Blumofe and C. E. Leiserson. Scheduling multithreaded computations by work stealing. *J. ACM*, 46(5):720–748, 1999.

[3] D. Chase and Y. Lev. Dynamic circular work-stealing deque. In *SPAA*, 2005.

[4] M. Frigo, C. E. Leiserson, and K. H. Randall. The implementation of the Cilk-5 multithreaded language. In *PLDI*, 1998.

[5] T. Gautier, X. Besseron, and L. Pigeon. KAAPI: A thread scheduling runtime system for data flow computations on cluster of multiprocessors. In *PASCO*, 2007.

[6] JTC1/SC22/WG14. *Programming languages – C, Committee Draft*. ISO/IEC, Apr. 2011.

[7] S. Mador-Haim, L. Maranget, S. Sarkar, K. Memarian, J. Alglave, S. Owens, R. Alur, M. M. K. Martin, P. Sewell, and D. Williams. An Axiomatic Memory Model for POWER Multiprocessors. In *CAV*, 2012.

[8] L. Maranget, S. Sarkar, and P. Sewell. A tutorial introduction to the ARM and POWER relaxed memory model, 2012. Draft. http://www.cl.cam.ac.uk/~pes20/ppc-supplemental/test7.pdf.

[9] P. E. McKenney and R. Silvera, 2011. http://www.rdrop.com/users/paulmck/scalability/!paper/N2745r.2011.03.04a.html.

[10] M. M. Michael, M. T. Vechev, and V. A. Saraswat. Idempotent work stealing. In *PPOPP*, 2009.

[11] S. Sarkar, K. Memarian, S. Owens, M. Batty, P. Sewell, L. Maranget, J. Alglave, and D. Williams. Synchronising C/C++ and POWER. In *PLDI*, 2012.

[12] S. Sarkar, P. Sewell, J. Alglave, L. Maranget, and D. Williams. Understanding POWER multiprocessors. In *PLDI*, 2011.

[13] P. Sewell, S. Sarkar, S. Owens, F. Zappa Nardelli, and M. O. Myreen. x86-TSO: a rigorous and usable programmer's model for x86 multiprocessors. *Commun. ACM*, 53(7):89–97, 2010.

[14] A. Terekhov. Brief tentative example x86 implementation for C/C++ memory model, 2008. http://www.decadent.org.uk/pipermail/~cpp-threads/2008-December/001933.html.

Data-Only Flattening for Nested Data Parallelism

Lars Bergstrom
John Reppy
Stephen Rosen
Adam Shaw

University of Chicago
{larsberg,jhr,sirosen,ams}@cs.uchicago.edu

Matthew Fluet

Rochester Institute of Technology
mtf@cs.rit.edu

Mike Rainey

Max Planck Institute for
Software Systems
mrainey@mpi-sws.org

Abstract

Data parallelism has proven to be an effective technique for high-level programming of a certain class of parallel applications, but it is not well suited to irregular parallel computations. Blelloch and others proposed *nested data parallelism* (NDP) as a language mechanism for programming irregular parallel applications in a declarative data-parallel style. The key to this approach is a compiler transformation that *flattens* the NDP computation and data structures into a form that can be executed efficiently on a wide-vector SIMD architecture. Unfortunately, this technique is ill suited to execution on today's multicore machines. We present a new technique, called *data-only flattening*, for the compilation of NDP, which is suitable for multicore architectures. Data-only flattening transforms nested data structures in order to expose programs to various optimizations while leaving control structures intact. We present a formal semantics of data-only flattening in a core language with a rewriting system. We demonstrate the effectiveness of this technique in the Parallel ML implementation and we report encouraging experimental results across various benchmark applications.

Categories and Subject Descriptors D.3.0 [*Programming Languages*]: General; D.3.2 [*Programming Languages*]: Language Classifications – Applicative (Functional) Programming, Concurrent, distributed, and parallel languages; D.3.4 [*Programming Languages*]: Processors – Compilers, Optimization

Keywords multicore, NESL, nested data parallelism, compilers

1. Introduction

Data-parallel computations are ones in which a function is applied to the elements of a collection (e.g., set or sequence) in parallel. Data parallelism is an effective technique to take advantage of parallel hardware and is especially suited to large-scale parallelism [10], but most languages that support data parallelism limit that support to *flat data parallelism* (FDP), where the computation being mapped over the collection does not contain nested parallel computation. While FDP is very effective for many regular-parallel applications, it is not well-suited for irregular parallel ap-

plications. To address this weakness, Blelloch and others proposed *nested data parallelism* (NDP) [4, 5, 8, 20].

The basic operation in both flat and nested data parallelism is the *parallel map operation*, which applies a function to the elements of a collection in parallel. What distinguishes NDP from FDP is that elements of the collection may themselves be collections, and the mapped computation may itself involve parallel maps over the nested collections. Because the nested collections in an NDP computation may vary in size, it is difficult to ensure a balanced partitioning of work across multiple processors and it is difficult to execute the parallel computation with Single-Instruction-Multiple-Data (SIMD) architectures.

Blelloch addressed these challenges with an approach that he called *flattening*. Flattening (also called *vectorisation*) is a technique for converting irregular nested computations into regular computations on flat arrays. This approach, which was invented for first-order NDP by Sabot and Blelloch [2, 5] and extended to full-featured higher-order functional languages by Keller, Chakravarty, and others [7, 8, 14, 16], transforms both the data representations and the code so that the computation can be executed by a SIMD machine. An alternative approach, which is used in the Manticore system, is to execute the parallel map operations as fork-join parallelism and to rely on efficient work-stealing techniques to handle load balancing [1, 23].

In this paper, we introduce a new approach to implementing NDP constructs that is based on the idea of flattening the nested data representations, but not vectorising the code [25]. In our prototype implementation, we build on the Manticore compiler for PML [11], a parallel dialect of Standard ML [17].

This paper makes the following contributions:

1. We introduce a novel approach to implementing NDP that is well suited to execution on MIMD architectures, such as modern multicore processors.

2. We provide a formalization of our approach using a core calculus.

3. We present empirical evidence that our approach improves the performance of code that executes over irregular data while also preserving performance on regular data.

2. Full flattening for NDP

As a motivating example, consider the NDP code to implement sparse-matrix times dense-vector multiplication. We represent a dense vector as a parallel array of floating-point values:

```
type dense_vec = float parray
```

and a sparse vector is a parallel array of index-value pairs:

$$\begin{bmatrix} 0.0 & 0.0 & 0.0 & 0.1 & 0.0 \\ 0.0 & 0.2 & 0.3 & 0.0 & 0.0 \\ 0.0 & 0.4 & 0.5 & 0.6 & 0.7 \\ 0.8 & 0.0 & 0.0 & 0.9 & 0.0 \end{bmatrix}$$

(a) a matrix

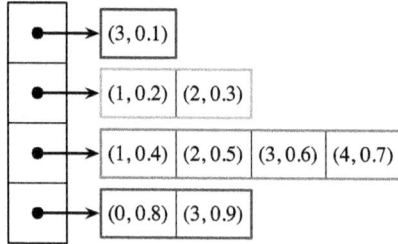

(b) its sparse representation

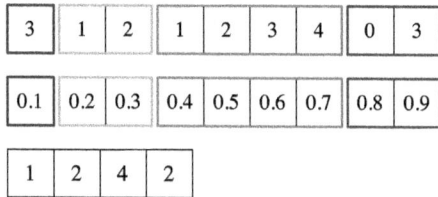

(c) its flat representation

Figure 1. Representations of a sparse matrix

```
type sparse_vec = (int * float) parray
```

In this representation, we record only the non-zero entries of the vector, paired with their indices. A sparse matrix is a parallel array of sparse vectors:

```
type sparse_mat = sparse_vec parray
```

Figure 1(a) and (b) illustrate a matrix and its sparse representation.

The sumP operator is a parallel reduction that computes the sum of the elements of a parallel array of floats:

```
val sumP : float parray -> float
```

We define multiplying a dense vector by a sparse-matrix as the following high-level NDP function:

```
fun smvm (sm : sparse_mat, v : dense_vec) =
  [| sumP [| x * v!i | (i,x) in sv |] | sv in sm |]
```

The technical challenge is to find the meeting point between this elegant declarative code and an efficient implementation that can exploit powerful multicore architectures.

As one solution to this challenge, Blelloch and Sabot introduced the NESL language and the *flattening transformation* to compile nested-data-parallel programs for wide-vector parallel machines [2, 5]. NESL is an ML-like language with nested-data-parallel features. NESL's provides only scalars and associated operators, sequences, simple datatypes, conditionals, let bindings, top-level function definitions, and a parallel *apply-to-each* construct. Blelloch's flattening transformation then substantially changes both the data structures and code. This transformation is especially effective in treating irregular parallelism: certain operations like the parallel *segmented sum* operation, where sums are computed over an array of arrays of numbers, complete in the same number of steps regardless of the irregularity of the shapes of the segments.

```
datatype 'a rope
  = Leaf of 'a seq
  | Cat of 'a rope * 'a rope

datatype shape
  = Lf of int * int
  | Nd of shape rope

datatype 'a farray
  = FArray of 'a rope * shape
```

Figure 2. Datatypes rope, shape and farray.

The flattening transformation yields flattened arrays consisting of two components: one or more flat data vectors (more than one in the case of unzipped tuples), containing the elements of the nested array in left-to-right order, and one or more *segment-descriptors*. In NESL, a segment-descriptor is always a flat vector of integers, and a flattened array carries with it one segment-descriptor for each level of nesting. Figure 1(c) illustrates the flat representation of the example sparse matrix.

2.1 Challenges for full flattening

Full flattening, while a successful innovation, can produce inefficient code in common cases, including conditionals and certain regular nested parallel programs.

When full flattening is applied to conditionals, the resulting code generates many intermediate vectors, as we demonstrate here in a simplified example. Here is a function that replaces the zeroes in a vector with ones:

```
fun g (xs : dense_vec) =
  [| if x=0.0 then 1.0 else x | x in xs |]
```

The transformed code (which uses standard split and combine operations [2]) builds intermediate vectors to handle partitioning the data elements, performs the appropriate conditional work on each partition of the data, and then combines them:

```
fun g_full_flat (xs : dense_vec) = let
  val flags = [| x=0.0 | x in xs |]
  val (zs, nzs) = split (xs, flags)
  val zs' = [| 1.0 | z in zs |]
in
  combine (zs', nzs, flags)
end
```

This approach makes sense for SIMD architectures with large penalties for failing to keep the vector registers full, but on multicore machines those benefits can be overwhelmed by the large number of memory operations. There are many more extended examples of this kind of transformation in the literature [2, 13]. Our approach, by contrast, will transform g to operate on a flattened dense vector, but will not otherwise transform the code; to the point, it will not necessitate generating any intermediates.

With respect to regular nested parallel programs, problems similar to dense matrix multiplication suffer from a polynomial space increase under full flattening, which is a known serious problem [26] also due to excessive data copying. The present work describes a system designed to address these problems with traditional full flattening by avoiding extra data copies, both due to splitting of conditional branches and duplication of vectors within nested parallel applications.

3. Data-Only Flattening

We present data-only flattening in the context of a broader system for *hybrid flattening*. Hybrid flattening is a program representation that allows both flat and nested representations of parallel arrays and which has coercions for transforming between representations.

This representation allows flexibility in choosing when it is profitable to use a flat representation vs. a nested representation. Hybrid flattening does not itself express or embody a particular transformation policy.

Whereas Manticore without flattening compiles nested parallel arrays to nested ropes [6], with flattening it compiles nested parallel arrays to flattened arrays. Flattened arrays, like nested arrays as compiled by NESL, consist of two pieces: a flat data vector, and a value representing the structure of the nested array called a *shape tree*. By means of standard unzipping transformations, nested arrays of tuples are compiled to tuples of flattened arrays. In our implementation, flattened arrays are represented by the polymorphic `farray` datatype. To represent the flat data vector part of flattened arrays, we use ropes, exploiting Manticore's existing rope infrastructure to compute in parallel with them. Figure 2 presents the PML datatype definitions for `rope`, `shape`, for shape trees, and `farray`. Note that ropes and shape trees are internal representations; the programmer uses them only indirectly.

Shape trees are our adaptation of segment descriptors in the NESL tradition. A `shape` is an n-ary tree whose leaves store integer pairs. Each leaf contains the starting index and the index of the element following the segment of data in an `farray`. The shape `Shape.Lf (i, i+n)` describes a length-n segment starting at i and ending at the last position before $i+n$.[1]

A simple, flat parallel array of integers such as

$$[| \; 1, \; 2, \; 3 \; |]$$

has the following `farray` representation:[2]

```
FArray (Rope.Leaf [1,2,3], Shape.Lf (0,3))
```

The data in the original sequence appears here in the original order as a `Rope.Leaf` and the accompanying `shape` indicates that the flattened array's only segment begins at position 0 and ends at position 2.

Nested parallel arrays are translated as follows. Consider the following nested array:

$$[| \; [| \; 1, \; 2 \; |], \; [| \; |], \; [| \; 3, \; 4, \; 5, \; 6 \; |] \; |]$$

Its flattened array representation is the following:

```
FArray (Rope.Leaf [1,2,3,4,5,6],
        Shape.Nd [Shape.Lf (0,2),
                  Shape.Lf (2,2),
                  Shape.Lf (2,6)])
```

The flat data appears in order in a `Rope.Leaf`. The shape is a `Nd` with three leaves: this means that the parallel array consists of three subsequences. The leaves tell us that the first sequence begins at position 0 and ends at 1, the second sequence is empty at position 2, and the third sequence begins at position 2 and ends at 5. This representation naturally scales to any nesting depth.

Literal values can be flattened at transformation time directly, with the representation change incurring no runtime cost. In general, however, the compiler must cope with arbitrarily nested arrays whose dimensions are known only at runtime. In such cases, the compiler needs to arrange for flattening to take place at runtime. We handle this issue, by inserting coercion operators that perform runtime flattening. When nested arrays are transformed into flattened arrays, all operations applied to those array values must be correspondingly transformed. Our approach to this problem is to provide a core group of type-indexed families of array operators, each of which performs its operation at every array type in its family.

---

[1] In practice, this choice of bounds is a convenient convention that guards against common fencepost errors.

[2] For brevity, we present the sequence in the `Rope.Leaf` node and the sequence of leaves in the `Shape.Nd` with list syntax.

$$
\begin{array}{llll}
\tau & ::= & g & \textit{ground types} \\
 & | & (\tau, \tau) & \textit{pairs} \\
 & | & \tau \rightarrow \tau & \textit{functions} \\
 & | & [\tau] & \textit{parallel arrays} \\
 & | & \{\tau \; ; \; \nu\} & \textit{flattened parallel arrays} \\
 & & & \\
\nu & ::= & \textit{lf} & \textit{structure of flat arrays} \\
 & | & nd(\nu) & \textit{structure of nested arrays} \\
 & & & \\
g & ::= & int \mid bool & \\
\end{array}
$$

Figure 3. Flatland: types.

$$
\begin{array}{llll}
t & ::= & e^\tau & \\
 & & & \\
e & ::= & b & \textit{ground terms} \\
 & | & x & \textit{variables} \\
 & | & \textbf{if } t \textbf{ then } t \textbf{ else } t & \textit{conditionals} \\
 & | & \textbf{let } x = t \textbf{ in } t & \textit{let expressions} \\
 & | & \textbf{fun } f\,x^\tau = t \textbf{ in } t & \textit{function expressions} \\
 & | & t \circ t & \textit{function composition} \\
 & | & t \; t & \textit{application} \\
 & | & (t, t) & \textit{pairs} \\
 & | & \pi_i \, t & \textit{projection } (i \in \{1, 2\}) \\
 & | & [t, \ldots, t] & \textit{arrays} \\
 & | & \{t, \ldots, t; s\} & \textit{flattened arrays} \\
 & | & t \,!_\tau\, t & \textit{array subscript} \\
 & | & \textbf{map}_{(\tau,\tau,\tau)} \, (t, t) & \textit{array map} \\
 & | & \textbf{filt}_{(\tau,\tau)} \, (t, t) & \textit{array filter} \\
 & | & \textbf{red}_{(\tau,\tau)} \, (t, t, t) & \textit{array reduction} \\
 & | & \tau \triangleright \tau & \textit{type coercions} \\
 & & & \\
s & ::= & \textbf{lf}(t, t) & \textit{leaves} \\
 & | & \textbf{nd}[s, \ldots, s] & \textit{nodes} \\
 & & & \\
b & ::= & \text{true} \mid \text{false} & \\
 & | & 0 \mid 1 \mid \ldots & \\
 & | & \text{not} \mid + \mid \ldots & \\
\end{array}
$$

Figure 4. Flatland: terms.

This group contains parallel array subscripting and parallel maps, filters, and reductions over parallel arrays. All operations on parallel arrays are either members of this core group or are built from members of this group. As such, transformation of the type-indexed operators matching the transformations of data structures is sufficient to preserve the program's behavior.

4. Formalization

The system presented here, *Flatland*, consists of a model language and a variety of rewriting systems and judgments. Its model language is an explicitly-typed, monomorphic, strict, pure functional language. Flattened and non-flattened terms commingle in Flatland: there is no inherent distinction between source language and target language.

Figure 3 presents Flatland's types, ranged over by the metavariable τ. We use subscript indices (τ_i) and overbars ($\bar{\tau}$) to distinguish types from one another. The type language consists of ground types *int* and *bool*, pairs, functions, parallel arrays, and flattened parallel arrays. Flattened-parallel types include *shape types* as subcomponents. Shape types, ranged over by the metavariable ν (for "nesting"), record an array's nesting depth.

$$\frac{\Gamma(x) = \tau}{\Gamma \vdash x^\tau\ ok} \qquad \frac{BE(b) = \tau \quad (BE = \text{basis env})}{\Gamma \vdash b^\tau\ ok}$$

$$\frac{\Gamma \vdash e_1{}^{bool}\ ok \quad \Gamma \vdash e_2{}^\tau\ ok \quad \Gamma \vdash e_3{}^\tau\ ok}{\Gamma \vdash (\textbf{if } e_1{}^{bool}\ \textbf{then } e_2{}^\tau\ \textbf{else } e_3{}^\tau)^\tau\ ok}$$

$$\frac{\Gamma \vdash e_1{}^\tau\ ok \quad \Gamma \vdash e_2{}^{int}\ ok \quad \tau' = (!\,\tau)}{\Gamma \vdash (e_1{}^\tau\ !_\tau\ e_2{}^{int})^{\tau'}\ ok}$$

$$\frac{\Gamma \vdash e_1{}^{\tau_1 \to \tau_2}\ ok \quad \Gamma \vdash e_2{}^{\tau_3}\ ok \quad \tau_3\ \mathbf{A}\ \tau_1 \quad \tau_4\ \mathbf{A}\ \tau_2}{\Gamma \vdash (\mathbf{map}_{(\tau_1,\tau_2,\tau_3,\tau_4)}\ (e_1{}^{\tau_1 \to \tau_2}, e_2{}^{\tau_3}))^{\tau_4}\ ok}$$

$$\frac{\Gamma \vdash e_1{}^{\tau_1 \to bool}\ ok \quad \Gamma \vdash e_2{}^{\tau_2}\ ok \quad \tau_2\ \mathbf{A}\ \tau_1}{\Gamma \vdash (\mathbf{filt}_{(\tau_1,\tau_2)}\ (e_1{}^{\tau_1 \to bool}, e_2{}^{\tau_2}))^{\tau_2}\ ok}$$

$$\frac{\Gamma \vdash e_1{}^{(\tau_1,\tau_1) \to \tau_1}\ ok \quad \Gamma \vdash e_2{}^{\tau_1}\ ok \quad \Gamma \vdash e_3{}^{\tau_2}\ ok \quad \tau_2\ \mathbf{A}\ \tau_1}{\Gamma \vdash (\mathbf{red}_{(\tau_1,\tau_2)}\ (e_1{}^{(\tau_1,\tau_1) \to \tau_1}, e_2{}^{\tau_1}, e_3{}^{\tau_2}))^{\tau_1}\ ok}$$

$$\frac{\vdash \tau \triangleright \bar{\tau}\ ok}{\Gamma \vdash (\tau \triangleright \bar{\tau})^{\tau \to \bar{\tau}}\ ok} \qquad \cdots$$

Figure 5. Well-typedness of terms (selected rules).

$$\overline{\vdash \tau \triangleright \tau\ ok}$$

$$\overline{\vdash [\tau] \triangleright \{\tau\ ;\ lf\}\ ok} \qquad \overline{\vdash \{\tau\ ;\ lf\} \triangleright [\tau]\ ok}$$

$$\overline{\vdash [(\tau_1,\tau_2)] \triangleright ([\tau_1],[\tau_2])\ ok} \qquad \overline{\vdash ([\tau_1],[\tau_2]) \triangleright [(\tau_1,\tau_2)]\ ok}$$

$$\frac{\vdash \tau_1 \triangleright \tau_2\ ok \quad \vdash \tau_2 \triangleright \tau_3\ ok}{\vdash \tau_1 \triangleright \tau_3\ ok} \qquad \cdots$$

Figure 6. Well-formedness of coercions (selected rules).

$$\frac{\Gamma \vdash e_1{}^{int}\ ok \quad \Gamma \vdash e_2{}^{int}\ ok}{\Gamma \vdash \mathbf{lf}(e_1{}^{int}, e_2{}^{int}) : lf}$$

$$\frac{\Gamma \vdash s_1 : \nu \quad \cdots \quad \Gamma \vdash s_n : \nu}{\Gamma \vdash \mathbf{nd}[s_1, \ldots, s_n] : nd(\nu)}$$

Figure 7. Calculation of shape types.

$$
\begin{aligned}
!\,[\tau] &= \tau \\
!\,\{\tau\ ;\ lf\} &= \tau \\
!\,\{\tau\ ;\ nd(\nu)\} &= \{\tau\ ;\ \nu\} \\
!\,(\tau_1,\tau_2) &= (!\,\tau_1, !\,\tau_2)
\end{aligned}
$$

Figure 8. Array-type subscripting.

$$\overline{\tau\ \mathbf{L}\ \tau}$$

$$\frac{\tau_1\ \mathbf{L}\ \tau_2}{\tau_2\ \mathbf{L}\ \tau_1} \qquad \frac{\tau_1\ \mathbf{L}\ \tau_2 \quad \tau_2\ \mathbf{L}\ \tau_3}{\tau_1\ \mathbf{L}\ \tau_3}$$

$$\overline{[(\tau_1,\tau_2)]\ \mathbf{L}\ ([\tau_1],[\tau_2])}$$

$$\overline{\{\{\tau\ ;\ \nu\}\ ;\ lf\}\ \mathbf{L}\ \{\tau\ ;\ nd(\nu)\}}$$

$$\overline{\{\{\tau\ ;\ \nu\}\ ;\ nd(\nu')\}\ \mathbf{L}\ \{\{\tau\ ;\ nd(\nu)\}\ ;\ \nu'\}}$$

$$\frac{\tau_1\ \mathbf{L}\ \tau_2}{[\tau_1]\ \mathbf{L}\ [\tau_2]} \qquad \frac{\tau_1\ \mathbf{L}\ \tau_2}{[\tau_1]\ \mathbf{L}\ \{\tau_2\ ;\ lf\}}$$

$$\frac{\tau_1\ \mathbf{L}\ \tau_2}{\{\tau_1\ ;\ \nu\}\ \mathbf{L}\ \{\tau_2\ ;\ \nu\}}$$

$$\frac{\tau_1\ \mathbf{L}\ \tau_1' \quad \tau_2\ \mathbf{L}\ \tau_2'}{(\tau_1,\tau_2)\ \mathbf{L}\ (\tau_1',\tau_2')} \qquad \frac{\tau_1\ \mathbf{L}\ \tau_1' \quad \tau_2\ \mathbf{L}\ \tau_2'}{\tau_1 \to \tau_2\ \mathbf{L}\ \tau_1' \to \tau_2'}$$

$$\frac{\tau_1\ \mathbf{L}\ [\tau_2]}{\tau_1\ \mathbf{A}\ \tau_2}$$

Figure 9. Definition of $\tau_1\ \mathbf{A}\ \tau_2$ and its auxiliary relation $\tau_1\ \mathbf{L}\ \tau_2$.

Figure 4 contains Flatland's term language. Every term t includes an explicit type as a superscript. The metavariable b ranges over constants, and x ranges over variables. As in the type language, parallel-array types are written with square brackets, and flattened-array types with curly braces. Every flattened array includes a shape tree. Since the language is monomorphic, array operators — in Flatland these are subscript, map, filter, and reduce — do not have polymorphic implementations. Instead, we assume there is a type-indexed family for each one.

Flattening and unflattening operators are represented in our system by *coercions*. For the coercion that transforms values of type τ_1 into values of type τ_2, we write $\tau_1 \triangleright \tau_2$. Except for identity coercions, these are potentially expensive representation-changing operations; during compilation, we try to eliminate as many of them as possible.

Well-formedness of coercions, so that nonsensical coercions like $int \triangleright (int, int)$ are rejected, is given in Figure 6. Well-typedness of terms is in Figure 5, and the rules for calculating shape types appear in Figure 7.[3] For array type τ, we use the notation

$(!\,\tau)$ to mean the type of the element selected by subscript out of a value of type τ. The return type of a particular subscript operator is calculated from its domain. Figure 8 gives the definition of $(!\,\tau)$. If $(!\,\tau)$ cannot be computed from these rules, it is undefined.

In order to understand the typing of the type-indexed operators, one needs to understand the relation $\mathbf{A}$. For a type τ, we cannot definitively write $[\tau]$ to mean "array of τ," because $\{\tau\ ;\ lf\}$ is also an array of τ, albeit in a different representation. Furthermore, if τ is a pair type (τ_1,τ_2), then $[(\tau_1,\tau_2)]$ and $([\tau_1],[\tau_2])$ (and more) are also arrays of τ, and so on. Thus we appeal to the relation $\tau_1\ \mathbf{A}\ \tau_2$ for "τ_1 is an array of τ_2." For arrays of (int, int), for example, all

---

[3] Due to space limitations, only selected rules are presented; the full rule sets appear in [25].

84

$$\overline{e^\tau \mapsto (\tau \triangleright \tau)\, e^\tau} \qquad \overline{(\tau \triangleright \tau)\, e^\tau \mapsto e^\tau}$$

$$\frac{\vdash \tau_1 \triangleright \tau_2\; ok \qquad \vdash \tau_2 \triangleright \tau_3\; ok}{\tau_1 \triangleright \tau_3 \mapsto (\tau_2 \triangleright \tau_3) \circ (\tau_1 \triangleright \tau_2)} \qquad \overline{(\tau_2 \triangleright \tau_3) \circ (\tau_1 \triangleright \tau_2) \mapsto \tau_1 \triangleright \tau_3}$$

$$\overline{(\mathbf{let}\; x = t_1 \;\mathbf{in}\; (\overline{\tau} \triangleright \tau)\, t_2)^\tau \mapsto ((\overline{\tau} \triangleright \tau)\, (\mathbf{let}\; x = t_1 \;\mathbf{in}\; t_2))^\tau}$$

$$\frac{\vdash \overline{\tau} \triangleright \tau\; ok}{x^\tau \mapsto ((\overline{\tau} \triangleright \tau)\, \overline{x^\tau})^\tau} \qquad \cdots$$

Figure 10. Coercion distribution (selected rules), by which coercions are introduced, eliminated and otherwise manipulated.

of the following are established by $\mathbf{A}$:

$$
\begin{aligned}
[(int, int)] &\quad \mathbf{A} \quad (int, int) \\
([int], [int]) &\quad \mathbf{A} \quad (int, int) \\
\{(int, int)\;;\; lf\} &\quad \mathbf{A} \quad (int, int) \\
(\{int\;;\; lf\}, \{int\;;\; lf\}) &\quad \mathbf{A} \quad (int, int)
\end{aligned}
$$

These types correspond to arrays of integer pairs and all equivalent representations under well-formed coercions. The relation $\mathbf{A}$ is defined in Figure 9. $\mathbf{A}$ is defined by defining an auxiliary relation $\mathbf{L}$ that verifies that two types are both representations of the same scalar or array type. We use the name $\mathbf{L}$ for the relation because it tells us that one type is "on the same level as" another. All arrays of type τ can be coerced between one another. Formally, if $\tau_1 \; \mathbf{A} \; \tau$, then $\tau_2 \; \mathbf{A} \; \tau \Leftrightarrow\; \vdash \tau_1 \triangleright \tau_2\; ok$ (proven elsewhere [25].)

We specify array operators by writing their type indices in a subscript. $!_\tau$ is the operator that selects elements from an array type τ. $\mathbf{map}_{(\tau_1, \tau_2, \tau_3, \tau_4)}$ takes two arguments, a function of type $\tau_1 \to \tau_2$ and a term of array type τ_3, and produces a term of array type τ_4. $\mathbf{filt}$ and $\mathbf{red}$ carry similar type subscripts. The typing rules of $\mathbf{map}$, $\mathbf{filt}$ and $\mathbf{red}$ all appeal to $\mathbf{A}$.

To perform a flattening step, we insert a coercion. A standard step in flattening transformations is to unzip arrays of pairs of scalars—that is, to reshape an array of pairs into a pair of arrays. The coercion that unzips an array of integer pairs is written $[(int, int)] \triangleright ([int], [int])$. Its inverse coercion $([int], [int]) \triangleright [(int, int)]$ is also part of the language of coercions. If it is ever the case that a pair of inverse coercions, like these two, are successively applied to a value, they may be rewritten to an identity coercion, which can in turn be removed from the program.

Well-formed programs are guaranteed to remain well-formed under any legal transformation in our rewriting system. The top-level type of the whole program remains fixed under transformation, but the types of the subexpressions within a program may change. The well-formedness guarantee is maintained by introducing inverse coercions for every coercion introduced into the program, to maintain the stability of the types in the program. For example, every time a coercion is applied to the value to which a variable x is bound, the inverse coercion is introduced at every use of coerced x. This ensures that no clients of x are put in a position to compute with a term of the wrong type, post-coercion. Type-indexed operators such as $\mathbf{map}$ and $\mathbf{filt}$ have the ability to absorb type coercions, since, for each one, there are many implementations from which to choose, and this helps reduce the number of type coercions in the transformed program.

To provide intuition about how this machinery works, here is an example of *Flatland* in action. Consider the following program:

$$\mathbf{let}\; ns = [1, 2, 3] \;\mathbf{in}\; (ns \,!_{[int]}\, 0)$$

$$\frac{\vdash \tau \triangleright \overline{\tau}\; ok}{(t_1 \,!_\tau\, t_2)^{(!\,\tau)} \mapsto ((!\,\overline{\tau} \triangleright\; !\,\tau)\, (((\tau \triangleright \overline{\tau})\, t_1) \,!_{\overline{\tau}}\, t_2)^{(!\,\overline{\tau})})^{(!\,\tau)}}$$

$$\frac{\overline{\tau}_2 \; \mathbf{A} \; \tau_1}{(\mathbf{filt}_{(\tau_1, \tau_2)}\, (t_1, t_2))^{\tau_2} \mapsto ((\overline{\tau}_2 \triangleright \tau_2)\, (\mathbf{filt}_{(\tau_1, \overline{\tau}_2)}\, (t_1, (\tau_2 \triangleright \overline{\tau}_2)\, t_2)))^{\tau_2}}$$

$$\frac{\overline{\tau}_3 \; \mathbf{A} \; \tau_1 \qquad \overline{\tau}_4 \; \mathbf{A} \; \tau_2}{\begin{array}{l}(\mathbf{map}_{(\tau_1, \tau_2, \tau_3, \tau_4)}\, (t_1, t_2))^{\tau_4} \\ \quad \mapsto ((\overline{\tau}_4 \triangleright \tau_4)\, (\mathbf{map}_{(\tau_1, \tau_2, \overline{\tau}_3, \overline{\tau}_4)}\, (t_1, (\tau_3 \triangleright \overline{\tau}_3)\, t_2)))^{\tau_4}\end{array}}$$

$$\frac{\overline{\tau}_2 \; \mathbf{A} \; \tau_1}{(\mathbf{red}_{(\tau_1, \tau_2)}\, (t_1, t_2, t_3))^{\tau_1} \mapsto (\mathbf{red}_{(\tau_1, \overline{\tau}_2)}\, (t_1, t_2, (\tau_2 \triangleright \overline{\tau}_2)\, t_3))^{\tau_1}}$$

Figure 11. Coercion introductions with type-indexed operators. Note how the indexing types change to accommodate the coercions introduced.

$$\frac{\vdash \tau_1 \triangleright \overline{\tau}_1\; ok \qquad \overline{x}\;\text{fresh} \qquad S = [x^{\tau_1} / ((\overline{\tau}_1 \triangleright \tau_1)\, \overline{x^{\overline{\tau}_1}})^{\tau_1}]}{(\mathbf{let}\; x = t_1 \;\mathbf{in}\; t_2)^{\tau_0} \mapsto (\mathbf{let}\; \overline{x} = (\tau_1 \triangleright \overline{\tau}_1)\, t_1 \;\mathbf{in}\; S\, t_2)^{\tau_0}}$$

$$\frac{\begin{array}{c}\vdash \tau_0 \triangleright \overline{\tau}_0\; ok \qquad \overline{f}, \overline{x}\;\text{fresh} \\ S = [f^{\tau_0 \to \tau_1} / (\overline{f}^{\overline{\tau}_0 \to \tau_1} \circ (\tau_0 \triangleright \overline{\tau}_0))^{\tau_0 \to \tau_1}] \\ S' = S[x^{\tau_0} / ((\overline{\tau}_0 \triangleright \tau_0)\, \overline{x^{\overline{\tau}_0}})^{\tau_0}]\end{array}}{(\mathbf{fun}\; f\, x^{\tau_0} = t_1 \;\mathbf{in}\; t_2)^{\tau_2} \mapsto (\mathbf{fun}\; \overline{f}\, \overline{x^{\overline{\tau}_0}} = S'\, t_1 \;\mathbf{in}\; S\, t_2)^{\tau_2}}$$

Figure 12. Coercion propagation rules. Coercions introduced at binding sites necessitate substitutions accordingly.

$$
\begin{aligned}
&\mathbf{let}\; ns = [1, 2, 3] \;\mathbf{in}\; (ns \,!_{[int]}\, 0) \\
\mapsto\quad &\mathbf{let}\; \overline{ns} =\, \downarrow\, [1, 2, 3] \;\mathbf{in}\; (\uparrow \overline{ns}) \,!_{[int]}\, 0 \\
\mapsto\quad &\mathbf{let}\; \overline{ns} =\, \downarrow\, [1, 2, 3] \;\mathbf{in}\; (int \triangleright int)\, ((\downarrow\, (\uparrow \overline{ns})) \,!_{\{int\;;\; lf\}}\, 0) \\
\mapsto\quad &\mathbf{let}\; \overline{ns} =\, \downarrow\, [1, 2, 3] \;\mathbf{in}\; (\downarrow\, (\uparrow \overline{ns})) \,!_{\{int\;;\; lf\}}\, 0 \\
\mapsto\quad &\mathbf{let}\; \overline{ns} =\, \downarrow\, [1, 2, 3] \;\mathbf{in}\; ((\downarrow \circ \uparrow)\, \overline{ns}) \,!_{\{int\;;\; lf\}}\, 0 \\
\mapsto\quad &\mathbf{let}\; \overline{ns} =\, \downarrow\, [1, 2, 3] \;\mathbf{in}\; ((\{int\;;\; lf\} \triangleright \{int\;;\; lf\})\, \overline{ns}) \,!_{\{int\;;\; lf\}}\, 0 \\
\mapsto\quad &\mathbf{let}\; \overline{ns} =\, \downarrow\, [1, 2, 3] \;\mathbf{in}\; (\overline{ns} \,!_{\{int\;;\; lf\}}\, 0)
\end{aligned}
$$

Figure 13. Transforming a program by $\mapsto$.

For brevity, we let

$$\downarrow\, = [int] \triangleright \{int\;;\; lf\}$$

and

$$\uparrow\, = \{int\;;\; lf\} \triangleright [int]$$

Think of $\downarrow$ as "flatten" and $\uparrow$ as "unflatten." The step-by-step transformation of this let-expression appears in Figure 13. The parallel array $[1, 2, 3]$ is transformed to its flattened array equivalent, $(\downarrow [1, 2, 3])$, which evaluates to $\{1, 2, 3; lf(0, 3)\}$. Furthermore, by rewriting, we exchange one type-indexed subscript operator for another, thereby eliminating coercion operations. The coercions $\downarrow$ and $\uparrow$ are inverse coercions. Note by the fourth rule in Figure 10 we have

$$([int] \triangleright \{int\;;\; lf\}) \circ (\{int\;;\; lf\} \triangleright [int]) \mapsto \{int\;;\; lf\} \triangleright \{int\;;\; lf\}$$

85

$$\mathbf{F}[\![g]\!] = g$$
$$\mathbf{F}[\![[g]]\!] = \{g \; ; \; \mathit{lf}\}$$
$$\mathbf{F}[\![\tau_1 \to \tau_2]\!] = \mathbf{F}[\![\tau_1]\!] \to \mathbf{F}[\![\tau_2]\!]$$
$$\mathbf{F}[\![(\tau_1, \tau_2)]\!] = (\mathbf{F}[\![\tau_1]\!], \mathbf{F}[\![\tau_2]\!])$$
$$\mathbf{F}[\![[\tau_1 \to \tau_2]]\!] = \{\mathbf{F}[\![\tau_1 \to \tau_2]\!] \; ; \; \mathit{lf}\}$$
$$\mathbf{F}[\![[(\tau_1, \tau_2)]]\!] = (\mathbf{F}[\![[\tau_1]]\!], \mathbf{F}[\![[\tau_2]]\!])$$
$$\mathbf{F}[\![[[\tau]]]\!] = \mathbf{N}[\![(\mathbf{F}[\![[\tau]]\!])]\!]$$

$$\mathbf{N}[\![(\tau_1, \tau_2)]\!] = (\mathbf{N}[\![\tau_1]\!], \mathbf{N}[\![\tau_2]\!])$$
$$\mathbf{N}[\![\{\tau \; ; \; \nu\}]\!] = \{\tau \; ; \; \mathit{nd}(\nu)\}$$

Figure 14. Type flattening.

$$\frac{\{\} \vdash e^\tau \searrow (\overline{\tau} \triangleright \tau) \diamond \overline{e}^{\overline{\tau}}}{e^\tau \Downarrow ((\overline{\tau} \triangleright \tau) \, \overline{e}^{\overline{\tau}})^\tau}$$

Figure 15. Top-level data-only flattening.

so the composition of $\downarrow$ and $\uparrow$ is mutually annihilating. Post-transformation, the representation of the array bound to ns is coerced exactly once, to the differently-typed fresh variable $\overline{ns}$.

4.1 Formal data-only flattening

We now present data-only flattening in the context of the *Flatland* system, as a transformation from a source language to a target language. A *source type* is a type that is neither a flattened-array type, nor contains any flattened-array types, generated by the grammar

$$\tau ::= g \mid \tau \to \tau \mid (\tau, \tau) \mid [\tau]$$

We define *source programs* as a term e^τ for source type τ, all of whose subterms have source types and contain no coercions. By this definition, we have made it illegal to write down flattened arrays anywhere in a source program. The transformation will introduce all flattened-array values and all coercions.

The target language is defined in terms of *flat types*. A type τ is *flat* if

- it is a ground type g,
- it is a function type $\tau_1 \to \tau_2$ and τ_1 and τ_2 are flat,
- it is a pair type (τ_1, τ_2) and τ_1 and τ_2 are flat, or
- it is an array type $\{\tau \; ; \; \nu\}$ and τ is a ground type or a flat function type.

If a type is not flat, we say it is *nonflat*. Note that source types and nonflat types are not the same. For example, $[(int, bool)]$ is a source type, and the related type $(\{int \; ; \; \mathit{lf}\}, \{bool \; ; \; \mathit{lf}\})$ is a flat type. But the related type $\{(int, bool) \; ; \; \mathit{lf}\}$ is neither a source type nor a flat type; it is disqualified as a source type since it is a flattened-array type and disqualified as a flat type since it includes a pair inside an array. A *target program* is an expression whose outermost type is a source type, yet all of whose subexpressions have flat types. The restriction on its outermost type is a consequence of the type-preservation property of *Flatland*'s rewriting. The restriction is enforced by the application of one last "unflattening" coercion to the transformed program at the top level. Within the program, all subexpressions are flattened.

Flattening of whole programs is written as a type-preserving relation $\Downarrow$. Figure 15 gives the sole judgment for $\Downarrow$, which immediately delegates its work to an auxiliary relation $\searrow$. Whole-program

$$\frac{}{\Delta \vdash b^\tau \searrow (\tau \triangleright \tau) \diamond b^\tau}$$

$$\frac{\Delta(x^\tau) = \overline{x}^{\overline{\tau}}}{\Delta \vdash x^\tau \searrow (\overline{\tau} \triangleright \tau) \diamond \overline{x}^{\overline{\tau}}}$$

$$\frac{\Delta \vdash e_1^{bool} \searrow (bool \triangleright bool) \diamond \overline{e}_1^{\,bool} \quad \Delta \vdash e_2^\tau \searrow (\overline{\tau} \triangleright \tau) \diamond \overline{e}_2^{\,\overline{\tau}} \quad \Delta \vdash e_3^\tau \searrow (\overline{\tau} \triangleright \tau) \diamond \overline{e}_3^{\,\overline{\tau}}}{\Delta \vdash (\mathbf{if}\ e_1^{bool}\ \mathbf{then}\ e_2^\tau\ \mathbf{else}\ e_3^\tau)^\tau \searrow (\overline{\tau} \triangleright \tau) \diamond (\mathbf{if}\ \overline{e}_1^{\,bool}\ \mathbf{then}\ \overline{e}_2^{\,\overline{\tau}}\ \mathbf{else}\ \overline{e}_3^{\,\overline{\tau}})^{\overline{\tau}}}$$

$$\frac{\Delta \vdash e_1^{\tau_1} \searrow (\overline{\tau}_1 \triangleright \tau_1) \diamond \overline{e}_1^{\,\overline{\tau}_1} \quad \Delta' = \Delta[x^{\tau_1} \mapsto \overline{x}^{\overline{\tau}_1}], \ \overline{x}\ \text{fresh} \quad \Delta' \vdash e_2^{\tau_2} \searrow (\overline{\tau}_2 \triangleright \tau_2) \diamond \overline{e}_2^{\,\overline{\tau}_2}}{\Delta \vdash (\mathbf{let}\ x = e_1^{\tau_1}\ \mathbf{in}\ e_2^{\tau_2})^{\tau_2} \searrow (\overline{\tau}_2 \triangleright \tau_2) \diamond (\mathbf{let}\ \overline{x} = \overline{e}_1^{\,\overline{\tau}_1}\ \mathbf{in}\ \overline{e}_2^{\,\overline{\tau}_2})^{\overline{\tau}_2}}$$

$$\frac{\Delta' = \Delta[f^{\tau_0 \to \tau_1} \mapsto \overline{f}^{\,\overline{\tau}_0 \to \overline{\tau}_1}], \ \overline{f}\ \text{fresh} \quad \Delta'' = \Delta'[x^{\tau_0} \mapsto \overline{x}^{\overline{\tau}_0}], \ \overline{x}\ \text{fresh} \quad \Delta'' \vdash e_1^{\tau_1} \searrow (\overline{\tau}_1 \triangleright \tau_1) \diamond \overline{e}_1^{\,\overline{\tau}_1} \quad \Delta' \vdash e_2^{\tau_2} \searrow (\overline{\tau}_2 \triangleright \tau_2) \diamond \overline{e}_2^{\,\overline{\tau}_2}}{\Delta \vdash (\mathbf{fun}\ f\ x^{\tau_0} = e_1^{\tau_1}\ \mathbf{in}\ e_2^{\tau_2})^{\tau_2} \searrow (\overline{\tau}_2 \triangleright \tau_2) \diamond (\mathbf{fun}\ \overline{f}\ \overline{x}^{\overline{\tau}_0} = \overline{e}_1^{\,\overline{\tau}_1}\ \mathbf{in}\ \overline{e}_2^{\,\overline{\tau}_2})^{\overline{\tau}_2}}$$

$$\frac{\Delta \vdash e_1^{\tau_1} \searrow (\overline{\tau}_1 \triangleright \tau_1) \diamond \overline{e}_1^{\,\overline{\tau}_1} \quad \Delta \vdash e_2^{\tau_2} \searrow (\overline{\tau}_2 \triangleright \tau_2) \diamond \overline{e}_2^{\,\overline{\tau}_2}}{\Delta \vdash (e_1^{\tau_1}, e_2^{\tau_2})^{(\tau_1, \tau_2)} \searrow ((\overline{\tau}_1, \overline{\tau}_2) \triangleright (\tau_1, \tau_2)) \diamond (\overline{e}_1^{\,\overline{\tau}_1}, \overline{e}_2^{\,\overline{\tau}_2})^{(\overline{\tau}_1, \overline{\tau}_2)}}$$

$$\frac{\Delta \vdash e^{(\tau_1, \tau_2)} \searrow ((\overline{\tau}_1, \overline{\tau}_2) \triangleright (\tau_1, \tau_2)) \diamond \overline{e}^{(\overline{\tau}_1, \overline{\tau}_2)}}{\Delta \vdash (\pi_1\ e^{(\tau_1, \tau_2)})^{\tau_1} \searrow (\overline{\tau}_1 \triangleright \tau_1) \diamond (\pi_1\ \overline{e}^{(\overline{\tau}_1, \overline{\tau}_2)})^{\overline{\tau}_1}} \quad (\pi_2\ \text{sim.})$$

Figure 16. Data-only flattening, group 1.

flattening consists of transforming a program e^τ of source type τ to a program $\overline{e}^{\overline{\tau}}$ of flat type $\overline{\tau}$ and then coercing the transformed program to original type τ at the top level. Note that in the cases where τ is, for example, a ground type (see Figure 13), the outermost coercion is an identity coercion and has no effect.

The auxiliary relation of data-only flattening is given in Figures 16 and 17. The syntax of $\searrow$ is as follows:

$$\Delta \vdash e^\tau \searrow (\overline{\tau} \triangleright \tau) \diamond \overline{e}^{\overline{\tau}}$$

Δ is a finite map from variable terms to variable terms; it is used to implement propagations through let-expressions and functions. On the right-hand side of the relation, a diamond ($\diamond$) is used to construct a pair out of a coercion and a transformed expression. The relation produces an unflattening coercion, along with the transformed expression, for use in one of the following ways. If the expression transformed is the whole program, the $\Downarrow$ relation applies the coercion to preserve the program's original type (as per the rule in Figure 15). If the expression is not the whole program, the accompanying coercion is used as a building block for further coercions as program transformation proceeds outward.

The important work in data-only flattening takes place at array terms; see the second rule in Figure 17 (which in turn appeals to

$$\frac{\Delta \vdash e_1{}^{\tau_1 \to \tau_2} \searrow (\overline{\tau}_1 \to \overline{\tau}_2 \triangleright \tau_1 \to \tau_2) \diamond \overline{e}_1{}^{\overline{\tau}_1 \to \overline{\tau}_2}}{\Delta \vdash e_2{}^{\tau_1} \searrow (\overline{\tau}_1 \triangleright \tau_1) \diamond \overline{e}_2{}^{\overline{\tau}_1}}{\Delta \vdash (e_1{}^{\tau_1 \to \tau_2}\, e_2{}^{\tau_1})^{\tau_2} \searrow (\overline{\tau}_2 \triangleright \tau_2) \diamond (\overline{e}_1{}^{\overline{\tau}_1 \to \overline{\tau}_2}\, \overline{e}_2{}^{\overline{\tau}_1})^{\overline{\tau}_2}}$$

$$\frac{\mathbf{F}[\![\tau]\!] = \overline{\tau}}{\Delta \vdash e^{[\tau]} \searrow (\overline{\tau} \triangleright [\tau]) \diamond (([\tau] \triangleright \overline{\tau})\, e^{[\tau]})^{\overline{\tau}}}$$

$$\frac{\Delta \vdash e_1{}^{\tau_2 \to \tau_3} \searrow (\overline{\tau}_2 \to \overline{\tau}_3 \triangleright \tau_2 \to \tau_3) \diamond \overline{e}_1{}^{\overline{\tau}_2 \to \overline{\tau}_3}}{\Delta \vdash e_2{}^{\tau_1 \to \tau_2} \searrow (\overline{\tau}_1 \to \overline{\tau}_2 \triangleright \tau_1 \to \tau_2) \diamond \overline{e}_2{}^{\overline{\tau}_1 \to \overline{\tau}_2}}{\Delta \vdash (e_1 \circ e_2)^{\tau_1 \to \tau_3} \searrow (\overline{\tau}_1 \to \overline{\tau}_3 \triangleright \tau_1 \to \tau_3) \diamond (\overline{e}_1 \circ \overline{e}_2)^{\overline{\tau}_1 \to \overline{\tau}_3}}$$

$$\frac{\Delta \vdash e_1{}^{\tau} \searrow (\overline{\tau} \triangleright \tau) \diamond \overline{e}_1{}^{\overline{\tau}} \qquad \Delta \vdash e_2{}^{int} \searrow (int \triangleright int) \diamond \overline{e}_2{}^{int}}{\Delta \vdash (e_1{}^{\tau}\, !_\tau\, e_2{}^{int})^{(!\,\tau)} \searrow ((!\,\overline{\tau}) \triangleright (!\,\tau)) \diamond (\overline{e}_1{}^{\overline{\tau}}\, !_{\overline{\tau}}\, \overline{e}_2{}^{int})^{(!\,\overline{\tau})}}$$

$$\frac{\Delta \vdash e_1{}^{\tau_1 \to \tau_2} \searrow (\overline{\tau}_1 \to \overline{\tau}_2 \triangleright \tau_1 \to \tau_2) \diamond \overline{e}_1{}^{\overline{\tau}_1 \to \overline{\tau}_2}}{\Delta \vdash e_2{}^{\tau_3} \searrow (\overline{\tau}_3 \triangleright \tau_3) \diamond \overline{e}_2{}^{\overline{\tau}_3}}{\mathbf{F}[\![\tau_4]\!] = \overline{\tau}_4}{\Delta \vdash (\mathbf{map}_{(\tau_1, \tau_2, \tau_3, \tau_4)}\, (e_1{}^{\tau_1 \to \tau_2}, e_2{}^{\tau_3}))^{\tau_4}}$$
$$\searrow (\overline{\tau}_4 \triangleright \tau_4) \diamond (\mathbf{map}_{(\overline{\tau}_1, \overline{\tau}_2, \overline{\tau}_3, \overline{\tau}_4)}\, (\overline{e}_1{}^{\overline{\tau}_1 \to \overline{\tau}_2}, \overline{e}_2{}^{\overline{\tau}_3}))^{\overline{\tau}_4}$$

$$\frac{\Delta \vdash e_1{}^{\tau_1 \to bool} \searrow (\overline{\tau}_1 \to bool \triangleright \tau_1 \to bool) \diamond \overline{e}_1{}^{\overline{\tau}_1 \to bool}}{\Delta \vdash e_2{}^{\tau_2} \searrow (\overline{\tau}_2 \triangleright \tau_2) \diamond \overline{e}_2{}^{\overline{\tau}_2}}{\Delta \vdash (\mathbf{filt}_{(\tau_1, \tau_2)}\, (e_1{}^{\tau_1 \to bool}, e_2{}^{\tau_2}))^{\tau_2}}$$
$$\searrow (\overline{\tau}_2 \triangleright \tau_2) \diamond (\mathbf{filt}_{(\overline{\tau}_1, \overline{\tau}_2)}\, (\overline{e}_1{}^{\overline{\tau}_1 \to bool}, \overline{e}_2{}^{\overline{\tau}_2}))^{\overline{\tau}_2}$$

$$\frac{\Delta \vdash e_1{}^{(\tau_1, \tau_1) \to \tau_1}}{\searrow ((\overline{\tau}_1, \overline{\tau}_1) \to \overline{\tau}_1 \triangleright (\tau_1, \tau_1) \to \tau_1) \diamond \overline{e}_1{}^{(\overline{\tau}_1, \overline{\tau}_1) \to \overline{\tau}_1}}{\Delta \vdash e_2{}^{\tau_1} \searrow (\overline{\tau}_1 \triangleright \tau_1) \diamond \overline{e}_2{}^{\overline{\tau}_1}}{\Delta \vdash e_3{}^{\tau_2} \searrow (\overline{\tau}_2 \triangleright \tau_2) \diamond \overline{e}_3{}^{\overline{\tau}_2}}{\Delta \vdash (\mathbf{red}_{(\tau_1, \tau_2)}\, (e_1{}^{(\tau_1, \tau_1) \to \tau_1}, e_2{}^{\tau_1}, e_3{}^{\tau_2}))^{\tau_2}}$$
$$\searrow (\overline{\tau}_2 \triangleright \tau_2) \diamond (\mathbf{red}_{(\overline{\tau}_1, \overline{\tau}_2)}\, (\overline{e}_1{}^{(\overline{\tau}_1, \overline{\tau}_1) \to \overline{\tau}_1}, \overline{e}_2{}^{\overline{\tau}_1}, \overline{e}_3{}^{\overline{\tau}_2}))^{\overline{\tau}_2}$$

Figure 17. Data-only flattening, group 2.

type flattening in Figure 14.) This rule introduces coercions from parallel arrays to flattened arrays. The variable rule (second rule, Figure 16) substitutes typed variables for their flattened replacements per the map carried by Δ. The array-operator rules exchange operators indexed by source type to operators indexed by the corresponding flat types. The other rules are administrative, recursively propagating transformations through expressions. There is exactly one rule for every distinct syntactic form, so the rules describes both a semantic specification and an algorithm.

5. Implementation

Data-only flattening in PML is accomplished in three successive phases: an *abstract flattening* phase, whereby abstract flattening operations — symbolic values that stand in for actual implementations — are inserted throughout the code; a *fusion* phase where canceling coercions (adjacent coercions that undo one another's work) are eliminated; and a *concrete flattening* phase, where symbolic flattening operations are replaced by monomorphic code. Due to space limitations, the detailed operations of these phases is not presented here and may be found elsewhere [25].

5.1 Optimizations

Flattened PML programs are amenable to various optimizations that cannot be applied to non-flattened ones. In this section, we discuss several such optimizations, each of which is responsible, in part, for the performance improvements we report in our benchmark results.

Monomorphization. Monomorphization is an optimization whereby a polymorphic data structure containing uniformly-represented (*i.e.*, boxed) elements is transformed to a representation containing raw (unboxed) elements in their place. The flattening transformation, by virtue of unzipping arrays of tuples, exposes more opportunities for monomorphization than otherwise. In PML, arrays of double pairs, for example, become pairs of double arrays, which in turn become farrays, each containing a specialized rope of doubles as its flat data vector. Monomorphization is well known to be valuable even outside the context of nested data parallel compilation. MLton [18], an optimizing whole-program SML compiler, performs monomorphization to generate better-performing sequential code. PML stands to benefit from monomorphization even without flattening (PML currently does no monomorphization unless flattening is enabled), although it will never be the case that, without unzipping tuples, non-flattened PML will have as many opportunities to do it.

Tab flattening. Nested parallel comprehensions over ranges have *regular* structure: at each dimension, the length of every array is fixed a constant. The regularity of such structures can be exploited by the *tab flattening* optimization, which performs simple integer arithmetic operations to collapse multidimensional tabulations into linear ones.

Every one-dimensional parallel comprehension of scalars is trivially regular:

```
val xs = [| Double.fromInt i | i in [| 0 to 9 |] |]
```

The straightforward, and inefficient, implementation of this parallel comprehension is to translate it to a map over the parallel array containing the integers from 0 to 9.

```
PArray.map Double.fromInt [| 0 to 9 |]
```

This naïve translation entails building an ephemeral data structure that is immediately computed with and discarded. To save the cost associated with this intermediate structure, the compiler rewrites parallel comprehensions over ranges as tabulations:

```
PArray.tabulate (10, Double.fromInt)
```

Tabulating over integer intervals requires no intermediate data structures, and realizes a performance improvement over the build-and-map strategy outlined above.

Nested parallel comprehensions naturally give rise to nested tabulations. The computation of xss in this excerpt

```
val xss = [| [| (i*10)+j | j in [| 0 to 9 |] |]
           | i in [| 0 to 9 |] |]
```

can be naturally expressed by a tabulate within a tabulate as follows:

```
PArray.tabulate (10, fn i =>
  PArray.tabulate (10, fn j =>
    (i*10) + j))
```

This translation is already better than using maps with ephemeral structures, but the shape of our flattened array representations allows us to use tab flattening to improve on nested tabulations. Recall our evaluation of xss results in an farray containing a flat data vector and a shape tree. We name the result xssF and sketch it as follows:

```
val xssF = FArray (Rope.Leaf [0, 1, 2, ..., 99],
                   Shape.Nd [Shape.Lf (0,10),
                             ...,
                             Shape.Lf (90,100)])
```

We can generate the flat data vector of `xssF` in one tabulation, over a single counter representing the total number of elements in the nested array, by performing the appropriate index arithmetic on the counter:

```
let fun f k = let
                  val (i, j) = (k div 10, k mod 10)
              in
                  (i*10) + j
              end
in
    PArray.tabulate (10*10, f)
end
```

The shape tree in rectangular cases has a simple regular structure as well, and be computed from the dimensions of a regular array in a straightforward way. Tab flattening operation scales to any number of dimensions for regular nested arrays.

Segmented reductions. NESL's fast segmented operations are an important element of NESL's ability to perform well on irregular nested data parallel programs, and an important one for PML to emulate. NESL's segmented sum operation, for example, is able to compute the sums of a nested array of numbers in a fixed number of steps regardless of the irregularity of the array's structure. This operation is critical to the performance of sparse-matrix/vector multiplication (see below). Here is an example of an irregular sum computation in PML:

```
let val nss = [| [| 1, 2 |],
                 [| |],
                 [| 3, 4, 5, 6 |] |]
in
    [| sum ns | ns in nss |]
end
```

If this parallel comprehension is rewritten such that the `sum` operation is simply mapped over the array-valued elements of `nss`, the irregularity of the structure of `nss`, if there is wide variation in the lengths of its elements, is bound to affect load balancing adversely. As such, the compiler replaces nested reductions like these

```
val ss = [| PArray.reduce add 0.0 ns | ns in nss |]
```

with "segmented reductions"

```
val ss = PArray.segreduce add 0.0 nss
```

The non-flattened implementation of `PArray.segreduce oper ident` is simply `PArray.map (PArray.reduce oper ident)`. As part of the flattening transformation, the non-flattened `segreduce` implementation is replaced by a faster `segreduce` written to exploit the shape of `farray` data structures.

6. Evaluation

These benchmarks compare the performance and scalability of Manticore's current implementation of parallel arrays [1] against data-only flattening. The baseline performance is from the sequential version of the benchmark, which runs on a single processor and eliminates all overhead from the parallel language constructs and associated runtime features. The sequential version does not take advantage of any of the data transformations provided by data-only flattening, relying on the default polymorphic array representation.

These benchmarks were selected to show that we gain performance on code that executes over irregular data, as in SMVM, while preserving most of the performance of benchmarks over

regular data. Flattening happens at compile time in the following sense: nested arrays such as those in the main expressions of `mandelbrot` and `raytracer` are created flat in the first place, not constructed nested and then flattened.

6.1 Experimental method

Our benchmark machine is a Dell PowerEdge R815 server, outfitted with 48 cores and 128 GB physical memory. This machine runs x86_64 Ubuntu Linux 10.04.2 LTS, kernel version 2.6.32-42. The 48 cores are provided by four 12 core AMD Opteron 6172 "Magny Cours" processors. Each core operates at 2.1 GHz and has 64 KB each of instruction and data L1 cache and 512 KB of L2 cache. There are two 6 MB L3 caches per processor, each of which is shared by six cores, for a total of 48 MB of L3 cache.

We ran each experiment configuration 30 times, and we report the average performance results in our graphs and tables. Times are reported in seconds.

6.2 Mandelbrot

We compute the Mandelbrot set by means of a function `elt` which consumes a pair of integers and produces an integer. The argument to `elt` represents a location in the complex plane. Its return value is the number of iterations required, according to the standard iterating Mandelbrot set membership test, for a given point to diverge outside the set (by having a modulus greater than 2). A point is a member of the Mandelbrot set if it fails to diverge before reaching a fixed upper limit of iterations (we use 1000). We execute this simple function in parallel over a 2048×2048 range using the following PML code:

```
fun mandelbrot n = let
    val rng = [| 0 to (n-1) |]
in
    [| [| elt (i, j) | j in rng |] | i in rng |]
end
```

Figure 18(a) shows PML speedups, with and without flattening, against the sequential baseline. Due to the relatively small amount of computation at each element, the benefits of the data-only flattening transformation provide only a 5% speedup at 48 cores. These benefits come from the reduced amount of memory traffic when using a monomorphic array representation, avoiding an extra allocation per result element and associated garbage collector pressure.

6.3 Raytracer

Our ray tracing benchmark computes the image of a scene graph consisting of a group of overlapping spheres with transparency and reflection. The code is translated from a parallel program in the implicitly-parallel language Id90 [19]. It is a brute-force implementation and does not use any acceleration data structures. The Raytracer benchmark renders a 2048×2048 image in parallel as a two-dimensional sequence.

Similar to the Mandelbrot benchmark, we write the body of the main function as a nested parallel comprehension:

```
fun raytracer n = let
    val ns = [| 0 to (n-1) |]
in
    [| [| trace (i, j) | j in ns |] | i in ns |]
end
```

In all versions of the program, the Manticore compiler transforms this nested parallel comprehension into a two-dimensional tabulation over fixed ranges, avoiding creation of an intermediate array of values to iterate over. In the data-only version of this program, that two-dimensional tabulation is instead performed as a

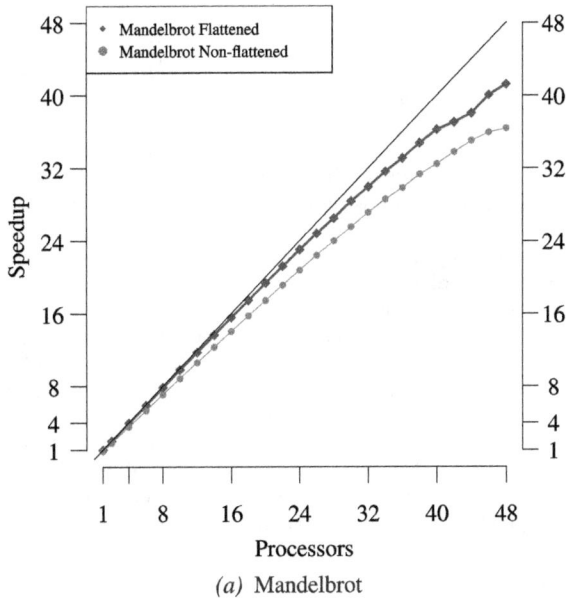

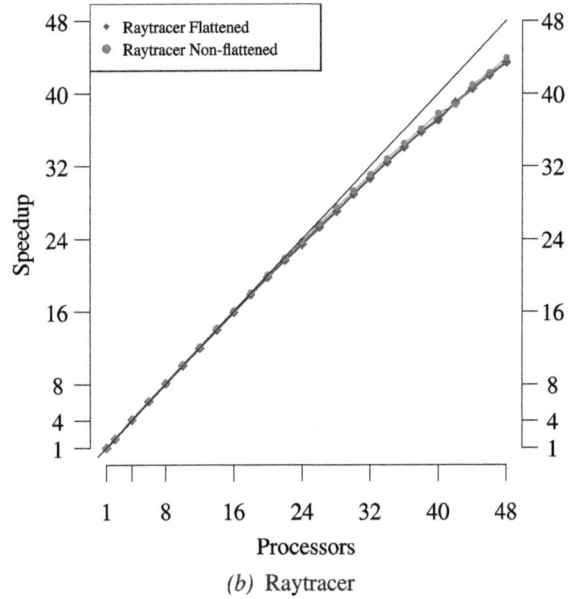

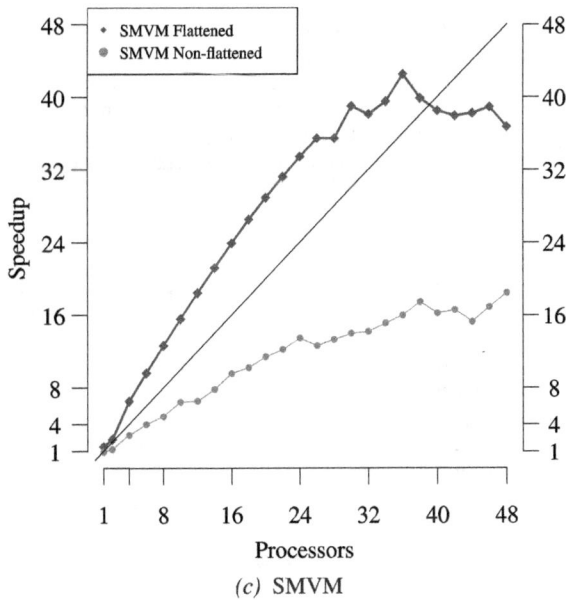

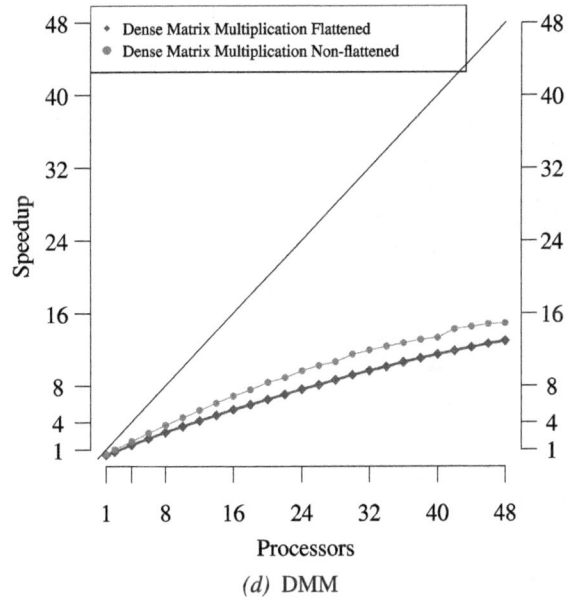

Figure 18. Comparison of flattened and non-flattened performance.

one-dimensional tabulation with adjusted indices. As is shown in Figure 18(*b*), this transformation slightly reduces the overhead required by the work-stealing scheduler to evenly balance the remaining work, since work on the one-dimensional data structure requires only splitting the index in half instead of the default finger-tree splitting required in the two-dimensional version [1].

6.4 Sparse-Matrix Vector Multiplication

Among our benchmarks, sparse-matrix vector multiplication profits most from the data-only flattening transformation. Sparse-matrix vector multiplication is expressed concisely in the following PML code:

```
fun smvm (sm, v) = let
  fun add (a,b) = a+b
  in
    [| PArray.reduce add 0.0
       [| x*(v!i) | (i,x) in sv |]
    | sv in sm |]
  end
```

The inner parallel array expression computes the dot-product of the sparse matrix and the vector. The outer parallel array then computes the sum of each of those resulting dot-products. The summation is implemented on top of `PArray.reduce`, which allows the runtime to processes the reduction in parallel.

In both versions of the benchmark, the Manticore compiler automatically optimizes the parallel reduction over multiple values

89

into a single segmented reduction. Segmented operators have been shown by Blelloch and others to result in more balanced chunks of parallel work, across a variety of platforms [3, 24]. All versions are transformed into the following PML code:

```
fun smvm (sm, v) = let
  val prods = products (sm, v)
  val sums = segsum prods
  in
    sums
  end
```

The flattened version of smvm uses monomorphic vectors for both the intermediate representation of the dot-products and the final result of the segmented reduction. Further, the implementation of segmented reduction over monomorphic vectors takes advantage of the layout, performing the segmented reduction with far less overhead than the sequential and non-flattened versions.

Figure 18(c) gives the speedups of PML over its sequential baseline, both with and without flattening. The sparse matrix is $10,000 \times 10,000$, with a random number of entries between 100 and 500 in each row. Flattened smvm is substantially faster than non-flattened smvm for all numbers of processors up to 48, and furthermore has much better performance with respect to the sequential baseline. The super-linear speedups are due to the relatively small amount of work performed on each element compared to the improvement due to the representation change. Above 36 processors, our performance improvement flattens due to having insufficient data to take advantage of the processors. Unfortunately, limitations in the Manticore runtime currently prevent us from further increasing the size of the data.

6.5 Dense Matrix Matrix Multiplication

The dense matrix multiplication (DMM) benchmark is a dense-matrix by dense-matrix multiplication in which each matrix is 600×600. As mentioned in Section 2, this benchmark has traditionally had extremely poor performance under flattening. As shown in Figure 18(d), our approach does still result in a slowdown in performance due to the creation of some intermediate arrays (resulting in a factor of 3 increase in memory usage). This penalty is roughly 13% and could be reduced through the introduction of additional fusion operations to avoid those intermediate arrays.

6.6 Conclusion

These benchmarks demonstrate that the data-only flattening transformation significantly improves a benchmark with irregular data (SMVM), does not experience the polynomial blowup typical to full flattening on DMM, and does not dramatically change the performance of other programs.

7. Related work

The incremental extension of NESL's foundation to a more feature-rich platform has ultimately taken the form of Data Parallel Haskell [9]. Chakravarty et al. first present the language Nepal in 2001 [8], characterized as a version of Haskell including nested data parallelism. Nepal is succeeded by Chakravarty et al.'s Data Parallel Haskell [9], bringing together Nepal-style nested data parallelism with Haskell as implemented in the Glasgow Haskell Compiler (GHC) [12]. In 2008, Peyton Jones et al. give a thorough overview of the Data Parallel Haskell language and its compilation [22], including an updated account of how Data Parallel Haskell uses the flattening transformation in their implementation. The especially germane question is this: what happens after a system has compiled a Data Parallel Haskell program in the manner of NESL, and yet executes on an SMP rather than a SIMD

machine? Their answer to this technical problem is to adapt the split and join mechanisms originally presented in Keller's dissertation [13] to implement NESL-style operations across the multiple processing elements on a multicore computer. Parallel computations are split across processing elements and subsequently joined on completion. To eliminate unnecessary synchronization points, GHC uses rewrite rules [21] to erase successive applications of split and join (per the identity equivalence rule originally given by Keller). (In addition to this, various advanced fusion techniques are employed to streamline the resulting post-flattened program, an overview of which is given in their paper.)

Though Data Parallel Haskell represents broad advances in NESL-style flattening in numerous ways, and although it has been adapted to run on multicore machines, its compilation strategy continues to reflect the SIMD orientation of its predecessors, though there has been recent work on vectorisation in DPH to avoid excessive flattening [15]. This work differs from that line of research by never performing the full vectorisation transformation on the code, though both approaches flatten nested data.

Acknowledgments

This material is based upon work supported by the National Science Foundation under Grants CCF-0811389 and CCF-1010568, and upon work performed in part while John Reppy was serving at the National Science Foundation. The views and conclusions contained herein are those of the authors and should not be interpreted as necessarily representing the official policies or endorsements, either expressed or implied, of these organizations or the U.S. Government.

References

[1] L. Bergstrom, M. Fluet, M. Rainey, J. Reppy, and A. Shaw. Lazy tree splitting. In *ICFP '10*, pages 93–104, New York, NY, September 2010. ACM.

[2] G. E. Blelloch. *Vector models for data-parallel computing*. MIT Press, Cambridge, MA, USA, 1990.

[3] G. E. Blelloch. Prefix sums and their applications. Technical Report CMU-CS-90-190, School of Computer Science, Carnegie Mellon University, Nov. 1990.

[4] G. E. Blelloch. Programming parallel algorithms. *CACM*, 39(3):85–97, Mar. 1996.

[5] G. E. Blelloch and G. W. Sabot. Compiling collection-oriented languages onto massively parallel computers. *JPDC*, 8(2):119–134, 1990.

[6] H.-J. Boehm, R. Atkinson, and M. Plass. Ropes: an alternative to strings. *SP&E*, 25(12):1315–1330, Dec. 1995. ISSN 0038-0644.

[7] M. M. T. Chakravarty and G. Keller. More types for nested data parallel programming. In *ICFP '00*, pages 94–105, New York, NY, Sept. 2000. ACM.

[8] M. M. T. Chakravarty, G. Keller, R. Leshchinskiy, and W. Pfannenstiel. Nepal – nested data parallelism in Haskell. In *Euro-Par '01*, volume 2150 of *LNCS*, pages 524–534, New York, NY, Aug. 2001. Springer-Verlag.

[9] M. M. T. Chakravarty, R. Leshchinskiy, S. Peyton Jones, G. Keller, and S. Marlow. Data Parallel Haskell. A status report. In *DAMP '07*, pages 10–18, New York, NY, Jan. 2007. ACM.

[10] J. Dean and S. Ghemawat. MapReduce: Simplified data processing on large clusters. In *OSDI '04*, pages 137–150, Berkeley, CA, Dec. 2004. USENIX Association.

[11] M. Fluet, N. Ford, M. Rainey, J. Reppy, A. Shaw, and Y. Xiao. Status Report: The Manticore Project. In *ML '07*, pages 15–24, New York, NY, Oct. 2007. ACM.

[12] GHC. The Glasgow Haskell Compiler. Available from http://www.haskell.org/ghc.

[13] G. Keller. *Transformation-based Implementation of Nested Data Parallelism for Distributed Memory Machines*. PhD thesis, Technische Universität Berlin, Berlin, Germany, 1999.

[14] G. Keller and M. M. T. Chakravarty. Flattening trees. In *Euro-Par '98: Proceedings of the 4th International Euro-Par Conference on Parallel Processing*, pages 709–719, London, UK, 1998. Springer-Verlag.

[15] G. Keller, M. M. T. Chakravarty, R. Leshchinskiy, B. Lippmeier, and S. Peyton Jones. Vectorisation Avoidance. In *HASKELL '12*, New York, NY, Sept. 2012. ACM. Forthcoming.

[16] R. Leshchinskiy, M. M. T. Chakravarty, and G. Keller. Higher order flattening. In V. Alexandrov, D. van Albada, P. Sloot, and J. Dongarra, editors, *ICCS '06*, number 3992 in LNCS, pages 920–928, New York, NY, May 2006. Springer-Verlag.

[17] R. Milner, M. Tofte, R. Harper, and D. MacQueen. *The Definition of Standard ML (Revised)*. The MIT Press, Cambridge, MA, 1997.

[18] MLton. The MLton Standard ML compiler. Available at `http://mlton.org`.

[19] R. S. Nikhil. *ID Language Reference Manual*. Laboratory for Computer Science, MIT, Cambridge, MA, July 1991.

[20] D. W. Palmer, J. F. Prins, and S. Westfold. Work-efficient nested data-parallelism. In *FoMPP5*, pages 186–193, Los Alamitos, CA, 1995. IEEE Computer Society Press.

[21] S. Peyton Jones, A. Tolmach, and T. Hoare. Playing by the rules: Rewriting as a practical optimization technique in GHC. In *Proceedings of the 2001 Haskell Workshop*, pages 203–233, Sept. 2001.

[22] S. Peyton Jones, R. Leshchinskiy, G. Keller, and M. M. T. Chakravarty. Harnessing the Multicores: Nested Data Parallelism in Haskell. In *APLAS '08*, pages 138–138, New York, NY, Dec. 2008. Springer-Verlag.

[23] M. Rainey. *Effective Scheduling Techniques for High-Level Parallel Programming Languages*. PhD thesis, University of Chicago, Aug. 2010. Available from `http://manticore.cs.uchicago.edu`.

[24] S. Sengupta, M. Harris, Y. Zhang, and J. D. Owens. Scan primitives for GPU computing. In *GH '07*, pages 97–106, Aire-la-Ville, Switzerland, Aug. 2007. Eurographics Association.

[25] A. Shaw. *Implementation techniques for nested-data-parallel languages*. PhD thesis, University of Chicago, Aug. 2011. Available from `http://manticore.cs.uchicago.edu`.

[26] D. Spoonhower, G. E. Blelloch, R. Harper, and P. B. Gibbons. Space profiling for parallel functional programs. In *ICFP '08*, pages 253–264, New York, NY, Sept. 2008. ACM.

Distributed Merge Trees

Dmitriy Morozov

Computational Research Division,
Lawrence Berkeley National Laboratory
One Cyclotron Road, MS 50F-1650,
Berkeley, CA 94720
dmitriy@mrzv.org

Gunther H. Weber

Computational Research Division,
Lawrence Berkeley National Laboratory
One Cyclotron Road, MS 50F-1650,
Berkeley, CA 94720 /
Department of Computer Science,
University of California, Davis
One Shields Avenue, Davis, CA 95616
GHWeber@lbl.gov

Abstract

Improved simulations and sensors are producing datasets whose increasing complexity exhausts our ability to visualize and comprehend them directly. To cope with this problem, we can detect and extract significant features in the data and use them as the basis for subsequent analysis. Topological methods are valuable in this context because they provide robust and general feature definitions.

As the growth of serial computational power has stalled, data analysis is becoming increasingly dependent on massively parallel machines. To satisfy the computational demand created by complex datasets, algorithms need to effectively utilize these computer architectures. The main strength of topological methods, their emphasis on global information, turns into an obstacle during parallelization.

We present two approaches to alleviate this problem. We develop a distributed representation of the merge tree that avoids computing the global tree on a single processor and lets us parallelize subsequent queries. To account for the increasing number of cores per processor, we develop a new data structure that lets us take advantage of multiple shared-memory cores to parallelize the work on a single node. Finally, we present experiments that illustrate the strengths of our approach as well as help identify future challenges.

Categories and Subject Descriptors D.1.3 [*Programming Techniques*]: Concurrent Programming; F.2.2 [*Analysis of Algorithms and Problem Complexity*]: Nonnumerical Algorithms and Problems.

Keywords topological data analysis, feature extraction, merge tree computation, parallelization, hybrid parallelization approaches

1. Introduction

Science and engineering increasingly rely on simulations to better understand natural phenomena. With the growing computational power available to these simulations, their results become more complex, and analysis becomes a challenge. Simultaneously, the improvements in the precision of physical instruments outpace our ability to process their measurements, creating a similar demand for tools capable of large-scale analysis. Traditional visualization techniques help gather new insights, but today's datasets achieve a level of complexity that hinders their direct understanding.

One way to reduce this complexity is to extract the salient features, subsequently using them for visualization and analysis. In this context, topological methods have proven useful as they supply flexible feature definitions for a range of scientific problems, including characterizing the mixing of fluids [14], analyzing combustion simulations [5, 6, 15, 23], and identifying states and transitions in chemical systems [3]. Often, topological features, such as isosurfaces and extrema, have a ready physical interpretation.

What makes topological analysis powerful is its principled approach. By drawing on algebraic insights, it establishes a connection between stability and persistence of topological features. Accordingly, it allows the user to zero in on what matters: to recognize the significance of the different parts of the input, to highlight its meaningful components, and to distinguish between important features and superficial noise. Feature detection provides a simpler, abstract view of the data.

But the increasing data sizes demand more computational power. While its growth was following Moore's law, serial computation was meeting this demand. Recently this growth has stalled. As a consequence, the need to speed up computation has put more emphasis on the use of parallelism. With modern supercomputers in mind, we aim to take full advantage not only of the large number of computational nodes, but also of the growing number of shared memory cores on each node.

To cope with the proverbial flood of data, we need to be able to run topological algorithms effectively on massively parallel machines. However, the analytical strength of topology is also its computational weakness. By definition, topology relies on global information: that's how it recognizes globally stable features. But global information is an obstacle to parallelization, which thrives on localized computation.

Accordingly, parallel approaches in topology are in their infancy. We are aware of only one result on parallel computation of merge trees [17], the main object of our study. Notable effort has gone into parallelizing Morse–Smale complex computation [13, 21, 22]. In all cases, the chief obstacle is the need to gather global information about the data. We propose to shift the focus from computation of topological descriptors in isolation and to consider their subsequent analysis. Our main contribution is a distributed representation of merge trees that can be quickly postprocessed. We believe such an emphasis on analysis would be useful for many topological descriptors.

Merge trees. In this paper, we focus on a 0-dimensional topological invariant, a merge tree. By keeping track of the evolution of components in sublevel sets of a scalar function, merge trees capture their global connectivity. This information, in turn, has been used for computation of contour trees [8] and the analysis of scientific datasets [6].

Because of their connection to persistent homology [10] — the branches of a merge tree are equivalent to a 0-dimensional persistence diagram — merge trees allow the user to examine the amplitude of noise in the data. Furthermore, they let us make minimal changes to the function while eliminating as many (noisy) extrema as possible [1, 2, 12]. Consequently, such a simplified, de-noised function can serve as an input to any visualization technique.

Reeb graphs [20] are descriptors closely related to merge trees. Instead of tracking components of sublevel sets, they track isosurfaces, i.e., components of level sets. Reeb graphs illuminate the stability of isosurfaces [4] by quantifying how small a perturbation eliminates any given component. When the domain is simply connected, Reeb graphs become trees, often called contour trees. The algorithm of Carr et al. [8] constructs contour trees from two merge trees: those of the function and of its negation. Flexible isosurfaces [7, 9] use these trees to manipulate individual contours.

In many data analysis applications, it is interesting how derived quantities change as we vary the classification threshold. For example, in combustion simulations one can classify regions as "burning" or "non-burning" by thresholding fuel consumption. Since superlevel sets correspond to segmentation of the domain above a threshold, it is possible to use merge trees to extract information, such as burning region size, for all possible thresholds [6]. Similarly, Mascarenhas et al. [15] use the merge tree to compute statistics about feature thickness depending on various scalar dissipation rate thresholds. Our own work is motivated by finding halos in astrophysical data. Here the goal is to identify clusters of high density without *a priori* knowledge of a suitable threshold. The merge tree provides a compact representation for all possible classifications, which not only lets us detect thresholds interesting for analysis, but also supports efficient computation of derived quantities such as the distribution of mass in a cluster. The salient point in all cases is that a merge tree is not an end goal in and of itself. Instead, it is a means to organize data for querying and post-processing.

Contribution. We attack the problem of computing merge trees on modern parallel computers on two fronts: (1) we develop a distributed representation of merge trees that not only improves their parallel computation, but also simplifies their subsequent analysis; (2) we develop a new algorithm for merging two trees. Specifically, after reviewing background and prior work in the next section, we present our contributions as follows:

- As a baseline, we assemble a global tree by performing in parallel a binary reduction. To fit the result on a single processor, we simplify the tree. In Section 3, we show that merging and simplification steps can be interleaved during the computation.

- Section 4 describes a distributed merge tree representation that not only speeds up the computation, but lets us parallelize subsequent queries. This representation is particularly interesting in the context of the so-called in-situ computation, where the input is partitioned among multiple processors by its producer, and any analysis must respect this partition, minimizing the movement of the data.

- Section 5 presents a new data structure for storing the merge tree. It not only speeds up the serial combination of two trees, a basic step both in our work and in prior work [17], but also lets this operation scale on multiple available shared-memory cores.

Section 6 illustrates our claims with experimental results.

2. Background

We begin by reviewing the relevant background, including related work.

Spaces, functions, and merge trees. In this paper we are concerned with triangulated domains that support continuous real-valued functions. Recall that a k-simplex is the convex hull of $k+1$ vertices. Its face is the convex hull of any subset of these vertices. A simplicial complex is a collection of simplices closed under taking faces. We assume that our input is a simplicial complex K together with a scalar function $\hat{f} : \mathrm{Vrt}\, K \to \mathbb{R}$ on its vertices. We extend this function to the underlying space $|K|$ of the simplicial complex, i.e., the union of its simplices, by linear interpolation and obtain $f : |K| \to \mathbb{R}$.

Merge trees capture the connectivity of the sublevel sets $K_a = f^{-1}(-\infty, a]$ of a real-valued function. (Symmetrically, they can keep track of the superlevel sets of a function, but it is convenient to think of this case as working with the negation, $-f$.) For a formal definition, we say that two points x and y in the domain $|K|$ of f are equivalent, $x \sim y$, if they belong to the same level set, $f(x) = f(y)$, and they belong to the same component of the sublevel set $f^{-1}(-\infty, f(x)]$. A *quotient space*, $|K|/\sim$, glues together points in $|K|$ that are equivalent under the relation $\sim$, i.e., it is the set of equivalence classes of $|K|$ with respect to $\sim$, equipped with the topology where open sets are those sets of equivalence classes whose unions are open sets in $|K|$. This quotient space is called a *merge tree*.

The following procedural description unravels the definition. As we sweep the function value from $-\infty$ to ∞, we create a new branch for each minimum. As its component in the sublevel set grows, we extend the branch until two of them merge (at a saddle). If the domain is connected, all the branches merge together by the time we reach the global maximum, which becomes the root of the tree. We can, thus, distinguish between three types of nodes in a merge tree: leaves represent the minima of the function; internal nodes correspond to the merge saddles; and the root of the tree captures the global maximum.

There is the fourth type of node, a *degree-two node*. These nodes are topologically trivial — they carry no information since the sublevel sets do not change as we pass the respective function value — but they are by far the most numerous. We prune such nodes from the tree, recording them in lists attached to the first non-trivial node below them.

For a linearly interpolated function only the 1-skeleton of the domain (vertices and edges) matters to the connectivity of the sublevel sets and, therefore, to the computation of the merge tree. We assume there are n vertices and m edges in the domain. The input function will be fixed throughout the paper. However, we will restrict it to different domains. We denote the merge tree of the function restricted to a set U by T_U.

Branch decomposition. To get a better handle on its structure, it is convenient to decompose a merge tree. At every internal node, we separate all but the deepest subtree. Here we mean the deepest in terms of the minimum function value. The result is a decomposition of the tree into half-open paths that start at an extremum and end just before a saddle, plus one closed path that starts at the global minimum and ends at the global maximum; see Figure 1. The intervals of function values covered by these paths nest into each other; they are precisely the persistence barcode [11]. Pascucci et al. [18] use a similar decomposition for the contour trees.

Computation. The standard approach to computing merge trees [8] is closely related to Kruskal's algorithm for finding minimum spanning trees. It maintains a disjoint-set data structure, initializing each vertex as its own set. Processing the vertices in order of increasing

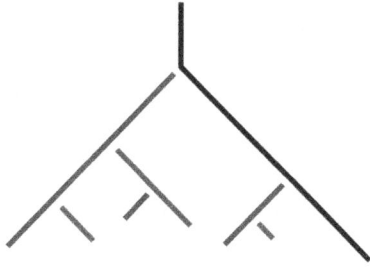

Figure 1: Branch decomposition.

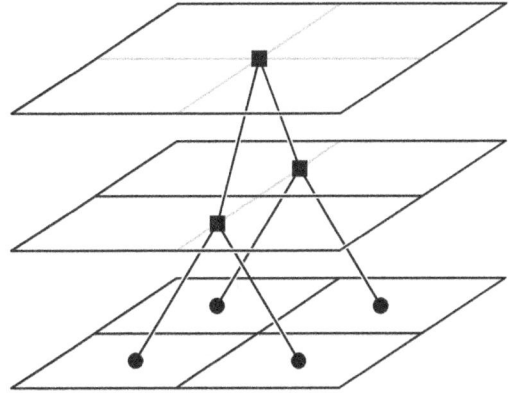

Figure 2: Hierarchy of merges resulting from a quadtree decomposition of the domain. The merges, represented by squares, follow in reverse the splitting of the sets in the quadtree.

function value, one finds the sets containing each lower neighbor v of the current vertex u. If the sets containing u and v are different, the highest-valued representative in the set of v is linked to u in the merge tree; the two sets are united. The procedure is dominated either by the initial sorting of the vertices or by the union–find algorithm; thus, it runs in time $O(n \log n + m\alpha(n))$[1], where $\alpha(n)$ is the inverse Ackermann function.

To avoid storing the entire input in memory, Bremer et al. [6] build merge trees by incrementally merging together paths. Processing the edges in arbitrary order, the authors merge together (in sorted order) the two paths in the tree that start from the vertices of an edge and go up to the root. It is not difficult to verify that the resulting tree is indeed the merge tree. (Here and throughout the paper, we abuse the terminology and refer to merge *trees* of disconnected domains, which are, in fact, forests.) The price for memory savings is speed: this construction technique is slower than the Kruskal's-like algorithm above.

Domain decomposition. Given multiple processors, the only existing technique [17] for parallel computation of merge trees follows the standard reduction strategy. The domain is covered by multiple sets; individual processors find merge trees of the function restricted to each of these sets. The resulting small trees are merged together in pairs — producing merge trees of the function restricted to larger and larger subsets of the domain — until all the covering sets are united. When this happens, we have the sought-after full merge tree.

It is convenient to think of the initial cover as the finest level in a hierarchical decomposition of the domain. The hierarchy follows in reverse the merging order of the sets; see Figure 2 for a two-dimensional example. The prototypical three-dimensional example of this construction is an octree subdivision of a cube. Because we are merging sets in pairs, we halve their number at each iteration and move higher up in the hierarchy: at level $3i$, we have 8^i smaller cubes. In this case, the intersection between two merging cubes is always a subset of their two-dimensional boundary. (In general, this need not be the case: for instance, if at the finest level the cubes were thickened by a layer of ghost cells.)

In the remainder of the paper we assume, for simplicity, that we are working with a hierarchy resulting from an octree subdivision of a cubical domain. In fact, we rely on no assumptions on the topology of the covering sets. This observation is irrelevant for cubical domains since the merged cubes remain contractible. However, it becomes beneficial on tori (periodic domains) and, especially, on adaptive mesh refinement (AMR) grids. In the latter case, higher-resolution grids refine subsets of the data at the coarser levels. This refinement, effectively, punches holes in coarser blocks

leaving us no control over the topology of their uncovered portions. Our results in the next two sections apply directly in these settings.

Merging. Pascucci and Cole-McLaughlin [17] follow the decomposition strategy outlined above. They merge the trees by repeating the Kruskal's algorithm with the union of the trees as the domain. The simplicity of this procedure is appealing: if you can compute a merge tree, you can merge two trees. But the entire approach is limited. As we merge more and more sets, fewer processors remain in use while the trees grow larger. As a result, the binary reduction underlying the merge is top-heavy, making this algorithm effective only for a small number of processors (relative to the size of the input).

The algorithm of Bremer et al. [6] can also be used for merging trees — after all, we just need the merge tree of the function on the union of the two trees. Although slower than [17], their technique serves as the foundation for our new merging algorithm in Section 5. Once we augment the underlying tree data structure, we get a merging algorithm that significantly outperforms the alternative.

3. Simplified Global Tree

For modern input sizes, the merge trees are too large to store in memory of a single node. That's the main motivation behind our work. It is also the main obstacle to a direct comparison of our work to prior approaches [6, 17], both of which try to compute the entire merge tree in one place. In this section we state auxiliary results and describe a scheme that serves as a comparison baseline for our main contribution.

The theory of persistent homology [10] suggests a way to limit the growth of the merge trees. Instead of computing the full tree, we could find a simplified tree that keeps only the stable branches. To distinguish between the unstable noise and the stable features, we need an extra parameter ε: any branch we can remove by changing the input by at most ε is noisy; every remaining branch is stable. When the threshold ε is sufficiently high, the simplified tree becomes small enough to fit in memory.

Simplification. A crucial realization is that we do not need to compute the full merge tree in order to simplify it[2]. Simplification and computation steps can be interleaved in the course of the reduction. Once we compute the merge tree for one of the regions

---

[1] In our implementation of union–find algorithm, we only use the path compression optimization, without the union-by-rank. Consequently, the running time is $O(m \log n)$.

[2] The idea of simplification is very natural in computational topology and has a long history. Gyulassy et al. [13] independently suggested to use it in the context of parallel computation of Morse–Smale complexes.

in the decomposed domain, we can remove all the branches of length at most ε that are completely internal to the domain, i.e., the ones without boundary nodes. The following theorem justifies this procedure.

THEOREM 3.1. *Given a function f, let T_U and $T_{U \cup V}$ be the merge trees of its restriction to sets U and $U \cup V$. If every node in a subtree of T_U lies outside $U \cap V$, then that subtree appears (unaltered) in $T_{U \cup V}$.*

PROOF. We prove the claim by induction on the size of the subtree. Let x be a node in T_U. If x is a leaf (i.e., a subtree of size one), it is a minimum of the function restricted to U. If it lies outside $U \cap V$, it remains a minimum in $U \cup V$. So it remains a leaf in $T_{U \cup V}$.

Assume the claim is true for all subtrees of size up to k. Let x be the root of a subtree of size $k+1$; let x and all of its descendants be outside $U \cap V$. From the inductive assumption, none of the subtrees of its children change in $T_{U \cup V}$. Therefore, the only way for the subtree of x to change is if its component of the sublevel set changes when we restrict the function to the union $U \cup V$. But this is impossible: since x and all of its descendants are outside $U \cap V$, its component in the sublevel set of the function restricted to $U \cup V$ lies entirely in $U - (U \cap V)$. □

The final merge tree has a convenient interpretation in light of the work on persistence-sensitive simplification [1, 2, 12]. We can find a function g, close to f in the sense that $\sup_x |f(x) - g(x)| \leq \varepsilon$, such that the simplified tree is really the merge tree of g. This view justifies our strategy: if the input was perturbed up to ε by noise, we can choose any nearby function without sacrificing precision — we might as well choose the function that gives the clearest view of the data.

Pruning. The efficiency of the merging and simplification procedures depends on the sizes of the trees involved. So we try to make them as small as possible. It is easy to prune the internal nodes: all degree-two nodes are redundant. The boundary nodes, on the other hand, present a problem. A degree-two boundary node in the restricted domain can end up a merge node once the two domains are united. The next lemma, however, grants us some freedom by elucidating which of the boundary nodes are definitely superfluous.

LEMMA 3.2. *Given a function f, suppose we have merge trees T_U and T_V of the restriction of f to sets U and V. If $x \in U \cap V$ is not a minimum of $f_{|U \cap V}$, then the path from x to the root in T_U is a sub-path of a path from y to the root for some node $y \in U \cap V$. The claim is true for the same pair of nodes in T_V.*

PROOF. Let x be a vertex in $U \cap V$ with a lower neighbor $y \in U \cap V$, $f(y) < f(x)$, i.e., x is not a minimum in the intersection. Then, since the function is piecewise-linearly interpolated on the interiors of the edges, y appears in the subtree of x both in T_U and T_V. Therefore, the paths from x to the roots in both trees are subsets of the paths from y. The claim follows. □

What is the implication? A degree-two node x that's not a minimum in the boundary of a cover set contributes no information about the connectivity of the sublevel sets in the union. Some other node y makes redundant x's only contribution, the evidence that the sublevel sets on its path to the root in the two trees are connected. In other words, if a boundary node is not a minimum (within the boundary), we are free to prune it away. On a $1,024^3$ grid we use for our experiments in Section 6, such an aggressive pruning reduces (already pruned) trees by an additional factor between three and four.

Limitation. The simplified-global-tree strategy has an obvious downside: we must know the simplification threshold ε in advance. Merge trees are interesting because they offer a comprehensive

view of the data. For example, the distribution of the branches lets us recognize the amplitude of the noise. But now we face a chicken-and-egg problem: we need a merge tree to choose a simplification threshold, and we need a threshold to get a merge tree. In the next section, we show that one need not choose: we can distribute the full merge tree among all the processors.

4. Local–Global Representation

No amount of simplification and pruning can save us from the sizes of the global trees, which grow in lockstep with the input. So instead of trying to assemble the entire output on a single processor, we distribute its representation.

There are many ways to do this. For instance, each processor could store those nodes in the tree that correspond to its local input data. Additionally, each such node could record its parent in the global tree. In principle, such a distribution represents the whole tree. But it is too expensive for analysis. Any non-trivial query requires a traversal of the tree, which, in turn, would generate too much communication: we may have to bounce between processors at every step.

With this consideration, we arrive at the main idea behind our work. By focusing on how a merge tree is used for analysis, we distribute it so as to minimize communication required to answer queries. To this end, each processor stores the detailed connectivity of the branches with its local input data, but keeps only a coarse view of the entire tree.

Sparsification. Instead of treating all the nodes equally, we bestow some with a special status. The chosen nodes are significant: we can answer detailed queries about them. We *sparsify* the tree as much as possible outside of these nodes. To do so, we remove all the branches not reachable from a special node by a monotonically increasing path; see Figure 3. Here we think of a branch as a minimum–saddle segment, open at the saddle. If the saddle loses enough branches to have only one child, i.e., when it becomes a degree-two node, we prune it from the tree. Such sparsification can be performed in linear time via a post-order traversal.

DEFINITION 4.1. *A merge tree T_X is sparsified with respect to $Y \subset X$ if all its branches $[m, s]$ that do not intersect ascending paths $[u, \text{ROOT}(T_X)]$ for any $u \in Y$ are removed. We refer to the removed branches as* ghost *and to the remaining branches as* live.

We note that in this definition the branches are open at the saddle. So if a path from a node in Y goes through a saddle, it does not preclude the removal of the branch that ends in that saddle (as well as the subsequent pruning of the saddle); see Figure 3.

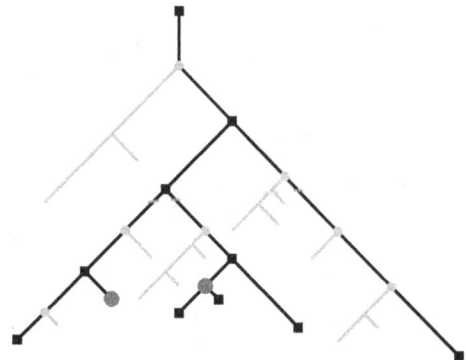

Figure 3: A tree sparsified with respect to the two nodes marked with red disks. Removed branches (and saddles) appear in gray. The remaining nodes are marked with black squares.

Our ultimate goal is to assemble on each processor the global tree sparsified with respect to the processor's local data. But to do so we need intermediate information. As before, our Algorithm 1, SPARSEEXCHANGE, grows the domain of the sparsified tree in iterations: starting from the finest sets in the cover, the trees are merged in pairs. After each iteration, each processor sparsifies its result with respect to the local data and the boundary of the larger domain; see Figure 4. The processors exchange data in pairs: they send to each other their local trees sparsified with respect to the boundary. After i iterations, 2^i nodes have the same outgoing information. In our implementation, they exchange it directly with their counterpart, a node with the same MPI rank except for the inverted i-th bit. Figure 5 illustrates the communication pattern.

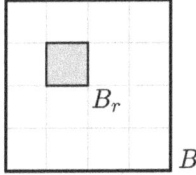

Figure 4: Special nodes in the tree after several iterations of merging are the vertices in the shaded local domain B_r and in the boundary of the larger domain ∂B.

Unlike in the previous section and in the prior work [17], the number of workers does not halve after each iteration. Every processor remains busy computing how its local data fits into the global (sparsified) tree.

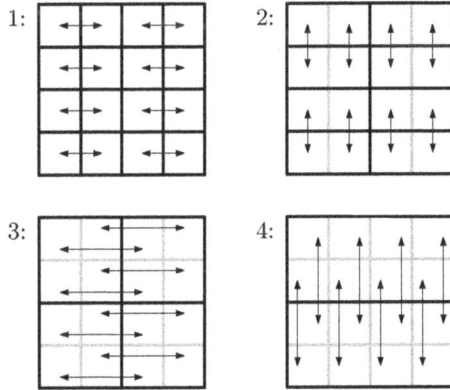

Figure 5: Communication pattern between 16 nodes. The nodes boxed together have the same outgoing information that corresponds to the boundary ∂B of the expanded domain in Figure 4.

The following theorem implies the correctness of our algorithm.

THEOREM 4.2. Ghost branches of T_U with respect to $Y_U \supseteq U \cap V$ remain ghosts in $T_{U \cup V}$ with respect to $Y_U \cup Y_V$ for any $Y_V \subset V$.

PROOF. Consider the merging of the trees T_U and T_V. It operates on the paths to the root that start from nodes in $U \cap V$. Since Y_U contains $U \cap V$, by definition, the ghost branches in T_U with respect to Y_U are not reachable from these paths. Therefore, they remain unreachable from $Y_U \cup Y_V$ in $T_{U \cup V}$. $\square$

In other words, once a branch is a ghost with respect to $X \cup \partial U$, it remains a ghost no matter how many other trees it is merged with. (Here we assume, for simplicity, that the sets in the cover intersect only along their boundaries.) Equivalently, sparsification and merge operations can be safely interleaved. So, once the SPARSE-EXCHANGE procedure terminates, we have the global tree sparsified with respect to the processor's local data.

Algorithm 1

SPARSEEXCHANGE(f):
(Assumes 2^k compute nodes. BOX(r) refers to the initial set assigned to the node r.)

  $r \leftarrow$ MPI-RANK
  $B \leftarrow B_r \leftarrow$ BOX(r)
  $T \leftarrow$ MERGETREE($f_{|B_r}$)
  for i **from** 0 **to** $k-1$ **do**
    $p \leftarrow r$ XOR 2^i # partner rank
    SEND($p, (T, B)$)
    $(T_p, B_p) \leftarrow$ RECEIVE(p)
    $T \leftarrow$ MERGE(T, T_p)
    $B \leftarrow B \cup B_p$
    $T \leftarrow$ SPARSIFY($T, B_r \cup \partial B$)
  $T \leftarrow$ SPARSIFY(T, B_r)

Post-processing. Usually merge tree computation serves as a preprocessing step; the real analysis is performed via subsequent queries. In this case, the local–global representation is especially powerful. The initial investment in its computation pays off: the queries can be answered in parallel employing all the available processors.

The simplest example of such post-analysis is the extraction of the persistence diagram, a completely parallel process requiring no communication: each node reports the branches started by the minima in its local domain. It is similarly simple to find which noisy minimum gets remapped into which persistent minimum when we simplify the function by a given threshold: all the information is available locally.

Histograms. A more interesting example is querying the distribution of volumes of sublevel set components containing a given point. Such analysis is useful, for example, in astrophysics when comparing simulated and observed data. Unlike the nodes of the merge tree, the sublevel sets are not localized; their different parts belong to different processors. Fortunately, we can find the sublevel set component of any given local node x without any communication. We identify each component with the point that started it, i.e., the lowest minimum it contains. This identification suggests an alternative view of the local–global representation: for every point in the local domain, it records all the sublevel set components that contain that point.

So for any point x we identify a sequence s_i of saddles that we encounter on the path from x to the root. Additionally, we get the sequence m_i of minima that identify the components of the sublevel sets, so that between $f(s_i)$ and $f(s_{i+1})$ point x belongs to the component identified with m_{i+1}; see Figure 6. Accordingly, the function values on these pairs nest into each other:

$$f(x) \in [f(m_1), f(s_1)] \subseteq [f(m_2), f(s_2)] \subseteq [f(m_3), f(s_3)] \subseteq \ldots$$

Now for any value $a \in [f(s_{k-1}), f(s_k)]$ we broadcast the minimum m_k to the rest of the processors, so that each one of them can find its contribution to the volume of the component of m_k in the sublevel set $f^{-1}(-\infty, a]$. The numbers are summed up by a single reduction. Similarly, for a histogram of volumes with bins defined by intervals I: we broadcast both sequences $f(s_i)$ and m_i; each processor finds its local contribution to each interval in I; the processors sum up all the contributions via a reduction.

Persistent components. Another common query is the location of components that cannot be removed by a small perturbation. Besides the merge tree, we are given two thresholds, m and t. The goal is to report all components of the sublevel set at t that contain a minimum lower than m. Typically, we want to find some additional

97

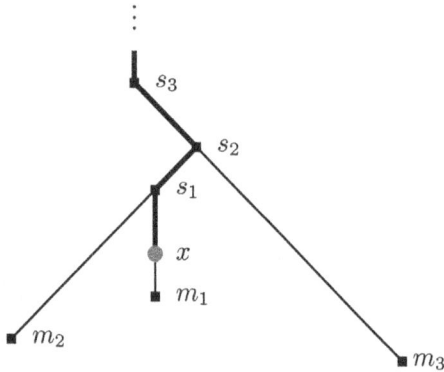

Figure 6: The saddles on the path from x to the root designate its membership in different sublevel set components, represented by the respective minima.

information for such components, for example, their volume or integral. In applications, such queries appear when we are looking for clusters in density functions; in cosmological simulations this problem is called "halo finding."

Here again the local–global representation proves convenient: every processor has complete information about all the components that intersect its local domain. Therefore, in a single traversal, it can identify both the persistent components and how much volume its local domain contributes to each one. Making each processor responsible for the minima local to its input, an exchange is still necessary to sum up the contributions from the different processors, but the required communication is minimal.

5. Skip Trees

Both in Sections 3 and 4 as well as in [17] the main computational step is the merging of two trees. The original approach of Pascucci and Cole-McLaughlin [17] finds the result by repeating the union–find procedure with the union of the two trees as the input. It is unsatisfying for two reasons: (1) the underlying union–find procedure is inherently serial; (2) the algorithm is not sensitive to the output. The former trait is particularly unfortunate for modern computer architectures where the number of cores on an individual node has been steadily rising. Sharing the same memory — the real limiting resource — these processing units could be simultaneously working on the same pair of trees. The goal of this section is to describe an alternative to the algorithm of Pascucci and Cole-McLaughlin that takes advantage of multiple shared-memory cores.

The work of Bremer et al. [6] can be used for merging just as well as for the initial construction. It would mitigate both of the above problems — their algorithm is easy to parallelize using shared memory, and it ignores the parts of the tree that remain unchanged — if only it was competitive with the union–find procedure. Below we adjust our data structure to gain both performance and scaling.

The algorithm of Bremer et al. creates n vertices (on-demand, if necessary) and then processes edges in an arbitrary order. Assuming we already have a merge tree for a domain K, the algorithm finds the merge tree for the domain $K \cup e$, where e is an arbitrary edge $e = (u, v)$ with $f(u) \leq f(v)$. This new edge indicates that all the sublevel set components containing vertex v also contain vertex u. The nodes on the path from v to the root represent all the former components; the nodes on the path from u to the root represent the latter. So all it takes to get the merge tree for $K \cup e$ is to merge these two paths in the sorted order.

The core of this algorithm is the merging of sorted paths. Unfortunately, we have no control over the order in which the edges arrive. Merging together n singleton paths can take quadratic time in the worst case. Although, in practice, the situation is not nearly as bad, profiling shows that the average node access is too high, indicating that the same nodes get traversed many times during the merge process. To alleviate this problem, we turn to skip lists [19] for inspiration and build additional shortcut levels over each parent pointer in the merge tree.

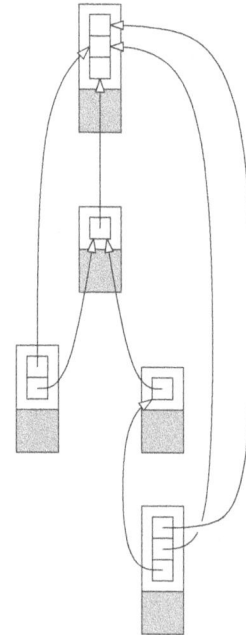

Figure 7: A skip tree with five nodes. The heights of parent stacks are randomized.

Like skip lists, the resulting data structure is randomized. Each node has a parent pointer stack, called a *finger*. The heights of these stacks follow the geometric distribution with probability parameter $1/2$: a node gets a stack of height at least i with probability $(1/2)^{i-1}$. Thus, the expected size of the stack is less than two. Together with the overhead to store the size and the location of the stack, our data structure grows by three words per node compared to the regular merge tree. At each available level i, the node stores the pointer to its first ancestor in the merge tree with the stack of height at least i; see Figure 7. In the resulting tree each path from a leaf to the root is a skip list.

To merge two skip trees, we proceed similarly to Bremer et al. Starting from the shared vertices (alternatively, from the user-provided extra edges), we merge the ascending paths in the two trees. Unlike their algorithm, we can use the additional levels to skip over many nodes at once — the ability responsible for the speedup in Figure 11. Although more involved, it is still simple to simultaneously perform multiple such merges in shared memory. (In fact, our implementation is lock-free.) The scaling results in Table 3 are encouraging.

Remark. We stress that our findings about skip trees apply only to the merging of two trees. When constructing two merge trees from scratch, the union–find-based construction outperforms the skip-tree approach.

6. Experimental Results

We perform experiments on four different datasets: **V** is a rotational angiography scan of a head with an aneurysm (a 512^3 image from http://volvis.org); **A1** and **A2** are two datasets of dark matter particle mass, results of astrophysics simulations ($1,024^3$ and $2,048^3$ fields, respectively); **C** is the rate of methane consumption during a combustion process ($1,024^2 \times 2,048$ flattened two-level AMR grid).

We ran all benchmarks on the "Hopper" system at the National Energy Research Scientific Computing Center (NERSC). "Hopper" is a Cray XE6 with 6,384 nodes connected by a proprietary "Cray Gemini Interconnect". Each node contains 24 cores — provided by two twelve-core AMD 'MagnyCours' 2.1GHz processors — with 32GB (6,000 nodes) or 64GB (384 nodes) of shared memory. Each core has its own L1 and L2 caches, of size 64KB and 512KB respectively, and six cores on the 'MagnyCours' processor share one 6MB L3 cache.

Figure 8 on the following page expresses the relationship between the computation of the local–global representation and of the global simplified trees. The salient point of the four graphs is clear: even when the computation of the most aggressively simplified tree is faster than the local–global representation, it is only slightly so. At the same time the local–global representation contains the same information as the entire unsimplified tree. As the graphs suggest, the less one simplifies the tree, the longer its global computation. We note that the algorithm of [17] computes the global unsimplified tree, which in our context is equivalent to the 0-simplification, meaning it is at least as slow as the slowest running times in those graphs.

To get a better idea about this behavior, we focus on one of the runs. Specifically, we examine the tree growth during the computation of the local–global representation and the global simplified trees for different thresholds using 512 processors on **A1** dataset. Table 1 shows the sizes of the largest tree on any processor during the different iterations of the algorithm, for varying thresholds. The tree growth reflects the memory demands on the processors, our most constraining resource. It also explains the slower computation of the global simplified trees: larger trees take longer to merge. Figure 9 displays the same information graphically. What do we observe? Although the local–global representation starts out larger than even the least aggressive simplification — indeed, it starts with the unsimplified tree — and even though the trees grow during the computation of the local–global representation, they do so significantly slower than during the computation of the global simplified tree. So much so that already before the final sparsification the local–global trees are smaller than the most aggressively simplified, '1e13', trees. The most simplified tree provides little detail about the underlying function. In contrast, the local–global representation gives access to the full merge tree, providing more detail than the most timid simplification, '8e11', which also happens to be several times slower. The situation becomes even more dramatic after the final sparsification: the sparsified local–global tree is not only significantly smaller than the global simplified trees, but it is barely larger than the initial local tree, 44,824 nodes at the end versus 42,594 nodes in the beginning.

Such shrinking of the final trees occurs in all our examples, most vividly illustrated in the bottom graph of Figure 10. This behavior highlights our main interest in the local–global representation. We can make the output of our algorithm (which is also the input to the subsequent analysis routines) small by increasing the number of processors we use. So even in the case of the **V** dataset, where, as the top graph in Figure 10 illustrates, it is disadvantageous to increase the number of processors past 512 — the problem size is too small, and the communication overhead becomes overwhelming — it is still advantageous to increase processor count to decrease the size of the per-processor input to the analysis routines.

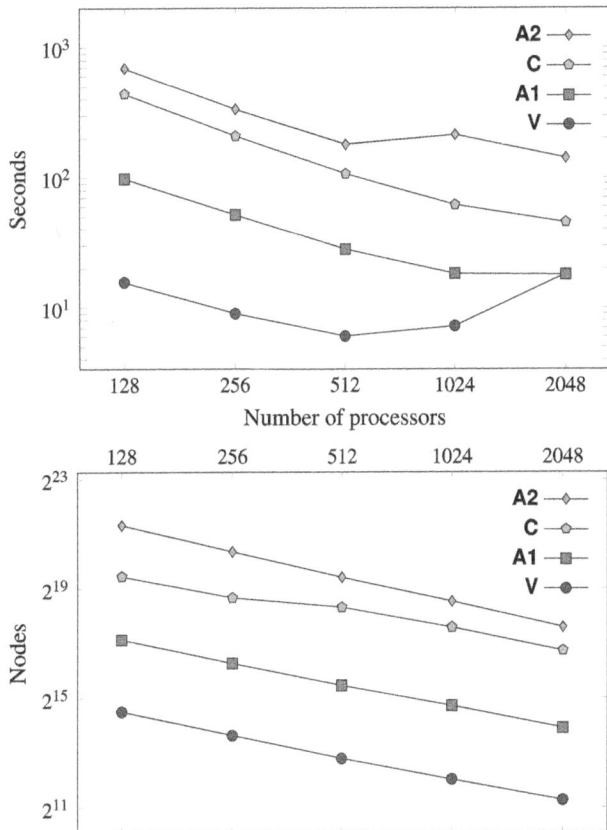

Figure 10: Times to compute the local–global representation (top) and its final (largest) tree sizes (bottom) for varying numbers of processors. Same data as in Table 2.

To get a sense of how the two methods influence analysis, we extract a persistence diagram for the **A1** dataset. When working with the local–global representation all 512 processors are participating in the computation; for the global simplified trees, we are limited to a single processor. It takes 3 seconds to get the persistence diagram in the former case versus 58 seconds in the latter (for the '8e11' threshold). Of course, the simplified diagram is less detailed. Although this comparison may seem strange — comparing one processor against 512 is hardly fair — it underlines our key message. Local–global representation lets us use all the available processors for post-processing. With global simplified trees we are stuck with a monolithic representation. It is worth noting that, in this case, the time to read the global simplified tree is about 14 seconds, i.e., it is significantly longer than the entire diagram extraction from the local–global representation.

In a sequel [16] we show how a more computationally intensive analysis routine (level set extraction) takes advantage of our representation and speeds up as the local–global trees shrink with the increasing number of processors.

Skip trees. Figure 11 and Table 3 below illustrate the time it takes to merge two trees restricted to adjacent $1024^2 \times 512$ subsets of a $1,024^3$ grid. The trees have 803,589 and 821,941 nodes.

Figure 11 shows how the merging time decreases as we increase the finger size. The run times stop improving once the finger size becomes larger than six, but naturally this depends on the size of the input trees. More importantly, the run times do not increase as we increase the finger size further. Thus, to be safe, we set this constant to 16 in our code. A skip tree with all fingers of size one

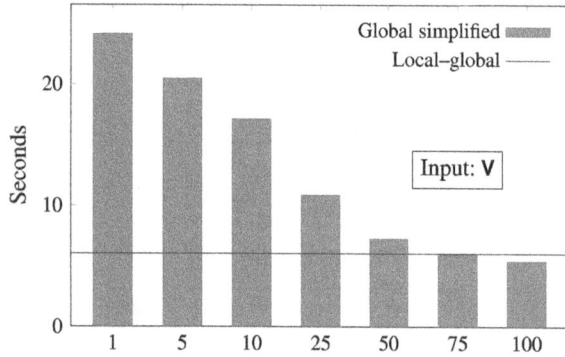

(a) Time to compute using 512 processors the global simplified trees, using different simplification thresholds, for the **V** dataset. It takes 6.04 seconds to compute the local–global representation of this dataset on 512 processors.

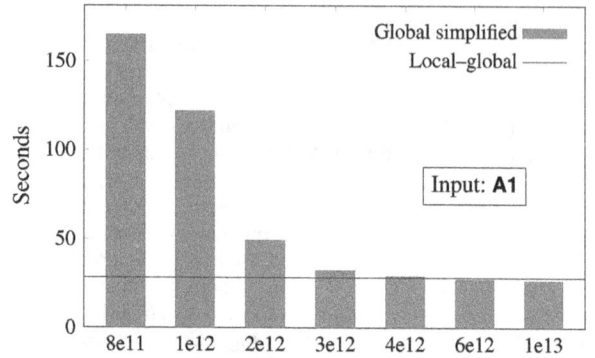

(b) Time to compute using 512 processors the global simplified trees, using different simplification thresholds, for the **A1** dataset. It takes 28.09 seconds to compute the local–global representation of this dataset on 512 processors.

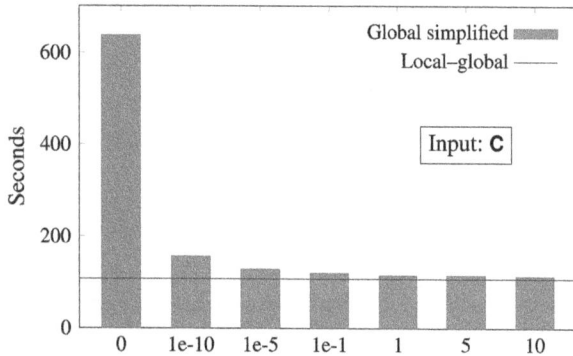

(c) Time to compute using 512 processors the global simplified trees, using different simplification thresholds, for the **C** dataset. It takes 106.92 seconds to compute the local–global representation of this dataset on 512 processors.

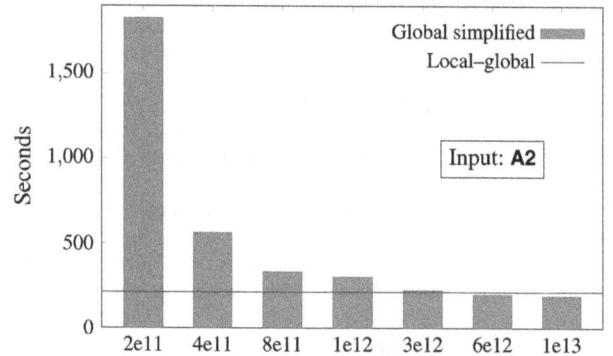

(d) Time to compute using 1,024 processors the global simplified trees, using different simplification thresholds, for the **A2** dataset. It takes 212.19 seconds to compute the local–global representation of this dataset on 1,024 processors.

Figure 8: Running times to compute global simplified trees for different simplification thresholds.

iteration	local–global	1e13	8e12	6e12	4e12	3e12	2e12	1e12	8e11
Initial	42,594	6,396	6,464	6,580	6,889	7,502	9,960	24,171	28,733
1	46,656	10,612	10,733	10,933	11,484	12,519	17,112	43,572	52,247
2	53,814	16,848	17,041	17,428	18,439	20,259	28,887	80,538	96,969
3	62,983	26,207	26,483	27,017	28,736	31,613	46,917	145,089	176,516
4	75,836	39,366	39,929	41,056	44,387	50,082	80,182	271,390	332,159
5	98,981	64,605	65,845	68,045	74,462	85,364	144,362	520,391	637,634
6	134,004	102,184	104,389	108,566	120,849	142,282	258,474	1,010,099	1,244,505
7	173,369	148,638	152,808	161,053	186,206	229,442	463,442	1,967,922	2,435,072
8	236,334	226,894	235,175	251,101	298,308	378,679	828,682	3,774,931	4,689,989
9	297,786	315,921	332,831	365,347	460,797	623,497	1,529,351	7,437,553	9,269,091
Final	44,824	247,755	264,829	297,705	393,969	557,679	1,467,172	7,392,027	9,228,241

Table 1: Maximum size of a tree on any processor at every iteration of the computation of the local–global representation and of the global simplified trees for different simplification thresholds for **A1** dataset, using 512 processors. Figure 9 displays the same numbers graphically.

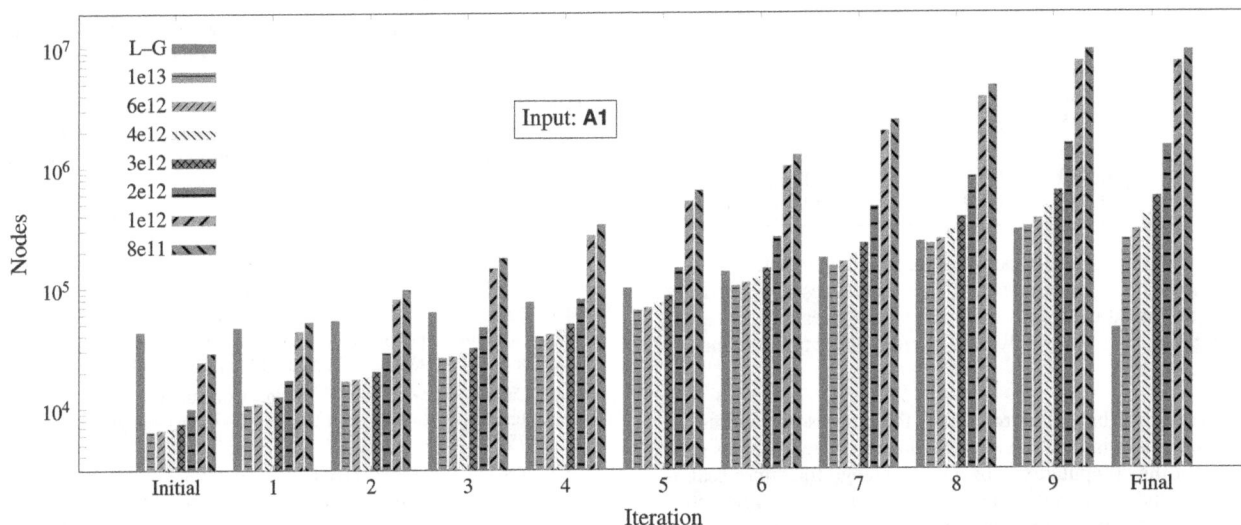

Figure 9: Maximum size of a tree on any processor at every iteration, using 512 processors. The raw data appears in Table 1.

| | V | | A1 | | C | | A2 | |
processors	seconds	nodes	seconds	nodes	seconds	nodes	seconds	nodes
128	15.72	23,258	98.36	143,371	438.88	713,998	692.46	2,595,954
256	9.03	12,721	51.88	78,665	208.49	415,927	334.48	1,328,602
512	6.04	7,093	28.09	44,824	106.92	325,708	179.20	694,689
1,024	7.22	4,179	18.20	26,895	61.75	196,009	212.19	376,917
2,048	18.04	2,480	17.88	15,330	45.23	108,937	141.01	197,579

Table 2: Times to compute the local–global representation and its final tree sizes, in terms of the largest number of nodes on any processor, for varying numbers of processors. Figure 10 displays the same numbers as graphs.

is the same as the ordinary merge tree. Accordingly, merging two such skip trees is equivalent to applying the algorithm of [6]. It is also notable that with the increased finger size our merging strategy becomes faster than the union–find-based approach in [17]. We stress that this statement is true only for merging of two trees and not for the initial construction, where the Kruskal's-like algorithm is still superior.

The main reason we look for alternative merging strategies that do not depend on the serial constraints of the union–find algorithm is to improve the running time on multiple shared memory cores. As Table 3 illustrates, the skip tree merging is able to benefit from multiple cores on a 2×12-core AMD MagnyCours processor. Although all 24 cores share the same memory, the non-uniformity of memory access is noticeable: we saw no real improvement past 12 threads as well as a significantly diminishing improvement past six threads. Nonetheless, the union-find algorithm took 5.39 seconds and could only utilize one core, while the skip tree merge took 1.74 seconds with one thread and dropped to 0.42 seconds with 12 threads.

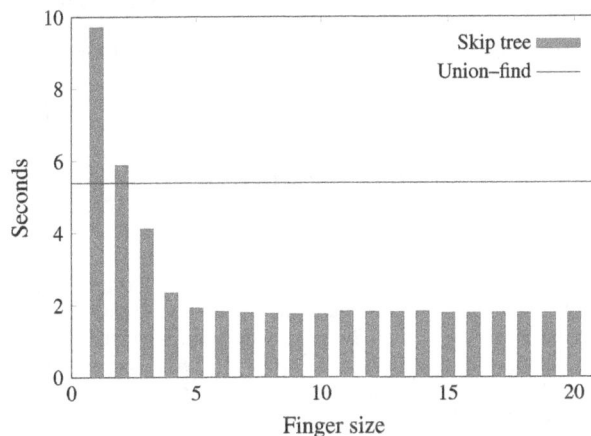

Figure 11: Merge time depending on the maximum size of the fingers in the skip tree. Finger size one is equivalent to applying the algorithm of [6] to an ordinary merge tree.

7. Conclusion

It is challenging to compute topological descriptors in parallel because they rely on global information. On the other hand, one of the main strengths of topological analysis is its ability to distinguish between stable and noisy features. We take advantage of this connection in Section 3 and reduce the size of the intermediate trees by interleaving computation and simplification.

We also benefit from taking a longer view by considering not just the computation of the individual descriptors, but also how we analyze them afterwards. To this end, we develop a local–global representation in Section 4. It is practical because it dramatically reduces the size of the trees during the computation. Even more useful is its output: instead of assembling all the information on

Threads	s	×	Threads	s	×
1	1.742	1.00	7	0.509	3.42
2	1.067	1.63	8	0.489	3.56
3	0.835	2.08	9	0.447	3.89
4	0.663	2.62	10	0.453	3.84
5	0.590	2.95	11	0.442	3.94
6	0.524	3.32	12	0.424	4.10

Table 3: Running times for skip tree merging using different number of threads. Columns labeled s show the times in seconds; $\times$ denotes the speed-up compared to the single thread. Merging the same dataset using the union–find algorithm takes 5.39 seconds.

one node, it distributes the tree across the processors, making the subsequent analysis fast. So even if the intermediate tree sizes grow throughout the computation, posing a challenge for future scaling — after all, individual nodes are still performing a binary reduction — we gain in the post-processing stage where the size of the input shrinks with the growing number of processors. Such an approach is likely to be useful for other topological descriptors.

On the shared-memory front, we present a parallel algorithm for merging two trees. It improves on the existing union–find-based techniques. Our experiments make it clear that new ideas will be necessary for the future architectures that will have many more cores with non-uniform memory access. Developing data structures that explicitly take this asymmetry into account is an important research direction.

Although our theoretical contributions apply in more general settings than the octree partitions we use as a running example in this paper, in practice, they require more work to deal with more complicated boundary and membership tests. We are currently focused on extending our implementation to adaptive mesh refinement grids.

Both because of the gains we find with the local–global representation and because of the challenges we discover along the way, we hope our contributions bring the community closer to the goal of parallel, scalable computation and analysis of topological descriptors.

Acknowledgments

This work was supported by the Director, Office of Science, Advanced Scientific Computing Research, of the U.S. Department of Energy under Contract No. DE-AC02-05CH11231 through the grant "Topology-based Visualization and Analysis of High-dimensional Data and Time-varying Data at the Extreme Scale," program manager Lucy Nowell, and by the use resources of the National Energy Research Scientific Computing Center (NERSC). The authors wish to thank Hank Childs, Terry Ligocki, Zarija Lukić, Peter Nugent, Casey Stark, and Matthew Turk for their encouragement and help.

References

[1] D. Attali, M. Glisse, S. Hornus, F. Lazarus, and D. Morozov. Persistence-sensitive simplification of functions on surfaces in linear time, 2009. Manuscript, presented at the Workshop on Topology In Visualization (TopoInVis'09).

[2] U. Bauer, C. Lange, and M. Wardetzky. Optimal topological simplification of discrete functions on surfaces. *Discrete and Computational Geometry*, 47(2):347–377, 2012.

[3] K. Beketayev, G. H. Weber, M. Haranczyk, P.-T. Bremer, M. Hlawitschka, and B. Hamann. Visualization of topology of transformation pathways in complex chemical systems. *Computer Graphics Forum (EuroVis 2011)*, pages 663–672, May/June 2011.

[4] P. Bendich, H. Edelsbrunner, D. Morozov, and A. Patel. Homology and robustness of level and interlevel sets. *Homology, Homotopy, and Application*, 2012. Accepted.

[5] P.-T. Bremer, G. H. Weber, V. Pascucci, M. S. Day, and J. B. Bell. Analyzing and tracking burning structures in lean premixed hydrogen flames. *IEEE Transactions on Visualization and Computer Graphics*, 16(2):248–260, 2010. doi: doi:10.1109/TVCG.2009.69.

[6] P.-T. Bremer, G. H. Weber, J. Tierny, V. Pascucci, M. S. Day, and J. B. Bell. Interactive exploration and analysis of large scale simulations using topology-based data segmentation. *IEEE Transactions on Visualization and Computer Graphics*, 17(9):1307–1325, 2011.

[7] H. Carr and J. Snoeyink. Path seeds and flexible isosurfaces using topology for exploratory visualization. In *Data Visualization 2003 (Proceedings VisSym 2003)*, pages 49–58, New York, NY, 2003.

[8] H. Carr, J. Snoeyink, and U. Axen. Computing contour trees in all dimensions. *Computational Geometry—Theory and Applications*, 24 (2):75–94, 2003.

[9] H. Carr, J. Snoeyink, and M. van de Panne. Simplifying flexible isosurfaces using local geometric measures. In *Proceedings IEEE Visualization 2004*, pages 497–504, Oct. 2004. doi: http://dx.doi.org/10.1109/VISUAL.2004.96.

[10] H. Edelsbrunner and J. Harer. *Persistent homology—a survey*, volume 453 of *Contemporary Mathematics*, pages 257–282. American Mathematical Society, 2008.

[11] H. Edelsbrunner and J. Harer. *Computational Topology. An Introduction*. American Mathematical Society, Providence, Rhode Island, 2010.

[12] H. Edelsbrunner, D. Morozov, and V. Pascucci. Persistence-sensitive simplification of functions on 2-manifolds. In *Proceedings of the Symposium on Computational Geometry*, pages 127–134, 2006.

[13] A. Gyulassy, V. Pascucci, T. Peterka, and R. Ross. The parallel computation of Morse–Smale complexes. In *Parallel & Distributed Processing Symposium (IPDPS)*, pages 484–495, 2012.

[14] D. Laney, P.-T. Bremer, A. Macarenhas, P. Miller, and V. Pascucci. Understanding the structure of the turbulent mixing layer in hydrodynamic instabilities. *IEEE Transactions on Visualization and Computer Graphics*, 12(6):1053–1060, 2006.

[15] A. Mascarenhas, R. Grout, P.-T. Bremer, V. Pascucci, E. Hawkes, and J. Chen. Topological feature extraction for comparison of length scales in terascale combustion simulation data. In V. Pascucci, X. Tricoche, H. Hagen, and J. Tierny, editors, *Topological Methods in Data Analysis and Visualization: Theory, Algorithms, and Applications*, pages 229–240, 2011.

[16] D. Morozov and G. Weber. Distributed contour trees. Manuscript, 2012.

[17] V. Pascucci and K. Cole-McLaughlin. Parallel computation of the topology of level sets. *Algorithmica*, 38(1):249–268, 2003. doi: 10.1007/s00453-003-1052-3.

[18] V. Pascucci, K. Cole-McLaughlin, and G. Scorzelli. *The Toporrery: Computation and Presentation of Multi-Resolution Topology*, pages 19–40. Springer-Verlag, 2009.

[19] W. Pugh. Skip lists: a probabilistic alternative to balanced trees. *Communications of the ACM*, 33(6):668–676, 1990.

[20] G. Reeb. Sur les points singuliers d'une forme de pfaff complètement intégrable ou d'une fonction numérique. *Comptes Rendus de l'Académie des Sciences de Paris*, 222:847–849, 1946.

[21] N. Shivashankar and V. Natarajan. Parallel computation of 3d Morse–Smale complexes. *Computer Graphics Forum (EuroVis 2012)*, 31(3): 965–974, 2012.

[22] N. Shivashankar, Senthilnathan M., and V. Natarajan. Parallel computation of 2d Morse–Smale complexes. *IEEE Transactions on Visualization and Computer Graphics*, 2012. To appear.

[23] G. H. Weber, P.-T. Bremer, M. S. Day, J. B. Bell, and V. Pascucci. Feature tracking using reeb graphs. In V. Pascucci, X. Tricoche, H. Hagen, and J. Tierny, editors, *Topological Methods in Data Analysis and Visualization: Theory, Algorithms, and Applications*, pages 241–253, 2011.

Fast Concurrent Queues for x86 Processors

Adam Morrison   Yehuda Afek

Blavatnik School of Computer Science, Tel Aviv University

Abstract

Conventional wisdom in designing concurrent data structures is to use the most powerful synchronization primitive, namely compare-and-swap (CAS), and to avoid contended hot spots. In building concurrent FIFO queues, this reasoning has led researchers to propose *combining-based* concurrent queues.

This paper takes a different approach, showing how to rely on fetch-and-add (F&A), a less powerful primitive that is available on x86 processors, to construct a *nonblocking (lock-free) linearizable concurrent FIFO queue* which, despite the F&A being a contended hot spot, outperforms combining-based implementations by 1.5× to 2.5× in all concurrency levels on an x86 server with four multicore processors, in both single-processor and multi-processor executions.

Categories and Subject Descriptors D.1.3 [*Programming Techniques*]: Concurrent Programming; E.1 [*Data Structures*]: Lists, stacks, and queues

Keywords concurrent queue, nonblocking algorithm, fetch-and-add

1. Introduction

Avoiding *contended hot spots* is a fundamental principle in the design of concurrent algorithms [13]. The concurrent FIFO queue, a fundamental and commonly used data structure, is a prime example of this principle in action: Both of Michael and Scott's classic algorithms [19], one lock-based and one nonblocking, do not scale past a small amount of concurrency because threads *contend* on the queue's tail and head [11, 13]. To get around this seemingly inherent bottleneck, researchers have recently applied *combining* approaches in which one thread gathers pending operations of other threads and executes them on their behalf [7, 8, 11].

Most non-combining concurrent algorithms synchronize using compare-and-swap (CAS) loops: a thread observes the shared state, performs a computation, and uses CAS to update the shared state. If the CAS succeeds, this read-compute-update sequence appears to be atomic; otherwise the thread must retry. Essentially, the idea behind combining is that the synchronization cost of a contended CAS hot spot (due to cache coherency traffic on the contended location) is so large that performing all the work *serially*, to save synchronization, performs better [11]. In this paper we show that the truth is more nuanced: it is *work wasted due to CAS failures*

PPoPP'13, February 23–27, 2013, Shenzhen, China.

	compare-and-swap	swap	test-and-set	fetch-and-add
ARM	LL/SC	deprecated	no	no
POWER	LL/SC	no	no	no
SPARC	yes	deprecated	yes	no
x86	**yes**	**yes**	**yes**	**yes**

Table 1: Synchronization primitives supported as machine instructions on dominant multicore architectures.

that largely causes the poor performance of algorithms with a CAS hot spot, not just the synchronization cost.

Observing this distinction, let alone exploiting it, is not possible on most commercial multicore architectures which only support the *universal* primitives CAS or load-linked/store-conditional (LL/SC). While in theory these can implement weaker primitives in a wait-free manner [12], such implementations are heavyweight and in practice vendors direct programmers to use CAS loops [1]. However, there is an interesting exception: the (64 bit) x86 architecture, which dominates the server and desktop markets, directly supports various theoretically weaker primitives whose crucial property for our purpose is that *they always succeed* (see Table 1).

Consider, for example, the fetch-and-add (F&A) primitive. Figure 1 shows the difference in the time it takes a thread to increment a contended counter on a modern x86 system when using F&A vs. a CAS loop. Avoiding the retries inherent and paying only the synchronization price leads to a 4×−6× performance improvement. In this paper we transfer this insight to the domain of FIFO queues, henceforth simply queues.

Our contribution We present **LCRQ**, a *linearizable nonblocking FIFO queue* that uses contended F&A objects to spread threads among items in the queue, allowing them to enqueue and dequeue quickly and in parallel, in contrast the inherently serial behavior of combining-based approaches. As a result, LCRQ outperforms prior queue implementations by 1.5× to 2.5× on a system with four Intel Xeon E7-4870 multicore processors, both on single-processor and on multi-processor executions. Because LCRQ is nonblocking, it maintains its performance in oversubscribed scenarios in which there are more threads than available hardware threads. In such workloads it outperforms by more than 20× lock-based combining queues, which cannot make progress if a combiner gets scheduled out.

Our LCRQ algorithm is essentially a Michael and Scott linked list queue [19] in which a node is a concurrent ring (cyclic array) queue, CRQ for short. A CRQ that fills up becomes *closed* to further enqueues, who instead append a new CRQ to the list and begin working in it. Most of the activity in the LCRQ occurs in the individual CRQs, making contention on the list's head and tail a non-issue. Within a CRQ, the head and tail are F&A objects which are used to spread threads around the slots of the ring, where they synchronize using (uncontended in the common case) CAS.

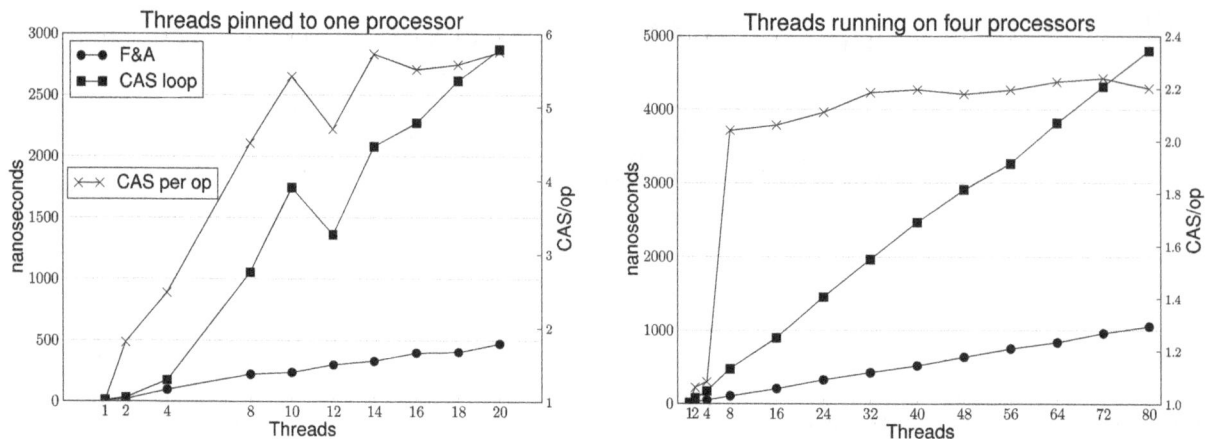

Figure 1: Time to increment a contended counter on a system with four Intel Xeon E7-4870 (Westmere EX) processors, each of which has 10 2.40 GHz cores that multiplex 2 hardware threads. The right vertical axis shows the number of CAS it takes to complete an increment.

One of the CRQ's distinctive properties compared to prior concurrent circular array queues [2–4, 9, 10, 22, 23] is that in the *common case* an operation accesses only the CRQ's head or tail but not both. This reduces the CRQ's synchronization cost by a factor of two, since the contended head and tail are the algorithm's bottleneck.

2. Related work

We refer the reader to Michael and Scott's extensive survey [19] for discussion of additional work that predates theirs.

List based queues Michael and Scott present two linked list queues, one nonblocking (henceforth MS queue) and one lock-based [19]. However, due to contention on the queue's head and tail, their algorithms do not scale past a low level of concurrency [7, 11]. Kogan and Petrank introduce a *wait-free* variant of the MS queue with similar performance characteristics [16]. Several works attempt to improve the MS queue's scalability, however all these still suffer from the CAS retry problem [15, 17, 20].

Cyclic array queues Prior concurrent cyclic array queues are *bounded* and can contain a fixed number of items. One of the challenges in these algorithms is correctly determining when the queue is full and empty. The queues of Gottlieb et al. [10] and of Freudenthal and Gottlieb [9] maintain a *size* counter that is updated using F&A. Such a F&A might bring the queue into an inconsistent state (e.g., *size* < 0) and the algorithm then tries to recover using a compensating F&A. Still, the inconsistent states make these queues non-linearizable [1]. Blelloch et al. [3] use *room synchronization*, which prevents enqueues from running concurrently to dequeues, to construct a queue that is linearizable despite temporarily entering inconsistent states when its head/tail are updated using F&A. Another queue by Blelloch et al. [2] avoids inconsistent states of the head and tail by updating these indices using hardware *memory block transactions* which are not supported by commercial hardware. Tsigas and Zhang [23], Colvin and Groves [4] and Shafiei [22] present cyclic array queues that avoid inconsistent head and tail states by performing the updates using CAS, but are therefore prone to the CAS failure effect.

In contrast to these prior designs, LCRQ is an unbounded queue formed by linking CRQs (array queues) in a list, with a new CRQ

added when an enqueue operation fails to make progress. The ability to *close* a CRQ, forcing enqueues to move to the next CRQ in the list, makes LCRQ nonblocking whereas prior F&A-based designs [2, 3, 9, 10] are blocking. In addition, since we do not need to determine when the queue is full in a linearizable way, we can recover from inconsistent states that result from using F&A for head/tail updates without compromising linearizability. Performance-wise, a CRQ operation accesses only one end of the queue in the common case, whereas the operations in the previous designs access both the head and tail indices.

Combining Researchers have recently shown that *combining-based* queues scale better than CAS-based list queues [7, 8, 11]. A combining algorithm is essentially a *universal construction* [12] that can implement any shared object. The idea is that a single thread scans a list of pending operations and applies them to the object. Such algorithms greatly reduce the synchronization cost of accessing the object, at the cost of executing work serially.

Hendler et al. describe a linked list queue based on *flat combining*, a lock-based combining construction [11]. Fatourou and Kallimanis present SimQueue [8], a queue based on a wait-free combining construction, and CC-Queue, a queue based on a blocking combining algorithm [7]. Section 5 details these algorithms.

Both of Fatourou and Kallimanis' algorithms use weak synchronization primitives (F&A and SWAP). However, they do so to reduce the synchronization cost of the combining algorithm, which still needs to perform serial work that is linear in the number of threads. In contrast, we use F&A to enable parallelism in the seemingly inherently sequential FIFO queue.

3. Preliminaries

System model Most concurrent algorithms work assumes a *sequentially consistent* shared memory system, particularly for correctness proofs, as this allows modeling the execution as a sequence of interleaved memory operations performed by the threads. While the x86 memory model is not sequentially consistent, the only difference is that on the x86 a write gets buffered in a *write buffer* before reaching the memory, allowing a read to be satisfied from memory before a write preceding it becomes globally visible [21].

However, in our algorithms threads write to shared data only with atomic operations, such as CAS and F&A. Atomic operations flush the write buffer and are globally ordered [21], allowing us to treat the system as sequentially consistent. Formally, we have a set

---

[1]Blelloch et al. [3] show a non-linearizable execution for Gottlieb et al.'s queue. A similar scenario applies to Freudenthal and Gottlieb's queue.

of T sequential *threads* that communicate by performing operations on the shared memory, as described below.

Memory operations The memory is an array of locations, each holding a 64-bit value. We use the notation $m[a]$ for the value stored in address a of the memory. Our algorithms use the following primitives supported by the x86 architecture: (1) read(a) which returns $m[a]$, (2) `fetch-and-add`, denoted F&A(a,x), which returns $v = m[a]$ and changes $m[a]$'s value to $v + x$, (3) `swap`, denoted SWAP(a,x), which returns $v = m[a]$ and changes $m[a]$'s value to x, (4) `test-and-set`, denoted T&S(a), which returns $v = m[a]$ and changes $m[a]$'s value to 1, (5) `compare-and-swap`, denoted CAS(a,o,n), which changes $m[a]$'s value to n if $m[a] = o$ and returns TRUE, or returns FALSE otherwise, (6) `compare-and-swap2`, denoted CAS2$(a, \langle o_0, o_1 \rangle, \langle n_0, n_1 \rangle)$, which changes $m[a]$'s value to n_0 and $m[a+1]$'s value to n_1 if $m[a] = o_0$ and $m[a+1] = o_1$ before returning TRUE, or else returns FALSE [2].

Concurrent objects The threads implement a high-level object defined by a *sequential specification*, a state machine specifying the object's *states* and the *operations* used to transition between the states. Here we are concerned with the *FIFO queue*, an object whose state, Q, is a (possibly empty) sequence of items. It supports an enqueue(x) operation that appends x to Q and returns OK, and a dequeue$()$ operation which removes the first item x from Q and returns x, or returns EMPTY if Q is the empty sequence.

Implementations, executions and linearizability We use the standard definitions of a high-level object implementation and its execution [14]. Our correctness condition is linearizability [14], which (informally) requires that a high-level operation appears to take place at one point in time during its execution interval.

Progress According to Herlihy's now standard definition [12], an implementation is *nonblocking* if it guarantees that some thread completes an operation in a finite number of steps. In other words, an individual operation may starve, but some operation always makes progress. This guarantee still allows some undesirable scenarios for queues, e.g., an execution in which enqueuers are starved by dequeuers returning EMPTY. Nonblocking queues in the literature [4, 19, 22, 23] actually provide a stronger guarantee, which we call *op-wise nonblocking* [3]: some enqueue$()$ completes in a finite number of steps by enqueuing threads, and some dequeue$()$ completes in a finite number of steps by dequeuing threads.

4. The LCRQ algorithm

LCRQ can be viewed as a practical realization of the following simple but unrealistic queue algorithm (Figure 2). The algorithm represents the queue using an *infinite* array, Q, with (unbounded) *head* and *tail* indices that identify the part of Q which may contain items. Initially, each cell $Q[i]$ is empty and contains a reserved value $\bot$ that may not be enqueued.

An enqueue(x) operation obtains a cell index t via a F&A on *tail*. The enqueue then atomically swaps the value in $Q[t]$ with x. If the swap returns $\bot$, the enqueue operation completes; otherwise, it repeats this process.

A dequeue, D, obtains a cell index h using F&A on *head* and atomically swaps the value in $Q[h]$ with another reserved value $\top$. If $Q[h]$ contained some $x \neq \bot$, D returns x. If D finds $\bot$ in $Q[h]$, the fact that D stored $\top$ in the cell guarantees that an enqueue operation which later stores an item in $Q[h]$ will not complete. D then returns EMPTY if $tail \leq h+1$ ($h+1$ is the value of *head* following D's F&A). If D cannot return EMPTY, it repeats this process.

```
1   enqueue(x : Object) {
2     while (true) {
3       t := F&A(&tail, 1)
4       if ( SWAP(&Q[t], x) = ⊥ ) return OK
5   } }
6   dequeue() {
7     while (true) {
8       h := F&A(&head, 1)
9       x := SWAP(&Q[h], ⊤)
10      if x ≠ ⊥ return x
11      if ( tail ≤ h+1) return EMPTY
12  } }
```

Figure 2: Infinite array queue.

While this algorithm is a linearizable FIFO queue [4] it has two major flaws that prevent it from being relevant in practice: using an infinite array and susceptibility to livelock (a dequeuer continuously swaps $\top$ into the cell an enqueuer is about to access). We obtain the practical LCRQ algorithm by solving these problems.

Our array queue, CRQ, transforms the infinite array to a cyclic array (*ring*) of R nodes. The *head* and *tail* indices still strictly increase, but now the value of an index modulo R specifies the ring node it points to. Since now more than one enqueuer and dequeuer can concurrently access a node, we replace the infinite array queue's SWAP-based exchange with a CAS2-based protocol. This protocol is unique in that, unlike prior work [2, 10], an operation does not have to *wait* for the completion of operations whose F&A returns smaller indices that also point to the same ring node.

The CRQ's crucial performance property is that in the common *fast path*, an operation accesses only *one* F&A. We use the additional synchronization in the ring nodes to detect corner cases, such as an empty queue. Since *head* and *tail* are heavily contended, our approach halves an operation's synchronization cost in the common case. We detail the CRQ algorithm in Section 4.1.

The LCRQ algorithm (Section 4.2) builds on CRQ to prevent the livelock problem. We represent the queue as a *linked list* of CRQs. An enqueue(x) operation failing to make progress in the tail CRQ *closes* it to further enqueues. Upon noticing the tail CRQ is closed, each enqueuer tries to append a new CRQ, initialized to contain its item, to the list. One enqueuer succeeds and completes; the rest move into the new tail CRQ, leaving the old tail CRQ with only dequeuers inside it, which allows the dequeuers to complete. The LCRQ is thus op-wise nonblocking.

4.1 The CRQ algorithm

The pseudocode of the basic CRQ algorithm appears in Figure 3. The CRQ represents the queue as a *ring* (cyclic array) of R nodes, with 64-bit *head* and *tail* indices (Figure 3a). An index with value i points to node $i \bmod R$, which we denote by $node(i)$. We reserve the most significant bit of *tail* to denote the CRQ's CLOSED state. We thus make the realistic assumption that both *head* and *tail* do not exceed 2^{63}.

The synchronization protocol in a CRQ ring node needs to handle more cases than the infinite array queue, which only needs to distinguish whether an enqueue or dequeue arrives first at the node. We proceed to describe this protocol and how it handles these cases.

Node structure (Figure 3a) Physically, a ring node contains two 64-bit words. Logically, a ring node is a 3-tuple (s, i, v) consisting of (1) a *safe* bit s (used by a dequeuer to notify the matching enqueuer that storing an item in the node is unsafe as the dequeuer will not be around to dequeue it; we explain the details below), (2) an *index* i, and (3) a *value* v. Initially, node u's state is $(1, u, \bot)$ for every $0 \leq u < R$.

```
13  struct Node {
14      safe : 1 bit (boolean)
15      idx : 63 bits (int)
16      val : 64 bits (int or pointer)
17      // padded to cache line size
18  }
19  struct CRQ { // fields are on distinct cache lines
20      head : 64 bit int
21      tail : struct { closed : 1 bit, t : 63 bits }
22      next : pointer to CRQ, initially null
23      ring : array of R Nodes, initially node u = <1,u,⊥>
24  }
```

(a) Globals

```
25  dequeue(crq : pointer to CRQ) {
26      // local variables
27      val, idx : 64 bit int
28      h, t : 64 bit int
29      node : pointer to Node
30      closed : boolean
31      safe : boolean
32
33      while (true) {
34          h := F&A(&crq.head, 1)
35          node := &crq.array [h mod R]
36          while (true) {
37              val := node.val
38              <safe, idx> := <node.safe, node.idx> // one 64−bit read
39              if (idx > h) goto Line 52
40              if (val ≠⊥) {
41                  if (idx = h) { // try dequeue transition
42                      if (CAS2(node, <safe, h, val>, <safe, h+R, ⊥>))
43                          return val
44                  } else { // mark node unsafe to prevent future enqueue
45                      if (CAS2(node, <safe, h, val>, <0, h, val>)) goto Line 52
46                  }
47              } else { // idx ≤ h and val =⊥: try empty transition
48                  if (CAS2(node, <safe, idx, ⊥>, <safe, h+R, ⊥>))
49                      goto Line 52
50              }
51          } // end of while loop, go back to Line 36
52          // failed to dequeue, check for empty
53          <closed, t> := crq. tail
54          if (t ≤ h+1) {
55              fixState (crq)
56              return EMPTY
57  } } }
```

(b) Dequeue

```
58  void fixState (crq : pointer to CRQ) {
59      // local variables
60      h, t : 64 bit int
61
62      while (true) {
63          h = F&A(&crq.head, 0)
64          t = F&A(&crq.tail, 0)
65
66          if (crq. tail ≠ t)
67              continue  // continue loop at Line 62
68
69          if (h ≤ t)
70              return  // nothing to do
71
72          if (CAS(&crq.tail, t, h))
73              return
74  } }
```

(c) fixState()

```
75  enqueue(crq : pointer to CRQ, arg : Object) {
76      // local variables
77      val, idx : 64 bit int
78      h, t : 64 bit int
79      node : pointer to Node
80      closed : boolean
81      safe : boolean
82
83      while (true) {
84          <closed, t> := F&A(&crq.tail, 1)  // F&A on all 64 bits of tail
85          if (closed)
86              return CLOSED
87          node = &crq.array [t mod R]
88          val := node.val
89          <safe, idx> := <node.safe, node.idx>  // one 64−bit read
90          if (val =⊥) {
91              if ((idx ≤ t) and
92                  (safe = 1 or crq.head ≤ t) and
93                  CAS2(node, <safe, idx, ⊥>, <1, t, arg>)) {
94                  return OK
95              }
96          }
97          h := crq. head
98          if (t − h ≥ R or starving ()) {
99              T&S(&crq.tail.closed)  // atomically set tail .closed to true
100             return CLOSED
101         }
102 } }
```

(d) Enqueue

Figure 3: Pseudocode of CRQ algorithm.

A node can be in one of two states: if its value is $\bot$ the node is *empty*; otherwise the node is *occupied*. A CRQ operation attempts to *transition* a node from empty to occupied or vice versa using CAS2. We say that an operation, *op*, *accesses node u using index i* if *op*'s F&A returns i and $u = i$ mod R, and refer to the operation as enq_i or deq_i as appropriate. An operation accessing a node uses the value of the node's safe bit and index, as described next, to determine whether it can attempt a transition or should obtain a new index and try accessing another node.

Dequeuing an item When a node is in an occupied state, (s,i,x), it holds the item x that has been stored by $enq_i(x)$. In this case, only deq_i, the dequeue operation accessing index i – exactly i and not just equal to i modulo R – can return x. Such a dequeue attempts to remove x by performing the transition $(s,i,x) \mapsto (s,i+R,\bot)$ using CAS2 (Figure 3b, Line 42). We refer to this as a *dequeue transition*.

Dequeue arrives before enqueuer while node is empty This case occurs when an empty node whose state is $(s,i,\bot)$ is accessed by deq_j with $j = i + kR$, i.e., before the matching enqueue enq_j completes. Similarly to the infinite array queue, deq_j prevents enq_j

from storing its item in the node by performing an *empty transition* $(s,i,\bot) \mapsto (s,j+R,\bot)$ (Line 48). In fact, the empty transition prevents *any* operation using some index $j - kR$ from performing a transition on the node. This stronger property was not needed in the infinite array queue, where only one enqueuer and one dequeuer ever access a node.

Dequeue arrives before enqueuer while node is occupied This case has no analog in the infinite array queue. It occurs when an occupied node (s,i,x) is accessed by deq_j with $j = i + kR$ ($k > 0$), i.e., before deq_i which is the dequeuer supposed to dequeue x. While deq_j cannot remove x, it must still mark the node somehow before moving on, so that enq_j knows not to enqueue an item in the node. deq_j uses the safe bit for this purpose, making an *unsafe* transition $(s,i,x) \mapsto (0,i,x)$ (Line 45). Once a node is unsafe, all dequeuer transitions keep the safe bit at 0. This prevents any enqueuer from storing its item in the node unless it first verifies that the corresponding dequeuer has not yet started, as explained next.

Enqueuing an item When a node is in an empty state $(s,i,\bot)$, any $enq_j(x)$ operation with $j = i + kR$ may attempt an *enqueue* *transition* to store x in the node. If $s = 1$, enq_j simply performs the transition $(1, i, \perp) \mapsto (1, j, x)$ (Figure 3d, Line 93). However, if $s = 0$, enq_j needs to make sure that deq_j is not the dequeuer that set s to 0, since then deq_j will not dequeue from the node. enq_j determines this by checking if $head \leq j$ (Line 92), which means that deq_j has not yet started. If so, then enq_j makes the transition $(0, i, \perp) \mapsto (1, j, x)$ (Line 93) which undoes the previous unsafe transition. If deq_j then starts after enq_j's check that $head \leq j$ and performs a transition on the node before enq_j's transition, then deq_j performs an empty transition (Line 49) which changes the node's index and causes enq_j's CAS2 to fail.

We now turn to a walk-through of the algorithm's pseudocode. For simplicity, we describe optimizations in Section 4.1.1, omitting them from the pseudocode.

Enqueue (Figure 3d) An enqueue *enq* repeats the following. It obtains an index to a ring node with a F&A on *tail* (Line 84). If the CRQ is closed, *enq* returns CLOSED (Lines 85-86). Otherwise, *enq* attempts an enqueue transition (Lines 87-96). If this fails (because the node is occupied or the CAS2 fails), *enq* decides to give up and closes the queue in one of two cases: (1) *enq*'s index has passed *head* by R places, indicating a possibly full queue, or (2) *enq* is failing to make progress for a long time (checked by `starving()`) (Lines 97-101).

Dequeue (Figure 3b) A dequeue *deq* repeats the following. It obtains an index, h, to a ring node using F&A on *head* (Lines 34-35). It then enters a loop in which it attempts to read a consistent state of the node and perform a transition. If $h < i$, where i is the node's index, then *deq* has been overtaken between its F&A and reading the node, and so it exits the loop (Line 39). If the node is occupied, *deq* attempts a dequeue transition (Lines 40-47). If the node is empty, *deq* attempts an empty transition (Line 48) and exits the loop if successful. Throughout this process, if *deq*'s CAS2 fails (implying the node's state changes) then *deq* restarts the loop of reading the node and performing a transition. Whenever *deq* exits the loop without successfully dequeuing an item, it verifies that the queue is not empty before trying to dequeue with a new index (Line 53-54). If the queue is empty, *deq fixes* (see below) the queue's state so that $head \leq tail$ before returning EMPTY (Lines 55-56).

Fixing the queue state (Figure 3c) A dequeuer F&A may bring the queue into an invalid state in which $head > tail$. In such a case, the dequeuer can just perform an empty transition and return EMPTY. However, doing so prevents the enqueuer with the same index from using the node, forcing it to F&A *tail* again and increasing contention. To avoid this problem, a dequeuer always verifies that $head \leq tail$ before returning EMPTY (Lines 62-74).

4.1.1 Optimizations

Bounded waiting for matching enqueues When an enqueue and dequeue operation using the same index are active concurrently, the dequeue may arrive at the node before the matching enqueuer. Performing an empty transition in such a case just leads to both operations restarting and accessing the F&A again, needlessly increasing contention on *head* and *tail*.

To avoid this, before performing an empty transition (Line 48), a dequeue operation checks whether $tail \geq h + 1$, where h is the dequeue's index. If so, then the matching enqueuer is active and the dequeuer spins for a short while, waiting for the enqueue transition to take place. Only after timing out on this spin loop does the dequeue perform an empty transition.

Hierarchy awareness Large servers are typically built hierarchically, with *clusters* of cores such that inter-core communication inside a cluster is cheap, but cross-cluster communication is expensive. For example, in a multiprocessor system a cluster consists of all the cores on a (multicore) processor. In these hierarchical machines, creating batches of operations that complete on the same cluster without interference from remote clusters reduces synchronization cost.

To achieve this, we add a `cluster` field to the CRQ, which identifies the current cluster from which most operations should complete. Before starting a CRQ operation, a thread checks if it is running on `cluster`. If not, the thread waits for a while, and then CASes `cluster` to be its cluster and enters the algorithm (even if the CAS fails). Similarly to prior NUMA-aware lock-based algorithms [5, 7], this divides the execution into segments such that in each segment most operations in the CRQ are from the same cluster. However, our optimization does not rely on locks nor does it introduce blocking, as every operation eventually enters the CRQ.

4.1.2 CRQ linearizability proof

The CRQ is not a standard FIFO queue because an enqueue can return CLOSED. To deal with this we give the CRQ the semantics of a *tantrum queue*: a queue in which an enqueue can nondeterministically refuse to enqueue its item, returning CLOSED instead and moving the queue to a CLOSED state. When a tantrum queue is in the CLOSED state, every enqueue operation returns CLOSED without enqueuing its item.

In the following, we prove that CRQ is a linearizable tantrum queue. Let $E = e_1, e_2, \ldots$ be a possibly infinite execution of CRQ. We assume every thread whose next local step is to complete does indeed complete in E. We denote an operation $op \in \{deq, enq\}$ that returns *ret* in E by $\langle op : ret \rangle$. We now describe a procedure P (Figure 4) to assign linearization points to the operations in E.

Essentially, the linearization order of $\langle enq(x) : OK \rangle$ operations is by the index the enqueuer uses when successfully enqueuing its item, and similarly $\langle deq() : x \rangle$ operations ($x \neq$ EMPTY) are linearized in the order of the index used to dequeue. The trick is to order enqueues and dequeues consistently, since for example a dequeuer's F&A returning index i can occur before the corresponding enqueuer's F&A.

To do this, we track the CRQ's state at each point in E using an auxiliary sequential queue. The auxiliary queue consists of an

```
103  Input:  CRQ execution, E = e_1, e_2, ...
104
105  for j = 1...
106    if e_j is a T&S by ⟨enq(x) : CLOSED⟩ that sets tail's closed bit
107       (Figure 3d, Line 99) then
108       Linearize ⟨enq(x) : CLOSED⟩ at e_j
109    elseif e_j = ⟨t := F&A(tail, 1)⟩ by ⟨enq(x) : CLOSED⟩ which
110       returns a closed value (Figure 3d, Line 84) then
111       Linearize ⟨enq(x) : CLOSED⟩ at e_j
112    elseif e_j = ⟨t := F&A(tail, 1)⟩ is the last F&A in E by ⟨enq(x) : OK⟩
113       (Figure 3d, Line 84) then
114       Q[t] := x
115       tail(Q) := t + 1
116       Linearize ⟨enq(x) : OK⟩ at e_j
117    elseif e_j = ⟨t := tail⟩, is a read returning t ≤ head by ⟨deq : EMPTY⟩
118       (Figure 3b, Line 53) then
119       Linearize ⟨deq : EMPTY⟩ at e_j
120    endif
121    while head(Q) < tail(Q)
122       h := min{i : Q[i] ≠ ⊥}
123       if dequeue whose F&A (Line 34) returns h not active in e_1, ..., e_j then
124          goto Line 130
125       endif
126       x := Q[h]
127       Q[h] := ⊥
128       head(Q) := h + 1
129       Linearize ⟨deq : x⟩ at e_j
130    endwhile
```

Figure 4: CRQ linearization procedure P. Operations linearized at the same event are ordered based on the order of P's steps.

infinite array, Q, coupled with indices $head(Q)$ and $tail(Q)$ representing Q's head and tail. (Note that Q is *not* cyclic.) Initially, $tail(Q) = head(Q) = 0$ and $Q[i] = \bot$ for all i.

We process the execution one event at a time, in order of execution, but using information about future events to decide when to linearize an operation. When we linearize an operation we also apply it to the auxiliary queue. We linearize an $\langle enq(x) : \text{OK} \rangle$ on its final F&A, the one returning index t such that the operation enqueues x in $node(t)$. At this point we also set $tail(Q)$ to $t+1$. We linearize the dequeue of item $x = Q[h]$ as soon as the dequeue becomes active and h is the lowest indexed non-$\bot$ cell in Q, and set $head(Q)$ to $h+1$ at this point. We linearize a $\langle deq : \text{EMPTY} \rangle$ on its read of *tail* that returns a value $\geq head$ (we later show that $head(Q) = tail(Q)$ at this point). The full pseudocode of P in Figure 4 also includes the straightforward cases of linearizing $\langle enq(x) : \text{CLOSED} \rangle$ operations.

By construction, the linearization point of an operation is within its execution interval, and all completed enqueues and all dequeues that return EMPTY are linearized. We now show that completed dequeues which do not return EMPTY are also linearized. Here we denote by $enq_i(x)$ the $\langle enq(x) : \text{OK} \rangle$ operation whose last F&A on *tail* in E returns i, causing P to set $Q[i] := x$ and linearize it. Similarly, we denote a dequeue operation whose last F&A on *head* in E returns i by deq_i.

Lemma 1. *Suppose P linearizes $enq_i(x)$. If there exists a dequeue operation deq that performs a F&A on head in E which returns i, then: (1) $deq = deq_i$ (i.e., deq performs no further F&As in E), (2) deq_i returns x if it completes, and (3) P linearizes $\langle deq_i : x \rangle$.*

Proof. Let $(s, j, \bot) \mapsto (1, i, x)$ be $enq_i(x)$'s enqueue transition storing x into $u = node(i)$ (Figure 3d, Line 93). Notice that $j \leq i$. If *deq* takes sufficiently many steps after obtaining i from its F&A on *head*, it performs a transition on u using index i. To see this, notice that *deq* moves on from u without performing a transition only if it reads an index $> i$ from u (Figure 3b, Line 39). Because enq_i's transition succeeds, *deq* is the only operation that can move u's index beyond i, so this is impossible.

Now, consider *deq*'s transition. It cannot be $(\cdot, k, \bot) \mapsto (\cdot, i + R, \bot)$ (Line 48) since that implies enq_i's transition fails. *deq*'s transition also cannot be of the form $(\cdot, k, v) \mapsto (0, k, v)$ (Line 45) because then, enq_i's transition succeeding implies that some enqueue (possibly enq_i) subsequently obtains index $t \leq i$ and then observes $head \leq t$, which is impossible since $head > i$. Thus, *deq*'s transition can only be a dequeue of x. Hence (1) and (2) hold.

We prove (3) using induction on k, the number of linearized enqueue operations. For $k = 0$ the claim is vacuously true. Suppose now that the k-th enqueue operation linearized is $enq_i(x)$. If deq_i exists in E, then it does not complete before $enq_i(x)$'s F&A which returns i, since otherwise deq_i does not return x, contradicting (2). Therefore, there exists a first event e in which $Q[i] = x$ and deq_i is active. Thus at some event e', at or after e, $Q[i] = x$ and deq_i has performed the F&A on *head* which returns i. Let $idx = \{j : j < i, Q[j] \neq \bot \text{ at } e'\}$. For all $j \in idx$, deq_j starts by e' (because deq_i's F&A has returned i) and does not complete before e' (as that implies it is not linearized before completing, contradicting the induction hypothesis). Therefore, at e' P linearizes deq_j for all $j \in idx$ and subsequently linearizes deq_i. $\square$

To complete the linearizability proof, we must show that our linearization order meets the tantrum queue specification. Because we enqueue to Q's tail, dequeue from Q's head, and following the first enqueue to return CLOSED all enqueues do so, this amounts to showing that the auxiliary queue is empty when we linearize a $\langle deq : \text{EMPTY} \rangle$ operation. Lemma 2 below implies this, because we linearize a $\langle deq : \text{EMPTY} \rangle$ when it reads a value t from *tail*

```
131   // shared variables on distinct cache lines :
132   tail : pointer to CRQ
133   head : pointer to CRQ
134   // initially :
135   tail = head = empty CRQ
```

(a) Globals

```
136   dequeue() {
137     // local variables
138     crq : pointer to CRQ
139     v : 64 bit value
140
141     while (true) {
142       crq := head
143       v := dequeue(crq)
144       if (v ≠ EMPTY) return v
145       if (crq.next = null) return EMPTY
146       CAS(&head, crq, crq.next)
147   } }
```

(b) Dequeue

```
148   enqueue(x : Object) {
149     // local variables
150     crq, newcrq : pointer to CRQ
151
152     while (true) {
153       crq := tail
154       if (crq.next ≠ null) {
155         CAS(&tail, crq, crq.next)
156         continue  // next iteration at Line 153
157       }
158       if (enqueue(crq, x) ≠ CLOSED)
159         return OK
160       newcrq := a new CRQ initialized to contain x
161       if (CAS(&crq.next, null, newcrq)) {
162         CAS(&tail, crq, newcrq)
163         return OK
164       }
165     }
166   }
```

(c) Enqueue

Figure 5: Pseudocode of the LCRQ algorithm, using a linearizable CRQ black box.

(Figure 3b, Line 53) such that $t \leq h + 1$, where $h < head$ is the value that the *deq*'s prior F&A returns (Line 34).

Lemma 2. *If at event e, $head \geq tail$, then $head(Q) = tail(Q)$.*

Proof. Suppose towards a contradiction that $head(Q) < tail(Q)$ at e. Then there exists a minimal i such that $Q[i] \neq \bot$ at e. Because we update $tail(Q)$ following the order of F&As on *tail*, $i < tail(Q) \leq tail \leq head$ at e. Thus, deq_i is active before e and should have been linearized by P, a contradiction. $\square$

In conclusion, we have shown the following.

Theorem 1. *CRQ is a linearizable implementation of a tantrum queue.*

4.2 The LCRQ algorithm

We now present LCRQ using the CRQ as a black box. The LCRQ is simply a linked list of CRQs in which dequeuing threads access the head CRQ and enqueuing threads access the tail CRQ (Figure 5a). An enqueue(x) operation that receives a CLOSED response from the tail CRQ creates a new CRQ, initialized to contain x, and links it after the current tail, thereby making it the new tail (Figure 5c). If the head CRQ becomes EMPTY and there is a node linked after it, dequeues move to the next node, after installing it as the new head (Figure 5b).

108

Memory reclamation A dequeue that successfully changes the head pointer cannot reclaim the memory used by the old CRQ because there may be concurrent operations about to access it (i.e., stalled just before Line 143 or Line 158). We address this problem by using *hazard pointers* [18] to protect an operation's reference to the CRQ it is about to access. We omit the details, which are standard.

Linearizability Assuming that the CRQ is a linearizable tantrum queue, proving that LCRQ is a linearizable queue implementation is straightforward:

Theorem 2. *If CRQ is a linearizable* tantrum queue *implementation, then LCRQ is a linearizable* queue *implementation.*

Proof. (Sketch) We linearize an enqueue that completes after appending a new CRQ to the list at the CAS which links the new CRQ (Figure 5c, Line 161). We linearize any other completed operation at the point in which its final CRQ operation takes place. The next pointer of a CRQ q changes from null only after q becomes CLOSED, and conversely, after a CRQ q becomes CLOSED no new enqueue completes until a new CRQ is linked after q. Thus, if q_0 precedes q_1 in the list, any q_1 enqueue is linearized after any q_0 enqueue. Similarly, any q_0 dequeue is linearized before any q_1 dequeue. Linearizability follows. □

4.2.1 LCRQ nonblocking proof

In this section, we sketch the proof of the following theorem:

Theorem 3. *LCRQ is op-wise nonblocking.*

An enqueuer that does not complete within a finite number of steps in the tail CRQ closes it. Once the CRQ is closed, every enqueuer taking enough steps tries to append a new CRQ to the LCRQ. The first one to CAS the CRQ's next pointer (Figure 5c, Line 161) succeeds and completes. Thus, an enqueue operation completes within a finite number of steps by enqueuing threads.

Now, consider a dequeuer *deq* taking an infinite number of steps without completing. Suppose first that *deq* remains in one LCRQ node, q. If enqueuers take infinitely many steps in q, then q does not close and so, because q's size is finite, dequeuers remove items from q. If enqueuers take only finitely many steps in q, then from some point only dequeuers take steps in q and so eventually q's *head* exceeds its *tail*. Then *deq* finds that q is empty (Lines 53–54), enters fixState() but never leaves. Thus, new dequeuers continue to enter q and increment *head*. Since the number of dequeuers is finite, this implies some dequeuer completes.

The other possibility is that *deq* returns EMPTY in each CRQ node q_i it enters but never reaches the LCRQ's tail. Each node q_i contains at least one item, and so there is a dequeuer d_i that holds the index to this item. After traversing through T nodes, where T is the number of threads in the system, it must be that $d_i = d_j$ for some $j > i$. This means d_i completes and returns. Overall, we have shown that a dequeue must complete within a finite number of steps by dequeuing threads.

5. Evaluation

Evaluated algorithms We compare LCRQ to the best performing queues reported in the recent literature, all of which are based on the *combining* principle: Hendler et al.'s **FC queue** [11] and Fatourou and Kallimanis' **CC-Queue** and **H-Queue** [7]. We also test Michael and Scott's classic nonblocking **MS queue** [19].

The FC queue is based on *flat combining*, in which a thread becomes a *combiner* by acquiring a global lock, and then applies the operations of the non-combining threads. The queue we test is a linked list of cyclic arrays, with a new tail array allocated when the old tail fills.

The CC-Queue replaces each of the two locks in Michael and Scott's *two-lock queue* [19], which serialize accesses to the queue's head and tail, with an instance of the *CC-Synch* universal construction [7]. The CC-Synch universal construction maintains a linked list to which threads add themselves using SWAP. The thread at the head of the list traverses the list and performs the requests of waiting threads. Since the enqueue and dequeue CC-Synch instances work in parallel, the CC-Queue outperforms the FC queue [7].

The H-Queue is a hierarchical version of the CC-Queue. It uses an instance of the *H-Synch* universal construction [7] to replace the two-lock queue's locks. The H-Synch construction consists of one instance of CC-Synch per cluster and a lock that synchronizes the CC-Synch instances. Each CC-Synch combiner acquires the lock and performs the operations of the threads on its cluster.

To obtain the most meaningful results, we use the queue implementations from Fatourou and Kallimanis' benchmark framework [7, 8], all of which are in C [5]. We incorporate the FC queue implementation into this framework.

LCRQ implementation We use CRQs whose ring size, R, is 2^{17}. (We include a sensitivity study of LCRQ to the ring size below.) In addition to baseline LCRQ, we also evaluate LCRQ+H, in which we enable our hierarchical optimization (with a timeout of 100 μs). To explore the impact of CAS failures, we test LCRQ-CAS, a version of LCRQ in which we implement the F&As using a CAS loop. All LCRQ variants include the overhead of pointing a hazard pointer at the CRQ before accessing it [6].

Methodology We follow the testing methodology of prior work [7, 19]. We measure the time it takes for every thread to execute 10^7 pairs of enqueue and dequeue operations, averaged over 10 runs.

As in prior work, in every test we avoid artificial *long run* scenarios [19], in which a thread zooms through many consecutive operations, by having each thread wait for a random number of nanoseconds (up to 100) between operations. Each thread is *pinned* to a specific hardware thread, to avoid interference from the operating system scheduler. Our tests use the jemalloc [6] memory allocator to prevent memory allocation from being a bottleneck. Results' variance is negligible (we use a dedicated test machine).

Platform We use a Fujitsu PRIMERGY RX600 S6 server with four Intel Xeon E7-4870 (Westmere EX) processors, which were launched by Intel in early 2011. Each processor has 10 2.40 GHz cores, each of which multiplexes 2 hardware threads, so in total our system supports 80 hardware threads. Each core has private write-back L1 and L2 caches; an inclusive L3 cache is shared by all cores.

Single processor executions (Figure 6a) Here we restrict threads to run on one of the server's processors. This evaluates the queues in a modern multicore environment in which all synchronization is handled on-chip and thus has low cost. We omit results of LCRQ+H and H-Queue, since they are relevant only for multi-processor executions.

LCRQ outperforms all other queues beyond 2 threads. From 10 threads onwards, LCRQ outperforms CC-Queue by 1.5×, the FC queue by > 2.5×, and the MS queue by > 3×. LCRQ-CAS matches LCRQ's performance up to 4 threads, but at that point its performance levels off. Subsequently, LCRQ-CAS exhibits the throughput "meltdown" associated with highly contended hot spots. Its throughput at maximum concurrency is 33% lower than its peak performance at 8 threads. Similarly, MS queue's performance peaks at 2 threads and degrades as concurrency increases.

Table 2 explains the above results. LCRQ, LCRQ-CAS and the MS queue all complete in a few instructions, but some of these

---

[5]We fixed a memory leak bug in the CC and H-Queue implementations, thereby improving their performance.

[6]This consists of a writing the CRQ's address to a thread-private location, issuing a memory fence, and rereading the LCRQ's *head/tail*.

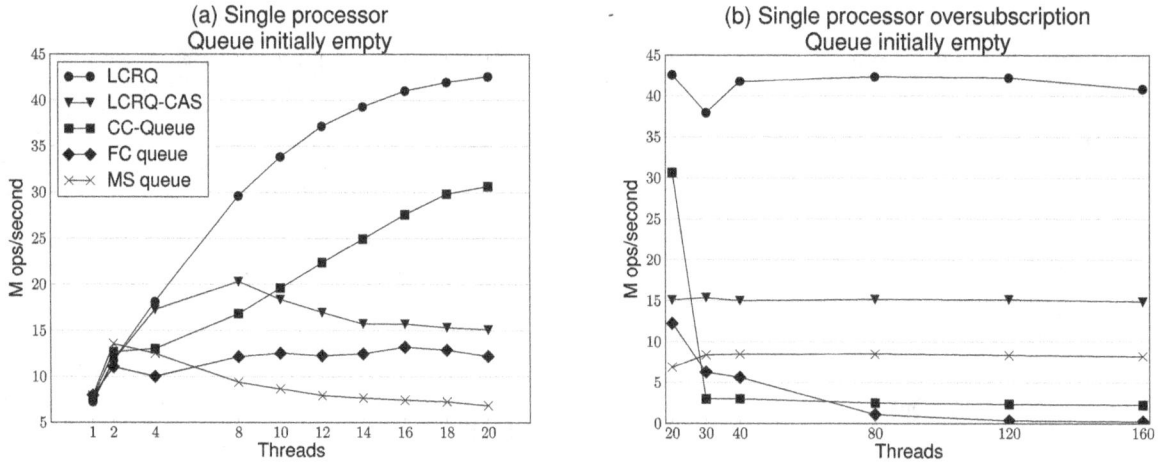

Figure 6: Enqueue/dequeue throughput on a single processor. The right plot shows throughput with more threads than available hardware threads; the first point, showing the throughput at maximal hardware concurrency, is included for reference.

	Single processor execution (queue initially empty)									
	1 thread					**20 threads**				
	LCRQ	**LCRQ-CAS**	**CC-Queue**	**FC queue**	**MS queue**	**LCRQ**	**LCRQ-CAS**	**CC-Queue**	**FC queue**	**MS queue**
Latency	0.13 μs	0.96 ×	0.95 ×	0.91 ×	0.88 ×	0.44 μs	2.70 ×	1.45 ×	3.51 ×	5.95 ×
Instructions	278.46	284.96	294.96	284.96	228.77	280.27	302.08	867.27	3846.29	321.05
Atomic operations	2	2	1	1	1.5	2	3.04	1	0.21	4.3
L1 misses	0.51	0.51	0	0.03	0	3.85	7.64	9.62	5.46	13.19
L2 misses	0.05	0.06	0	0	0	3.86	7.23	6.91	3.81	13.15

Table 2: Single processor average per-operation statistics. Latency numbers are relative to LCRQ. There are no L3 misses because the workload fits into the shared L3 cache.

are expensive atomic operations on contended locations. LCRQ-CAS and the MS queue suffer from CAS failures, which also lead to more cache misses as the algorithm wastes work. In the combining algorithms, communication between combiners and waiting threads causes more cache misses compared to LCRQ.

Oversubscribed workloads (Figure 6b) Problems related to blocking usually occur in *oversubscribed* scenarios, in which the number of software threads exceeds the hardware supported level and forces the operating system to context switch between threads. If a thread holding a lock is scheduled out, the algorithm cannot make progress until it runs again. We show this by increasing the number of threads in a single processor execution beyond 20. The throughput of the lock-based combining algorithms plummets, with FC queue dropping by 40× and CC-Queue by 15×, whereas both LCRQ and the MS queue maintain their peak throughput. As a result, LCRQ outperforms the CC-Queue by 20×.

Four processor executions (Figure 7) To measure the effect of the increased synchronization cost between processors, we pin the threads across the processors in a round-robin manner, so that the cross-processor cache coherency cost always exists. One can see how, in contrast to the single processor experiment, when going from 1 to 2 threads the throughput of all algorithms drops due to cross-processor synchronization, except for LCRQ and LCRQ+H.

Figure 7a shows the results when the queue is initially filled with 2^{16} elements, thus keeping the queue's head and tail apart [7]. This causes the throughput of CC-Queue to degrade by ≈ 10%

---

[7] On a single processor this test yields similar results to an initially empty queue and so we did not discuss it earlier.

compared to the initially empty case (Figure 7b), due to reduced *locality*: in an initially empty queue, the queue's state keeps hovering around empty and so there is a 1 in 4 chance that dequeued items will have just been enqueued on the same processor by the enqueuing combiner. In contrast, switching to an initially filled queue *improves* LCRQ's throughput by ≈ 5%. The reason is that when the queue is not empty an LCRQ dequeuer does not wait for an enqueuer to arrive at its ring node. (Table 3 shows that LCRQ operations take less instructions to complete.) The reduced locality does not hurt LCRQ because dequeued items are fetched *in parallel* by all operations, and not sequentially by a single combiner. Overall, using an initially filled queue increases LCRQ's advantage over CC-Queue from ≈ 1.5× to ≈ 1.8×.

Heavy synchronization cost due to lack of locality also explains why only the hierarchical LCRQ+H and H-Queue scale past 16 threads. These algorithms amortize the synchronization cost by running batches of operations on a single processor while operations on other processors wait. However, H-Queue suffers much more from the reduced locality caused when switching to an initially filled queue: it triples the number of L3 misses (Table 3), which must be satisfied from off-chip resources and so its throughput drops by ≈ 40%. In contrast, LCRQ+H maintains its performance, increasing its advantage over H-Queue from 1.5× to 2.5×.

Latency of operations (Figure 8) Examining the latency distribution of queue operations at maximum concurrency provides more refined insight on the performance of the algorithms. For instance, while the average latency of an LCRQ+H operation is 2.19 μs (Table 3), 96% of the operations complete in ≤ 0.5 μs and 98% in ≤ 1 μs. The remaining operations are those that complete only

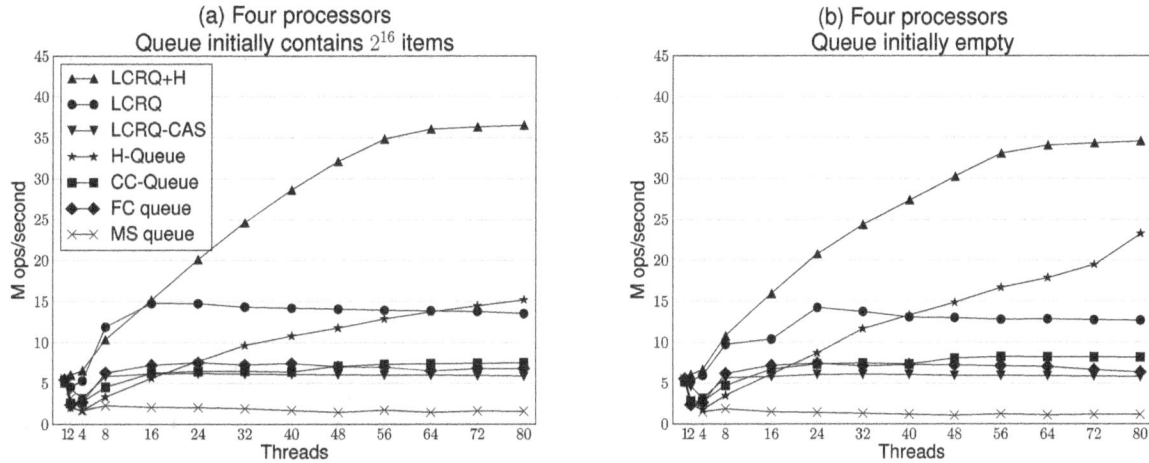

Figure 7: Enqueue/dequeue throughput on four processors (threads run on all processors from the start).

| | Four processor execution (80 threads) | | | | | | | | | |
| | Queue initially empty | | | | | Queue initially full | | | | |
	LCRQ+H	LCRQ	LCRQ-CAS	H-Queue	CC-Queue	LCRQ+H	LCRQ	LCRQ-CAS	H-Queue	CC-Queue
Latency	2.19 μs	6.20 μs	13.50 μs	3.28 μs	9.70 μs	2.05 μs	5.81 μs	13.45 μs	5.19 μs	10.55 μs
Instructions	1456.65	307.15	338.98	5670.17	16249.94	1515.60	278.62	293.86	9173.94	18224.62
Atomic operations	2	2	2.88	1.05	1	2	2	2.95	1.05	1
L1 misses	4.12	2.91	4.15	9.99	10.70	3.43	3.01	4.31	10.60	11.33
L2 misses	4.15	2.83	4.01	7.10	8.65	3.54	2.90	4.17	7.74	9.07
L3 misses	0.51	1.47	2.23	0.34	5.90	0.81	1.43	2.22	0.95	6.19

Table 3: Four processor average per-operation statistics.

after the timeout expires. The spinning these operations do while waiting accounts for the increased average instruction count of LCRQ+H compared to LCRQ shown in Table 3. In general, LCRQ operations have better latency than combining-based operations, which spend time either servicing other threads or waiting for the combiner. On a single processor, 42% of LCRQ operations finish in ≤ 0.1 μs while none of the combining operations do. On four processors, 80% of LCRQ operations finish in ≤ 4 μs compared to 50% of CC-Queue operations. Similarly, 80% of LCRQ+H operation finish in ≤ 0.2 μs compared to 30% of H-Queue operations.

Ring size sensitivity study (Figure 9) The ring size plays an important role in the performance of LCRQ. Intuitively, as the ring size decreases an LCRQ operation needs more tries before it succeeds in performing an enqueue/dequeue transition.

To quantify this effect, we test LCRQ on an initially empty queue at maximum concurrency with various ring sizes. On a single processor, taking $R \geq 32$ is enough for LCRQ to outperform the CC-Queue by 1.33×. As R increases LCRQ's throughput increases up to $\approx 1.5\times$ that of the CC-Queue. In other words, as long as an individual CRQ has room for all running threads, LCRQ obtains excellent performance.

On the four processor benchmark the results are similar, but due to the higher concurrency level, LCRQ outperforms CC-Queue starting with $R = 128$ and the advantage becomes $\approx 1.5\times$ starting with $R = 1024$. LCRQ+H requires $R = 512$ to match H-Queue and $R = 4096$ to outperform H-Queue by 1.5×.

6. Conclusion

We have presented **LCRQ**, a concurrent nonblocking linearizable FIFO queue that outperforms prior combining-based queue imple-

mentations by 1.5× to more than 2× in all concurrency levels on an x86 server with four multicore processors. LCRQ uses contended F&A objects to spread threads around items in the queue, allowing them to complete in parallel. Because the hardware guarantees that every F&A succeeds, we avoid the costly failures that plague CAS-based algorithms.

Our results show a couple of ways in which modern x86 multicore architecture requires reevaluating conventional wisdom about concurrent programming. First, LCRQ shows that on modern hardware an algorithm with a contended hot spot can scale quite well. Instead, it is CAS retries that are often the cause for notorious "contention meltdowns." Second, the conventional wisdom in the literature, of avoiding F&A or CAS2 since they are not widely supported, is outdated. We believe these principles can guide the design of future concurrent algorithms.

More practically, the LCRQ algorithm is simple to implement and offers excellent and robust performance on one of today's dominant multicore architecture. We therefore hope it gets adopted and used in practice.

Acknowledgments

This work was supported by the Israel Science Foundation (grant 1386/11), by the Israeli Centers of Research Excellence (I-CORE) program (Center 4/11), and by Intel's lab support program.

References

[1] Power ISA Version 2.06. http://www.power.org/resources/downloads/PowerISA_V2.06B_V2_PUBLIC.pdf, January 2009.

[2] G. E. Blelloch, P. B. Gibbons, and S. H. Vardhan. Combinable memory-block transactions. In *SPAA 2008*.

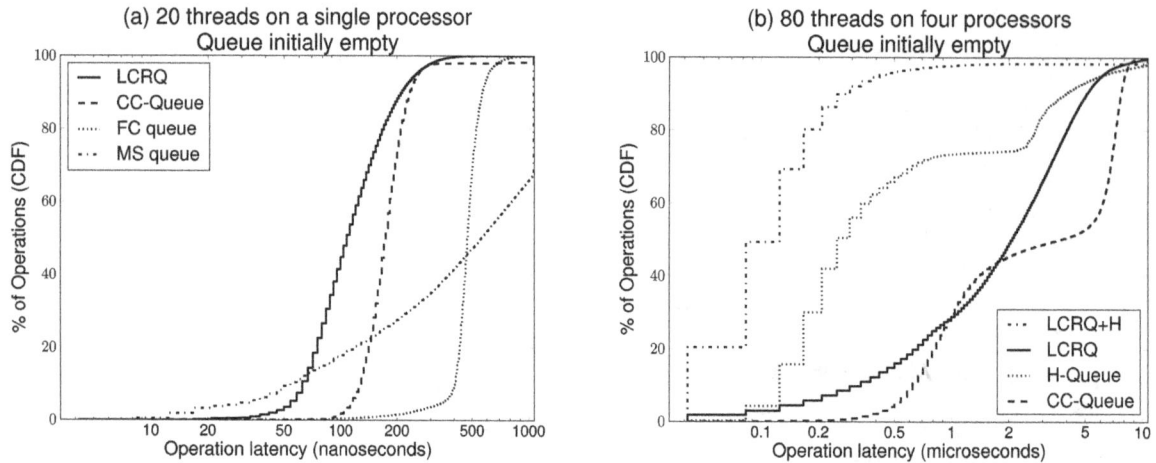

Figure 8: Cumulative distribution of queue operation latency at maximum concurrency.

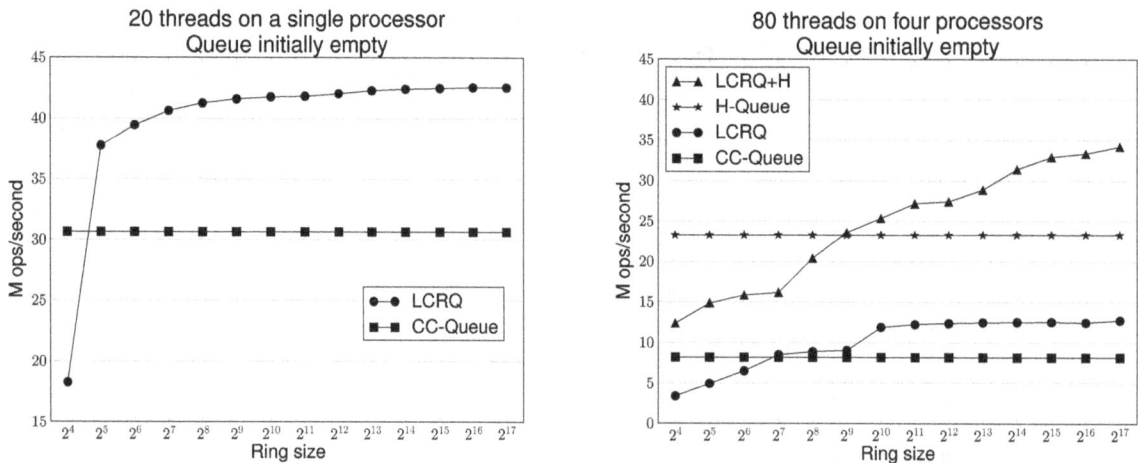

Figure 9: Impact of ring size on LCRQ throughput (CC-Queue and H-Queue results are shown for reference).

[3] G. E. Blelloch, P. Cheng, and P. B. Gibbons. Scalable room synchronizations. *Theory of Computing Systems*, 36, 2003.

[4] R. Colvin and L. Groves. Formal verification of an array-based nonblocking queue. In *ICECCS 2005*.

[5] D. Dice, V. J. Marathe, and N. Shavit. Lock cohorting: a general technique for designing numa locks. In *PPoPP 2012*.

[6] J. Evans. Scalable memory allocation using jemalloc. http://www.facebook.com/notes/facebook-engineering/scalable-memory-allocation-using-jemalloc/480222803919, 2011.

[7] P. Fatourou and N. D. Kallimanis. Revisiting the combining synchronization technique. In *PPoPP 2012*.

[8] P. Fatourou and N. D. Kallimanis. A highly-efficient wait-free universal construction. In *SPAA 2011*.

[9] E. Freudenthal and A. Gottlieb. Process coordination with fetch-and-increment. In *ASPLOS 1991*.

[10] A. Gottlieb, B. D. Lubachevsky, and L. Rudolph. Basic techniques for the efficient coordination of very large numbers of cooperating sequential processors. *TOPLAS*, 5(2), Apr. 1983.

[11] D. Hendler, I. Incze, N. Shavit, and M. Tzafrir. Flat combining and the synchronization-parallelism tradeoff. In *SPAA 2010*.

[12] M. Herlihy. Wait-free synchronization. *TOPLAS*, 13:124–149, January 1991.

[13] M. Herlihy and N. Shavit. *The Art of Multiprocessor Programming*. Morgan Kaufmann Publishers Inc., San Francisco, CA, USA, 2008.

[14] M. P. Herlihy and J. M. Wing. Linearizability: a correctness condition for concurrent objects. *TOPLAS*, 12:463–492, July 1990.

[15] M. Hoffman, O. Shalev, and N. Shavit. The baskets queue. In *OPODIS 2007*.

[16] A. Kogan and E. Petrank. Wait-free queues with multiple enqueuers and dequeuers. In *PPoPP 2011*.

[17] E. Ladan-Mozes and N. Shavit. An optimistic approach to lock-free FIFO queues. In *DISC 2004*.

[18] M. M. Michael. Hazard pointers: Safe memory reclamation for lock-free objects. *IEEE TPDS*, 15(6):491–504, June 2004.

[19] M. M. Michael and M. L. Scott. Simple, fast, and practical non-blocking and blocking concurrent queue algorithms. In *PODC 1996*.

[20] M. Moir, D. Nussbaum, O. Shalev, and N. Shavit. Using elimination to implement scalable and lock-free FIFO queues. In *SPAA 2005*.

[21] P. Sewell, S. Sarkar, S. Owens, F. Z. Nardelli, and M. O. Myreen. x86-TSO: a rigorous and usable programmer's model for x86 multiprocessors. *Communications of the ACM*, 53(7):89–97, July 2010.

[22] N. Shafiei. Non-blocking array-based algorithms for stacks and queues. In *ICDCN 2009*.

[23] P. Tsigas and Y. Zhang. A simple, fast and scalable non-blocking concurrent FIFO queue for shared memory multiprocessor systems. In *SPAA 2001*.

FASTLANE: Improving Performance of Software Transactional Memory for Low Thread Counts

Jons-Tobias Wamhoff
Christof Fetzer

Technische Universität Dresden,
Germany
first-last@tu-dresden.de

Pascal Felber
Etienne Rivière

Université de Neuchâtel,
Switzerland
first.last@unine.ch

Gilles Muller

INRIA,
France
first.last@inria.fr

Abstract

Software transactional memory (STM) can lead to scalable implementations of concurrent programs, as the *relative* performance of an application increases with the number of threads that support it. However, the *absolute* performance is typically impaired by the overheads of transaction management and instrumented accesses to shared memory. This often leads STM-based programs with low thread counts to perform worse than a sequential, non-instrumented version of the same application.

In this paper, we propose FASTLANE, a new STM algorithm that bridges the performance gap between sequential execution and classical STM algorithms when running on few cores. FASTLANE seeks to reduce instrumentation costs and thus performance degradation in its target operation range. We introduce a novel algorithm that differentiates between two types of threads: One thread (the master) executes transactions pessimistically without ever aborting, thus with minimal instrumentation and management costs, while other threads (the helpers) can commit speculative transactions only when they do not conflict with the master. Helpers thus contribute to the application progress without impairing on the performance of the master.

We implement FASTLANE as an extension of a state-of-the-art STM runtime system and compiler. Multiple code paths are produced for execution on a single, few, and many cores. The runtime system selects the code path providing the best throughput, depending on the number of cores available on the target machine. Evaluation results indicate that our approach provides promising performance at low thread counts: FASTLANE almost systematically wins over a classical STM in the 1-6 threads range, and often performs better than sequential execution of the non-instrumented version of the same application starting with 2 threads.

Categories and Subject Descriptors D.1.3 [*Programming Techniques*]: Concurrent Programming

General Terms Algorithms, Performance.

Keywords Transactional Memory, Concurrency.

1. Introduction

Transactional memory (TM) has received much attention over the last decade as it provides a scalable and easy-to-use approach to concurrent programming. Developers simply enclose critical sections within transactions[1] that execute speculatively and abort when conflicting accesses to shared data are detected at runtime.

In a short term, software-based implementations of TM (STM) will remain in the focus for optimizations as processors with dedicated hardware TM (HTM) instructions are not commonly available yet or require a software fallback. Many applications make use of few threads only: They either run on a large fraction of computers that provide only a small number of processor cores (e.g., mobile devices), or they expose only little parallelism, which hardly exceeds a level of 3 threads for general purpose applications [1]. Therefore, our focus in this paper is on STM for few threads.

While STM implementations often exhibit excellent scalability with high thread counts [5, 6, 8, 9], the overheads related to transaction management and instrumentation of memory accesses[2] are the main limitation when executing with few threads. In fact, the performance of a single-threaded non-instrumented application is generally higher than when using STM on a small number of cores [2, 4, 6, 17]. An in-depth study has shown that, with compiler instrumentation of transactions, on average more than four cores are necessary to outperform sequential code [7]. Let x be the threshold on the number of cores necessary for STM to pay off. The goal of this work is to enable an application to outperform sequential code already with less than x cores, i.e., to bridge the gap between single-threaded performance of the non-instrumented code and multi-threaded performance of the STM-based code on x cores. To that end we propose FASTLANE, a novel synchronization strategy and runtime system designed to optimize performance of STM on $1 < n < x$ cores. Depending on the target architecture, the runtime system can select an optimal synchronization strategy for the application: sequential for 1 core, FASTLANE for 2 to x cores, or STM for more than x cores. Figure 1 depicts schematically the expected behavior of the three execution strategies and the zone where FASTLANE can boost performance as compared to the state-of-the-art STM algorithms.

The basic idea of FASTLANE is to have threads operate in one of two modes. One pessimistic *master* thread runs at nearly sequential speed with only minimal instrumentation, while all other threads execute speculatively and try to help the master whenever

---

[1] TM-aware compilers typically provide higher-level *atomic block* language constructs that are transparently mapped to transactions.

[2] Reads and writes to shared memory are replaced by transactional accesses, which trigger execution of complex operations (conflict detection, maintenance of the read/write sets, etc.) requiring hundreds of additional cycles.

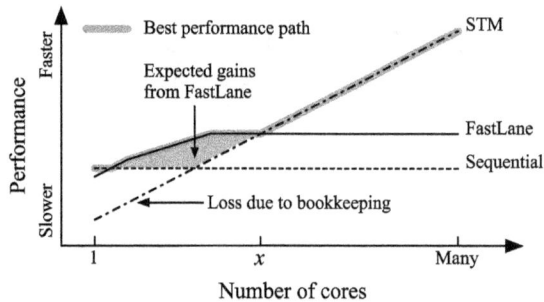

Figure 1. Our objective is to develop an algorithm that bridges the gap between sequential and STM performance at low thread counts.

they can. The latter threads, called *helpers*, typically run slower than STM threads, because in addition to performing the extra bookkeeping associated with memory accesses they should not hamper progress of the master. The roles of master and helper can be changed dynamically by the runtime system during execution of the concurrent application, e.g., if a thread requests to perform irrevocable operations and must execute as master.

An application compiled for FASTLANE includes the different synchronization strategies (sequential, STM, and FASTLANE) to allow the selection of the appropriate strategy depending on the number of cores available on the target machine. For this, we have extended the DTMC compiler [2] so as to generate all the synchronization strategies within the application binary.

We have evaluated the performance of FASTLANE on a number of synthetic and realistic benchmarks, and compared them against STM and sequential executions. Our results show that FASTLANE performs competitively with sequential execution for a single thread, and perform most of the time better with already two threads. Further, FASTLANE often continues to scale well and generally outperforms STM algorithms up to six threads, which corresponds to the number of cores per processor on our test machine. When the workload can be partitioned, FASTLANE can execute one master thread per partition and performs significantly better than other STM algorithms even for high thread counts.

The rest of this paper is organized as follows. Section 2 discusses related work. Section 3 describes the FASTLANE algorithm and the design choices that led to several optimizations. Section 4 evaluates the performance of the algorithm on various synthetic and realistic benchmarks. Finally, Section 5 concludes.

2. Related Work

A wide variety of efficient software transactional memory implementations have been proposed over the last few years [5, 6, 8, 9, 11, 25]. The main focus has been on exploiting the available disjoint access parallelism with high thread counts. It has also been shown in previous work that dynamic tuning of the STM runtime system depending on the workload can significantly improve the throughput [20, 22, 26], e.g., the bookkeeping overhead can be reduced when no contention is present. Instead of tuning, FAST-LANE focuses on optimizing the synchronization algorithm for few threads.

We are aware of only few STM designs that explicitly target small thread counts. Transactional mutex locks (TML) [4] use a versioned reader-writer lock: read-only transactions can concurrently execute and commit but, as soon as a transaction wants to write, it must acquire the lock, which will lead to an abort of all other active transactions. While no other transaction can execute concurrently when an update transaction is active, the benefit is that instrumentation overhead is minimal. Transactions only have

to save the context upon start to support retries. No write or undo logs are needed, and transactional loads only have to check the status of the versioned reader-writer lock.

We compared FASTLANE to several optimistic STM implementations known for their efficiency and low instrumentation overhead. NOREC [5] extends the idea of TML with a read-set and value-based validation to deal with concurrent updates. This allows read transactions to execute concurrently with an update transaction. Value-based validation requires a consistent state, i.e., the versioned lock must not be owned by an update transaction during the validation. If combined with FASTLANE, the master would hold the lock very frequently and for long periods, which hinders other threads to validate and would result in a poor performance. TINYSTM [8] is a word-based implementation of the lazy snapshot algorithm [19] that uses a shared array of revocable locks and time-based validation. The shared array allows a fine granular synchronization scheme that scales up to a high number of threads. It allows multiple update transactions to proceed in parallel if not in conflict. Therefore, FASTLANE uses such a shared array to allow the master and helpers to execute in parallel. TINYSTM can be configured in direct update mode (WT) or with buffered updates and encounter time locking (ETL).

Pessimistic transactions, like the master in FASTLANE, have been proposed in different flavors. A fully pessimistic STM [14] executes every transaction once and never aborts, enabling the execution of irrevocable operations and simpler debugging at the cost of limiting concurrent updates. ROBUSTM [27] starts to execute transactions speculatively but gives transactions that aborted a certain number of times a priority privilege. This privilege lets a transaction pessimistically win all conflicts, even in the presence of crashes and non-terminating transactions, making it practically wait-free. Similarly, the authors of [13] propose to execute a transaction subject to a deadline in increasingly pessimistic modes as that deadline nears.

Runtime systems for parallelization often use speculation. Software lock elision [21] processes critical sections speculatively in parallel but will fall back to lock acquisition upon frequent conflicts or irrevocable operations, which always wins over speculation. Other runtime systems auto-parallelize programs by thread-level speculation [18] or profile-guided automatic loop parallelization [15]. Fastpath [24] uses pessimistic and speculative modes to parallelize loops. Each iteration starts in speculative mode, using NOREC for synchronization, but can switch to a pessimistic mode that requires only entry and exit instrumentation whenever preceding iterations have finished.

3. FASTLANE Algorithms

The high-level objective of FASTLANE is to perform (1) approximately identically to sequential execution, and (2) better when leveraging a few additional threads. To meet the first goal, we rely on a pessimistic and lightly-instrumented master thread that never aborts and, hence, should provide performance similar to sequential execution on a single core. The role of the helper threads is to address the second objective, i.e., improve performance by committing transactions that do not conflict with those of the master.

We start by describing the global data structures used by FAST-LANE and the behavior of the master thread, before describing the helper threads and the optimizations we applied.

3.1 Data Structures

The shared data structures used by the FASTLANE algorithms are summarized in Table 1. They essentially consist of: a shared counter, $cntr$, that is incremented each time a transaction commits updates; a shared array of integers, $dirty[]$, that protects a set of memory addresses and stores the value of the counter at the last

Variable	Description
cntr	Counter that tracks updates of the master and helpers. The value is odd when a transaction performs updates and even otherwise. This variable is used for validation by the helpers.
dirty[]	Array of monotonically increasing integers. Each memory address is mapped to one entry in the array (by hashing the address modulo the size of the array). The entry contains the value of the counter cntr at the last time the address was written.
helpers	Lock to serialize commit attempts of helpers. It is implemented as a MCS list-based queue lock [16] and provides FIFO guarantees.
master	Lock to synchronize the master with the helper. Helpers must acquire helpers first. It is implemented as a TTAS (test-and-test-and-set) lock [12] and protects all shared variables.
masterID	Identity of the current master thread. It must only be modified after the master has been acquired.

Table 1. Shared variables used by FASTLANE algorithms.

time one of these addresses was updated; a FIFO lock, helpers, implemented using the scalable MCS[3] algorithm [16], to serialize helpers that intend to commit update transactions; a lock, master, implemented using the low-overhead TTAS[4] protocol [12], which must be acquired before any shared data can be modified; and a variable, masterID, that holds the current master.

3.2 Code Path Selection

We have extended the DTMC open-source C/C++ TM compiler [2] to generate multiple code paths for each transaction (see Figure 2): (1) a sequential path without instrumentation of reads and writes, (2) a pessimistic master path with a lightweight instrumentation of writes, (3) a speculative helper path with instrumentation for reads and deferred writes, and (4) an optimistic fully-fledged STM path with instrumentation of reads and writes.

The selection of the code path is performed dynamically at the beginning of a transaction. As long as only a single thread is registered with the runtime system, the sequential code path will be executed. The FASTLANE mode with the master and helper code paths is enabled after a second thread is active. When more than a specified number of threads are registered, the STM mode is selected. This number is currently fixed empirically based on observations of the average number of threads after which STM outperforms FAST-LANE. Switching to STM mode requires the acquisition of a quiescence lock that prevents further helper transactions from starting, as well as the acquisition of the master lock to stop the master. When no threads execute transactions, it is safe to set the code path for all subsequent transactions to the STM algorithm.

Algorithm 1 shows the selection of the master and helper in the FASTLANE mode. Initially, the thread that registered first with the runtime system becomes the master. When the master calls START to begin a transaction (lines 1-2) it must first acquire master using TTAS to synchronize with the helpers (line 3). As the master transaction will apply updates in-place during its execution, the

---

[3] An MCS lock uses a list-based queue to grant access to the lock in FIFO order. Threads only spin on cacheable local memory, thus achieving high scalability.

[4] A TTAS (test-and-test-and-set) lock scales better than a simpler test-and-set spin lock. TTAS first reads the state of the lock using a normal memory access and, if is it free, tries to acquire it using an atomic operation. This helps avoid unnecessary traffic on the bus because the requesting thread will spin on its local cache if the lock is not free. A TTAS lock can be released by a simple write to memory.

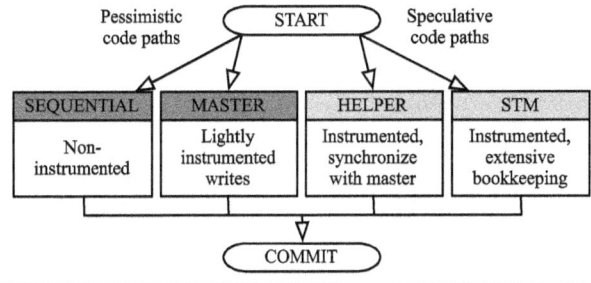

Figure 2. Multiple code paths are generated for each transaction and can be selected at transaction start by the runtime system.

master must be owned during that time. If another thread was meanwhile promoted to master, the thread releases master and continues as helper (lines 7-10, Section 3.4). For the common case that the master remains unchanged, one can assume that masterID is cached, hence, the overhead of the additional check is negligible. The thread can continue as master (lines 4-6, Section 3.3). Note that transactions that have an explicit abort request (cancel) cannot be executed as master. The compiler identifies such transactions and generates code that always selects the helper code path.

Helper threads will acquire master during their HELPER-COMMIT because they execute speculatively in parallel with the pessimistic master. They directly jump to the helper code path (lines 15-17, Section 3.4).

Helper threads can also request to gain master privilege, e.g., to perform irrevocable operations such as I/O or system calls (see Section 3.5). Upon such an event, the thread aborts and sets the pessimistic flag when the transaction is restarted (line 11). A thread that wants to become master first acquires master using TTAS (line 12). It can now execute in isolation and set masterID to its thread identifier to reflect the change (line 13). It then continues with the master code path (line 14).

Algorithm 1: Code path selection at transaction start.

```
1  function START(pessimistic)              // Begin or restart a transaction
2      if masterID = threadID then          // Is thread currently master?
3          ttas-lock(master)                // Acquire master
4          if masterID = threadID then      // Is thread still master?
5              MASTERSTART                   // Start transaction as master
6              return CP_MASTER              // Jump to master code path
7          else                             // Thread is helper now
8              ttas-unlock(master)          // Release master
9              HELPERSTART                   // Start transaction as helper
10             return CP_HELPER             // Jump to helper code path
11     else if pessimistic then             // Master privilege requested?
12         ttas-lock(master)                // Acquire master
13         masterID ← threadID              // Set current thread as master
14         return CP_MASTER                 // Jump to master code path
15     else                                 // Thread is helper
16         HELPERSTART                       // Start transaction as helper
17         return CP_HELPER                 // Jump to helper code path
```

3.3 Master Thread

The operation of the master thread is described in Algorithm 2. After the selection of the master code path in Section 3.2 the thread already owns master at MASTERSTART (line 2) and has exclusive privilege to directly update shared data during the pessimistic transaction.

Instrumentation of memory accesses is minimal on the master thread so as to obtain performance as close as to a single thread

Algorithm 2: Master code path.

```
1  function MASTERSTART
2  |                                    // Thread owns master at this point, no context saved
3  function MASTERREAD(addr)
4  |   return *addr                     // No instrumentation
5  function MASTERWRITE(addr, val)
6  |   if ¬(cntr & 0x01) then           // Is cntr already odd?
7  |   |   cntr ← cntr + 1              // Master sets odd cntr once
8  |   dirty[hash(addr)] ← cntr         // Mark as modified
9  |   addr ← val                       // No additional bookkeeping
10 function MASTERCOMMIT
11 |   if cntr & 0x01 then              // Is cntr odd from write?
12 |   |   cntr ← cntr + 1              // Master sets cntr even
13 |   ttas-unlock (master)             // Release master
```

Algorithm 3: Helper code path

```
1  function HELPERSTART
2  |   setjmp (ctx)                     // Store the current context
3  |   start ← cntr & ∼1               // Take even counter value
4  function HELPERREAD(addr)
5  |   if CONTAINS(write-set, addr) then    // Already written?
6  |   |   return GET(write-set, addr)      // Return written value
7  |   val ← *addr                      // Read from memory
8  |   if dirty[hash(addr)] > start then     // Validate read
9  |   |   ABORT                        // Abort and restart
10 |   ADD(read-set, addr)              // Add address to read set
11 |   return val
12 function HELPERWRITE(addr, val)
13 |   if dirty[hash(addr)] > start then    // Validate write
14 |   |   ABORT                        // Abort and restart
15 |   PUT(write-set, addr, val)        // Add to (or update) write set
16 function VALIDATE                    // Validate read and write sets
17 |   if cntr ≤ start then
18 |   |   return true                  // No updates since start
19 |   foreach addr ∈ (read-set ∪ write-set) do
20 |   |   if dirty[hash(addr)] > start then
21 |   |   |   return false             // Concurrent update
22 |   return true
23 function HELPERCOMMIT
24 |   if EMPTY(write-set) then         // Read-only transaction?
25 |   |   return                       // Commit immediately
26 |   mcs-lock (helpers)               // Acquire helpers
27 |   ttas-lock (master)               // Acquire master
28 |   if ¬VALIDATE then
29 |   |   ttas-unlock (master)         // Release master
30 |   |   mcs-unlock (helpers)         // Release helpers
31 |   |   ABORT                        // Abort and restart
32 |   cntr ← cntr + 1                  // Helper sets cntr odd
33 |   foreach (addr, val) ∈ write-set do
34 |   |   dirty[hash(addr)] ← cntr     // Update dirty[]
35 |   |   *addr ← val                  // Update memory
36 |   cntr ← cntr + 1                  // Helper sets cntr even
37 |   ttas-unlock (master)             // Release master
38 |   mcs-unlock (helpers)             // Release helpers
39 function ABORT
40 |   CLEAR(read-set, write-set)       // Clear read and write-set
41 |   longjmp (ctx)                    // Jump back to start
```

case. MASTERREAD operations are not instrumented (line 4) because the master does not need to ever validate the read set, while MASTERWRITE operations are augmented of a store of the value of the counter in the corresponding entry of the `dirty[]` array (line 8). No undo logging is required because the pessimistic master never aborts. On the first write only, `cntr` must be incremented to an odd value (line 7). Finally, upon MASTERCOMMIT, the master simply reverts the counter to an even value in case it has performed writes (line 12) and releases `master` (line 13).

In most cases, the master has very low overhead. The `masterID` variable is infrequently modified and thus remains in the CPU cache. At transaction START only one atomic *test-and-set* operation is needed to implement the TTAS lock. Between the TTAS lock and unlock operations, only the master can write shared data and thus we do not need any additional atomic operations or barriers. MASTERREAD operations are not instrumented and MASTERWRITE operations go directly to memory. Upon the first write `cntr` is incremented using a simple store, which may cause invalidation messages if `cntr` is cached in other cores. Note that `cntr` cannot be updated by other threads while `master` is owned, thus subsequent MASTERWRITE operations have lower overhead because `cntr` is cached and unmodified. If the transaction is read-only we completely avoid the invalidation of `cntr`. Finally, one update to the `dirty[]` array is necessary for every write. Upon MASTERCOMMIT, the `master` lock is released in order to serialize all changes made by the transaction. In Section 3.6 we show how the contention on `master` and `cntr` can be reduced.

3.4 Helper Thread

The price to pay for having a lightly instrumented master thread becomes clear when considering the algorithm of the helpers. Extra work must be performed to speculatively execute transactions and try to commit changes without slowing down the master.

The functions of the FASTLANE helper code path are shown in Algorithm 3. Upon HELPERSTART, the current value of `cntr` is stored for subsequent validation purposes, discarding the least significant bit to force the value to be even (line 3).

For HELPERREAD operations, the helper first checks whether it has already written to the same address. If so, it returns the value of the previous write (lines 5–6). Otherwise, it reads the value and conservatively checks if the address has been concurrently written, by validating the associated entry of `dirty[]`; if so, the transaction simply aborts (lines 7–9). This guarantees opacity [10]. Otherwise, the read can successfully complete: the address is added to the read set and the previously read value is returned (lines 10–11).

Upon HELPERWRITE, we check if the written address has possibly been updated concurrently, like for reads, and if so, the transaction aborts (lines 13–14). Otherwise, we simply add or update the

address and the written value in the write set (line 15), delaying the actual update of the shared memory to the commit phase.

The HELPERREAD and HELPERWRITE operations must both perform lookups on the write set for each invocation. The write set is a vector with an index to reduce the lookup time, following the same general principle as in [23].

The main idea of HELPERCOMMIT is to perform the validation of the read and write sets, resulting in either an abort or a successful commit, while holding `master`. If the transaction is read-only (lines 24–25), all memory accesses have already been validated by the HELPERREAD operation and the transaction can commit immediately. Otherwise, the helper must ensure mutual exclusion for its commit phase. To that end, it first acquires the MCS queue lock `helpers` (line 26) to synchronize with other helpers and then acquires `master` using TTAS (line 27) to synchronize with the master. The rationale behind using the additional `helpers` lock is to reduce the contention on `master`, i.e., minimize the negative impact of the helpers on the master. In Section 3.6 we use the `helpers` for a lock handover optimization.

The validation is performed while holding `master` and no other thread (even the master) can interfere. VALIDATE verifies if any address stored in the read and write set may have been concurrently updated, by looking into the `dirty[]` array (lines 16–22), and if so HELPERCOMMIT conservatively aborts after releasing `helpers` and `master` (lines 28–31). Upon successful validation, all pending updates stored in the write set are sent to shared memory (line 35) and the associated entries of the `dirty[]` array are updated with the current odd `cntr` (lines 32 and 34). Finally, `cntr` is increased to the next even value (line 36) and `master` and `helpers` are released (lines 37–38).

3.5 Irrevocability And Privatization

Some operations cannot be executed speculatively because they cannot be reverted, e.g., system calls or other operations with externally visible side effects. If a thread encounters such an operation and is currently executing speculatively, it requests to enter pessimistic mode to ensure that the transaction must not abort. Depending on the current code path, this requires for a helper thread to become the master and for an STM thread to execute exclusively in sequential mode. Note that switching to the pessimistic modes can also be used when the progress of a thread is at stake, with the benefit of the master to allow parallel helpers in contrast to the exclusive sequential mode.

A thread in STM mode that requests irrevocability must acquire a quiescence lock, a common approach described in detail in the literature [28]. In short, it will prevent other threads from starting transactions. It then waits until all active transactions are either committed or aborted. After that it can execute the transaction in isolation, using a non-instrumented code path, and release the quiescence lock after commit.

In FASTLANE mode, the pessimistic master is used to execute irrevocable operations that cannot be rolled back. Helpers must abort the transaction when they encounter irrevocable operations, switch to the master code path (presented in Section 3.2) to re-execute the transaction. Other helpers can continue to execute transactions speculatively in parallel. Note that the operations of the master must not contain non-transactional code that does not reflect updates to shared memory in `dirty[]`.

Threads can request to privatize data in order to access it outside of transactions afterwards. Privatization safety [11] requires that no other threads are accessing the data after the privatizing transaction committed. This is supported natively for the master because, once it has started its privatizing transaction, no helper can commit concurrently before it is finished. The helpers will abort when their validation encounters data privatized by the master. Helper threads that request privatization must wait after they committed until all earlier helper transactions are either committed or aborted. This is determined by looping through all transaction descriptors and waiting if they are active and still have a start counter value less than the privatizing transaction.

3.6 Optimizations

The goal of FASTLANE is to reduce the overhead for master transactions in order to achieve a performance close to sequential non-instrumented execution. The lightweight instrumentation of the master presented in Section 3.3 combined with a distinct compiler generated code path is key to a range of optimizations: all master-specific instrumentation can be inlined to remove call overheads; because the master only updates global data, it does not need access to a transaction descriptor during its read or write operations; and at transaction start, the master can omit saving the context because it never aborts.

Helper threads that execute in parallel will have an impact on the master because `master`, `cntr` and `dirty[]` are shared resources. While the contention on `dirty[]` is spread over the elements of the array, the contention on `master` and `cntr` can have a negative impact because they will be modified by each update transaction.

With high likelihood, `cntr` will be in the cache of the helper threads for validation purposes, thus the modifications will cause invalidation traffic.

We applied a number of specific optimizations to the FAST-LANE algorithm to further reduce the overheads of the master and helper threads:

1. **Keep-lock** — The master thread can keep the `master` lock if no helper requests it to avoid unnecessary updates to shared variables.

2. **Pre-validate** — Helper threads can validate before attempting to acquire the `master` lock, to stop the master only if they have a high likelihood of a successful commit.

3. **Hand-over** — Helper threads can hand over the `master` lock if a successor exists in the `helpers` MCS queue to increase the commit chance.

The first optimization (*keep-lock*) can save the master the cost of releasing and reacquiring `master`, along with incrementing `cntr`, as long as no helper requests it. After each MASTERCOMMIT, the master checks if `helpers` was acquired.[5] If this is not the case, the master keeps `master` and does not increment `cntr` to the next even value (line 3 in Algorithm 1 and lines 11–13 in Algorithm 2 will not be executed). A helper acquires `helpers` when it needs to commit and must acquire `cntr`, or when the helper aborts because it cannot validate. In the latter case, the helper needs the counter to be incremented to eventually commit. Indeed, assume that a shared variable has been written by the master when the value of the counter is x (odd) without the counter being subsequently incremented. A helper that later reads the same variable will remember $x-1$ (even) as start value of the counter and will systematically fail validation until `cntr` becomes greater than x (see Algorithm 3, lines 3 and 20).

Helper threads can reduce the contention on `cntr` by validating before they attempt to acquire `master` with the second optimization (*pre-validation*). After acquiring `helpers` (Algorithm 3, line 26) the thread calls VALIDATE and keeps the current value of `cntr`. Upon successful validation it acquires `master` (line 27) and must only validate again (line 28) if `cntr` was incremented because another thread committed in the meantime. This is expected to reduce contention with the master, as a transaction that is known to abort will not compete for `master`. We prevent multiple helpers from committing concurrently using the `helpers` lock in order to avoid interference with the pre-validation from other helpers.

Finally, the third optimization (*hand-over*) allows the helper threads to hand over the `master` lock if a successor is waiting in the `helpers` MCS queue at HELPERCOMMIT. In that case, the helper does not increment `cntr` to the next even value and skips releasing the `master` lock (Algorithm 3, lines 36–37). It only releases `helpers` (line 38) and the succeeding owner in the queue of `helpers` can skip the acquisition of `master` (line 27) and will increment `cntr` by two to the next odd value (instead of line 32). Besides a reduction of the contention on `master`, this optimization is expected to improve the chance for helper threads that have already reached the commit phase to complete it. This is particularly interesting when combined with the second optimization: pre-validation holds because no other thread can commit in the meantime.

---

[5] It is sufficient to check if the head node of the `helpers` MCS queue is not null.

4. Evaluation

In this section, we evaluate and analyze the performance of FASTLANE. We compare the FASTLANE algorithm against non-instrumented sequential execution; two STM variants that are based on the lazy snapshot algorithm [19]: TINYSTM [8] operating either in write-through mode (WT), i.e., direct updates to memory, or in write-back mode with encounter time locking (ETL), i.e., buffered updates with eager conflict detection; and two STMs based on a single versioned lock, either exclusively directly updating memory (TML [4]) or performing buffered updates and value-based validation (NOREC [5]). For FASTLANE, we measured the plain algorithm (FL, see Sections 3.3 and 3.4) as well as the optimizations described in Section 3.6. All evaluated configurations are summarized in Table 2.

For our test applications, we use the synthetic *intset* micro-benchmarks, realistic applications from the STAMP [17] benchmark suite, and a new benchmark that we designed to analyse the benefits and limitations of FASTLANE and which computes communities of interest for communication networks (see Section 4.5).

The *intset* benchmarks perform randomly queries and updates on integer sets implemented as a *red-black tree* (RB), a *linked list* (LL), a *skip list* (SL), or a *hash set* (HS). We use a working set of 8,192 elements for RB; 2,048 and 1,024 elements for LL; and 1,024 elements for SL and HS. We use update-to-lookup ratios of 5% and 20%, and the execution time for each run is 10 seconds.

The STAMP benchmark suite consists of the following applications: bayes learns the structure of Bayesian networks in a directed acyclic graph; genome performs gene sequencing using hash sets and string search; intruder emulates a signature-based network intrusion detection system by matching packets against signatures stored in self-balancing trees; labyrinth finds the shortest-distance paths between pairs of points using breadth-first search; kmeans clusters a set of partitioned points in parallel; ssca2 constructs an efficient graph data structure using adjacency arrays; vacation emulates a travel reservation system, reading and writing different tables that are implemented as red-black trees; finally, yada performs mesh refinement of triangles in a work queue.

Using FASTLANE, there is a very unbalanced workload distribution between threads because the master is able to process transactions much faster than the helpers. Therefore we have adapted the STAMP benchmarks with a partitioning-based dynamic work balancing that introduces only very little overhead and allows adapting the amount of work for each thread and account for differences in throughput between the master and helpers. Otherwise, all STAMP benchmarks are configured accordingly to the documentation with parameters for non-simulator runs and high contention.

Our tests have been carried out on a dual-socket server with two 6-core Intel Xeon Westmere-EP X5650 running 64-bit Linux 3.0. All 6 cores of a processor share the L3 cache. The CPU affinity was configured such that the penalty of moving data between sockets is as limited as possible, i.e., for up to 6 threads only a single processor is used. All benchmarks were compiled with the DTMC open-source TM C/C++ compiler [2].

In the rest of this section, we first analyze the scalability of FASTLANE against existing STM algorithms for a low number of thread. Then we study the comparative contribution of the master and the worker threads. We later study the impact of optimizations. Finally, we present the new benchmark that computes communities of interest for communication networks.

4.1 Scalability for Low Thread Counts

Our main goal is to achieve better scalability for a low thread counts than traditional STM approaches. Figure 3 presents the throughput obtained in millions of transactions per second for the duration of each of the *intset* benchmarks. Figure 4 presents completion times

Name	Description
Seq	Non-instrumented sequential execution.
WT	TINYSTM operating in write-through mode (direct updates to memory) [8].
ETL	TINYSTM operating in write-back mode with encounter time locking (buffered updates with eager conflict detection) [8].
TML	Single versioned lock with exclusive direct updates to memory [4].
NOREC	Single versioned lock with buffered updates and value-based validation [5].
FL	Basic version of FASTLANE with no optimizations (Sections 3.3 and 3.4).
FL-PV	FASTLANE with *pre-validation* before the helpers stop the master (Section 3.6).
FL-HO	FASTLANE with *hand-over* of locks for helper threads and *keep-lock* for master threads (Section 3.6).
FL-O3	FASTLANE with all three optimizations enabled: *keep-lock*, *pre-validation*, and *hand-over* (Section 3.6).
FL-P	FASTLANE with support for partitions (one master per partition, see Section 4.5).

Table 2. STMs and FASTLANE configurations used in the tests.

for STAMP applications, which have a fixed number of transactions depending on the input parameters. The STAMP graphs show execution times instead of scalability to allow an easy comparison with the sequential baseline Overall, FASTLANE scales well for a number of threads up to 6 and is on average more efficient than STM approaches for that number of threads. The sequential baseline corresponds to an implementation of transactions using a global lock because all benchmarks spend most of their time inside transactions and no scalability can be achieved.

On the *intset* micro-benchmarks, the minimal overhead of the master thread gives it a head start and the helpers contribute their share when the number of threads increases. FASTLANE is only outperformed on the RB micro-benchmark by TML, because of the instrumentation overhead to access $dirty[]$ in FASTLANE. TML is typically very efficient for workloads that contain mostly transactions that are either short, read-only, or have a short period of updates at the end, but cannot exploit parallelism as long as a single update transaction is active.

The *intset* micro-benchmarks have a drop in throughput when more than 6 threads are active and the second socket is in use. This due to the more expensive cache coherence traffic over the interconnect, for up to 6 threads the L3 cache can handle the coherence. Here, the main source of cache contention, common to all STMs and FASTLANE, is the shared clock used for versioning that must be incremented upon each update transaction.

The STAMP benchmarks do not exhibit this behavior because they have larger transactions and, hence, the relative impact of the cache contention bottleneck is lower. Here, FASTLANE wins over all STMs for up to 6 threads with the exception of labyrinth, intruder and ssca2 for which ETL is more efficient. With the two latter benchmarks, the master performs short update transactions at a high rate that prevent the helpers from committing.

Note that the performance of some algorithms is not shown for bayes and labyrinth because the DTMC compiler instruments loading of regions, which is currently not supported by NOREC and results in prohibitively long execution times for WT. Hence, both variants are omitted from the graphs. The other algorithms serialize transactions upon such an operation: FASTLANE switches to master mode; ETL acquires the quiescence lock and executes the non-instrumented sequential code path; and TML acquires its reader-writer lock. As a result, labyrinth does not exhibits scalability and the plot only shows the constant instrumentation

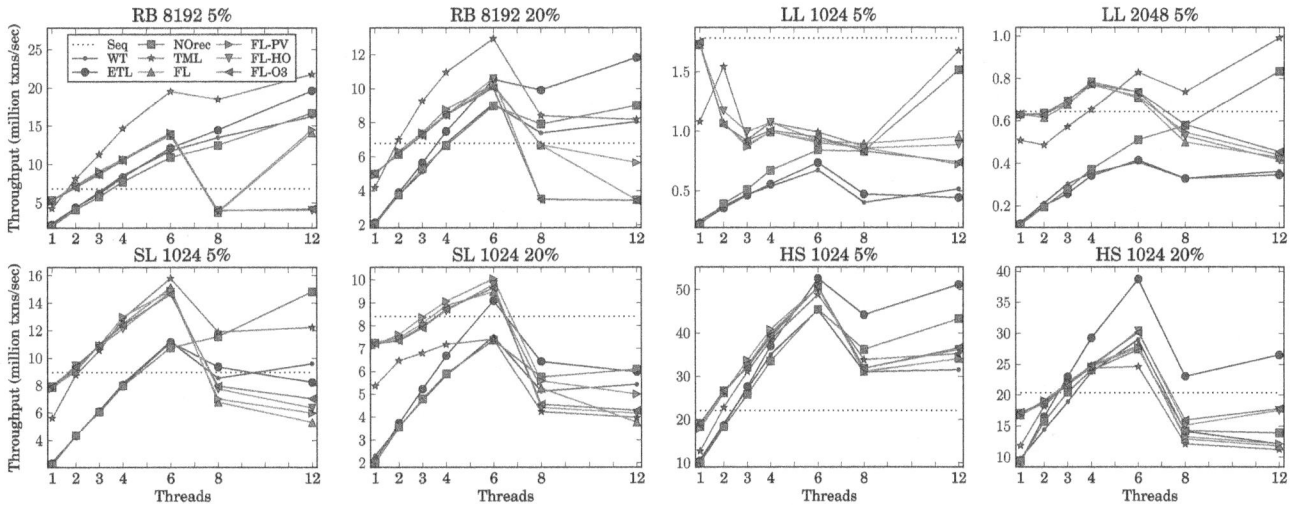

Figure 3. Throughput of the *Intset* benchmarks (higher is better).

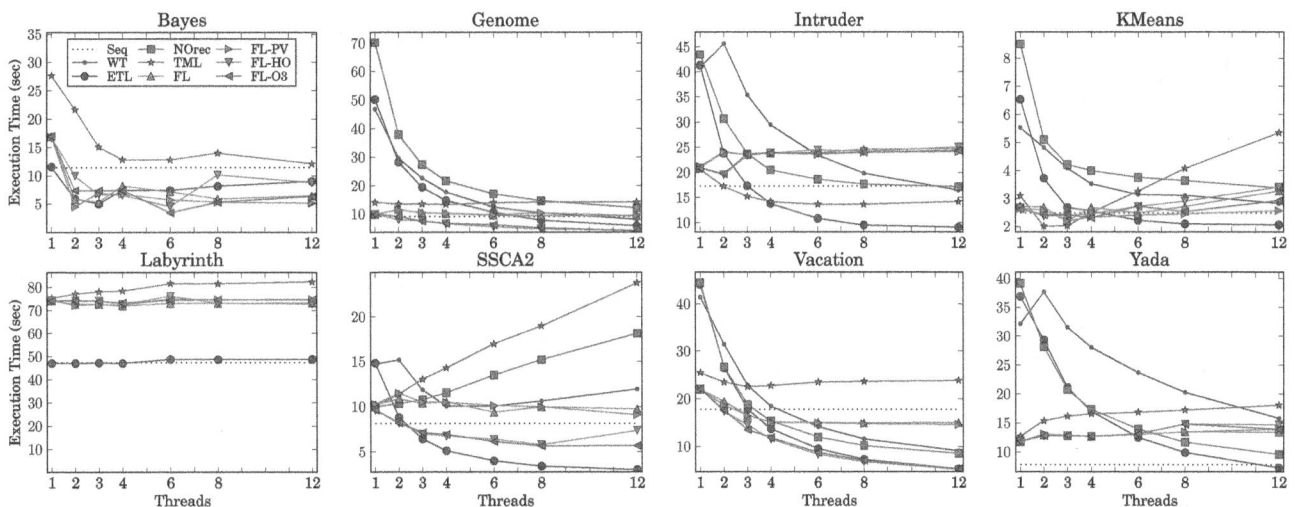

Figure 4. Completion times of the STAMP benchmarks [17] (all with high contention configuration, lower is better).

overhead for the FASTLANE master and TML, while ETL executes non-instrumented code. Bayes scales beyond sequential execution because not all time is spent inside serialized transactions, leaving a portion of the application where parallelism can be exploited.

Even if FASTLANE shows better performance than STMs on yada, it does not scale. The reason is that yada spends most of its time in long-running transactions and that FASTLANE serializes transactions of the master thread and commits of helper transactions by the `master` lock. As long as the master executes a transaction, no helper can commit and when a helper wants to commit it must stop the master.

4.2 Contribution of the Master

To better understand the performance of FASTLANE, we first evaluate the overhead of the master thread with respect to the non-instrumented sequential execution. Since we run the plain FASTLANE algorithm without dynamic switching of code paths, using one thread amounts to using only the master thread. In that case, instrumentation is lightweight: it only needs to acquire and release `master` upon beginning and committing a transaction, re-

spectively. Loads have no instrumentation at all, while writes only require an additional update to the `dirty[]` array and the first write additionally increments `cntr`.

The one thread results in Figure 3 and Figure 4 show that the master can indeed achieve single-threaded throughput close to that of sequential execution. For *intset*, the performance is very close to sequential: less than 2% slower for LL, at most 34% for RB, and 16% on average. For STAMP, the overhead ranges from 5% for kmeans to 52% for yada, with an average of 29%.

This good performance can be explained because `master` and `cntr` are cached and have only a marginal impact on the overhead. With an increasing update rate the overhead slightly increases because `dirty[]` must be updated more often. Since the optimization that keeps `master` does not perform noticeably faster than the basic algorithm, the updates to `dirty[]` are the main source of overhead for the master.

When comparing FASTLANE to the state-of-the-art STM algorithms, the latter require non-trivial algorithms to be executed for every transactional operation. While runtime systems could decide to choose the sequential non-instrumented path if only a

119

| | Worker commits (%) | | | | | | | |
| | FL | | FL-PV | | FL-HO | | FL-O3 | |
Benchmark	2 thr.	6 thr.	2 thr.	6 thr.	2 thr.	6 thr.	2 thr.	6 thr.
rb 8k 05%	29.9	70.4	30.0	70.2	29.8	70.7	29.9	70.7
rb 8k 20%	30.1	73.1	29.6	72.4	28.9	74.3	28.9	74.6
ll 1k 05%	20.5	67.3	20.6	67.6	17.8	66.7	19.8	65.7
ll 2k 05%	16.6	60.1	16.2	59.4	14.9	58.8	15.1	59.4
sl 1k 05%	23.9	65.1	23.3	64.7	24.2	64.9	24.6	66.2
sl 1k 20%	22.7	68.1	24.2	65.8	22.5	70.3	23.5	69.0
hs 1k 05%	37.4	77.6	37.4	77.6	35.7	77.2	35.8	77.3
hs 1k 20%	39.5	84.5	39.3	84.2	36.6	85.0	36.2	85.1
bayes	1.7	2.3	1.7	5.0	1.1	2.5	1.1	7.3
genome	3.8	6.3	3.8	6.3	18.4	50.9	24.1	53.2
intruder	1.3	1.6	1.4	2.9	0.0	1.5	0.0	3.6
labyrinth	22.9	51.8	23.6	47.3	19.8	63.6	21.5	62.1
kmeans	12.2	1.4	14.5	29.0	0.3	1.5	0.3	22.1
ssca2	12.5	44.8	21.9	26.0	34.4	58.3	34.4	58.3
vacation	28.1	50.0	25.0	49.0	31.2	69.8	31.2	72.9
yada	0.2	0.0	0.2	0.0	0.1	0.3	0.1	0.3

Table 3. Contribution of helpers to the global commit throughput.

single thread is active, we are interested in the general overhead introduced by an algorithm during its normal operation, i.e., the instrumented code path but without contention. STMs must typically copy the current CPU context at transaction START to support restart upon abort, keep track of read and write sets upon memory accesses, and perform validation and memory copy operations upon commit. FASTLANE's objective is to streamline these costs for the master thread.

TINYSTM and NOREC suffer from high transactional management costs that are mainly depending on the number of transactional memory accesses, e.g., LL has the largest transaction sizes and the biggest performance degradation. TML has slightly higher overhead than FASTLANE because it must additionally save the context at START and instrument reads to check for concurrent writers. These observations are also visible in the STAMP measurements. Only bayes and labyrinth differ, because they contain compiler instrumented regions that will be executed in irrevocable mode by ETL (non-instrumented) and by the master with constant overhead in FASTLANE.

4.3 Contribution of the Workers

To understand the importance of helpers in the global commit throughput of applications, we show in Table 3 the percentage of commits that have been achieved by helpers for all FASTLANE variants and all applications, with 2 and 6 threads. For the *intset* micro-benchmarks the contribution of the helpers varies from approximately 15-40% with 2 threads, to 60-85% with 6 threads. There is no noticeable difference between the FASTLANE variants. This can be explained by the fact that transactions are short and all identical, which limits the benefits of pre-validation and lock hand-over.

For the STAMP benchmark, one can observe important differences between the applications and the FASTLANE variants. Workers contribute almost nothing with the bayes, intruder, and yada applications because of the size of transactions that leave almost no opportunity for helpers to commit without conflicts. One should also point out that bayes and labyrinth have very few transactions (less than 2,000 for the whole execution) and, hence, results are not very representative.

With genome, ssca2, and vacation, we observe the benefits of the *hand-over* optimization. When executing with 6 threads, the contribution of helpers in genome increases from 6.3% to 50.9%, i.e., almost one order of magnitude. Gains are also significant with the other two applications.

| | Failed PV (%) | | | PV holds (%) | | | HO used (%) | | |
Benchmark	2 thr.	6 thr.	12 thr.	2 thr.	6 thr.	12 thr.	2 thr.	6 thr.	12 thr.
rb 8k 05%	0.0	0.0	0.1	1.5	2.6	0.9	0.0	0.5	3.0
rb 8k 20%	0.0	0.1	1.4	3.7	6.3	1.7	0.0	4.9	13.0
ll 1k 05%	0.0	0.1	2.9	2.1	2.3	2.2	0.0	0.1	0.8
ll 2k 05%	0.0	0.1	1.3	2.0	2.3	2.3	0.0	0.1	0.6
sl 1k 05%	0.0	0.0	0.5	1.3	3.0	1.8	0.0	0.6	3.0
sl 1k 20%	0.0	0.6	4.0	2.3	6.8	2.5	0.0	7.8	19.3
hs 1k 05%	0.0	0.0	0.0	1.1	1.5	0.9	0.0	0.4	1.3
hs 1k 20%	0.0	0.0	0.0	3.4	3.4	0.9	0.0	4.9	9.3
bayes	0.0	45.3	68.6	86.4	12.1	12.2	0.0	67.1	72.5
genome	0.0	0.0	0.2	9.5	6.9	3.8	0.0	55.7	84.4
intruder	0.0	54.9	86.8	0.7	10.9	8.8	0.0	62.4	63.7
labyrinth	0.0	6.2	53.1	19.6	4.7	12.5	0.0	86.9	99.7
kmeans	0.0	50.6	72.8	33.3	1.3	1.0	0.0	97.4	95.4
ssca2	0.0	0.0	0.0	2.6	2.1	0.0	0.0	97.0	99.7
vacation	0.0	0.0	0.0	7.0	5.3	3.6	0.0	36.5	76.9
yada	0.0	0.0	89.7	0.1	0.0	0.5	0.0	63.4	62.0

Table 4. Impact of optimizations for FL-O3: percentage of failed pre-validations; percentage of pre-validations that hold after acquisition of the master lock; and hand-overs of helpers.

Interestingly, kmeans appears to suffer from the *hand-over* optimization but benefits from *pre-validation*. Indeed, with 6 threads, the contribution of the helpers increases from 1.4% to 29% when activating the latter optimization. This is because pre-validation helps detect early that a transaction is doomed and must abort, without needing to acquire the locks and slow down other threads. This optimization is particularly important given the level of contention in kmeans.

4.4 Impact of Optimizations

We now focus on the the impact of optimizations. Table 4 shows, for FL-O3, the following metrics for 2, 6, and 12 threads: (1) percentage of failed pre-validations, i.e., helper transactions abort before even trying to acquire the master lock and hence do not slow down the master; (2) percentage of pre-validations that still hold after acquisition of the master lock, i.e., helper transactions do not need to validate again; and (3) percentage of committed helper transactions that benefited from the hand-over optimization.

One can first notice that pre-validation almost never fails for the *intset* benchmarks and several of the STAMP benchmarks. It only fails at a significant rate with bayes, intruder, and kmeans, as well as with labyrinth and yada but only when many threads are used. These numbers are consistent with the nature of the workloads: pre-validation is more likely to fail when conflicts with concurrent transactions are frequents. This optimization saves the cost of acquiring the master lock and slowing down the other threads.

For most benchmarks, pre-validation does not hold often. This is because helper threads typically request the master lock while the master thread is active. Once they succeed in acquiring it, the master has committed and incremented cntr, which requires helpers to validate again. Only for some STAMP applications (bayes, labyrinth, and kmeans) does pre-validation hold more than 10% of the time, and essentially in the case of 2 threads. These benchmarks have long-running transactions that reduce the likelihood of a concurrent commit.

Finally, we observe that the *hand-over* optimization is very effective in STAMP benchmarks that have workloads with transactions of different sizes, but less so for the *intset* benchmarks because transactions are short and identical, hence the master commits at a high rate and prevents helpers handling over the lock to one another. As expected, hand-overs are generally more frequent when increasing the number of threads.

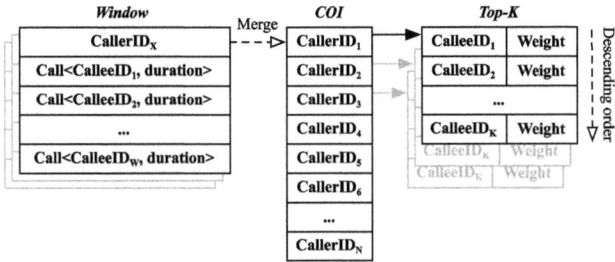

Figure 6. Windows are merged into the communities of interest. Each caller has an ordered Top-K list of callees.

4.5 Communities of Interest Benchmark

In many applications, data can be naturally partitioned such that transactions operating on different partitions do not conflict and threads rarely access the same partition at the same time. Such applications can take full advantage of the FASTLANE algorithm because each partition can conceptually have its own master. If several threads try to access a partition at the same time, all but the first one will do it speculatively as a helper.

To evaluate the benefits of FASTLANE in such settings, we developed a new benchmark implementing an operator from the field of streaming and batch systems that calculates the communities of interest (COI) for communication networks [3, 29]. The COI operator processes telephone calls and calculates the callees that are most often called by a caller. Figure 6 schematically illustrates the operator. One transaction will merge a given sequence of calls ("window") into the COI. The window has a configurable size W and is generated randomly before each transaction. The identities of callers and callees are randomly distributed between 1 and N, and the duration of each call between 1 and 60 seconds.

The COI is computed for each caller that placed a call. The operator maintains a top-k list of size $K = 9$ in which callees are ordered by weight. The weight is calculated as a moving average with factor θ ($0 \leq \theta \leq 1$): ($weight\_of\_callee\_in\_top\text{-}k * \theta$) + ($duration\_in\_window * (1 - \theta)$). Thus, θ defines how much a new record influences the data. As the transaction iterates over the window, it updates the weights of callees (possibly inserting new entries) and moves them in the right position in the top-k list.

The partitioning of the data is based on the identity of the caller in the COI. We extended FASTLANE to support partitions in the following way: (1) each partition has its own `master`, `cntr`, and `helpers`; (2) the hash function to find the `dirty[]` entry was adapted to be aware of the partition and keeps disjoint partitions in `dirty[]` during the mapping; (3) at START each thread becomes master if there is no other master, and releases the master privilege on MASTERCOMMIT; (4) all optimizations are disabled. Note that the approach taken in this benchmark differs from related work on TM partitioning, e.g., [20], because we do not rely on tuning to determine which synchronization mechanisms to use in each partition, and we can benefit from more parallelism than a shared lock (a secondary thread can access the partition as a helper) and less overhead than multiple locks as used by many STMs.

Figure 5 shows the experimental results for FASTLANE with partition support (FL-P) for different values of N (2^{10} and 2^{15}) and W (1, 10, 20). FL-P is configured with 8 partitions. The window size essentially defines the size of a transaction, i.e., how many callees have to be merged.

A first observation is that, for $W = 1$, FL-P has a higher single-threaded overhead than FL because of the extra indirection to select the partition has an high impact with short transactions. Except for that configuration, FL-P performs and scales systematically better than FL and other STMs thanks to having one master per

	Worker commits (%)							
	FL				FL-P			
Benchmark	3 thr.	6 thr.	8 thr.	12 thr.	3 thr.	6 thr.	8 thr.	12 thr.
N=1024 W=01	41.8	54.7	50.3	49.4	13.7	27.5	33.4	42.7
N=1024 W=10	33.0	49.9	56.7	56.2	12.8	23.8	30.1	39.5
N=32768 W=10	32.9	49.9	53.5	55.0	12.0	24.0	30.7	40.2
N=32768 W=20	30.1	49.3	55.8	54.9	10.7	22.2	28.5	37.9

Table 5. Contribution of helpers to the global commit throughput.

partition. If more threads are active than partitions (12 threads vs. 8 partitions), FL-P is still able to scale because the threads execute transactions as helpers. This contribution of helper threads is shown in Table 5, which lists the percentage of commits achieved by FL and FL-P for 3, 6, 8, and 12 threads. Without partitioning, the contribution of helpers grows from 30% to 55%. When using partitions, it remains in the 12% to 42% range because more threads execute as master, but it continues to grow when using more threads than partitions.

Note that using partitions with other STMs would not produce the same benefits as it would not suppress the overheads associated with transaction management (context saving, instrumentation). Table 6 shows the abort rates for all STMs and FASTLANE when 12 threads are active. TINYSTM and NOREC have very low abort rates that would not diminish much if one instance per partition would be used; only the contention on their shared counter would be reduced. TML has a very high abort rate because almost all transactions perform updates and hence are practically serialized. Having one instance per partition would correspond to having a shared counter per partition, enabling parallelism as long as not two threads try to access the same partition. FL has an abort rate that increases with large transaction sizes because the fast master will invalidate slow helper transactions more often. Finally, FL-P has a moderate abort rate due to the fact that more threads are active than partitions. As compared to having a shared lock per partition, the speculative helpers can execute concurrently with masters and allow for more parallelism.

One can notice a drop in the throughput of FL-P after 6 threads for $W = 1$ and, to a lesser extend, for $W = 10$. As previously said, this is due to fact that when more than 6 threads are active, the second socket of our experimental machine is in use, which creates expensive cache coherence traffic over the interconnect. For longer transactions ($W = 20$), there is no noticeable degradation because the cache is less effectively used even on a single processor.

Interestingly, FL-P provides significant improvements over sequential with 2 threads already, and scales remarkably well, making the switch to STM less crucial even for 12 threads (except for $W = 1$ where ETL wins starting with 8 threads).

As a final remark, this benchmark is representative of applications with low latency requirements, e.g., for stream processing. Having one master per partition allows us to guarantee fast processing with almost predictable execution times, comparable to non-instrumented execution.

	Aborts (%, 12 threads)					
Benchmark	WT	ETL	NOREC	TML	FL	FL-P
N=1024 W=01	0.0	0.0	0.0	91.4	0.0	0.2
N=1024 W=10	1.5	3.0	0.1	90.9	0.5	1.6
N=32768 W=10	0.1	0.4	0.0	90.9	7.1	3.1
N=32768 W=20	0.6	0.9	0.0	90.9	19.0	8.1

Table 6. Abort rates for STMs and FASTLANE (12 threads).

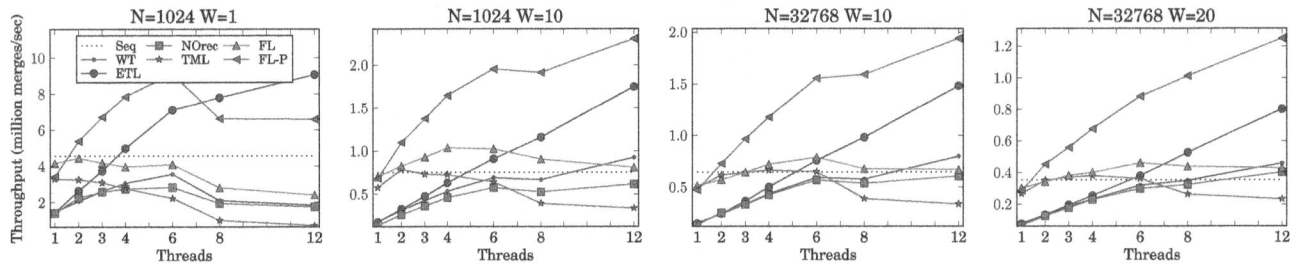

Figure 5. Throughput of the *COI* benchmark (higher is better).

5. Conclusion

In this paper, we have addressed one of the main drawbacks of STM: its limited performance at low thread counts, as compared to the execution of the sequential original application without the overheads of TM.

We have proposed a novel synchronization strategy, FAST-LANE, designed to perform best at low thread counts, where classical STM implementations are slower than sequential execution—typically between 2 and 4 threads. FASTLANE relies on a single pessimistic master thread with light instrumentation that never aborts, and one or more speculative helper threads that perform additional work as they try to commit their transactions without hampering the progress of the master. We have presented several variants that differ mainly by the optimizations they introduce in the commit function of the helper threads.

We have introduced a new benchmark that computes communities of interest, with a transactional workload that can be partitioned such that multiple masters can execute in distinct partitions. Results from experimental evaluation show that our new algorithms performs well in their target operation range of low thread counts, and provide a real performance boost if combined with partitioning.

Currently, the decision of when to change between the different code paths (sequential, FASTLANE, and STM) is based on the number of physical cores available on the target machine when starting the application. In the future, we would like to investigate dynamic schemes by periodically switching modes for short durations to gather samples of the commit rate and taking decision pon than basis. This simple sampling-based approach could obviously be combined with more sophisticated strategies, e.g., using modeling-based techniques, depending on the workload nature.

References

[1] G. Blake, R. G. Dreslinski, T. Mudge, and K. Flautner. Evolution of thread-level parallelism in desktop applications. *SIGARCH Comput. Archit. News*, 38(3):302–313, 2010.

[2] D. Christie, J.-W. Chung, S. Diestelhorst, M. Hohmuth, M. Pohlack, C. Fetzer, M. Nowack, T. Riegel, P. Felber, P. Marlier, and E. Riviere. Evaluation of AMD's advanced synchronization facility within a complete transactional memory stack. In *Eurosys*, Apr. 2010.

[3] C. Cortes, D. Pregibon, and C. Volinsky. Communities of interest. In *Advances in Intelligent Data Analysis*, IDA. Springer, 2001.

[4] L. Dalessandro, D. Dice, M. Scott, N. Shavit, and M. Spear. Transactional mutex locks. In *Euro-Par*, 2010.

[5] L. Dalessandro, M. F. Spear, and M. L. Scott. NOrec: Streamlining STM by abolishing ownership records. In *PPoPP*, 2010.

[6] D. Dice, O. Shalev, and N. Shavit. Transactional locking II. In *DISC*, 2006.

[7] A. Dragojević, P. Felber, V. Gramoli, and R. Guerraoui. Why STM can be more than a research toy. *CACM*, 54(4):70–77, Apr. 2011.

[8] P. Felber, C. Fetzer, and T. Riegel. Dynamic performance tuning of word-based software transactional memory. In *PPoPP*, 2008.

[9] S. M. Fernandes and J. Cachopo. Lock-free and scalable multi-version software transactional memory. In *PPoPP*, 2011.

[10] R. Guerraoui and M. Kapalka. On the correctness of transactional memory. In *PPoPP*, 2008.

[11] T. Harris, J. Larus, and R. Rajwar. *Transactional Memory, 2nd edition*. Morgan and Claypool Publishers, December 2010.

[12] C. P. Kruskal, L. Rudolph, and M. Snir. Efficient synchronization of multiprocessors with shared memory. *ACM Trans. Program. Lang. Syst.*, 10(4):579–601, Oct. 1988.

[13] W. Maldonado, P. Marlier, P. Felber, J. Lawall, G. Muller, and E. Riviere. Deadline-aware scheduling for software transactional memory. In *DSN*, 2011.

[14] A. Matveev and N. Shavit. Towards a fully pessimistic STM model. In *TRANSACT*, New Orleand, LA, USA, 2012.

[15] M. Mehrara, J. Hao, P.-C. Hsu, and S. Mahlke. Parallelizing sequential applications on commodity hardware using a low-cost software transactional memory. In *PLDI*, 2009.

[16] J. M. Mellor-Crummey and M. L. Scott. Algorithms for scalable synchronization on shared-memory multiprocessors. *ACM Trans. Comput. Syst.*, 9(1):21–65, Feb. 1991.

[17] C. C. Minh, J.-W. Chung, C. Kozyrakis, and K. Olukotun. STAMP: Stanford transactional applications for multi-processing. In *IISWC*, 2008.

[18] C. E. Oancea, A. Mycroft, and T. Harris. A lightweight in-place implementation for software thread-level speculation. In *SPAA*, 2009.

[19] T. Riegel, P. Felber, and C. Fetzer. A lazy snapshot algorithm with eager validation. In *DISC*, 2006.

[20] T. Riegel, C. Fetzer, and P. Felber. Automatic data partitioning in software transactional memories. In *SPAA*, 2008.

[21] A. Roy, S. Hand, and T. Harris. A runtime system for software lock elision. In *EuroSys*, 2009.

[22] M. F. Spear. Lightweight, robust adaptivity for software transactional memory. In *SPAA*, 2010.

[23] M. F. Spear, L. Dalessandro, V. J. Marathe, and M. L. Scott. A comprehensive strategy for contention management in software transactional memory. In *PPoPP*, 2009.

[24] M. F. Spear, K. Kelsey, T. Bai, L. Dalessandro, M. L. Scott, C. Ding, and P. Wu. Fastpath speculative parallelization. In *LCPC*, 2009.

[25] J. Sreeram, R. Cledat, T. Kumar, and S. Pande. RSTM: A relaxed consistency software trans. memory for multicores. In *PACT*, 2007.

[26] T. Usui, R. Behrends, J. Evans, and Y. Smaragdakis. Adaptive locks: Combining transactions and locks for efficient concurrency. In *PACT*, 2009.

[27] J.-T. Wamhoff, T. Riegel, C. Fetzer, and P. Felber. RobuSTM: a robust software transactional memory. In *SSS*, 2010.

[28] C. Wang, W.-Y. Chen, Y. Wu, B. Saha, and A.-R. Adl-Tabatabai. Code generation and optimization for transactional memory constructs in an unmanaged language. In *CGO*, 2007.

[29] S. Weigert, M. Hiltunen, and C. Fetzer. Community-based analysis of netflow for early detection of security incidents. In *LISA*, 2011.

From Relational Verification to SIMD Loop Synthesis

Gilles Barthe[1]   Juan Manuel Crespo[1]   Sumit Gulwani[2]   César Kunz[1,3]   Mark Marron[1]

[1]IMDEA Software Institute, [2]Microsoft Research, [3]Technical University of Madrid

{gilles.barthe, juanmanuel.crespo, cesar.kunz, mark.marron}@imdea.org, sumitg@microsoft.com

Abstract

Existing pattern-based compiler technology is unable to effectively exploit the full potential of SIMD architectures. We present a new program synthesis based technique for auto-vectorizing performance critical innermost loops. Our synthesis technique is applicable to a wide range of loops, consistently produces performant SIMD code, and generates correctness proofs for the output code. The synthesis technique, which leverages existing work on relational verification methods, is a novel combination of deductive loop restructuring, synthesis condition generation and a new inductive synthesis algorithm for producing loop-free code fragments. The inductive synthesis algorithm wraps an optimized depth-first exploration of code sequences inside a CEGIS loop. Our technique is able to quickly produce SIMD implementations (up to 9 instructions in 0.12 seconds) for a wide range of fundamental looping structures. The resulting SIMD implementations outperform the original loops by $2.0\times$-$3.7\times$.

Categories and Subject Descriptors   D.2.4 [*Software Engineering*]: Software/Program Verification;   D.3.4 [*Programming Languages*]: Processors-Optimization;   C.1.1 [*Single Data Stream Architectures*]: VLIW architectures

Keywords   Program Vectorization, Program Synthesis, Deductive Synthesis, Inductive Synthesis, Relational Program Verification

1. Introduction

Single Instruction Multiple Data (SIMD) instructions sets (such as SSE on x86 or NEON on ARM) provide high throughput and power efficient data-parallel operations. These operations can process 128 bits in a single instruction and can often do so in the same number of cycles (and power usage) needed to process a single 32 bit value via the standard ALU execution path. These features have proven invaluable in accelerating multimedia and high performance computing applications, and are critical to achieving both good application performance and battery life in many mobile computing environments. Despite these advantages and their proven value in practice, the use of SIMD operations has been limited to a relatively small set of (often hand optimized) applications. Extending these benefits to a wider range of programs via automatic compiler vectorization has, in practice, been limited by three major challenges: the presence of pointers, sub-optimal data layout, and complex data driven control flow. In this paper we explore a new approach to

```
// Simple widget struct with a tag and a score value
struct { int tag; int score; } widget;

int exists(widget* vals, int len, int tv, int sv) {
  for (int i = 0; i < len; ++i) {
    int tagok = vals[i].tag == tv;
    int scoreok = vals[i].score > sv;
    int andok = tagok & scoreok;
    if (andok) return 1;
  }
  return 0;
}
```

Figure 1. Initial Loop.

```
int exists_sse(widget* vals, int len, int tv, int sv) {
  m128i vectv = [tv, tv, tv, tv];
  m128i vecsv = [sv, sv, sv, sv];

  int i = 0;
  for (; i < (len - 3); i += 4) {
    m128i blck1i = load_128(vals + i);
    m128i blck2i = load_128(vals + i + 2);

    int tvswizzle = SHF_ORDER(0, 2, 0, 2);
    int svswizzle = SHF_ORDER(1, 3, 1, 3);

    m128i tagvs = shuffle_i32(blck1i, blck2i, tvswizzle);
    m128i scorevs = shuffle_i32(blck1i, blck2i, svswizzle);

    m128i cmprl = cmpeq_i32(vectv, tagvs);
    m128i cmprh = cmpgt_i32(vecsv, scorevs);
    m128i cmpr = and_i128(cmprl, cmprh);

    int match = !allzeros(cmpr);
    if (match) return 1;
  }

  for (; i < len; i++) {
    int tagok = vals[i].tag == tv;
    int scoreok = vals[i].score > sv;
    if (tagok & scoreok) return 1;
  }
  return 0;
}
```

Figure 2. SIMD Implementation.

auto-vectorization that is intended to address the last two of these challenges. This approach allows us to produce efficient SIMD implementations for many loops that are present in foundational libraries such as the STL for C++ or the BCL for C#.

Motivating Example.   Consider the program fragment in Figure 1, which consists of a loop that traverses an array of `widget` structs (of length `len`). The loop body checks if the values in the `tag` and `score` fields satisfy certain properties and if so returns 1 immediately. If no such `widget` is found then 0 is returned.

(variables)			$a : $ Array $\mid i, x : $ Int32 $\mid s : $ Struct$\mid \mathbf{v} : \mathbf{Vector}$
(fields)			$f \in $ Field
(constants)	c	$::=$	$\mathbb{Z} \mid \mathbf{SHF\_ORDER}(\mathbf{c}, \mathbf{c}, \mathbf{c}, \mathbf{c})$
(expr)	e	$::=$	$c \mid x \mid a[i] \mid e.f \mid x \circ x$, where $\circ \in \{+, =, \&, \ldots\} \mid \mathbf{allzeros(v)}$
(vector expr)	$\mathbf{ve}$	$::=$	$\mathbf{v} \mid \langle \mathbf{e}, \mathbf{e}, \mathbf{e}, \mathbf{e} \rangle \mid \mathbf{load\_128(a, i)} \mid \mathbf{shuffle\_i32(v, v, c)}$
			$\mid \mathbf{op(v, v)}$, where $\mathbf{op} \in \{\mathbf{add\_i32, cmpeq\_i32, and\_i128}, \ldots\}$
(stmts)	st	$::=$	$x := e \mid a[i] := x \mid e.f := x \mid \mathsf{skip} \mid \mathbf{v := ve} \mid \mathbf{store\_128(a, i, v)}$
(block)	b	$::=$	$st \mid b; b \mid \mathsf{if}\ x\ \mathsf{then}\ b\ \mathsf{else}\ b$
(flowblock)	f	$::=$	$b \mid \mathsf{return}\ x \mid \mathsf{break} \mid f; f \mid \mathsf{if}\ x\ \mathsf{then}\ f\ \mathsf{else}\ f$
(loop)	ℓ	$::=$	$\mathsf{for}\ i := e;\ i \bowtie e';\ i = i \pm c;\ \mathsf{do}\ f$, where $\bowtie \in \{=, \neq, <, >, \leq, \geq\} \land e' : $ Int32 $\land e'$ is invariant in f
(fragment)	δ	$::=$	$f; \ell; \ell *; f$

Figure 3. Program Fragment Language and SIMD extensions (in bold)

This loop contains two major challenges from the viewpoint of automatic vectorization. First is that since the loop can exit on any iteration (*i.e.* `return 1`) the loop carries a control flow dependence on all previous iterations. Second is the fact that the data is poorly laid out for SIMD processing – it is in an *array of structs*. Thus, doing a block load from the array will get a mixture of the `tag` and `score` fields. Since these fields are processed differently in the loop body (`tag == tv` vs. `score > sv`) the mixture prevents the direct use of SIMD operations (which apply the same operation to each value). Thus, this loop body does not fit into a standard vectorization template form. Attempting to write a compiler that recognizes and transforms this loop appropriately based on a set of pattern matching rules is unattractive from both an implementation effort and complexity standpoint.

Despite these complications it is possible to construct an efficient SIMD implementation using the SSE instructions found in x86 processors (see Figure 2). The program first loads two data blocks of 128 bits each (two `widget` structs per load) from the array via the `load_128` operation. The SSE implementation handles the array-of-struct issue by *swizzling* [14] the four `tag` values into one SSE register (`tagvs`) and the four `score` fields into a second SSE register (`scorevs`). This is done by computing two swizzle masks, `tvswizzle` and `svswizzle`, and using them to control how the data that was loaded from the array is unpacked by the `shuffle_i32` operations. The `tvswizzle` mask indicates that the 0th and 2nd entries, which contain the `tag` fields, should be loaded from `blck1i` and `blck2i`, and these four values should be placed into `tagvs`. Similarly the 1st and 3rd values, which contain the `score` fields, should be placed into `scorevs`. Once these values are unpacked it is then simple to apply the appropriate SIMD equality (`cmpeq_i32`) and greater than (`cmpgt_i32`) operations to compare the four `tag` fields and the four `score` fields. These comparison operations produce bitmasks in the result vector, all 1's if the test result is true and all 0's if the result is false, for each 32 bit value. The results of these comparisons are then bitwise anded in one step via the `and_i128` operation. The final test (`!allzeros(cmpr)`) checks if any of the `widgets` processed satisfy the constraints and if one does then the `match` value will be 1. Since the original loop simply returns on finding a matching `widget` the SSE loop returns 1 if any of the four `widgets` being processed match (*i.e.* the `allzeros` value is 0). The resulting SSE implementation outperforms the simple loop by well over a factor of $2\times$ for large numbers of iterations and is 25% faster even on small iteration counts.

There are a number of challenges present when designing a system to automatically vectorize loops, such as the one in Figure 1. The first challenge is structuring the vectorization algorithm such that it is *applicable* to a wide range of loops and variations in how they are implemented [21]. This is critical to ensuring that the auto-vectorization is consistently able to find optimized implementations for loops in the input programs and thus improve performance in practice. The next challenge is that the process of vector-

izing code often adds complexity and overhead. In order to avoid slowing down the program instead of speeding it up, it is useful to be able to predict if (and when) the SIMD implementation will *reliably improve* the performance of the program relative to the initial implementation. Finally, a fundamental issue in any compiler optimization is *correctness*. Since compiler bugs may introduce errors into every program that is compiled, it is critical to ensure that the resulting SIMD code is equivalent to the input program.

Contributions. To construct an auto-vectorization algorithm that achieves the desired *applicability*, *reliable improvement*, and *correctness* objectives, this paper makes the following contributions:

- A new methodology for program optimization (Section 4) based on a novel combination of: *deductive* rewriting of loop and control-flow structures, *inductive* synthesis of the desired code blocks, and a novel construction based on relational program verification to connect the deductive and inductive steps.

- The methodology is applied to the problem of auto-vectorization of irregular loops that have sub-optimal data layouts and complex data driven control flow. In particular we look at library code from the C++ STL or the C# Base Class Libraries.

- An efficient technique for inductive synthesis of loop-free code fragments, based on a novel combination of concrete program execution, bounded search techniques, and symbolic counter example generation methods (Section 5).

- An experimental evaluation of the auto-vectorizer on a set of challenge loops and real-world applications (Section 7). The results show that the technique performs well in practice: producing SIMD implementations which outperform the original implementations by $2.0\times$-$3.7\times$. We also apply the technique to vectorize loops in the SPEC 483.Xalan benchmark to obtain a 5.5% reduction in runtime.

2. Relational Verification

We begin by reviewing *relational verification* [8, 42] and explain how this technique can be used to reason about the equivalence of two implementations of a loop. We will then introduce two novel forms of *equivalence relations* on program variables for showing the equivalence of a scalar and a vectorized loop.

2.1 Relational Verification Background

The key insight in relational verification is that given two similar programs one does not need to know the exact functionality of the two programs in order to show that they are equivalent. It is sufficient to show that, at the appropriate *synchronization points* during their execution, the states of the two programs are equivalent under some relation. Consider the loops:

```
int sum = 0;                int j = -1;
for(int i = 0; i < n; i++)  int sum = 0;
   sum += i;                for(int i = 0; i < n; i++) {
                               j++;
                               sum += j;
                            }
```

We begin by renaming any variables v which appear in both programs as $v_{\langle 1 \rangle}$ for the value of the variable in the first program on the left and $v_{\langle 2 \rangle}$ for the value of the variable in second program on the right. After this renaming then the equality relation for the states of the two programs is $i_{\langle 1 \rangle} = i_{\langle 2 \rangle} \wedge j = i_{\langle 1 \rangle} - 1 \wedge sum_{\langle 1 \rangle} = sum_{\langle 2 \rangle}$.

Using this relationship we can show these two loops compute the same value. We begin by checking that, when the loop iterations are run in lockstep, at every iteration the states of the programs are equivalent under the relation. Once we have shown that the equivalence relations hold at every loop iteration we can show that they hold after the exit of the loop as well. Thus, we can generate a proof that the two loops compute the same values for the final sums and are observationally equivalent, i.e. $sum_{\langle 1 \rangle} = sum_{\langle 2 \rangle}$.

A critical step in this process is obtaining suitable equality relations. Techniques for obtaining some of these relations, particularly relating to loop structure and conditional control flow, have been developed in previous work [4]. Loop splitting and unrolling are standard transformations which make latent data-parallelism in the loop body more easily exploitable. As SIMD operations operate on k values at a time we need to restructure the loop so that (1) the iteration count of the loop is a multiple of k and (2) that there are k exposed values to operate on. Similarly we can separate the expected hot path in the loop body from the branches that may lead to abnormal loop exits. This restructuring can be viewed as a variation on the *hot-trace* with a *guarded trace-exit* flow restructuring that is commonly done in *Tracing Just-In-Time Compilers* [1, 7].

2.2 Relational Verification of SIMD Loops

In this work we are primarily interested in showing the equivalence of a scalar loop and a loop using SIMD instructions. Thus, to leverage the relational verification machinery we need to identify a suitable set of equivalence relations that may hold between a scalar loop and the corresponding SIMD implementation. We have identified two commonly occurring forms for these equivalence relations, invariant and reduction expressions Section 4, which are sufficient to enable the scalar/SIMD loop equivalence verifications we are interested in. Consider the following loops which illustrate the needed equivalence relations:

```
int x = ...;                int x = ...;
int hash, i = 0;            int hash, i = 0;
                            m128i hv = [0, 0, 0, 0];
                            m128i xv = [x, x, x, x];

for(; i < n; i += 4) {      for(; i < n; i += 4) {
   hash ^= A[i] & x;           m128i d = load_128(A + i);
   hash ^= A[i+1] & x;         m128i t = and_i128(d, xv);
   hash ^= A[i+2] & x;         hv = xor_i32(hv, t);
   hash ^= A[i+3] & x;      }
}                           hash = (hv.r0 ^ hv.r1 ^
                                    hv.r2 ^ hv.r3);
```

The first loop on the left contains several variables with live ranges that span multiple iterations of the loop. The variable x is an invariant value in the loop on the left and a vectorized invariant version xv is used in the second loop on the right. The variable hash is a reduction variable in the first loop. The loop on the right represents these accumulated values in four i32 values in the vector variable hv and adds a final reduction at the exit of the loop. Thus, the relations needed to show these loops are equivalent on each lockstep iteration are: $i_{\langle 1 \rangle} = i_{\langle 2 \rangle} \wedge xv = [x_{\langle 1 \rangle}, x_{\langle 1 \rangle}, x_{\langle 1 \rangle}, x_{\langle 1 \rangle}] \wedge hash_{\langle 1 \rangle} = (hv.r0 \char`^ hv.r1 \char`^ hv.r2 \char`^ hv.r3)$.

Given these relations it is straight forward to use a relational verification technique to show the program fragments are equiva-

lent. In practice we use a *product program construction* [4] with off the shelf SMT solvers to solve the generated verification conditions. The equivalence relation is clearly satisfied on the first entry to the loop. Then inductively we can see that if the equivalence holds on iteration k then in iteration $k + 1$ it will again hold after executing both loop bodies. The final step is then simply to show that when the loop exits, and after executing the final reduction after the loop when the relational equivalence invariant holds, that $hash_{\langle 1 \rangle} = hash_{\langle 2 \rangle}$.

In practice these new relations, *invariant expression vectorization* and *reduction variable vectorization*, along with previously known relations (Section 2.1) for reasoning about loop control-flow restructuring are sufficient to verify the equivalence of the loops that are of interest in this work. In Section 4 we will formalize the definitions for the invariant and reduction vectorization equivalence relations. Additionally, we show how to leverage the relational verification methodlogy to construct the constraints needed to synthesize a vectorized body given a scalar implemention of a loop.

3. Problem Description & Algorithm Overview

This section presents a formalization of the program fragment language that we want to vectorize and the language with SIMD instructions that the auto-vectorization algorithm produces as output. We also provide an overview of the auto-vectorization algorithm.

3.1 Input and Output Loop Languages

Input Language. The work in this paper operates on a core imperative language shown in the non-bold portion of Figure 3. For simplicity, this language consists of variables and operations on three types: 32-bit integers, user defined structures (with named fields) and arrays of either structures or integers. This language extends naturally to include other integer sizes, floating point values, etc. The expressions e in the language cover the standard sets of arithmetic, bitwise, comparison, and access operations. The language admits the standard suite of assignments to locals, array locations, and fields in structs.

To focus on blocks of code that are suitable for vectorization, we distinguish between blocks consisting of simple assignments with conditional flow inside a single iteration b, and blocks of statements that may contain non-local control flow f. The grammar describes the structure of the loops that we are interested in vectorizing and which are likely to benefit most from the conversion to a SIMD implementation – innermost loops that are free of function calls. However, in practice the technique can be applied more aggressively by explicit inlining of function calls or by providing explicit pre/post semantics for an inner loop or method call.

To ensure that the loop is amenable to vectorization, we also impose some semantic restrictions: (1) the loop limit expression e' is invariant, (2) the iteration variable is only updated by linear operations, and (3) the updates are done uniformly on all paths of the loop. Finally, we define a program fragment δ as a single loop with possible loop initialization and clean-up code.

SIMD Output Language. The output of the auto-vectorization algorithm is a program in the SIMD extended language shown in Figure 3, including the terms in bold. The output language extends the input language with a set of SIMD instructions similar to what is present in the Intel SSE4 instruction set. For simplicity, we assume that all of the vectors ($v \in V$) are 128 bits which can contain 4 integers of 32 bits each. We extend the constant set with macros for shuffle constants and add the **allzeros** operation to the set of expressions that produce integer values (e). The SIMD expressions (**ve**) treat each 128 bit vector either as a single bit set of 128 bits for logical operations (*e.g.* **or_i128** or **and_i128**) and as four 32 bit integer values for arithmetic and comparison operations (*e.g.* `add_i32` or `cmpgt_i32`). We add operations to load (`load_128`) and store (`store_128`) 128 bits at a time. Finally, we allow the fragment to contain a sequence of loops.

3.2 Algorithm Overview

The auto-vectorization algorithm is depicted in Figure 4. This flow diagram shows how we first apply deductive restructuring to the loop to expose data parallelism using deductive rewritings. From this restructured loop and the associated equivalence relations from Section 2 we extract a loop-free block of code from the loop body which will be replaced with a sequence of synthesized SIMD instructions. This synthesized code is then patched back into the loop. Finally we compute a cost scoring function and a proof of correctness for the final code fragment.

Restructuring and Pre/Post Generation. The loop is first restructured via standard loop splitting/unrolling and if-conversion. We also introduce vector variables (Section 4) which are used in the synthesis phase. The condition generator examines the restructured program and equivalence relations that are built up during the restructuring to construct the needed synthesis pre/post conditions.

Inductive Concolic Synthesis. The synthesis phase (Section 5) takes the pre/post conditions produced by the previous step and produces a sequence of instructions that realize the specified behavior. The synthesizer uses a novel combination of concrete program execution and counter example generation, which we call *concolic synthesis*. This combined search approach quickly produces an efficient sequence of instructions that satisfies the pre/post conditions and this sequence of instructions is the output of this phase.

Merge and Cost Ranking Function. The final step in the algorithm is to patch in the synthesized code for the hole in the program and to clean up any dead or loop invariant code that may have been created in the vectorization step. The final program is passed to the cost ranking computation (Section 6), and a proof of correctness is computed for the program.

Output. The output of the algorithm is (1) the SIMD optimized program, (2) a proof of equivalence between the SIMD implementation and the original program, and (3) a cost ranking function.

This approach provides the ability to use deductive heuristic rules to quickly rewrite a loop to expose parallelism and enables the reduction of the synthesis problem to small blocks of code. The synthesis component provides a simple inductive method to construct efficient code blocks that is robust to a wide range of structures, and variations on these structures, that appear in the loop bodies. The relational verification methodology provides a connection between the inductive and deductive approach allowing them to co-operate to maximize the strengths of each approach. As an additional benefit the correctness certificate enables the pre-compilation of code in a managed language, such as C#, to assembly code which can be deployed and JITed without violating the safety guarantees of the language [26, 27].

4. From Relational Verification to Synthesis

We borrow the general concept of turning an appropriate verification methodology into a synthesis algorithm from [38] and extend the core idea to apply it to our problem domain. The approach in [38] requires a specification of the program to be synthesized as a pre/post condition pair (ϕ, ψ) and a template T (with only first-order holes) that form the full-correctness proof for the program. In our setting there are two natural possibilities for constructing the pre/post conditions: (1) the minimal loop invariant required for correctness and (2) the precondition and postcondition for the loop

body. Unfortunately, both of these options are unsatisfactory. The computation of loop invariants (even with the limited language in Figure 3) is an undecidable problem. Conversely, pre/post conditions based on only the loop body can be computed efficiently. However, the resulting conditions are highly restrictive and cannot be used for loops that require certain vector registers to be live across loop iterations (such as reduction variables).

We use results from the area of *Relational Program Verification* [4, 8, 30] and the transformation/verification rules outlined in Section 2 to generate the synthesis pre/post conditions. To expose or create data parallelism which can be exploited in the SIMD synthesis step we utilize standard loop restructuring rules (splitting, unrolling, and if-conversion) and rules for introducing vectorized variables or constants. Each rule consists of (1) a loop rewriting template and (2) a template for the equivalence relation between the original loop and the rewritten version. The equivalence relations are used to generate the desired synthesis condition and an equivalence proof between the original loop and the vectorized version (or to reject the vectorized version if a proof cannot be generated).

4.1 Introduction of Vectorized Variables/Constants

Vectorization of Loop Invariant Expressions. We identify variables and expressions e that are invariant across loop iterations in the standard manner – either none of the values used in e are modified in the loop body or they are assigned the result of another loop invariant expression. For each invariant expression, e of type Int32, we introduce the corresponding *vectorized* version, `vece` := $\langle e, e, e, e \rangle$, where `vece` is a fresh variable name and the initialization is done before the loop. We accumulate the loop invariant expressions and the corresponding vector variables as tuples (e, vece) in the set V_e. The equality relationship that should exist between the scalar and vector forms is given by:

$$\text{Inv}(V_e) = \bigwedge_{(e,v) \in V_e} v = [e_{\langle 1 \rangle}, e_{\langle 1 \rangle}, e_{\langle 1 \rangle}, e_{\langle 1 \rangle}]$$

Vectorization of Reduction Variables. We define a reduction variable x as a candidate for reduction variable vectorization when: x is not used as an array index and all paths through the loop contain an assignment of the form $x := x \bullet e$ where $\bullet$ is commutative. This definition heuristically identifies a reduction variable x, introduces a vector version `vecx`, and adds the appropriate initialization before the loop with reduction at loop exit. This definition is unsafe to use in general as we have ignored the effects of the rest of the loop body and their interaction with the reduction operator. However, in the case where the transformation is unsafe we will not be able to produce a proof of equivalence in the relational verification step and will reject the resulting program. The equality relationship that should exist between the scalar and vector forms is given by:

$$\text{Reduce}(V_r) = \bigwedge_{(x,v,\bullet) \in V_r} \left(\begin{array}{l} v = [r_0, r_1, r_2, r_3] \wedge \\ x_{\langle 1 \rangle} = x_{\langle 2 \rangle} \bullet (r_0 \bullet r_1 \bullet r_2 \bullet r_3) \end{array} \right)$$

4.2 Final Equivalence Relation

Once we have the identified the loop invariant expressions, the reduction variables, and the input and output variables (I and O) for the loop, the next step is to construct the final equivalence relations at the desired synchronization points.

In our setting the synchronization points correspond to the program points at the normal control-flow entries and exits of the loop bodies. By definition the variables in V_e or V_r are in scope at both the loop body entry and exit points so the special equality conditions for them are the same at both points. For the variables not in the V_e or V_r sets we check if they are in the input or output variable sets (I or O) and if so add an equality condition between the versions in the two programs. We say a variable x is *simple* at a

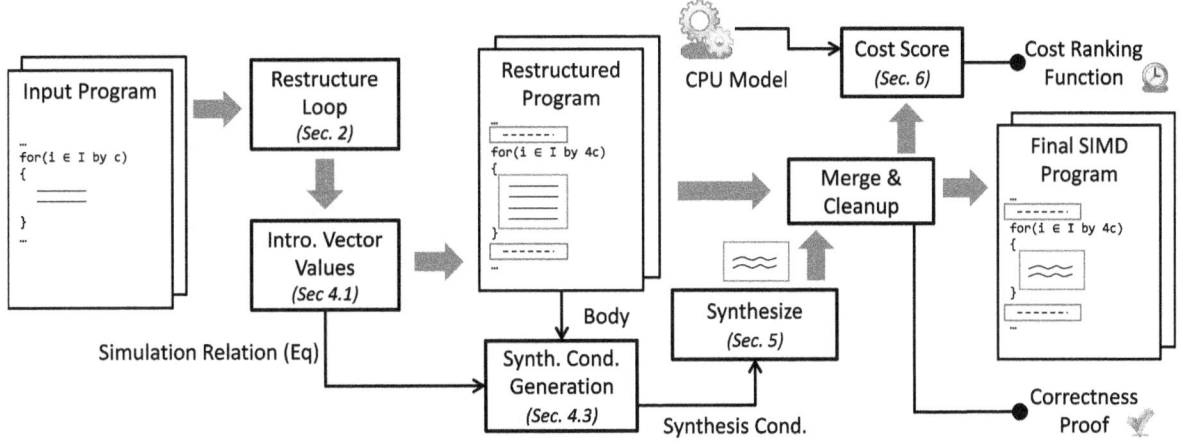

Figure 4. Overview of the auto-vectorization algorithm.

program point if it is defined at that point and it is not an invariant or reduction variable. We define the equivalence relation for the loop entries E_{pre} and exits E_{post} as:

$$E_{pre} = \mathsf{Inv}(V_e) \wedge \mathsf{Reduce}(V_r) \wedge \bigwedge_{x \in X} x_{\langle 1 \rangle} = x_{\langle 2 \rangle}$$

where $X = \{x \in I | x \text{ simple at the loop entries}\}$

$$E_{post} = \mathsf{Inv}(V_e) \wedge \mathsf{Reduce}(V_r) \wedge \bigwedge_{x \in X} x_{\langle 1 \rangle} = x_{\langle 2 \rangle}$$

where $X = \{x \in I \cup O | x \text{ simple at the loop exits}\}$

4.3 Partial Program and Condition Generation

As the natural candidate code for conversion to a SIMD implementation is the normal control-flow block of the loop body. We replace the normal control-flow block between the loop entry and exit with a *hole* [36]. Using the equality relations from E_{pre} and E_{post}, along with the *weakest preconditions* computed with them, we can construct pre/post conditions ϕ and ψ for the hole which are used to construct replacement code to fill the hole.

Given our choice synchronization points as the loop normal control-flow entries/exits, the required verification condition is of the form $E_{pre} \Rightarrow \mathsf{wp}(b_1, \mathsf{wp}(b_2, E_{post}))$ where b_1, b_2 are the loop bodies from the left and right programs respectively and wp computes weakest preconditions. If b_2 is a *hole* then this verification condition is a specification for the required code. We compute the synthesis pre/post conditions (ϕ, ψ) for our synthesis hole by taking the code for the block we want to replace and compute:

$$\phi = \exists I_{\langle 1 \rangle} E_{pre} \text{ where } I_{\langle 1 \rangle} = \{x_{\langle 1 \rangle} | x \in I\}$$
$$\psi = \exists I_{\langle 1 \rangle} (E_{pre} \wedge \mathsf{wp}(b_1, E_{post})) \text{ where } I_{\langle 1 \rangle} = \{x_{\langle 1 \rangle} | x \in I\}$$

This construction lifts the relational program verification methodology to a synthesis condition generation methodology. Further, it reduces the problem of synthesizing loopy programs to the problem of synthesizing straight line code. However, it does so in a way that preserves cross loop information as well as context from before/after the loop body. This context ensures that the generated conditions are as *relaxed* as possible, enabling the generation of optimized code in the synthesizer, while still ensuring the equivalence of the original and optimized programs.

4.4 Running Example

Figure 5 shows the result of applying these transformations to the input code from Figure 1. The resulting fragment has two loops,

the first one has a loop guard that ensures the loop iteration count is a multiple of 4 while the second loop handles the remaining iterations. The first loop has been unrolled 4 times and the variables have been uniquely renamed to expose 4 independent sets of values for the vectorization. The if-conversion step has swept the conditional guards and abnormal loop exit to the single flow block at the end of the loop.

After the loop restructuring and introduction of vector variables, `vectv` and `vecsv` for `tv` and `sv` respectively, we have the following following equivalence post relation for the body:

$$E_{post} = match_{\langle 1 \rangle} = match_{\langle 2 \rangle} \wedge vals_{\langle 1 \rangle} = vals_{\langle 2 \rangle}$$
$$\wedge i_{\langle 1 \rangle} = i_{\langle 2 \rangle} \wedge tv_{\langle 1 \rangle} = tv_{\langle 2 \rangle} \wedge sv_{\langle 1 \rangle} = sv_{\langle 2 \rangle}$$
$$\wedge vectv = [tv_{\langle 1 \rangle}, tv_{\langle 1 \rangle}, tv_{\langle 1 \rangle}, tv_{\langle 1 \rangle}]$$
$$\wedge vecsv = [sv_{\langle 1 \rangle}, sv_{\langle 1 \rangle}, sv_{\langle 1 \rangle}, sv_{\langle 1 \rangle}]$$

The code shown in Figure 6 has had the normal control flow code in the loop, from the first statement to the `if`, replaced with a `[HOLE]` as a place holder for the code we want to synthesize. The pre/post conditions we want to generate (ϕ and ψ) for use in the synthesis step are shown before/after the hole.

The only assignments to externally visible variables that can be made by the synthesized code are specified by the set O. Thus, we simplify the computed post condition, ψ, by assuming that all variables not in O have the same values before/after the synthesized code. As the only variable in O is `match`, the interesting parts of the generated synthesis pre/post conditions are:

$$\phi = (vectv = \langle tv, tv, tv, tv \rangle \wedge vecsv = \langle sv, sv, sv, sv \rangle)$$
$$\psi = (match = ((vals[i].tag = tv \wedge vals[i].score > sv)$$
$$\vee (vals[i+1].tag = tv \wedge vals[i+1].score > sv)$$
$$\vee (vals[i+2].tag = tv \wedge vals[i+2].score > sv)$$
$$\vee (vals[i+3].tag = tv \wedge vals[i+3].score > sv)))$$

After synthesizing the SIMD code for these conditions and substituting it in for the hole we get the final program shown in Figure 2. Using the equivalence relations E_{pre} and E_{post} we can compute and discharge a set of verification conditions for the original input loop and the final SIMD implementation which serve as a correctness proof for the transformation. Finally, using the construction in Section 6 we can produce a cost function for the relative performance of the input and SIMD loops.

127

```
int i;
for (i = 0; i < len −3; i+=4) {
  int tagok0 = vals[i].tag == tv;
  int scoreok0 = vals[i].score > sv;
  int andok0 = tagok0 & scoreok0;

  ...

  int tagok3 = vals[i+3].tag == tv;
  int scoreok3 = vals[i+3].score > sv;
  int andok3 = tagok3 & scoreok3;

  match = andok0 | andok1 | andok2 | andok3;
  if (match) return 1;
}

for (; i < len; ++i) {
  int tagok = vals[i].tag == tv;
  int scoreok = vals[i].score > sv;
  int andok = tagok & scoreok;
  if (andok) return 1;
}
```

Figure 5. Running example after structural transformation.

```
int i;
for (i = 0; i < len −3; i+=4) {
  φ
  [HOLE]
  ψ
  if (match) return 1;
}

for (; i < len; ++i) {
  int tagok = vals[i].tag == tv;
  int scoreok = vals[i].score > sv;
  int andok = tagok & scoreok;
  if (andok) return 1;
}
```

Figure 6. Running example after hole insertion and pre/post condition locations shown.

5. Inductive SIMD Synthesis

The synthesis algorithm takes a pre/post condition pair (ϕ, ψ), a set of instructions to select from $Stmts$, the set of input variables I and outputs O, and a maximum cost for the program to be synthesized ($cost_m$). The output is a program p which is a sequence of statements such that for any state valuation s that satisfies the precondition ϕ, the execution of p starting in s yields a state valuation s' that satisfies the postcondition ψ. Inspired by work on *concolic testing* [9, 32] our concolic synthesis algorithm uses a combination of a top-level counter-example driven loop (based on symbolic methods) to find interesting values for the inputs I and an efficient search for candidate programs p (based on concrete execution over these input values). The symbolic reasoning in the top-level loop (Algorithm 1) ensures that each new input provides useful information, which forces behavioral differences, while the use of concrete values in the program search subroutine (Algorithm 2) provides an efficient method for generating candidate programs.

5.1 Counter-Example Generation Loop

The top-level *CEGIS* (Counter-Example Guided Inductive Synthesis [35]) loop in Algorithm 1 iteratively constructs a set of *concrete state valuations* (a mapping of values to variables) and searches for a candidate program p that satisfies the postcondition ψ when run on these state valuations, line 6. On line 4 the algorithm attempts to symbolically construct a new input state valuation s that is a counter-example for the correctness of the program p – i.e. ψ does not hold on the result of running p on s. If such an example can be found it is added to the set on line 5 and the loop is repeated,

if we can prove that no such example exists then p is the desired program and we return on line 8, and if we cannot decide if such an example exists then the synthesis fails. The initialization of the concrete state valuations set, the underlined call to *GenInitialStates* on line 2 is an optimization, described in Section 5.3, to minimize the number of iterations of the CEGIS loop.

Algorithm 1: Top-Level CEGIS Loop

input : pre ϕ, post ψ, statements $Stmts$,
             inputs I, outputs O, max. cost $cost_m$,
             disjunctive precondition χ
output: program p
1   $p \leftarrow \text{skip}$;
2   $S \leftarrow GenInitialStates(\chi)$;
3   **while** $\text{GenModel}(\exists \vec{V}, \phi \wedge \neg wp(p, \psi)) \notin \{\text{unsat}, \text{fail}\}$ **do**
4      $s \leftarrow GenModel(\exists \vec{V}, \phi \wedge \neg wp(p, \psi))$;
5      $S \leftarrow S + s$;
6      $p \leftarrow Search(\langle\rangle, S, \psi, \emptyset, \emptyset, Stmts, I, O, cost_m)$;
7   **if** $p = \bot$ **then return** fail;
8   **return** $(\text{GenModel}(\exists \vec{V}, \phi \wedge \neg wp(p, \psi)) = \text{unsat})$ *? p : fail*;

5.2 Candidate Program Search

The *Search* method, Algorithm 2, performs the search for a program p_{res} that when run on the input list of state valuations S produces a list of state valuations that satisfy the post condition ψ. The *naive search*, i.e., the algorithm excluding the underlined code, is a depth first enumeration of possible sequences of instructions from the set $Stmts$. If we reach a point where every state valuation in S satisfies ψ then we have a candidate program and can return it, line 9. Otherwise the current program is extended with another instruction from $Stmts$, yielding p_i, and this statement is applied to each of the state valuations in S, yielding S_i. The new values, p_i and S_i, are then used in the recursive search call on line 14. As this naive search approach is computationally intractable for instruction sequences of length greater than four [12, 16, 23] we introduce several optimizations below.

5.3 Synthesis Optimizations

Initial State Valuations. The set of input state valuations S in the top-level CEGIS loop (Algorithm 1) plays a critical role in the number of iterations required for the loop to terminate. Every new state valuation that is added to S is, by construction, a counter-example and when no further counter-examples can be generated the loop terminates. Thus, we initialize S with a number of input valuations that are likely to provide good initial constraints and as a result we will need to generate very few additional counter-examples. As in concolic testing we note that different paths through the program are likely to exercise different behaviors. Thus, we alter the synthesis algorithm to take a *disjunctive pre-condition* χ, which is a disjunction of *per path* weakest preconditions from the input program. The *GenInitialStates* method produces a state valuation for each clause in the disjunctive pre-condition and we use these to initialize S on line 2.

Search Merging. The naive search builds redundant instruction sequences that repeatedly generate the same program state valuations, *e.g.* repeatedly add and then subtract a constant. We also observe that the search re-explores equivalent state valuations that are reachable on different instruction paths, *e.g.* $(a + (b + c)) − d$ and $(a + b) + (c − d)$. We can eliminate this redundant exploration by merging branches in the instruction sequence search tree that are actually exploring the same set of state valuations. This is done by adding a set, *Seen*, of state valuations that have been seen during previous search steps (checked on line 2). If we encounter a state valuation that has been previously seen it means that either (1) the current instruction sequence has redundant instructions, in which case it is suboptimal, or (2) we have already explored the state valuations reachable from the current valuation, and so continuing exploration on this sequence of instructions merely re-visits previously seen state valuations. In these cases, pending a check on cost information described below, we simply abort the current branch of the search on line 3.

Cost Bounds. In our application we are only interested in minimal cost code sequences. Using the cost model from Section 6 we score the initial program fragment that is being replaced and compute cost scores for each program generated during the search. With this information we can immediately stop searching, line 1, if the current program has a larger score, $cost_m$, than the input program or current best solution. This bound is updated as needed to be the best found so far in a standard branch-and-bound manner, line 17.

We further refine how the search handles state valuations that have been seen previously by noting that computational cost is monotone. Thus, repeating the exploration of a previously visited state with a higher cost program will not discover a faster program. However, if the current instruction sequence was able to produce the current state valuation more efficiently than previous instruction sequences then it may be possible to reach target state valuations satisfying ψ without exceeding the cost bound $cost_m$. Thus, on line 3 we check if we have found a less costly instruction sequence, if not we return immediately but if the new instruction sequence is less costly we update the min cost for this state valuation on line 4 and continue the search (re-exploring as needed).

Stack Machine. In order to limit the introduction and lifetime of intermediate values, as well as to reduce the combinatorial problems of selecting which variables to use/modify in each instruction, we extend the concrete execution state valuation with an evaluation stack. The use of an evaluation stack is a common way to simplify the operation of an abstract machine (*e.g.* the .Net and Java virtual machines) by removing the need to explicitly refer registers or to introduce explicit temporary variables. In the instruction selection step, line 11, we assume instructions take their arguments from the evaluation stack and place the result on the stack. We also extend the instruction set with operations to load input variable values on the stack and to pop values off of the stack into output variables. The introduction of an explicit evaluation stack allows us to place a bound on stack depth, line 8. This biases the search to avoid instruction sequences that produce large numbers of intermediate values which would produce code with high register pressure.

Incremental Search Expansion. We can obtain additional performance by using incremental expansion of the search parameters. In general the operations used by the original program (==, &, ...) are the same type of operations that will be needed in the SIMD version. Thus, we start with only the corresponding vector operations and basic load/store operations in the set of instructions (*Stmts*). If we fail to find a suitable program we extend this set with additional operations such as the `shuffle` and other bitmasking operations. Finally, if this larger set fails we let *Stmts* be the set of all instructions. Similarly, we start with a small eval stack, in our case depth 4 increasing to 6 if the first search fails. This allows us to improve the performance of the synthesizer in many cases but still allows the incremental exploration of the full program space as desired.

6. Cost Ranking Function

The computation of absolute costs for arbitrary blocks of code is a challenging problem [39]. However, we do not need to compute the

---

Algorithm 2: Concrete Program State Search

input : program p, state valuations S, post ψ,
        seen set *Seen*, seen cost *Cost*, instructions *Stmts*,
        inputs I, outputs O, max. cost $cost_m$

output: program p_{cand}

1 **if** $\text{cost}(p) \geq cost_m$ **then** **return** $\bot$;
2 **if** $S \in Seen$ **then**
3   **if** $cost(p) \geq Cost(S)$ **then** **return** $\bot$;
4     $Cost \leftarrow Cost + [S \rightarrow cost(p)]$;
5 **else**
6     $Seen \leftarrow Seen \cup \{S\}$;
7     $Cost \leftarrow Cost + [S \rightarrow cost(p)]$;
8 **if** $\text{Stack}_{depth}(S) > \text{Max}_{stack}$ **then** **return** $\bot$;
9 **if** $\forall s \in S . \psi$ *holds for* s **then return** p;
10 $p_{res} \leftarrow \bot$;
11 **foreach** stmt $\in$ Stmts$\cup\{\text{ldv}(v)|v \in I\} \cup \{\text{stv}(v)|v \in O\}$ **do**
12     $p_i \leftarrow p + inst$;
13     $S_i \leftarrow ApplyInstToAll(inst, S)$;
14     $p_o \leftarrow Search(p_i, S_i, \psi, Seen, Cost, Stmts, I, O, cost_m)$;
15   **if** $p_o \neq \bot \wedge cost(p_o) < cost_m$ **then**
16         $p_{res} \leftarrow p_o$;
17         $cost_m \leftarrow cost(p_o)$;
18 **return** p_{res};

---

absolute costs of the programs. As we are only interested in identifying the best performing program from a set of candidates we only need to model cost in a way that allows relative comparison of two programs. Further, our more restricted program fragment language and vectorization application possess a number of simplifying features. The impacts of branch mis-prediction are parameterized as described below while the the uniform array accesses required for vectorization imply that the caching/prefetching in the processor will behave in a consistent and uniform manner.

We assume that we are given a model of the processor architecture, M, which contains the standard information on execution unit resources and latencies as well as branch mis-predict costs M_{miss}. We parametrize the remaining program fragment behaviors based on the conditionals C (*i.e.* `if` statements) and the loops L that appear in the program fragment:

$B_p : C \mapsto [0, 1)$ The mis-predict probability of each branch.
$B_t : C \mapsto [0, 1)$ The probability that the true path is taken.
$L_c : L \mapsto \mathbb{N}$ The number of times a loop is executed.

From these parameters we construct a cost ranking function $Perf^M : (\delta, B_p, B_t, L_c) \mapsto \mathbb{R}$. The cost of a straight line block of code is simply the sum of each statement as reported by the underlying processor model M. The cost of a branch statement, β with true branch β_t and false branch β_f is:

$$Perf^M(\beta, B_p, B_t, L_c) =$$
$$B_p(\beta) * M_{miss} + B_t(\beta) * Perf^M(\beta_t, B_p, B_t, L_c)$$
$$+ (1 - B_t(\beta)) * Perf^M(\beta_f, B_p, B_t, L_c)$$

The cost of a loop statement, ℓ with the body ℓ_{body} is simply $M_{miss} + L_c(\ell) * Perf^M(\ell_{body}, B_p, B_t, L_c)$. We can compute the cost ranking function for a fragment where $\delta = f_{init}; \ell_1 \ldots \ell_k; f_{exit}$ in the natural way as the sum of all the costs:

$$Perf^M(\delta, B_p, B_t, L_c) = Perf^M(f_{init}, B_p, B_t, L_c)$$
$$+ (\Sigma_{\ell_1 \ldots \ell_k} Perf^M(\ell_i, B_p, B_t, L_c)) + Perf^M(f_{exit}, B_p, B_t, L_c)$$

In this paper we report results when running the code on an Intel i7 processor. We can construct a (very) simple model M for this processor with: a normalized latency of 1 per operation, a 3 wide execution unit, a mis-predict cost $M_{mis} = 12$, a uniform mis-predict probability of 5% for forward conditional branches, and a 1% mis-predict rate for loop back and exit branches. Using this model the cost ranking function for the SIMD loop in Figure 2 is $Perf_\delta^M(\delta_{opt}, n_1, n_2) = 24 + n_1 * 5.16 + n_2 * 3.16$ and for the original loop in Figure 1 the function is $Perf_\delta^M(\delta_{orig}, n_1') = 12 + n_1' * 3.16$.

The estimated asymptotic speedup can be computed by observing that as n_1' becomes large the costs of the loops are proportional to $n_1' * 3.16$ for the original loop and $n_1' * 1.29$ for the SIMD loop (since the SIMD loop processes 4 elements per iteration). Thus, the cost ranking functions predict a speedup of $2.44\times$, closely matching the empirically observed speedup of $2.5\times$. To find the predicted break even point we solve for the values where the cost ranking functions for the original loop and SIMD loop are equal, $n_1' = 8$ for our functions. As we see in Section 7 this matches well with the experimentally seen break-even of between 4 and 8.

Even with our simple processor model, which can be built using readily available information, the resulting static cost predictions are both precise and, as we would like in a static compiler, conservative. This simple model can be further improved via either more detailed architecture descriptions [39] or autotuning [41] to identify key performance parameters in the processor models. As the cost estimation functions are parametrized on branch mis-predict, branch taken, and loop count information it is also possible to evaluate them and select the best implementation based on run-time data, as in a Tracing JIT [1, 7].

7. Experimental Evaluation

To evaluate the approach presented in this paper we selected 18 loops which represent fundamental classes of algorithms (find, exists, accumulate, map, etc.) that are found in standard libraries such as the STL for C++ or the base class libraries for C# (or Java). These algorithms cover many common loop idioms that appear in real world code. In this section we examine 6 benchmarks in detail. Four benchmarks – CountIf, Find, Lexo, Equals – come from the C++ STL (specialized for random access iterators). Two benchmarks – FindIf and the running example Exists – are from the .Net base class libraries (BCL) and are implementations of methods in the List<T> class. Finally, the CyclicHash comes from production C++ code and implements a hash code function for data blocks. For the methods that take user defined lambda expressions – CountIf, FindIf, and Exists – we used non-trivial instantiations for the lambda code, e.g. the running example in Figure 1.

7.1 Transformation and Synthesis Performance

Table 1 shows the time required to vectorize each program fragment (memory is always less than 100MB). In practice the synthesis step accounts for 90% or more of this time. Thus, the table shows the number of input states the synthesis started with, the number of additional iterations the CEGIS loop needed, and the number of instructions in the final synthesized block. As we can see in this table the resource requirements vary greatly even for similarly sized code blocks. This variability is not surprising as the synthesis is fundamentally a search in a very large state space. However, in all of the cases the synthesizer was able to produce an optimized SIMD program. These programs consisted of up to 9 instructions and covered a diverse set of comparison, bitwise, and swizzling operations. The results also show the impact the *disjunctive precondition* generation heuristic has on the total number of iterations (taking only 1 iteration for all but one case).

Benchmark	Time(s)	Init./Iters.	Insts.
CountIf	0.136s	16/1	8
Find	0.053s	6/1	4
Lexo	0.056s	6/1	5
Equals	0.667s	10/1	5
Exists	0.120s	6/2	9
CyclicHash	0.998s	16/1	5

Table 1. *Time* required by the synthesizer. *Init* number of examples in S and *Iters* of the CEGIS loop. *Insts* in the final SIMD code.

7.2 Performance of SIMD Loops

To compare the performance of the synthesized SIMD loops and the original scalar implementations we implemented a driver loop which executes each loop, on inputs of various sizes, 5 million times in a simple timing loop. The evaluation was done on an Intel i7 running Windows 7 (32 bit) and Visual Studio C++ compiler (Version 16 for x86) with the default optimization settings.

Figure 7 contains a chart for each of the benchmark loops. This chart shows the experimentally measured performance improvement seen with the synthesized SIMD implementation and the performance improvements predicted by the analytical cost functions in Section 6. The logarithmic x-axis is the number of iterations that the original loop expected to execute. For fixed count loops like CountIf and CyclicHash this is the size of the input array. For loops with abnormal returns (the remaining four loops) this is the expected number of iterations before the loop exits. As we use a uniform distribution for where the element of interest is in the input the expected number of iterations is half the length of the input array. The y-axis is the speedup of the SSE implementation relative to the original scalar implementation. Finally we mark the break-even line where the performance of the SSE implementation and original implementation are equal.

The results in Figure 7 show that in general the SIMD implementations start to outperform the baseline implementations almost immediately (the *Actual* plot). For an iteration count of 8 only the Lexo loop is slower than the baseline implementation while CyclicHash is slightly better than break-even and the remaining loops show a 10% to 40% reduction in runtime. As the input size gets larger the performance differences get larger in favor of the SIMD loops. Once the iteration counts approach 32 the Lexo has passed the predicted break even point and is now faster than the baseline implementation. At iteration counts of 512 all the loops outperform the baseline by a factor of $2\times$ or more. Finally by iteration counts of 2048 the loops performance ratios are near their asymptotic speedup and now outperform the baseline implementations by between $2.0\times$ and $3.7\times$, which is near the $4\times$ maximum speedup we would expect from using 4 wide SSE instructions. These results demonstrate that the approach to vectorization described in this paper is *applicable* to a wide range of loops and produces SIMD implementations that consistently provide large performance increases (even on relatively small inputs).

The *Predicted* plots in Figure 7 show that in general the speedups predicted by the analytic cost model from Section 6 correlate well with the observed speedups – despite the relatively crude model used for the processor. The major exception to this trend is the Equals program where the predicted and actual performance diverge significantly for large iteration counts. Further investigation indicates that in this case the processor is able to optimize the loop execution in ways that are not captured by the simple processor model, M, used when constructing the cost functions. Thus there is room for improvement via either more detailed architecture descriptions [39] or autotuning [41] to identify key performance parameters in the processor models.

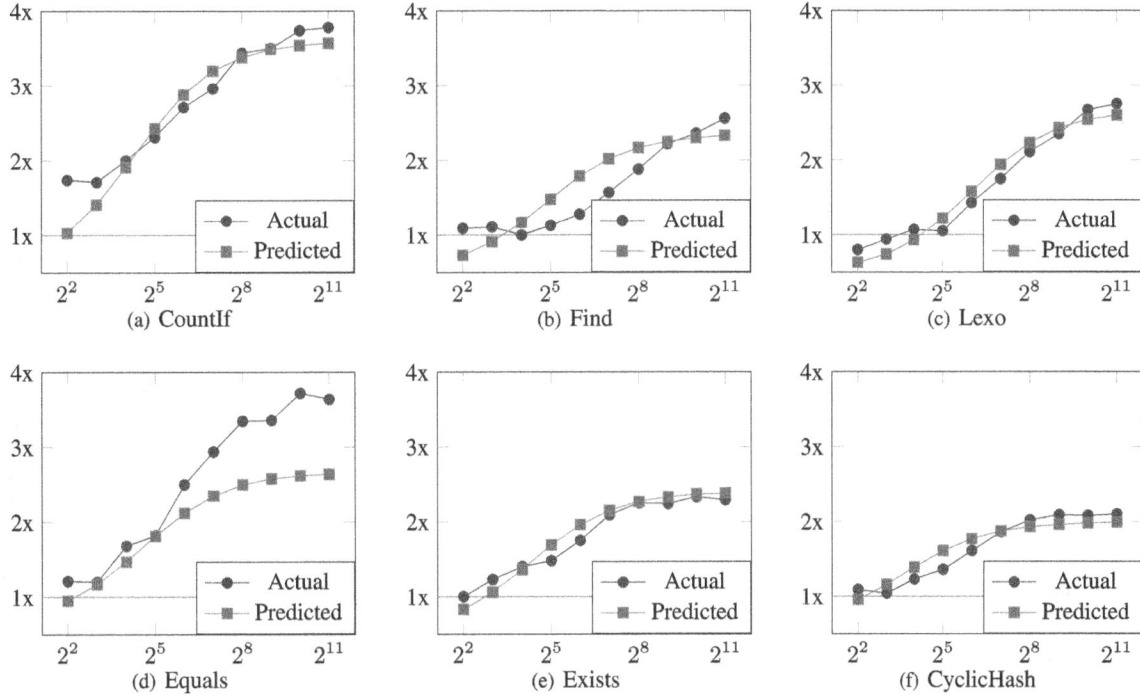

Figure 7. Speedup (Original Time / SSE Time) on Y axis ranging over the expected number of iterations in original loop on X axis.

To avoid performance degradations it is critical that the cost model is able to predict the break-even number of iterations (where the SIMD loop begins to outperform the original loop). In all our benchmarks we see that this number is well predicted by the cost model and in all cases is a conservative estimate (*i.e.* overestimating the number of iterations needed to break-even). Thus, these results demonstrate that the cost model defined in this work is an effective predictor for the relative performance of the loops and provides an effective means to check that a SIMD implementation will *reliably improve* the performance of the program in practice.

To validate that these results were not an artifact of the evaluation environment [25] we ran the evaluation on a second platform. This environment consisted of an Intel Core2 running Mac OS X (Tiger) and GNU C++ compiler (Version 4.2.1 x86). The results were, with one notable exception, consistent with the performance improvements seen on the Intel i7 platform. The outlier benchmark, *Exists*, had a break-even cost of 16 on the Core2 compared to a break-even of 8 on the i7. This increase is mainly a result of the `shuffle` operation being more expensive on the Core2 and the increased break-even is correctly predicted by our cost function.

7.3 Synthesis with Specialized Operations

In order to evaluate how the synthesis technique handles SIMD operations with unusual semantics we synthesized three common string operations from the C# `System.String` class: StringEquals, IndexOf and IndexOfAny. These can be implemented using the specialized *Packed Compare Strings* (PCMPESTRI) operation from SSE 4.2. The synthesis algorithm produces SIMD implementations for these loops using the specialized packed compare strings operation in less than 1 second for each benchmark. The speedups obtained ranged from $3.4\times$ for StringEquals to $9.5\times$ for IndexOfAny. These results demonstrate how the synthesis approach can be easily extended to make use of new, or unusual, instructions to produce optimized loop implementations.

7.4 Impact on 483.Xalan

The results in Section 7.1 show that the synthesized loop implementations consistently improve performance across a range of loops and input data sizes. To validate that the performance gains seen on the micro-benchmarks translate into similar performance gains in practice, we selected the 483.Xalan benchmark from SPEC CPU2006 [37] as a case study. This program makes heavy use of `std::vector<string*>` as a cache for commonly used strings and it uses the STL `find` algorithm (our Find benchmark) to find string pointers in the cache.

The cache behavior is very sensitive to the data that is being processed as shown in recent work on automatic data structure selection [17]. Replacing the `std::vector` with a `std::set` (or a `hashset`) resulted in performance improvements of up to 20% on the SPEC provided `train` input but when run with the SPEC provided `test` input the alternative data structure representation actually *degrades* performance by up to 20%. This swing from performance improvement to performance degradation is driven by the sensitivity of the cache to particular features of the input data set. Thus, this program tests both the performance impact of the SIMD code our synthesis produces and the robustness of the performance improvements on the various benchmark inputs.

Performance profiling of the 483.Xalan program shows that approximately 14% of the total runtime is spent executing the `find` algorithm on the cache. As our loop micro-benchmarks indicate that the SIMD `find` code is between $1.08\times$ and $2.4\times$ faster than the baseline implementation we would expect to see between a 1% (worst case) and 8% (best case) reduction in total runtime.

Table 2 shows the performance results obtained by replacing (by hand) the calls to the `find` algorithm with calls to our synthesized SIMD code. We show for each input provided in the SPEC test suite the size of the input and the percentage reduction in the total program execution time. The speedup indicates that the calls to the synthesized SIMD code are, depending on the inputs, 1.15

131

Input Data	Input Size	Improve(%)
test	28KB	5.5%
train	39MB	2%
ref	56MB	5%

Table 2. Runtime improvement(%) for 483.Xalan.

to 1.5 times faster than the standard implementations (matching our expectations from the micro-benchmark results). In contrast to the widely variable speedup (and slowdown) seen by changing the underlying data structure, the use of the vectorized find loop showed consistent improvements of 2%-5% across the inputs.

8. Related Work

Vectorization. Automatic program vectorization is a challenging problem which requires the application of a wide range of techniques for effective vectorization including: loop transformation [18, 29], control flow dependency elimination [18], alignment optimizations [28, 40], and finding sets of operations that can be executed in parallel [19, 33]. However, previous work on compiler auto-vectorization has focused on what are traditionally considered *regular* applications (e.g., scientific codes, multimedia applications, encode/decode algorithms) and on special purpose libraries (codecs, encryption, etc.), where loops have well behaved termination conditions, data sets are of a fairly regular/large size, and data layouts are suited to SIMD computation.

In contrast, the work in this paper seeks to apply SIMD instructions to *irregular* loops from standard library implementations which often have poor data layouts, small iteration count loops, and extensive data dependent control flow. These types of programs present different and in many ways more difficult problems to the automatic construction of vectorized code. These difficulties are highlighted in a recent study by Maleki et. al. [21] which examines a number of state of the art vectorizing compilers and their ability to vectorize a range of loops. They conclude that modern compilers fail to vectorize many loop patterns due to a lack of development resources needed to build a compiler that can identify and treat all the needed loop and computation patterns.

The work in this paper focuses on the issues of sub-optimal data layouts and complex data driven control flow but does not examine issues involving indirect memory accesses via pointers. Recent work has begun to explore how to reorganize and traverse pointer based structures into flat structures which are amenable to SIMD computation [31]. In particular work on unique pointer referencing [3, 20] and object lifetime, either as a global invariant or in a localized section of code, based on static [20, 22] is a critical first step dealing with the challenges posed by pointers.

Verification. Translation validation is a general method for checking a posteriori that compiler runs are correct, i.e output target programs that are semantically equivalent to input programs [30, 43]. Product programs reduce relational verification to functional verification of a single program: instances include self-composition [6], cross-products [42], and their combination [4, 5]. These methods are able to validate a wide range of loop optimizations, including those needed by our method. In this work, we use product programs to generate synthesis conditions for loop bodies.

Relational Hoare Logic is a generalization of Hoare logic in which judgments involve two programs, and pre- and post- conditions are denoting relations on states [8]. Relational Hoare Logic is effective for proving the correctness of structure-preserving optimizations, and simple optimizations that alter the control flow of programs. However, the core logic of [8] does not support the kind of loop optimizations required for our examples.

Synthesis The area of program synthesis is gaining renewed interest [10, 11, 35]. Srivastava et.al. introduced the notion of *proof-theoretic synthesis* where the problem of synthesizing a loopy program, given a pre/post condition, is reduced to the problem of simultaneously synthesizing loop-free fragments and loop invariants [38]. This approach is limited to synthesis of simple programs whose total correctness proofs or loop invariants can be expressed as simple templates. In contrast, we reduce the problem of vectorizing a given loopy program, to the problem of synthesizing only a loop-free fragment (without the need to synthesize any sophisticated loop invariants). This reduction is enabled by our use of the powerful relational verification methodology, which allows us to separate the process of verification and synthesis by generating an over approximation of the equalities required for equivalence proof.

The problem of synthesizing loop-free programs has been addressed in a variety of domains including bit-vector algorithms [12, 15, 36], ruler/compass based geometry constructions [13], text transformations [24], and algebraic proof problems [34]. One class of technique is based on *constraint solving*, which involves reducing the synthesis problem to that of solving a SAT/SMT formula (inside a CEGIS loop) and let an off-the-shelf SAT/SMT solver efficiently explore the search space. The applicability of this technique has been limited to semi-automatic settings, where the user provides templates [36] or reasonable over-approximation of the number of times each base component is used in the desired program [12]. Another class of technique is based on *brute-force search*, which involves systematically exploring the entire state space of artifacts and checking the correctness of each candidate. This approach often requires use of non-trivial optimizations and performs best when the specification consists of examples as opposed to a formal relational specification. Past work has included optimizations such as goal-directed search [13], clues based on textual features of examples [24], and common subexpression evaluation [34]. In this work, we combine the CEGIS loop from constraint-solving approaches with brute force search approach and novel optimizations.

Superoptimization is the task of finding an optimal code sequence for a straight-line target sequence of instructions, and it is used in optimizing performance-critical inner loops. One approach to superoptimization has been to constrain the search space to a set of equality-preserving transformations [2, 16], and then select the one with the lowest cost. This approach is limited by the kind of transformations that it can generate. Another approach to superoptimization has been to use brute-force search and enumerate sequences of increasing length or cost, testing each for equality with the target specification [23]. We also use brute-force search, but combined with a CEGIS loop and non-trivial optimizations.

9. Conclusion

This work presents a new approach to addressing the challenges that are present when attempting to harness the performance and power advantages available from data-parallel SIMD operations. In particular we looked at the problem of auto-vectorizing loops that have sub-optimal data layouts and complex data driven control flow, as is frequently the case in general purpose library code from the C++ STL or the C# Base Class Libraries. Our approach is driven by three core objectives: to produce an auto-vectorizer that is *applicable* to a wide range of *irregular* loops, that produces code which *reliably improves* the performance of the loop, and that guarantees the *correctness* of the resulting SIMD code.

These objectives led us to a novel auto-vectorization approach based on *deductive* loop rewriting and *inductive* synthesis of loop-free code. The use of inductive synthesis for constructing the loop body makes it particularly robust when dealing with the multitude of variations on the basic loop forms (find, map, reduce, etc.) that appear in practice. In addition this approach allows us to produce correctness proofs for the resulting code. We believe that this underlying approach of combining deductive code restructuring with inductive code generation represents a general and promising way forward in research on program compilation. Thus, this work is an important step in both expanding the set of programs that can be automatically SIMDized and in the larger problem of effective compilation for specialized hardware.

Acknowledgments

We would like to thank the PPoPP reviewers and Rastislav Bodik for their constructive comments and thoughts on this work. This work was supported in part by: European Projects FP7-318337 ENTRA, FP7-231620 HATS and FP7-256980 NESSoS, Spanish project TIN2009-14599 DESAFIOS 10, Madrid Regional project S2009TIC-1465 PROMETIDOS. César Kunz is funded by Spanish Juan de la Cierva programme (JCI-2010-08550). Juan Manuel Crespo is funded by FPI Spanish programme (BES-2010-031271).

References

[1] M. Arnold, S. Fink, D. Grove, M. Hind, and P. F. Sweeney. Adaptive optimization in the Jalapeño JVM. In *OOPSLA*, 2000.

[2] S. Bansal and A. Aiken. Automatic generation of peephole superoptimizers. In *ASPLOS*, 2006.

[3] E. Barr, C. Bird, and M. Marron. Collecting a Heap of Shapes. Technical Report MSR-TR-2011-135, Microsoft Research, Dec. 2011.

[4] G. Barthe, J. M. Crespo, and C. Kunz. Relational verification using product programs. In *FM*, 2011.

[5] G. Barthe, J. M. Crespo, and C. Kunz. Beyond 2-safety: Asymmetric product programs for relational program verification. In *LFCS*, 2013.

[6] G. Barthe, P. R. DArgenio, and T. Rezk. Secure information flow by self-composition. In *CSFW*, 2004.

[7] M. Bebenita, F. Brandner, M. Fahndrich, F. Logozzo, W. Schulte, N. Tillmann, and H. Venter. SPUR: A trace-based JIT compiler for CIL. In *OOPSLA*, 2010.

[8] N. Benton. Simple relational correctness proofs for static analyses and program transformations. In *POPL*, 2004.

[9] P. Godefroid, N. Klarlund, and K. Sen. Dart: Directed automated random testing. In *PLDI*, 2005.

[10] S. Gulwani. Dimensions in program synthesis. In *PPDP*, 2010. Invited talk paper.

[11] S. Gulwani. Synthesis from examples: Interaction models and algorithms. *SYNASC*, 2012. Invited talk paper.

[12] S. Gulwani, S. Jha, A. Tiwari, and R. Venkatesan. Synthesis of loop-free programs. In *PLDI*, 2011.

[13] S. Gulwani, V. A. Korthikanti, and A. Tiwari. Synthesizing geometry constructions. In *PLDI*, 2011.

[14] Intel Optimization Manual (June 2011) – Section 6.5.1. http://www.intel.com/content/dam/doc/manual/64-ia-32-architectures-optimization-manual.pdf.

[15] S. Jha, S. Gulwani, S. Seshia, and A. Tiwari. Oracle-guided component-based program synthesis. In *ICSE*, 2010.

[16] R. Joshi, G. Nelson, and K. H. Randall. Denali: A goal-directed superoptimizer. In *PLDI*, 2002.

[17] C. Jung, S. Rus, B. P. Railing, N. Clark, and S. Pande. Brainy: Effective selection of data structures. In *PLDI*, 2011.

[18] K. Kennedy and J. Allen. *Optimizing compilers for modern architectures: a dependence-based approach*. Morgan Kaufmann Publishers Inc., 2002.

[19] S. Larsen and S. Amarasinghe. Exploiting superword level parallelism with multimedia instruction sets. In *PLDI*, 2000.

[20] K.-K. Ma and J. Foster. Inferring aliasing and encapsulation properties for java. In *OOPSLA*, 2007.

[21] S. Maleki, Y. Gao, M. Garzarán, T. Wong, and D. Padua. An evaluation of vectorizing compilers. In *PACT*, 2011.

[22] M. Marron. Structural analysis: Shape information via points-to computation. Technical Report 1201.1277, arXiv, Jan. 2012.

[23] H. Massalin. Superoptimizer - a look at the smallest program. In *ASPLOS*, 1987.

[24] A. Menon, O. Tamuz, S. Gulwani, B. Lampson, and A. Kalai. A machine learning framework for programming by example. In *ICML*, 2013.

[25] T. Mytkowicz, A. Diwan, M. Hauswirth, and P. F. Sweeney. Producing wrong data without doing anything obviously wrong! In *ASPLOS*, 2009.

[26] G. Necula. Proof-carrying code. In *POPL*, 1997.

[27] G. Necula and P. Lee. Safe kernel extensions without run-time checking. In *OSDI*, 1996.

[28] D. Nuzman, I. Rosen, and A. Zaks. Auto-vectorization of interleaved data for SIMD. In *PLDI*, 2006.

[29] D. Nuzman and A. Zaks. Outer-loop vectorization: Revisited for short SIMD architectures. In *PACT*, 2008.

[30] A. Pnueli, M. Siegel, and F. Singerman. Translation validation. In *TACAS*, 1998.

[31] B. Ren, G. Agrawal, J. Larus, T. Mytkowicz, T. Poutanen, and W. Schulte. SIMD parallelization of applications that traverse irregular data structures. In *CGO*, 2013.

[32] K. Sen, D. Marinov, and G. Agha. CUTE: A concolic unit testing engine for C. In *ESEC/FSE-13*, 2005.

[33] J. Shin, M. Hall, and J. Cha. Superword-level parallelism in the presence of control flow. In *CGO*, 2005.

[34] R. Singh, S. Gulwani, and S. Rajamani. Automatically generating algebra problems. In *AAAI*, 2012.

[35] A. Solar Lezama. *Program Synthesis By Sketching*. PhD thesis, EECS Department, University of California, Berkeley, Dec 2008.

[36] A. Solar-Lezama, R. M. Rabbah, R. Bodík, and K. Ebcioglu. Programming by sketching for bit-streaming programs. In *PLDI*, 2005.

[37] SPEC. Standard Performance Evaluation Corporation (SPEC). http://www.spec.org/cpu2006/.

[38] S. Srivastava, S. Gulwani, and J. S. Foster. From program verification to program synthesis. In *POPL*, 2010.

[39] R. Wilhelm, J. Engblom, A. Ermedahl, N. Holsti, S. Thesing, D. Whalley, G. Bernat, C. Ferdinand, R. Heckmann, T. Mitra, F. Mueller, I. Puaut, P. Puschner, J. Staschulat, and P. Stenström. The worst-case execution-time problem: Overview of methods and survey of tools. *ACM TECS*, 7(3), 2008.

[40] P. Wu, A. Eichenberger, and A. Wang. Efficient SIMD code generation for runtime alignment and length conversion. In *CGO*, 2005.

[41] K. Yotov, X. Li, G. Ren, M. Garzaran, D. Padua, K. Pingali, and P. Stodghill. Is search really necessary to generate high-performance BLAS? *Proceedings of the IEEE*, 93(2), 2005.

[42] A. Zaks and A. Pnueli. Covac: Compiler validation by program analysis of the cross-product. 2008.

[43] L. D. Zuck, A. Pnueli, and B. Goldberg. Voc: A methodology for the translation validation of optimizing compilers. *J. UCS*, 9(3), 2003.

Ligra: A Lightweight Graph Processing Framework for Shared Memory

Julian Shun

Carnegie Mellon University
jshun@cs.cmu.edu

Guy E. Blelloch

Carnegie Mellon University
guyb@cs.cmu.edu

Abstract

There has been significant recent interest in parallel frameworks for processing graphs due to their applicability in studying social networks, the Web graph, networks in biology, and unstructured meshes in scientific simulation. Due to the desire to process large graphs, these systems have emphasized the ability to run on distributed memory machines. Today, however, a single multicore server can support more than a terabyte of memory, which can fit graphs with tens or even hundreds of billions of edges. Furthermore, for graph algorithms, shared-memory multicores are generally significantly more efficient on a per core, per dollar, and per joule basis than distributed memory systems, and shared-memory algorithms tend to be simpler than their distributed counterparts.

In this paper, we present a lightweight graph processing framework that is specific for shared-memory parallel/multicore machines, which makes graph traversal algorithms easy to write. The framework has two very simple routines, one for mapping over edges and one for mapping over vertices. Our routines can be applied to any subset of the vertices, which makes the framework useful for many graph traversal algorithms that operate on subsets of the vertices. Based on recent ideas used in a very fast algorithm for breadth-first search (BFS), our routines automatically adapt to the density of vertex sets. We implement several algorithms in this framework, including BFS, graph radii estimation, graph connectivity, betweenness centrality, PageRank and single-source shortest paths. Our algorithms expressed using this framework are very simple and concise, and perform almost as well as highly optimized code. Furthermore, they get good speedups on a 40-core machine and are significantly more efficient than previously reported results using graph frameworks on machines with many more cores.

Categories and Subject Descriptors D.1.3 [*Programming Techniques*]: Concurrent Programming—Parallel Programming

General Terms Algorithms, Performance

Keywords Shared Memory, Graph Algorithms, Parallel Programming

1. Introduction

There has been significant recent interest in processing large graphs, and recently several packages have been developed for pro-

cessing such large graphs on parallel machines including the parallel Boost graph library (PBGL) [19], Pregel [34], Pegasus [24], GraphLab [29, 30], PowerGraph [17], the Knowledge Discovery Toolkit [8, 31], GPS [40], Giraph [16], and Grace [39]. Motivated by the need to process very large graphs, most of these systems (with the exception of the original GraphLab [29] and Grace) have been designed to work on distributed memory parallel machines.

In this paper, we study Ligra, a lightweight interface for graph algorithms that is particularly well suited for graph traversal problems. Such problems visit possibly small subsets of the vertices on each step. The interface is lightweight in that it supplies only a few functions, the implementation is simple, and it is fast.

Our work is motivated in part by Beamer et. al.'s recent work on a very fast BFS for shared memory machines [3, 4]. They use a hybrid BFS which uses a sparse representation of the vertices when the frontier is small and a dense representation when it is large. Our interface supports hybrid graph traversal algorithms and for BFS, we achieve close to the same efficiency (time and space) as the optimized BFS of Beamer et. al., and our code is much simpler than theirs. In addition, we apply it to many other applications including betweenness centrality, graph radii estimation, graph connectivity, PageRank and single-source shortest paths.

Ligra is designed for shared memory machines. Compared to distributed memory systems, communication costs are much cheaper in shared memory systems, leading to performance benefits. Although shared memory machines cannot scale to the same size as distributed memory clusters, current commodity single unit servers can easily fit graphs with well over a hundred billion edges in memory[1], large enough for any of the graphs reported in the papers mentioned above.[2] Shared memory along with the existing support for parallel code (CilkPlus [27] in our case) on multicores allows for our lightweight implementation. Furthermore, these multicore servers have sufficient memory bandwidth to get quite good speedups over sequential codes (up to 39 fold on 40 cores in our experiments). Shared memory algorithms tend to be simpler than their distributed counterparts. Unlike in distributed memory, race conditions can occur in shared memory, but as we later show, this can be dealt with in our system with appropriate uses of the atomic compare-and-swap instruction. Compared to the distributed memory systems mentioned above, our system is over an order of magnitude faster on a per-core basis for the benchmarks

---

[1] For example, the Intel Sandy Bridge based Dell R910 has 32 cores (64 hyperthreads) and can be configured with up to 2 Terabytes of memory, and the AMD Opteron based Dell R815 has 64 cores and can be configured with up to 1 Terabyte of memory.

[2] The largest graph in the papers cited is a synthetic 127 billion edges in the Pregel paper [34]. The rest of the papers do not use any graphs larger than 20 billion edges. The largest non-synthetic graph described is the Yahoo graph with 6.6 billion directed edges [42].

```
1:  Parents = {−1, . . . , −1}                      ▷ initialized to all -1's
2:
3:  procedure UPDATE(s, d)
4:      return (CAS(&Parents[d], −1 , s ))
5:
6:  procedure COND(i)
7:      return (Parents[i] == −1)
8:
9:  procedure BFS(G, r)                              ▷ r is the root
10:     Parents[r] = r
11:     Frontier = {r}          ▷ vertexSubset initialized to contain only r
12:     while (SIZE(Frontier) ≠ 0) do
13:         Frontier = EDGEMAP(G, Frontier, UPDATE, COND)
```

Figure 1. Pseudocode for Breadth-First Search in our framework. The compare-and-swap function CAS(*loc,oldV,newV*) atomically checks if the value at location *loc* is equal to *oldV* and if so it updates *loc* with *newV* and returns *true*. Otherwise it leaves *loc* unmodified and returns *false*.

we could compare with, and typically faster even on absolute terms to the largest systems run, which sometimes have two orders of magnitude more cores. Finally, commodity shared memory servers are quite reliable, often running for up to months or possibly years without a failure.

Ligra supports two data types, one representing a graph $G = (V, E)$ with vertices V and edges E, and another for representing subsets of the vertices V, which we refer to as *vertexSubsets*. Other than constructors and size queries, the interface supplies only two functions, one for mapping over vertices (VERTEXMAP) and the other for mapping over edges (EDGEMAP). Since a vertexSubset is a subset of V, the VERTEXMAP can be used to map over any subset of the original vertices, and hence its utility in traversal algorithms—or more generally in any algorithm in which only (possibly small) subsets of the graph are processed on each round. The EDGEMAP also processes a subset of the edges, which is specified using a vertexSubset to indicate the valid sources, and a Boolean function to indicate the valid targets of each edge. Abstractly, a vertexSubset is simply a set of integer labels for the included vertices and the VERTEXMAP simply applies the user supplied function to each integer. It is up to the user to maintain any vertex based data. The implementation switches between a sparse and dense representation of the integers depending on the size of the vertexSubset. In our interface, multiple vertexSubsets can be maintained and furthermore, a vertexSubset can be used for multiple graphs with different edge sets, as long as the number of vertices in the graphs are the same.

With this interface a breadth-first search (BFS), for example, can be implemented as shown in Figure 1. This version of BFS uses a Parents array (initialized all to −1, except for the root r where Parents[r] = r) in which each vertex will point to its parent in a BFS tree. As with standard parallel versions of BFS [28, 41], on each step i (starting at 0) the algorithm maintains a frontier of all vertices reachable from the root r in i steps. Initially a vertexSubset containing just the root vertex is created to represent the frontier (line 11). Using EDGEMAP, each step checks the neighbors of the frontier to see which have not been visited, updates those to point to their parent in the frontier, and adds them to the next frontier (line 13). The user supplied function UPDATE (lines 3–4) atomically checks to see if a vertex has been visited using a compare and swap (CAS) and returns true if not previously visited (Parents[i] == −1). The COND function (lines 6–7) tells EDGEMAP to consider only target vertices which have not been visited (here, this is not needed for correctness, but is used for efficiency). The EDGEMAP function returns a new vertex set containing the target vertices for which UPDATE returns true, i.e., all the vertices in the next frontier

(line 13). The BFS completes when the frontier is empty and hence no more vertices are reachable.

The interface is designed to allow the edges to be processed in different orders depending on the particular situation. This is different from many of the interfaces mentioned in the first paragraph (e.g. Pregel, GraphLab, GPS and Giraph) which are vertex based and have the user hardcode how to loop over the out-edges or in-edges. Our implementation supports a few different ways to traverse the edges. One way is to loop over each vertex in a sparse representation of the active source vertices applying the function to each out-edge (this is basically the order Pregel, GPS and Giraph supports). This loop over the out-edges can either be parallel or sequential depending on the degree of the vertex (Pregel and the others do not support parallel looping over out-edges, although the most recent version of GraphLab does [17]). A dense representation of the set of source vertices could also be used. Another way to map over the edges is to loop over all destination vertices sequentially or in parallel, and for each in-edge check if the source is in the source vertex set and apply the edge function if so. Finally, we can simply apply a flat map over all edges checking which need to be applied.

In this paper, we apply the Ligra framework to a collection of problems: breadth-first search, betweenness centrality, graph radii estimation, graph-connectivity, PageRank, and Bellman-Ford single-source shortest paths. All of these applications have the property that they work in rounds and each round potentially processes only a subset of the vertices. In the case of BFS, each vertex is only processed once but in the others they can be processed multiple times. For example, in the shortest paths algorithm a vertex only needs to be added to the active vertex set if its distance has changed. Similarly in a variant of PageRank, a vertex needs to be processed only if its PageRank value has changed by more than some delta since it was last processed.

Betweenness centrality, a technique for measuring the "importance" of vertices in a graph, is basically a version of BFS that accumulates statistics along the way and propagates first in the forward direction and then backward direction. In betweenness centrality, one needs to keep around the frontiers during the forward traversal to facilitate the backward traversal. In Ligra, this is easily done by storing the vertexSubsets in each iteration during the forward traversal. In contrast, this cannot be easily expressed in Pregel and GraphLab, because although vertices can be made inactive in Pregel and GraphLab, the state is associated with the vertices as opposed to being separate.

Our contributions are threefold:

1. We provide an abstraction based on edgeMaps, vertexMaps and vertexSubsets for programming a class of parallel graph algorithms.

2. We provide an efficient and lightweight implementation of our framework, and applications using the framework.

3. We provide experimental evaluation of using the framework and timing results of our applications on various input graphs.

The Ligra code and applications can be found at www.cs. cmu.edu/~jshun/ligra/.

2. Related Work

Beamer et. al [3, 4] recently developed a very fast BFS for shared-memory machines. They use a hybrid BFS consisting of the conventional top-down approach, where each vertex on the current frontier explores all of its neighbors and adds unvisited neighbors to the next frontier (write-based), and a bottom-up approach, where each unvisited vertex in the graph tries to find any parent (visited vertex) among its neighbors (read-based). While the neighbor visits in the top-down approach will mostly be to unvisited vertices when the frontier is small, for large frontiers many of the edges will be to neighbors already visited. The edges to visited neighbors can be avoided in the bottom-up approach because an unvisited vertex can stop checking once it has found a parent; this makes it more efficient than the top-down approach for large frontiers. The disadvantage of the bottom-up approach is that it processes all of the vertices, so is more expensive than the top-down approach for small frontiers. Beamer et. al.'s hybrid BFS switches between the two approaches based on the size of the frontier, and the representation of the active set of vertices also switches between sparse and dense accordingly. They show that for small-world and scale-free graphs, the hybrid BFS achieves a significant speedup over previous BFS implementations based on the top-down approach. We use this same idea in a more general setting.

Pegasus [24] and the Knowledge Discovery Toolbox (KDT) [15, 31] process graphs by using sparse matrix operations with generalized matrix operations. Each row/column corresponds to a vertex and each non-zero in the matrix represents an edge. Pegasus uses the Hadoop implementation of MapReduce in the distributed-computing setting, and includes implementations for PageRank, random walk with restart, graph diameter/radii, and connected components. It does not allow a sparse representation of the vertices and therefore is inefficient when only a small subset of vertices are active. Also, because it is built on top of MapReduce, it is hard to make it perform well. KDT provides a set of generalized matrix-vector building blocks for graph computations. It is built on top of the the Combinatorial BLAS [8], a lower-level generalized sparse matrix library for the distributed setting. Using the building blocks, the KDT developers implement algorithms for breadth-first search, betweenness centrality, PageRank, belief propagation and Markov Clustering. Since the abstraction allows for sparse vectors as well as sparse matrices, it is suited for the case when only a small number of vertices are active. However, it does not switch representations of the vertex sets based on its density. We give some performance comparisons with both systems in Section 6.

Pregel is an API for processing large graphs in the distributed setting [34]. It is a vertex-centric framework, where vertices can loop over their edges and send messages to all their out-neighbors. These messages are then collected at the target vertex, possibly using associative combining. The system is bulk-synchronous so the received value is not seen until the next round. The reported performance of Pregel is relatively slow, likely due to the overhead of the framework and the use of a distributed memory machine. The GPS [40] and Giraph [16] systems are public source implementations of the Pregel interface with some additional features. The GPS system allows for graph partitioning and reallocation during the computation. This improves performance over Pregel, but only marginally.

GraphLab is a framework for asynchronous parallel graph computations in machine learning. It works in both shared-memory and distributed-memory architectures [29, 30]. It differs from Pregel in that it does not work in bulk-synchronous steps, but rather allows the vertices to be processed asynchronously based on a scheduler. The vertex functions can run at any time as long as specified consistency rules are obeyed. It is therefore well-suited for the machine learning types of applications for which it is defined, where each vertex accumulates information from its neighbors states and updates its state, possibly asynchronously. The recent PowerGraph framework combines the shared-memory and asynchronous properties of GraphLab with the associative combining concept of Pregel [17]. In contrast to our vertexSubset data type, both Pregel and GraphLab assume a single graph, and do not allow for multiple vertex sets, since state is associated with the vertices.

Grace is a graph management system for shared-memory [39]. It uses graph partitioning techniques and batched updates to exploit locality. Updates to the graph are done transactionally. Their reported times are slower than that of our system for applications like BFS and PageRank, after accounting for differences in input size and machine specifications.

GraphChi is a system for handling graph computations using just a PC [26]. It uses a novel parallel sliding windows method for processing graphs from disk. Although their running times are slower than ours, their system is designed for processing graphs out of memory, whereas we assume the graphs fit in memory.

Galois is a graph system for shared-memory based on set iterators [38]. Unlike our EDGEMAP and VERTEXMAP functions, their set iterator does not abstract the internal details of the loop from the user. Their sets of active elements for each iteration must be generated directly by the user, unlike our EDGEMAP which generates a vertexSubset which can be used for the next iteration.

Green-Marl is a domain-specific language for writing graph algorithms for shared-memory [21]. Graph traversal algorithms using Green-Marl are written using built-in breadth-first search (BFS) and depth-first search (DFS) primitives whose implementations are built into the compiler. Their language does not support operations over arbitrary sets of vertices on each iteration of the traversal, and instead the user must explicitly filter out the vertices to skip. This makes it less flexible than our framework, which can operate on arbitrary vertexSubsets. In Green-Marl, for traversal algorithms which cannot be expressed using a BFS or DFS (e.g. radii estimation and Bellman-Ford shortest paths), the user has to write the for-loops themselves. On the other hand, such algorithms are naturally expressed in our framework.

Other high-performance libraries for parallel graph computations include the Parallel Boost Graph Library (PBGL) [19] and the Multithreaded Graph Library (MTGL) [5]. The former is developed for the distributed-memory setting and the latter is developed for massively multithreaded architectures. These libraries provide few higher-level abstractions beyond the graphs themselves.

3. Preliminaries

A variable *var* with type *type* is denoted as $var : type$. We denote a function f by $f : X \mapsto Y$ if each $x \in X$ has a unique value $y \in Y$ such that $f(x) = y$. We denote the Cartesian product of sets A and B by $A \times B$ where $A \times B = \{(a, b) : a \in A \land b \in B\}$. We define the Boolean value set *bool* to be the set $\{0, 1\}$ (equivalently {*false*,*true*}).

We denote a directed unweighted graph by $G = (V, E)$ where V is the set of vertices and E is the set of (directed) edges in the graph. Graphs have type *graph*, vertices have type *vertex* and edges have type *vertex* × *vertex*, where the first vertex is the source of the edge and the second the target. We will use the convention of denoting the number of vertices in a graph by $|V|$ and number of edges in a graph by $|E|$. We denote a weighted graph by $G = (V, E, w)$, where w is a function which maps an edge to a real value ($w : vertex \times vertex \mapsto \mathbb{R}$), and each edge $e \in E$ is associated with the weight $w(e)$. $N^+(v)$ denotes the set of out-neighbors of vertex v in G and $deg^+(v)$ denotes the out-degree of v in G. Similarly, $N^-(v)$ and $deg^-(v)$ denote the in-neighbors and in-degree of v in G.

A ***compare-and-swap*** (CAS) is an atomic instruction that takes three arguments—a memory location (*loc*), an old value (*oldV*) and a new value (*newV*); if the value stored at *loc* is equal to *oldV* it atomically stores *newV* at *loc* and returns *true*, and otherwise it does not modify *loc* and returns *false*. In our implementations, we use CAS's both directly and as a subroutine to other atomic functions, such an as atomic increment. Throughout the paper we use the notation $\&x$ to refer to the memory location of variable x.

4. Framework

4.1 Interface

For an unweighted graph $G = (V, E)$ or weighted graph $G = (V, E, w(E))$, our framework provides a ***vertexSubset*** type, which represents a subset of vertices $U \subseteq V$. Note that V, and hence U, may be shared among graphs with different edge sets. Except for some constructor functions and some optional arguments described in Section 4.4, the following describes our interface.

1. SIZE(U: *vertexSubset*) : $\mathbb{N}$.

   Returns $|U|$.

2. EDGEMAP(G : *graph*,
             U : *vertexSubset*,
             F : (*vertex* $\times$ *vertex*) $\mapsto$ *bool*,
             C : *vertex* $\mapsto$ *bool*) : *vertexSubset*.

   For an unweighted graph $G = (V, E)$ EDGEMAP applies the function F to all edges with source vertex in U and target vertex satisfying C. More precisely, for an active edge set

   $$E_a = \{(u, v) \in E \mid u \in U \wedge C(v) = true\},$$

   F is applied to each element in E_a, and the return value of EDGEMAP is a vertexSubset:

   $$\text{Out} = \{v \mid (u, v) \in E_a \wedge F(u, v) = true\}.$$

   In this framework, F can run in parallel, so the user must ensure parallel correctness. F is allowed to side effect any data that it is associated with (and does so when used in the graph algorithms we discuss later), so F, C, E_a and Out can depend on order. The function C is useful in algorithms where a value associated with a vertex only needs to be updated once (i.e. breadth-first search). If the user does not need the this functionality, a default function C_{true} which always returns true may be supplied.

   For weighted graphs, F takes the edge weight as an additional argument.

3. VERTEXMAP(U : *vertexSubset*,
             F : *vertex* $\mapsto$ *bool*) : *vertexSubset*.

   Applies F to every vertex in U. Its returns a vertexSubset:

   $$\text{Out} = \{u \in U \mid F(u) = true\}$$

   As with EDGEMAP, the function F can run in parallel.

4.2 Implementation

We index the vertices V of a graph from 0 to $|V| - 1$. A vertexSubset $U \subset V$ is therefore a set of integers in the range $0, \ldots, |V| - 1$. In our implementation this set is either represented sparsely as an array of $|U|$ integers (not necessarily sorted) or as a Boolean array of length $|V|$, *true* in location i if and only if $i \in U$. For example, for a graph with 8 vertices the sparse representation of a vertex subset $\{0, 2, 3\}$ could be $[0, 2, 3]$ or $[3, 0, 2]$ and the corresponding dense representation would be $[1, 0, 1, 1, 0, 0, 0, 0]$. The implementation of vertexSubset contains routines for converting its sparse representation to a dense representation and vice versa. In the following pseudocode we assume unweighted graphs, but it can easily be extended to weighted graphs. Also we overload notation and use U and Out both to denote subsets of vertices and also to denote the vertexSubsets representing them.

For a given graph $G = (V, E)$, a vertexSubset representing a set of vertices $U \subseteq V$ and functions F and C, the EDGEMAP function (pseudocode shown in Algorithm 1) calls one of **EDGEMAPSPARSE** (Algorithm 2) and **EDGEMAPDENSE** (Algorithm 3) based on $|U|$ and the number of outgoing edges of U (if this quantity is greater than some threshold, it calls EDGEMAPDENSE, and otherwise it calls EDGEMAPSPARSE). EDGEMAPSPARSE loops through all

vertices present in U in parallel and for a given $u \in U$ applies $F(u, \text{ngh})$ to all of u's neighbors ngh in G in parallel. It returns a vertexSubset that is represented sparsely. The work performed by EDGEMAPSPARSE is proportional to $|U|$ plus the sum of the out-degrees of U. On the other hand, EDGEMAPDENSE loops through all vertices in V in parallel and for each vertex $v \in V$ it sequentially applies the function $F(\text{ngh}, v)$ for each of v's neighbors ngh that are in U, until $C(u)$ returns *false*. It returns a dense representation of a vertexSubset. For EDGEMAPSPARSE, since a sparse representation of a vertexSubset is returned, duplicate vertex IDs in the output vertexSubset must be removed. Intuitively EDGEMAPSPARSE should be more efficient than EDGEMAP-DENSE for small vertexSubsets, while for larger vertexSubsets EDGEMAPDENSE should be faster. The threshold of when to use EDGEMAPSPARSE versus EDGEMAPDENSE is set to $|E|/20$, which we found to work well across all of our applications.

Algorithm 1 EDGEMAP

```
1: procedure EDGEMAP(G, U, F, C)
2:     if (|U| + sum of out-degrees of U > threshold) then
3:         return EDGEMAPDENSE(G, U, F, C)
4:     else return EDGEMAPSPARSE(G, U, F, C)
```

Algorithm 2 EDGEMAPSPARSE

```
1: procedure EDGEMAPSPARSE(G, U, F, C)
2:     Out = {}
3:     parfor each v ∈ U do
4:         parfor ngh ∈ N⁺(v) do
5:             if (C(ngh) == 1 and F(v, ngh) == 1) then
6:                 Add ngh to Out
7:     Remove duplicates from Out
8:     return Out
```

Algorithm 3 EDGEMAPDENSE

```
1: procedure EDGEMAPDENSE(G, U, F, C)
2:     Out = {}
3:     parfor i ∈ {0, ..., |V| - 1} do
4:         if (C(i) == 1) then
5:             for ngh ∈ N⁻(i) do
6:                 if (ngh ∈ U and F(ngh, i) == 1) then
7:                     Add i to Out
8:                 if (C(i) == 0) then break
9:     return Out
```

The VERTEXMAP function (Algorithm 4) takes as inputs a vertexSubset representing the vertices U and a Boolean function F, and applies F to all vertices in U. It returns a vertexSubset representing subset Out $\subseteq U$ containing vertices u such that $F(u)$ returns *true*.

Algorithm 4 VERTEXMAP

```
1: procedure VERTEXMAP(U, F)
2:     Out = {}
3:     parfor u ∈ U do
4:         if (F(u) == 1) then Add u to Out
5:     return Out
```

4.3 Graph Representation

Our code represents in-edges and out-edges as arrays. In particular the in-edges for all vertices are kept in one array partitioned by their target vertex and storing the source vertices. Similarly, the out-edges are in an array partitioned by the source vertices and storing the target vertices. Each vertex points to the start of their in-edge and out-edge partitions and also maintains their in-degree and out-degree. Note that EDGEMAPSPARSE only uses the out-edges and

EDGEMAPDENSE only uses the in-edges. To transpose a graph (i.e. switch the direction of all edges), which is needed in betweenness centrality, we swap the roles of the in-edges and out-edges. When a graph is symmetric (or undirected) the in-neighbors and out-neighbors are the same so only one copy needs to be stored. For weighted graphs, the weights are interleaved with the edge targets in the edge array for cache efficiency.

4.4 Optimizations

Here we discuss several optimizations to our interface and implementation. These optimizations affect only performance and not correctness.

Note that EDGEMAPSPARSE applies F in parallel to target vertices (second argument), while EDGEMAPDENSE applies F sequentially given a target vertex. Therefore the F in EDGEMAPDENSE does not need to be atomic with respect to the target vertex. An optimization is for EDGEMAP to accept two version of its function F, the first of which must be correct when run in parallel with respect to both arguments, and the second of which must be correct when run in parallel only with respect to the first argument (source vertex). Both functions should behave exactly the same if EDGEMAP were run sequentially. If this optimization is used, then EDGEMAPSPARSE would use the first version of F as before, but EDGEMAPDENSE would use the second version of F (which we found to be slightly faster for some applications).

The default threshold of when to use EDGEMAPSPARSE versus EDGEMAPDENSE is $|E|/20$, but if the user discovers a better threshold, it can be passed as an optional argument to EDGEMAP.

If the user is careful in defining the F and C functions passed to EDGEMAP to guarantee that no duplicate vertices will appear in the output vertexSubset of EDGEMAP, then the remove-duplicates stage of EDGEMAPSPARSE can be bypassed. Our EDGEMAP function takes a flag indicating whether duplicate vertices need to be removed.

For EDGEMAPDENSE, the inner for-loop is sequential (see Algorithm 3) because the behavior of C may allow it to break early (e.g., in BFS, breaking after the first valid parent is found). If instead the user wants to run the inner for-loop in parallel and give up the option of breaking early, a flag can be passed to EDGEMAP to indicate this.

Since EDGEMAPDENSE is read-based, we also provide a write-based version of EDGEMAPDENSE called **EDGEMAPDENSE-WRITE** (shown in Algorithm 5). This write-based version loops through all vertices in V in parallel and for vertices contained in U it applies F (now required to correct when run in parallel with respect to both arguments) to all of its neighbors in parallel, as in EDGEMAPSPARSE. It returns a dense representation of a vertexSubset. We found EDGEMAPDENSE-WRITE to be more efficient than EDGEMAPDENSE only for two of our applications—PageRank and Bellman-Ford shortest paths. In our framework, the user may pass a flag to EDGEMAP specifying whether to use EDGEMAPDENSE (default) or EDGEMAPDENSE-WRITE when the vertexSubset is dense. The user would need to figure out experimentally which version is more efficient.

Algorithm 5 EDGEMAPDENSE-WRITE

```
1: procedure EDGEMAPDENSE-WRITE(G, U, F, C)
2:     Out = {}
3:     parfor i ∈ {0, ..., |V| − 1} do
4:         if (i ∈ U) then
5:             parfor ngh ∈ N⁺(i) do
6:                 if (C(ngh) == 1 and F(i, ngh) == 1) then
7:                     Add ngh to Out
8:     return Out
```

For VERTEXMAP, if the user knows that the input and output vertexSubsets are the same, an optimized version of VERTEXMAP that avoids creating a new vertexSubset can be used.

5. Applications

Here we describe six applications of our framework. In the following discussions, the "frontiers" of the algorithms are represented as vertexSubsets.

5.1 Breadth-First Search

A **breadth-first search** (BFS) algorithm takes a graph $G = (V, E)$ and a starting vertex $r \in V$, and computes a breadth-first search tree rooted at r containing all nodes reachable from r. A simple parallel algorithm processes each level of the BFS in parallel. The number of iterations required is equal to the (unweighted) distance of the furthest node reachable from the starting vertex, and the algorithm processes each edge at most once. There has been recent work on developing fast parallel breadth-first search algorithms for shared-memory machines [3, 4, 28, 41] and these algorithms have been shown to be practical for many real-world graphs.

In our framework, a breadth-first search implementation is very simple as we described in Section 1. To make the computation more efficient for dense frontiers for which EDGEMAPDENSE is used, we can also provide a version of UPDATE, which is not atomic with respect to d and does not use a CAS. The code for BFS is shown in Figure 1.

5.2 Betweenness Centrality

Centrality indices for graphs have been widely studied in social network analysis because they are useful indicators of the relative importance of nodes in a graph. One such index is the betweenness centrality index [13].

To precisely define the betweenness centrality index, we first introduce some additional definitions. For a graph $G = (V, E)$ and some $s, t \in V$, let σ_{st} be the number of shortest paths from s to t in G. For vertices $s, t, v \in V$, define $\sigma_{st}(v)$ to be the number of shortest paths from s to t that pass through v. Define $\delta_{st}(v) = \frac{\sigma_{st}(v)}{\sigma_{st}}$ to be the **pair-dependency** of s, t on v. The **betweenness centrality** of a vertex v, denoted by $C_B(v)$ is equal to $\sum_{s \neq v \neq t \in V} \delta_{st}(v)$. A naive method to compute the betweenness centrality scores is to perform a BFS starting at each vertex to compute the pair-dependencies, and then sum the pair-dependencies for each $v \in V$. There are $O(|V|^2)$ pair-dependency terms associated with each vertex, hence this method requires $O(|V|^3)$ operations.

Brandes [6] presents an algorithm which avoids the explicit summation of pair-dependencies and runs in $(|V||E| + |V|^2 \log |V|)$ operations for weighted graphs and $O(|V||E| + |V|^2)$ operations for unweighted graphs. Brandes' defines the **dependency** of a vertex r on a vertex v as follows:

$$\delta_{r\bullet}(v) = \sum_{t \in V} \delta_{rt}(v) \qquad (1)$$

For any given r, Brandes' algorithm computes $\delta_{r\bullet}(v)$ for all v in linear time for unweighted graphs, by using the following two equations, where $P_r(v)$ is defined to contain all immediate parents of v in the BFS tree rooted at r:

$$\sigma_{rv} = \sum_{u \in P_r(v)} \sigma_{ru} \qquad (2)$$

$$\delta_{r\bullet}(v) = \sum_{w : v \in P_r(w)} \frac{\sigma_{rv}}{\sigma_{rw}} \times (1 + \delta_{r\bullet}(w)) \qquad (3)$$

The algorithm works in two phases: the first phase of the algorithm computes the number of shortest paths from r to each vertex using Equation 2, and the second phase computes the dependency scores via Equation 3. The first phase is similar to a forward BFS from vertex r and the second phase works backwards from the last frontier of the BFS. This algorithm can be parallelized in two way—(1) for each vertex, the traversal can be done in parallel, and (2) each vertex can perform their individual computations independently in parallel with other vertices' computations. Although much more efficient than the naive algorithm, Brandes' algorithm still requires at least quadratic time, and is thus prohibitive for large graphs. To address this problem, there has been work on computing approximate betweenness centrality scores based on using the pair-dependency contributions from just a sample of the vertices of the vertices and scaling the betweenness centrality scores appropriately [2, 14]. The KDT package provides a parallel implementation of batched computation of betweenness centrality scores by running multiple individual computations independently in parallel [31].

We describe the betweenness centrality computation from a single root vertex—these computations can be run independently in parallel for any sample of the vertices. The computation here is different from the BFS described in Section 5.1 in that instead of finding a parent, each vertex v needs to maintain a count of the number of shortest paths passing through it. This means the number of updates to v is equal to its number of parents in the BFS tree, instead of just one update as in BFS.

The psuedocode for our implementation is shown in Algorithm 6. The frontier is initialized to contain just r. For the first phase we use an array of integers *NumPaths*, which is initialized to all 0's except for the root vertex which has NumPaths[r] set to 1. By traversing the graph in a breadth-first manner and updating the NumPaths value for each v that is traversed, we obtain the number of shortest paths passing through each v from r (NumPaths[v] will remain 0 if v is unreachable from r). The PATHSUPDATE function passed to EDGEMAP is shown in lines 13–18. As there can be multiple updates to some NumPaths[v] in parallel, the update attempt is repeated with a compare-and-swap until successful. Line 18 guarantees that a vertex is placed on the frontier only once, since the old NumPaths value will be 0 for at most one update. Each frontier of the search is stored in a *Levels* array for use in the second phase.

To keep track of vertices that have been visited (and avoid having to remove duplicates in EDGEMAPSPARSE), we also maintain a Boolean array *Visited*. Visited is initialized to all 0's (except for the root vertex whose entry is set to 1), and we set a vertex's entry in Visited to 1 after it is first visited in the computation. To do this, we use a VERTEXMAP and pass the VISIT function shown in lines 9–11 of Algorithm 6 to VERTEXMAP. The COND function in lines 27–28 makes EDGEMAP only consider unvisited target vertices. The psuedocode for the first phase starting at a root vertex is shown in lines 32 to 36.

For the second phase, we use a new array *Dependencies* (initialized to all 0.0) and reuse the Visited array (reinitialized to all 0). Also we transpose the graph (line 40), since edges now need to point in the reverse direction. The algorithm operates on the vertexSubsets in the Levels array returned from the first phase in reverse order, uses the same VISIT and COND functions as in the first phase, and passes the DEPUPDATE function shown in lines 20 to 25 of Algorithm 6 to EDGEMAP. Psuedocode for the second phase of the betweenness-centrality computation is shown in lines 42–46.

5.3 Graph Radii Estimation and Multiple BFS

For a graph $G = (V, E)$, the ***radius*** of a node $v \in V$ is the shortest distance to the furthest reachable node of v. The ***diameter*** of the graph is the maximum radius over all $v \in V$. For unweighted graphs, one simple method for computing the radii of all nodes (and hence the diameter of the graph) is to run $|V|$ BFS's, one starting at each vertex. However, for large graphs this method is impractical

---

Algorithm 6 Betweenness Centrality

```
1:  NumPaths = {0, ..., 0}                      ▷ initialized to all 0
2:  Visited = {0, ..., 0}                        ▷ initialized to all 0
3:  NumPaths[r] = 1
4:  Visited[r] = 1
5:  currLevel = 0
6:  Levels = [ ]
7:  Dependencies = {0.0, ..., 0.0}            ▷ initialized to all 0.0
8:
9:  procedure VISIT(i)
10:     Visited[i] = 1
11:     return 1
12:
13: procedure PATHSUPDATE(s, d)
14:     repeat
15:         oldV = NumPaths[d]
16:         newV = oldV + NumPaths[s]
17:     until (CAS(&NumPaths[d], oldV, newV) == 1)
18:     return (oldV == 0)
19:
20: procedure DEPUPDATE(s, d)
21:     repeat
22:         oldV = Dependencies[d]
23:         newV = oldV + NumPaths[d]/NumPaths[s] × (1 + Dependencies[s])
24:     until (CAS(&Dependencies[d], oldV, newV) == 1)
25:     return (oldV == 0.0)
26:
27: procedure COND(i)
28:     return (Visited[i] == 0)
29:
30: procedure BC(G, r)
31:     Frontier = {r}          ▷ vertexSubset initialized to contain only r
32:     while (SIZE(Frontier) ≠ 0) do                        ▷ Phase 1
33:         Frontier = EDGEMAP(G, Frontier, PATHSUPDATE, COND)
34:         Levels[currLevel] = Frontier
35:         Frontier = VERTEXMAP(Frontier, VISIT)
36:         currLevel = currLevel + 1
37:
38:     Visited = {0, ..., 0}               ▷ reinitialize to all 0
39:     currLevel = currLevel − 1
40:     TRANSPOSE(G)                               ▷ transpose graph
41:
42:     while (currLevel ≥ 0) do                             ▷ Phase 2
43:         Frontier = Levels[currLevel]
44:         VERTEXMAP(Frontier, VISIT)
45:         EDGEMAP(G, Frontier, DEPUPDATE, COND)
46:         currLevel = currLevel − 1
47:     return Dependencies
```

---

as each BFS requires $O(|V| + |E|)$ operations, leading to a total of $O(|V|^2 + |V||E|)$ operations (see [11]). This approach can be parallelized by running the BFS's independently in parallel, and also by parallelizing each individual BFS, but currently this is still impractical for large graphs.

There has been work on techniques to estimate the diameter of a graph. Magnien et. al. [33] describe several techniques for computing upper and lower bounds on the diameter of a graph, using BFS's and spanning subgraphs. They describe a method called the *double sweep lower bound*, which works by first running a BFS from some node v and then a second BFS from the furthest node from v (call it w). The radius of w is then taken to be a lower bound on the diameter of the graph. Their method can be repeated by picking more vertices to run BFS's from. Ferrez et. al. [12] perform experiments with parallel implementations of some of these methods. Another approach based on counting neighborhood sizes was described by Palmer et. al. [37]. Their algorithm approximates the neighborhood function for each vertex in a graph, which is more general than computing graph radii. Kang et. al. [23] parallelize this algorithm using MapReduce. Cohen [10] describes an algorithm for approximating neighborhood sizes, which requires $O(|E|\log|V|)$ expected number of operations for undirected graphs.

We implement the simple method for estimating graph radii by performing BFS's from a sample of K vertices. Its accuracy can be improved by using the double sweep method of Magnien et. al. [33]. Instead of running the BFS's in parallel independently, we run multiple BFS's together. In the ***multiple-BFS*** algorithm, each vertex maintains a bit-vector of length K. Initially K vertices are chosen randomly to act as "source" vertices and each of these K vertices has exactly one unique bit in their bit-vector set to 1; all other vertices have their bit-vectors initialized to all 0's. The K sampled vertices are placed on the initial frontier of the multiple-BFS search. In each iteration, each frontier vertex bitwise-ORs its vector into each of its neighbors' vectors. Vertices whose bit-vectors changed in an iteration are placed on the frontier for the next iteration. The algorithm iterates until none of the bit-vectors change.

For a sample of size K this algorithm simulates running K BFS's in parallel, but without computing the BFS tree (which is not needed for the radii computation). Storing the iteration number in which a vertex v's bit-vector last changed is a lower-bound on the radius of v since at least one of the K sampled vertices took this many rounds to reach v. If K is set to be the number of bits in a word (32 or 64) this algorithm is more efficient than naively performing K individual BFS's in two ways: (1) the frontiers of the K BFS's could overlap in any given iteration and this algorithm stores the union of these frontiers usually leading to fewer edges traversed per iteration and (2) performing a bitwise-OR on bit-vectors can pass information from more than one of the K BFS's while only requiring one arithmetic operation. Note that this algorithm only estimates the diameter of the connected components of the graph which contain at least one of the K sampled vertices; if there are multiple connected components in the graph, one would first compute in parallel the components of the graph and then run the multiple-BFS algorithm in parallel on each component.

To implement the multiple-BFS algorithm in our framework (pseudocode shown in Algorithm 7), we maintain two bit-vectors, *Visited* and *NextVisited*, which are initialized to all 0's, except for the K sampled vertices each of which has a unique bit in their Visited bit-vector set to 1. We also maintain an array *Radii*, which for each vertex stores the iteration number in which the bit-vector of the vertex last changed. It is initialized to all ∞ except for the K sampled vertices which have a Radii entry of 0. At the end of the algorithm, Radii contains the estimated (lower-bound) radius of each vertex, the maximum of which is a lower-bound on the graph diameter. In the pseudocode, we use "|" to denote the bitwise-OR operation. The initial frontier contains the K sampled vertices. The update function RADIIUPDATE passed to EDGEMAP is shown in lines 6–12 of Algorithm 7. ATOMICOR(x, y) performs a bitwise-OR of y with the value stored at x and atomically updates x with this new value. It is implemented using a compare-and-swap. The reason we have both Visited and NextVisited is so that new bits that a vertex receives in an iteration do not get propagated to its neighbors in the same round, otherwise the values in Radii would be incorrect. The compare-and-swap on line 11 guarantees that any Radii entry is updated at most once (and returns *true*) per iteration. Therefore any vertex will be placed at most once on the next frontier, eliminating the need for removing duplicates. As in the other implementations, we can provide a version of RADIIUPDATE non-atomic with respect to d to EDGEMAP.

The ORCOPY function (lines 14–16) passed to VERTEXMAP simply takes an index i, performs a bitwise-OR of NextVisited[i] and Visited[i] and stores the result in NextVisited[i]. We use this because the roles of NextVisited and Visited are switched between

iterations. The while loop in lines 22–26 is executed until the entries of the Radii array do not change (or equivalently, none of the bit-vectors change).

Algorithm 7 Radii Estimation

1: Visited $= \{0, \ldots, 0\}$ ▷ initialized to all 0
2: NextVisited $= \{0, \ldots, 0\}$ ▷ initialized to all 0
3: Radii $= \{\infty, \ldots, \infty\}$ ▷ initialized to all ∞
4: round $= 0$
5:
6: **procedure** RADIIUPDATE(s, d)
7:     **if** (Visited[d] $\neq$ Visited[s]) **then**
8:        ATOMICOR(&NextVisited[d], Visited[d] | Visited[s])
9:        oldRadii $=$ Radii[d]
10:        **if** (Radii[d] $\neq$ round) **then**
11:           **return** CAS(&Radii[d], oldRadii, round)
12:     **return** 0
13:
14: **procedure** ORCOPY(i)
15:     NextVisited[i] $=$ NextVisited[i] | Visited[i]
16:     **return** 1
17:
18: **procedure** RADII(G)
19:     Sample K vertices and for each one set a unique bit in Visited to 1
20:     Initialize Frontier to contain the K sampled vertices
21:     Set the Radii entries of the sampled vertices to 0
22:     **while** (SIZE(Frontier) $\neq$ 0) **do**
23:        round $=$ round $+ 1$
24:        Frontier $=$ EDGEMAP$(G,$ Frontier, RADIIUPDATE, $C_{true})$
25:        Frontier $=$ VERTEXMAP(Frontier, ORCOPY)
26:        SWAP(Visited, NextVisited)   ▷ switch roles of bit-vectors
27:     **return** Radii

5.4 Connected Components

For an undirected graph $G = (V, E)$, a connected component $C \subseteq V$ is one in which all vertices in C can reach one another. The ***connected components*** problem is to find $C_1, \ldots, C_k$ such that each C_i is a connected component, $\bigcup_i C_i = V$, and there is no path between vertices belonging to different components.

One method of computing the connected components of a graph is to maintain an array *IDs* of size $|V|$ initialized such that IDs[i] $= i$, and iteratively have every vertex update its IDs entry to be the minimum IDs entry of all of its neighbors in G. The total number of operations performed by this algorithm is $O(d(|V|+|E|))$ where d is the diameter of G. For high-diameter graphs, this algorithm can perform much worse than standard edge-based algorithms which require only $O(|V|+|E|)$ operations [11, 22], but for low-diameter graphs it runs reasonably well. We show this algorithm as a simple application of our framework.

The pseudocode for our implementation is shown in Algorithm 8. The initial frontier contains all vertices in V. In addition to the IDs array, we maintain a second array *prevIDs* (used to check whether a vertex has been placed on the frontier in a given iteration yet), and pass the CCUPDATE function shown in lines 4–8 of Algorithm 8 to EDGEMAP. WRITEMIN(x, y) atomically updates the value at location x to be the minimum of x's old value and y, and is implemented with a compare-and-swap. It returns *true* if the value at location x was changed, and *false* otherwise. Line 7 places a vertex on the next frontier if and only if its ID changed in the iteration. To synchronize the values of prevIDs and IDs after every iteration, we pass the COPY function to VERTEXMAP. The while loop in lines 16–18 is executed until IDs remains the same as prevIDs. When the algorithm terminates, all vertices in the same component will have the same value stored in their IDs entry.

Algorithm 8 Connected Components

```
1: IDs = {0, . . . , |V| − 1}              ▷ initialized such that IDs[i] = i
2: prevIDs = {0, . . . , |V| − 1}      ▷ initialized such that prevIDs[i] = i
3:
4: procedure CCUPDATE(s, d)
5:     origID = IDs[d]
6:     if (WRITEMIN(&IDs[d], IDs[s])) then
7:         return (origID == prevIDs[d])
8:     return 0
9:
10: procedure COPY(i)
11:     prevIDs[i] = IDs[i]
12:     return 1
13:
14: procedure CC(G)
15:     Frontier = {0, . . . , |V| − 1}    ▷ vertexSubset initialized to V
16:     while (SIZE(Frontier) ≠ 0) do
17:         Frontier = VERTEXMAP(Frontier, COPY)
18:         Frontier = EDGEMAP(G, Frontier, CCUPDATE, C_true)
19:     return IDs
```

5.5 PageRank

PageRank is an algorithm that was first used by Google to compute the relative importance of webpages [7]. It takes as input a graph $G = (V, E)$, a damping factor $0 \le \gamma \le 1$ and a convergence constant ϵ. It initializes a PageRank vector PR of length $|V|$ to have all entries set to $\frac{1}{|V|}$, and iteratively applies the following equation for all indices v, until the sum of the differences of PR values between iterations drops to below ϵ:

$$PR[v] = \frac{1 - \gamma}{|V|} + \gamma \sum_{u \in N^-(v)} \frac{PR[u]}{deg^+(u)} \qquad (4)$$

This leads to a very simple implementation in our framework. We also describe a variant of PageRank (PageRank-Delta) which applies Equation (4) to only a subset of V in an iteration. By choosing the subset to contain only vertices whose PageRank entry that changed by more than a certain amount, we can speed up the computation.

The pseudocode for our implementation of PageRank is shown in Algorithm 9. In every iteration, the frontier contains all vertices. Our implementation maintains two arrays p_{curr} and p_{next} each of length $|V|$. p_{curr} is initialized to $\frac{1}{|V|}$ for each entry and p_{next} is initialized to all 0.0's. The PRUPDATE function passed to EDGEMAP is shown in lines 5–7. ATOMICINCREMENT(x, y) atomically adds y to the value at location x and stores the result in location x; it can be implemented with a compare-and-swap. Each iteration of the while loop (lines 18–22) applies an EDGEMAP, uses a VERTEXMAP to process the result of the EDGEMAP, computes the error for the iteration and switches the roles of p_{next} and p_{curr}. The PRLOCALCOMPUTE function (lines 9–13) passed to VERTEXMAP normalizes the result of the EDGEMAP by γ, adds a constant, computes the absolute difference between p_{next} and p_{curr}, and resets p_{curr} to 0.0 for the next iteration (since the roles of p_{next} and p_{curr} become switched). The while loop is executed until the error drops below ϵ.

PageRank-Delta is a variant of PageRank in which vertices are active in an iteration only if they have accumulated enough change in their PR value. This idea is used in GraphLab for computing PageRank [30]. In our framework, in each EDGEMAP vertices pass their changes (deltas) in PR value to their neighbors, and all vertices accumulate a sum of delta contributions from their neighbors. Each VERTEXMAP only updates and returns vertices whose accumulated delta contributions from neighbors is more than a δ-fraction of its PR value since the last time it was active. Such an implementation allows for vertices which do not influence the PR values much to stay inactive, thereby shrinking the frontier. We

Algorithm 9 PageRank

```
1: p_curr = {1/|V|, . . . , 1/|V|}          ▷ initialized to all 1/|V|
2: p_next = {0.0, . . . , 0.0}               ▷ initialized to all 0.0
3: diff = {}                                ▷ array to store differences
4:
5: procedure PRUPDATE(s, d)
6:     ATOMICINCREMENT(&p_next[d], p_curr[s]/deg^+(s))
7:     return 1
8:
9: procedure PRLOCALCOMPUTE(i)
10:     p_next[i] = (γ × p_next[i]) + (1−γ)/|V|
11:     diff[i] = |p_next[i] − p_curr[i]|
12:     p_curr[i] = 0.0
13:     return 1
14:
15: procedure PAGERANK(G, γ, ε)
16:     Frontier = {0, . . . , |V| − 1}    ▷ vertexSubset initialized to V
17:     error = ∞
18:     while (error > ε) do
19:         Frontier = EDGEMAP(G, Frontier, PRUPDATE, C_true)
20:         Frontier = VERTEXMAP(Frontier, PRLOCALCOMPUTE)
21:         error = sum of diff entries
22:         SWAP(p_curr, p_next)
23:     return p_curr
```

can implement PageRank-Delta in our framework by modifying the function passed to EDGEMAP to pass the deltas instead of the PR values, and modifying the function passed to VERTEXMAP to only perform updates and return true for the vertices whose accumulated delta contributions from neighbors since it was last active is more than a δ-fraction of its PR value. Due to space limitations, we do not show the pseudocode for this algorithm.

5.6 Bellman-Ford Shortest Paths

The single-source shortest paths problem takes as input a weighted graph $G = (V, E, w(E))$ and a root vertex r, and either computes the shortest path distance from r to each vertex in V (if a vertex is unreachable from r, then the distance returned is ∞), or reports the existence of a negative cycle.

If the edge weights are all non-negative, then the single-source shortest paths problem can be solved with Dijkstra's algorithm [11]. Parallel variants of Dijkstra's algorithm have been studied [36], and have been shown to work well on real-world graphs [32]. However, Dijkstra's algorithm does not work with negative edge weights, and the Bellman-Ford algorithm can be used instead in this case. Although in the worst case the Bellman-Ford algorithm requires $O(|V||E|)$ operations, in contrast to the $O(|E| + |V| \log |V|)$ worst-case operations of Dijkstra's algorithm, in practice it can require many fewer than the worst case since on every step only some of the vertices might change distances. It is therefore important to take advantage of this fact and only process vertices when they actually change distance.

We first describe the standard Bellman-Ford algorithm [11] and then show how it can be implemented in our framework. The algorithm initializes the shortest paths array SP to all ∞ except for the root vertex which has an entry of 0. A **RELAX** procedure is repeatedly invoked by Bellman-Ford. RELAX takes G as an input and checks for each edge (u, v) if $SP[u] + w(u, v) < SP[v]$; if so, it sets $SP[v]$ to $SP[u] + w(u, v)$. If a call to RELAX does not change any SP values then the algorithm terminates. If RELAX is called $|V|$ or more times, then there is a negative cycle in G and the Bellman-Ford algorithm reports the existence of one.

To implement the Bellman-Ford algorithm in our framework (pseudocode shown in Algorithm 10) we maintain a *Visited* array in addition to the SP array. Since only vertices whose SP value has changed in an iteration need to propagate its SP value to its neighbors, the Visited array (initialized to all 0's) keeps track of which vertices had their SP value changed in an iteration. The update function passed to EDGEMAP is shown in lines 4–7 of Algorithm 10 (note that since this algorithm works on weighted graphs, the update function has the edge weight as an additional argument). It uses WRITEMIN (as described in Section 5.4) to posssibly update SP with a smaller path length. The compare-and-swap on line 6 guarantees that a vertex is placed on the frontier at most once per iteration. The initial frontier contains just the root vertex r. Each iteration of the while loop in lines 17–20 applies the EDGEMAP, which outputs a vertexSubset containing the vertices whose SP value changed. In order to reset the Visited array after an EDGEMAP, the BFRESET function (lines 9–11) is passed to VERTEXMAP. The algorithm either runs until no SP values change or runs for $|V|$ iterations and reports the existence of a negative-weight cycle. An iteration here differs from the RELAX procedure in that RELAX processes all vertices each time.

Algorithm 10 Bellman-Ford

1: SP = $\{\infty, \ldots, \infty\}$ ▷ initialized to all ∞
2: Visited = $\{0, \ldots, 0\}$ ▷ initialized to all 0
3:
4: **procedure** BFUPDATE(s, d, edgeWeight)
5:     **if** (WRITEMIN(&SP[d], SP[s] + edgeWeight)) **then**
6:         **return** CAS(&Visited[d], 0, 1)
7:     **else return** 0
8:
9: **procedure** BFRESET(i)
10:     Visited[i] = 0
11:     **return** 1
12:
13: **procedure** BELLMAN-FORD(G, r)
14:     SP[r] = 0
15:     Frontier = $\{r\}$ ▷ vertexSubset initialized to contain just r
16:     round = 0
17:     **while** (SIZE(Frontier) $\neq$ 0 and round < $|V|$) **do**
18:         round = round + 1
19:         Frontier = EDGEMAP(G, Frontier, BF-UPDATE, C_{true})
20:         Frontier = VERTEXMAP(Frontier, BF-RESET)
21:     **if** (round == $|V|$) **then return** "negative-weight cycle"
22:     **else return** SP

---

6. Experiments

All of the experiments presented in this paper were performed on a 40-core Intel machine (with hyper-threading) with 4×2.4GHz Intel 10-core E7-8870 Xeon processors, a 1066MHz bus, and 256GB of main memory. The parallel programs were compiled with Intel's `icpc` compiler (version 12.1.0) using CilkPlus [27] with the −O3 flag. The sequential programs were compiled using g++ 4.4.1 with the −O2 flag. We also ran experiments on a 64-core AMD Opteron machine, but the results are slower than the ones from the Intel machine so we only report the latter.

The input graphs used in our experiments are shown in Table 1. **3D-grid** is a grid graph in 3-dimensional space in which every vertex has six edges—one connecting it to each of its two neighbors in each dimension. **Random-local** is a synthetic graph in which every vertex has edges to five randomly chosen neighbors, where the probability of an edge between two vertices is inversely correlated with their distance in the vertex array (vertices tend to have edges to other vertices that are close in memory). The **rMat** graphs are synthetic graphs with a power-law distribution of degrees [9]. **RMat24** (scale 24) contains 1.68×10^7 vertices and was generated with parameters $a = 0.5, b = c = 0.1, d = 0.3$. **RMat27** (scale 27) is one of the Graph500 benchmark graphs [18], and generated with parameters $a = 0.57, b = c = 0.19, d = 0.05$.

Twitter is a real-world graph of the Twitter social network containing 41.7 million vertices and 1.47 billion directed edges [25] . **Yahoo** is a real-world graph of the Web containing 1.4 billion vertices and 6.6 billion directed edges (12.9 billion after symmetrizing and removing duplicates) [42]. With the exception of Pregel, Yahoo is the largest real-world graph reported by other graph processing systems.

The number of edges reported is the number of directed edges in the graph with duplicate edges removed. The synthetic graphs are all symmetric, and we symmetrized the Yahoo graph for our experiments so that we have a larger graph. We used the original asymmetric Twitter graph. For the synthetic weighted graphs, the edge weights were generated randomly and were verified to contain no negative cycles. We used unit weights on the Twitter and Yahoo graphs for our Bellman-Ford experiments.

Input	Num. Vertices	Num. Directed Edges
3D-grid	10^7	6×10^7
random-local	10^7	9.8×10^7
rMat24	1.68×10^7	9.9×10^7
rMat27	1.34×10^8	2.12×10^9
Twitter	4.17×10^7	1.47×10^9
Yahoo*	1.4×10^9	12.9×10^9

Table 1. Graph inputs. *The original asymmetric graph has 6.6×10^9 edges.

Table 2 shows the running times for our implementations on each of the input graphs using a single thread and 40 cores with hyper-threading. All of the implementations used EDGEMAP-DENSE for the dense iterations with the exception of Bellman-Ford, PageRank and PageRank-Delta, which used EDGEMAPDENSE-WRITE, an optimization described in Section 4.4 (we found it to be more efficient in these cases). Figure 2 shows that all of our implementations scale well with the number of threads ("80" on the x-axis is 40 cores with hyper-threading).

For BFS, we achieve a 10–28 fold speedup. Using our framework we are able integrate the ideas of [3] to give a simple implementation of BFS, which is almost as fast as their highly optimized implementation. Our running times are better than those reported in [1, 28, 41], which do not take advantage of changes in the frontier density. Compared to the sequential BFS implementation in [41], we are faster on two or more threads.

For betweenness centrality (performing the two-phase computation for a single source) we achieve a 12–32 fold speedup on 40 cores. The KDT system [31] reports that on 256 cores (2.1 GHz AMD Opteron) their batched implementation of betweenness centrality (performs the two-phase computation for multiple sources in parallel) traverses almost 125 million edges per second on an rMat graph with 2^{18} vertices and 16×2^{18} edges. On rMat27 our implementation traverses 526 million edges per second using 40 cores on the Intel Nehalem machine, but it is difficult to directly compare because our machine is different and we do not do a batched computation. For the Twitter graph, since we transpose the graph for the second phase, the in-degree of some of the vertices increases dramatically, so we found that using a parallel inner loop in EDGEMAPDENSE, an optimization described in Section 4.4, was more efficient.

We ran our graph radii estimation implementation using a 64-bit vector for each vertex ($K = 64$) and achieve a 23–35× speedup on 40 cores. Kang et. al. [23] implement a slightly different algorithm for estimating the radii distribution using MapReduce, and run experiments on the Yahoo M45 Hadoop cluster (480 machines with 2 quad-core Intel Xeon 1.86 GHz processors per machine). Using 90 machines their reported runtime for 3 iterations on a 2 billion-edge graph is almost 30 minutes. Using a 40-core machine we are

Application	3D-grid			random-local			rMat24			rMat27			Twitter			Yahoo		
	(1)	(40h)	(SU)	(1)	(40h)	(SU)	(1)	(40h)	(SU)	(1)	(40h)	(SU)	(1)	(40h)	(SU)	(1)	(40h)	(SU)
Breadth-First Search	2.9	0.28	10.4	2.11	0.073	28.9	2.83	0.104	27.2	11.8	0.423	27.9	6.92	0.321	21.6	173	8.58	20.2
Betweenness Centrality	9.15	0.765	12.0	8.53	0.265	32.2	11.3	0.37	30.5	113	4.07	27.8	47.8	2.64	18.1	634	23.1	27.4
Graph Radii	351	10.0	35.1	25.6	0.734	34.9	39.7	1.21	32.8	337	12.0	28.1	171	7.39	23.1	1280	39.6	32.3
Connected Components	51.5	1.71	30.1	14.8	0.399	37.1	14.1	0.527	26.8	204	10.2	20.0	78.7	3.86	20.4	609	29.7	20.5
PageRank (1 iteration)	4.29	0.145	29.6	6.55	0.224	29.2	8.93	0.25	35.7	243	6.13	39.6	72.9	2.91	25.1	465	15.2	30.6
Bellman-Ford	63.4	2.39	26.5	18.8	0.677	27.8	17.8	0.694	25.6	116	4.03	28.8	75.1	2.66	28.2	255	14.2	18.0

Table 2. Running times (in seconds) of algorithms over various inputs on a 40-core machine (with hyper-threading). (SU) indicates the speedup of the application (single-thread time divided by 40-core time).

able to process the rMat27 graph of similar size until completion (9 iterations) in 12 seconds.

Our connected components implementation achieves a 20–37 fold speedup on 40 cores. The Pegasus library [24] also has a connected components algorithm implemented for the MapReduce framework. For a graph with 59,000 vertices and 282 million edges, and using 90 machines of the Yahoo M45 cluster, they report a runtime of over 10 minutes for 6 iterations. In contrast, for the much larger rMat27 graph (also requiring 6 iterations) our algorithm completes in about 10 seconds on the 40-core machine.

For a single iteration, our PageRank implementation achieves a 29–39 fold speedup on 40 cores. GPS [40] reports a running time of 144 minutes for 100 iterations (1.44 minutes per iteration) of PageRank on a web graph with 3.7 billion directed edges on an Amazon EC2 cluster using 30 large instances, each with 4 virtual cores and 7.5GB of memory. In contrast, our PageRank implementation takes less than 20 seconds per iteration on the larger Yahoo graph. For PageRank on the Twitter graph [25], our system is slightly faster per iteration (2.91 seconds vs. 3.6 seconds) on 40 cores than PowerGraph [17] on 8×64 cores (processors are 2.933 GHz Intel Xeon X5570 with 3200 MHz bus). We also compared our implementations of PageRank and PageRank-Delta, run to convergence with a damping factor of $\gamma = 0.85$ and parameters $\epsilon = 10^{-7}$ and $\delta = 10^{-2}$. Figure 2(e) shows that PageRank-Delta is faster (by more than a factor of 6 on rMat24) because in any given iteration it processes only vertices whose accumulated change is above a δ-fraction of its PageRank value at the time it was previously active. We do not analyze the error (which depends on δ) of our PageRank-Delta implementation in this work—the purpose of this experiment is to show that our framework also works well for non-graph traversal problems.

Our parallel implementation of Bellman-Ford achieves a 18–28× speedup on 40 cores. In Figure 2(f) we compare this implementation with a naive one which visits all vertices and edges in each iteration, and our more efficient version is almost twice as fast. The single-source shortest paths algorithm of Pregel [34] for a binary tree with 1 billion vertices takes almost 20 seconds on a cluster of 300 multicore commodity PCs. We ran our Bellman-Ford algorithm on a larger binary tree with $2^{27} (\approx 1.68 \times 10^7)$ vertices, and it completed in under 2 seconds (time not shown in Table 2). Compared to our implementation of the standard sequential algorithm described in [11], our parallel implementation is faster on a single thread.

Since the Yahoo graph is highly disconnected, we computed the number of vertices and directed edges traversed for BFS and betweenness centrality and found it to be 701 million and 12.8 billion respectively (this is the largest connected component of the graph). The number of vertex and edge traversals for the graph radii algorithm ($K = 64$) on the Yahoo graph were 2.7 billion and 50 billion respectively. Note that doing 64 individual BFS's to compute the same thing would require many more vertex and edge traversal; our implementation of radii estimation (multiple-BFS) reduces the number of traversals (and hence running time) by combining the operations of multiple BFS's into fewer operations.

Figure 3 shows scalability plots for the various applications. The experiments were performed on random graphs of varying size with the number of directed edges being ten times the number of vertices. We see that the implementations scale quite well with increasing graph size, with some noise due to the variability in the structures of the different random graphs.

Figure 4 shows plots of the size of the frontier plus the number of outgoing edges for each iteration and each application on rMat24. The rMat24 graph is a scale-free graph and hence able to take advantage of the hybrid BFS idea of Beamer et. al. [4]. The y-axes are shown in log-scale. We also plot the threshold, above which EDGEMAP uses the dense implementation and below which EDGEMAP uses the sparse implementation. For BFS, betweenness centrality (same frontier plot as that of BFS), radii estimation and Bellman-Ford, the frontier is initially sparse, switches to dense after a few iterations and then switches back to sparse later. For connected components and PageRank-Delta, the frontier starts off as dense (the vertexSubset contains all vertices), and becomes sparser as the algorithm continues. See [4] for a more detailed analysis of frontier plots for BFS.

7. Conclusions

We have described Ligra, a simple framework for implementing graph traversal algorithms on shared-memory machines. Furthermore, our implementations of several graph algorithms using the framework are efficient and scalable, and often achieve better running times than ones reported by other graph libraries/systems. In addition to the algorithms discussed in this paper, we believe other algorithms such as maximum flow, biconnected components, belief propagation, and Markov clustering can also benefit from our framework. Currently, Ligra does not support algorithms based on modifying the input graph, and extending Ligra to support graph modification is a direction for future work. Recently, GPU systems have been explored for implementing graph traversal problems [20, 35]. It is possible that our framework can be extended to this context.

Acknowledgments. This work is partially supported by the National Science Foundation under grant number CCF-1018188, and by Intel Labs Academic Research Office for the Parallel Algorithms for Non-Numeric Computing Program.

References

[1] V. Agarwal, F. Petrini, D. Pasetto, and D. A. Bader. Scalable graph exploration on multicore processors. In *SC*, 2010.

[2] D. A. Bader, S. Kintali, K. Madduri, and M. Mihail. Approximating betweenness centrality. In *WAW*, 2007.

[3] S. Beamer, K. Asanović, and D. Patterson. Searching for a parent instead of fighting over children: A fast breadth-first search implementation for graph500. *Technical Report UCB/EECS-2011-117, EECS Department, University of California, Berkeley*, 2011.

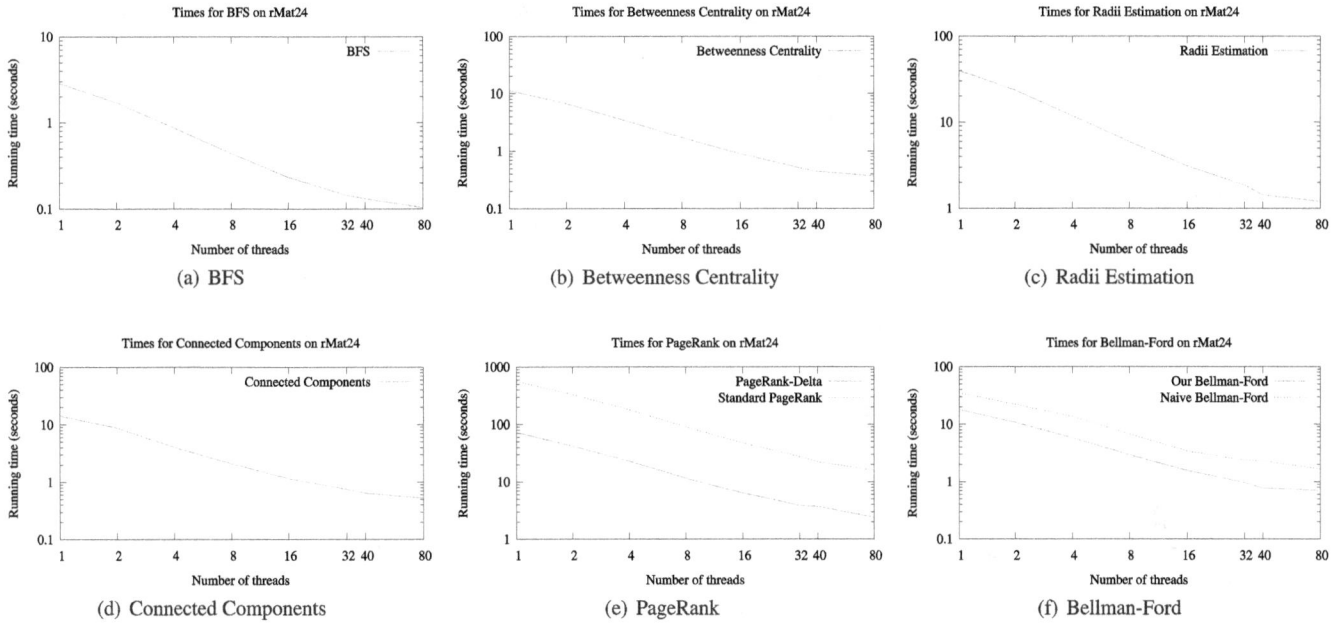

Figure 2. Log-log plots of running times on rMat24 on a 40-core machine (with hyper-threading).

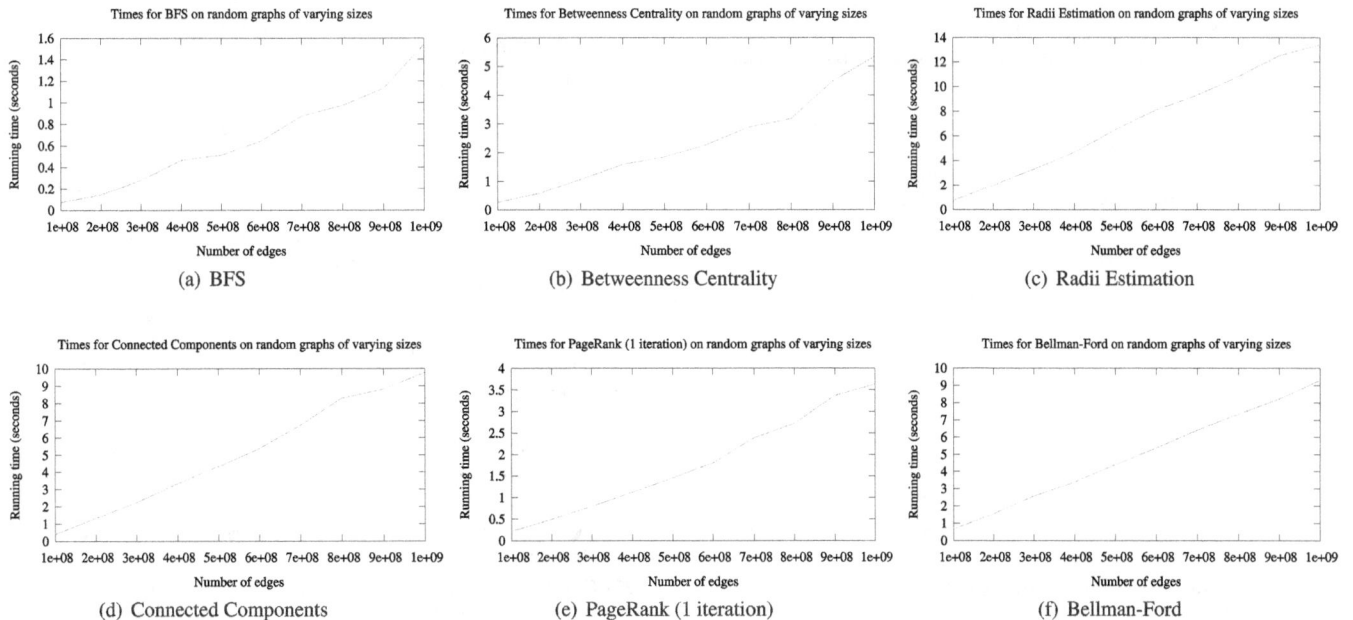

Figure 3. Plots of running times versus edge counts in random graphs on a 40-core machine (with hyper-threading).

[4] S. Beamer, K. Asanović, and D. Patterson. Direction-optimizing breadth-first search. In *SC*, 2012.

[5] J. Berry, B. Hendrickson, S. Kahan, and P. Konecny. Software and algorithms for graph queries on multithreaded architectures. In *In IPDPS*, 2007.

[6] U. Brandes. A faster algorithm for betweenness centrality. *Journal of Mathematical Sociology*, 25, 2001.

[7] S. Brin and L. Page. The anatomy of a large-scale hypertextual web search engine. In *WWW*, 1998.

[8] A. Buluç and J. R. Gilbert. The Combinatorial BLAS: Design, implementation, and applications. *The International Journal of High Performance Computing Applications*, 2011.

[9] D. Chakrabarti, Y. Zhan, and C. Faloutsos. R-MAT: A recursive model for graph mining. In *SDM*, 2004.

[10] E. Cohen. Size-estimation framework with applications to transitive closure and reachability. *J. Comput. Syst. Sci.*, 55, December 1997.

[11] T. H. Cormen, C. E. Leiserson, R. L. Rivest, and C. Stein. *Introduction to Algorithms (3. ed.)*. MIT Press, 2009.

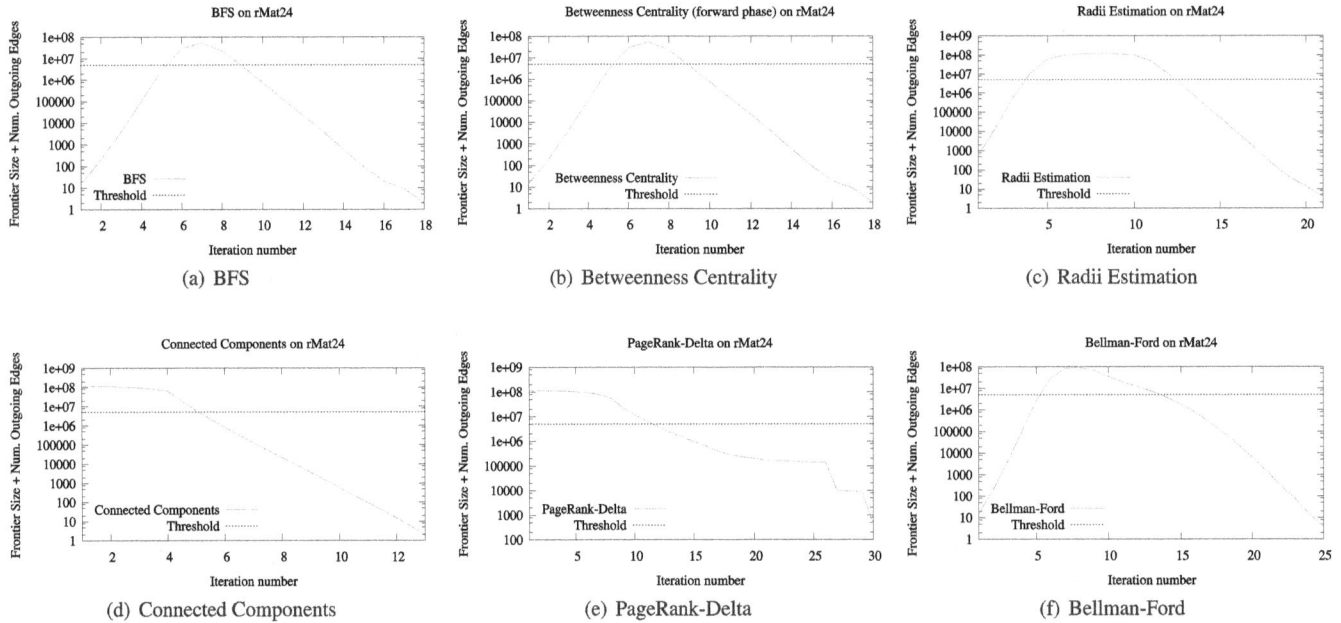

Figure 4. Plots of frontier size plus number of outgoing edges (y-axis in log scale) versus iteration number for rMat24.

[12] J.-A. Ferrez, K. Fukuda, and T. Liebling. Parallel computation of the diameter of a graph. In *HPCSA*, 1998.

[13] L. Freeman. A set of measures of centrality based upon betweenness. *Sociometry*, 1977.

[14] R. Geisberger, P. Sanders, and D. Schultes. Better approximation of betweenness centrality. In *ALENEX*, 2008.

[15] J. R. Gilbert, S. Reinhardt, and V. B. Shah. A unified framework for numerical and combinatorial computing. *Computing in Sciences and Engineering*, 10(2), Mar/Apr 2008.

[16] Giraph. "http://giraph.apache.org", 2012.

[17] J. Gonzalez, Y. Low, H. Gu, D. Bickson, and C. Guestrin. Power-Graph: Distributed graph-parallel computation on natural graphs. In *OSDI*, 2012.

[18] Graph500. "http://www.graph500.org", 2012.

[19] D. Gregor and A. Lumsdaine. The Parallel BGL: A generic library for distributed graph computations. In *POOSC*, 2005.

[20] S. Hong, T. Oguntebi, and K. Olukotun. Efficient parallel graph exploration on multi-core CPU and GPU. In *PACT*, 2011.

[21] S. Hong, H. Chafi, E. Sedlar, and K. Olukotun. Green-Marl: a DSL for easy and efficient graph analysis. In *ASPLOS*, 2012.

[22] J. Jaja. *Introduction to Parallel Algorithms*. Addison-Wesley Professional, 1992.

[23] U. Kang, C. E. Tsourakakis, A. P. Appel, C. Faloutsos, and J. Leskovec. Hadi: Mining radii of large graphs. In *TKDD*, 2011.

[24] U. Kang, C. E. Tsourakakis, and C. Faloutsos. PEGASUS: mining peta-scale graphs. *Knowl. Inf. Syst.*, 27(2), 2011.

[25] H. Kwak, C. Lee, H. Park, and S. Moon. What is Twitter, a social network or a news media? In *WWW*, 2010.

[26] A. Kyrola, G. Blelloch, and C. Guestrin. GraphChi: Large-scale graph computation on just a PC. In *OSDI*, 2012.

[27] C. E. Leiserson. The Cilk++ concurrency platform. *J. Supercomputing*, 51(3), 2010. Springer.

[28] C. E. Leiserson and T. B. Schardl. A work-efficient parallel breadth-first search algorithm (or how to cope with the nondeterminism of reducers). In *SPAA*, 2010.

[29] Y. Low, J. Gonzalez, A. Kyrola, D. Bickson, C. Guestrin, and J. M. Hellerstein. GraphLab: A new parallel framework for machine learning. In *Conference on Uncertainty in Artificial Intelligence*, 2010.

[30] Y. Low, J. Gonzalez, A. Kyrola, D. Bickson, C. Guestrin, and J. M. Hellerstein. Distributed GraphLab: A Framework for Machine Learning and Data Mining in the Cloud. *PVLDB*, 2012.

[31] A. Lugowski, D. Alber, A. Buluç, J. Gilbert, S. Reinhardt, Y. Teng, and A. Waranis. A flexible open-source toolbox for scalable complex graph analysis. In *SDM*, 2012.

[32] K. Madduri, D. A. Bader, J. W. Berry, and J. R. Crobak. An experimental study of a parallel shortest path algorithm for solving large-scale graph instances. In *ALENEX*, 2007.

[33] C. Magnien, M. Latapy, and M. Habib. Fast computation of empirically tight bounds for the diameter of massive graphs. *J. Exp. Algorithmics*, 13, February 2009.

[34] G. Malewicz, M. H. Austern, A. J. Bik, J. C. Dehnert, I. Horn, N. Leiser, and G. Czajkowski. Pregel: a system for large-scale graph processing. In *SIGMOD*, 2010.

[35] D. Merrill, M. Garland, and A. Grimshaw. Scalable GPU graph traversal. In *PPoPP*, 2012.

[36] U. Meyer and P. Sanders. Δ-stepping: a parallelizable shortest path algorithm. *J. Algorithms*, 49(1), 2003.

[37] C. R. Palmer, P. B. Gibbons, and C. Faloutsos. ANF: a fast and scalable tool for data mining in massive graphs. In *ACM SIGKDD*, 2002.

[38] K. Pingali, D. Nguyen, M. Kulkarni, M. Burtscher, M. A. Hassaan, R. Kaleem, T.-H. Lee, A. Lenharth, R. Manevich, M. Méndez-Lojo, D. Prountzos, and X. Sui. The tao of parallelism in algorithms. In *PLDI*, 2011.

[39] V. Prabhakaran, M. Wu, X. Weng, F. McSherry, L. Zhou, and M. Haridasan. Managing large graphs on multi-cores with graph awareness. In *USENIX ATC*, 2012.

[40] S. Salihoglu and J. Widom. GPS: A graph processing system. Technical Report InfoLab 1039, Stanford University, 2012.

[41] J. Shun, G. E. Blelloch, J. T. Fineman, P. B. Gibbons, A. Kyrola, H. V. Simhadri, and K. Tangwongsan. Brief announcement: the Problem Based Benchmark Suite. In *SPAA*, 2012.

[42] Yahoo! Altavista web page hyperlink connectivity graph, 2012. "http://webscope.sandbox.yahoo.com/catalog.php?datatype=g".

Morph Algorithms on GPUs

Rupesh Nasre[1]   Martin Burtscher[2]   Keshav Pingali[1,3]

[1]Inst. for Computational Engineering and Sciences, University of Texas at Austin, USA
[2] Dept. of Computer Science, Texas State University, San Marcos, USA
[3] Dept. of Computer Science, University of Texas at Austin, USA
nasre@ices.utexas.edu, burtscher@txstate.edu, pingali@cs.utexas.edu

Abstract

There is growing interest in using GPUs to accelerate graph algorithms such as breadth-first search, computing page-ranks, and finding shortest paths. However, these algorithms do not modify the graph structure, so their implementation is relatively easy compared to general graph algorithms like mesh generation and refinement, which *morph* the underlying graph in non-trivial ways by adding and removing nodes and edges. We know relatively little about how to implement morph algorithms efficiently on GPUs.

In this paper, we present and study four morph algorithms: (i) a computational geometry algorithm called Delaunay Mesh Refinement (DMR), (ii) an approximate SAT solver called Survey Propagation (SP), (iii) a compiler analysis called Points-to Analysis (PTA), and (iv) Boruvka's Minimum Spanning Tree algorithm (MST). Each of these algorithms modifies the graph data structure in different ways and thus poses interesting challenges.

We overcome these challenges using algorithmic and GPU-specific optimizations. We propose efficient techniques to perform concurrent subgraph addition, subgraph deletion, conflict detection and several optimizations to improve the scalability of morph algorithms. For an input mesh with 10 million triangles, our DMR code achieves an $80\times$ speedup over the highly optimized serial *Triangle* program and a $2.3\times$ speedup over a multicore implementation running with 48 threads. Our SP code is $3\times$ faster than a multicore implementation with 48 threads on an input with 1 million literals. The PTA implementation is able to analyze six SPEC 2000 benchmark programs in just 74 milliseconds, achieving a geometric mean speedup of $9.3\times$ over a 48-thread multicore version. Our MST code is slower than a multicore version with 48 threads for sparse graphs but significantly faster for denser graphs.

This work provides several insights into how other morph algorithms can be efficiently implemented on GPUs.

Categories and Subject Descriptors   D.1.3 [*Programming Techniques*]: Concurrent Programming—Parallel Programming

General Terms   Algorithms, Languages, Performance

Keywords   Morph Algorithms, Graph Algorithms, Irregular Programs, GPU, CUDA, Delaunay Mesh Refinement, Survey Propagation, Minimum Spanning Tree, Boruvka, Points-to Analysis

1. Introduction

Graphics Processing Units (GPUs) have been shown to be very useful in many application domains outside of graphics. GPU hardware is designed to process blocks of pixels at high speed and with wide parallelism, so it is well suited for executing regular algorithms that operate on dense vectors and matrices. We understand much less about how to use GPUs effectively to execute *irregular* algorithms that use dynamic data structures like graphs and trees. Harish and Narayanan [10] pioneered this field with their CUDA implementations of algorithms such as breadth-first search and single-source shortest paths. BFS has recently received much attention in the GPU community [9, 12, 17, 20]. Barnat *et al.* [3] implemented a GPU algorithm for finding strongly-connected components in directed graphs and showed that it achieves significant speedup with respect to Tarjan's sequential algorithm. Other irregular algorithms that have been successfully parallelized for GPUs are *n*-body simulations and dataflow analyses [5, 18, 25].

An important characteristic of most of the irregular GPU algorithms implemented to date is that they are graph analysis algorithms that do not modify the structure of the underlying graph [3, 10, 12, 17, 20]. When they do modify the graph structure, the modifications can be predicted statically and appropriate data structures can be pre-allocated [5, 25]. However, there are many important graph algorithms in which edges or nodes are dynamically added to or removed from the graph in an unpredictable fashion, such as mesh refinement [7] and compiler optimization [1]. Recently, Mendez-Lojo *et al.* described a GPU implementation of Andersen-style points-to analysis. In this algorithm, the number of edges strictly increases during the computation. However, we are unaware of a high-performance GPU implementation of an irregular graph algorithm that adds and removes nodes and edges. In TAO analysis [24] – an algorithmic classification for irregular codes – these are called *morph* algorithms. Implementation of a morph algorithm on a GPU is challenging because it is unclear how to support dynamically changing graphs while still achieving good performance.

In this paper, we describe efficient GPU implementations of four morph algorithms: (i) Delaunay Mesh Refinement (DMR) [7], which takes a triangulated mesh as input and modifies it in place by adding and removing triangles to produce a triangulated mesh satisfying certain geometric constraints; (ii) Survey Propagation (SP) [4], an approximate SAT solver that takes a *k*-SAT formula as input, constructs a bipartite factor graph over its literals and constraints, propagates probabilities along its edges, and occasionally deletes a node when its associated probability is close enough to 0 or 1; (iii) Points-to Analysis (PTA) [1], which takes a set of points-to constraints derived from a C program, creates a constraint graph whose nodes correspond to program variables and whose directed edges correspond to the flow of points-to information, and iteratively computes a fixed-point solution by propagating the points-to information and adding the corresponding edges; and (iv) Boruvka's Minimum Spanning Tree algorithm (MST), which operates on an undirected input graph and relies on the process of minimum edge contraction, which involves merging of the adjacency lists of the edge's endpoints, until an MST is formed. Each of these algorithms poses different and varying levels of challenges for a massively parallel architecture like a GPU, as we discuss next.

- In DMR, triangles are added and deleted on the fly, thus requiring careful attention to synchronization. Another challenge is memory allocation as the number of triangles added or deleted cannot be predicted *a priori*. Allocating storage statically may result in over-allocation whereas dynamic allocation incurs runtime overhead. Further, the amount of work tends to be different in different parts of the mesh, which may lead to work imbalance. During refinement, new bad triangles may be created, which can lead to an unpredictable work distribution.

- In SP, the situation is simpler as the number of nodes only decreases. Deletion of a node involves removal of a node and its edges. However, implementing subgraph deletion in a highly concurrent setting is costly due to synchronization overhead.

- Although the number of nodes is fixed in PTA (it is equal to the number of variables in the input program), the number of edges in the constraint graph increases monotonically and unpredictably. Therefore, we cannot use a statically allocated storage scheme to represent the dynamically growing graph.

- In MST, the adjacency lists of two nodes need to be merged during each edge contraction. While edge merging can be done explicitly in small graphs, it is too costly for large graphs, especially in the later iterations of the algorithm. Edge merging can also skew the work distribution.

We address these challenges by proposing several mechanisms that are novel in the context of irregular algorithms; many of them are applicable to the implementation of other morph and non-morph algorithms on GPUs. We contrast our approach with alternative ways of addressing these challenges. The contributions of this paper are as follows.

- Many morph algorithms have to deal with neighborhood conflicts. For efficient execution, the corresponding implementation needs to be cautious [19]. We propose a GPU-friendly mechanism for conflict detection and resolution.

- Addition and deletion of arbitrary subgraphs can be implemented in several ways. We present a qualitative comparison of different mechanisms and provide guidelines for choosing the best implementation.

- Neighborhood conflicts lead to aborted work, resulting in wasted parallelism. We propose an adaptive scheme for changing the kernel configuration to reduce the abort ratio, thus leading to improved work efficiency.

- Information can be propagated in a directed graph either in a *push* or a *pull* manner, *i.e.*, from a node to its outgoing neighbors or from the incoming neighbors to the node, respectively. We compare the two approaches and observe that a *pull* model usually results in reduced synchronization.

- The amount of parallelism present in morph algorithms often changes considerably during their execution. A naive work distribution can lead to load imbalance. We propose better ways to distribute tasks across threads, which improves system utilization and, in turn, performance.

- To avoid the bottleneck of a centralized worklist and to propagate information faster in a graph, we propose using local worklists, which can be efficiently implemented in shared memory.

- Our GPU codes, written in CUDA, outperform existing state-of-the-art multicore implementations. Our DMR code is faster than a 48-core CPU version of the same algorithm [16], achieving up to $2.3\times$ speedup. With respect to the highly optimized and widely-used sequential CPU implementation of the Triangle program [28], our implementation achieves up to $80\times$ speedup. Our SP code is $3\times$ and the PTA code is $9.3\times$ faster than their multicore counterparts. Our GPU implementation of MST is slower for sparse graphs (like road networks) but significantly faster for denser graphs (like RMAT).

The rest of this paper is organized as follows. We introduce Delaunay Mesh Refinement, Survey Propagation, Points-to Analysis and Boruvka's Minimum Spanning Tree algorithm and discuss the sources of parallelism in these algorithms in Sections 2 through 5. We describe our graph representation and its memory layout in Section 6. We discuss efficient implementations of morph algorithms in Section 7, where we explain generic techniques for subgraph addition and deletion, conflict detection and resolution, improving work efficiency, and using local worklists. The experimental evaluation comparing the performance of the GPU, multicore and sequential implementations is discussed in Section 8. We compare and contrast with related work in Section 9 and conclude in Section 10.

2. Delaunay Mesh Refinement

Mesh generation and refinement are important components of applications in many areas such as the numerical solution of partial differential equations and graphics.

DMR Algorithm The goal of mesh generation is to represent a surface or a volume as a tessellation composed of simple shapes like triangles, tetrahedra, *etc.* Although many types of meshes are in use, Delaunay meshes are particularly important since they have a number of desirable mathematical properties [7]. The Delaunay triangulation for a set of points in the plane is the triangulation such that none of the points lie inside the circumcircle of any triangle.

In practice, the Delaunay property alone is not sufficient, and it is necessary to impose quality constraints governing the shape and size of the triangles. For a given Delaunay mesh, this is accomplished by iterative mesh refinement, which successively fixes *bad* triangles (triangles that do not satisfy the quality constraints) by adding new points to the mesh and re-triangulating the affected areas. Figure 1 illustrates this process; the shaded triangle is assumed to be bad. To fix it, a new point is added at the circumcenter of this triangle. Adding this point may invalidate the empty circumcircle property for some neighboring triangles. Therefore, the affected triangles around the bad triangle are determined. This region is called the *cavity* of the bad triangle. The cavity is re-triangulated, as shown in Figure 1(c) (in this figure, all triangles lie in the cavity of the shaded bad triangle). Re-triangulating a cavity may generate new bad triangles, but the iterative refinement process will ultimately terminate and produce a guaranteed-quality mesh. Different orders of processing bad elements lead to different meshes, but all of them satisfy the quality constraints [7].

Amorphous data-parallelism in DMR The natural unit of work for parallel execution is the processing of a bad triangle. Because a cavity is usually just a small neighborhood of triangles around the bad triangle (typically 4 to 10 triangles), two bad triangles that are far apart in the mesh typically have cavities that do not overlap. Furthermore, the entire refinement process (expansion, retriangulation, and graph updating) for the two triangles is completely independent. Thus, the two triangles can be processed in parallel. This approach obviously extends to more than two triangles. However, if the cavities of two triangles do overlap, the triangles can

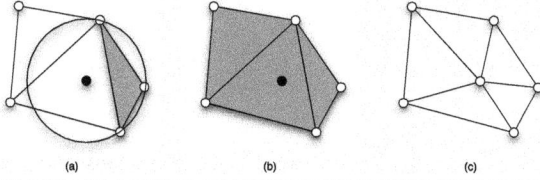

Figure 1. Refinement: Fixing a bad triangle by modifying its cavity. (a) A bad triangle (shaded) and its circumcircle indicating the overlapping triangles that form the cavity. (b) Cavity of the bad triangle and new point. (c) Refined cavity formed using the new point.

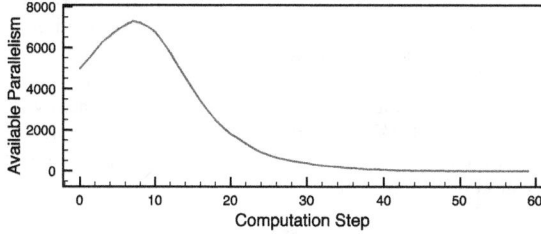

Figure 2. Parallelism profile of Delaunay Mesh Refinement

```
main():
  read input mesh                      // CPU
  transfer initial mesh                // CPU → GPU
  initialize_kernel()                  // GPU
  do {
    refine_kernel()                    // GPU
    transfer changed                   // GPU → CPU
  } while changed
  transfer refined mesh                // GPU → CPU

refine_kernel():
  foreach triangle t in my worklist {
    if t is bad and not deleted {
      create and expand cavity around t
      mark all triangles in the cavity with my thread id
      __global_sync()
      check and re-mark with priority    // Section 7.3
      __global_sync()
      if all cavity-triangles are marked with my thread id {
        create new cavity by retriangulating
        delete triangles in old cavity from mesh
        add triangles from new cavity to mesh
        if any new triangle is bad {
          changed = true
        }
      } else {                           // back-off
        changed = true
      }
    }
  } }
```

Figure 3. Pseudo code of our DMR implementation

be processed in either order but only one of them can be processed at a time. Whether or not two bad triangles have overlapping cavities depends entirely on the structure of the mesh, which changes throughout the execution of the algorithm. Figure 2 shows a parallelism profile for DMR produced by the ParaMeter tool [15]. The profile was obtained by running DMR on a randomly generated input mesh consisting of 100K triangles, half of which are initially bad. The amount of parallelism changes significantly during the execution of the algorithm, and this has an impact on how we implement DMR as we discuss in Section 7.4. Initially, there are about 5,000 bad triangles that can be processed in parallel. This number increases as the computation progresses, peaking at over 7,000 triangles, after which point the available parallelism drops slowly. The amount of parallelism is higher for larger inputs.

GPU Implementation The DMR algorithm we use on the GPU is slightly different from the multicore algorithm described above. The pseudo code of our implementation is shown in Figure 3. The comments indicate if the relevant code is executed on the CPU or the GPU, or whether it is a data transfer between the two devices.

The main program starts with the host code (on the CPU) reading an input mesh from a file. The mesh is initially stored in the CPU's memory and has to be transferred to the GPU via an explicit call to the cudaMemcpy() function. Then the GPU performs a few initialization steps. These include resetting the deletion flag of each triangle, identifying if a triangle is bad, and computing the neighborhood of each bad triangle. Next, the host code repeatedly invokes the refinement kernel, which re-triangulates the mesh. In each invocation, a thread operates on a bad undeleted triangle, creates a cavity around that triangle, re-triangulates the cavity, marks the triangles in the old cavity as deleted, and adds the new triangles to the mesh. If any of the new triangles are bad, the thread sets a flag *changed* to inform the host that another kernel invocation is necessary. Thus, the host code only stops invoking the GPU kernel once there are no more bad triangles to process. At this stage, the refined mesh is transferred back to the CPU using another call to cudaMemcpy(). We emphasize that all of the refinement code executes on the GPU. The CPU is responsible only for reading the input mesh, transferring it to the GPU, repeatedly invoking the GPU kernel, and transferring the refined mesh back.

Our approach is *topology-driven* [24], *i.e.,* threads process both good and bad triangles. In contrast to a *data-driven* approach [24], which processes only the bad triangles, a topology-driven approach may perform more work and threads may not have useful work to do at every step. However, a data-driven approach requires maintenance of a worklist that is accessed by all threads. A naive implementation of such a worklist severely limits performance because work elements must be added and removed atomically. Therefore, we use a topology-driven approach and add optimizations to improve work efficiency (*cf.* Section 7.4). Topology-driven approaches have also been used in GPU implementations of other algorithms [18].

3. Survey Propagation

Survey Propagation is a heuristic SAT solver based on Bayesian inference [4]. The algorithm represents a Boolean SAT formula as a *factor graph*, which is a bipartite graph with literals on one side and clauses on the other. An undirected edge connects a literal to a clause if the literal participates in the clause. The edge is given a value of -1 if the literal in the clause is negated, and +1 otherwise. The general strategy of SP is to iteratively update each literal with the likelihood that it should be assigned a truth value of *true* or *false*. The amorphous data-parallelism in this algorithm arises from the literals and clauses that need to be processed. Although there are no ordering constraints on processing the elements, different orders may lead to different behavior. An example 3-SAT formula and the corresponding factor graph are given in Figure 4.

SP has been shown to be quite effective for hard SAT instances [4]. For $K = 3$, *i.e.,* when the number of literals per clause is three, a SAT instance becomes hard when the clause-to-literal ratio is close to 4.2. We focus on hard SAT problems in this work.

SP Algorithm The SP algorithm proceeds as follows. Each phase of the algorithm first iterates over the clauses and the literals of the formula updating 'surveys' until all updates are below some small epsilon. Then, the surveys are processed to find the most biased literals, which are fixed to the appropriate value. The fixed literals are then removed from the graph. If only trivial surveys remain or

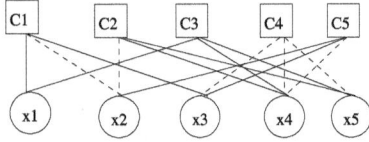

Figure 4. Factor graph of $(x_1 + \overline{x_2} + x_3)(\overline{x_2} + x_4 + x_5)(x_1 + x_4 + x_5)(\overline{x_3} + \overline{x_4} + \overline{x_5})(x_2 + x_3 + \overline{x_4})$. Dotted edges are negated.

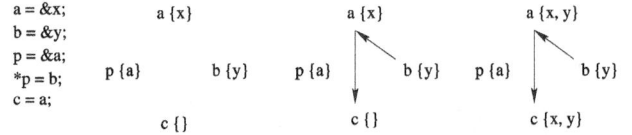

Figure 5. Points-to constraints and states of the constraint graph

the number of literals is small enough, the problem is passed on to a simpler solver. Otherwise, the algorithm starts over with the reduced graph as input. It performs as many such phases as are necessary until no more literals can be fixed. If there is no progress after some number of iterations, the algorithm gives up.

Amorphous data-parallelism in SP The active nodes are the literals in the factor graph. Initially every literal node is active. If the surveys on some edges change during processing, the nodes' neighbors' neighbors (*i.e.*, other literals in common clauses) become active. Thus, the neighborhood of each active node encompasses the neighbors and neighbors' neighbors.

Each iteration of SP touches a single node's neighborhood in the factor graph. Iterations conflict with one another if their neighborhoods overlap. The structure of the graph is mostly constant, except that nodes are removed occasionally when their values become stable (*i.e.*, biased towards 0 or 1). Thus, the available parallelism reflects the connectivity of the graph and remains roughly constant, dropping infrequently as nodes are removed from the graph. SP is a heuristic SAT solver, and it behaves non-deterministically.

GPU Implementation Our implementation of SP first generates a random SAT formula based on the input number of clauses and literals. After initialization, the surveys are propagated through the edges in the factor graph until the surveys stabilize or until a fixed number of iterations has been performed. Next, the literals are updated to reflect their bias towards their neighbors (the clauses) for satisfiability. If the kernel updates the bias of any literals, a process of decimation kicks in, which removes any literals whose bias is close to *true* or *false*. Once the biased literals have been removed, the reduced factor graph is processed again, continuing with the current state of the surveys and biases.

4. Points-to Analysis

Points-to analysis is a key static compiler analysis. We implement a variant of the flow-insensitive, context-insensitive, inclusion-based points-to analysis [1]. It works on the points-to constraints obtained from the input program's statements and computes a fixed-point points-to solution based on the constraints.

PTA Algorithm PTA operates on a constraint graph in which nodes correspond to pointers and each directed edge between two nodes represents a subset relationship between the points-to sets of the corresponding two pointers. In other words, the points-to information *flows* from the source to the target node along an edge. There are four kinds of constraints: address-of ($p = \&q$), copy ($p = q$), load ($p = *q$) and store ($*p = q$). The address-of constraints determine the initial points-to information in the constraint graph and the other three types of constraints add edges. The points-to information is then propagated along these edges until convergence. Due to the accumulation of new points-to information at some nodes, the load and the store constraints add more edges to the constraint graph and create additional opportunities for propagation. This process continues until a fixed-point is reached. The final points-to information is then available at the pointer nodes. An

example set of constraints and the state of the constraint graph in different stages of the algorithm are shown in Figure 5.

Amorphous data-parallelism in PTA PTA has been shown to exhibit a moderate amount of parallelism [18, 26]. Its source of parallelism is the optimistic propagation of points-to information along edges that do not have common nodes. Although the amorphous data-parallelism in PTA is input dependent, it usually increases gradually at first, remains high for some time and then slowly decreases (similar to DMR). Although conflicts can be handled using atomics, we employ a novel pull-based approach that avoids synchronization (*cf.* Section 6.4).

GPU Implementation Our PTA implementation first extracts points-to constraints from an input C/C++ program and transfers them to the GPU. The initialization kernel initializes each pointer with a 'null' points-to set. Processing of each constraint happens in two phases. In the first phase, the constraints are evaluated to determine their source and destination. In the second phase, the points-to information is actually updated/propagated. First, the address-of constraints are processed in this two-phase manner. Then, the remaining three kinds of constraints are also processed in a two-phase manner. In the first phase, the constraints add edges to the graph. In the second phase, the points-to information is propagated along these edges. This process repeats until a fixed-point is reached. Finally, the points-to information is copied to the CPU.

5. Boruvka's Minimum Spanning Tree Algorithm

Boruvka's algorithm computes a minimum spanning tree of an edge-weighted undirected graph (without self-loops) through successive applications of *edge contraction*. Edge contraction is a general operation on a graph in which an edge is chosen and the two end points of that edge are fused to form a new node that is connected to all nodes incident on either of the two original nodes.

MST Algorithm Boruvka's algorithm is an *unordered* algorithm [24]: if an edge (a, b) is the lightest edge connecting its end point a to its end point b, it can be contracted. This is in contrast to Kruskal's algorithm, which is an *ordered* algorithm in which edge contractions are performed in increasing weight order. For efficiency, our implementation of edge contraction does not literally merge the incident edges on the two nodes being fused; instead, we maintain groups of endpoints that form a partition over nodes. Only edges whose endpoints lie in distinct components are eligible for contraction. The number of partitions (which we call components) decreases and the partition sizes grow as edges are contracted. The algorithm stops when there is only one component left. The contracted edges form the MST of the original graph.

Amorphous data-parallelism in MST Initially, there is a lot of parallelism in Boruvka's minimum spanning tree algorithm as half the nodes can perform independent edge contractions. After each edge contraction, the graph becomes denser with fewer nodes, lowering the available parallelism. This is why many parallel MST implementations begin with Boruvka's algorithm but switch algorithms as the graph becomes dense.

150

GPU Implementation Initially, each node forms its own component in our MST implementation. Then, it repeatedly performs pseudo edge contractions. The process is divided into multiple kernels. The first kernel identifies the minimum edge of each node whose other endpoint is in another component. The second kernel isolates the minimum inter-component edge for each component. Since the sequence of the identified edges can form cycles over components (due to common edge weights), the third kernel finds the partner component with which each component needs to be merged to break these cycles. This is done by choosing the component with minimum ID as a cycle representative. All components in a cycle are then merged with the cycle representative in the fourth kernel. The process repeats until there is a single component. The inter-component minimum-weight edges are the MST.

6. Graph Representation on the GPU

We store the graphs in compressed sparse row (CSR) format. Thus, all edges are stored contiguously with the edges of a node stored together. Each graph node records a start offset into the edge array. This representation makes it easy to find a node's outgoing neighbors and improves locality since the edges of a node are stored together. By default, we store outgoing edges, but the same representation can be used to store incoming edges (*e.g.*, PTA). This representation assumes directed edges. For undirected graphs (*e.g.*, MST and SP), we store each edge twice, once for each direction.

6.1 Memory Layout Optimization

In many graph algorithms, computation 'flows' from a node to its neighbors. For instance, in DMR, the refinement process works by identifying a cavity around a bad triangle. Therefore, neighboring graph elements that are logically close to each other should also be close to each other in memory to improve spatial locality. We optimize the memory layout in this way by performing a scan over the nodes that swaps indices of neighboring nodes in the graph with those of neighboring nodes in memory. This optimization is similar in spirit to the data reordering approach by Zhang *et al.* [33].

6.2 Graph Specialization for DMR

We focus on 2D DMR, which operates on a triangulated mesh and modifies it in place to produce a refined triangulated mesh. Each triangle is represented by a set of three coordinates and each coordinate is simply an ordered pair <x, y>. The triangle vertices are stored in two associative arrays for the x and y coordinates, and the n triangles are stored in an n×3 matrix, where the three entries per line designate indices into the x and y coordinate arrays.

This simple representation is, in theory, sufficient for performing mesh refinement. However, for performance reasons, it is essential to also keep connectivity information with each triangle to accelerate the formation of a cavity, which requires the determination of the neighbors of a given triangle.

One possible representation for the neighbor information is a Boolean adjacency matrix in which an entry [i, j] is true if triangles i and j are adjacent to each other in the mesh. However, since meshes are very sparse, an adjacency matrix representation would waste a lot of space. As is well known, a more compact way of storing sparse graphs is using adjacency lists or sparse bit vectors. However, since we are dealing with a triangulated mesh, it is easy to see that each triangle can have at most three neighbors. Therefore, the neighborhood information of the n triangles can be represented by an n×3 matrix. Boundary triangles may have only one or two neighbors. We further record which edge is common between a triangle and its neighbor. Additionally, we maintain a flag with each triangle to denote if it is bad. Note that all of this information needs to be computed when a new triangle is added to the mesh during refinement.

6.3 Graph Specialization for SP

SP is based on a factor graph with two kinds of nodes: one for literals and one for clauses. We split the graph nodes into two arrays and store the clauses separately from the literals. This simplifies the processing since one kernel only works on clause nodes whereas two other kernels only work on literal nodes. Note that the edges connect both kinds of nodes.

Since the factor graph is undirected, surveys flow freely from clause nodes to literal nodes and vice versa. Therefore, it is essential to be able to easily find the neighbors of a type, given a node of the other type. To make neighbor enumeration efficient, we store mappings from each clause to all the literals it contains and from each literal to all the clauses it appears in. Fortunately, each clause has a small limit on the number of literals it can contain, which is the value of K in the K-SAT formula. As in DMR, this allows accessing literals in a clause using a direct offset calculation instead of first having to read the starting offset. Note, however, that this optimization is only possible for the clause-to-literal mapping. Since a literal may appear in an unpredictable number of clauses, the literal-to-clause mapping uses the standard CSR format.

6.4 Graph Specialization for PTA

In its iterative processing, PTA operates in two synchronized phases: one to add new directed edges between nodes and another to propagate information along the edges. There are two ways to manage propagation: *push*-based and *pull*-based. In a push-based method, a node propagates points-to information from itself to its outgoing neighbors, whereas in a pull-based method, a node pulls points-to information to itself from its incoming neighbors. The advantage of a pull-based approach is that, since only one thread is processing each node, no synchronization is needed to update the points-to information. Although some other thread may be reading the points-to information, due to the monotonicity of flow-insensitive points-to analysis (*i.e.*, new edges may be added but no edges are deleted), it is okay to read potentially stale points-to information as long as the up-to-date information is eventually also read [26]. In contrast, in a push-based approach, multiple threads may simultaneously propagate information to the same node and, in general, need to use synchronization.

To implement a pull-based approach, each node keeps a list of its incoming neighbors. Unfortunately, since the number of edges is not fixed, we cannot rely on a single static list of incoming edges but need to maintain a separate list for each node to allow for dynamic growth (*cf.* Section 7.1).

6.5 Graph Specialization for MST

The MST algorithm repeatedly merges components (disjoint sets of nodes) until a single component remains. Conceptually, these components are similar to the clauses in SP. Thus, our MST implementation also maintains a many-to-one (nodes-to-component) mapping and a one-to-many (component-to-nodes) mapping. The key differences are that a literal may be part of multiple clauses in SP whereas a node is part of only a single component in MST, which simplifies the implementation. However, in SP, the number of literals in a clause is bounded by K (a small number) whereas in MST the size of a component can change in each iteration. These changes require dynamic updates to the two mappings, which complicate the MST implementation.

7. Accelerating Morph Algorithms on GPUs

Many morph algorithms involve common operations and depend upon efficient strategies to implement these operations. Such strategies often work across a range of algorithms and can be tailored to special needs. We now discuss several techniques for different scenarios we encountered while implementing our morph algorithms.

7.1 Subgraph Addition

Addition of a subgraph is a basic operation in graph algorithms that increases the number of graph elements. For instance, in DMR, the number of triangles in the mesh increases, in PTA, the number of edges increases, and in MST, the number of nodes in a component increases. Subgraph addition can be performed in various ways.

Pre-allocation If the maximum size of the final graph is bound by a reasonably small factor of the original graph size, one may simply choose to pre-allocate the maximum amount of memory required. For instance, a PTA implementation may choose to pre-allocate memory for all the address-taken variables in the input constraints for each pointer to avoid allocating on the fly. Pre-allocation often results in a simpler implementation and higher performance. However, due to wasted space, the implementation may quickly run out of memory for larger inputs. MST is a special case: the components are graphs without edges (*i.e.,* sets) and, although the component sizes grow, the sum of the nodes in all components is constant. Therefore, the newly formed components can be handled by reshuffling the nodes in an array.

Host-Only Another way of identifying additional memory requirements is by pre-calculation, where the host code performs some computation to determine the amount of memory that will be needed in the next kernel. It then either allocates the additional storage (using cudaMalloc()) or re-allocates the existing plus additional storage. For example, in each iteration of DMR, our host code pre-calculates the maximum number of new triangles that can be added by the next kernel invocation depending upon the current number of bad triangles in the mesh and performs the corresponding memory reallocation. Although reallocation can be costly due to memory copying, by choosing an appropriate over-allocation factor, the number of reallocations can be greatly reduced. Similarly, in PTA, the host code can compute the additional number of points-to facts to be propagated in the next iteration and allocate additional storage accordingly.

Kernel-Host An alternative to host-side pre-calculation is to calculate the future memory requirement in the kernel itself and inform the host about it. The host can then either allocate additional storage or perform a re-allocation. The advantage of Kernel-Host over Host-Only is that the computation of the amount of memory needed may be able to piggyback on the main kernel processing.

Kernel-Only The most complicated way of dealing with subgraph addition is to allocate memory in the kernel itself. CUDA 2.x devices support mallocs in kernel code with semantics similar to CPU heaps. Thus, a malloced region can span kernel invocations, can be pointed to by pointers from different threads, *etc.* We employ this strategy in PTA to allocate storage for the incoming edges of a node. Each node maintains a linked list of chunks of incoming neighbors. Each chunk contains several nodes. The best chunk size is input dependent and, in our experiments, varies between 512 and 4096. Chunking reduces the frequency of memory allocation at the cost of some internal fragmentation. To enable efficient lookups, we sort the nodes in the chunks by ID.

Clearly, the best way to perform subgraph addition is application-dependent. Pre-allocation usually performs better but can suffer from over-allocation. The host-only approach is suitable when it is relatively easy for the host to compute the additional memory requirement, which may not be the case because the data often only reside on the device. If the calculation of the additional memory requires a non-trivial computation based on the current state of the graph, a kernel-host approach is probably preferable.

The host-only and kernel-host strategies should be used when memory allocation is global with respect to the graph, as is the case for DMR. The kernel-only approach is well-suited when memory allocation is local to a part of the graph. For instance, PTA may require additional memory for individual pointer nodes.

7.2 Subgraph Deletion

Marking If a morph algorithm operates mostly on a fixed graph where nodes and edges are only deleted occasionally, it may be best to simply mark the corresponding nodes and edges as deleted. We employ this strategy in SP since the decimation process is called infrequently. The marking approach is simple to implement, reduces synchronization bugs, and usually performs well as long as only a small fraction of the entire graph is deleted.

Explicit Deletion When an application performs both deletions and additions of subgraphs, simple marking may rapidly increase the unused space. In such codes, explicit freeing of the deleted memory may be necessary (*e.g.,* using free or cudaFree) to ensure that the deleted memory can be reused for graph additions. This approach is particularly suitable for local deletions. Otherwise, the implementation may have to compact the storage to obtain a contiguous data layout, resulting in high overheads.

Recycle An implementation may also choose to manage its own memory. It can then reuse the deleted memory of a subgraph for storing a newly created subgraph. This strategy works well if the memory layout is such that the new data fit within the memory of the old data. We use this strategy in DMR. Memory recycling offers a useful tradeoff between memory-compaction overhead and the cost of allocating additional storage.

There is no single best subgraph addition and deletion strategy; the choice should be guided by the application and the scale of the underlying problem. However, the above classification of these well-known techniques can help a morph-algorithm implementer select an appropriate strategy.

7.3 Probabilistic 3-Phase Conflict Resolution

Activities that require disjoint neighborhoods necessitate conflict resolution mechanisms across threads. One way to deal with conflicts is using mutual exclusion (implemented with atomic instructions), but this approach is ill-suited for GPUs due to the large number of threads. Therefore, we have developed an efficient 3-phase strategy to detect and resolve conflicts (*cf.* Figure 3). We explain it in the context of DMR, but it is generally applicable.

We exploit the parallelism in DMR by optimistically assuming that cavities around bad triangles do not overlap. When this assumption is valid, multiple bad triangles can be processed and refined in parallel. However, this strategy requires a mechanism to check for conflicts between threads and for resolving them.

Conflict checking A naive way to check for conflicts (*i.e.,* cavity overlap) is to use the two-phase procedure *race-and-check*. In the *race* phase, each thread marks the triangles in the cavity that it wants to refine, and in the *check* phase, the thread checks if its markings still exist. If all markings of thread t_1 exist, t_1 can go ahead and refine the cavity. Otherwise, some other thread t_2 has succeeded in marking (part of) the cavity and t_1 must back off. For correct execution, it is essential that the *race* phase of all threads finishes before the *check* phase of any thread starts. This requires a global barrier between the two phases.

Barrier implementation Current GPU architectures do not directly support global barriers in hardware, so barriers need to be implemented in user code. One way to implement a global barrier inside a kernel is using atomic operations on a global variable. Each thread atomically decrements the variable, initially set to the number of threads, and then spins on the variable until it reaches zero. Unfortunately, this method is particularly inefficient on GPUs because of the large number of threads, because atomic operations are significantly slower than non-atomic accesses [29], and because of the high memory bandwidth requirement of the spinning code.

A better way of implementing a global barrier is to use a hierarchical approach in which threads inside a block synchronize using the __syncthreads() primitive and block representatives (*e.g.*, threads 0) synchronize using atomic operations on a global variable. The hierarchical barrier significantly improves performance over the naive barrier implementation.

Xiao and Feng developed an even more efficient global barrier that does not require atomic operations [31]. However, their code was developed for pre-Fermi GPUs, which do not have caches, so writes to global variables directly update the global memory. Fermi GPUs have incoherent L1 caches and a coherent L2 cache, which may optimize global writes by not writing them through to global memory. Therefore, Xiao and Feng's barrier code needs to be augmented with explicit __threadfence() calls after writes to global memory to make the writes visible to all threads.

Avoiding live-lock Assuming conflict detection is implemented using a marking scheme coupled with a global barrier, the detected conflicts still need to be resolved. This can easily be achieved by backing off conflicting transactions. Thus, if the cavities created by two or more threads overlap, all affected threads back off, which guarantees conflict-free refinement but may result in live-lock.

One way to address live-lock is by reducing the number of threads, thereby reducing the probability of conflicts. However, avoiding live-lock cannot be guaranteed unless only one thread is running. Thus, when live-lock is detected, *i.e.*, when no bad triangle is refined during a kernel invocation, the next iteration can be invoked with just a single thread to process the current bad triangles serially. The following kernel invocation can resume parallel execution. However, running a single-threaded GPU kernel to avoid conflicts is an inefficient way of addressing this issue.

A better solution is to avoid live-lock with high probability by prioritizing the threads, *e.g.*, using their thread IDs. A thread with a higher ID gets priority over another thread with a lower ID. This approach changes the two-phase *race-and-check* procedure into *race-and-prioritycheck*. The *race* phase works as before, *i.e.*, each thread marks the triangles in its cavity with its thread ID. In the *prioritycheck* phase, thread t_i checks the marking t_m on each triangle in its cavity and uses the following priority check.

1. if $t_i == t_m$ then t_i owns the triangle and can process the cavity if the remaining triangles in the cavity are also owned by t_i.

2. if $t_i < t_m$ then t_m has priority and t_i backs off.

3. if $t_i > t_m$ then t_i has priority and t_i changes the marking on the triangle to its thread ID.

Note that it is not necessary for a thread to remove its markings when it backs off. Whereas the above modification greatly alleviates the probability of live-lock, it introduces another. Two threads may process overlapping cavities simultaneously due to a race in the *prioritycheck* phase. The following scenario illustrates the issue. Two cavities that share a triangle are processed by threads t_i and t_j. Let $t_i > t_j$. In the *race* phase, both threads mark the common triangle. Let the lower priority thread t_j write its ID last. Thus, the common triangle is marked by t_j at the end of the *race* phase. After the global synchronization, both threads check if they own all the triangles in their cavities. Let thread t_j check the marking of the common triangle first. It finds the triangle marked with its ID. Assuming that it also owns all the remaining triangles, t_j is ready to process its cavity. Now the higher priority thread t_i starts its *priori-*

tycheck phase and finds that the common triangle has been marked by a lower priority thread. Therefore, t_i changes the marking to its own ID. Assuming that it owns the remaining triangles, t_i is also ready to process its cavity. Thus, both threads start processing their cavities even though they overlap with one another.

The race condition occurs due to unsynchronized reads and writes of IDs in the *prioritycheck* phase. It can be avoided by adding a third phase. Thus, the two-phase *race-and-prioritycheck* mechanism becomes the three-phase *race-prioritycheck-check* procedure. In the third phase, each thread checks if its markings from the previous two phases still exist. If a thread owns all the triangles in its cavity, it is ready to process the cavity, otherwise it backs off. Because the *check* phase is read-only, the race condition mentioned above does not arise, thus guaranteeing correct conflict detection. As long as overlaps involve only two cavities, this approach is also guaranteed to avoid live-lock. However, with three or more overlapping cavities, it is possible that all conflicting threads abort due to a race in step 3 of the *prioritycheck* phase. To handle this rare instance, one thread may be allowed to continue either in the same kernel invocation or as a separate kernel launch.

7.4 Adaptive Parallelism

In some morph algorithms, the degree of parallelism changes considerably during execution. For example, Figure 2 shows that the amount of parallelism in DMR increases at first and then gradually decreases. Boruvka's MST algorithm exhibits high parallelism initially, but the parallelism drops quickly. To be able to track the amount of parallelism at different stages of an algorithm, we employ an adaptive scheme rather than fixed kernel configurations.

For DMR and PTA, we double the number of threads per block in every iteration (starting from an initial value of 64 and 128, respectively) for the first three iterations. This improves the work efficiency as well as the overall performance (by 14% and 17%). In SP, the number of threads per block is fixed at 1024 because the graph size mostly remains constant.

The number of thread blocks is set once per program run for all kernel invocations. It is proportional to the input size. Depending upon the algorithm and the input, we use a value between $3 \times SM$ and $50 \times SM$, where SM is the number of streaming multiprocessors in the GPU. Note that these are manually tuned parameters.

7.5 Local Worklists

For large inputs, performance increases when each thread processes more than one graph element per iteration (bad triangles in DMR, pointer nodes in PTA, clause nodes in SP, and components in MST). However, due to the large number of threads, it is inefficient to obtain these graph elements from a centralized work queue. Hence, we use a local work queue per thread.

In local queues, work items can be dequeued and newly generated work enqueued without synchronization, which improves performance. Local work queues can be implemented by partitioning the graph elements into equal-sized chunks and assigning each chunk to a thread. It is often possible to store the local work queues in the fast shared memory of GPUs. Due to the memory layout optimization discussed in Section 6.1, neighboring graph elements tend to be near one another in memory. Thus, when assigning a range of consecutive triangles to a thread in DMR, the cavity of a bad triangle has a good chance of falling entirely into this range, which reduces conflicts. Intuitively, the combination of the memory layout optimization and the local work queues forms a pseudo-partitioning of the graph that helps reduce conflicts and boosts performance.

7.6 Reducing Thread Divergence

To minimize thread divergence in DMR, we try to ensure that all threads in a warp perform roughly the same amount of work by

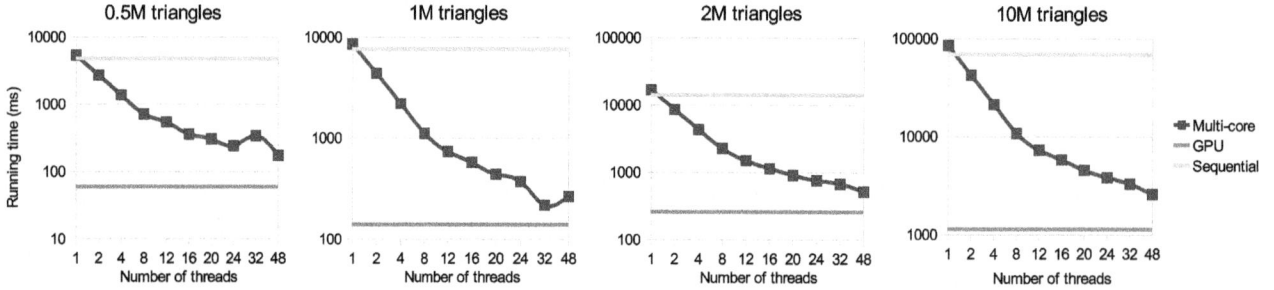

Figure 6. DMR runtime of the GPU, sequential CPU (Triangle), and multicore CPU (Galois) codes for different inputs

Triangles		Speedup	
Total $\times 10^6$	Bad $\times 10^6$	Galois-48	GPU
0.5	0.26	27.6	80.5
1	0.48	28.6	54.6
2	0.95	27.2	54.8
10	4.75	26.5	60.6

Figure 7. Speedup obtained using multicore (Galois) and GPU implementations of DMR over the sequential version (Triangle)

	Optimization	Time (ms)
1	Topology-driven with mesh-partitioning	68,000
2	3-phase marking	10,000
3	2 + Atomic-free global barrier	6,360
4	3 + Optimized memory layout	5,380
5	4 + Adaptive parallelism	2,200
6	5 + Reduced thread-divergence	2,020
7	6 + Single-precision arithmetic	1,020
8	7 + On-demand memory allocation	1,140

Figure 8. Effect of optimizations on the running time of DMR using an input mesh with 10 million triangles

moving the bad triangles to one side of the triangle array and the good triangles to the other side. This way, the threads in each warp (except one) will either all process bad triangles or not process any triangles. Note that this distribution is not perfect since the amount of work depends upon the cavity size. Nevertheless, the sorting assigns roughly equal amounts of work to each warp-thread. We perform sorting at the thread-block level in each iteration. In PTA, we similarly move all pointer nodes with enabled incoming edges to one side of the array. An edge is enabled if the points-to information of its source has changed, thus requiring its destination to be processed. Since each clause node is connected to a fixed number of literal nodes in SP, the work distribution is largely uniform even without sorting. There is also no sorting in MST.

8. Experimental Evaluation

We evaluate the performance of our CUDA implementations on a 1.15 GHz NVIDIA Tesla C2070 GPU with 14 SMs (448 processing elements, *i.e.,* CUDA cores) and 6 GB of main memory. This Fermi GPU has a 64 KB L1 cache per SM. We dedicate 48 KB to shared memory (user-managed cache) and 16 KB to the hardware-managed cache. The SMs share an L2 cache of 768 KB. We compiled the code with *nvcc* v4.1 RC2 using the *-arch=sm_20* flag.

To execute the CPU codes, we used a Nehalem-based Intel Xeon E7540 running Ubuntu 10 with 8 hex-core 2 GHz processors. The 48 CPU cores share 128 GB of main memory. Each core has two 32 KB L1 caches and a 256 KB L2 cache. Each processor has a 18 MB L3 cache that is shared among its six cores.

8.1 Delaunay Mesh Refinement

We compare the GPU DMR performance to two CPU implementations: the sequential Triangle program [28] and the multicore Galois version 2.1.4 [16].

The input meshes are randomly generated. We use the quality constraint that no triangle can have an angle of less than 30 degrees. The mesh sizes range from 0.5 million to 10 million triangles, and roughly half of the initial triangles are bad.

The relative performance of the three implementations for four different inputs is depicted in Figure 6. The x-axes show the number of threads used in the multicore version and the y-axes give the

running time in milliseconds on a logarithmic scale. The two horizontal flat lines correspond to the sequential and the GPU runtime. The reported GPU runtime is for the execution of the do-while loop in Figure 3. Similarly, we only report the mesh-refinement runtime for the sequential and multicore codes.

It is evident that our GPU implementation is significantly faster than the serial and multicore codes are. It takes the GPU 1.14 seconds to refine the largest mesh consisting of 10 million triangles, out of which 4.7 million triangles are initially bad.

The speedups of the multicore and GPU implementations over the sequential implementation are shown in Figure 7. The multicore version running with 48 threads achieves a speedup between 26.5 and 28.6 on our data sets. The GPU version is 2× to 4× faster and achieves a speedup between 54.6 and 80.5 over the sequential code. Figure 8 shows the effect of individual optimizations on DMR.

8.2 Survey Propagation

Figure 9 shows the SP runtimes for $K = 3$ and a clause-to-literal ratio of 4.2 (*i.e.,* hard SAT problems). The number of literals ranges from 1 million to 4 million. The GPU code is almost 3× faster than the 48-thread Galois code.

Both codes implement the same algorithm with one exception. The GPU code caches computations along the edges to avoid some repeated graph traversals. The importance of this optimization is more pronounced for larger K, as Figure 9 shows. Note that the hard SAT ratios differ (we obtained them from Mertens *et al.* [21]). The multicore version does not scale with the problem size and requires hours to complete. In contrast, the GPU version scales linearly and successfully completes within a few minutes.

8.3 Points-to Analysis

The PTA runtimes on six SPEC 2000 inputs are shown in Figure 10. The CPU codes perform optimizations like online cycle elimination and topological sort that are not included in our GPU code. Yet, the GPU implementation is 1.9 to 34.7 times faster. Major performance gains are obtained by separating the phases for constraint evalua-

M $\times 10^6$	N $\times 10^6$	K	Time (s) Galois-48	GPU
4.2	1	3	108	35
8.4	2	3	230	73
12.6	3	3	336	117
16.8	4	3	445	157
4.2	1	3	108	35
9.9	1	4	3,033	85
21.1	1	5	40,832	178
43.4	1	6	*OOT*	368

Figure 9. Performance of Survey Propagation

Benchmark	Vars	Cons	Time (ms) Serial	Galois-48	GPU
186.crafty	6,126	6,768	595	86	44.4
164.gzip	1,595	1,773	456	73	7.1
256.bzip2	1,147	1,081	396	94	2.7
181.mcf	1,230	1,509	382	59	8.7
183.equake	1,317	1,279	436	49	3.3
179.art	586	603	485	72	7.4

Figure 10. Performance of Points-to Analysis

tion and propagation and by transforming the code from a push- to a pull-based approach to avoid costly synchronization.

8.4 Boruvka's Minimum Spanning Tree

We evaluate the GPU and multicore Galois MST codes on a range of graphs as shown in Figure 11. The graphs other than the road networks are randomly generated. The Galois version 2.1.4 implements edge contraction by explicitly merging adjacency lists. The GPU code implements it using components as discussed above. Note that we run the multicore MST version with up to 48 threads and report the runtime for the best-performing number of threads.

For road networks and grids, the multicore code achieves up to 7.0 million edges/sec and generally outperforms our GPU code, which only reaches up to 2.5 million edges/sec. For the RMAT and random graphs, however, the multicore rate drops to 0.014 million edges/sec, whereas the GPU achieves 0.85 million edges/sec, greatly outperforming the CPUs. This behavior is due to differing graph densities that affect the edge-contraction performance. Road networks and grids are relatively sparse, *i.e.,* have small degrees, whereas the RMAT and random graphs are denser. The cost of merging adjacency lists in the Galois version is directly proportional to the node degrees. Therefore, denser graphs are processed more slowly. Moreover, the cost increases for later iterations as the graph becomes smaller and denser. In contrast, the GPU implementation maintains the original adjacency list for each node and performs edge traversals per node. The cost of merging increases with the number of nodes rather than with the number of edges because each component only contains nodes, and component merging requires node merging rather than edge merging.

Based on this observation, we modified the Galois implementation (in version 2.1.5) to also use a component-based approach. Additionally, the new multicore code incorporates a fast union-find data structure that maintains groups of nodes, keeps the graph unmodified, and employs a bulk-synchronous executor. The resulting CPU code is much faster and, in fact, outperforms the GPU code. It would be interesting to see whether including these optimizations in the GPU code would result in a similar performance boost.

9. Related Work

There are many implementations of parallel graph algorithms on a variety of architectures, including distributed-memory supercomputers [32], shared-memory supercomputers [2], and multicore machines [16]. DMR in particular has been extensively studied in sequential [8], multicore [6] and distributed-memory settings [14].

Irregular programs have only recently been parallelized for GPUs. Harish and Narayanan [10] describe CUDA implementations of graph algorithms such as BFS and single-source shortest paths computation. BFS has received significant attention [9, 12, 17, 20]. In these algorithms, the structure of the graph remains unchanged, simplifying the implementation. Hong *et al.* [11] propose a warp-centric approach for implementing BFS, which is related to

our solution for distributing work among threads. Vineet *et al.* [30] and Nobari *et al.* [23] propose computing the minimum spanning tree and forest, respectively, on GPUs. Both implementations use statically allocated memory.

There are relatively few GPU implementations of *morph* algorithms. Burtscher and Pingali [5] describe an implementation of an *n*-body simulation (Barnes Hut algorithm) based on unbalanced octrees. Whereas tree building is a morph operation, the vast majority of the runtime is spent in the force calculation, which does not modify the octree. Prabhu *et al.* [25] describe a GPU implementation of a 0-CFA analysis and Mendez-Lojo *et al.* [18] implemented an Andersen-style points-to analysis on the GPU. In these two algorithms, the number of nodes in the graph is invariant, and the number of edges grows monotonically until a fixed-point is reached. Our work deals with more general morph algorithms.

Our conflict-detection scheme has some similarity to the coloring heuristic of Jones *et al.* [13]. However, their distributed memory algorithm involves no aborting threads; hence, there is no issue with live-lock. Delaunay triangulation (not refinement) has been studied by several researchers [27]. A refinement algorithm based on edge-flipping has been proposed by Navarro *et al.* [22]. Although it is a morph algorithm, it does not exhibit the same challenges because the number of nodes and edges in the mesh do not change during execution. Instead, edges are flipped to obtain a better triangulation.

To the best of our knowledge, ours is the first paper on general morph algorithms for GPUs that describes efficient arbitrary subgraph addition and deletion and provides general techniques for implementing other morph algorithms.

10. Conclusions

Using a GPU to accelerate morph algorithms is very challenging. In this paper, we describe various aspects of efficiently implementing such algorithms on GPUs and discuss techniques for subgraph addition and deletion, conflict detection and resolution, and improving load distribution and work efficiency. We illustrate our techniques on efficient GPU implementations of four graph algorithms that modify the underlying graph in different ways: Delaunay Mesh Refinement, Survey Propagation, Points-to Analysis, and Boruvka's MST algorithm. We evaluate the effectiveness of our implementations on a range of inputs and show that our techniques lead to large speedups compared to multicore and sequential versions of these algorithms. We hope that this work proves useful for other GPU implementations of general morph algorithms.

Acknowledgments

This work was supported by NSF grants 0833162, 1062335, 1111766, 1141022, 1216701, 1217231 and 1218568 as well as gifts from NVIDIA, IBM, Intel and Qualcomm Corporations.

References

[1] L. O. Andersen. *Program Analysis and Specialization for the C Programming Language*. PhD thesis, DIKU, University of Copenhagen,

Graph	N $\times 10^6$	M $\times 10^6$	Time (s) Galois v2.1.4	Galois v2.1.5	GPU
USA	23.9	57.7	8.2	3.0	35.8
W	6.3	15.1	2.3	0.8	9.5
RMAT20	1.0	8.3	1,393.6	0.4	26.8
Random4-20	1.0	4.0	281.9	0.4	4.7
grid-2d-24	16.8	33.6	14.3	5.0	71.8
grid-2d-20	1.0	2.0	0.7	0.2	0.9

Figure 11. Performance of Boruvka's MST Algorithm. Time shown for Galois is the best time obtained with up to 48 threads.

May 1994. (DIKU report 94/19).

[2] David A. Bader and Kamesh Madduri. Designing multithreaded algorithms for breadth-first search and st-connectivity on the cray mta-2. In *Proceedings of the 2006 International Conference on Parallel Processing*, ICPP '06, pages 523–530, Washington, DC, USA, 2006. IEEE Computer Society.

[3] J. Barnat, P. Bauch, L. Brim, and M. Češka. Computing Strongly Connected Components in Parallel on CUDA. In *Proceedings of the 25th IEEE International Parallel & Distributed Processing Symposium (IPDPS'11)*, pages 541–552. IEEE Computer Society, 2011.

[4] A. Braunstein, M. Mèzard, and R. Zecchina. Survey propagation: An algorithm for satisfiability. *Random Structures and Algorithms*, 27(2):201–226, 2005.

[5] Martin Burtscher and Keshav Pingali. An efficient CUDA implementation of the tree-based barnes hut n-body algorithm. In *GPU Computing Gems Emerald Edition*, pages 75–92. Morgan Kaufmann, 2011.

[6] Andrey N. Chernikov and Nikos P. Chrisochoides. Three-dimensional delaunay refinement for multi-core processors. In *Proceedings of the 22nd annual international conference on Supercomputing*, ICS '08, pages 214–224, New York, NY, USA, 2008. ACM.

[7] L. Paul Chew. Guaranteed-quality mesh generation for curved surfaces. In *Proc. Symp. on Computational Geometry (SCG)*, 1993.

[8] Panagiotis A. Foteinos, Andrey N. Chernikov, and Nikos P. Chrisochoides. Fully generalized two-dimensional constrained delaunay mesh refinement. *SIAM J. Sci. Comput.*, 32(5):2659–2686, 2010.

[9] Abdullah Gharaibeh, Lauro Beltro Costa, Elizeu Santos-Neto, and Matei Ripeanu. A yoke of oxen and a thousand chickens for heavy lifting graph processing. In *The 21st International Conference on Parallel Architectures and Compilation Techniques*, PACT '12, 2012.

[10] Pawan Harish and P. J. Narayanan. Accelerating large graph algorithms on the gpu using cuda. In *HiPC'07: Proceedings of the 14th international conference on High performance computing*, pages 197–208, Berlin, Heidelberg, 2007. Springer-Verlag.

[11] Sungpack Hong, Sang Kyun Kim, Tayo Oguntebi, and Kunle Olukotun. Accelerating cuda graph algorithms at maximum warp. In *Proceedings of the 16th ACM symposium on Principles and practice of parallel programming*, PPoPP '11, pages 267–276, New York, NY, USA, 2011. ACM.

[12] Sungpack Hong, Tayo Oguntebi, and Kunle Olukotun. Efficient parallel graph exploration on multi-core cpu and gpu. In *20th International Conference on Parallel Architectures and Compilation Techniques*, PACT'11, 2011.

[13] Mark T. Jones and Paul E. Plassmann. A parallel graph coloring heuristic. *SIAM J. Sci. Comput.*, 14(3):654–669, May 1993.

[14] Andriy Kot, Andrey Chernikov, and Nikos Chrisochoides. Effective out-of-core parallel delaunay mesh refinement using off-the-shelf software. In *Proceedings of the 20th international conference on Parallel and distributed processing*, IPDPS'06, pages 125–125, Washington, DC, USA, 2006. IEEE Computer Society.

[15] Milind Kulkarni, Martin Burtscher, Rajasekhar Inkulu, Keshav Pingali, and Calin Casçaval. How much parallelism is there in irregular applications? In *Proc. Symp. on Principles and practice of parallel programming (PPoPP)*, pages 3–14, New York, NY, USA, 2009.

[16] Milind Kulkarni, Keshav Pingali, Bruce Walter, Ganesh Ramanarayanan, Kavita Bala, and L. Paul Chew. Optimistic parallelism requires abstractions. *SIGPLAN Not. (PLDI)*, 42(6):211–222, 2007.

[17] Lijuan Luo, Martin Wong, and Wen-mei Hwu. An effective gpu implementation of breadth-first search. In *Proceedings of the 47th Design Automation Conference*, DAC '10, pages 52–55, New York, NY, USA, 2010. ACM.

[18] Mario Mendez-Lojo, Martin Burtscher, and Keshav Pingali. A gpu implementation of inclusion-based points-to analysis. In *Proceedings of the 17th ACM SIGPLAN symposium on Principles and Practice of Parallel Programming*, PPoPP '12, pages 107–116, New York, NY, USA, 2012. ACM.

[19] Mario Méndez-Lojo, Donald Nguyen, Dimitrios Prountzos, Xin Sui, M. Amber Hassaan, Milind Kulkarni, Martin Burtscher, and Keshav Pingali. Structure-driven optimizations for amorphous data-parallel programs. In *Proceedings of the 15th ACM SIGPLAN Symposium on Principles and Practiceof Parallel Programming (PPoPP'10)*, pages 3–14, January 2010.

[20] Duane G. Merrill, Michael Garland, and Andrew S. Grimshaw. Scalable gpu graph traversal. In *17th ACM SIGPLAN Symposium on Principles and Practice of Parallel Programming*, PPoPP'12, 2012.

[21] Stephan Mertens, Marc Mézard, and Riccardo Zecchina. Threshold values of random k-sat from the cavity method. *Random Struct. Algorithms*, 28(3):340–373, May 2006.

[22] Cristobal A. Navarro, Nancy Hitschfeld-Kahler, and Eliana Scheihing. A parallel gpu-based algorithm for delaunay edge-flips. In *The 27th European Workshop on Computational Geometry*, EuroCG '11, 2011.

[23] Sadegh Nobari, Thanh-Tung Cao, Panagiotis Karras, and Stéphane Bressan. Scalable parallel minimum spanning forest computation. In *Proceedings of the 17th ACM SIGPLAN symposium on Principles and Practice of Parallel Programming*, PPoPP '12, pages 205–214, New York, NY, USA, 2012. ACM.

[24] Keshav Pingali, Donald Nguyen, Milind Kulkarni, Martin Burtscher, M. Amber Hassaan, Rashid Kaleem, Tsung-Hsien Lee, Andrew Lenharth, Roman Manevich, Mario Méndez-Lojo, Dimitrios Prountzos, and Xin Sui. The tao of parallelism in algorithms. In *Proceedings of the 32nd ACM SIGPLAN conference on Programming language design and implementation*, PLDI '11, pages 12–25, New York, NY, USA, 2011. ACM.

[25] Tarun Prabhu, Shreyas Ramalingam, Matthew Might, and Mary Hall. Eigencfa: accelerating flow analysis with gpus. In *Proceedings of the 38th annual ACM SIGPLAN-SIGACT symposium on Principles of programming languages*, POPL '11, pages 511–522, New York, NY, USA, 2011. ACM.

[26] Sandeep Putta and Rupesh Nasre. Parallel replication-based points-to analysis. In *Proceedings of the 21st international conference on Compiler Construction*, CC'12, pages 61–80, Berlin, Heidelberg, 2012. Springer-Verlag.

[27] Meng Qi, Thanh-Tung Cao, and Tiow-Seng Tan. Computing 2d constrained delaunay triangulation using the gpu. In *Proceedings of the ACM SIGGRAPH Symposium on Interactive 3D Graphics and Games*, I3D '12, pages 39–46, New York, NY, USA, 2012. ACM.

[28] Jonathan Richard Shewchuk. Triangle: Engineering a 2d quality mesh generator and Delaunay triangulator. In *Applied Computational Geometry: Towards Geometric Engineering*, volume 1148 of *Lecture Notes in Computer Science*, pages 203–222. Springer-Verlag, 1996.

[29] Jeff A. Stuart and John D. Owens. Efficient synchronization primitives for gpus. *CoRR*, abs/1110.4623, 2011.

[30] Vibhav Vineet, Pawan Harish, Suryakant Patidar, and P. J. Narayanan. Fast minimum spanning tree for large graphs on the gpu. In *Proceedings of the Conference on High Performance Graphics 2009*, HPG '09, pages 167–171, New York, NY, USA, 2009. ACM.

[31] Shucai Xiao and Wu chun Feng. Inter-block gpu communication via fast barrier synchronization. In *IPDPS*, pages 1–12. IEEE, 2010.

[32] Andy Yoo, Edmond Chow, Keith Henderson, William McLendon, Bruce Hendrickson, and Umit Catalyurek. A scalable distributed parallel breadth-first search algorithm on bluegene/l. In *Proceedings of the 2005 ACM/IEEE conference on Supercomputing*, SC '05, pages 25–, Washington, DC, USA, 2005. IEEE Computer Society.

[33] Eddy Z. Zhang, Yunlian Jiang, Ziyu Guo, Kai Tian, and Xipeng Shen. On-the-fly elimination of dynamic irregularities for gpu computing. In *Proceedings of the sixteenth international conference on Architectural support for programming languages and operating systems*, ASPLOS '11, pages 369–380, New York, NY, USA, 2011. ACM.

NUMA-Aware Reader-Writer Locks

Irina Calciu
Brown University
irina@cs.brown.edu

Dave Dice
Oracle Labs
dave.dice@oracle.com

Yossi Lev
Oracle Labs
yossi.lev@oracle.com

Victor Luchangco
Oracle Labs
victor.luchangco@oracle.com

Virendra J. Marathe
Oracle Labs
virendra.marathe@oracle.com

Nir Shavit
MIT
shanir@csail.mit.edu

Abstract

Non-Uniform Memory Access (NUMA) architectures are gaining importance in mainstream computing systems due to the rapid growth of multi-core multi-chip machines. Extracting the best possible performance from these new machines will require us to revisit the design of the concurrent algorithms and synchronization primitives which form the building blocks of many of today's applications. This paper revisits one such critical synchronization primitive – the reader-writer lock.

We present what is, to the best of our knowledge, the first family of reader-writer lock algorithms tailored to NUMA architectures. We present several variations which trade fairness between readers and writers for higher concurrency among readers and better back-to-back batching of writers from the same NUMA node. Our algorithms leverage the *lock cohorting* technique to manage synchronization between writers in a NUMA-friendly fashion, binary flags to coordinate readers and writers, and simple distributed reader counter implementations to enable NUMA-friendly concurrency among readers. The end result is a collection of surprisingly simple NUMA-aware algorithms that outperform the state-of-the-art reader-writer locks by up to a factor of 10 in our microbenchmark experiments. To evaluate our algorithms in a realistic setting we also present performance results of the kccachetest benchmark of the *Kyoto-Cabinet* distribution, an open-source database which makes heavy use of pthread reader-writer locks. Our locks boost the performance of kccachetest by up to 40% over the best prior alternatives.

Categories and Subject Descriptors D.1.3 [*Programming Techniques*]: Concurrent Programming

General Terms Algorithms, Design, Performance

Keywords NUMA, hierarchical locks, mutual exclusion, reader-writer locks

1. Introduction

As microprocessor vendors aggressively pursue the production of bigger multi-core multi-chip systems (Intel's Nehalem-based and Oracle's Niagara-based systems are typical examples), the computing industry is witnessing a shift toward distributed and cache-coherent Non-Uniform Memory Access (NUMA) architectures. [1] These systems contain multiple nodes where each node has locally attached memory, a local cache and multiple processing cores. Such systems present a uniform programming model where all memory is globally visible and cache-coherent. The set of cache-coherent communications channels between nodes is referred to collectively as the interconnect. These inter-node links normally suffer from higher latency and lower bandwidth compared to the intra-node channels. To decrease latency and to conserve interconnect bandwidth, NUMA-aware policies encourage intra-node communication over inter-node communication.

Creating efficient software for NUMA systems is challenging because such systems present a naive uniform "flat" model of the relationship between processors and memory, hiding the actual underlying topology from the programmer. The programmer must study architecture manuals and use special system-dependent library functions to exploit the system topology. NUMA-oblivious multithreaded programs may suffer performance problems arising from long access latencies caused by inter-node coherence traffic and from interconnect bandwidth limits. Furthermore, inter-node interconnect bandwidth is a shared resource so coherence traffic generated by one thread can impede the performance of other unrelated threads because of queueing delays and channel contention. Concurrent data structures and synchronization constructs at the core of modern multithreaded applications must be carefully designed to adapt to the underlying NUMA architectures. One key synchronization construct is the reader-writer (RW) lock.

A RW lock relaxes the central property of traditional mutual exclusion (mutex) locks by allowing multiple threads to hold the lock simultaneously in *read mode*. A thread may also acquire the lock in *write mode* for exclusive access. RW locks are used in a wide range of settings including operating system kernels, databases, high-end scientific computing applications and software transactional memory implementations [6].

RW locks have been studied extensively for several decades [1, 2, 11, 13–16], with proposals ranging from simple counter- or semaphore-based solutions [2], to solutions leveraging centralized wait-queues [14, 16], to solutions that use more sophisticated data structures such as Scalable Non-Zero Indicators (SNZI) [15]. Of these, all but the SNZI-based solutions rely on centralized structures to coordinate threads, and thus encounter scalability impediments [15]. The SNZI-based algorithms keep track of readers – threads acquiring the RW lock in read mode – with each reader arriving at a leaf in the "SNZI tree". Readers can be made NUMA-aware by partitioning the leaves of the SNZI-tree among the NUMA nodes, with threads arriving at SNZI leaves associated with their node. Writers, however, remain NUMA-*oblivious*, which can impair scalability.

---

[1] We use the term NUMA broadly to include Non-Uniform Communication Architecture (NUCA) [17] machines as well.

Hsieh and Weihl [11] and Vyukov [20] independently suggested a simple *distributed*[2] approach to building scalable RW locks. Each distributed RW lock contains N RW locks where N is the number of processors in the system. Each reader is mapped to a single RW lock, and must acquire that lock in read mode in order to execute its critical section. A writer must acquire *all* the underlying RW locks in write mode to execute its critical section. Deadlocks between writers are avoided by forcing a specific locking order. The approach can be made NUMA-aware by restricting N to the number of NUMA nodes in the system, and mapping each reader to the lock dedicated to its node. This variant algorithm which we call DV (representing the initials of Vyukov), is partially NUMA-aware, just like the SNZI-based RW locks. Absent any writers, readers on different nodes can obtain and release read permission without generating any inter-node write coherence traffic. However, every writer incurs the overhead of acquiring write permission for the RW lock of every node, potentially generating significant coherence traffic. Thus, the performance of DV plummets with increased writer activity. Also, because of the canonical locking order used to avoid deadlock, readers on nodes that appear late in the order may enjoy an unfair performance advantage over readers running on nodes that appear earlier.

In this paper we present a novel family of RW locks that are designed to leverage NUMA features and deliver better performance and scalability than any prior RW lock algorithm. We take a three-pronged approach in our lock designs. First, similar to DV, we maintain a distributed structure for the readers metadata such that readers denote their intent by updating only locations associated with their node. By localizing updates to read indicators we reduce coherence traffic on the interconnect. Second, writers preferentially hand off access permission to blocked writers on the same node, enhancing reference locality in the node's cache for both the lock metadata and data accessed in the critical section it protects. Finally, our algorithms maintain tight execution paths for both readers and writers, reducing latency of the lock acquisition and release operations.

Our RW lock algorithms build on the recently developed *lock cohorting* technique [7], which allows for the construction of NUMA-aware mutual exclusion locks. Briefly, writers use a cohort lock to synchronize with each other and to maintain writer-vs-writer exclusion. Using the cohort locking approach, a writer releasing the lock generally prefers to transfer ownership to a pending local writer (if there is one), thus reducing *lock migrations*[3] between nodes.

Our RW locks also contain distributed implementations of *read indicators*, a data structure that tracks the existence of readers [15]. Readers "arrive" at these read indicators during lock acquisition and "depart" from them during lock release. Writers query the read indicators to detect concurrently active readers. Because of the distributed nature of our read indicators, the readers need to access just the node-specific metadata of the lock. We additionally use simple flags and checks for coordination between readers and writers. The result is a family of surprisingly simple algorithms that push the performance envelope of RW locks on NUMA systems far beyond the prior state-of-the-art algorithms.

Our various RW locks can be differentiated on the basis of the fairness properties they provide as recognized by Courtois et

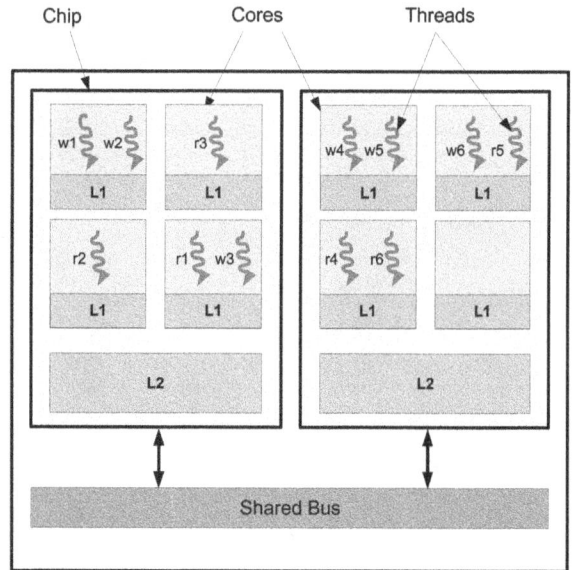

Figure 1. An example multi-core multi-chip NUMA system containing 2 chips with 4 cores per chip. Each chip is a NUMA node. Each core can have multiple hardware thread contexts (not shown in the figure). Each core has its individual $L1$ cache, and all cores on a chip share an $L2$ cache. Inter-thread communication via local caches ($L1$ and $L2$) is significantly faster than via remote caches because the latter involve coherence messages across the interconnect. In the figure, threads $r1..r6$ intend to acquire a RW lock in *read* mode, and threads $w1..w6$ intend to acquire the same lock in *write* mode.

al. [2]. In particular, we present locks exhibiting different "preference" policies: reader-preference, writer-preference, and neutral-preference. The reader-preference policy dictates that readers should acquire (be granted) the lock as early as possible, regardless of arrival order, whereas the writer-preference policy has a symmetric bias towards writers. More concretely, these preference policies allow readers or writers to "bypass" prior pending writers or readers (respectively) in the race to acquire the lock. The preference policies—except for the neutral policy—may lead to starvation of threads engaged in the non-preferred lock acquisition operation. We avoid such situations by allowing the lock mechanism to temporarily override the preference policy so as to allow forward progress of starving threads. Starving threads become "impatient" and transiently change the preference policy.

We present an empirical evaluation of our RW locks, comparing them with each other and with prior RW lock implementations. Our evaluation, conducted on a 256-way 4-node Oracle SPARC T5440^{TM} server, shows that our locks significantly outperform all prior RW locks on a diverse set of workloads. In our microbenchmark experiments, our locks outperform the prior best RW lock (the SNZI-based *ROLL* lock [15]) by up to a factor of 10.

We discuss our RW lock design approach in Section 2. In Section 3, we present our lock algorithms in detail. We present our empirical evaluation in Section 4, and conclude in Section 5.

2. Lock Design Rationale

NUMA-aware mutex locks have been explored in depth [3, 7, 17, 19]. However, to the best of our knowledge, there has been no prior effort toward constructing NUMA-aware RW locks. NUMA-aware mutex lock designs pursue only one goal – reduction of the lock

---

[2] The term "distributed" was coined by Vyukov for his algorithm [20], but this algorithm appears to be the same as Hsieh and Weihl's "static algorithm" [11]

[3] We say that *lock migration* occurs when the lock is consecutively acquired by threads residing on distinct NUMA nodes. On a cache-coherent NUMA system, lock migration leads to the transfer of cache lines–both for lines underlying the lock metadata as well as for lines underlying mutable data accessed in the critical section protected by the lock—from the cache associated with the first thread to that of the second thread.

(a) Naïve reader-writer lock schedule

(b) Lock schedule with aggressive reader batching

(c) Lock schedule with aggressive reader and writer batching

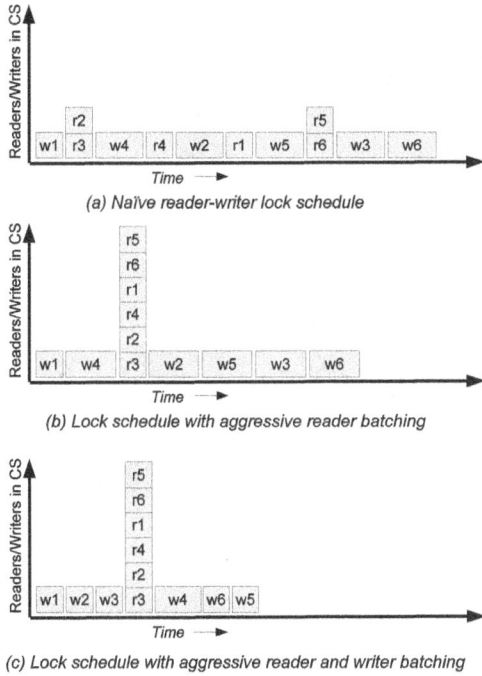

Figure 2. Execution scenarios depicting possible locking schedules for Figure 1

migration frequency so as to generate better node-local locality of reference for the lock and the critical section it protects. NUMA-aware mutex locks act to reduce the rate of write invalidations and coherence misses satisfied by cache-to-cache transfers from remote caches via the interconnect. We believe that, just like general RW locks, NUMA-aware RW lock designs must additionally consider the complementary goal of maximizing reader-reader concurrency.

We observe an interesting tension between these two goals: promoting concurrent reader-reader sharing across NUMA nodes tends to lead to designs that "spread" the lock metadata and critical section data across these nodes, whereas reducing the lock migration rate tends to significantly curtail this spread. However, this apparent contradiction between our goals can be effectively reconciled by using a policy that tries to reduce lock migrations only between writers while at the same time maximizing concurrency between readers. For this strategy to be most effective, we must aggressively "batch" the concurrent writer locking requests coming from a single NUMA node and maintain a high local writer-to-writer lock hand off rate. We note that this aggressive writer batching approach is not completely out-of-place. To the contrary, it nicely complements the goal of maximizing reader-reader concurrency because the latter can benefit significantly by aggressively aggregating (co-scheduling) reader locking requests. We illustrate the potential benefits of these design goals using an example.

Figure 1 depicts a NUMA system with six threads attempting to acquire a lock L in read mode, and six threads attempting to acquire L in write mode. We assume that the critical sections protected by the lock access the same data. Figure 2 shows possible critical section execution schedules for these readers and writers when the critical section is protected by different kinds of RW locks. Figure 2(a) shows a possible critical section execution schedule arbitrated by a naive RW lock that does not aggressively aggregate readers or provide back-to-back consecutive batching of writers from a given NUMA node. The schedule shows that the lock does not provide good reader-reader concurrency, and hence

it takes more time to execute all the critical sections. Assuming a backlog of pending readers, higher rates of alternation between read and write modes yields lower levels of reader-reader concurrency. Figure 2(b) shows a scheduling policy that yields improved reader-reader concurrency. By aggressively aggregating read requests the lock successfully co-scheduled a large group of readers, allowing them to execute the critical section concurrently. However, the order of writers alternates between the two NUMA nodes from Figure 1. This leads to significant coherence traffic that slows down the writers. The width of the boxes reflects the relative time taken to complete a critical section invocation, with broader boxes showing the overheads associated with inter-node communication latencies. Figure 2(c) addresses this problem by batching together writers from the same NUMA node in a consecutive back-to-back fashion. As a result, writers $w2$, $w3$, $w5$, and $w6$ will incur fewer coherence misses during the execution of their critical sections. As we shall see in Section 4, these savings translate to significant performance gains for our locks.

3. RW Lock Algorithms

We use *lock cohorting* [7] as a starting point for our RW lock designs. Each of our RW lock instances contains a single central cohort mutual exclusion lock that is used to synchronize writers – we resolve writer-vs-writer conflicts via the cohort lock. Writers must first acquire this cohort lock in order to gain exclusive (write) ownership of the RW lock. Before executing the critical section, the writer owning the cohort lock must also reconcile reader-vs-writer conflicts by ensuring that there are no concurrent readers executing or about to execute their respective critical sections. The readers counterpart of our RW locks use distributed *read indicators* (ReadIndr for short). To acquire a RW lock in read mode, a reader must *arrive* at the lock's ReadIndr. ReadIndr is implemented as a distributed counter, with a counter per NUMA node. Each reader increments its local counter during arrival and decrements the local counter during *depart*. Crucially, writers update the central lock but only query and do not update the multiple reader indicators.

In this section we describe the cohort lock used to provide write-write exclusion and then present three RW lock algorithms, each of which implements one of the three preference policies: neutral-, reader- or writer-preference. We first present these algorithms at a high level (Sections 3.2 through 3.4). We then make an important observation that implementors can substitute almost any type of mutex lock and reader indicator mechanism into their implementation of our RW locks. Finally, we describe the scalable read indicator implementations used in our RW locks.

3.1 The Writer Cohort Lock

Lock cohorting is a technique to compose NUMA-aware mutex locks from NUMA-oblivious mutex locks. It leverages two key properties of mutex lock implementations – (i) *cohort detection*, where a lock owner can determine whether there are additional threads waiting to acquire the lock; and (ii) *thread-obliviousness*, where the lock can be acquired by one thread and released by any other thread. Cohort locks are hierarchical in structure, with one top-level lock and multiple locks at the second level, one for each node in the NUMA system. The top-level lock is thread-oblivious and the second-level locks must have the property of cohort detection. A cohort lock is said to be owned by a thread when that thread owns the top-level lock.

To acquire the cohort lock, a thread must first acquire ownership of the lock assigned to its node and then acquire ownership of the top-level lock. After executing its critical section, the cohort lock owner uses the cohort detection property of the node-local lock to determine if there are any local successors, and hands off ownership of the local lock to a successor. With this local lock hand off, the owner also implicitly passes ownership of the top-

159

level lock to that same successor. If the lock owner determines that there are no local successors then it must release the top-level lock. The top-level lock's thread-obliviousness property comes into play here – the lock's ownership can be acquired by one thread from a node, then implicitly circulated among several threads in that node, and eventually released by some (possibly different) thread in that node. To avoid starvation and provide long-term fairness, cohort lock implementations typically bound the number of back-to-back local lock transfers. (We used a bound of 64 in all our experiments described in this paper). Our algorithm intentionally trades strict short-term FIFO/FCFS fairness for improved aggregate throughput. Specifically, we leverage unfairness – where admission order deviates from arrival order – in order to reduce lock migrations and improve aggregate throughput of a set of contending threads. Unfairness, applied judiciously, and leveraged appropriately, can result in reduced coherence traffic and improved cache residency.

The primary goal of cohort locks is to reduce interconnect coherence traffic and coherence misses. In turn the hit rate in the local cache improves. We presume that critical section invocations under the same lock exhibit reference similarity – acquiring lock L is a good predictor that the critical section protected by L will access data that was accessed by recent prior critical sections protected by L. After a local hand off, data to be written by the next lock owner is more apt to be in the owner's local cache, already in *modified* coherence state, as it may have been written by the prior owner. As such, the critical section may execute faster than if the prior owner resided on a different node. Cohort locks provide benefit by reducing coherence traffic on both lock metadata and data protected by the locks. If a cache line to be read is in *modified* state in some remote cache then it must currently be *invalid* or not present in the local cache. The line must be transferred to the local cache from the remote cache via the interconnect and downgraded to *shared* state in the remote cache. Similarly, if a cache line to be written is not already in *modified* state in the local cache, all remote copies must be invalidated, and, if the line is not in *shared* state, the contents must be transferred to the writer's cache. Read-read is the only form of sharing that does not require coherence communication. We are less concerned with classic NUMA issues such as the placement of memory relative to the location of threads that will access that memory and more interested in which caches shared data might reside in, and in what coherence states. Cohort locking works to reduce write invalidation and coherence misses satisfied from remote caches and does not specifically address remote capacity, conflict, and cold misses, which are also satisfied by transfers over the interconnect.

For use in our RW locks, we have developed a new cohort lock that uses classic ticket locks [12] for the NUMA node-local locks and a partitioned ticket lock [5] for the top-level lock. We call this lock C-PTL-TKT, short for *Partitioned-Ticket-Ticket* cohort lock. We expose a new isLocked interface that allows readers to determine if the write lock is held. This function is implemented by comparing the *request* and *grant* indices of the top-level partitioned ticket lock. We elected to use C-PTL-TKT in our RW locks as it is competitive with the best of the cohort locks, avoids the node management overheads inherent in classic queue-based locks such as MCS but still provides local spinning. The top-level and node-level locks are FIFO although the resultant C-PTL-TKT lock is not itself necessarily FIFO.

3.2 The Neutral-Preference Lock

Our neutral-preference lock, called C-RW-NP (Cohort; Read-Write; Neutral-Preference) for short, attempts to ensure fairness between readers and writers. By fairness here we mean that the readers or writers do not get any preferential treatment over the writers or readers, respectively. To do so, all threads – including readers and writers – are "funnelled" through the central cohort

```
1:  reader:
2:      CohortLock.acquire()
3:      ReadIndr.arrive()
4:      CohortLock.release()
5:      <read-critical-section>
6:      ReadIndr.depart()

7:  writer:
8:      CohortLock.acquire()
9:      while NOT(ReadIndr.isEmpty())
10:         Pause
11:     <write-critical-section>
12:     CohortLock.release()
```

Figure 3. The Neutral-Preference Lock (C-RW-NP). The top half is executed by a reader and the bottom half by a writer. For simplicity, the pseudo-code lists the entirety of lock acquisition, critical section execution, and lock release operations in sequential order. In their lock acquisition steps, both readers and writers acquire the cohort lock, while readers also arrive at the ReadIndr. ReadIndr arrival and departures must be atomic.

```
1:  reader:
2:      while RBarrier != 0
3:          Pause
4:      ReadIndr.arrive()
5:      while CohortLock.isLocked()
6:          Pause
7:      <read-critical-section>
8:      ReadIndr.depart()

9:  writer:
10:     bRaised = false // local flag
11: start:
12:     CohortLock.acquire()
13:     if NOT(ReadIndr.isEmpty())
14:         CohortLock.release()
15:         while NOT(ReadIndr.isEmpty())
16:             Pause
17:             if RanOutOfPatience AND ~bRaised
18:                 // erect barrier to stall readers
19:                 atomically increment RBarrier
20:                 bRaised = true
21:         goto start
22:     if bRaised
23:         atomically decrement RBarrier
24:     <write-critical-section>
25:     CohortLock.release()
```

Figure 4. The Reader-Preference Lock (C-RW-RP).

lock, an approach that has been used in the past [15, 16]. Figure 3 depicts the high-level pseudo-code of C-RW-NP. Each thread must first acquire CohortLock. The reader uses the central lock to obtain permission to arrive at ReadIndr (the implementation details of which appear in Section 3.6), then immediately releases the lock, and proceeds to execute its critical section. The fact that readers execute their critical sections *after* releasing CohortLock enables the potential for reader-reader concurrency. After acquiring the cohort lock, the writer must ensure that there are no concurrent conflicting readers. This is done by spinning on ReadIndr (lines 9 and 10) waiting for any readers to depart. This algorithm is clearly very simple and also ensures neutral preference since both the readers and the writers have to acquire the cohort lock. However, requiring readers to acquire the cohort lock can be detrimental to the scalability of C-RW-NP, and also increases the latency of each read acquisition request. C-RW-NP preserves some cache locality benefits for accesses to the lock metadata and the critical section because all operations funnel through the central cohort lock.

We note that C-RW-NP does not guarantee FIFO semantics. Rather, admission ordering is determined by the prevailing policy imposed by the underlying CohortLock.

3.3 The Reader-Preference Lock

As noted above, C-RW-NP has a crucial drawback arising from the requirement that readers are forced to acquire the central Cohort-Lock. Acquiring the CohortLock incurs extra path length and overheads for read operations, even if the cohort lock is uncontended. Under load, contention on the central lock can result in extra coherence traffic and contention for available interconnect bandwidth although this bottleneck is mitigated to some degree by our choice of lock cohorting which acts to reduce inter-node coherence traffic. Furthermore, the extra serialization related to the CohortLock critical section in the read path – albeit very brief – can constitute a scalability bottleneck. Finally, the algorithm's ordering of reader and writer requests based on the cohort lock acquisition order restricts the achievable degree of reader-reader concurrency. In the worst case, there will be no reader-reader concurrency if readers and writers alternate in the cohort lock acquisition order. We overcome both these problems in our reader-preference lock algorithm (called C-RW-RP for short).

Intuitively it makes sense to more aggressively aggregate reader lock acquisition requests to maximize reader-reader concurrency for better scalability. This, however, requires the ability to allow newly arriving readers to bypass writers that arrived earlier but that are still waiting to acquire the lock. This observation was made in the earliest work on RW locks by Courtois et al. [2], and then followed by other works that make the same trade off between fairness and scalability [11, 15, 16]. Our C-RW-RP algorithm also entails the same trade off.

Figure 4 depicts the pseudo-code of C-RW-RP. Readers and writers interact with each other in a way that is reminiscent of the classic Dekker locking idiom [8, 10], where each first declares its existence to the other, and then checks for the other's status. To detect and resolve conflicts, readers must be visible to writers, and writers visible to readers and other potential writers. C-RW-RP readers do not acquire the cohort lock. Instead, they directly arrive at the lock's ReadIndr (line 4). However, each reader can make forward progress only when there are no "active" writers queued on the cohort lock (lines 5–6) Thereafter readers can execute their critical sections and release the lock by departing from ReadIndr.

Writers first acquire CohortLock (line 12) and then verify that there are no concurrent "active" readers. If there are any concurrent readers (indicated by the ReadIndr), the writer releases CohortLock (lines 13–14) and then waits for the readers to drain (line 15). Note that there is a danger of starvation of the writers if they simply wait for no readers to be present but there is a steady stream of arriving readers. To avoid this problem, we have introduced a special reader barrier (called RBarrier) that lets the writer temporarily block all new readers from acquiring read ownership of C-RW-RP. Lines 17–20 show the writer raising the barrier (which is then lowered on line 23), and lines 2–3 show the new readers being blocked by the barrier[4]. The reader barrier is implemented as a single central counter. The writer waits for a pre-determined amount of time before running out of patience on line 17. The writer's "patience threshold" is fairly long so that the barrier is raised rarely and as a result we do not expect it to become a contention bottleneck. In our experiments we used a writer patience threshold of 1000 iterations of the busy-wait loop. The threshold is a tunable parameter. After the writer raises the barrier, the readers steadily drain and when all readers have departed the writer may execute its critical section (line 24) and then finally relinquish write permission by simply releasing CohortLock (line 25).

While the above algorithm is simple, it has a significant performance flaw because of an interesting interaction between contending readers and writers and the succession policy of the CohortLock: Consider an execution scenario where N writers W_1, W_2, W_3, ..., W_N are queued on the cohort lock. W_1 is the lock owner

---

[4] There may be another pathology that lets readers starve in the case where writers continuously keep raising the reader barrier and do not allow any readers to make forward progress. We consider such a situation to be even more rare than the rare case where writers run out of patience and raise the reader barrier, and as a result, do not address it in our algorithm.

but it has not yet reached line 13. This means that the isLocked function called on line 5 will return true, and block all the readers. A multitude of readers arrive at that time, atomically incrementing ReadIndr, and then spin-wait for isLocked to return false. Next, W_1 executes line 13, detects concurrent readers, and releases CohortLock on line 14. In the process, W_1 hands off CohortLock to W_2, which in turn similarly hands off CohortLock to W_3, and so on. All this while, CohortLock remains in the *locked* state though the lock owner keeps changing, and isLocked returns true for all the readers spinning on it. This circulation of CohortLock ownership between the writers leads to superfluous coherence activity on the lock metadata as well as long and unnecessary waiting periods for readers. In our experiments we have observed that this undesirable interaction between readers and writers leads to significant performance degradation. Furthermore, circulation voids any ordering imposed between writers by the underlying CohortLock.

To avoid this problem we add a new WActive field to C-RW-RP that reflects the *logical* state of the CohortLock. We modify the reader-writer conflict detection logic in line 5 of Figure 4 to spin while WActive is true, instead of spinning on CohortLock. Meanwhile, for the writers, the code between lines 11 and 21 changes to the following:

```
CohortLock.acquire()
loop:
    while NOT(ReadIndr.IsEmpty())
        if RanOutOfPatience AND ~bRaised
        // erect barrier to stall readers
        atomically increment RBarrier
        bRaised = true
    WActive = true // set flag for readers to spin
    if NOT(ReadIndr.IsEmpty())
        // there exist some active readers
        WActive = false // reset the flag
        goto loop
```

Writers acquire CohortLock in the usual fashion and then enter a loop. The code in the loop first waits for ReadIndr to show that there are no pending or active readers, optionally erecting RBarrier if the writer becomes impatient. After ReadIndr indicates that there are no active readers, the code sets WActive to true, and then validates that there are no active or pending readers. If this is the case then control exits the loop and passes into the write critical section. If ReadIndr indicates the existence of readers, however, the code sets WActive to false and passes control back to the top of the the loop which again waits for extant readers to depart. The writer continues to hold CohortLock while it waits for the readers to vacate, avoiding superfluous lock hand offs between writers. After completing its critical section the writer releases the lock by setting WActive to false and then releasing CohortLock. Readers can be blocked by writers only in the brief window where the writer sets WActive and then resets it after detecting the pending readers. We refer to this form as C-RW-RP-opt. Notice that WActive is modified only under CohortLock, and reflects the lock's state: true if CohortLock is acquired, and false otherwise. There is no analogous writer-preference "-opt" form as readers can efficiently rescind publication of their intent to take read permission and then defer to pending writers.

3.4 The Writer-Preference Lock

Conventional wisdom suggests that the reader-preference policy would perform better than both the writer and the neutral-preference policies. Since the application developer has selected a RW lock instead of a mutual exclusion lock, we expect the workload to be read-dominated. The intuition is that packing together as many readers as possible generally leads to better reader-reader concurrency, and hence better throughput. Though we agree with the intuition, we contend that, assuming that a RW lock is acquired by threads in read mode most of the time, the writer-preference policy indirectly leads to the same result – packing together large numbers of reader requests. This is because preferential treatment

```
1:  reader:
2:      bRaised = false // local flag
3:    start:
4:      ReadIndr.arrive()
5:      if CohortLock.isLocked()
6:          ReadIndr.depart()
7:          while CohortLock.isLocked()
8:              Pause
9:              if RanOutOfPatience AND ~bRaised
10:                 atomically increment WBarrier
11:                 bRaised = true
12:         goto start
13:     if bRaised
14:         atomically decrement WBarrier
15:     <read-critical-section>
16:     ReadIndr.depart()

17: writer:
18:     while WBarrier != 0
19:         Pause
20:     CohortLock.acquire()
21:     while NOT(ReadIndr.isEmpty())
22:         Pause
23:     <write-critical-section>
24:     CohortLock.release()
```

Figure 5. The Writer-Preference Lock (C-RW-WP).

of writers leads to a build up of pending reader requests which are then granted en masse when all the writers complete their critical sections. Furthermore, we have observed that the reader-preference policy actually leads to an interesting performance pathology, which we describe in Section 4.3, that can seriously undermine the lock's scalability potential.

Figure 5 depicts the pseudo-code for our writer-preference lock, which we call C-RW-WP. Our C-RW-WP algorithm is clearly symmetric to our C-RW-RP algorithm, the only difference being that the roles of readers and writers in their interactions are switched. Readers arrive at the lock's ReadIndr (line 4), check for a writer (line 5), and if there is one, they depart from the ReadIndr and wait for the writers to drain. If a reader runs out of patience – which is a tunable parameter set to 1000 in our experiments – it can raise a writer barrier (line 10) to block out new writers from acquiring CohortLock (lines 18–19). Writers first verify that the writer barrier has not been raised (line 18–19), then acquire CohortLock (line 20) and ensure that there are no concurrent readers (lines 21–22) before executing the critical section.

3.5 RW Lock Generalization

We observe that our RW lock algorithms are oblivious of the underlying read indicator (ReadIndr) and mutex lock (CohortLock) implementations. Our RW locks require the read indicator data structure to provide just the *arrive*, *depart*, and *isEmpty* operations, and the mutex lock to provide *acquire*, *release*, and *isLocked* operations. Any read indicators and mutex locks that support these operations can be trivially plugged into our algorithms. Furthermore we expect that most implementations of read indicators and mutex locks can support all these operations with at most trivial modifications.

The design flexibility afforded by our RW locks grants programmers significant leverage to build RW locks that are best suited for their applications. For instance, in this paper, we have proposed NUMA-aware RW locks that leverage known NUMA-aware mutex locks and scalable read indicators. In our empirical evaluation (Section 4), we also present performance results of a RW lock that uses distributed counters in the read indicator, and the MCS lock [12] for writer-writer mutual exclusion. Such a lock may be appropriate for applications where writing is exceptionally rare.

3.6 Tracking Readers

Lev et al. [15] observed that readers of a RW lock can be tracked with just the *read indicator* abstraction. Writers checking for the existence of conflicting readers do not need an exact count of readers, but instead need only determine if there are any extant readers.

This read indicator can be implemented as a simple counter, updated atomically, which tracks the number of readers that are executing or intend to execute their respective critical sections. However, a simple counter does not scale on a NUMA system. Having made this observation, Lev et al. proposed a SNZI-based [9] solution in their RW locks [15]. The SNZI-based solution significantly scales the read indicator, however the algorithm is complex and readers incur significant overheads at low and moderate contention levels (as we shall see in Section 4). As a result, we have adopted a simple strategy where we "split" a logical counter into multiple physical counters, one per NUMA node. The main goal of our approach is to have a solution that has low latency at low to moderate read arrival rates and scales well at high arrival rates.

A reader thread always manipulates its node-local reader counter. This ensures that counter manipulations do not lead to inter-node coherence traffic. However, after acquiring the internal cohort lock, the writer must peruse through all the reader counters of the RW lock to determine if it is safe to proceed executing the critical section. This adds overhead to the writer's execution path. There is a clear trade off here, and assuming that a RW lock will be acquired in read mode most often, we have opted to simplify the reader's execution path (which involves an increment of just the local reader counter) at the cost of making the writer's execution path longer. Furthermore, most multi-core multi-chip systems available today have relatively small number of NUMA nodes (4 in the system used in our experiments), and we believe the overhead on the writer's execution path is not a major performance concern on these systems. Future NUMA systems with larger numbers of nodes may pose a problem, but we leave the exploration of possible solutions to future work.

The decentralized split-counter can itself be implemented in multiple ways. We discuss two approaches. First is the trivial split-counter, where each node-specific counter is an integer counter. Each reader atomically increments the counter assigned to the reader's node during lock acquisition (arrival), and atomically decrements that same counter during lock release (departure). Using alignment and padding, each node-specific counter is sequestered on its own cache line to avoid false sharing. Each writer, during lock acquisition, verifies that each node-specific counter is 0, and spin-waits on any non-zero counter.

The simple split-counter approach, though effective in reducing inter-node coherence traffic for readers, still admits intra-node contention. Our second approach reduces this contention by employing a pair of *ingress* and *egress* counters in place of each node-specific counter. A reader atomically increments the ingress counter during lock acquisition, and atomically increments the egress counter during lock release. By splitting the logical node-level counter into two variables we divide contention arising from rapid intra-node arrival and departure of readers. On a given node, arriving threads can update ingress independently of concurrently departing threads that are incrementing egress. The ingress and egress counters for a given node may reside on the same cache line. The counter is logically 0 when ingress and egress are equal. Interestingly, the approach of using per-node counters or per-node split-egress-egress counters appears to outperform SNZI-based reader counters, at least for the platforms on which we have taken performance data. We believe this outcome to be platform-specific. Given a sufficiently large number of nodes, the burden of work required to scan those nodes by writers when resolving reader-vs-writer conflicts could become prohibitive. But on current platforms split ingress-egress counters are our preferred implementation for reader counters.

During lock acquisition, a writer verifies that each node-specific ingress-egress pair is equal. This cannot be done atomically, and special care needs to be taken to avoid any races with concurrent readers that are manipulating the counters. More specifically, in our C-RW-WP algorithm, the writer must first read the egress counter and then the ingress counter in order to correctly determine if the two are equal. Note that both these counters are monotonically increasing, and it is always guaranteed that $egress \leq ingress$ at any given time.

4. Empirical Evaluation

We now present the empirical evaluation of our NUMA-aware RW locks, comparing them with each other and also with other state-of-the-art RW locks. We first present scalability results of these locks on a synthetic microbenchmark. Our results cover a wide range of configurations on varying critical and non-critical section lengths and distributions of read-only and read-write critical sections. We also report what we believe to be a fundamental performance pathology in reader-preference locks. We thereafter show how read indicator implementations affect the scalability of our RW locks. Finally, we present performance results of the kccache-test benchmark of the Kyoto-Cabinet open-source database package, when used with different RW locks. Our empirical evaluation shows that our NUMA-aware RW locks deliver far superior performance than all prior RW locks.

We present performance results of all our locks: the C-RW-NP lock, both the variants of the C-RW-RP lock (the basic C-RW-RP lock, and its optimized form, C-RW-RP-opt, which eliminates the writer ownership circulation problem), and the C-RW-WP lock. Unless specified otherwise, we use the split ingress-egress counter for ReadIndr in our algorithms. We compare our locks with the SNZI-based ROLL lock, the distributed RW lock (DV), and the recently published NUMA-oblivious RW lock by Shirako et al. [18]. Since our locks are built on top of cohort locks, we add a simple mutual-exclusion cohort lock in the mix to understand the benefits our RW locks give above and beyond cohort locks. Finally, to quantify the benefits of using a cohort lock in our RW locks, we compare them with a variant of C-RW-WP that uses an MCS lock for writer-writer exclusion. We call this the DR-MCS lock (short for Distributed Readers, MCS writers).

We implemented all of the above algorithms in C compiled with GCC 4.4.1 at optimization level -O3 in 32-bit mode. The experiments were conducted on an Oracle T5440 series system which consists of 4 Niagara T2+ SPARC chips, each chip containing 8 cores, and each core containing 2 pipelines with 4 hardware thread contexts per pipeline, for a total of 256 hardware thread contexts, running at a 1.4 GHz clock frequency. Each chip has locally connected memory, a 4MB L2 cache, and each core has a shared 8KB L1 data cache. Each T2+ chip is a distinct NUMA node, and the nodes are connected via a central coherence hub. The Solaris 10 scheduler is work-conserving and to maintain cache residency will try to avoid migrating threads. Thread migration was observed to be minimal for all our experiments. While not shown in our pseudocode, explicit memory fences were inserted as necessary.

We implemented all the above locks within LD_PRELOAD interposition libraries that expose the standard POSIX *pthread_rwlock_t* programming interface. This allows us to change lock implementations by varying the LD_PRELOAD environment variable and without modifying the application code that uses RW locks.

We use the Solaris *schedctl* interface to efficiently query the identity of the CPU on which a thread is running, requiring just two load instructions on SPARC and x86 platforms. In turn the CPU number may be trivially and efficiently converted to a NUMA node number. In our implementation a thread queries its NUMA node number each time it tries to acquire a lock. We record that number and ensure that readers depart from the same node. The RDTSCP instruction may be a suitable alternative to schedctl on other x86-based platforms where the kernel has arranged to return the CPUID.

4.1 RWBench

To understand the performance characteristics of our locks, and compare them with other locks, we implemented a synthetic multi-threaded microbenchmark that stresses a single RW lock by forcing threads to repeatedly execute critical sections in read or write mode. The microbenchmark, which we call RWBench, is a flexible framework that lets us experiment with various workload characteristics such as varying critical and non-critical section lengths, distribution of read and write mode operations, number of distinct cache lines accessed, etc., all of which are configurable parameters. It uses the pthreads RW lock interface to acquire and release the lock, and we use our LD_PRELOAD interposition library to select various lock implementations.

RWBench spawns the configured number of concurrent threads, each of which loops continuously for 10 seconds. Each top-level iteration starts by casting a biased Bernoulli dice via a thread-local random number generator to determine if the particular iteration should execute a read-only or read-write critical section. The probability with which each loop iteration selects read-write critical sections is a configurable parameter. The critical section touches a single shared array of 64 integers which is protected by a single global RW lock instance. The read-only operation iterates through an inner loop for RCSLen times (a configurable parameter) where each iteration fetches 2 randomly selected integers from the shared array. The read-write operation iterates through an inner loop for WCSLen times (another configurable parameter) where each iteration selects two integers from the shared array, and adds a random value to one integer and subtracts that same value from the other integer. The non-critical section of the main loop similarly updates another thread-private array of 64 integers for NCSLen iterations. At the conclusion of the 10 second run the benchmark verifies that the sum of all the values in the shared array is 0.

The benchmark reports aggregate throughput at the end of a 10 second run, expressed as iterations of top-level loop executed by the worker threads. We ran 3 trials for each configuration and report their median result. The observed variance was extremely low. In order to adhere as much as possible to real-world execution environments, we do not artificially bind threads to hardware contexts, and instead rely on the default Solaris kernel scheduler to manage placement of the benchmark's threads in the NUMA system [4]. Unlike some other NUMA-aware locks, our locks tolerate ambient thread placement instead of requiring explicit binding.

4.2 RWBench **Scalability Test**

Figure 6 reports throughput of RWBench with the different locks, and different read/write percent distributions. We believe the read-write distribution mix covers a broad swath of workloads that appear in real application settings. We collected data for higher write percent configurations (up to 50% writes), and found the results to be qualitatively similar to that of Figure 6 (d). The critical and non-critical section sizes in these experiments were deliberately kept small to help us better understand the behavior of all the RW locks under high arrival rates.

First, C-RW-WP is clearly the best performer across the board. Interestingly, DR-MCS performs the second best at 2% writes, but deteriorates considerably with increasing write load. This is because the writes start to play an increasingly important role in performance and DR-MCS experiences excessive coherence traffic due to the NUMA-oblivious queuing of writers on its internal MCS lock. DV is competitive at low thread counts, but deteriorates significantly with high contention, presumably because writers must acquire all the NUMA-node RW locks, which increases both the coherence traffic and delays in lock acquisition in both read and write modes.

ROLL initially scales slowly with increasing thread count. This is because the threads in our test harness are dispersed by the

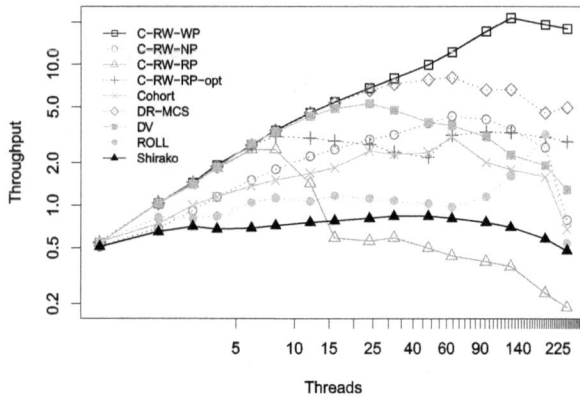

(a) 98% Reads, 2% Writes

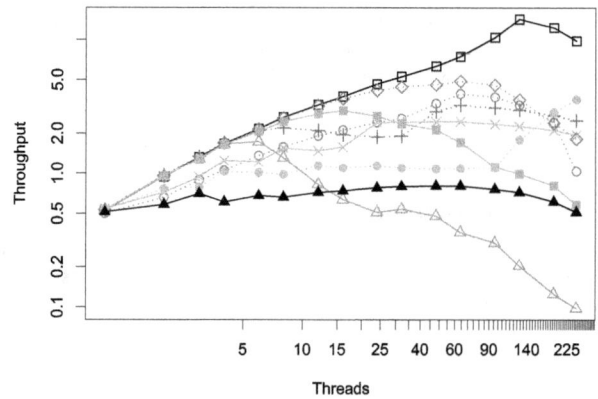

(b) 95% Reads, 5% Writes

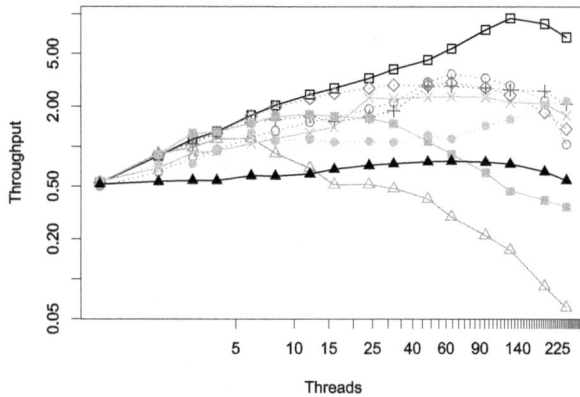

(c) 90% Reads, 10% Writes

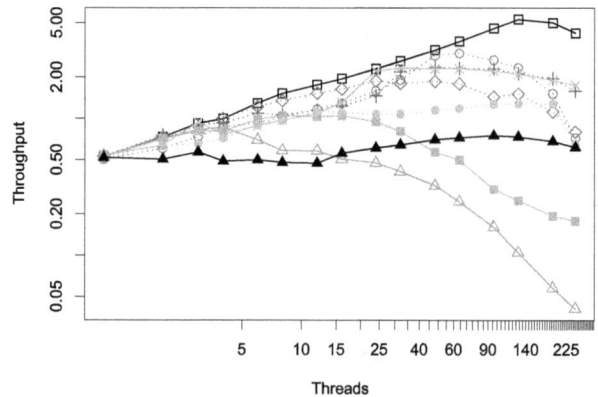

(d) 80% Reads, 20% Writes

Figure 6. RWBench scalability results of various RW locks for varying read/write distributions: 2%, 5%, 10%, and 20% of write mode lock acquisitions. All graphs are in *loglog* scale. Here RCSLen = 4, WCSLen = 4, and NCSLen = 32. We vary the number of threads from 1 to 255 on the X-axis. Y-axis throughput is expressed in terms of aggregate million loop iterations performed per second.

Solaris scheduler over the entire system [4], and as a result, there are fewer threads dedicated to a SNZI-tree leaf node of the ROLL lock. The end result is that more threads tend to "climb" up the SNZI-tree and compete at the top level (root) node, which is shared across the entire system and consequently leads to an increase in coherence traffic. ROLL starts to scale more quickly at high thread counts, presumably because the load at each leaf of the SNZI-tree is sufficient to reduce the number of threads visiting the root node, thus reducing the coherence traffic over the system. However, this scaling is constrained even at 20% write load, where writers, which are NUMA-oblivious, begin to play a noticeable role in the scalability of the lock. The Shirako lock, which is another recent NUMA-oblivious lock, does not scale on our NUMA system.

Cohort exhibits interesting performance characteristics. Since it does not provide any reader-reader concurrency, Cohort does not scale as well as the best RW locks. However, as the write rate increases, Cohort starts to close its performance gap with our other RW locks, and is quite competitive with all but C-RW-WP at 20% write loads. This demonstrates that even at modestly high write loads, the writer-writer exclusion component of a RW lock becomes an important scalability factor, and since Cohort is extremely efficient and scalable at writer-writer exclusion on NUMA systems, it tends to be competitive with the best RW locks.

Relative to a simple mutual exclusion lock, RW locks usually have longer path lengths (latency) and access more shared metadata. The latter can detract from scalability. Comparing Co-

hort to true RW locks is interesting as the benefits of potential reader-reader concurrency do not necessarily overcome the additional overheads inherent in RW locks, particularly when critical sections are relatively short or the thread count is low. C-RW-NP appears to leverage additional reader-reader concurrency benefit only marginally over Cohort when the write load is low (2%). In all other cases, it performs similarly to Cohort because even the readers have to acquire the cohort lock in order to arrive at the ReadIndr.

Lastly, the difference in performance of C-RW-RP and C-RW-RP-opt clearly demonstrates the pitfalls of the superfluous writer ownership circulation problem in C-RW-RP. However, C-RW-RP-opt does not scale as well as C-RW-WP because of its reader-preference performance pathology, which we describe next.

4.3 Reader-Preference Performance Pathology

As is clear from Figure 6, our reader-preference locks perform considerably worse than our writer-preference lock. It is well-known that a *strict* reader-preference policy may allow writers to starve. However, we have observed that a reader-preference policy can also result in a secondary phenomenon where readers themselves may underutilize available concurrency.

Say we have a fixed set of threads that loop, deciding randomly whether to take a central RW lock for either reading (query) or writing (update). We will assume that reading is more frequent than writing – access to the RW lock is read-dominated. We will assume that most of the threads are initially readers. Over time

164

those readers will complete their operation and some fraction will evolve into writers, while the majority will remain readers. Those writers will block in deference to the extant readers given the reader-preference policy. Finally, when no readers remain active, a writer is allowed admission. But when that writer completes its operation it may quickly turn into a reader again, thus obstructing the large set of blocked writers. This undesirable mode can persist. At any given time most threads are blocked trying to acquire write permission while either one writer is active or a small number of readers are active. This results in underutilizing the system by failing to leverage potential reader-reader concurrency that could be realized with a different lock admission schedule. Even though our workload is read-dominated, we have sufficient threads, and we have a reader-preference lock policy, we achieve very low reader throughput and experience diminished reader-reader concurrency. The writer starvation effect that arises from the reader-preference policy prevents a sufficient number of writers from evolving back into readers, thus restricting reader-reader concurrency. While we observed this behavior in RWBench we note that a pool of server threads accepting query or update requests on a data structure protected by an RW lock are also exposed to this pathology.

One might wonder if the writer-preference policy could also lead to a similar pathology. Though incoming writers may obstruct concurrent readers, we do not expect the problem to be as severe with a writer-preference policy. We assume that RW locks will be predominantly acquired in read mode. Hence, even if a set of writers block concurrent readers, their threads will usually return to reacquire the lock in read mode. As a result the readers will be stalled for short intervals. Furthermore, a group of waiting readers can proceed concurrently once all the writers get out of their way.

Strict reader/writer-preference policies may lead to the starvation of the threads engaged in the non-preferred lock acquisition operation. Consequently, to avoid such issues, we believe that a general-purpose RW lock algorithm should detect and recover from policy-based starvation. If the base policy is writer-preference, for example, then if readers languish for too long then the lock can block incoming writers and allow the backlog of readers to enter. And in fact this mechanism can promote aggregation of readers, yielding increased reader-reader concurrency. Effectively, the lock can switch transiently from writer-preference to either neutral-preference or reader-preference. Similarly, if the base lock policy is reader-preference, when writers starve the lock could take remedial action to ensure that writers make progress by transiently shifting to neutral- or writer-preference. This mechanism is illustrated in the anti-starvation facility shown in Figure 5. As an alternative to erecting barriers to block the flow of incoming writers, we also experimented with having impatient readers acquire the CohortLock as shown in the neutral-preference lock in Figure 3. Readers first attempt to use the fast path, but if they fail to make reasonable progress, they instead use a more pessimistic approach and pass through the CohortLock. This approach also yields reasonable performance.

4.4 ReadIndr Implementations

As described in Section 3.6, ReadIndr can be implemented in multiple ways. We now compare the performance of each of the three implementations we discussed – a simple integer counter, a split counter with one integer counter per NUMA node, and a split ingress-egress counter with one pair of ingress-egress counters per NUMA node. Figure 7 depicts the performance of C-RW-WP when equipped with these counter implementations when run with 98% reads and 2% writes. C-RW-WP-1RC represents the version of C-RW-WP with a single central reader counter. This central counter is clearly a scalability bottleneck and results in significant performance deterioration with increasing thread count. C-RW-WP-4RC is a variant of C-RW-WP that uses 4 simple counters, one per

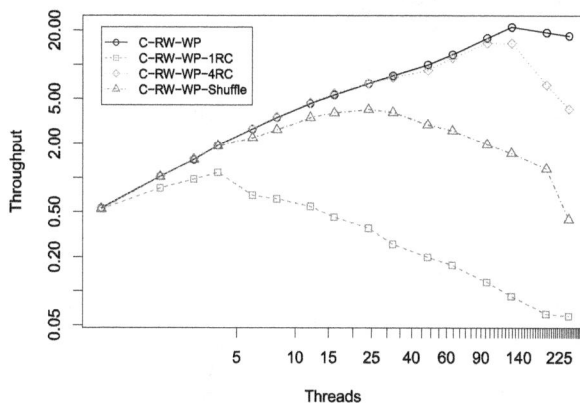

Figure 7. Scalability of the various reader counter implementations used in the same RWBench test configuration as Figure 6(a).

NUMA node on our experimental platform. The improvement with this split counter is significant and tracks the performance of C-RW-WP (which uses 4 ingress-egress counter pairs, one pair per NUMA node) to about 96 threads, but subsequently deteriorates because of excess contention on each of the node-local counters. The ingress-egress pair halves such contention, and scales better than the split counter implementation.

The scalable performance exhibited by C-RW-WP could arise in part by virtue of NUMA-locality via node-specific counters and in part by simply distributing accesses over the set of 4 reader indicator instances. C-RW-WP-Shuffle is a variation of C-RW-WP where we randomly shuffle reader indicator indices associated with threads. The number of threads accessing each counter remains the same, but those threads can reside on different nodes. As can be seen in the figure, a significant fraction of the benefit in C-RW-WP comes from NUMA-locality.

4.5 kccachetest Performance

kccachetest is provided with the Kyoto-Cabinet distribution, a popular open-source database package. It serves as a stress test and performance benchmark for the in-memory "cache hash" (CacheDB) database. CacheDB makes heavy use of standard pthread_rwlock_t operators, and performance of the benchmark is sensitive to the quality of the lock implementation. We ran the program with the "wicked" argument, which constructs an in-memory non-persistent database and then runs randomly selected transactions against that database. Both the benchmark and database reside in the same process and communicate via calls and shared memory. The benchmark is internally constrained to at most 64 threads. The number of threads can be specified on the command line, and each of the worker threads loops, selecting a random operation to be performed on the database. In some cases the operations are simple lookups or deletes, while others are more complex transactions. Each thread performs the same number of operations, and the program reports the interval between the time the first thread starts and the time the final thread completes. Unfortunately the size of the key range, and thus the footprint of the in-memory database, is a function of the number of threads. So as we increase the number of threads we also increase the key range and the footprint, which means that the results of runs with different numbers of threads are not easily comparable. As a result, we do not plot kccachetest results on a graph, but rather use a tabular representation.

Figure 8 shows the performance of kccachetest when used with the different RW locks. While all the locks are competitive at low threading levels, their performance diverges significantly with increasing thread counts. kccachetest contains a diverse mix of crit-

165

Locks	1T	2T	3T	4T	6T	8T	12T	16T	24T	32T	48T	64T
C-RW-WP	.510	1.20	1.78	1.95	3.08	4.24	6.99	9.24	14.5	18.0	26.7	37.7
C-RW-NP	.521	1.09	1.64	2.16	3.09	4.26	6.58	9.22	14.3	17.6	25.4	36.4
C-RW-RP	.550	1.12	1.77	2.23	3.31	4.53	7.09	10.4	13.3	18.9	34.5	52.5
C-RW-RP-opt	.531	1.15	1.76	2.19	3.30	4.54	7.45	10.5	13.5	27.0	41.2
Cohort	.516	1.25	1.74	2.35	3.41	4.36	7.03	8.55	13.3	18.2	29.6	44.3
DR-MCS	.531	1.13	1.58	1.94	3.17	4.19	6.79	10.2	17.6	26.7	49.6	77.1
DV	.511	1.18	1.75	2.14	3.18	4.12	6.59	9.88	12.8	21.3	52.0	56.8
ROLL	.547	1.25	1.55	1.99	3.32	4.50	7.79	11.3	20.2	29.0	46.4	63.3
Shirako	.554	1.16	1.61	2.07	3.33	4.53	7.30	10.7	18.5	27.0	35.5	55.2

Figure 8. Scalability results of the Kyoto Cabinet kccachetest benchmark (with the command line arguments: wicked -th Thrds -capsiz 2000000 100000). Each entry in the table reports wall clock time to completion in seconds.

ical sections, including short read-only and read-write ones, and long and complex read-write ones. Overall, the workload is dominated by read-write critical sections, where the threads acquire the RW locks in write mode. As a result, Cohort performs comparably to our NUMA RW locks, and much better than all other locks that contain NUMA-oblivious writers – DR-MCS, DV, ROLL, and Shirako. DR-MCS scales poorly because the underlying MCS lock acquired by writers forces the cache lines of the lock and the data it protects to bounce between NUMA nodes more often than other locks. Since Cohort significantly curtails lock migration, it performs much better. Our NUMA-aware RW locks, except C-RW-RP, further extend the *cohorting* advantage because of NUMA-friendly reader-reader concurrency. C-RW-RP succumbs to the superfluous writer ownership circulation performance problem described earlier, and, as a result, does not scale as well as our other locks. It does however scale better than all prior locks. Overall, C-RW-WP and C-RW-NP, which perform the best, outperform the best of the prior locks (DV and Shirako) by about 40%.

5. Conclusion

The rapid growth of multi-core multi-chip systems is making NUMA architectures commonplace, and fundamental data structures and synchronization primitives must be redesigned to adapt to these environments. We introduced a new family of surprisingly simple NUMA-aware reader-writer locks that outperform prior lock algorithms by a large margin. Writers use centralized lock metadata and readers use decentralized metadata. Microbenchmark experiments suggest that our best lock exceeds the performance of the prior state-of-the-art by up to a factor of 10, and our experiments on a real-world application, the Kyoto Cabinet database, show our locks can boost the application's performance by up to 40%.

Acknowledgments

We thank Doug Lea for useful discussions. Nir Shavit was supported in part by NSF grant 1217921.

References

[1] B. B. Brandenburg and J. H. Anderson. Spin-based Reader-Writer Synchronization for Multiprocessor Real-time Systems. *Real-Time Syst.*, 46(1):25–87, 2010.

[2] P. J. Courtois, F. Heymans, and D. L. Parnas. Concurrent control with "readers" and "writers". *Communications of the ACM*, 14(10):667–668, 1971.

[3] D. Dice, V. J. Marathe, and N. Shavit. Flat Combining NUMA Locks. In *Proceedings of the 23rd ACM Symposium on Parallelism in Algorithms and Architectures*, 2011.

[4] D. Dice. Solaris Scheduling: SPARC and CPUIDs. URL https://blogs.oracle.com/dave/entry/solaris_scheduling_and_cpuids.

[5] D. Dice. A Partitioned Ticket Lock. In *Proceedings of the 23rd ACM Aymposium on Parallelism in Algorithms and Architectures*, pages 309–310, 2011.

[6] D. Dice and N. Shavit. TLRW: Return of the Read-Write Lock. In *Proceedings of the 22nd ACM Symposium on Parallelism in Algorithms and Architectures*, pages 284–293, 2010.

[7] D. Dice, V. J. Marathe, and N. Shavit. Lock Cohorting: A General Technique for Designing NUMA Locks. In *Proceedings of the 17th ACM SIGPLAN symposium on Principles and Practice of Parallel Programming*, pages 247–256, 2012.

[8] E. W. Dijkstra. The origin of concurrent programming. chapter Cooperating sequential processes, pages 65–138. 2002.

[9] F. Ellen, Y. Lev, V. Luchangco, and M. Moir. SNZI: Scalable NonZero Indicators. In *Proceedings of the 26th Annual ACM Symposium on Principles of Distributed Computing*, pages 13–22, 2007.

[10] E. Freudenthal and A. Gottlieb. Process coordination with fetch-and-increment. In *Proceedings of the 4th International Conference on Architectural Support for Programming Languages and Operating Systems*, pages 260–268, 1991.

[11] W. C. Hsieh and W. E. Weihl. Scalable Reader-Writer Locks for Parallel Systems. In *Proceedings of the Sixth International Parallel Processing Symposium*, 1991.

[12] J. M. Mellor-Crummey and M. L. Scott. Algorithms for Scalable Synchronization on Shared-Memory Multiprocessors. *ACM Transactions on Computer Systems*, 9(1):21–65, 1991.

[13] J. M. Mellor-Crummey and M. L. Scott. Synchronization without Contention. In *Proceedings of the 4th International Conference on Architectural Support for Programming Languages and Operating Systems*, pages 269–278, 1991.

[14] O. Krieger, M. Stumm, R. Unrau, and J. Hanna. A Fair Fast Scalable Reader-Writer Lock. In *Proceedings of the 1993 International Conference on Parallel Processing*, pages 201–204, 1993.

[15] Y. Lev, V. Luchangco, and M. Olszewski. Scalable Reader-Writer Locks. In *Proceedings of the 21st Annual Symposium on Parallelism in Algorithms and Architectures*, pages 101–110, 2009.

[16] J. M. Mellor-Crummey and M. L. Scott. Scalable Reader-Writer Synchronization for Shared-Memory Multiprocessors. In *Proceedings of the 3rd ACM SIGPLAN Symposium on Principles and Practice of Parallel Programming*, pages 106–113, 1991.

[17] Z. Radović and E. Hagersten. Hierarchical Backoff Locks for Nonuniform Communication Architectures. In *HPCA-9*, pages 241–252, Anaheim, California, USA, Feb. 2003.

[18] J. Shirako, N. Vrvilo, E. G. Mercer, and V. Sarkar. Design, verification and applications of a new read-write lock algorithm. In *Proceedinbgs of the 24th ACM symposium on Parallelism in algorithms and architectures*, pages 48–57, 2012.

[19] Victor Luchangco and Dan Nussbaum and Nir Shavit. A Hierarchical CLH Queue Lock. In *Proceedings of the 12th International Euro-Par Conference*, pages 801–810, 2006.

[20] D. Vyukov. Distributed Reader-Writer Mutex. URL http://www.1024cores.net/home/lock-free-algorithms/reader-writer-problem/distributed-reader-writer-mutex.

Online-ABFT: An Online Algorithm Based Fault Tolerance Scheme for Soft Error Detection in Iterative Methods

Zizhong Chen

University of California, Riverside
chen@cs.ucr.edu

Abstract

Soft errors are one-time events that corrupt the state of a computing system but not its overall functionality. Large supercomputers are especially susceptible to soft errors because of their large number of components. Soft errors can generally be detected offline through the comparison of the final computation results of two duplicated computations, but this approach often introduces significant overhead. This paper presents Online-ABFT, a simple but efficient online soft error detection technique that can detect soft errors in the widely used Krylov subspace iterative methods in the middle of the program execution so that the computation efficiency can be improved through the termination of the corrupted computation in a timely manner soon after a soft error occurs. Based on a simple verification of orthogonality and residual, Online-ABFT is easy to implement and highly efficient. Experimental results demonstrate that, when this online error detection approach is used together with checkpointing, it improves the time to obtain correct results by up to several orders of magnitude over the traditional offline approach.

Categories and Subject Descriptors D.1.3 [*Programming Techniques*]: Concurrent Programming— Parallel programming

General Terms Design, Reliability, Performance

Keywords Algorithm-Based Fault Tolerance (ABFT), Checkpoint, Iterative Methods, Online Error Detection, Soft Error

1. Introduction

The extreme scale high performance computing (HPC) systems available before the end of this decade are expected to have 100 million to 1 billion CPU cores[1]. Due to the large number of components in these platforms, the probability that a failure occurs during the execution of an extreme scale application is expected to be much higher than today. Resilience has been widely viewed as a necessity for the exascale HPC applications [1, 8]. Fault tolerance techniques have been identified to be critical to the effective use of these HPC systems [8, 13, 22].

Soft errors are one-time events that corrupt the state of a computing system but not its overall functionality. Large supercomputers are especially susceptible to soft errors because of their large number of components. If a soft error causes the crash of a process in a HPC system, the process stops working and the soft error

becomes a fail-stop process failure which can often be tolerated using the standard checkpointing/restart technique [5, 13, 25, 30]. If a soft error does not cause the crash of a process, it becomes a fail-continue failure and does not interrupt the normal program execution. However the computation results from the computing can not be trusted any more. This paper restricts its scope to silent soft errors that do not cause the crash of a process. In what follows, for simplicity, soft errors are used to refer to such silent soft errors.

While soft errors in storage such as DRAM may be tolerated using error correction codes, soft errors in computing (e.g., errors such as $1 + 1 = 3$) are often more difficult to detect and correct. The idea of the triple modular redundancy (TMR) can be employed to ensure a very high soft error reliability. However, the overhead for TMR is high.

For iterative methods to solve linear equations, a standard approach to detect soft errors in the computation is to verify whether the computed solution satisfies the original equations or not. If the verification indicates that the computed solution does not satisfy the original equations, then a soft error may have occured. This approach can detect the errors but can not correct errors. In order to obtain the correct results, the computing has to be performed again. This approach is an offline approach which performs the error detection after the computation is finished. Therefore, even if the soft error occurs early in the computation, the corrupted computation will still continue until the end of the computation. Soft errors in iterative methods can also significantly increase the number of iterations (i.e., the amount of computation) to finish corrupted computation due to the loss or slow down of the convergence.

In this paper, we present a highly efficient online soft error correction technique for Krylov subspace iterative methods that can detect and correct soft errors in the middle of the program execution so that computation efficiency can be significantly improved through the termination of the corrupted computation in a timely manner in the middle of the program execution. Krylov subspace methods are among the most popular techniques today to solve sparse linear systems and eigenvalue problems. All Krylov subspace methods employ projections in one way or another and therefore often maintain an orthogonality relationship between vectors during the whole computation process. Furthermore, a residual vector is also often calculated independently of the residual relationship. The proposed technique in this paper is based on a simple verification of the above orthogonality and residual relationships and, therefore, is easy to implement and highly efficient. Experimental results demonstrate that, when this soft error detection technique is used together with the checkpoint technique, the computational efficiency can be improved by up to several orders of magnitude over the standard offline solution verification and recomputing approach. To the best of our knowledge, no previous research explored the detection of soft errors in iterative methods through orthogonality verification.

Permission to make digital or hard copies of all or part of this work for personal or classroom use is granted without fee provided that copies are not made or distributed for profit or commercial advantage and that copies bear this notice and the full citation on the first page. To copy otherwise, or republish, to post on servers or to redistribute to lists, requires prior specific permission and/or a fee.
PPoPP'13, February 23–27, 2013, Shenzhen, China.
Copyright © 2013 ACM 978-1-4503-1922-5/13/02...$15.00.

167

The rest of the paper is organized as following. Section 2 introduces related work. Section 3 presents our failure models. In Section 4, we develop fault tolerant versions of several iterative algorithms. Section 5 analyzes the performance of the proposed technique theoretically. In Section 6, we experimentally compare our online error correction technique with existing soft error correction techniques. Section 7 concludes the paper.

2. Related Work

Soft errors usually do not interrupt the program execution. In HPC, soft errors are often handled by checking the computation results after the computation is finished. Triple modular redundancy (TMR) is one of the general approaches to tolerate such failures. For matrix operations, Huang and Abraham developed the algorithm-based fault tolerance (ABFT) technique [24] to detect (and sometimes locate and correct) soft errors. Huang and Abraham proved that, for many matrix operations, the checksum relationship in the input checksum matrices is still held in the *final computation results*. Therefore, if the failed process is able to continue their work and finish the computation, the miscalculations can be detected by verifying whether or not the checksum relationship is still held in the final computation results. ABFT has been extended by [11, 12, 16, 17]. In [6], Bronevetsky et al. developed useful techniques to predict the soft error vulnerability for scientific applications. Techniques for correcting soft errors are also explored for iterative methods in [23, 26, 27]. In [4, 20], cooperative application/OS recovery was developed to correct DRAM soft errors. Considerable researches have been also done to provide fault tolerance for hard errors [2, 3, 5, 7, 9–19, 21, 25, 28, 30] during the past thirty years.

3. Failure Models

When an error occurs during an application execution, if the affected process stops working, we define the error as a hard error. When a hard error occurs, all data associated with the affected process are permanently lost. Hard errors may be caused by the crash of operating systems, underlying hardware, or interconnection networks. Hard errors are often tolerated by checkpoint/restart.

When an error occurs during an application execution, if the affected process continues working, we define the error as a soft error. Soft errors include computation errors by logic circuit and bit-flips in memory. They may be caused by many reasons including alpha particles from package decay, cosmic rays, thermal neutrons, and random noises. Soft errors do not interrupt the program execution. But the computation results cannot be trusted any more. Soft errors can often be tolerated by TMR. *The focus of this paper is on soft errors.*

4. Tolerating Soft Errors Online

Sparse matrices often arise during the solution of partial differential equations. Krylov subspace methods are often used to solve sparse linear systems and eigenvalue problems.

Soft errors in Krylov subspace methods can be detected by verifying whether the computed solution generates a small enough residual or not. However, this approach detects soft errors **offline** after the computation is finished. If an error is detected, the whole computation has to be performed again. Even if a soft error occurs in the early stage of the computation, the corrupted computation still continue until the end of the computation. Soft errors in iterative methods can significantly increase the number of iterations due to the slow down or loss of the convergence.

In this section, we present a highly efficient **online** soft error correction technique for Krylov subspace methods that detects and

corrects soft errors at the early stages in the middle of the program execution so that computation efficiency can be significantly improved through the termination of the corrupted computation in a timely manner in the middle of the program execution.

The key idea for our soft error detection techniques is based on the fact that projections are used in all Krylov subspace methods in one way or another and therefore orthogonality between vectors often exists the computation process. Based on this fact, soft errors in Krylov subspace methods can often be detected online during the program execution by dynamically verifying the orthogonality in the middle of the program execution. Compared with the offline error detection approach, the proposed online error detection approach improves the computation efficiency significantly because the unfinished corrupted computation can now be terminated in a more timely manner in the middle of the program execution.

To further improve efficiency, checkpoint can be used to save a copy of the verified computation locally so that the terminated computation does not have to be restarted from the beginning. More improvements of efficiency can be achieved by reducing the size of checkpoint through the residual relationship (e.g., Theorem 2) in most iterative methods. Because the checkpoints are saved **locally in parallel** and no communications are involved in our chechpointing, the approach is highly scalable.

Due to page limit, in what follows, without loss of generality, only CG, BiCG, and Lanczos biorthogonalization will be used as examples to demonstrate how orthogonality relationships can be used to detect soft errors dynamically during the program execution in Krylov subspace methods. However, the ideas developed here can also be used in other Krylov subspace methods including, but not limited to, Generalized Minimal Residual method (GMRES), BiConjugate Gradient Stabilized method (Bi-CGSTAB), Arnoldi's method for eigenvalue problems, Lanczos method for symmetric eigenvalue problems, and Lanczos biorthogonalization for non-symmetric eigenvalue problems, because all Krylov subspace methods employ projections and maintain similar orthogonality relationships during computation.

4.1 Preconditioned Conjugate Gradient Method

The *Preconditioned Conjugate Gradient (CG)* method is one of the most commonly used iterative methods to solve the sparse linear system $Ax = b$ when the coefficient matrix A is symmetric positive definite. The method computes successive approximations to the solution, residuals corresponding to the approximate solutions, and search directions used to update both the approximate solutions and the residuals. The length of these vector sequences can be large, but only a small number of the vectors needs to be maintained in memory. It involves one sparse matrix vector multiplication three vector updates, and two vector inner products in every iteration of the method. For more details of the algorithm, we refer readers to [29].

4.1.1 Detecting Fail-Continue Soft Errors in CG

In the preconditioned conjugate gradient algorithm, in addition to the explicit relationships among different variables and constants specified in Figure 1, there are also implicit relationships among different variables and constants. In what follows, we give two important implicit relationships that can be used to detect fail-continue soft errors in the preconditioned conjugate gradient algorithm.

Theorem 1. *In the preconditioned conjugate gradient algorithm in Figure 1, at each iteration i, the vectors $p^{(i+1)}$ and $q^{(i)}$ satisfy the following orthogonality relationship*

$$p^{(i+1)^T} q^{(i)} = 0. \tag{1}$$

Proof. See [29]. □

Theorem 2. *In the preconditioned conjugate gradient algorithm in Figure 1, at each iteration i, the vectors $r^{(i+1)}$, $x^{(i+1)}$, b, and the matrix A satisfy the following equality relationship*

$$r^{(i+1)} + Ax^{(i+1)} = b. \tag{2}$$

Proof. See [29]. □

```
 1 : Compute r^(0) = b - Ax^(0), z^(0) = M^(-1)r^(0), p^(0) = z^(0),
       and ρ_0 = r^(0)^T z^(0) for some initial guess x^(0)
 2 : checkpoint: A, M, and b
 3 : for i = 0, 1, ...
 4 :    if ( (i>0) and (i%d = 0) )
 5 :       if ( (p^(i+1)^T q^(i))/(||p^(i+1)||.||q^(i)||) > 10^(-10)
             or (||r^(i+1) + Ax^(i+1) - b||)/(||b||.||A||) > 10^(-10) )
 6 :          recover: A, M, b, i, ρ_i,
                          p^(i), x^(i), and r^(i).
 7 :       else if ( i%(cd) = 0 )
 8 :          checkpoint: i, ρ_i, p^(i), and x^(i)
 9 :       endif
10 :    endif
11 :    q^(i) = Ap^(i)
12 :    α_i = ρ_i / p^(i)^T q^(i)
13 :    x^(i+1) = x^(i) + α_i q^(i)
14 :    r^(i+1) = r^(i) - α_i q^(i)
15 :    solve Mz^(i+1) = r^(i+1), where M = M^T
16 :    ρ_{i+1} = r^(i+1)^T z^(i+1)
17 :    β_i = ρ_{i+1}/ρ_i
10 :    p^(i+1) = z^(i+1) + β_i p^(i)
19 :    check convergence; continue if necessary
20 : end
```

Figure 1. Fault tolerant preconditioned conjugate gradient algorithm.

Theorem 1 can be used to detect fail-continue soft error occurs in A, M, b, ρ_i, $p^{(i)}$, or $r^{(i)}$. When there is a fail-continue soft error occurs in the ith iteration in A, M, b, ρ_i, $p^{(i)}$, or $r^{(i)}$, the error will be propagated to $p^{(i+2)}$ or $q^{(i+1)}$, which often damage the orthogonality relationship between $p^{(i+2)}$ and $q^{(i+1)}$. Even if orthogonality relationship between $p^{(i+2)}$ and $q^{(i+1)}$ is not damaged, due to the continue propagation of errors to $p^{(i+2+k)}$ or $q^{(i+1+k)}$, where $k = 1, 2, \ldots$, the orthogonality relationship will be violated eventually.

Theorem 1 can not be used to detect fail-continue soft errors occur in the solution vector $x^{(i)}$. It is because any fail-continue soft error occurs in $x^{(i)}$ will not be propagated to $p^{(i+k+1)}$ or $q^{(i+k)}$, therefore will not affect the orthogonality relationship between $p^{(i+k+1)}$ and $q^{(i+k)}$.

However, fail-continue soft errors occur in the solution vector $x^{(i)}$ can be often detected through verifying the equality relationship in Theorem 2. This is because the damage of the vector $x^{(i)}$ will damage the residual relationship $r^{(i+k)} + Ax^{(i+k)} = b$, where $k = 1, 2, \ldots$.

The verification of the orthogonality and residual relationship involves one vector inner product and one matrix vector multiplication. In a parallel environment, both the vector inner product and the matrix vector multiplication involves global communications which may affect the performance the algorithm especially when the matrix vector multiplication is the dominant time in each iteration.

However, the impact of the error detection on performance can be greatly reduced by performing error detection every several iterations. The optimal number of iterations d between two error detection depends on the failure rate of the computation platform, which will be addressed in Section 5.

Note that, in practical computations, all calculations are performed using floating-point arithmetics with round-off errors. Therefore, when Theorems 1 and 2 are used to detect errors, the effect of round-off errors have to be considered. As shown in Figure 1, we use 10^{-10} as the error bar for detecting soft errors. If a soft error is too close to the machine epsilon, we will not be able to detect and correct it. Actually, if a soft error is too close to machine epsilon, it does not have to be detected and corrected because it will not be drastically enlarged in a practical numerically stable algorithm. If an algorithm is not numerically stable enough, round-off errors may also be drastically enlarged, which may make the correct computation without soft errors also useless. This paper restricts its scope to well-conditioned problems and numerically stable algorithms .

4.1.2 Correcting Fail-Continue Soft Errors in CG

After a soft error is detected, a natural error correction approach is to terminate the computation damaged by the error immediately and restart the computation from the beginning again. However, the drawback of this approach is that all previous computation is lost.

In this subsection, we propose to use an algorithm based checkpointing approach to correct the error. Our algorithm based checkpointing approach will be different from the existing checkpointing approach. The key difference is that the size of checkpoint is reduced by 33% over the existing checkpointing approach.

The preconditioned conjugate gradient algorithm depends on the following eight variables: i, A, M, b, $r^{(i)}$, ρ_i, $p^{(i)}$, and $x^{(i)}$.

When a soft error is detected at the iteration j, if there is a correct copy of the variables i, A, M, b, $r^{(i)}$, ρ_i, $p^{(i)}$, and $x^{(i)}$ at the ith iteration, where $i < j$, then the computation can be restarted from the ith iteration.

A, M, b are constants. i and ρ_{i-1} are scalars. Therefore the size of the *periodical* checkpoint is dominated by three vectors: $r^{(i)}$, $p^{(i)}$, and $x^{(i)}$.

However, according to Theorem 2, the vectors $r^{(i)}$ and $x^{(i)}$ are not independent. A, b, $r^{(i)}$, and $x^{(i)}$ satisfy the following relationship

$$r^{(i)} + Ax^{(i)} = b.$$

Therefore, it is not necessary to checkpoint $r^{(i)}$.

In our checkpoint, we do not checkpoint $r^{(i)}$. After a soft error is detected, $r^{(i)}$ is recovered not through a checkpoint. We recover $r^{(i)}$ through the following relationship

$$r^{(i)} = b - Ax^{(i)}.$$

By eliminating $r^{(i)}$ from the periodical checkpoint, the size of the periodical checkpoint is reduced about 33%.

In order to reduce the impact of error detection and periodical checkpoint on performance, we perform error detection every d iterations and perform periodical checkpoint every cd iterations. Both the optimal checkpoint interval cd and the optimal error detection interval d depends on the time for one checkpoint, the time for one error detection, and the failure rate. The details of the optimal checkpoint interval and optimal error detection interval will be addressed in Section 5. Figure 1 is the complete fault tolerant preconditioned conjugate gradient algorithm with both error detection and error correcting.

4.2 Biconjugate Gradient Method

The biconjugate gradient method is an algorithm that can be used to solve nonsymmetric linear systems. Figure 2 (black part) shows the biconjugate gradient algorithm. More details of the algorithm can be found in [29].

4.2.1 Detecting Fail-Continue Soft Errors in BiCG

In the biconjugate gradient algorithm in Figure 2, there are two important implicit relationships among different variables and constants that can be used to detect fail-continue soft errors.

Theorem 3. *In the biconjugate gradient algorithm in Figure 2, the vectors $\tilde{p}^{(i+1)}$ and $q^{(i)}$ satisfy the following orthogonality relationship $\tilde{p}^{(i+1)^T} q^{(i)} = 0$.*

Proof. See *Proposition* 7.2 in [29]. □

Theorem 4. *In the biconjugate gradient algorithm in Figure 2, the vectors $r^{(i+1)}$, $x^{(i+1)}$, b, and the matrix A satisfy the following equality relationship $r^{(i+1)} + Ax^{(i+1)} = b$.*

Proof. See [29]. □

Theorem 3 can be used to detect fail-continue soft error occurs in A, A^T, b, i, ρ_i, $p^{(i)}$, $\tilde{p}^{(i)}$, $r^{(i)}$, and $\tilde{r}^{(i)}$. When there is a fail-continue soft error occurs in the ith iteration in A, A^T, b, i, ρ_i, $p^{(i)}$, $\tilde{p}^{(i)}$, $r^{(i)}$, and $\tilde{r}^{(i)}$, the error will be propagated to $\tilde{p}^{(i+k+1)}$ or $q^{(i+k)}$, where $k = 1, 2, \ldots$, which often damage the orthogonality relationship between $\tilde{p}^{(i+k+1)}$ and $q^{(i+k)}$. Theorem 3 can NOT be used to detect fail-continue soft errors occur in the solution vector $x^{(i)}$. It is because any fail-continue soft error occurs in $x^{(i)}$ will not be propagated to $\tilde{p}^{(i+k+1)}$ or $q^{(i+k)}$, therefore will not affect the orthogonality relationship between $\tilde{p}^{(i+k+1)}$ and $q^{(i+k)}$.

But fail-continue soft errors occur in the solution vector $x^{(i)}$ can often be detected through verifying the equality relationship in Theorem 4. This is because the damage of the vector $x^{(i)}$ will damage the residual relationship $r^{(i+k)} + Ax^{(i+k)} = b$, where $k = 1, 2, \ldots$.

In order to reduce the impact of the error detection on performance, error detection can be performed every several iterations. The optimal number of iterations between error detection will be addressed in Section 5.

4.2.2 Correcting Fail-Continue Soft Errors in BiCG

The biconjugate gradient algorithm depends on the following ten variables: A, A^T, b, i, ρ_i, $p^{(i)}$, $\tilde{p}^{(i)}$, $r^{(i)}$, $\tilde{r}^{(i)}$, and $x^{(i)}$. Note that A, A^T, and b are constants and i and ρ_i are scalars. Therefore the size of the *periodical* checkpoint is dominated by five vectors: $p^{(i)}$, $\tilde{p}^{(i)}$, $r^{(i)}$, $\tilde{r}^{(i)}$, and $x^{(i)}$.

However, according to Theorem 4, the vectors $r^{(i)}$ and $x^{(i)}$ are not independent. A, b, $r^{(i)}$, and $x^{(i)}$ satisfy

$$r^{(i)} + Ax^{(i)} = b.$$

Therefore, it is not necessary to checkpoint $r^{(i)}$. In our soft error correcting algorithm, $r^{(i)}$ will be recovered through

$$r^{(i)} = b - Ax^{(i)}.$$

By eliminating $r^{(i)}$ from the periodical checkpoint, the size of the periodical checkpoint is reduced by about 20%.

In the fault tolerant biconjugate gradient algorithm in Figure 2, we perform error detection every d iterations and perform periodical checkpoint every cd iterations. The optimal values for d and c will be discussed in Section 5.

```
1 : Compute r^(0) = b - Ax^(0). Choose r̃^(0) = r^(0).
      Set p^(0) = r^(0), p̃^(0) = r̃^(0), and ρ_0 = r^(0)^T r̃^(0)
2 : checkpoint: A, A^T, and b
3 : for i = 0, 1, ...
4 :     if ( (i>0) and (i%d = 0) )
5 :         if ( (p̃^(i+1)^T q^(i))/(||p̃^(i+1)||.||q̃^(i)||) > 10^-10
             or (||r^(i+1) + Ax^(i+1) - b||)/(||b||.||A||) > 10^-10 )
6 :             recover: A, A^T, b, i, ρ_i, p^(i),
                         p̃^(i), x^(i), r^(i), and r̃^(i)
7 :         else if ( i%(cd) = 0 )
8 :             checkpoint: i, ρ_i, p^(i), p̃^(i),
                            r̃^(i), and x^(i)
9:          endif
10:     endif
11:     q^(i) = Ap^(i)
12:     q̃^(i) = A^T p̃^(i)
13:     α_i = ρ_i/q^(i)^T p̃^(i)
14:     x^(i+1) = x^(i) + α_i p^(i)
15:     r^(i+1) = r^(i) - α_i q^(i)
16:     r̃^(i+1) = r̃^(i) - α_i q̃^(i)
17:     ρ_{i+1} = r^(i+1)^T r̃^(i+1)
18:     β_i = ρ_{i+1}/ρ_i
19:     p^(i+1) = r^(i+1) + β_i p^(i)
20:     p̃^(i+1) = r̃^(i+1) + β_i p̃^(i)
21:     check convergence; continue if necessary
22: end
```

Figure 2. Fault tolerant biconjugate gradient algorithm.

4.3 Lanczos Biorthogonalization Algorithm

The Lanczos biorthogonalization algorithm is proposed by Lanczos to extend the symmetric Lanczos algorithm to **nonsymmetric** matrices. The goal is to build a pair of biorthogonal bases for the two subspaces $span\{v_1, Av_1, \ldots, A^{m-1}v_1\}$ and $span\{v_1, Av_1, \ldots, A^{m-1}v_1\}$. The Lanczos biorthogonalization algorithm is the base of quasi-minimal residual (QMR) algorithm, biconjugate gradient (BiCG) algorithm, conjugate gradient squared (CGS) algorithm, and biconjugate gradient stabilized (BiCGSTAB) algorithm. More details of the algorithm can be found in [29].

4.3.1 Detecting Fail-Continue Soft Errors in Lanczos Biorthogonalization

In the Lanczos biorthogonalization algorithm in Figure 3 (black part), there is an implicit relationships between $w^{(i)}$ and $v^{(i)}$ that can be used to detect fail-continue soft errors.

Theorem 5. *In the Lanczos biorthogonalization algorithm in Figure 3, the vectors $w^{(i+1)}$ and $v^{(i)}$ satisfy the following orthogonality relationship $w^{(i+1)^T} v^{(i)} = 0$.*

Proof. See *Proposition* 7.1 in [29]. □

Theorem 5 can be used to detect fail-continue soft error occurs in A, A^T, i, β_i, δ_i, $v^{(i)}$, $v^{(i-1)}$, $w^{(i)}$, and $w^{(i-1)}$. When there is a fail-continue soft error occurs in the ith iteration in A, A^T, i, β_i, δ_i, $v^{(i)}$, $v^{(i-1)}$, $w^{(i)}$, and $w^{(i-1)}$, the error will be propagated to $w^{(i+k+1)}$ or $v^{(i+k)}$, where $k = 1, 2, \ldots$, which often damage the orthogonality relationship between $w^{(i+k+1)}$ and $v^{(i+k)}$.

In order to reduce the impact of the error detection on performance, error detection can be performed every several iterations. The optimal number of iterations between error detection will be addressed in Section 5.

4.3.2 Correcting Fail-Continue Soft Errors in Lanczos Biorthogonalization

```
 1 : Set v^(0) = w^(0) = 0, β_1 = δ_1 = 0. Choose two
         vectors v^(1) and w^(1) such that v^(1)w^(1) = 1.
 2 : checkpoint: A and A^T
 3 : for i = 1,2,...
 4 :     if ( (i>0) and (i%d = 0) )
 5 :         if ( (w^(i+1)^T v^(i)) / (||w^(i+1)||.||v^(i)||) > 10^(-10) )
 6 :             recover: A, A^T, i, β_i, δ_i, v^(i),
                                    v^(i-1), w^(i), and w^(i-1)
 7 :         else if ( i%(cd) = 0 )
 8 :             checkpoint: i, β_i, δ_i, v^(i), v^(i-1),
                                    w^(i), and w^(i-1)
 9 :         endif
10 :     endif
11 :     p^(i) = Av^(i)
12 :     q^(i) = A^T w^(i)
13 :     α_i = p^(i)^T w^(i)
14 :     ṽ^(i+1) = p^(i) - α_i v^(i) - β_i v^(i-1)
15 :     w̃^(i+1) = q^(i) - α_i w^(i) - δ_i w^(i-1)
16 :     β_{i+1} = √(ṽ^(i+1)^T w̃^(i+1)). If β_{i+1} = 0 stop.
17 :     δ_{i+1} = ṽ^(i+1)^T w̃^(i+1) / δ_{i+1}
18 :     v^(i+1) = ṽ^(i+1) / β_{i+1}
19 :     w^(i+1) = w̃^(i+1) / δ_{i+1}
20 :     check convergence; continue if necessary
21 : end
```

Figure 3. Fault tolerant Lanczos biorthogonalization algorithm.

The Lanczos biorthogonalization algorithm depends on A, A^T, i, β_i, δ_i, $v^{(i)}$, $v^{(i-1)}$, $w^{(i)}$, and $w^{(i-1)}$. Note that A and A^T are constants. Therefore, in our the *periodical* checkpoint, we only checkpoint i, β_i, δ_i, $v^{(i)}$, $\tilde{v}^{(i)}$, $w^{(i)}$, and $\tilde{w}^{(i)}$.

In the fault tolerant algorithm in Figure 3, we perform error detection every d iterations and perform periodical checkpoint every cd iterations. The optimal values for d and c will again be addressed in Section 5.

5. Performance Analysis

This section analyzes the expected execution time of our iterative methods on unreliable computing systems and compare the proposed online soft error detection and correcting scheme with the traditional offline error detection and recomputing scheme.

Assume the time to failure of all processes follows an independent and identically distributed exponential distribution. Let λ denote the failure rate for an application with p processes. Assume the time for an error detection is t_d, the time to perform a checkpoint is t_c, and the time to recover from a checkpoint is t_r. Assume the iterative method converges and it takes I iterations to converge. Let t denote the time for each iteration and $T = It + t_d$ denote the time to finish all iterations plus the time to perform a error detection at the end.

5.1 Offline Error Detection with Recomputation

When computing systems are not reliable, a standard approach to detect whether or not there is any error occur during the computation is to verify whether the residual $||b - Ax||/(||b||.||A||)$ is in the same order of magnitude as the machine ϵ. Note that, in this paper, we only analyze the case where the iterative method converges when there are no errors. Therefore, if the residual is too large, it indicates there must be an error during the computation. After errors are detected, the application can be restarted from the beginning.

Because the detection of the errors are performed after the computation is finished, in this paper, we call this error detection approach *offline error detection*.

Iterative methods sometimes may still converge even if there is an error occurs during the computation. However, whether the iterative method converges to the correct solution or not depends on which part of the data is corrupted. For example, if the coefficient matrix of the equation to be solved is corrupted, even if the iterative method converges, it will not converge to the correct solution. For Krylov subspace iterative methods, if there is an error, the orthogonality relationships are often damaged. Therefore, even if they converge, they often need significantly more iterations.

Let M denote the number of iterations and $T_M = Mt + t_d$ denote the execution time when an error occurs during the computation. When the failure rate is λ, the probability that there are no errors during the whole execution time T is $e^{-\lambda T}$. The probability that there are at least one error during the whole execution time T is $1 - e^{-\lambda T}$.

Let $E_{\text{offline-recp}}$ denote the expected time to obtain the correct solution when computing systems are not reliable. By taking a conditional expectation on whether there is an error or not, we have

$$
E_{\text{offline-recp}} = Te^{-\lambda T} + (T_M + E_{\text{offline-recp}})(1 - e^{-\lambda T}).
$$

Therefore

$$
E_{\text{offline-recp}} = T + T_M(e^{\lambda T} - 1). \tag{3}
$$

The expression (3) indicates that the expected program execution time will increase exponentially as the number of the processes increases.

5.2 Online Error Detection with Timely Termination

With the help of the proposed online error detection technique, when an error occurs during the computation, it is possible to detect the error before the damaged computation finishes and terminate the damaged computation in a timely manner.

Let d denote the number of iterations between two consecutive error detections and $k = I/d$ denote the total number error detections during the computation. Let T_d denote the error detection interval. Let s denote the probability that no errors occur during the interval T_d and f denote the probability that there is at least one error occurs during the interval T_d. Then we have

$$
T_d = d \cdot t + t_d \tag{4}
$$
$$
s = e^{-\lambda T_d} \tag{5}
$$
$$
f = 1 - e^{-\lambda T_d} \tag{6}
$$

Let $E_{online-recp(d)}$ denote the expected time to obtain the correct solution when the error detection is performed every d iterations. By taking a conditional expection on the number of errors occur during the computation, we have

$$
\begin{aligned}
E_{\text{online-recp}}(d) &= f(1.T_d + E_{\text{online-recp}}(d)) + \\
&\quad sf(2.T_d + E_{\text{online-recp}}(d)) + \\
&\quad s^2 f(3.T_d + E_{\text{online-recp}}(d)) + \\
&\quad \vdots \\
&\quad s^{k-1} f(k.T_d + E_{\text{online-recp}}(d)) + \\
&\quad s^k(k.T_d) \\
&= f(1 + s + s^2 + \ldots + s^{k-1})E_{\text{online-recp}}(d) \\
&\quad + f(1 + 2s + 3s^2 + \ldots + ks^{k-1})T_d \\
&\quad + s^k(k.T_d) \\
&= f\frac{1 - s^k}{1 - s}E_{\text{online-recp}}(d) \\
&\quad + f\left(\frac{1 - s^k}{(1 - s)^2} - \frac{ks^k}{1 - s}\right)T_d + s^k(k.T_d) \\
&= (1 - s^k)E_{\text{online-recp}}(d) + \frac{1 - s^k}{1 - s}T_d
\end{aligned}
$$

Therefore

$$
\begin{aligned}
E_{\text{online-recp}}(d) &= \frac{1}{s^k}\frac{1 - s^k}{1 - s}T_d \\
&= (e^{\lambda I(t + \frac{t_d}{d})} - 1)\frac{d \cdot t + t_d}{1 - e^{-\lambda(d \cdot t + t_d)}}. \quad (7)
\end{aligned}
$$

Let $E_{\text{online-recp}}$ denote the minimum value of $E_{\text{online-recp}}(d)$, then

$$
E_{\text{online-recp}} = \min_d \left\{ (e^{\lambda I(t + \frac{t_d}{d})} - 1)\frac{d \cdot t + t_d}{1 - e^{-\lambda(d \cdot t + t_d)}} \right\}.
$$

There are no explicit analytical expressions for the optimal values of both the error detection interval d and the time $E_{\text{online-recp}}$. Optimal values of d and $E_{\text{online-recp}}$ will be explored numerically in the Section 6.

5.3 Online Error Detection with Restart from Checkpoints

When an error is detected, if the whole computation is restarted from the beginning, then all the finished computation will be lost. When error detection procedure does not detect any errors, if we can save a checkpoint periodically, then it is possible to restart the computation from a checkpoint so that the finished computation before the latest checkpoint do not have to be repeated.

When a periodical checkpoint scheme is also used in the application, let c denote the number of error detections between two consecutive checkpoints, then cd is the number of iterations between two consecutive checkpoints. Let $n = I/(cd)$ denote the number of checkpoints during the whole application. Let T_c denote the length of the checkpoint interval and E_c denote the expected execution time for one checkpoint interval. If we assume there are no failures occur during the checkpoint and recovery, then we have

$$
\begin{aligned}
T_c &= c(d \cdot t + t_d) + t_c. \quad (8) \\
E_c &= (e^{\lambda cd(t + \frac{t_d}{d})} - 1)\frac{d \cdot t + t_d}{1 - e^{-\lambda(d \cdot t + t_d)}} \\
&\quad + (e^{\lambda cd(t + \frac{t_d}{d})} - 1)t_r + t_c. \quad (9)
\end{aligned}
$$

Therefore, the expected time to finish all intervals (i.e the whole application) is

$$
\begin{aligned}
E_{\text{online-ckpt}}(c, d) &= \frac{I}{cd}\left[(e^{\lambda cd(t + \frac{t_d}{d})} - 1)\frac{d \cdot t + t_d}{1 - e^{-\lambda(d \cdot t + t_d)}} \right. \\
&\quad \left. + (e^{\lambda cd(t + \frac{t_d}{d})} - 1)t_r + t_c\right]. \quad (10)
\end{aligned}
$$

The expected execution time $E_{\text{online-ckpt}}(c, d)$ depends on the number of checkpoints c and the number of error detections d. Let $E_{\text{online-ckpt}}$ denote the optimal expected time to obtain the correct solution, then

$$
\begin{aligned}
E_{\text{online-ckpt}} &= \min_{c,d} \left\{ \frac{I}{cd}\left[(e^{\lambda cd(t + \frac{t_d}{d})} - 1)\frac{d \cdot t + t_d}{1 - e^{-\lambda(d \cdot t + t_d)}} \right.\right. \\
&\quad \left.\left. + (e^{\lambda cd(t + \frac{t_d}{d})} - 1)t_r + t_c\right]\right\}.
\end{aligned}
$$

No explicit analytical expressions exist for the optimal values c, d and $E_{\text{online-ckpt}}$. Optimal values of c, d and $E_{\text{online-ckpt}}$ will be studied in the Section 6 using a numerical approach.

6. Experimental Evaluation

In this section, we first evaluate the error detection capability of the following four soft error detection techniques: the offline residual checking at the end of the computation (denoted by **Offline-Residual**), the online residual checking in the middle of the computation (denoted by **Online-Residual**), the online matrix-vector-multiplication checking using the ABFT idea in[24] (denoted by **Online-MV**), and the proposed technique in this paper (denoted by **Online-ABFT**), and then evaluate the performance of these techniques. For demonstration purposes, we focus our evaluation on using the preconditioned conjugate gradient method to solve the following sparse linear system (arising from discretizing a 3D Poisson's equation) on Jaguar at ORNL.

$$
A_{n^3 \times n^3}\ u_{n^3 \times 1} = b_{n^3 \times 1},
$$

where

$$
A_{n^3 \times n^3} = \begin{pmatrix}
M_{n^2 \times n^2} & I_{n^2 \times n^2} & & & \\
I_{n^2 \times n^2} & M_{n^2 \times n^2} & I_{n^2 \times n^2} & & \\
& \ddots & \ddots & \ddots & \\
& & I_{n^2 \times n^2} & M_{n^2 \times n^2} & I_{n^2 \times n^2} \\
& & & I_{n^2 \times n^2} & M_{n^2 \times n^2}
\end{pmatrix},
$$

$$
M_{n^2 \times n^2} = \begin{pmatrix}
T_{n \times n} & I_{n \times n} & & & \\
I_{n \times n} & T_{n \times n} & I_{n \times n} & & \\
& \ddots & \ddots & \ddots & \\
& & I_{n \times n} & T_{n \times n} & I_{n \times n} \\
& & & I_{n \times n} & T_{n \times n}
\end{pmatrix},
$$

$$
T_{n \times n} = \begin{pmatrix}
-6 & 1 & & & \\
1 & -6 & 1 & & \\
& \ddots & \ddots & \ddots & \\
& & 1 & -6 & 1 \\
& & & 1 & -6
\end{pmatrix}.
$$

6.1 Error Detection Capability

In this subsection, we experimentally evaluate the error detection capability of the Offline-Residual technique, the Online-Residual technique, the Online-MV technique, and the Online-ABFT technique on Jaguar by incorporating these four techniques into a preconditioned conjugate gradient solver we developed. Except the loop variable i, our preconditioned conjugate gradient solver involves 11 variables A, M, b, ρ, α, β, z, q, r, p, and x. Forty four experiments are performed to answer the following four questions:

1. Which of the 11 variables can be protected if the residual is checked **offline** and errors are reported when the norm of the residual indicates divergence?

2. Which of the 11 variables can be protected if the norm of the residual is checked **online** and errors are reported when the norm of the residual increases?

3. Which of the 11 variables can be protected if the Online-MV technique is used to detect errors?

4. Which of the 11 variables can be protected if the proposed Online-ABFT technique is used to detect errors?

At each experiment, one significant soft error (i.e., adding 1.0 to original value) was introduced into one of the 11 variables to test one of the four error detection techniques. The experimental results are summarized in Figure 4. A "yes" in Figure 4 means that the injected errors are successfully detected. A "no" in Figure 4 means that the injected errors are not detected. Figure 4 indicates that all soft errors in all 11 variables can be detected when the residual is checked offline. However, none of the soft errors can be detected when the norm of the residual is checked online periodically during the computation. This is because the norm of the residual is not strictly decreasing during the computation and errors are reported no matter there are errors occur or not. When online-MV is used to detect errors, experimental results indicate that errors in variables b, ρ, α, and β can not be detected. When the proposed Online-ABFT technique is used, all soft errors in all variables can be detected. Figure 4 indicates that only the Offline-Residual technique and the proposed Online-ABFT technique can detect all soft errors in all 11 variables. Therefore, in what follows, we will only compare the performance of these two techniques.

Figure 4. Error Detection Capability for Different Techniques with CG on Jaguar at ORNL.

Variables with Error	Offline-Residual	Online-Residual	Online-MV	Online-ABFT
A	yes	no	yes	yes
M	yes	no	yes	yes
b	yes	no	no	yes
ρ	yes	no	no	yes
α	yes	no	no	yes
β	yes	no	no	yes
z	yes	no	yes	yes
q	yes	no	yes	yes
r	yes	no	yes	yes
p	yes	no	yes	yes
x	yes	no	yes	yes

6.2 Error Correction Overhead

In order to quantify the overhead of the proposed technique, we ran both the Offline-Residual based fault tolerant preconditioned conjugate gradient solver and the Online-ABFT based fault tolerant preconditioned conjugate gradient solver for 100 iterations on Jaguar at ORNL using 5000 cores. For the Online-ABFT based solver, we performed error detection every 10 iterations and checkpoint every 20 iterations. For the Offline-Residual based solver, we performed the error detection through residual checking after the computation is finished. In both experiments, one significant soft error was introduced into the variable β at the 50th iteration. For

Figure 5. Error Correction Overhead for Different Techniques with CG on Jaguar at ORNL.

Time-Overhead	Offline-Residual	Online-ABFT
Time per Detection (s)	0.20	0.21
Time per Checkpoint (s)	N/A	1.02
Time for Rollback (s)	99.58	9.01
Time per Recovery (s)	N/A	0.99
Total Time Overhead (s)	99.78	17.41
Total Exec. Time (s)	200.26	119.00

the Online-ABFT based solver, the introduced soft error was successfully detected at the beginning of the 51st iteration and the computation was rolled back to the checkpoint at the 40th iteration. For the Offline-Residual based solver, the introduced soft error was successfully detected after the computation is finished and the computation was restarted from the beginning.

Figure 5 summarizes the experimental results. Note that neither checkpoint nor recovery is involved in the Offline-Residual based solver, therefore, the corresponding time is "N/A" in Figure 5. The total execution time for the first execution of the Offline-Residual based solver takes 99.58 seconds. Due to the detection of an error, the computation has to be restarted from (i.e., rolled back to) the beginning, which caused a rollback overhead of 99.58 seconds. Because of the re-computation, the total execution time for the Offline-Residual-based solver is 200.26 seconds. For the Online-ABFT based solver, the number of iterations rolled back is only 10, which introduced a rollback overhead of 9.01 seconds. Because there are 5 checkpoints (5.1 seconds) and 10 detections (2.1 seconds) involved for the Online-ABFT based solver plus some random noise in timing, the total overhead for this solver is 17.41 seconds. The total measured execution time for the Online-ABFT based solver is 119.00 seconds, which is much smaller than total execution time for the Offline-Residual based solver (200.26 seconds).

6.3 Expected Execution Time and Overhead

In the previous subsection, because we do not know the probability distribution for the underlying failures, both the error detection interval (10 iterations) and the checkpoint interval (20 iterations) are chosen in a subjective way. The iteration index (50) that we inject the soft error is also subjective.

In this subsection, we evaluate the performance improvement of the proposed technique over the Offline-Residual technique by simulation assuming: (1). the underlying failures follow Poisson distribution; (2). both the optimal error detection interval and the optimal checkpoint interval are used in the proposed Online-ABFT technique. The evaluation is based on the performance analysis model in Section 5.

Extensive simulation experiments have been performed to evaluate the optimal error detection interval, the optimal checkpoint interval, and the optimal expected execution time to obtain correct solution on various combinations of parameters. For demonstration purposes, in what follows, we report an example set of our experimental results with the following parameter configuration: When the computing platform is error-free, the solver converges to the correct solution within 100 iterations; The time for each iteration is 1 hour; The time to perform each error detection is 0.2 hours; The time for each recovery is 1 hour; The time for each checkpoint is 1 hour; The failure rates (i.e., the number of errors per hour) are $\lambda = 0.01, 0.02, 0.03, 0.04, 0.05, 0.06, 0.07, 0.08, 0.09$, and 0.10. Note that a failure rate of $\lambda = 0.01$ equals to, on average, one soft

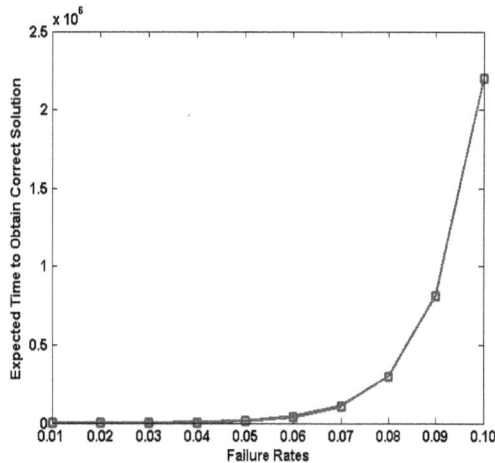

Figure 6. Expected execution time for offline residual checking error detection with recomputation.

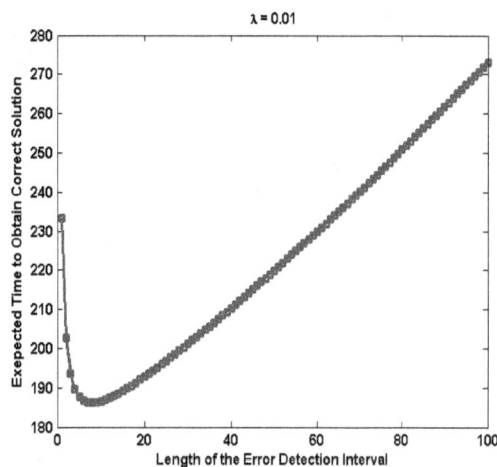

Figure 7. Expected execution time for online error detection with timely execution termination.

error per 100 hours. In what follows, for simplicity, we ignore the time unit hour.

6.3.1 Offline Error Detection with Recomputation

Offline error detection with recomputation is the standard technique that can detect all soft errors in all critical variables on a unreliable computing platform. Due to the fact that the error detection is performed offline after all computation is finished, it is impossible for this technique to find out when the error occurs. Therefore, if a error is detected in the final solution, the technique has to restart the whole computation from the beginning. Figure 6 demonstrates the expected execution time to obtain the correct solution as the failure rate changes. Figure 6 indicates, due to recomputation, the expected execution time to obtain correct solution will increase exponentially as the failure rate increases.

6.3.2 Online Error Detection with Timely Termination

When errors can be detected online, applications can be terminated before they finish if an error was detected. This subsection explores the impact of the timely termination and compares the performance

Figure 8. Optimal error detection interval and execution time.

λ	Opt Detect Intv	Opt Time
0.01	8	186
0.02	7	366
0.03	7	774
0.04	7	1732
0.05	7	4053
0.06	7	9808
0.07	7	24342
0.08	7	61590
0.09	7	158190
0.10	7	411400

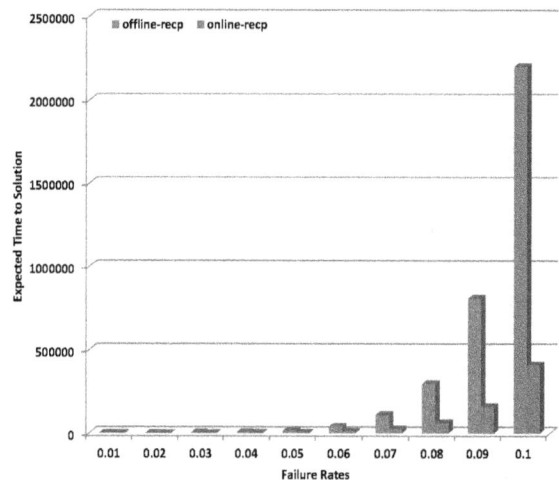

Figure 9. Expected execution time: offline residual checking error detection vs online orthogonality checking error detection.

of the proposed online detection technique with the standard offline residual checking technique. Figure 7 shows the relationship between the error detection interval and the expected execution time for $\lambda = 0.01$ when applications can be terminated in a timely manner after an error occured. Figure 7 indicates that the expected execution time first decrease and then increase. There is an optimal value for the error detection interval. Figure 8 demonstrates the optimal value for the error detection interval and the corresponding expected execution time when $\lambda = 0.1, 0.2, \ldots, 0.10$. Figure 9 compares the performance of the proposed online error detection technique with the standard offline residual checking technique when the optimal error detection interval is used. Figure 9 indicates that early detection and termination of the corrupted computation can improve the performance by several times.

6.3.3 Online Error Detection with Checkpointing

When the correctness of the finished part of the computations can be verified in the middle of the program execution, checkpointing technique can be used to save the finished part of the computation into a reliable disk. Through restart from a checkpoint that has been verified to be correct, we can avoid repeating the correct part of the finished computation. Formula (10) in Section 5 gives the expected execution time when the error detection interval is d and the checkpoint interval is cd. However, there are no explicit analytical solutions for the optimal error detection interval and optimal checkpoint interval. This subsection studies the relationship among the error detection interval, the checkpoint interval, and the expected execution time numerically.

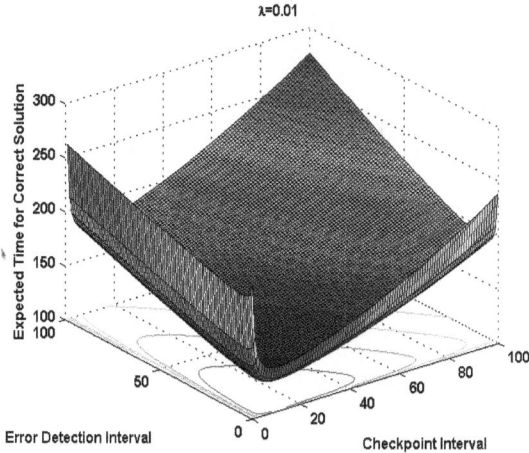

Figure 10. Expected execution time for online error detection with checkpointing with $\lambda = 0.01$.

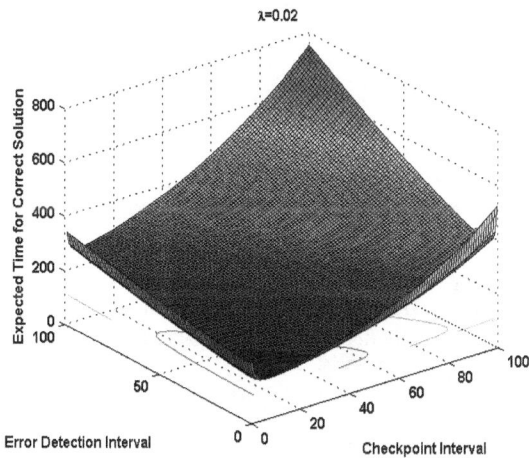

Figure 11. Expected execution time for online error detection with checkpointing with $\lambda = 0.01$.

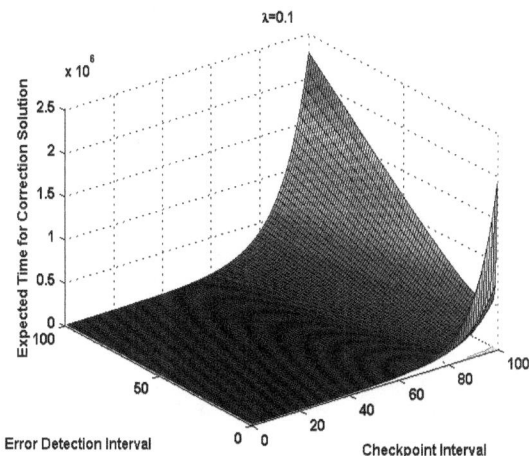

Figure 12. Expected execution time for online error detection with checkpointing with $\lambda = 0.1$.

Figure 13. Optimal error detection interval, checkpoint interval, and expected execution time.

λ	Opt Ckpt Intv	Opt Detect Intv	Opt Time
0.01	12	6	122
0.02	8	4	134
0.03	8	4	143
0.04	6	3	151
0.05	6	3	159
0.06	4	2	167
0.07	4	2	173
0.08	4	2	179
0.09	4	2	186
0.10	4	2	193

Figure 14. offline error detection with recomputing vs online error detection with recomputing vs online error detection with checkpointing.

λ	$E_{\text{offline-recp}}$	$E_{\text{online-recp}}$	$E_{\text{online-ckpt}}$
0.01	271	186	122
0.02	738	366	134
0.03	2008	774	143
0.04	5459	1732	151
0.05	14841	4053	159
0.06	40342	9808	167
0.07	109663	24342	173
0.08	298095	61590	179
0.09	810308	158190	186
0.10	2202646	411400	193

Figure 10, 11, and 12 demonstrate the relationships of the error detection interval, the checkpoint interval, and the expected execution time when $\lambda = 0.01, 0.02$ and 0.10. Figure 10, 11, and 12 indicate: (1). The expected execution time changes as the error detection interval and checkpoint interval change; and (2). The expected execution time has an optimal value. Figure 13 shows the optimal error detection interval, the optimal checkpoint interval, and the optimal expected execution time. Figure 14 compares the expected execution time when both the optimal error detection interval and the optimal checkpoint interval are used. Figure 14 indicates that the proposed online soft error correction technique improves the performance by at least $\times 2$ when the failure rate is one error every 100 hours and more than $\times 10^4$ when the failure rate is one error every 10 hours.

7. Conclusion

This paper presented Online-ABFT, an online soft error detection technique for today's most widely used iterative methods: Krylov subspace methods. Based on a simple verification of orthogonality and residual, the technique is easy to implement and highly efficient. The technique is online and, therefore, allows the corrupted computation to be terminated in a timely manner soon after a soft error occurs. When the technique is used together with checkpointing, it is able to improve the time to obtain correct results under unreliable computing platforms by up to several orders of magnitude over the standard offline residual checking and recomputing approach.

Acknowledgment

This research is partly supported by National Science Foundation under grants #CCF-1305622, #OCI-1305624, and #CNS-1118037.

We would also like thank the following institutions for the use of their computing resources:

- Oak Ridge National Laboratory: Jaguar
- The National Institute for Computational Sciences: Kraken
- The Golden Energy Computing Organization: Ra

References

[1] The International Exascale Software Project. http://www.exascale.org.

[2] Coordinated Infrastructure for Fault Tolerant Systems. http://www.mcs.anl.gov/research/cifts.

[3] MPICH-V. http://mpich-v.lri.fr.

[4] P. Bridges, M. Hoemmen, K. Ferreira, M. Heroux, P. Soltero and R. Brightwell. Cooperative Application/OS DRAM Fault Recovery. In *Proceedings of the 4th International Workshop on Resiliency in High Performance Computing (Resilience 2011)*, Bordeaux, France, August 29 - September 2, 2011.

[5] G. Bronevetsky, D. Marques, K. Pingali, and P. Stodghill. Automated Application-level Checkpointing of MPI Programs. In *Proceedings of the 2003 ACM SIGPLAN Symposium on Principles and Practice of Parallel Programming (PPoPP03)*, San Diego, California, June 11-13, 2003.

[6] G. Bronevetsky and B. R. Supinski Soft Error Vulnerability of Iterative Linear Algebra Methods. In *Proceedings of the 22nd annual international conference on Supercomputing (ICS2008)*, Island of Kos, Aegean Sea, Greece, June 7-12, 2008.

[7] G. Burns, R. Daoud, and J. Vaig. LAM: An Open Cluster Environment for MPI. *Proceedings of Supercomputing Symposium*, 1994.

[8] F. Cappello, A. Geist, B. Gropp, L. V. Kal, B. Kramer, and M. Snir. Toward Exascale Resilience. *International Journal of High Performance Computing Applications*, Vol. 23, No. 4, Page 374-388, 2009.

[9] Z. Chen and J. Dongarra. Numerically stable real number codes based on random matrices. In *Proceeding of the 5th International Conference on Computational Science (ICCS2005)*, Atlanta, Georgia, USA, May 22-25, 2005. LNCS 3514.

[10] Z. Chen and J. Dongarra. Condition Numbers of Gaussian Random Matrices. *SIAM Journal on Matrix Analysis and Applications*, Volume 27, Number 3, Page 603-620, 2005.

[11] Z. Chen, and J. Dongarra. Algorithm-Based Checkpoint-Free Fault Tolerance for Parallel Matrix Computations on Volatile Resources. *Proceedings of the 20th IEEE International Parallel & Distributed Processing Symposium (IPDPS 2006)*, Rhodes Island, Greece, April 25-29, 2006.

[12] Z. Chen, and J. Dongarra. Algorithm-Based Fault Tolerance for Fail-Stop Failures. *IEEE Transactions on Parallel and Distributed Systems*, Vol. 19, No. 12, December, 2008.

[13] Z. Chen, and J. Dongarra. Highly Scalable Self-Healing Algorithms for High Performance Scientific Computing. *IEEE Transactions on Computers*, July, 2009.

[14] Z. Chen, G. E. Fagg, E. Gabriel, J. Langou, T. Angskun, G. Bosilca, and J. Dongarra. Fault tolerant high performance computing by a coding approach. In *Proceedings of the ACM SIGPLAN Symposium on Principles and Practice of Parallel Programming (PPOPP 2005)*, June 14-17, 2005, Chicago, IL, USA.

[15] Z. Chen. Optimal Real Number Codes for Fault Tolerant Matrix Operations. *Proceedings of the ACM/IEEE SC09 Conference*, Portland, OR, November 14-20, 2009.

[16] T. Davies, C. Karlsson, H. Liu, C. Ding, and Z. Chen. High Performance Linpack Benchmark: A Fault Tolerant Implementation without Checkpointing. *Proceedings of the 25th ACM International Conference on Supercomputing (ICS 2011)*, Tucson, Arizona, May 31 - June 4, 2011.

[17] D. Hakkarinen and Z. Chen. Algorithmic Cholesky Factorization Fault Recovery. *Proceedings of the 24th IEEE International Parallel & Distributed Processing Symposium*, Atlanta, GA, USA, April 19-23, 2010.

[18] Z. Chen. Algorithm-Based Recovery for Iterative Methods without Checkpointing. *Proceedings of the 20th ACM International Symposium on High-Performance Parallel and Distributed Computing (HPDC 2011)*, San Jose, California, June 8-11, 2011.

[19] J. Daly. A higher order estimate of the optimum checkpoint interval for restart dumps. *Future Generation Comp. Syst.*, 22(3): 303-312 (2006).

[20] D. Fiala, K. Ferreira, F. Mueller, and C. Engelmann A Tunable, Software-based DRAM Error Detection and Correction Library for HPC. In *Proceedings of the 4th International Workshop on Resiliency in High Performance Computing (Resilience 2011)*, Bordeaux, France, August 29 - September 2, 2011.

[21] Open MPI: www.open-mpi.org/.

[22] G. A. Gibson, B. Schroeder, and J. Digney. Failure Tolerance in Petascale Computers. *CTWatch Quarterly*, Volume 3, Number 4, November 2007.

[23] P. Bridges, K. Ferreira, M. Heroux, and M. Hoemmen Fault-tolerant linear solvers via selective reliability. http://arxiv.org/abs/1206.1390.

[24] K.-H. Huang and J. A. Abraham. Algorithm-based fault tolerance for matrix operations. *IEEE Transactions on Computers*, vol. C-33:518–528, 1984.

[25] J. S. Plank, K. Li, and M. A. Puening. Diskless checkpointing. *IEEE Trans. Parallel Distrib. Syst.*, 9(10):972–986, 1998.

[26] K. Malkowski, P. Raghavan, and M. Kandemir. Analyzing the soft error resilience of linear solvers on multicore multiprocessors. *Proceedings of the 24th IEEE International Parallel & Distributed Processing Symposium*, Atlanta, GA, USA, April 19-23, 2010.

[27] M. Shantharam, S. Srinivasmurthy, and P. Raghavan. Characterizing the impact of soft errors on iterative methods in scientific computing. *Proceedings of the 25th ACM International Conference on Supercomputing (ICS 2011)*, Tucson, Arizona, May 31 - June 4, 2011.

[28] V. S. Sunderam. PVM: a framework for parallel distributed computing. *Concurrency: Pract. Exper.*, 2(4):315–339, 1990.

[29] Y. Saad. *Iterative Methods for Sparse Linear Systems*. Society for Industrial and Applied Mathematics. Second Edition. April 30, 2003.

[30] C. Wang, F. Mueller, C. Engelmann, and S. Scot. Job Pause Service under LAM/MPI+BLCR for Transparent Fault Tolerance. In *Proceedings of the 21st IEEE International Parallel and Distributed Processing Symposium*, March, 2007.

Ownership Passing: Efficient Distributed Memory Programming on Multi-core Systems

Andrew Friedley

Indiana University
Bloomington, IN
afriedle@indiana.edu

Torsten Hoefler

ETH Zurich
Zurich, Switzerland
htor@inf.ethz.ch

Greg Bronevetsky

Lawrence Livermore National
Laboratory
Livermore, CA
bronevetsky@llnl.gov

Andrew Lumsdaine

Indiana University
Bloomington, IN
lums@indiana.edu

Ching-Chen Ma

Rose-Hulman Institute of Technology
Terre Haute, IN
mac@rose-hulman.edu

Abstract

The number of cores in multi- and many-core high-performance processors is steadily increasing. MPI, the de-facto standard for programming high-performance computing systems offers a distributed memory programming model. MPI's semantics force a copy from one process' send buffer to another process' receive buffer. This makes it difficult to achieve the same performance on modern hardware than shared memory programs which are arguably harder to maintain and debug. We propose generalizing MPI's communication model to include ownership passing, which make it possible to fully leverage the shared memory hardware of multi- and many-core CPUs to stream communicated data concurrently with the receiver's computations on it. The benefits and simplicity of message passing are retained by extending MPI with calls to send (pass) ownership of memory regions, instead of their contents, between processes. Ownership passing is achieved with a hybrid MPI implementation that runs MPI processes as threads and is mostly transparent to the user. We propose an API and a static analysis technique to transform legacy MPI codes automatically and transparently to the programmer, demonstrating that this scheme is easy to use in practice. Using the ownership passing technique, we see up to 51% communication speedups over a standard message passing implementation on state-of-the art multicore systems. Our analysis and interface will lay the groundwork for future development of MPI-aware optimizing compilers and multi-core specific optimizations, which will be key for success in current and next-generation computing platforms.

Categories and Subject Descriptors D.1.3 [*Programming Techniques*]: Concurrent Programming

Keywords Ownership Passing; Distributed Memory; Shared Memory; Message Passing; Multi-core

1. Introduction and Motivation

The most commonly used programming model for large-scale parallel applications is the Message Passing Interface (MPI [13]). This model generally assumes a one-dimensional distribution of P processes, where each process has its own (private) memory space and data is solely exchanged through explicit messages.

The message passing style of programming enables easy abstraction and code composition. Its *shared nothing* semantics and the SPMD programming simplify reasoning about the program's state and avoid complex problems that are often encountered in shared memory programming models [10]. Composition is achieved through communication contexts (called *communicators* in MPI) that enable multiple parallel libraries or objects to be combined into a single program without interference [8]. Those features have made MPI the predominant programming model for parallel scientific applications. However, this abstraction comes at a cost: all message transmissions have copy semantics, that is, the implementation requires a single copy from a buffer at the source process to a buffer at the destination process. Typical MPI libraries even require more copies, either through intermediate shared memory buffers or for the serialization and deserialization of complex data structures.

All modern parallel computing systems consist of network nodes with multiple processing elements (or cores). Processing elements (PEs) on a single node commonly have access to a cache-coherent hardware shared memory system. MPI was originally designed for distributed memory computers with either single-core or small SMP nodes. On today's architectures, the current copy-based message-passing model is suboptimal in terms of *memory* (send and receive buffers), *energy* (data movement consumes most energy [2]), and *time* (busses are used twice which reduces performance). To avoid those issues, many software developers switched to hybrid programming techniques, combining MPI for inter-node communication with shared memory programming models such as OpenMP [20] for intra-node communication. However, achieving the same level of performance is a tedious and complex task and often requires major code restructuring to work in the shared memory world [21].

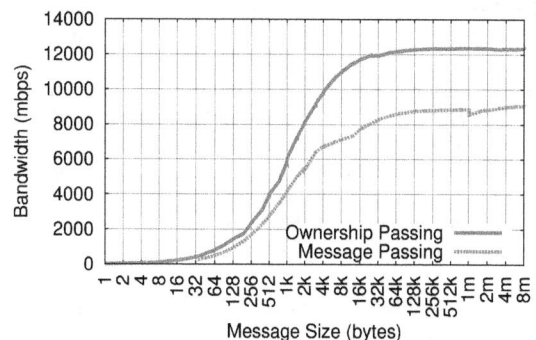

Figure 1: Bandwidth of Ownership Passing vs. Message Passing.

In this work, we use an ownership passing technique to easily and safely transform message-passing parallel applications to utilize shared memory hardware more efficiently. Instead of re-writing existing applications, we simply change them to pass a pointer from the sender to the receiver instead of copying the data. In fact, the production and consumption of buffers in our system automatically aligns in a pipelined fashion so that both stages can overlap.

As a motivating example, we show the effective bandwidth when passing a memory buffer instead of copying its contents on a modern HPC architecture in Figure 1. The measurement was done with the well-known NetPIPE [23] ping-pong benchmark on the Cab system (described later). To ensure fair comparison we extended NetPIPE to read the received data, thus accounting for the cost of transferring the data using ownership passing. We see that the standard copy approach is limited by the memory copy bandwidth and synchronization costs while ownership passing essentially requires only synchronization and reading from (potentially remote) memory. Thus, ownership passing is usually significantly faster than standard message passing on today's multicore systems.

Our approach is true zero-copy (zero-touch, in fact) because the buffer contents are neither read nor written during the communication. We develop a novel memory pooling technique to re-use communication buffers and avoid synchronization.

The main contributions of this work are:

- We design an interface for ownership passing that is compatible with MPI and allows for easy porting from MPI codes.
- We propose a static analysis technique to transform codes automatically to use ownership passing.
- We analyze the performance of ownership passing in realistic environments.
- We demonstrate practical results of important HPC micro-applications and application kernels that have been improved with our technique.

In the next section, we describe our Hybrid MPI implementation that spawns MPI processes as threads, creating the shared address space necessary for ownership passing. Section 3 describes the ownership passing technique and introduces our Ownership Passing Interface (OPI) library and API. We describe and give examples for applying ownership passing to point-to-point message passing codes in Section 3.3 and collective communication in Section 3.5. We propose a technique for automatically transforming parallel codes to ownership passing in Section 4. Finally, Section 5 provides a performance analysis of ownership passing using a micro-benchmark and several applications.

2. Hybrid MPI—A Threaded MPI Implementation

Before any shared memory communication can be introduced alongside MPI, processes need a method to directly access each others' memory. We use a thread-based MPI approach [16, 22] which replaces the common process-based rank design with a thread-based design (i.e., an MPI process is a thread). All MPI processes (threads) on a node are grouped into one operating system process[1]. Hereafter, we use the term *rank* to refer to an MPI process as defined by the MPI standard, which may be an operating system process or thread depending on the MPI implementation. We use the terms *process* and *thread* as defined in the context of the operating system.

The benefit of a thread-based MPI implementation is portability—no additional support is required from the operating

system. However, the application must be made thread-safe due to sharing of a single address space (global variables become shared by all MPI ranks). Solutions exist to perform privatization of global variables automatically [14, 16], minimizing the required developer effort. Such thread-based hybridization approaches are indeed used routinely in practice, for example in CHARM++'s AMPI [14].

We have developed a portable library called Hybrid MPI (HMPI) that implements the thread-based rank design on top of any standard MPI library. HMPI intercepts messages destined for ranks within the same node and uses a faster single memory copy communication path (MPI often performs two copies via shared memory segments), while utilizing an existing MPI for inter-node communication. Although we use HMPI in this paper to demonstrate results, our proposed ownership passing optimization would work with any thread-based MPI library or other scheme enabling direct memory access between MPI processes, such as XPMEM [25].

3. Ownership Passing

MPI's distributed memory design ensures that only one rank can access a buffer (any arbitrary memory region). That is, exactly one rank *owns* a buffer, and that is the only rank that may read or write that buffer. Using a shared memory technique with MPI (explained in Section 2), ownership can be *passed* from one rank to another via message passing. When a rank gives away ownership of a buffer, that rank can no longer access that buffer. Likewise, taking ownership of a buffer enables exclusive read and write access.

Ownership passing reinterprets the concept of distributed memory in a way that retains its simplicity while taking advantage of shared memory hardware. Traditional distributed memory partitions the application's address space into static private memory blocks. In contrast, ownership passing allows this partition to be dynamic, with memory regions moving from one private space to another while maintaining the invariant that each memory region is privately owned by exactly one thread of execution. The resulting flexibility makes it possible for message passing applications to utilize shared memory hardware in ways similar to native shared memory applications but without concern about data races and other complications of the shared memory model. Not only is our approach beneficial on cache-coherent architectures (e.g., commodity x86), it also works on non-cache-coherent and non-uniform memory architectures (NUMAs).

3.1 Ownership Passing Programming Interface

Transferring ownership of a buffer only requires sending a pointer instead of the entire message data. When the new owner of a buffer begins reading the message from its original location, the shared memory hardware will begin to stream data from the sender rank's cache and/or memory to the receiver. Standard architectural CPU features such as snoop caches and memory prefetching improve the performance and enable efficient communication/computation overlap in hardware. Since the communication library never accesses the buffer data, true zero-copy communication is achieved.

We define a small extension API, referred to as the Ownership Passing Interface (OPI), to simplify the use of ownership passing in applications. The C interface is shown in Figure 2 and Figure 3 shows a MPI simple example and its OPI counterpart. All routines are thread-safe with respect to one another.

OPI_Alloc and OPI_Free allocate and deallocate new communication buffers, calling `malloc` and `free` and performing additional management of buffer memory pools, as described in Section 3.2. Ownership passing is performed using the OPI_Give and OPI_Take routines, which are analogous to MPI_Send and MPI_Recv (nonblocking versions are also available in analogy to nonblocking MPI calls). OPI_Give consumes the provided buffer. If the destination rank is in the same address space (on the same

---

[1] The term "MPI Process" is abstractly defined in the MPI standard and does not necessarily mean operating system process.

`OPI_Alloc(void** ptr,` `    size_t length)`	Allocate a communication buffer of some length.
`OPI_Free(void** ptr)`	Release a buffer allocated by `OPI_Alloc`.

`OPI_Igive(void** ptr, int count,`
`    MPI_Datatype datatype,`
`    int rank, int tag,`
`    MPI_Comm comm, MPI_Request req)`
	Pass ownership of a buffer to another MPI rank.

`OPI_Itake(void** ptr, int count,`
`    MPI_Datatype datatype,`
`    int rank, int tag,`
`    MPI_Comm comm, MPI_Request req)`
	Receive ownership of a buffer from another MPI rank.

Figure 2: Nonblocking Ownership Passing Interface (OPI).

MPI Code	OPI Code

double buf[...];
if(rank==0)
    MPI_Send(buf, 1, ...)
 	
else if(rank==1)
    MPI_Recv(buf, 0, ...)
	double* buf;
	if(rank==0) {
	    buf=OPI_Alloc(...);
	    OPI_Give(&buf, ...);
	} else if(rank==1) {
	    OPI_Take(&buf, ...);
	    OPI_Free(&buf);
	}

Figure 3: Example of MPI to OPI conversion

node), then the source rank synchronizes with the destination and passes the buffer. If the destination is in a different address space, then the source rank invokes a normal `MPI_Send` call with the given arguments and returns the buffer to the buffer pool after the send completes. `OPI_Take` returns a new buffer to the receiver. If the buffer comes from a rank in the same address space, then it will simply return the pointer to the buffer. If the source is a rank from a different address space then it allocates memory of the required size, invokes `MPI_Recv` on this buffer, and returns the buffer upon completion of the remote receive. Figure 4 depicts the ownership passing mechanism, flow control, and buffers.

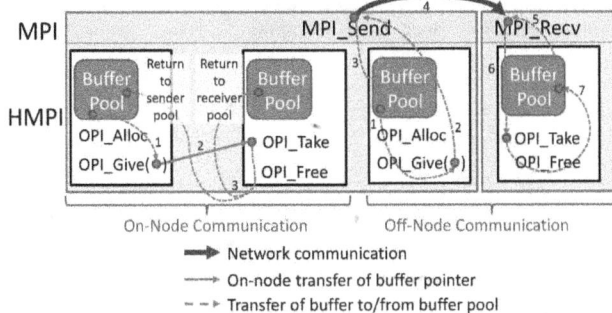

Figure 4: Flow of Control and Buffers in Ownership Passing.

Note that `OPI_Alloc` and `OPI_Take` introduce new buffers, while `OPI_Give` and `OPI_Free` relinquish ownership of a buffer. For safety and to promote the *ownership* concept, the latter two routines clear the provided pointer to `NULL` before returning.

3.2 Communication Buffer Management

Once a rank has taken ownership of a buffer and consumed its contents, that buffer must be disposed of. We could simply free the buffer back to the heap, but this is not ideal. `Malloc` and `free` must be implemented in a thread-safe manner, which in our case implies a lock shared between all ranks on a node. Furthermore `malloc` and `free` are costly library calls, and ownership passing encourages allocating a new buffer for every message sent.

We can alleviate the costs of `malloc` and `free` by caching buffers in a memory pool. When allocating, we search the pool for the first buffer large enough for the requested size and reuse it. If

no such buffer exists, a new one is allocated. When freeing a buffer, we return it to a memory pool instead of the heap.

Using one memory pool per node would require a lock shared between all ranks on a node, which is not an improvement over using the heap. Instead, we maintain one memory pool per rank. Now, a choice must be made—buffers can be returned to either the sender's or the receiver's memory pool. Returning buffers to the sender's pool requires a lock, since multiple ranks may simultaneously return a buffer to the pool, perhaps also while the sender is allocating. However, this approach distributes contention over many locks rather than one, yielding an improvement.

On the other hand, no lock is required if we return buffers to the receiver's local pool—each rank only accesses its own memory pool. However if one rank receives more messages than others, buffers accumulate in one memory pool and never get reused, wasting memory. To solve this problem, we introduce a check when a buffer is added to a memory pool. If the number of unused buffers exceeds a threshold, some buffers are freed back the heap. This memory will eventually be reused in later `malloc` calls, potentially on other ranks.

To evaluate the performance of these different buffer management schemes, we measure the time to perform the code "`OPI_Free(OPI_Alloc(8))`" (8 byte buffer size), averaged over 5,000 runs. The results, shown in Figure 5 demonstrate that returning buffers to the receiver's pool has the lowest cost—this solution has no synchronization between ranks, and reduces the frequency of expensive `malloc` and `free` calls. We use this scheme for all experimental results shown later in the paper.

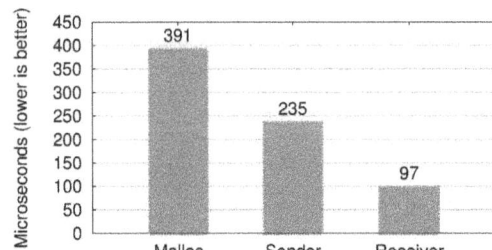

Figure 5: Average time of the different buffer management schemes to allocate and free eight bytes.

3.3 Point to Point Ownership Passing

Transforming an application to use ownership passing consists of three steps:

1. Replace `MPI_Send` and `MPI_Recv` and related communication functions with `OPI_Give` and `OPI_Take`, respectively. OPI makes this trivial; except for the additional referencing in the first argument (buffer pointers) `OPI_Give` and `OPI_Take` accept the same arguments as `MPI_Send` and `MPI_Recv`.

2. Insert a call to `OPI_Alloc` before packing a communication buffer for sending. Since giving away ownership consumes the communication buffer, a new one must be allocated every time a message is sent.

3. Insert a call to `OPI_Free` after receiving and unpacking a communication buffer. Since taking ownership produces a new communication buffer, every received message must be freed.

Although communication buffers can be allocated at any time before they are packed and can be freed any time after they are unpacked, the best buffer reuse is achieved by allocating send buffers as 'late' as possible in the application (immediately before they're packed), and freeing received buffers as 'early' as possible (immediately after they're unpacked).

To illustrate the changes needed to perform ownership passing with MPI, we present a two-dimensional molecular dynamics (MD) example, where space is divided into regions and each processor is responsible for computing forces on and positions of particles within its region. Particles on the boundary of each processor's region are communicated to processors responsible for adjacent space regions. Figure 6(a) shows how this is performed using MPI for a single boundary exchange (the same is done with other neighbors). Boundary particles are serialized into a buffer, which is then sent via MPI (copied) and deserialized on the receiver. Ownership passing, shown in Figure 6(b), speeds up the process by replacing the MPI copy with a transfer of ownership of the packed buffer.

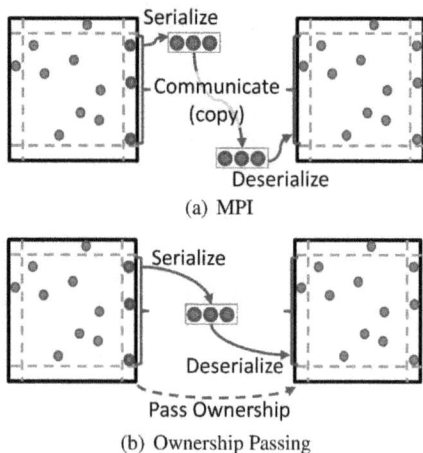

(a) MPI

(b) Ownership Passing

Figure 6: Molecular dynamics overlap communication. The boundary particles must be serialized into contiguous buffers.

Figure 7 presents pseudo-code for the MPI and the ownership passing implementation. The skeleton and code flow (computation of the directions and the computations) are identical in both codes. The ownership passing version allocates a buffer from the local memory pool just before packing, regardless of whether the destination is local or remote. Ownership is passed if the neighbor rank is local; otherwise the message is passed as would normally be done with negligible overheads. After unpacking, the received buffer is returned to the receiver's memory pool.

3.4 MPI Datatypes

MPI datatypes allow strided sequences of elements or arbitrary memory layouts to be sent and received. The ownership passing principle can be adapted to communication of disjoint sets of elements. Since MPI datatypes must be specified at both the sender and the receiver, ownership to the elements specified by the datatype can be easily transferred as long as the datatypes on both sides have the same memory layout. In cases where the receiver only consumes part of a buffer or when the sender wishes to reuse the data after passing ownership, the receiver can pass ownership back. Such an approach is analogous to protecting access to the buffer with a mutex. Compiler support for this technique is part of our future work. MPI also allows applications to provide different datatypes on the sender and receiver that place data in memory in different orders (e.g. matrix row on the sender and matrix column on the receiver). Copying is required to support this use-case and is the most efficient way to provide this specialized functionality.

3.5 Collective Ownership Passing

Although this paper specifically focuses on ownership passing for point-to-point communication, it can also be used effectively for collective communication. Here, we discuss how ownership passing can be used to implement scatter, gather, and all-to-all. Further

MPI

```
pack_particle_buffer(send_buffer, particle_data);

MPI_Isend(send_buffer, count, datatype,
    neighbor_rank, TAG, MPI_COMM_WORLD, &reqs[0]);

MPI_Irecv(&recv_buffer, count, datatype,
    neighbor_rank, TAG, MPI_COMM_WORLD, &reqs[1]);

MPI_Waitall(2, reqs, MPI_STATUSES_IGNORE);

unpack_particle_buffer(recv_buffer, particle_data);
```

Ownership Passing

```
OPI_Alloc(&send_buffer, max_particles);

pack_particle_buffer(send_buffer, particle_data);

// Pass ownership of our send buffer.
OPI_Igive(&send_buffer, count, datatype,
    neighbor_rank, TAG, MPI_COMM_WORLD, &reqs[0]);

// Take ownership of a new receive buffer.
OPI_Itake(&recv_buffer, count, datatype,
    neighbor_rank, TAG, MPI_COMM_WORLD, &reqs[1]);

MPI_Waitall(2, reqs, MPI_STATUSES_IGNORE);

unpack_particle_buffer(recv_buffer, particle_data);

// Always return the receive buffer.
OPI_Free(&recv_buffer);
```

Figure 7: Boundary exchange communication between a pair of neighbors.

techniques are possible, such as allowing read access for multiple ranks, though are not the focus of this paper.

First, consider the MPI scatter operation in which applications allocate and pack into one send buffer, with respective portions to be scattered to each rank. Ownership of this buffer can be passed to the receive ranks as a collective, but this approach raises the question of which rank should release the buffer, and when. Synchronization (e.g. a barrier) is required to solve this problem, but negates the performance benefits of ownership passing.

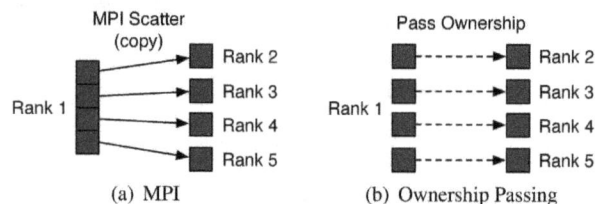

(a) MPI

(b) Ownership Passing

Figure 8: Scatter collective communication. MPI copies out of one buffer, while ownership passing gives separate buffers to each rank.

A better solution is to allocate a separate buffer for each destination rank, as illustrated in Figure 8. OPI_Igive is used to pass ownership of each buffer to its respective rank. Each receiver can then return its buffer to the sender's memory pool without a global synchronization.

Figure 9 demonstrates ownership passing for scatter communication in code form. Note that we have used point-to-point communication, although ownership could also be transferred using an MPI_Scatter routine or OPI equivalent. Gather operations are performed in a similar manner to scatter; the root rank gathers an array of buffer pointers to take ownership. When finished with the data, the root can release each buffer back to the respective memory pools. An ownership passing all-to-all can be constructed by combining scatter and gather. This work focuses on point-to-point ownership passing; more advanced collective techniques for collective ownership passing will be investigated in the future.

```
if(my_rank == root) {
  for(int i = 0; i < mpi_size; i++) {
    // Allocate a buffer and pack data for rank i
    OPI_Alloc(&buffer, buffer_size);

    pack_buffer(buffer, i);

    // Pass ownership of the buffer.
    OPI_Igive(&buffer, count, datatype,
        i, TAG, shared_mem_comm, &reqs[i]);
  }
}

OPI_Itake(&buffer, count, datatype,
    root, TAG, shared_mem_comm, &recv_req);

// Wait to take ownership or receive from the root.
MPI_Wait(&recv_req, MPI_STATUS_IGNORE);

unpack_buffer(buffer);

// Always return the buffer to where it came from.
OPI_Free(&buffer);

// Complete the send requests.
MPI_Waitall(mpi_size, reqs, MPI_STATUSES_IGNORE);
```

Figure 9: Ownership passing in scatter collective communication.

4. Compiler Analysis

To simplify the deployment of OPI in legacy applications, we have designed a novel compiler analysis. Our analysis detects code patterns to which OPI is applicable and automatically transforms the code to use the OPI extensions. We have implemented our analysis using the ROSE framework [19], although several analyses we depend on are not yet available in ROSE. Our implementation functions on simple codes and will support complex codes when the analyses we depend on are available in ROSE.

We examined the NAS Parallel Benchmarks (NPB) for applicability of OPI. Almost all point-to-point communication fits the OPI pattern and can be converted by our analysis. The exception is CG's row reduction, which reads the send buffer immediately after MPI_Send. Many NPB codes communicate different non-overlapping regions of the same buffer, requiring an analysis that identifies these regions and presents them to our analysis as separate buffers. BT uses pointer-based data structures that require a simple points-to analysis to disambiguate.

Our analysis works in two phases. First, it analyzes the code around each MPI_Send, MPI_Recv and related calls via a backwards data flow analysis to determine if the application accesses each buffer used in these operations in a way that is compatible with ownership passing. Then, associations between MPI_Send and MPI_Recv operations are made using either previously published analyses [3] or user annotations. If a given operation and all of its possible associated operations are OPI-Compatible, we use a second forward analysis to identify the points where OPI operations need to be inserted and original operations need to be removed. Since each MPI send must match at least one MPI receive, every given buffer must be taken by its receiver.

4.1 Outline of Analyses and Transformations

The sender transformation is illustrated in Figure 10. The left graph describes the pattern of operations that may be performed on an OPI-compatible buffer as a control flow graph and the left code example provides an example of matching code. The right graph and

code example describe how such code is transformed, with dashed arrows identifying locations in the original code where the new operations or replacements are inserted. The graphs correspond to just the operations that refer to a single buffer and may be interleaved with operations that refer to other memory regions. After a buffer is allocated (e.g., static buffer declaration or dynamic malloc or new) the application must pack and send that buffer zero or more times before it is deallocated (e.g., scope exit of static buffer or dynamic free or delete). During packing, the application must overwrite the buffer without reading its prior contents; reads are allowed as long as they are preceded by a write to the same location. The buffer is sent via MPI_Send or an equivalent function. Code that follows this pattern is transformed as follows: (i) the buffer's allocation is replaced with an assignment to a uniquely named integer that stores the buffer's size, (ii) OPI_Alloc is inserted at CFG locations where control transitions from Allocate or Send to Pack and takes the buffer's size variable as input, (iii) MPI_Send is replaced with OPI_Give, and (iv) the buffer's deallocation is removed.

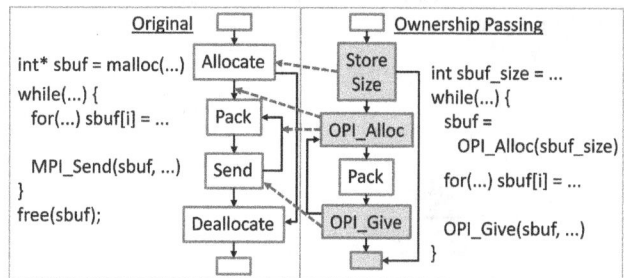

Figure 10: Sender code pattern and transformation

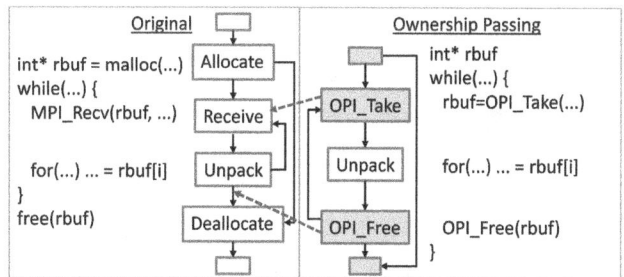

Figure 11: Receiver code pattern and transformation

Figure 11 illustrates the receiver transformation. After a buffer is allocated, the application must receive and unpack it zero or more times before it is deallocated. The buffer's data is received via MPI_Recv or an equivalent function, which overwrites its contents. During unpacking the application may read from or write to the portions of the buffer overwritten by MPI_Recv. Matching code is transformed as follows: (i) the buffer's allocation is removed, (ii) MPI_Recv is replaced by OPI_Give, the return value of which is assigned to the buffer's pointer, (iii) OPI_Free is placed at CFG locations where control transitions from Unpack to Receive or Deallocate, and (iv) the buffer's deallocation is removed.

Both analyses operate by maintaining at each location in the application's control flow graph (CFG) a mapping from live memory regions to one of the states of a finite automaton that captures the patterns shown in Figures 10 and 11. The backward analysis also includes state Fail, indicating that the buffer's use does not fit the OPI pattern. This mapping can use information from any alias or points-to analysis [1] that indicates whether the buffers referred to by two pointers are always-same (must-equal) or never-same (not may-equal). If at any CFG node there exist two buffers that are

181

not always-same or never-same (e.g., one pointer refers to different buffers in different executions), their state is set to Fail. This conservatively handles cases where one portion of the OPI sender or receiver pattern holds for a given buffer and another portion holds for a different buffer (e.g., one buffer is packed but another is sent but in both cases the same pointer variable is used).

4.2 Pattern detection analyses

Figures 12 and 14 present the transfer and meet functions used by the backwards analyses that determine whether sender and receiver code fits the OPI pattern. Transfer functions are shown as finite automata where nodes correspond to the possible states of a buffer during the analysis and edges indicate how these states are transferred through operations. Each edge represents an operation relevant to the analysis. When the buffer is in the edge's source state and an operation is encountered, the buffer's transitions to the edge's destination state. Snd and Rcv edges denote `MPI_Send` and `MPI_Recv` of the buffer, respectively (or equivalent operation). Allocate and Deallocate correspond to the buffer's allocation and deallocation points. R identifies buffer reads and W buffer writes.

Transfer Function

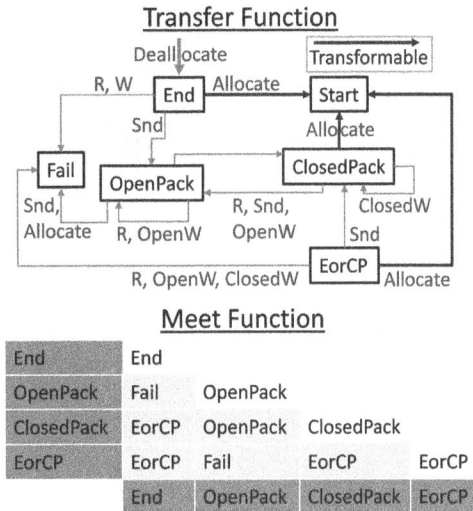

Meet Function

End	End			
OpenPack	Fail	OpenPack		
ClosedPack	EorCP	OpenPack	ClosedPack	
EorCP	EorCP	Fail	EorCP	EorCP
	End	OpenPack	ClosedPack	EorCP

Figure 12: Sender pattern detection backward analysis

Our analysis relies on an external array region analysis to indicate if the buffers adhere to the following required properties:

1. In the sender code pattern, all reads in the Pack must be preceded by prior writes to the same buffer location (i.e., reads cannot be upwardly-exposed), which includes the reads from `MPI_Send`.

2. In the receiver pattern, the Unpack code can only read the subregion of a buffer that was overwritten by the prior `MPI_Recv`.

This information is represented by replacing R and W with more focused operations. In the sender transfer function, OpenW indicates a write that is followed by some upwardly-exposed reads along the path between the write and the following `MPI_Send` (including the reads by `MPI_Send`. ClosedW denotes a write not followed by such reads. In the receiver transfer function, InR and InW denote a read or write to a buffer region overwritten by the prior `MPI_Recv` (in-buffer) and OutR and OutW indicate a read and write to a region not overwritten by the `MPI_Recv` (out-of-buffer).

Since the pattern detection analyses work backwards through the application's CFG, they begin to consider a given buffer at the point immediately before its deallocation in state End. The sender analysis transitions from End to OpenPack if it observes a send operation, to Send if it observes Allocate and to Fail if it observes

reads or writes after the final send. Once in OpenPack, the analysis stays in this state until it observes a ClosedW operation. Whan that occurs, it transitions to ClosedPack, indicating that the code region between this code location and the next send is well-formed and has no upwardly-exposed reads. It returns from ClosedPack to OpenPack on any R or OpenW operations. If the analysis observes a Snd while in OpenPack state it transitions to Fail since the pack code between two adjacent sends is not well-formed. Snds observed while in ClosedPack state fit the OPI pattern and return the analysis to the OpenPack state. Finally, if Allocate is observed while in ClosedPack state, the analysis transitions to the Start state, indicating that the buffer's use fits the OPI pattern. If Allocate is observed in other states, the analysis transitions to Fail.

The meet function takes as input two states from two different control-flow paths that converge at a given CFG node and outputs the state at this meet point. It is a table with the input states on the horizontal and vertical axes and the output state at their intersection. The Fail state is omitted since the meet of any state with Fail is Fail. The meet of any state with itself is itself. The first property of the meet function is that the meet of OpenPack with either OpenPack or ClosedPack is OpenPack since this means that the meet point is followed by upwardly-exposed reads. Further, the meet of End with ClosedPack produces a new state EorCP, which captures the fact that a buffer fits the OPI pattern if it is either communicated according to the pattern or not communicated at all. On Allocate operations EorCP transitions to Start, indicating the buffer's use fits the OPI pattern.

Figure 13 shows an example of the sender analysis operating on two code examples. The left example has two statically distinct buffers, one of which follows the OPI pattern and one that does not. This example shows how the analysis state evolves to conclude that `buf1` fits the pattern. Starting at the deallocation of `buf1` and `buf2` it proceeds backwards around the `while` loop (steps 2, 3 and 4) to reach state ClosedPack for `buf1` (the buffer is fully packed before being sent) and OpenPack for `buf2` (the buffer is sent without being packed). At the loop's entry (step 5) the states evolve to EorCP for `buf1` (it is either packed/sent correctly or not used) and Fail for `buf2` (its communication in the loop doesn't follow the OPI pattern). At the end `buf1` transitions from EorCP to Start at its allocation site, indicating that it fully fits the OPI pattern, while `buf2` remains at Fail, indicating that it does not. In the code example on the right, the identity of the buffer pointed to by p is not statically unique. As discussed in the last paragraph of Section 4.1 if there exists ambiguity about the identity of buffers involved in OPI operations (reads, writes, sends, receives) their state is set to Fail. This is done at the `MPI_Send` operation where the referent of p is either `buf1` or `buf2` but it is statically not known which one.

Example Evolution of Sender-Side Pattern Detection Analysis

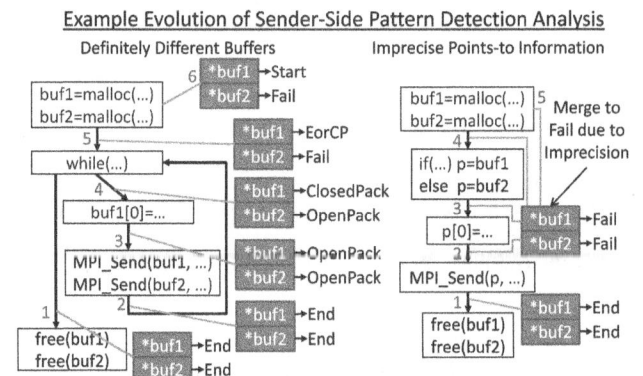

Figure 13: Example of sender pattern detection analysis

182

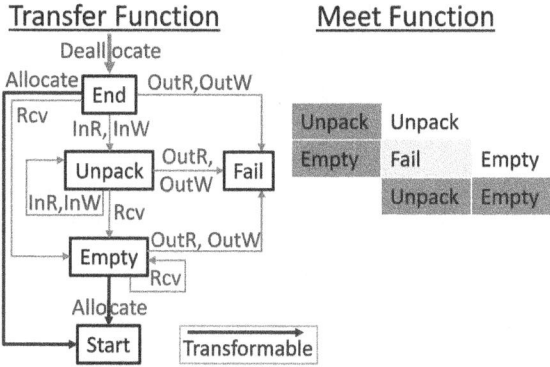

Figure 14: Receiver pattern detection backward analysis

Figure 14 presents the receiver analysis. Like the sender analysis, it starts from state End. When a receive occurs, it transitions to Empty to indicate an unused buffer. On Allocate it transitions to Start and on InR and InW to Unpack. The analysis stays in Unpack while it observes only InR and InW operations and stays in Dead while it observes receives. It transitions to Fail whenever OutR or OutW are observed in any state. This is a conservative decision; while some applications with such accesses can be made to use OPI (e.g. where communication is not inside a loop), this is too complex in general. If Allocate is observed in state Unpack, the analysis transitions to Start to indicate that the receiver OPI pattern holds for this buffer. Otherwise, if Allocate is observed while in another state, the analysis transitions to Fail. The meet of Unpack and Empty is Unpack since this corresponds to applications that stop unpacking on one side of a branch (looking forward in the code) and continue unpacking on another side.

4.3 Transformation Analyses

If the backward pattern detection analysis indicates that a buffer's use follows the OPI code pattern, we use a forward transformation analysis to identify the code locations that must be transformed to use OPI. The left parts of Figures 15(a) and 15(b) show the transfer functions of the sender and receiver analyses, respectively. Since these are forward analyses, they begin at each buffer's allocation and terminate at its deallocation. Transformations are performed when the transfer function transitions along an edge, as shown the graphs on the right sides of the figures. When the original operation must be removed, it is crossed out in each graph. When it is to be replaced with alternate code, the replacement code is specified. In the receiver transformation, transitions from Unpack and Init to Init correspond to replacing MPI_Recv with an OPI_Free; OPI_Take sequence.

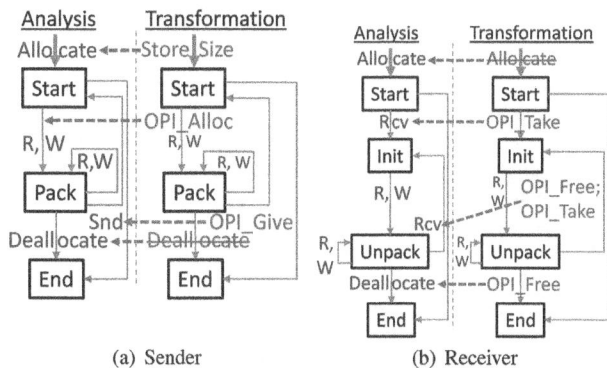

(a) Sender (b) Receiver

Figure 15: Transformation forward analysis

5. Experimental Results

Experimental results were obtained using the LLNL Sierra and Cab systems. Sierra has two Xeon X5660 (six core, 2.8 GHz) processors (12 cores total) and 24 GiB of RAM, while Cab has two Xeon ES-2670 (eight core, 2.6 GHz) processors (16 cores total) and 32 GiB of RAM. MVAPICH2 v1.8 was used for all results. Since ownership passing is a shared memory optimization, we show performance results for varying numbers of ranks executed on a single node to avoid a network complicating the results. As discussed in Section 4, our compiler analysis only works on simple codes. All codes shown here were transformed manually.

5.1 Microbenchmark Analysis

We developed OPBench to analyze the performance characteristics of ownership passing (as implemented by the OPI interface) and compare them to MPI and HMPI. OPBench implements a simple nearest-neighbor stencil, performing the following steps:

1. Computation time is simulated and measured by performing a simple calculation on each of the elements of an array.

2. A pack loop copies the data from the 'application' data structure to a communication buffer.

3. The communication buffers are exchanged between two ranks.

4. An unpack loop copies the data from the received communication buffer back to the application data structure.

For each iteration of the benchmark we perform step 1 once, then repeat steps 2-4 four times to simulate multiple neighbors. We ran our benchmark in two configurations on the Cab system: (i) ranks are located on different cores within the same processor and (ii) ranks are located on different processors. Each data point in the results is an average of 5,000 benchmark iterations, with timings acquired from both ranks.

Figure 16 shows the bandwidth achieved when packing, communicating, and unpacking a message (the sum of time taken by steps 2, 3, 4 of OPBench) within and across processors. Figure 16(a) shows the total bandwidth achieved when packing, communicating, and unpacking a message (the sum of time taken by steps 2, 3, 4 of OPBench) on cores within the same processor. OPI (2.8 GB/s) significantly improves on HMPI (2.5 GB/s) and MPI (1.75 GB/s). Here, OPI performance is bounded by the memory bandwidth achieved during the pack and unpack phases.

Figure 16(b) shows the same measurement when both processes are on distant cores on different sockets. Here, we see that HMPI (2 GB/s) has a negligible benefit over MPI (2 GB/s) because MPI's pipelined copy is essentially using the on-board interconnect as well as HMPI can. MPI's bandwidth is slightly higher than in the previous case because the copy uses two NUMA domains and thus gets twice the write bandwidth. OPI (2.7 GB/s) improves the bandwidth significantly by streaming the data directly from the source buffer, avoiding the additional copy completely.

To understand the performance properties of OPI in detail, we measured cache behavior during OPBench execution. Figure 17(a) shows the number of L1 cache misses incurred while packing, communicating and unpacking a message. The data shows that MPI incurs several times more misses than HMPI or OPI for communicating the same message. This is because MPI must copy data across memory spaces, which involves the sender copying into a common shared buffer and the receiver copying back from this buffer. In contrast, HMPI and OPI only perform a single direct data transfer from one core to another. A key difference between the algorithms used by the approaches is their effect on the cache itself, demonstrated in Figure 17(b), which shows the number of L1 cache misses during the execution of the simulated application code (step 1 of OP-

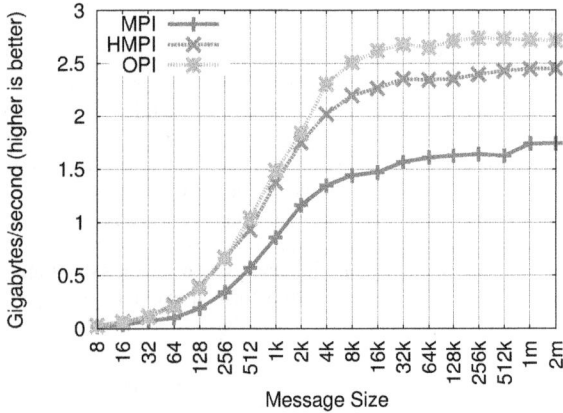

(a) Same-socket throughput

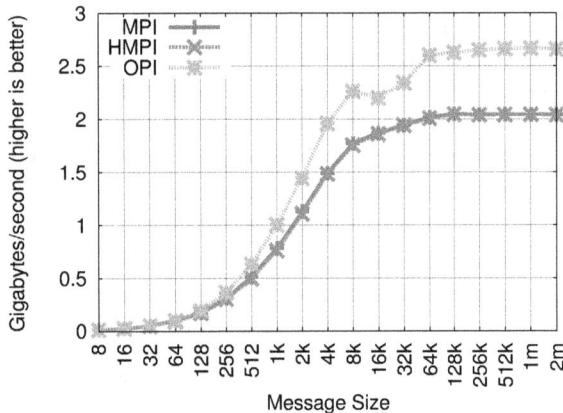

(b) Cross-socket throughput

Figure 16: Bandwidth for pack + communication + unpack on the Cab system.

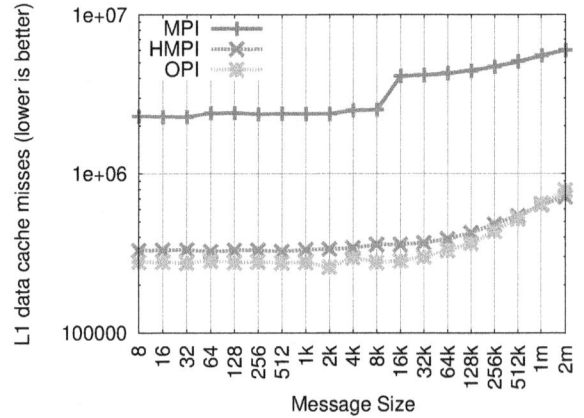

(a) Total pack + communicate + unpack misses

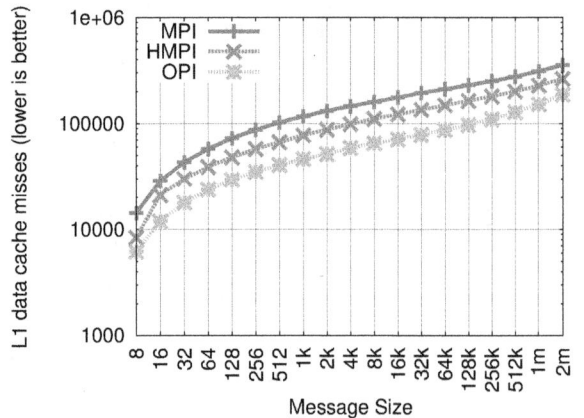

(b) Application misses

Figure 17: L1 Cache misses for different components of OPBench on the Cab system.

Bench). Since HMPI must copy the entire buffer into the receiver's cache before allowing it to read the data, it can pollute the cache by evicting the application's state. During subsequent computation this state must be brought back into the cache, causing additional misses. In contrast, OPI interleaves application reads and transfers of message data, so it is less disruptive to the cache, resulting in fewer cache misses for OPI than for HMPI or MPI.

5.2 MiniMD

MiniMD is part of the Mantevo [7] mini-application suite, which consists of several mini-applications representing larger application classes. Such mini-applications are increasingly used in exascale research for their combination of simplicity and relevance. MiniMD is a molecular dynamics simulation that computes atom movement over a 3D space decomposed into a processor grid. The primary work loop performs the following steps every iteration:

1. Every 20th iteration, migrate atoms to different ranks depending on atom locations.

2. Exchange position information of atoms in boundary regions to neighboring ranks.

3. Compute forces from both local atoms and those in boundary regions from neighboring ranks.

4. Exchange force information of atoms in boundary regions to neighboring ranks.

5. Update local atom velocities and positions.

MiniMD is an example of a stencil communication pattern that exchanges irregular data with point-to-point messages during steps 2 and 4. We transformed these communication phases to use ownership passing in the same manner as was done for the two-dimensional stencil example described in Section 3.3.

Performance results are shown in Figure 18. Computation of forces between atoms dominates execution time, so optimizing communication has a smaller affect on overall application time. When the communication time alone is considered, significant speedups are observed—up to 43% on Sierra, and 51% on Cab.

5.3 Fast Fourier Transform

Fast Fourier Transforms (FFTs) are among the most important operations in use today. Numerous algorithms and parallel applications use FFTs in their core computations [6, 9]. A one-dimensional FFT transforms a one-dimensional array of N complex numbers from real space to N complex numbers in frequency space. Such a one-dimensional FFT can be expressed in terms of multi-dimensional FFTs with additional application of *twiddle factors* [17, §12]. A multi-dimensional FFT with d dimensions can be computed by applying one-dimensional FFTs in all d dimensions. Multi-dimensional FFTs are very important in practice; image analysis often requires two-dimensional FFTs and transformations in real-space require three-dimensional FFTs [6, 9].

We perform our experiments using a two-dimensional FFT kernel. The original 2D FFT code is implemented using MPI and transforms an $N_x \times N_y$ domain. The initial array is stored in x-major

184

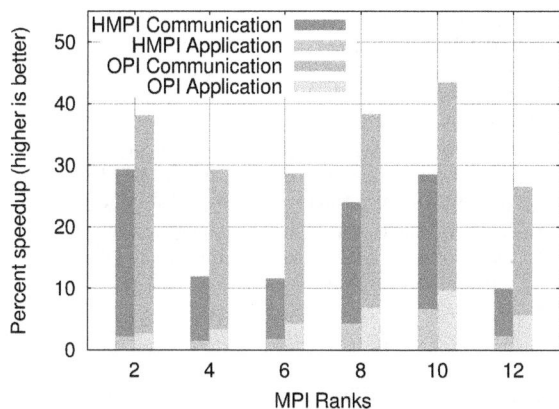

(a) Sierra System

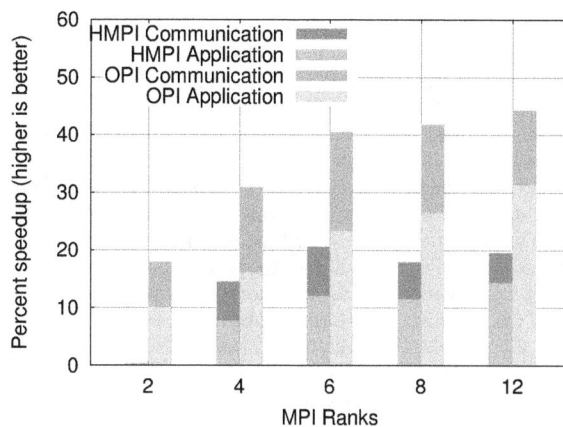

(b) Cab System

Figure 18: MiniMD speedup using ownership passing and HMPI, relative to MVAPICH2. A 4,000-atom problem size was used. Application times include communication time.

order and distributed in y-dimension such that each process has N_x/P y-pencils. The steps to perform the 2D FFT are:

1. Perform N_x/P 1D FFTs in y-dimension (N_y elements each).

2. Serialize the array into a buffer for the all-to-all.

3. Perform a global all-to-all.

4. De-serialize the array to be contiguous in the x-dimension (each process now has N_y/P x-pencils).

5. Perform N_y/P 1D FFTs in the x-dimension (N_x elements each).

6. Serialize the array into a send buffer for the all-to-all.

7. Perform a global all-to-all.

8. De-serialize the array into its original layout.

The all-to-all communications in steps 3 and 6 make 2D FFTs an interesting application for ownership passing. We perform the all-to-all ownership passing transformation described in Section 3.5. Each sender has one memory pool, from which it allocates and packs one buffer for each other rank. As each rank is packed, ownership is transferred to the receiver. Buffers are unpacked as ownership control arrives from each other rank.

The 2D FFT execution time is dominated by all-to-all communication, which in turn is dominated by message copying overhead in MPI. Ownership passing eliminates this overhead, leading to large speedups. The remaining communication time is dominated by the

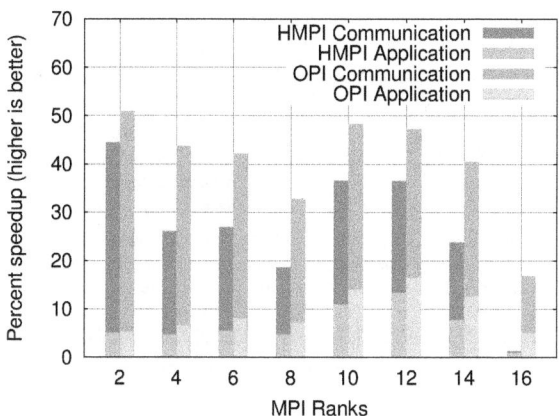

(a) Sierra System

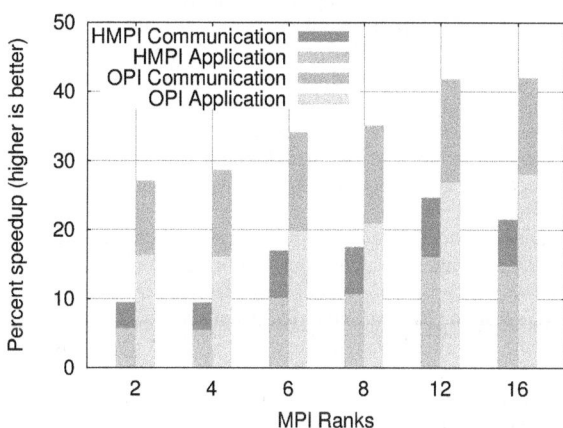

(b) Cab System

Figure 19: 2D FFT speedup using ownership passing and HMPI, relative to MVAPICH2. A 6,144x6,144 problem size was used. Application times include communication time.

pack and unpack routines, which transpose the two-dimensional matrix of FFT data points. Figure 19 shows the results, with communication time speedups of up to 48% on Sierra and 35% on Cab.

6. Related Work

In Section 2, we introduced the concept of a thread-based MPI for enabling direct memory access between ranks. An alternative approach is to use virtual memory extensions to directly map memory from one process into another [24, 25]. The advantage of this approach is that the MPI process-rank design (i.e., a rank is a process) remains intact. However, extensions to the operating system are required and are not generally available on existing installations, limiting availability and portability.

The idea of ownership passing draws upon techniques that can be found in distributed shared memory (DSM) systems [18] and early cache coherence protocols [5]. In either case, *ownership* is defined in the same manner—only one process is entitled to read or write a particular block of memory (e.g., a page or cache line). In this work, we use the concept of ownership to present a clean interface to improved shared memory performance in the context of MPI's distributed memory model.

The Generic Message Passing Framework [11, 12] implements a message passing interface for C++ that is reminiscent of MPI, with an extension for doing ownership passing using the auto_ptr reference counting pointer class. Our approach integrates with existing MPI, making it possible to incorporate ownership passing into legacy applications written in FORTRAN, C, and C++.

Multi-Version Variables (MVVs) [4, §8] are a language extension to Co-Array FORTRAN for supporting a producer-consumer communication channel. A memory pool concept similar to our own is used to provide a form of streaming message passing in a partitioned global address space (PGAS) language. Though similar, our work describes a path for modifying legacy MPI applications for improved performance on shared-memory hardware.

Ownership passing has been used to speed up other parallel programming frameworks such as the actor-based framework *Actor-Foundry* [15]. Significant performance benefits have been demonstrated in this context. However, C or Fortran with MPI codes have a more complex structure than *ActorFoundry* and complete static analysis is thus not always possible.

7. Discussion and Conclusions

We show how the principle of ownership passing can be used with MPI applications in order to utilize shared memory (multi-core) hardware more efficiently. This principle is often used implicitly in cache-coherency protocols and we extend it with a software interface to be used explicitly. Our ownership passing interface (OPI) is a simple extension to MPI and keeps MPI's ease of programming and abstraction (as opposed to shared memory programming with critical sections) while providing true zero-touch intra-node communication.

We address the challenge of returning the buffers with several pooling techniques. Our lock-free receiver pooling technique shows best results for practical applications where messages (buffers) are often passed symmetrically between MPI ranks.

Our interface allows the porting of legacy MPI applications to support "fat" shared memory nodes with simple transformations. Our examples show that the transformation is indeed simple. We provide a static compiler transformation that detects transformable code patterns and replaces them with appropriate OPI calls.

Our performance studies with microbenchmarks and real applications show that ownership passing is an effective technique for achieving better performance on shared memory hardware. Communication time speedups of up to 51% in a molecular dynamics application and 44% are realized in a two-dimensional FFT code.

Acknowledgments

This work was supported in part by the Department of Energy X-Stack program and the Early Career award program. It was partially performed under the auspices of the U.S. Department of Energy by Lawrence Livermore National Laboratory under Contract DE-AC52-07NA27344. (LLNL-CONF-609538)

References

[1] A. V. Aho, M. S. Lam, R. Sethi, and J. D. Ullman. *Compilers: Principles, Techniques, and Tools*. Addison-Wesley, 2 edition, 2007.

[2] S. Borkar. Will interconnect help or limit the future of computing. Presented as the 19th IEEE Conference on Hot Interconnects, 2011.

[3] G. Bronevetsky. Communication-sensitive static dataflow for parallel message passing applications. In *International Symposium on Code Generation and Optimization (CGO)*, Mar. 2009.

[4] Y. Dotsenko. Expressiveness, programmability and portable high performance of global address space languages. Technical report, 2006.

[5] S. J. Frank. Tightly Coupled Multiprocessor System Speeds Memory-Access Times. *Electronics*, 57(1):164–169, Jan. 1984.

[6] X. Gonze et al. A brief introduction to the ABINIT software package. *Zeitschrift fr Kristallographie*, 220(5-6-2005):558–562, 2005.

[7] M. A. Heroux, D. W. Dorfler, P. S. Crozier, J. M. Willenbring, H. C. Edwards, A. Williams, M. Rajan, E. R. Keiter, H. K. Thornquist, and R. W. Numrich. Improving performance via mini-applications. 2009.

[8] T. Hoefler and M. Snir. Writing Parallel Libraries with MPI - Common Practice, Issues, and Extensions. In *18th European MPI Users' Group Meeting, EuroMPI, Proc.*, volume 6960, pages 345–355, Sep. 2011.

[9] S. Kumar, C. Huang, G. Zheng, E. Bohm, A. Bhatele, J. C. Phillips, H. Yu, and L. V. Kalé. Scalable molecular dynamics with NAMD on the IBM Blue Gene/L system. *IBM J. Res. Dev.*, 52:177–188, January 2008.

[10] E. A. Lee. The problem with threads. *Computer*, 39(5):33–42, May 2006.

[11] L.-Q. Lee and A. Lumsdaine. Generic programming for high performance scientific applications. In *Proc. of the 2002 Joint ACM Java Grande – ISCOPE Conference*, pages 112–121. ACM Press, 2002.

[12] L.-Q. Lee and A. Lumsdaine. The generic message passing framework. In *Proceedings of the International Parallel and Distributed Processing Symposium (IPDPS)*, page 53, April 2003.

[13] MPI Forum. MPI: A message-passing interface standard. version 2.2, September 4th 2009.

[14] S. Negara, G. Zheng, K.-C. Pan, N. Negara, R. E. Johnson, L. V. Kale, and P. M. Ricker. Automatic MPI to AMPI Program Transformation using Photran. In *3rd Workshop on Productivity and Performance (PROPER 2010)*, number 10-14, Ischia/Naples/Italy, August 2010.

[15] S. Negara, R. K. Karmani, and G. Agha. Inferring ownership transfer for efficient message passing. In *Proceedings of the 16th ACM symposium on Principles and practice of parallel programming*, PPoPP '11, pages 81–90, New York, NY, USA, 2011. ACM.

[16] M. Pérache, P. Carribault, and H. Jourdren. MPC-MPI: An MPI implementation reducing the overall memory consumption. In *Proc. of the 16th European PVM/MPI Users' Group Meeting*, pages 94–103, Berlin, Heidelberg, 2009. Springer-Verlag.

[17] W. H. Press, S. A. Teukolsky, W. T. Vetterling, and B. P. Flannery. *Numerical recipes in C (2nd ed.): the art of scientific computing*. Cambridge University Press, 1992.

[18] J. Protic, M. Tomasevic, and V. Milutinovic, editors. *Distributed Shared Memory: Concepts and Systems*. IEEE Computer Society Press, Los Alamitos, CA, USA, 1st edition, 1997.

[19] D. J. Quinlan. Rose: Compiler support for object-oriented frameworks. *Parallel Processing Letters*, 10(2/3):215–226, 2000.

[20] R. Rabenseifner. Hybrid parallel programming on HPC platforms. In *In proceedings of the Fifth European Workshop on OpenMP, EWOMP'03*, Aachen, Germany, 2003.

[21] R. Rabenseifner, G. Hager, and G. Jost. Hybrid mpi/openmp parallel programming on clusters of multi-core smp nodes. In *Proceedings of the 2009 17th Euromicro International Conference on Parallel, Distributed and Network-based Processing*, PDP '09, pages 427–436, Washington, DC, USA, 2009. IEEE Computer Society.

[22] H. Tang and T. Yang. Optimizing threaded MPI execution on SMP clusters. In *ACM International Conference on Supercomputing (ICS)*, pages 381 – 392, 2001.

[23] D. Turner and X. Chen. Protocol-dependent message-passing performance on linux clusters. In *Proceedings of the IEEE International Conference on Cluster Computing*, CLUSTER '02, pages 187–, Washington, DC, USA, 2002. IEEE Computer Society.

[24] S.-Y. Tzou and D. P. Anderson. The performance of message-passing using restricted virtual memory remapping. *Software - Practice and Experience*, 21:251–267, 1991.

[25] M. Woodacre, D. Robb, D. Roe, and K. Feind. The SGI Altix 3000 global shared-memory architecture. 2005.

Parallel Schedule Synthesis for Attribute Grammars

Leo A. Meyerovich, Matthew E. Torok, Eric Atkinson, Rastislav Bodík

University of California, Berkeley *

{lmeyerov,mtorok,ericatkinson,bodik}@eecs.berkeley.edu

Abstract

We examine how to synthesize a parallel schedule of structured traversals over trees. In our system, programs are declaratively specified as attribute grammars. Our synthesizer automatically, correctly, and quickly schedules the attribute grammar as a composition of parallel tree traversals. Our downstream compiler optimizes for GPUs and multicore CPUs.

We provide support for designing efficient schedules. First, we introduce a declarative language of schedules where programmers may constrain any part of the schedule and the synthesizer will *complete* and *autotune* the rest. Furthermore, the synthesizer answers debugging queries about how schedules may be completed.

We evaluate our approach with two case studies. First, we created the first parallel schedule for a large fragment of CSS and report a 3X multicore speedup. Second, we created an interactive GPU-accelerated animation of over 100,000 nodes.

Categories and Subject Descriptors   I.2.2 [*Artificial Intelligence*]: Automatic Programming—Program Synthesis; D.1.3 [*Programming Techniques*]: Concurrent Programming—Parallel programming

Keywords   CSS, layout, sketching, attribute grammars, scheduling

1. Introduction

Programmers struggle to map applications into parallel algorithms. We examine attribute grammars, which are a declarative formalism for defining tree processors such as document layout engines. A grammar is high-level because it does not specify a tree traversal order that computes all node attributes. Algorithm designers optimize parallel tree traversals, so our approach is to stage the problem by first finding a schedule of traversals for a grammar.

We present a synthesizer that automatically schedules an attribute grammar as a tuned choice of tree traversals. For example, if our synthesizer schedules a grammar as a sequence of parallel preorder tree traversals, our more traditional GPU compiler can then implement them as level-synchronous breadth-first tree traversals. As another example, we present a case study of synthesizing

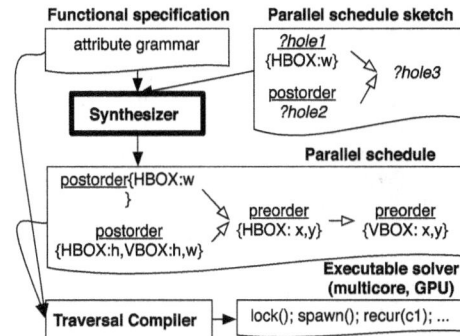

Figure 1: Synthesizer input/output: The synthesizer completes a schedule sketch and gives it to a traditional parallel compiler.

a schedule for a multicore CSS [3] webpage layout engine. CSS is a long-standing sequential bottleneck in web browsers that consumes 15-22% of the CPU time [9, 21]. We found the need to guide the choice of schedule, so we extend grammars with a language of schedules where programmers may specify parts of the schedule and let the synthesizer fill in the rest.

Our synthesizer explores the space of scheduling decisions:

- **Decomposing a sequential traversal.** Many computations contain sequential dependencies between nodes. One correct traversal over the full tree might then be sequential. However, if the sequential dependencies can be isolated to a subtree, an overall parallel traversal would be possible if it invokes a sequential traversal for just the isolated subtree. Our synthesizer therefore explores multiple non-obvious alternatives.

- **Composition of traversals.** Programs such as browsers perform many traversals. Traversals might run one after another, concurrently, or be fused into one. These choices optimize for different aspects of the computation. Running two traversals in parallel improves scaling, but fusing them into one parallel traversal avoids overheads: the choice may depend on both the hardware and tree size. Our synthesizer selects by autotuning.

- **Distribution of computations across traversals.** Even for a fixed schedule, i.e., a composition of traversals, node computations might commute across traversals. Redistributing them may improve memory use and avoid sequential bottlenecks.

These decisions explode the space of schedules. Today, programmers manually navigate the space by selecting a parallel schedule, judging its correctness, and comparing its efficiency to alternative schedules. The tasks are expensive: programmers globally reason about dependencies, develop prototypes for profiling, and whenever the functional specification changes, restart the process.

---

* Research supported by Microsoft (Award #024263) and Intel (Award #024894) funding and by matching funding by U.C. Discovery (Award #DIG07-10227). Additional support comes from Par Lab affiliates National Instruments, Nokia, NVIDIA, Oracle, and Samsung.

We present three techniques for automatically synthesizing a parallel schedule for an attribute grammar (Figure 1):

1: A scheduling language of parallel tree traversals that is explicit, orthogonal, and safe. A program can fully specify a *schedule* to simplify code generation. It identifies the available parallelism (composition of traversal types). The schedule is still high-level: it is specified alongside the functional specification and compilers handle the actual translation into lower-level code. We adapt attribute grammar dependence analysis [13] to statically verify that a schedule respects dependencies in the attribute grammar.

2: Schedule sketching for automatic parallelization. Fully automatic scheduling obstructs programmer guidance. We extend our scheduling language with a *sketching* [25] construct for partial specification of schedules. A *hole* is a symbolic variable that can be put in place of any term of an otherwise fully specified schedule. As an extreme example, the entire schedule may be specified as a hole. Our synthesizer fills in any holes to achieve a fully specified schedule. It finds a correct completion, and if there are multiple functionally correct ones, autotunes for the fastest. The same sketching language acts as a query language for parallelism debugging. Our synthesizer outputs sketch completions, and if the sketch and functional specification are mutually inconsistent, it shows the earliest stage in which the sketched schedule is incompletable.

3: Fast and extensible schedule synthesis. We struggled to implement a synthesizer that is fast and can be extended with new traversal types. Ours supports inputs and outputs beyond those of current grammar compilers, such as schedule sketches as input constraints, returning multiple schedules as outputs, and parameterization by multiple traversal types and composition operators.

Synthesis is a simple search: A) *enumerate* increasingly complete schedules and B) invoke individual traversal verifiers to *check* every partial schedule. We optimize both steps so synthesis is $O(n^3)$ in the number of attributes. To synthesize exponential-time extensions such as nesting schedules, we use incrementalization, sketching, and greedy heuristics.

In summary, we present a synthesizer that automatically schedules an attribute grammar as a tuned choice of tree traversals. First, we introduce a language of *structured* traversal schedules that can be sketched and verified (Section 2). Second, we describe our extensible $O(n^3)$ algorithm for synthesizing a correct schedule (Section 3). Finally, we use the synthesizer for schedule autotuning, parallelism debugging, and new primitives (Section 4).

We evaluate our approach with two case studies (Section 5). First, we synthesized a parallel schedule for a fragment of the CSS webpage layout language. CSS has long challenged parallelization [21]. We report multicore speedups of 3X. Second, we implemented a GPU-accelerated interactive visualization of 10^5 nodes.

2. Parallel Programming with Synthesis

Our system can be understood in terms of our case study of synthesizing a webpage layout engine. Accordingly, we present a running example of synthesizing the schedule for a simple layout language.

Its architecture is in Figure 1. A webpage is a tree with style constraints over attributes on each node, which the layout engine solves during tree traversals. Given the attribute grammar specifying a layout language, our synthesizer finds a parallel schedule. Next, our compiler that optimizes for different traversal patterns reads the schedule and outputs a browser layout engine that executes the traversals. In summary, our system uses several functions:

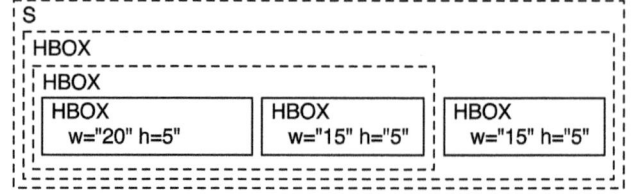

(a) Input tree. Only some of the x, y, w, and h attributes are specified.

$S \rightarrow HBOX$
$\quad \{ HBOX.x = 0; HBOX.y = 0 \}$

$HBOX \rightarrow \epsilon$
$\quad \{ HBOX.w = input_w(); HBOX.h = input_h() \}$

$HBOX_0 \rightarrow HBOX_1\ HBOX_2$
$\quad \{ HBOX_1.x = HBOX_0.x;$
$\quad\quad HBOX_2.x = HBOX_0.x + HBOX_1.w;$
$\quad\quad HBOX_1.y = HBOX_0.y;$
$\quad\quad HBOX_2.y = HBOX_0.y;$
$\quad\quad HBOX_0.h = \max(HBOX_1.h, HBOX_2.h);$
$\quad\quad HBOX_0.w = HBOX_1.w + HBOX_2.w \}$

(b) Attribute grammar for a language of horizontal boxes.

$AG \rightarrow (Prod \{ Stmnt? \})*$

$Prod \rightarrow V \rightarrow V*$

$Stmnt \rightarrow Attrib = id(Attrib*) \mid Attrib = n \mid Stmnt ; Stmnt$

$Attrib \rightarrow id.id$

(c) Language of attribute grammars.

Figure 2: (a) input tree (b) attribute grammar specifying the layout language (c) specification language of attribute grammars

$$\text{Synthesizer: } AG \rightarrow Sched \quad (1)$$
$$\text{Compiler: } AG \times Sched \rightarrow LayoutEngine \quad (2)$$
$$\text{LayoutEngine: } ConstraintTree \rightarrow ConcreteTree \quad (3)$$

This section describes specifying a layout language as an attribute grammar and the synthesized parallel schedule. We found implementing more complicated layout languages benefits from support in controlling and reasoning about the schedule. Thus, we conclude this section by extending the input language to support *sketching* (partial specification) of the schedule. A sketch is a full schedule, except any term (e.g., a choice of traversal type) can be left as a hole (symbolic variable) that the synthesizer will fill in:

$$\text{Synthesizer}_{sketch}: AG \times Sched_{sketch} \rightarrow Sched \quad (4)$$

2.1 Attribute Grammars

Consider solving the tree of horizontal boxes shown in Figure 2 (a). As input, a webpage author provides a constraint tree. Only some node attribute values are provided: the widths and heights of leaf nodes. The meaning of a horizontal layout is that, as is also depicted, the boxes will be placed side-by-side. The layout engine must solve for all remaining x, y, width, and height attributes.

The layout language of horizontal boxes, H-AG (Figure 2 (b)) can be declaratively specified as an attribute grammar [15, 21, 24]. First, the specification defines the set of well-formed input trees as the derivations of a context-free grammar. In this case, a document is an unbalanced binary tree of arbitrary depth where the root node has label S and intermediate nodes have label HBOX. Second, the specification defines semantic functions that relate

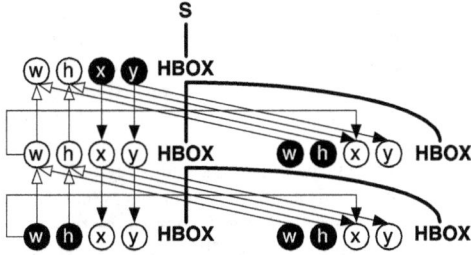

Figure 3: Data dependencies. Shown for constraint tree in Figure 2 (a). Circles denote attributes, with black circles being input () sources. Thin lines show data dependencies and thick lines show production derivations.

attributes associated with each node. For example, the width of an intermediate horizontal node is the sum of its children widths. Likewise, the width of a leaf node is provided by the user, which is encoded by nullary function call $input_w()$:

$$HBOX \to \epsilon \ \{ \ HBOX.w = input_w(); \ldots \ \} \qquad \text{/* leaf */}$$

$$HBOX_0 \to HBOX_1 \ HBOX_2 \qquad \text{/* binary node */}$$
$$\{ \ldots HBOX_0.w = HBOX_1.w + HBOX_2.w \ \}$$

Note that the evaluation order is not specified. For example, while the above statements will be executed within different tree traversals, the mapping is not specified. Likewise, an executable implementation may need to reorder the statements within a traversal. Whatever evaluation order is used to solve for the attribute values, the statements are constraints that must hold over them. Attribute grammars can therefore be thought of as a single assignment language where attributes are dataflow variables.

The language of attribute grammars is defined in Figure 2 (c). Our example assumes the following encoding. Semantic functions are uninterpreted, so, for example, the addition of widths can be rewritten as "$HBOX_0.w = f(HBOX_1.w, HBOX_2.w)$". Likewise, constant values are equivalent to nullary function calls. To specify grammars more complicated than H-AG, we provide extensions (Section 4) whose scheduling reduces to attribute grammars.

2.2 Language of Schedules

Given an attribute grammar, our synthesizer statically finds a schedule of tree traversals that will, for any tree described by the grammar, solve all of its attributes. For example, the width and height attributes of any H-AG tree can be solved in an initial *postorder* tree traversal, after which the x and y attributes can be computed with a *preorder* tree traversal. This two-pass schedule respects all data dependencies possible in an input tree. For example, it respects the data dependencies for Figure 2 (a), which are shown in Figure 3. Finally, both traversals exhibit structured parallelism that a compiler can exploit: parallel preorder allows a top-down wavefront, and postorder allows bottom-up.

Our synthesizer targets a language of traversals. A schedule for H-AG that exercises different types of traversals is in Figure 4 (a). It declares what simple tree traversals to use (parallel preorder and parallel postorder); how to combine them (here, serially); and what attributes to compute when a production is visited in each of these traversals. This section also describes parallel and nested combination as well as sequential recursive traversals. Our synthesizer is designed to support adding even more variants (Section 3).

A schedule is fed to simple compilers that produce evaluation code. An evaluator has two parts, as Figure 4 (c) shows for H-AG:

```
1  parPost
2    HBOX₀ → HBOX₁ HBOX₂ { HBOX₀.w HBOX₀.h }
3    HBOX → ε { HBOX.w HBOX.h }
4  ;
5  parPre
6    S → HBOX { HBOX.x HBOX.y }
7    HBOX₀ → HBOX₁ HBOX₂
8      { HBOX₁.x HBOX₂.x HBOX₁.y HBOX₂.y }
```

(a) One explicit parallel schedule for H-AG.

```
1  void parPre(void (*visit)(Prod &), Prod &p) {
2    visit(p);
3    for (Prod rhs in p)
4      spawn parPre(visit, rhs);
5    join;
6  }
7  void parPost(void (*visit)(Prod &), Prod &p) {
8    for (Prod rhs in p)
9      spawn parPost(visit, rhs);
10   join;
11   visit(p);
12 }
```

(b) Naïve traversal implementations with Cilk's [2] **spawn** and **join**.

```
1  void visit1 (Prod &p) {
2    switch (p.type) {
3      case S → HBOX: break;
4      case HBOX → ε:
5        HBOX.w = input(); HBOX.h = input(); break;
6      case HBOX → HBOX₁ HBOX₂:
7        HBOX₀.w = HBOX₁.w + HBOX₂.w;
8        HBOX₀.h = MAX(HBOX₁.h, HBOX₂.h);
9        break;
10   }
11 }
12 void visit2 (Prod &p) {
13   switch (p.type) {
14     case S → HBOX:
15       HBOX.x = input(); HBOX.y = input(); break;
16     case HBOX → ε: break;
17     case HBOX → HBOX₁ HBOX₂:
18       HBOX₁.x = HBOX₀.x
19       HBOX₂.x = HBOX₀.x + HBOX₁.w;
20       HBOX₁.y = HBOX₀.y
21       HBOX₂.y = HBOX₀.y
22       break;
23   }
24 }
25 parPost(visit1, start); parPre(visit2, start);
```

(c) Scheduled and compiled layout engine for H-AG.

$Sched \rightarrow Sched \,;\, Sched \mid Sched \parallel Sched \mid Trav$

$Trav \rightarrow TravAtomic \ Visit*\{(TravAtomic \mapsto Visit*)*\}?$

$TravAtomic \rightarrow \textbf{parPre} \mid \textbf{parPost} \mid \textbf{recursive}$

$Visit \rightarrow Prod \ \{ \ Step* \ \}$

$Step \rightarrow Attrib \mid \textbf{recur} \ V$

(d) Language of schedules (without holes)

Figure 4: Scheduled and compiled layout engine for H-AG.

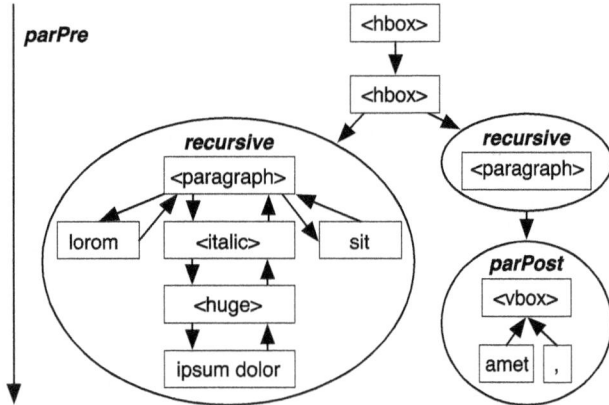

Figure 5: Nested traversal for line breaking. The two paragraph are traversed in parallel as part of a preorder traversal and a sequential recursive traversal is used for words within a paragraph.

1. **The traversals to execute.** Line 25 shows the sequence of two traversals for H-AG . An individual traversal can be parallel, as shown for the naïve implementations for preorder and postorder traversals in Figure 4 (b). Our compilers use the traversal structure to safely apply further optimizations (Section 5.2).

2. **Statements to execute within a traversal.** Lines 17-22 show the statements run for intermediate nodes in the second traversal. Every attribute in the schedule corresponds to a unique statement's left-hand side attribute. The compiler automatically infers the order of statements by topologically sorting them according to their dependency graph (Section 3.2).

Multiple schedules may be correct. For example, the initial **parPost** traversal for H-AG can instead be scheduled as two concurrent **parPost** traversals:

```
1  (    parPost
2        HBOX_0 → HBOX_1 HBOX_2 { HBOX_0.w }
3        HBOX → ε { HBOX.w }
4   ||
5        parPost
6        HBOX_0 → HBOX_1 HBOX_2 { HBOX_0.h }
7        HBOX → ε { HBOX.h })
8   ; parPre ... /* same as before */
```

Prior attribute grammar compilers would partition attributes into independent sets [13], but not as part of a greater schedule.

We provide two traversal types in addition to **parPre** and **parPost**. The first is a sequential **recursive** traversal. We use it, for example, in our case study of document layout. Consider inserting line breaks into the following stylized paragraph of XML strings:

```
lorom <italic><huge>ipsum dolor</huge></italic> sit
```

Due to <huge>, the paragraph may need a line break between "ipsum" and "dolor." Identifying the line break position involves visiting the subtree <italic>...</italic>; the resulting line break position is a data dependency influencing line breaks in the remainder of the text. The sequence of arrows in the big circle of Figure 5 show a trace of performing a recursive traversal over the paragraph. The traversal visits a node n, then visits n's first child, revisits n, and repeats this process for the remaining children before returning to the parent.

Our second traversal type is a *nested* traversal. With it, the tree is partitioned into an outer region and disjoint inner regions. The outer and inner regions are evaluated with different traversals, and both may exploit parallelism. We can think of the inner regions as macro-nodes that are evaluated in full (with their particular traversal type) when the outer traversal encounters them.

To motivate the need for the nested traversal type, we revisit line breaking. Even though line breaking of a single paragraph is sequential, distinct paragraphs of text can be handled in parallel. To avoid locally sequential computations from forcing the entire tree traversal to be sequential, we allow the outer region to be paralle, while each paragraph forms an inner region that is handled with the sequential recursive traversal. Figure 5 shows how parallel evaluation may be used to compute across different **recursive** paragraphs and within individual **parPost** regions for this example.

To partition a tree into regions, each grammar production (and thus each node of the tree) is mapped to a traversal type in the synthesized schedule. A subtree composed from nodes of the same traversal types form an inner region. For example, a nested traversal of paragraphs with sequential traversals of nested text subtrees is described as follows:

```
1  parPre
2    P → W { W.relativeX }
3    { recursive ↦
4        W_0 → W_1 W_2 {
5            W_1.relativeX recur W_1
6            W_2.relativeX recur W_2 } }
```

Overall, we see that schedules are explicit, orthogonal, and safe. They are explicit in that a custom code generator can be invoked without further high-level analysis. They are orthogonal in that they sit alongside the grammar: changes to one are often made independent of the other. Finally, they are safe. Traditional attribute grammar analyses can be used to check that a schedule does not violate a dependence in the attribute grammar (Section 3). If there is a bug, it is in the functional specification as an attribute grammar or somewhere in the implementation of the compiler toolchain.

2.3 Sketching

Specifying a full schedule is difficult. There are many attributes to schedule within a traversal, and often times, it is unclear whether a schedule is possible. We introduce a sketching language where programmers can specify parts of the schedule they care about and leave a hole, *?hole*, anywhere else. The synthesizer will fill in the hole, even if the hole is the entire schedule.

We can concisely specify the preceding schedules as follows:

$$\textbf{parPost} \; ?hole_1 \; ; \; \textbf{parPre} \; ?hole_2 \qquad (5)$$
$$(\textbf{parPost} \; ?hole_3 \; ; \; \textbf{parPost} \; ?hole_4) \; ; \; ?hole_5 \qquad (6)$$
$$?hole_6 \qquad (7)$$

In the first example, the synthesizer finds that the width and height attributes can be computed in $?hole_1$ and the remaining in $?hole_2$. The second example can be completed in several ways. Most prominently, $?hole_5$ may be a **parPost** or a sequential **recursive** traversal. By default, our synthesizer picks the first parallel traversal it finds, and our autotuner (Section 4.1) can optimize the choice.

Sketching has various uses. The third variant, $?hole_6$, enables automatic parallelization, which helps with prototyping. As an attribute grammar grows and is shared by programmers, sketches enable static checks that program edits do not break the parallelization scheme. Finally, sketches speed up synthesis time (Section 3.1).

3. Schedule Synthesis Algorithm

Our synthesizer takes an attribute grammar and a sketch as input, and outputs a set of schedules. It is designed to support multiple traversal types, multiple solutions, and rich attribute grammar and schedule sketching languages. Our initial implementation used the dependency analysis of Kastens [15], but it was too inflexible. Our new algorithm is designed for modularity and speed:

Line			
1	**parPre** {x,y,w,h}		**incorrect: unsat {x,w,h}**
2	**parPre** {y}		correct: continue
	... /* expand subtree to schedule x, w, h */ ...		
3	**parPost** {x,y,w,h}		**incorrect: unsat {x,y}**
4	**parPost** {w,h}		correct: continue
5	_ ; **parPre** {x,y}		**correct: complete**
6	_ ; **parPost** {x,y}		**incorrect: unsat {x,y}**
7	_ ; (**parPre** {x} ‖ _)		correct: continue
8	_ ; (_ ‖ **parPre** {y})		**correct: complete**
9	_ ; (_ ‖ **parPost** {y})		**incorrect: unsat {y}**
10	_ ; (**parPre** {y} ‖ _)		correct: continue
11	_ ; (_ ‖ **parPre** {x})		**correct: complete**
12	_ ; (_ ‖ **parPost** {x})		**incorrect: unsat {x}**
13	_ ; (**parPost** {y} ‖ _)		**incorrect: unsat {y}**
14	_ ‖ **parPre** {x,y}		**incorrect: unsat {x}**
15	_ ‖ (**parPre** {y} ; _)		correct: continue
16	_ ‖ (_ ; **parPre** {x})		**incorrect: unsat {x}**
17	_ ‖ (_ ; **parPost** {x})		**incorrect: unsat {x}**
	...		
18	**parPost** {w}		correct: continue
19	_ ‖ **parPre** {x,y,h}		**incorrect: unsat {x,h}**
	...		

Figure 6: Trace of synthesizing schedules for H-AG. Note that scheduling of "‖" does not use the optional greedy heuristic.

Simple enumerate-and-check The algorithm enumerates schedules and checks which are correct. Checking is for individual traversal types and for traversal compositors, and checkers are written independently of one another. Enumeration is simply syntactic. Adding a new traversal type involves adding a checker and syntax.

Optimization Naïve enumerate-and-check is too slow. Without significantly changing the interface for adding checkers, we optimize synthesizing one schedule to be $O(n^3)$. Some features are still slow, such as nested traversals, so we introduce optimizations of incrementalization, greediness, and sketching.

We now overview our high-level algorithm. After, we describe how to check the correctness of an overall schedule and individual traversal, and then analyze the correctness of our optimizations.

3.1 The Algorithm

We split discussion of optimizations between finding one schedule and finding many. Figure 6 demonstrates an algorithm trace for enumerating schedules of H-AG . Figure 9 shows the full algorithm.

Synthesizing one schedule is $O(A^3)$ in the number of attributes. The algorithm finds an increasingly long and correct prefix of the schedule (*prefix expansion*). At each step, it tries different suffixes until one succeeds, where a suffix "**parPre**{x,y}" is a traversal type and attributes to compute in it. When a correct suffix is found, it is appended to the prefix and the loop continues on to the next suffix. Finding one suffix involves trying different traversal types, and for each one, different attributes. Only the suffix needs to be checked (*incremental checking*), and checking a suffix is fast (*topological sort*). Finally, finding a set of attributes computable by a particular traversal type only requires $O(A)$ attempts (*iterative refinement*).

We consider each optimization in turn:

1. **Prefix expansion.** The synthesizer searches for an increasingly large *correct* schedule prefix. Every line of the trace represents a prefix. If a prefix is incorrect, no suffix will yield a correct schedule. Therefore, the only prefixes that get expanded are those that succeed (lines 2, 4, 7, 10, 15, 18).

   To synthesize only one schedule, only one increasingly large prefix is expanded. Line 2 has a correct prefix, so only "**parPre**{y}"

would be explored. Either no schedule is possible at all, or if there are any, one is guaranteed to exist in the expansion. In this case, "**parPre**{y} ; **parPost**{w,h} ; **parPre**{x}" would be found.

2. **Incremental checking.** Line 4 checks prefix "**parPost**{w,h}" for attributes "w" and "h." Therefore, lines 5-17 can check the suffix added at each line without rechecking "**parPost**{w,h}".

3. **Topological sort.** We optimize checking a suffix by topologically sorting the dependency graph of its attributes (rule check$_\beta$ in the next subsection). Topologically sorting a graph is $O(V + E)$. It is $O(A)$ in this case because $V = A$, and as the arity of semantic functions is generally small, E is $O(A)$.

4. **Iterative refinement.** The algorithm iteratively refines an over-approximation of what attributes can be computed in a suffix by removing under-approximations of what cannot. For example, the check in line 1 for **parPre**{x,y,w,h} fails with error {x,w,h}, which details the attributes with unsatisfiable dependencies. Computing fewer attributes cannot satisfy more dependencies, so no subset of {x,w,h} has satisfiable dependencies either. Therefore, the next check is on a set without them: {y}.

   Subtraction of attributes can be performed at most A times before reaching the empty set. Checking one refinement invokes the $O(A)$ topological sort. Put together, finding attributes computable by a suffix is $O(A^2)$.

Every traversal computes at least one attribute, so there are at most A traversals. A constant number of traversal types are examined for each suffix, and synthesizing each one is $O(A^2)$. Synthesizing one schedule is therefore $O(A^3)$.

Features such as nesting regions and enumerating all schedules are exponential, which we address with three further optimizations:

1. **Backtracking.** To emit multiple schedules, prefix expansion is modified to backtrack. After a schedule is completed or a suffix fails, the synthesizer backtracks to the most recent correct prefix. For example, line 8 is a complete and correct schedule. Backtracking returns to the earlier correct prefix of line 7 and tries an alternative suffix in line 9.

2. **Interleaved sketch unification.** Sketching prunes the search. For example, "**parPost** *?hole* ‖ *?hole*" enables skipping lines 1-3 because they do not start with a **parPost** traversal. Lines 5-13 could also be skipped because the compositor is not "‖".

   A sketch that provides a full schedule reduces synthesis to checking, which is $O(A)$. Sketching also enable features that otherwise require exponential search to still synthesize in $O(A^3)$. For example, scheduling nested regions is exponential in the number productions, but if just the production partitioning is sketched, synthesis is still only $O(A^3)$.

3. **Greedy heuristic.** For any schedule "p ; q", solving fewer attributes in p will not enable solving q with fewer traversals. Thus, to minimize the number of traversals, all such subsets are pruned. For example, as line 4 found **parPost**{w,h}, line 19 skips "**parPost**{w} ; _ " and proceeds to "**parPost**{w} ‖ _".

   Greediness reduces enumerating all schedules to only being exponential in the number of traversals. This is significant because, for example, our schedule for CSS has only 9 traversals.

In summary, synthesizing one schedule is $O(A^3)$, while emitting all of them is exponential. Finally, constructs such as nested traversals are still efficient when guided by sketches.

$$\frac{\{A\}\,p\,\{B\} \quad \{B\}\,q\,\{C\}}{\{A\}\,p\,;\,q\,\{C\}} \quad \text{(seq)}$$

$$\frac{\{A\}\,p\,\{B\} \quad \{A\}\,q\,\{C\}}{\{A\}\,p\,\|\,q\,\{B \cup C\}} \quad \text{(par)}$$

$$Regions = \{\alpha \mapsto Visit*_\alpha\} \ \cup \ \bigcup_i \{\beta_i \mapsto Visit_i*\}$$

$$\frac{\forall\,(\gamma \mapsto Visit*) \in Regions:}{C_\gamma = \texttt{alwaysCommunicate}_\alpha(\gamma, B, Regions)} \ \frac{\{A, C_\gamma\}\ \gamma\ Visit*\ \{A \cup B_\gamma\}}{\{A\}\ \alpha\ Visit*_\alpha\ \{(\beta_i \mapsto Visit_i)*\}?\ \{A \cup \bigcup B_\gamma\}} \quad \text{(nest}_\alpha\text{)}$$

$$\frac{P = \cup Prod_i \quad Steps = \cup Step_j}{B = \bigcup_i \texttt{reachable}_\beta(Prod_i, P, A, Steps, C)}{\{A, C\}\ \beta\ (Prod_i\ \{\ Step_j*\ \})*\ \{A \cup B\}} \quad \text{(check}_\beta\text{)}$$

$$\frac{\{A\}\,p\,\{B\} \quad unify(sketch, p)}{\{A\}\,p \wedge sketch\,\{B\}} \quad \text{(sketch)}$$

Figure 7: Correctness axioms for checking a schedule

```
1  alwaysCommunicate_parPre(β, B, M) =
2    {a_{W,W→X} | (W→X B_β) ∈ M[β]
3       ∧         ⋀           a_{W,V→W} ∈ B ∪ A}
          (V→W B_γ)∈M[γ≠β]
```

(a) Communication check for region boundaries in a **parPre** traversal

```
1  set reachable_parPre(W→X, P, A, B, C):
2    reach :=
3        {a_{*,W→X} | a_{*,W→X} ∈ A}
4      ∪ (C ∩ {a_{W,W→X} |      ⋀      W.a_{V→W} ∈ B})
                              V→W∈P
5      ∪ (C ∩ {a_{X,W→X} | ¬∃X→Y ∈ P})
6    while true:
7        progress := {a_{*,W→X} | a_{*,W→X} = f(b_0,...,b_n) ∈ F
                        ∧ a_{*,W→X} ∈ B ∧ ⋀ b_i ∈ reach}
8        reach := reach ∪ progress
9        if progress = ∅:
10           break
11   return reach
```

(b) Unoptimized production visit check for **parPre** traversal

Figure 8: Inter- and intra-region checkers for **parPre**.

3.2 Correctness Checking Axioms

Correctness axioms for checking an entire schedule are in Figure 7. The judgements recursively check a composition of traversals until reaching the traversal-specific checks of Figure 8. This procedure is inefficient and monolithic; the next subsection will why our optimizations correctly interleave the checks presented here.

Variables p and q denote schedules (<Sched>), A and B are sets of attributes, and α and β are traversal types (<travAtomic>). Attribute $a_{W,V \to W}$ is decorated with its production ($V \to W$) and

the non-terminal within it (W). We write $a_{*,V \to W}$ if a can be associated with a non-terminal on either side of the production.

The composition and traversal rules are as follows:

Sequential and parallel composition: ";" and "‖" The simplest composition check is for sequencing: Hoare triple "$\{A\}\,p\,;\,q\,\{C\}$" (rule seq). If attributes A are solved before traversal "p ; q", then attributes C will be solved after. The conditions above the judgement bar state this is true if p can always compute attributes B given attributes A, and q can always then compute C. The judgement is recursive. Analogous reasoning explains "‖" (rule par).

Nested composition Rule nest$_\alpha$ checks outer traversal type α over regions where each one may have its own traversal type γ. Consider an outer traversal type of **parPre**: as it progresses top-down, every region might be guaranteed to have attributes of its root node solved before evaluation proceeds within it. For each region (the set of productions mapped to region traversal type γ), the rule calls $\texttt{alwaysCommunicate}_{\text{parPre}}$ to find the set C_γ of attributes that are externally set before the region is traversed. Rule nest$_\alpha$ calls checks for every region under the assumption that C_γ is already solved.

The first line of rule nest$_\alpha$ means that, for any outer traversal α, attributes scheduled for the outer region are treated as if they were in their own region ($\gamma = \alpha$). Traversals that do not use nesting are degenerate: all the productions belong to one region ($\gamma = \alpha$).

Traversal over a region The schedule for a traversal of type β over a region is correct if every production visit schedule is correct (rule check$_\beta$). A production visit schedule $Prod_i\ \{\ Step_j\ \}$ is correct when there is an order for computing its scheduled attributes $Step_j*$ along which all of the data dependencies of the corresponding semantic functions are satisfied.

Production visit Figure 8 (b) shows an unoptimized reachability computation for visiting a production inside a **parPre** region. It is the standard transitive closure, except for two subtleties:

First, only attributes that are meant to be scheduled are considered reachable (B membership check in line 7). Incorrectly including unscheduled attributes would erroneously allow attributes with unresolved dependencies to also be included.

Second, attributes computed by visits to adjacent productions must be distinguished. Adjacent productions may be in the same region or in another. In a **parPre** region, consider when W is always an intermediate node of the region and attribute $a_{W,W \to X} \in B$ is always set by a parent production $V \to W$ in the same region. For this intra-region case, $a_{W,W \to X}$ is guaranteed to be reachable at the beginning of the visit to $W \to X$. However, if W can be the root node of the region, we must also check $a_{W,V \to W}$ is set by adjacent regions before the root is visited. The checks for the intra-region case and the $\texttt{alwaysCommunicate}$ inter-region case are in lines 4-5 of nest$_\alpha$.

Sketches Rule sketch separates checking the correctness of a schedule from whether a sketch matches it. First, a schedule must be correct irrespective of the accompanying sketch. Second, the schedule must syntactically match the schedule ($unify$). Later, we provide semantically constrained sketches that are checked by Prolog's more general unifier (Section 4.2).

3.3 Correctness of the optimizations

The optimization are *sound* and *complete* with respect to the axioms in Figure 7. Soundness means there is a derivation tree for a synthesized schedule, and completeness mean the optimizations do not preclude sound schedules. Most of our optimizations prune schedules from consideration by moving checks earlier, which is sound, so we only manually analyze completeness here.

Prefix expansion Prefix expansion prunes schedules $p \otimes q$ if p does not check. Completeness has two important cases. First, pruning a failing prefix p does not prune sound schedules. Any expansion $p \otimes q$ would have been rejected because composition operator check would fail. Second, to synthesize only one schedule, only one increasingly long prefix p needs to be expanded. Assume some alternative prefix q succeeds. A sound completion to p would be q modified to not include attributes already solved by p. If a sound schedule exists, prefix expansion will return one.

Incremental checking Incremental checking is sound and complete because it is the memoization of checking p for all completions $p \otimes q$.

Iterative refinement Refinement is complete because it only removes attributes from consideration that cannot be scheduled. Consider refining unreachable attribute a found by rule check$_\beta$:
$$a \in B - \bigcup_i \mathtt{reachable}_\beta(Prod_i, P, A, Steps, C)$$
If an alternative traversal computes a subset of *Steps* and a, the assumption of what is reachable before a is weakened. Attribute a will again be unreachable, and the schedule will fail. Refinement prunes such schedules, and therefore does not affect completeness.

Interleaved unification with sketches Interleaving is complete because any rejected schedule would have failed for the corresponding unification check.

Greedy heuristic By design, the greedy heuristic is not complete. Instead, classical attribute grammar languages [15] use greediness to guarantee that a node is visited a minimum number of times. We support traversal types of varying strengths, so this property is not immediate. For example, "**recursive** ; **parPre**" can often (but not always) be replaced by "**parPre** ; **parPost**; **parPre**", which is longer but more parallel. We instead guarantee that if there is a shorter schedule, it uses different traversal types.

4. Extensions

We outline three extensions that use the attribute grammar synthesizer: a schedule autotuner, a parallelism debugger, and grammar extensions for classes, loops, and schedule constraints. These extensions are important because they influenced the architectural design of the synthesizer.

4.1 Autotuning

We use the synthesizer to autotune for a fast schedule. For example, sketch "?*hole*$_1$; parPre ?*hole*" is underconstrained so the autotuner has freedom in choosing how to fill ?*hole*$_1$. The synthesizer provides two correct choices:

$$?hole_1 \in \{ \ \mathbf{parPost}\{\text{w,h}\}, \ \mathbf{parPost}\{\text{w}\} \ || \ \mathbf{parPost}\{\text{h}\} \ \}$$

Which schedule is faster depends on both the hardware and the size of expected trees. The first completion exposes more parallelism. However, on webpage-sized trees for multicore hardware, the overheads of a single traversal are high so the second completion is better. In general, the choice is not obvious because the selection of attributes for early traversals impacts the traversals possible later, and performance varies depending on hardware and trees.

Our autotuner design is simple. First, the developer provides input trees and hardware to test on. Second, the synthesizer enumerates all correct schedules. Finally, the autotuner compiles the schedules, profiles them on the inputs, and returns the fastest one.

4.2 Embedding the scheduling DSL in Prolog for first-class sketches and symbolic constraints

We implemented the synthesizer as a standard Prolog [6] relation. Doing so enables schedules to be unified with arbitrary Prolog programs rather than just sketches with holes. For an intuition, holes

```
1  def synthFast(sketch):
2    yield synth(∅, Attributes, sketch)

4  def synth(prev, rest, sketch):
5    choose ⊗ ∈ { ";", "||" }
6    if ⊗ = ";":
7      choose α ∈ { "parPre", "parPost", ... }
8      A := iterativeRefine(α, prev, rest)
9      if A = rest:
10       unify(sketch, α A)
11       yield α A
12     else if A = ∅:
13       backtrack
14     else:
15       unify(sketch, α A ; rhs₁)
16       yield α A ; synth(prev ∪ A, rest − A, rhs₁)
17   else:
18     unify(sketch, lhs₂ || rhs₂)
19     choose A ⊂ rest
20     p := synth(prev, A, lhs₂)
21     q := synth(prev, rest   A, rhs₂)
22     yield p || q

24 def iterativeRefine(α, prev, rest):
25   overapproxA = rest
26   do:
27     X = checkα(prev, overapproxA)
28     overapproxA = overapproxA − X
29   while X ≠ ∅
30   yield overapproxA
31   if nonGreedy:
32     choose overapproxA' ⊂ overapproxA
33     yield iterativeRefine(α, prev, overapproxA')
```

Figure 9: Optimized synthesis algorithm. Lines 10,15,18: early unification with sketches. Lines 8,27: incremental checking. Line 26: iterative refinement. Line 31: toggle minimal length schedules. Lines 12,28: pruning of traversals with unsatisfiable dependencies.

now simply map to the Prolog convention of using "_" for anonymous variables to automatically unify. Arbitrary Prolog programs can be used to further constrain them.

Our embedding treats schedule terms as first-class citizens that can be constrained with standard Prolog programs. For example:

```
1  Sched = [(T₁,A₁), recursive, (T₂,A₂)],
2  subset([x,y],A₁),
3  (T₂ = parPre ; T₂ = parPost)
```

The first line defines the schedule as a sequence of two traversals. The second line requires that the first traversal solves for, at least, x and y attributes. It demonstrates that schedules are first-class values. The final line specifies that the second traversal is either a parallel preorder traversal or a parallel postorder traversal. These last two lines demonstrate symbolic constraints beyond simple holes.

Our synthesizer provides constants **recursive** (";"), **parPre**, and **parPost**. Prolog provides operators [ ], ( ), subset, =, ; (disjunction), and "," (conjunction). Furthermore, it intreprets identifiers with capital first letters as variables to unify (e.g., Sched, T_1, A_1, ...).

We implemented the DSL with two techniques. First, we implemented the synthesizer as a search in Prolog. This enables us to reuse Prolog's unification algorithm and, for the sketching language, arbitrary Prolog programs. Second, as in Section 3, the algorithm unifies each prefix rather than just the final schedule.

193

4.3 Parallelism Debugging

We reuse the sketching language as an interface for three schedule debugging tasks: exploring, analyzing, and testing schedules.

Exploring underconstrained schedules The synthesizer can show different completions to the programmer. This provides concrete understanding of the space of opportunities.

Analyzing bottlenecks Our embedding in Prolog enables queries that analyze one or more schedules. The insight is that each schedule is a first-class Prolog value. For example, the diff of two schedule expression trees provides a lightweight change impact analysis. If a set of attributes can be synthesized as a **recursive** traversal but only a subset as **parPre**, the programmer knows that there is a problematic dependency for attributes in the difference of the two sets.

Testing schedules The synthesizer can be used to try new schedule ideas. If the sketch cannot be filled in, the synthesizer returns an informative error. In particular, it describes the "first" unsynthesizable tree traversal in the sketch, meaning the bottom leftmost failing traversal in a failing schedule's expression tree.

We found support for exploring, analyzing, and testing schedules enabled a productive workflow. Early on, a developer examines possible schedules and fixes a subset using a sketch. Then, as ideas form on how to remove bottlenecks in the schedule, a developer can iterate between checking and analyzing schedules. Meanwhile, development focused on the functional specification can rely on the checker to detect any changes that violate the parallel schedule.

4.4 Loops, Interfaces, and Traits for Attribute Grammars

Our experiences with document layout languages led to extending attribute grammars with several features: recurrence relations (loops), information hiding (interfaces), and code reuse (traits).

The synthesizer does not need to be modified to support these constructs. Instead, we reduce the scheduling the extensions to that of plain attribute grammars. Subsequent code generation inverts the reduction to recover the used features. The following high-level implementation strategies illustrate how this can be done:

Loops A tree may have a statically unbounded number of children. We support recurrence relations for computing over them. To demonstrate synthesis over non-trivial array expressions, consider an intentionally obfuscated way to count the number of chidlren:

```
1  HBOX0  →  HBOX1 * {
2    HBOX0.numChildren = HBOX1*[last].rollLen1;
3    HBOX1*[init].rollLen1 = 0;
4    HBOX1*[i].rollLen1 = HBOX1*[i-1].rollLen2 + 1;
5    HBOX1*[init].rollLen2 = 0;
6    HBOX1*[i].rollLen2 = HBOX1*[i-1].rollLen1 + 1 }
```

The synthesizer finds a loop interleaving rollLen1 and rollLen2 calls.

Loops resemble the uniform recurrence relations of Karp et al. [7, 14]. Ours are more expressive in that loops support escaping. For example, global sequential dependencies require **recursive** traversals to recur mid-iteration. We restrict the language of array indices to guarantee that the schedule for a few unrolled steps of the recurrences generalizes to recurrences of any length.

Traits Traits support code sharing. They share declarations across productions. For example, trait paintRect can be added to any production with attributes $\{x_V, y_V, w_V, h_V, fill_V\}$ via "$V \rightarrow W$ (paintRect) {...}". Traits are implemented with macros.

Interfaces Interfaces support information hiding. The programmer associates every non-terminal with a set of attributes: its public interface. For production $V \rightarrow W$, semantic functions may read and write any attribute of V but only interface ones of W.

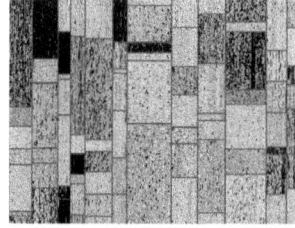

(a) Votes Five-pass parallel treemap visualizing Russian election data.

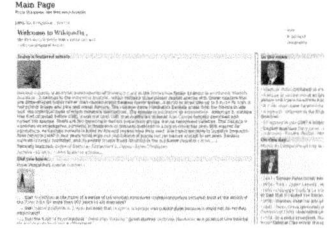

(b) CSS 9-pass parallel CSS engine run on Wikipedia.

Figure 10: Visualizations rendered with two grammars

name	loc	1st	sketch	found	avg
hbox++	305	5.6s	9.6s	54	2.7s
spiral	144	0.7s	0.9s	12	0.4s
votes	327	15.4s	22.0s	36	8.0s
css	1132	1919.6s	65.1s	100	445.4s

Figure 11: Synthesizer speed: 1st is the time to first schedule without using a sketch. sketch is the time to first schedule using a sketch of the traversal sequence. found is the number of schedules found. avg is the average time to find a sketch.

We found that information hiding provides an opportunity for optimization. The synthesizer only needs to schedule interface-level attributes. The availability of the rest can be inferred locally.

5. Evaluation

We evaluated the key aspects of our synthesizer. First, our algorithm synthesizes one or more schedules in a reasonable amount of time. Second, by exposing traversal structure information to a parallel runtime, we see 2-7X speedups over other approaches. Third, we describe the ability to add new traversal types. Finally, we performed two case studies of being able to apply our synthesizer: a multicore implementation of the CSS webpage layout language achieves 3X speedups on 4 cores, and a GPU implementation of a visualization of the 2011 Russian elections supports real-time interactions with over 96,000 polling stations.

5.1 Synthesis Speed

We measured the time to synthesize several attribute grammars:

1. **HBOX++** H-AG extended with more node types and styling
2. **Spiral** A radial visualization of space taken in a file system
3. **Votes** An interactive treemap of the 2011 Russian elections
4. **CSS** A CSS subset with floats, tables, and nested text

Figure 11 shows the lines of code for each one and various timings on a 2.66GHz Intel Core i7 with 4GB of RAM.

Generally, synthesizing a schedule, whether an arbitrary one (1st) or from a traversal sketch (sketch), takes less than 30 seconds. The exception was CSS, which we discuss in its own subsection and was still fast.

Emitting all schedules is even faster per emitted schedule (avg) than just finding the first. While the total time to emit all schedules can be slow, we note that enumeration is for offline autotuning. Finally, the greedy heuristic was necessary for enumerating schedules. Even after one day of running the non-greedy algorithm for CSS, most of the greedy CSS schedules were still not reached.

	Total speedup				Parallel speedup		
	Cores				Cores		
Configuration	1	2	4	8	2	4	8
TBB, server	1.2x	0.6x	0.6x	1.2x	0.5x	0.5x	1.0x
FTL, server	1.4x	2.4x	5.2x	9.3x	1.8x	3.8x	6.9x
FTL, laptop	1.4x	2.1x			1.6x		
FTL, mobile	1.3x	2.2x			1.7x		

Figure 12: Speedups and strong scaling across different backends (Back) and hardware. Baseline is a sequential traversal with no data layout optimizations. FTL is our multicore tree traversal library. Left columns show total speedup (including data layout optimizations by our code generator) and right columns show just parallel speedup. Server = Opteron 2356, laptop = Intel Core i7, mobile = Atom 330.

5.2 Parallel Speedups From Structured Traversals

By statically exposing traversal structure (e.g., **parPre**) to our code generators, we observe sequential and parallel speedups. Our code generator performs pointer compression [17] and tiling [12] to improve sequential and parallel memory access, and beyond the scope of this paper, a new semi-static variant of work stealing to schedule tiles. We compare to using the Intel's TBB [23] dynamic task scheduler that performs work stealing [2] over the tiles.

For random 500-1000 node documents in the `hbox++` language, we saw 6.9X parallel speedups on 8 cores with our custom scheduler (FTL). For TBB, we saw slowdowns until 8 cores. The results are consistent across hardware (Figure 12). Finally, we also report sequential speedups of 1.2X-1.4X due to the memory optimizations, yielding a combined superlinear speedup of 9.3X on 8 cores. Static scheduling yielded significant speedups.

5.3 Autotuning

We evaluated schedule autotuning speedups for `hbox++` (`laptop`):

Greedy schedules We enumerated greedy schedules for `hbox++` and compared performance on 1 and 2 cores. The relative standard deviation for performance of different schedules (σ/μ) is 8%. The best schedules for 1 and 2 cores are different. Swapping them leads to 20-30% performance degradation, and the difference between the best and worst schedules for the two scenarios are 32% and 42%, respectively. Autotuning schedules improves performance.

Greedy vs. non-greedy Our schedule enumeration is not exhaustive because of the greedy heuristic, and therefore may miss fast schedules (Section 3.2). For a fixed schedule of traversals with a greedy attribute schedule, non-greedy attribute schedules were 0-6% faster. On average, however, non-greedy schedules were 5% slower. Greedy scheduling was safe for `hbox++` .

5.4 Adding New Scheduling Primitives

Adding new scheduling primitives is simple. The average length of our primitives is 61 lines of commented Prolog code. For example, our nested traversal primitive was actually conceived of late into the CSS case study and took only 82 lines of code.

As another example, consider adding the scheduling primitives of spawn and join [2]. Their use is theoretically possible by generalizing the approach of FNC-2 [13] to extend our **recursive** traversal. Explicit schedules would include spawn and join points, which requires extending the syntactic enumerator. Any recursion point is a legal spawn but, if a statement depends on an attribute set by a preceding spawn, a join must be scheduled beforehand. To check this property, we can modify topological sorting ($reachable_{taskRecursive}$) to check reads. We did not add this feature because, as Jourdan [13] report, its reliance on dynamic scheduling suggests poor strong scaling (Section 5.2).

Backend	Input	Parallel speedup		
		Cores		
		2	4	8
TBB	Wikipedia	1.5x	1.6x	1.2x
TBB	xkcd Blog	1.5x	1.8x	1.2x
FTL	Wikipedia	1.6x	2.8x	3.2x
FTL	xkcd Blog	1.5x	2.3x	3.1x

Figure 13: Parallel CSS layout engine. Run on a 2356 Opteron.

5.5 GPU Case Study: Interactive Treemap of Elections

We examined synthesizing GPU-accelerated code for an interactive and animated treemap of the 2011 Russian legislative elections for exploring anomalous voting activity. To run it, we created a GPU backend that generates level-synchronous breadth-first tree traversal [20] in OpenCL. Figure 10 (a) shows a real-time rendering of the entire data set of 94,601 polling stations. A surprising result was that parallelization was fully automated: the visualization programmer did not know the traversal schedule.

On a laptop-grade GPU (GeForce GT 650M with 384 cores), we measured end-to-end performance on three data sets: 10,000, 100,000 and 1,000,000 nodes. They achieved 27.6 fps, 27.6 fps, and 4.5 fps, respectively. We compared to running in our JavaScript backend, representing another high-level language. On Chrome 21.0 and `laptop`, JavaScript ran at most 500 nodes at 27 fps. Finally, we compared layout time between the GPU a multicore CPU (`server`). The laptop GPU had a 1.6X speedup over the server for layout, and not measured, directly invoked rendering without transferring layout data.

5.6 Multicore Case Study: CSS Webpage Layout

We synthesized a multicore implementation of the CSS language for webpage layout. The official CSS standard [3] is informal, written assuming an implementation using sequential tree traversals, and notoriously hard to implement even without considering parallelism. Further challenging supporting CSS is its many interacting features. For example, tables and nested text were not discussed in previous work [21] and required a new schedule.

Figure 10 (b) shows our grammar's result for laying out Wikipedia. We implemented features suggested by Mozilla developers (floats, automatic tables, nested blocks and inlines), as well as others seen in our tested websites, such as margins, padding, borders, relative positioning, and lists. Additional features, such as clearance and generated content, are ongoing targets for concurrent work in a tested, mechanized, and verified semantics of CSS.

For parallelization, the developer sketched to explore scheduling ideas. Usefully, edits to the grammar were checked for unsatisfiable dependencies and against the parallel schedule sketch. Our current schedule is a sequence of 9 parallel traversals, including one nested traversal with a sequential region for nested text. With a sketch similar to this description, synthesizing the schedule takes one minute. During development, the programmer typically experienced even faster synthesis times. He would manually incrementalize by only synthesizing edited classes.

We report a 3.1X speedup on layout (Figure 13). Our case study presents two milestones: the largest executable yet declarative specification of CSS and the first case of strong scaling.

6. Related work

Parallel document layout Parallel layout is a difficult challenge. Browsers load independent resources in parallel, which can be used for parallel layout by decomposing a page into independent units. Concurrent work by Mai et al. [19] lays out a page on a proxy server, rewrites it as visually disjoint documents, and sends them to a client incorporating shared memory parallelism optimizations similar to those of Meyerovich and Bodík [21] for parallel rendering. We instead parallelize by optimizing just the layout engine.

Brown [4] propose applying task parallelism, which Meyerovich and Bodík [21] implement using Cilk [2] and TBB [23] to weakly scale a CSS subset. Burckhardt et al. [5] likewise apply task parallel Revisions. We achieve strong scaling and on a bigger subset.

Attribute grammars Attribute grammars, first introduced by Knuth [16] to define language semantics, are tractable for static analysis and optimization. Saraiva and Swierstra [24] specify non-automatic HTML table layout with attribute grammars and Meyerovich and Bodík [21] first examine CSS.

Kastens [15] presents a sequential schedule synthesizer based on a global dependency analysis. Jourdan [13] surveys parallel attribute grammar evaluators that largely extend this idea. Most similar to our work are systems that find completely independent sets of attributes, corresponding to parallel composition ("||"), and those that treat each node as a dynamically schedulable unit. The former is too coarse-grained to expose significant parallelism, while, as reported by Jourdan for FNC-2, the latter rely upon runtime schedulers such as work stealers and thus only weakly scale.

Synthesis Data structure synthesis is an old problem. Early on, Low [18] examined multiple set implementations for an ALGOL-60 variant. Recent work by Hawkins et al. examines tuning over data structures for relational code [11]. Our paper leaves decisions of how to implement tree data structures to our optimizing backends and instead focuses on how to determine what tree traversal types characterize the computations.

Our autotuning compiler backend is similar to the ATLAS [26] framework for linear algebra in that we tune parameters such as block size to optimize for a particular device. Autotuning is actively being applied to further domains, such as work in stencils [8] by Datta et al.: our backend examines the case of traversals over trees.

Similar to our schedule autotuner, FFTW [10] and PetaBricks [1] select algorithms, not just parameters. However, programmers must state what algorithms to try in those systems. Our synthesizer infers what is possible. Elixir [22] infers dynamic task scheduling optimizations for a single for-loop. Assuming extensions for structured traversals, Elixir might replace our code generators for concrete schedules. Hypothetically, our system would synthesize schedule "**parPost**{w,y};**parPre**{x,y}" and could then ask Elixir for dynamic task scheduling optimizations for traversal "**parPre**{x,y}".

Finally, our language extension for programming with holes, which we use for scheduling, is inspired by Sketch [25].

7. Conclusion

We presented a synthesizer that can schedule an attribute grammar as a composition of parallel tree traversals. The synthesizer's enumerate-and-check design simplifies adding new traversal types and extensions such as debugging. For $O(n^3)$ synthesis and practical autotuning, we optimized its algorithm. Furthermore, to enable control of schedules, we introduced a declarative language and extended it with sketches. Finally, we successfully performed two non-trivial case studies: multicore parallelization of a large fragment of the CSS webpage layout language and GPU acceleration of a Russian election animation. Put together, we demonstrate a path to more productive and effective parallel programming.

Acknowledgments

We thank anonymous reviewers for presentation suggestions. Adam Jiang and Edward Lu contributed to early versions of this work. Discussions with Krste Asanovic, Boris Zbarsky, Robert O'Callahan, Wolfram Schulte, Todd Mytkowicz, David Sheffield, Shoaib Kamil, Scott Beamer, and others helped guide our case studies.

References

[1] J. Ansel, C. Chan, Y. L. Wong, M. Olszewski, Q. Zhao, A. Edelman, and S. Amarasinghe. Petabricks: A language and compiler for algorithmic choice. In *PLDI'09*, June 2009.

[2] R. D. Blumofe, C. F. Joerg, B. C. Kuszmaul, C. E. Leiserson, K. H. Randall, and Y. Zhou. Cilk: an efficient multithreaded runtime system. In *PPOPP'95*, pages 207–216, 1995.

[3] B. Bos, H. W. Lie, C. Lilley, and I. Jacobs. Cascading style sheets, level 2 CSS2 specification, 1998.

[4] H. Brown. Parallel processing and document layout. *Electron. Publ. Origin. Dissem. Des.*, 1(2):97–104, 1988.

[5] S. Burckhardt, D. Leijen, C. Sadowski, J. Yi, and T. Ball. Two for the price of one: a model for parallel and incremental computation. In *OOPSLA'11*, pages 427–444, 2011.

[6] A. Colmerauer. An introduction to Prolog III. *CACM*, 33, July 1990.

[7] A. Darte and F. Vivien. Revisiting the decomposition of Karp, Miller and Winograd. In *ASAP*, pages 13–25, 1995.

[8] K. Datta, M. Murphy, V. Volkov, S. Williams, J. Carter, L. Oliker, D. Patterson, J. Shalf, and K. Yelick. Stencil computation optimization and auto-tuning on state-of-the-art multicore architectures. In *SC'08*.

[9] S. Dubey. AJAX Performance Measurement Methodology for Internet Explorer 8 Beta 2. *CODE Magazine*, 5(3):53–55, 2008.

[10] M. Frigo and S. G. Johnson. The design and implementation of FFTW3. *IEEE*, 93(2):216–231, 2005. Special issue on "Program Generation, Optimization, and Platform Adaptation".

[11] P. Hawkins, A. Aiken, K. Fisher, M. Rinard, and M. Sagiv. Data representation synthesis. In *PLDI'11*, June 2011.

[12] F. Irigoin and R. Triolet. Supernode partitioning. In *POPL'88*.

[13] M. Jourdan. A survey of parallel attribute evaluation methods. In *Attribute Grammars, Applications and Systems*, volume 545 of *LNCS*, pages 234–255. Springer Berlin / Heidelberg, 1991.

[14] R. M. Karp, R. E. Miller, and S. Winograd. The organization of computations for uniform recurrence equations. *J. ACM*, July 1967.

[15] U. Kastens. Ordered attributed grammars. *Acta Informatica*, 1980.

[16] D. E. Knuth. Semantics of context-free languages. *TOCS*, 2(2):127–145, June 1968.

[17] C. Lattner and V. Adve. Automatic pool allocation: Improving performance by controlling data structure layout in the heap. In *PLDI'05*.

[18] J. Low. Automatic data structure selection: an example and overview. *CACM*, 21(5):376–385, 1978.

[19] H. Mai, S. Tang, S. T. King, C. Cascaval, and P. Montesinos. A case for parallelizing web pages. In *HotPar'12*, 2012.

[20] D. Merrill, M. Garland, and A. Grimshaw. Scalable GPU graph traversal. In *PPOPP '12*, pages 117–128, 2012.

[21] L. A. Meyerovich and R. Bodík. Fast and parallel webpage layout. In *WWW'10*, pages 711–720, 2010.

[22] D. Prountzos, R. Manevich, and K. Pingali. Elixir: a system for synthesizing concurrent graph programs. In *OOPSLA '12*, October 2012.

[23] J. Reinders. *Intel threading building blocks*. O'Reilly, 2007.

[24] J. a. Saraiva and D. Swierstra. Generating spreadsheet-like tools from strong attribute grammars. In *GPCE'03*, pages 307–323, 2003.

[25] A. Solar-Lezama, L. Tancau, R. Bodik, S. Seshia, and V. Saraswat. Combinatorial sketching for finite programs. In *ASPLOS-XII*, pages 404–415, 2006.

[26] R. C. Whaley, A. Petitet, and J. J. Dongarra. Automated empirical optimization of software and the ATLAS project. *Parallel Computing*, 27(1–2):3–35, 2001.

Parallel Suffix Array and Least Common Prefix for the GPU

Mrinal Deo

Advanced Micro Devices, Inc.
Mrinal.Deo@amd.com

Sean Keely

Advanced Micro Devices, Inc.,
University of Texas, Austin
Sean.Keely@amd.com

Abstract

Suffix Array (SA) is a data structure formed by sorting the suffixes of a string into lexicographic order. SAs have been used in a variety of applications, most notably in pattern matching and Burrows-Wheeler Transform (BWT) based lossless data compression. SAs have also become the data structure of choice for many, if not all, string processing problems to which suffix tree methodology is applicable. Over the last two decades researchers have proposed many suffix array construction algorithm (SACAs). We do a systematic study of the main classes of SACAs with the intent of mapping them onto a data parallel architecture like the GPU. We conclude that *skew algorithm* [12], a linear time recursive algorithm, is the best candidate for GPUs as all its phases can be efficiently mapped to a data parallel hardware. Our OpenCL implementation of *skew algorithm* achieves a throughput of up to 25 MStrings/sec and a speedup of up to 34x and 5.8x over a single threaded CPU implementation using a discrete GPU and APU respectively. We also compare our OpenCL implementation against the fastest known CPU implementation based on *induced copying* and achieve a speedup of up to 3.7x. Using SA we construct BWT on GPU and achieve a speedup of 11x over the fastest known BWT on GPU.

Suffix arrays are often augmented with the longest common prefix (LCP) information. We design a novel high-performance parallel algorithm for computing LCP on the GPU. Our GPU implementation of LCP achieves a speedup of up to 25x and 4.3x on discrete GPU and APU respectively.

Categories and Subject Descriptors D.1.3 [*Programming Techniques*]: Concurrent programming — Parallel Programming

General Terms Algorithms, Performance

Keywords Suffix Array, Suffix Tree, BWT, Longest Common Prefix, OpenCL, GPU, Prefix Sum, Accelerated Processing Unit (APU)

1. Introduction

Suffix array (SA) was introduced by Manber & Myers [18] as a space saving alternative for suffix trees [21, 35]. SA is a lexicographic sorted list of all suffixes of a string. This implies that using a comparison based sorting algorithm e.g. quicksort or merge-

sort, with complexity $O(n \log n)$ will give us a solution with complexity $O(n^2 \log n)$. However, SAs can be seen as a special case of string sorting. Sorting suffixes differ from ordinary string sorting in that the elements to sort are overlapping strings of length linear in the input size n. Over the last two decades researchers have used this fact that the strings being sorted are related to each other, and proposed several optimisations [29] including some linear time SACAs [12, 13]. Abouelhoda [1] introduced a related data structure called the Enhanced Suffix Array (ESA), which is primarily a SA augmented with another table of longest common prefix (LCP). They are able to replace every string processing algorithm that is based on a bottom-up traversal of a suffix tree using a corresponding algorithm based on ESA. Another important application of suffix array is the Burrows-Wheeler transform (BWT) [5]. The BWT is a reversible permutation of the characters of a string, which enables very powerful lossless data compression, and is the basis of practical compression tools such as *bzip2* [33]. SAs have also been used as the basis for advanced data structures to construct succinct full text indexes [8]. Thus an efficient implementation of SA on the GPU is a prerequisite for offloading all these important applications mentioned above. We summarize the contribution of our paper below.

- Suffix array construction algorithms (SACAs) have not been studied with an intent to map them onto GPUs. We do a detailed analysis of the main class of SACAs [29] and reason about each one's applicability to a data parallel architecture like GPUs. Specifically, we show that the method which delivers fastest CPU implementations is not easily parallelized because of dependencies and that any attempt at decomposing the problem into chunks leads to irregular structure not fit for the GPUs.

- We show that *skew algorithm*, a linear time recursive algorithm, is the most suitable for GPUs by providing an efficient implementation which scales well across small GPUs (using APUs) to discrete GPUs. In our implementation we are able to avoid all communication between the CPU and GPU except the decision to recurse further. We argue that with the advancements in GPU hardware such as, *dynamic parallelism* [27] we will be able to launch kernels from within the GPU eliminating last piece of communication and synchronization between the CPU and GPU improving the performance further.

- Suffix arrays are often augmented with the longest common prefix (LCP) table. We provide a novel method to parallelize the linear time algorithm proposed by Kasai [15] to compute LCP. Our implementation, though it scales well across APUs and GPUs, suffers from thread divergence for inputs with high maximum LCP. We argue that this is more an artifact of the GPU hardware rather than our approach towards parallelization.

- APU provides a notion of *zero copy memory* which allows the CPU and GPU to access the same buffer without having to copy the buffer explicitly from host to device or vice versa. This opens up a new design space for programmers to consider and optimize around it. We do a cost-benefit analysis for the *skew algorithm* to find an optimal balance of work between CPU and GPU. We look at the return on investment for parallelizing each subpart of the algorithm and choose to either parallelize or leave it untouched on the CPU. This kind of flexibility is unique to heterogeneous systems like the APUs because of 'zero copy' buffers and low synchronizations cost between CPU and GPU.

The rest of the paper is organized as follows. Related work in this area is discussed in section 2. Section 3 provides the background knowledge and section 4 discusses different SACAs. In section 5 we discuss *skew algorithm* and BWT. Section 6 provides details about our parallel implementation of the *skew algorithm*. Section 7 discusses parallel LCP construction. Section 8 presents the experimental results. Finally in section 9 we conclude.

2. Related Work

One of the earliest works on parallel implementation of suffix arrays was by Futamura [26]. They start by choosing a window-size w and separate the suffixes into buckets according to its first w characters. This step is parallel and each suffix can be inserted into their relevant bucket. However, the next step of sorting the suffixes within each bucket is done in serial. Also in the second step they are sorting a subset of the suffixes in each bucket; therefore any suffix sorting algorithm which takes advantage of the structure in suffixes cannot be applied. Instead each bucket is sorted using a ternary search-tree based general string sorting algorithm [4]. On traditional multi-core architectures this implementation achieves good results as the CPU cores are optimized for single threaded performance resulting in very fast runtime for the second step. But due to the serial second step, this method does not work well on GPUs. Another problem with this approach is that since they use a general string sorting algorithm they could end up doing quadratic work in the worst case as seen in some real world inputs with long common prefixes [20].

In the work done by Homann [10], the authors choose to parallelize Deep-Shallow SACA [20]. They achieve a speedup of less than 2x using 16 threads. This is not surprising, as the authors of Deep-Shallow algorithm regard their work as an "algorithmic engineering" paper where they have used many tricks to speed up special cases which are serial in nature. Abouelhoda [24] provides a parallel implementation of bucket pointer refinement algorithm (BPR) [31] and achieves a speedup of less than 2x but claims to be faster than [10]. Both these approaches try to parallelize what is called as the *two-stage* or *induced copying* algorithm [29]. Later in section 4 we discuss the general structure of these algorithms and reason why they are difficult to parallelize.

Recent work by Patel et al. [28] provides an implementation of BWT on the GPU. This is done as a part of a larger goal to study the feasibility of lossless data compression e.g *bzip2* on the GPU. For their BWT implementation on the GPU they report a 3x slowdown as compared to a single thread CPU implementation by Seward [32]. The implementation by Seward is another example of *two-stage* or *induced copying* SACA. It uses a radix sort to create buckets and then follows it up with a ternary quick-sort. The challenging part with these algorithms is to find a good data-parallel solution to ternary quicksort. Patel et al. choose to implement BWT using an entirely new approach, based on merge sort. They report extreme degradation in performance in the later stages of merge sort mainly due to branch divergence and global memory access. Another issue with using merge sort to compute BWT is that it cannot take advantage of the fact that suffixes of a string are related and their algorithm has a complexity of $O(n^2 \log n)$. Our imple-

Figure 1. SI-GPU block diagram

Term	Description
work-item	A unit of computation representing one input data point. Sometimes referred to as a "thread" or a "vector lane".
wavefront	A collection of 64 work-items grouped for efficient processing on the CU. Each wavefront shares a single program counter.
work-group	A collection of work-items working together, capable of sharing data and synchronizing with each other. Can comprise of more than one wavefront, but is always on a single CU.

Table 1. AMD APP and OpenCL related terms

mentation and choice of the algorithm does not suffer from any such problems and we are able to achieve speed up as compared to the implementation by Seward. We do a further analysis of their approach and provide experimental results in section 8.

The work that most closely relates to ours is by Kulla et al. [16]. They do a parallel implementation of DC3 [13] which is very similar to the *skew algorithm* with some generalization. Their work was done on a distributed architecture using MPI on an Itanium cluster. A lot of the ideas presented by them are applicable to us but our work is novel as it is the first and only implementation of *skew algorithm* on the GPU and there are significant differences in optimization strategies for a cluster and a GPU. Since we do not have access to their source code nor to an Itanium cluster we do not provide any direct performance comparison.

Finally to the best of our knowledge there is no prior art in parallelizing the linear time LCP algorithm by Kasai et al. [15]. We provide novel techniques to efficiently parallelize this algorithm.

3. GPU architecture and programming model

We briefly describe the micro-architecture of modern graphics processors (GPUs) and the OpenCL programming model [2, 9] for using them. Although we discuss AMD Southern Island GPUs (SI-GPU) [3], concepts discussed here are applicable to other GPU architectures in general. SI-GPUs implement a parallel micro-architecture suitable for both graphics and general purpose data-parallel compute applications (Figure 1). The SI-GPU consists of a command processor that communicates with the host and schedules on chip workloads. The ultra-threaded dispatch processor accepts commands from the command processor and distributes work across the compute units. Each compute unit contains instruction logic (fetch, buffer, decode, issue), scalar and vector ALU units with registers, a high-bandwidth low-latency shared memory, and a read/write L1 cache equipped with general load/store/atomic and

i	Suffix	$SA[i]$	$\overline{SA}[i]$	$LCP[i]$	Sorted Suffix
1	abeacadabea$	121	4	–	$
2	beacadabea$	11	8	0	a$
3	eacadabea$	8	12	1	abea$
4	acadabea$	1	5	4	abeacadabea$
5	cadabea$	4	9	1	acadabea$
6	adabea$	6	6	1	adabea$
7	dabea$	9	10	0	bea$
8	abea$	2	3	3	beacadabea$
9	bea$	5	7	0	cadabea$
10	ea$	7	11	0	dabea$
11	a$	10	2	0	ea$
12	$	3	1	2	eacadabea$

Table 2. Suffix array example

texture addressing/filtering capabilities. The compute units are supported by a multi-banked read/write L2 memory cache, a global shared memory and a memory controller.

A compute unit (CU) is the basic unit of computation and different SI-GPUs have a different number of CUs. Each CU contains scalar ALUs and scalar GPRs, 4 SIMD, each consisting of vector ALU and vector GPRs, local memory or LDS and a read/write access to vector memory through L1 cache. Table 1 summarizes the terms related to OpenCL and SI-GPU. CU executes various user-developed programs, known as *kernels* to compute programmers and *shaders* to graphics programmers. Work is assigned to a CU in blocks of 64 items, called a *wavefront*. A *wavefront* has a single program counter and is the minimum granularity of work. Scalar instructions in the kernel operate on a single value common to all *work-items* in the *wavefront*. Vector instructions operate on all of the *work-items* in a *wavefront*, but each *work-item* has a unique data value. There can be many *wavefronts* resident on a CU. They are used to hide memory latency by having the scheduler switch the active *wavefront* in a given CU whenever the current *wavefront* is waiting for a memory access to complete. This context switch is typically done by the hardware and is very fast. This low-cost approach to hiding memory latency allows the GPU to maximize memory bandwidth and ultimately performance.

4. Suffix Array Algorithm

Consider a text input $T = t_1 t_2 \ldots t_{n-1}$\$ of length $n \geq 1$. In what follows we assume that T ends with a special end marker \$, that occurs nowhere else in T and is the lexicographically smallest character. Let $T_i = t_i t_{i+1} \ldots t_{n-1}$\$ denote the suffix of T that starts at position i. To store the suffix T_i we only store the starting position number i. Then the suffix array is a sorted array $SA[1..n]$ of all the suffixes of T, i.e., $SA[k] = i$ if T_i is lexicographically the kth smallest suffix. We also define the inverse suffix array (ISA), $\overline{SA}[1..n]$, such that $\overline{SA}[i] = k$, iff $SA[k] = i$. Thus $\overline{SA}$ provides the lexicographic rank of $T[i..n]$ in constant time. We denote by $lcp(A, B)$ the length of the longest common prefix between strings A and B. Now, we consider the following problem: compute the LCP between Suffix T_i and its adjacent suffix in the suffix array. This is computed and maintained in the LCP array. Table 2 gives an example of SA, $\overline{SA}$, LCP for a given text $T = abeacadabea$\$. The authors refer the readers to survey paper on SACAs by Puglisi et al. [29]. We now discuss each of the class of SACA algorithms briefly with the intent of extracting parallelism and mapping it onto GPU.

4.1 Prefix Doubling

The *prefix-doubling* technique was first applied to suffix array by Manber & Myers inspired by the earlier work of Karp et al. [14] in string matching. The most efficient implementation is that of

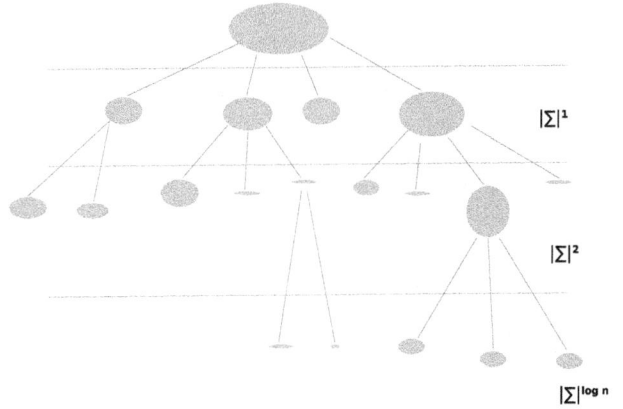

Figure 2. Parallelism profile of *prefix-doubling*

	Type A if $T[i] > T[i+1]$											
	Type B if $T[i] \leq T[i+1]$											
		1	2	3	4	5	6	7	8	9	10	11	12
T	=	b	a	d	d	a	d	d	a	c	c	a	$
Type	=	A	B	B	A	B	B	A	B	B	A	A	B

Table 3. Illustration of *Type A & Type B*

Larsson [17]. The first step of the algorithm places the suffixes – represented as numbers 0 to N, into an array I, sorted according to the first symbol of each suffix. This step consists of integer sorting, where the keys are drawn from the input alphabet. This step can be efficiently parallelized using any integer sorting routine, preferably a radix sort. After the 1st step, I is in h-order with $h = 1$. A maximal sequence of adjacent suffixes in I which have the same initial h-symbols is a group. A group containing at least two suffixes is an unsorted group. Then a number of passes for further sorting follow, possibly done in parallel. At the beginning of jth such pass, I is in h-order, where $h = 2^{j-1}$. The algorithm will finish in a maximum of $\log N$ passes and we will be left with zero unsorted groups. We sort the unsorted groups using the group number of suffix $i + h$ as the key for the suffix i, which places I in $2h$-order. Larsson [17] used ternary-split quicksort to sort the unsorted groups. For GPUs can we can instead use radix sort.

The key property of this algorithm that makes it unsuitable for GPU is the fact that after each pass we get an increasing number of unsorted buckets. Let T, the input string be over an alphabet Σ, then in subsequent passes each unsorted bucket can potentially produce as many child buckets as $|\Sigma|$ (see Figure 2). Moreover the amount of work in each unsorted bucket is not uniform. This algorithm exhibits a behaviour very similar to MSB radix sort, very efficient in theory for sorting strings but is difficult to implement in practice, more so on a GPU. In figure 2 each oval represents an unsorted bucket. The number of unsorted bucket (unit of work) increases at each level and can be a maximum of $|\Sigma|^{\log N}$. This method has enough parallelism but is difficult to manage on a GPU.

4.2 Two-Stage or Induced Copying

The algorithms in this class are arguably the most diverse [11, 19, 31]. These algorithms are all based on the central idea that (usually) a complete sort of a selected subset of suffixes can be used to induce a fast sort of the remaining suffixes. We choose to discuss the original algorithm by Itoh [11] in detail. Following this paper there were other algorithms proposed, which improved upon the memory usage and also proposed techniques for faster implementation in practice, but they all had the same asymptotic time complexity of $O(n^2 \log n)$ [20]. Therefore we believe it is sufficient to discuss the original work by Itoh et al[11].

The algorithm proceeds as follows:

Step 1 Initial bucket sort assigns a bucket to each suffix according to its first character to either *Type A* or *Type B* (Table 3). Then, each index of the *Type B* suffix is actually put into its bucket. The bucket for suffix of *Type A* remains empty. This step can be efficiently parallelized.

Step 2 Buckets of *Type B* which contain more than two indexes are sorted using a string sorting algorithm. Itoh & Tanaka use MSB radix sort [22] for sorting large group of suffixes, Bentley-Sedgewick Multikey quicksort [4] for medium size groups and insertion sort for small groups. All the three algorithms used are either serial in nature or difficult to parallelize on GPUs. This is also the most time consuming step. Another point worth noting is that Itoh & Tanaka could not take advantage of the special structure of suffixes in this step.

Step 3 Sort buckets of *Type A*. The crucial observation of algorithm *two-stage* is that once all *Type B* suffixes are sorted we can derive the ordering of *Type A* suffixes by direct comparison. This is done with a single pass over the input array i.e. in linear time $O(n)$. We pick up an index i in buckets one by one in lexicographic ascent order, and if $T_{i-1} > T_i$, i.e. *Type A*, then we put index i into the bucket of *Type A* correspondono to the first character of T_{i-1}. This sequential scan is thus data dependent. We need to keep track of the last position on the bucket where the *Type A* suffix was inserted. Parallelizing this would entail explicit communication between the compute units.

Over the years many researchers have improved upon Step 2, the task of sorting *Type B* suffixes in what they call as an "algorithmic engineering" paper [20]. Variants of *two-stage* or *induced copying* are currently the highest performing CPU implementation and we compare our results with the best variant, *libdivsufsort* [25].

5. Skew Algorithm

Skew algorithm is a linear time recursive algorithm for constructing SA. It follows the same pattern as Farach's linear time suffix tree construction algorithm [7]. The algorithm has 3 basic steps:

Step 1 Construct the suffix array of the suffixes starting at positions $i \mod 3 \neq 0$, we call these suffixes *Type A*. This is done by reducing the problem to the SA construction of a string of two thirds the length, which is solved recursively to obtain SAA.

Step 2 Construct the suffix array of the remaining suffixes $i \mod 3 = 0$, we call these *Type B* suffixes, using the result of the first step. This gives us SAB.

Step 3 Merge the two suffix arrays, SAA and SAB, to get the full suffix array SA.

Here we briefly review the workings of *skew algorithm*, following the notation of Kärkkäinen and Sanders[12]. The first step of the algorithm contains the recursion and is the most expensive. In this step the algorithm ignores every third suffix and attempts to sort the remaining 2/3, those suffixes S_i with $i \mod 3 \neq 0$. Sorting is performed by examining the first three characters of each selected suffix and assigning a sorting key, or "lexicographic name", to each unique triplet. This is done by radix sorting the triplets, writing one in the key array if the triplet is different from its predecessor (zero otherwise), and scanning the key array. In this way the suffix contributing the kth different triplet recieves a lexicographic name, s'_i, equal to k. Importantly these keys sort to the same order as their

Suffixes	ID	Sorted Suffixes	SA	Sorted Rotations	BWT
banana$	1	$	7	$banana	a
anana$	2	a$	6	a$banan	n
nana$	3	ana$	4	ana$ban	n
ana$	4	anana$	2	anana$b	b
na$	5	banana$	1	banana$	$
a$	6	na$	5	na$bana	a
$	7	nana$	3	nana$ba	a

Table 4. BWT for an example string T=banana

triplets taken from the suffixes. If all the names are different step one is finished. Otherwise ambiguity remains between two or more strings and we must recurse to complete the sorting. The algorithm recurs using the array of lexicographic names for the recursive input. So it computes the suffix array, SA^{12}, of the string

$$s^{12} = [s'_i : i \mod 3 = 1] \circ [s'_i : i \mod 3 = 2]$$

resulting in a fully sorted set of lexicographic names for the suffixes of S_i with $i \mod 3 \neq 0$.

Step 2 is the task of sorting the suffixes S_i with $i \mod 3 = 0$ is relatively easy. Here the remaining suffixes with $i \mod 3 = 0$ are sorted by sorting the pairs $(s[i], S_{i+1})$. This pair is just the suffix S_i taken as its first character paired with its remainder, which is a suffix sorted during step 1. Because the sort order of the remainders is already known, stored in SA^{12}, it remains only to perform a stable sort on the entries $SA^{12}[j]$ that represent remainders, S_{i+1}, with respect to $s[i]$. This is done with a single pass of radix sort.

The authors of the *skew algorithm* highlight the simplicity of the last step as their greatest contribution. The task is to merge the two suffix arrays to obtain the complete suffix array SA. To compare the suffix S_j, with $j \mod 3 = 0$ with a suffix S_i, with $i \mod 3 \neq 0$, there are two cases to consider: if $i \mod 3 = 1$, take S_i as $(s[i], S_{i+1})$ and S_j as $(s[j], S_{j+1})$. Since $i + 1 \mod 3 = 2$ and $j + 1 \mod 3 = 1$, the order of S_{j+1} and S_{i+1} is contained in SA^{12}, as these are strings which were sorted during step 1. Their position can be quickly determined using an array, $\overline{SA}^{12}$, which holds an inverse of the suffix array SA^{12}, $\overline{SA}^{12}[i] = j + 1$ when $SA^{12}[j] = i$. For $i \mod 3 = 2$, the triples $(s[i], s[i + 1], S_{i+2})$ and $(s[j], s[j+1], S_{j+2})$ are considered and similarly replace S_{i+2} and S_{j+2} by their lexicographic names in $\overline{SA}^{12}$.

5.1 Burrows-Wheeler Transform

Burrows-Wheeler transform starts out by producing a list of strings which are all the cyclic rotations of the original string. This list is then sorted lexicographically and the last character of each transformed string forms the BWT. It is straightforward to calculate BWT once we have SA. Given an input string T and its SA, BWT can be computed as follows:

$$BWT[i] = \begin{cases} T[SA[i] - 1] & \text{if } SA[i] \neq 1 \\ T[n - 1] = \$ & \text{otherwise} \end{cases}$$

Given this we can safely choose to ignore BWT and only discuss SA and its parallel implementation. We will be able to derive the BWT trivially once we have computed SA. Table 4 shows the relationship between the input T, its SA and BWT.

6. Parallel skew algorithm

Table 5 presents the pseudocode for the *skew algorithm*. We explain the working of each of the kernels below. The first step is sorting the triplets from suffixes starting at position $i \mod 3 \neq 0$. This can be computed using the classic LSB radix sort. We use the optimizations techniques used in the work from Merrill [23]. One

```
      computeSA(int *T, int *SA, int length)
1.    {
2.        initMod12(); // form triplet s12: i mod ≠ 0, s0:i   mod 3= 0
3.        radixSort(s12); // lsb radix 1st Character          kernel1
4.        radixSort(s12); // lsb radix 2nd Character
5.        radixSort(s12); // lsb radix 3rd Character
6.        lexicRankOfTriplets();                              kernel2
7.        if (!allUniqueRanks)
8.            computeSA();                                    recursion
9.            storeUniqueRanks();                             kernel3
10.       else
11.           computeSAFromUniqueRank();                      kernel4
12.       radixSort(s0) //                                    kernel1
13.       mergeSort(s0, s12) //                               kernel5
14.   }
```

Table 5. *skew algorithm* pseudocode

```
      // SA [] suffix array
      // ISA [] inverse suffix array
      // T [] input string
      // n input length
      // LCP [] output lcp array
1.    h = 0
2.    for i in 1 ... n
3.        if ISA[i] > 1
4.            j := SA[ISA[i]-1]
5.            while T[i+h] = T[j+h]
6.                h := h+1
7.            LCP[ISA[i]] := h
8.            if h > 0 then h := h-1
```

Table 6. The LCP algorithm from Kasai et al[15].

thing worth noting is that after the very first triplets are sorted in the first recursion the subsequent ones are use ranks as the value, for the key-value sort. For a 32-bit value, sorting on GPU means 4 passes of radix sort as we sort 8 bits in each pass to limit the memory needed to store histograms [23]. For sorting triplets, we make 12 kernel launches. Since radix sort is very efficient on the GPU, as shown by Merrill et al. [23], we still manage to get considerable speedup, even though we are doing more work.

The second step is to compute the ranks of the sorted triplets. The function lexicRankOfTriplets(), appears to be serial at first glance. This function is essentially counting the unique elements in a list. Therefore, given a list of items (in this case triplet) the first step is to compare and find the positions where we have a unique element or triplet. We compare each element against its predecessor and store a value of 1 (flag) whenever they are unequal. Now, to be able to find the ranks of each triplet it is a matter of doing a prefix sum of the stored flags. Both the comparison step and prefix sum computation can be spread across all the compute units of the GPU. We use local memory to store the flags and compute the prefix sum per workgroup. Later we launch a second kernel to sum up all the values across workgroups and assign ranks to each triplets.

The functions on line 9 and line 11 are trivially parallelized. If we know the rank of each suffix triplet and if that is unique, we can directly compute the SA. This is what computeSAFromRank() does. Line 12 is where we sort the suffixes with $j \mod 3 = 0$ within itself. This is done by a two step radix sort of string formed by the first character of S_j and appending it with the rank of S_{j+1} with the rank of S_{j+1} from the sorted suffixes s12. We use the same LSB radix code used for sorting triplets.

The final step is merging the two sorted suffix lists, s0 and s12 of unequal sizes with s12 being twice as large then s0. This can be treated as the final step of a classic merge sort routine with two sorted sub-lists to merge at the end. We use the technique by Satish [30] to parallelize the merge. Note that this step is not as work-efficient as the early stages of merge sort. The inefficiency comes from the fact that we need to find the smallest possible range in the other sorted list to compare with, to find the final position in the merged list. The algorithm proceeds by dividing the two sorted lists into small chunks. We keep elements of s0 in the registers and read in elements of s12 in local memory. Each block of s0, is assigned to a different workgroup. To find the relevant block in s12 we can do a binary search. Each block is then further sub divided and assigned to each *work-item* within a workgroup. Each *work-item* does a binary search in the s12 block to pick up the index to start comparing from. This step leads to bank conflicts in local memory but is essential to avoid doing a lot of extra comparison. We amortize the cost of this search by having each *work-item* work on large number of elements. We use the optimization strategy by

Davidson [6] of keeping two windows, one in registers and one in local memory. We refer the reader to the original paper [12] for details. Finally, at each step we create just one more chunk of work of 2/3rd the original size which is easy to manage without any elaborate load balancing scheme.

7. Longest Common Prefix

LCP is defined as the length of the longest common prefix between every pair of lexicographically consecutive suffixes. Note that $LCP[1]$ is undefined as since $T[SA[1], n]$ is the lexicographic smallest suffix and therefore has no predecessor. Kasai [15] described a simple linear time algorithm to compute the LCP given the input array and the suffix array. The algorithm is derived from the following observation.

$$\text{If } LCP[p] = LCP(T_j; T_{i-1}) > 1 \text{ then}$$

$$LCP[q] = LCP(T_k; T_i) \geq LCP[p] - 1$$

This states that when the LCP between the suffix T_{i-1} and its adjacent suffix is h, suffix T_i and its adjacent suffix on SA has a common prefix of length at least $h - 1$. Therefore it suffices to compare from the hth characters for computing the LCP between T_i and its adjacent suffix. If h is less than or equal to 1, the comparison will begin with the first character. We refer the readers to the original paper [15] for proof and correctness of this statement.

We now describe the working of the algorithm in table 6. The algorithm starts out by preparing the ISA, if not already given as input. Line 1 initializes the value of h to 0. The main loop is a linear scan of the ISA picking up the suffixes in increasing order. Line 4 looks up the position in the SA and find the suffix preceding it. Line 5 & 6 is comparing the suffixes one character at a time starting from the offset h until a mismatch. The fact that we start comparing the suffixes starting from the hth character and not the first character makes it a linear time algorithm. The value h at the time of mismatch is the LCP.

7.1 Parallelizing LCP

There is a dependency in the algorithm of table 6, where we take advantage of the LCP value computed previously to skip character comparisons when computing LCP of the subsequent suffix pairs. The first observation that we make is that when $h \leq 1$, the algorithm starts out comparing from the first character, thus not taking advantage of the previously computed values. This essentially breaks up the dependency chain. Therefore, we can safely conclude that there are as many groups of independent suffixes as there are number of suffix index with $lcp = 0$. We know for a fact that $lcp(S_i, S_{i-1}) = 0$, only when the suffixes differ in their first character. Therefore the first task is to identify the suffixes whose LCP is 0. This can be trivially parallelized, and we can compare each

m	i	s	s	i	s	s	i	p	p	i	$	T []
$	i$	ippi$	issippi$	ississippi$	mississippi$	p$	ppi$	sippi$	sisissippi$	ssippi$	ssissippi$	Suffixes
11	10	7	4	1	0	9	8	6	3	5	2	SA []
	≠			≠	≠		≠					
--	10	--	--	--	0	9		6	--	--	--	

Sorted Ranges {0,5} {6,8} {9,10} {10,11}

Figure 3. kernel1 - Parallel LCP implementation

character in the string T with its previous character. If there is a mismatch then we store the suffix id. If the string T is over the alphabet Σ, we can have a maximum of $|\Sigma|$ suffixes with LCP as 0. Thus $|\Sigma|$ is the upper limit of the amount of parallelism we are left with after kernel1. Figure 3 explains the computation of kernel1 of LCP.

Before we dispatch the final kernel to compute lcp values we need to sort these suffix ids into ranges, to be able to simulate a linear scan of ISA from the original algorithm. The input string T and $|\Sigma|$ governs the number of independent suffix ranges after Kernel1 and it can be anywhere between 1 (string is a repeat of a single character) to a maximum of $|\Sigma|$. Moreover, the number of suffixes in each range is non-uniform. We have measured the ratio of sizes between the largest range to the smallest range to be 100000:1 for some real life inputs. Thus a straight forward approach of launching each range as a separate workgroup is inefficient. For GPUs this kind of non-uniform chunks of parallel tasks leads to severe load imbalance between workgroups. Therefore we need the 2nd kernel which is responsible for load balancing.

There are 2 cases (Figure 4) that we need to worry about which leads to load imbalance. First, when we don't have enough independent ranges after kernel1, e.g. when processing a genome file with characters (A,T,C,G). In this case we will have a maximum of 4 ranges. To extract maximum performance from a GPU we need to have maximum occupancy which cannot be achieved with 4 workgroups. Therefore we need a scheme to increase the number of workgroups. We choose to break up the ranges into sub-ranges to get maximum occupancy on the GPU. Second, when we have sufficient number of ranges, but the number of suffixes in each range is non-uniform. If not redistributed, the running time will be governed by the workgroup that has the largest range. We need to carefully balance the work done in kernel2 for load balancing with the actual benefit. Fortunately for strings over ASCII and UTF-8 we need to rebalance a maximum of 256 ranges which is not computationally expensive. We start by sorting the ranges by their size and also compute the average over all the range sizes. The end goal is to make each range close to average. To this end, we scan the sorted list in an ascending order, if the range size is below average, we pick up more work from the range at the end of the list (largest range). We keep a running counter to indicate the range from which to steal from. We stop the scan when we pick up a range that is close to the average governed by a threshold. Since we are dealing with small number of bins we think this static load balancing scheme works best.

Kernel3 (Figure 5) computes the lcp. Let us say the number of suffixes or size of a range is R. We divide R into B blocks. Each *work-item* is assigned one block to process. The processing of the block by *work-item* is done in 2 steps. First, each *work-item* starts out by computing the lcp of first suffix in its block. This is done by comparing suffixes starting from the first character. In this step, we are doing more work than serial version of the algorithm. Once we

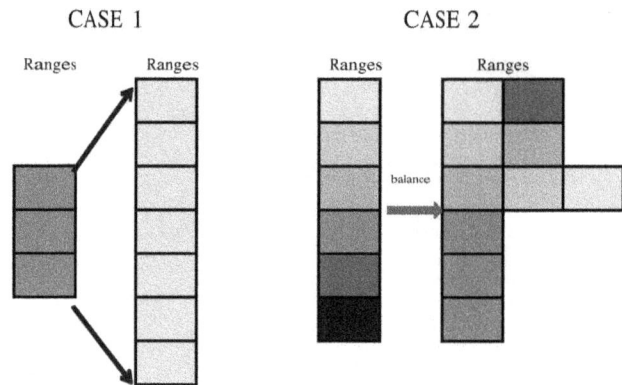

Figure 4. Kernel2 – Load Balancing. Size is denoted using a color map - light to dark denotes increasing sizes.

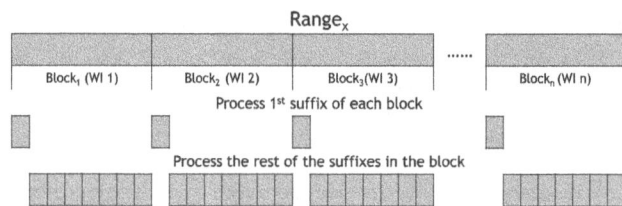

Figure 5. Kernel3 – ComputeLCP. (WI is work-item)

have the lcp i.e. 'h' each thread can use the value computed to speed up the second step i.e processing B-1 suffixes of the block. We use the same trick by Kasai where each subsequent lcp computation starts comparing from $(h-1)$th character.

Note that the lcp of S_i and S_{i+1} are not necessarily strictly decreasing, even though the lcp computation of S_{i+1} starts comparing from $h-1$, it could very well be higher than h, the lcp of S_i. Therefore the amount of work done by each *work-item* in processing its block is non-uniform, thus leading to thread divergence. The severity of thread divergence can be gauged by two lcp based metric – maximum lcp and average lcp. If the ratio between the maximum lcp and average lcp is large then we expect a large amount of thread divergence. In our experiments with some real life input strings we observe this behavior for few inputs.

7.2 Optimization

Kernel1 in figure 3 does not need to launch as a separate kernel and can be merged with the computation of SA. If we know for sure that we wish to compute the lcp after having computed the SA, we can include the functionality of Kernel1 in mergeKernel of SA. When we are doing the final merge of suffix S_j, with $j \mod 3 = 0$ with a suffix S_i, with $i \mod 3 \neq 0$, we can add one more comparison to find the ranges. To compute the suffixes that define the boundary of ranges, we need to compare with the suffix preceding itself in SA. Therefore at the merge step, we cache the previous suffix id, inserted into the merged SA and at the time we decide to merge the next suffix, we compare against the cached value. If it is not equal we store the suffix id we are about to merge and also update the cached id for the next comparison. We provide experimental results with this optimization in section 8.

We emphasize that the approach discussed in section 7.1 is an important technique to implement lcp and can be used independently of SA computation. This is crucial for cases where the user chooses a different algorithm to compute SA or chooses to defer the lcp computation.

Name	paper5	paper1	bib	news	mj	hi	himj	sc	bible	sao	dickens	samba	Chr22.dna	howto	mozilla	jdk13c
Size	11k	52K	110K	375K	440K	510K	958K	2.9M	4M	7M	10M	21M	33M	39M	50M	69M
Max LCP	52	104	156	1029	175	446	446	2106	551	15	10263	31670	120k	70720	41326	37334
Avg LCP	5	8	11	18	4	4	4	12	13	4	56	38	114	49	43	1

Table 7. Max and Average LCP for test corpus

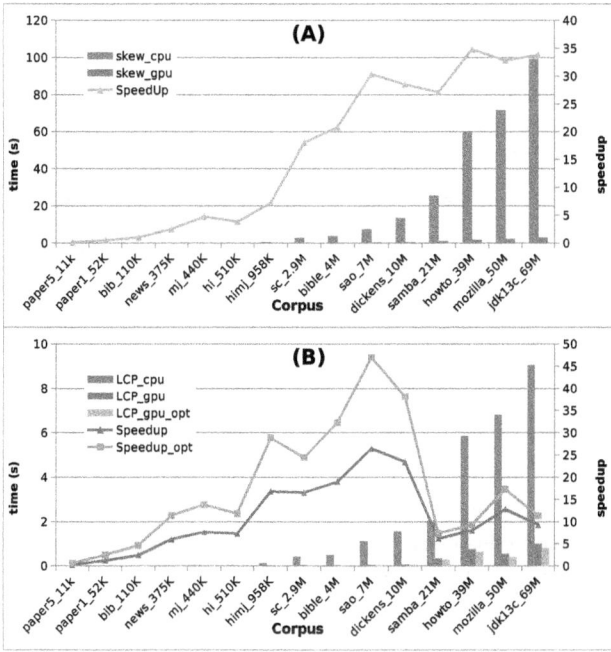

Figure 6. Time (seconds) and speedup for *skew algorithm* (SA) and LCP on GPU using AMD Phenom with Radeon 7970.

8. Experiments and Analysis

We provide experimental results of our implementation of *skew* and LCP algorithms using OpenCL. We compare our results with the single thread version available from the author's website, referred to as "KS" in [25]. We also compare our implementation with the fastest known single thread implementation, *libdivsufsort*, which is an extreme example of algorithmic engineering.

We describe the inputs that we use for all our experiments (Table 7). The input strings are collected from Calgary Corpus, Large Canterbury Corpus, Manzini's Corpus, Protein Corpus and Silesia Corpus [25]. We choose to pick up strings from a variety of corpuses so that we can get a good mix of inputs with different properties. The files are carefully selected to provide us a good span of string length from 10KB to 70MB. One of the key properties of interest to us is the maximum lcp and the average lcp of each input string. Maximum lcp has a direct impact on the SA runtime as it governs the maximum number of characters that needs to be compared between any two suffixes to arrive at a lexicographic order. The ratio of the maximum lcp and average lcp is a good indication of thread divergence in our GPU implementation of Kasai algorithm. These corpuses have been used by most of the researchers in this field.

The measurements done in figure 6 are using AMD Phenom X6 1090T, which has 6 CPU cores running at 3.2 GHz with a turbo frequency of 3.6GHz. The chip has a 6MB shared L3 cache. The GPU code is run on Radeon 7970 discrete GPU. The GPU has 32

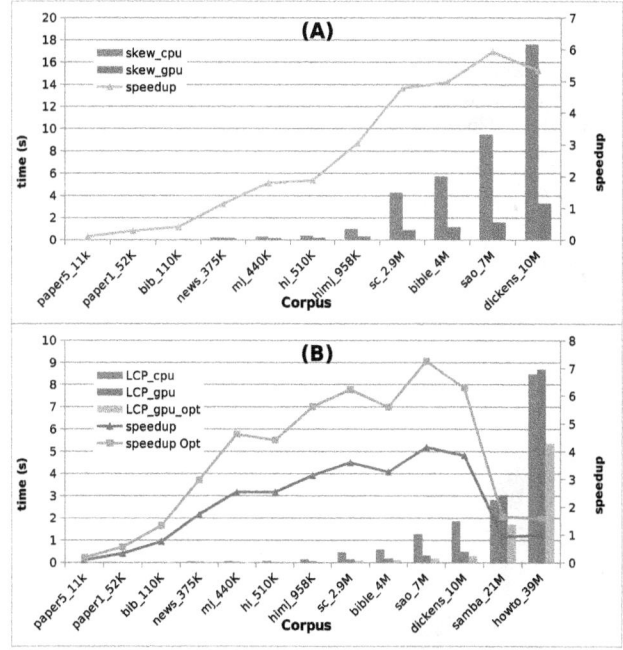

Figure 7. Experimental results of *skew algorithm* and LCP on APU

compute units with a maximum frequency of 925MHz. Each compute unit has a 32KB local memory shared by all the *work-items* in a *workgroup*. 7970 also includes a 768KB L2 read/write data cache. The GPU features GDDR5 memory with a peak theoretical bandwidth of 264GB/s. Figure 6a. presents the performance results when comparing our parallel *skew algorithm* running on the GPU to the serial version running on the CPU.

Our OpenCL version starts to outperform the CPU version at a file size of 110KB (bib). For smaller files there is not enough work for the GPU to run efficiently. GPU needs a large amount of threads to hide the large memory latency and to extract maximum bandwidth. We achieve a speedup of 35x for sufficiently large input strings (greater than 30MB characters). We include the cost of data copy in all our measurements when using a discrete GPU. Figure 6 shows the performance chart for parallel LCP implementation. Here we compare the algorithm from Kasai to our parallel version in OpenCL. LCP-gpu is the version with kernel1 included as part of the timing. LCP-gpu-opt is the version where the computation in kernel 1 is done along with the merge step in *skew algorithm*. Here too, we see similar behavior with GPU starting to perform well as we increase the size of the character strings. At best LCP-gpu and LCP-gpu-opt achieves a speedup of 25x and 45x respectively. The drop in speedup that we see towards the right of the chart for files *samba*, *howto*, *Mozilla* and *jdk13c* can be attributed directly to the maximum LCP values for these files. The ratio of maximum lcp to averge lcp for these four files is approximately 1000:1. On SIMD architectures like GPUs, when individual SIMD lanes are assigned different amount of work the total time is governed by the longest running lane. This is exactly what we see happening in these 4 input strings.

Figure 7 plots the performance results running on Accelerated Processing Units (APU). The APU has a CPU clocked at 2.4GHz and a GPU clocked at 600 MHz. The GPU has 5 compute units and a maximum theoretical memory bandwidth of 17GB/s. The CPU has a 4 MB cache shared between the 4 cores. Figure 7 plots the speedup for the *skew algorithm*. The OpenCL version running on the GPU achieves a maximum speed up of 5.8x. For

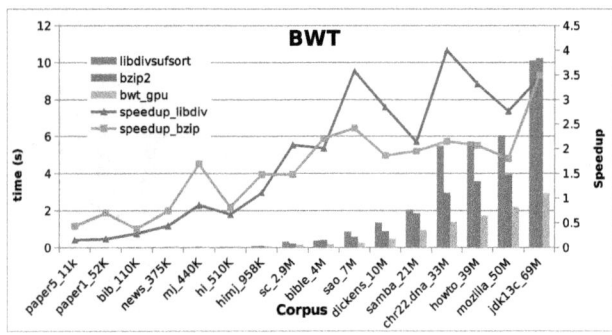

Figure 8. BWT on Phenom and discrete GPU

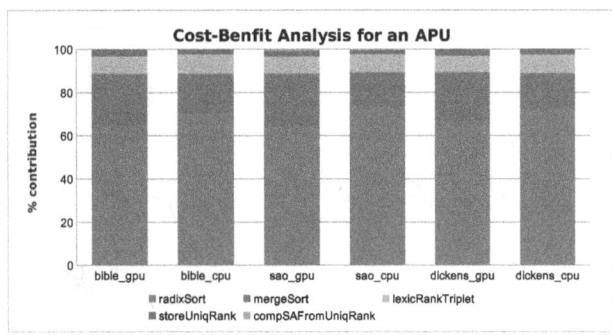

Figure 9. Cost-benefit analysis for APUs

an APU the cross over point i.e. where the GPU code starts to outperform CPU shifts to the right – (bib 375KB). LCP_gpu and LCP_gpu_opt achieves a speed up of 4x and 7x respectively. Files *samba* and *howto* suffer the same degradation in performance as seen on discrete GPU. We run a smaller number of tests on the APU as it has memory limitations and we cannot run our largest input set.

We provide experimental results for our BWT implementation based on parallel *skew algorithm*, and compare it against libdivsifsort [25] and *bzip2* [33] (Figure 8). We choose *bzip2* as a proxy for comparing against the work done by Patel et al. [28] since we do not have access to their implementation. Computing BWT using *bzip2* needs further clarification. BWT is typically computed over the entire string, but *bzip2* works in block sizes of 900KB. Breaking up the file into smaller chunks has an effect on performance. One, the maximum lcp decreases, which decreases the amount of comparisons done in sorting suffixes. Secondly, smaller working set means better cache hit rate on the CPU. This is evident for files chr22.dna and *howto* where BWT based on *bzip2* outperforms *libdivsufsort*. However, we believe that this will not be the case if we compute BWT of the entire file. We instrument the sources of *bzip2* to add timing information and sum up the time over all blocks. We do not attempt to change the *bzip2* sources to work with larger block sizes due to its complexity. Our BWT implementation achieves a speedup of up to 4x over *libdivsufsort* and up to 3.5x over BWT based on *bzip2*. Patel [28] reports a 3x slowdown as compared to *bzip2* which makes us up to 10x faster than their implementation.

8.1 Cost-Benefit Analysis

The key to performance optimization is identifying the true bottleneck and invest in speeding that up. Many a times programmers are faced with a difficult choice between performance, code maintenance and project schedule. The onus is on them to find a balance and make the correct trade-offs. This makes a case for doing some

cost-benefit analysis. When programming for heterogeneous architectures, programmers need to decide which portion is best suited to be offloaded to the GPU. For a discrete GPU there is not much flexibility to break the problem into fine granularity and decide the best target for each block. This is primarily because the cost of copying the data across the PCIe bus from host to device or vice versa is prohibitive. APU provides us a unique opportunity and the ability to break up the problem into small functions and decide the best target for each one. This is made feasible by a shared address space, small launch latency of kernels and small synchronization cost.

In figure 9 we provide a breakdown of the total time for running *skew algorithm* on CPU and GPU into its functions or kernels (OpenCL). We do this for a sample of 3 input strings. There are two guiding principles for this analysis. First, start by parallelizing the kernel which consumes the maximum time. Second, decide the optimal target for your function based on scalability of its parallel implementation. From figure 9 it is clear that we can get 65% of the performance by choosing to parallelize just one function radixSort() and close to 85% if we code up second function, mergeSort(). In our particular example, since all the functions scale equally well, the second principle does not help us in deciding a target for our functions.

With the industry converging towards heterogeneous architectures with shared address space and coherent memory across CPU and GPUs, we believe that we will see more of this cost-benefit analysis in the future.

9. Conclusions and future work

We present GPU-based parallel implementation of one of the key data structures used in string processing algorithms. Our choice of SACA, the *skew algorithm* provides us good scalability and performance across APUs and discrete GPUs. To efficiently map any SACA based on "two-stage" or "induced copying" we need to tackle two problems, first finding parallelism in the "inducing" step and second implementing an efficient string sorting routine for irregularly sized strings.

We also present a novel scheme to parallelize LCP computation. The algorithm by Kasai needs the ISA which increases the memory requirement. One possible extension of our work could be to look at algorithms which require less memory for computing LCP [19]. We believe our work lays the foundation for offloading some new and important applications like pattern matching and lossless data compression on the GPU. We demonstrate the first two stages of a pattern matching pipeline i.e. computing SA and LCP which when combined with work done by Soman [34] on range minimum queries completes the pattern matching pipeline. Similarly using our BWT implementation may also make the lossless data compression a viable option for GPU offload. Another possible extension of our work could be to explore advanced data structures for building compressed indexes [8].

Acknowledgments

We thank Takahiro Harada and Lee Howes for providing the initial implementaion of radix sort. We would also like to thank our colleagues for their support with this work.

References

[1] M. I. Abouelhoda, S. Kurtz, and E. Ohlebusch. Replacing suffix trees with enhanced suffix arrays. *J. of Discrete Algorithms*, 2(1):53–86, Mar. 2004.

[2] AMD. AMD accelerated parallel processing programming guide. http://developer.amd.com/sdks/amdappsdk/assets/amd_

accelerated_parallel_processing_opencl_programming_guide.pdf, 2012.

[3] AMD. AMD Southern Island instruction set architecture. http://developer.amd.com/sdks/amdappsdk/assets/AMD_Southern_islands_Instruction_Set_Architecture.pdf, 2012.

[4] J. L. Bentley and R. Sedgewick. Fast algorithms for sorting and searching strings. In *Proceedings of the eighth annual ACM-SIAM symposium on Discrete algorithms*, SODA '97, pages 360–369, Philadelphia, PA, USA, 1997.

[5] M. Burrows and D. J. Wheeler. A block-sorting lossless data compression algorithm. Technical Report 124, Digital Equipment Corporation, Palo Alto, California, 1994.

[6] A. Davidson, D. Tarjan, M. Garland, and J. Owens. Efficient parallel merge sort for fixed and variable length keys. In *Innovative Parallel Computing (InPar), 2012*, pages 1 –9, may 2012.

[7] M. Farach. Optimal suffix tree construction with large alphabets. In *Foundations of Computer Science, 1997. Proceedings., 38th Annual Symposium on*, pages 137 –143, oct 1997.

[8] P. Ferragina and G. Manzini. Opportunistic data structures with applications. In *Foundations of Computer Science, 2000. Proceedings. 41st Annual Symposium on*, pages 390 –398, 2000.

[9] K. O. W. Group. Opencl 1.2 specifications. http://www.khronos.org/registry/cl/specs/opencl-1.2.pdf, 2012.

[10] R. Homann, D. Fleer, R. Giegerich, and M. Rehmsmeier. mkESA: enhanced suffix array construction tool. *Bioinformatics*, 25(8):1084–1085, 2009.

[11] H. Itoh and H. Tanaka. An efficient method for in memory construction of suffix arrays. In *Proceedings of the String Processing and Information Retrieval Symposium & International Workshop on Groupware*, SPIRE '99, pages 81–88, Washington, DC, USA, 1999.

[12] J. Kärkkäinen and P. Sanders. Simple linear work suffix array construction. In *Automata, Languages and Programming*, volume 2719 of *Lecture Notes in Computer Science*, pages 943–955. 2003.

[13] J. Kärkkäinen, P. Sanders, and S. Burkhardt. Linear work suffix array construction. *J. ACM*, 53(6):918–936, Nov. 2006.

[14] R. M. Karp, R. E. Miller, and A. L. Rosenberg. Rapid identification of repeated patterns in strings, trees and arrays. In *Proceedings of the fourth annual ACM symposium on Theory of computing*, STOC '72, pages 125–136, New York, NY, USA, 1972.

[15] T. Kasai, G. Lee, H. Arimura, S. Arikawa, and K. Park. Linear-time longest-common-prefix computation in suffix arrays and its applications. In *Proceedings of the 12th Annual Symposium on Combinatorial Pattern Matching*, CPM '01, pages 181–192, London, UK, UK, 2001.

[16] F. Kulla and P. Sanders. Scalable parallel suffix array construction. *Parallel Computing*, 33(9):605612, 2007.

[17] N. J. Larsson and K. Sadakane. Faster suffix sorting. Technical Report LU-CSTR: 99-214, Dept. of Computer Science, Lund University, Sweden, 1999.

[18] U. Manber and G. W. Myers. Suffix arrays: a new method for on-line string searches. In *Proceedings of the first ACM-SIAM Symposium on Discrete Algorithms*, pages 319–327, 1990.

[19] G. Manzini. Two space saving tricks for linear time LCP array computation. In *Algorithm Theory - SWAT 2004*, volume 3111 of *Lecture Notes in Computer Science*, pages 372–383. 2004.

[20] G. Manzini and P. Ferragina. Engineering a lightweight suffix array construction algorithm. In *Proc. 10th Annual European Symposium on Algorithms*, volume 2461 of *Lecture Notes in Computer Science*, pages 698–710. 2002.

[21] E. M. McCreight. A space-economical suffix tree construction algorithm. *J. ACM*, 23(2):262–272, Apr. 1976.

[22] P. Mcllroy, K. Bostic, and M. Mcllroy. Engineering radix sort. *Computing systems*, 6(1):5–27, 1993.

[23] D. Merrill and A. Grimshaw. Revisiting sorting for gpgpu stream architectures. Technical Report CS2010-03, Department of Computer Science, University of Virginia, 2010.

[24] H. Mohamed and M. Abouelhoda. Parallel suffix sorting based on bucket pointer refinement. In *Biomedical Engineering Conference (CIBEC), 2010 5th Cairo International*, pages 98 –102, dec. 2010.

[25] Y. Mori. libdivsufsort, version 2.0.1. http://code.google.com/p/libdivsufsort/, 2010.

[26] S. A. N. Futamura and S. Kurtz. Parallel suffix sorting. In *Proceedings 9th International Conference on Advanced Computing and Communications*, pages 76–81, 2001.

[27] NVIDIA. NVIDIAs next generation CUDA compute architecture: Kepler GK110. http://www.nvidia.com/content/PDF/kepler/NVIDIA-Kepler-GK110-Architecture-Whitepaper.pdf, 2012.

[28] R. Patel, Y. Zhang, J. Mak, A. Davidson, and J. Owens. Parallel lossless data compression on the gpu. In *Innovative Parallel Computing (InPar), 2012*, pages 1–9, may 2012.

[29] S. J. Puglisi, W. F. Smyth, and A. H. Turpin. A taxonomy of suffix array construction algorithms. *ACM Comput. Surv.*, 39(2), July 2007.

[30] N. Satish, M. Harris, and M. Garland. Designing efficient sorting algorithms for manycore gpus. In *Parallel Distributed Processing, 2009. IPDPS 2009. IEEE International Symposium on*, pages 1 –10, may 2009.

[31] K. Schürmann and J. Stoye. An incomplex algorithm for fast suffix array construction. In *Proc. 7th Workshop on Algorithm Engineering and Experiments and 2nd Workshop on Analytic Algorithmics and Combinatorics (ALENEX/ANALCO)(2005)*, pages 77–85, 2005.

[32] J. Seward. On the performance of bwt sorting algorithms. In *Data Compression Conference, 2000. Proceedings. DCC 2000*, pages 173 –182, 2000.

[33] J. Seward. http:\www.bzip2.org, 2012.

[34] J. Soman, M. Kumar, K. Kothapalli, and P. Narayanan. Efficient discrete range searching primitives on the gpu with applications. In *High Performance Computing (HiPC), 2010 International Conference on*, pages 1 –10, dec. 2010.

[35] P. Weiner. Linear pattern matching algorithms. In *Switching and Automata Theory, 1973. SWAT '08. IEEE Conference Record of 14th Annual Symposium on*, pages 1 –11, oct. 1973.

Scalable Deterministic Replay in a Parallel Full-system Emulator [*]

Yufei Chen [†]   Haibo Chen [‡]

†School of Computer Science, Fudan University   ‡Institute of Parallel and Distributed Systems, Shanghai Jiao Tong University
chenyufei@fudan.edu.cn   haibochen@sjtu.edu.cn
http://ipads.se.sjtu.edu.cn/coremu

Abstract

Full-system emulation has been an extremely useful tool in developing and debugging systems software like operating systems and hypervisors. However, current full-system emulators lack the support for deterministic replay, which limits the reproducibility of concurrency bugs that is indispensable for analyzing and debugging the essentially multi-threaded systems software.

This paper analyzes the challenges in supporting deterministic replay in parallel full-system emulators and makes a comprehensive study on the sources of non-determinism. Unlike application-level replay systems, our system, called ReEmu, needs to log sources of non-determinism in both the guest software stack and the dynamic binary translator for faithful replay. To provide scalable and efficient record and replay on multicore machines, ReEmu makes several notable refinements to the CREW protocol that replays shared memory systems. First, being aware of the performance bottlenecks in frequent lock operations in the CREW protocol, ReEmu refines the CREW protocol with a seqlock-like design, to avoid serious contention and possible starvation in instrumentation code tracking dependence of racy accesses on a shared memory object. Second, to minimize the required log files, ReEmu only logs minimal local information regarding accesses to a shared memory location, but instead relies on an offline log processing tool to derive precise shared memory dependence for faithful replay. Third, ReEmu adopts an automatic lock clustering mechanism that clusters a set of uncontended memory objects to a bulk to reduce the frequencies of lock operations, which noticeably boost performance.

Our prototype ReEmu is based on our open-source COREMU system and supports scalable and efficient record and replay of full-system environments (both x64 and ARM). Performance evaluation shows that ReEmu has very good performance scalability on an Intel multicore machine. It incurs only 68.9% performance overhead

on average (ranging from 51.8% to 94.7%) over vanilla COREMU to record five PARSEC benchmarks running on a 16-core emulated system.

Categories and Subject Descriptors   D.1.3 [*Programming Techniques*]: Concurrent Programming—Parallel programming;   D.2.5 [*Software Engineering*]: Testing and Debugging—Debugging aids

General Terms   Algorithms, Performance, Reliability

Keywords   Scalable Deterministic Replay, Full-system Emulator

1. Introduction

Full-system emulation is very useful for a number of usage scenarios, including pre-silicon system software development, characterizing performance issues, exposing and analyzing software bugs. Compared to a real machine, a full-system emulator saves lengthy machine rebooting by completely running in user-mode, can have much richer runtime information via introspection, and can flexibly provide an execution environment completely different from the host platform in scales and even ISAs (Instruction Set Architecture). For these reasons, many system software developers have chosen to use a full-system emulator in the major cycle of system developing and debugging.

Ideally, a full system emulator should provide true parallelism so that it can produce a comparable set of access interleavings as a real machine. This enables it to expose many concurrency bugs in an early stage. Further, by leveraging the abundant multicore resources, the performance and scalability of a full-system emulator can be significantly boosted. Hence, there have been several efforts in building parallel full-system emulators, including Parallel SimOS [13], COREMU [22], PQEMU [6] and HQEMU [9]. Unfortunately, adding parallelism to a full-system emulator makes its execution even more non-deterministic, due to the additionally introduced racy memory accesses. To enable reproducibility of guest software stack, it is vitally important to add deterministic replay features to parallel full-system emulators.

Previous researchers have proposed various schemes for deterministic replay in both application and full-system level. There are a number of software-based approaches that can provide relatively low overhead to replay a multi-threaded application [21]. However, they may not be easily adopted to efficiently support full-system replay as system and device emulation in full-system emulators cannot be trivially rerun and a number of racy execution will significantly degrade performance. SMP-ReVirt [8] incorporates the CREW protocol [14] to replay a virtual machine running atop a virtualized platform (i.e., Xen). However, the difference between a virtualized platform and an emulation platform makes it non-trivial to directly apply their approach to a full-system emulator. Besides, according to our analysis, the previous CREW protocols

[*] This work was done when Yufei Chen was a visiting student in Institute of Parallel and Distributed Systems, Shanghai Jiao Tong University. This work was funded by China National Natural Science Foundation under grant numbered 61003002, A grant from Shanghai Science and Technology Development Funds (No. 12QA1401700) and A Foundation for the Author of National Excellent Doctoral Dissertation of PR China.

suffer from performance and scalability issues when replaying a relative large number of cores.

One possible approach to providing deterministic replay to a full-system emulator is treating it as an application for application-level replay systems. However, such an approach loses the capability of incorporating debugging tools to introspect or manipulate internal information regarding guest software stack [19], as this may change the execution behavior of the emulator and the guest software stack.

This paper makes the first attempt to provide deterministic replay capability to parallel full-system emulators. Our goal is to efficiently support scalable record and replay of a relative large number of emulated cores running the entire software stack.

Our analysis indicates that there are several unique differences between a native or virtualization platform and an emulator, which creates both opportunities and challenges. First, there are only software MMUs instead of hardware MMUs in an emulator, which provides more flexibility as well as performance overhead. Second, there is no convenient way to uniquely identify a memory instruction in an emulator[1], making it costly to record the shared memory accesses. Finally, the dynamic binary translator in an emulator can behave differently during record and replay, yet its execution affects the state of the emulated system.

As shared memory accesses are the key factor in a replay system, we carefully study possible schemes that can be adopted in a full-system emulator. We choose the CREW (concurrent-read, exclusive-write) protocol, which was proposed by Courtois et al. [5] and was first used by Leblanc and Mellor-Crummey [14] to replay loosely-coupled message-passing applications. It has been also used by recent systems such as SMP-Revirt [8] and Scribe [12], to record and replay shared memory accesses. Essentially, the CREW protocol serializes racy memory accesses including write-after-write, read-after-write and write-after-read and logs the serialized order of accesses during replay run.

To improve the performance and scalability of ReEmu, we make a comprehensive analysis on possible issues in the previous CREW protocols. First, previous CREW protocols either acquire a huge system-wide lock (e.g., SMP-Revirt [8]) or a spinlock multiple times to serialize shared memory accesses. This severely limits the performance and scalability of a replay system. Finally, adopting a read-write lock scheme [5, 14] may further cause write starvation under heavy contention over a shared memory object. To address this issue, we observe that the design of seqlock[2] essentially matches the design of CREW protocols as both design uses a version number to indicate whether a memory object is contended or not and to serialize the access order to a shared memory object. Based on this observation, ReEmu reuses and extends the design of seqlock to serialize and log access orders of shared memory accesses. The resulting design allows complete lock-free read accesses and non-blocking write access to shared memory objects, thus significantly boost performance and scalability in record and replay runs.

Second, previous CREW protocols usually result in an excessive number of redundant logs, which not only increase the log size, but also cause runtime overhead in record run. Further, some previous CREW protocols requires accesses [8] to remote CPU information, and thus may limit their performance scalability. Finally, some schemes may result in logging overconstained access orders, which may limit parallelism and thus performance in replay run.

To reduce unnecessary logs and improve logging efficiency, ReEmu dynamically detects version changes and only takes logs when necessary. Further, it only requires accesses to mostly local CPU information for logging, but instead relies on an offline log processing tool to infer shared memory dependence.

Third, though ReEmu has tried to minimize the amount of lock operations, per-update lock acquisition may still be a limiting factor to performance. To address this issue, ReEmu design and implement a lock clustering mechanism that clusters multiple uncontended memory accesses together into a bulk, which requires only one lock operation. This noticeably reduces expensive lock operations.

To demonstrate the effectiveness and efficiency of our proposals, we have implemented our techniques based on the open-source COREMU and support deterministic replay of full software stack based on both x86 and ARM. Performance evaluation shows that ReEmu incurs around an average of 68.9% (ranging from 51.8% to 94.7%) performance overhead over COREMU to record five PARSEC applications with different characteristics on a 16-core emulated machine. Using the racy benchmark [23], we show that ReEmu can faithfully reproduce concurrency bugs.

In summary, this paper makes the following contributions:

1. The first attempt to add the full-system deterministic replay feature to parallel full-system emulators, as well as a comprehensive analysis of the sources of non-determinism.

2. A comprehensive analysis on issues with prior CREW protocols and a set of novel refinements that provide efficient and scalable record and replay of a full-system software stack wtih contemporary workloads.

3. A working prototype that demonstrates both effectiveness and efficiency of ReEmu.

In the rest of this paper, we first describe the overall design of ReEmu and how ReEmu tracks different sources of non-determinism. Then, we describe the key part of ReEmu by illustrating how ReEmu logs shared memory dependence for faithful replay. Next, we describe how ReEmu is implemented in an open-source full-system emulator. Section 5 then evaluates the performance overhead and scalability of ReEmu and how the refinements to CREW contribute to the performance. We then relate ReEmu to prior work (section 6) and conclude this paper with a brief discussion on current limitation and possible future work (section 7).

2. ReEmu Overview

ReEmu is designed to support record and replay the execution of whole guest software stack running atop, including a hypervisor, an operating system and the applications. ReEmu can checkpoint the states of guest software stack, start execution while logging all sources of non-determinism and then replay the execution from the checkpointed states. Like other full-system emulators such as QEMU, ReEmu runs completely in user space and thus it is very convenient to start and terminate its execution.

ReEmu records and replays sources of non-determinism by using dynamic fine-grained instrumentation. This contrasts with some previous systems [8, 12] by leveraging hardware-based memory protection (e.g., MMU). Using dynamic instrumentation enables ReEmu to choose the granularities of shared memory objects. Fine-grained tracking can avoid false sharing at the cost of increased memory consumption due to the associated metadata, while coarse-grained tracking may just be opposite. Further, not relying on a specific hardware memory protection scheme makes ReEmu easily portable among different platforms (e.g., x86 and ARM).

In the following sections, we will first review the general architecture of full-system emulators and illustrate the sources of non-

---

[1] Native systems usually leverage performance counters such as program counter and branch counter [7, 8] to uniquely identify an instruction.

[2] Seqlock is short for sequential lock, which is special locking scheme in Linux kernel that allows fast writes to a shared memory location among multiple racy accesses.

determinism. Then, we will describe how ReEmu records and replays them accordingly.

2.1 Full-system Emulator

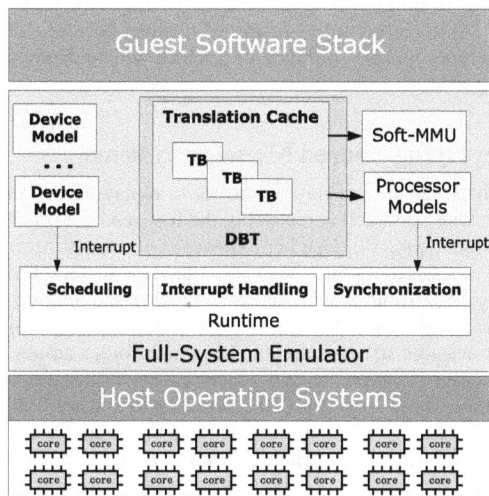

Figure 1. General architecture of full-system emulators using dynamic binary translation.

Figure 1 shows an overview of the general architecture of typical full-system emulators. The emulator usually runs as a user-level program in the host operating system and emulates multiple cores and devices for the guest software stack. State-of-the-art emulators usually use a dynamic binary translator (DBT) to first translates the guest machine code into a common intermediate format, which is then translated into the host machine code. Here, an instruction in guest machine code may be decomposed and reorganized into several host machine instructions. The guest processor states are also mapped into a portion of memory in the emulator. To avoid re-translation of target code, a DBT usually maintains a translation cache that caches translated blocks (TBs). For the sake of performance, a DBT usually supports chaining its translation blocks (TBs) to allow directly jumping from one TB to another TB, without the need to jump out of the translation cache.

Unlike user-level emulators, a full-system emulator also needs to emulate the address translation from guest virtual address to guest physical address and then to host virtual address. A software MMU is usually used to assist such a process. A soft-TLB that resembles a real TLB caching such address translation. Upon misses in the soft-TLB, the emulator will traverse guest page table to do address translation and raise page faults if the address mapping is not present. In addition, the emulator needs to emulate devices such as network interface cards and disks, as well as interrupt mechanism to notify the receiving virtual cores. As a full-system emulator is itself a multi-threaded program, it may also need to handle synchronization and scheduling among virtual cores.

2.2 Sources of Non-determinism

Some sources of non-determinism are common among application-level replay schemes. In addition, the record and replay code of ReEmu lie in and may interact with the full-system emulator, which is non-deterministic. Hence, other than the sources of non-determinism inside the guest software stack, we also need a careful examination on which sources of non-determinism in the emulator may affect a faithful replay of guest software stack. The followings list the sources of non-determinism:

Interrupts: Interrupts in guest software stack are asynchronous events, whose delivery timing will affect the execution of guest software stack. Hence, ReEmu needs to record when an interrupt occurs and to inject the interrupt at the right time during replay.

DMA handling: Handling a typical DMA involves the following steps: 1) CPU issues a DMA command by writing to device registers; 2) The device starts executing the DMA command, which reads or writes memory; 3) When the DMA operation is done, the device will send an interrupt to CPU. Here, the timing of interrupt and the access orders to the DMA memory between the device and CPU cores may both affect guest execution, which need to be recorded as well.

Orders of Guest Page Table Walking: The orders to walking a shared guest page table by multiple cores may affect the execution of guest software stack. The walking order is caused by the internal races among multiple cores walking the same page table. If two cores encounter TLB misses on the same address not present in the guest page table, there will be only one core handling the page fault. Hence, if a different core from that in the record run handles the page fault in the replay run, the execution behavior of guest software stack will diverge, which may lead to either unfaithful replay or even replay failures.

Non-deterministic Instructions: The guest software stack may also issue some non-deterministic instructions, including synchronous accesses to device states (e.g., I/O instructions such as in/out and accesses to memory mapped region), and reading non-deterministic CPU states (e.g., "rdtsc"). These instructions will happen in fixed point in guest instruction stream. However, the execution result is non-deterministic.

Shared Memory Accesses: ReEmu also needs to handle memory accesses from the translation cache. The access orders from multiple cores to a shared memory object may affect the execution of guest software stack, especially for racy accesses.

Unnecessary Non-determinism: The accesses to guest state from the DBT may be different between the record and the replay run. Such accesses include code translation and guest page table walking in soft-MMU. Code translation needs to read guest memory to translate guest instruction stream. However, the code generation strategy may be different due to optimization policies and code cache flush behavior are not the same. It could happen that some guest code is translated only once during recording, but is translated twice during replay. As translation need to read guest memory, this will affect the state of soft-TLB. Hence, the soft-TLB state may also be different between record and replay. Fortunately, code translation only reads guest memory states, and the soft-TLB state should be transparent to guest software stack. Hence, such accesses need not to be handled.

2.3 Record and Replay Non-determinism

Identifying Guest Execution: Previous native or virtualized systems usually use some performance counters to accurately identify the location of guest execution. For example, SMP-ReVirt [8] leverages a combination of the program counter and branch counters to uniquely identify the timing of an interrupt and memory instructions. However, the program counters are not updated upon the execution of every instruction and there is no branch counter maintained to save performance overhead in a full-system emulator.

ReEmu uses two mechanisms to identify guest execution. First, as most full-system emulators using binary translator only inject interrupts in a basic block (i.e., translation block or TB in QEMU) boundary. Hence, ReEmu maintains a per-core counter (BB Counter) that counts the number of executed basic blocks in software and use the BB Counter to record the timing for interrupts. Second, to identify a memory instruction, ReEmu maintains a per-core memory counter that counts the number of memory instructions executed in each emulated core. Note that, as these two counters are per-core based, updates to these counters are normal memory operations, instead or being protected using either locks or atomic instructions.

Handling Interrupts: ReEmu logs the timing of interrupts by recording the BB counter of the corresponding virtual core. In addition, ReEmu records the interrupt number as well. In replay run, ReEmu checks whether the number of executed TBs reaches the recorded number before jumping to the successive translated block. If an interrupt should be injected, ReEmu jumps to the corresponding interrupt handler code and unchains the translated blocks.

Handling DMA: The interrupt can be recorded and replayed using the mechanism described above. As DMA also has memory operations, the access order between the device and cores also need to be recorded.

Typically, during the execution of a DMA command, the DMA memory region should only be accessed by the device, otherwise the memory content may be corrupted because of concurrent memory accesses. One way to record memory orders between device and CPU cores is to treat DMA device as a special core, which only accesses memory when it receives DMA commands [8, 23]. This will record the order between memory accesses for CPU and devices. However, this may prevent the opportunity of using a replay scheme to detect DMA related bugs as the memory accesses between CPU and device to the DMA memory region are serialized. If the operating system is buggy and allows concurrent accesses to DMA memory region, such concurrent accesses will not manifest during the record run.

Instead, ReEmu does not enforce such an order but instead add checking code to detect such parallel accesses. ReEmu utilizes the memory order recording mechanism (see section 3) to detect concurrent accesses to the DMA memory region. If the operating system is correct and guarantees no concurrent access to DMA memory region, by correctly replaying the execution of the operating system, the order of memory access for CPU and device should be exactly the same with the original run. Hence, we just need to ensure that the interrupt indicating the completion of a DMA operation happens after the corresponding DMA has completed. If the OS does not enforce such a DMA access order, then the record and replay run may diverge and thus we can detect such a bug.

To detect such bugs during recording, a DMA read request (which writes memory) will first acquire write locks for each shared object which it is trying to access, and mark the shared object as being under DMA operations. Any memory accesses to the shared objects with DMA operations marked are concurrent accesses to DMA memory regions. In such cases, ReEmu will report the problem and continue recording.

To track when a DMA request completes, ReEmu maintains a DMA completion counter for each DMA device. The counter is updated each time a DMA operation completes. When recording a DMA interrupt, we also record the corresponding device's DMA completion counter. During replay, before injecting a DMA interrupt, ReEmu should wait until the corresponding device's DMA completion counter reaches the recorded value.

Access order to MMU: To enforce the same order of page faults during record and replay runs, ReEmu logs each page fault by recording the memory count, the faulting address and the core ID. In replay run, ReEmu checks if the core ID corresponding to a page fault matches the current running core ID when the memory count and fault address match. If the core ID matches, ReEmu will inject the page fault. Otherwise, this core should wait until another core has handled the page fault before it can proceed.

Non-deterministic Instructions: For non-deterministic instructions, ReEmu simply logs the return results of the correspond-ing emulation functions in the DBT in record run. In replay run, ReEmu just returns the logged results to the calling functions and does not actually execute the functions for most applications. However, there are some functions like reading some device register may have side effects. ReEmu still needs to execute such functions.

Shared Memory Accesses: ReEmu leverages the CREW protocol [5, 14] to record orders of shared memory accesses, but with a notable redesign and optimizations, which will be detailed in the following section.

3. Replaying Shared Memory Systems

A key challenge in a replay system is to replay shared memory accesses. One approach is recording the first read values of memory locations (e.g., BugNet[17]). However, it cannot infer shared memory access orders and thus cannot provide much information for debugging. Another approach is serializing and logging the order of read and write accesses to each shared memory object, so that it is possible to infer the partial or total order among memory accesses to a shared memory object among different cores. The CREW protocol [5, 14] serializes accesses to a shared object by enforcing and logging a total order among writers and a total order of readers with respect to writers. However, it places no constraints among multiple readers. We choose such a protocol as it is very suitable for dynamic instrumentation (e.g., InstantReplay [14]).

However, most previous software-based work only applies the CREW protocol on a few number of cores (e.g., 4 cores in SMP-Revirt [8] and 2 cores (4 threads) in Scribe [12]), without the consideration of scalable record and replay of running on a machine with a relatively large number of cores with non-trivial racy execution[3].

In this section, we first examine the performance and scalability issues with the original CREW protocol and its variants. Then, we propose our refinements and optimizations that significantly boost performance and scalability.

3.1 Previous CREW Protocols

Generally, there are two states for each shared memory object in the CREW protocol: 1) *concurrent-read*, where all cores can read but none can write; 2) *exclusive-write*, where only one core can read and write, while other cores cannot access that shared object. Algorithm 1 shows the original design of the CREW protocol in Instant Replay [14]. The essence of the protocol is the incorporation of the Read-Write Lock with the logging of object versions, and leverage the object versions to infer and enforce access orders of read/write accesses to a shared memory object. This design protects every read and write instruction with a read-write lock. One interesting point of the CREW protocol in Instant Replay is that version information itself is enough to define orders between read-after-write and write-after-write memory accesses.

Our analysis shows that such a protocol has significant performance and scalability issues when replaying contemporary multi-threaded applications on commodity multicore processors. First, it requires taking a log on every memory access, which will cause a huge per-access overhead for memory instructions. Second, the locks and atomic instructions associated with instrumentation may incur huge runtime overhead and scalability issues when replaying systems with multiple cores. Third, as the writer needs to wait until there is no reader accessing the memory object, it will be easily

---

[3] Though Instant Replay reported the results on a machine with a relatively large number of processors. The target applications are based on message-passing, which have very little contention on shared memory. Further, it is based on a machine in 25 years ago, at which the memory wall was not a problem.

```
1  Read object begin
2  │  P (object.lock)
3  │  AtomicAdd (object.activeReader, 1)
4  │  V (object.lock)
   │  // Write to core local log file
5  │  WriteLog (object.version)
6  │  Do Actual Read
7  │  AtomicAdd (object.totalReaders, 1)
8  │  AtomicAdd (object.activeReaders, −1)
9  end
10 Write object begin
11 │  P (object.lock)
12 │  while object.activeReaders ≠ 0 do delay
13 │  WriteLog (object.version)
14 │  WriteLog (object.totalReaders)
15 │  Do Actual Write
16 │  object.totalReaders ← 0
17 │  object.version ← object.version
18 │  V (object.lock)
19 end
```

Algorithm 1: InstantReplay Record Algorithm [14]

starved, especially given the fact that the reader-side critical section in this protocol is quite lengthy.

```
1  Read object begin
2  │  version ← ReadLog
   │  // wait write to this object
3  │  while object.version ≠ version do delay
4  │  Do Actual Read
5  │  AtomicAdd (object.totalReaders, 1)
6  end
7  Write object begin
   │  // Read recorded version and totalReaders
8  │  version ← ReadLog
9  │  totalReaders ← ReadLog
   │  // wait write to this object
10 │  while object.version ≠ version do delay
   │  // wait reads to this object
11 │  while object.totalReaders ≠ totalReaders do delay
12 │  Do Actual Write
13 │  object.totalReaders ← 0
14 │  AtomicAdd (object.version, 1)
15 end
```

Algorithm 2: InstantReplay Replay Algorithm

To reduce the per-access overhead associated with each memory access, recent virtualization-based [8] and application-level [12] replay systems have leveraged hardware MMUs to enforce and track access orders among shared memory accesses. When a memory page is in the concurrent-read state, the page table entry of that page in each core has read-only permission. When a memory page is in exclusive-write state, only one core's page table entry has read-write permission to that page, while all other cores have no permission to that page. A CREW fault will be raised if a memory write has no sufficient permission, where the memory access ordering constraints (i.e., "happen-before" relationships) can be logged.

For example, as shown in Figure 2, a shared object X is first concurrently read by three cores. At time t7, Core0 wants to write the shared object, at which a CREW fault happens as Core1 does

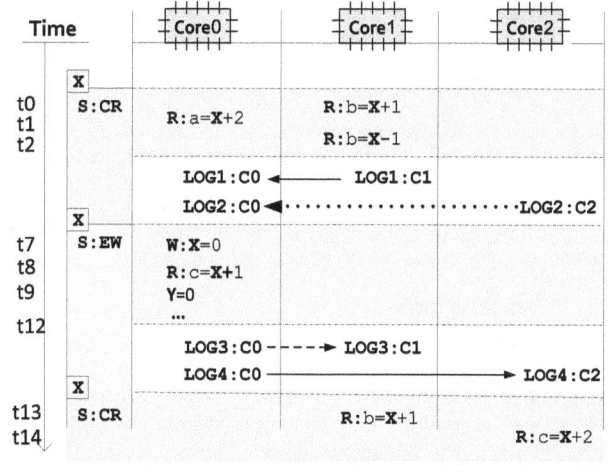

Figure 2. An overview of the CREW protocol based on MMU protection: left squares are a shared object in different states: concurrent-read (CR) and exclusive-write (EW); top squares are CPU cores accessing the shared object. The solid arrows indicate the captured "happen-before" relationship between two memory operations. Log2 is a redundant log and LOG3 is an overcontrained log.

not have sufficient permission. Hence, the record system has to first decrease permission on Core1 and Core2 and then increase the permission on Core0. The record system then logs that the permission decrease happens before the permission increases and the replay system enforces such orders during replay. Once Core0 has both read and write permission with the shared object, the following read operation at t8 can go without further CREW faults. However, when Core1 tries to read the object at time t13, a CREW fault again happens due to insufficient permission. Here, Core0 will decrease its permission before Core1 can increase their permissions. Core1 needs to notify all other cores to increase their permission after Core0 decreases its permission. As Core2 has already increased its permission in t3, subsequent read access at t4 can proceed without CREW faults.

It should be noted that upon a CREW fault, though only the faulting core needs to acquire a lock and remove other cores' permission, it needs to send IPIs (Inter-Processor Interrupts) to all other cores to take logs and flush TLB, as it is uncertain whether other cores are sharing the current object or not. Hence, such a design may cause scalability issues for a large number of cores and may cause frequent CREW faults upon non-trivial racy execution.

Further, it may also record over-constrained order as well as unnecessary logs. For example, LOG3 in the above example records that the read instruction at t13 of Core1 should happen after the instruction in t12, which actually should happen after t7 precisely. This is because there is no easy way for the MMU to identify the last writer of a shared object. Though the logged order is sufficient to ensure correct replay, this decreases parallelism as instructions between t7 and t13 can be executed in parallel for all cores, but is unfortunately serialized by this overconstrained log.

As the above MMU-based CREW protocol has no idea of which core may access a shared memory object, it may also take a lot of unnecessary logs. For the above example, LOG2 is unnecessary as core2 is not sharing X at that time. Suppose there are 16 cores in the above example and only 3 cores will share X, all other cores will have to be interrupted and take unnecessary logs. This will greatly impact performance.

3.2 A Scalable CREW Protocol

Being aware of the performance and scalability with prior CREW protocols, we propose a scalable and efficient CREW protocol. As ReEmu is based on a full-system emulator, where hardware MMU is not available, we mainly rely on dynamic binary instrumentation to enforce and log orders among concurrent accesses to a shared memory object.

The key idea under the new CREW protocol is that the seqlock used in Linux essentially matches the design of the CREW protocol. Hence, we redesign the CREW protocol by reusing the seqlock.

3.2.1 Data Structures

For each core, ReEmu maintains a *memop* describing the total number of memory accesses in each core. This can uniquely identify the timestamp of a memory access. For each memory object, ReEmu maintains a version number, which remains even and unchanged for a read access, but is increased twice for a write access. The first increment during a write access indicates that a write operation is in progress, while the second increment indicates that the write operation has finished. Thus, the odd or even value of the version number indicates whether there is a write access in progress.

For each memory object on each (virtual) core, ReEmu maintains a *last_seen* structure that describes the last access to a shared memory object, including the version number (i.e., version) and the timestamp (i.e., memop). The *last_seen* structure is used to avoid unnecessary and overconstained logs mentioned in previous CREW protocols.

ReEmu divides log entries into two types: *wait-version* log, and *wait-read* log. As shown in the LogOrder function, each wait-version log item is a tuple of (*memop, version*). Each core has such a version log recording every memory access that needs to obey the write/read-after-write order. During replay, when the memop reaches a recorded memop, the virtual core must wait until the accessing object's version reaches the recorded version.

Each wait-read log entry contains a tuple of (*object id, version memop, coreid*). For example, a log tuple (3, 141, 59, 2) means that, if there is any write to a shared object with ID 3 at version 141 on other cores, it must wait until core 2 has done 59 memory accesses. Hence, this log ensures the write-after-read order.

3.2.2 Record Phase

Algorithm 3 illustrates the main algorithm of the record phase in ReEmu. Line 1 to line 16 in the *Read* function show how ReEmu logs read accesses to a shared memory object. ReEmu reads the global object version and checks if there is a pending write access by checking if the version number is odd or not. ReEmu repeats this process until the version number becomes even (line 4-7). Then ReEmu performs the actual read (line 8) and checks if there is or has been any write access during the read operation and retries the read if so (line 9).

If the memory object has been updated by other cores since last access in this core (line 10), ReEmu needs to log the shared memory dependence (line 11) and refresh the version last seen by this core for the object (line 12). Finally, ReEmu updates the last access memory operation count (memop) (line 14) and increases the memory operation count (line 15).

To track and log a write access, ReEmu first acquires the per-object lock to prevent concurrent write accesses to an object (line 18) and takes a snapshot of current version of the memory object (line 19). It then increases the object version to an odd value to exclude a potential read access (line 20), performs the actual write (line 21), increase the object version to an even value so that a potential read can proceed, and finally release the per-object lock. ReEmu checks if there is any other write access to this object (line 24) and takes a log on such a write/read-after-write dependence

if so (line 25). ReEmu finally flips the memop in the *last_seen* to indicate that this access is a write operation, updates the version number seen by this core to the object, and increases the memory operation count.

The LogOrder function takes logs by writing the memory operation count and version to the per-core wait-version log file (line 32). If the last access to this object is a read operation (line 33), ReEmu takes an additional wait-read log that records the write-after-read dependence as well.

```
1   Read (object, last_seen) begin
        // last_seen contains info about last access, local to core
2       repeat
3           version ← object.version
4           while version is odd do
5               version ← object.version
6               delay
7           end
8           Do Actual Read
9       until version = object.version
        // Version change means modified by other core
10      if last_seen.version ≠ version then
11          LogOrder (object, last_seen)
12          last_seen.version ← version
13      end
        // memop is also local to core
14      last_seen.memop ← memop
15      memop ← memop + 1
16  end
17  Write (object, last_seen) begin
18      SpinLock (object.lock)
19      version ← object.version
        // Odd version locks reader
20      object.version ← object.version + 1
21      Do Actual Write
22      object.version ← object.version + 1
23      SpinUnlock (object.lock)
24      if last_seen.version ≠ version then
25          LogOrder (object, last_seen)
26      end
        // Complement to be negative, mark last access as write
27      last_seen.memop ← ∼ memop
28      last_seen.version ← version + 2
29      memop ← memop + 1
30  end
31  LogOrder (object, last_seen) begin
32      WriteVersionLog (memop, version)
33      if last_seen.memop ≥ 0 then
34          WriteReadLog (object.id, last_seen.version,
                last_seen.memop)
35      end
36  end
```

Algorithm 3: ReEmu Record Algorithm

3.2.3 Log Processing

As ReEmu takes a per-core log scheme and each log only contains local access information, an offline log processing algorithm is necessary to combine log files and infer access orders of a shared memory object. ReEmu only needs to process the wait-read log as each core only needs to read its local wait-version log sequentially.

ReEmu first sorts the wait-read log of each core and then merges all logs together into a single file ordered by object ID and version. ReEmu will also generate another index file that contains the starting location of the wait-read log for each object. During replay, a core performing a write access only needs to do a single sequential search to find the dependent read accesses by other cores to this object.

3.2.4 Replay Phase

Algorithm 4 shows the replay algorithm in ReEmu. For each read access, ReEmu needs to wait until the version of the object has reached to a logged version (line 2). This ensures that a read access can get the same value as in record run. Then, it performs the actual read operation (line 3) and updates the memory operation count (line 4). For each write access, ReEmu needs to first wait until other write accesses before this access have happened (line 7). Then, it needs to ensure all other dependent readers have done the read accesses (line 8). Finally, ReEmu performs the actual write and updates object version and memory operation count.

```
1   Read (object) begin
2   │  WaitVersion(object)
3   │  Do Actual Read
4   │  memop ← memop + 1
5   end
6   Write (object) begin
7   │  WaitVersion(object)
8   │  WaitRead(object)
9   │  Do Actual Write
10  │  object.version ← object.version + 2
11  │  memop ← memop + 1
12  end
13  WaitVersion(object) begin
14  │  version ← ReadLog()
    │  // wait write to this object
15  │  while object.version ≠ version do delay
16  end
17  WaitRead(object) begin
    │  // wait all reads to the object at the current version
18  │  for each tuple in the form of
    │     (object.id, object.version, readmemop, readcoreid)
    │     in read log do
19  │  │  while readcoreid's memop ≤ readmemop do
    │  │     delay
20  │  end
21  end
```

Algorithm 4: ReEmu Replay Algorithm

3.2.5 Performance and Scalability Analysis

As shown in the previous algorithms, ReEmu has several good properties that make it efficient and scalable. First, there is only one variable (i.e., object.version) shared among multiple cores, which may reduce unnecessary cache ping-ponging. Second, all logs are taken with only local information (except object.version) to per-core log files, this makes the logging process pretty fast and scalable. Third, there is only one lock to serialize multiple writers and the read side is completely lock-free. Fourth, the logs are taken only when necessary and the logged order contains no overconstained order but is precise to reflect the exact access orders.

3.3 Lock Clustering

Even though ReEmu has been designed to minimize synchronization operations, there is still some overhead related to each memory access, especially write accesses. In some cases, it is possible that for some periods of time, some memory objects are only accessed by one core. In such cases, it would be beneficial to acquire the shared object with exclusive write permission, then do all the following access directly without the need to acquire the lock again.

To enable such an optimization, ReEmu associates an owner information to each shared object. The owner information indicates which core is currently holding the write lock. On acquiring a write lock, a virtual core can hold the lock and set the owner to itself. Each memory access first checks if the owner of the shared object is itself. If so, it then can access the shared memory directly with only the need to update the memop and update last seen information. Otherwise, it goes through the original recording algorithm.

ReEmu needs to avoid possible deadlocks. Deadlock will occur if Core1 holds the lock of shared object A, and then try to access shared object B, whose lock is hold by Core2 and Core2 is trying to access shared object A. To avoid such a deadlock, each core has a mailbox. When a core tries to access a shared object that is hold by other cores, it will send a message to the owner's mailbox with the contending shared object ID, and then wait until the lock is released. Each core will check this mailbox and release the contending shared objects at the end of each basic block or when it is contending shared memory objects with other cores.

A successive access from another core to a shared object cannot release the lock, as the owning core may be doing memory access at that time. However, waiting for the owner to release the lock would incur performance overhead when there are many shared accesses. To reduce this overhead, each core is only allowed to hold a predefined number of shared objects and ReEmu tries to detect contention and disable lazy lock release when there is heavy contention.

ReEmu currently sets the maximum number of shared object each core can hold to 32. Setting this value too low may miss the opportunity to reduce overhead of lock operations, while a large value may incur excessive waiting overhead.

ReEmu tries to detect contention by recording the memop in a contending point for each shared object for each core. The contending memop is recorded whenever a core sends a shared object ID to the mailbox of the owning core, or when the owning core releases contending objects. This contending memop acts like a timestamp of last contention. A core performing write access will release the lock lazily only if the current memop is greater than the contending memop by a predefined number (e.g., 10 in our implementation). This means that some certain time has elapsed since last contention.

4. Implementation

We have implemented ReEmu based on COREMU 0.1.2 [22], an open-source parallel full-system emulator based on QEMU [2]. The implementation adds around 2500 SLOCs to COREMU. ReEmu checkpoints the guest stack by leveraging the qcow [16] support in QEMU to checkpoint guest states. ReEmu divides memory into equally-sized memory chuncks, each chunk maps to an object ID. The memory access recording algorithm uses this ID to identify a shared object. The chunk size can be changed at compile time. As object ID is accessed very frequently, ReEmu uses fixed mapping from memory address for fast object ID calculation. The object ID is calculated as $(address \gg \text{CHUNK\_BITS}) \& \text{OBJID\_MASK}$. For a 4 KB chunk size, the CHUNK_BITS is 12. To bound the number of object id used, ReEmu fixes the OBJID_MASK to be an integer with the lowest 21-bit set. When chunk size is small, it is possible that multiple memory chunk may map to the same ID. However, this will not affect the correctness of the order recording algorithm as those chunks will be considered as a single combined shared object.

Port to ARM: To demonostrate the portability of ReEmu, we further port ReEmu to support deterministic replay of ARM. As the algorithms and instrumentation code is almost the same for ARM and x86, only around 120 SLOCs are added, which mainly lie in the atomic instruction emulation in ARM to support memory order recording.

Validating Correctness: During development, ReEmu records the PC of each executed basic block. This log defines an execution path that must be identical between record and replay. During replay, ReEmu reads the recorded PC before executing a basic block and checks if the PC are the same. Hence, we can check if the replay run is the same with the record run.

ReEmu also uses memory value verification that records the value of each read/write instruction and verifies the value during replay, which validates that shared memory accesses are recorded correctly.

5. Evaluation

Performance evaluation is done on a 20-core Intel x64 machine (2 GHZ, 2 processors with each having 10 cores with 32KB L1, 256KB private L2 and 24MB shared L3 cache) running Debian 6 with Linux kernel version 2.6.38.5. The guest OS is also a Debian 6 with kernel version 2.6.32.5. The host machine has 64GB memory and the guest is configured with 2GB memory.

For the x86 guest machine, we use `int $0x77` as a backdoor instruction marking the start and end of timing. For the ARM guest machine, we use the atomic instruction `swp` as the backdoor instruction because it's not used normally. (Neither Linux kernel or the tested application uses `swp` instruction.) All tests were executed at least four times and we report the arithmetic average of them.

5.1 Workload Characteristics

For x86 architecture, we choose five applications from the PARSEC benchmark suite (version 2.1) [3]: *blackscholes*, *bodytrack*, *canneal*, *fluidanimate*, *swaptions*. All applications are tested with the simlarge input size. PARSEC can be treated as worst-case applications due to pervasive shared memory accesses, causing larger overhead and log size. (For system applications like kernel build, ReEmu has about 50% overhead on average compared to COREMU.)

application	#sync	#shared memop	working set
blackscholes	very few	a few	grow with #core
canneal	a few	a few	large
swaptions	a few	many	small
bodytrack	medium	large	small
fluidanimate	large	very few	large

Table 1. Selected PARSEC applications characteristics

As shown in Table 1, the five applications are chosen based on their differences in the amount of synchronization primitives, shared memory accesses and the working set size: blackscholes has very few synchronization primitives, a number of shared memory accesses among two threads and a small working wet; canneal has a few number of synchronization primitives, a few amount of shared memory access and a relatively large working set; swaptions has a few number of synchronization primitives, many shared memory accesses, and a small working set; bodytrack has a medium amount of synchronization primitives, a large amount of shared memory accesses and a small working set; fluidanimate has a very large number of synchronization primitives, very few shared memory access and a large working set.

Unless otherwise noted, we use 1KB as the default memory chunk size. As we assign 2 Gbyte memory to the guest, and use

the 21-bit object ID mask, there is exactly one memory chunk mapped to the same shared object ID. As some applications require the number of threads to be the power of 2, we only report the performance results for an emulated system with the number of cores be power of 2.

5.2 Performance Slowdown

Slowdown in Record Run: Figure 3 shows performance slowdown in record run compared to COREMU. The average slowdowns are 60.2%, 74.8%, 77.7%, 74.5%, 68.9% for recording these applications on 1, 2, 4, 8, and 16 cores. Among them, swaptions has a relatively large overhead (94.7% at 16 cores) due to the relatively large amount of shared write memory accesses [3], which is a limiting factor to performance. For other four applications, the performance overhead is relatively small and mostly less than 80%. The small overhead is attributed to the efficient and scalable design in the recording algorithm of ReEmu.

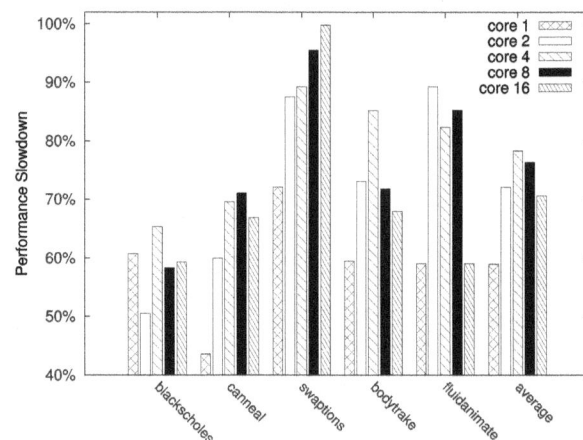

Figure 3. Record slowdown compared to COREMU

Slowdown in Replay Run: Figure 4 shows replay performance slowdown compared to COREMU. Currently, we have not done any optimization for replay. Hence, some applications are still with a very large performance overhead during replay. The main reason may be that a relatively large number of waiting operations get aggregated together to degrade the replay performance. Swaptions is with a relatively large overhead on 16 cores, probably due to the fact that a large number of shared write accesses need to wait for its dependent readers to finish.

Scalability: To see whether ReEmu has a good performance scalability on a multicore machine, we also plot the execution time of ReEmu and COREMU with the increasing amount of cores. As shown in figure 5, we can see that ReEmu in record run has similar performance scalability with COREMU. ReEmu in replay run also has good performance scalability before 8 cores but stops scaling in 16 cores due to performance degradation caused by aggregated waiting, which we will optimize in our future work.

Slowdown to Native Execution: We also compare the performance of ReEmu to native execution. The average record and replay slowdown for 1, 2, 4, 8 and 16 cores are 17X, 16X, 14X, 14X, 18X and 16X, 15X, 14X, 17X and 33X accordingly, while the slowdown caused by COREMU is 11X, 10X, 8X, 8X and 12X accordingly. Though the slowdown is still relatively large, it is still much smaller than prior user-level replay system such as PinPlay [19], which more than 80X even for recording an application with a small number of cores. Further, the performance slowdown can be further reduced if the overhead of COREMU/QEMU has been reduced. Actually, recent work over QEMU shows that, by integrating an

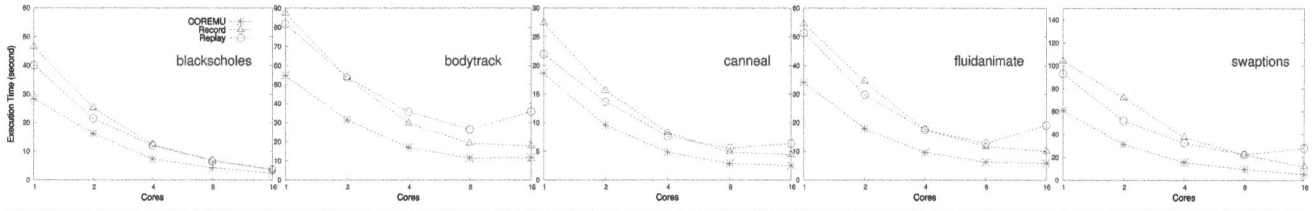

Figure 5. Performance and scalability of the PARSEC benchmark

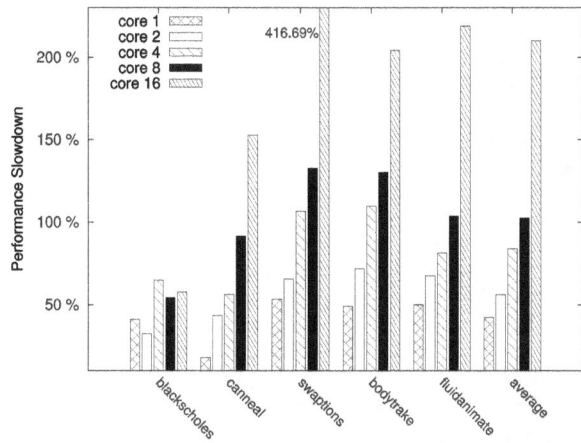

Figure 4. Replay slowdown compared to COREMU

optimized backend compiler (e.g., LLVM) with optimizations, the performance of QEMU can be reduced by 2.4X to 4X. With a more optimized DBT, the overhead of ReEmu can be similarly reduced.

5.3 Benefits of Performance Optimization

Compared with Prior CREW Protocols: To compare the CREW protocol in ReEmu with prior ones, we implement the CREW protocol in SMP-Revirt [8] in ReEmu with a few changes: 1) retrieving remote core information for logging is done by directly accessing the fields in remote cores, instead of sending IPIs; 2) a read-write lock is used to guarantee that the remote core information is unchanged, instead of using a system-wide lock (i.e., shadow_lock). We tried to implement the original CREW protocol in Instant Replay [14], but it turns to be too slow to boot Linux.

ReEmu with this CREW protocol takes around 122.6s, 343.6s 912.3s 1343.5s to record the execution of blackscholes on 1, 2, 4 and 8 cores. When using 16 cores, the system runs too slowly that it still fails to boot Linux after 1 hour. In contrast to the CREW protocol in ReEmu, it has significantly worse performance and scalability.

Benefits of Lock Clustering: Due to space constraints, we present three applications that are with performance speedup and slowdown due to the lock clustering algorithm. As shown in Table 2, the execution time of swaptions is reduced from 27.3% to 19.2% when the number of cores increased from 1 to 16. When there is contention on an object, lock clustering will not be applied for that object. This explains why the improvement is reduced when the number of cores increases. blackscholes also gets some speedup with lock clustering, but not that much as swaptions. canneal is the only tested application with performance slowdown with lock clustering. Though lock clustering can avoid repeatedly acquiring the same lock, it needs extra work like recording which locks are hold by self and releasing hold locks when there is contention. To avoid holding too much locks and hurt performance when there's

contention on many shared object, each emulated core can hold at most 32 locks. When this number increases to 64, canneal will also show a little speedup running 1 emulated core, but more slowdown when running more emulated cores.

app	#core	w/o opt	with opt	reduction
swaptions	1	143.38	104.18	27.3%
	2	75.10	59.42	20.9%
	4	38.56	30.76	20.2%
	8	24.23	18.39	24.1%
	16	13.08	10.57	19.2%
blackscholes	1	52.57	46.43	11.7%
	2	27.28	25.08	8.1%
	4	13.72	12.30	10.3%
	8	8.12	6.90	15.0%
	16	4.02	3.67	8.5%
canneal	1	26.92	27.44	-1.9%
	2	14.56	15.68	-7.7%
	4	7.61	8.24	-8.4%
	8	4.56	4.86	-6.6%
	16	4.02	4.41	-9.9%

Table 2. Optimization effect of lock clustering

5.4 Impact of Object Size

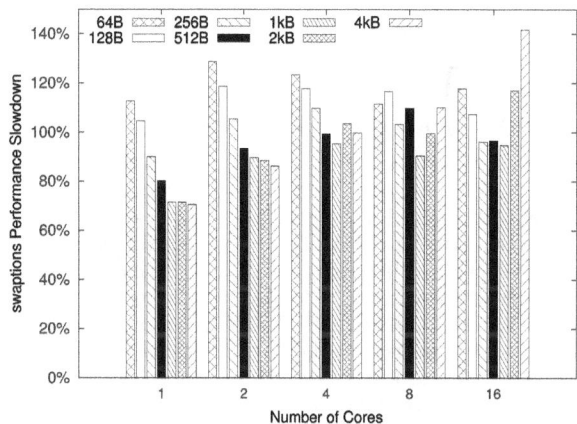

Figure 6. Impact of memory chunk size (record performance slowdown compared to COREMU)

Figure 6 shows the performance impact of different memory chunk sizes for the swaptions application. (swaptions has many shared memory operations thus the impact would be bigger.) This result is tested with lock clustering enabled. For 1 core configuration, a larger memory chunk size reduces the number of lock operations thus setting it to 4K has the smallest slowdown (70.5%), while 64byte has the largest slowdown (112.7%). For 16-core configuration, as there are more concurrent accesses to the same page, the performance of 4 Kbyte memory chunk size degrades, and the slowdown increases to 141.6% (while the lowest slowdown is 94.7%). To get a consistent performance, we set the default memory chunk size to 1 KByte, which shows good performance from small number of of emulated cores to larger number of emulated cores. We will apply an adaptive approach by assigning the chunk size according to the number of cores in future.

5.5 Log Size

To collect log size for an application, we modified ReEmu to start take log after the timing backdoor has triggered. So the data here are only for the log taken when executing region of interest.

Table 3 shows low size for all the benchmarks applications and Linux kernel boot. For single core recording, as no memory ordering needs to be logged, the log size is very small. The log size grows as number of cores grows. The log size for bodytrack and swaptions grows much slower than other applications. These 2 applications has small working sets, they touch less memory chunks and thus less memory ordering logs are required. While canneal and fluidanimate has very large working set, as the number of cores grow to 16, the log size grows to more than 20MB. blackscholes' working set size grows with core number thus the log size also grows a lot.

Note that working set size is not an accurate indicator of log size. Memory access pattern is also a deciding factor to log size. In the worst case, two cores writing to a single shared object in turn, every write needs to take log. So even for working set as small as a single page, the runtime overhead and log size could still be big.

application	1 core	2 cores	16 cores
blackscholes	123K	398K	18M
canneal	346K	1.5M	26M
swaptions	67K	149K	2.3M
bodytrack	12K	209K	2.7M
fluidanimate	54K	687K	24M
kernel boot	1.2M	1.5M	6M

Table 3. Log size of ReEmu (compressed with gzip)

5.6 ARM Performance

We ported one MapReduce application in the Phoenix test suite [20] to ARM platform to study the performance and scalability of ReEmu on ARM record and replay. The guest version of Linux is 2.6.28 which is provided by ARM corporation. We tested Word-Count with 10 Mbyte file running on a 1, 2, 4 core configuration[4]. The average slowdowns caused by ReEmu in record and replay run are 2.1X, 1.9X, 1.9X and 3.3X, 3.4X, 3.8X accordingly. It also exhibits good performance scalability: the execution time is 32.1s, 12.6s, 5.8s and 50.5s, 21.8s, 11.4s to record and replay WordCount under 1, 2, and 4 core configuration accordingly.

5.7 Bug Reproducibility

To evaluate the bug reproducibility of ReEmu, we record and replay the racy benchmark [23] on ReEmu. We validate the signature generated from record and replay runs and find that the signature is the same. Hence, ReEmu can faithfully reproduce concurrency bugs.

---

[4] The maximum number of cores supported in ARM Cortex-A9 is 4.

6. Related Work

Replaying in the Virtual World: There has been some prior work in supporting execution replay of virtual machines. Bressoud et al. [4] are the first to provide execution replay for virtual machines, but their techniques target at single-core VM and are used for fault-tolerance in between a primary machine and the backup. Revirt [7] logs external inputs and source of non-determinism in a single-core VM and replays the execution mainly for intrusion analysis. The time-travel VM [11] and ReTrace [24] leverages execution replay of single-core virtual machines to debug operating systems and collect execution trace respectively, which can also be similarly applied to ReEmu. SMP-Revirt [8] is the first to provide execution replay of multiprocessor VMs by leveraging the CREW protocol [5] to record orders of shared memory accesses. ReEmu also leverages the CREW protocol, but with notable refinements that enable ReEmu to be scalable and efficient to replay multicore systems.

Leap [10] and ORDER [25] are two recent systems supporting deterministic replay in Java virtual machines (JVMs). Like ReEmu, replaying in JVM can do fine-grained instrumentation and track memory accesses in fine-granularity. For example, ORDER takes an object-centric approach that records shared memory accesses in object-level. However, execution in a full-system emulator has no such good locality with objects, for which reasons ReEmu tracks memory objects at a fixed size.

Replaying Natively in the User Land: Similarly to ReEmu, Scribe [12] also leverages the CREW protocol to record shared memory accesses. However, Scribe defers page ownership transition at sync points (e.g., system calls), which is not appealing for ReEmu as the delayed memory access interleaving may hide many data races that occurs in a real machine. Compared to Scribe, the CREW protocol in ReEmu has been refined to be scalable and efficient by precise and scalable tracking of access orders to shared memory objects. Finally, tracking memory accesses in page granularity in Scribe may suffer from false sharing, while ReEmu is more flexible in choosing tracing granularity. DoublePlay takes an approach called uniparallelism that uses serialized execution to check the memory ordering of parallel execution. However, uni-parallelism may be hard to be efficient for a full-system emulator, which may cause frequent rollback and it is not easily to efficiently rollback the execution of a full-system stack.

There are also efforts in trading determinism and recording overhead. ODR [1] reduces the overhead by only guaranteeing output deterministic at the benefit of ignoring the outcomes of data-races, while takes more time and space to search the execution path during replay to ensure output-determinism. PRES [18] also only records a "sketches" during record run, and instead leverages the replayer to explore possible execution spaces to reproduce bugs. Respec [15] combines speculative execution for logging and replies on the replayer to detect and recover if the replay session diverges. There techniques should also be able to be integrated into ReEmu to further reduce the overhead of ReEmu, which will be our future work.

7. Conclusion and Future Work

In this paper, we made the first attempt to provide deterministic replay features to parallel full-system emulators. Based on a comphrensive analysis on issues with prior CREW protocols, we make several refinements that made ReEmu scalable on multicore platforms and efficient. Evaluation showed that ReEmu incurs modest runtime and space overhead and can faithfully replay the whole software stack.

There are still plentiful research opportunities for us to explore in future. First, we plan to incorporate debugging and analysis tools into ReEmu so that it can seamlessly work with existing tools like gdb. Second, we will study the performance and scalability of our refined CREW protocol to record and replay user-level system such as user-mode QEMU and Pin, which should bennefit from the scalable design. Third, as we currently only evaluate ReEmu on a small amount of cores, we plan to study the performance and scalability of ReEmu on a machine with hundreds of cores.

References

[1] G. Altekar and I. Stoica. ODR: output-deterministic replay for multi-core debugging. In *Proc. SOSP*, 2009.

[2] F. Bellard. Qemu, a fast and portable dynamic translator. In *Proc. USENIX ATC*, 2005.

[3] C. Bienia, S. Kumar, J. Singh, and K. Li. The PARSEC benchmark suite: Characterization and architectural implications. In *Proc. PACT*, 2008.

[4] T. C. Bressoud and F. B. Schneider. Hypervisor-based fault tolerance. In *Proc. SOSP*, 1995.

[5] P. Courtois, F. Heymans, and D. Parnas. Concurrent control with readers and writers. *Comm. of the ACM*, 14(10):667–668, 1971.

[6] J. Ding, P. Chang, W. Hsu, and Y. Chung. PQEMU: A parallel system emulator based on QEMU. In *Proc. ICPADS*, 2011.

[7] G. W. Dunlap, S. T. King, S. Cinar, M. A. Basrai, and P. M. Chen. ReVirt: enabling intrusion analysis through virtual-machine logging and replay. In *Proc. OSDI*, 2002.

[8] G. W. Dunlap, D. G. Lucchetti, M. A. Fetterman, and P. M. Chen. Execution replay of multiprocessor virtual machines. In *Proc. VEE*, 2008.

[9] D. Hong, C. Hsu, P. Yew, J. Wu, W. Hsu, P. Liu, C. Wang, and Y. Chung. HQEMU: a multi-threaded and retargetable dynamic binary translator on multicores. In *Proc. CGO*, 2012.

[10] J. Huang, P. Liu, and C. Zhang. LEAP: lightweight deterministic multi-processor replay of concurrent java programs. In *Proc. SIG-SOFT FSE*, 2010.

[11] S. T. King, G. W. Dunlap, and P. M. Chen. Debugging operating systems with time-traveling virtual machines. In *Proc. USENIX ATC*, 2005.

[12] O. Laadan, N. Viennot, and J. Nieh. Transparent, lightweight application execution replay on commodity multiprocessor operating systems. In *Proc. SIGMETRICS*, 2010.

[13] R. Lantz. *Parallel SimOS - Performance and Scalability for Large System*. PhD thesis, Stanford University, 2007.

[14] T. Leblanc and J. Mellor-Crummey. Debugging Parallel Programs with Instant Replay. *Computers, IEEE Transactions on Computers*, C-36(4):471–482, 1987.

[15] D. Lee, B. Wester, K. Veeraraghavan, S. Narayanasamy, P. M. Chen, and J. Flinn. Respec: efficient online multiprocessor replayvia speculation and external determinism. In *Proc. ASPLOS*, 2010.

[16] M. McLoughlin. The qcow image format, 2008.

[17] S. Narayanasamy, G. Pokam, and B. Calder. BugNet: Continuously Recording Program Execution for Deterministic Replay Debugging. In *Proc. ISCA*, 2005.

[18] S. Park, Y. Zhou, W. Xiong, Z. Yin, R. Kaushik, K. Lee, and S. Lu. PRES: probabilistic replay with execution sketching on multiprocessors. In *Proc. SOSP*, 2009.

[19] H. Patil, C. Pereira, M. Stallcup, G. Lueck, and J. Cownie. PinPlay: a framework for deterministic replay and reproducible analysis of parallel programs. In *Proc. CGO*, 2010.

[20] C. Ranger, R. Raghuraman, A. Penmetsa, G. Bradski, and C. Kozyrakis. Evaluating mapreduce for multi-core and multiprocessor systems. In *Proc. HPCA*, pages 13–24, 2007.

[21] K. Veeraraghavan, D. Lee, B. Wester, J. Ouyang, P. M. Chen, J. Flinn, and S. Narayanasamy. DoublePlay: parallelizing sequential logging and replay. In *Proc. ASPLOS*, 2011.

[22] Z. Wang, R. Liu, Y. Chen, X. Wu, H. Chen, Z. W., and B. Zang. Coremu: a scalable and portable parallel full-system emulator. In *Proc. PPoPP*, 2011.

[23] M. Xu, R. Bodik, and M. Hill. A "flight data recorder" for enabling full-system multiprocessor deterministic replay. In *Proc. ISCA*, 2003.

[24] M. Xu, V. Malyugin, J. Sheldon, G. Venkitachalam, and B. Weissman. Retrace: Collecting execution trace with virtual machine deterministic replay. In *Proceedings of the Third Annual Workshop on Modeling, Benchmarking and Simulation*, 2007.

[25] Z. Yang, M. Yang, L. Xu, H. Chen, and B. Zang. ORDER: object centric deterministic replay for java. In *Proc. USENIX ATC*, 2011.

Scheduling Parallel Programs by
Work Stealing with Private Deques

Umut A. Acar

Department of Computer Science
Carnegie Mellon University
umut@cs.cmu.edu

Arthur Charguéraud

Inria Saclay – Île-de-France
& LRI, Université Paris Sud, CNRS
arthur.chargueraud@inria.fr

Mike Rainey

Max Planck Institute
for Software Systems
mrainey@mpi-sws.org

Abstract

Work stealing has proven to be an effective method for scheduling parallel programs on multicore computers. To achieve high performance, work stealing distributes tasks between concurrent queues, called deques, which are assigned to each processor. Each processor operates on its deque locally except when performing load balancing via steals. Unfortunately, concurrent deques suffer from two limitations: 1) local deque operations require expensive memory fences in modern weak-memory architectures, 2) they can be very difficult to extend to support various optimizations and flexible forms of task distribution strategies needed many applications, e.g., those that do not fit nicely into the divide-and-conquer, nested data parallel paradigm.

For these reasons, there has been a lot recent interest in implementations of work stealing with non-concurrent deques, where deques remain entirely private to each processor and load balancing is performed via message passing. Private deques eliminate the need for memory fences from local operations and enable the design and implementation of efficient techniques for reducing task-creation overheads and improving task distribution. These advantages, however, come at the cost of communication. It is not known whether work stealing with private deques enjoys the theoretical guarantees of concurrent deques and whether they can be effective in practice.

In this paper, we propose two work-stealing algorithms with private deques and prove that the algorithms guarantee similar theoretical bounds as work stealing with concurrent deques. For the analysis, we use a probabilistic model and consider a new parameter, the branching depth of the computation. We present an implementation of the algorithm as a C++ library and show that it compares well to Cilk on a range of benchmarks. Since our approach relies on private deques, it enables implementing flexible task creation and distribution strategies. As a specific example, we show how to implement task coalescing and steal-half strategies, which can be important in fine-grain, non-divide-and-conquer algorithms such as graph algorithms, and apply them to the depth-first-search problem.

Categories and Subject Descriptors D.3.4 [*Programming Languages*]: Processors – Run-time environments

Keywords work stealing, nested parallelism, dynamic load balancing

PPoPP'13, February 23–27, 2013, Shenzhen, China.
Copyright © 2013 ACM 978-1-4503-1922-5/13/02...$15.00

1. Introduction

As multicore computers (i.e., computers with chip-multiprocessors) become mainstream, techniques for writing and executing parallel programs have become increasingly important. By allowing parallel programs to be written in a style similar to sequential programs implicit parallelism, as elegantly exemplified by languages such as Cilk [23], NESL [7], parallel Haskell [32], and parallel ML [22] has emerged as a promising technique for parallel programming [33]. In such languages, the programmer expresses all opportunities for parallelism and leaves it to the language and its run-time system to create and manage the parallel tasks needed to take advantage of the opportunities for parallel execution.

Since implicit parallel programs expose all opportunities for parallelism, they can create an overabundance of tasks, including tiny ones. Executing such fine-grained parallel programs with high-performance therefore requires overcoming a key challenge: efficient scheduling. Scheduling costs include the cost creating a potentially very large number of parallel tasks each of which can contain a tiny amount of actual work (e.g., several thousands of cycles), and distributing such parallel tasks among the available processors to minimize the total run time. In the course of the last decade, the randomized work-stealing algorithm as popularized by Cilk [9, 23] has emerged as an effective scheduler for implicitly parallel programs. (The idea of work stealing goes back to 80's [11, 25].)

In work stealing each processor maintains a *deque* (doubly-ended queue) of ready tasks to execute. By operating at the "bottom" end of its own deque, each processor treats its deque as a stack, mimicking sequential execution as it works locally. When a processor finds its deque empty, it acts globally by stealing the task at the top end of the deques of a *victim*, a randomly chosen processor. In theory, work stealing delivers close to optimal performance for a reasonably broad range of computations [10]. Furthermore, these theoretical results can be matched in practice by carefully designing scheduling algorithms and data structures. Key to achieving practical efficiency is a non-blocking deque data structures that prevents contention during concurrent operations. Arora et al [3] proposed the first such data structure for fixed-sized deques. Hendler et al [26] generalized that data structure to support unbounded deques; however, the algorithm could result in memory leaks. Chase and Lev [12] used circular buffers to obtain deques whose size can grow without memory leaks. Most current parallel programming systems that support this form of work stealing critically utilize these data structures.

While randomized work stealing with concurrent queues has been shown to be effective in many applications, previous research has also identified both algorithmic and practical limitations with it. A number of studies show that in scheduling, it can be important to be flexible in choosing the task(s) to transfer during a steal.

These studies show experimentally [14, 17, 27, 38, 39] and the-oretically [4, 36, 37], that, for certain important irregular graph computations, it is advantageous to transfer not just a single task at every steal, but multiple tasks. For instance, previous research found the *steal-half* strategy [27], where a steal transfers half of tasks from the victim's deque, can be more effective [14, 17, 39] compared to the "steal-one" approach. Another important practi-cal limitation concerns the interaction between concurrent deque data structures used in the implementation of work stealing and modern memory models, which provide increasingly weaker con-sistency guarantees. On weak memory models, concurrent deques require expensive memory-fences, which can degrade performance significantly [19, 23, 34]; for example, Frigo et al. found that Cilk's work-stealing protocol spends half of its time executing the memory fence [23]. The final limitation concerns flexibility and generality. Due to their inherent complexity, the non-blocking de-ques are difficult to extend to support sophisticated algorithms for creating and scheduling parallel tasks. For example, Hiraishi et al. [29] and Umatani et al. [44] used non-concurrent, private de-ques to implement their techniques for reducing task-creation over-heads; Hendler et al.'s non-blocking, concurrent deques for steal-half work stealing require asymptotically non-constant atomic op-erations, and works only for bounded, fixed-size deques [27]; Cong et al. found that a batching technique can reduce task-creation over-heads but were not able to combine it with the flexibility of steal-half strategy using private deques [14].

Due to these limitations, there has been a lot of interest in work-stealing algorithms where non-concurrent, *private* deques replace the concurrent, *shared* deques, and processors explicitly commu-nicate to balance load. In such algorithms, each processor keeps its deque private, operating on its bottom end as usual. When a pro-cessor finds its deque to be empty, instead of manipulating a remote deque in a concurrent fashion, the processor sends a message to a randomly chosen victim processor and awaits for a response, which either includes one or more tasks or indicates that victim's deque is empty. In order to respond to messages, each processor polls its message queue on a regular basis.

This message-passing approach to work stealing has been re-ceiving significant attention in multicore computers. In early work, Feeley [19] investigates the use of work stealing with private de-ques to accellerate task creation. Hendler et al. [28] use a private deques to implement a load distribution strategy for improved lo-cality. Hiraishi et al [29] and Umatani et al [44] use private deques to reduce task-creation overheads. The Manticore system for Par-allel ML uses private deques, because they simplify the parallel-garbage-collection problem by minimizing pointers between the memory of different processors [22]. Using simulation studies, Sanchez et al [39] show that minimal hardware support for mes-sage passing and interrupts can further improve the performance of work stealing, even if the private deques and the work stealing algorithm itself is implemented in software.

While previous work highlights the benefits of work stealing with private deques in terms of enabling key optimizations, algo-rithms, and flexible distribution strategies, relatively little is known about whether the approach can, in general, perform as well as work stealing with concurrent deques. Theoretically, it is not known whether private deques can yield similar theoretical guarantees as the work stealing algorithm with concurrent deques. Practically, it is not known whether private deques can yield as good performance as state of the art systems, such as Cilk, that use concurrent deques. To the best of our knowledge no thorough comparison between the two approaches exist.

In this paper, we study the theoretical and the practical effective-ness of work stealing with private deques. We propose two algo-rithms, a sender- and a receiver-initiated algorithm for work steal-

ing. Using private deques, our algorithms eliminate memory fences from the common scheduling path. To balance load, our algorithms rely primarily on explicit communication between processors. In implicitly parallel programs, such communication is naturally easy to support, because the scheduler is invoked frequently due to small task sizes. Thus, most of polling needed for communication can be performed by the scheduler without (hardware or software) inter-rupts, which, depending on the platform, may not be able to de-liver interrupts frequently and cheaply enough. Although we do not consider coarse-grain parallel programs in this paper, we report on some preliminary investigations on the use of interrupts to make our algorithms robust even with large tasks.

We give a proof of efficiency for both the sender- and receiver-initiated work-stealing algorithms using private deques. For our analysis, we consider a probabilistic model, which takes into ac-count the delays due to the interval between polling operations. We present a bound in terms of the work and depth (traditional parame-ters used in the analysis of work stealing), and a new parameter, the *branching depth*, which measures the maximal number of branch-ing nodes in the computation DAG. The branching depth is similar to traditional notions of depth but is often significantly smaller be-cause it counts only the number of fork nodes along the path, ig-noring sequential work performed in between. The branching depth parameter enables us to bound tightly the effect of the polling de-lays on performance, showing that the algorithm performs close to a greedy scheduler, even when the communication delay is quite large. Due to space restrictions we could not provide all the details of the proof, which can be found in the accompanying technical report accessible online [1].

We present an implementation of our algorithm as a C++ library. To evaluate the effectiveness of our implementation, we consider a number of parallel benchmarks, including standard Cilk bench-marks, as well as more recently proposed graph benchmarks from the PBBS [6] benchmark suite. Using these benchmarks, we com-pare our algorithms with Cilk (more precisely, Cilk Plus [30]). Fur-thermore, in order to isolate the differences due to the use of private deques from the differences due to the representation of tasks and other implementation details, we compare our algorithms against an implementation of the standard Chase Lev work stealing algo-rithm [12] in our framework. Our experiments show that our algo-rithms are competitive with both Cilk and to our own implementa-tion of work stealing with concurrent deques.

A key benefit of the proposed approach with private deques is that it eliminates all concurrency operations from local deque oper-ations. More precisely, our algorithms require only a simple, non-concurrent deque data structure, because all other load balancing actions are performed via explicit communication. This approach allows implementing sophisticated task-creation and scheduling al-gorithms as may be needed by the application at hand, e.g., those that do not fit into the divide-and-conquer or nested data paral-lel paradigm. As an important example, we show how to coalesce small tasks into larger tasks while also supporting the steal-half policy for load balancing. We show, in particular, how to apply our approach to solve a challenging graph-reachability problem and demonstrate good scaling with our implementation.

2. Algorithms

Our sender-initiated and receiver-initiated algorithms both follow the same skeleton but differ in how they perform the load balancing actions. Figure 1 shows the parts that are shared by both algorithms. Each of the P processors owns a deque (doubly-ended queue of tasks). The deque is accessible by its owner only. The function `main` implements main scheduling loop. The loop starts by check-ing if the deque is empty. If so, it calls the function `acquire`, which obtains a task to execute. Otherwise, it pops the bottom

```
deque<task*> q[P] = {EMPTY, ..} // deques

// entry point for the workers
void main(int i) // i = ID of the worker
  repeat
    if (empty(q[i]))
      acquire(i)
    else
      task* t = pop_bottom(q[i])
      update_status(i)
      communicate(i)
      execute(t)

// called for scheduling a ready task t
void add_task(int i, task* t)
  push_bottom(q[i], t)
  update_status(i)
```

Figure 1. Scheduler code for work stealing with private deques

```
bool a[P] = {false, .. } // status flag
int NO_REQU = -1
int r[P] = {NO_REQU, .. } // requests cells
task* NO_RESP = 1 // any non-null pointer
task* t[P] = {NO_RESP, .. } // tranfer cells

// update the status flag
void update_status(int i)
  bool b = (size(q[i]) > 0)
  if a[i] != b then a[i] = b

// called by workers when running out of work
void acquire(int i)
  while true
    t[i] = NO_RESP
    int k = random in {0, .., P-1}\{i}
    if a[k] && compare_and_swap(&r[k], NO_REQU, i)
      while (t[i] == NO_RESP)
        communicate(i)
      if (t[i] != null)
        add_task(i, t[i])
        r[i] = NO_REQU
        return
    communicate(i)

// check for incoming steal requests
void communicate(int i)
  int j = r[i]
  if j == NO_REQU then return
  if empty(q[i])
    t[j] = null
  else
    t[j] = pop_top(q[i])
  r[i] = NO_REQU
```

Figure 2. Receiver-initiated algorithm

task from the deque and executes it. When executed, a task can create new subtasks, which are then pushed at the bottom of the deque with function add_task. Between the execution of every two tasks, the function communicate is called, for the purpose of load balancing, to communicate with other processors. Observe that the call to communicate takes place after the pop operation, ensuring that a processor never sends away the last task that it owns. The receiver-initiated algorithm and the sender-initiated algorithm differ only in the design of the function acquire and communicate. The auxiliary function update_status, which appears in the the function main, is used by the receiver-initiated algorithm only.

```
task* DUMMY_TASK = 1 // any non-null pointer
task* INCOMING = 2 // another non-null pointer
task* s[P] = {DUMMY_TASK, .. } // communication cells
double d[P] = { 0, ...} // date of next deal attempt

// called by workers when running out of work
void acquire(int i)
  s[i] = null
  while (s[i] == null)
    noop
  add_task(i, s[i])

// attempt to deal a task to an idle processor
void deal_attempt(int i)
  if empty(q[i]) then return
  int j = random in {0, .., P-1}\{i}
  if s[j] != null then return
  bool r = compare_and_swap(&s[j], null, INCOMING)
  if r then s[j] = pop_top(q[i])

// call try_send if it is time to do so
void communicate(int i)
  if now() > d[i]
    deal_attempt(i)
    d[i] = now() - delta * ln (rand(0,1))
```

Figure 3. Sender-initiated algorithm

Receiver-initiated algorithm Figure 2 shows the pseudo-code for the receiver-initiated algorithm. Processors communicate via two kinds of cells: *request cells*, stored in the array r, and *transfer cells*, stored in the array t. Each processor has its own request and transfer cell. In addition, each processor uses the array a to indicate that its deque contains more than one task (i.e., that the processor has work to offer). The function update_status updates the value stored in this cell.

In the receiver-initiated algorithm, when an idle processor calls the function acquire, it picks a random target "victim" processor. The idle processor then reads the status cell of the victim processor to determine whether the victim processor has some work to offer. If not, it starts over with another random target. If, however, the victim processor has some work to offer, then the idle processor makes a steal request. To that end, it writes atomically (with a compare-and-swap operation) its id in the request cell of its victim processor. The atomic write guarantees a processor receives at most one steal request at once. If the atomic write fails, the processor starts over; if it succeeds, then the idle processor simply waits for an answer from its victim, by repeatedly reading its transfer cell.

Whenever a busy processor calls the function communicate, it checks whether its request cell contains the processor id of a thief. If so, then it responds to the thief by writing the top task in its deque to the transfer cell of the thief. Otherwise, if the processor has no more than one task then it declines the request by sending the null pointer. Since write operations can take some time to become visible to all processors, a processor may receive steal requests while it is already idle and running the function acquire. There are two ways to ensure that the steal request receives a response in such a case. One possibility, which we follow in this paper, is to have the idle processor call communicate regularly while looping in the function acquire. Another possibility, which we implement and which is described in the long version of the paper [1], is to have the idle processor atomically write its own id in its request cell, thereby blocking incoming requests.

Sender-initiated algorithm Figure 3 shows the pseudo code for the sender-initiated algorithm. Each processor uses a *communication cell*, both to indicate its status and to receive tasks. These cells are stored in the array s. Each processor additionally keeps track of the next date at which it should make a deal attempt, using the array d. We will explain later why these dates are needed.

In the sender-initiated algorithm, when an idle processor calls the function `acquire`, it simply declares itself as idle by writing the value null in its communication cell. It then waits until a busy processor delivers work in this cell. A busy processor uses the function `deal_attempt` to attempt to deal a task to an idle processor. To make a deal attempt, the busy processor first checks whether its deque is empty. If so, the busy processor returns immediately because it cannot send a task. Otherwise, the busy processor picks a random target, and checks whether this target is idle, by testing whether the communication cell of the target contains the value null. If the target is not idle, then the busy processor gives up, that is, it does not try to find another target. If the target is idle, then the busy processor tries to atomically update the communication cell of the target by writing the constant INCOMING into it, so as to prevent other processors from concurrently delivering a task. If the atomic operation succeeds, the busy processor pops the task from the top of its deque, and writes the corresponding pointer into the communication cell of the target. If the atomic operation fails, indicating that the busy processor has been out-raced by another busy processor, the busy processor simply aborts.

In the particular case of the steal-one policy, which is being described here, we can save the intermediate write of the constant INCOMING and instead directly send a task pointer. This optimization can be obtained by replacing in Figure 3 the last two lines of the function `deal_attempt` with the following code.

```
task* t = peek_top(q[i])
bool r = compare_and_swap(&s[j], null, t)
if r then pop_top(q[i])
```

The two-step process described in Figure 3 is, however, required to support policies such as steal-half, as discussed in Section 5.

Consider the execution of a processor i that is working on a collection of small tasks. If the tasks owned by i are smaller on average than those owned by other processors, then i would have more chances of dealing tasks than other processors. Because the tasks that i deals are small, many more task migrations would be needed than in a fair situation, where processors owning big pieces of the computation have similar chances of dealing them.

To ensure fairness, we could impose that busy processors make deal attempts only at regular intervals. We have observed in practice slightly better and much more regular results when we introduce randomness in the intervals between deal attempts. There are many possible ways of introducing randomness. Our approach, which follows the assumption that we make in the proof of efficiency, consists is making the delay between two deal attemps follow a Poisson distribution with parameter δ, for some δ larger than the typical duration of a task. With this approach, deal attempts take place on average slightly more than every δ, because a processor needs to complete a task before it is able to check whether the time has come to make a deal attempt.

Once a deal attempt is made, to determine the time for the next deal attempt according to the Poisson distribution, we use Knuth's formula $-\delta \ln(x)$, where x is a random variable uniformly picked in the range $[0, 1]$. As an optimization, we do not reset the date d[i] to the value now() at the end of the function `acquire`, meaning that we typically allow a processor that receives a task in `acquire` to make a deal attempt immediately after it has executed this task. This optimization significantly helps in distributing the work quickly in the initial phase of a parallel algorithm.

3. Analysis

When using concurrent deques, idle processors are able to almost immediately acquire some work by stealing it from the deque of one of the busy processors. On the contrary, when using private de-ques, idle processors need to wait for a busy processor to communicate with them. A central aspect of work stealing algorithms based on private deques is therefore to quantify the amount of additional idle time induced by the communication delays. In this section, we prove a bound showing that the amount of idle time is bounded by $O(\delta F)$, where δ denotes the average communication delay and where F denotes the branching depth, that is, the maximal number of branching nodes in a path from the computation DAG.

To model the communication pattern in the proof, we use a probabilistic model. For the sender-initiated algorithm, we assume that deal attemps follow a Poisson distribution with parameter δ. This model is faithful to the behavior of the actual algorithm whenever δ is larger than the duration of a few tasks. Note that the larger is δ compared with the typical size of sequential tasks, the more faithful is the model.

For the receiver-initiated algorithm, we assign a different interpretation to the variable δ: we assume that the interval between two polling operations made by a given processor follow a Poisson distribution with parameter δ. The parameter δ here corresponds to the average duration of a sequential task. In the actual algorithms, some polling operations actually happen more frequently, because of the "fork tasks" and the "join tasks" which perform only a tiny amount of work. In the receiver-initiated algorithm, these additional polling operations can only help the algorithm by accelerating the distribution of tasks. The direct cost of these additional polling operations, which consists simply in reading a local variable, is negligible in front of the costs associated with the creation and the manipulation of tasks. Note that the receiver-initiated algorithm has no issue with fairness like that of the sender-initiated one, because, in the receiver-initiated algorithm, all the random decisions are made by the idle processors.

Our proof establishes a bound on the execution time for both the receiver- and the sender-initiated algorithms. Before stating our bound, we briefly recall the bounds from the literature for work stealing with concurrent deques. The proof given by Blumofe and Leiserson [8], later simplified and generalized by Arora, Blumofe, Plaxton in [3], is $\mathbb{E}[T_P] \leq \frac{T_1}{P} + 32T_\infty$, where T_P denotes the execution time with P processors, T_1 denotes the sequential execution time, and T_∞ denotes the length of the critical path (which corresponds to the minimal execution time with infinitely-many processors). This bound is established using an potential analysis based on *phases*: at each phase, the relative decrease in potential exceeds $\frac{1}{4}$ with probability greater than $\frac{1}{4}$. Tchiboukdjian et al [42] tightened this bound to $\mathbb{E}[T_P] \leq \frac{T_1}{P} + 3.65T_\infty$, using an analysis based on a bound of the expected decrease in potential at each time step. This bound shows that work stealing is not far from matching Brent's bound $\frac{T_1}{P} + \frac{P-1}{P}T_\infty$, which applies to all greedy schedulers.

Our proof is also based on the expected decrease in potential, however it uses a different potential function, which depends on the value of δ and which distinguishes the contribution of T_∞ from that of the branching depth. In first approximation, the bound that we establish for both receiver-initiated and sender-initiated work stealing with private deques is:

$$\mathbb{E}[T_P] \leq_\approx \left(1 + \frac{1}{\delta - 1}\right) \cdot \left(\frac{T_1}{P} + T_\infty + O(\delta F)\right).$$

The bound above includes a factor $1 + \frac{1}{\delta-1}$, which corresponds to the overhead associated with polling. The constant 1 that appears in the denominator should be interpreted as the round-trip time for a message to go back and forth between two processors. The bound also includes the term $O(\delta F)$, which corresponds to the idle time associated with task migrations. The formal lower bound that we prove on $\mathbb{E}[T_P]$ involves a constant c, defined as 1.0 in the sender-initiated algorithm and $\frac{1}{1-1/e} \approx 1.58$ in the receiver-initiated

	Concur. deques (speedup)	Concur. deques (sec)	Recv.-init. (%)	Sender-init. (%)	Cilk Plus (%)
matmul	21.7	2.61	-18	-18	-3
cilksort(exptintseq)	18.6	1.32	-2	-0	-7
cilksort(randintseq)	21.7	1.51	-2	+0	-7
fibojnnacci	26.2	4.11	-2	+1	-3
matching(eggrid2d)	19.6	0.44	+9	+12	+9
matching(egrlg)	20.0	0.72	-1	+2	+5
matching(egrmat)	20.1	0.90	+0	+4	+6
MIS(grid2d)	17.5	0.19	+2	-0	+5
MIS(rlg)	17.9	0.21	-4	-2	+7
MIS(rmat)	18.5	0.16	+1	+4	+7
hull(plummer2d)	18.0	0.27	+6	+4	-5
hull(uniform2d)	19.1	0.55	+2	+2	-3
sort(exptseq)	23.2	1.90	-4	-4	+29
sort(randdblseq)	23.5	2.84	-7	-6	+25

Figure 4. Comparison of the schedulers.

algorithm. It also involves a factor $\frac{\mu}{1-e^{-\mu}}$, where μ is defined as $\frac{0.63}{c\delta}$. Since $\frac{\mu}{1-e^{-\mu}} \approx 1 + \frac{\mu}{2} \approx 1 + \frac{0.31}{c\delta}$, the factor $\frac{\mu}{1-e^{-\mu}}$ can be approximated as 1.0 for any practical purpose. The formal bound is:

$$\left(1 + \frac{1}{\delta - 1}\right) \cdot \left(\frac{T_1}{P} + \frac{P-1}{P} \cdot \frac{\mu}{1 - e^{-\mu}} \cdot \left(T_\infty + 2.68 \cdot c\delta F\right)\right).$$

The fact that c is larger in the receiver-initiated algorithm corresponds to the fact that idle processors may need some time to find a busy target. Note that this difference does not imply that the receiver-initiated algorithm is slower than the sender-initiated one, because the former algorithm is associated with a smaller value for δ. The main arguments of the proof can be found in the appendix of this paper. The complete proof can be found in the online appendix [1].

4. Evaluation

We implemented a C++ library to provide a framework for evaluating our algorithms. The library creates one POSIX thread (i.e., one *pthread*) for each core available. We implemented the receiver-initiated and the sender-initiated algorithms with private deques, as well as the standard Chase-Lev algorithm based on concurrent deques [12]. We also compare against Cilk Plus, an extension of GCC, that is the result of many years of careful engineering. Our goal is to evaluate whether private deques can be competitive with our own implementation of concurrent deques, and whether this baseline is competitive with the state of the art technology.

Comparison. We evaluated the schedulers on several programs. First, we ported three classic Cilk programs: *cilksort*, which is based on a parallel version of merge-sort; *matmul*, which multiplies two dense matrices in place using a cache-efficient, divide-and-conquer algorithm [23]; and *fibonacci*, which computes Fibonacci number using the exponential algorithm. This last benchmark is useful to perform analyses without observing interference from the memory. We also ported four benchmarks from the recent Blelloch et al's problem-based benchmark suit (PBBS) [6], which consists of internally-deterministic parallel programs targeting Cilk. We ported: *matching*, which computes the maximal matching of an undirected graph; *hull*, which computes a 2-dimensional convex hull; and *sample-sort*, which is a low-depth, cache-efficient version of the classic sample sort algorithm.

In order to reuse some parts of Cilk Plus, and in order to ease the comparison, we use the same heap allocator (*miser* [41]), the same random number generator, and the same compiler as Cilk. We left the benchmarks programs exactly as they were implemented orig-

inally, only increasing slightly the sequential cutoff value in the three Cilk benchmarks programs to adapt to the speed of our test machine. One difference, though, concerns the implementation of Cilk's parallel for-loops, which is used by the three PBBS benchmarks. The strategy of Cilk consists in statically partitionning loops in $8P$ subtasks. This approach results in the creation of large sequential tasks, which is problematic for schedulers based on private deques. Instead, we use a divide-and-conquer approach to scheduling parallel loops, simply cutting off at a number of iterations that roughly corresponds to 10 microseconds worth of work. The difference in the number of subtasks generated explains the significant difference in execution time observed on some benchmarks between Cilk Plus and our implementation of concurrent deques.

Our test machine hosts four eight-core Intel Xeon X7550 [31] chips with each core running at 2.0GHz. Each core has 32Kb each of L1 instruction and data cache and 256 Kb of L2 cache. Each chip has an 18Mb L3 cache that is shared by all eight cores. The system has 1Tb of RAM and runs Debian Linux (kernel version 3.2.21.1.amd64-smp). We consider just 30 out of the 32 total cores in order to reduce interference with the operating system. All of our code is compiled by the Cilk Plus GCC (v4.8.0 20120625) with the -O2 option. For the sender-initiated algorithm, we set the delay parameter δ to 30 microseconds, which we have found to yield good performance on our machine. The input sizes are as follows: *cilksort*: random and exponentially-distributed, 240m integers, *matmul*: square matrix of size 3500, *fibonacci*: n = 48, *matching*: 3-d grid with 40m nodes, random graph with 40m nodes and 200m edges, and rMat graph with 40m nodes and 200m edges, *hull*: uniform and plummer with 100m points, *sample-sort*: random and exponentially-distributed, 240m doubles. To tame the variance observed in the measures when running with 30 cores (there is usually between 5% and 10% difference between a fast and a slow run), we averaged the measures over 20 runs.

Figure 4 gives the speedup and the absolute execution time for our baseline (Chase-Lev concurrent-deques algorithm), and gives the relative value of the execution time of the other schedulers: our receiver-initiated, our sender-initiated algorithms, and Cilk Plus. Several interesting conclusions can be drawn from this figure. First, the receiver-initiated algorithm and the sender-initiated algorithm perform almost exactly the same (usually within 2% of each other). This similarity confirms the intuition that, at a high-level, these algorithms are dual of one another. Second, we observe that, on many benchmarks, private deques are performing close to concurrent deques, sometimes a little worse and sometimes a little better. In one particular benchmark, such as maximal matching on a grid, private deques shows poorer performance than concurrent deques. This benchmark involves some phases where parallelism is so scarce that the communication delay becomes visible. In some other benchmarks, such as *matmul* and *sample-sort*, private deques seem to perform significantly better. We believe that, in these memory-intensive benchmarks, saving the cost of the memory fence brings a significant improvement. Third, we observe that our baseline is competitive with Cilk Plus. Our library is never more than 7% slower, and it is often about 7% faster. Moreover, due to our different treatment of for-loops, we are able to outperform Cilk by over 25% on the sample sort benchmark. From these results, we conclude that the private-deque approach to work stealing is competitive with state of the art, concurrent-deques algorithms.

Although having competitive performance in practice is crucial, the true benefits of the private-deque approach relate to flexibility and generality. In Section 1, we discussed the benefits, but here, we provide further evidence to back these claims. The development of state-of-the-art concurrent-deque algorithms dates back to the non-blocking algorithm of Arora et al. [3], which went through a few revisions due to concurrency bugs. Several years later, the nonblock-

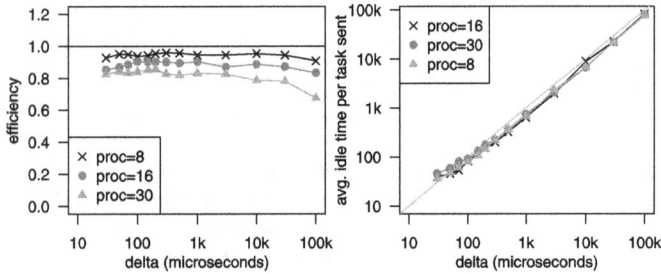

Figure 5. Impact of δ in the sender-initiated algorithm (Fibonacci).

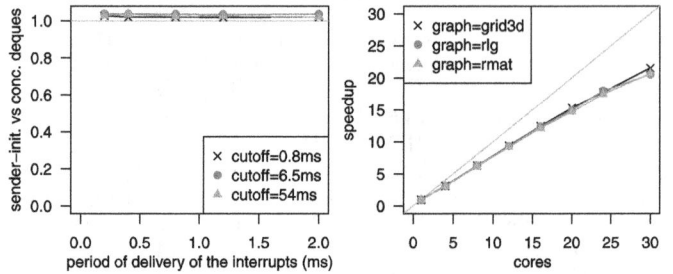

Figure 6. (a) Handling of large sequential tasks using interrupts, and (b) Speedup curves for pseudo-DFS on three graphs.

ing algorithm was extended by Chase and Lev to support dynamic resizing [12]. Their first and, to our knowledge, only proof of correctness of a nonblocking work-stealing algorithm is not trivial: it spans over thirty pages [13]. Moreover, there is, in the literature, no nonblocking algorithm which combines resizeability with other extensions, such as steal half, possibly owing to the complexity involved in extending the proof of correctness. Although we had to omit the proof of correctness for our sender- and receiver-initiated algorithms due to space limitations, the proofs are trivial because in both cases the concurrency is limited to accesses on a single shared cell. The private-deque algorithms support steal half as well as other extensions that are not yet supported by concurrent deques.

Analysis of the impact of δ in the sender-initiated algorithm.
In the evaluation, we have been setting δ to 30 microseconds. In benchmarks where the branching depth is large, typically in algorithms that have an outer sequential loop and an inner parallel loop, the value of δ needs to remain relatively small in order to efficiently distribute tasks. However, in benchmark where the branching depth is small, the value of δ can be safely increased without noticeably affecting on the execution time. According to our theorem, it is perfectly fine to use any δ such that $2.68 \cdot \delta F \ll \frac{T_1}{P}$. For example, for *fibonacci* with $n = 48$ and sequential cutoff at $n = 18$, the fork depth is 30. Given that $T_1 = 56$ seconds and $P = 30$, $\frac{T_1}{2.68 \cdot F P} = 23$ milliseconds. Therefore, up to $\delta = 1$ millisecond, we do not expect to see any effect on the execution time. This theoretical prediction is confirmed by the first chart shown in Figure 5.

To better understand the impact of δ on the idle time involved in an execution, we measure the ratio between the total amount of idle time and the number of tasks being migrated between processors. At high load, when a processor runs out of work, there are $P - 1$ processors that may send work to it; each of these busy processors performs a deal attempt on average every δ, and find the idle processor with probability $\frac{1}{P-1}$. As a result, the expected time before a processor receives some work is exactly δ. The second chart in Figure 5 confirms that the average idle time per task migration is indeed extremely close to δ. Because the number of task migrations is typically small when the deque discipline of work stealing is followed, the total amount of idle time is relatively small and grows only linearly with δ.

Handling of large sequential tasks If we cannot assume that the tasks have a bounded execution time, then we need to adapt the algorithms so as to ensure that the control is handed back to the scheduler regularly enough. Several approaches are possible. One possibility, in the receiver-initiated algorithm, is for idle processors to send interrupts to their targets. However, this approach does not apply to the sender-initiated algorithm. We could resort to compiler-assisted software polling, where the compiler inserts into the program operations to check for incoming messages [20, 21], or to the use of periodic interrupts. In order to make our C++ library more generally applicable, we do not use software polling. Ideally,

we would use interrupts triggered by some form of hardware down-counter. For now, we have instead been using a more basic approach that consists in running an additional pthread that issues interrupts at regular intervals. With this approach, we are able to get interrupts delivered as frequently as every 200 microseconds.

When interrupting tasks during their execution, we need to prevent races between the interrupt handler and the action of the running task. In particular, we need to prevent a race from corrupting the deque. Such races are much simpler to handle than that involved in concurrent deques, because interrupts happen on the same core, and therefore with a consistent view of the memory. Futhermore, their execution is not arbitrarily interleaved with that of the running task. If suffices for the actions on the deque to be protected by a local lock, which can be implemented without atomic operation. If an interrupt is raised during a critical section, then it can be ignored because the scheduler has the control during these critical sections, so it is able to execute a polling operation anyway.

As explained earlier on, for all programs with limited branching depth, δ can be set to 200 microseconds or even more without noticeable effect on the execution time. To evaluate the overheads associated with interrupts, we considered the dense matrix multiplication benchmark (on a parallel run of 3.7s), and varied the sequential cutoff so as to generate sequential tasks of size either 0.8ms, or 6.5ms, or 54ms. We measured the efficiency of our sender-initiated algorithm equipped with periodically-delivered interrupts relative to our implementation of concurrent deques. The results appear in the the first plot in Figure 6. For all periods tested between 200 microseconds and 2 milliseconds, and for any of the three sequential cutoff, we observe that the execution time is only 3.7 % slower than the baseline. On other benchmarks, we also observed overheads of the same order of magnitude. These results suggest that even the sender-initiated algorithm extended with interrupts can achieve competitive performance in the context of corse-grained parallelism.

5. Going beyond divide-and-conquer parallelism

In this section, we investigate the benefits of using private deques for programs falling outside of the fork-join model. We explain why concurrent deques are limited when it comes to supporting the steal-half policy and task coalescing. We show that, on the contrary, private deques can easily accomodate these two features. We demonstrate this ability by implementing a pseudo-DFS algorithm, which computes reachability in a graph from a given source.

Steal half The steal-half policy consists in transferring, during one steal operation, half of the tasks in the deque, instead of only one task. A number of researchers have argued for the benefit of the steal-half policy, in particular in the context of irregular graph applications [4, 14, 17, 36, 37, 39]. Intuitively, the weakness of the steal-one policy in a non fork-join computation is that, when a processor receives a single task, it is likely to run out of work soon afterwards. Hendler et al. have developed a concurrent deque able to support the steal-half strategy, but only at the cost of logarithmically many atomic operations in the total number of deque accesses [27]. Furthermore, Hendler et. al.'s data structure supports only fixed-sized deques, and it is not known if the data structure can be generalized to support resizable deques. When using private deques, however, implementing the steal-half policy requires only a trivial change to the algorithm. For example, in the sender-initiated pseudo-code, it suffices to change the type of the communication cells to `vector<task*>*` and to update the code from Figure 3 so that the busy processor sends a vector of tasks carved out of its own deque.

```
// change the last line of deal_attempt to:
int half_size = (size(q[i]) + 1) / 2
if r then s[j] = q[i].extract_items(half_size)

// change the last line of acquire to:
delete(q[i]) // q[i] is empty here
q[i] = s[i]  // use the incoming vector
```

Remark: when vectors are used to represent deques, the splitting operation has a linear cost. This cost is usually well amortized, because the average number of times that a task is transfered from a processor to another is usually tiny. Furthermore, if needed, the cost of splitting can be made logarithmic instead of linear by using more advanced data structures, such as binomial trees, which achieve logarithmic-time splitting and amortized constant-time push and pop operations.

More generally, work stealing with private deques can easily accomodate a wide range of transfer policies and accomodate efficient data structures to implement these policies, without requiring the development, for each policy, of a specific concurrent data structure.

Task coalescing To achieve good speedups, the task-creation costs need to be well amortized. In divide-and-conquer programs, this type of amortization is obtained by sequentializing the execution of subtasks smaller than some threshold. However, this technique does not apply to less structured applications such as irregular graph algorithms. To make matters worse, in this type of applications, the amount of work associated with each individual task is usually tiny. For example, in pseudo-DFS, if one task corresponds to the treatment of a single node from the graph, then the task-creation overheads are overwhelming. We conducted experiments showing that these overheads typically slow down the program by a factor 3 or more.

Task coalescing is a classic approach to reducing the overheads. It consists in grouping similar tasks into one, in order to reduce the work associated with task creation. In the case of pseudo-DFS, one coalesced task describes not just one node but a batch of nodes to visit. Let us explain why task coalescing is incompatible with the use of concurrent deques. If the size of the batches (number of nodes contained in each task) is constant, then it can happen that never more than one task is created, resulting in a purely sequential run. To see why, consider the case where the graph is a complete binary tree: the size of the stack of nodes to visit never contains more than a logarithmic number of nodes at once. To overcome this problem, Cong et al [14] suggest the following policy: if the number of nodes in the batch of the currently-running task is about to exceed $\min(2^Q, S)$, where Q is the size of the local deque and S is a constant large-enough to amortize scheduling costs, then the current batch is packed into a new task and pushed into the deque. While this approach can be effective for relatively regular graphs, it suffers from prohibitive overheads on all the graphs where the size of the stack of nodes to visit remains small (typically, in balanced trees and graphs with hierarchical clusters), because in this case one task typically contains a small number of the nodes. Moreover, Cong et al's approach cannot be combined with steal half.

By contrast, when using private deques, task coalescing is straightforward to implement and can be combined with steal half. For pseudo-DFS, each processor can use a single task, which contains a vector of nodes to visit. When executed, the task processes no more than a constant number of S nodes, where S is large enough to amortize the scheduling overhead. Before it continues, the task hands the control back to the scheduler. If the scheduler needs to transfer some work to another processor, then it may call on the task a splitting function that returns a new task containing half of the nodes.

We have implemented pseudo-DFS with task coalescing and the steal-half policy, using simple vectors to represent set of nodes. We implement efficient termination detection by having each processor keep a local count of the difference between the number of tasks received and the number of tasks sent. Termination occurs when the sum of the per-processor counts equals zero. One processor, assigned arbitrarily, performs the check when idle. We benchmarked our program on the three kinds of graphs that Blelloch et. al. [6] used to benchmark their BFS program: *3d-grid* (40m nodes, $T_1 = 11.5$s), *rlg* (40m nodes, 150m edges, $T_1 = 12.8$s), and *rmat* (40m nodes, 90 edges, $T_1 = 9.1$s). The second plot in Figure 6 shows that, on each of the three graphs, we achieve over 20x speedup with 30 cores.

In summary, the use of private deques offer a lot of flexibility. They allow for simple implementations of various scheduling techniques, without having to worry about the performance and the correctness of ad-hoc concurrent data structures.

6. Related work

We have discussed closely related work in relevant sections, in particular in Sections 1 and 5; here, we briefly review other more remotely related work, specifically the work on distributed systems. In distributed systems (without shared memory), scheduling algorithms usually rely on explicit communication between processors rather than concurrent data structures. Our algorithms therefore share some properties of distributed scheduling algorithms. Our algorithms also differ from distributed ones, because we perform communication via hardware shared memory and use atomic operations to maintain certain critical invariants.

Using the logp model, Sanders [40] analyzes a receiver-initiated load-balancing algorithm for a subclass of tree-shaped computations, presenting bounds that show the approach to be theoretically efficient. In contrast to the literature on hardware shared-memory systems where there is relatively little discussion of the sender-initiated approach, many studies on distributed scheduling compare the receiver- and sender-initiated approaches. Eager et al. [18] compare sender-initiated policies under different job scheduling policies, finding that performance depends on the system load as well as cost of certain operations, such as task transfers. Followup work refines these comparisons by considering the delays in the system [35], and different job scheduling policies [15]. More recently Dinan et al [16] compare work stealing (receiver initiated) and work sharing (sender initiated) when implemented on top of the MPI interface for message passing by using the unbalanced tree-search benchmark. These papers find that the algorithms both perform quite well—there are no clear winners—and the specifics such as the delays, the system load, and the job scheduling and preemption policies can make one preferable over the other.

Our empirical results also show that the two algorithms perform similarly on shared memory architectures. That said, workload characteristics and future advances in hardware and can make one more effective than the other. For example, receiver-initiated algorithms may be not as well suited to multiprogrammed environments because an idle processor takes exclusive access to a specific victim, which can delay execution if the sender is swapped out. Also, in receiver-initiated systems, processors can spin while looking for work, thereby making it difficult for the job scheduler to identify idle processors [24]. In contrast, in the sender-initiated approach, any sender can send work to an idle processor, and idle processors do not spin to look for work.

Tzannes proposes an algorithm in which each processor keeps all tasks in a private deque, except for the topmost one, which is exposed in a shared cell [43]. Although slightly simpler than our receiver-initiated algorithm, Tzannes' algorithm could show worst-case behavior when given certain computation graphs that lead the algorithm to access the topmost task at a high frequency, because the scheduler would have to repeatedly push and pop using compare and swap on the shared cell. (The Chase-Lev algorithm has a similar problem.)

The work presented in this paper was partly motivated by a desire to design scheduling algorithms for improved data locality (e.g., [2, 5]), which we expect to be a promising research direction.

7. Conclusion

In this paper, we design, analyze, and empirically evaluate two work-stealing algorithms for executing implicitly parallel programs on modern multicores. Both algorithms use private, non-concurrent deques to store parallel tasks and rely on explicit communication for load balancing. Our analysis shows the algorithms to be competitive with optimal bounds. Our implementation and experiments show that they are competitive with Cilk Plus, a state-of-the-art, highly optimized software system. We show that, thanks to eliminating concurrency from local deque operations, our approach enables designing and implementing sophisticated task-coalescing and scheduling techniques that accellerate irregular problems. As a challenge benchmark, we consider depth first search and obtain encouraging results.

Acknowledgments

We would like to thank the anonymous referees, editor, and Alexandros Tzannes for their helpful comments and suggestions.

References

[1] Umut A. Acar, Arthur Charguéraud, and Mike Rainey. Technical report associated with the present paper. http://arthur.chargueraud.org/research/2013/ppopp/full.pdf

[2] Umut A. Acar, Guy E. Blelloch, and Robert D. Blumofe. The data locality of work stealing. *Theory of Computing Systems (TOCS)*, 35(3):321–347, 2002.

[3] Nimar S. Arora, Robert D. Blumofe, and C. Greg Plaxton. Thread scheduling for multiprogrammed multiprocessors. In SPAA '98, pages 119–129. ACM Press, 1998.

[4] Petra Berenbrink, Tom Friedetzky, and Leslie Ann Goldberg. The natural work-stealing algorithm is stable. *SIAM J. Comput.*, 32:1260–1279, May 2003.

[5] Guy E. Blelloch, Rezaul A. Chowdhury, Phillip B. Gibbons, Vijaya Ramachandran, Shimin Chen, and Michael Kozuch. Provably good multicore cache performance for divide-and-conquer algorithms. In *In the Proceedings of the 19th ACM-SIAM Symposium on Discrete Algorithms*, pages 501–510, 2008.

[6] Guy E. Blelloch, Jeremy T. Fineman, Phillip B. Gibbons, and Julian Shun. Internally deterministic parallel algorithms can be fast. In PPoPP '12, pages 181–192, NY, USA, 2012. ACM.

[7] Guy E. Blelloch and John Greiner. A provable time and space efficient implementation of NESL. In ICFP '96, pages 213–225. ACM, 1996.

[8] R.D. Blumofe and C.E. Leiserson. Scheduling multithreaded computations by work stealing. *Foundations of Computer Science, IEEE Annual Symposium on*, 0:356–368, 1994.

[9] Robert D. Blumofe, Christopher F. Joerg, Bradley C. Kuszmaul, Charles E. Leiserson, Keith H. Randall, and Yuli Zhou. Cilk: an efficient multithreaded runtime system. In PPoPP, pages 207–216, 1995.

[10] Robert D. Blumofe and Charles E. Leiserson. Scheduling multithreaded computations by work stealing. *J. ACM*, 46:720–748, September 1999.

[11] F. Warren Burton and M. Ronan Sleep. Executing functional programs on a virtual tree of processors. In *Functional Programming Languages and Computer Architecture (FPCA '81)*, pages 187–194. ACM Press, October 1981.

[12] David Chase and Yossi Lev. Dynamic circular work-stealing deque. In SPAA '05, pages 21–28, 2005.

[13] David Chase and Yossi Lev. Dynamic circular work-stealing deque. Technical report, Sun Microsystems, 2005.

[14] Guojing Cong, Sreedhar B. Kodali, Sriram Krishnamoorthy, Doug Lea, Vijay A. Saraswat, and Tong Wen. Solving large, irregular graph problems using adaptive work-stealing. In *ICPP*, pages 536–545, 2008.

[15] Sivarama P. Dandamudi. The effect of scheduling discipline on dynamic load sharing in heterogeneous distributed systems. *Modeling, Analysis, and Simulation of Computer Systems, International Symposium on*, 0:17, 1997.

[16] J. Dinan, S. Olivier, G. Sabin, J. Prins, P. Sadayappan, and C.-W. Tseng. Dynamic load balancing of unbalanced computations using message passing. In IPDPS '07. IEEE International, march 2007.

[17] James Dinan, D. Brian Larkins, P. Sadayappan, Sriram Krishnamoorthy, and Jarek Nieplocha. Scalable work stealing. In *Proceedings of the Conference on High Performance Computing Networking, Storage and Analysis*, SC '09, pages 53:1–53:11. ACM, 2009.

[18] Derek L. Eager, Edward D. Lazowska, and John Zahorjan. A comparison of receiver-initiated and sender-initiated adaptive load sharing. *Perform. Eval.*, 6(1):53–68, 1986.

[19] Marc Feeley. A message passing implementation of lazy task creation. In *Parallel Symbolic Computing*, pages 94–107, 1992.

[20] Marc Feeley. *An efficient and general implementation of futures on large scale shared-memory multiprocessors*. PhD thesis, Brandeis University, MA, USA, 1993. UMI Order No. GAX93-22348.

[21] Marc Feeley. Polling efficiently on stock hardware. In *Proceedings of the conference on Functional programming languages and computer architecture*, FPCA '93, pages 179–187, NY, USA, 1993. ACM.

[22] Matthew Fluet, Mike Rainey, John Reppy, and Adam Shaw. Implicitly threaded parallelism in Manticore. *Journal of Functional Programming*, 20(5-6):1–40, 2011.

[23] Matteo Frigo, Charles E. Leiserson, and Keith H. Randall. The implementation of the Cilk-5 multithreaded language. In *PLDI*, pages 212–223, 1998.

[24] David Grove, Olivier Tardieu, David Cunningham, Ben Herta, Igor Peshansky, and Vijay Saraswat. A performance model for x10 applications: what's going on under the hood? In *Proceedings of the 2011 ACM SIGPLAN X10 Workshop*, pages 1:1–1:8, NY, USA, 2011. ACM.

[25] Robert H. Halstead, Jr. Implementation of multilisp: Lisp on a multiprocessor. In *Proceedings of the 1984 ACM Symposium on LISP and functional programming*, LFP '84, pages 9–17. ACM, 1984.

[26] Danny Hendler, Yossi Lev, Mark Moir, and Nir Shavit. A dynamic-sized nonblocking work stealing deque. *Distrib. Comput.*, 18:189–207, February 2006.

[27] Danny Hendler and Nir Shavit. Non-blocking steal-half work queues. In *PODC*, pages 280–289, 2002.

[28] Danny Hendler and Nir Shavit. Work dealing. In SPAA '02, pages 164–172. ACM, 2002.

[29] Tasuku Hiraishi, Masahiro Yasugi, Seiji Umatani, and Taiichi Yuasa. Backtracking-based load balancing. In PPoPP '09, pages 55–64. ACM, 2009.

[30] Intel. Cilk Plus. http://software.intel.com/en-us/articles/intel-cilk-plus/.

[31] Intel. Intel Xeon Processor X7550. Specifications at http://ark.intel.com/products/46498/Intel-Xeon-Processor-X7550-(18M-Cache-2_00-GHz-6_40-GTs-Intel-QPI).

[32] Gabriele Keller, Manuel M.T. Chakravarty, Roman Leshchinskiy, Simon Peyton Jones, and Ben Lippmeier. Regular, shape-polymorphic, parallel arrays in haskell. In ICFP '10, pages 261–272, 2010.

[33] Sanjeev Kumar, Christopher J. Hughes, and Anthony Nguyen. Carbon: architectural support for fine-grained parallelism on chip multiprocessors. *SIGARCH Computer Architecture News*, 35:162–173, June 2007.

[34] Maged M. Michael, Martin T. Vechev, and Vijay A. Saraswat. Idempotent work stealing. In PPoPP '09, pages 45–54, 2009.

[35] R. Mirchandaney, D. Towsley, and J.A. Stankovic. Analysis of the effects of delays on load sharing. *Computers, IEEE Transactions on*, 38(11):1513–1525, nov 1989.

[36] Michael Mitzenmacher. Analyses of load stealing models based on differential equations. In SPAA '98, pages 212–221, NY, USA, 1998. ACM.

[37] Larry Rudolph, Miriam Slivkin-Allalouf, and Eli Upfal. A simple load balancing scheme for task allocation in parallel machines. In SPAA '91, pages 237–245, NY, USA, 1991. ACM.

[38] Bratin Saha, Ali-Reza Adl-Tabatabai, Anwar Ghuloum, Mohan Rajagopalan, Richard L. Hudson, Leaf Petersen, Vijay Menon, Brian Murphy, Tatiana Shpeisman, Jesse Fang, Eric Sprangle, Anwar Rohillah, and Doug Carmean. Enabling scalability and performance in a large scale chip multiprocessor environment. *Technical Report. Intel Corp.*, 2006.

[39] Daniel Sanchez, Richard M. Yoo, and Christos Kozyrakis. Flexible architectural support for fine-grain scheduling. In ASPLOS '10, pages 311–322, NY, USA, 2010. ACM.

[40] Peter Sanders. Randomized receiver initiated load-balancing algorithms for tree-shaped computations. *Comput. J.*, 45(5):561–573, 2002.

[41] Barry Tannenbaum. Miser - a dynamically loadable memory allocator for multi-threaded applications. *Intel Software Network*, 2009.

[42] Marc Tchiboukdjian, Nicolas Gast, Denis Trystram, Jean-Louis Roch, and Julien Bernard. A tighter analysis of work stealing. In *Algorithms and Computation - 21st International Symposium, ISAAC 2010*, volume 6507 of LNCS, pages 291–302. Springer, 2010.

[43] Alexandros Tzannes. *Enhancing Productivity and Performance Portability of General-Purpose Parallel Programming*. PhD thesis, University of Maryland, 2012.

[44] Seiji Umatani, Masahiro Yasugi, Tsuneyasu Komiya, and Taiichi Yuasa. Pursuing laziness for efficient implementation of modern multithreaded languages. In *ISHPC*, pages 174–188, 2003.

A. Proof of efficiency

Assumptions We say that a processor makes a *transfer attempt* when, in the sender-initiated algorithm, it makes a deal attempt, or, in the receiver-initiated algorithm, when it polls on its reception cell and possibly answer a steal request. We assume that a transfer attempt always completes in one time step, and that, at any given time step, a non-idle processor makes a transfer attempt happens with probability $\frac{1}{\delta}$, for some constant $\delta > 1$. For the receiver-initiated algorithm, we assume that, in one time step, an idle processor is able to send a request to a busy processor and receive a response from this busy processor in case it is polling for requests in the same time step. For the sender-initiated algorithm, we assume that, in one time step, a busy processor is able to query the state of the idle processor and to deliver a task to this processor.

Consider a unit computation DAG describing a binary fork-join computation. In this DAG, each node is uniquely identified and corresponds to a task that takes one time step to complete. Each edge indicates a dependency between two tasks. Let T_1 be the total work (number of nodes) and T_∞ be the total depth (maximal length of a path in the DAG). We call a node a *fork node* if its out-degree is two. We define the *branching depth*, written F, as the maximal number of fork nodes in a path contained in the DAG.

Configurations Consider an execution of the computation DAG using P processors. A *configuration*, written s, represents the state of the processors during this execution. Concretely, it maps each processor to the list of nodes contained in its deque, in the deque order. In the initial configuration, called s_i, the initial task is in the deque of the processor 0, while all the other processors have empty deques. In the terminal configuration, called s_e, all the deques are empty. At each time step, the algorithm makes a transition from a configuration to another configuration (possibly the same). Let $\rho(s, s')$ denote the probability that, from configuration s, the algorithm makes a transition to the configuration s'. For any non-terminal configuration, the probabilities of the outgoing transitions add up to one, i.e., $\sum_{s'} \rho(s, s') = 1$ for any $s \neq s_e$.

Consider a particular computation DAG and let s_i denote the initial configuration of its execution. The *configuration graph* is a finite graph whose nodes correspond to the set of possible configurations reachable from s_i, and whose edges correspond to the possible transitions. More precisely, the configuration graph contains an edge from a configuration s to a configuration s' if s' is reachable in one time step from s, that is, if $\rho(s, s') > 0$. The configuration graph has s_i for source and s_e for sink. Each path in the configuration graph joining s_i to s_e describes one possible parallel execution of the computation DAG considered.

Tokens We analyse the execution time using tokens. At each time step, the algorithm makes a transition from a configuration to another, following an edge of the configuration graph. In a time step, P tokens are created: one *work token* is produced by each processor executing a task, one *communication token* is produced by each processor making a transfer attempt, and one *idle token* is produced by each idle processor. We introduce four variables to analyse the number of tokens produced during an execution path joining a given configuration s to the terminal configuration s_e. Let $W(s)$ be the number of work tokens issued starting at configuration s. (Note that the amount of work does does not depend on the execution path followed.) Let $K(s)$ be a random variable that denotes the number of communication tokens generated from s, Let $I(s)$ be a random variable that denotes the number of idle tokens generated from s. Let $T_P(s)$ be a random variable that denotes the length (in number of time steps) of the execution path taken from s. Note that, once the terminal configuration has been reached, no more tokens are produced, therefore $W(s_e) = K(s_e) = I(s_e) = T_P(s_e) = 0$. Note also that, since the total amount of work is T_1, we have $W(s_i) = T_1$. We let T_P be a shorthand for $T_P(s_i)$, which is a random variable that denotes the parallel execution time.

Throughout the proof, we write $\alpha(s)$ to denote the number of processors with an empty deque at configuration s. The value $\alpha(s)$ corresponds to the number of token produced when making a transition starting from configuration s. Note that, for any non-terminal configuration s, we have $\alpha(s) \leq P - 1$ because at least one processor has a non-empty deque.

Analysis We bound the expected execution time with P processors, $\mathbb{E}[T_P] = \mathbb{E}[T_P(s_i)]$, in terms of the total work T_1, the expected number of communication tokens $\mathbb{E}[K(s_i)]$, and the expected number of idle tokens $\mathbb{E}[I(s_i)]$. Using the fact that communication is only performed by busy processors, we then show that $\mathbb{E}[K(s_i)]$ does not exceed a fraction of T_1. To bound $\mathbb{E}[I(s_i)]$, we introduce a potential function Φ, which maps each configuration s to a natural number $\Phi(s)$. The potential function is defined in such a way that the potential decreases along any execution path. Moreover, the potential decreases significantly either when a processor has a single task to work on or when a processor succeeds in dealing a task. We conduct an inductive proof to establish that the expected number of idle tokens issued from a configuration s does not exceed $r \cdot \ln \Phi(s)$, for some constant r. A key lemma used in this proof establishes that the potential decreases by a factor at least $\frac{\alpha(s)}{r}$ during a time step that starts in a configuration s where $\alpha(s)$ processors are idle. Once the inductive proof is completed, we are able to deduce a bound on $\mathbb{E}[I(s_i)]$. Combining all these results yields a bound on the expected execution time $\mathbb{E}[T_P]$.

LEMMA A.1.
$$\mathbb{E}[T_P] = \frac{T_1}{P} + \frac{1}{P}\mathbb{E}[K(s_i)] + \frac{1}{P}\mathbb{E}[I(s_i)]$$

LEMMA A.2.
$$\mathbb{E}[K(s_i)] = \frac{T_1}{\delta - 1}$$

LEMMA A.3. *For any non-terminal configuration s,*
$$\mathbb{E}[I(s)] = \alpha(s) + \sum_{s'} \rho(s, s') \cdot \mathbb{E}[I(s')].$$

The definition of the potential function involves a few auxiliary definitions. The *depth potential* of a node u, written $d(u)$, is defined as T_∞ (the total depth) minus the minimal length of a path that reaches the node u from the root node (in the unit-cost DAG). The *fork potential* of a node u, written $f(u)$, is defined as F (the total branching depth) minus the minimal number of fork nodes in a path that reaches the node u from the root node. Given a task u and a deque s, we let $b(u, Q)$ be equal to 0 if u is at the bottom of Q and to 1 otherwise. We let c be 1.0 in sender-initiated algorithm and $\frac{1}{1-1/e} \approx 1.58$ in receiver-initiated algorithm. We define $\mu = \frac{1-2e^{-\kappa}}{c\delta}$ and κ to be any constant such that $\kappa > \ln 2$, which ensures $\mu > 0$. We define the potential $\Phi(Q)$ of a deque Q as follows.

$$\Phi(Q) \equiv \begin{cases} 0 & \text{if } Q \text{ is empty} \\ e^{\mu D(Q) + \kappa F(Q)} & \text{otherwise} \end{cases}$$
$$\text{where} \quad D(Q) \equiv \max_{u \in Q} d(u)$$
$$F(Q) \equiv \max_{u \in Q} f(u) + b(u, Q)$$

We then define the potential $\Phi(s)$ of a configuration s as the sum of the potential of all the deques, i.e. $\Phi(s) = \sum_{i \in I} \Phi(Q_i(s))$, where I denotes the set of all processors and where $Q_i(s)$ denotes the deque of processor i in the configuration s. Note that a potential is always greater or equal to zero and that the terminal configuration s_e is the only configuration whose potential is equal to zero.

Our algorithm follows the same *deque discipline* as in work stealing: processors push and pop tasks at the bottom of their deque when working locally, and migrate tasks taken from the top of their deque.

LEMMA A.4 (Deque discipline). *If u and u' are two nodes contained in a same deque Q in such a way that u is located above u', then $d(u') \leq d(u) - 1$ and $f(u') \leq f(u) - 1$.*

LEMMA A.5 (Decrease in potential). *The total potential never increases: if $\rho(s, s') > 0$ then $\Phi(s') \leq \Phi(s)$.*

LEMMA A.6. *Consider a configuration s, where $\alpha(s)$ processors are idle. Consider a busy processor with more than one task in its deque in this configuration. If this processor makes a transfer attempt, then a task migration happens with probability at least $\frac{\alpha(s)}{P-1} \cdot \frac{1}{c} \cdot (1 - \frac{1}{\delta})$.*

Let s and s' be two configurations such that $\rho(s, s') > 0$. Let i be a busy processor in s. We define $\Delta_i(s, s')$ to be equal to: 0 if i sends no task during the transition from s to s', and to $\Phi(\{u\})$ if u is the unique task sent by i in this transition.

LEMMA A.7. *Let r be equal to $\frac{P-1}{(1-1/\delta) \cdot (1-e^{-\mu})}$. Let s be a non-terminal configuration, and let i be the index of a busy processor in s. Then,*
$$\sum_{s'} \rho(s, s') \cdot \frac{\Phi(Q_i(s)) - \Phi(Q_i(s')) - \Delta_i(s, s')}{\Phi(Q_i(s))} \geq \frac{\alpha(s)}{r}.$$

LEMMA A.8. *For any non-terminal configuration s,*
$$\sum_{s'} \rho(s, s') \cdot \frac{\Phi(s) - \Phi(s')}{\Phi(s)} \geq \frac{\alpha(s)}{r}.$$

LEMMA A.9. *For any non-terminal configuration s,*
$$\alpha(s) \leq r \cdot \sum_{s' \neq s_e} \rho(s, s') \ln \frac{\Phi(s)}{\Phi(s')}.$$

We have just bounded the expected relative decrease in potential. This result will help us prove the inequality $\mathbb{E}[I(s)] \leq r \cdot \ln \Phi(s)$. We conduct this proof by induction on a well-founded relation, written $\prec$. The relation $\prec$ is defined below, as a lexicographical order that first compares the amount of remaining work and then compares the number of idle processors.
$$s' \prec s \equiv W(s') < W(s) \lor \left(W(s') = W(s) \land \alpha(s') < \alpha(s)\right)$$

LEMMA A.10. *For any configurations s and s',*
$$\rho(s, s') > 0 \implies s' \prec s \lor s' = s.$$

LEMMA A.11. *For any non-terminal configuration s,*
$$\mathbb{E}[I(s)] \leq r \cdot \ln \Phi(s).$$

LEMMA A.12.
$$\mathbb{E}[I(s_i)] \leq \left(1 + \frac{1}{\delta-1}\right) \cdot (P-1) \cdot \frac{\mu}{1-e^{-\mu}} \cdot \left(T_\infty + \frac{\kappa}{\mu}F\right)$$

Proof. We apply Lemma A.11 to the initial configuration s_i. In this configuration, there is a single task u_0 placed in the deque of processor with index 0. Its potential is $\Phi(s_i) = \Phi(Q_0(s_i)) = e^{\mu d(u_0) + \kappa f(u_0)} = e^{\mu T_\infty + \kappa F}$. So, we have: $\mathbb{E}[I(s_i)] \leq r \cdot (\mu T_\infty + \kappa F)$. Unfolding the definition $r = \frac{P-1}{(1-\frac{1}{\delta}) \cdot (1-e^{-\mu})}$ gives
$$\mathbb{E}[I(s_i)] \leq \frac{P-1}{1-\frac{1}{\delta}} \cdot \frac{\mu}{1-e^{-\mu}} \cdot \left(T_\infty + \frac{\kappa}{\mu}F\right). \qquad \square$$

LEMMA A.13. *The expected parallel execution time, $\mathbb{E}[T_P]$, is less than*
$$\left(1 + \frac{1}{\delta-1}\right) \cdot \left(\frac{T_1}{P} + \frac{P-1}{P} \cdot \frac{\mu}{1-e^{-\mu}} \cdot (T_\infty + 2.68 \cdot c\delta F)\right).$$

Proof. The proof is as follows.
$$\mathbb{E}[T_P] = \frac{1}{P}\left(T_1 + \mathbb{E}[K(s_i)] + \mathbb{E}[I(s_i)]\right)$$
by Lemma A.1
$$\leq \frac{1}{P}\left(T_1 + \frac{1}{\delta-1}T_1 + \left(1 + \frac{1}{\delta-1}\right)\frac{P-1}{1}\frac{\mu}{1-e^{-\mu}}\left(T_\infty + \frac{\kappa}{\mu}F\right)\right)$$
by Lemma A.2 and Lemma A.12
$$\leq \left(1 + \frac{1}{\delta-1}\right) \cdot \left(\frac{T_1}{P} + \frac{\mu}{1-e^{-\mu}}\frac{P-1}{P}\left(T_\infty + \frac{\kappa}{1-2e^{-\kappa}}c\delta F\right)\right)$$
rearranging terms and unfolding the definition of μ

At this point, we are still completely free to instantiate κ with any value such that $\kappa > \ln(2) \approx 0.69$. We take $\kappa \approx 1.67835$, which minimizes the value of $\frac{\kappa}{1-2e^{-\kappa}}$. We then have $1 - 2e^{-\kappa} \approx 0.626637$ and $\frac{\kappa}{1-2e^{-\kappa}} \approx 2.67835 < 2.68$. $\qquad \square$

StreamScan: Fast Scan Algorithms for GPUs without Global Barrier Synchronization

Shengen Yan[1,2,3]   Guoping Long[1]   Yunquan Zhang[1,2]

[1]Lab. of Parallel Software and Computational Science, Institute of Software, Chinese Academy of Sciences
[2]State Key Laboratory of Computing Science, the Chinese Academy of Sciences
[3]Graduate University of Chinese Academy of Sciences
yanshengen@gmail.com, guoping@iscas.ac.cn, zyq@mail.rdcps.ac.cn

Abstract

Scan (also known as prefix sum) is a very useful primitive for various important parallel algorithms, such as sort, BFS, SpMV, compaction and so on. Current state of the art of GPU based scan implementation consists of three consecutive Reduce-Scan-Scan phases. This approach requires at least two global barriers and 3N (N is the problem size) global memory accesses. In this paper we propose StreamScan, a novel approach to implement scan on GPUs with only one computation phase. The main idea is to restrict synchronization to only adjacent workgroups, and thereby eliminating global barrier synchronization completely. The new approach requires only 2N global memory accesses and just one kernel invocation. On top of this we propose two important optimizations to further boost performance speedups, namely thread grouping to eliminate unnecessary local barriers, and register optimization to expand the on chip problem size. We designed an auto-tuning framework to search the parameter space automatically to generate highly optimized codes for both AMD and Nvidia GPUs. We implemented our technique with OpenCL. Compared with previous fast scan implementations, experimental results not only show promising performance speedups, but also reveal dramatic different optimization tradeoffs between Nvidia and AMD GPU platforms.

Categories and Subject Descriptors   D.1.3 [**Concurrent Programming**]: Parallel programming

Keywords   Scan, prefix-sum, OpenCL, CUDA, GPU, Parallel algorithms

1. Introduction

Scan, also known as prefix-sum, is a very important problem in parallel computing. Blelloch [1] first introduced scan as a fundamental primitive and discussed its possible applications [2].Later on, more and more parallel applications of scan emerged, such as sort [6, 7, 8, 9, 10, 11], BFS [12, 13], SpMV [13, 14], parallel compaction [15],minimal spanning tree [16] and linked list prefix computations [17], etc. The (inclusive) scan problem is defined as follows:
Given a sequence with n input elements:

$$[a_0, a_1, ..., a_{n-2}, a_{n-1}]$$

Return a sequence with n output elements:

$$[a_0, (a_0 \oplus a_1), ..., (a_0 \oplus a_1 \oplus ... \oplus a_{n-2} \oplus a_{n-1})]$$

The $\oplus$ symbol denotes a binary reduction operator, which satisfies the associative law and commutative law. The sequential algorithm to compute prefix sums is simple. Over the years several well known parallel scan algorithms have been proposed [3, 4, 5]. However, it is still surprisingly challenging for high performance parallel implementation, especially when considering target hardware architecture specifics.

In recent years, GPUs emerge as a promising platform for various computation intensive applications. At the same time a lot of optimization skills proposed on GPUs [29]. Compared with CPUs, GPUs have much higher computation density and off chip memory bandwidth. For both Nvidia and AMD GPUs, the ultra high computing power comes from many processing cores organized in a highly hierarchical manner. On the high level, although scan has relatively low computation density, there is ample inherent parallelism. This, combined with the high memory bandwidth of GPUs, makes it possible to achieve promising speedups. Hence, over the years many fast scan algorithms [20, 21, 24, 28] have been proposed on GPU platforms.

Current state of the art scan algorithms [20, 21] on GPUs consist of three Reduce-Scan-Scan phases. The idea is to partition the computation into three consecutive steps. Threads of all workgroups work together to complete each step one by one. Therefore, global barrier synchronization is needed between successive steps. Because of this, this approach requires at least 3N (N is the problem size) global memory accesses, which is detrimental to scan like memory intensive algorithms.

At the micro-architecture level, there are two major flavors of designs for the instruction pipelines. One is the scalar approach on Nvidia GPUs. The other is VLIW on AMD GPUs. To the best of our knowledge, current state of the art implementations only explored the optimization space for scalar architectures, neglecting the fact that the same set of optimization techniques may have drastic different implications on different hardware platforms.

In this paper, we propose StreamScan, a novel scan algorithm for GPUs. Compared to current state of the art, StreamScan has two unique features. First, by restricting synchronization only to adjacent workgroups, we eliminate global barriers completely (Section 3.1). This reduces global memory traffic from at least 3N to only ~2N. On top of this we propose two important optimizations to further improve performance, namely thread grouping to eliminate unnecessary local barriers, and register optimization to expanding the on chip problem size (Section 3.3). Second, we explore the optimization space across both Nvidia and AMD

GPUs. To facilitate this task, we implement our algorithm with OpenCL. Our experimental results show not only superior performance speedups, but also reveal very different optimization tradeoffs on both platforms (Section 4.2).

Specifically, we make the following contributions:

a) We propose StreamScan, a novel scan algorithm on GPUs which requires only ~2N global memory accesses;

b) We propose thread grouping, an optimization to eliminate redundant local barriers while loading data to local memory. Instead of arranging local memory data as a 2D matrix as MatrixScan [21], we organize the data in 3D manner;

c) We propose register optimization to exploit register file space to enlarge the solvable problem size on chip.

d) We propose a performance auto-tuning framework to explore the parameter space for optimal implementations for both Nvidia and AMD GPUs automatically.

The terminology used in our work is based on the OpenCL specification [30]. This paper is organized as follows. Section 2 discusses research background and motivations of our work. Section 3 presents the StreamScan algorithm. Section 4 presents experimental results and our main findings. Section 5 discusses related works. The final section concludes our work.

2. Background & Motivation

Parallel scan algorithms on CPU architectures are well known [1, 2]. Compared to CPUs, GPUs have much higher computation density and off-chip memory bandwidth. Therefore there is strong incentive to parallelize scan on GPU platforms. However, because of the complex, deep memory hierarchies and week memory consistency models, high performance parallel scan implementations on GPUs are much more challenging. In this section, we review current state of the art of parallel scan algorithms on GPUs and motivate our approach.

2.1 Existing scan algorithms on GPUs

Existing fast scan implementations on GPUs all exploit the hierarchical parallelism of the algorithm. On the high level, the workspace is partitioned into multiple workgroups (or blocks) of work-items. The design space is twofold. The first is the design of an inter-block orchestration mechanism. The second is intra-block scan implementation.

2.1.1 Inter-block orchestration mechanism

An intuitive, yet memory consuming way to perform scan is a three phase Scan-Scan-Add approach[23], as shown in Figure 1. In the first phase, the input array is partitioned into a number of blocks and each block is scanned locally. After this, the last element of each block is stored into an intermediate array I according to the block order. The second phase is to perform exclusive scan on the intermediate array I. In the last phase, for the k-th block

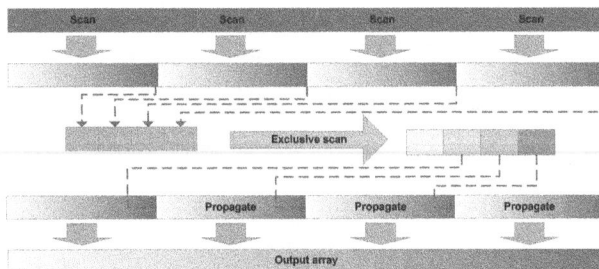

Figure 1. Scan-Scan-Add inter-block orchestration mechanism.

(except the first block), each element within the block is added by $I[k]$ of the intermediate array. Global barriers are needed between successive phases. This approach requires at least 4N global memory accesses. If the barrier is implemented by a kernel invocation, it also suffers from kernel invocation overheads.

A better three-phase approach is the Reduce-Scan-Scan [21], as shown in Figure 2. In the first phase, the input array is partitioned into multiple blocks, and each block is reduced rather than scanned. The result of each block is stored in the intermediate array I, according to the block order. The second phase is the same, to perform exclusive scan on the intermediate array I. In the

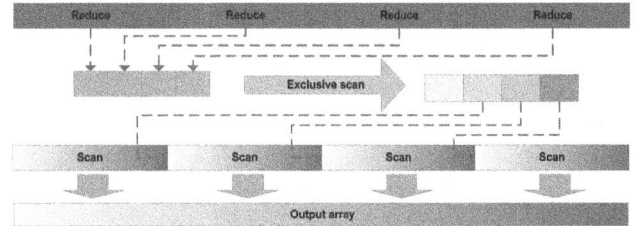

Figure 2. Reduce-scan-Scan inter-block orchestration mechanism.

last phase, each block is scanned. After this, for the k-th block (except the first block), each element within the block is added by $I[k]$. By moving the block local scan from the first phase to the third phase, the number of global accesses is reduced from 4N to 3N.

The size of the intermediate array depends on the number of partitions of the input array. In the original implementation [21], the size can be so large that it is impossible to perform scan on intermediate array with on workgroup. In this case recursive partitioning of the array is needed, and thus can incur further implementation complexity and performance overheads. This issue can be addressed by fixing the size of the intermediate array by using static threads [24].

2.1.2 Intra-block scan implementation

One common intra-block scan implementation is the tree based approach, which realizes a well known two-phase work-efficient algorithm [25]. On GPU platforms, the challenge is load balance and potential bank conflicts (if on-chip local memory (shared memory in CUDA) is used for data buffering).

A better approach for intra-block implementation is MatrixScan [21], which is in essence another three phase Reduce-Scan-Scan in local memory, as shown in Figure 3. The input 1D array is arranged as a 2D matrix in local memory. The number of rows is the same as the number of threads in a workgroup. In the first phase, each thread performs reduce on a row in the matrix sequentially and stores results into an auxiliary array C. A local barrier is necessary to ensure that all threads have finished before proceed to the next phase. In the second phase, the auxiliary array C is scanned using several threads for best performance. Another local

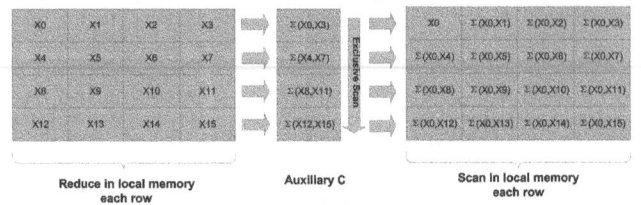

Figure 3. 2D Matrix Scan.

Table 1. Comparison of Our Work to Previous Works.

Strategy	Global memory accesses	Global Barriers	Cross Platform Analysis
Scan-Scan-Add[23]	~4N	>=2	No
Reduce-Scan-Scan[20]	~3N	>=2	No
StreamScan	**~2N**	**None**	**Yes**

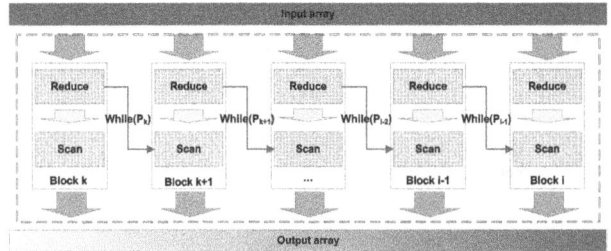

Figure 4. StreamScan Architecture (P is the sync condition).

barrier is needed here. Finally in the last phase, each thread scans its corresponding row again taking the corresponding results of array C to the first element. Potential local memory bank conflicts can be reduced substantially by appropriate column padding to the matrix.

2.2 Motivation of this work

All fast scan implementations on GPUs partition the input array into multiple blocks, and perform computation and synchronization at block granularity. However, the main issue with all variants of the three-phase approach is the global barrier synchronization. Because of the limitation of the on-chip memory, global barrier will suffer global memory traffic overheads. If the global barrier is implemented via kernel invocations, there are also extra runtime overheads.

There is another perspective to understand the scan problem, especially when the problem size is large. Instead of partitioning the computation horizontally into three phases, it's possible to partition the data into multiple blocks, and perform scan at block granularity sequentially. Although the parallelism at the block level is decreased (there is data dependence between adjacent blocks), there is ample parallelism while scanning within the block. In this case, synchronization occurs only between adjacent blocks, global barriers are not necessary. In this algorithm, we need to cache the processing data in the on-chip memory until the whole work completed in the same block. However, we only need to invoke one kernel and since the early exit workgroups will free the on-chip resources, the number of global memory accesses can be reduced to approximate 2N. There are two major challenges to this approach. First, how to fully exploit the parallel computation power of the GPU while scanning one block? Second, how to determine the optimal block size in order to balance between synchronization overheads and kernel performance?

The design space of the intra-block scan implementation also deserves detailed exploration. First, is the traditional intra-block scan approach still suitable for the StreamScan? Second, since the algorithm is memory intensive, how to access the global memory efficiently? Third, due to the large register file size of modern GPUs, how to fully leverage its space to increase the solvable problem size on-chip for the scan problem? Fourth, optimal implementations on different GPUs depend on a set of key parameters. An automatic parameter searching and tuning framework is necessary to generate optimal code versions for various GPU platforms. Table1 summarizes key features of our approach. We will all challenges in detail in the next section.

3. StreamScan

In this section, we present StreamScan, our approach for fast scan implementation on GPUs. We first review StreamScan architec-

ture, and especially how this organization can fully exploits the parallel computation capability of modern GPUs. We then discuss the synchronization mechanism between adjacent blocks. In Section 3.3 we present various intra-block scan algorithms within the StreamScan framework.

3.1 Inter-Block orchestration

Figure 4 illustrates the high level architecture of StreamScan. The input data array is partitioned into multiple blocks. Then each block is scanned with a three-phase Reduce-Scan-Scan intra-block algorithm. After all blocks have been scanned, results are written to the output array.

However, there are data dependences between adjacent blocks. That is, scan of block i must take the accumulated result of all previous blocks as input. Luckily this accumulated result can be generated after the first reduce phase of the intra-block scan. Thus inter-block synchronization happens only after the first phase. Note that the first reduce phases of all blocks can proceed simultaneously. Abundant inter-block parallelism is available.

Modern GPUs have a hierarchy of parallel processing units. For AMD GPUs, one chip has multiple compute units (CU), with each CU containing a number of processing cores. For StreamScan to work on practical problem sizes, typically the number of blocks is much larger than the number of CUs. We therefore map all intra-block scans on blocks to all CUs. Since adjacent block synchronization occurs only after the first phase, there is still ample parallelism to keep all CUs busy.

The mapping of intra-block scan to all cores within the compute unit is critical to performance. In order to eliminate global barriers completely, we assign one workgroup for each block scan. Parallelism in all three phases is mapped uniformly among all cores. The thread organization within the workgroup is tuned automatically to ensure proper computation overlap and latency hiding. Design details are in Section 3.3. Note that the parallelization and computation mapping framework can be applied to Nvidia GPUs in a similar way.

3.2 Block synchronization

Inter-block synchronization is performed via shared global memory. Like previous algorithms [20], we also need an intermediate array I to store reduction results of all workgroups. The difference is that in our approach, the array I not only stores reduction results but also serves as a flag variable array for adjacent block synchronization. At the beginning, we initialize all elements of the flag array to a fixed value F. Since we can't guarantee the execution order of different workgroups, we initialize the array on the host side before upload it to GPU memory. Compared to the input array to be scanned, the size of the intermediate array is very small (~2K elements for the input array with 16M elements). Thus the upload overhead of the initial intermediate array is negligible.

```
gid: workgroup id.

lid: thread local id.

I: intermediate array.

r:The reduction value of current workgroup;

s: The reduction value of the previous workgroups.

F: The initial value of the intermediate array I.

void   ADJACENT_SYNCHRONIZATION(int  gid,  int  lid,  __global
volatile int  *I, int r, __local int *s)

{

    if(lid==0) {

        int p=0;

        if(gid == 0)  I[0] = r;

        else{

            while((p=I[gid - 1])== F){}

            I[gid] = p + r;

        }

        *s = p;

    }

    barrier(CLK_LOCAL_MEM_FENCE);

}
```

Figure 5. Adjacent synchronization.

The inter-block synchronization algorithm is shown in Figure 5. For each workgroup, only the first thread (lid=0) is necessary to execute the while loop. A local barrier is needed to make sure that only after the first thread has obtained the reduction result of the previous workgroup, other threads in the same workgroup can continue execution. In order to broadcast the reduction value of the previous workgroup to all threads in the workgroup, we use the on-chip local memory (shared memory in CUDA) to store the reduction result. The purpose of the *volatile* keyword is to prevent the compiler from caching stale results to the register file. This guarantees that each workgroup can get the latest value from the intermediate array once the previous workgroup has produced the result.

This algorithm works fine when the on-chip cache capability is disabled. In some platforms, the cache is enabled by default. If the cache between the register file and global memory is enabled, it's still possible to get stale cached copies in each iteration of the while loop. One possible way to address this issue is using atomic primitives to fetch the reduction value of the previous workgroup.

3.3   Intra-Block scan algorithm

In principle, any local scan algorithm can fit into the StreamScan framework. There are three basic approaches for our purpose. A simple one is the classical tree based scan [25], but suffers from the issues like load imbalance among all threads and potential bank conflicts if on-chip local memory is used as data buffers.

A better approach is the three-phase Scan-Scan-Add algorithm. Although it does not suffer from issues faced by the tree based scan, there are two other issues, which may throttle its efficiency. As discussed in Section 3.1, each workgroup (except the starting workgroup) synchronizes with its previous one to retrieve the reduction result at the end of the first phase. While the first scan phase can generate a reduction result, it is much more time consuming than a direct reduction phase. The result is that the delayed inter-block synchronization delays the freedom of dynamic

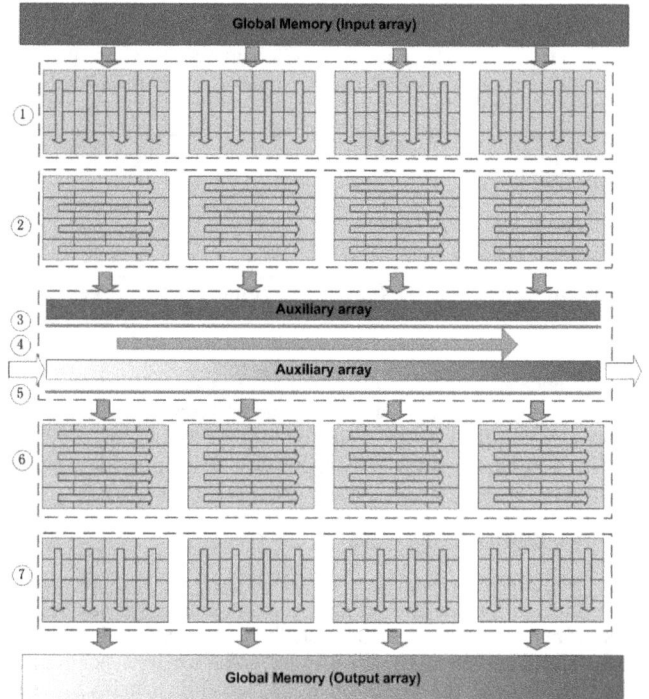

Steps of 3D MatrixScan. ① Loads data from global memory to local memory. The arrow direction shows the access order of a thread. ② Performs reduction on the row of the matrix. Each thread is in charge of a row. ③ Local Barrier, which ensures all threads have written their reduction results to the auxiliary array. ④ Scan of the on-chip auxiliary array and add the accumulation value of the previous workgroups. The reduction result is sent to the next workgroup via adjacent synchronization. ⑤ Local Barrier, which ensures the scan on auxiliary array is finished. ⑥ Propagates the auxiliary array to the first element of each row in the matrix, and then performs scan on each row of the matrix. ⑦ Store scanned results back to global memory

Figure 6. 3D MatrixScan.

parallelism. Another issue is the on-chip local memory traffic. The data array needs to be updated in place in both the first scan and the third add phases.

The third approach is the Reduce-Scan-Scan algorithm. Compared with Scan-Scan-Add, since Reduce is much faster than Scan, adjacent block synchronization can complete as early as possible. Moreover in the first phase, only the reduction result is needed. It's not necessary to update any element of the data array in local memory. We therefore base our intra-block scan implementation on the Reduce-Scan-Scan algorithm.

An efficient way to implement the three-phase scan algorithm is matrix based scan [21]. In StreamScan, the matrix based intra-block scan consists of three basic steps. In the first step, the input data is loaded from global memory to on-chip space (local memory and registers) and organized as a multidimensional matrix. Next we perform reduction on each row of the matrix and store the reduction result to an auxiliary array and perform a scan on the auxiliary array. In the second step, we propagate the reduction value of current workgroup to the next one and each workgroup except the first one synchronizes with its previous workgroup to retrieve the reduction result. In the last step, we perform a scan on each row after propagating the accumulation result of the previous rows and the previous workgroups to the first elements in the row.

The primary challenge with intra-block scan is how to balance three performance critical tradeoffs. This includes: (1) Optimal matrix dimension, 2D or 3D? (2) The tradeoff between memory efficiency and implementation complexity; (3) What's the sweet spot by using register space to enlarge the solvable on chip problem size? In the rest of the subsection we discuss each tradeoff in detail.

3.3.1 2D Matrix VS. 3D Matrix

In order to coalesce off chip memory accesses as much as possible, the traditional 2D matrix based intra-block scan will load the data in the local memory as a transposed manner compared with storing them. This discrepancy of access ordering necessitates a local barrier between loading data from global memory and actual computation. This hurts performance, especially so when we use the register file space to enlarge the on chip working set.

Instead of 2D matrix arrangement, we propose a novel organization to eliminate unnecessary local barriers, as shown in Figure 6. We call this technique thread grouping in this paper. The basic idea is to arrange threads of the same workgroup into several no more than wavefront (warp) size groups. Each group loads and processes a sub-block of the input array independently, following the 2D matrix arrangement approach. By treating the thread group as a third dimension, we transform the input array into a logical 3D matrix. For each group, in order to coalesce off chip memory accesses as much as possible, there still exist access transpose of the matrix. However, no explicit local barrier is needed because the hardware will ensure that all threads within the same wavefront (warp) will complete loading data into local memory in a synchronized manner. This is important if we use the register to further enlarge the on chip working set (section 3.3.4).

In our 3D arrangement, each group is responsible for a 2D array. Each thread within the group processes a row. This access pattern is prone to bank conflicts. By appropriately padding extra columns, the number of bank conflicts can be reduced quit a lot.

3.3.2 Expanding working set via register space

On modern GPUs, the register file size is much larger than the local memory size. One advantage of large register file size is to hold as many thread contexts on chip as possible. While more thread contexts may enable more potential for latency hiding, it also increases the thread management overhead. A balanced implementation achieves latency hiding with a reasonable number of threads. In this case, it makes sense to expand the solvable problem size on chip by exploiting register storage.

As discussed in the previous section, we partition all threads within the workgroup into multiple groups. Each group processes a data segment arranged as a 2D array. This array is a logical structure, because physically we partition it into two components: one in the register file, and the other in local memory.

With this partitioned array structure, an immediate issue is how to load data into the register space. In OpenCL, we can declare thread local static arrays to allocate space in the register file. A simple approach is for each thread to load its own data from global memory into its on-chip space directly. While this approach works, memory requests of all threads exhibits strided (hard to coalesce in hardware) access pattern, which is not efficient on modern GPUs.

Another approach to load data into the register space is via local memory. First, data is loaded from global memory in fully coalesced way into the local memory. After this each thread read the row corresponding to itself to its local register space. While this approach fully exploits off chip memory bandwidth, the kernel implementation is relatively complex (Section 3.3.3).

Since the 2D matrix is partitioned in a column major way, each thread needs to access both the register file and the local memory

```
__kernel void StridedStreamScan(__global VEC_TYPE *src, __global
volatile int *I, __global VEC_TYPE *dst)
{
    int gid = get_group_id(0), lid = get_local_id(0),c, p=0,src_id;
    __local int C[GROUP_SIZE], s;
    __local VEC_TYPE lm[GROUP_SIZE][L];
    VEC_TYPE re[R],temp;
    src_id = gid * GROUP_SIZE * (R+L) + lid * (R+L);
    for(i=0;i<L;i++){
        temp = src[src_id+i];
        p = SCAN_ON_VECTOR(temp, p);
        lm[lid][i] = temp;
    }
    for(i=0;i<R;i++){
        re[i] = src[src_id + i + L];
        p = SCAN_ON_VECTOR(re[i],p);
    }
    C[lid] = p;
    barrier(CLK_LOCAL_MEM_FENCE);
    EXCLUSIVE_TREE_BASED_SCAN(C, lid);
    if(lid==0)  c = C[GROUP_SIZE - 1];
    ADJACENT_SYNCHRONIZATION( gid, lid, I, c, &s);
    for(i=0; i<R; i++){ dst[src_id + i + L] = re[i] + s + C[lid]; }
    for(i=0;i<L;i++){
        temp=lm[lid][i];
        dst[src_id + i] = temp + s + C[lid];
    }
}
```

VEC_TYPE: vector type, such as int4, int8.

GROUP_SIZE: The number of threads in a workgroup.

R: The number of the used vector registers per thread.

L: Used local memory size per thread.

SCAN_ON_VECTOR (): Scan on all components of the vector. The second parameter is the propagation value. Return the reduction value.

EXCLUSIVE_TREE_BASED_SCAN(): Perform a exclusive scan on the auxiliary array C using the tree-based scan algorithm.

ADJACENT_SYNCHRONIZATION(): Fetching the accumulation result of previous workgroups from the intermediate array I to s, and write c to I.

Figure 7. Strided StreamScan (Access the global memory in strided way).

to reduce or scan a row of the 2D matrix. As discussed earlier, inter-block synchronization happens after the first reduce phase of each workgroup. One possible optimization here is for each thread to reduce in place while loading data into its local register array.

3.3.3 Memory efficiency VS. Kernel complexity

As discussed in section 3.3.1, in order to access global memory in coalesced manner, regardless of the matrix dimension (2D or 3D), the access order for producing data to and consuming data from the local memory matrix is different. Specifically, all threads write the same row of the matrix at the same time while producing data, and all read the same column at the same time while consuming data. Introducing register space to further expand on-chip working set size further complicates this issue. In order to access the global memory in coalesced manner, data must be loaded into local memory first and then transferred into the register space. However, since local memory space is much smaller, such data transfers may happen multiple times. Arranging local memory data in 3D manner eliminates local barriers between producing data to and consuming data from local memory buffers. This is more useful if the register space is used, because of the increased memory traffic between global memory and the register file through local memory. However, both optimizations are not free. They increase the OpenCL kernel implementation complexity accordingly.

Note that in the Reduce and Scan computation phases, each thread within a workgroup processes only one row of the matrix. The simple approach is to let each thread read its own portion of data, resulting in strided global memory access patterns. This is much less efficient than coalesced access, but there is no access order discrepancy. Therefore it is not necessary either to arrange data in 3D manner. Also there is no need to transfer data into registers through local memory.

This is the delicate tradeoff between memory efficiency and implementation complexity. Does the improved global memory access speed outweigh the overhead of more complex implementation? We will explore this in more detail in the experimental evaluation section.

3.3.4 Putting it all together

We implemented two families of intra-block scan algorithms, with varying considerations on memory efficiency and kernel complexity. The one with smaller overhead uses strided memory access using register as transmit buffer. The one most sophisticated algorithm takes advantage of the coalesced memory access, but using local memory as transmit buffer. In this paper, we use *Strided* and *Coalesced* to denote the two algorithms outlined above, respectively. Details for *Strided* and *Coalesced* algorithms are shown in Figure 7 and Figure 8, respectively.

Another problem is the potential deadlock due to the unguaranteed runtime scheduling order of workgroups. The underlying assumption of this concern is that we distribute the work of input sequence based on the static workgroup ID defined by the static function "get_group_id()". To solve this problem we can allocate all workgroup IDs dynamically. Work distribution among all workgroups is done based on this dynamically allocated runtime workgroup ID. Figure 9 illustrates the idea. Compared to the static allocation mechanism, performance overhead of the dynamic approach is less than 2%.

3.4 Auto-tuning framework

We implemented StreamScan with OpenCL. We designed an auto-tuning framework to search the parameter space automatically. It explores all possible parameter configurations to generate optimal implementations for each algorithm on both NVIDIA and AMD platforms. Table 2 shows all tunable parameters in our auto-tuning framework. These parameters are not independent. For each kernel, the framework explores the entire space for all possible combinations of the rest parameters. A common optimization while loading from global memory is using vectors. This vector length is also tunable. The group size parameter selects optimal dimensions for the 3D matrix, as discussed in section 3.3.1. For each parameter we list the possible values in table 2, but note that the actual value assignment depends on resource constraints of specific GPU platforms. The tuning process starts with initialization, which includes basic configuration of the OpenCL environment and the parameter space. Then for each kernel, it

```
__kernel void CoalescedStreamScan(__global int *src, __global volatile
int *I, __global int *dst)
{
    int gid = get_group_id(0), lid = get_local_id(0);
    __local int lm [BUNCH_NUM][BUNCH_SIZE][LOCAL_SIZE];
    __local int C[GROUP_SIZE], s;
    int re[R*BUNCH_SIZE],i=0, p=0, c;
    for(i=0;i<R; i++){
        LOAD_GLOBAL_ TO_LOCAL(src, lm, gid, lid, i);
        LOAD_LOCAL_TO_REGISTER ( lm, re,  lid ,i); }
    // the reduction value stores in p.
    p = ROW_REDUCE_ON_REG (re,  lid, R, p);
    for(i=0;i<L;i++)
        LOAD_GLOBAL_TO_LOCAL(src,lm,gid, lid,i+R);
    //p: input is the previous reduction value. return reduction value.
    p = ROW_REDUCE_ON_LOCAL (lm,  lid, L, p);
    C[lid] = p;
    barrier(CLK_LOCAL_MEM_FENCE);
    EXCLUSIVE_TREE_BASED_SCAN( C, lid);
    if(lid==0)   c = C[GROUP_SIZE - 1];
    ADJACENT_SYNCHRONIZATION( gid, lid, I, c, &s);
    p=ROW_SCAN_ON_REG (re,  lid, R, c, s, p);
    p=ROW_SCAN_ON_LOCAL (lm,  lid, L, c, s, p);
    for(i=0;i<L;i++)
        PUSH_LOCAL_TO_GLOBAL(lm, dst, gid, lid,i+R);
    for(i=0;i<R;i++){
        PUSH_REGISTER_TO_LOCAL(re,lm,lid,i);
        PUSH_LOCAL_TO_GLOBAL(lm, dst,gid, lid,i);  }
}
```

BUNCH_NUM: The number of thread groups in a workgroup.

BUNCH_SIZE: The number of the threads in a group.

GROUP_SIZE: The number of the threads in a workgroup.

R: The number of register pieces.   L: The number of local memory pieces.

LOCAL_SIZE: L * BUNCH_SIZE + 1.

LOAD_GLOBAL_TO_LOCAL(): Load data from global memory to the local memory and organized as a 3D matrix; Each thread group in charge of a flat.

LOAD_LOCAL_TO_REGISTER(): Load data from local memory to the registers.

ROW_REDUCE_ON_LOCAL(): Perform a reduction on every local row.

ROW_REDUCE_ON_REG (): Perform a reduction on every register row.

ROW_SCAN_ON_LOCAL(): Perform a scan on every local row.

ROW_SCAN_ON_REG (): Perform a scan on every register row.

EXCLUSIVE_TREE_BASED_SCAN(): Perform a exclusive scan on the auxiliary array C using the tree-based scan algorithm.

ADJACENT_SYNCHRONIZATION(): Fetching the accumulation result of previous workgroups from the intermediate array I to s, and write c to I.

PUSH_REGISTER_TO_LOCAL(): Push the data in registers to the local memory, each thread in charge of a row.

PUSH_LOCAL_TO_GLOBAL():Push the data in local memory to global memory, each thread in charge of a column.

Figure 8. Coalesced StreamScan (Access the global memory in coalesced way)

```
int lid = get_local_id(0), gid;
    __local int gid_;
    if(lid == 0) gid_=atom_add(S,1); // S is initialized to 0 in global memory
    barrier(CLK_LOCAL_MEM_FENCE);
    gid=gid_;
```

Figure 9. Dynamical allocation of runtime workgroup ID.

enumerates the parameter space and generates an OpenCL kernel instance. Compilation may fail due to illegal parameter combinations. If compilation succeeds, the tuning process runs the kernel, records the performance statistics, and updates the optimal parameter configuration if necessary. The whole tuning process finishes when the entire parameter space has been explored.

4. Experimental results

In this section, we present experimental results and the analysis of StreamScan. We first discuss our experimental environments, which include one AMD GPU and one Nvidia GPU. Next we report all our performance results and insights.

4.1 Experimental setup

In order to experiment the implementation space on both NVIDIA and AMD GPUs, we implemented StreamScan with OpenCL. For performance comparison purposes, we use two open source scan implementations: CUDPP_Scan [19] and Merrill_scan [13, 20]. CUDPP_Scan is the most popular open source scan implementation. And to the best of our knowledge, Merrill_Scan is the fastest open source scan implementation. We also implemented the 2D MatrixScan [21] within our auto-tuning framework.

We evaluated StreamScan on two platforms, namely NVIDIA Tesla C2050 and AMD Radeon HD5850. We varied the input array size from 1M 4-byte elements to 64M 4-byte elements to experiment a wide range of parameter space. Table 3 lists important system parameters for the two GPU platforms.

Tesla C2050 has hardware ECC support. Unless stated explicitly, all our execution times in this work assume enabled ECC, since this reflects true production running environments. There is no such issue on AMD HD5850 because it does not have ECC support.

4.2 Results

4.2.1 Memory efficiency VS. Kernel complexity

Table 4 shows optimal parameters, and corresponding OpenCL kernel execution time for two algorithms on both hardware platforms. The problem size is 16M(4-byte elements).In our experiments, we varied the problem size from 1M to 64M.The basic trend for optimal parameter configurations across all problem sizes on the same platform is similar.

On Tesla C2050, coalesced kernel performs much better than strided kernel. This means the performance is very sensitive to global memory access patterns, and relatively less sensitive to kernel complexity. Nvidia GPUs have highly optimized mechanisms for memory request coalescing [22]. The sophisticated scalar instruction pipeline is also capable of discovering parallelism for programs with irregular control flow.

On AMD HD5850, strided kernel performs better (7.6%) than coalesced kernel. The system is more sensitive to kernel complexity than global memory access patterns. The main reason is that AMD GPUs employ VLIW design for the instruction pipeline.

Table 2. Tunable parameter space.

Name	Value Domain
Kernel	StridedStreamScan
	CoalescedStreamScan
Workgroup Size (WS)	64, 128, 256, 512, 1024
Vector Length (VL)	1,2, 4, 8, 16
Group Size (GS)	8, 16, 32, 64
Local Memory Size (LMS)	0K~32K
Register Size (RS)	0K ~ 142K

Table 3. System configurations.

GPUs	Tesla C2050	HD 5850
Operation System	Ubuntu 9.04	Ubuntu 10.10
Runtime	CUDA 4.0	AMD SDK 2.6
Compute Unit (CU)	14	18
Cores	448	288*5
Flops	1.03TFlops	2.09TFlops
Global Memory	3GB GDDR5	1GB GDDR5
Theoretical bandwidth	144GB/s	128GB/s
Local memory banks	32	32
Local memory limits/CU	48KB	32KB
Register file size/CU	128KB	256KB

Table 4. Optimal parameters on two platforms.

Parameters		Tesla C2050	HD5850
Coalesced Kernel	WS	128	256
	GS	32	16
	VL	2	1
	LMS	16KB	16KB
	RS	16KB	48KB
	Kernel Time	1.42ms	1.83ms
Strided Kernel	WS	256	128
	VL	4	4
	LMS	12KB	26KB
	RS	4KB	46KB
	Kernel Time	2.43ms	1.71ms

The optimal on chip problem size (RS+LMS) for C2050 is much smaller than HD5850. Smaller size means more workgroups, which in turn implies more adjacent synchronization. It seems sync overhead on C2050 is less prominent than HD5850.

4.2.2 Performance results

Here we compare performance results of StreamScan with prior fast scan implementations on both platforms. Figure 10.a shows the throughputs (measured as 10^9 elements/sec.) of different sequence lengths on NVIDIA Tesla C2050 (CUDPP_Scan can't support 64M elements). As Figure 10.b shows, StreamScan has achieved notable performance speedups. Specifically, when the

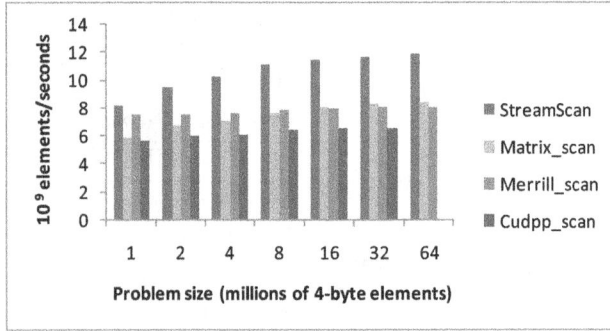

a) Throughput for different problem sizes

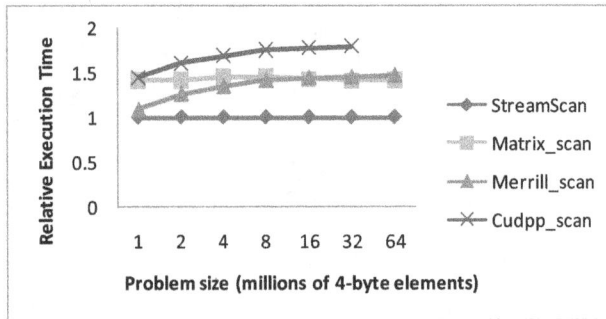

b) Relative execution time for different problem sizes.

Figure 10. Performance on NVIDIA Tesla C2050.

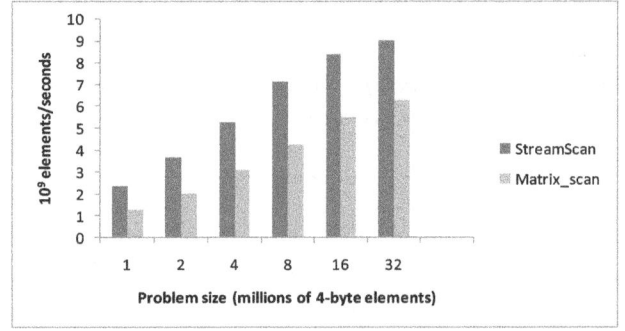

a) Throughput for different problem sizes

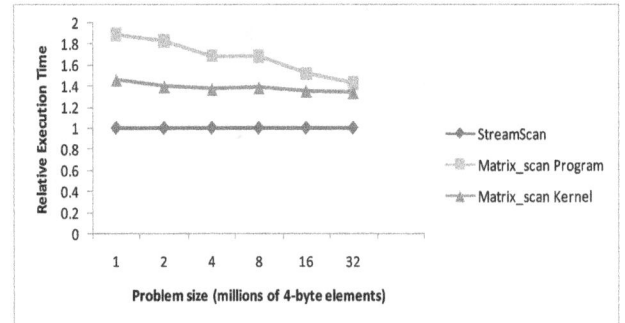

b) Relative execution time for different problem sizes.

Figure 11. Performance on AMD Radeon HD5850.

problem size is 16M, speedups of StreamScan, compared to CUDPP_Scan, Merrill_scan and MatrixScan, are 1.8x, 1.46x and 1.41x, respectively. There are two reasons for this. First, compared with all other algorithms, StreamScan only needs only ~2N global memory accesses. Second, optimizations like 3D data arrangement and register space exploitation further boost the performance.

Figure 11 shows the test results on AMD Radeon HD 5850 for various problem sizes (Because of the global memory limits, we can't test the 64M 4-byte input sequence on this GPU). Since CUDPP_Scan and Merrill_Scan only have CUDA versions, we implemented MatrixScan in OpenCL for comparison. Figure 11.a shows throughputs (measured as 109 elements/sec.) of different sequence lengths on this platform. Because of high kernel launch overhead, the throughput on AMD Radeon HD 5850 lower much than on NVIDIA Tesla C2050 when the problem size is small. Since AMD GPUs have relatively large kernel launch overheads (~0.3ms), we measure both the kernel execution time and total program execution time in our experiments. As Figure 11.b shows, compared to the program execution time, the speedups at problem sizes of 1M and 32M are 1.9x and 1.4x, respectively. Compared to the kernel execution time, the speedups at 1M and 32M are 1.46x and 1.35x, respectively.

In our experiments, the OpenCL kernel launch overhead on NVIDIA GPUs (~0.02ms) is approximately fifteen times lower than AMD GPUs (~0.3ms). Recall that CUDPP_Scan, Merrill_Scan and MatrixScan all require global barriers. If implemented with kernel invocations, as been studied extensively in previous works [19, 20, 21], the kernel launch overhead may cause notable performance loss on AMD GPUs. Our StreamScan algorithm addresses this issue neatly by eliminating global barriers completely.

4.2.3 Speedup breakdown analysis

As discussed in the previous section, three factors contribute to the performance speedup, namely reduction of off chip I/O traffic from at least 3N to 2N, 3D on chip data arrangement, and register space exploitation. Figure 12 illustrates a further breakdown of relative contributions of these three factors to the overall performance speedup.

On Tesla C2050, among the overall performance speedup, contributions of traffic reduction, 3D arrangement, and the register optimization are 48%, 6%, and 46%, respectively. As can be seen, using register space is a very important optimization. The contribution of thread grouping is relatively small, but still useful. Optimizations on AMD Radeon HD5850 are even more important for performance improvement. As discussed in section 4.2.1, the optimal configuration requires 72KB on chip storage to hold the working set. Shrinking the working set size to smaller than local memory size (32KB) hurts the performance dramatically. Note that for strided kernel, thread grouping is not necessary. In order to illustrate contributions of all three factors, Figure 12 shows relative contributions of three factors for the best coalesced kernel. On Radeon HD5850, among the overall performance speedup, contributions of traffic reduction, 3D arrangement, and the register optimization are 22%, 7%, and 71%, respectively.

4.2.4 Working Set Sensitivity Analysis

For StreamScan, there is another important tradeoff between the working set size (on chip problem size) and the performance. Figure 13 shows the throughput (measured in 10^9 elements/second) variations with different working set size (measured in KB) on Tesla C2050. There are three factors underlying this tradeoff. The smaller the working set size, the faster the intra-block scan. However, as discussed in section 3.1, small working

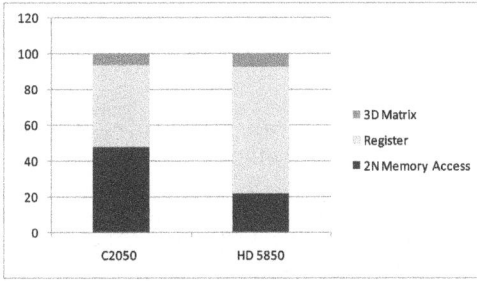

Figure 12. Speedup breakdown.

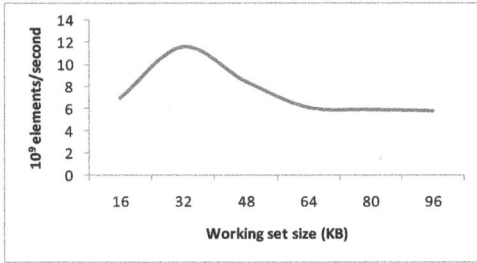

Figure 13. Throughput results of varying working set sizes on NVIDIA Tesla C2050 (Problem Size: 16M).

Figure 14. Throughput results of varying working set sizes on AMD HD 5850 (Problem size: 16M).

set also implies more inter-block synchronization overheads. There is one more resource constraint. Tesla C2050 only has 48KB local memory and 128KB register space per compute unit. The larger the working set, due to resource constraints, the less the exploitable dynamic parallelism between workgroups. The sweet spot is 32KB, with 16KB of local memory and 16KB of register space.

Figure 14 shows the tradeoff between throughput and working set size on AMD HD5850. The profile is very different. Compared to Tesla C2050, each compute unit of AMD HD5850 has much larger register space (256KB), but smaller local memory size (32KB). The implications are twofold. First, the optimal working set size is 72KB, with 26KB of local memory and 46KB of register space (as on-chip cache), due to the large register file. Second, while there are variations, the throughput maintains approximately at the same level when the working set is less than 120KB. There is a balance between the inter-block synchronization overhead and intra-block scan performance when working set size varies. Performance drops sharply when the working set goes beyond 120KB, because register consumption is so high that the system has to spill some registers to global memory.

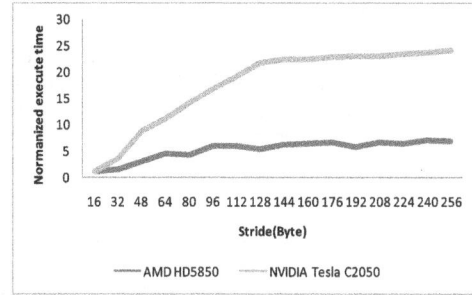

Figure 15. Execution time for different stride sizes (Normalized to coalesced memory access).

4.2.5 Memory system sensitivity analysis

As discussed in previous sections, while Tesla C2050 is more sensitive to memory system performance, AMD HD5850 is more sensitive to kernel complexity. A legitimate question to ask is, for each platform, how much is the performance gap between the coalesced memory access pattern and the strided pattern? Figure 15 shows this result for both GPUs.

For each platform, Figure 15 shows the I/O performance for different stride sizes. The test kernel simply loads 64MB of data from global memory and stores the data back to global memory. For each platform, the execution time is normalized to the performance of the coalesced kernel. As can be seen clearly, the performance gap between these two access patterns is much more prominent on Tesla C2050 than AMD HD5850. This, combined with AMD's VLIW instruction pipeline design, further explains why AMD HD5850 favors the strided kernel.

5. Related works

The scan problem has been studied for decades. Iverson [3] first proposed the problem in APL. Kogge and Stone[4] designed a work inefficient parallel prefix network, which requires exactly $N\log_2 N - (N-1)$ binary operations. Brent and Kung[5] improved this result by devising a tree-based strategy with only $2N - \log_2 N - 2$ binary operations. Horn [27] first implemented the scan algorithm on GPUs. This implementation used the streaming model for the scan operation. Similar to Brent's approach, Sengupta et al [25] first implemented a work-efficient and step-efficient algorithm for scan on GPUs. Harris et al [28] proposed detailed steps on how to implement scan with CUDA. Yuri Dotsenkoet et al [21] first proposed the matrix based scan algorithm on GPUs. The matrix based approach is much more efficient than tree based algorithms. They also proposed the three-phase Reduce-Scan-Scan approach for scan implementation. Duane G. Merrill [13] studied various scan implementation alternatives. In his thesis, he proposed three scan algorithms on GPUs and implemented these three algorithms as an open source library (B40C). In this paper we refer it to Merrill_Scan. Jens Breitbart [24] proposed a scan algorithm on GPUs with a fixed number of threads. Nan Zhang [14] proposed a novel parallel scan for multicore processors. In this work, the input sequence is first divided into several blocks, then one thread is assigned to scan a block. Compared to previous scan algorithms on multicore processors, this work did not require the number of processors to be a power of two. Shucai Xiao et al [26] proposed a fast global barrier implementation on GPUs. Different to them, we proposed the adjacent synchronization to replace global barriers.

6. Conclusion

For all existing GPU scan algorithms, there is a serial dependence between adjacent workgroups. In this work, we've shown that this can be exploited to eliminate global barriers by introducing adjacent synchronization between consecutive thread blocks only. We believe that the idea could be generalized to other algorithms with similar dependence structures.

Based on the adjacent synchronization, we propose StreamScan, a novel scan algorithm on both Nvidia and AMD GPUs. Compared with current state of the art, StreamScan eliminates global barrier synchronization completely. This reduces the global memory I/O traffic from at least 3N to only ~2N. On top of this, we propose thread grouping and register optimization to further boost the performance. Our experimental results show promising speedups on both Tesla C2050 and AMD HD5850.

Besides propose the adjacent synchronization and design a novel scan algorithm on GPUs, our work reveals very different optimization tradeoffs on the two hardware platforms. For Nvidia GPUs, coalesced memory access is critical to performance speedups. Due to the scalar micro-architecture, less compiler and programmer effort is necessary to exploit parallelism. Compared to memory efficiency, optimization efforts on AMD GPUs are more sensitive to kernel complexity. This is largely due to VLIW design of the instruction pipeline. The large register space is very useful for expanding on-chip working set size, which proves to be critical for performance speedups.

Acknowledgments

We would like to thank Yan Li for his collection of materials in the early stage of our work. We thank all the anonymous reviewers for their valuable comments. This paper is supported by National Natural Science Foundation of China (No.61133005, No.61272136, No.61100073), the National High-tech R&D Program of China (No.2012AA010902, No. 2012AA010903). Dr. Guoping Long is supported by National Natural Science Foundation of China (Grant No. 61100072)

References

[1] Blelloch, G. E. Scans as Primitive Parallel Operations. IEEE Trans. Comput, 1989.

[2] Blelloch, G.E. Prefix Sums and Their Applications. Synthesis of Parallel Algorithms, 1990.

[3] Iverson, K. E. A Programming Language. AIEE-IRE '62, 1962.

[4] Kogge, P. M. and Stone, H. S. A Parallel Algorithm for the Efficient Solution of a General Class of Recurrence Equations. IEEE Trans. Comput, 1973.

[5] Brent, R. P. and Kung, H. T. A Regular Layout for Parallel Adders. IEEE Trans. Comput, 1982.

[6] D. Merrill, and A. Grimshaw Revisiting Sorting for GPGPU Stream Architectures. Tech. Rep. CS2010-03, Department of Computer Science, University of Virginia, 2010.

[7] Cederman, D. and Tsigas, P. On Sorting and Load Balancingon GPUs. SIGARCH Comput. Archit. News, 2008.

[8] D. Merrill and A. Grimshaw. High Performance and Scalable Radix Sorting: A case study of implementing dynamic parallelism for GPU computing. Parallel Processing Letters, 2011.

[9] Cederman, D., and Tsigas, P. GPU-Quicksort: A practical Quicksort algorithm for graphics processors. Journal of Experimental Algorithmics. 2009.

[10] H. Peters, O. Schulz-Hildebrandt, and N. Luttenberger. Fast in-place sorting with cuda based on bitonic sort. PPAM 09: Proceedings of the International Conference on Parallel Processing and Applied Mathematics, 2009.

[11] N. Satish, M. Harris, and M. Garland. Designing Efficient Sorting Algorithms for Manycore GPUs. In Proc. Int'l Symposium on Parallel and Distributed Processing (IPDPS), 2009.

[12] D. Merrill, M. Garland, and A. Grimshaw. Scalable GPU Graph Traversal. Proceedings of the 17th ACM SIGPLAN symposium on Principles and Practice of Parallel Programming (PPoPP '12), 2012.

[13] D. Merrill. Allocation-oriented Algorithm Design with Application to GPU Computing. PhD thesis, University of Virginia, 2011.

[14] Nan Zhang. A Novel Parallel Scan for Multicore Processors and Its Application in Sparse Matrix-Vector Multiplication. Parallel and Distributed Systems, IEEE Transactions, 2012.

[15] Markus Billeter, Ola Olsson and Ulf Assarsson. Efficient stream compaction on wide SIMD many-core architectures, Proceedings of the Conference on High Performance Graphics, 2009.

[16] Vibhav Vineet, Pawan Harish, Suryakant Patidar, and P. J. Narayanan. Fast minimum spanning tree for large graphs on the GPU. In Proc. of High Performance Graphics, 2009.

[17] Zheng Wei, Joseph JaJa. Optimization of linked list prefix computations on multithreaded GPUs using CUDA. In Parallel & Distributed Processing (IPDPS), 2010.

[18] Mark Harris. State of the Art in GPU Data-Parallel Algorithm Primitives. Tech. Rep. GPU Technology Conference, 2010.

[19] M. Harris, J. Owens, S. Sengupta, Y. Zhang, and A. Davidson. CUDPP: CUDA Data Parallel Primitives Library. http://gpgpu.org/developer/cudpp.

[20] D. Merrill. Parallel Scan for Stream Architectures. Technical Report CS2009-14, Department of Computer Science, University of Virginia, 2009.

[21] Y. Dotsenko, N. K. Govindaraju, P.-P. Sloan, C. Boyd, and J. Manferdelli. Fast Scan Algorithms on Graphics Processors. In ICS'08: Proc. 22nd Annual International Conference on Supercomputing, 2008.

[22] NVIDIA Corporation. Nvidia Cuda C Programming Guide. http://developer.download.nvidia.com/compute/DevZone/docs/html/C/doc/CUDA_C_Programming_Guide.pdf, 2012.

[23] S. Sengupta, M. Harris, and M. Garland. Efficient Parallel Scan Algorithms for GPUs. NVIDIA Tech. Rep, 2008.

[24] Jens Breitbart. Static GPU threads and an Improved Scan Algorithm. In Euro-Par 2010 Work-shop Proceedings, Lecture Notes in Computer Science, 2010.

[25] Sengupta S., Lefohn A. and Owens, J. A work-efficient step-efficient prefix-sum algorithm. Proceedings of the Workshop on Edge Computing Using New Commodity Architectures, 2006.

[26] S. Xiao and W. chun Feng. Inter-block GPU Communication via Fast Barrier Synchronization. In Parallel & Distributed Processing (IPDPS), 2010.

[27] Horn D. Stream Reduction Operations for GPGPU Applications. In GPU Gems 2, Pharr M., (Ed.).Addison Wesley, ch. 36, pp. 573–589, 2005.

[28] Harris M., Sengupta S. and Owens J. D. Parallel Prefix sum (scan) with CUDA. In GPU Gems 3, Nguyen H., (Ed.).Addison Wesley, ch. 39, 2007.

[29] Haipeng Jia, Yunquan Zhang, Guoping Long, Jianliang Xu, and Shengen Yan. GPURoofline: A Model for Guiding Performance Optimizations on GPUs. Euro-Par 2012 Parallel Processing, 2012.

[30] Khronos OpenCL Working Group, The OpenCL Specification Version: 1.2, 2012.

The Tasks with Effects Model for Safe Concurrency

Stephen T. Heumann   Vikram S. Adve   Shengjie Wang

University of Illinois at Urbana-Champaign

{heumann1,vadve,wang260}@illinois.edu

Abstract

Today's widely-used concurrent programming models either provide weak safety guarantees, making it easy to write code with subtle errors, or are limited in the class of programs that they can express. We propose a new concurrent programming model based on *tasks with effects* that offers strong safety guarantees while still providing the flexibility needed to support the many ways that concurrency is used in complex applications. The core unit of work in our model is a dynamically-created task. The model's key feature is that each task has programmer-specified *effects*, and a run-time scheduler is used to ensure that two tasks are run concurrently only if they have non-interfering effects. Through the combination of statically verifying the declared effects of tasks and using an effect-aware run-time scheduler, our model is able to guarantee strong safety properties, including data race freedom and atomicity. It is also possible to use our model to write programs and computations that can be statically proven to behave deterministically. We describe the tasks with effects programming model and provide a formal dynamic semantics for it. We also describe our implementation of this model in an extended version of Java and evaluate its use in several programs exhibiting various patterns of concurrency.

Categories and Subject Descriptors   D.3.2 [*Software*]: Language Classifications—Concurrent, distributed, and parallel languages; D.3.3 [*Software*]: Language Constructs and Features—Concurrent Programming Structures;   D.1.3 [*Software*]: Concurrent Programming

General Terms   Languages, Verification, Design, Performance

Keywords   Tasks, effects, task scheduling, concurrent and parallel programming, task isolation, data race freedom, atomicity, determinism

1. Introduction

Concurrency is used for many purposes in modern programs. To exploit the full capabilities of today's multicore processors, parallel algorithms must be used. But concurrency is also used for other purposes. This is perhaps particularly true of interactive programs, both on end-user devices and servers, where the behavior of the user or client is inherently concurrent with the program. In GUI programs, long-running operations should be run concurrently with user interface event processing in order to preserve responsiveness.

It can also be convenient to express a full program as a set of of modules or actors [3] that can operate concurrently and communicate with each other. This can be a natural fit, for example, to the model-view-controller design of interactive programs.

Large programs often combine multiple types of concurrency. For example, an interactive application may separate long computations from the UI thread or use multiple concurrent modules, but also sometimes perform data-parallel computations. We believe a widely-applicable concurrent programming model should seek to support all of these forms of concurrency, since they are all widely used and are often combined within a single application.

Today, parallel and concurrent programs are commonly written using threads, with low-level mechanisms such as locks used for synchronization (or with carefully designed lock-free data structures). Such a programming model is flexible enough to express many forms of concurrency, but it does not guarantee any safety properties such as data race freedom, atomicity, deadlock-freedom, or determinism. It also provides little well-defined structure for the concurrent control flow and synchronization in programs, making it difficult to reason about them manually or automatically. In addition, complicated low-level details such as processor memory models [2] can affect the semantics of programs written in this style, further complicating the task of reasoning about them.

Many previous systems have attempted to address aspects of these problems. Some offer more structured parallel control and synchronization constructs, but sometimes with limitations that prevent them from expressing general, event-driven concurrency, and often without strong safety guarantees. Cilk [11] and Thread Building Blocks (TBB) [22], for example, provide structured parallelism constructs, but they do not offer checked guarantees of strong safety properties such as data race freedom.

Some other systems do seek to offer stronger guarantees. The Deterministic Parallel Java (DPJ) language [13, 14] offers a strong set of guarantees for programs that can be expressed in it. These include data race freedom, strong atomicity [1], deadlock freedom, and deterministic semantics with full sequential equivalence for parallel computations that do not explicitly use nondeterministic parallel constructs. These guarantees are very strong, but DPJ's parallelism model does not provide the flexibility that we seek. Most critically, DPJ is restricted to fork-join parallelism structures, which are not suitable for many concurrent programs.

In this paper, we propose a new model for concurrent programming, which gives strong safety guarantees while providing the flexibility needed to express a wide range of concurrent programs in it. We call our model *tasks with effects*.[1] It uses tasks that can execute concurrently as the fundamental units of work. Tasks are lighter-weight constructs than threads and support only limited operations for inter-task communication and synchronization. Concurrent work is launched by creating a new task, and it is possi-

---

[1] Two workshop papers gave preliminary descriptions of the tasks with effects model [20, 21].

ble for one task to await the completion of another. A scheduler is responsible for executing tasks in an efficient manner. Tasks provide a structured mechanism for concurrent control flow, while still preserving the flexibility to express a wide variety of concurrency patterns and parallel algorithms.

Several existing systems support task-based programming models, including Intel's TBB, Apple's Grand Central Dispatch and operation queues [6], Microsoft's Task Parallel Library in .NET [30], the ForkJoinTask framework in Java 7 [33], and the tasking operations in OpenMP 3.x [32]. However, they do not offer strong safety guarantees. It is possible for two concurrent tasks to perform conflicting accesses that give rise to data races or violations of intended atomicity properties, and it is generally the programmer's responsibility to manually reason that such accesses do not occur or are benign, or else to protect them using low-level synchronization mechanisms such as locks.

We propose instead to associate a checked effect specification with each task. The run-time system then schedules tasks so as to ensure that only tasks with non-interfering effects can run concurrently. Effect specifications can take many forms, but in this work we adopt the statically-checked effect system developed for Deterministic Parallel Java [13]. In this system, the compiler statically verifies that the memory accesses in each task or method are covered by its programmer-specified effects. By combining these static checks with our dynamic effect-based task scheduling system, we are able to guarantee the basic *task isolation* property that no two tasks with interfering effects may run concurrently with each other. This guarantee leads to a guarantee of data race freedom, and to a guarantee of atomicity for tasks or portions of tasks that do not create or wait for any other tasks.

We also define mechanisms based on *effect transfer* between tasks to further enhance the utility of our model. One mechanism is used to avoid a class of deadlocks, and also enables certain useful programming paradigms. Another form of effect transfer is used for nested parallel computations. It enables us to provide a compile-time guarantee of determinism for a class of deterministic programs and algorithms similar to those supported by DPJ. We are aware of no other programming model which provides equally strong safety guarantees while supporting the flexible control flow needed for general concurrent programs such as interactive applications and actor-like programs.

This paper makes the following contributions:

- We define the tasks with effects programming model, which supports flexible task-based concurrency while providing a strong set of safety guarantees.

- We describe the TWEJava language which implements this model, and describe our compiler and runtime system for it.

- We provide a formal dynamic semantics of tasks with effects, and describe how it guarantees task isolation, data race freedom, atomicity, and (for certain computations) determinism.

- We evaluate the expressiveness and performance of our language and implementation. We show that TWEJava can be used to write a variety of concurrent and parallel programs, including two interactive applications, and that we can achieve substantial parallel speedups.

The rest of this paper proceeds as follows. Section 2 presents the TWEJava language and describes the task-related operations used in it. Section 3 gives a dynamic semantics of tasks with effects. Section 4 describes the safety properties of our model. Section 5 discusses our implementation of TWEJava in a compiler and runtime system, and section 6 evaluates it on several benchmark programs. Finally, section 7 discusses related work and section 8 concludes.

```
1  public abstract class Task<type TRet, TArg, effect E> {
2    // Code to be run when task is executed.
3    public abstract TRet run(TArg arg) effect E;
4
5    // Execute a task at some point in the future
6    public final TaskFuture<TRet> executeLater(TArg arg);
7    // Spawn a subtask of the current task, with effect transfer
8    public final SpawnedTaskFuture<TRet, effect E> spawn(TArg arg);
9  }
10
11 public class TaskFuture<type TReturn> {
12   // Await completion and get return value (no effect transfer)
13   public TReturn getValue();
14   // Check if task is done
15   public boolean isDone();
16 }
17
18 public class SpawnedTaskFuture<type TReturn, effect E>
19         extends TaskFuture<TReturn> {
20   // Await completion and get return value, with effect transfer
21   public TReturn join();
22 }
```

Figure 1. Operations supported by TWEJava. The abstract method `run` must be implemented in concrete subclasses of `Task`, giving the code to be run as a task. The other operations, although using the syntax of Java methods, are in fact new task-related language operations supported by our compiler and runtime system.

2. The TWEJava language

We implement the tasks with effects model for safe, flexible concurrency in an extended version of Java, which we call TWEJava. (TWEJava programs can use almost all Java language features, but they should not use Java's thread-based concurrency mechanisms or lock-based synchronization, which TWEJava is designed to replace.) Figure 1 shows the new operations supported by TWEJava.

Figure 2 shows how our task system can be used in an image editing program, which we will use as as running example. It illustrates a simplified version of a programming pattern used in the ImageEdit program that we have implemented in TWEJava (see section 6). The example code shows a class `Image` representing an image, with the pixel values held in two arrays, `topHalf` and `bottomHalf`. We would like to support operations in parallel on these two halves of the image. (We adopt this arrangement for simplicity. In the actual ImageEdit application, it is possible to use finer-grained parallelism.) We also want to support a variety of operations to read and manipulate the image, which may be invoked as asynchronous tasks. This is useful, for example, when the user directs the program to perform a lengthy operation that should not block the user interface while it runs.

We show the task `increaseContrast` (lines 6–16), which can be executed to increase the contrast of the image. It relies on the separate method `increasePixelContrast` (lines 18–26) to actually update the pixel values in each array. This enables the `increaseContrast` operation to work on the top and bottom halves of the image in parallel, by spawning a child task to work on the top half while the parent task works on the bottom half.

Figure 3 shows the tasks created in this computation. The GUI system executes the `increaseContrast` task in response to user input. That task in turn spawns a child task so that the two halves of the image can be processed in parallel, and then joins that child task after it completes. Meanwhile, the GUI system might execute additional tasks in response to further user input. (In this example, we show the GUI system as a task, responsible for processing low-level input data and launching tasks in response to UI events. This architecture would be possible, but for ease of implementation we have so far used Java's Swing GUI framework, with wrappers to launch tasks in response to Swing events.)

```
1   class Image {
2     region Top, Bottom;
3     final int[]<Top> topHalf;        // pixel values
4     final int[]<Bottom> bottomHalf;
5     ...
6     public final Task<Void, Void, writes Top,Bottom>
7     increaseContrast =
8       new Task<>() {
9         public Void run(Void _) {
10          SpawnedTaskFuture<Void, writes Top> f =
11            increasePixelContrast(topHalf).spawn(null);
12          increasePixelContrast(bottomHalf).run(null);
13          f.join();
14          return null;
15        }
16      };
17
18    private static <region runtime R> Task<Void, Void, writes R>
19    increasePixelContrast(final int[]<R> pixels) pure {
20      return new Task<>() {
21        public Void run(Void _) {
22          modify values in pixels array
23          return null;
24        }
25      };
26    }
27  }
```

Figure 2. Example computation.

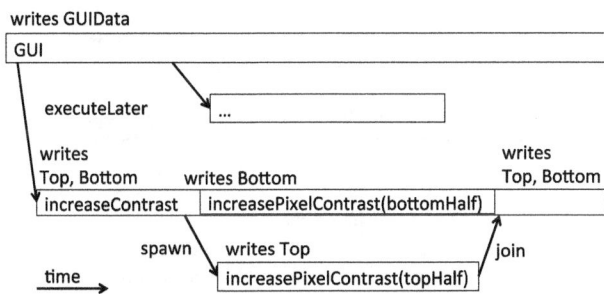

Figure 3. Tasks in example computation.

2.1 Tasks

In TWEJava, potentially concurrent work is made by creating a *task*, which will then be executed at some point when execution resources are available. It is possible to check if a task is completed or block awaiting its completion. A program written in TWEJava is started by invoking an initial task, and creating new tasks is the sole means of performing concurrent work. Tasks can also take parameters as input and return a result. (Wrapper classes support tasks with multiple parameters.) Three fundamental operations implement this basic tasking model: executeLater adds a task to the queue of tasks to be executed, getValue waits until a task is done and gives its return value, and isDone checks whether a task is done, without blocking.

Each type of task is specified by a subclass of the Task class, which takes type parameters giving its input and output types, and an effect parameter giving its effect (described below). An executeLater operation performed on a Task instance returns a TaskFuture object, which represents an actual execution of the task; getValue and isDone operations can be performed on this task future. In our example, the increaseContrast task is created by an executeLater operation in the GUI. (The spawn and join operations used within it will be described in section 2.5.)

The structure described above is similar to other existing task systems, but TWEJava has a key difference. In other systems, a

task can generally be run at any time after it is queued for execution, without regard to what other tasks are running concurrently. Because of this, the programmer must take care to ensure that there are no data races between potentially concurrent tasks. This can be done by using synchronization mechanisms such as locks within tasks to guard access to shared data, or by carefully designing the pattern in which tasks are executed and joined in such a way that no two tasks accessing the same data might be executed concurrently. Using these mechanisms to guard against data races is often complex and error-prone, and traditional thread-based systems for concurrent programming generally do not provide a mechanism to automatically check that they have been used correctly.

Our system solves this problem by using *effects* to control the scheduling of tasks. Each task has an effect specification, which is checked at compile time to ensure that it accurately (conservatively) reflects the task's memory accesses. These effect specifications of tasks are in turn used at run time by the task scheduler, which will ensure task isolation—that is, that no two tasks with interfering effects can be running concurrently.

2.2 Effects and Regions

In order to perform effect-based scheduling of tasks, our system must know the effects of each task, and be able to check whether the effects of two different tasks interfere with each other. Intuitively, two tasks interfere if they could both access the same memory location and at least one of those accesses could be a write. Two tasks can only be run concurrently if their effects do not interfere, which is the core property enforced by the scheduler in our system.

In TWEJava, we use the effect system originally developed for the Deterministic Parallel Java (DPJ) language [13]. DPJ is an extended version of Java that uses type and effect annotations to enable the compiler to statically prove strong safety properties for programs written using its fork-join parallel constructs. In this work, however, we adopt its type and effect system for use in combination with our effect-based task scheduling system.

The DPJ type and effect system is based on a partitioning of memory into *regions*. The programmer can declare each object field and array cell to be in a specified region. Region-parameterized types and methods are also supported. This permits different instances of a class to have their fields in different regions by giving different region arguments when instantiating the class. In addition, nested hierarchies of regions are supported by using *region path lists* (RPLs), and *index-parameterized arrays* allow each element of an array to be placed in a distinct region. A wildcard * can be used in RPLs to specify effects covering a set of regions.

Using this partitioning of memory into regions, the effects of any operation in the program can be specified in terms of read and write effects on memory regions. The programmer declares the effects of each method as part of its method signature. The compiler can then statically verify that the declared effects of each method actually cover the effects of every operation in it. The DPJ type and effect system also defines formally under what circumstances two effects can be proven to be non-interfering. In DPJ, this information is used purely statically to verify that programs using simple fork-join parallelism constructs have no interference of effect between portions of code that can run concurrently.

TWEJava adopts DPJ's region-based type and effect system, but couples it with a runtime representation of effects that is used by a run-time scheduler to guarantee noninterference of effect between concurrent tasks. This allows it to support a much wider range of programs than DPJ can handle, including those that are inherently nondeterministic and do not use a fork-join style of concurrency.

We also use an extension of the basic DPJ type system to support effect parameters to types (in addition to region parameters), which was introduced in [12]. This allows us to use an effect parameter E in our definition of the abstract class Task, which will be extended by each actual task defined in the user's code. The definition of each actual type of task will instantiate this parameter with that task's effects, and the compiler will then be able to ensure statically that the effects of the supplied run method for that task are actually covered by the effect parameter E. Thus, our runtime system can safely use that effect parameter as a (possibly conservative) summary of the actual effects of the task.

In our example code, we declare two region names, Top and Bottom (line 2). We then declare the cells of the topHalf and bottomHalf arrays to be in those two regions, respectively. The increaseContrast task is declared with the effects writes Top, Bottom, meaning it can read and write the pixel values in both halves of the image. The increasePixelContrast method has a region parameter R corresponding to the region containing the cells of the array passed to it. Since the declared effect of the task it returns is writes R, increasePixelContrast(topHalf) will produce a task with the effect writes Top.

Like DPJ, we use purely static checks to ensure that each method and task complies with its effect declaration and that region- and effect-parameterized types are used soundly. TWEJava never requires runtime checks associated with individual memory accesses, which avoids a major source of overhead in some other systems such as STMs. However, our system does need to have information on the effects of tasks available at run time so that it can be used by the scheduler. We make this information available by introducing a set of internal runtime classes that represent dynamic regions and effects, and internally adding extra fields to classes which hold the runtime instantiation of their region and effect parameters, as well as extra arguments to constructors and methods corresponding to the region and effect parameters passed to them.

The scheduler only directly needs information about the effect parameters of task objects, but these may depend on other region and effect parameters in scope at the places where task classes are declared and instantiated, making it necessary to also track those additional parameters at run time. To minimize the overhead of this run-time tracking, we require programmers to annotate region parameters that need to be tracked at run time. This allows us to avoid generating run-time tracking code for the many region parameters that are used only in the compiler's static analysis. (Failing to provide such an annotation where needed will cause a compile-time error.)

2.3 Effect-Based Task Scheduling

The key property that our run-time task scheduler must enforce is that two tasks with interfering effects will not be run concurrently. To do this, the scheduler will have to delay the execution of tasks that are created while another task with interfering effects is already executing. It may also delay tasks for other reasons, e.g. waiting until execution resources are available.

In Figure 3, the increaseContrast task with effects writes Top, Bottom is run while the GUI task with effect writes GUIData continues to execute. To determine if the new task may be run concurrently with the already-executing task, the scheduler will check if these two sets of effects interfere with each other. In this case, the region GUIData is disjoint from Top and Bottom, so the two tasks have non-interfering effects and may be run concurrently.

If a third task is run with executeLater while these two tasks are executing, its effects will be checked against those of both existing tasks. Thus, another task trying to access the image data in the regions Top and Bottom would have to wait until the increaseContrast task is done, but a task accessing different regions might be able to run concurrently. (The increasePixelContrast(topHalf) task is run with the spawn

operation, which uses effect transfer to avoid the need for these run-time checks; see section 2.5.)

Considerable variation is possible in the design of an effect-aware task scheduler. Our initial prototype implementation uses an approach based on a linear queue of tasks, which is described in section 5.2. For greater performance and scalability, the effect checking could be structured around regions, so that tasks accessing unrelated regions do not need to be explicitly checked against each other. A scheduler may also provide additional properties related to fairness or task ordering, in addition to the basic property of noninterference. For interactive programs, it is valuable to preserve responsiveness through fairness properties that avoid delaying the execution of one task excessively while other tasks execute ahead of it. But for efficiency in many parallel codes, it would be desirable to use algorithms similar to Cilk's work-stealing scheduler [11], which preferentially execute recently-created tasks on each processor. We believe that the design of high-performance effect-based task schedulers is a valuable area for future work.

2.4 Effect Transfer When Blocked

The model we have described so far envisions the effects of each task remaining unchanged while it runs, and says that two tasks with interfering effects may not run concurrently. This will lead to deadlock if one task blocks waiting for another task that has yet to run and which has effects that interfere with those of the first task. For example, if task A creates task B using executeLater, then blocks on B using getValue, and the effects of tasks A and B interfere, deadlock results because B cannot begin execution until A is complete.

We wish to prevent this form of deadlock and enable certain useful programming patterns involving this sort of blocking, so we introduce a mechanism for *effect transfer* from a blocked task to the task it is blocked on. The key idea is that a getValue or a join operation (described later) "transfers" enough effects from the blocking task to the target task to allow the target task to begin execution. For example, if a task A is blocked on another task B using getValue, we record this fact and ignore any effect conflict between A and B in deciding whether B can be executed. We also extend this to indirect blocking through chains of blocking operations. Note that a task that blocks will always remain blocked until all the tasks it directly or indirectly blocks on are done. Therefore, this mechanism does not enable two tasks with conflicting effects to be actively running at the same time.

This form of effect transfer prevents the type of deadlock described above, and it also allows some useful programming patterns. One of these is for one module of the program with effects on a certain region to launch and block on a task in another module, which may "call back" to the first module by launching and blocking on another task whose effects interfere with those of the first task. Another useful programming pattern enabled by this mechanism is similar to a locked or atomic block in other programming models. One task can launch a second task with a superset of its effects, and then use a getValue operation to wait for the second task. This transfers the first task's effects to the second task (allowing it to access the same regions as the first task), and leaves the second task to wait until it can acquire access to the regions covered by its other effects, which may correspond to a shared resource.

2.5 Effect Transfer for Nested Parallelism

Our system supports an additional form of effect transfer which is particularly suitable for nested parallelism, as used in fork-join style computations. It is a mechanism to transfer some of the effects of a parent task to a newly-created child task, and later transfer those effects back to the parent task when the child task completes. We call these operations spawn and join, respectively. A child task created with spawn may run immediately, since "ownership" of its effects is transferred directly from the parent to the child task, and thus no other tasks with conflicting effects may be running concurrently.

In Figure 2, these mechanisms are used to operate in parallel on the two halves of the image. We use the spawn operation to run the increasePixelContrast(topHalf) task (line 11). This transfers the effect writes Top directly from the parent increaseContrast task to the new child task, which means the new task can be enabled for execution immediately. The parent task also continues executing concurrently, with its remaining effect writes Bottom. The increasePixelContrast(bottomHalf) operation is run as a method within the parent task, which is possible since its remaining effect writes Bottom covers the effect of the method call. After that computation finishes, the parent task joins the spawned child task. This join operation also transfers the child task's effect writes Top back to the parent task. After this, both halves of the image will have been updated, so any other task that waits for the increaseContrast task to finish will know that the full operation is complete.

2.5.1 Spawning and joining child tasks

The spawn operation executes a new task, whose effects must be entirely covered by the effects of the parent task calling spawn. It immediately transfers those effects to the spawned task, which allows that task to be enabled for execution immediately, without going through the normal effect-based scheduling process required when using executeLater. Since the effects are transferred directly from the parent task to the child task, data in regions covered by those effects cannot be modified by any other task in the interim, so the child task reading that data is guaranteed to see the values last seen or written by the parent task.

The join operation permits effect transfer back to the parent task at the end of a child task. Apart from effect transfer, join behaves like getValue: it will await the completion of the joined task, and return the result value produced by it, if any. The difference is that join will transfer effects directly from a completed task to the task that joins it. This permits the task that called join to perform subsequent operations covered by the effects of the joined task. One application of this is that data written by the completed child task can be read by its parent task after the child task is done.

Only tasks executed with spawn are joinable, and this is reflected by the fact that spawn returns a SpawnedTaskFuture, which supports the join operation. Furthermore, only the parent task that spawns a task may join it, and a task may only be joined once (violating these rules causes an exception to be thrown). Also, the system implements an implicit join operation prior to returning from each method for all the tasks spawned by that method that have not already been explicitly joined. These measures ensure that all spawned tasks get joined, and that all the effects transferred from a method with spawn are returned to it through join operations before the method returns. This simplifies our static effect analysis, since a method never "gives up" effects from the perspective of its callers.

2.5.2 Covering Effect Analysis for Effect Transfer

Implementing effect transfer makes the static analysis of covering effects more complex, since a spawn or join operation subtracts or adds effects to the task in which it is executed, thereby changing the covering effects applicable to subsequent code in that task. This would be easy to address if we used dynamic checks to determine whether the effect of each memory operation is covered by the current effects of the task in which it appears, but we want to use a static analysis to determine this in order to minimize runtime overheads and detect as many errors as possible at compile time.

To do so, we added a dataflow analysis algorithm in the compiler to conservatively compute the *current covering effect* applicable to each expression in the program. The current covering effect at the beginning of a method is given by its declared method effect summary. When spawn operations are encountered, the statically declared effects of the spawned task are subtracted from the current covering effect, and a SpawnedTaskFuture parameterized by the effects of the spawned child task is returned. At join operations, the effects given by the static type of the joined SpawnedTaskFuture are added to the current covering effect. At control flow join points, a minimum of the current covering effects from the different control flow paths is used. Using an iterative dataflow analysis, we can thus conservatively compute the current covering effect applicable to each expression in the program. The effects of each expression can then be compared against its current covering effect to ensure the expression's effects will be covered.

In our example the covering effect of the increaseContrast task is initially writes Top, Bottom. When it spawns a child task (line 11), its covering effect then becomes writes Bottom, since the writes Top effect has been transferred to the spawned child task. When that task is joined (line 13), the covering effect of the parent task once again becomes writes Top, Bottom.

One detail that must be accounted for in this analysis is that effect-parameterized types in the static program code are in general only a conservative summary of the actual effects of tasks at run time, and they may contain wildcard elements in their region specifiers. The actual effects of the Task object used at run time may be smaller than the effects given in the static type, e.g. by omitting some of the effects that are included in the static type or replacing effects on RPLs containing wildcards (which can cover a set of regions) with effects on a fully-specified RPL designating a single region in that set. We generally use a conservative static analysis: spawns are treated as transferring away all the effects in the static type of the spawned task, including ones with wildcards. Subsequent operations in the parent task may not interfere with those transferred-away effects, which conservatively ensures that they cannot interfere with any of the actual effects of the child task at run time.

As an exception in this conservative analysis, however, we allow spawn operations even if we cannot be certain at compile time whether or not the effects of the spawned task will actually be covered at run time. In this case, we generate code to keep track of the run-time covering effects in the method containing the spawn operation (updated only when a spawn or join operation is performed). An exception will be thrown if the effects of the spawned task are not actually covered at run time. This limited dynamic checking is useful for cases where we do not have full information on the effects of spawned tasks at compile time. For example, a loop may spawn tasks to operate on different elements of an index-parameterized array, but our compiler cannot determine statically whether each of the elements is distinct, so this mechanism effectively enables the check to be performed dynamically instead.

For joins, we need to be sure that the actual run-time effects of the task being joined are not less than those specified in the static type. To do this, we statically treat joins as performing effect transfer only if the effect parameter of the joined task's static type is fully-specified (i.e. contains no wildcards). We also adopt the typing rule that an effect-parameterized type A is only treated as a subtype of another effect-parameterized type B if either the corresponding effect parameters are exactly equivalent, or the effect parameters in B are *not* fully-specified. This ensures that fully-specified effect parameters in the static types of SpawnedTaskFutures exactly match the actual parameters used when instantiating the task object at run time, so we may safely use those parameters in the static analysis of join operations.

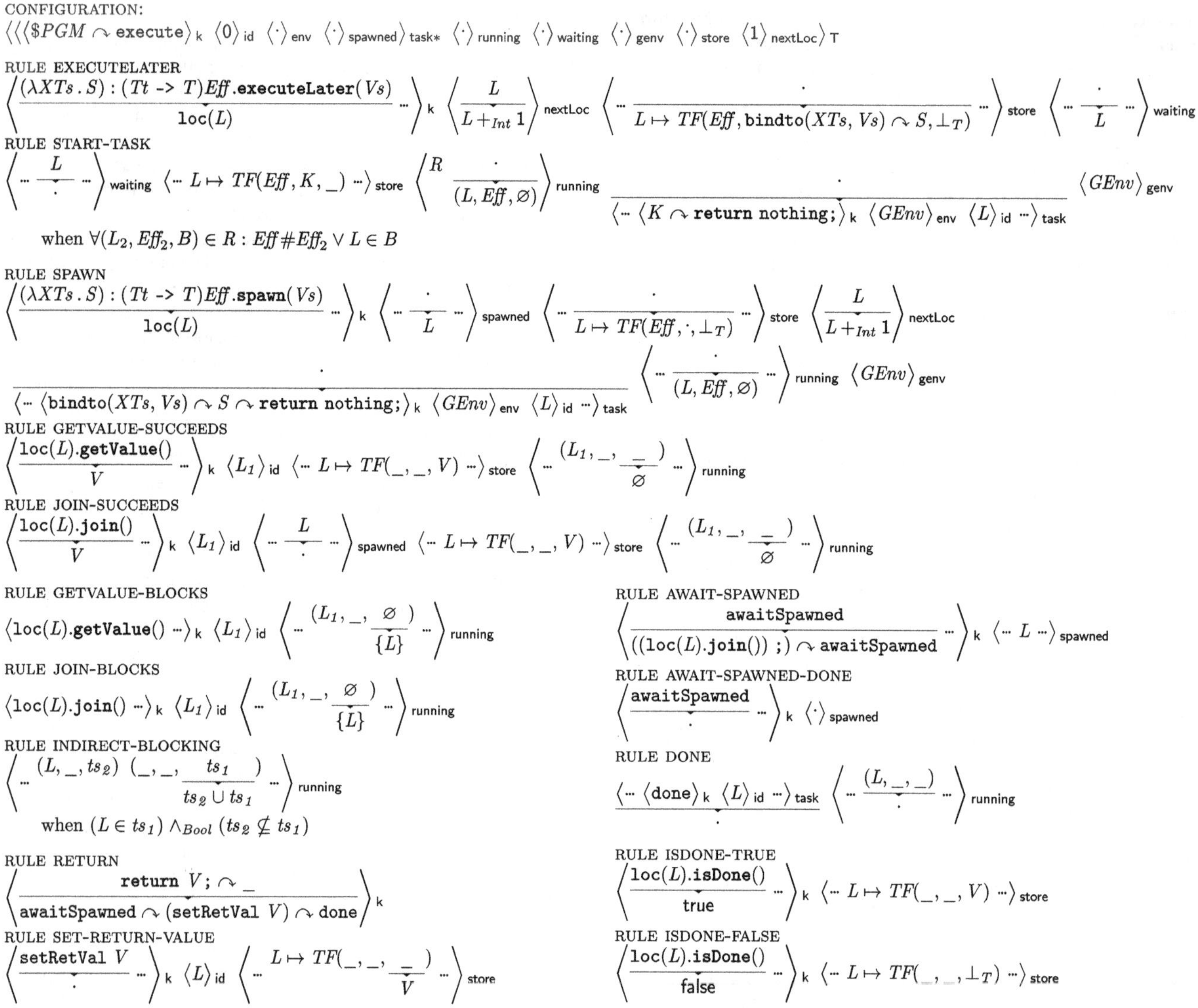

CONFIGURATION:

$\langle\langle\langle \$PGM \curvearrowright \texttt{execute}\rangle_k \ \langle 0\rangle_{id} \ \langle\cdot\rangle_{env} \ \langle\cdot\rangle_{spawned}\rangle_{task*} \ \langle\cdot\rangle_{running} \ \langle\cdot\rangle_{waiting} \ \langle\cdot\rangle_{genv} \ \langle\cdot\rangle_{store} \ \langle 1\rangle_{nextLoc}\rangle_T$

RULE EXECUTELATER

$\left\langle \dfrac{(\lambda XTs . S) : (Tt \rightarrow T)\mathit{Eff}.\texttt{executeLater}(\mathit{Vs})}{\texttt{loc}(L)} \cdots \right\rangle_k \ \left\langle \dfrac{L}{L +_{Int} 1}\right\rangle_{nextLoc} \ \left\langle \cdots \dfrac{\cdot}{L \mapsto TF(\mathit{Eff}, \texttt{bindto}(XTs, \mathit{Vs}) \curvearrowright S, \bot_T)} \cdots\right\rangle_{store} \ \left\langle \cdots \dfrac{\cdot}{L} \cdots\right\rangle_{waiting}$

RULE START-TASK

$\left\langle \cdots \dfrac{L}{\cdot} \cdots\right\rangle_{waiting} \ \left\langle \cdots L \mapsto TF(\mathit{Eff}, K, \_) \cdots\right\rangle_{store} \ \left\langle \dfrac{R}{(L, \mathit{Eff}, \varnothing)}\right\rangle_{running} \ \dfrac{\cdot}{\langle \cdots \langle K \curvearrowright \texttt{return nothing;}\rangle_k \ \langle GEnv\rangle_{env} \ \langle L\rangle_{id} \cdots\rangle_{task}} \ \langle GEnv\rangle_{genv}$

when $\forall (L_2, \mathit{Eff}_2, B) \in R : \mathit{Eff} \# \mathit{Eff}_2 \vee L \in B$

RULE SPAWN

$\left\langle \dfrac{(\lambda XTs . S) : (Tt \rightarrow T)\mathit{Eff}.\texttt{spawn}(\mathit{Vs})}{\texttt{loc}(L)} \cdots\right\rangle_k \ \left\langle \cdots \dfrac{\cdot}{L} \cdots\right\rangle_{spawned} \ \left\langle \cdots \dfrac{\cdot}{L \mapsto TF(\mathit{Eff}, \cdot, \bot_T)} \cdots\right\rangle_{store} \ \left\langle \dfrac{L}{L +_{Int} 1}\right\rangle_{nextLoc}$

$\dfrac{\cdot}{\langle \cdots \langle \texttt{bindto}(XTs, \mathit{Vs}) \curvearrowright S \curvearrowright \texttt{return nothing;}\rangle_k \ \langle GEnv\rangle_{env} \ \langle L\rangle_{id} \cdots\rangle_{task}} \ \left\langle \cdots \dfrac{\cdot}{(L, \mathit{Eff}, \varnothing)} \cdots\right\rangle_{running} \ \langle GEnv\rangle_{genv}$

RULE GETVALUE-SUCCEEDS

$\left\langle \dfrac{\texttt{loc}(L).\texttt{getValue}()}{V} \cdots\right\rangle_k \ \langle L_1\rangle_{id} \ \langle \cdots L \mapsto TF(\_, \_, V) \cdots\rangle_{store} \ \left\langle \cdots \dfrac{(L_1, \_, \dfrac{\_}{\varnothing})}{} \cdots\right\rangle_{running}$

RULE JOIN-SUCCEEDS

$\left\langle \dfrac{\texttt{loc}(L).\texttt{join}()}{V} \cdots\right\rangle_k \ \langle L_1\rangle_{id} \ \left\langle \cdots \dfrac{L}{\cdot} \cdots\right\rangle_{spawned} \ \langle \cdots L \mapsto TF(\_, \_, V) \cdots\rangle_{store} \ \left\langle \cdots \dfrac{(L_1, \_, \dfrac{\_}{\varnothing})}{} \cdots\right\rangle_{running}$

RULE GETVALUE-BLOCKS

$\langle \texttt{loc}(L).\texttt{getValue}() \cdots\rangle_k \ \langle L_1\rangle_{id} \ \left\langle \cdots \dfrac{(L_1, \_, \dfrac{\varnothing}{\{L\}})}{} \cdots\right\rangle_{running}$

RULE JOIN-BLOCKS

$\langle \texttt{loc}(L).\texttt{join}() \cdots\rangle_k \ \langle L_1\rangle_{id} \ \left\langle \cdots \dfrac{(L_1, \_, \dfrac{\varnothing}{\{L\}})}{} \cdots\right\rangle_{running}$

RULE INDIRECT-BLOCKING

$\left\langle \cdots (L, \_, ts_2) \ (\_, \_, \dfrac{ts_1}{ts_2 \cup ts_1}) \cdots\right\rangle_{running}$

when $(L \in ts_1) \wedge_{Bool} (ts_2 \nsubseteq ts_1)$

RULE RETURN

$\left\langle \dfrac{\texttt{return } V; \curvearrowright \_}{\texttt{awaitSpawned} \curvearrowright (\texttt{setRetVal } V) \curvearrowright \texttt{done}} \right\rangle_k$

RULE SET-RETURN-VALUE

$\left\langle \dfrac{\texttt{setRetVal } V}{\cdot} \cdots\right\rangle_k \ \langle L\rangle_{id} \ \left\langle \cdots L \mapsto TF(\_, \_, \dfrac{\_}{V}) \cdots\right\rangle_{store}$

RULE AWAIT-SPAWNED

$\left\langle \dfrac{\texttt{awaitSpawned}}{((\texttt{loc}(L).\texttt{join}()) \ ;) \curvearrowright \texttt{awaitSpawned}} \cdots\right\rangle_k \ \langle \cdots L \cdots\rangle_{spawned}$

RULE AWAIT-SPAWNED-DONE

$\left\langle \dfrac{\texttt{awaitSpawned}}{\cdot} \cdots\right\rangle_k \ \langle\cdot\rangle_{spawned}$

RULE DONE

$\langle \cdots \langle \texttt{done}\rangle_k \ \langle L\rangle_{id} \cdots\rangle_{task} \ \left\langle \cdots \dfrac{(L, \_, \_)}{\cdot} \cdots\right\rangle_{running}$

RULE ISDONE-TRUE

$\left\langle \dfrac{\texttt{loc}(L).\texttt{isDone}()}{\texttt{true}} \cdots\right\rangle_k \ \langle \cdots L \mapsto TF(\_, \_, V) \cdots\rangle_{store}$

RULE ISDONE-FALSE

$\left\langle \dfrac{\texttt{loc}(L).\texttt{isDone}()}{\texttt{false}} \cdots\right\rangle_k \ \langle \cdots L \mapsto TF(\_, \_, \bot_T) \cdots\rangle_{store}$

Figure 4. Dynamic semantics of tasks with effects.

3. Dynamic Semantics of Tasks with Effects

We have formalized the dynamic semantics for the core operations of the tasks with effects model in the context of a basic imperative language. A program in this language consists of a set of global variable declarations and task declarations (which are similar to function declarations in a traditional language, but include an effect specification for each task). Here we present and describe only those semantic rules related to tasks, which are shown in Figure 4.

These rules are written using the K semantic framework [36], which is based on rewriting logic and operates on a configuration of nested cells which corresponds at any point to the current state of the execution. (Although the K framework is less common than the standard approach for operational semantics, it has significant advantages, especially in that it is more modular and flexible.) Each rule may apply when it can match the configuration elements on the top of it, and when it applies any elements with a horizontal line under them are replaced by what is below the line. K supports lists, sets, and maps, and a rule may match a single element from these structures, either anywhere in them or at the front of a list; in these cases, the remainder of the structure is denoted by ellipses. A dot

represents the identity element of these structures, and an underline is a 'don't-care' element that can match anything. K rules also obey a locality principle, saying that a rule matching two subcells that appear within the same outer cell must match only two subcells within the same *instance* of that outer cell.

At the top of Figure 4, we show the initial configuration of the program. It consists of a *task* cell (of which there may later be more than one, indicated by the *); a *running* cell which will hold a set containing information on running tasks; a *waiting* cell which will contain a set of IDs of tasks waiting to execute; a *genv* cell holding the global environment (mapping identifiers to locations in the store); a *store* cell which will map locations (integers) to various objects; and a *nextLoc* cell giving the next available location in the store. Each *task* cell contains code to be executed in its *k* subcell; an ID in its *id* subcell (corresponding to a location in the store); the current environment in its *env* subcell; and a set of IDs of spawned child tasks in its *spawned* subcell. The initial configuration will pass the program code to a special operation `execute` (not shown) which initializes the store and global environment based on the declarations in the program and then runs the task named `main`.

244

Note that we present here only a dynamic semantics, which presupposes that the program has passed all static checks, including type checking and checking that the current covering effects at each point in each task correctly cover all the memory accesses it may perform. (Dynamic computations of current covering effects are not needed in this formalism, because the effects of each task are fully defined statically and there is no provision for dynamic instantiation of region or effect parameters.) These semantics are agnostic to the specific effect system used, but a formalism of the DPJ type and effect system used in TWEJava is presented in [13].

3.1 Starting Tasks

The first major class of rules in our semantics relates to starting tasks. The EXECUTELATER rule implements the executeLater operation. It will apply once the executeLater operation is the next piece of code to execute, after a task name in the code has been evaluated to a lambda expression (comparable to a Task object in TWEJava) and its arguments have been evaluated to values (simple rules not shown). The EXECUTELATER rule will allocate a new location L in the store, and store a *TF* tuple (corresponding to a TaskFuture in TWEJava). This tuple contains the effect of the task, the code to be executed when it is run, and the task's return value (initially $\bot_T$, indicating it has not yet been set). The rule adds the ID (location) of this task to the set of tasks waiting to run, and the result of the operation is a reference to that location.

The START-TASK rule is then responsible for actually starting one of the tasks in the *waiting* set. When it applies, it will create a new *task* cell in the configuration, containing the code of the new task to be run. (This cell may exist side-by-side with other *task* cells.) The rule also adds a tuple (L, *Eff*, $\varnothing$) to the *running* cell. This indicates that the task L is now running, and holds its effects and an initially-empty set of tasks that it is blocked on. Finally, the key element of this rule is the condition relating to the existing contents R of the *running* cell. This will contain information about all the other currently-running tasks, and we use it to ensure our model's basic property of task isolation. Specifically, the new task L cannot be started unless for every already-running task L_2, either the effects of L are non-interfering with those of L_2 (denoted by #) or L is in the set of tasks on which L_2 is blocked. This latter case implements our mechanism for effect transfer when blocked.

The SPAWN rule is similar to a combination of the EXECUTE-LATER and START-TASK rules, since it allows a task to start immediately without the need for the effect checking in the START-TASK rule. One addition, however, is that the ID of the spawned task is added to the *spawned* set of its parent task, which keeps track of child tasks that have been spawned and not yet joined.

3.2 Awaiting Completed Tasks and Blocking

The next group of rules relates to the potentially blocking operations getValue and join. They both can be applied to a reference to a location containing a *TF* tuple. The GETVALUE-SUCCEEDS rule addresses the case where the task in question is complete, and as such has a return value V stored in its *TF* tuple. In this case, the result of the operation is that value. Since the task that executed the getValue operation (L_1) will no longer be blocked, we empty the blocked-on set in its *running* tuple. The JOIN-SUCCEEDS rule is similar, but also requires that the task being joined was in the current task's *spawned* set, and removes it. This reflects the fact that a task can only be joined once, and only by the task that spawned it. (If a join operation violates these rules, the task that executes it will hang in our formalism. In TWEJava, an exception is thrown.)

The next two rules, GETVALUE-BLOCKS and JOIN-BLOCKS, handle the case where the task L may not yet be done. These rules put L in the blocked-on set for the task L_1 that does a getValue or join operation on L. This potentially allows L to be started based on effect transfer, using the START-TASK rule. The INDIRECT-BLOCKING rule propagates entries in the blocked-on sets when there is a chain of blocked tasks, allowing effect transfer to be applied in the case of indirect blocking. (In the TWEJava implementation, this propagation is fully performed at the time a getValue or join operation is evaluated.)

3.3 Finishing Tasks and Checking If Tasks are Done

The next group of rules relates to finishing a task. The RETURN rule handles a return statement (which may be in the program's code, or the return nothing; that we insert at the end of each task when starting it, in case it does not explicitly return a value). The rule says to first await any spawned children of the current task that have not yet been joined, then set the task's return value in its *TF* tuple (which will signal that the task may be considered done), and finally erase its *task* cell and its entry in the *running* set. The next several rules implement these operations.

Finally, the last two rules implement the isDone operation. A task is considered done once its return value has been set to a value. If it is still undefined (indicated by $\bot_T$), then the task is not done.

4. Safety Properties

Our model guarantees strong safety properties, including our basic task isolation property, plus data race freedom and atomicity properties stemming from it. We also avoid a significant class of deadlocks and can prove that many computations are deterministic.

4.1 Task isolation

The task isolation property of our system is that no two tasks may be actively running concurrently with interfering covering effects. The basic check used to guarantee this is to record the effects of each running task in the *running* set, and compare the effects of new tasks against the effects of all existing tasks before allowing them to start in the START-TASK rule.

There are two cases where we can start tasks even though they might appear to have effects interfering with those of another running task. One is that a task A may be allowed to start while a task B with conflicting effects is in the *running* set if A is in the blocked-on set for B. In this case, our rules guarantee that B cannot resume execution until A has completed, so we allow A to run based on our first effect transfer mechanism.

The other case is the spawn operation. In this case, our covering effects analysis ensures that the spawned task's effects are subeffects of its parent task's effects (so they may not conflict with anything that the parent's effects do not) and that the parent task will not execute any operations that conflict with the effects of the spawned task between where it is spawned and where it is joined.

4.2 Data race freedom

Data race freedom follows from the combination of the task isolation property and the guarantee provided by our static checks that the specified effects of each task cover all its memory accesses.

The formalism in section 3 implicitly uses a sequentially-consistent memory model, but in fact the tasks with effects model requires memory updates to be visible only between operations ordered by a limited set of happens-before edges. Our model imposes some order on any two tasks with interfering effects. This gives rise to happens-before edges between the end of one task and the start of any subsequent task with interfering effects, analogous to those between a lock release and subsequent acquisition in other systems. A full happens-before relation for our model is given by the transitive closure over these edges as well as edges for task creation, waiting or checking for task completion, and the sequential program order within each task. Any two accesses to a memory location where at least one is a write will be ordered by this happens-before relation.

4.3 Atomicity

A task or portion of a task that does not create or wait for any other tasks behaves atomically. It has fixed effects that cover all the memory locations it can access, and the scheduler will ensure that no other tasks performing conflicting accesses run concurrently with it, which ensures it is atomic. This atomicity property also extends to portions of tasks that contain task creation operations, in the sense that the semantics are equivalent to those given by creating the new tasks only at the end of the parent task or just before the next `getValue` or `join` operation in it.

Atomicity does not always extend across `getValue` or `join` operations, as our mechanism for effect transfer when blocked may allow other tasks with conflicting effects to run before the blocking operation completes. However, this potential for non-atomicity is limited to running the task(s) that are directly or indirectly blocked on, and it does not occur in cases where those tasks have definitely finished prior to the `getValue` or `join` operation. Also, a deterministic computation (discussed below) effectively executes atomically, as it is semantically equivalent to a sequential execution with no task-related operations. As in languages with explicit atomic constructs, it remains the programmer's responsibility to identify sections of code that should behave atomically and write the code in a way that ensures they do so, e.g. by not using `getValue` or `join` operations within such sections.

4.4 Deadlock avoidance

Our model avoids deadlocks in the case that a task A directly or indirectly blocks on another task B whose effects conflict with A's effects, using the effect transfer mechanism discussed in section 2.4. While we do not prevent all deadlocks, we believe this class of deadlocks is significant, and we found our effect transfer mechanism to be useful in practice, particularly in the interactive FourWins program (see section 6).

4.5 Determinism

Many parallel algorithms are deterministic. That is, they always produce the same output given the same input state. Since this is an expected property of many algorithms, detecting violations of it is a useful way of finding bugs. Moreover, knowing that a program or an algorithm is deterministic makes it much easier to reason about: the user of the program or algorithm knows that it will always produce the same output given the same input, so they need not be concerned that different parallel interleavings of operations may produce different results. Determinism also makes a program or algorithm much simpler to debug, since one knows that the same result will be produced every time it is run with a given input.

DPJ [13] can provide a compile-time guarantee of determinism using the combination of its type and effect system and simple parallelism constructs supporting only fork-join patterns of parallelism. We provide a similar static guarantee of determinism for deterministic algorithms or programs written in TWEJava. All programming patterns for which DPJ can give a guarantee of determinism can also be expressed and proven deterministic using the tasks with effects model. Our model also allows us to give a static guarantee of determinism for certain computations in a program while still allowing the rest of the program to use the full flexibility of TWEJava (including non-fork-join concurrency structures), and guaranteeing our other safety properties for the whole program. Thus, our feature for guaranteed determinism can be used within programs that could not be expressed with DPJ.

To request that the compiler check and enforce the determinism of a certain task or method, the programmer can annotate it as `@Deterministic`. In code that has this annotation, the compiler will enforce that the only task-related operations used in the code are the `spawn` and `join` operations described in section 2.5. Also, code annotated as deterministic may only call other deterministic methods and spawn other deterministic tasks.

These restrictions ensure that the code invoked from a deterministic task or method (including through the creation of other tasks) accesses memory only as specified by its declared effects. Moreover, there is a defined order by which control of each region covered by those effects is transferred between tasks, as determined by `spawn` and `join` operations. (Note that the form of effect described in section 2.4 will never be needed for `join` operations within a deterministic computation, and thus will not occur.) Therefore, for a given input state of the memory in regions covered by the effects of the deterministic task or method, there is a deterministic output state that will not vary between executions of the code. This state is the same as the state produced if the code were executed sequentially with each task's code run at the point where the task is spawned. These deterministic computations are also deadlock-free.

5. Compiler and Runtime System

Our implementation of TWEJava consists of a compiler and a runtime system, which we briefly describe here.

5.1 Compiler

The compiler is based on the DPJ compiler, which checks that effect declarations are correct and that types are used correctly. Our extended version also supports the new features of TWEJava described in Section 2. These include generating code to record effect parameters and some region parameters for use at run time; performing a data flow analysis to determine the covering effects for each operation (accounting for operations that do effect transfer); and checking the use of the `@Deterministic` annotation.

To enable interoperation with existing Java code and libraries that do not have region and effect annotations (including the Java standard libraries), the compiler allows methods without effect annotations to be called within methods that have effect annotations. This produces a warning, but that warning can be suppressed for individual methods. Since we have not written an extensive standard library for TWEJava, we take advantage of this capability to use Java standard library features such as the Swing GUI system, I/O routines, and math functions. The compiler cannot give a full guarantee about the correctness of code making such calls, so the programmer has to manually reason about it, but that reasoning can be encapsulated by writing annotated wrapper methods that internally call unannotated library routines.

5.2 Runtime System

Code generated by our compiler can be run using our runtime system, which implements the various task-related operations in TWEJava. We use an effect-based scheduler to enforce our model's key property of task isolation. Our current prototype implementation uses a queue of tasks protected by a single lock to manage the effect-checking phase of task scheduling. The effect-based scheduler enables a task for execution only once it is safe to do so based on its effects. Once a task is enabled for execution by our scheduler, it is handed off to a version of the Java `ForkJoinPool` framework, which is responsible for actually executing tasks using a thread pool.

When attempting to execute a task, our implementation generally works by scanning from a task's position forward toward the head of the queue (which includes both running and waiting tasks), checking if the task's effects conflict with those of each task ahead of it. If a conflicting task is found when attempting to schedule a task, then the later task is marked as waiting for the earlier one to complete. This approach will generally run conflicting tasks in the order that they were enqueued, but there is also a mechanism for prioritizing tasks that a running task is blocked on.

We show below that with this relatively simple scheduling approach we can achieve substantial speedups on a range of benchmarks. However, the tasks with effects model could also be implemented with other more scalable scheduling approaches. In particular, if we associated information about enqueued tasks with regions, then tasks with effects on unrelated regions would not need to have their effects explicitly compared against each other, and we could also avoid the need for a single global task queue lock.

6. Evaluation

We have carried out an evaluation of the tasks with effects model and our TWEJava language by porting several concurrent programs to it and writing one new one from scratch. We are principally concerned with demonstrating that TWEJava and the tasks with effects model can express a variety of concurrent programming styles used in real-world applications, but we also show that substantial parallel speedups can be achieved with our current TWEJava implementation.

6.1 Expressiveness

We ported four existing concurrent programs to TWEJava and wrote one new application in it. The first ported program is an interactive Connect Four game implementation called FourWins, which was ported from an original code that used JCoBox [37], an actor-like concurrent programming system for Java. The FourWins code is structured in terms of modules that behave similarly to actors, including the game state, board state, game controller, GUI view, and human and computer players. These modules communicate by sending messages between each other, sometimes, but not always, blocking until the message is processed. Our general approach in most parts of this code was to introduce a region holding the data for each module, and to define a number of types of tasks corresponding to each message that may be sent to that module. Those tasks have either read or write effects on the module's region, as needed. This code also includes a parallel computation in the computer player's AI, to explore the tree of possible future moves. That recursive parallel computation consumes most of the execution time, and it is the portion for which we report performance results below. We note that the complex concurrency structure of this program, with code from multiple actors running concurrently and sending messages between each other, cannot be expressed in many more restrictive parallelism models that require structured parallelism (e.g. fork-join) or involve a single conceptual flow of control.

The other interactive GUI application we implemented is an image editing application called ImageEdit, which we wrote from scratch in TWEJava. It allows the user to open one or more images and apply various image editing filters to them. Each of the images is displayed in a separate window and updated as filters are applied to it. Each image has a region associated with it, and the actual pixel data for the image is broken up into a 2-D grid of blocks, with the data for each block placed in a separate region using index-parameterized arrays. (By default, and in our benchmarks, a block is simply a group of adjacent lines totaling about 100,000 pixels, but the user may specify other block dimensions.) Concurrency is possible both by doing concurrent operations on different images and by operating in parallel on one image at the level of blocks. ImageEdit currently includes filters for Gaussian blur, sharpening (unsharp mask), detecting edges in the image (based on the Canny edge detection algorithm [15]), darkening or brightening the image, and converting it to grayscale. All of the filters can use parallelism

at the level of blocks, sometimes using several computation steps in sequence with parallelism in each step. The only non-parallel step in any of them is a short final step in the edge detection filter to identify edges in the input image that cross between two different blocks. Computation in this program is driven by user input events, so the program as a whole does not follow the fork-join computation model required by systems like DPJ. It could be written in other task-based concurrency models that do not use effects, but these would not provide the strong safety guarantees of TWEJava and would require the programmer to manually ensure that tasks performing conflicting memory operations cannot run concurrently.

The other three benchmarks were previously written in DPJ [13], and we ported our versions from the DPJ versions, following a similar pattern of regions and effects. These are the force computation from a Barnes-Hut n-body simulation; a k-means clustering algorithm (originally adapted from STAMP); and a Monte Carlo financial simulation, originally from the Java Grande parallel benchmarks. These three benchmarks allow us to evaluate the impact of the run-time scheduling overheads in our system by comparing against the original DPJ versions, which do not have any overheads related to effect-based scheduling at run time.

The Barnes-Hut force computation involves a parallel loop over a set of bodies, computing and adding up the forces on each body due to the other bodies. We create one task per thread using the spawn operation, each operating on a portion of the total set of bodies, which is divided using an index-parameterized array. The resulting computation is deterministic and has good parallelism.

The Monte Carlo simulation includes a deterministic parallel loop to compute an array of results, followed by a reduction step that updates globally shared data. In the DPJ version, this reduction step used DPJ's commutative annotation, which represents an unchecked assertion from the programmer that two invocations of a certain method are commutative and that it internally uses the necessary locking to correctly synchronize concurrent invocations. In the TWEJava version, this commutative method is replaced by a task, and our system automatically guarantees that this task behaves atomically. Thus, TWEJava offers a stronger safety guarantee than DPJ, since it does not require the programmer to correctly insert manual locking operations. As with Barnes-Hut, we create one task per thread in the parallel loop.

The k-means computation involves a parallel loop with a reduction step. In the original STAMP code, this reduction step is an atomic block, but in the DPJ version it is a commutative method with internal locking. In TWEJava, it is a task. As in Monte Carlo, the DPJ version relied on unchecked, manual locking, so TWEJava offers a stronger safety guarantee than DPJ. The structure of the reduction computation in k-means requires that we create many reduction tasks, independent of the number of threads.

We were able to express all the parallelism that was present in the original codes that we ported. Both the executeLater/getValue operations and structured parallelism with spawn are used in our benchmarks. The former are necessary for unstructured parallelism such as messaging between actors or modules, and for defining tasks that behave like atomic or synchronized blocks, while the latter can be used in parallel loops or recursive parallel computations.

6.2 Performance

We measured the performance of our benchmark codes on a machine with four Intel Xeon E7-4860 processors (40 total cores, 80 hardware threads using Hyper-Threading) and 128 GB of memory, running Scientific Linux 6.3 with kernel 2.6.32 and 64-bit Oracle JDK 7u9. Figures 5 and 6 report the speedups achieved in the parallel portion of each code. For ImageEdit, we report speedups for

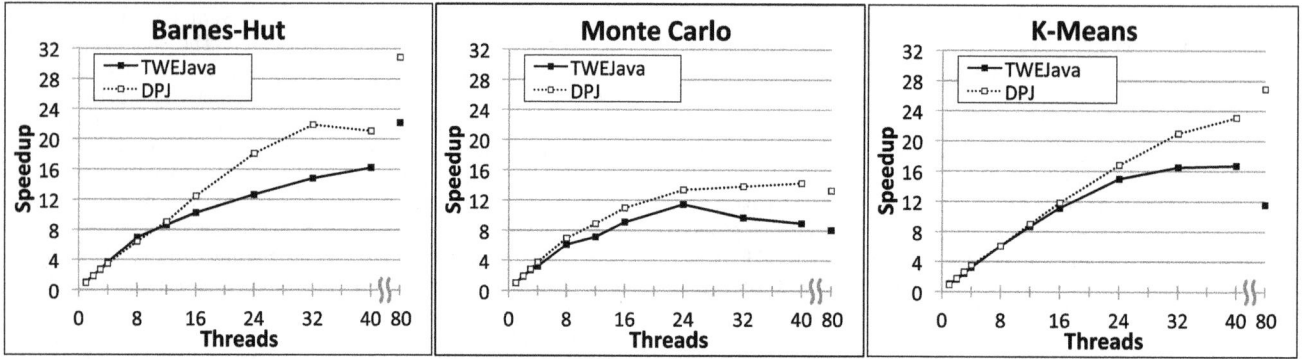

Figure 5. Parallel speedups of benchmarks ported from DPJ, showing performance of TWEJava and DPJ versions. These speedups are for the parallel portion of each code and are relative to the DPJ code compiled and run in sequential mode, in which the DPJ parallelism constructs are erased by the compiler, creating a sequential program with no run-time overheads related to parallelism constructs.

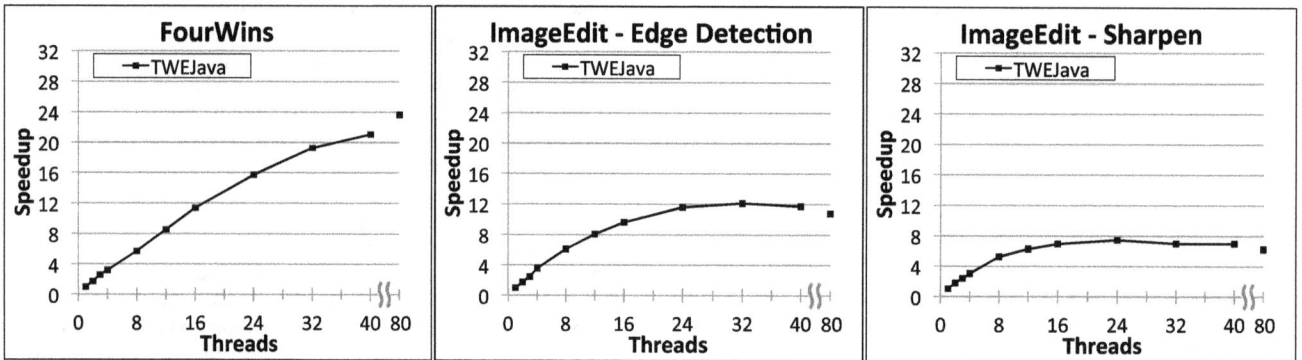

Figure 6. Speedups for the FourWins AI computation and two filters in the ImageEdit application. We did not have pure sequential versions of these programs available for comparison, so we give speedups relative to the TWEJava codes run using one worker thread and configured so that the major potentially-parallel computations in the codes each run as a single task, thereby minimizing task-related overheads.

both the edge detection filter and the sharpening filter. We also compared the parallel running times to DPJ for the codes where there is a DPJ version. The multi-threaded DPJ version internally executes tasks on a thread pool, but it does not have the overhead of runtime effect-based task scheduling, and previous work has shown it is generally quite efficient [13].

Each of our TWEJava benchmarks achieves significant speedups, with maximum speedups on the various benchmarks ranging from 7.5x to 23.6x. The Barnes-Hut and FourWins benchmarks continue scaling substantially up to 80 threads (with the gains going from 40 to 80 threads attributable to Hyper-Threading). The other benchmarks show good scaling at lower numbers of threads, but do not continue scaling above 24 to 32 threads.

The benchmarks for which we have DPJ versions perform very similarly to the DPJ versions up to at least eight threads, but show worse scaling at high numbers of threads. Several types of overhead in the TWEJava system may be responsible for these performance differences. The overheads of our effect-based run-time task scheduling system include the need to check the effects of tasks against each other to see whether they conflict, and the need to track some region parameters and all effect parameters at run time, rather than erasing them during compilation. These overheads can become larger with larger numbers of threads, because there will generally be more tasks active at once in such configurations. Another important factor limiting the scalability of our current implementation is that our effect-based scheduler uses a single queue

protected by a single lock, so all the effect-based scheduling operations in the system are essentially serialized. Also, the DPJ runtime system can use recursive subdivision to split the iterations of parallel loops into tasks, while in TWEJava we converted these constructs to loops that sequentially spawn off child tasks. This may also contribute to the inferior scalability of the TWEJava codes. It would be possible to implement this sort of recursive subdivision in the tasks with effects model, but TWEJava currently does not have convenient language constructs for it.

We believe the overheads of effect-based task scheduling are particularly important factors in explaining the inferior scaling of our version of KMeans compared to the DPJ version on large numbers of threads, because the TWEJava version uses a task rather than a locked block for the reduction step. This is called a large number of times, regardless of the number of threads (550,000 times in our benchmark configuration). Since task scheduling is a heavier-weight procedure than simple locking around a short block, and particularly since (as noted above) the scheduling of each task is effectively sequentialized in our current implementation, this leads to poorer scalability for the TWEJava version of the code.

In the case on ImageEdit, one factor limiting the speedups achieved is that each time the image is updated, some sequential operations are necessary to actually change the image displayed in the GUI, which is implemented with Java's Swing framework and therefore needs to do GUI operations on a single thread, in accordance with Swing's architecture. This is a larger factor for the

248

sharpening operation than for the edge detection operation, since the core parallel computation for sharpening is faster than for edge detection. We believe this at least partially accounts for the poorer scalability of sharpening compared to edge detection, as well as the overall scalability limits of the ImageEdit computations.

While our system has run-time overheads related to task scheduling and dynamic tracking of region and effect parameters, it still delivers significant parallel speedups, sometimes comparable to the DPJ versions of the codes (particularly on relatively low numbers of threads). We believe the scalability and performance of our system could be improved by implementing a scheduler that does not use a single lock and a compiler and scheduler that work together to minimize the number of dynamic effect comparisons (e.g. by avoiding the need for run-time checking of covering effects when child tasks are spawned in a loop). However, we think our current implementation without these optimizations still gives good enough performance to be used in many applications, particularly in desktop and mobile systems with relatively low numbers of cores.

7. Related Work

Traditional multithreaded systems such as Java or Posix threads are more flexible than TWEJava in the sense that they allow almost any desired concurrency and synchronization structure to be expressed, but they provide no guarantees about the absence of concurrency errors, and also have few or no facilities that simplify reasoning about such errors. Some systems, including OpenMP [32], Cilk [11], Threading Building Blocks (TBB) [22] (except for the "lower-level" task interfaces), and Java's ForkJoinTask [33] are more structured and easier to reason about than traditional threads. However, these systems still do not provide any correctness guarantees such as data race freedom or determinism. The programmer still has to reason manually to ensure that data sharing patterns are correct and synchronization is present when needed. These systems simplify such reasoning by limiting programs to use a particular parallelism structure (e.g. fork-join), but in doing so, can no longer express the forms of concurrency required by many programs such as interactive applications, servers, and actor-style programs. TWEJava is able to express all these kinds of programs and yet provides strong correctness guarantees.

RCCJava [18] can ensure data race freedom, but it does not provide structured concurrency constructs or guarantee other safety properties such as determinism. SharC [5] allows flexible concurrent control flow while providing a guarantee of data race freedom, but it also does not provide structured concurrency constructs and cannot guarantee stronger properties like determinism. CoreDet [8], Kendo [31], Grace [9], and DMP [16] allow multithreaded programs to be executed with a deterministic execution order that does not vary from run to run, but they do not provide structured parallelism constructs, and the deterministic execution order they provide is not related in an obvious way to the program code and may change if the code or input changes, which limits their utility as tools for reasoning about program behavior.

Many parallel and concurrent programming systems provide various correctness guarantees but have weaker expressive power than TWEJava. These include Jade [35], Prometheus [4], DPJ [13, 14], OoOJava [23], Dynamic Out-of-Order Java (DOJ) [17], Pāṇini [27], SvS [10], Legion [7], and Ke et al.'s system for parallelization with dependence hints [25]. Several of these systems, including Jade, Prometheus, OoOJava, DOJ, and Pāṇini, guarantee deterministic semantics (often with equivalence to a unique sequential program) but these systems are unable to express inherently nondeterministic algorithms, or programs where concurrency is due to external requests or user input and the input and its timing may affect the program's results. SMPSs [34] is also designed to provide sequential-equivalent semantics and uses a form of effect annotations for task scheduling, but these annotations are not verified, so the programmer is responsible for ensuring that the annotations are correct in order to ensure proper program behavior. Several systems, including (at least) Jade, SvS, Legion, DOJ, SMPSs, and Aida [28], have used effects in some form to guide run-time scheduling decisions, but TWEJava provides the ability to express programs not supported by any of these other languages and gives stronger safety guarantees than some of them.

DPJ, Legion and SvS can express nondeterministic programs, but not programs requiring flexible concurrency structures, identified above. DPJ supports programs with both deterministic and nondeterministic algorithms, and provides the strongest parallel correctness guarantees we know of, but because it is limited to fork-join parallel structures, it is not suitable for many concurrent programs. TWEJava supports a much broader class of programs than DPJ, and provides almost as strong correctness guarantees: its primary weakness compared to DPJ is that it only provides limited protection from deadlocks. Like DPJ, Legion cannot express programs with general concurrency and synchronization patterns because there are no mechanisms for explicit "join" synchronization between tasks (tasks block for other tasks only due to interfering effects, enforced by the scheduler) and the effects of a parent task must be a superset of the effects of its child tasks. Legion also provides significantly weaker correctness guarantees than DPJ or TWEJava, although it allows more dynamic assignment of data to regions, and explicit program management of locality via region maps. SvS executes tasks according to a statically-defined task graph, which limits the language to a narrower range of concurrent applications than TWEJava. SvS allows both deterministic and nondeterministic algorithms, and guarantees data race freedom to such programs. One key difference is that SvS *infers* potential conflicts due to implicit sharing of data between tasks, and uses an approximate run-time analysis of the memory possibly accessed by a task. While these features reduce the annotation burden on the programmer, they increase the likelihood of spurious dependences ("false positives") that prevent two tasks from executing in parallel. TWEJava does not suffer from such false positives when checking for effect interference between tasks.

Transactional memory systems [19] use speculative execution to enforce correctness guarantees such as atomicity. These systems guarantee that atomic blocks declared by the programmer execute in isolation from each other, performing rollback and retry if necessary. To date, implementations have often relied on software transactional memory (STM). STM systems generally have high overheads, stemming from the need to track memory accesses and check for conflicts, combined with wasted computation when rollbacks occur. In contrast, TWEJava only requires conflict checks (on task effect summaries) before a task begins execution and never rolls back partially-completed tasks. Also, to avoid exorbitantly high overheads, many STM systems only guarantee isolation between two atomic blocks (weak isolation). In these systems, statements outside atomic blocks may still race with other statements inside or outside atomic blocks, so there is not a full guarantee of data race freedom.

Several other systems also use optimistic parallelism. Galois [26] focuses on irregular algorithms and requires the programmer to specify which operations are semantically commutative and define inverse methods for use on rollback. Non-deterministic algorithms in DPJ also use atomic blocks implemented via an STM system, which has fairly poor absolute performance [14]. Aida [28] also focuses on irregular parallelism. It guarantees the absence of data races, deadlock and livelock, via a mechanism called "delegated isolation," where a task that conflicts with another concurrent task is rolled back and then "delegates" all its computation and data to the latter task. Galois, DPJ and Aida are all limited to highly structured, fork-join concurrency.

A more flexible style of concurrent programming is *actors* [3]. In the basic actor model, a concurrent system is composed of several actors, each potentially having local state, but no shared state between the actors. Actors communicate by sending messages to other actors, and computation is done at each actor in response to the messages received. Each actor processes only one message at a time, so all concurrency is due to the simultaneous execution of different actors. Actor-style programs are natural to express using our system: a region can be defined to correspond to each actor, and tasks with effects on that region can be thought of as equivalent to messages sent and processed by that actor. Several actor-like programming models for shared memory systems [24, 29, 37] broaden the basic actor model to include some form of shared state between actors, but these systems are generally less flexible than our effect system, and in some cases do not guarantee data race freedom. Our system, when used to write actor-style programs, can express both shared state between actors and internal concurrency within actors, while guaranteeing data race freedom as well as, where desired, deterministic, sequential-equivalent semantics for parallel algorithms used within an actor.

8. Conclusion

We have described and defined the semantics of a new concurrent programming model based on tasks with effects, and presented a language called TWEJava that implements it. TWEJava can express a wide range of concurrent and parallel programs, while delivering very strong safety properties including task isolation, data race freedom, atomicity, and optionally determinism. We have implemented several concurrent programs in TWEJava and shown that our present implementation can give substantial parallel speedups.

Acknowledgments

This work was funded by the Illinois-Intel Parallelism Center at the University of Illinois at Urbana-Champaign. The Center is sponsored by the Intel Corporation.

References

[1] M. Abadi, A. Birrell, T. Harris, and M. Isard. Semantics of transactional memory and automatic mutual exclusion. In *POPL*, 2008.

[2] S. V. Adve and K. Gharachorloo. Shared memory consistency models: A tutorial. *IEEE Comp., Special Issue on Shared-Mem. Multiproc.*, pages 66–76, December 1996.

[3] G. Agha. *Actors: A model of concurrent computation in distributed systems*. MIT Press, 1986.

[4] M. D. Allen, S. Sridharan, and G. S. Sohi. Serialization sets: A dynamic dependence-based parallel execution model. In *PPOPP*, 2009.

[5] Z. Anderson, D. Gay, R. Ennals, and E. Brewer. SharC: Checking data sharing strategies for multithreaded C. In *PLDI*, 2008.

[6] Apple. Concurrency Programming Guide. `http://developer. apple.com/library/mac/documentation/General/ Conceptual/ConcurrencyProgrammingGuide/`, Dec. 2012.

[7] M. Bauer, S. Treichler, E. Slaughter, and A. Aiken. Legion: Expressing locality and independence with logical regions. In *SC'12*, 2012.

[8] T. Bergan, O. Anderson, J. Devietti, L. Ceze, and D. Grossman. CoreDet: A compiler and runtime system for deterministic multithreaded execution. In *ASPLOS*, 2010.

[9] E. D. Berger, T. Yang, T. Liu, and G. Novark. Grace: Safe multithreaded programming for C/C++. In *OOPSLA*, 2009.

[10] M. J. Best, S. Mottishaw, C. Mustard, M. Roth, A. Fedorova, and A. Brownsword. Synchronization via scheduling: Techniques for efficiently managing shared state. In *PLDI*, 2011.

[11] R. D. Blumofe, C. F. Joerg, B. C. Kuszmaul, C. E. Leiserson, K. H. Randall, and Y. Zhou. Cilk: An efficient multithreaded runtime system. In *PPOPP*, 1995.

[12] R. L. Bocchino and V. S. Adve. Types, regions, and effects for safe programming with object-oriented parallel frameworks. In *ECOOP*, 2011.

[13] R. L. Bocchino, V. S. Adve, D. Dig, S. V. Adve, S. Heumann, R. Komuravelli, J. Overbey, P. Simmons, H. Sung, and M. Vakilian. A type and effect system for Deterministic Parallel Java. In *OOPSLA*, 2009.

[14] R. L. Bocchino, S. Heumann, N. Honarmand, S. V. Adve, V. S. Adve, A. Welc, and T. Shpeisman. Safe nondeterminism in a deterministic-by-default parallel language. In *POPL*, 2011.

[15] J. Canny. A computational approach to edge detection. *IEEE Trans. Pattern Analysis and Machine Intelligence*, 8(6):679–698, June 1986.

[16] J. Devietti, B. Lucia, L. Ceze, and M. Oskin. DMP: Deterministic shared memory multiprocessing. In *ASPLOS*, 2009.

[17] Y. h. Eom, S. Yang, J. C. Jenista, and B. Demsky. DOJ: Dynamically parallelizing object-oriented programs. In *PPoPP*, 2012.

[18] C. Flanagan and S. N. Freund. Type-based race detection for Java. In *PLDI*, 2000.

[19] T. Harris, J. Larus, and R. Rajwar. *Transactional Memory, 2nd Edition (Synthesis Lectures on Comp. Arch.)*. Morgan & Claypool, 2010.

[20] S. Heumann and V. Adve. Disciplined concurrent programming using tasks with effects. In *HotPar*, 2012.

[21] S. Heumann and V. Adve. Tasks with effects: A model for disciplined concurrent programming. In *WoDet*, 2012.

[22] Intel. Intel Thread Building Blocks Reference Manual. `http: //software.intel.com/sites/products/documentation/ hpc/tbb/referencev2.pdf`, Aug. 2011.

[23] J. C. Jenista, Y. h. Eom, and B. C. Demsky. OoOJava: software out-of-order execution. In *PPOPP*, 2011.

[24] R. K. Karmani, A. Shali, and G. Agha. Actor frameworks for the JVM platform: A comparative analysis. In *Principles and Practice of Programming in Java (PPPJ)*, 2009.

[25] C. Ke, L. Liu, C. Zhang, T. Bai, B. Jacobs, and C. Ding. Safe parallel programming using dynamic dependence hints. In *OOPSLA*, 2011.

[26] M. Kulkarni, K. Pingali, B. Walter, G. Ramanarayanan, K. Bala, and L. P. Chew. Optimistic parallelism requires abstractions. In *PLDI*, 2007.

[27] Y. Long, S. L. Mooney, T. Sondag, and H. Rajan. Implicit invocation meets safe, implicit concurrency. In *Generative Programming and Component Engineering (GPCE)*, 2010.

[28] R. Lublinerman, J. Zhao, Z. Budimlić, S. Chaudhuri, and V. Sarkar. Delegated isolation. In *OOPSLA*, 2011.

[29] Microsoft. Axum. `http://msdn.microsoft.com/en-us/ devlabs/dd795202`.

[30] Microsoft. Task Parallel Library (TPL). `http://msdn.microsoft. com/en-us/library/dd460717.aspx`.

[31] M. Olszewski, J. Ansel, and S. Amarasinghe. Kendo: Efficient deterministic multithreading in software. In *ASPLOS*, 2009.

[32] OpenMP Architecture Review Board. OpenMP Application Program Interface, Version 3.1. `http://www.openmp.org/mp-documents/ OpenMP3.1.pdf`, 2011.

[33] Oracle. Java Platform, Standard Edition 7 API specification. `http: //download.oracle.com/javase/7/docs/api/`.

[34] J. M. Perez, R. M. Badia, and J. Labarta. A dependency-aware task-based programming environment for multi-core architectures. In *IEEE International Conference on Cluster Computing*, 2008.

[35] M. C. Rinard and M. S. Lam. The design, implementation, and evaluation of Jade. *TOPLAS*, 20(3):483–545, May 1998.

[36] G. Roşu and T. F. Şerbănuţă. An overview of the K semantic framework. *Journal of Logic and Algebraic Programming*, 79(6), 2010.

[37] J. Schäfer and A. Poetzsch-Heffter. JCoBox: Generalizing active objects to concurrent components. In *ECOOP*, 2010.

TigerQuoll: Parallel Event-based JavaScript

Daniele Bonetta   Walter Binder   Cesare Pautasso

Faculty of Informatics, University of Lugano – USI
Lugano, Switzerland
{name.surname}@usi.ch

Abstract

JavaScript, the most popular language on the Web, is rapidly moving to the server-side, becoming even more pervasive. Still, JavaScript lacks support for shared memory parallelism, making it challenging for developers to exploit multicores present in both servers and clients. In this paper we present TigerQuoll, a novel API and runtime for parallel programming in JavaScript. TigerQuoll features an event-based API and a parallel runtime allowing applications to exploit a mutable shared memory space. The programming model of TigerQuoll features automatic consistency and concurrency management, such that developers do not have to deal with shared-data synchronization. TigerQuoll supports an innovative transaction model that allows for eventual consistency to speed up high-contention workloads. Experiments show that TigerQuoll applications scale well, allowing one to implement common parallelism patterns in JavaScript.

Categories and Subject Descriptors   D.1.3 [*Concurrent Programming*]: Parallel Programming

General Terms   Languages, Performance

Keywords   JavaScript, Event-based Programming, Parallelism, Eventual Transactions

1. Introduction

JavaScript was initially designed as a single-threaded programming language for executing small client-side scripts within Web browsers. To support increasingly complex Web applications such as Facebook or GMail, recent research has focused on increasing the performance of JavaScript engines. As a result, modern engines such as Google's V8 and Mozilla's SpiderMonkey feature advanced optimizations such as just-in-time compilation and inline caching.

Despite of these advancements, one fundamental issue with JavaScript-based applications remains unsolved, that is, the poor support for parallelism. As the Web continues evolving towards a mature application-hosting platform, the lack of parallelism in JavaScript would eventually correspond to a serious technological barrier. Furthermore, the wide-spread deployment of JavaScript-based frameworks for server-side development has increased the pervasiveness of the language, making JavaScript a central language for the entire Web development stack. As a result, frameworks such as Microsoft Azure and Node.JS [2] offer a convenient solution to develop Cloud-hosted Web applications using JavaScript as the sole language for both the client and the server.

The limited support for parallelism in JavaScript constrains the class of applications which can be executed in the browser, thus preventing Web developers from fully exploiting parallel infrastructures such as multicore machines commonly available both on the client and on the server. Current actor-based solutions such as WebWorkers [1] limit the way developers can exploit parallelism, as they force them to reason in terms of parallel processes, message passing, and share-nothing parallelism. Although well suited for master-worker parallelism, the Actor model of concurrency appears to be too limited for algorithms and applications that can benefit from more complex parallel patterns [24]. Moreover, share-nothing parallelism represents a strong limitation for JavaScript developers, as it clashes with the programming style of JavaScript, based on single-threaded asynchronous programming and shared memory for accessing the Document Object Model (DOM) of a Web page.

We advocate a different solution, claiming that the parallel support for JavaScript should come *without* violating the programming style of JavaScript, that is, asynchronous programming [16]. To substantiate our claim, in this paper we present TigerQuoll, a fully JavaScript-compatible execution engine which allows scripts to be executed in parallel using a flexible event-based API.

TigerQuoll makes the following contributions to advancing the state-of-the-art in the field of parallel programming for the Web:

(1) *Programming Model.* The TigerQuoll API extends single-threaded event-based JavaScript programming with support for parallelism. The resulting programming model allows the developer to exploit parallelism by means of *parallel event handlers*. Executing multiple event handlers in parallel allows the JavaScript developer to adopt a familiar programming style based on asynchronous callback invocation.

(2) *Eventual Transactions.* Parallel execution is protected using a software transactional memory (STM). In addition, TigerQuoll introduces a novel form of transactions called *eventual transactions* which ensure that the parallel execution of event handlers accessing mutable global shared state through a controlled mechanism always succeed. Eventual transactions help improve scalability for certain workloads.

(3) *Parallel JavaScript Engine.* JavaScript applications are executed by the TigerQuoll parallel execution engine. Its run-

time executes multiple event handler functions in parallel, ensuring a consistent view of the shared memory.

To the best of our knowledge, TigerQuoll is the first parallel JavaScript engine supporting mutable shared state. Furthermore, we are the first introducing eventual transactions for software transactional memory.

This paper is structured as follows. Section 2 introduces the main design goals of TigerQuoll. Section 3 introduces the event-based API, while Section 4 describes how events can be used to build high-level parallel constructs. Section 5 provides a detailed description of the TigerQuoll memory model. Section 6 provides details about the architecture of the TigerQuoll engine. Section 7 presents an initial performance evaluation of the engine, whose results are discussed in Section 8. Section 9 presents related work, and Section 10 concludes.

2. Parallelizing JavaScript

Introducing parallelism in a language that has not been designed for it is a challenging task. Our solution preserves compatibility with existing JavaScript applications allowing developers to write parallel code adopting a programming style familiar with the one of single-threaded sequential asynchronous programming. In more detail, TigerQuoll has been designed to meet the following requirements:

(1) **Backward compatibility**. Existing applications designed to run on single-threaded JavaScript engines shall be fully compatible with TigerQuoll. To guarantee strict compatibility the sequential semantics shall be enforced by the runtime, which needs to execute existing legacy code strictly sequentially (i.e., in the same thread).

(2) **Forward compatibility**. Applications developed for parallel execution on the TigerQuoll parallel engine shall also be executable by existing single-threaded JavaScript engines (at the cost of losing the performance benefits coming from parallelism).

(3) **Implicit parallel entities**. The complexity of the programming model of JavaScript shall not be increased by adding explicit parallel entities such as threads or processes. Therefore, no coordination mechanisms (e.g., locks, barriers, or message queues) need to be exposed to the developer.

(4) **Event-based concurrency**. The only concurrency control mechanism supported by the programming model shall be the one already present in single-threaded JavaScript, that is, event-based concurrency. Asynchronous event-based programming is therefore extended (through a novel API) to express parallel computations.

(5) **Shared memory space**. To preserve the existing single-threaded JavaScript programming model, a mutable global state shall be supported by the programming model. However, the developer shall not be responsible for ensuring thread-safety and liveness. Instead, the programming model shall automatically guarantee atomicity, consistency, and isolation. Such properties shall be guaranteed transparently, as the developer shall not be in charge of adding explicit atomic blocks.

The main difference of the TigerQuoll programming model over existing solutions for parallel JavaScript is that it is conveniently compatible with the programming style JavaScript developers are already familiar with, not requiring developers to reason in terms of either share-nothing parallelism (as in WebWorkers [1]) or immutable shared state (as in Intel's River Trail [19] or Parallel Closures [23]). Indeed, the TigerQuoll programming model allows developers to write parallel JavaScript applications adopting a parallelism model with mutable shared-memory and asynchronous event-based concurrency, allowing applications to transparently benefit from the presence of multiple cores.

3. The Programming Model of TigerQuoll

The programming model of TigerQuoll is based on event production and consumption. Every JavaScript object in TigerQuoll can produce and consume events. The resulting event-based model is a set of low-level APIs which can be directly used for parallel programming, or as basic building blocks for developing convenient higher-level parallel primitives. This is discussed in the next section, where common high-level parallel constructs are illustrated.

3.1 Core Event API

The two main primitives for event-based programming in the TigerQuoll API are on and emit. Using the on primitive, any object can specify an event handler callback function to be associated with any event. Events are specified using strings (called event labels). The emit primitive is used to notify the runtime that an event has happened. It is a non-blocking primitive which immediately returns. The on primitive is memory-less, meaning that it is not triggered by any event emitted before the callback was registered. Events can also be associated with parameters, like in this example callback registration:

```
obj.on('connection', function(fd) {
    // open the 'fd' descriptor and handle the request
});
```

which can be triggered by the following event emission:

```
// somewhere in the connection handling code...
obj.emit('connection', 33)
```

The two pieces of code correspond to how incoming connections are handled by a JavaScript server (e.g., the Node.JS socket server). An object responsible for accepting the incoming request (obj) is registered to listen for an incoming connection using on. When the runtime receives a new connection on a listening socket the 'connection' event is emitted, and the socket descriptor on which the connection has been accepted is passed to the event handler. The callback associated with the 'connection' event is then invoked with the actual value of the fd variable as argument (i.e., 33 in the example). Multiple calls to emit correspond to multiple invocations of the callback function handling the event.

To ensure that a callback is executed only once, and is then immediately unregistered, the API provides the once() primitive:

```
obj.once('fireAndForget', function() {
    // do something...
})
obj.emit('fireAndForget')
obj.emit('fireAnotherEvent')
obj.emit('fireAndForget')
```

The once() primitive registers the callback to be executed only once. Hence, the second time emit is called with 'fireAndForget' as argument (line 6) it will not cause the callback to be re-executed again. The emit primitive is asynchronous and does not offer any ordering guarantees. As a consequence, the two events ('fireAndForget' and 'fireAnotherEvent') in the example may be executed in any order.

The dual primitive is `never()`:

```
obj.never('ev')
```

which is used to remove the callback handler for a specific event identifier.

3.2 Event-based Parallelism

The `on`/`emit` API is similar to the one found in server-side event-based frameworks *à la* Node.JS as well as many client-side libraries for JavaScript (e.g., JQuery or Async.JS). Differently from such frameworks, event handlers (i.e., callbacks) are executed by the runtime *in parallel*. Consider the following example:

```
var stats = { tot : 0, found : [] }
obj.on('data', function(n) {
    if(isPrime(n)) {
        stats.tot++
        stats.found.push(n)
    }
})

var inArr = new Array(1, 2, 3, 4, ...)
for(var i=0; i<inArr.length; i++)
    obj.emit('data', inArr[i])
```

The example corresponds to a simple primes checker. The checker operates on an array of numbers (`inArr`) and asynchronously evaluates for every element whether the given number is prime by calling the `isPrime(n)` function. When a prime number is found, it is saved.

When executed by an event-driven JavaScript framework such as Node.JS, the code above will process all the elements of the array sequentially, because JavaScript is single-threaded by design, and so are the existing JavaScript execution engines. Conversely, the code in the example is executed in parallel by the TigerQuoll runtime, using all the cores in the system. This is made possible by the TigerQuoll engine, which executes multiple event handlers (i.e., the callback for the `'data'` event) in parallel. Furthermore, event handlers are guaranteed to run atomically with respect to other handlers. Therefore, the counter in the example is guaranteed to have a consistent value at the end of the computation. As the whole event emitter is guaranteed to execute atomically, also the array keeping track of all the prime numbers found during the parallel computation will eventually be consistent.

3.3 Event Handler Synchronization

Asynchronous, event-based programming is the default abstraction for dealing with I/O in JavaScript. Thanks to the event-based programming model, a single-threaded application can trigger multiple downloads sequentially and wait for multiple transfers to happen in parallel, thus overlapping the download of multiple remote resources thanks to mechanisms such as `select` or `epoll` (implemented either by the OS Kernel or by the browser). With single-threaded JavaScript, the asynchronous interaction with multiple resources (for instance, multiple ongoing downloads) requires that the single JavaScript thread never blocks.

The ability to execute multiple event handlers asynchronously and in parallel introduces a more stronger need for event synchronization. In such a context it makes sense to provide the developer with a mechanism to automatically synchronize specific event execution with other events completion. Such mechanism could then be exploited to schedule the execution of certain event handlers upon the completion of other events. This is made possible in TigerQuoll through the `waitall` primitive, which can be used to register *event guards*. Consider the following example:

```
// register an event handler for 'compute'
obj.on('compute', function() {
    // do something...
})

// trigger the 'compute' event N times
for(var i=0; i<N; i++)
    obj.emit('compute')

// register an event guard for 'compute'
obj.waitall('compute', function() {
    // all the 'compute' events have been emitted
    // and all the corresponding event handlers
    // have returned
})
```

In the code above an event is emitted several times, causing the engine to execute the corresponding callbacks in parallel. The `waitall` primitive is used to register another event handler which is executed *after* all the `compute` events have been processed (i.e., when all the parallel callbacks have been executed and have returned). One important consideration about the `waitall` primitive is that it allows to wait for any number of events emitted by the currently running event handler, thus allowing for event composition.

As for the `on` primitive, `waitall` is memory-less: if the event it is required to wait for has been emitted and executed before a call to `waitall`, the event emission cannot be tracked, and the callback associated with the event guard will not be executed. In particular, event guards are guaranteed to track the event emission of all the events emitted by the currently running event handler. As a consequence, event guards cannot guarantee to track events emitted by multiple event handlers concurrently.

4. High-level Parallelism

The TigerQuoll Core Event API offers a relatively low abstraction level. This low-level substrate can be conveniently used to build high-level mechanisms and constructs that Web developers can use to exploit parallelism in their everyday life. In this section we introduce some of the possible high-level constructs (i.e., asynch, finish, map/reduce) that can be built upon the Core Event API of TigerQuoll.

4.1 Futures and Task Parallelism

Many programming languages feature a notion of future tasks [17]. These can be introduced in JavaScript with the `spawn` method :

```
// Execute the 'fun' function with argument 'arg'
// in parallel, and get a future as the result
var future = spawn(fun, arg)
// register a callback to get the result
future.get(function(result) {
    // 'result' contains the return value
    // for 'fun(args)'
})
```

In the example, the `fun` function is executed asynchronously in parallel, and the result is fetched calling `get`, which will call the given callback with the function return value once its execution has completed.

Another task parallelism construct many languages feature is lightweight tasks for immediate parallel execution. Such tasks are usually spawned through an asynchronous function call, and the runtime provides a way for synchronizing on task completion. For example, in X10 [7] such primitives are called `async` and `finish`. Having such primitives in JavaScript would simplify the way parallel computations can be developed. They can be used as in the following ex-

```
1   var spawn = function(f, arg) {
2       // Create an object to track the state of the async call
3       var _A = {}
4       // Register the function for async execution
5       _A.on('go!', function() {
6           // Call the function
7           _A.result = f(arg)
8       })
9       // Register the future callback
10      .on('get!', function(cb) {
11          cb(_A.result)
12      })
13      // Fire the event to call the function
14      .emit('go!')
15      // Return the future object
16      return {
17          get: function(callback) {
18              // Register the callback to be called once the
19              // result has been computed, or return it
20              if (_A.result)
21                  return callback(_A.result)
22              _A.emit('get!', callback)
23      } }
24  }
```

```
1   var async = function(fun, a, b) {
2       // schedule 'fun' for asynchronous execution
3       // using the 'finish' global object as the
4       // event emitter
5       finish.emit('go', fun, a, b)
6   }
7   var finish = function(f) {
8       // register a callback for executing functions
9       // in parallel using the 'finish' (this) object
10      finish.on('go', function(fun, a, b) {
11          fun(a, b)
12      })
13      // execute the function, which will call
14      // async multiple times
15      f()
16      // Return the ondone function
17      return {
18          ondone : function(callback) {
19              // register a wait guard for the
20              // 'go' event
21              finish.waitall('go', function() {
22                  callback()
23              })
24      }}
```

Figure 1. Simplified implementation of spawn, async, and finish using the TigerQuoll API

ample, which applies a function fun to all the elements of an array (data) in parallel:

```
1   var data = [...] // the array to be processed
2
3   var fun = function(index) {
4       data[index] = someProcessing(data[index])
5   }
6   finish(function() {
7       for(var i in data)
8           async(fun, i)
9   }).ondone(function() {
10      // since all the parallel tasks have completed,
11      // now the data array contains the result
12  })
```

As shown in Figure 1, the JavaScript version of spawn makes use of the TigerQuoll API by means of an auxiliary object to keep track of the state of the parallel tasks' execution (called _A). The spawn primitive makes use of the auxiliary object to register an event to trigger the asynchronous invocation of the function ('go!'), and returns an object representing the future. When the get method of the future is called, a callback is registered which will eventually be called with the result of the asynchronous function execution.

The implementation of the async and finish primitives uses another shared object (i.e., the finish function itself) to associate the emission of all the parallel tasks being executed by async with a same event emitter object. In this way, the waitall primitive can be used to postpone the ondone callback execution until all the tasks have been executed. Support for nested finish invocations could be achieved by using a stack of shared objects instead of the finish function itself (not shown in the Figure).

4.2 Structured Parallelism

Another example of high-level parallelism constructs which can be built with the event-based API is represented by some very common structured parallelism patterns (a.k.a. Algorithmic Skeletons [9, 24]). Such patterns simplify the way common parallel patterns can be programmed by introducing the notion of structured parallel patterns. Very popular examples of such patterns are Map/Reduce [11] and Scatter/Gather [8].

Building such patterns on top of the TigerQuoll API is straightforward. Consider the following implementation of a MapReduce-like computation for processing all the elements of a given array in parallel:

```
1   Array.prototype.mapred = function(map, reduce) {
2       var obj = {}
3       obj.waitall('go', function() {
4           var result = reduce(this)
5           obj.emit('donePar', result)
6       })
7       // register an event for parallel processing
8       obj.on('go', function(fun, x) {
9           fun(x)
10      })
11      // emit an event for
12      for(var v=0; v<this.length; v++)
13          obj.emit('go', map, this[v])
14
15      return {
16          ondone : function(fincb) {
17              obj.on('donePar', fincb)
18      }}
19  }
```

As in common MapReduce computations, the example above applies a given map function to all the elements of a fixed size array, and eventually calls a reduction function returning the result. The event-based parallel MapReduce can be easily invoked in the following way:

```
1   // declare an array
2   var a = new Array(1,2,...)
3
4   // execute the mapreduce using two arbitrary functions
5   a.mapred(map, reduce)
6   .ondone(function(result) {
7       // the variable 'result' contains the
8       // result of the computation
9   })
```

5. Shared Memory Model

Unlike existing approaches to parallelize JavaScript which are either based on message-passing (i.e., share-nothing) or on shared but immutable data, TigerQuoll parallel event handlers can access and also modify shared data. Global uncontrolled heap access requires the developer to deal with synchronization mechanisms (e.g., locks or barriers [21]) which often result in complex and error-prone programming techniques. Access to heap objects can be mediated by using atomic blocks, usually implemented through Software Transactional Memory (STM) or Lock Inference, but such approaches would again require the developer to explicitly identify which portion of the code is to be protected with an atomic block, and data races or race conditions would still be possible for unprotected code.

TigerQuoll adopts a radically simplified solution, with the goal of keeping the programming model as close as possible to the one of single-threaded JavaScript. The goal is not to completely hide parallelism from the developer. Instead, the developer must be aware of the fact that event handlers are executed in parallel, but all the data consistency issues are automatically handled by the runtime. To this end, TigerQuoll executes automatically and transparently every parallel event handler shielded behind an STM-mediated atomic block. This has the advantage of giving the developer the impression that every handler has a consistent view of the global shared state as it would have when being executed by a single-threaded execution engine. As opposed to introducing an explicit atomic block construct, we chose to associate atomic semantics with the event handlers, which are already the basic unit of parallelization in TigerQuoll.

5.1 Eventual Transactions

Despite the benefit of keeping the programming model of TigerQuoll as close as possible to the one of single-threaded JavaScript, STMs offer poor performance for certain workload types [18]. Apart from the fixed cost of managing a transaction's metadata, one of the problems with STM's performance lies in the fact that for high-contention workloads transactions are forced to abort frequently, reducing efficiency and wasting computing resources. Although the debate on the maturity of STMs is still ongoing [6, 14], there is some general consensus that STM-based solutions have scalability limits. For certain workloads, TigerQuoll offers the possibility to relax the default transactional isolation allowing to modify shared data using a different, more efficient transactional mechanism. This novel mechanism, called *eventual transactions*, corresponds to a class of transactions which never fail to commit, and always succeed in updating the global state after their execution.

The key consideration for speeding up transactional workloads in TigerQuoll is that some algorithms do not require shared data to be consistent *during* the execution of the transaction, but only *after* commit has happened. For instance, this is the common case when parallel tasks are performing computations on partial results on a shared data structure. This consideration can be used to implement transactions which never fail to commit, as data inconsistencies on the same shared value during the transaction do not mean any incorrect semantics, as long as the transactional system is given a way to solve the conflict when the transaction completes.

Consider the case of a JavaScript word counter, that is, a function to count the frequency of the words within a text. The function consumes a stream of data by tokenizing each input chunk in order to count the number of occurrences of each word. Such functions are very common in server-side applications for buildings systems such as Web crawlers or to generate trending topics for services such as Twitter.

As every event handler is executed atomically and with isolation, there is no way to let event handlers communicate

```
1   // shared object to collect the statistics
2       var stats = {
3           total : 0           // total number of words
4           word : new Array()  // occurrences of each word
5       }
6       finish(function() {
7   // open and scan the input file
8           open(url, function(chunk) {
9   // spawn a parallel task for each chunk
10              async(function() {
11                  var tokens = tokenize(chunk)
12  // for each token update the statistics
13                  for(var i=0; i<tokens.length; i++) {
14                      var word = tokens[i]
15                      if( ! stats.word[word]) {
16                          stats.total++
17                          stats.word[word] = 0
18                      }
19                      stats.word[word]++
20  } }) }) })
21  .ondone(function() {
22  // once all chunks have completed return the statistics
23      console.log(stats.total)
24  })
```

Figure 2. Parallel word count function in TigerQuoll

partially computed values. In other words, the result of the execution of any event handler (including eventual transactions) become visible to other handlers only when the handler terminates (and commits its result). This execution semantics can be combined with the `waitall` primitive, which guarantees that a given event handler is executed once a set of other parallel events have been successfully executed. For instance, this is the case for the MapReduce example in Section 4.2 where the `result` variable is always guaranteed to be consistent.

The code in the example (Figure 2) reads from a data stream by opening a URL (which could correspond to a remote Web resource or a file stored locally). The URL is opened through the `open` function, which invokes its callback as soon as a data chunk is available. As the callback uses `async`, the chunks will be processed in parallel. For each chunk, the parallel callbacks will tokenize the string and will update the global shared object containing the statistics (`stats`).

One important consideration about the example is that the `stats` object (more precisely, its fields) is not required to be consistent during the execution of the parallel event handlers, as what really matters for the word counter is to produce a consistent result, i.e., to return a consistent (and correct) value of `stats`. In other words, the fields of the `stats` object need to be consistent only eventually, i.e., after all parallel callbacks have completed.

This property can be explicitly specified by the developer by marking certain fields of an object as *eventual*. In the example this can be done using the `markEventual()` primitive provided by the TigerQuoll API:

```
1   // The 'total' field is eventual
2   stats.markEventual('total', sum)
3   // All the elements of the array are eventual
4   stats.word.markEventual('*', sum)
```

Marking a field as eventual tells the runtime not to fail in case it detects an inconsistent value of the field at commit-time. This implies that the runtime needs to know how to deal with inconsistent values. More precisely, it needs to know how to *accumulate* the partial value of an eventual field when committing its value to the global shared state. This

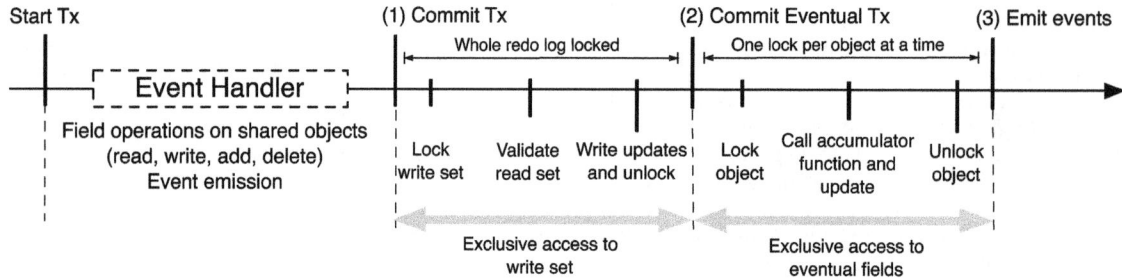

Figure 3. Overview of the commit phase of the TigerQuoll runtime.

is done by passing another argument to `markEventual()`, called the *accumulator function*. In the example above the accumulator function only has to add the partially computed value of field to the global value. This can be specified as follows:

```
1   function sum(global, initial, final) {
2       return global+(final-initial)
3   }
```

Accumulator functions receive three arguments as input, and return the new value to be stored in the global object. The three input arguments are (1) the value of the global field at the moment the accumulator function is called, (2) the initial value of the field before the parallel event handler was called, and (3) the final value of the field at the end of the execution of the event handler.

In the example, eventual fields are used to count, and therefore the accumulator function corresponds to a simple sum function adding the partial result as evaluated by the event handler to the global value. This is natural for fields with numeric values. Since the TigerQuoll programming model does not constrain the type of fields which can be marked eventual, other kinds of accumulator functions may be specified by the developer. The only constraint for accumulator functions is that they must be side-effect free and they should not access any shared object different from the ones they are passed as arguments.

6. Architecture

In this section we describe the principal design decisions behind the TigerQuoll parallel engine architecture. The engine is a prototype JavaScript engine derived from Mozilla SpiderMonkey [4]. The most relevant changes include modifications to the native implementation of the JavaScript `Object` class to associate every object with the needed transactional metadata. Moreover, the `Object` class has also been modified to enable objects with support for event emission, consumption and synchronization through the `on`, `emit` and `waitall` primitives. Every object also holds a private table of event handlers registration. The TigerQuoll runtime runs multiple threads accessing the same memory heap mediated by an STM layer.

The TigerQuoll runtime features an event-based execution system based on a simple master-worker pattern for processing multiple events in parallel. The system is composed of multiple threads holding a pointer to a shared double-ended queue containing references to event objects. Events are consumed nondeterministically by the threads, therefore allowing for parallelism.

To guarantee compatibility with existing JavaScript applications, the TigerQuoll engine behaves as a standard non-parallel engine as long as the TigerQuoll runtime is not explicitly activated. Once active, JavaScript applications can run parallel tasks only through the event-based API (e.g., through `on`/`emit`) or through higher-level constructs already present in the TigerQuoll runtime (for instance `async`). This ensures that existing applications that use neither the event-based API nor the TigerQuoll runtime will always run sequentially.

To guarantee TigerQuoll applications to run in non-parallel JavaScript engines, the TigerQuoll event-based API can be implemented in pure JavaScript by extending the prototype of the `Object` object. All the event emissions and consumptions can be therefore made asynchronous just by using a global queue shared by all the objects within the same application. Indeed, this is the same execution model as in Node.JS, which handles event consumption and emission in the JavaScript space.

6.1 Transactional Support

The TigerQuoll runtime features a STM with global versioning clock, lazy version management, and commit-time locking [18]. Conflicts are detected both at commit-time and during transactions' execution. The versioning management algorithms implemented by the TigerQuoll STM are similar to the ones of the TL2 STM [12], with the main difference that TigerQuoll features per-field versioning (as opposed to per-object versioning) with per-object locking.

The commit-time locking with redo logs fits well with the event-based design of the TigerQuoll engine, as state changes are made persistent only after the transaction has completed. This also guarantees that read-only transactions (i.e., read-only event handlers) can operate in parallel without any lock acquisition. The per-field version management prevents transactions operating on different fields of the same object from failing because of versioning conflicts.

Transactions are committed in three distinct steps, namely (1) non-eventual fields commit, (2) eventual fields commit, and (3) deferred event emission. The whole process is summarized in Figure 3, while the three phases are described in detail in the following sections.

6.1.1 Non-eventual Fields Commit

Read and write operations on non-eventual fields are mediated through a redo log and two sets tracking field reads and field writes, respectively. The redo log keeps a thread-local copy of global objects as locally computed by each parallel event handler. The redo log is managed with a lazy strategy,

```
1    // tx struct which holds all the logs
2    Transaction tx;
3    // start the transaction
4    do {
5        // event handler execution: the redo_log
6        // is created and modified as well as the
7        // read set, the write set, the eventual log
8        // and the events log
9    } while ( ! Tx_Commit_redo(&tx) );
10   // redo_log committed: eventual fields can be processed
11   foreach(JS_OBJECT obj in eventual_log)
12       // Get a reference to the global shared object
13       JSObject *global = tx->eventual[obj]->global;
14       // --- (1) Lock the object --- //
15       Lock(&global)
16       // scan all its eventual fields
17       foreach(EV_FIELD f in global->ev_fields) {
18           // Get the accumulator for this field
19           jsval accFun = global->acc_fun[f];
20           // prepare the arguments for the accumulator
21           jsval *argv;
22           argv[0] = JS_ReadField(global, f)
23           argv[1] = tx->eventual[iter]->delta
24           argv[2] = tx->eventual[iter]->snapshot
25           // --- (2) Execute the accumulator function --- //
26           jsval result = JS_Execute(&accFun, argv)
27           // store back the result
28           JS_WriteField(global, f, result)
29       }
30       // Release the lock
31       UnLock(&global)
32   }
```

Figure 4. Eventual transactions commit-phase pseudocode.

meaning that global object fields are copied to the redo log only when accessed for the first time.

Conflicts are resolved using per-field versioning. Each time a transaction is executed, it reads the most recent value of a shared global clock (a 64-bit integer), obtaining a Read Version number (RV) which is used to validate both the read and write sets. Both during the transaction and at commit time, the RV of the transaction is compared against the version of the fields as stored in the corresponding global state field. When a field with a more recent version is found, the transaction is aborted, as the current value of the field has been changed by another transaction in the meanwhile. Modifications to the object structure (i.e., field additions and deletions) are treated as special cases of transactional write operations. At commit-time, the STM (1) acquires all the per-object locks of all the fields in the write set; (2) validates the the read set against the RV; (3) in case of no conflicts (either with lock acquisition or read version management), commits and updates the shared objects writing the new values. (4) Eventually it releases all the locks.

6.1.2 Eventual Fields Commit

Eventual transactions have the property of never failing. They always commit by accumulating data in shared fields marked as eventual through a user-given function called accumulator. This is made possible by operating on a thread-local copy of the value of local fields which is managed by the STM runtime through a separate log, called eventual log.

During an event handler execution, all the accesses of eventual fields are mediated by the eventual log, and no actual access to the global object's fields is performed. Similarly to regular transactions, the eventual log keeps track of all the operations performed on eventual fields. Conversely, the log is not used for validating the consistency of the field neither during the transaction's execution nor at commit-time. As

any operation happens on the local copy of every eventual field, any operation on such data structures happens with snapshot isolation from the event handler perspective.

At the end of the event handler execution, the eventual log holds the locally computed value of the eventual field (called the *delta*) plus the initial value of the field, called *snapshot*. Together with the current global value, these two values are then passed to the accumulator function as arguments.

The commit phase for eventual fields (Figure 4) is performed in two steps:

(1) *Locking of objects with eventual fields.* The eventual log is scanned and for every eventual field, a lock is acquired on the corresponding objects. Locks on different objects are not acquired all-at-once, as in the commit phase of the standard STM. Instead, it is safe to acquire only one lock at a time, as eventual fields do not need to guarantee atomicity. The eventual log is sorted so as to acquire only one lock per object, thus allowing to commit all the eventual fields belonging to the same object at the same time.

(2) *Accumulator function execution.* Once the lock is acquired, the accumulator function corresponding to the eventual field is called passing as arguments the current value of the global object, the delta value, and the snapshot value. The value returned by the function is written back to the global value. The lock on the object can be released once all its eventual fields have been updated.

6.1.3 Deferred Event Emission and I/O

In a system with everything mediated by an STM it becomes crucial to properly treat all the deterministic blocking operations which cannot be re-executed in case of commit failure. This is usually the case with I/O operations such as blocking file read/write operations as well as standard output operations. Fortunately, the case for JavaScript is simpler, as all the I/O operations already happen asynchronously. Therefore, all I/O operations in JavaScript naturally play well with the transactional system, as they are already happening outside of event handlers.

The asynchronous nature of JavaScript is of great advantage for including an STM support in the runtime, as the only operation which has to be treated as a special case is event emission. In fact, a failed transaction which emits an event immediately before committing will be re-executed by the runtime and will likely re-emit the same event. This could easily lead to inconsistencies. To avoid this, the TigerQuoll event-based programming model does not assume that events are actually emitted immediately after emit is called. The emission of events is asynchronous by design (there is no guarantee that a thread will be ready for executing the corresponding callback at the moment the event is emitted), and therefore event emission can be safely postponed. Hence, during the execution of an event handler, emitted events are buffered in another thread-local log, called event log. Only after the transaction has successfully committed the event log is processed and deferred events are safely emitted for parallel processing.

7. Evaluation

To evaluate the performance of the TigerQuoll engine we have performed two distinct classes of experiments. First, we evaluated the performance of the engine to assess the performance overhead of the TigerQuoll engine compared to the most popular existing share-nothing parallelism solution (i.e., WebWorkers). Second, we evaluated the engine in the context of shared-memory applications, to observe

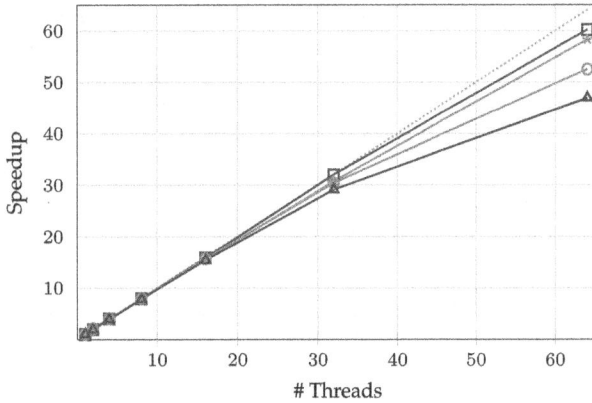

Figure 5. Share-nothing scalability. The graph shows the scalability of TigerQuoll for the Primes (—□—) and Mandelbrot (—○—) benchmarks compared with the equivalent WebWorkers Primes (—*—) and Mandelbrot (—▲—) benchmarks.

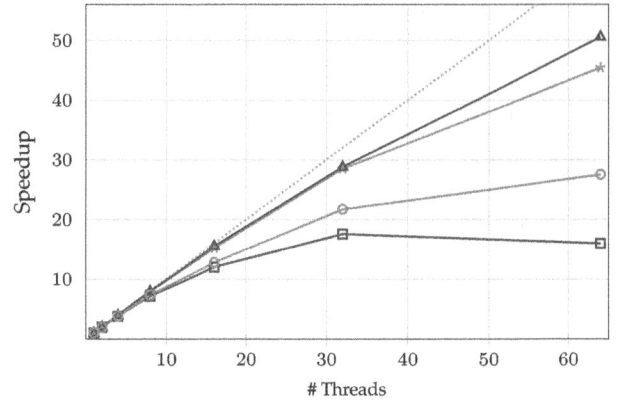

Figure 6. Shared Memory Scalability: Primes checker with shared counter. The graph presents TigerQuoll scalability in case of high contention with regular transactions (—□—) and eventual transactions (—○—), as well as low contention with regular transactions (—*—) and eventual transactions (—▲—).

the performance of eventual transactions for high- and low-contention workloads. All the experiments have been executed on a 32 cores AMD-Bulldozer machine with support for 64 parallel (hyper-threaded) threads. The machine has a total of four CPUs connected to four NUMA nodes. All the results presented in this Section are average values computed over five independent runs of each experiment. The standard deviation is negligible.

7.1 Share-nothing Scalability

To assess the performance of the engine in comparison with existing share-nothing solutions, we have parallelized some existing JavaScript benchmarks using TigerQuoll and Web-Workers, and we have measured how the execution time decreases when adding more parallel threads to the engine. Results are depicted in Figure 5.

The algorithms selected for the evaluation are the parallel calculation of a 1024x1024 Mandelbrot Set and a parallel primes checker scanning 10^6 integers looking for prime numbers. As clearly depicted in the figure, the TigerQuoll engine has performance comparable to the ones of WebWorkers, and scales linearly with almost ideal scalability up to the number of physical cores (32) in the system (lines —○— and —□—). This shows that the event-emission, routing and consumption mechanism of the engine as well as its transactional support do not prevent share-nothing applications from scaling. This also means that share-nothing algorithms can be parallelized using the `on`/`emit` primitives of TigerQuoll in addition to using explicit parallel entities such as WebWorkers and message passing coordination.

7.2 Shared Memory Scalability

Of the algorithms presented in the previous section one can be easily modified to become a shared memory algorithm. In fact, the primes number calculator can be modified to use a shared object to keep track of the prime numbers it has found. In more detail, the algorithm implements a traditional divide-and-conquer scheme by partitioning the space of integer numbers to check, and by assigning each parallel event handler a partition of the space for processing. Each handler thus receives an interval to scan and searches for primes in its local partition only, eventually updating the global object with the number of prime numbers it has found once done with its job.

As in many data-parallel computations with shared state, the size of the task assigned to parallel workers is a crucial performance parameter. In fact, tasks with a too small size can easily degrade performance because of data contention, while tasks with an outsized dimension tend to degrade scalability (especially when the tasks are not homogeneous in terms of processing time). To measure the impact of task size in the case of the primes checker we have performed an additional experiment measuring the performance of the algorithm using the shared counter with different task size. Results depicted in Figure 6 describe how with a small task size (10^2 numbers per event) the STM is forced to abort very often (see line —□—, where the STM aborts are on average more than 10% of the total started transactions), while with a bigger task size (10^3 numbers per event) the STM is still able to scale (line —*—, with a failure rate of less than 5%).

Fortunately, this is the classic case in which the partial result of the computation (i.e., updating the counter) is not needed by the parallel task. Therefore, we could mark the field of the shared object counting the number of primes as eventual, and specify that we need an accumulator function which just sums the delta to the global value of the counter. The performance of the TigerQuoll runtime using the eventual counter are depicted in the same figure (lines —○— and —▲—). Using eventual fields significantly out-performs the version using regular transactions, since the presence of the eventual field saves the transaction from aborting and restarting.

The impact of contention on shared-memory algorithms can in some cases dramatically affect the performance of an STM system. This is the case for the experiment depicted in Figure 7, where a data intensive workload with high and low contention has been evaluated. The experiment corresponds to the word-counter example presented in Figure 2. In the experiment, the parallel word-counter is given a text file of 4MB to parse. The file contains a variety of equally distributed words which corresponds to the creation of thousands of items on the shared array. The experiment has been executed with two chunk sizes to vary the contention on the shared array. As expected, using regular transactions will not scale, since the abort rate of the transactions is very high as soon as multiple threads are handling events in parallel (lines —□— and —*—). With almost certain probability two parallel event

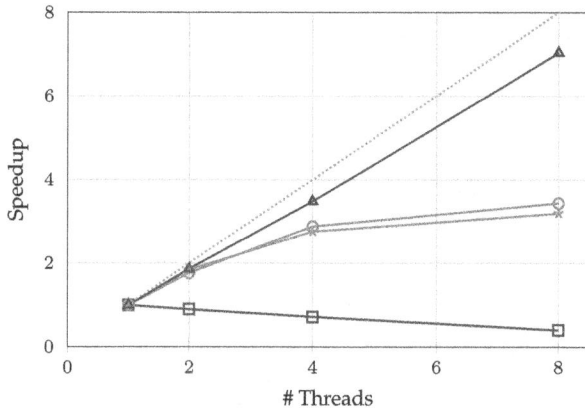

Figure 7. Shared Memory Scalability: word counter. The graph presents TigerQuoll scalability in case of high contention with regular transactions (—□—) and eventual transactions (—⊖—), as well as low contention with regular transactions (—∗—) and eventual transactions (—▲—).

handlers will try to create or update the same element of the shared array, and all but one transaction will have to be aborted and re-executed. By marking all the fields of the array as eventual, this effect is mitigated and the system scales when adding more parallel threads (lines —⊖— and —▲—).

8. Discussion

The results from the initial evaluation of our VM confirm that shared-memory parallelism can be safely brought to JavaScript with an event-based model of parallelism. Our approach succeeds in keeping the programming model as close as possible to existing single-threaded JavaScript and in maintaining compatibility with existing applications. These two goals represent key factors for introducing parallelism in the domain of JavaScript, as the language has a very wide and heterogeneous user community spanning from client-side Web application developers to server-side developers.

Our event-based approach to parallelism is not competing with emerging parallel solutions for JavaScript (e.g., Web-Workers and RiverTrail), but instead should be considered as complementary. In particular, our approach does not prevent developers from using such solutions, but offers them an alternative for developing applications using a parallel programming model other than message passing or immutable shared data, still without introducing the complexity of programming with locks, and giving good speedup (ideal speedup, indeed, when falling back to the case of share-nothing computations). Other solutions such as WebWorkers can still be used in all the circumstances in which a master-worker parallelism pattern is more natural to be expressed. However, we think that shared-memory event-based parallelism represents a suitable solution for parallelizing several problems peculiar to the domain of JavaScript, like for instance the real-time parallel processing of data streams from sources such as RESTful services [5] or WebSockets. In terms of programming model, it would be interesting to explore how to combine multiple models, having for instance Web-Workers which internally execute multiple events in parallel.

The design decisions underlying eventual transactions have similar rationale. Our goal is to propose a novel, convenient programming-model abstraction, which provides transactions which never abort, at the cost of ensuring only

eventual consistency. As implemented in TigerQuoll, the model is complementary to existing STM-based approaches and allows us to speed-up transactional event handlers when strong consistency is not needed. The metadata overhead for managing eventual fields is equivalent to the overhead of standard transactions, as all the operations on each field have to be tracked. Similarly, the consistency management overhead of eventual fields is similar to the one of transactions, as eventual fields are made consistent by acquiring a lock. Performance benefits come from the fact that the commit phase never forces a transaction to re-execute, therefore eventual transaction's performance is comparable to the one of regular transactions which always commit.

The TigerQuoll engine has been developed and tested with the workloads presented in Section 7, and is being currently improved. As of now, the overhead introduced by the event-based system is negligible. In other words, a single-threaded event-based execution performs almost identically to the equivalent code executed on a unmodified engine. The overhead introduced by STM metadata is proportional to the size of the transaction's logs.

9. Related Work

Several efforts are being directed towards overcoming current limitations of JavaScript concerning its support for parallelism. As part of the HTML5 standardization, WebWorkers [1] offer a simple message-passing abstraction for implementing the Actor model in JavaScript. This technology has been used in [15] to develop an event-based programming model for parallelizing JavaScript applications, which hides WebWorkers from the developer's perspective but still assumes a share-nothing memory model. On the server-side, Cluster [2] is a process-based parallelism library for Node.JS implementing a programming model similar to Actor-based concurrency. On the client-side, River Trail [19] offers an API for developing data-parallel computations by means of automatic compilation of JavaScript code to OpenCL [3] so that parts of the computation is offloaded on the GPU. Only applications using static immutable data structures are supported. Another interesting solution for parallelizing JavaScript is Parallel Closures [23]. The approach attempts to bring fork/join-like parallelism to JavaScript through constructs similar to `async` and `finish`. Differently from TigerQuoll, Parallel Closures operate on immutable (read-only) shared data, and support only fork/join parallel patterns [22].

All of these approaches show the importance and the need for offering simple parallelism support in JavaScript applications. The TigerQuoll engine is based on an alternative, complementary approach, which allows developers to exploit a protected, shared, mutable, global address space. Furthermore, TigerQuoll can express share-nothing parallelism (as with WebWorkers) without messages and explicit parallel entities, and allows to implement any arbitrary data-parallel algorithm over mutable shared-memory. Developers used to asynchronous programming can directly use the TigerQuoll Core Event API, while others can take advantage of the higher level constructs that are built on top of it.

Out of the realm of JavaScript, other languages feature a task-parallelism programming model. Some notable examples are X10 [7], F# [28] and [20]. Each language provides different ways of controlling and interacting with parallel tasks, but none of them is based on explicit event emission and consumption.

Software Transactional Memory is the most prominent way of enabling atomic blocks-based programming. STMs are used in several languages and libraries (e.g., the Akka framework in Scala [26] or [10, 13]). A notable attempt to bring STM-based solutions to JavaScript has been presented in [25] where the authors describe a system for automatic parallelization of existing legacy single-threaded applications through STM-based speculation. The approach differs from TigerQuoll in that our goal is not to parallelize existing applications, but instead to offer a programming model for building new parallel applications.

To the best of our knowledge, we are the first to introduce eventual transactions. Out of the realm of transactions associative and commutative operations are used in some parallel programming languages and models to speed-up certain computations. Piccolo [27], for instance, allows to specify lightweight associative functions to be automatically applied by the runtime when modifying the parallel elements in a shared table.

10. Conclusion

In this paper we introduced TigerQuoll, an execution engine and an event-based API for parallel programming in JavaScript. TigerQuoll features transactional support for programming using a mutable shared memory model through the execution of multiple asynchronous parallel event handlers. TigerQuoll brings an alternative to share-nothing parallelism to JavaScript with a programming model already familiar to JavaScript developers, ensuring compatibility. TigerQuoll features an STM-based protection of shared memory accesses, and features an innovative class of transaction, called eventual transactions, to speed-up high-contention workloads. Our initial evaluation confirms that the engine is able to fully exploit the underlying parallelism in modern multicore machines while preserving the programming model of single-threaded JavaScript.

Acknowledgments

The research presented in this paper has been supported by the Swiss National Science Foundation (SINERGIA grant nr. CRSI22_127386) and by the European Commission (Seventh Framework Programme grant 287746).

References

[1] HTML5 Web Worker API specification draft. URL http://dev.w3.org/html5/workers/.

[2] Node.JS: evented programming for networked services in JS. URL http://www.nodejs.org.

[3] OpenCL, the standard for parallel programming of GPU. URL http://developer.amd.com.

[4] Mozilla SpiderMonkey JS engine. URL www.mozilla.org/js/spidermonkey/.

[5] D. Bonetta, P. Achille, C. Pautasso, and W. Binder. S: a scripting language for high-performance RESTful Web services. In *Proc. of PPoPP*, pages 97–106, 2012.

[6] C. Cascaval, C. Blundell, M. Michael, H. W. Cain, P. Wu, S. Chiras, and S. Chatterjee. Software Transactional Memory: Why Is It Only a Research Toy? *Queue*, 6(5):46–58, Sept. 2008.

[7] P. Charles, C. Grothoff, V. Saraswat, C. Donawa, A. Kielstra, K. Ebcioglu, C. von Praun, and V. Sarkar. X10: an object-oriented approach to non-uniform cluster computing. In *Proc. of OOPSLA*, OOPSLA '05, pages 519–538, 2005.

[8] M. Cole. *Algorithmic skeletons: structured management of parallel computation*. MIT Press, Cambridge, MA, USA, 1991.

[9] M. Cole. Bringing skeletons out of the closet: a pragmatic manifesto for skeletal parallel programming. *Parallel Comput.*, 30(3):389–406, Mar. 2004.

[10] P. Damron, A. Fedorova, Y. Lev, V. Luchangco, M. Moir, and D. Nussbaum. Hybrid transactional memory. In *Proceedings of the 12th international conference on Architectural support for programming languages and operating systems*, ASPLOS-XII, pages 336–346, 2006.

[11] J. Dean and S. Ghemawat. MapReduce: simplified data processing on large clusters. *Commun. ACM*, 51(1):107–113, Jan. 2008.

[12] D. Dice, O. Shalev, and N. Shavit. Transactional locking II. In *Proceedings of the 20th international conference on Distributed Computing*, DISC'06, pages 194–208, 2006.

[13] A. Dragojević, R. Guerraoui, and M. Kapalka. Stretching transactional memory. In *Proceedings of the 2009 ACM SIGPLAN conference on Programming language design and implementation*, PLDI '09, pages 155–165, 2009.

[14] A. Dragojević, P. Felber, V. Gramoli, and R. Guerraoui. Why STM can be more than a research toy. *Commun. ACM*, 54(4): 70–77, Apr. 2011.

[15] A. Erbad, N. C. Hutchinson, and C. Krasic. DOHA: scalable real-time Web applications through adaptive concurrent execution. In *Proceedings of the 21st international conference on World Wide Web*, WWW '12, pages 161–170, 2012.

[16] D. Flanagan. *JavaScript. The Definitive Guide*. O'Reilly, 5th rev. edition, 2006.

[17] R. H. Halstead, Jr. Multilisp: a language for concurrent symbolic computation. *ACM Trans. Program. Lang. Syst.*, 7(4):501–538, Oct. 1985.

[18] T. Harris, J. Larus, and R. Rajwar. *Transactional Memory*. Morgan and Claypool, 2nd edition, 2010.

[19] S. Herhut, R. L. Hudson, T. Shpeisman, and J. Sreeram. Parallel programming for the Web. In *Proceedings of the 4th USENIX conference on Hot Topics in Parallelism*, HotPar'12, pages 1–6, 2012.

[20] M. Isard and A. Birrell. Automatic mutual exclusion. In *Proceedings of the 11th USENIX workshop on Hot topics in operating systems*, HOTOS'07, pages 3:1–3:6, 2007.

[21] D. Lea. *Concurrent Programming in Java. Second Edition: Design Principles and Patterns*. Addison-Wesley, Boston, MA, USA, 2nd edition, 1999.

[22] D. Lea. A Java fork/join framework. In *Proceedings of the ACM 2000 conference on Java Grande*, JAVA '00, pages 36–43, 2000.

[23] N. D. Matsakis. Parallel closures: a new twist on an old idea. In *Proceedings of the 4th USENIX conference on Hot Topics in Parallelism*, HotPar'12, pages 1–6, 2012.

[24] M. D. McCool. Structured parallel programming with deterministic patterns. In *Proceedings of the 2nd USENIX conference on Hot topics in parallelism*, HotPar'10, pages 1–6, 2010.

[25] M. Mehrara, P.-C. Hsu, M. Samadi, and S. A. Mahlke. Dynamic parallelization of JavaScript applications using an ultra-lightweight speculation mechanism. In *17th International Conference on High-Performance Computer Architecture*, HPCA-17, pages 87–98, 2011.

[26] M. Odersky, S. Micheloud, N. Mihaylov, M. Schinz, E. Stenman, M. Zenger, and et al. An overview of the Scala programming language. Technical Report IC/2004/64, EPFL Lausanne, Switzerland, 2004.

[27] R. Power and J. Li. Piccolo: building fast, distributed programs with partitioned tables. In *Proceedings of the 9th USENIX conference on Operating systems design and implementation*, OSDI'10, pages 1–14, 2010.

[28] D. Syme, T. Petricek, and D. Lomov. The F# asynchronous programming model. In *Proceedings of the 13th international conference on Practical aspects of declarative languages*, PADL'11, pages 175–189, 2011.

Using Hardware Transactional Memory to Correct and Simplify a Readers-Writer Lock Algorithm

Dave Dice Yossi Lev
Victor Luchangco Mark Moir

Oracle Labs

{dave.dice,yossi.lev,victor.luchangco,mark.moir}@oracle.com

Yujie Liu

Lehigh University

lyj@lehigh.edu

Abstract

Designing correct synchronization algorithms is notoriously difficult, as evidenced by a bug we have identified that has apparently gone unnoticed in a well-known synchronization algorithm for nearly two decades. We use hardware transactional memory (HTM) to construct a corrected version of the algorithm. This version is significantly simpler than the original and furthermore improves on it by eliminating usage constraints and reducing space requirements. Performance of the HTM-based algorithm is competitive with the original in "normal" conditions, but it does suffer somewhat under heavy contention. We successfully apply some optimizations to help close this gap, but we also find that they are incompatible with known techniques for improving progress properties. We discuss ways in which future HTM implementations may address these issues. Finally, although our focus is on how effectively HTM can correct and simplify the algorithm, we also suggest bug fixes and workarounds that do not depend on HTM.

Categories and Subject Descriptors D.1.3 [*Programming Techniques*]: Concurrent Programming

Keywords readers-writer lock, hardware transactional memory

1. Introduction

We recently observed incorrect behavior in a test using the readers-writer lock (RW-lock) algorithm of Krieger et al. [8] (which we call KSUH). This led us to discover a subtle bug in KSUH that has apparently gone unnoticed for almost two decades. The bug involves synchronization for removing a node from a doubly-linked list. It turns out that a node can be modified by a late update after it has already been reused; this bug can manifest in a variety of ways.

It was straightforward to devise an HTM-based variant of the KSUH algorithm that is significantly simpler than the original, eliminates the bug, and eliminates inconvenient (and implicit) requirements for client code. For evaluation, we used a system based on the prototype Rock chip developed by Sun Microsystems [2, 13], which supports HTM. This evaluation shows that our HTM-based algorithms perform competitively with (a corrected version of) KSUH under reasonable workloads.

While this is encouraging, there are two issues with this simple algorithm. First, "best effort" HTM such as Rock supports does not guarantee to be able to commit transactions, so threads can starve, even running alone. Second, one variable of the algorithm (the tail of the list) is frequently modified in transactions, raising concerns about performance under contention (even in read-dominated workloads). Although the RW-lock might arguably have been designed differently in the first place to avoid contention on a single variable, we decided to retain the basic structure and approach of the KSUH algorithm in order to evaluate the effectiveness of HTM to improve and simplify an algorithm even if the use of HTM has not been anticipated in the original design.

The first issue can be addressed by using Transactional Lock Elision (TLE) [1, 11], whereby a thread that repeatedly fails to commit a transaction acquires a lock, and then executes the code of its transaction nontransactionally. To preserve correctness, all transactions are modified so that they cannot commit when the lock is held. It was straightforward to apply TLE to our transactional RW-lock, and our evaluation confirmed that the overhead was low.

To address the second issue, we have explored a variety of techniques for transforming the algorithm to reduce contention. Many of these transformations preserve the semantics of the code, and thus could potentially be applied by compilers. Others depend on knowledge of the algorithm, but still could be used in a fairly systematic way by programmers.

Unfortunately, some of the optimizations we have explored to reduce contention are not compatible with the simple TLE technique for ensuring progress. While we were able to use similar, but algorithm-specific, techniques to accommodate at least one such optimization, doing so in general quickly complicates the algorithm, thereby at least partially defeating the purpose of using HTM in the first place. We discuss ways in which future HTM implementations could reduce or eliminate these drawbacks.

Our main focus is on the ability of HTM to simplify synchronization algorithms. However, we also discuss ways to address the bug we identified with the KSUH algorithm without using HTM; these include solutions that do not modify the RW-lock implementation, but impact how clients use it, and vice versa.

In Section 2, we describe the KSUH algorithm, explain how the bug in it arises, and describe the changes we made to eliminate it. In Section 3, we describe our basic transactional variant of KSUH, as well as several optimizations aimed at reducing contention on the Tail variable. In Section 4, we contrast the difficulty of reasoning about the correctness of KSUH and of our basic transactional variant, highlighting how HTM makes algorithms simpler. We present performance results in Section 5, discuss alternative solutions to the bug we identified in Section 6, and conclude in Section 7.

2. The KSUH Algorithm

The KSUH RW-lock algorithm is derived from Mellor-Crummey and Scott's well-known mutual exclusion algorithm (MCS) [10]. Before discussing details, it is useful to describe abstract versions of these algorithms, both to convey intuition about the algorithms, and to provide useful reference points for correctness proofs, as discussed further in Section 4.

2.1 Abstract algorithm descriptions

We begin with an abstract description of MCS, which maintains an ordered list of client-provided nodes—one for each thread that is in the critical section or is waiting to enter. When invoking a lock procedure, a thread must pass a node that is not already being used by any thread (including the invoking thread), and when invoking an unlock procedure, it must pass the same node that it passed to the corresponding lock procedure. We say that the thread *owns* this node from the time it invokes the lock procedure until it returns from the corresponding unlock procedure. If a thread inserts its node into an empty list, it enters the critical section; otherwise it waits until its node is first in the list. When leaving the critical section, a thread removes its node from the list. Thus, a thread in the critical section always owns the first node in the list.

The abstract description for KSUH is similar, but supports acquiring the lock in read or write mode, and allows a reader to enter the critical section provided all of the nodes ahead of its node in the list belong to readers. Because readers might not exit the critical section in the same order they entered, the algorithm allows the removal of reader nodes from within the list (in MCS, only the first node is ever removed).

2.2 Details of KSUH

Figure 1 shows KSUH (with our fix marked by ***); we discuss important details below. As in MCS, the Tail variable (called L in [8, 10]) identifies the most recently added node, and if the next field of a node n is non-NULL, it identifies the node that was added after n. To enable departing readers to remove their nodes from within the list, each reader node is linked to its predecessor (if any) in the list via a new prev field, and a per-node lock is used for node removal, as described below; henceforth we refer to these per-node locks as *mutexes* to avoid confusion with the RW-lock being implemented. KSUH also adds a state field to each node, which contains READER or WRITER when the node is added to the list, indicating the mode of the lock request; a reader changes its state to ACTIVE_READER before entering the critical section (line 29) to allow its successor to follow it into the critical section. As in MCS, the waiting described in the abstract algorithm is achieved by a thread spinning on a spin field in its node; another thread informs it that it can enter the critical section by resetting this field.

A node is inserted into the list by using SWAP to record the previous value of Tail while simultaneously storing a pointer to the new node into Tail (lines 5 and 21). This establishes the order in which nodes are added, but additional steps are needed to link added nodes into the list (lines 7, 23, and 24). Because these steps may be delayed, sometimes a thread must wait until such linking has been performed (lines 13, 44, and 53).

We approximate the property that a reader can enter the critical section if all the nodes before its node in the list belong to readers by propagating the information that the first reader in the list has entered the critical section down the list. Before entering, a reader r releases its successor if it is a reader (line 28), and then sets its state to ACTIVE_READER (line 29), so that a subsequently arriving reader can determine that it does not need to wait (line 25). Such a successor may arrive too late for r to release it, and start spinning before r sets its own state to ACTIVE_READER. To ensure progress

```
1   procedure writerLock( Tail , I)
2       I→state = WRITER;
3       I→spin = 1;
4       I→next = NULL;
5       pred = SWAP(Tail, I);
6       if (pred != NULL)
7           pred→next = I;
8           while (I→spin);

10  procedure writerUnlock( Tail , I)
11      if (! I→next && CAS(Tail, I, NULL))
12          return;
13      while (! I→next);
14      I→next→prev = NULL;
15      I→next→spin = 0;

17  procedure readerLock( Tail , I)
18      I→state = READER;
19      I→spin = 1;
20      I→next = I→prev = NULL;
21      pred = SWAP(Tail, I);
22      if (pred != NULL)
23          I→prev = pred;
24          pred→next = I;
25          if (pred→state != ACTIVE_READER)
26              while (I→spin);
27      if (I→next && I→next→state == READER)
28          I→next→spin = 0;
29      I→state = ACTIVE_READER;

31  procedure readerUnlock( Tail , I)
32      pred = I→prev;
33      if (pred)
34          LOCK(pred);
35          while (pred != I→prev)
36              UNLOCK(pred);
37              pred = I→prev;
38              if (! pred) break;
39              LOCK(pred);
40          if (pred)
41              LOCK(I);
42              pred→next = NULL;
43              if (! I→next && !CAS(Tail, I, I→prev))
44                  while (! I→next);
45              if (I→next)
46                  I→next→prev = I→prev;
47                  I→prev→next = I→next;
48              UNLOCK(I);
49              UNLOCK(pred);
50              return;
51      LOCK(I);
52      if (! I→next && !CAS(Tail, I, NULL))
53          while (! I→next);
54      if (I→next)
55          succIsWriter = (I→next→state == WRITER);   ***
56          I→next→spin = 0;
57          if (! succIsWriter )                        ***
58              I→next→prev = NULL;                     // see caption
59      UNLOCK(I);
```

Figure 1. KSUH algorithm with fix (marked by ***). In [8], line 58 reads "I→prev→prev = NULL". We believe this is a typo, as it does not make sense and the algorithm is easily seen to be incorrect with this version. The corrected code usually makes sense, but does not avoid the bug we have discovered; to address this bug, we introduced the two lines marked with ***.

in this case, the successor is eventually released by the owner of its predecessor exiting the critical section (line 56).

When a thread t removes a reader node r that has a predecessor node p and a successor node s, t acquires the mutexes of p and r, and then updates links in p and s in order to splice r out of the list (lines 32–50). If r has a successor s but no predecessor, t acquires the mutex only for r (line 51). After removing r from the list in this case, t releases the owner of s by setting its spin field to 0 (line 56), and then clears s's prev field (line 58). This is important if s is a reader node, because the subsequent removal of s should not access the removed node r. Because r's mutex is held while s's prev field is reset, s cannot be removed before this occurs.

If s is a writer node, however, there is a problem. Because r's owner has cleared s's spin field, the owner of s can enter and exit the critical section, and then call writerUnlock. This procedure does not check s's predecessor in the list, so the owner of s may return from writerUnlock even though r's mutex is still held. Now there is a pending write to the prev field of s, which can occur at any time, including after s has been recycled. This is the root of the problem that manifests in at least four different ways, depending on when the late store happens: a read-write exclusion violation, a write-write exclusion violation, a segmentation fault, and an infinite loop. For example, if s is reused as a reader node, the late store to reset its prev field can break the list, so that a departing reader can believe it is the last one, and therefore release a writer into the critical section, causing a read-write exclusion violation.

We initially thought that the bug could be fixed by reversing the order of the stores performed in lines 56 and 58. However, this does not work: it allows a successor reader to believe it is at the head of the list, so it can remove itself without coordinating with its predecessor, which may be poised to set the successor's spin flag, even after the successor's node is recycled.

We explored several fixes for KSUH, settling on the one indicated by *** in Figure 1, whereby we reset the successor's prev field (line 58) only if it is not a writer. To enable this, we record whether the successor is a writer (line 55) before releasing its owner into the critical section (line 56); this ensures that the node has not been recycled before recording whether the successor node is a writer. (Recall that, if the successor node is a reader, the mutex protocol prevents it from being recycled prematurely.)

Finally, we note a critical issue regarding how clients manage the nodes they use with the KSUH algorithm. (We assume an environment without garbage collection.) MCS allows nodes to be stack allocated, so that explicit recycling of nodes is unnecessary. This is not possible with KSUH because nodes can be modified arbitrarily long *after* they have been removed from the list; if the memory used for a node has been reallocated for another purpose, such late updates can lead to arbitrary behavior. Thus, KSUH requires clients to store nodes in Type Stable Memory (TSM) [7], i.e., ensure that they are never deallocated or reused for a different purpose.

The corrected KSUH must still keep nodes in TSM because readerUnlock (line 34) attempts to acquire the mutex of a node it previously identified as the predecessor of the node to be removed. There is no guarantee that this node is not removed from the list before the mutex is acquired. The transactional RW-lock algorithms presented next eliminate this issue, so that—as with MCS—nodes can be stack allocated, a significant advantage for developers.

3. Transactional RW-lock algorithms

In this section, we first present a basic transactional RW-lock algorithm TxLock, which retains the structure of KSUH, but uses transactions to simplify and improve the algorithm. Then we introduce a variant that seeks to reduce contention on Tail, while retaining much of the simplicity of TxLock. Finally, we discuss a number of optimizations and variations on these algorithms.

3.1 Basic transactional algorithm: TxLock

Our first transactional RW-lock algorithm, TxLock, shown in Figure 2, retains KSUH's overall approach. However, using transactions to update the list (and to record state needed to determine actions to be taken after a transaction commits), simplifies the algorithm and eliminates the need for the per-node locks used by KSUH. Shared variables are accessed only within transactions, with the following exceptions. Initialization of a node's fields before it is made "pub-

lic" by inserting it into the list are performed without synchronization. Accesses to spin variables, both by threads waiting for these variables to change, and by threads changing them, are performed nontransactionally. This is for two reasons.

First, if a thread inserts a node and spins on its spin field within the same transaction, it will never exit the spin, because the node will not become visible so no thread will reset its spin field. We could perform the spinning in a separate transaction after the transaction that inserts the node into the list has committed. However, a waiting transaction would be caused to abort by the event for which it is waiting, so it would have to retry, harming performance. Furthermore, it does not complicate the algorithm significantly to perform the spinning nontransactionally.

Second, waiting threads are also released using nontransactional stores, because a transaction attempting to modify a variable on which another thread is spinning may have its transaction aborted due to the spinning thread. Again, updating spin variables nontransactionally did not significantly complicate the algorithm.

The writerLock and writerUnlock procedures are fairly self-explanatory. The first transaction in readerLock (lines 26–32) inserts a new node into the list and also records (in predState) the state of the node previously pointed to by Tail, if any. If that node exists and its status is not ACTIVE_READER, the thread then spins, waiting for its predecessor to release it. After this, it uses another transaction (lines 36–38) to atomically change its state to ACTIVE_READER and to record the next node in the list, if any. If there is a next node and it is a reader, the thread releases the thread that owns the next node (line 40).

The readerUnlock procedure uses a transaction (lines 44–54) to remove the departing thread's node from the list. If the removed node has no predecessor, the transaction records the state of the next node, and if it is a writer, its thread is released into the critical section (line 55) as the departing thread is the last reader before it.

Our use of transactions makes this algorithm simpler and easier to reason about than KSUH in several ways. First, the locks used in KSUH are no longer needed, which both saves space and eliminates the need to reason about the locks.

Next, note that TxLock resets the successor's prev field without regard to whether it is a reader or a writer (line 49). This may be surprising, as it was exactly this behavior that caused the bug in KSUH. This does not compromise TxLock's correctness or require it to use TSM because the write to the prev field is in a transaction that confirms that the node being written is still the successor of the writing thread's node, which itself is still in the list.

There is no analogue in TxLock for the first loop in the readerUnlock procedure of KSUH, which is needed because the list may change after a thread determines its node's predecessor and before it is able to lock the predecessor. If this occurs in TxLock, the transaction will abort and be retried, and this is hidden by the transaction construct. This is the reason that our algorithm allows nodes to be freed after use.

In both readerLock and writerLock, the next field of the node previously pointed to by Tail is set to point to the newly introduced node, atomically with setting Tail to point to this node. Therefore, there is no "intermediate" state in which Tail already points to a new node, but the previous node's next field has not yet been set to point to the new node. (KSUH has two loops to deal with this case.)

Finally, our use of transactions ensures that, when a reader r sets its status to ACTIVE_READER before entering the critical section, either r will see a successor reader s and thus reset its spin field so s can also enter the critical section, or s will see r's status as ACTIVE_READER when it links in its node, and thus can enter the critical section. As a result, s never has to wait while r is in the critical section. In contrast, this can happen with KSUH, as

```
1   procedure writerLock(Tail, I)
2     I→state = WRITER;
3     I→spin = 1;
4     I→next = NULL;
5     atomically
6       pred = Tail;
7       Tail = I;
8       if (pred) pred→next = I;

10    if (pred) while (I→spin) Pause();

12  procedure writerUnlock(Tail, I)
13    atomically
14      next = I→next;
15      if (!next)

17        Tail = NULL;
18      else
19        next→prev = NULL;
20    if (next) next→spin = 0;

22  procedure readerLock(Tail, I)
23    I→state = READER;
24    I→spin = 1;
25    I→next = I→prev = NULL;
26    atomically
27      pred = Tail;
28      Tail = I;
29      if (pred)
30        I→prev = pred;
31        pred→next = I;
32        predState = pred→state;

34    if (pred != NULL && predState != ACTIVE_READER)
35      while (I→spin) Pause();
36    atomically
37      I→state = ACTIVE_READER;
38      next = I→next;
39      if (next && next→state == READER)
40        next→spin = 0;

42  procedure readerUnlock(Tail, I)
43    succState = UNDEF_STATE;
44    atomically
45      pred = I→prev;
46      next = I→next;
47      if (pred) pred→next = next;
48      if (next)
49        next→prev = pred;
50        if (!pred)
51          succState = next→state;
52      else

54        Tail = pred;
55    if (succState == WRITER) next→spin = 0;
```

Figure 2. The basic transactional RW-lock algorithm `TxLock`.

```
1   procedure writerLock(Tail, I)
2     I→state = WRITER;
3     I→spin = 1;
4     I→next = NULL;
5     while (Tail == POISON || (pred = SWAP(Tail, POISON)) == POISON)
6       Pause();

8     if (pred) pred→next = I;
9     Tail = I;
10    if (pred) while (I→spin) Pause();

12  procedure writerUnlock(Tail, I)
13    atomically
14      next = I→next;
15      if (!next)
16        if (Tail == POISON) retry;
17        Tail = NULL;
18      else
19        next→prev = NULL;
20    if (next) next→spin = 0;

22  procedure readerLock(Tail, I)
23    I→state = READER;
24    I→spin = 1;
25    I→next = I→prev = NULL;
26    while (Tail == POISON || (pred = SWAP(Tail, POISON)) == POISON)
27      Pause();
28    I→prev = pred;
29    if (pred)
30      atomically
31        pred→next = I;
32        predState = pred→state;
33    Tail = I;
34    if (pred !=NULL && predState != ACTIVE_READER)
35      while (I→spin) Pause();
36    atomically
37      I→state = ACTIVE_READER;
38      next = I→next;
39      if (next && next→state == READER)
40        next→spin = 0;

42  procedure readerUnlock(Tail, I)
43    succState = UNDEF_STATE;
44    atomically
45      pred = I→prev;
46      next = I→next;
47      if (pred) pred→next = next;
48      if (next)
49        next→prev = pred;
50        if (!pred)
51          succState = next→state;
52      else
53        if (Tail == POISON) retry;
54        Tail = pred;
55    if (succState == WRITER) next→spin = 0;
```

Figure 3. Final `PoisonTheTail` algorithm.

explained in Section 2.2. For the same reason, in our algorithm, `readerUnlock` resets the spin of the successor only if it is a writer, because the above-described scenario in which reader s may wait for reader r to release it even though r has already entered the critical section cannot happen.

While `TxLock` (Figure 2) is simpler than KSUH and does not require nodes to be stored in TSM, it performs considerably worse than (corrected versions of) KSUH under heavy contention. We have explored a number of ways to improve its performance. In the remainder of this section, we discuss algorithmic changes we have explored, in which we sacrifice some of the simplicity of `TxLock` in order to improve performance.

3.2 Poison the Tail

In `TxLock`, `Tail` is modified by every lock operation and some unlock operations. Heavy contention on a single shared variable can lead to livelock with simple "requester wins" conflict resolution

mechanisms, such as Rock uses [2, 3]. We were therefore motivated to try to reduce contention on `Tail`, while continuing to exploit HTM to keep the algorithm simpler than the KSUH algorithm.

To avoid retries in cases that always modify `Tail` (`writerLock` and `readerLock`), we changed these procedures to use nontransactional atomic instructions (such as SWAP and CAS) to modify `Tail`. In other cases, we sought to make transactions access `Tail` less frequently and to be vulnerable to conflicts on this variable for shorter periods of time, and in some cases to access `Tail` without using a transaction. (This approach assumes that the HTM supports strong atomicity, allowing `Tail` to be concurrently accessed both by CAS and within transactions; Rock supports this behavior.) This effort led us to the `PoisonTheTail` algorithm, which we describe via a series of modifications to `TxLock`, using the `writerLock` procedure as an example. The final algorithm appears in Figure 3.

We first change `writerLock` and `readerLock`, which always modify `Tail`, to "claim" the right to insert the next node by modifying `Tail` with a nontransactional atomic instruction, and then complete the insertion using a transaction. To limit the complexity introduced by separating these steps, we prevent any transaction that accesses `Tail` from completing between them. To do so, the "claiming" is achieved by changing `Tail` from a node pointer to a special value POISON, recording the replaced pointer to enable the subsequent transaction to link the new node into the list. The resulting `writerLock` procedure is:

```
procedure writerLock( Tail , I )
    I→state = WRITER;
    I→spin = 1;
    I→next = NULL;
    while ( Tail == POISON || (pred = SWAP(Tail, POISON) == POISON))
        Pause ();
    atomically
        Tail = I;
        if (pred)
            pred→next = I;
    if (pred) while (I→spin) Pause();
```

As a result of this change, the previous value of `Tail` is known before the transaction that links in the node is executed. Therefore, the analogous change in `readerLock` allows the new node's `prev` field to be initialized before the transaction (line 28 in Figure 3) because the node is "private" until it is linked in, so it does not matter if its `prev` field is set before the node is linked into the list.

We further modify the algorithm so that, whenever a transaction accesses `Tail` it also checks if `Tail` contains POISON, retrying if so. The only differences between the `writerUnlock` and `readerUnlock` procedures in Figure 2 and their counterparts in Figure 3 are due to this change. This ensures that, when `Tail` contains POISON, it is accessed only by the thread that most recently set it to POISON performing its transaction to finish linking in its node. This way, contention on `Tail` is avoided for the transaction that links in the node, while keeping the algorithm simple.

Next various transformations are used to make transactions smaller, or otherwise more likely to succeed, as well as replacing some transactions with nontransactional accesses, thus avoiding the overhead of a executing—and possibly retrying—a transaction.

The path through a transaction can sometimes be determined by local variables, allowing this path to be factored out into its own transaction. For example, the transaction in the `writerLock` code shown above can be replaced with the following:

```
if (pred)
    atomically
        Tail = I;
        pred→next = I;
else
    atomically
        Tail = I;
```

This transformation allows the separate transactions to be optimized independently. Furthermore, eliminating conditional branches within transactions can be beneficial with HTM such as in Rock, which can fail due to misspeculating.

Another transformation we apply moves an assignment to `Tail` to the end of the transaction. (Other threads do not observe partial effects of the transaction, so the order in which updates happen within the transaction does not affect the correctness of the algorithm.) However, it reduces the time a transaction spends after modifying `Tail` and before committing, thus reducing the likelihood of such transactions aborting due to contention on `Tail`. Furthermore, a transaction that will access only a single shared variable—such as the one in the else clause above—can be replaced by code that performs this access nontransactionally. Applying these two changes to the transaction shown above yields the following code:

```
if (pred)
    atomically
        pred→next = I;
        Tail = I;
else
    Tail = I;
```

All of the transformations described above are easily seen to preserve the semantics of the algorithm, and could be performed automatically, for example by an optimizing compiler. Next we discuss two transformations that require knowledge of the algorithm.

After `Tail` is set to POISON by a thread t, no transaction accesses `Tail` until t updates `Tail` to a non-POISON value. Thus, t's update to `Tail` need not be performed atomically with linking in t's node: this access can be performed nontransactionally after that transaction commits. This allows us to refactor the code so that the assignment to `Tail` is performed nontransactionally, regardless of whether `pred` is non-NULL. Furthermore, this change results in a transaction that accesses only a single shared variable; therefore this access too can be performed nontransactionally. As a result of all of these changes, there is no longer a transaction in the `writerLock` procedure of the final `PoisonTheTail` algorithm shown in Figure 3. This progression is reminiscent of that used by Dice et al. [4] to eliminate the use of transactions from common paths of their HTM-based work stealing algorithm, while still exploiting transactions elsewhere in the algorithm to simplify it.

Finally, we note that some care is required in applying some of these optimizations, especially those that make transactional accesses nontransactional, because of issues related to the memory consistency model. For our target platform (Rock, which supports the TSO consistency model [12]), there was no need to insert any additional memory fence instructions due to the transformations we applied, but this may not be the case for some platforms.

3.3 Variations and optimizations

Some of the variations and optimizations we have explored are related to idiosyncrasies of Rock's HTM implementation discussed by Dice et al. [2, 3]. Others are not Rock-specific and are more likely to be relevant with future HTM implementations.

Prefetching As reported by Dice et al., it is sometimes possible to make transactions more likely to succeed on Rock by prefetching some variables to be accessed in the transaction before starting the transaction. After some experimentation, we have settled on prefetching the `Tail` variable before retrying transactions that will access it. We do so unconditionally before retrying transactions that always access `Tail`, and conditionally before retrying transactions that conditionally access `Tail`. Implementations of all transactional algorithms evaluated in Section 5 use this technique.

Shortcut transaction The key idea behind this technique is to precede a transaction with a short transaction that applies the same effects as the original transaction in a case that is expected to be common, so it can be optimized for that case, while having no effect in other cases. When the common case occurs, the original transaction need not be executed. Even when the common case is not encountered, the shortcut transaction can serve to prefetch some of the variables to be accessed when the original transaction is executed. For this paper, we experimented with the following shortcut transaction at the beginning of `readerUnlock`:

```
atomically
    pred = I→prev;
    next = I→next;
    if (pred && next)
        next→prev = pred;
        pred→next = next;
    if (pred && next) return;
```

CAS-based `writerUnlock` We can use CAS to modify `Tail` in the `writerUnlock` procedure of `TxLock` (Figure 2), as we do for `writerLock` and `readerLock` in `PoisonTheTail` (Figure 3). In fact, this was our first attempt to use a nontransactional instruction (CAS) to modify `Tail` to reduce contention on `Tail` and resulting retries. We used the following code:

```
procedure writerUnlock( Tail , I)
    next = I→next;
    if (!next) {
        if (CAS (Tail, I, NULL)) return;
        next = I→next;
        next→prev = NULL;
        next→spin = 0;
```

The correctness of this version depends on knowledge of the algorithm. In particular, when a writer is releasing the lock, its node—call it n—has no predecessor (if it existed, it was removed before the writer entered the critical section). If the node's `next` field is NULL, then it also has no successor. In this case, removing the writer's node from the list amounts to setting `Tail` to NULL.

However, because the read of n's `next` field and update of `Tail` are not guaranteed to be atomic, the algorithm must allow for the possibility that `Tail` no longer points to n when `Tail` is modified. For this reason, we use a CAS instruction to set `Tail` to NULL only if it still points to n. If this succeeds, then there is no subsequent node to be released, and the unlock operation is complete.

If the CAS fails, on the other hand, then another node has been inserted into the list, and n is no longer the last node in the list; because the new node was inserted using a transaction, n's `next` field is already set, so there is no need to wait for it to be set, as is the case in KSUH. In this case, just as if n had not been the last node when its `next` field was first read, the unlocking thread simply unlinks its node by setting the next node's `prev` field to NULL, and then releases the thread spinning on that node. These can be performed with simple nontransactional stores because only the writer releasing the lock can access these fields until the next thread is released; note that it is important that these stores happen in the order shown, because otherwise, if the owner of the next node enters the critical section, it may subsequently leave and remove its node before the store to its `prev` field occurs.

While this change complicates the algorithm and correctness argument somewhat, the algorithm is still considerably simpler and easier to reason about than KSUH, and it still does not require TSM for nodes. We call the version of `TxLock` with this `writerUnlock` procedure `TxLock+CAS`. We can apply a similar technique to `PoisonTheTail`, resulting in the `PoisonTheTail+CAS` algorithm. The only change is that, if the CAS fails, we must wait until `next` is not null, because a writer may be poised to perform the write at lines 8 in Figure 3. The resulting `writerUnlock` code is essentially the same as that of KSUH.

The CAS-based `writerUnlock` procedure improves performance considerably in workloads with moderate to high numbers of write operations (Section 5) because it avoids delaying a writer that is attempting to release the lock, which is on the critical path.

Improving simple algorithms via transformations As the above discussion shows, there are many possibilities for optimizing HTM-based algorithms, but using them often makes the algorithms more complex. We have commented that some of these possibilities preserve semantics and could be applied by a compiler, while others can likely be shown to preserve semantics provided some simple properties of the algorithm are known. Together, these observations suggest that a useful strategy for designing such algorithms may be to start with simple transactional versions with relatively large transactions, and to then apply transformations in a disciplined and perhaps (partially) automated way.

Transactional Lock Elision (TLE) The well-known TLE technique [1] aims to achieve reasonable progress properties for algorithms that use best-effort HTM (such as Rock's), which do not guarantee to be able to commit transactions. Briefly, the idea is to augment transactions so that they read a lock and check that it is not held before committing the rest of the transaction. This way, an operation that is unable to make progress by committing its transaction can give up trying, acquire the lock, and perform its operation nontransactionally. Because all transactions check the lock to ensure they do not commit while the lock is held, this approach preserves the semantics of the transaction while overcoming the weak progress guarantees made by best-effort HTM. We have applied TLE to `TxLock`, resulting in the `TxLock+TLE` algorithm.

However, TLE is *not* compatible with all of the variations and optimizations we have explored. In particular, for algorithms that mix transactions with nontransactional atomic operations such as CAS (`TxLock+CAS` and all variants of `PoisonTheTail`), we do not have an effective way to prevent the instructions from taking effect while the lock is held, so we cannot ensure that transactions executed while holding the lock are atomic with respect to these operations. Consequently, enhancing an algorithm's progress properties by using TLE precludes the use of optimizations that are valuable, as shown in Section 5.

If future processors that support HTM were to also provide variants of simple synchronization operations such as CAS that are able to confirm the expected value of a separate memory location and are as fast as the underlying operation (CAS, in this case), then the "best of both worlds" would be possible: we could apply these optimizations while still using TLE for progress.

4. How transactions simplify algorithms

Clearly, `TxLock` is considerably simpler than KSUH. In this section, we underscore this gap by discussing how the use of transactions impacts careful reasoning about the algorithms. This discussion is based on our experiences reasoning in detail about `TxLock` and the (corrected) KSUH algorithm. (Note: outlines of correctness arguments, including all needed invariants, are available in [5].)

Models and proof obligations Verifying correctness of a concurrent algorithm requires a careful model of the algorithm and the environment in which it operates. It is important that the granularity of the model match that of the target execution platform. For example, it may be tempting to model the execution of a statement such as line 15 in Figure 1 as a single action. However, this ignores the fact that the two shared memory accesses in this statement are executed separately—so actions of other threads may occur between these steps—and thus fails to consider all possible behaviors. A model of KSUH that addresses this issue has over 60 actions in total.

In contrast, a transaction can be modeled by a single action. As a result, a model of `TxLock` requires only about 20 actions. Fewer actions means fewer cases to consider, reducing the potential for error. Furthermore, the properties needed to establish correctness are simpler because they do not have to account for the additional behaviors that are possible with finer-grained actions.

Bugs can also be overlooked by failing to faithfully model the environment or failing to check properties that are important for correct operation in that environment. For example, if a model for KSUH does not allow for the possibility of nodes being reused, then it will not exhibit the incorrect behavior we have identified. (Krieger et al. used a model checker to "do a full search of the state space for small numbers of requesters" [8], but did not uncover this bug, which can manifest with three requesters. One possible explanation is that their model did not allow reuse of nodes.) Similarly, to verify that `TxLock` does not require TSM for recycling nodes, the model must allow deallocated nodes to be reused for any purpose.

Exclusion properties The abstract algorithm in Section 2.1 guarantees the exclusion properties. Two writers cannot be in the critical section concurrently: this would imply that both of their nodes are first in the list (recall that threads must use distinct nodes). Similarly, if a reader and a writer were concurrently in the critical section, the writer's node would be first in the list, while all nodes before the reader's node in the list would be owned by readers, a contradiction. Thus, it suffices to show that each algorithm behaves equivalently to the abstract algorithm. Below we discuss two key reasons why this is substantially harder for KSUH than for TxLock.

Defining the list We relate the concrete data structures maintained by each algorithm to the list used in the abstract algorithm description by identifying the steps that add and remove nodes from the list, describing how to derive the abstract list from any reachable state of the algorithm, and showing that this derived list is changed by the identified steps according to the abstract algorithm.

For TxLock, this is relatively straightforward. A node is added to the list by transactions at lines 5–8 and 26–32, and removed from the list by transactions at lines 13–19 and 44–54. These transactions update Tail, and the next and prev pointers of the nodes to maintain the doubly linked list structure, except that a writer does not initialize the prev pointer of its node, which is never read (the prev field of a node is read only at line 45). Thus, we can determine whether a node is in the list by the program counter of its owner, and we can order the nodes in the list by their next pointers. Tail points to the last node in the list, unless the list is empty, in which case Tail is NULL. Also, the prev field of a reader node in the list is NULL iff it is the first node in the list.

For KSUH, a node is added to the list when Tail is modified on line 5 or 21, and it is removed from the list by a successful CAS on line 11, 43 or 52, when its predecessor's next field is written on line 47, or when its successor's spin field is set to 0 on line 15 or 56. If the next field of a node in the list is not NULL, then it points to the node's successor in the list. But unlike in TxLock, a node in the list with a NULL next field need not be the last node; it has a successor if the local pred variable of some thread at line 6–7, 22–24 or 43–47 points to that node. Such a thread will either update that node's prev field, or make that node the last node in the list by removing its own node (by a successful CAS on line 43). It must be shown that this definition of the nodes in the list and the successor of each such node indeed defines a list (e.g., that the successor of a node in the list is also in the list, and there is no cycle).

One key property concerns the prev fields of reader nodes in the list. (As in TxLock, the prev field of a node is only read by its owner in readerUnlock, so the prev field of a writer node is never read.) In TxLock, this is simple: the prev field of a reader node in the list (other than the first) points to its predecessor. However, in KSUH, the prev field of a reader node does not point to its predecessor immediately after it is added to a nonempty list (i.e., when its owner is at line 23), just before its predecessor is removed when its predecessor is not the first reader node in the list (i.e., when its predecessor's owner is at line 15 or 47), or just after its predecessor is removed when its predecessor is the first reader node in the list (i.e., when its predecessor's owner is at line 57–58). These "exceptions" complicate the algorithm and invariants considerably.

Memory lifecycle issues As we have seen, it is important to clearly understand "memory lifecyle" issues, such as how nodes are recycled, and whether and how they can be accessed when not in use. For example, to show that TxLock does not require nodes to be stored in TSM, it suffices to show that a thread does not access a node that it does not own unless that node is in the list. This is easily seen for all accesses within transactions because Tail and every prev or next field of a node in the list points to a node in the list (unless it is NULL), except for prev fields of writer nodes,

which are never read. Outside transactions, such nodes are accessed only at lines 20, 39–40 and 55. For lines 39–40, the thread's node is still in the list, and the thread's local next variable points to its successor (if any), which must therefore also be in the list. For lines 20 and 55, the thread just removed its node from the list, and the thread's local next variable points to the node that was its node's successor (if any). In these cases, the invariants relating nodes in the list to program counters of the threads that own them imply that the owner of the successor node cannot enter the critical section before the owner of the preceding node sets its spin field to zero. Thus, lines 20 and 55 do not modify a node that is not in the list.

In contrast, memory lifecyle issues are much more difficult for KSUH. In particular, it is not possible to prove the simple property discussed above because it is not true: threads *can* modify nodes that are not in the list and not owned; this is central to the bug we have identified. This is true even with our fix, because a thread can acquire the mutex of a node previously observed to be the predecessor of its node, even after that node has been recycled. Thus, once again, the invariants used to verify KSUH are complicated by the need to capture subtle behaviors that cannot occur with TxLock.

5. Performance experiments

Next we evaluate our HTM-based RW-lock algorithms and the version of KSUH shown in Figure 1 (including the corrections labeled with ***). The algorithms are implemented in C and compiled with the GCC 4.4.1 compiler at optimization level -O3 in 32-bit mode (except the kccachetest, which requires 64-bit libraries). The experiments were conducted on the Rock-based system described in [2, 3]. We use both a synthetic benchmark (rwbench) and a more realistic benchmark that employs RW-locks (kccachetest) to compare the performance of KSUH, TxLock, TxLock+CAS, TxLock+TLE, PoisonTheTail, and PoisonTheTail+CAS.

5.1 Synthetic Workloads

In rwbench, each thread repeatedly attempts to acquire and release a single RWLock object for reading or for writing. Benchmark parameters cs and ncs control the amount of work performed in the critical and non-critical sections, respectively. We use rwbench to examine the performance of the algorithms under a variety of workload scenarios, including maximum-contention "torture tests" (cs=0 and ncs=0), as well as workloads with short critical sections and a range of longer non-critical sections. The writer parameter controls the fraction of lock acquisitions that are for writing.

In Figure 4, each column has a fixed fraction of writers: in the left column, all acquisitions are for reading, and in the right, all are for writing. The middle two columns have 10% and 50% of acquisitions for writing, respectively. The top row is the "torture test" configuration, with no delay between lock acquisitions and releases. In the other rows, a short critical section (cs=4) is used, and the non-critical section length increases towards the bottom.

Some of the extreme cases may seem unimportant, because a well-designed application would not use RW-locks with empty critical sections, would not use them so frequently, and would not use an RW-lock when most acquisitions are for write. However, the focus of our paper is not only on RW-locks, but on the ability of HTM to simplify synchronization algorithms. Therefore, it is important to examine performance under heavy contention, and to explore how changes to software and/or hardware might improve performance. Furthermore, workload behavior can often be influenced by input data, so performance of an RW-lock in heavily write-dominated workloads is not unimportant. We first observe that:

- Comparing TxLock+CAS to TxLock and PoisonTheTail+CAS to PoisonTheTail, we see that the CAS-based writerUnlock

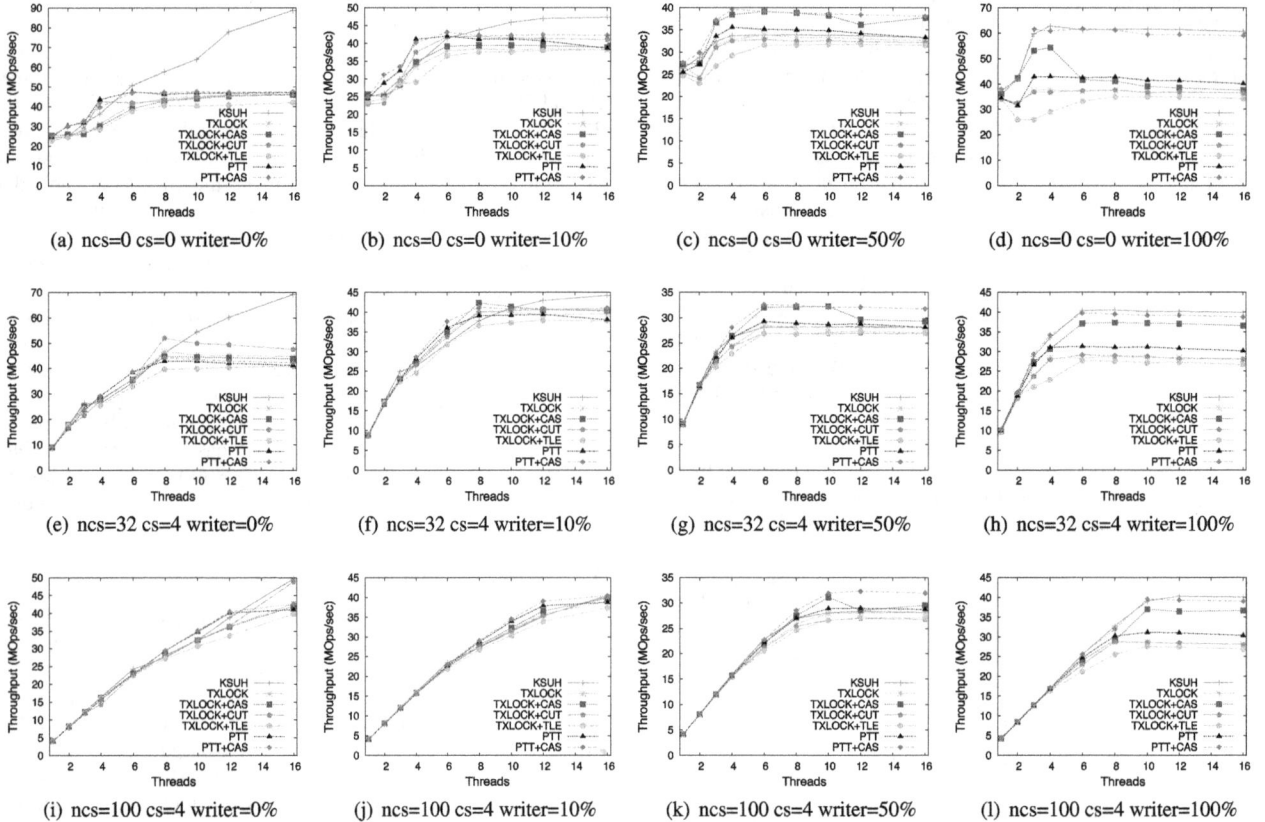

Figure 4. Performance comparison between KSUH and HTM-based RW-locks.

variant provides significant benefit as the fraction of acquisitions for writing increases.

- The `PoisonTheTail` variants almost always perform competitively with or better than their `TxLock` counterparts, and sometimes significantly better, particularly when the fraction of write acquisitions is higher. `PoisonTheTail+CAS` in particular performs well in these scenarios, as it eliminates transactions from both the `writerLock` and `writerUnlock` procedures.

- Comparing `TxLock+TLE` to `TxLock`, we see that the price of using TLE to avoid starvartion is noticeable, but usually small.

- The shortcut transaction provides a small but noticeable improvement in some cases, mostly in read-heavy workloads; we explore this issue in more detail later.

In the most realistic configurations—with longer non-critical sections, and a small fraction of acquisitions being for writing (e.g., Figures 4(i) and 4(j))—there is relatively little difference between the RW-lock algorithms, showing that HTM-based algorithms can be much simpler than the non-HTM-based algorithms on which they are based, while still delivering competitive performance.

Next we discuss the read-only torture test (Figure 4(a)), where KSUH wins by the widest margin. KSUH increases throughput up to 16 threads, but the transactional variants do not scale past 8 threads. All of the transactional algorithms use transactions in `readerLock` and `readerUnlock`, and high contention between them in this test results in retrying and backoff, limiting the throughput.

The best hope to avoid this contention is via the shortcut transaction described in Section 3.3. Indeed, `TxLock+CUT` outperforms `TxLock` noticeably in a number of read-dominated cases. For exam-

ple, it provides about 36% higher throughput at four threads in Figure 4(a). However, with increasing contention (more threads and/or shorter non-critical sections), its benefit fades.

Although the shortcut transaction does not access the highly-contended `Tail` variable, it eliminates the original transaction only when removing a reader from between two nodes, and is still subject to contention with transactions removing neighboring nodes. We believe it may provide greater benefit in workloads in which readers execute longer and more diverse critical sections, resulting in longer reader chains in the list, and making it less likely for a departing reader to conflict with a departing neighbor.

The shortcut transaction (Section 3.3) is compatible with all other optimizations and with TLE. A variant (not shown) that uses *both* the shortcut transaction and the CAS-based `writerUnlock` generally gets the benefit of whichever optimization is most relevant (shortcut transaction in read-heavy cases and CAS-based `writerUnlock` in write-heavy cases). However, in the case of 50% writers, the shortcut transaction imposes overhead for little benefit, as chains of readers build up rarely, so there are few opportunities to remove a reader's node from between two neighbors.

We studied the behavior of the read-only torture test in more detail, collecting statistics on how often transactions are retried and for what reasons, as well as how often `readerUnlock` returns after executing only the shortcut transaction. First, we observed that the shortcut transaction significantly reduced the retry rate for the transactions in `readerLock` *and* `readerUnlock`, as we had hoped. However, as we have noted, the performance improvement was modest. This is primarily because shortcut transaction in most cases did *not* avoid the need to execute the original `readerUnlock`

(a) Shortcut Transaction Disabled

(b) Shortcut Transaction Enabled

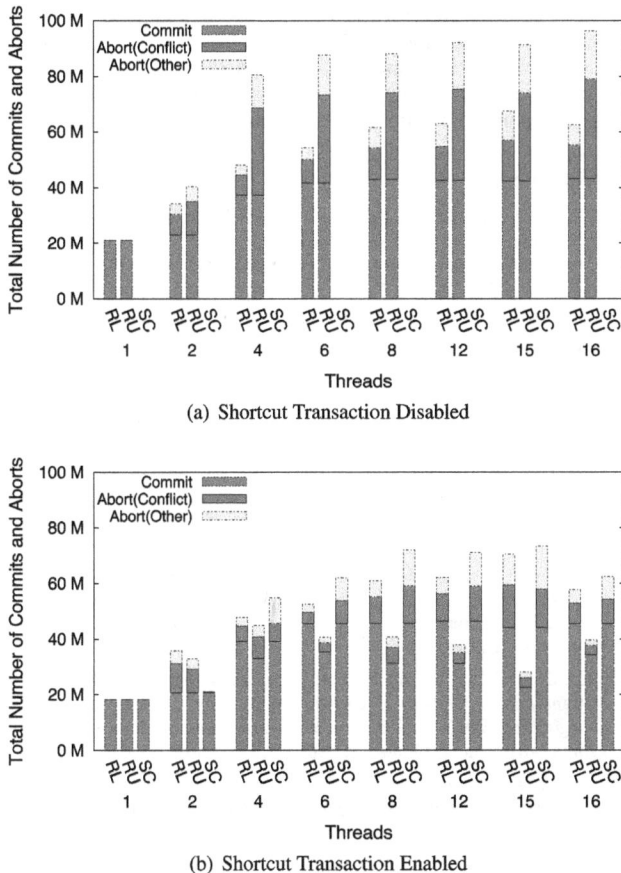

Figure 5. Abort Statistics of Read-only Torture Test (RWBench with NCSLen = CSLen = 0)

transaction. It is interesting, therefore, that the shortcut does not *reduce* performance. The reason is that, if the original transaction is executed, the shortcut transaction prefetches some variables, thus making the original transaction faster and less vulnerable to abort.

Although some techniques successfully improve performance somewhat in the read-only torture test, and further improvements may be possible (for example with better backoff tuning), it is clearly difficult to match the performance of the more complex non-HTM-based algorithm under heavy contention on Rock. This is consistent with the observations of Dice et al. [2, 3], who described several implementation-specific idiosyncrasies with Rock's HTM.

To examine this issue in more depth, we also collected statistics on the reasons that transactions aborted. A noticeable fraction were due to Rock idiosyncrasies. Importantly, however, in most cases 50-75% of aborts were due to conflicts (Figure 5). This suggests that any future HTM implementation that has a "requester-wins" conflict resolution policy [2, 3] is likely to similarly make it difficult to achieve good performance in the face of heavy contention. We hope that designers will seek to improve transaction success rates, even in the face of contention, so that software built using it will be more robust to unexpected or transient contention.

With 100% writers, KSUH is equivalent to the MCS algorithm, and uses only one atomic instruction per lock or unlock operation, giving KSUH a clear advantage over the transactional algorithms that may suffer from transaction aborts and retrying. PoisonTheTail closes the gap somewhat, and TxLock+CAS closes it even more. In both cases, the reason is that transactions are replaced with atomic

CAS instructions that do not abort. PoisonTheTail+CAS, which combines both techniques, achieves almost identical performance to KSUH in the writer-only workloads, using a simpler algorithm. (Recall that many of the changes made to the simple and easy-to-prove TxLock algorithm in order to achieve PoisonTheTail were via transformations that could be applied systematically.)

It is interesting to note that, in workloads with mixed readers and writers (in particular, the 50% writer case), TxLock+CAS and especially PoisonTheTail+CAS noticeably outperform KSUH. To understand why, note that the writerLock and writerUnlock procedures are very similar to those of KSUH in this case, while the readerLock and readerUnlock procedures of KSUH entail significant overhead for the complicated synchronization, including acquiring node locks in readerUnlock. On the other hand, because of the 50%-writer workload, departing readers will typically have a successor but no predecessor in the list. Thus, readers departing using the HTM-based algorithms perform a simple transaction that is unlikely to encounter contention because it will not access Tail and will not have any neighboring readers in the list.

Finally, we reiterate that, while TLE adds only modest overhead to TxLock, it is not possible to use the PoisonTheTail and the CAS optimizations together with TLE, because of their mixed use of transactions and non-transactional atomic instructions such as CAS. At the end of Section 3, we mentioned some possibilities for overcoming this barrier to using HTM to simplify synchronization algorithms while achieving performance competitive with the complex non-HTM-based alternative.

5.2 Kyoto Cabinet: A More Realistic RWLock Application

kccachetest serves as a stress test and performance benchmark for the in-memory "cache hash" (CacheDB) database. It is part of the Kyoto-Cabinet distribution, a popular open-source database package. CacheDB uses RWlocks heavily. We ran the program with the "wicked" argument, which constructs an in-memory non-persistent database and then runs randomly selected database transactions against it. A parameter specifies the number of threads. Each worker thread repeatedly performs a randomly selected operation on the database. Some operations are simple lookups or deletes, while others are more complex transactions. Each thread performs the same number of operations, and we measure completion time. The size of the key range, and thus the memory footprint, is a function of the number of threads. Results of runs with different numbers of threads are therefore not easily comparable. As a result, we do not report absolute performance of kccachetest, but rather the normalized performance compared to KSUH.

We ran kccachetest with 1 to 16 threads, taking the median of 12 trials in each case. At all thread levels, the transactional algorithms are fairly competitive with KSUH. TxLock overhead compared to KSUH ranges from 0.7% to 4.8%, but is usually less than 3%. The CAS optimization usually provides a small improvement (for both TxLock and PoisonTheTail). PoisonTheTail+CAS is particularly competitive, paying at most 2.5% overhead, but usually less than 2%, and in one case even slightly outperformed KSUH. The shortcut transaction mostly hurt performance by at least a small margin, but in one case it provided the best performance, outperforming KSUH by about 1%. Finally, to achieve better progress guarantees, TxLock+TLE imposes noticeable overhead compared to KSUH, ranging from 1.25% to over 6.75%, and it is usually over 3.5%. This show that HTM allows much simpler algorithms to be used without substantially harming performance, and that optimizations can help close the small gap. If future HTM implementations impose lower overhead and deal with contention better, such optimizations may not be as important. Nonetheless, as discussed in Section 3.3, future HTMs could support the use of TLE with such optimizations using fast conditional atomic operations.

6. Discussion

The focus of this paper has been on the use of HTM to simplify algorithms, and the KSUH algorithm and the bug we found in it served as a good example to study. However, in this section, we briefly discuss alternative solutions that do not depend on HTM.

First, other RW-lock algorithms that have been published since KSUH was published should be considered. Some of them deliver signifcantly better scalability; see [9], for example.

Next, we discuss several possible approaches that we believe allow use of (variants of) the KSUH algorithm while avoiding the incorrect behavior we have identified, without depending on HTM. First, we believe our fix (see *** in Figure 1) corrects the algorithm.

Alternatively, if it is not possible or desirable to modify the implementation of KSUH, we believe it will behave correctly if the client separates nodes into two TSM domains: one for read requests and one for write requests. The reason is that this would ensure that the problematic late store described in Section 2 would only ever target nodes used for store requests, and the prev field that gets overwritten by the late store is used only in nodes used for read requests. (This would also allow for an optimization in which the state field is written once when a node is allocated, allowing the initialization of the field during each request to be elided, but of course this would require the KSUH implementation to be modified.)

The solutions mentioned above do not change the fact that nodes must be kept in TSM, which again imposes considerable inconveniences on programmers. We believe that, given our fix to the KSUH algorithm, the only reason TSM is still required is because the locks are stored in nodes, and could be accessed after a node has been removed, as discussed in Section 2. It is interesting to note that known techniques can be used to remove this dependence. In particular, rather than having a lock per node, we could have a persistent array of locks, hashing nodes into the array to determine which lock protects a node. Care must be taken, however, to avoid deadlock, because the hashing loses the properties that ensure deadlock does not arise in KSUH. This is not difficult: if a thread's attempt to acquire the lock to which its own node hashes times out, it can release the lock on its predecessor and retry.

Finally, we note that such a solution has significant overlap with a more direct solution in which we use software transactional memory (STM) to implement the TxLock; by using a privatization-safe STM, we could still achieve a solution that does not require nodes to be kept in TSM. This raises interesting possible research directions, such as making STM compatible with single-location nontransactional accesses like those we used to reduce transaction aborts due to contention on Tail for the PoisonTheTail algorithm. It is also interesting to consider whether techniques such as those presented by Dragojevic and Harris [6] may be used to improve performance of algorithms achieved in this manner.

7. Concluding remarks

We have demonstrated the power of hardware transactional memory (HTM) to simplify and improve synchronization algorithms. We used HTM to significantly simplify a well-known synchronization algorithm, while correcting an error in it that has escaped notice for decades. The resulting algorithm is dramatically easier to prove correct, and furthermore eliminates usage constraints that apply to the original algorithm, making it more convenient to use, and improving its space requirements. We have also presented optimized versions of this algorithm using transformations for making transactions shorter, and in some cases, eliminating them entirely.

Our HTM-based algorithms perform competitively with the original algorithm under reasonable conditions. However, the transactional algorithms are not as competitive under extreme contention. We also find that using Transactional Lock Elision (TLE)

to enhance the algorithm's progress properties precludes the use of some valuable optimizations. We have discussed ways in which future HTM implementations might alleviate both isuses.

We have also identified several fixes and workarounds for the original algorithm that do not depend on HTM.

References

[1] D. Dice, M. Herlihy, D. Lea, Y. Lev, V. Luchangco, W. Mesard, M. Moir, K. Moore, and D. Nussbaum. Applications of the adaptive transactional memory test platform. Transact 2008 workshop, 2008. URL http://labs.oracle.com/projects/scalable/pubs/TRANSACT2008-ATMTP-Apps.pdf.

[2] D. Dice, Y. Lev, M. Moir, and D. Nussbaum. Early experience with a commercial hardware transactional memory implementation. In Proceeding of the 14th international conference on Architectural support for programming languages and operating systems, ASPLOS '09, 2009.

[3] D. Dice, Y. Lev, M. Moir, D. Nussbaum, and M. Olszewski. Early experience with a commercial hardware transactional memory implementation. Technical Report TR-2009-180, Sun Microsystems Laboratories, 2009.

[4] D. Dice, Y. Lev, V. J. Marathe, M. Moir, D. Nussbaum, and M. Oleszewski. Simplifying concurrent algorithms by exploiting hardware transactional memory. In Proceedings of the 22nd ACM symposium on Parallelism in algorithms and architectures, SPAA '10, 2010.

[5] D. Dice, Y. Lev, Y. Liu, V. Luchangco, and M. Moir. Using hardware transactional memory to correct and simplify a readers-writer lock algorithm, 2013. URL http://labs.oracle.com/projects/scalable/pubs/PPoPP2013-HTM-RWlocks-appendix.pdf.

[6] A. Dragojević and T. Harris. STM in the small: trading generality for performance in software transactional memory. In Proceedings of the 7th ACM european conference on Computer Systems, EuroSys '12, pages 1–14, New York, NY, USA, 2012. ACM. ISBN 978-1-4503-1223-3. doi: 10.1145/2168836.2168838. URL http://doi.acm.org/10.1145/2168836.2168838.

[7] M. Greenwald and D. Cheriton. The synergy between non-blocking synchronization and operating system structure. In Proceedings of the second USENIX symposium on Operating systems design and implementation, OSDI '96, pages 123–136, New York, NY, USA, 1996. ACM. ISBN 1-880446-82-0. doi: 10.1145/238721.238767. URL http://doi.acm.org/10.1145/238721.238767.

[8] O. Krieger, M. Stumm, R. Unrau, and J. Hanna. A fair fast scalable rea,der-writer lock. In Proceedings of the 1993 International Conference on Parallel Processing - Volume 02, ICPP '93, pages 201–204, Washington, DC, USA, 1993. IEEE Computer Society. ISBN 0-8493-8983-6. doi: 10.1109/ICPP.1993.21. URL http://dx.doi.org/10.1109/ICPP.1993.21.

[9] Y. Lev, V. Luchangco, and M. Olszewski. Scalable reader-writer locks. In Proceedings of the twenty-first annual symposium on Parallelism in algorithms and architectures, SPAA '09, pages 101–110, New York, NY, USA, 2009. ACM. ISBN 978-1-60558-606-9. doi: 10.1145/1583991.1584020. URL http://doi.acm.org/10.1145/1583991.1584020.

[10] J. M. Mellor-Crummey and M. L. Scott. Algorithms for scalable synchronization on shared-memory multiprocessors. ACM Trans. Comput. Syst., 9(1):21–65, Feb. 1991. ISSN 0734-2071. doi: 10.1145/103727.103729. URL http://doi.acm.org/10.1145/103727.103729.

[11] R. Rajwar and J. R. Goodman. Speculative lock elision: Enabling highly concurrent multithreaded execution. In Proc. 34th International Symposium on Microarchitecture, pages 294–305, Dec. 2001.

[12] I. Sparc International. The sparc architecture manual, version 8, 1991. URL http://www.sparc.com/standards/V8.pdf.

[13] M. Tremblay and S. Chaudhry. A third-generation 65nm 16-core 32-thread plus 32-scout-thread CMT SPARC® processor. In IEEE International Solid-State Circuits Conference, Feb. 2008.

ZOOMM: A Parallel Web Browser Engine for Multicore Mobile Devices

Călin Caşcaval   Seth Fowler   Pablo Montesinos Ortego   Wayne Piekarski   Mehrdad Reshadi

Behnam Robatmili   Michael Weber   Vrajesh Bhavsar

Qualcomm Research Silicon Valley

zoomm@qualcomm.com

Abstract

We explore the challenges in expressing and managing concurrency in browsers on mobile devices. Browsers are complex applications that implement multiple standards, need to support legacy behavior, and are highly dynamic and interactive. We present ZOOMM, a highly concurrent web browser engine prototype and show how concurrency is effectively exploited at different levels: speed up computation performance, preload network resources, and preprocess resources outside the critical path of page loading. On a dualcore Android mobile device we demonstrate that ZOOMM is two times faster than the native WebKit based browser when loading the set of pages defined in the Vellamo benchmark.

Categories and Subject Descriptors   D.1.3 [*Programming Techniques*]: Concurrent Programming - Parallel Programming

Keywords   Parallel Browser, Mobile Multicore

1. Introduction

Smartphones and tablet computers are seeing tremendous adoption by consumers. These devices are replacing laptops and desktop machines as the platform of choice for many users. Mobility and permanent connectivity have driven initial adoption and as the devices become more capable, most users can accomplish their daily tasks with ease and convenience. Many of these tasks involve web browsing, whether using a browser or native applications that provide a customized view of web content.

In this paper we present a browser architecture targeted toward exploiting the hardware capabilities of modern mobile devices: multicore parallelism and hardware acceleration, increased network bandwidth and long network latencies. The majority of current smartphones and tablets have SoCs with 2 or 4 cores, aggressively optimized for power – power gated, voltage and frequency scaled. On the network side, LTE brings 100 Mbps bandwidth, however, latency continues to be high [1].

Web browser designers have to address several challenges: fast response time for page load, even in the presence of long network latencies [22], high performance to enable interactivity for web applications, and user interface responsiveness to provide good expe-

rience [18]. In this paper we demonstrate how our browser architecture allows exploitation of multicore concurrency to hide network latency and improve performance. When tested using the publicly available Vellamo [20] benchmark suite, our ZOOMM browser completed the run in 55 seconds, compared to 113 seconds using the standard WebKit [23] available on a commercial HTC Jetstream device. This is an approximately 2× improvement in performance, demonstrating the benefits of our browser architecture.

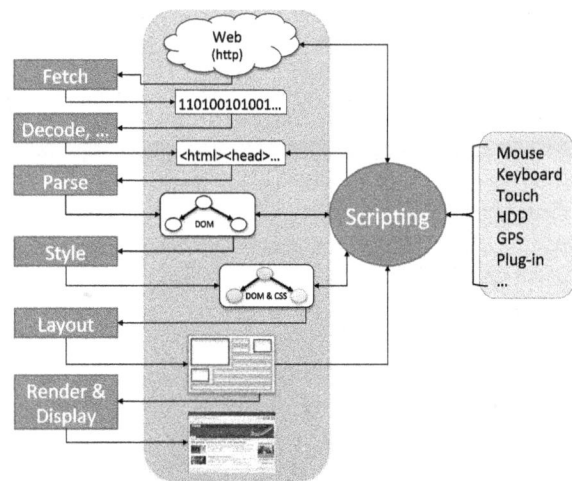

Figure 1. Typical browser processing steps.

Exploiting concurrency to improve browser experience is a relatively new approach. Most existing browsers, such as the WebKit based Chrome [4] and Safari [19], along with the Firefox [8] browser, have a long history of development and are fundamentally architected as sequential engines, using event driven models to help with interactivity. Such design admits some limited parallelization; however, full parallelism requires thread safe data structures and synchronization between components that is hard to graft on an existing design. These browsers have been exploiting process multicore concurrency, using on process per tab, and relying on the OS to map processes to different cores.

As the Web is evolving, we see a remarkable increase in complexity and dynamic behavior. For example, in [13] the authors measured WebKit execution and observed that JavaScript took around 5% of the execution time. About one year later, the fraction of JavaScript execution has increased to 30%. Even more significantly, we observe a major trend to support application development using web technologies, such as HTML5, CSS, and JavaScript. Poor browser performance is one of the most important factors hampering the move towards web apps.

271

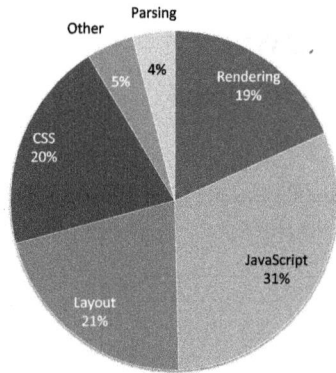

Figure 2. Browser processing times by component, excluding network load time. Profiling results obtained using the WebKit browser on an ARM Cortex A9 processor. Results are an aggregate of the top Alexa 30 sites as of March 2010.

Therefore our main challenge, and the focus of this paper, is to build a high-performance modern browser engine that works for a realistic set of web pages and web apps. In this paper we make the following contributions:

- A parallel browser architecture designed for fast web page loading and performant web applications; our hierarchical architecture exploits concurrency by overlapping the execution of major components as well as implementing parallel algorithms for some of the processing steps (Section 2);

- We demonstrate the use of concurrency to hide latency by discovering resources ahead of time, downloading and processing them in parallel (Section 3);

- We present a novel CSS matching and styling algorithm that scales linearly (Section 4);

- We describe briefly a parallel JavaScript engine to improve the performance of long running web applications (Section 5).

We briefly describe the other browser components and their interaction in Section 6 and discuss performance results in Section 8.

2. A Parallel Browser Architecture

Figure 1 shows a typical browser architecture and illustrates the steps required to render a web page. JavaScript interacts with the page during the page load, as well as after the page is loaded to provide interactivity. Figure 2 shows the breakdown of execution time by component, excluding the network time. Our measurements, similar to [22] show the network time being 30%-50% of the total execution time. Given this breakdown of computation, it is clear that in order to optimize the execution of the browser, one has to address all components.

2.1 Design goals

Our goal is to exploit concurrency at multiple levels: parallel algorithms for individual passes to speed up processing of each component, and overlapping of passes to speed up total execution time. In addition, we must respect the HTML and JavaScript semantics, even during concurrent execution. The main data structure that is used by all browser passes is the *Document Object Model* (DOM). The DOM is a tree representing all the HTML elements: their contents, relationships, styles, and positions. Web programmers use JavaScript to manipulate the DOM, producing interactive web pages and web apps. Most communication between browser passes and components happens through the DOM. Unfortunately, even in

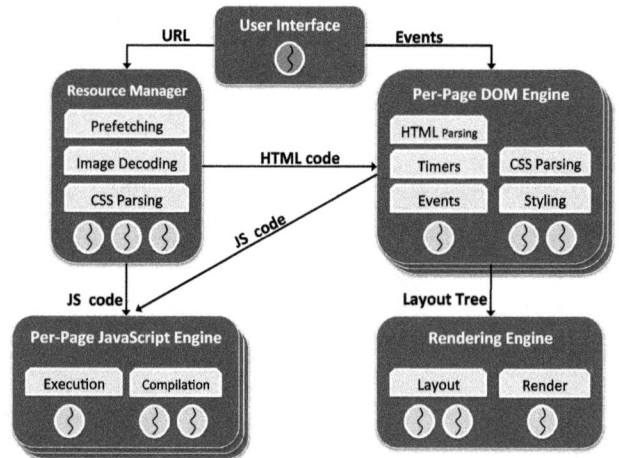

Figure 3. ZOOMM Browser Architecture. Concurrency is exploited both across components and within each component.

a concurrent browser, access to the DOM tree (constructed by the *HTML5 parser*) must be serialized, to conform to the HTML5 specification [11]. This is the biggest limitation ZOOMM must contend with, and it has influenced the design significantly. In our architecture, we manage access to the DOM through a dispatcher; most passes have their own private concurrent data structures to allow for greater parallelism inside components, and they send DOM updates to be processed by the dispatcher. Figure 3 shows the high level components of the architecture. We discuss the details in the following sections.

2.2 ZOOMM Browser Architecture

The ZOOMM browser consists of a number of loosely-coupled subsystems, which are all designed with concurrency in mind. With the exception of the browser-global *resource manager* and the *rendering engine*, all sub-systems are instantiated once for each page (shown as a separate *tab* in the user interface).

Resource Manager. The *resource manager* is responsible for managing and preprocessing all network resources, including fetching resources from the network, cache management for fetched resources, and notifications for the arrival of data from the network to other browser components. In our first implementation, all resources are fetched in the order in which they appear, without imposing any priorities. In addition, the *resource manager* includes other components, such as the *HTML prescanner* and *image decoder*. The HTML prescanner quickly determines all external resources in an HTML document, requests their downloading, and, depending on the type of resources, request further processing (Section 3.1). The Image decoder component consists of a thread pool that decodes images for later use as they are received by the resource manager. These operations are fully concurrent, as each image decode is an independent task.

DOM Engine. In ZOOMM, each page (tab) instantiates a *DOM engine* which consists of the *DOM dispatcher, HTML parser, CSS parsing and styling*, and *timers and events*. The *DOM dispatcher* thread is responsible for scheduling DOM updates; it serves as the page event loop. It serializes access to the DOM and manages the interaction between components. The rest of the browser infrastructure dispatches *work items* into the concurrent DOM dispatcher queue, which are then handled one at a time. Work items represent browser passes as well as events like from timers events and the user interface. The *HTML parser* receives incoming (partial) data chunks for an HTML document via a DOM dispatcher work item, and constructs the *DOM tree* by executing the HTML5 parsing algorithm [11]. The parser adds external resources referenced from the HTML document to the resource manager's fetch queue. The parser also initiates execution of JavaScript code by calling the *JavaScript engine* at appropriate times during parsing. The CSS engine is responsible for calculating the look and feel of the DOM elements for the later layout and rendering stages. Similar to image decoding, the resource manager hands off CSS stylesheets to the *CSS engine* for parsing and for discovering new resources to be requested (Section 4).

Rendering engine. Whenever the DOM or the CSS stylesheets change, whether because the fetcher delivered new resources, the HTML parser updated the DOM, or as a result of JavaScript computations, this change needs to be reflected on the screen so that the user can view and interact with it. The *layout engine* is responsible for transforming the styled DOM tree into geometry and content which the *rendering engine* can turn into a bitmap (Section 6). Ultimately this bitmap is *displayed* on the screen by the user interface as a viewable web page. Normally, the layout and rendering engine takes a snapshot of the DOM information it needs and performs the rest of the work asynchronously; however, it can also be invoked synchronously when JavaScript makes use of APIs that query layout information.

JavaScript Engine. The ZOOMM *JavaScript engine* executes all JavaScript code. The engine's novel design is outside the scope of this paper. Instead, we focus on the integration with the rest of the browser architecture (Section 5).

User Interface. The ZOOMM browser is currently available on Android, Linux, and Mac OS X platforms, and is mainly implemented in platform agnostic C++. For concurrency, we use a custom asynchronous task library, that provides similar functionality to Intel Thread Building Blocks [16]. On Android, a thin Java wrapper is used to create the user interface. User interactions such as touching a link on the display are translated into JNI method calls, which ultimately create work items in the DOM dispatcher. Drawing to the display is performed using the Android NDK, which provides direct access to Android bitmaps. On Linux and Mac OS X, a similar wrapper is implemented in C++ using the Qt interface toolkit [15]. Although our deployment targets are Android devices, the Qt implementation allows much easier debugging and testing on desktop based machines, and the ability to evaluate concurrency beyond what Android devices offer today.

In the following sections, we discuss some of ZOOMM's components in more detail.

3. Aggressive Resource Prefetching

Mobile devices commonly experience high latency when requesting the resources that form an HTML document. In order to reduce the overall time taken to load a page, fetching all of the dependencies from the network as early as possible is very important. This section describes the techniques we employ to prefetch resources discovered in HTML and CSS content.

3.1 HTML Prescanning

Due to idiosyncrasies in the HTML5 specification, the HTML5 parser must wait for `<script>` blocks to finish executing before it can continue parsing. Thus, if a web page references an external resource *after* a script element, fetching the resource cannot be overlapped with the waiting. Potentially, this can delay the completion of page loading. The Mozilla Firefox browser [8] mitigates such situations by speculatively parsing ahead of script blocks to

discover new resources. (It may then be forced to throw away some of that work if, for example, JavaScript inserts new content into the DOM tree via the `document.write()` API.) Once resources are discovered, network latency can be masked by requesting multiple resources to be fetched in parallel. This strategy also helps to utilize all available bandwidth. In either case, it reduces the overall time spent waiting for resources to arrive.

In ZOOMM, we favor concurrency to achieve the same goal by running an HTML *prescanning* component in parallel to a (non-speculative) HTML parser. The main objective of the HTML prescanner is to quickly determine all external resources in an HTML document and trigger their fetching from the network. The most commonly referenced resources are images, CSS stylesheets, and JavaScript sources. In addition, stylesheets and JavaScript sources can themselves reference further external resources. Furthermore, the prescanner obtains all `id`, `class` and `style` attributes used in the document.

As network packets of an HTML document arrive, they are given to the prescanner and the actual HTML parser independently. The prescanner is able to run ahead of the HTML parser because it only has to approximately parse HTML in order to find resources, thus skipping the complex DOM tree construction phase. More importantly, the prescanner does not have to wait for the execution of `<script>` blocks to finish.

The processing of prefetched resources works as follows. Images are fetched concurrently with the rest of the page processing. Once downloaded, image data is given to a thread pool for decoding, concurrently. The decoded image is added to the *DOM dispatcher queue*, which updates the corresponding `img` tree node. Then, the image is removed from the set of pending images.

3.2 CSS Prefetching

CSS stylesheets are dispatched to a thread pool responsible for parsing CSS concurrently. If a CSS rule contains further external resources, the parser makes a decision whether to initiate prefetching for them, based on the likelihood that they are actually referenced in the HTML document.

It is crucial to download just enough of the referenced resources. Downloading too little means that new resources are discovered only when styling the DOM tree later on, which incurs additional latency penalties. It is common practice among websites to reference many more resources than are actually needed for any given document, for example by using a site-wide common style file. Downloading all resources invariably consumes too much bandwidth and slows down page loading.

In ZOOMM, the CSS parser employs the `id` and `class` attributes discovered by the HTML prescanner to determine if a rule is likely to be matched. If all of the attribute values referenced in a CSS rule selector have been seen by the HTML prescanner, we assume that the rule will match at least one DOM tree element, and initiate downloading its resources. This heuristic is simple, but effective (Table 1). Note that wrong decisions here do not affect correctness; any missed resources will be discovered during the styling phase, at the cost of additional latency.

3.3 Limitations

ZOOMM's prescanner is limited to discovering resources which can be determined without having to execute JavaScript. Furthermore, the CSS parser may erroneously initiate prefetching of a resource (*false positive*). For example, this occurs if all class IDs were detected by the HTML prescanner individually, but in the HTML document they do not appear nested in the same way as described by any CSS rule. The CSS prefetching algorithm does not generate *false negatives*, except when JavaScript dynamically changes the DOM tree.

4. The CSS engine

Cascading Style Sheets (CSS) is a language used to describe the look and formatting of web sites, thus separating the presentation of a document from its content. Each style sheet consists of an ordered collection of rules with the following format:

> selector {
> $property_1$: value;
>   ...
> $property_n$: value;
> }

For example, the following CSS code makes the browser render all `<cite>` elements whose direct ancestor is a `<p>` element using a white foreground:

```
p>cite { color: white; }
```

It is common for web sites to use several thousand such rules.

ZOOMM's CSS engine performs three jobs: CSS resource prefetching, CSS parsing, and DOM styling. We describe CSS prefetching in Section 3.2. We now describe the other two.

4.1 Concurrent CSS Parsing

During CSS parsing, the CSS engine reads the CSS code and creates a collection of data structures that we call *in-memory rules*. CSS code can be embedded in HTML or linked as separate files, perhaps stored on different servers. Traditional CSS engines — like the ones in WebKit or Firefox— parse CSS sequentially in the main browser thread. Thus, if a page uses embedded CSS, the HTML parser cannot parse the rest of the HTML document until the CSS engine has parsed the style element in the document's header. Moreover, if a page uses several CSS files, they will all be parsed sequentially, even though idle CPU cores are available. Such serialization is particularly noticeable in sites using large CSS files; for example, the main CSS file for BBC News[1] is 250 KBytes in size.

ZOOMM's CSS parser is re-entrant so that it is possible to invoke it from asynchronous, concurrent tasks. During page load, ZOOMM's HTML parser spawns a CSS parsing task for each style element in the DOM tree. Similarly, the resource manager spawns a CSS parsing task for each CSS file it receives. Effectively, this means that a CSS parser instance executes as soon as any new CSS is available, regardless of whether the HTML parser or other instances are already executing. However, ZOOMM must ensure that the total order of the in-memory rules is equal to the one that would have been generated by a sequential CSS engine. Each parsing task receives a unique, sequential ID that is later used to recreate the ordering of the style sheets in the original document.

4.2 Parallel DOM Styling

DOM styling is the means by which the CSS engine uses in-memory rules to determine the style of the nodes in the DOM tree. For each node, the CSS engine must first find all the rules whose selectors match the node, or *rule matching*. Rule matching often returns many — and usually conflicting — rules per node. Using *cascading*, the CSS engine assigns weights to rules and chooses only the ones with the greatest weight. During *style creation*, the CSS engine creates the style data structure using the rules selected by the cascading algorithm and attaches it to the node.

A key insight is that it is possible to concurrently style several DOM nodes as long as certain dependencies are enforced, and we developed a new parallel DOM styling algorithm that leverages it.

Algorithm 1 shows that the CSS engine uses two types of tasks per node to style the DOM tree: *matching tasks* and *styling tasks*.

---
[1] http://www.bbc.co.uk/news/

Algorithm 1 Parallel DOM Styling Algorithm

```
 1: function STYLENODE(node, ruleset)
 2:     finalRuleset ← Cascade(ruleset, node)
 3:     node.style ← BuildStyle(finalRuleset, node)
 4: end function
 5:
 6: function MATCHNODE(node, ruleset, styling)
 7:     child ← node.FirstChild()
 8:     while child ≠ NULL do
 9:         r ← NewRuleset()
10:         ts ← NewTask(StyleNode(child, r))
11:         tm ← NewTask(MatchNode(child, r, ts))
12:         tm.SetSuccessor(ts)
13:         styling.SetSuccessor(ts)
14:         tm.Spawn()
15:         ts.Spawn()
16:         child ← child.NextSibling()
17:     end while
18:     Match(node, ruleset)
19: end function
20:
21: function STYLEDOMTREE(tree)
22:     root ← tree.root()
23:     ruleset ← NewRuleset()
24:     ts ← NewTask(StyleNode(root, ruleset))
25:     tm ← NewTask(MatchNode(root, ruleset, ts))
26:     tm.SetSuccessor(ts)
27:     tm.Spawn()
28:     ts.Spawn()
29:     WaitForTasks()
30: end function
```

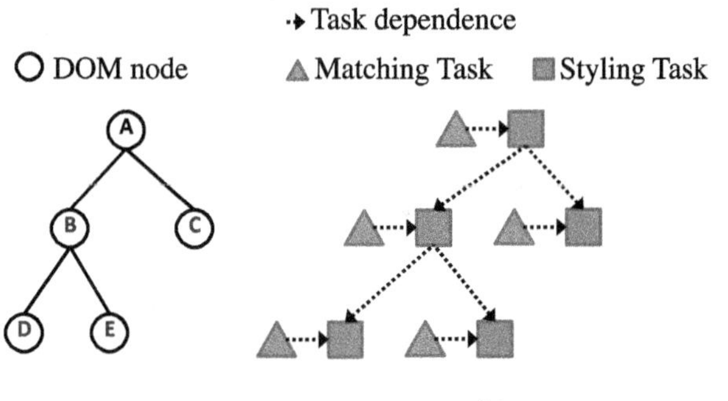

Figure 4. DOM tree (a) and corresponding task DAG (b).

Matching tasks start by spawning new matching and styling tasks for each of the node's children. Then, they rule-match the node. Their output is a set of rules that are applicable to the node. They spawn children tasks before they do the actual work because styling tasks are fully independent, and it is desirable to have as many of them executing as possible.

Styling tasks apply the cascading algorithm and create the final style data structure for each node. A styling task must satisfy two dependencies before it can execute. First, it can only execute after the matching task working on the same node has completed execution, since the cascading algorithm uses the rules selected by the matching task. Second, a styling task working on a node can only execute after the styling task working on the node's parent has completed execution. This is because some style properties of a node may be inherited from its parent. By using two types of tasks, our algorithm can rule-match a node before its parent is styled. Figures 4a and 4b show a DOM tree and its corresponding task DAG, respectively.

This basic version of the algorithm limits style sharing to parent-child sharing. However, we subdivide style objects into substyles containing related properties, and allow sharing at the substyle level, which increases the degree of available sharing (see Section 6.1). For example, if a child node uses the same font properties as its parent, then they can share the font substyle. To add support for sibling style sharing, the matching task must speculate whether a child node may be able to share its style with a previous child node before spawning tasks for it. If the answer is yes, it does not spawn new tasks for the second child.

Matching tasks can be expensive because the rule matching algorithm must decide whether each selector applies to the node or to any of its ancestors. This may require traversing the tree all the way to the root. For example, rule-matching BBC News requires more than 400,000 of such walks. WebKit saves 90% of them by using a Bloom filter [3] that stores information about the ancestors of a DOM node. In Safari 5.0, a Bloom filter instance amounts to a space overhead of 4 KB. ZOOMM cannot use the same data structure because it would require a new Bloom filter instance per matching task. Instead, ZOOMM utilizes *matching bitmaps*. Matching bitmaps are fixed size (64 byte) and record whether an ID, a class or a tag has been seen in one of the node ancestors.

Section 3.2 describes how ZOOMM uses element `id`, `tag` and `class` attributes to predict whether an image referenced in the CSS file should be prefetched. These attributes are stored in a database that sorts them according to the number of times each one appears in the document. Before the rule matching algorithm starts, the CSS engine assigns a bit to each of them in a bitmap data structure. If the number of ids and classes is larger than the bitmap size, a single bit can be assigned to multiple items. During rule matching, each matching task receives a matching bitmap from its parent. Matching tasks use the matching bitmap to filter out rules that could never match: if the bit corresponding to a tag, id or class is not set, that means that no ancestor has it. Therefore, there is no need to traverse the tree. After matching is completed, matching tasks add their node's id, class, and tag to the bitmap and send a copy to their descendants.

5. JavaScript Engine

The ZOOMM browser includes a JavaScript engine that is optimized for parallel execution. In particular, our engine expoits concurrency by compiling multiple scripts in parallel, as well as compiling scripts asynchronously with the rest of the browser passes. To achieve this, the JavaScript engine uses a thread pool and the JIT compiler uses separate state for each script.

Due to JavaScript semantics, execution of scripts is performed sequentially in the main engine thread. When the HTML parser or the DOM dispatcher (e.g., for user interface events) requests the execution of a JavaScript script that has not been compiled already, compilation is initiated. In either case, the engine waits for the compiled result, and then executes the script. The goal of the engine is to use available resources on the platform to improve the generated code for JavaScript execution.

For adaptive compilation and execution of the JavaScript code, the JavaScript engine consists of an interpreter, and two compilers:

Interpreter. The interpreter is used for fast startup execution of small JavaScript scripts. It is mainly invoked on page load, since many pages have inline JavaScript code that is executed only once and mainly calls into the browser bindings.

Light compiler. This compiler is optimized for page load and generates executable code for infrequently reused JavaScript code. We have a parametrized threshold that triggers the invocation of the light compiler.

Full compiler. This compiler is optimized for interactivity and *web apps*, and generates higher quality code for heavily reused JavaScript code. The slower code generation of the full compiler is amortized between multiple runs of the reused code. Compared to the light compiler, this compiler achieves significant speedup for iterative web apps. For example, using this compiler, an *N-body simulation* web app runs six times faster than the same application compiled with the light compiler.

A full description and evaluation of the JavaScript engine is outside the scope of this paper.

6. Layout, Rendering, and Display

Once styles have been applied to the DOM tree by the CSS engine, it is necessary to use this information to produce a bitmap image that will be displayed to the user. This job is performed in four steps:

1. The *layout tree* is created or updated by the page event loop. This tree captures all the information from the DOM that is relevant for the subsequent steps; each node represents a visual element on the web page. Only this step needs to run on the page event loop; after the layout tree is created, the remaining steps are independent of the DOM, and can run concurrently with tasks like JavaScript.

2. The *layout engine* is responsible for solving the system of constraints expressed by the layout tree's styles and structure; it implements the CSS layout algorithm [6]. Ultimately it annotates each layout tree node with width, height, margins, and other spatial information which determines how it will be displayed on the screen.

3. The *rendering engine* walks the annotated layout tree nodes and draws them, along with any text or other content they may contain, into a bitmap. The resulting bitmap is again independent of the previous steps, and further manipulation of it can happen concurrently.

4. The *user interface*, running on its own thread to assure responsiveness to user input, accepts the bitmap produced by the rendering engine and displays it on the screen. The user interface is also responsible for scrolling; once a bitmap has been displayed, the user can scroll freely even if all of the other threads in the system are busy.

Layout, rendering, and display thus involve three different tasks in a pipeline-like structure, although as we discuss below, there are subtleties that may increase its complexity. This arrangement isolates both the page event loop and the user interface from the delays caused by layout and rendering, allowing JavaScript and interactive events like scrolling to run as fast as possible.

In the following subsections we explore the detailed design of each step in this process.

6.1 Layout Tree

The layout tree's purpose is to decouple layout, rendering, and display from the page event loop, allowing JavaScript and other types of tasks to run freely. The main obstacle to this goal is JavaScript's ability to change DOM nodes and CSS rules at will; these changes may cause inconsistent layout results or rendering artifacts if they are not protected against.

The CSS layout rules do not create a one-to-one mapping between DOM nodes and layout nodes; this means that a distinct tree must be created for the layout nodes[2] regardless of our concurrency goals. To eliminate any possible interference from JavaScript, we augment the information normally found in the layout tree in such a way that there is no longer any need to refer back to the DOM or the CSS rules.

We use different strategies for different types of information, as follows:

CSS Styles. Because of their large size, we divide style objects into a number of substyles, each containing properties that usually vary together. Each substyle can be shared with many style objects using copy-on-write semantics; a style object thus consists of a set of references to potentially-shared substyles. In addition to greatly reducing memory usage, this approach has the advantage that we do not need to worry about modification to styles when building the layout tree; as long as our style object has a reference to a substyle, we know that it will remain unchanged, regardless of any concurrent style changes that may occur.

DOM Text Content. It would be feasible to use a copy-on-write approach for text as well, but because text content was so small compared to other types of data on our test sites, we simply copy the text into the layout tree.

DOM Image Content. Images are immutable in ZOOMM, so all we need to place in the layout tree is a reference.

Canvas Elements. Canvas elements need to be treated specially because their contents are often changed rapidly by JavaScript. Given that they contain image data that is fairly expensive to copy and that the old contents of a canvas element are only occasionally needed, a copy-on-write approach is not appropriate here. Instead, it proves cheaper to copy the contents of the canvas into a corresponding buffer in the layout tree. These buffers are reused to minimize memory allocation, and we use dirtiness annotations in the DOM to avoid copying if the canvas element contents have not changed.

An alternate strategy would be to avoid copying the canvas contents at all and simply paint whatever contents the canvas has at render time; this has the disadvantage that tearing will be visible to the user. Effectively, copying the canvas contents amounts to double buffering.

HTML Attributes. Only a small subset of HTML attributes matter to layout; these are presentational values like `border`. In most cases these map directly to CSS properties, and when these attributes are set on a node we translate them into changes to that node's style. Certain presentational HTML attributes have no CSS equivalents; for these, we make use of special ZOOMM-only CSS properties.

One interesting case concerns the HTML `height` and `width` attributes; although in many cases these are equivalent to the corresponding CSS properties, for canvas elements the HTML attributes control the dimensions of the canvas's internal coordinate system, while the CSS properties control the scaling of the canvas on the page. This difference requires that we record both values in the style for canvas elements.

Conceptually, a new layout tree is generated whenever the DOM or CSS are updated. This is usually triggered by JavaScript, but may also be the result of the arrival of new resources. However, in practice we do not need to generate a new layout tree unless we are going to use it, so we defer the work until either we reach the point of displaying the previous tree and detect that the page's contents have changed, or we must compute layout to determine a value that JavaScript is requesting.

We have found that in practice, JavaScript often makes numerous references to values computed by layout during page load. Current browsers typically only allow one layout tree to exist at a time, synchronizing it with the DOM according to some policy. This is not a problem if layout blocks the page event loop anyway, but in ZOOMM we run layout asynchonously; if we were forced to wait for layout and rendering to finish to update the layout tree, we might block the event loop for the time required to run layout twice – one time to be able to update the layout tree, and a second time to actually run the layout algorithm. We avoid this problem by allowing multiple layout trees to exist at the same time, and running layout in the page event loop thread if up-to-date layout information is not available when JavaScript requests it.

To minimize the costs of copying or updating our layout trees – indeed, these are the same operation for us – we treat the layout trees as an immutable data structure. Information that is likely to change frequently is factored out of the layout tree nodes and stored in separate data structures at the root; the nodes themselves only store keys or indices into these data structures. This arrangement means that we often only need to update a small portion of the overall data in the layout tree when something changes; though we only handle certain common cases at present, this approach can be taken quite far. As a concrete example, we store the contents of canvas elements in a list, while canvas nodes in the layout tree contain only an index into this list. When the canvas contents are updated, the new layout tree can share all of the layout nodes with the old tree; only the list of canvas contents must be duplicated.[3] Note that there are some data structures in the layout tree that are not truly immutable until the layout algorithm has already been run; we take note of whether this has happened and decide whether to copy those data structures on that basis.

Creating or copying the layout tree is the only step that must take place in the page event loop. This prevents JavaScript and CSS from running concurrently and ensures that the resulting layout tree is consistent. Once the layout tree is ready, we transfer its ownership to the task responsible for layout and rendering and the event loop can continue processing without any further delay.

6.2 Layout Engine

When the layout engine, running concurrently with the page event loop, receives a layout tree, it consults metadata stored in the layout tree to decide whether to perform CSS layout [6]. This information is stored as part of the process of creating or updating the layout tree, since inferring it after the fact is much more difficult.

Currently we use coarse-grain *dirty bits* to record which aspects of the page have changed, allowing us to determine whether a layout is necessary. In some cases, such as when only images or the contents of canvas elements have changed, the information in the layout tree will be up to date and there will be no need to perform layout at all. In all other cases we currently run a full layout. It is possible to determine the scope of the effect of particular DOM changes and only run the layout algorithm on the subtrees affected; we leave this for future work.

The particular algorithm used to compute layout is orthogonal to our asynchronous layout approach. We use asynchrony to move layout and rendering out of the critical path of the page event loop; a parallelized layout algorithm complements our current design by reducing the delay until layout changes are visible on the screen. Additionally, JavaScript queries like those we mention above sometime force layout to be performed in the page event loop; this case

---

[2] Although in some implementations, a single node can serve both purposes when a one-to-one mapping is possible.

[3] Indeed, using standard immutable data structure techniques, only updating part of the list is necessary. Our current implementation uses a coarser granularity, however.

would also benefit from a parallelized layout algorithm. We leave this extension for future work.

Regardless of the layout implementation, after the layout engine is finished each node in the layout tree is annotated with spatial information such as its final x and y position and layer. This annotated layout tree is then transferred to the rendering engine.

6.3 Rendering Engine

The rendering engine also runs concurrently with the page event loop, after the layout task has executed. It walks the annotated layout tree and paints the contents of the page into a bitmap. We use a simple sequential algorithm that performs rendering according to the CSS standard [6]. It would be possible to use many parallel walks over the layout tree to render into independent tiles simultaneously, but we leave an investigation of this approach for future work; because it does not block the page event loop, rendering is currently not a bottleneck in ZOOMM.

Beyond parallelism, an additional advantage of the layout tree design in ZOOMM is that we can treat layout and rendering as a service which is shared between web pages. Since layout trees do not refer back to the DOM or CSS they were constructed from, it's no problem for the same layout and rendering thread to handle all layout trees regardless of their source. This means that expensive, finite rendering-related resources like bitmaps only need one instance per browser window.

We reuse the same bitmap as long as change to the environment like a resize of the browser window does not invalidate it. This greatly reduces ZOOMM's memory requirements, but it means that we must ensure that the bitmap is copied into graphics memory before any further rendering is performed. This is accomplished by temporarily transferring control of the bitmap to the user interface. When the user interface finishes processing the bitmap, rendering is complete and the layout and rendering thread notifies the page event loop that it is ready to accept any updated layout trees that become available.

6.4 User Interface

The user interface runs on its own thread. The layout and rendering thread transfers control of the bitmap representing the current page contents to the user interface, and then blocks while the user interface uploads the bitmap into graphics memory. This task is performed in the user interface thread only because of platform-related restrictions on which thread must perform this action. After this is complete, the user interface thread notifies the layout and rendering thread that it may continue working, and displays the new content to the user.

The user interface thread is also responsible for processing events caused by user interaction. Most events are handled by JavaScript; these are packaged and delivered to the appropriate page event loop. However, certain events can be handled by the user interface directly. For example, because a page's contents are stored in graphics memory, the user interface can scroll the contents directly. This means that even if the page event loop or layout and rendering thread are busy, scrolling continues to be smooth and responsive.

7. Related Work

There is a wide variety of existing studies on browser parallelism and concurrency in the literature. We summarize the most relevant of these here.

Process-Per-Page Browsers. Chrome [17], the WebKit2 [24] engine, and Gazelle [21] exploit parallelism by using separate processes for the event loop of each open page, essentially delegating the responsibility of using multiple cores to the OS. This is simple to implement and provides isolation between different sites. However, processes are heavyweight in terms of both memory and startup overhead, and page-level parallelism doesn't address the needs of mobile browsers, where single-page performance is often inadequate and users do not open many tabs at once.

Chrome additionally performs display in a separate process [5]; layout and rendering take place in the page event loop, and the resulting rendered segments of the page are transferred to a separate process, allowing the segments to be displayed and scrolled without blocking the event loop. In contrast, our model moves layout and rendering almost entirely out of the page event loop, allowing more time for handling UI events and executing JavaScript.

OP and OP2. Grier et al. [10] developed browsers designed for security and isolation. The OP and OP2 browsers use a per-page multiprocess architecture that places several browser components, such as networking, in different processes. They observed speedups from the ability to overlap operations at the process level. While a multicore/parallelism study was not their primary goal, the observations made are a good indication of the potential of overlapping browser components. We improve on their multiprocess model by adding algorithm-level parallelism and separating out more components, such as layout and rendering, which can run asynchronously in parallel with other activity on the page.

Adrenaline. Mai et al. [12] speed up page processing by splitting the original page in minipages. Each minipage contains only a subset of the CSS and HTML of the original page. This makes CSS and layout faster because the DOM trees have fewer nodes and the style sheets have fewer rules. Additionally, this work can happen in parallel with JavaScript, which runs in a process associated with the main page; Adrenaline is the only other browser we are aware of that allows this. However, Adrenaline must merge other mini pages into the master page if JavaScript makes any reference to their content, preventing any further parallelism for that mini page. In contrast, JavaScript's DOM access in our browser is unrestricted and does not penalize parallelism or trigger the overhead of page merging. Our method also does not require server-side support as Adrenaline does.

The Berkeley Parallel Browser Project. Meyerovich and Bodik have looked at the problem of parallelizing the CSS and layout algorithms [13]. Their initial results are very promising, offering $80\times$ speed-up in some instances. However, their CSS algorithm only supports a subset of the CSS standard, and it is a standalone component that only performs selector matching. ZOOMM's parallel styling algorithm is CSS 2.1 compliant and combines parallel matching with parallel cascading. Their study also addresses the problem of parallel layout. Their work is orthogonal to ours – we address performing layout entirely outside of the page event loop and could use their parallel algorithm.

Although they target only a well-behaved subset of the specification, their experience shows that browser processing algorithms can be made highly concurrent if one could modify the standard. We expect that many of their optimizations would be beneficial if combined with our approach, although we leave this for future work.

Parallel CSS in Firefox. Badea et al. [2] profiled Firefox and found that, in most cases, rule matching a node requires rule matching all the node's ancestors. They propose using helper threads to speed up matching of ancestor selectors. In their implementation, each helper thread is assigned a number of ancestors to process. WebKit and ZOOMM avoid most of those traversals by using bloom filters and matching bitmaps, respectively, addressing this issue in a sequential fashion.

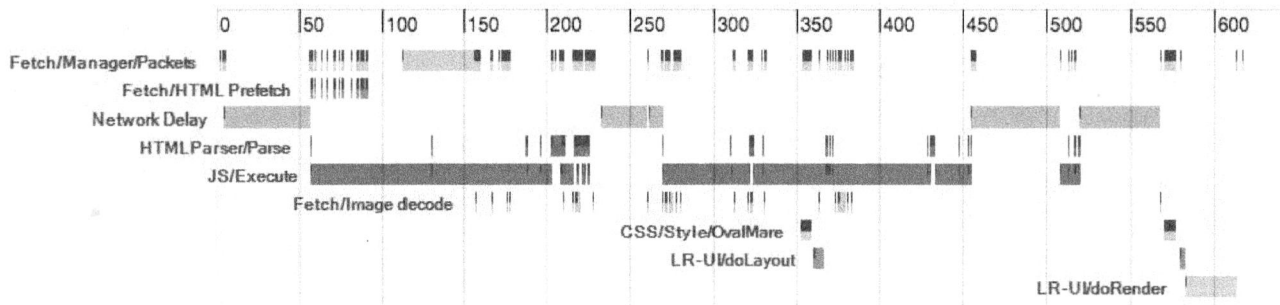

Figure 5. Gantt chart of loading the Yahoo! web page with ZOOMM from a mirror: concurrency among components are visible through overlapping bars; intra-component concurrency is not shown here.

Prefetching. There is a long history in web browsers of resource prefetching. A variety of schemes has been developed over the years, with and without server support, with and without prefetch directives, augmented with features like learning components, etc.. We refer to Duchamps and Fisher et al. for summaries [7, 9].

The HTML parser in Mozilla Firefox 4 and later supports *speculative parsing* [14]: instead of waiting for the execution of JavaScript to finish, the parser scans ahead for external resources (scripts, style sheets and images) and downloads them. The approach is different than in ZOOMM, in that Firefox also continues to construct the DOM tree. This work is necessarily speculative in nature, since the currently executing JavaScript can alter the parsing context (e.g., by emitting new content via `document.write()`). In that case, the speculative work has to be undone. In ZOOMM, we chose to make the HTML prescanner independent from the parser, thus simplifying the architecture of both. Furthermore, it allows the prefetcher to be moved into a separate thread, thereby hiding any overhead incurred as long as enough compute resources are available. However, our approach precludes speculative construction of the DOM tree. As future work, it would be interesting to compare the benefits of the Firefox approach in more detail to ZOOMM's approach, and investigate whether it can be incorporated into ZOOMM's architecture.

Compared to Firefox and earlier approaches, the novelty in our approach lies not in the prefetching itself, but in the additional funneling of information from the HTML prefetcher to the CSS parser, thereby allowing resources referenced in CSS documents to be requested ahead of time.

8. Experimental Results

In this section we present data to demonstrate the benefits of concurrency with respect to hiding the network latency, parallel CSS styling, and image decoding. We show two sets of data, one set to demonstrate effectiveness on a mobile platform (an HTC Jetstream device using a dual-core Snapdragon processor) and another set (on an Intel 6-core Xeon) that demonstrates the scalability of our design targeted at future mobile devices.

Performance. In order to test the overall performance of the ZOOMM browser, we used the publicly available Vellamo [20] benchmark suite. Vellamo tests the overall page load time, from the initial fetch to showing pixels on the display for a set of web sites: CNN, BBC, Yahoo!, Guardian, New York Times, Facebook, Engadget, and QQ (also shown in Table 1). Vellamo uses the user agent of a desktop browser to ensure that the HTML is not simplified for a mobile device. Pages are loaded and displayed twice: first time with a cold cache, and second using the browser cache. We measured Zoomm against the standard WebKit-based browser

included with Android on the HTC Jetstream device. The Vellamo test was performed using a local network proxy to ensure that the network conditions were consistent between both browsers. Overall, the ZOOMM browser completed the test run in 55 seconds, while WebKit completed it in 113 seconds. Figure 6 shows the time for loading each page in the two browsers. The load times are the average over 5 runs of the non-cached round. While there is a large variability between sites, ZOOMM is always faster, with an overall improvement of approximately 2×, demonstrating the effectiveness of the techniques uses in ZOOMM to improve browser performance.

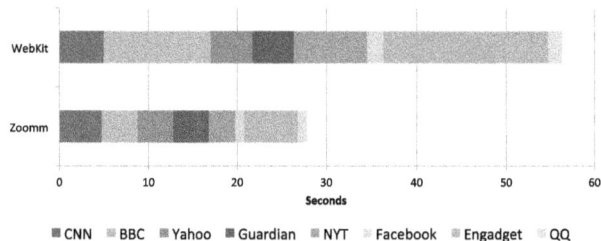

Figure 6. WebKit vs. Zoomm page load time on HTC Jetstream

Concurrency. Figure 5, illustrates the concurrency among the major components in ZOOMM while loading the Yahoo! web page from a mirror over a high-bandwidth/high-latency network connection representative of future 4G networks (Gigabit ethernet with artificial 50ms network latency). In addition, there also intra-component concurrency which is not shown; for example, image decoding and CSS styling internally run with multiple threads.

The "Network Delay" row indicates times when the DOM dispatcher loop sleeps because there are no events (network activity, user interaction, timers, etc.) to process due to waiting for external resources. The first network delay is between the request of the HTML document and the first packets arriving. Then the HTML parser processes the packets and kicks off execution of JavaScript code. The HTML parser waits with further processing until the JavaScript finishes. However, in parallel, further packets arrive and images are being decoded. We note that even for a single run, styling and rendering happens twice, the first time triggered by a call to the `getComputedStyle` function from JavaScript.

Compared to the 2010 WebKit numbers in Figure 2, JavaScript has become more prevalent. Also, ZOOMM's JavaScript engine is comparatively less mature than WebKit's and hence shows up more prominently in the chart.

Prefetching. Figure 7 shows the speed-up gains from early resource discovery on two different networks: the 4G Verizon net-

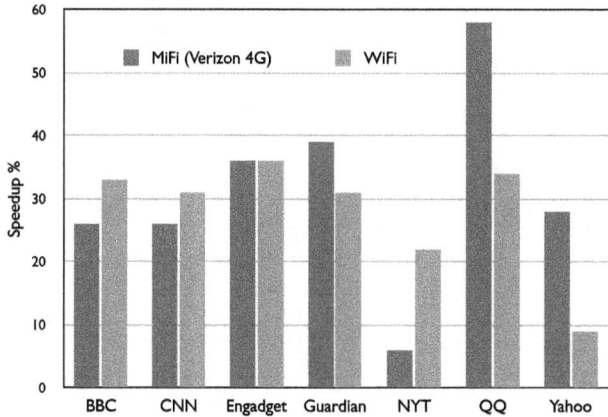

Figure 7. Prefetching speed-up on 4G and WiFi networks (higher numbers are better). The bars show the percentage reduction in page load time when prefetching is enabled in the ZOOMM browser vs. a baseline page load without prefetching enabled.

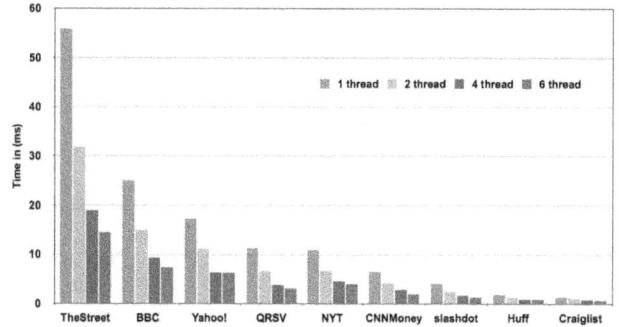

Figure 8. Large and complex web sites benefit from the scalability of the parallel DOM styling algorithm, here running on an Intel Xeon with 6 hyper-threaded cores. The first five web sites were retrieved using a desktop user agent, making the HTML more complex. The last five web sites were retrieved using a mobile user agent, where the server sends simpler HTML for display on a small mobile device. Desktop-based HTML experiences larger improvements in performance due to the size of the content.

Site	% Avoided Walks	% False Positives
CNN	88.94	0
BBC	88.02	0.021
Yahoo!	86.83	0.080
Guardian	94.19	0
NYT	98.74	0.035
Engadget	82.77	0
QQ	92.46	0.031
Average	90.28	0.024

Table 2. Accuracy of the matching bitmaps technique for the Vellamo benchmark with desktop user agent. Higher number of avoided walks is better, and lower number of false positives is better.

work through a MiFi device, and a WiFi wireless network. In both cases, devices were connected wirelessly to these access points. The pages are fetched from the real servers on the Internet. Experiments were run with a cleared cache. The speed-up is measured on total page load, with and without prefetching enabled. While there is significant variability in the results due to Internet latencies, we improve page load time in all cases, up to 58% (25% geometrical mean).

Table 1 shows the number of resources that are successfully requested by the prefetching stage, and the number of resources are missed due to use of JavaScript. Note that resources would also count as "missed" if the prefetching algorithms would fall behind the actual HTML and CSS parsers. However, we found this to be never the case in all our experiments. The prefetching components are fast enough to always finish much earlier than the parsers.

Despite the heuristic nature of some of the prefetching decisions, they are quite accurate: in our experiments, 80–95% of all externally referenced resources in a document are prefetched correctly, with only a small error rate. Due to bandwidth and power considerations, our heuristics are still conservative, i.e., they rather prefetch too little than too much: "Missed Prefetch" (not prefetched, but needed for rendering the web page) numbers are higher than "Mistaken Prefetch" (prefetched, but not needed for rendering).

CSS Performance. In Figure 8 we present scalability results for the parallel CSS algorithm. The algorithm scales well for complex sites, with large numbers of rules and many DOM nodes. Because the testing machine has 6 hyper-threaded cores, we observe limited scalability beyond 6 cores. Our measurements indicate that ZOOMM spends 97% of CSS styling time executing matching tasks, and only 3% executing node styling tasks.

Table 2 shows the accuracy of ZOOMM's matching bitmaps technique for a set of websites. On average, ZOOMM avoids 90% of the walks to the root of the DOM tree, with only 0.024% of false positives. False positives occur because matching bitmaps do not record the order in which labels and ids are encountered. For example, suppose ZOOMM wants to know whether the following rule applies to a `<p>` node: `h1>h2 p {color: red}`.

Assume that the matching bitmap indicates that both `<h1>` and `<h2>` are `<p>`'s ancestors. ZOOMM's matching algorithm must traverse up the tree to check whether there is a `<h1>` node that is a direct ancestor of a `<h2>`'s. If that is not the case, then it is

a false positive. Note that false positives do not cause the page to render incorrectly, they just waste CPU cycles.

Parallel Image Decoding. Figure 9 shows the scalability of offline image decoding when increasing the number of threads in the shared thread pool used for CSS prefetching and image decoding. In the figure we average the total time over 5 runs on a test page that consists of 36 images of 1.6 Megapixels each. These plots demonstrate that with enough work, we can take advantage of multiple cores for image decoding. However, other factors, like memory and network bandwidth, as well as server latency, and number of allowable connections per server, can lead to diminishing returns. In our experiment, we did not observe speed-ups beyond six cores, due to the hyper-threaded nature of our test CPU, and the browser computations unrelated to image decoding.

9. Conclusions

In this paper we presented ZOOMM, a parallel browser engine designed to exploit multicore concurrency. We demonstrated how concurrency helps hide up to 60% of the network latency when loading web pages. We also demonstrated that scalable concurrency exists and can be efficiently exploited for a number of browser algorithms — CSS styling and image decoding are only two such examples. When loading pages, we demonstrate that ZOOMM is twice as fast as a native WebKit browser on a dual-core Android platform. The technologies demonstrated in ZOOMM are being adapted for production browsers.

Web site	Correct Prefetch				Missed Prefetch		Mistaken Prefetch				Total Resources	
	HTML		CSS				HTML		CSS			
	Files	Bytes	Files	Bytes	Files	Bytes	Files	Bytes	Files	Bytes	Files	Bytes
cnn.com	34	979,695	52	409,377	2	372	0	0	5	3,371	93	1,392,815
bbc.co.uk/news	54	610,479	24	407,819	16	468,371	0	0	1	1,277	95	1,487,946
yahoo.com	44	672,595	13	264,603	2	2,016	1	0	0	0	60	939,214
guardian.co.uk	49	1,018,738	14	92,997	7	102,087	1	0	3	11,305	74	1,225,127
nytimes.com	73	1,046,636	9	73,487	13	228,162	1	10,837	1	89	97	1,359,211
engadget.com	128	2,023,135	84	651,030	5	104,320	0	0	9	34,824	226	2,813,309
qq.com	45	485,264	22	167,078	7	39,361	0	0	0	0	74	691,703

Table 1. Combined HTML & CSS Prefetching initiates download of most external resources ahead of their discovery by the HTML and CSS parsers with high accuracy ("Correct Prefetch") and small error ("Missed/Mistaken Prefetch"); web sites from *Vellamo* benchmark. "Total Resources" denotes the number of *referenced resources* in a web page.

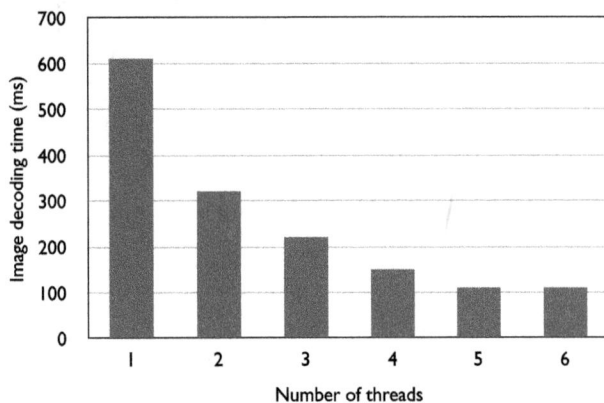

Figure 9. Image-heavy web site benefit from the scalability of the parallel image decoding algorithm, running on an Intel Xeon with 6 hyper-threaded cores.

Acknowledgments

We would like to thank Nayeem Islam and the Qualcomm Research Executive team for the opportunity to build the ZOOMM prototype. We thank Alex Shye, Greg Wright, Dario Gracia, Christoph Kerschbaumer, and Madhukar Kedlaya for their contributions. We also thank the reviewers for their thoughtful comments.

References

[1] D. Astely, E. Dahlman, A. Furuskar, Y. Jading, M. Lindstrom, and S. Parkvall. LTE: the evolution of mobile broadband. *IEEE Communications Magazine*, 47(4):44–51, Apr. 2009.

[2] C. Badea, M. R. Haghighat, A. Nicolau, and A. V. Veidenbaum. Towards parallelizing the layout engine of firefox. In *Proceedings of the Second USENIX Workshop on Hot topics in Parallelism, HotPar*, pages 1–6, 2010.

[3] B. H. Bloom. Space/time trade-offs in hash coding with allowable errors. *Communications of the ACM*, 13(7):422–426, 1970.

[4] The Google Chrome web browser. https://www.google.com/chrome.

[5] The chromium projects: Compositor thread architecture. http://dev.chromium.org/developers/design-documents/compositor-thread-architecture.

[6] Cascading style sheets level 2 revision 1 (css 2.1) specification. http://www.w3.org/TR/CSS2.

[7] D. Duchamp. Prefetching hyperlinks. In *USENIX Symposium on Internet Technologies and Systems*, pages 12–23, October 1999.

[8] The Mozilla Firefox web browser. https://www.mozilla.org/firefox.

[9] D. Fisher and G. Saksena. Web content caching and distribution. chapter Link prefetching in Mozilla: a server-driven approach, pages 283–291. Kluwer Academic Publishers, Norwell, MA, USA, 2004.

[10] C. Grier, S. Tang, and S. T. King. Designing and implementing the OP and OP2 web browsers. *ACM Transactions on the Web (TWEB)*, 5(2), May 2011.

[11] I. Hickson. HTML5 specification, March 2012. http://whatwg.org/html.

[12] H. Mai, S. Tang, S. T. King, C. Cascaval, and P. Montesinos. A case for parallelizing web pages. In *Proceedings of the 4th USENIX conference on Hot Topics in Parallelism*, HotPar'12, Berkeley, CA, USA, June 2012. USENIX Association.

[13] L. A. Meyerovich and R. Bodík. Fast and parallel webpage layout. In *Proc. of the Intl. Conf. on the World Wide Web*, pages 711–720, 2010.

[14] Mozilla Developer Network. Optimizing your pages for speculative parsing. https://developer.mozilla.org/en-US/docs/HTML/Optimizing_Your_Pages_for_Speculative_Parsing, 2012.

[15] Nokia. Qt - cross-platform application UI framework. http://qt.nokia.com/, 2012.

[16] J. Reinders. *Intel Threading Building Blocks: Multi-core parallelism for C++ programming*. O'Reilly, 2007.

[17] C. Reis and S. D. Gribble. Isolating web programs in modern browser architectures. In *Proceedings of the 4th ACM European conference on Computer systems*, EuroSys '09, pages 219–232, New York, NY, USA, March 2009. ACM.

[18] V. Roto. *WEB BROWSING ON MOBILE PHONES - CHARACTERISTICS OF USER EXPERIENCE*. PhD thesis, Helsinki University of Technology, 2006.

[19] The Safari web browser. http://www.apple.com/safari/.

[20] The Vellamo mobile web benchmark. http://www.quicinc.com/vellamo/.

[21] H. J. Wang, C. Grier, A. Moshchuk, S. T. King, P. Choudhury, and H. Venter. The multi-principal os construction of the gazelle web browser. In *Proceedings of the 18th conference on USENIX security symposium*, SSYM'09, pages 417–432, Berkeley, CA, USA, August 2009. USENIX Association.

[22] Z. Wang, X. Lin, L. Zhong, and M. Chishtie. Why are web browsers slow on smartphones? In *Proc. ACM Intl. Workshop on Mobile Computing Systems and Applications (HotMobile)*, March 2011.

[23] The WebKit open source project. http://www.webkit.org.

[24] WebKit2. http://trac.webkit.org/wiki/WebKit2.

Automatic Problem Size Sensitive Task Partitioning on Heterogeneous Parallel Systems

Ivan Grasso   Klaus Kofler   Biagio Cosenza   Thomas Fahringer

Institute of Informatics, University of Innsbruck, Austria

{grasso, klaus, cosenza, tf}@dps.uibk.ac.at

Abstract

In this paper we propose a novel approach which automatizes task partitioning in heterogeneous systems. Our framework is based on the Insieme Compiler and Runtime infrastructure [1]. The compiler translates a single-device OpenCL program into a multi-device OpenCL program. The runtime system then performs dynamic task partitioning based on an offline-generated prediction model. In order to derive the prediction model, we use a machine learning approach that incorporates static program features as well as dynamic, input sensitive features.

Our approach has been evaluated over a suite of 23 programs and achieves performance improvements compared to an execution of the benchmarks on a single CPU and a single GPU only.

Categories and Subject Descriptors D.3.2 [*Programming Languages*]: Language Classifications; D.3.4 [*Programming Languages*]: Processors; C.1.3 [*Processor Architectures*]: Other Architecture Styles

General Terms Languages, Algorithms, Performance

Keywords heterogeneous computing, compilers, GPU, task partitioning, code analysis, machine learning, runtime system

1. Introduction

The transition from homogeneous to heterogeneous architectures is challenging with respect to the efficient utilization of the hardware resources and the reuse of the software stack. This problem has drawn great interest from researchers and industry, leading to the proposal of several programming models including HMPP, OpenACC, CUDA and OpenCL [6]. OpenCL (Open Computing Language) is the first open standard for cross-platform parallel computing that supports a wide range of hardware through a low-level high performance abstraction layer.

As heterogeneous computing opens many new opportunities for developing parallel algorithms, our work is motivated by the additional challenges and complexity that it also introduces. One of the challenges is the distribution of tasks (i.e. task partitioning) among the available OpenCL devices in order to maximize the system performance. Task partitioning defines how the total workload is distributed among several computational resources. It is important to

understand that the best-performing task partitioning changes with different applications, different (input) problem sizes, and different hardware configurations.

Another important aspect of heterogeneous computing is the difficulty of writing *multi-device* programs (i.e. a single program which can be executed on multiple devices concurrently).

In this paper we present an automatic, problem size sensitive method for task partitioning of OpenCL programs on heterogeneous systems. Our work is based on machine learning which effectively combines compile time analysis with runtime feature evaluation to predict the optimal task partitioning for every combination of program, problem size and hardware configuration.

2. Framework Overview

The proposed approach, based on the Insieme Compiler and Runtime infrastructure [1], is composed by two main phases: *training* and *deployment*.

The goal of the training phase is to build a task partitioning prediction model. To build the model, a set of OpenCL programs are provided to the system and translated by the code analyzer into the *Insieme Parallel Intermediate Representation* (INSPIRE). From this representation, the features of the program (*static program features*) are extracted and stored in a database. The intermediate representation of the program is then passed to the backend which generates multi-device OpenCL code. Once generated, the new program will be executed with various problem sizes and the available task partitionings. The obtained performance measurements, together with the problem size dependent features of the program (i.e. *runtime features*), are collected and added to the database. After these steps have been accomplished for all programs, a machine learning task partitioning model is generated using the features and the performance measurements stored in the database.

In the deployment phase a new OpenCL program is provided to the analyzer, the static features are extracted and the intermediate representation is passed to the backend which generates a multi-device OpenCL program. When the program is executed, the static code features along with the runtime features are provided to the previously trained model, which predicts the best task partitioning for the current program with the selected problem size. Finally, the runtime system executes the program on the given hardware using the predicted task partitioning.

2.1 Predicting the Optimal Partitioning

Our overall approach requires building a model using machine learning in order to predict a task partitioning p from a vector of features that describes the essential characteristics of a program as well as the current problem size. The predicted task partitioning p should be as close as possible to the best task partitioning in terms

PPoPP'13, February 23–27, 2013, Shenzhen, China.
ACM 978-1-4503-1922-5/13/02.

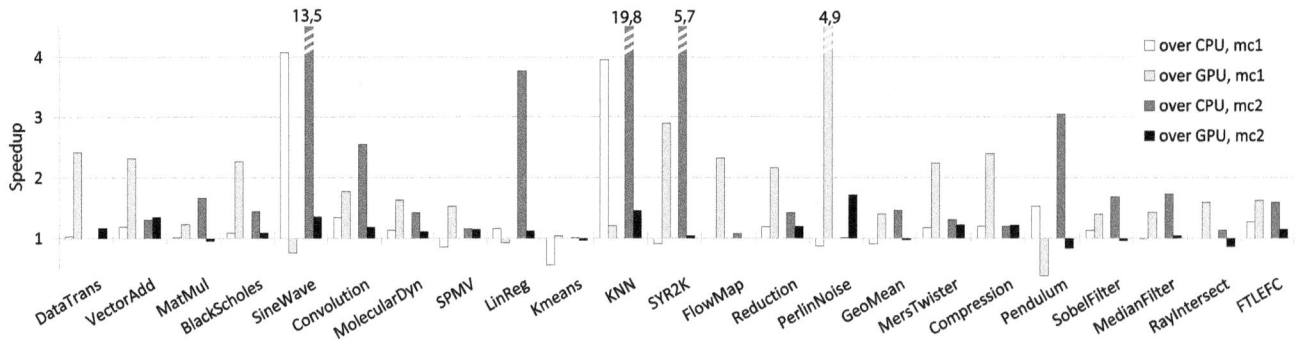

Figure 1. Speedup of our machine leaning guided task partitioning approach over execution on CPU/GPU only for different programs on two target architectures with different problem sizes.

of performance. p is selected from a discretized partitioning space with a stepsize of 10%.

3. Evaluation

To evaluate the performance of our approach we used a selection of 23 programs drawn from OpenCL vendors' example codes, applications from our department or partner universities, and benchmark suites [2–4]. After processing the OpenCL input program with the Insieme source-to-source compiler, the Gnu Compiler Collection (GCC) version 4.6.3 was used to convert the resulting code to binary.

In order to examine the impact of problem sizes on task partitioning we executed each benchmark with varying problem sizes on two heterogeneous target platforms composed of three OpenCL devices: two GPUs and two multi-core CPUs in a dual-socket infrastructure. While both GPUs represent a separate device, the two CPUs are reported as a single OpenCL device. The first platform, *mc1*, consists of two AMD Opteron CPUs and two Ati Radeon HD 5870 GPUs, while the second, *mc2*, holds two Intel Xeon CPUs and two NVIDIA GeForce GTX 480 GPUs.

Each training pattern consists of the static features of a program, its runtime features for a certain problem size as well as the best task partitioning for the given program with the current input size. To ensure a fair comparison between different task partitionings, we measured the execution time of the kernels including the memory transfer overhead [5].

In Figure 1 we compare the performance of the task partitionings predicted by the Insieme framework based on a machine learning approach, with the performance delivered by the CPU/GPU-only strategy for each code and each target architecture individually. Of these two default strategies, in almost all test cases, the CPU-only strategy delivers a higher performance on *mc1*, while on *mc2* the GPU-only strategy usually performs better. This is a result of the weaker performance of the GPU in *mc1*. The VLIW architecture with a very wide instruction width and high branch miss penalty would require specific fine-tuning of each code to perform well [7]. However, none of our test cases was tuned for a specific device.

On average considering both target architectures, our approach delivers a significantly better performance than the two default strategies for most test cases. Our models are capable of representing the target architecture's characteristics in order to find performance efficient task partitionings and determine which device is to be favored on a specific target architecture.

4. Conclusion

In this paper we proposed a novel approach which can automatically distribute OpenCL programs on heterogeneous CPU-GPU systems. It consists of a source-to-source compiler, which translates a single-device OpenCL program into a multi-device OpenCL program and a runtime system which distributes the workload over all heterogeneous resources using a machine learning based, offline generated prediction model.

Our measurements demonstrate that the optimal task partitioning does depend on the program, the target architecture, as well as the problem size. To accommodate this observation, we use two classes of features: static program features, whose values can be extracted from the source code at compile time, and problem size dependent runtime features, whose values are collected during program execution.

To demonstrate the portability and the performance of the system, all tests were performed on two different target architectures showing that our approach outperforms the two default strategies that use only the CPU or only the GPU, respectively.

Acknowledgment

This project was funded by the FWF Austrian Science Fund as part of project TRP 220-N23 "Automatic Portable Performance for Heterogeneous Multi-cores".

References

[1] Insieme compiler and runtime infrastructure. - Distributed and Parallel Systems Group, University of Innsbruck. http://insieme-compiler.org, 2012.

[2] S. Che, M. Boyer, J. Meng, D. Tarjan, J. W. Sheaffer, S.-H. Lee, and K. Skadron. Rodinia: A benchmark suite for heterogeneous computing. In *IISWC*, pages 44–54, 2009.

[3] A. Danalis, G. Marin, C. McCurdy, J. S. Meredith, P. C. Roth, K. Spafford, V. Tipparaju, and J. S. Vetter. The scalable heterogeneous computing (shoc) benchmark suite. In *GPGPU*, pages 63–74, 2010.

[4] S. Grauer-Gray, L. Xu, R. Searles, S. Ayalasomayajula, , and J. Cavazos. Auto-tuning a high-level language targeted to gpu codes. In *InPar*, 2012.

[5] C. Gregg and K. M. Hazelwood. Where is the data? why you cannot debate cpu vs. gpu performance without the answer. In *ISPASS*, pages 134–144, 2011.

[6] Khronos OpenCL Working Group. The OpenCL 1.2 specification. http://www.khronos.org/opencl, 2012.

[7] P. Thoman, K. Kofler, H. Studt, J. Thomson, and T. Fahringer. Automatic opencl device characterization: guiding optimized kernel design. In *Euro-Par*, pages 438–452, 2011.

Data Layout Optimization for GPGPU Architectures

Jun Liu, Wei Ding, Ohyoung Jang, Mahmut Kandemir

The Pennsylvania State University, University Park, PA 16802, USA

{jxl1036, wzd109, oyj5007, kandemir}@cse.psu.edu

Abstract

GPUs are being widely used in accelerating general-purpose applications, leading to the emergence of GPGPU architectures. New programming models, e.g., Compute Unified Device Architecture (CUDA), have been proposed to facilitate programming general-purpose computations in GPGPUs. However, writing high-performance CUDA codes manually is still tedious and difficult. In particular, the organization of the data in the memory space can greatly affect the performance due to the unique features of a custom GPGPU memory hierarchy. In this work, we propose an automatic data layout transformation framework to solve the key issues associated with a GPGPU memory hierarchy (i.e., *channel skewing*, *data coalescing*, and *bank conflicts*). Our approach employs a widely applicable strategy based on a novel concept called *data localization*. Specifically, we try to optimize the layout of the arrays accessed in affine loop nests, for *both* the device memory and shared memory, at *both* coarse grain and fine grain parallelization levels. We performed an experimental evaluation of our data layout optimization strategy using 15 benchmarks on an NVIDIA CUDA GPU device. The results show that the proposed data transformation approach brings around 4.3X speedup on average.

Categories and Subject Descriptors D.3.4 [*Processors*]: Code generation, Compilers, Optimization

General Terms Algorithms, Design, Performance, Experimentation

Keywords GPGPU, Data Layout Transformation, CUDA, Optimization

1. Introduction

The CUDA [1, 5] programming model can greatly improve the programmer productivity. However, fully utilizing the specific features of the underlying architecture can be very challenging. One of the most important reasons for this is that the customized memory hierarchy in GPGPUs needs to be explicitly managed at an application level by the CUDA programmer. We believe that automated compiler support can play a critical role in exploiting the memory hierarchy of emerging GPGPU systems. It is also to be noted that loop nests constitute a significant fraction of application execution time in high performance computing. The unique characteristics of the GPGPU architectures pose new challenges as well as opportunities

PPoPP'13, February 23–27, 2013, Shenzhen, China.
Copyright © 2013 ACM 978-1-4503-1922/13/02... $10.00

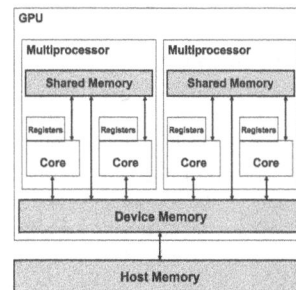

Figure 1. Memory hierarchy of a GPU architecture.

for traditional loop optimization techniques. As shown in Figure 1, the CUDA GPU memory hierarchy consists of a (global) device memory and shared memories on the streaming multiprocessors. Clearly, patterns exhibited by data accesses to different memory components can greatly affect the overall performance of the applications running on this architecture.

In this work, we target the codes already parallelized for CUDA GPGPUs, and focus on *data layout transformations* to improve application performance by taking into account the underlying memory hierarchy. Our approach employs a *general* data layout optimization strategy based on a novel concept called *data localization*. Specifically, we first consider the data access patterns exhibited by the parallel processing units (thread blocks/threads), followed by identifying localized arrays and partitioning them into data blocks that are mostly accessed by corresponding processing units. We then apply both an affine data transformation and a non-affine data transformation to change the layout of the localized arrays to solve three specific problems associated with the GPGPU memory hierarchy: *channel skewing*, *memory coalescing* and *shared memory bank conflicts*.

2. Problem Definition

As shown in Figure 1, the device memory of the GPU can be accessed by all thread blocks mapped to different streaming multiprocessors. Each multiprocessor has its own shared memory, which can only be accessed by the threads assigned to that multiprocessor. The device memory can be accessed through different memory channels at the same time to increase memory level parallelism. In addition, if the data accessed by different threads on the same multiprocessor are aligned and continuous in the device memory, they can be coalesced into a single memory operation to increase memory bandwidth. On the other hand, the most frequently reused data are likely to be copied into the shared memory to reduce access latency, and the banks of the shared memory provide parallel data accesses. However, there exist three issues as follows regarding this GPU memory hierarchy that need to be addressed in order to exploit its full potential.

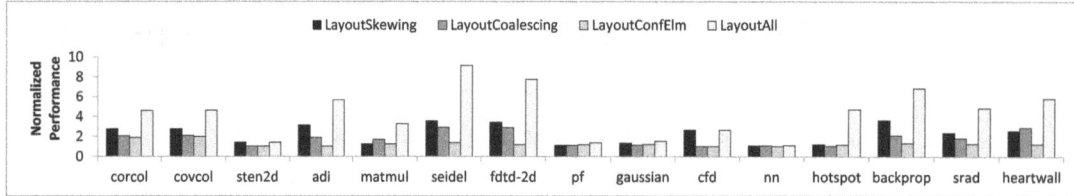

Figure 2. Performance of our data layout transformations normalized to the Original version.

- **Channel Skewing** If the accesses to the memory channels of the device memory are not well balanced, some of the channels may be congested, and as a result, bandwidth utilization can be affected.

- **Coalescing** Threads from the same warp may access the data elements stored non-contiguously in the device memory. In such cases, the memory coalescing instructions provided by the underlying architecture cannot be utilized.

- **Bank Conflicts** If at the same time, different data accessed by different threads to the shared memory are located in the same bank, conflicts occur and the accesses involved need to be serialized.

3. Data Layout Optimization

3.1 Parallelization

In this work, we mainly target at optimizing the CUDA kernels that are transformed from *affine loop nests*. We assume that the array references and loop bounds are affine functions of the enclosing loop indices and loop-independent variables. Our optimizations are thus based on polyhedral model and mainly focus on optimizing direct/regular data accesses, which are more common in most applications. We further assume that our target loop nests have already been parallelized for the CUDA. Specifically, how the computations are divided into thread blocks and how each thread block is partitioned into threads, are assumed to be known to our approach.

3.2 Layout Optimization

For a kernel extracted from an affine loop nest under the parallelization described above, to achieve high performance, we need to solve the three problems discussed above. Considering the unique features of the CUDA programming model and memory hierarchy, each layout optimization applied in our work mainly consists of two basic steps, *localization* and *data relocation*. The basic idea of the first step (data localization) is to divide the entire data space of an array into *data blocks*, such that the data elements in each data block are mostly accessed by only one processing unit (thread block/thread). In other words, data localization ensures that the data elements accessed by the same processing unit are not spread over the entire data space. The second step then performs the actual transformation that maps the data from its current layout to the desired layout. Overall, our layout optimization employs a two-level transformation, i.e., coarse level (thread block) and finer level (thread). Specifically, the data optimization at the coarse level is used to minimize channel skewing in the device memory. Our goal of this optimization is to obtain a data layout so that the data accesses made by different thread blocks will go to different memory channels of the device memory. In this way, the thread blocks mapped to different multiprocessors will have balanced accesses to the memory channels of the device memory, lessening the channel skewing problem. Our data optimization at the finer level tries to increase the opportunities for data coalescing in the device memory and reduce the number of bank conflicts in the shared memory. Intuitively, in the device memory, we apply affine transformation

to obtain a data access pattern such that the threads of a warp will access (at each time step) data elements that are stored in consecutive memory locations. In other words, our layout transformation targets at improving data locality among the threads of a warp, i.e., *inter-thread locality*. In the shared memory, we apply strip-mining and permutation to obtain the desired data layout where data accessed by a thread will be only stored in its own associated bank.

4. Experimental Evaluation

We implemented our proposed data layout optimization strategy in Pluto 0.6.2-CUDA [2, 3], a source-to-source transformation framework for affine loop nests based on the polyhedral model with CUDA support. The optimized kernel code is then compiled with the CUDA compiler (nvcc release 4.0, V0.2.1221) into binaries for execution on the GPU. We performed our experiments on an NVIDIA Tesla C2050 GPU device. The device is equipped with 2.8 GB of device (global) memory and 14 streaming multiprocessors clocked at 1.15 GHz.

We evaluated our strategy on 15 benchmarks from Pluto [2] and Rodinia [4]. Each benchmark is compiled into five versions, namely, *Original*, *LayoutSkewing*, *LayoutCoalescing*, *LayoutConfElm*, and *LayoutAll*. Specifically, the *Original* version is the original parallel CUDA kernel code without our data layout optimization; the *LayoutSkewing* version is obtained by applying our data optimization (to the Original version) for reducing channel skewing in the device memory; the *LayoutCoalescing* version is generated by applying our data optimization (to the Original version) for increasing coalescing instructions; the *LayoutConfElm* version is formed by applying our data optimization (to the Original version) for reducing bank conflicts in the shared memory; and the *LayoutAll* version is obtained by applying all of our three optimizations to the Original version. Figure 2 gives performance numbers for different versions, *normalized* with respect to the Original version. The average normalized performance values (when all 15 applications are accounted for) of LayoutSkewing, LayoutCoalescing, LayoutConfElm and LayoutAll versions are 2.3, 1.8, 1.3 and 4.3, respectively.

Acknowledgments

This research is supported in part by NSF grants #1213052, #1152479, #1147388, #1139023, #1017882, #0963839, #0811687 and a grant from Microsoft Corporation.

References

[1] CUDA. http://www.nvidia.com/object/cuda_home_new.html.

[2] PLUTO. http://pluto-compiler.sourceforge.net/.

[3] U. Bondhugula et al. A practical automatic polyhedral parallelizer and locality optimizer. *Proc. of PLDI*, 2008.

[4] S. Che et al. Rodinia: A benchmark suite for heterogeneous computing. *IISWC*, 2009.

[5] M. Garland et al. Parallel computing experiences with CUDA. *MICRO*, 2008.

Decomposition Techniques for Optimal Design-Space Exploration of Streaming Applications

Shobana Padmanabhan, Yixin Chen, and Roger D. Chamberlain

Dept. of Computer Science and Engineering, Washington University in St. Louis

{spadmanabhan, ychen25, roger}@wustl.edu

Abstract

Streaming data programs are an important class of applications, for which queueing network models are frequently available. While the design space can be large, decomposition techniques can be effective at design space reduction. We introduce two decomposition techniques called convex decomposition and unchaining and present implications for a biosequence search application.

Categories and Subject Descriptors   B.8.2 [*Performance and Reliability*]: Performance Analysis and Design Aids

General Terms   Design, Performance, Theory

Keywords   Optimization, Domain-specific branch and bound

1. Introduction

High performance streaming data applications are frequently deployed on architecturally diverse or hybrid systems (employing chip multiprocessors, graphics engines, and reconfigurable logic). Searching the design space of possible configurations, commonly referred to as design-space exploration, is challenging because: a) the number of configurations is exponential in the number of design parameters; b) the design parameters may interact nonlinearly; and c) the goals of the exploration are often multiple and conflicting.

We approach the design-space exploration of streaming applications as an optimization problem that searches for a globally optimal configuration. Cost functions are derived from queueing network (QN) models of the application, in particular, BCMP networks. Consider Figure 1. A four-stage pipelined application is modeled with a QN consisting of four *service centers*. A service center comprises a queue and one or more servers. The application stages represent functions in the biosequence search application BLAST [1]. It is conventional to denote the mean arrival rate at service center j as $\lambda_j \in \mathbb{R}$ and the mean service rate as $\mu_j \in \mathbb{R}$.

The optimization problem formulations tend to be mixed-integer, nonlinear and NP-hard. We have developed domain-specific branch and bound techniques that exploit topological information about the application's pipelining embodied in the QNs [3, 4]. More precisely, we identify Jordan block form and solve the blocks independently. We define a block as the group of variables associated with a single service center. We call these vari-

Supported by NSF under grants CNS-0905368 and CNS-0931693.

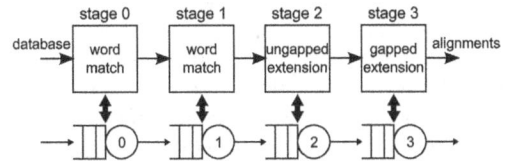

Figure 1. BLAST application and its queueing network model.

ables *single* variables and the ones associated with more than one block as *complicating* variables.

After such decomposition, however, the search space size can still be considerable. To reduce the search space further, here we present two decomposition techniques that we call *convex decomposition* (extended from [4]) and *unchaining* (novel here). We analyze the impact of these decomposition techniques by quantifying the reduction in the number of configurations (leaf nodes) to be evaluated during branch and bound search.

2. Convex Decomposition

We define a *convex variable* as a design parameter for which the optimization problem's objective function is convex when all other parameters are held constant (even when the problem itself is non-convex). In convex decomposition, we decompose the optimization problem to exclude the convex variable and solve for the remaining variables as a new problem (with a new objective function). The solution is substituted back in the original problem which is then solved for the convex variable. We guarantee that the resulting configuration is globally optimum.

Previously [4], we identified sufficient conditions for a convex variable to result in convex decomposition when each normalized performance measure remains the same or improves ("not worsen") with increasing any μ_j in Equation (2) below. Below, we present sufficient conditions for a convex variable to lead to convex decomposition when some normalized measures do not worsen and others remain the same or worsen ("not improve"), as expressed in (1). An increase in the value of a measure is not always the desired goal. An example is power usage. We denote the measures that we wish to decrease by $\vec{\rho}$ and the ones that we wish to increase by $\vec{\tau}$.

Notation. When an optimization problem satisfies the sufficient conditions for a convex variable (an example of which is λ_{in} denoting the application's data ingest rate) to lead to convex decomposition, it takes the form shown below. We denote such a problem as P. n_m denotes the number of measures in the objective function. Let there be n variables in $\vec{v}$ (corresponding to the design parameters); these variables may be integer or real-valued. Let us denote variables other than λ_{in} in $\vec{v}$ by $\vec{v'}$. $\vec{\lambda}$ denotes the vector of the mean job arrival rates at the different stages of the queueing network and $\vec{\mu}$, that of the mean service rates. Functions $\vec{g}$ and $\vec{h}$ are any user-specified constraints; $\vec{\rho}, \vec{\tau}, \vec{u}, \vec{l}, \vec{g}$, and $\vec{h}$ may not be convex, differentiable, or continuous but are assumed to have closed-form. The problem formulation of P is:

$$\min_{\vec{v}} \quad \sum_{k=1}^{x} W_k \cdot \rho_k\left(\vec{v'}\right) - \sum_{k=x+1}^{n_m} W_k \cdot \tau_k\left(\lambda_{in}\right) \quad (1)$$

$$\text{subject to} \quad \vec{\mu} = \vec{u}\left(\vec{v'}\right) \quad (2)$$

$$\lambda_j = l_j\left(\vec{v'}\right) \cdot \lambda_{in}, \; j = 1, 2, \ldots, n \quad (3)$$

$$\vec{\lambda} < \vec{\mu}; \; \vec{g}\left(\vec{v'}\right) \leq 0; \; \vec{h}\left(\vec{v'}\right) = 0$$

The sufficient conditions for a convex variable to result in convex decomposition are: a) each ρ_k in (1) is independent of λ_{in} and $\vec{\lambda}$ while each τ_k depends only on λ_{in}; b) each ρ_k does not improve with increasing any μ_j while each τ_k does not worsen; c) variables in $\vec{\mu}$ are independent of λ_{in} and $\vec{\lambda}$ as shown in (2) whereas variables in $\vec{\lambda}$ depend on $\vec{v'}$ and λ_{in} as shown in (3); and d) variables in λ_{in} and $\vec{\lambda}$ are not involved in the bound of any other design variable, while these variables can be bounded themselves.

Reduction in the number of configurations: If each variable in $\vec{v}$ has d values, the number of leaves in a branch and bound tree is d^n. However, with a convex variable, the number reduces to d^{n-1}.

3. Unchaining

When there is chaining of service centers in a queueing network, the corresponding Jordan blocks (JBs) get chained as well. We define a *chaining variable* as a derived variable (one that depends on one or more of the design parameters) that connects two adjacent JBs that are otherwise independent. A set of $k-1$ chaining variables would then chain k adjacent JBs. Our unchaining solves the blocks independent of each other, while preserving feasibility. We require only a feasible solution here because we expect to have branched on all the parameters not associated with the chained blocks and we expect this to determine the value of the objective function.

To apply unchaining, we identify the following sufficient conditions: a) the only variables remaining in the optimization problem are the single variables associated with each of the chained blocks; and b) the value of the objective function is known.

Notation. Let k adjacent Jordan blocks be *chained*. We index these JBs as $JB_i, i = 1, 2, \cdots, k$. Let P_F be the feasibility (a.k.a. satisfiability) problem in the general form shown below. Design variables are denoted as $\vec{v} = (\vec{y}_1, \vec{y}_2, \ldots, \vec{y}_k)$. Each $\vec{y}_i = (y_{1i}, y_{2i}, \ldots, y_{in_i})$; n_i denotes the number of elements in each $\vec{y}_i$ and the variables may be real or integer valued. $\vec{\mu} = (\mu_1, \mu_2, \ldots, \mu_k)$ are derived variables and are real-valued. $\vec{\mu}$, with the exception of μ_1, are the variables that chain the blocks as shown in P_F below. An example of this is illustrated using three blocks in Figure 2 where μ_3 chains JB_3 and JB_2 while μ_2 chains JB_2 and JB_1. Functions $\vec{g}$ and $\vec{h}$ are any user-specified constraints; $\vec{u}, \vec{g}$, and $\vec{h}$ may not be convex, differentiable, or continuous but are assumed to have closed-form. The form of P_F is:

Find a feasible solution for $\vec{v}$

$$\text{subject to} \quad \mu_i = u_i(\vec{y}_i, \mu_{i+1}), \; i = 1, 2, \ldots, k-1$$

$$\mu_k = u_k(\vec{y}_k)$$

$$\mu_i > L_i, \; i = 1, 2, \ldots, k; L_i \text{ are given constants}$$

$$\vec{g}_i(\vec{y}_i) \leq 0; \; \vec{h}_i(\vec{y}_i) = 0, \quad i = 1, 2, \ldots, k$$

We refer to the block where a chaining variable gets defined as its *right-block* and the block where it gets used as its *left-block*. E.g., in Figure 2, the right-block of μ_3 is JB_3 and its left-block is JB_2.

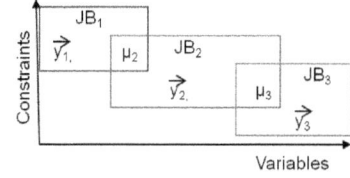

Figure 2. Chaining of blocks.

We unchain the blocks as follows. We begin by finding the upper and lower bounds of every chaining variable in its right-block and using the bounds to constrain the selection of a range of feasible values of the chaining variable in its left-block. Bounds are determined by formulating a pair of maximization and minimization problems for each of $\mu_k, \mu_{k-1}, \ldots, \mu_2$. Then, we assign feasible values for the single variables of JB_1. We then proceed with assigning values to variables associated with each of $JB_2, JB_3, \ldots, JB_k$, using the solution of the chained variable selected in its left-block to assign feasible values for the variables of its right-block. We guarantee that these solutions together constitute a feasible assignment to all variables $\vec{v}$ in P_F.

Reduction in the number of configurations: When there are chaining variables, the number of subproblems to solve is linear in the number of chained blocks (denoted by k) (i.e., $3k - 1$). Without unchaining, the number of configurations is the product of the number of values of each variable in $\vec{v}$.

4. Empirical Results

For the BLAST models in [2, 3], the number of configurations from the single variables of Jordan blocks 0, 1, 2, and 3, and the complicating variables are $15^5 \times 100 \times 100 \times 4 \times 72 \times 10^6 \approx 2 \times 10^{18}$. Our earlier techniques [3] reduce the number to $15 \times 5 \times (100 + 100 + 4) \times 72 \times 10^6 \approx 10^{12}$. The reduction in JB_0 comes from the assumption that the substages have infinite buffers making the servers independent [2].

In this work, convex decomposition of λ_{in} (in the BLAST model of [2]) reduces 72×10^6 configurations to 72×10^4. The total search space size is reduced to about 10^{10} configurations.

Accounting for dependency arising from finite buffering among the service centers within stage 0 [3], the number of configurations reverts to the original product of configurations at each service center rather than their sum. Even using the techniques described in [3], the search space is only reduced to approximately 10^{16} configurations. Unchaining, however, allows the 15^5 configurations within JB_0 to be reduced to $15 \times 5 \times 2$. The multiple of 2 is because at each step one must solve for both a minimum and a maximum value of the chaining variable. This results in a search space size of approximately 2×10^{12}, and we have almost returned to the search space size of the model in [2].

References

[1] S. F. Altschul and W. Gish. Local alignment statistics. *Methods: a Companion to Methods in Enzymology*, 266:460–80, 1996.

[2] R. Dor et al. Using queuing theory to model streaming applications. In *Symp. on Application Accelerators in High Perf. Computing*, 2010.

[3] S. Padmanabhan, Y. Chen, and R. D. Chamberlain. Optimal design-space exploration of streaming applications. In *Int'l Conf. on Application-specific Systems, Architectures and Processors*, Sept. 2011.

[4] S. Padmanabhan, Y. Chen, and R. D. Chamberlain. Convexity in Non-convex Optimizations of Streaming Applications. In *IEEE Int'l Conf. on Parallel and Distributed Systems*, Dec. 2012.

Exploring Different Automata Representations for Efficient Regular Expression Matching on GPUs

Xiaodong Yu

Dept. of Electrical and Computer Engineering
University of Missouri
Columbia, MO
Email: xymt3@mail.missouri.edu

Michela Becchi

Dept. of Electrical and Computer Engineering
University of Missouri
Columbia, MO
Email: becchim@missouri.edu

Abstract

Regular expression matching is a central task in several networking (and search) applications and has been accelerated on a variety of parallel architectures. All solutions are based on finite automata (either in deterministic or non-deterministic form), and mostly focus on effective memory representations for such automata. Recently, a handful of work has proposed efficient regular expression matching designs for GPUs; however, most of them aim at achieving good performance on small datasets. Nowadays, practical solutions must support the increased size and complexity of real world datasets. In this work, we explore the deployment and optimization of different GPU designs of regular expression matching engines, focusing on large datasets containing a large number of complex patterns.

Categories and Subject Descriptors C.2.0 [**Computer Communication Networks**]: General – Security and protection (e.g., firewalls).

General Terms Algorithms, Design, Experimentation, Performance, Security.

Keywords CUDA; GPGPU; deep packet inspection; finite automata; regular expression matching.

1. Introduction

Regular expression matching is an important task in several application domains (bibliographical search, networking, and bioinformatics) and has received particular consideration in the context of deep packet inspection, a fundamental network security operation. Regular expression matching is traditionally performed using deterministic and non deterministic finite automata — DFAs and NFAs, respectively. DFAs can achieve optimal matching speed at the cost of high memory space requirements; NFAs are space-efficient but exhibit high memory bandwidth requirements, potentially leading to inferior processing speeds. As a result, to meet the requirements of networking applications, the exploration space of a regular expression matching engine is characterized by a trade-off between the size of the automaton and the worst-case bound on the amount of per character processing.

2. Related Work

Previous work has focused on accelerating regular expression matching on a variety of parallel architectures: general purpose multi-core processors, network processors, FPGAs, ASIC- and TCAM-based systems. In all these proposals, particular attention has been paid to providing efficient logic- and memory-based representations of the underlying automata (namely, DFAs, NFAs and equivalent abstractions). Because of their massive parallelism and computational power, in recent years GPUs have been considered a viable platform for this application. However, existing work has mostly evaluated specific solutions on small datasets consisting of a few tens of patterns, which are far behind today's applications with typically thousands of rules.

Recently Cascarano *et al* [1] proposed iNFAnt, a NFA-based regex matching engine for GPUs. Since NFAs do not suffer from state explosion (which occurs when converting NFAs into DFAs), iNFAnt is the first solution that can be easily applied to rule-sets of arbitrary size and complexity. In fact, this work is, to our knowledge, the only GPU-oriented proposal which presents an evaluation on large, real-world datasets (from 120 to 543 regular expressions). In the iNFAnt proposal, the transition table is encoded using a *symbol-first* representation: transitions are represented through a list of (*source*, *destination*) pairs sorted by their triggering symbol. Different threads process different transitions, whereas different thread-blocks are assigned different packets. Global memory accesses are coalesced, and shared memory accesses are conflict-free. The main disadvantage of iNFAnt is its unpredictable performance and its poor worst-case behaviour.

3. Our Contributions

Our contributions can be summarized as follows:
1. We analyse and overcome the limitations of iNFAnt [1], a recently proposed NFA-based design for GPU;
2. We map DFA solutions using state-of-the-art memory compression schemes to GPUs;
3. We evaluate both automata representations on datasets of practical size and complexity.

4. Designs and Implementations

4.1 NFA-Based Solution

The iNFAnt [1] design presents inefficiencies in the way the input characters are processed. We introduce two optimizations aimed at reducing the amount of computation needed to fully process the input stream. In particular, our optimizations concern the way the state transitions are organized and laid out in memory, and are based on the following observations: (i) in most traversal steps, only a minority of the NFA states are active; and (ii) NFA states

Table 1. Throughput (in Mbps) obtained with different implementations on a variety of datasets and traffic traces.

	C-DFA	NFA	O-NFA	C-DFA	NFA	O-NFA	C-DFA	NFA	O-NFA	C-DFA	NFA	O-NFA
	$P_M=0.35$			$P_M=0.55$			$P_M=0.75$			$P_M=0.95$		
Spyware	11.5	40.1	46.4	11.6	37.5	43.5	9.3	35.3	35.9	8.2	33.2	29.0
E-M	182.9	14.3	27.3	173.3	11.4	26.3	162.2	10.0	24.9	148.4	9.9	19.2
Range1	180.3	18.6	25.7	170.5	15.4	24.7	158.9	13.3	23.3	145.3	10.2	17.2
nnl.05	23.9	18.3	25.0	22.4	16.3	23.9	20.3	14.6	22.8	19.4	12.9	17.9
Dotstar.05	13.7	20.0	25.8	13.6	17.1	24.5	13.4	13.2	17.6	12.5	13.1	15.7

can be easily clustered into groups of states that cannot be active at the same time. By using convenient grouping and sorting schemes, we are able to sharply reduce the processing performed on each input character, which is especially beneficial on large and complex datasets leading to many NFA transitions. In Figure 1 we show the memory layout and the operation of our optimization schemes for NFAs.

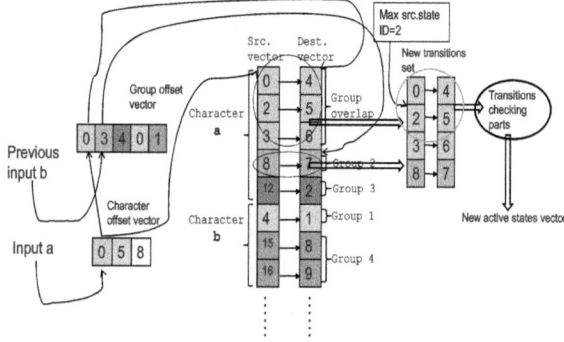

Figure 1. Exemplification of our optimization schemes for NFAs.

4.2 DFA-Based Solution

To limit the potentially prohibitive memory requirements of DFAs, we adopt the default transition compressed DFA representation [2] and group regular expressions into multiple DFAs [3, 4]. Our design aims at fully utilizing the parallelism offered by GPUs. In particular, by mapping multiple input streams to different streaming multiprocessors (SMs) and by splitting the DFA traversal among cores on the same SM, we exploit both the coarse- and the fine-grained parallelism offered by the GPU hardware.

```
kernel compressed-DFA
1:    current_sv[tid.y] ← initial_sv[tid.y]
2:    idx[tid.y] ← 0
3:    while (idx[tid.y] ≠ PACKET_SIZE) do
4:        future_sv[tid.y] ← INVALID
5:        c ← input[idx[tid.y]]
6:        tx_offset ← offset[current_sv[tid.y]]
7:        while current state has unprocessed transitions
8:            symbol ← char_array[tid.y][tx_offset][it_offset+tid.x]
9:            dst ← dest_array[tid.y][tx_offset][it_offset+tid.x]
10:           if (symbol = c)
11:               future_sv[tid.y] ← dst
12:               idx[tid.y]++
13:        if (future_sv[tid.y] = INVALID)
14:            future_sv [tid.y] ← default_tx[tid.y][current_sv[tid.y]]
15:        current_sv[tid.y] ← future_sv[tid.y]
16:        initial_sv[tid.y] ← current_sv[tid.y]
end;
```

The pseudo-code above represents a kernel implementing multiple-DFA traversal in the presence of default transition compression. In a default transition-compressed DFA, each state has a default transition and a variable number of labeled transitions. Default transitions can be therefore stored in a one-dimensional array (*default_tx*) with as many entries as DFA states. Labeled transitions can be represented through a list of (*input character*, *destination state*) pairs, and an ancillary data structure (*offset array*) indicating, for each state, the offset in the transition list. In our implementation, the transition list is represented through two equally sized vectors, *char_array* and *dest_array*, containing, for every transition, the input character and the destination state, respectively. These data structures are stored in global memory. The data structures stored in shared memory are: (i) the active state vector *current_sv*, (ii) the future state vector *future_sv*, and (iii) the vector *idx* containing a pointer to the next character to be processed. Each of these three arrays contains one entry per DFA, which must be shared along the x-dimension by all threads processing the same DFA. For efficiency, variables *c*, *tx_offset*, *symbol* and *dst* reside in (per-thread) registers.

5. Evaluation

We evaluated our implementations (O-NFA and C-DFA) and compared them with iNFAnt (NFA) using synthetic pattern-sets [4] consisting of 1,000 rules with various complexity and synthetic input streams characterized by different matching probabilities (p_M) [4]. Table 1 shows the throughput (in Mbps) of all implementations. As can be seen, the compressed DFA achieves very good performance on moderately complex datasets; in addition, the optimizations for the NFA-based solution lead to good improvements over the original iNFAnt implementation.

6. Conclusion

In this work, we have explored advantages and limitations of NFAs and DFAs for GPU-based regular expression matching.

Acknowledgments

This work has been supported by National Science Foundation grant CNS-1216756, and by equipment donation from Nvidia Corporation.

References

[1] N. Cascarano *et al.* iNFAnt: NFA Pattern Matching on GPGPU Devices. In ACM SIGCOMM Computer Communication Review, vol. 40 Num. 5, pp. 21-26, 2010.

[2] M. Becchi *et al.* An Improved Algorithm to Accelerate Regular Expression Evaluation. In Proc. of ANCS 2007, pp. 145-154, 2007.

[3] F. Yu *et al.* Fast and Memory-Efficient Regular Expression Matching for Deep Packet Inspection. In Proc. of ANCS 2006, pp. 93-102, 2006.

[4] M. Becchi *et al.* A Workload for Evaluating Deep Packet Inspection Architectures. In Proc. of IISWC 2008, pp. 79-89, 2008.

Expressing Graph Algorithms Using Generalized Active Messages

Nick Edmonds

Indiana University
Bloomington, IN 47405
ngedmond@cs.indiana.edu

Jeremiah Willcock

Indiana University
Bloomington, IN 47405
jewillco@cs.indiana.edu

Andrew Lumsdaine

Indiana University
Bloomington, IN 47405
lums@cs.indiana.edu

Abstract

Recently, graph computation has emerged as an important class of high-performance computing application whose characteristics differ markedly from those of traditional, compute-bound, kernels. Libraries such as BLAS, LAPACK, and others have been successful in codifying best practices in numerical computing. The data-driven nature of graph applications necessitates a more complex application stack incorporating runtime optimization. In this paper, we present a method of phrasing graph algorithms as collections of asynchronous, concurrently executing, concise code fragments which may be invoked both locally and in remote address spaces. A runtime layer performs a number of dynamic optimizations, including message coalescing, message combining, and software routing. Practical implementations and performance results are provided for a number of representative algorithms.

Categories and Subject Descriptors D.1.3 [*Programming Techniques*]: Concurrent Programming—Parallel Programming

Keywords Parallel Graph Algorithms; Active Messages; Parallel Programming Models

1. Introduction

Graph problems have a number of inherent characteristics that distinguish them from traditional scientific applications [1]. Graph computations are often completely *data-driven*: they are dictated by the vertex and edge structure of the graph rather than being expressed directly in code. Execution paths and data locations are therefore highly unpredictable. Moreover, the connectivity of many graphs is not determined by 3D space (as is the case for discretized PDEs), resulting in data dependencies and computations with *poor locality*. Partitioning in such situations is computationally impractical since no good separators may exist [2, 3] and scalability can be significantly limited by the resulting unbalanced computational loads. Finally, graph algorithms are often based on exploring the structure of a graph rather than performing large numbers of computations on the graph data, which results in *fine-grained data accesses* and a *high ratio of data accesses to computation*. Memory and communication latency can dominate such computations.

The standard parallelization approach for scientific applications follows the SPMD model which partitions the problem data among a number of processes and then uses a bulk-synchronous-parallel [4] pattern to effect the overall computation. Although this approach has been tremendously successful for scientific applications based on discretized PDEs, it is not well-suited for graph-based, data-intensive applications [1]. To address these issues, we have developed an approach for portably expressing high-performance graph algorithms based on fine-grained generalized active messages, as provided by the Active Pebbles programming model [5].

Formulating graph algorithms using active messages has the dual advantages of being both conceptually simple while not over-constraining implementations. Active messages allow the user to modify algorithm code in an understandable fashion (individual vertex and edge op-

erations) rather than requiring the use of complicated, vendor-tuned primitives which operate at a coarser level.

With this approach, we are able to capture the fine-grained dependency structure of graph computations at runtime, exposing maximal parallelism. Separating the expression of an algorithm (the code in the active messages) from the implementation (the messages themselves) enables performance portability across a variety of platforms without modifying the algorithm specification. This allows the runtime system to adapt algorithms to the hardware using coalescing and other transformations. Deferring these decisions until runtime is especially appropriate for graph algorithms as the structure of the graph determines the computational structure of the algorithm and thus both are discovered dynamically.

Finally, the active message phrasing permits both shared- and distributed-memory parallelism, and is amenable to acceleration. A single algorithm specification may be executed using an active message library in a distributed memory environment, a threading library (possibly combined with work-stealing) in a shared memory environment, and a hardware-specific programming environment targeting various kinds of accelerators. Most importantly, arbitrary combinations of these hardware environments are supported.

2. Programming Model

Message passing, an effective programming model for regular HPC applications, provides a clear separation of address spaces and makes all communication explicit. The Message Passing Interface (MPI) is the de facto standard for programming such systems. However, graph applications need shared access to data structures which naturally cross address spaces. A number of choices exist for how to implement fine-grained, irregular remote memory access. The key requirement with regard to graph applications is that the remote memory updates performed by one process must be atomic with regard to those performed by other processes and must support "read-modify-write" operations (e.g., compare-and-swap, fetch-and-add, etc.). More importantly, only the process performing the updates has knowledge of which regions of memory are being updated and thus the process whose memory is the target of these updates cannot perform any sequencing or arbitration of the updates. Finally, some algorithms require dependent updates to multiple, non-contiguous locations in memory, which provides perhaps the greatest challenge to a programming model.

MPI-2 One-Sided operations and Partitioned Global Address Space (PGAS) models attempt to fill the gap left by two-sided MPI message passing by allowing transparent access to remote memory in an emulated global address space. However, mechanisms for concurrency control are limited to locks and critical sections; some models support weak predefined atomic operations (e.g., *MPI_Accumulate()*). Stronger atomic operations (e.g., compare and swap, fetch and add) and user-defined atomic operations are either not supported in current versions or do not perform well. Thus, we claim that these approaches do not provide the appropriate primitives for fine-grained graph applications. The designers of those approaches have also realized these limitations in the original models, leading to proposals such as UPC queues [6] and Global Futures [7] to add more sophisticated primitive operations (including active messages in some cases) to otherwise PGAS programming models. The Chapel and X10 languages in particular have direct support for active messages.

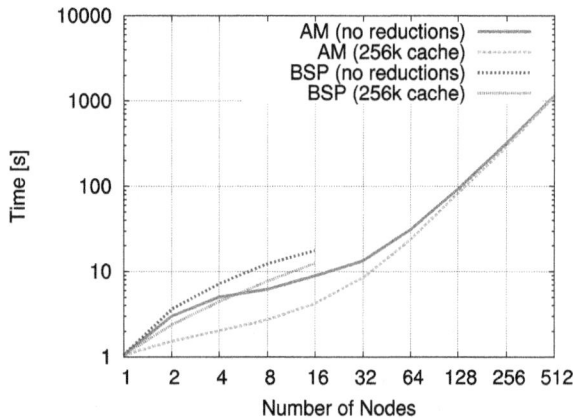

Figure 1. Δ-stepping shortest paths (Graph 500, 2^{16} vertices per node, average degree 16, 2^{18}-element reduction caches).

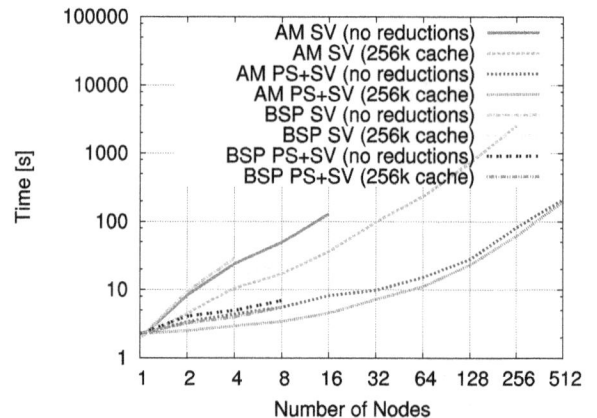

Figure 2. Shiloach-Vishkin connected components (Erdős-Rényi, 2^{18} vertices per node, average degree 2, 2^{18}-element reduction caches).[1]

3. Evaluation

We have applied the active message abstraction to the design a library of graph algorithms utilizing the Active Pebbles (AP) programming and execution model. We used Challenger, a 13.6 TF/s, 1 rack Blue Gene/P with 1024 compute nodes. Each node has 4 PowerPC 450 CPUs and 2 GiB of RAM. Our experiments used Version 1.0 Release 4.2 of the Blue Gene/P driver, IBM MPI, and g++ 4.3.2 as the compiler (including as the back-end compiler for MPI).

For our evaluation, we chose algorithms from each of four representative algorithm classes—wavefront expansion (label-setting and label-correcting), coarsening and refinement, and iterative methods—however in the interest of brevity we present only a subset of the results here. We compare algorithms written in an active message (AM) style to the same algorithms written in a BSP [4] style. Both implementations use AP for the sake of comparison including routing and, where specified, message reductions provided in AP. Our results demonstrate reasonable weak-scaling performance, and more importantly, the ability to complete computations where the BSP form of the algorithm fails due to memory exhaustion (which is indicated by a missing data point). This is due to the fact that in the AM algorithms messages can be executed and retired whereas, in the BSP cases data communicated must be retained until the end of a computation phase *even if it is received earlier*.

Figure 1 shows the weak scaling performance of the Δ-stepping single-source shortest paths algorithm [8], an example of a label-correcting wavefront. Here, the BSP algorithms fail to complete due to memory exhaustion for more than 16 nodes. In addition, the AM formulations out-perform their BSP counterparts in the region where both algorithms run to completion.

The Shiloach-Vishkin connected components algorithm is an example of a coarsening and refinement algorithm. It consists of contraction of components to rooted "stars" via iterative hooking and pointer-doubling steps. We also implement an optimized algorithm which does a parallel exploration from the highest degree vertex (which is likely to be in the giant component), and then applies the Shiloach-Vishkin connected components algorithm to the undiscovered portion of the graph to label the remaining components. We call this variant "Parallel Search + Shiloach-Vishkin" (PS+SV). Figure 2 shows the weak scaling performance of the AM and BSP implementations of both algorithms. The AM implementation out-performs the corresponding BSP implementation in all cases, in addition to completing successfully on more nodes.

Increasingly poor scaling in both sets of experiments as the processor counts increase could be ameliorated by making the choice of coalescing factors and cache sizes dynamic. Additionally, removing routing at smaller scales would improve performance there. Incorporating dynamic variation of these features at runtime is interesting future work.

4. Conclusion

Phrasing graph algorithms as collections of asynchronous, concurrently executing, message-driven fragments of code allows for natural expression of algorithms, flexible implementations leveraging various forms of parallelism, and performance portability—all without modifying the algorithms themselves. Active messages are an effective abstraction for expressing graph applications because they allow the fine-grained dependency structure of the computations to be expressed directly in a form that can be observed dynamically at runtime as it is discovered. At this point a variety of optimizations are available (coalescing, reductions, etc.) that are difficult or impossible to apply effectively at compile time. The active message abstraction allows the specification of graph algorithms to be separated from the details of their execution, yielding flexible and expressive semantics and high performance.

Acknowledgments

This work was supported by NSF grant CCF-11118882. Resources of the Argonne Leadership Computing Facility at Argonne National Laboratory were used, which is supported by the Office of Science of the U.S. Department of Energy under contract DE-AC02-06CH11357.

References

[1] A. Lumsdaine, D. Gregor, B. Hendrickson, and J. Berry, "Challenges in parallel graph processing," *Parallel Processing Letters*, vol. 17, no. 1, pp. 5–20, 2007.

[2] K. Lang, "Fixing two weaknesses of the spectral method," in *Neural Information Processing Systems*, 2005.

[3] P. Erdős, R. L. Graham, and E. Szemeredi, "On sparse graphs with dense long paths," Stanford Univ., Tech. Rep. CS-TR-75-504, 1975.

[4] L. G. Valiant, "A bridging model for parallel computation," *Communications of the ACM*, vol. 33, no. 8, pp. 103–111, 1990.

[5] J. Willcock, T. Hoefler, N. Edmonds, and A. Lumsdaine, "Active Pebbles: Parallel programming for data-driven applications," in *International Conference on Supercomputing*, Tucson, Arizona, May 2011.

[6] J. Jose, S. Potluri, M. Luo, S. Sur, and D. K. Panda, "UPC Queues for scalable graph traversals: Design and evaluation on InfiniBand clusters," in *Conference on PGAS Programming Models*, Oct. 2011.

[7] D. Chavarria-Miranda, S. Krishnamoorthy, and A. Vishnu, "Global Futures: A multithreaded execution model for Global Arrays-based applications," in *CCGRID*, 2012, pp. 393–401.

[8] U. Meyer and P. Sanders, "Δ-stepping: A parallelizable shortest path algorithm," *J. Algorithms*, vol. 49, no. 1, pp. 114–152, 2003.

---

[1] The missing data point for "AM SV (1M cache)" is due to the wall clock time limit on the machine expiring before the algorithm completed, not memory exhaustion as with the missing data points for the BSP algorithms.

Multi-Level Parallel Computing of Reverse Time Migration for Seismic Imaging on Blue Gene/Q

Ligang Lu and Karen Magerlein
IBM Watson Research Center, Yorktown Heights, USA

Categories and Subject Descriptors J.2 [Physical Sciences and Engineering]: Earth and Atmospheric Sciences
Keywords Multi-level Parallelism, Parallel Computing, High Performance Computing, Performance Optimization, Reverse Time Migration, Seismic Imaging

1. Introduction

Blue Gene/Q (BG/Q) has large counts of nodes, cores, and threads; and a rich programming environment with many degrees of freedom in optimization. So it is both a challenge and an opportunity to use it to accelerate the seismic imaging applications to a new level that will significantly advance the technologies for the oil and gas industry. In this work we aim to address two important questions: how such HPC system will perform in real applications; and how the many degrees of freedom in parallel programming can be calibrated to achieve optimal performance. Based on BG/Q's architecture features and RTM workload characteristics, we developed massive domain partition, MPI, and SIMD. Our detailed deep analyses in various aspects of optimization also provide valuable findings and insights in how BG/Q can be utilized to facilitate the advance of seismic imaging technologies. The BG/Q RTM solution achieved a 14.93x speedup over the BG/P implementation. applications to a new level.

2. Reverse Time Migration

3D Reverse Time Migration (RTM) is a computationally intensive seismic imaging algorithm increasingly used in the oil and gas exploration to locate hydrocarbon reserves in complex subsurface domains because of its superior imaging accuracy. The RTM algorithm [1] is based on the physical intuition that pressure waves should be correlated at reflection boundaries; so RTM proceeds by correlating two pressure waves (called the forward and backward waves) to find those boundaries. To generate the waves for correlation, RTM simulates wave propagation using the wave equation below for a wave U(x,y,z,t) with a source term S(x,y,z,t):

$$(1) \quad \frac{1}{C^2}\frac{\partial^2 U}{\partial t^2} = \frac{\partial^2 U}{\partial x^2} + \frac{\partial^2 U}{\partial y^2} + \frac{\partial^2 U}{\partial z^2} + S$$

The **forward wave** is the wave generated from a source and propagating forward in time using a **"velocity model"** represented by C(x,y,z), which specifies the wave velocity at each point in space and represents the various material properties and boundaries of the volume being imaged. The **backward wave** is generated by using shot data recorded by a hydrophone array as the source term for the wave equation and propagating backward in time. These two waves are then multiplied pointwise at each time step to generate an image. This process is repeated for all shots in the seismic survey. Figure 1 describes RTM's computation workload flow for a single shot.

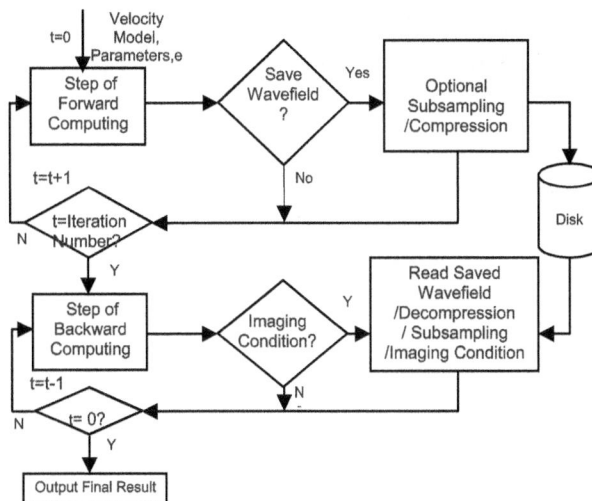

Figure 1. RTM workload flowchart

3. Overview of the Blue Gene/Q System

Each BG/Q compute node has 16 processor cores, a clock speed of 1.6 GHz, up to 16 GB SDRAM memory, and a 4-wide floating point vector unit to deliver a peak performance of 204.8 gigaflops [2]. Each node has a memory bandwidth of 42.6 GB/s to its 16 GB of main store. The nodes are connected through a 5D torus network and the inter-node communication has an aggregated bandwidth of 40 GB/s. Each BG/Q core supports execution of four independent hardware threads. On any cycle, one of the 4 hardware threads per core may issue a floating point operation, while another may issue a load/store operation. With 16 cores and 4 hardware threads per core, the BG/Q node provides a programming environment with up to 64 application threads. A full, 1024-node BG/Q rack has 16,384 cores, 65,536 hardware threads and a peak performance of 204.8TF/s.

4. Multi-Level Paralleliel Computing of RTM on BG/Q

We implemented an end-to-end isotropic finite-difference time-domain RTM algorithm, including application of source and receiver signals, 8th-order spatial stencil calculations, 2nd-order time update, absorbing boundary condition calculation[3], boundary data exchange to support domain partitioning, snapshot handling and image condition calculation. Our RTM solution uses the domain–partition parallel strategy at the node level to take advantage of BG/Q's architecture characteristics in large in-node memory and fast inter-node communication. Furthermore, our domain partition method allows us to reduce the wave field snapshot I/O need and improve data locality thus the cache hit ratio. At the core/thread level, we seek for the best combination of MPI processes and OpenMP threads to maximize the throughput. At the data level parallelism, we make full use of 4-way SIMD in all floating-point calculations, such as stencil stepping, boundary absorbing, and imaging condition. For performance evaluation, we use a 1024^3 large size velocity model and 1408+1408 iterations in the forward and backward pass. As shown in Figure 2, our multi-level parallel RTM computing solution on BG/Q achieved a speedup of 14.93x out of a theoretic 15.03x over the performance obtained on BG/P[4,5]. The RTM performance also scales very well on BG/Q as shown in Figure 3.

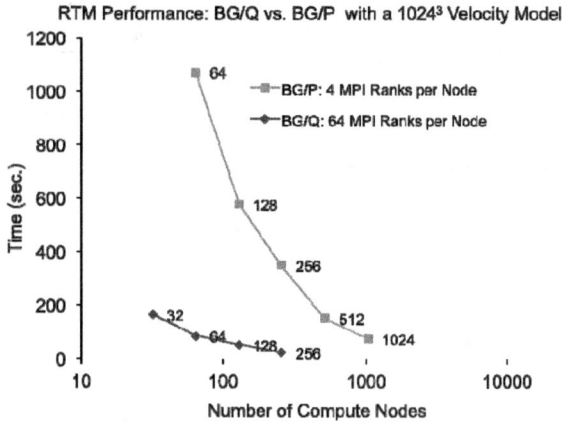

Figure 2. RTM runtimes on BG/Q and BG/P. The numbers of nodes are indicated on the curves.

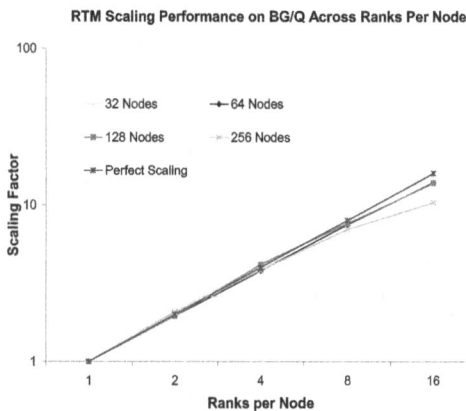

Figure 3. Scaling performance on ranks per node

To evaluate the efficiency of our SIMD implementation, we measured the percentage of total quad floating point (QFP) instructions against the total number of floating point (FP) instructions. Results show that the QFP instructions count over 99% of all FP instructions. We also investigated and analyzed many other aspects of performance optimization, including cache tiling, non-uniform partition, throughput, cache hit rate, instruction issue rate, peak memory bandwidth usage, and I/O performance. For examples, Figure 4 and Figure 5 show that our optimization strategies achieved up to 580 million stencils per second per node and near 100% cache hit ration with L1, L2, and L1 pre-fetch.

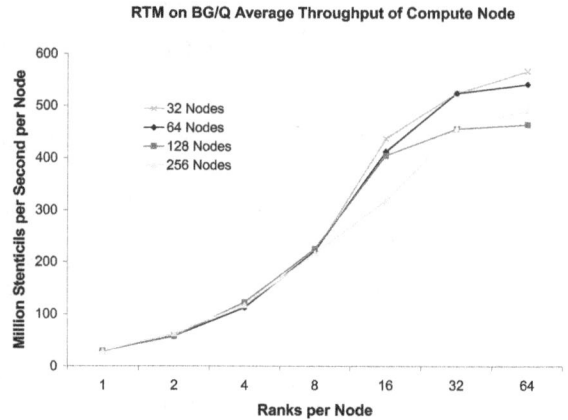

Figure 4. Average throughput vs. ranks per node

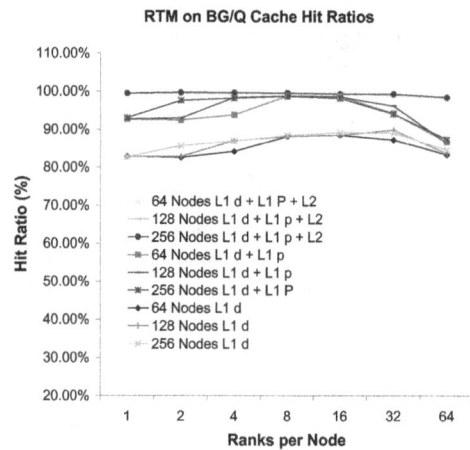

Figure 5. Cache hit ratio analysis

5. Conclusions

Our multi-level parallel computing of RTM on BG/Q provides a valuable example how HPC systems with many degrees of freedom in optimization like BG/Q can be used to accelerate seismic imaging applications to an unplecedented level to meet the demand from the advance the technologies and scence in the oil and gas industry.

References

[1] Baysal, E., Kosloff, D., and Sherwood, J., Reverse-time migration: Geophysics, **48**, pp. 1514-24, 1983.

[2] *IBM System Blue Gene Solution: Blue Gene/Q Application Development, IBM Redbooks.*

[3] Higdon, R. L. Numerical Absorbing Boundary Conditions for the Wave Equation. *Math. of Computation*, Vol. 49:179, pp. 65-90, July, 1987.

[4] Perrone, M., Lu, L., Liu, L., Fedulova, I., Semenikhin, A., and Gorbik, V., "High Performance RTM Using Massive Domain Partitioning", *EAGE*, May, 2011.

[5] Perrone, M., Liu, L., Lu, L., Magerlein, K., Kim, C., Fedulova, I., and Semenikhin, A., "Reducing Data Movement Costs—Scalable Seismic Imaging on Blue Gene", *IPDPS*, Shanghai, China, May 2012.

Parallel Programming with Big Operators

Changhee Park
KAIST
changhee.park@kaist.ac.kr

Guy L. Steele Jr.
Oracle Labs
guy.steele@oracle.com

Jean-Baptiste Tristan
Oracle Labs
jean.baptiste.tristan@oracle.com

Abstract

In the sciences, it is common to use the so-called "big operator" notation to express the iteration of a binary operator (the reducer) over a collection of values. Such a notation typically assumes that the reducer is associative and abstracts the iteration process. Consequently, from a programming point-of-view, we can organize the reducer operations to minimize the depth of the overall reduction, allowing a potentially parallel evaluation of a big operator expression. We believe that the big operator notation is indeed an effective construct to express parallel computations in the Generate/Map/Reduce programming model, and our goal is to introduce it in programming languages to support parallel programming. The effective definition of such a big operator expression requires a simple way to generate elements, and a simple way to declare algebraic properties of the reducer (such as its identity, or its commutativity). In this poster, we want to present an extension of Scala with support for big operator expressions. We show how big operator expressions are defined and how the API is organized to support the simple definition of reducers with their algebraic properties.

Categories and Subject Descriptors D.1.3 [*Programming Techniques*]: Concurrent Programming—Parallel Programming

Keywords Parallelism, Mathematical notation, Scala

1. A useful parallel programming tool

In mathematics, in the sciences, it is sometimes convenient to express the iteration of an operator to a collection of values using a "big operator". As an example, $\sum$ is a big operator that denotes the iterated application of the binary operator $+$ over a collection of numbers. This operator can be used as part of what we call in this a paper a "big expression" such as:

$$\sum_{x \in [1..n]} e^{ix}$$

This expression is a compact (and declarative) way to denote the sum of all the complex numbers e^{ix} for all values of x comprised between 1 and n. We can think of such a big operator as a lifting of an operator to a collection of values. Typically, the lifted operator is binary and associative. This last property explains why we can abstract away the order in which we apply the lifted operator to our collection of values, resulting in a declarative expression. In our work, we also require the lifted operator to possess an identity: it is

often convenient to have an identity element at hand and it allows for big expression to be defined even when the iterated collection is empty.

In a typical programming language, a big expression could be implemented with a loop, a recursive function definition, or simply as a call to a function such as `fold` if the collection has one. The drawback of these definitions is that they typically enforce a particular evaluation order. As an example, summing the list of numbers $[x_1, x_2, x_3, x_4]$ may correspond to the evaluation of the expression $((x_1 + x_2) + x_3) + x_4$. While this is semantically correct, we are missing an opportunity to exploit the associativity of $+$, which could allow for a balanced parallel evaluation of the expression, as in $(x_1 + x_2) + (x_3 + x_4)$. This is what makes big operator notation interesting for parallel programming. As an example it was in some form a feature of `Fortress` [1], a programming language oriented towards parallel programming. The more a programmer expresses application of an operator over a collection using this notation, the less he arbitrarily enforces an evaluation order where it is not semantically necessary.

Before adding big expressions to a language, it is useful to identify and name what constitutes such an expression. As an example, the big expression mentioned at the beginning of this section has four important constituents:

- The collection of integers $[1..n]$: It is the collection from which we generate values, we call it the *generator*. In general, the generator can be composed from other generators by taking their cross product, nesting them, or filtering them. These are fairly standard operations in any language that provides support for collection-comprehension or for-comprehension.

- The function from integers to complex numbers e^{ix}: we call it the *mapping*. It is also standard in any language that supports collection-comprehension or for-comprehension.

- The type of the values we are reducing, which does not appear explicitly in our example. In this case, it corresponds to the type of complex numbers. We refer to this type as the type of the big expression.

- Finally, $\sum$, the big operator itself. We refer to it as the *reducer*.

A big expression therefore needs to specify a big operator, a generator –perhaps defined by composing simpler generators–, and a mapping. Aside from the big operator, this is very similar to comprehension notations such as $\{\ f(x) \mid x \in [1..n]\ \}$. In fact, the big expression is a generalization of such comprehension notations. As an example, the previous set-comprehension can be rewritten as the big expression: $\bigcup_{x \in [1..n]} \{\ f(x)\ \}$.

2. An implementation in Scala

To experiment with big expressions, we introduce them into the Scala programming language [2]. There are at least two reasons that make Scala an appropriate language to support big expressions.

First, Scala supports for-comprehensions, and provides a means to compose generators. Second, Scala has a parallel collection library that we can build on to evaluate big expressions in parallel.

Let us assume for now that we have `sum`, a big operator that sums integers. We program the summation of the square of all even integers between 1 and n as

```
BIG sum (i <- 0 to n if i % 2 == 0) i * i
```

Our big expression is introduced by the keyword "BIG", and followed by the big operator, the generator, and the mapping. The type of this big expression is `Int` and the type of the big operator is `Reducer[Int]`.

2.1 The definition of big operators

To define a big operator, the end user must extend the class `Reducer` whose definition is similar to (the actual definition is slightly different, but this is an implementation detail):

```
trait Associative

trait Identity[T] { val identity: T }

trait Reducer[T] extends Function2[T,T,T]
                 with Associative
                 with Identity[T]
```

A reducer should have a binary operator (the `apply` method inherited from `Function2`), be associative, and possess an identity, as inherited from trait `Identity`. For instance, we can define `sum` as follows:

```
val sum = new Reducer[Int] {
    def apply(x: Int, y: Int): Int = x + y;
    val identity = 0
}
```

2.2 Compilation of big expressions

Big expressions are compiled by desugaring. In the simplest case, a big expression of the form

```
BIG big_op (i <- g) mapping
```

can simply be desugared into

```
g.generate(big_op, i => mapping)
```

We require every collection that is to be used as a generator to mix in the trait `Generator`. We define this trait as follows:

```
trait Generator[A] {
  def generate[B](bin_op: (B,B) => B,
                  mapping: A => B)
}
```

It contains a single function `generate` that expects a binary operator and the mapping. It is up to the library writer to implement this function. As an example, he could implement it by mapping `mapping` on the collection and then calling method `reduce` with `bin_op` as an argument.

We explain in the next section why we do not require `bin_op` to be a `Reducer`. To evaluate a big operator in parallel, the library writer may define function `generate` as follows:

```
def generate[B](bin_op: (B,B) => B, mapping: A => B) =
  bin_op match {
    case b: Reducer[B] => self.par.aggregate ...
  }
```

where method `par` is the method provided by Scala collections that converts serial collections to their parallel counterpart, allowing parallel evaluation of the big expression.

2.3 Inline definition of big operators

To improve the use of big expressions, we would like to allow the end user to be able to simply define a big operator within the big expression. For example, the end user can avoid pre-defining `sum` and write the previous big expression as

```
BIG (fn with { val identity = 0 } (x,y) => x + y)
    (i <- 0 to n if i % 2 == 0) i * i
```

or even

```
BIG + with { val identity = 0 }
    (i <- 0 to n if i % 2 == 0) i * i
```

Also, an end user who doesn't want to provide the identity element can define the big expression as

```
BIG + (i <- 0 to n if i % 2 == 0) i * i
```

This is for that reason that method `generate` is declared with such generality. In such a case, our desugarer will compile the method name into an object of type `Function2` which is not a subtype of `Reducer`. If the collection is empty, the implementation of `generate` may handle such a binary operator by throwing an exception.

Finally, not all type and binary operator have a simple identity. Think for instance of the binary operator set-intersection. In this case, we provide the end-user with a simple way of lifting the type `Set[...]` to `Option[Set[...]]` where None represents the universe.

3. Configuration of the big operator

As presented above, the class `Reducer` mixes in the trait `Associative` and the trait `Identity`. Trait `Associative` is only informative, it does not provide or require any definition. Yet, we "attach" this information to the binary operator, since it is assumed that the binary operator is associative. This extra piece of information is a means to communicate to the compiler and the runtime a property that could used to increase performance.

Following this idea, we add to our API other algebraic traits, allowing the programmer to attach as much information as possible to the binary operator underlying the big operator. For instance, on a cluster, the runtime may make good use of the fact that a binary operator is commutative to distribute appropriate workloads to different nodes. Such algebraic could include, among other things:

```
trait Commutative

trait Absorber[T] { val absorber: T }
```

4. Conclusion

To conclude, we think that big operators and their associated big expressions are a useful tool to write better parallel programs. Also, we think that it is useful to tell the compiler and the runtime of properties we know about the big operator. The design questions remain largely open. We are experimenting with some designs in Scala, but deciding on the syntax of big expressions, especially inlined one, and on an API to support simple description of algebraic properties of big operators requires more practice and feedback.

References

[1] E. Allen, D. Chase, J. Hallett, V. Luchangco, J.-W. Maessen, S. Ryu, G. L. Steele Jr., and S. Tobin-Hochstadt. *The Fortress Language Specification.* Sun Microsystems, March 2008.

[2] M. Odersky. *The Scala Language Specification.* EPFL, May 2011.

Programming with Hardware Lock Elision

Yehuda Afek   Amir Levy   Adam Morrison

Blavatnik School of Computer Science, Tel Aviv University

Abstract

We present a simple yet effective technique for improving performance of lock-based code using the *hardware lock elision* (HLE) feature in Intel's upcoming Haswell processor.

We also describe how to extend Haswell's HLE mechanism to achieve a similar effect to our lock elision scheme entirely in hardware.

Categories and Subject Descriptors   D.1.3 [*Programming Techniques*]: Concurrent Programming

Keywords   Haswell, hardware lock elision, speculative execution

1. Introduction

Hardware lock elision (HLE), a hardware mechanism to dynamically remove unnecessary lock-induced serialization, will soon be available with the release of Intel's Haswell processor microarchitecture. Haswell introduces two *transactional synchronization extensions* (TSX) to the x86 architecture [1], both of which allow a thread to execute a *memory transaction* [3] whose sequence of memory operations appears to occur instantaneously as an atomic update when viewed by other threads.

In this paper we focus on Haswell's *hardware lock elision* (HLE) feature, which is aimed at removing unnecessary lock-induced serialization. The idea behind lock elision [7] is to transactionally execute lock-protected critical sections, and serialize them if an actual data conflict occurs. (Two memory operations *conflict* if they concurrently access the same cache line and one of them is a write.) This allows programmers to use coarse-grained locking, which is easier to program and reason about, while getting the performance of fine-grained locking.

Using HLE is quite simple in principle, as Figure 1 shows. One uses a new instruction prefix, XACQUIRE, before the write that acquires the lock, and another prefix, XRELEASE, before the write which releases the lock. The processor then *elides* the XACQUIRE write and does not expose it to the rest of the system. Instead, the executing thread begins executing the critical section speculatively. If the speculative run finishes without conflict and exits the critical section by performing the XRELEASE write, its memory updates are made globally visible. Thus, Haswell's HLE mechanism works for lock implementations whose releasing write restores the lock to its original state prior to the acquire [1]. Unfortunately, not all lock algorithms meet this demand; as part of our contribution we adapt

---

Algorithm 1 TTAS (Test&Test&Set) Lock using HLE

TTAS Lock

```
1: while true do
2:     while (lock == 1) do
3:         {busy-wait}
4:     end while
5:     ret = XACQUIRE test&set(lock)
6:     if (ret == 0) then
7:         return
8:     end if
9: end while
```

TTAS Unlock

```
1: XRELEASE lock = 0
```

Figure 1: HLE-enabled TTAS lock. The instruction prefix hints, XACQUIRE and XRELEASE, activate the HLE mechanism.

---

ticket locks [5] (which are used in the Linux kernel [6]) and CLH locks [2, 4] for use under HLE.

However, our main contribution concerns HLE's *avalanche behavior*. In a smooth conflict free run HLE indeed provides better performance by allowing concurrent execution of protected code sections. Yet HLE suffers from an avalanche behavior if one thread aborts, e.g., due to a conflict. After an HLE thread aborts it re-enters the critical section non-speculatively. The non-speculative lock acquisition *causes all speculatively executing threads to abort*. In addition, new threads that arrive at the critical section see that the lock is taken and are either delayed or prevented from entering speculative execution. The phenomenon is intensified when *fair locks* [5] are used. Due to the fairness guarantees that a fair lock provides, it "remembers" conflict events and makes it harder to resume a speculative execution. As a result, an HLE fair lock offers little if any speedup over a standard fair lock, even when there is little underlying contention.

In Section 2 we present a method that guards the HLE based speculative execution from this avalanche of aborting threads. We develop a lock elision technique wrapping Haswell's HLE that allows the non-conflicting threads to continue their speculative HLE-based run without interference from the conflicting threads. To do this we add a *serializing path* to the lock implementation, in which an aborted thread acquires a distinct *auxiliary lock* (without using lock elision) and then *rejoins the speculative execution with the other threads*. Our scheme can be applied to any type of lock.

In Section 3 we discuss how to extend (what we believe to be) Haswell's HLE implementation to achieve a similar effect to our lock elision scheme entirely in hardware, by distinguishing between conflicts on the lock and on other data cache lines. We show how such a mechanism can be used to allow speculative

PPoPP'13,   February 23–27, 2013, Shenzhen, China.
ACM 978-1-4503-1922-5/13/02.

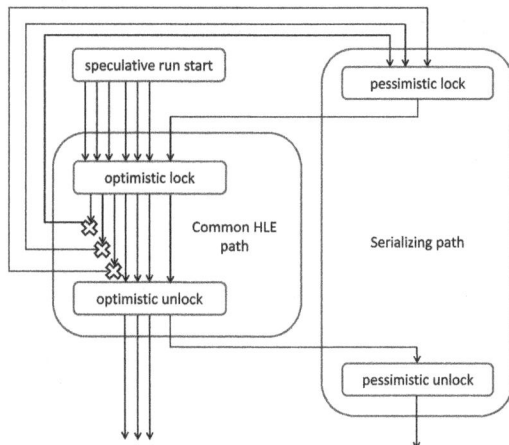

Figure 2: A block diagram of a run using our software scheme. The entry point of a speculative section is the 'speculative run' rectangle. All threads acquire the original optimistic lock using the lock-elision mechanism. If a conflict occurs (described by 'x'), the conflicting threads are sent to the serializing path. Once a thread acquires the auxiliary standard lock in a non-speculative manner, it rejoins the speculative run.

sections that do not conflict on data lines to continue with their speculative runs even in the presence of conflicting threads that abort, acquire the lock, and serialize.

2. Lock Elision with Fast Speculation Reentry

Our scheme uses two locks, the original optimistic lock which is taken using the lock-elision mechanism and an auxiliary standard lock which is taken only in a standard non-speculative manner.

The auxiliary lock groups all the threads that are involved in a conflict and serializes them (see Figure 2). Any conflicting thread has to acquire the auxiliary lock in a standard manner before rejoining the speculative run. Hence, the conflicting threads rejoin the speculative run one at a time. Thus, a conflict event does not abort the entire speculative run, nor does it prevent new threads from starting speculative runs. The process of acquiring the auxiliary lock in order to rejoin the speculative run is referred to as the serializing path.

The elected thread among the conflicting threads (holding the auxiliary lock) might repeatedly abort while speculatively executing. To prevent starvation, we bound the number of repeated failures per thread until completing its speculative execution while holding the auxiliary lock. After a given number of failures, the thread holding the auxiliary lock acquires the original optimistic lock in a standard non-speculative manner. The lock acquisition causes all other speculatively executing threads to abort. The auxiliary lock holders is now the only thread that can make progress, and so it completes its critical section. Fairness among the conflicting threads in the serializing path is kept by the fairness capabilities of the auxiliary lock itself.

Notice that grouping the conflicting threads in one group is, in principle, too strict since a single conflicting thread does not have to conflict with the entire group. A natural extension (left for future work) to explore is dividing the conflicting threads to different groups, each containing only threads that conflict among themselves.

3. Architectural Approach for Increasing Lock Elision Concurrency

Here we present an alternative hardware-based solution to cope with the avalanche phenomenon. We suggest extending HLE's conflict detection to distinguish between conflicts on the lock and conflicts on the data cache lines, allowing speculative threads to progress even when encountering a held lock. In turn, this allows speculative sections that do not conflict on data lines to continue with their speculative runs while the conflicting ones do serialize. Our proposal does not require cache-coherence protocol changes.

Our proposal is based on the following observation. In contrast to a conflict on the *data* in the critical section, which means the conflicting sections need to be serialized, a conflict on the lock's cache line is merely a *synchronization signal*. It indicates that some thread T has acquired the lock, but T does not necessarily conflict with all running speculative threads. Yet allowing a speculative thread to ignore a conflict on the lock and continue running concurrently with T (until either it experiences a data conflict with T or commits) can lead to incorrect executions. That is why the Haswell processor implements a *conservative* approach that guarantees correctness, terminating all speculative threads when the lock is non-speculatively acquired.

In our approach, a speculatively executing thread that experiences a conflict on the lock does not automatically abort. Instead, it tries to complete its speculative execution as follows: As long as the speculative thread accesses only data which is already in its caches, it can safely continue. If the speculative execution encounters a cache miss (due to a read or a write operation), it reads the lock address again. If the lock is free, the optimistic execution can continue, otherwise, it is suspended. Hence, while the lock is taken, speculative threads can proceed as long as they do not incur a cache miss in order to expand their read or write sets. When the lock is released, the resulting cache coherency operation releases the suspended speculative threads which continue the speculative run by executing the memory operation that caused the cache miss.

The processor can identify the lock cache line since it is written to by the instruction prefixed with XACQUIRE. The lock cache line is placed in the read/write-set only if it gets accessed for data. If the lock's cache line gets evicted, either (1) it is in the read/write-set, and we abort, or (2) it is not (only the lock got accessed so far), so we proceed with the above protocol.

References

[1] Intel Architecture Instruction Set Extensions Programming Reference. http://software.intel.com/file/41604, 2012.

[2] T. S. Craig. Building FIFO and priority-queuing spin locks from atomic swap. Technical Report 93-02-02, Department of Computer Science and Engineering, University of Washington, 1993.

[3] M. Herlihy and J. E. B. Moss. Transactional memory: architectural support for lock-free data structures. In *ISCA 1993*.

[4] P. S. Magnusson, A. Landin, and E. Hagersten. Queue locks on cache coherent multiprocessors. In *Proceedings of the 8th International Symposium on Parallel Processing*, pages 165–171, Washington, DC, USA, 1994. IEEE Computer Society.

[5] J. M. Mellor-Crummey and M. L. Scott. Algorithms for scalable synchronization on shared-memory multiprocessors. *ACM Transactions on Computer Systems*, 9(1):21–65, Feb. 1991.

[6] N. Piggin. x86: FIFO ticket spinlocks. http://lkml.org/lkml/2007/11/1/125, 2007.

[7] R. Rajwar and J. R. Goodman. Speculative Lock Elision: enabling highly concurrent multithreaded execution. In *MICRO 2001*.

RaceFree: An Efficient Multi-Threading Model for Determinism

Kai Lu   Xu Zhou   Xiaoping Wang   Wenzhe Zhang   Gen Li

National University of Defense Technology

{kailu, zhouxu, xiaopingwang, zhangwenzhe, ligen}@nudt.edu.cn

Abstract

Current deterministic systems generally incur large overhead due to the difficulty of detecting and eliminating data races. This paper presents RaceFree, a novel multi-threading runtime that adopts a *relaxed deterministic model* to provide a data-race-free environment for parallel programs. This model cuts off unnecessary shared-memory communication by isolating threads in separated memories, which eliminates direct data races. Meanwhile, we leverage the happen-before relation defined by applications themselves as one-way communication pipes to perform necessary thread communication. Shared-memory communication is transparently converted to message-passing style communication by our Memory Modification Propagation (MMP) mechanism, which propagates local memory modifications to other threads through the happen-before relation pipes. The overhead of RaceFree is 67.2% according to our tests on parallel benchmarks.

Categories and Subject Descriptors   D.1.3 [*Programming Techniques*]: Concurrent Programming—Parallel programming;   D.2.5 [*Software Engineering*]: Testing and Debugging—Debugging Aids; D.4.1 [*Operating Systems*]: Process Management—Threads

Keywords   deterministic multi-threading, debug, synchronization, relaxed deterministic model, happen-before

1. Introduction

Parallel programs of shared-memory multi-threading are inherently nondeterministic due to the unpredictable thread interleavings, which brings difficulties to software debugging, testing and fault tolerance [1, 2]. Current techniques that could solve the nondeterministic problem contain *Deterministic Replaying* [6–9] and *Deterministic Multi-Threading* (DMT) [1–5]. These approaches apply different methods to eliminate the nondeterministic sources. However, due to the difficulty of detecting and eliminating the nondeterministic data races, current deterministic approaches are generally low-efficiency.

Thread concurrency exposes two kinds of nondeterminism to user programs: data race and synchronization race. In shared-memory multi-threading, threads could communicate with each other by directly reading and writing shared memories. The unprotected shared memory accesses may incur data race, which is the most common nondeterminism of parallel programs. Eliminating data races is difficult as they may occur at any memory access. In order to eliminate data race, we have to check every memory access to make sure the memory access will not conflict with another concurrent memory access. Compared with data race, synchronization race is much easier to handle. The reason is that synchronization race could only occur at well-defined synchronizations, which are (1) explicit in user programs, and (2) much fewer than memory accesses.

1.1 Relaxed Determinism

To address the performance problem of current deterministic systems, we introduce a novel threading model: *relaxed deterministic model*. The relaxed deterministic model provides a data-race-free multi-threading environment, in which only synchronization race could affect the determinism of parallel programs. Since this model does not guarantee strong determinism unless we ensure a deterministic synchronization order, the deterministic semantics this model promises is called *relaxed determinism*.

Relaxed determinism could be easily changed to strong determinism if the synchronization order is guaranteed to be deterministic. We deliberately leave this nondeterminism to other techniques (e.g., deterministic replay [6–8] and weak determinism [2]) to provide a spectrum of determinism choices for different application scenarios, as discussed in Section 1.4 .

1.2 Design

Data race is considered as unnecessary shared-memory communication between threads. The basic design of our relaxed deterministic model is to identify necessary communication from unnecessary communication, and cut off all the unnecessary shared-memory communication. Since the programmer knows exactly whether a communication is necessary or not, we leverage what the programmer writes in the codes as a clue—user-inserted synchronizations. We assume that any necessary thread communication is noticed and thus synchronized by the programmers. Hence, we could use the happen-before relation [10] defined by synchronizations to distinguish necessary communication and unnecessary communication. As shown in Figure 1, if two memory accesses do not have a happen-before relation, they are treated as unnecessary communication. Otherwise, they are necessary communication, and they should communicate in their original way. To preserve the original communication semantics, we ensure the following semantics invariant for our model:

A Read should always see the value of a Write if it is the last Write that happens before the Read.

To cut off unnecessary thread communication, we isolate threads in separated shared memories. However, this could also block the necessary communication. To address this problem, we propagate memory modifications among threads to simulate the original nec-

PPoPP'13,   February 23–27, 2013, Shenzhen, China.
ACM 978-1-4503-1922-5/13/02.

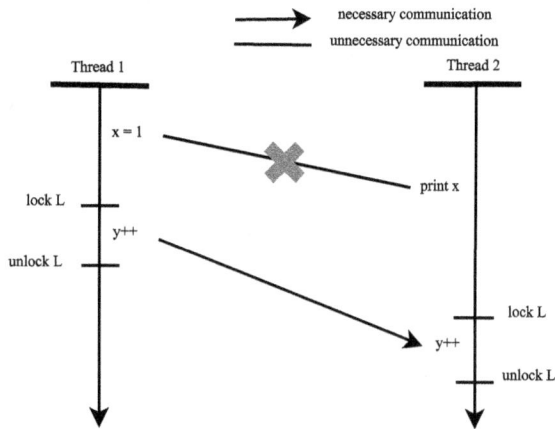

Figure 1. Shared-memory communication in relaxed deterministic model. Unnecessary communication is cut off while necessary communication is preserved.

essary communication. First, we interpose the synchronizations to capture the happen-before relation of the program. Then we perform necessary thread communication according to the happen-before relation, which is converted to one-way communication pipes between threads. Shared-memory communication could be converted to message-passing style communication by our Memory Modification Propagation (MMP) mechanism. MMP cuts thread execution into slices using synchronizations, collects the local memory modifications using the page protection mechanism, and propagates the modifications to other threads at the synchronization boundaries through the happen-before pipes. By this means, the original programs could run correctly and transparently on our model. Meanwhile, we constrain the nondeterministic data races to the boundaries of user-defined synchronizations. The characteristic of relaxed deterministic model is that it does not introduce extra synchronization schemes, thus threads could synchronize in the same way as their original design.

1.3 Results

We implemented a runtime system RaceFree to evaluate the relaxed deterministic model. We tested RaceFree in two aspects: determinism and performance. Since RaceFree only ensures relaxed determinism, we used the deterministic-replay approach to ensure a deterministic synchronization order for RaceFree. We checked whether this modified system could ensure determinism for parallel programs. Performance was evaluated by comparing RaceFree with the nondeterministic pthread library. The results on *racey* and parallel benchmarks (from Splash-2, Parsec and Phoenix) show that RaceFree could ensure relaxed determinism and the average overhead is 67.2% compared to pthread.

1.4 Application Scenario

Relaxed determinism that RaceFree ensures could be used to implement a spectrum of determinism for different applications. Here we discuss several application scenarios of RaceFree.

Implementing DMT. A DMT system is useful in many domains, such as debugging, testing and fault-tolerance [1–4]. Since only the synchronization order affects determinism, RaceFree could be upgraded to a DMT system with little effort. We note that *weak determinism* only ensures the deterministic synchronization order of a program [2], which is exactly complementary to our system. Hence, to build a DMT system, we only need to change the implementation of synchronizations in RaceFree, and use logical time to arbitrate the lock contentions [2].

Facilitating Deterministic Replay. Deterministic replay could be used for parallel debugging and intrusion analysis [11]. The most difficult part of deterministic replay is to identify and record data races, which often leads to complicated system design, large recording overhead and large disk-space overhead [9, 11]. With RaceFree, deterministic replay is simple and efficient: we only need to interpose synchronizations to record their execution order.

Reproducing Bugs. In parallel debugging, it is acceptable to reproduce a hidden bug in a few re-execution tries [6]. The data-race-free environment can be leveraged to implement such a system. As only synchronization race exists, the nondeterministic interleaving space is reduced. Hence, RaceFree is able to increase the probability of reproducing bug. Moreover, the reproducing of nondeterministic bugs could be directed by calculating the detailed scheduling information from the sketchy information of the original run (e.g., program outputs) to further increase the reproducing probability [6, 7].

Acknowledgments

This work is partially supported by National High-tech R&D Program of China (863 Program) under Grants 2012AA010901, 2012AA01A301, NCET, and National Science Foundation (NSF) China 61272142, 61103082, 61003075, 61170261, 61103193.

References

[1] D. Joseph, L. Brandon, C. Luis, and O. Mark, "DMP: deterministic shared memory multiprocessing," in Proceeding of the 14th international conference on Architectural support for programming languages and operating systems Washington, DC, USA: ACM, 2009.

[2] M. Olszewski, J. Ansel, and S. Amarasinghe, "Kendo: efficient deterministic multithreading in software," in Proceeding of the 14th international conference on Architectural support for programming languages and operating systems, 2009, pp. 97-108.

[3] X. Zhou, K. Lu, X. Wang, and X. Li, "Exploiting parallelism in deterministic shared memory multiprocessing," J.ParallelDistrib.Comput., pp. 72(2012)716-727, 2012.

[4] B. Tom, A. Owen, D. Joseph, C. Luis, and G. Dan, "CoreDet: a compiler and runtime system for deterministic multithreaded execution," in Proceedings of the fifteenth edition of ASPLOS on Architectural support for programming languages and operating systems Pittsburgh, Pennsylvania, USA: ACM, 2010, pp. 53-64.

[5] T. Liu, C. Curtsinger, and E. D. Berger, "DTHREADS: Efficient Deterministic Multithreading," in Proceedings of the 22nd ACM Symposium on Operating Systems Principles, 2011.

[6] S. Park, Y. Zhou, W. Xiong, Z. Yin, R. Kaushik, K. H. Lee, and S. Lu, "PRES: probabilistic replay with execution sketching on multiprocessors," in Proceedings of the ACM SIGOPS 22nd symposium on Operating systems principles, 2009, pp. 177-192.

[7] G. Altekar and I. Stoica, "ODR: output-deterministic replay for multicore debugging," in Proceedings of the 22nd ACM Symposium on Operating Systems Principles, 2009.

[8] D. Subhraveti and J. Nieh, "Record and transplay: partial checkpointing for replay debugging across heterogeneous systems," 2011, pp. 109-120.

[9] H. Patil, C. Pereira, M. Stallcup, G. Lueck, and J. Cownie, "Pinplay: a framework for deterministic replay and reproducible analysis of parallel programs," in Proceedings of the 8th annual IEEE/ACM international symposium on Code generation and optimization, 2010, pp. 2-11.

[10] L. Lamport, "Time, clocks, and the ordering of events in a distributed system," Communications of the ACM, vol. 21, pp. 558-565, 1978.

[11] G. W. Dunlap, S. T. King, S. Cinar, M. A. Basrai, and P. M. Chen, "ReVirt: enabling intrusion analysis through virtual-machine logging and replay," ACM SIGOPS Operating Systems Review, vol. 36, pp. 211-224, 2002.

Reducing Contention Through Priority Updates (Poster Paper)

Julian Shun*   Guy E. Blelloch*   Jeremy T. Fineman[†]   Phillip B. Gibbons[‡]

*Carnegie Mellon University   [†]Georgetown University   [‡]Intel Labs, Pittsburgh

jshun@cs.cmu.edu   guyb@cs.cmu.edu   jfineman@cs.georgetown.edu   phillip.b.gibbons@intel.com

1. Introduction

Memory contention can be a serious performance bottleneck in concurrent programs on shared-memory multicore architectures. Having all threads write to a small set of shared locations, for example, can lead to orders of magnitude loss in performance relative to all threads writing to distinct locations, or even relative to a single thread doing all the writes. Shared write access, however, can be very useful in parallel algorithms, concurrent data structures, and protocols for communicating among threads. In our ongoing work [8], we study a generalization of the test-and-set operation, which we call *priority update*. This operation has many applications and, as with test-and-set, it can greatly reduce write contention in parallel and concurrent programs for shared memory.

2. Priority Updates

A *priority update* takes as arguments a memory location containing a value of type T, a new value of type T to write, and a binary comparison function **comp** : $T \times T \rightarrow bool$ that enforces a total order over values. The operation atomically compares the two values using the provided comparison function and replaces the current value with the new value if the new value has higher priority according to the comparison function. We require that all priority updates to a given location use the same comparison function. In the simplest form, called a *write-with-min* (or write-with-max), T is a number type, and the comparison function is standard numeric less-than (or greater-than). In general, the type T and the comparison function may be arbitrary. A test-and-set is a special case of priority update over two values, where the value is initialized to 0, the new value to be written is 1, and the comparison function is ">", meaning that 1 has higher priority than 0.

The intended programming abstraction for priority updates is to avoid conflicting concurrent mutations to the same memory locations. Any number of concurrent priority updates to the same location are permitted (provided they use the same comparison function), but those operations should complete before the value is reinitialized. Section 4 discusses many applications of this abstraction.

Categories and Subject Descriptors   D.1.3 [*Programming Techniques*]: Concurrent Programming

General Terms   Experimentation, Performance

Keywords   Parallel Programming, Contention

A priority update may be implemented in software as follows using compare-and-swap (CAS) as an atomic hardware primitive.

```
1: procedure PRIORITY UPDATE(addr, newval, comp)
2:     oldval ← *addr
3:     while comp(newval, oldval) do
4:         if CAS(addr, oldval, newval) then return
5:         else oldval ← *addr
```

We note that even though a CAS might only work on a single word, this implementation can be applied to arbitrary types (e.g. structures with one of the fields being compared, or variable-length character strings) by using a pointer to the type.

In the best case, the given implementation of priority update completes immediately after a single application of the comparison function (line 3), determining that the value already stored in the location has higher priority than the new value. Otherwise an update attempt occurs with a compare-and-swap operation (line 4). If successful, then the priority update finishes (line 4), and otherwise it rereads the value at the memory location (line 5) and retries. It completes only when the value currently stored has higher priority than the new value, or when its CAS succeeds. This implementation greatly reduces write contention on the shared location because most accesses read the location once and do not require a CAS attempt, especially if the order of the updates is randomized.

3. Contention in Memory Operations

We define *sharing* to be the degree of concurrent access to a shared memory resource by multiple cores, and *contention* to be the performance penalty associated with sharing.

Although contention can be a problem in any system that serializes accesses to a shared resource, the problem is amplified for memory updates on most cache coherent shared-memory machines because of the need to acquire a cache line in exclusive mode. In the standard MESI (Modified, Exclusive, Shared, Invalid) protocol and its variants, a reader can acquire a cache line in shared mode and any number of other caches can simultaneously acquire the line for reading. Concurrent reads to shared locations therefore tend to be reasonably efficient. On the other hand, concurrent updates to a shared location can be very inefficient because the desired cache line ends up ping-ponging around the caches.

To study the effects of contention on contemporary multicore machines, we ran experiments under various degrees of sharing for a variety of memory operations—write-with-min, test-and-set, fetch-and-add, compare-and-swap, (plain) write, and read. For the experiments, we use a 40-core Intel Nehalem machine with E7-8870 processors. We perform 10^8 concurrent operations on a varying number of locations (various degrees of sharing), chosen randomly from 10^8 locations. As shown in Figure 1, fetch-and-add, compare-and-swap, and plain write all suffer from high contention under high sharing, while write-with-min, test-and-set (implemented as a test-and-test-and-set), and read do not. The difference can be over two orders of magnitude! Write-with-min

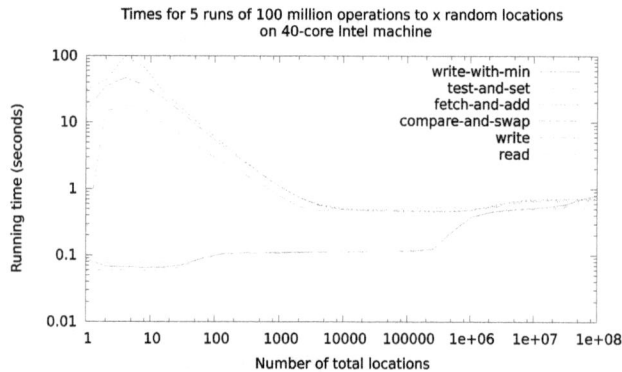

Figure 1. Times for performing different operations (log-log scale). The number of operations is fixed, so fewer locations implies more operations sharing those locations.

nearly matches the performance of test-and-set (because the CAS is almost always avoided under modest to high sharing), while providing many beneficial properties that test-and-set does not have. We obtained similar results on an AMD K10 machine and an Intel SandyBridge machine, and for other priority update operations.

4. Applications of Priority Update

On the algorithms side, priority updates have many applications. In addition to being used directly to take the minimum or maximum of a set of values, they can be used to prioritize threads in order to avoid non-determinism and/or guarantee progress.

Priority updates can be used in a technique called deterministic reservations to implement a speculative for-loop [2]. This technique allows for parallel execution of any prefix of the iteration space. It involves a two-phase procedure, where in the first phase loop iterates use priority updates with unique priorities to reserve shared data, and in the second phase iterates check to see whether their reservations were successful. If successful, an iterate proceeds with any updates to the shared state. This approach guarantees the same order of execution of the iterates as in the sequential order and also guarantees progress since at least the earliest iterate will succeed.

Priority updates have applications in many graph algorithms. They can be used in parallel minimum-spanning-forest algorithms to select the minimum-weight edge between components. They can be used in Bellman-Ford shortest paths to update the neighbors of a vertex with a potentially shorter path. They can also be used in certain graph algorithms to guarantee determinism. In particular, any conflicts can be broken using priorities so that they are always broken in the same way. For example, in breadth-first search (BFS), they can be used to deterministically generate a BFS tree.

In BFS, many vertices may compete to place the same neighbor on to the next frontier, so there may be high sharing. We implemented a serial version of BFS (serialBFS) and two parallel versions of BFS, one which uses a write-with-min (writeMinBFS) as the atomic operation to place neighbors on the frontier, and the other which uses a plain write (writeBFS). We ran experiments comparing these implementations, using a family of comb graphs which have varying degrees of sharing. The *comb* graph is a three layered graph with the first layer containing only the root vertex r of the BFS, the second layer containing $n - k - 1$ vertices and the third layer containing k vertices. The root vertex has an edge to all vertices in the second layer, and each vertex in the second layer has an edge to a randomly chosen vertex in the third layer. There are a total of $4(n - k - 1)$ directed edges in this graph. The sharing comes from the $n - k - 1$ vertices in the second layer placing the k vertices in the third layer on to the next frontier. A lower value of k corresponds to higher sharing. In our experiments, $n = 10^7$

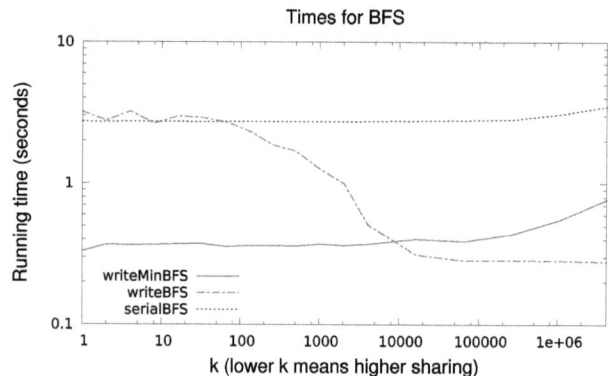

Figure 2. BFS times on different comb graphs (log-log scale)

and we used all 40 cores of the machine. Figure 2 shows that for values of k up to about 10^4, writeMinBFS outperforms writeBFS by an order of magnitude. For higher values of k where there is low sharing, writeMinBFS is slightly slower than writeBFS due to its overhead, but has the benefit of being deterministic. For values of k less than 100, writeBFS is worse than even serialBFS.

5. Related Work

In the PRAM literature, a ***priority write*** is a concurrent write where the highest-priority processor wins on a shared location. This is a special case of priority update.

Lock-free data structures alleviate memory contention, but such solutions only partially solve issues of contention as even the simplest lock-free shared write access to a memory location can create severe performance problems. Researchers have suggested other approaches to reduce memory contention. One approach is to use hardware combining [1, 4], however no current machines support it. The idea of software combining [3, 7] is to simulate in some way what hardware combining would do. However, these techniques may suffer from high overhead or limited scalability. Finally, the test-and-test-and-set operation can be used to reduce contention [5, 6] because only a single update is needed and the remaining operations just perform reads. However, it does not have as broad applicability as the priority update.

Acknowledgments. This work is partially supported by the National Science Foundation under grants CCF-1018188 and CCF-1218188, by Intel Labs Academic Research Office for the Parallel Algorithms for Non-Numeric Computing Program, and by the Intel Science and Technology Center for Cloud Computing.

References

[1] G. E. Blelloch, P. B. Gibbons, and H. V. Simhadri. Combinable memory-block transactions. In *SPAA*, 2008.

[2] G. E. Blelloch, J. T. Fineman, P. B. Gibbons, and J. Shun. Internally deterministic algorithms can be fast. In *PPoPP*, 2012.

[3] P. Fatourou and N. D. Kallimanis. Revisiting the combining synchronization technique. In *PPoPP*, 2012.

[4] A. Gottlieb, B. D. Lubachevsky, and L. Rudolph. Basic techniques for the efficient coordination of very large numbers of cooperating sequential processors. *ACM Trans. Program. Lang. Syst.*, 5(2), 1983.

[5] J. M. Mellor-Crummey and M. L. Scott. Synchronization without contention. *SIGPLAN Not.*, 26(4), 1991.

[6] L. Rudolph and Z. Segall. Dynamic decentralized cache schemes for MIMD parallel processors. In *ISCA*, 1984.

[7] N. Shavit and A. Zemach. Combining funnels: a dynamic approach to software combining. *J. Parallel Distrib. Comput.*, 60(11), 2000.

[8] J. Shun, G. E. Blelloch, J. T. Fineman, and P. B. Gibbons. Priority update as a parallel primitive. *Technical Report CMU-CS-13-101*, 2013.

Relational Algorithms for Multi-Bulk-Synchronous Processors

Gregory Diamos

Nvidia Research
Santa Clara, CA, USA
gdiamos@nvidia.com

Haicheng Wu

Georgia Institute of Technology
Atlanta, GA, USA
hwu36@gatech.edu

Jin Wang

Georgia Institute of Technology
Atlanta, GA, USA
jin.wang@gatech.edu

Ashwin Lele

Georgia Institute of Technology
Atlanta, GA, USA
alele3@gatech.edu

Sudhakar Yalamanchili

Georgia Institute of Technology
Atlanta, GA, USA
sudha@ece.gatech.edu

Abstract

Relational databases remain an important application infrastructure for organizing and analyzing massive volumes of data. At the same time, processor architectures are increasingly gravitating towards Multi-Bulk-Synchronous processor (Multi-BSP) architectures employing throughput-optimized memory systems, lightweight multi-threading, and Single-Instruction Multiple-Data (SIMD) core organizations. This paper explores the mapping of primitive relational algebra operations onto such architectures to improve the throughput of data warehousing applications built on relational databases.

Categories and Subject Descriptors H.2.4 [*Database Management*]: System—Relational Database, Query Processing

Keywords Relational Algebra, GPGPU

1. Introduction

Modern relational database systems and languages are built on efficient implementations of relational algebra (RA) operators combined with specialized data structures that are used to store relations. These systems have been deployed with success on single-core processors and clusters. However, as power-constrained processor architectures move towards multiple cores with fine grained SIMD parallelism and non-uniform or user-managed memory hierarchies (e.g. modern GPGPUs), new algorithms are needed that can harness the massive parallelism provided by these processors.

Relational operations capture the high level semantics of an application in terms of a series of bulk operations on relations. The data intensive nature of relations might suggest that a high degree of data parallelism could be discovered in RA operations. Unfortunately, this parallelism is generally more unstructured and irregular than other domain specific operations complicating the design of efficient parallel implementations. In particular, we identify a fundamental conflict between the structure of algorithms with good computational complexity and that of algorithms with memory ac-

cess patterns and instruction schedules that achieve peak machine utilization. To reconcile this conflict, our design space exploration converges on a hybrid multi-stage algorithm that devotes a small amount of the total runtime to prune input data sets using an irregular algorithm with good computational complexity. The partial results are then fed into a regular algorithm that achieves near peak machine utilization. These algorithms can be used directly to implement a relational database system in a single node using a single GPU blade, or as building blocks in higher level distributed algorithms that scale to multiple processors within a node or across multiple nodes.

2. Data Structure and Algorithm Design

RA consists of a set of fundamental transformations that are applied to relations. A relation consists of n-ary tuples that map attributes (or dimensions) to values. Each attribute consists of a finite set of possible values and an n-ary tuple is a list of n values, one for each attribute. Each transformation included in RA performs an operation on a relation, producing a new relation. Many operators divide the tuple attributes into key attributes and value attributes. In these operations, the key attributes are considered by the operator and the value attributes are treated as payload data which are not considered. In this work, relation is stored as a weakly ordered densely packed array of tuples for efficient access in GPUs.

A relational database application is specified as a dataflow graph of operators, making for a natural mapping to a variety of parallel execution models, for example, by mapping operators to Multi-BSP kernels and relations to data structures. RA operators include SET family (*UNION, INTERSECTION, DIFFERENCE*), *CROSS PRODUCT, JOIN, SELECT*, and *PROJECT*. All operators are designed to have the same sequence of stages (**partition, compute,** and **gather**) where each stage has a Multi-BSP structure, which eases further cross-operator optimization [1]. The philosophy of the algorithm design is to increase core utilizations (achievable throughput) until the computation becomes memory bound, and then achieve near peak utilization of the memory interface. This paper only introduces the implementation of the most complex operator, *JOIN*. The implementation of the other operators can be found in a technical report [2].

Figure 1 shows the three stages of a *JOIN*. The initial **partition** stage (Figure 1(a)–(b)) operates on a sorted list and is performed in-place and the partitions are sized as follows. One of the input relations is partitioned into N parts bounded by pivot elements. Each partition will be processed by a single cooperative thread

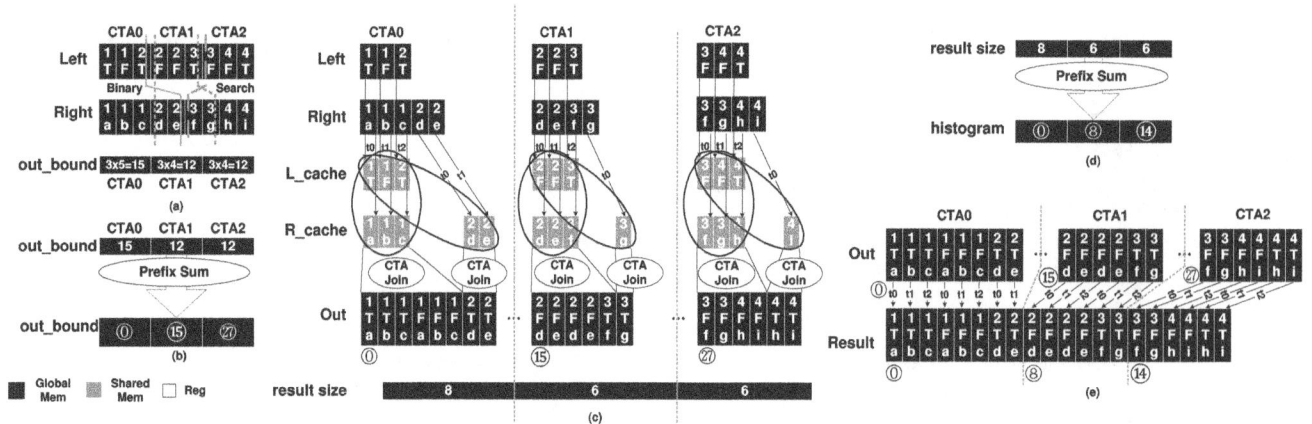

Figure 1. Example of the *JOIN*.

array (CTA). A binary search is used to lookup the tuples in the other input corresponding to the pivots creating a corresponding series of partitions in the second array. The partitions in the two inputs now have overlapping index ranges of tuples. This stage is critical for sparse data sets because it quickly discards large segments of the input relations that do not overlap.

The **compute** stage (Figure 1(c)) is the most complex stages of the three. It identifies subsets of the partitioned relations with overlapping attributes and performs the cross product for each subset. This presents a significant problem to parallel implementations of the algorithm that eventually write to a statically allocated dense array. Namely, the number of tuples in each partition of the output relation is unknown until very late in the computation. The algorithm is that once the inputs have been partitioned, each pair of partitions is assigned to a separate CTA to perform the merge operation independently. The merge operation is implemented by scanning one of the input partitions one *chunk* of tuples at a time where a chunk is a number of tuples that can be processed by a fixed number of threads in a CTA. This chunk is loaded into shared memory for fast access. A corresponding chunk from the second input partition is also loaded into shared memory and a CTA-JOIN is performed upon two chunks within a CTA. Chunks from the second input partition are scanned until they go out of range of the first chunk, at which time a new chunk is loaded from the first partition and the process is repeated. The results of CTA-JOIN are gathered into shared memory until a threshold is reached and eventually written out to a preallocated temporary array. The chunk copy operations into and out of shared memory are carefully designed such that they maximize DRAM bandwidth. The default CTA-JOIN algorithm is referred as Binary-Search CTA-JOIN. Other alternative implementations are described in the technical report [2].

Binary-Search CTA-JOIN is based on a parallel binary search, similar to the **partition** stage of the complete join algorithm. Each thread accesses a tuple from one of the input relations and computes the upper bound and lower bound of that tuple's key in the other relation. The elements between the two bounds match the tuple's key and are joined together. Results generated are aggregated using the stream compaction algorithm and buffered until a threshold number of tuples is reached. At this time, the buffer is written out completely to global memory. Even though this implementation has good algorithmic complexity, it suffers in terms of work-efficiency and processor utilization. It includes a chain of data-dependent loads to shared memory and control-dependent branches. Furthermore, the binary search result of different threads may overlap presenting an opportunity for shared memory bank conflicts and instruction replays when combining two tuples. The

other CTA-JOIN algorithms make different trade-off decisions to address these problems.

The final **gather** stage requires first computing the position of each partition of the result in the final array. This is performed by updating a histogram during the **compute** stage, followed by an out-of-place scan operation over the histogram buckets (Figure 1(d)). Again, the number of partitions is sized such that this operation is relatively inexpensive compared to the **compute** phase. Once the position of each section in the output relation is determined, elements need to be copied from a temporary buffer for each section into the final array (Figure 1(e)).

3. Performance

We ran a set of experiments on Tesla C2050 GPU to examine the performance of each RA operator algorithm. The size of each input relation is swept from 8192 to 16 million tuples. The tuple attributes are randomly generated 32-bit integers. These algorithms are expected to be memory bound, and the results are presented in achieved bandwidth. The most efficient algorithms (*PRODUCT*, *PROJECT*, and *SELECT*) achieve $86\% - 92\%$ of peak machine performance (achieved bandwidth of an optimized stream-copy benchmark) across all input data sets. The least efficient algorithm (*JOIN*) achieves $57\% - 72\%$ of peak machine performance depending on the density of the input. The detailed analysis is in the technical report [2]. To the best of our knowledge, our algorithms represent the best known published results to date for any implementations.

Acknowledgments

This research was supported in part by the National Science Foundation under grants IIP-1032032 & CCF 0905459, by LogicBlox Corporation, and by equipment grants from NVIDIA Corporation. We also acknowledge the detailed and constructive comments of the reviewers.

References

[1] H. Wu, G. Diamos, S. Cadambi, and S. Yalamanchili. Kernel weaver: Automatically fusing database primitives for efficient gpu computation. In *Proceedings of the 45th Annual IEEE/ACM International Symposium on Microarchitecture*, MICRO-45 '12, pages 107–118, 2012.

[2] G. Diamos, H. Wu, A. Lele, J. Wang, and S. Yalamanchili. Efficient relational algebra algorithms and data structures for gpu. Technical Report GIT-CERCS-12-01, CERCS, Georgia Institute of Technology, 2012.

Runtime Elision of Transactional Barriers for Captured Memory *

Fernando Miguel Carvalho[1,2]

[1] ADEETC, Lisbon Polytechnic Institute (ISEL)
mcarvalho@cc.isel.ipl.pt

João Cachopo

[2] INESC-ID Lisboa/Technical University of Lisbon
joao.cachopo@ist.utl.pt

Abstract

In this paper, we propose a new technique that can identify transaction-local memory (i.e. *captured memory*), in managed environments, while having a low runtime overhead. We implemented our proposal in a well known STM framework (Deuce) and we tested it in STMBench7 with two different STMs: TL2 and LSA. In both STMs the performance improved significantly (4 times and 2.6 times, respectively). Moreover, running the STAMP benchmarks with our approach shows improvements of 7 times in the best case for the Vacation application.

Categories and Subject Descriptors D.1.3 [*Programming Techniques*]: Concurrent Programming - Parallel Programming

General Terms Performance, Transactions

Keywords Software Transactional Memory, Runtime Optimizations

1. Introduction

Over-instrumentation [8] is one of the major sources of overhead in concurrent applications that are synchronized with STMs and, thus, several researchers proposed optimization techniques to elide useless barriers. Many of the existing approaches decompose the STM's API in heterogeneous parts that allow the programmer to convey application-level information about the behavior of the memory locations to the instrumentation engine. Yet, this approach conflicts with one of the main advantages of an STM, which is to provide a transparent synchronization API, meaning that programmers just need to specify which operations are atomic, without knowing which data is accessed within those operations. That is the approach taken by Deuce [5], which provides a simple API based on an `@Atomic` annotation to mark methods that must have a transactional behavior.

So, approaches such as those proposed in [1, 3], which perform runtime or static analysis to identify whether memory locations being accessed are transaction-local, are better suited to the overall goal of STMs. Yet, none of these approaches accomplishes the performance of the proposals based on heterogeneous APIs. Our work is based on the proposal of Dragojevic et al. [3], which introduces the concept of *captured memory* as memory allocated inside a transaction that cannot escape (i.e., is *captured* by) its allocating transaction.

In this paper, we propose a new technique for *runtime capture analysis* in managed environments that is the first one to achieve performance results similar to those obtained with heterogeneous APIs, but without reducing the transparency of an STM. A distinctive aspect of our approach is that it performs a lightweight analysis when compared to other capture analysis implementations (e.g. [3]) and it has almost no overhead when the benchmark presents no opportunities for optimization, such as on the Kmeans and Ssca2 benchmarks from STAMP [6]. We implemented our technique in the Deuce STM framework, incorporating our capture analysis approach, which thus becomes available for any STM supported by Deuce, such as LSA [7] and TL2 [2] STMs.

2. Lightweight Capture Analysis

In Figure 1, we depict the code skeleton of a read and a write barrier using runtime capture analysis, which was adapted from the seminal proposal of Dragojevic et al. [3] to the Deuce environment. The new delegator—`ContextDelegatorCapturedState`—performs the capture analysis for each STM barrier (for simplification we just depict the code for the `int` type). There is a singleton `Context` object per thread that keeps track of the transaction data and that is part of the arguments of each STM barrier. As in Deuce, object fields are updated in place using the `sun.misc.Unsafe` pseudo-standard internal library.

```
static int onReadAccess(Object ref, int val, long addr,
    Context ctx){
    if (isCaptured(ref, ctx)) return val;
    return onFullReadAccess(ref, val, addr);
}
static void onWriteAccess(Object ref, int val, long addr,
    Context ctx){
    if (isCaptured(ref, ctx))
        UnsafeHolder.getUnsafe().putInt(ref, addr, val);
    else onFullWriteAccess(ref, val, addr);
}
```

Figure 1. The code skeleton of a read and a write barrier when using capture analysis.

Our capture analysis approach consists in labeling objects with something that uniquely identifies their creating transaction, and later if the accessing transaction corresponds to that label then we can avoid barriers. For this purpose, we keep a *fingerprint* in every

* This work was partially supported by FCT, both via INESC-ID multi-annual funding through the PIDDAC Program funds and via the RuLAM project (under contract number PTDC/EIA-EIA/108240/2008).

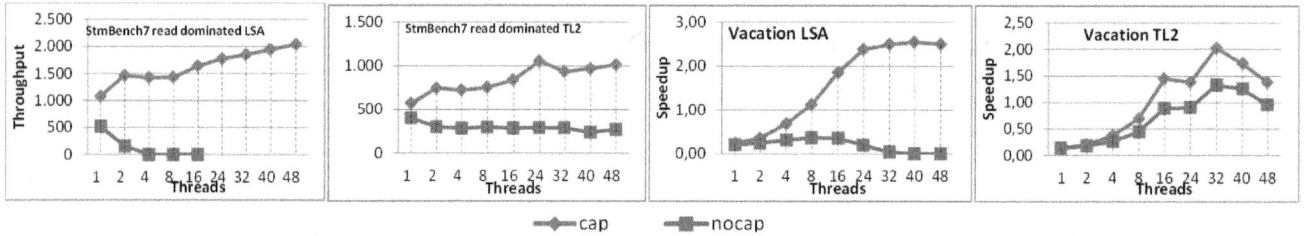

Figure 2. Performance results of the STMBench7 and Vacation for the LSA and TL2 STMs, comparing the execution with and without the capture analysis support, identified by the label *cap* and *nocap*, respectively. In the Vacation application we show the speedup relative to its sequential execution by one thread without instrumentation.

transaction, which is recorded in objects instantiated by a transaction, representing its *owner* transaction. Thus, the `isCaptured` algorithm just needs to check if the owner of the accessed object corresponds to the fingerprint of the executing transaction, which is accomplished with a simple identity comparison.

We use a newly allocated instance of class `Object` as a fingerprint and we let the garbage collection subsystem provide uniqueness and the ability to recycle unused fingerprints. Despite the additional memory management burden imposed by this solution, the fingerprint is just created when the transaction starts and corresponds to a very small cost of the entire transaction. So, the benefits of this approach overcome the associated overhead in memory.

In Figure 3, we show an example of three different transactions sharing a `Counter` object instantiated by one of those transactions—transaction 1. The bar bellow each thread has a number representing the `id` of each transaction. In this example thread A performs transactions 1 and 3, while thread B performs transaction 2. In this case, only transactions 2 and 3 perform full barriers, whereas transaction 1 returns and updates the `Counter` object in place. On the other hand, thread A has the same fingerprint of the `Counter` object, only during the execution of transaction 1, avoiding in this case a full barrier. After the completion of transaction 1, no other transaction will have the same fingerprint of the `Counter` object and all subsequent transactional accesses must perform a full barrier, as happens for transactions 2 and 3.

3. Performance evaluation

All the tests were performed on a machine with 4 AMD Opteron(tm) 6168 processors, each one with 12 cores, resulting in a total of 48 cores. The JVM version used was the 1.6.0 33-b03, running on Ubuntu with Linux kernel version 2.6.32.

In Figure 2 we can observe the performance improvement in the STMBench7 and the Vacation applications due to the capture analysis support. Many of the STMBench7 operations traverse a large graph of objects, leading to an intensive use of collection iterators. These iterators are transaction local and they have a large overhead when they are instrumented and performed with STM barriers. On the other hand, the Vacation performs an *initialization* phase (non transactional) where it instantiates several parameterized arrays that provide the required arguments for the execution of the Vacation operations. By moving this initialization into the *execution* phase, which is already atomic, we can turn the parameterized arrays in transaction local objects avoiding most of the arrays' barriers with the capture analysis support.

References

[1] Y. Afek, G. Korland, and A. Zilberstein, *Lowering STM overhead with static analysis*, LCPC'10, Springer-Verlag, 2011, pp. 31–45.

[2] D. Dice, O. Shalev, and N. Shavit, *Transactional locking II*, DISC'06, Springer-Verlag, 2006, pp. 194–208.

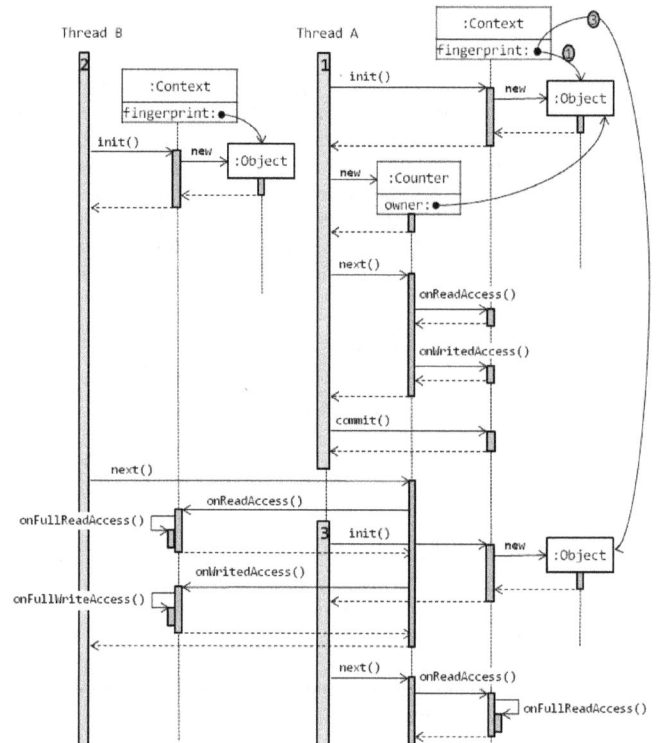

Figure 3. Three different transactions accessing a shared object `Counter` that was previously instantiated by transaction 1, which is the only one that avoids the execution of the full barriers when accessing that object.

[3] A. Dragojevic, Y. Ni, and A. Adl-Tabatabai, *Optimizing transactions for captured memory*, SPAA '09, ACM, 2009, pp. 214–222.

[4] R. Guerraoui, M. Kapalka, and J. Vitek, *STMBench7: a benchmark for software transactional memory*, EuroSys '07, ACM, 2007, pp. 315–324.

[5] G. Korland, N. Shavit, and P. Felber, *Noninvasive concurrency with java STM*, MultiProg 2010, 2010.

[6] C. Minh, J. Chung, C. Kozyrakis, and K. Olukotun, *STAMP: Stanford transactional applications for multi-processing*, Workload Characterization, 2008. IISWC 2008. IEEE International Symposium on, sept. 2008, pp. 35 –46.

[7] T. Riegel, P. Felber, and C. Fetzer, *A lazy snapshot algorithm with eager validation*, DISC'06, Springer-Verlag, 2006, pp. 284–298.

[8] R. Yoo, Y. Ni, A. Welc, B. Saha, A. Adl-Tabatabai, and H. Lee, *Kicking the tires of software transactional memory: why the going gets tough*, SPAA '08, ACM, 2008, pp. 265–274.

Scaling Data Race Detection for Partitioned Global Address Space Programs

Chang-Seo Park   Koushik Sen

University of California Berkeley
{parkcs,ksen}@eecs.berkeley.edu

Costin Iancu

Lawrence Berkeley National Laboratory
cciancu@lbl.gov

Categories and Subject Descriptors   D.2.4 [*Software/Program Verification*];   D.2.5 [*Testing and Debugging*]

Keywords   scalable data race detection; hierarchical sampling

1.   Introduction

Attaining good performance and efficacy on contemporary and future large scale High Performance Computing systems requires using hybrid programming models: OpenMP+MPI, UPC+MPI, Intel TBB + MPI or OpenMP+UPC. With multiple levels, *intra-node* parallelism is usually exploited using shared memory programming models, while *inter-node* parallelism is exploited using message passing or shared memory abstractions.

Bugs due to non-deterministic execution and conflicting memory accesses are fairly common and notoriously hard to detect in a parallelism rich environment. Previous work demonstrates the ability of dynamic program analyses to find concurrency bugs (data race, atomicity violations, deadlock) in shared memory programs. Dynamic program analyses have been also used to find *heisenbugs* in distributed memory programs: DAMPI [5] for MPI wildcard receives and UPC-Thrille [4] for data races in Unified Parallel C [2].

Data race detectors for shared memory programming trace individual memory references (load/store instructions) and reason about program semantics using a centralized analysis. The implementations are heavily optimized to reduce the instrumentation overhead and reportedly function with overhead lower than 10×. Bug finding for distributed memory programming models is made scalable by using a distributed analysis, but the current approaches illustrated by DAMPI and UPC-Thrille track only the calls into communication libraries. Thus, distributed memory tools need to be extended with tracking of memory references in order to handle hybrid programming. Furthermore, while acceptable when testing programs on workstations, the current overhead of dynamic program analyses is hard to stomach at the contemporary HPC concurrencies of tens of thousands of cores. Large scale analyses face the additional challenge to provide the lowest achievable overhead while still providing good coverage. While the adoption criteria for shared memory tools is "acceptable overhead", more stringent optimality criteria are desired at scale.

We present the first complete dynamic analysis for distributed memory programs able to track both memory references and communication calls. We extend the UPC-Thrille data race detection tool with tracking of individual memory references and discuss techniques to achieve low overhead for scientific applications running at scale. The results are validated for implementations of the NAS Parallel Benchmarks [1], as well as other fine-grained dynamic programming and tree search applications. We believe that our findings are widely applicable to any tool for data race detection in Partitioned Global Address Space languages: Chapel, Titanium, Co-Array Fortran, X10.

PPoPP'13,   February 23–27, 2013, Shenzhen, China.
ACM 978-1-4503-1922-5/13/02.

				Overhead				
Bench	LoC	Time(s)	#Races	NL	HA.5	IA	FA0	I
guppie	271	19.070	2 + 0	54.9%	54.2%	53.7%	DNF	74.9%
psearch	803	0.697	3 + 2	2.48%	10.8%	666%	8.01%	6490%
BT 3.3	9698	189.48	7 + 3	0.574%	1.16%	77.6%	DNF	-
CG 2.4	1654	39.573	0 + 1	1.09%	27.6%	57.6%	DNF	2579%
EP 2.4	678	54.453	0	-0.618%	0.805%	2.09%	4.74%	111%
FT 2.4	2289	62.663	2 + 0	0.601%	30.1%	121%	DNF	2744%
IS 2.4	1R36	5.130	0	0.376%	119%	159%	DNF	1201%
LU 3.3	6348	155.997	0 + 44	-0.425%	-	75.7%	DNF	-
MG 2.4	2229	18.687	2 + 4	0.336%	176%	632%	DNF	2020%
SP 3.3	5740	247.937	10 + 3	0.160%	0.861%	29.1%	DNF	-

Table 1: *Statistics for the NAS Parallel Benchmarks class C, guppie and psearch running on 16 cores. We report the races found as A + B, where A represents the number of races detected by the original UPC-Thrille tool (column NL: No-Local) and B represents the additional number of races detected with our extensions. Some execution overheads are omitted (-), due to configuration errors.*

2.   Scalable Data Race Detection

UPC-Thrille implements a dynamic program analysis running in two phases. In the first phase the program is executed with additional instrumentation and data about memory accesses, communication and synchronization operations is gathered and analyzed. For the purposes of this paper we distinguish three types of overhead: 1) *instrumentation overhead* is introduced by the checks to prune the non-interesting data accesses; 2) *computation overhead*, by the operations on internal data structures to manage the accesses and compute conflicting accesses; and 3) *communication overhead*, by the exchange of conflicting accesses between threads.

Analysis Overhead: The most widely used technique to reduce overhead is sampling of the program execution. Tools for shared memory use instruction level sampling while the distributed memory tools [4, 5] implement its equivalent by sampling the communication operations. For shared memory, Marino et al [3] recently introduced LiteRace which coarsens the granularity of the sampling at function boundaries: functions are compiled in two versions, instrumented and uninstrumented, each version being selected at runtime using heuristics. LiteRace showed better scalability and coverage than instruction level sampling when applied on several Microsoft programs, as well as Apache and Firefox.

We have experimented with both instruction level sampling and function level sampling on a Cray XE6 system composed of nodes containing two twelve-core AMD MagnyCours 2.1 GHz processors. The results in Table 1 indicate that instruction level sampling (IA) performs better than (FA) function level sampling for scientific programs. Instruction level sampling adds runtime overhead as high as 65× while many runs using function level sampling did not terminate, even when instrumenting only the first execution of a function (FA0). This result contradicts the trends reported for LiteRace and it is caused by a combination of two factors: 1) determining the locality of a reference is expensive in PGAS programs; and 2) scientific programs have long running loops, with billions of memory accesses per invocation in our benchmarks. Our results also indicate that in most settings instrumentation overhead dominates the computation and communication overhead during the analysis. The typical behavior is illustrated in Figure 1 (left). Note that with func-

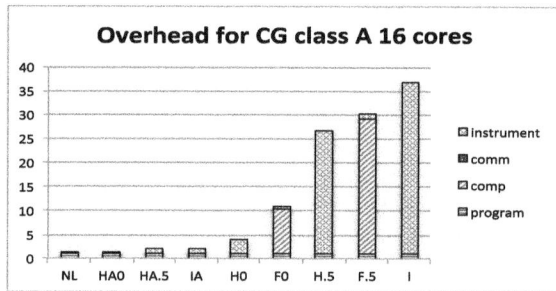

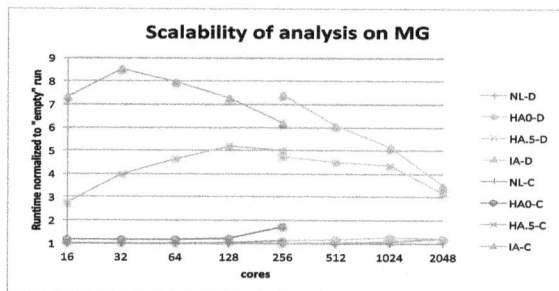

Figure 1: *Breakdown of data race detection overhead running on 16 cores (left). Scalability of the different sampling methods on NPB 2.4 MG, classes C and D (right).*

tion sampling (F.5, F0) the computation overhead increases due to the very large number of memory locations accessed in loops.

Reducing Overhead: For every memory reference there are two sources of runtime overhead. Instrumentation overhead is introduced to decide whether the reference should be recorded and computation overhead is introduced when recording the reference in the tool internal data structures. We employ a combination of techniques to improve the analysis performance: 1) we use program semantic information such as aliasing to prune un-interesting memory accesses; and 2) we use a hierarchical sampling approach where instrumentation is dynamically controlled both at the function level and at the instruction level.

The first optimization redüces the overhead of instrumentation by exploiting the insight that aliases are persistent in PGAS programs: once one is created it will point in the same memory region (private or global) for a long period of time. Using this we can eliminate the overhead introduced by looking up the physical memory layout inside the language runtime. Adding the aliasing heuristics to any of the tool methods greatly improves performance. For example, the overhead of instruction sampling (I) is reduced from 3600% to 105% with (IA) for CG class A running on 16 cores. The overhead of hierarchical sampling (H) is reduced from 2550% with (H.5) to 99% with (HA.5) and from 294% with (H0) to 17% with (HA0). The lowest overhead of data race detection is obtained by the HA approach.

Function sampling ((F) or (FA)) is faster than instruction sampling ((I) or (IA), respectively) for problems using small datasets, such as class A of the NAS Parallel Benchmarks. When increasing the data set size to B, C and D, function sampling in any flavor does not terminate, while the highest overhead observed for instruction sampling is $65\times$. From all benchmarks considered, the only exception happens for *psearch* and EP where (F) is roughly twice as fast as (I). *psearch* is a tree search benchmark which performs a constant and small amount of work per function, independent of the problem size: this is a common characteristic to many commercial applications. EP is an "Embarrassingly Parallel" benchmark where no global memory accesses are made and thus none need to be tracked. The performance reversal observed for most benchmarks contradicts the common intuition that function sampling performs better than instruction sampling.

Hierarchical sampling (H) performs better than both instruction sampling (I) and function sampling (F) as it reduces all three type of overhead: instrumentation, computation and communication. With hierarchical sampling we observe slowdowns as high as $20\times$ which is still unacceptable when running at scale. Applying the aliasing heuristic reduces the overhead of data race detection for both instruction level and hierarchical sampling. The maximum slowdown observed by (IA) is $10\times$ while the maximum slowdown for (I) is $65\times$. Similar results are observed for (HA) when compared to (H).

3. Results

Figure 1 (right) shows the performance of our approach when performing strong scaling experiments for the classes C and D of the

MG NAS Parallel Benchmark. For all experiments, the lowest overhead is introduced by the (HA) configuration and we are able to find all the races with less than 50% runtime overhead when running up to 2048 cores. In the case of the NAS Parallel Benchmarks class C on 16 cores, the weighted average overhead for all the benchmarks with (HA.5) was 11.9%.

For scalable data race detection, we needed to combine the two techniques: hierarchical sampling and aliasing heuristics. In the scalable versions of (IA) and (HA), the computation overhead is small. At large scale the communication overhead is also small due to the techniques presented in [4]. Overall, instrumentation overhead contributes the most to the slowdown caused by data race detection.

Races Found: In [4] we present a detailed discussion of the races found in the current program workload. Our extended implementation finds all these and, in addition, uncovers several other races. For a summary please see Table 1. For example, we detect a previously unknown race in NAS CG introduced by the presence of aliasing: memory is initialized using "local" pointers and distributed without synchronization to other threads using global pointers. In NAS BT, LU, and SP we uncover 50 additional races. Four of these races are real and confirmed by the tool; they occur when executing custom synchronization code similar to:

$$\texttt{signal(v = 1);} \quad \| \quad \texttt{wait(while(v == 0););.}$$

The remaining new data races are caused by data references separated by custom synchronization code. Identifying races in the presence of custom synchronization code is a common limitation of data race detection tools.

4. Conclusion

We present the first implementation of a data race detector for distributed memory programs that tracks all memory references. The goal of our implementation is to provide low overhead with good program coverage when running at scale. We propose two techniques to improve the scalability of data race detection in UPC programs: 1) hierarchical function and instruction level sampling; and 2) exploiting the runtime persistence of aliasing and locality in UPC applications. The results indicate that both techniques are required in practice.

References

[1] D. Bailey, T. Harris, W. Saphir, R. Van Der Wijngaart, A. Woo, and M. Yarrow. The NAS Parallel Benchmarks 2.0. *Technical Report NAS-95-010, NASA Ames Research Center*, 1995.

[2] W. W. Carlson, J. M. Draper, D. E. Culler, K. Yelick, and K. W. E. Brooks. Introduction to UPC and Language Specification, 1999.

[3] D. Marino, M. Musuvathi, and S. Narayanasamy. LiteRace: Effective Sampling for Lightweight Data-Race Detection. In *PLDI*, 2009.

[4] C.-S. Park, K. Sen, P. Hargrove, and C. Iancu. Efficient Data Race Detection for Distributed Memory Parallel Programs. In *Supercomputing (SC11)*, 2011.

[5] A. Vo, S. Aananthakrishnan, G. Gopalakrishnan, B. R. d. Supinski, M. Schulz, and G. Bronevetsky. A Scalable and Distributed Dynamic Formal Verifier for MPI Programs. In *Supercomputing (SC10)*, 2010.

Scalable Statistics Counters

Dave Dice

Oracle Labs
dave.dice@oracle.com

Yossi Lev

Oracle Labs
yossi.lev@oracle.com

Mark Moir

Oracle Labs
mark.moir@oracle.com

Abstract

Naive statistics counters that are commonly used to monitor system events and performance become a scalability bottleneck as systems become larger and more NUMA; furthermore some are so inaccurate that they are not useful. We present a number of techniques to address these problems, evaluating solutions in terms of performance, scalability, space overhead, and accuracy.

1. Problem

Large software systems may include thousands of statistics counters, often implemented using an operation such as compare-and-swap (CAS) in a retry loop, usually with random exponential backoff to mitigate contention for a given counter.

Practioners sometimes use "unsynchronized" counters that avoid the overhead of a CAS retry loop, reasoning that "occasional" lost updates due to concurrent unsynchronized updates is an acceptable price to pay for the resulting performance improvement. Unfortunately, as we show below, none of these techniques is effective in larger and increasingly NUMA systems.

Our experimemnts were conducted on an Oracle T5440 series machine running Solaris 10; this system comprises four Niagara T2+ SPARC chips, each with eight cores, each of which contains two pipelines with four hardware thread contexts per pipeline. Thus, there is a total of 256 hardware thread contexts; they run at 1.4 GHz. Each Niagara T2+ chip is a NUMA node, and the nodes are connected via a central coherence hub.

Each thread alternates between incrementing a counter chosen at random from 7,500 counters and incrementing a specific one of them. This arrangement models a system with many counters, of which only one experiences high contention. Between increments, threads perform "external work" (by pausing for an amount of time determined by a parameter), modeling other application activity. We reflect the effect of this parameter as the fraction of time spent performing external work in a single-thread run using a simple CAS retry loop to increment counters.

The results shown in Figure 1 are for 99% external work: relatively low contention. The simple CAS-based counter (CAS) does not scale well beyond 8 threads, and scales negatively beyond 32 threads. Random exponential backoff (RBO) mitigates the effects of contention, but still scales negatively beyond 32 threads. The unsynchronized solution (Serial) scales much better, but as the table shows, the fraction of updates lost by the contended counter due to

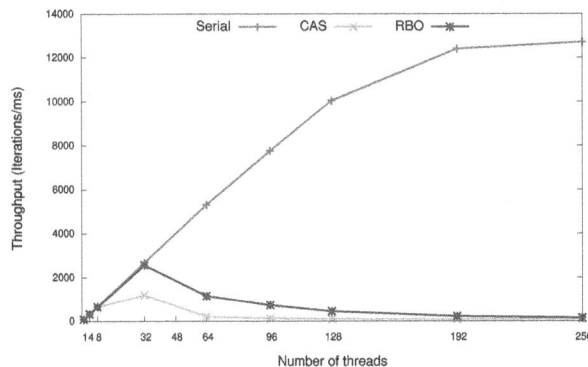

#T	1	4	8	32	64	128	256
% lost	0.00	3.01	6.11	22.65	42.42	78.68	98.13

Figure 1. Naive statistics counters, 99% external work. Table shows fraction of updates lost by Serial counter.

the lack of synchronization grows much more quickly than naive reasoning about "occasional" upates suggests. Therefore, we claim that the Serial approach is useless on NUMA machines because it loses most of the information for the most important counters, i.e., those incremented most frequently.

A common suggestion is to use per-thread counter components that are combined when reading the counter. This approach can dramatically improve scalability, but increases space consumption considerably (especially when per-thread components are padded to avoid false sharing), and imposes significant overhead and constraints on read operations. Perhaps more importantly, while in some monolithic systems it is straightforward to map thread IDs to per-thread components, in many other contexts (e.g., dynamically scheduled tasks) this approach is inconvenient or inapplicable.

2. Our contributions

We have explored scalable statistics counter algorithms that differ in space overhead and accuracy properties. Unlike the naive Serial solution, even our approximate counters have well understood and controlled error behavior. In this short paper, we briefly overview some of the counters we have explored; interested readers may contact the authors for more detailed descriptions.

2.1 Precise counters

Some techniques we explored that require zero or very little additional space overhead were inspired by previous NUMA-aware locks, such as [2]. These techniques improve throughput by encouraging consecutive increments by threads on the same NUMA node, for example by giving one node priority and having threads

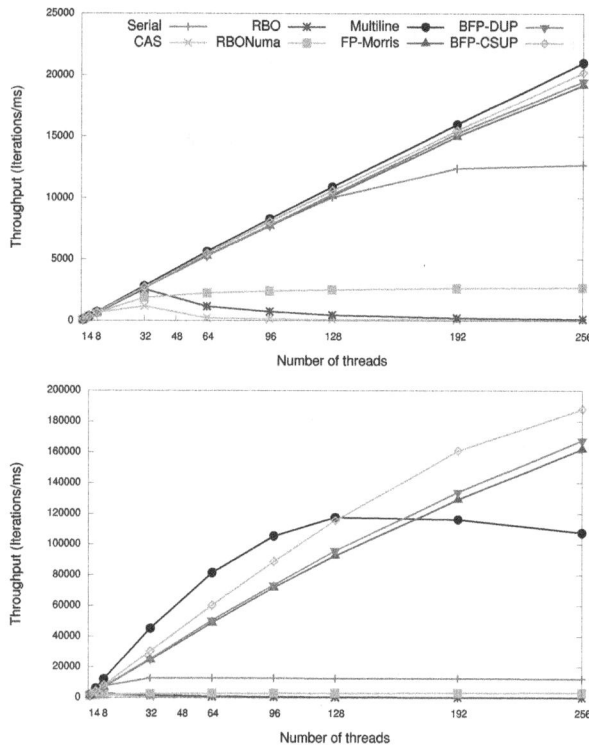

Figure 2. Top: 99% external work, bottom: 70% external work.

on that node attempt to increment the counter more aggressively than threads on non-priority nodes.

One way to identify the current priority node is by using a few middle bits in the counter, chosen so that a node keeps priority for some number of increments, but not for too long. One of our contributions is a more flexible algorithm that gives priority to the node that last modified the counter, with some additional mechanisms to control fairness. With 99% external work, this solution outperforms the commonly-used non-NUMA-friendly RBO solution by a factor of 20 with large numbers of threads.

If higher space overhead is acceptable, we can allocate a counter component per NUMA node, with threads incrementing the "local" component (Multiline). Unlike solutions that use per-thread components, such solutions can easily be used with dynamically scheduled tasks, dynamic numbers of threads, etc. Although components for different NUMA nodes should be in different cache lines to avoid inter-node false sharing, the components of different counters for the same NUMA node can be colocated within a cache line. Furthermore, it is not difficult to dynamically allocate the additional space only for counters that turn out to be contended, thus avoiding the overhead for the vast majority of counters.

2.2 Approximate counters

Our first approximate counter is inspired by ideas due to Morris [1] in 1978 to enable (single threaded) counting to values larger than 2^8 using only 8 bits, with controlled relative error. Briefly, if the 8-bit variable stores a value $C < 256$, the *projected value* $f(C)$ estimates the number of increments that have been performed. Each increment operation adds one to the stored value with probability $1/(f(C + 1) - f(C))$, where C is the current stored value. Because we add one to the stored value with probability inversely proportional to the amount added to the projected value, the expected projected value is the number of increment operations performed.

To keep the relative error low, Morris chose f such that the probability to update the stored value decreases exponentially with every update. This way, when the projected value is low, we almost always increment, and thus keep the relative error low, but when it is high, we increment less frequently (and increase the projected value by a higher value). The faster the update probability decreases, the higher the expected relative error is. To avoid expensive probability calculations for every increment operation, Morris's algorithm uses a precalculated 256-entry probability table.

We implemented several counters that use a similar technique to reduce the update frequency for counters that are frequently incremented. Our first variant (FP-Morris) is more efficient than the original Morris algorithm and does not require precalculating a table of probabilities for all values of C (which would be impractical given that we use 32-bit counters to allow much larger counter values than Morris did). Each increment operation simply compares a random number to a stored floating point value (to decide whether to update it), and in case the stored value is to be updated, it is simply multiplied by a precalculated floating point constant.

FP-Morris counters are scalable, efficient and compact, but floating point operations cannot be used in some contexts. We therefore developed counters that are based on a similar approach to FP-Morris, but use a "binary floating point" representation, restricting update probabilities to always be a negative power of two (i.e., we add 2^i to the projected value with probability of $1/2^i$). This avoids the need to use floating point operations. With this restriction, decreasing the update probability every time the stored value is updated would cause the update probability to decrease too quickly, allowing the relative error to become too large. Instead, multiple updates are performed with the same probability (by increasing the mantissa of the binary floating point stored value) before the probability is reduced (by increasing the exponent).

One variant—Determinisitic Update Policy (DUP)—increases the mantissa until it reaches a threshold before increasing the exponent, thereby reducing the update probability for subsequent increment operations. Another variant—Contention-Sensitive Update Policy (CSUP)—usually decreases the update probability only in case of contention for the counter. This way, when the update probability becomes low enough to avoid further contention, it stops decreasing, resulting in lower relative error in practice. All of our probabilistic counting algorithms use only 32 bits per counter.

With 99% external work, Multiline and all of the probabilistic counters (with accuracy parameters chosen for a desired 1% bound on relative standard deviation) scale well up to 256 threads (see Figure 2). However, with 70% external work, contention on Multiline's per-NUMA-node components causes a bottleneck, while the probabilistic counters continue to scale well, even under maximum contention (zero external work, not shown). CSUP outperforms the other methods, primarily because the uncontended counters remain accurate and are always updated with probability one, thus avoiding the need to generate a random number. The highest relative standard deviation we have observed for any probabilistic counter is less than 3%, and for CSUP, it never exceeded 0.25%.

This shows that we can build scalable and efficient statistics counters with low space overhead and good accuracy properties.

References

[1] R. Morris. Counting large numbers of events in small registers. *Commun. ACM*, 21(10):840–842, Oct. 1978. ISSN 0001-0782. doi: 10.1145/359619.359627. URL http://doi.acm.org/10.1145/359619.359627.

[2] Z. Radovic and E. Hagersten. Hierarchical backoff locks for nonuniform communication architectures. In *Proceedings of the 9th International Symposium on High-Performance Computer Architecture*, HPCA '03, 2003.

Swift/T: Scalable Data Flow Programming
for Many-Task Applications

Justin M. Wozniak

Argonne National Laboratory &
University of Chicago
wozniak@mcs.anl.gov

Timothy G. Armstrong

University of Chicago
tga@uchicago.edu

Michael Wilde

Argonne National Laboratory &
University of Chicago
wilde@mcs.anl.gov

Daniel S. Katz

Argonne National Laboratory &
University of Chicago
d.katz@ieee.org

Ewing Lusk

Argonne National Laboratory
lusk@mcs.anl.gov

Ian T. Foster

Argonne National Laboratory &
University of Chicago
foster@mcs.anl.gov

Abstract

Swift/T, a novel programming language implementation for highly
scalable data flow programs, is presented.

Categories and Subject Descriptors D.3.2 [*Programming Languages*]: Language Classifications— Concurrent, distributed, and
parallel languages; Data-flow languages

General Terms Languages

Keywords MPI; ADLB; Swift; Turbine; exascale; concurrency;
dataflow; futures

1. Introduction

Many important application classes that are driving the requirements for extreme-scale systems—branch and bound, stochastic
programming, materials by design, uncertainty quantification—can
be productively expressed as many-task data flow programs. The
data flow programming model of the Swift parallel scripting language [6] can elegantly express, through implicit parallelism, the
massive concurrency demanded by these applications while retaining the productivity benefits of a high-level language.

However, the centralized single-node evaluation model of
the previously developed Swift implementation limits scalability.
Overcoming this important limitation is difficult, as evidenced by
the absence of any massively-scalable data flow languages in current use.

We present here Swift/T, a new data flow language implementation designed for extreme scalability. Its technical innovations include a distributed data flow engine that balances program evaluation across massive numbers of nodes using data-flow-driven
task execution and a distributed data store for global data access.
Swift/T extends the Swift data flow programming model of external executables with file-based data passing to finer-grained applications using in-memory functions and in-memory data.

PPoPP'13, February 23–27, 2013, Shenzhen, China.
ACM 978-1-4503-1922-5/13/02.

We have evaluated the performance and programmability of
Swift/T for a collaboration graph analysis and optimization application, a branch-and-bound game solver, and synthetic stress
tests of language constructs. Our tests show that Swift/T can already scale to 128K compute cores with 85% efficiency for 100-
second tasks. Thus, Swift/T provides a scalable parallel programming model for productively expressing the outer levels of highly-
parallel many-task applications. The benefits of these advances are
illustrated by considering the Swift code fragment in Figure 1.

```
1    int X = 1000, Y = 1000;
2    int A[][];
3    int B[];
4    foreach x in [0:X-1] {
5      foreach y in [0:Y-1] {
6        if (check(x, y)) {
7          A[x][y] = g(f(x), f(y))
8        } else {
9          A[x][y] = 0;
10       }}
11   B[x] = sum(A[x]);
12   }
```

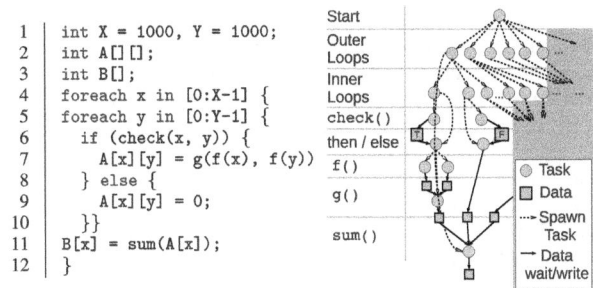

Figure 1. Simple data flow application.

The implicit parallelism of this code generates 1 million concurrent executions of the inner block of expressions, invoking as many
as 4M function calls (3M within conditional logic). Previously, the
single-node Swift engine would perform the work of sending these
leaf function tasks to distributed CPUs at <500 tasks/sec. The new
Swift/T architecture, in contrast, can distribute the evaluation of the
outer loop to *many* CPUs, each of which can in turn distribute the
inner loop to many additional CPUs. The diagram on the right illustrates how evaluation of the entire program — not just the external
tasks at the leaves of the call graph — can utilize many nodes to
rapidly generate massive numbers of leaf tasks. Tasks in this model
are managed by Turbine and ADLB, described below.

2. Applications

Ensemble studies involving different methodologies such as uncertainty quantification, parameter estimation, graph pruning, and
inverse modeling all require the ability to generate and dispatch

tasks on the order of millions to the distributed resources. *Regional watershed analysis and hydrology* are investigated by the Soil and Water Assessment Tool (SWAT), which analyzes hundreds of thousands of data files via MATLAB scripts on hundreds of cores. This application will utilize tens of thousands of cores and more data in the future. SWAT is a motivator for our work because of the large number of data files. *Biomolecular analysis* by using ModFTDock results in a large quantity of available tasks [3], and represents a complex, multi-stage workflow.

3. Programming Model

We seek to provide a system that allows code written by non-experts to run at extreme scale. This goal may be infeasible in a general model for computation. However, we focus on many-task applications, which exhibit simpler coordination patterns.

Hierarchical programming: We assume that much performance-critical code will remain in lower level languages such as C, Fortran, or even assembly, using threads or MPI for fine-grained parallelism. Data flow scripting provides a powerful mechanism for coordinating these high-performance components, as it enables fault-tolerance, dynamic load balancing and flexible, rapid composition of components. In Swift, each lower-level component is viewed as a black box with well-defined inputs and outputs.

Implicit parallelism: Swift makes parallelism implicit, similarly to other data flow programming languages such as Sisal [2] and Id [5]. When control enters a code block, any Swift statement in that block can execute concurrently with other statements. This concurrent execution is feasible because of the functional nature of Swift, where we avoid mutable state and use write-once variables pervasively to schedule execution based on data dependencies. Each operation, down to basic arithmetic, can be realized as an asynchronous task, eligible to be executed anywhere in the distributed-memory computer.

For implicit and pervasive parallelism to be manageable, we need a simple model for language semantics. It has been argued [1] that parallel languages should have a deterministic sequential interpretation for most language features, with non-determinism introduced only through explicit non-deterministic constructs. All core data types in Swift, *including arrays*, are guaranteed to be deterministic and referentially transparent.

Turbine execution model: Turbine enables distributed execution of large numbers of user functions and of control logic used to compose them. Turbine requires the compiler to break user program code into many discrete *fragments*, to enable all work to be load balanced as discrete tasks. These fragments are either user-defined *leaf functions*, such as external compiled procedures or executables, or *control fragments* for data flow coordination logic. Turbine engines execute control tasks, while workers execute leaf functions, as shown in Figure 2. Execution of a Turbine control logic fragment may produce additional control fragments that are redistributed via ADLB. Turbine tracks data dependencies between tasks in order to know when each is eligible to run. Turbine provides a globally-addressable *distributed future store* [7], which drives data-dependent execution and allows typed data operations.

The Asynchronous Dynamic Load Balancer (ADLB) is an MPI library for distributing tasks (work units) among worker processes [4]. ADLB is a highly scalable system without a single bottleneck, and has been successfully used physics applications.

Mapping Swift functions onto Turbine tasks: Computationally intensive non-Swift functions such as compiled functions or command-line applications execute as Turbine leaf functions, while control flow in the Swift language is implemented by using Turbine control tasks. If, as is often the case, control flow in a Swift function requires multiple waits for data, that Swift function must be compiled to multiple control fragments.

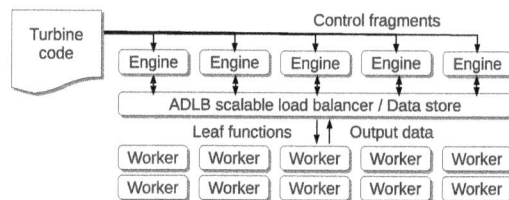

Figure 2. Architecture of Swift/T runtime: Engines evaluate Swift language semantics; workers execute leaf-task applications.

Limited non-determinism: Some patterns are difficult to express efficiently with write-once variables, for example, branch pruning in branch and bound algorithms and shared counters. *Updatable* variables can better support such patterns. An updatable variable is initialized to a fixed number, and can then be updated with one of several commutative update operations. The value retrieved by each read will not be deterministic, but the commutativity property makes the non-determinism more usable than a variable supporting arbitrary mutation.

Swift/T extension functions: Since Swift/T is a many-task computing language, making external code callable from Swift is crucial. Currently we support applications that call C/C++/Fortran functions from Swift scripts, by using SWIG to automatically generate wrappers.

4. Future Work

We are aware of many potential optimizations to improve Swift/T performance, such as caching, relaxing consistency, and coalescing Turbine operations at compile or run time. We intend to explore other load balancing methods and data-aware scheduling and expect that advances in this area will yield many improvements.

Acknowledgments

This research is supported by the U.S. DOE Office of Science under contract DE-AC02-06CH11357, FWP-57810. Computing resources were provided by the Argonne Leadership Computing Facility. This material was based on work (by DSK) supported by the National Science Foundation, while working at the Foundation. Any opinion, finding, and conclusions or recommendations expressed in this material are those of the authors and do not necessarily reflect the views of the National Science Foundation.

References

[1] R. L. Bocchino, Jr., V. S. Adve, S. V. Adve,, M. Snir. Parallel programming must be deterministic by default. In *Workshop Hot Topics in Parallelism: HotPar'09*.

[2] J. T. Feo, D. C. Cann,, R. R. Oldehoeft. A report on the Sisal language project. *J. Parallel and Distributed Computing*, 1990.

[3] M. Hategan, J. Wozniak,, K. Maheshwari. Coasters: uniform resource provisioning and access for scientific computing on clouds and grids. In *Proc. Utility and Cloud Computing*.

[4] E. L. Lusk, S. C. Pieper,, R. M. Butler. More scalability, less pain: A simple programming model and its implementation for extreme computing. *SciDAC Review*, 2010.

[5] K. R. Traub. A compiler for the MIT tagged-token dataflow architecture. Tech. rep., Massachusetts Institute of Technology, 1986.

[6] M. Wilde, M. Hategan, J. M. Wozniak, B. Clifford, D. S. Katz,, I. Foster. Swift: A language for distributed parallel scripting. *Par. Comp.*, 2011.

[7] J. M. Wozniak, T. G. Armstrong, E. L. Lusk, D. S. Katz, M. Wilde,, I. T. Foster. Turbine: A distributed memory data flow engine for many-task applications. In *Int'l Workshop Scalable Workflow Enactment Engines and Technologies (SWEET) 2012*.

TeamWork: Synchronizing Threads Globally to Detect Real Deadlocks for Multithreaded Programs

Yan Cai[†], Ke Zhai[‡], Shangru Wu[†], and W.K. Chan[†*]

† Department of Computer Science
City University of Hong Kong
Tat Chee Avenue, Hong Kong
{yancai2, shangruwu2}@student.cityu.edu.hk
wkchan@cityu.edu.hk

‡ Department of Computer Science
The University of Hong Kong
Pokfulam Road, Hong Kong
kzhai@cs.hku.hk

Abstract

This paper presents the aim of TeamWork, our ongoing effort to develop a comprehensive dynamic deadlock confirmation tool for multithreaded programs. It also presents a refined object abstraction algorithm that refines the existing stack hash abstraction.

Categories and Subject Descriptors D.2.5 [**Software Engineering**]: Testing and Debugging – testing tools. D.4.1 [**Operating Systems**]: Processing Management –deadlocks, synchronization, threads.

General Terms Reliability, Verification

Keywords deadlock detection, object abstraction, thread scheduling

1. Introduction

Deadlocks in multithreaded programs are difficult to both expose and reproduce, and yet they are critical bugs that should be fixed. Existing dynamic detection techniques that rely on systematic thread scheduling only guarantee a low probability to trigger real deadlocks [2]. Dynamic randomized deadlock confirmation techniques [3][6] that attempt to heuristically trigger a real deadlock in a new run with respect to some predictive run show their promise to significantly improve the deadlock detection probability over the systematic thread scheduling approach. Nonetheless, the current generation of randomized deadlock confirmation actively manipulate thread schedules of an execution *only when* a thread is about to acquire a lock at a position (site) predicted to form a deadlock in a predictive run that has been run beforehand. These techniques have no ability to coordinate threads (that are predicted to form a deadlock occurrence) and yet deadlock is a *global* property that threads should be carefully synchronized (instead of in a randomized manner) to trigger them.

This paper reports the status of our ongoing project for the dynamic confirmation of *resource deadlocks* in large-scale multithreaded programs. This work has not been generalized to consider deadlocks that involve communication primitives (e.g., the *wait−notify* primitives in Java) or conditional variables (e.g., to implement user-defined synchronization idioms).

In a program execution, a resource deadlock occurs if every thread in a set waits for a lock that another thread in the same set holds. Existing predictive techniques usually either identify cyclic subgraphs in lock-order graphs [1] or infer cyclic dependency

chains from a lock dependency set [3][6]. We refer to their reported cases as *tentative deadlocks*.

Figure 1 is a resource deadlock example: Two threads t_1 and t_2 compete for two locks l_1 and l_2. A deadlock occurs when (1) t_1 has acquired l_1 at line 2 and requests to acquire l_2 at line 3 and (2) t_2 has acquired l_2 at line 9 and requests to acquire l_1 at line 10. On the other hand, if t_1 executes lines 1−6 followed by t_2 executing lines 7−12, then the execution produces no deadlock occurrence. Based on the second execution, deadlock prediction technique such as [3] is able to report a tentative deadlock in the form of cyclic lock dependency chain [3]: $\langle\langle t_1, l_2, \{l_1, m\}\rangle, \langle t_2, l_1, \{l_2\}\rangle\rangle$, which means that the thread t_1 requests the lock l_2 while holding the set of locks $\{l_1, m\}$ and the thread t_2 requests the lock l_1 while holding a set of locks $\{l_2\}$.

In the rest of this paper, we present a brief overview of our ongoing effort to trigger resource deadlocks hidden in multithreaded programs. It also presents an object abstraction algorithm that our framework is expected to use.

2. Our Framework

2.1 The Aim of the TeamWork Component

We are developing a framework to supports the dynamic detection of concurrency bugs in multithreaded programs. The first two components of the framework include a lock trace reduction component [4] for predictive data race detection [5] and a dynamic predictive deadlock detector [3] to produce tentative deadlocks. We are developing TeamWork as its third component, which is for dynamic confirmation of the tentative deadlocks if such deadlocks are real deadlocks. All these three components share the common theme that the casual dependencies among threads with respect to the threading and locking operations can be harvested to significantly improve the cost-effectiveness of the framework.

In this section, we outline our onging work on TeamWork.

We conjecture that in real-world applications, a program execution visits a series of critical states before reaching a tentative deadlocked state. We are investigating methods to identify such critical states. In general, a critical state over multiple threads forms a thread synchronization condition, which this paper refers to it as a *barrier*.

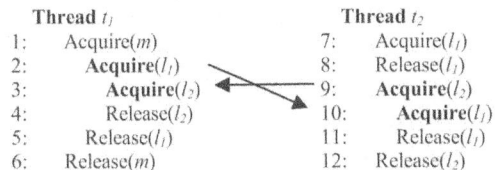

This work is supported in part by the General Research Fund of the Research Grant Council of Hong Kong (project nos. 111410 and 123512).

```
        Thread t₁                    Thread t₂
1:      Acquire(m)            7:     Acquire(l₁)
2:        Acquire(l₁)         8:     Release(l₁)
3:          Acquire(l₂)       9:     Acquire(l₂)
4:          Release(l₂)       10:      Acquire(l₁)
5:        Release(l₁)         11:    Release(l₁)
6:      Release(m)            12:    Release(l₂)
```

Figure 1. An example deadlock scenario (the deadlock is highlighted)

Once they could be identified, we plan to synchronize selected threads at selected barriers so that the operations performed by these threads could be executed by stages. TeamWork aims at escorting threads to concurrently pass through all the selected barriers before reaching the deadlocked state. If this is successful, TeamWork will be novel in its barrier-based strategy to confirm real concurrency bugs in general and real deadlocks in particular.

There are some considerations that we are studying for this component of our framework. For instance, a subset (possibly a singleton set) of all identified barriers can be used to synchronize threads at the same time. The same subset may be used multiple times to manipulate the same execution before the execution reaching the deadlocked state. Moreover, the number of threads selected among different occurrences of the same subset (or different subsets) of all the selected barriers can be non-identical. The thread selection strategy with respect to each barrier will be investigated. We will also study the complexity of large-scale real-world multithreaded programs to make TeamWork both scalable and effective to deal with this interesting class of program. As such, TeamWork is an umbrella of techniques instead of one technique.

2.2 Object Frequency Abstraction

Our framework relies on an effective but abstract representation to both effectively and efficiently models various entities (e.g., a program state needed in the barriers).

For dynamic confirmation of concurrency bugs, one key challenge is to compute an *object abstraction* [3][6] so that a thread or an event in a confirmation run is able to approximately map to the "same" thread or the "same" event occurred in another (e.g., predictive) run. An exact mapping may not be able to be developed.

We have developed an *instance* form of object abstraction [3][6][8] with a reference to *memory indexing* [7]. This form of object abstraction used the hash value for the program stack content (refer to as *stack hash*) [8] for matching efficiency. It also refines the precision of the existing proposal [3][6] by distinguishing the number of times that the same combination of a particular *thread* (and *lock*) *abstraction* (in the sense of existing form [3][6]) and a particular *stack hash value* has been used for the creation of the abstraction. We refer to it as the ***object frequency abstraction***:

- For a lock object or a thread object o, its abstraction $abs(o)$ is denoted by $\langle thread\_abs, call\_stack\_hash, newObj_{counter}\rangle$, where the couple $\langle call\_stack\_hash, newObj_{counter}\rangle$ is the site (i.e., $site(o)$) of the object.

- For a lock acquisition event e, the abstraction $abs(e)$ is denoted by $\langle thread\_abs, lock\_abs, call\_stack\_hash, acq_{counter}\rangle$, where the couple $\langle call\_stack\_hash, acq_{counter}\rangle$ is the site (i.e., $site(e)$) of the event.

In the above two abstraction definitions, $thread\_abs$ is the abstraction of the thread [3] to produce the *new object* or *lock acquisition* events, $lock\_abs$ is a lock abstraction [3], and $call\_stack\_hash$ is the *hash value* [8] for the combination of call stack value and a program statement $stmt$ being executed by the thread. Both $acq_{counter}$ and $newObj_{counter}$ are thread-local mappings from $thread\_abs$ and $call\_stack\_hash$ and from $thread\_abs$, $lock\_abs$, and $call\_stack\_hash$ to an integer, respectively. Algorithm 1 shows the algorithm to compute the object frequency abstraction for object and locking event creations. The object frequency abstractions for the other events and objects can be defined and computed similarly.

In the algorithm, each call to a function `getProgramCall-Stack` (k) at lines 3 and 8 returns the sequence of the top k (inputted at line 1) values of the program call stack (or the whole call stack if there are less than k values). Line 2 initializes the abstraction of the

---

Algorithm 1: Object Frequency Abstraction

Initialization

1:    $k := input()$; //a user specified value, by default, it is 8 according //to [8].
2:    $abs\,(main\_thread) := \langle -1, -1, -1\rangle$;

OnCreateAnObject (Thread t, Object o, Statement $stmt$):

3:    Vector $st := getProgramCallStack(k)$;
4:    st.push $(stmt)$;
5:    $call\_stack\_hash := hash(st)$;
6:    $newObj_{counter} = Occurrence_{counter1}\,(abs(t), call\_stack\_hash)$;
7:    $abs(o) := \langle \boldsymbol{abs}(t), \boldsymbol{call\_stack\_hash}, \boldsymbol{newObj_{counter}}\rangle$;

OnAcquireALock (Thread t, Lock m, Statement $stmt$, Event e):

8:    Vector $st := getProgramCallStack(k)$;
9:    st.push $(stmt)$;
10:   $call\_stack\_hash := hash(st)$;
11:   $acq_{counter} := Occurrence_{counter2}\,(abs(t), abs(m),$
                     $call\_stack\_hash)$;
12:   $abs(e) := \langle \boldsymbol{abs}(t), \boldsymbol{abs}(m), \boldsymbol{call\_stack\_hash}, \boldsymbol{acq_{counter}}\rangle$

---

main thread (denoted by `main_thread`) by arbitrary values as its abstraction. The procedure `OnCreateAnObject` (lines 3–7) computes $abs(o)$ for an object o. It firstly computes the above-mentioned hash value, finds out the number of times that the couple of this hash value and the thread associated with o have previously been mapped via $Occurrence_{counter1}()$ (which is a map from the inputted pair to the occurrence times of this pair). It then constructs $abs(o)$. The procedure `OnAcquireALock` (lines 8–12) computes $abs(e)$ for a lock acquisition event e, which can be interpreted similar to `OnCreateAnObject`. The function $Occurrence_{counter2}()$ can be interpreted similar to $Occurrence_{counter1}()$.

Using Algorithm 1, in our experimentation, the executions for deadlock confirmation only encounters very few occurrences of object mismatches. We leave the report of the experimental results as a future work.

3. Conclusion

In this paper, we have presented the aim of TeamWork. We have also presented a refined object abstraction algorithm. Future work includes the formulation of the concrete strategy of TeamWork.

References

[1] R. Agarwal, L. Wang, and S. D. Stolle, 2005. Detecting potential deadlocks with static analysis and run-time monitoring. In *Proceedings of the 2005 IBM Verification Conference*.

[2] S. Burckhardt, P. Kothari, M. Musuvathi, and S. Nagarakatte, 2010. A randomized scheduler with probabilistic guarantees of finding bugs. In *Proceedings of ASPLOS'10*, 167–178.

[3] Y. Cai and W.K. Chan, 2012. MagicFuzzer: Scalable deadlock detection for large-scale applications. In *Proceedings of ICSE'12*, 606–616.

[4] Y. Cai and W.K. Chan, to appear. Lock trace reduction for multithreaded programs. *IEEE Transactions on Parallel and Distributed Systems*.

[5] Y. Cai and W.K. Chan, 2011. LOFT: Redundant synchronization event removal for data race detection. In *Proceedings of ISSRE'11*, 160–169.

[6] P. Joshi, C.S. Park, K. Sen, and M. Naik, 2009. A randomized dynamic program analysis technique for detecting real deadlocks. In *Proceedings of PLDI'09*, 110–120.

[7] W. N. Sumner and X. Zhang, 2010. Memory indexing: Canonicalizing addresses across executions. In *Proceedings of FSE '10*, 217–226.

[8] H. Jula, D. Tralamazza, C. Zamfir, and G. Candea, 2008. Deadlock Immunity: enabling systems to defend against deadlocks. In *Proceedings of OSDI'08*, 295–308.

Towards an Energy Estimator for Fault Tolerance Protocols

Mohammed el Mehdi Diouri
Olivier Glück   Laurent Lefèvre

INRIA Avalon Team
Laboratoire de l'Informatique du Parallélisme
CNRS, ENS Lyon, INRIA, Université Lyon 1
{Mehdi.Diouri,Olivier.Gluck,Laurent.Lefevre}@ens-lyon.fr

Franck Cappello

Laboratoire de Recherche en Informatique - NCSA
INRIA and University of Illinois at Urbana-Champaign

cappello@illinois.edu

Abstract

Checkpointing protocols have different energy consumption depending on parameters like application features and platform characteristics. To select a protocol for a given execution, we propose an energy estimator that relies on an energy calibration of the considered platform and a user description of the execution settings.

Categories and Subject Descriptors   D.4.5 [*Operating Systems*]: Reliability - Checkpoint/restart, Fault-tolerance.

Keywords   Fault tolerance protocols; Checkpointing; Energy Consumption; Estimation.

1. Introduction

Currently, in order to evaluate the power consumption of a fault tolerant protocol for any particular execution, the only approach is to pre-execute the application and monitor the energy consumption. This approach is not practical for protocol selection since it does not allow to evaluate power consumption before the execution. To address this problem, this paper[1] proposes an estimator of the energy consumed by a particular fault tolerant protocol for a large variety of execution configurations. It can also be used to compare fault tolerant protocols from given execution configurations.

Our study focuses on the fault free execution of coordinated, uncoordinated, and hierarchical [3] protocols. Checkpointing consists in storing a snapshot image of the current application state that can be later on used for restarting the execution in case of failure. In uncoordinated protocols, message logging consists in saving on each sender process the messages sent on a given storage media. In coordinated protocols, a coordination consists in synchronizing the processes before taking the checkpoints. If some processes have inflight messages at the coordination time, all the other ones are actively polling until these messages are sent.

Our energy estimation relies on an energy calibration of the considered platform and a user description of the execution settings. Section 2 presents the calibration approach while Section 3

---

[1] This research is partially supported by the INRIA-Illinois Joint Laboratory on Petascale Computing.

presents the estimation methodology. Section 4 concludes the paper and presents some future works.

2. Calibration approach

Estimating the energy consumption of a given high-level operation *op* (message logging, coordination, or checkpointing) is really complex as it depends on a large set of parameters. In message logging, the basic operation is to write the message on a given media storage. In checkpointing, the basic operation is to write the checkpoint on a reliable media storage. In coordination, the basic operations are the active polling during the transmission of inflight messages and the synchronization that occurs when there is no more inflight message. These operations are associated to parameters that depend not only on the protocols (checkpointing interval, checkpointing storage destination, etc.) but also on the application features (volume of messages exchanged between processes, etc.), and on the hardware used (number of nodes, network technology, etc.).

In order to estimate accurately the energy consumption of a high-level operation, our estimator needs to take into consideration all the parameters. Our framework integrates an automated calibration. The goal of this calibration is to gather energy knowledge of all the identified operations according to the hardware used in the platform. At this end, we developed a set of simple benchmarks that extracts for each node i, the energy consumption e_{op}^i for each operation *op* encountered in fault tolerance protocols: $e_{op}^i = p_{op}^i \cdot t_{op}^i$ where t_{op}^i is the time required to perform *op* and p_{op}^i the power consumption during t_{op}^i.

2.1 Power consumption p_{op}

For a node i, the power consumption of an operation *op* is:
$$p_{op}^i = p_{idle}^i + \Delta p_{op}^i$$
p_{idle}^i is the power consumption when the node i is idle and Δp_{op}^i is the extra power cost due to *op*. In [1], we showed that p_{idle}^i may be different even for identical nodes. Thus, we gather p_{idle}^i by measuring the power consumption of each node while it is idle. We also showed in [1] that for a given operation, Δp_{op}^i is the same on identical nodes, and that Δp_{op}^i depends only on the hardware used on the node. In order to take into account the impact of parallelism, Δp_{op}^i is calibrated by varying the number of cores that perform the same *op*. In order to measure Δp_{op}^i experimentally, we isolate each basic operation by instrumenting the implementation of each fault tolerance protocol that we consider, and by using an external power meter for gathering the power measurements.

2.2 Execution time t_{op}

For each operation *op*, t_{op}^i depends on different parameters. For each node i, t_{op}^i is calibrated by considering different numbers of processes per node. The time required for checkpointing a volume of data or for logging a message is:

$$t^i_{ckpt/logging} = t^i_{access} + t^i_{transfer} = t^i_{access} + \frac{V_{data}}{R^i_{transfer}}$$

t^i_{access} is the time needed to access the storage media where the checkpoint will be stored or where the message will be logged. $t^i_{transfer}$ is the time needed to write a data on a given storage media. To calibrate $t^i_{ckpt/logging}$, our framework automatically runs a simple benchmark that measures the execution time for different values of V_{data}. This calibration process is performed for the different storage medium (RAM, HDD, etc.) available in the platform. For instance, Figure 1 presents calibration results for checkpointing on HDD for a cluster composed of 64 nodes of 2 CPU cores each. For different data sizes, we measure the checkpointing time for each node of the considered cluster, by considering one or both CPU cores. For each data size, we represent in Figure 1, the mean checkpointing time and the standard deviation over all the nodes.

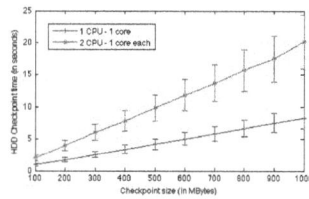

Figure 1. Calibration of the HDD Checkpointing time

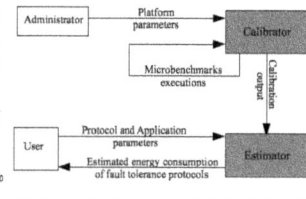

Figure 2. Energy estimator framework components

First, the curve shapes consolidate our linear approach to calibrate checkpointing. Then, the significant differences between the checkpointing times of nodes from a same cluster demonstrate why we need to calibrate execution times for all the nodes.

Since checkpointing is considered at the system level, the coordinated checkpointing requires an extra synchronization between the processes. The time required for a process coordination is:

$$t^i_{coordination} = t^i_{synchro} + t^i_{polling} = t^i_{synchro} + \frac{V_{data}}{R^i_{transfer}}$$

$t_{synchro}$ is the time needed to exchange a marker among all the processes. It is calibrated by measuring the time required to perform a synchronization barrier among processes that are already synchronized meaning $t^i_{polling}$ is equal to zero (the best case). $t^i_{polling}$ is the time necessary to finish transfers of inflight messages. It is calibrated by measuring for different message size values, the mean transfer time of this message. $R^i_{transfer}$ is the transfer rate of the network infrastructure used.

3. Estimation methodology

Once this calibration is completed, the energy framework can estimate the energy consumption of fault tolerance protocols. The user provides information related to the execution context and to the application he wants to run. This information is taken as an input by the calibrator. As an output, the calibrator provides the calibration data on which the framework relies on to estimate the energy consumed by fault tolerance protocols. Figure 2 shows the components of our framework and their interactions.

To estimate the energy consumed by checkpointing, the estimator collects from the user the total memory size required by the application to run, the total number of nodes and the number of processes per node. From this information, the estimator computes the mean memory size V^{mean}_{mem} required by each node. The estimator collects also the number of checkpoints to perform during the application execution. Besides, it collects from the calibrator the checkpoint times corresponding to the calibrated checkpoint sizes.

The estimator calculates the checkpoint times t^i_{ckpt} corresponding to V^{mean}_{mem}. If V^{mean}_{mem} is not a size recorded by the calibrator, the estimator computes the equation that gives t^i_{ckpt} according to V^{mean}_{mem}, and adjusts the equation using the method of least squares.

To estimate the energy consumed by message logging, the estimator collects from the user the number of processes per node, the total number and size of the messages sent during the application. From this information, it computes the mean volume of data V^{mean}_{data} sent (so logged) by each node. Similarly to checkpointing, it collects from the calibrator the logging time $t^i_{logging}$ corresponding to V^{mean}_{data} for each node and according to the number of processes per node.

To estimate the energy consumed by coordination, the estimator uses the mean message size $V^{mean}_{message}$ as the total size of messages divided by the total number of messages. It also uses the number of checkpoints C, the total number of nodes N and the number of processes per node that are provided for message logging and checkpointing estimations. From the calibration output, it collects the synchronization time $t_{synchro}$ corresponding to the number of processes per node and the total number of nodes specified by the user. $t_{synchro}$ corresponds to one synchronization among all the processes. Similarly to checkpointing, the estimator calculates the message transfer time $t^i_{polling}$ corresponding to the mean message size $V^{mean}_{message}$.

The estimated energy of one basic operation op (checkpointing, logging, polling or synchronization) is:

$$E_{op} = \sum_{i=1}^{N} e^i_{op} = \sum_{i=1}^{N} p^i_{op} \cdot t^i_{op}$$

The total estimated energy consumption of checkpointing is obtained by multiplying E_{ckpt} by the number of checkpoints C. The estimator calculates the estimated energy of all coordinations as follows: $E_{coordinations} = C \cdot (E_{polling} + E_{synchro})$.

To estimate the energy consumed by hierarchical checkpointing, the estimator collects from the user the composition of each cluster (i.e the list of processes in each cluster).

4. Conclusion

This paper presents a framework that estimates the energy consumption of three families of fault tolerance protocols: coordinated, uncoordinated and hierarchical protocols. To provide accurate estimations, it relies on an energy calibration of the considered platform and a user description of the execution settings. Thanks to our approach based on a calibration process, this framework can be used in any monitored platform.

To obtain a coherent global state, checkpointing is combined with message logging in uncoordinated protocols and with coordination in coordinated protocols. Therefore, to compare the energy consumed by coordinated and uncoordinated protocols, we compare the energy cost of coordinations to message logging. By providing energy estimations before pre-executing the HPC application, we can select the less energy consuming fault tolerant protocol. As a future work, we plan to extend our framework to more services needed at extreme-scale [2] such as data management protocols.

References

[1] MM. Diouri et al. Energy considerations in checkpointing and fault tolerance protocols. In *FTXS 2012*, Boston, MA, USA, June 2012.

[2] MM. Diouri, O. Glück and L. Lefèvre. Towards a novel smart and energy-aware service-oriented manager for extreme-scale applications. In *PFGC 2012*, San Jose, CA, USA, June 2012.

[3] T. Ropars et al. On the use of cluster-based partial message logging to improve fault tolerance for MPI HPC applications. In *Euro-Par 2011*, Bordeaux, France, 2011.

Work-stealing with Configurable Scheduling Strategies

Martin Wimmer   Jesper Larsson Träff

Faculty of Informatics, Research Group Parallel
Computing
Vienna University of Technology
1040 Vienna/Wien, Austria
{wimmer,traff}@par.tuwien.ac.at

Daniel Cederman   Philippas Tsigas

Computer Science and Engineering
Chalmers University of Technology
412 96 Göteborg, Sweden
{cederman,tsigas}@chalmers.se

Abstract

Work-stealing systems are typically oblivious to the nature of the tasks they are scheduling. They do not know or take into account how long a task will take to execute or how many subtasks it will spawn. Moreover, task execution order is typically determined by an underlying task storage data structure, and cannot be changed. There are thus possibilities for optimizing task parallel executions by providing information on specific tasks and their preferred execution order to the scheduling system.

We investigate generalizations of work-stealing and introduce a framework enabling applications to dynamically provide hints on the nature of specific tasks using *scheduling strategies*. Strategies can be used to independently control both local task execution and steal order. Strategies allow optimizations on specific tasks, in contrast to more conventional *scheduling policies* that are typically global in scope. Strategies are *composable* and allow different, specific scheduling choices for different parts of an application simultaneously. We have implemented a work-stealing system based on our strategy framework. A series of benchmarks demonstrates beneficial effects that can be achieved with scheduling strategies.

Categories and Subject Descriptors   D.4.1 [*Operating Systems*]: Process Management—Scheduling; D.3.2 [*Programming Languages*]: Language Classifications—concurrent, distributed, and parallel languages

General Terms   Algorithms

Keywords   Work-stealing, scheduler hints, strategies, priorities

1. Introduction

Work-stealing is a popular way to schedule parallel work-loads of independent tasks [4] and is used by well-known frameworks such as Cilk [3], Cilk++ [9], Intel Threading Building Blocks [8], X10 [5] and others. Standard work-stealing schedulers are oblivious to most properties of individual tasks and treat tasks equally. When this is a drawback, specialized work-stealing systems can apply specific optimizations, taking knowledge of the tasks into account. Such systems can be useful for specific applications, but may be difficult to compose with other applications running at the same time.

The execution order for local tasks in a work-stealing system is determined by the data structures used for storing the tasks. While the execution order provided by work-stealing deques [1] is good for some applications, there are application kernels for which other execution orders are better. Search-based algorithms can profit from prioritization to explore the most promising branches early. Other applications benefit from giving preference to tasks that access data already in the cache [12]. Locality-aware scheduling policies are also often used [7]. Another heuristic is to prioritize tasks on the critical path [11].

2. Scheduling Strategies

We introduce the concept of *scheduling strategies* as a way of informing the scheduling system about properties of *individual tasks*. Strategies also provide means to prioritize tasks without losing any generality of the scheduler. In addition, strategies are composable, so regardless of which strategies/types of strategies are combined, the scheduling behavior is always well-defined.

2.1 Spawn to call

Strategies make it possible to perform a conversion of task spawns to synchronous function calls based on properties of the task to be spawned and the state of the system. Our system maintains a *transitive weight* estimate of the work that will be generated by a task and its descendants. Below a certain threshold the spawn is converted to a function call. This can depend dynamically on, for example, the number of tasks in the local task queue.

2.2 Number of tasks to steal

Using the transitive weight the number of tasks stolen can be chosen to better reflect the amount of work that will be generated by these tasks, which can improve load balance [2]. Strategies can control the steal operation in this fashion.

2.3 Priority

Strategies can be used to suggest an execution order to the scheduling system, by giving the user a means to prioritize tasks. An application specific execution order of tasks leads to higher efficiency (performance, memory usage, quality of the results) compared to a fixed execution order like *last-in-first-out*.

2.4 Locality

Together with the notion of a *place*, which denotes an execution unit together with its supporting data-structures, the prioritization mechanism can be used to implement per task (spatial and temporal) locality optimizations.

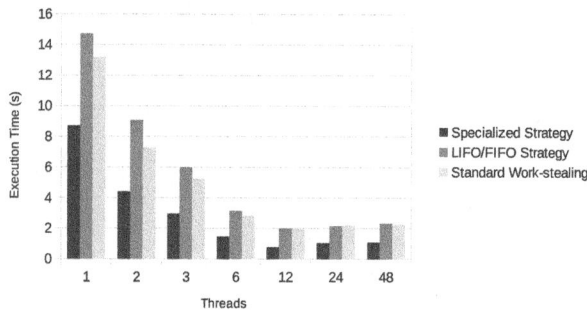

Figure 1. Graph bipartitioning for unweighted graphs. Problem size $n = 39$, density 50%. Results obtained on a 4×12-core AMD Opteron 6168.

2.5 Composability

We achieve *composability* of algorithms that use different (per task) strategies by organizing strategies into a hierarchy, which imposes an order on strategies of different types. Tasks with different strategies are prioritized by the strategy of their common ancestor.

3. Applications and Results

We have used a number of (kernel) applications to illustrate advantages and flexibility of scheduling strategies.

3.1 Graph Bipartitioning

Branch-and-bound algorithms can be implemented in a task-parallel fashion, and benefit from an execution order determined by a weight assigned to each subproblem task. We used strategies to solve the graph-bipartitioning problem using an easily computable lower bound. Figure 1 shows the effect of prioritization vs. a non-prioritized task-execution (LIFO/FIFO), as well as a standard work-stealing system without strategy support.

3.2 Prefix sum

For the prefix-sums problem strategies can be used to make a parallel algorithm (which performs about a factor two more operations than the trivial sequential algorithm) adapt towards the sequential performance when other applications are running at the same time. Strategies lead to better performance when the prefix-sums computation is performed concurrently as part of a larger application.

3.3 Unbalanced Tree Search

The fine-grained Unbalanced Tree Search (UTS) benchmark [10] reduces the scheduler overhead using the more flexible spawn to call conversion that is possible with strategies.

3.4 Triangle strip generation

Using an implementation of the so called SGI algorithm [6], this benchmark explores the simultaneous use of two different prioritization strategies to achieve better results faster.

3.5 Single-source shortest path

The straight-forward parallelization of Dijkstra's single-source shortest path algorithm requires prioritization and can be parallelized in a simple way with strategies.

3.6 Quicksort

This standard example can also benefit from strategies. Good cache behavior is expected if locally spawned tasks are executed depth-first, and the shorter subsequence is processed first. When stealing tasks, the largest subsequences should be stolen first to reduce interference. When enough tasks have been generated, further spawns should be converted to calls. This can all be achieved with strategies.

4. Conclusion

We introduced a dynamic scheduling strategy framework for work-stealing schedulers in order to enable application dependent scheduling decisions. This includes decisions on the execution and stealing order of tasks, as well as on when to merge tasks at runtime. These decisions can reduce scheduling overhead, as well as make the execution more efficient and adaptive. We found considerable improvements to a series of kernel benchmarks.

Acknowledgments

This research was partly funded by the European Union Seventh Framework Programme (FP7/2007-2013) under grant agreement no. 248481 (project PEPPHER, www.peppher.eu).

References

[1] U. A. Acar, G. E. Blelloch, and R. D. Blumofe. The data locality of work stealing. *Theory of Computing Systems*, 35(3):321–347, 2002.

[2] P. Berenbrink, T. Friedetzky, and L. A. Goldberg. The natural work-stealing algorithm is stable. In *Proceedings of the 42nd IEEE Symposium on Foundations of Computer Science (FOCS)*, pages 178–187, 2001.

[3] R. D. Blumofe, C. F. Joerg, B. C. Kuszmaul, C. E. Leiserson, K. H. Randall, and Y. Zhou. Cilk: An efficient multithreaded runtime system. *Journal of Parallel and Distributed Computing*, 37(1):55–69, 1996.

[4] R. D. Blumofe and C. E. Leiserson. Scheduling multithreaded computations by work stealing. *Journal of the ACM*, 46(5):720–748, 1999.

[5] P. Charles, C. Grothoff, V. Saraswat, C. Donawa, A. Kielstra, K. Ebcioglu, C. von Praun, and V. Sarkar. X10: an object-oriented approach to non-uniform cluster computing. In *Proceedings of the 20th annual ACM SIGPLAN conference on Object-oriented programming, systems, languages, and applications*, OOPSLA, pages 519–538, New York, NY, USA, 2005. ACM.

[6] F. Evans, S. Skiena, and A. Varshney. Optimizing triangle strips for fast rendering. In *Proceedings of the 7th conference on Visualization'96*, pages 319–326. IEEE, 1996.

[7] Y. Guo, J. Zhao, V. Cavé, and V. Sarkar. SLAW: A scalable locality-aware adaptive work-stealing scheduler. In *24th IEEE International Symposium on Parallel and Distributed Processing (IPDPS)*, pages 1–12, 2010.

[8] A. Kukanov and M. J. Voss. The foundations for scalable multi-core software in Intel Threading Building Blocks. *Intel Technology Journal*, 11(4), 2007.

[9] C. E. Leiserson. The Cilk++ concurrency platform. *The Journal of Supercomputing*, 51(3):244–257, 2010.

[10] S. Olivier, J. Huan, J. Liu, J. Prins, J. Dinan, P. Sadayappan, and C. Tseng. UTS: An unbalanced tree search benchmark. *Languages and Compilers for Parallel Computing*, pages 235–250, 2007.

[11] F. Song, A. YarKhan, and J. Dongarra. Dynamic task scheduling for linear algebra algorithms on distributed-memory multicore systems. In *Proceedings of the Conference on High Performance Computing Networking, Storage and Analysis*, SC '09, pages 19:1–19:11, New York, NY, USA, 2009. ACM.

[12] B. Weissman. Performance counters and state sharing annotations: a unified approach to thread locality. In *Proceedings of the eighth international conference on Architectural support for programming languages and operating systems*, ASPLOS-VIII, pages 127–138, New York, NY, USA, 1998. ACM.

WuKong: Effective Diagnosis of Bugs at Large System Scales

Bowen Zhou   Milind Kulkarni   Saurabh Bagchi

Purdue University

{bzhou, milind, sbagchi}@purdue.edu

Abstract

A key challenge in developing large scale applications (both in system size and in input size) is finding bugs that are latent at the small scales of testing, only manifesting when a program is deployed at large scales. Traditional statistical techniques fail because no error-free run is available at deployment scales for training purposes. Prior work used *scaling models* to detect anomalous behavior at large scales without being trained on correct behavior at that scale. However, that work cannot localize bugs automatically. In this paper, we extend that work in three ways: (i) we develop an automatic diagnosis technique, based on *feature reconstruction*; (ii) we design a heuristic to effectively prune the feature space; and (iii) we validate our design through one fault-injection study, finding that our system can effectively localize bugs in a majority of cases.

Categories and Subject Descriptors   D.2.4 [*Software Engineering*]: Software/Program Verification—Statistical Methods; D.2.5 [*Software Engineering*]: Testing and Debugging—Diagnostics

General Terms   Reliability, Verification

Keywords   Scale-dependent Bug, Program Behavior Prediction, Feature Reconstruction

1. Introduction

One of the key challenges of developing large-scale software, intended to run on many processors or with very large data sets, is detecting and diagnosing *scale-dependent* bugs. Most bugs manifest at both small and large scales, and as a result, can be identified and caught during the development process, when programmers are typically working with both small-scale systems and small-scale inputs. However, a particularly insidious class of bugs are those that predominantly arise at deployment scales. These bugs appear far less frequently, if at all, at small scales, and hence are often not caught during development, but only when a program is released into the wild and is deployed at large scales. As a result, these bugs are unlikely to be caught by regular software testing and debugging techniques.

Our previous work VRISHA [4] has attempted to address this particular type of bugs where existing debugging techniques fails. VRISHA is a statistical-model-based debugging tool that exploits *scale-determined* features to detect bugs in large-scale program runs even if the statistical model was only trained on small-scale behavior. Note that in this paper, we adopt the same convention as

VRISHA, and use "scale" as a generic term to refer to the number of executing entities (threads, processes, peers, etc.) or input data size (or both). Unfortunately, while the detection of bugs is automatic, VRISHA is only able to identify that the scaling trend has been violated; it cannot determine *which* program feature violated the trend, *i.e.*, where in the program the bug manifested.

1.1   Our approach: WuKong

This paper presents WuKong[1], an *automatic, scalable approach to detecting and diagnosing bugs that manifest at large system scales*. WuKong is based on the same high level concepts as VRISHA, but provides three key contributions over the previous work:

Automatic bug localization   WuKong, in contrast to VRISHA, provides an *automatic* diagnosis technique. The key insight driving our localization technique is that a regression model built across multiple training scales can be used to *predict* the expected bug-free behavior at larger scales. By building per-feature scaling models, WuKong is able to infer what the value of each feature *would have been* were a run bug-free, and hence identify which feature(s) deviate most from expected behavior. With carefully chosen program features that can be linked to particular regions of code (WuKong uses calling contexts rooted at conditional statements, as described in Section 2), identifying the most deviant features can pinpoint which lines of code result in particularly unexpected behavior, providing a roadmap the programmer can use in tracking down the bug.

Feature pruning   Not all program behaviors are well-correlated with scale, and hence cannot be predicted by scaling models. Examples of such behaviors include truly random conditionals (*e.g.*, `if (x < rand())`) or, more commonly, data-dependent behaviors (where the *values* of the input data, rather than the *size* of that data determine behavior). When *diagnosing* bugs, the existence of such hard-to-model features can dramatically reduce the effectiveness of localization: a feature whose behavior seems aberrant may be truly buggy, or may represent a modeling failure.

To address this shortcoming, we introduce a cross-validation-based *feature pruning* technique. This mechanism provides a "knob" that can effectively prune features that are hard to model accurately from the feature set, allowing programmers to trade off reduced detectability for improved localization accuracy.

2. Bug Localization Via Feature Reconstruction

The fundamental approach of WuKong is to build a statistical model of program behavior that incorporates scale. Essentially, we would like a model that infers the relationship between *control features*, *i.e.*, scale attributes (*e.g.*, number of processes, or input

---

[1] WuKong, the Monkey King, is the main character in the epic Chinese novel *Journey to the West*, and possesses the ability to recognize evil in any form.

size) and *observational features, i.e.,* program behavior (*e.g.,* the number of iterations taken by a particular loop).

WUKONG models application behavior with a collection of base models, each of which characterizes a single observational feature. The base model is a log-transformed regression where all control features are included in a log-transformed regression model to predict each observational feature. The log transformation accounts for higher-order relationships between behavior and scale (consider the many algorithms that are $O(n^2)$).

$$\log(Y) = \beta_0 + \sum_{i=1}^{N} \beta_i \log(X_i) \quad (1)$$

Following the procedure of Barnes *et al.* [2], the regression model in Equation 1 allows us to readily compute the relative prediction error, as in Equation 2.

$$E_i = |e^{\log(Y_i') - \log(Y_i)} - 1| \quad (2)$$

To provide a "roadmap" for developers to follow when tracking down the bug, WUKONG ranks all observational features by relative error.

3. Feature Pruning

To eliminate bad features, *i.e.,* features that cannot be modeled accurately, WUKONG employs cross validation. Cross validation uses a portion of the training data to test models built using the remainder of the training data. More specifically, WUKONG employs k-fold cross validation. It splits the original training data by row into k folds, treats each one of the k folds in turn as the test data and the remaining $k-1$ folds as the training data, then trains and evaluates a model using each of the k sets of data. In this way, cross validation is able to estimate the mean reconstruction error for each feature using the original training data.

If a particular feature cannot be modeled well during cross validation, WUKONG assumes that the feature is unpredictable and will filter it out from the roadmaps generated during the localization phase. Those features with an error higher than a preset threshold h are removed from the input. The threshold is configurable by users and usually set to be a positive number less than 100%, as it is trivial to achieve 100% relative error by using 0 as the prediction.

4. Evaluation

We conducted a large scale fault injection experiment on a benchmark applications from the Sequoia benchmark suite [1]: AMG2006. AMG2006 is a parallel algebraic multigrid solver for linear systems arising from problems on unstructured grids. We began by building a model for each observational feature of AMG2006, using as training runs program executions ranging from 8 to 128 nodes. The control features were the X, Y, Z dimension parameters of the 3D process topology, and the observational features were the number of times each branch is taken at a unique calling context, resulting in 3 control features and 1633 observational features. Then we prune all observational features whose reconstruction error during cross validation is greater than 0.5. We are left with 1466 features for which WUKONG builds the final models. We use Pin [3] to collect the observational features from our training runs and testing runs.

We ran 100 instances of the 1024-node execution, each time injecting a fault into rank 0 process by choosing (randomly) one conditional test (selected from the set of all observational features) to "flip" throughout the rest of the execution. Of the 100 injected runs, 47 resulted in non-crashing bugs.

We found that in 70.2% of cases, the source of the bug (the conditional that was flipped) was among the top 10 aberrant fea-

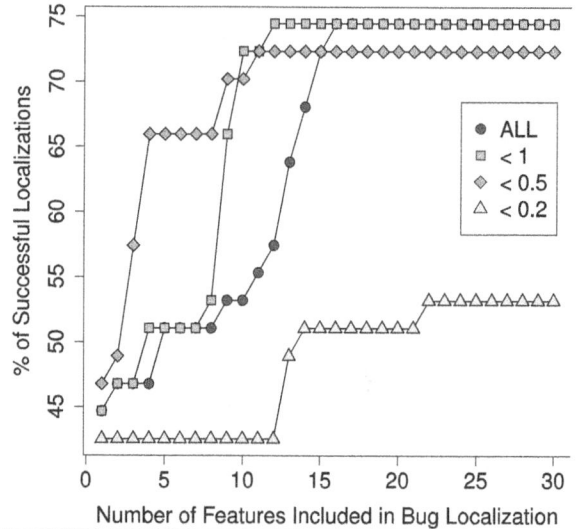

Figure 1. Comparison of different feature pruning thresholds. "ALL" means no pruning. "$< \eta$" means only keeping features with reconstruction error less than η.

tures. Furthermore, 46.8% of the time the faulty feature was the first feature identified by WUKONG. We then examined the sensitivity of WUKONG's localization to the filtering threshold used by the feature pruning algorithm described in Section 3. We used four different pruning thresholds: none, 1.0, 0.5 and 0.2. Figure 1 shows the percentage of buggy runs where the faulty feature appears in the top x features for different x. We see that performing a small amount of feature pruning can dramatically improve the quality of WUKONG's roadmap: at a threshold of 0.5, over 66% of the faulty features appear in the top 5 features suggested by WUKONG.

5. Conclusions

With the increasing scale at which programs are being deployed, both in terms of input size and system size, techniques to automatically detect and diagnose bugs in large-scale programs are becoming increasingly important, especially if bugs are scale-dependent. To address these problem, we developed WUKONG, which leverages novel statistical modeling and feature reconstruction techniques to automatically diagnose bugs in large scale systems, even when trained only on data from small-scale runs. This approach is well-suited to modern development practices, where developers may only have access to small scales, and bugs may manifest only rarely at large scales. With a fault injection study, we showed that WUKONG is able to automatically, scalably and effectively diagnose bugs.

References

[1] ASC Sequoia Benchmark Codes. https://asc.llnl.gov/sequoia/benchmarks/.

[2] B. J. Barnes, B. Rountree, D. K. Lowenthal, J. Reeves, B. de Supinski, and M. Schulz. A regression-based approach to scalability prediction. In *Proceedings of the 22nd annual international conference on Supercomputing*, pages 368–377, 2008.

[3] C.-K. Luk, R. Cohn, R. Muth, H. Patil, A. Klauser, G. Lowney, S. Wallace, V. J. Reddi, and K. Hazelwood. Pin: building customized program analysis tools with dynamic instrumentation. In *Proceedings of the 2005 ACM SIGPLAN conference on Programming language design and implementation*, pages 190–200, 2005.

[4] B. Zhou, M. Kulkarni, and S. Bagchi. Vrisha: using scaling properties of parallel programs for bug detection and localization. In *Proceedings of the 20th ACM international symposium on High performance distributed computing*, pages 85–96, 2011.

Author Index